Guide to Congress

Guide to Congress

FIFTH EDITION • VOLUME I

CQ PRESS

A Division of Congressional Quarterly Inc.
Washington, D.C.

CQ Press
A Division of Congressional Quarterly Inc.
1414 22nd Street, N.W.
Washington, D.C. 20037
(202) 822-1475; (800) 638-1710

www.cqpress.com

Book design and production by Kachergis Book Design,
Pittsboro, North Carolina

Printed in the United States of America

03 02 01 00 99   5 4 3 2 1

The paper used in this publication meets the minimum requirements of the American National Standard for Information Science—Permanence of Paper for Printed Library Materials, ANSI Z 39.48-1984.

Illustration credits and acknowledgments appear on pages 1353–1354, Volume II, which constitutes a continuation of the copyright page.

LIBRARY OF CONGRESS CATALOGING-IN-PUBLICATION DATA
Congressional Quarterly's guide to Congress.—5th ed.
    p. cm.
    Includes bibliographical references and index.
    ISBN 1-56802-476-2 (v. 1) — ISBN 1-56802-436-3 (v. 2)
— ISBN 1-56802-477-0 (set)
    1. United States. Congress. I. Title: Guide to Congress.
II. Congressional Quarterly, Inc.
  JK1021.C565 1999
  328.73—dc21   99-053914

Summary Table of Contents

Table of Contents

Preface

The Congress of the United States in 1999, on the threshold of the twenty-first century, found itself mired in one of the most partisan eras of the twentieth century. More than usual, Congress had become an object of derision by commentators, academicians, and—if polls are to be believed—the voting public. And yet, behind the image of ineffectiveness, even incompetence, that Congress sometimes projected to the world, there were positive developments suggesting that the roles intended for this institution were still in place and functioning.

Longtime observers of Congress saw the partisanship as more razor sharp than at any time in their memory. The pinnacle came in late 1998 and early 1999, when Congress for only the third time in two hundred years debated the impeachment and removal from office of the president of the United States. The House, largely along partisan lines, voted to impeach President Bill Clinton, but the Senate, in the ensuing trial, found him not guilty. Later in the year the Senate, again largely along party lines, rejected ratification of a nuclear test ban treaty, the most prominent of a number of congressional actions on foreign policy that prompted Clinton to charge Republicans with returning the nation to the isolationism of past generations.

These events and others put on display a deep animosity between the parties at the end of century, fed by enormous Republican distrust of and hostility toward Clinton. But conflict between the parties that had been developing at least since the 1980s. Various strands of public policy controversy, social conflict, and institutional malaise had converged in preceding decades to feed this animosity.

To a considerable extent this state of affairs grew out of the longtime Democratic Party control of Congress, which had been almost continuous since the New Deal era of the 1930s. The situation was aggravated by the Democrats' proclivity to treat their Republican counterparts as annoying nuisances rather than as part of the legitimate governing structure.

But it was more than internecine warfare between the two parties. Volatile social issues, such as abortion, gay and sexual equality rights, racial divisions, economic dislocations, and personal conduct, had been simmering for decades. By the 1990s opposing sides were closely matched in strength and legislative strategy, often reflecting voters' division on the controversies. Until the late-1990s, when a booming economy poured tax revenue into the Treasury to ease the problem, a huge federal budget deficit and the fiscal constraints of seemingly uncontrollable entitlement programs left legislators with few options to deal with economic and social concerns. Added to this was the resurgence of a vigorous Republican Party under the control of its most conservative elements that did not accept the legitimacy of a large activist federal government and was willing to use new aggressive tactics to change that philosophy. The GOP's opportunity came in 1994 when the party captured full control of Congress for the first time in forty years by winning the House and retaking the Senate after being in the minority since 1987. This election, especially in the House, brought to power a conservative congressional leadership determined to reverse decades of Democratic policy and programs. The focus and the tone of debate in Congress did indeed change, but the Republicans battled—at best—to a standstill with the Democratic president who occupied the White House. The GOP's performance and rhetoric so burned the party that Republicans actually lost seats in the House in both the 1996 and 1998 elections. The latter was particularly notable because not since 1934 had the party not controlling the White House lost seats in a midterm election.

As a result, the twentieth century set on a U.S. Congress stalemated between the parties and political philosophies, an image that contributed to the public's view of Congress as an institution of comic relief and bumbling, especially when contrasted to resurgent and vigorous state governments led by governors with programs that addressed real voter concerns.

And yet, in spite of Congress's troubled years in the last decades of the century, there were positive developments. The 1994 Republican House victory broke a mold that even some Democrats conceded was deformed by an arrogance born of holding power too long. The victory allowed Republicans to set an agenda that challenged the long-dominant view of the primacy of the federal government's role in social and economic issues and relations with the states. It also allowed the Republicans to make important procedural changes and reorganize committees and jurisdictional powers. In the process the Republicans recentralized leadership in the Speaker in a form not seen since the first decade of the century, a development that could lead to a more focused and functional Congress in the future—regardless of which party holds the majority. The personalities and strengths of future Speakers will have much to do with the role that this highest House official plays.

Although the spotlight was on change, there was much more

that did not change. Committees still developed and reported legislation, although in the House they had less power than in the past. Procedures and rules still were employed to maintain order and set priorities, even though some traditional practices were altered. Leaders still had to make sensible decisions and lead their followers in wise strategic and tactical ways or risk paying a heavy political price—as the Republicans learned at the polls. In the Senate, which regards itself as a continuing body because only a third of the membership is elected every two years, the historical accommodative and cooperative spirit of that chamber continued even while being strained by the growing partisanship that became increasingly public during President Clinton's second term. The institution of Congress still mattered.

The *Guide to Congress,* fifth edition, will help readers understand this vital institution in American political life. The editors of Congressional Quarterly hope the reader will come away with a better appreciation of Congress as a continuing institution that has functioned for more than two hundred years in a generally beneficial way for a changing nation. The *Guide,* offered for the first time in two volumes to allow more convenient use of the book, is organized in eight sections to help readers through different aspects of understanding Congress. The core of the book is contained in the first three sections: history; powers; and procedures of the institution. These are followed by more detailed examination of related subjects such as pressures on Congress; pay, housing, qualifications, and ethics of members; and how Congress is elected. Volume II has an extensive Appendix providing a myriad of factual details about the institution, members, and elections, and each volume contains the comprehensive index that covers both volumes.

All chapters and tables in the work have been thoroughly updated to reflect developments since the fourth edition was published in 1991. Literally hundreds of individuals have lent their time, knowledge, and advice to this work since the first edition was published in 1971. The fifth edition was prepared under the direction of David Tarr, CQ Press executive editor, Patricia Ann O'Connor, former director of CQ book publishing, and Jon Preimesberger, CQ Press senior editor. Authors who contributed to this edition include Rhodes Cook, Ron dePaolo, Phil Duncan, David Hosansky, Kenneth Jost, Melissa Kaye, Christine C. Lawrence, Bert Levine, Colleen McGuiness, Patricia Ann O'Connor, Betsy Palmer, Matthew Pinkus, and Richard Worsnop. The bibliographies were compiled by Fenton Martin of Indiana University. The Appendix was under the supervision of Chris Karlsten, who was assisted in research by Grace Hill, who compiled and updated the biographical index of members of Congress. Assisting with the editing were Sandy Chizinsky, Chris Karlsten, Kerry Kern, Sabra Ledent, Nola Lynch, and Tom Roche. Jan Danis created the index.

The editors wish also to thank congressional experts who gave generously of their time to comment on material as it was in preparation: Walter J. Oleszek, Paul E. Dwyer, and Paul Rundquist, all of the Congressional Research Service; Christopher J. Deering of George Washington University; Michael Nelson of Rhodes College; and John Cranford, former senior economics reporter for Congressional Quarterly.

Lastly, the editors must acknowledge and thank the many persons who created the first *Guide to Congress* and kept it current in subsequent editions. Most important are two persons who were present at the creation in 1971: William Korns, who conceived the plan for the first edition and wrote a number of its chapters, and Mary Wilson Cohn, who was a major contributor to the first and subsequent editions and served as editor of the fourth edition. Other major contributors to previous editions include Irwin B. Arieff, Thomas J. Arrandale, Prentice Bowsher, Michael Carson, William Gerber, Martha V. Gottron, Sari Horwitz, Ed Johnson, Nancy Lammers, Mary McNeil, Jack McWethy, John L. Moore, Warden Moxley, John Pierson, James Phillips, Georgiana Rathbun, Park Teter, Margaret C. Thompson, James R. Wagner, Elder Witt, and Michael Wormser.

CQ Press Editors

Origins and Development of Congress

CHAPTER 1

Constitutional Beginnings

WHEN THE FEDERAL convention met in Philadelphia in 1787 to consider revising the Articles of Confederation, the reasons for seeking a more effective form of national government for the newly independent United States of America seemed manifest and pressing. The exact form that government should take was by no means clear, however, and substantial compromise was required before agreement could be reached. What finally emerged as the Constitution of the United States nevertheless reflected in good measure the shared experience of men who had grown up in a colonial America that was predominantly English in origin and who had finally rebelled against English sovereignty when that seemed the only way to preserve the basic rights and freedoms they had come to expect as a part of their English heritage.

Colonial Background: Growing Friction with England

Private initiative was the prime mover behind the settlement of America by the English during the seventeenth century, when all of the original thirteen colonies except one were founded. Several were started by promoters with an eye to profits or the creation of new feudal domains. Religious strife underlay the "Great Migration" of Puritans to New England (and the West Indies) during the repressive reign of Charles I (1625–1649). Poverty drove many others to take a chance on America. Whatever the motive for settlement, it was entirely a private undertaking, receiving little help from the state other than a charter to the land to be settled.

The English achieved their dominant position along the Atlantic seaboard in two waves of colonization. Virginia, Maryland, and the New England colonies were founded before 1642, when the outbreak of civil war in England absorbed Britain's energies.

After restoration of the monarchy in 1660, the English added New York, New Jersey, Pennsylvania, Delaware, and the Carolinas. Georgia, the thirteenth colony, was founded in 1733. By 1700 the colonies had a population of two hundred thousand—largely of English origin—stretched along a thousand miles of coast from Maine to the Carolinas.

ROOTS OF SELF-GOVERNMENT

By the time Jamestown was founded in 1607, the English had already attained significant rights and privileges. English justice was grounded on a solid body of common law that included the right to trial by jury. No English subject could be deprived of life, liberty, or property without due process in the courts. The first colonists brought with them the models of English courts and other organs of local government.

The long struggle in England for the right of self-government also was well advanced by the beginning of the seventeenth century. The Crown still was supreme, and it would take the beheading of Charles I in 1649 and the dethroning of James II in 1688 to ensure Parliament ascendancy over the king. Already, though, the two houses of Parliament—the Lords and the Commons—symbolized the principle of government by law and representative assembly, and this principle, too, was soon transplanted to America. In 1619 the Virginians (then numbering about one thousand) elected twenty-two "burgesses"—the first English elected representatives in the New World—to a general assembly. After Virginia became a royal colony in 1624, the governor and his council were appointed by the king, but popular representation in the lower house of the Virginia Assembly—the House of Burgesses—was retained.

The organizers of the Massachusetts Bay Company carried governing matters considerably further when they voted to transfer the entire enterprise and its charter as "one body politique and corporate" to New England. On their arrival in 1630, the officers promptly established themselves as the government of the Bay Colony, subject only to annual election thereafter by the stockholder-colonists. The founders of Massachusetts thereby asserted a right to full self-government that neither the king nor Parliament had contemplated or would be prepared to challenge for another fifty years.

The great distance that separated England from America was itself a major factor in promoting a spirit of independence and self-reliance among the early colonists. Many of those drawn to America were predisposed to resist authority in any event, and this attitude was reinforced by the free availability of land and the harshness of frontier living. In New England, where entire congregations of Puritans had often emigrated and settled together in a town of their own, the town meeting became a unique instrument of self-government that was exceptionally democratic for the times.

Origins of Conflict

England left the colonies largely to themselves initially, but it was not for lack of a concept of the role they would be expected to play. Under the prevailing economic doctrine of the times—mercantilism—the central goal of any nation-state was self-

3

COLONIAL SETTLEMENTS IN THE SEVENTEENTH AND EIGHTEENTH CENTURIES

Virginia. The Virginia Company of London, a joint stock company with a charter from James I, founded the first permanent English settlement in America at Jamestown in 1607. After severe setbacks, the company found tobacco to be a thriving crop and profitable export and began to attract new settlers with "head rights" to fifty acres of land. The company was dissolved in 1624, when Virginia became a royal colony. Its population had reached fifteen thousand by 1648.

Massachusetts. A small band of Pilgrims founded Plymouth in 1620. Few others came until 1630, when John Winthrop and other Puritan organizers of the Massachusetts Bay Company arrived with one thousand colonists to settle Boston and nearby towns. The Bay Colony, which had attained a population of sixteen thousand by 1643, remained a self-governing Puritan commonwealth until its charter was annulled in 1684. In 1691 Massachusetts became a royal colony, incorporating Plymouth and Maine as well.

New Hampshire. Various groups of Antinomians, Puritans, and Anglicans began a number of settlements between 1623 and 1640 on land granted to John Mason by Charles I. Massachusetts annexed these settlements briefly, and border disputes between the two continued even after New Hampshire became a royal colony in 1679. The governor of Massachusetts served also as governor of New Hampshire from 1699 to 1741.

New York. The Dutch West Indies Company founded New Netherland with posts at Albany (1624) and Manhattan (1626). Confined largely to the Hudson River Valley, the colony was seized by the English in 1664 and renamed New York as part of a grant by Charles II to his brother, the Duke of York, of all land between the Connecticut and Delaware rivers. The duke attempted to run the colony without an assembly until 1683; as James II, he made it a royal colony in 1685.

Delaware. The town of Lewes, on the shore of Delaware Bay, was settled by the Dutch in 1631. They were followed by Swedish settlers, who called it New Sweden, until overcome by Dutch forces in 1655. The area was conquered by the English in 1664 and was included in the grant to the Duke of York, who sold it to William Penn in 1682. Known as the "Lower Counties," Delaware had its own assembly after 1704 but had the same proprietary governor as Pennsylvania until 1776.

Maryland. In 1632 Charles I gave a proprietary charter to Maryland (originally a part of Virginia) to Sir George Calvert, who wanted a feudal domain for his family that would serve also as a refuge for English Catholics. Settlement began at St. Mary's in 1634. Protestants soon outnumbered Catholics, leading to continuing friction between settlers and the proprietor. Maryland became a royal colony in 1692 but was restored to the Calvert family in 1715.

Connecticut. Thomas Hooker led a group of Puritans from the Massachusetts Bay Colony to found Hartford in 1636. About the same time, other groups of Puritans settled Saybrook and New Haven. Modeled along the theocratic lines of Massachusetts, these and other settlements were joined when Connecticut in 1662 obtained from Charles II its own charter as a self-governing colony. The colony retained that status until 1776.

Rhode Island. Providence was founded in 1636 by Roger Williams, a strong believer in religious freedom who had been banished from the Bay Colony for opposing the intolerant and conformist rule of Governor Winthrop and the Puritans. The area drew other freethinkers and nonconformists, and in 1644 the settlements federated as Rhode Island and Providence Plantations. They obtained a royal charter of their own in 1663 and remained a self-governing colony until the Revolution.

New Jersey. In 1665 the Duke of York gave the land between the Hudson and Delaware rivers to Lord John Berkeley and Sir George Carteret (a former governor of the Isle of Jersey), who named the area New Jersey. The two proprietors later sold East and West Jersey separately, and although the two were reunited as a royal colony in 1702, confusion of land titles continued to plague New Jersey. The colony had the same governor as New York until 1738.

Carolinas. Charles II gave proprietary title to all land between Virginia and Florida in 1663 to the Carolina proprietors, a group of promoters led by Sir John Colleton and the Earl of Shaftesbury. Charleston was founded in 1670 by settlers from England and Barbados. Later, French Huguenots and Scots came to settle. South Carolina became a plantation colony like Virginia. North Carolina became an area of small farms. The two became royal colonies in 1729.

Pennsylvania. William Penn, a Quaker convert, received proprietary title to Pennsylvania from the Duke of York in 1681. Penn attracted settlers from the Continent as well as England with promises of political and religious liberty and the offer of land on generous terms. German Mennonites were among the first groups to come, settling Germantown in 1683. Pennsylvania prospered under Penn's tolerant rule, and it remained a proprietary colony until the Revolution.

Georgia. General James Oglethorpe and other English philanthropists envisioned the territory known as Georgia as a refuge for debtors. They founded Savannah in 1733 and in the next eight years brought over approximately eighteen hundred charity colonists. Many of these settlers moved on to South Carolina, however, and Georgia had a total population of little more than two thousand residents when it became a royal colony in 1752.

sufficiency, and it was taken for granted that all profits of empire should accrue to the benefit of the mother country. Thus the English were quick to try to monopolize the trade in Virginia tobacco, the first American product to find a wide market. And in 1660 they initiated systematic efforts to exploit colonial trade with the first of a series of Acts of Trade and Navigation.

These laws were designed to maximize English profits on the transport of imports to and exports from the colonies and on the marketing of major colonial products. They required all trade between England and the colonies to be carried by English or colonial-built ships manned by English subjects; stipulated that imports of goods to the colonies from other countries in Europe first had to be landed and reloaded at English ports; and prohibited the export of certain colonial products to countries other than England. Tobacco was the first of these enumerated items, and eventually every important American export except salt fish was added to the list.

The trade acts were not without some benefit to the colonies. But in exchanging their raw products for English manufactures, the colonists rarely found the terms of trade to their advantage. When tobacco prices collapsed in the 1660s, for example, Virginians had no recourse against the English merchants who raised the prices of goods sent in exchange. This situation was aggravated by England's continuing refusal to permit its coins to circulate in the colonies. To get specie (gold or silver), the colonists had to sell their products in the West Indies or other markets.

The trade acts were met with widespread evasion in the colonies. Smuggling, bribery, and the use of false documents were commonplace. New Englanders, who ran a chronic deficit in their balance of trade with England, were especially resourceful in evading the trade acts. Massachusetts went so far as to refuse to obey them, asserting that the laws of England "do not reach America" because the colonies were unrepresented in Parliament. For this and similar acts of defiance against English authority, the Bay Colony's charter was annulled in 1684.

When James II came to the throne in 1685, England moved to strengthen its colonial administration by consolidating the New England colonies, New York, and New Jersey into one Dominion of New England. For three years these colonies were ruled by Sir Edmund Andros as governor-general with the aid of an appointed council but no representative assembly. The colonists bridled at being taxed without their consent and were quick to oust Andros and other dominion officials as soon as they received word of the Glorious Revolution of 1688 and the expulsion of James from England. The concept of the Dominion of New England was promptly abandoned.

The accession of William and Mary in 1689 marked the beginning of a transfer of power from the British Crown to Parliament and a series of colonial wars that ended in 1763 with the English in control of all of North America east of the Mississippi River. Mercantilist aims continued to dominate English colonial policy throughout this period, and new restrictions were placed on colonial trade. But the American colonies continued to grow in population, economic strength, and political assertiveness.

Growth of the Colonies

Between 1700 and 1760 large families and new immigrants boosted the colonial population from 200,000 to about 1.7 million. Persons of English stock were in the majority overall and among the colonial leaders. The first Adams arrived in 1636, the first Washington in 1656, the first Franklin in 1685. Other major ethnic groups in 1760 were the Scots-Irish (estimated at 280,000) and Germans (170,000), whose forebears had started coming to America toward the end of the seventeenth century. Finding the best land along the seaboard already taken, most of them had moved on to settle the back country.

Even more numerous in the American population of 1760 were an estimated 310,000 black slaves. The Spaniards brought the first African slaves to the New World in the sixteenth century; a Dutch ship brought the first twenty to Virginia in 1619. The English saw nothing wrong in slavery, and the Puritans regularly took Indians as slaves and sold them in the West Indies.

Slaves helped to meet a chronic shortage of labor in colonial America at a time when most colonists wanted and usually could obtain their own land. Slavery eventually declined in the North, where it became unprofitable, but it flourished in the plantation economy of the South. The number of slaves in Virginia, the Carolinas, and Georgia grew rapidly during the eighteenth century. Americans vied with the English slave traders in meeting the demand. Yankee slavers were especially successful in trading New England rum for Africans, who then were sold in the West Indies for sugar and molasses with which to make more rum.

Profits from slave labor and the slave trade thus added to a prosperity that was sustained by a rise in prices for colonial goods in England and the rest of Europe. In 1731 exports leaving Charleston included 42,000 barrels of rice, 14,000 barrels of pitch, tar, and turpentine, and 250,000 deerskins. Virginia and Maryland shipped more tobacco, while Pennsylvania found a growing market for its wheat and flour. The fur trade was centered in New York. The New England colonies exported large quantities of ship timber and lumber of all types along with fish and meat.

Most of the colonial products were not competitive with those of England, but when competition did appear, restrictions followed. The Woolens Act of 1699 barred sale of colonial cloth outside the place where it was woven. Parliament in 1732 banned the export of hats from one colony to another. To protect English exports of iron and steel products, the colonies in 1750 were ordered to stop building various kinds of mills. After the British West Indies complained that the Americans were buying cheaper sugar and molasses from the French, Parliament passed the Molasses Act of 1733, placing a stiff duty on imports from the French islands. For the most part, however, these restrictions were poorly enforced and easily evaded by the Americans.

Governors versus Assemblies

As the American population and economy grew, so did the problems of English colonial administration. All of the colonies were permitted to elect their own assemblies after the Dominion of New England collapsed in 1689, but only Connecticut and Rhode Island retained the right to elect their governors as well.

The governors of the eight royal colonies were appointed by the king and those of the five proprietary colonies served with the king's approval. It was these royal and proprietary governors who had primary responsibility for enforcing English laws and regulations in America. The governors were armed with great legal authority. Long after the Crown had been stripped of such prerogatives in England, the colonial governors had the right of absolute veto over colonial legislation, the authority to terminate and dissolve assemblies, and the power to dismiss judges and create courts. But the real power of the governors was effectively limited by their dependence on the colonial assemblies in almost all cases for their salaries and operating revenues.

In this situation, many governors chose simply not to "consider anything further than how to sit easy" and to be careful "to do nothing, which upon a fair hearing . . . can be blamed." Because the surest way to "sit easy" was to reach a political accommodation with local interests, they very frequently aligned themselves with dominant political factions in the colonies. Such governors sought to avoid disputes with the lower houses by taking especial care not to challenge their customary privileges and, if necessary, even quietly giving way before their demands.[1]

The powers of the assemblies, though nowhere carefully defined by charter or statute, grew steadily. In time they claimed and exercised the right to lay taxes, raise troops, incur debts, issue currency, and otherwise initiate all legislation. They commonly passed only short-term revenue bills, stipulated in detail how appropriations were to be spent, tacked riders on essential money bills, and vied with the governors for control of patronage.

Claiming prerogatives similar to those of the British House of Commons, the assemblies made the most of their power of the purse to extract concessions from the governors. When one governor asked for a fixed revenue for five years, the assembly demanded the right to appoint every official to be paid from the grant.

If the governors found it impolitic to veto certain colonial measures, such legislation still could be killed by royal decree. Acts so vetoed included those that discriminated against the various religious minorities, assessed duties on the products of neighboring colonies, authorized unbacked issues of paper currency, and restricted the burgeoning slave trade. But preventing the assemblies from taking unwanted action was not the same as winning their support for imperial projects, as the English found out during the wars they waged against the French. During these wars, English requisitions on the colonies for men, money, and supplies were honored by the assemblies slowly, if at all, especially in those colonies that did not feel threatened. The larger states, such as New York and Pennsylvania, were notori-

ous for continuing to trade with the French while France was warring with England. All of the colonies resisted imperial direction to some degree, however, and cherished their independence one from another. Not one of the state assemblies ratified the Albany Plan of Union of 1754, although it had been drafted primarily by Benjamin Franklin with the approval of representatives from seven of the thirteen colonies. The Albany Plan of Union was designed to create "one general government" in America. *(See box, The Albany Plan of Union, this page.)*

Colonial Frustrations

The French and Indian War (1754–1763) doubled the national debt of England (to £130 million) and quadrupled the prospective cost (to £300,000 a year) of administering the greatly enlarged empire in America. The result was to put the government of King George III, crowned in 1760, on a collision course with the colonies. To the mercantilists in Parliament, it now seemed logical to plug the loopholes in England's trade controls on the

---

THE ALBANY PLAN OF UNION

The Albany Congress of 1754 was initiated by the British in an effort to nail down the wavering friendship of their longtime allies, the six Indian nations of the Iroquois Confederacy. The Iroquois had come under increasing French pressure on the western frontier. The Americans who represented the seven colonies that took part—Massachusetts, New Hampshire, Connecticut, Rhode Island, New York, Pennsylvania, and Maryland—were more ambitious and adopted a Plan of Union drafted largely by Benjamin Franklin.

The plan called on Parliament to create "one general government" in America, to be administered by a president-general appointed by the Crown and a grand council of representatives from all of the colonies (in proportion to their financial contributions) elected by the assemblies. This government was to have the sole authority to regulate Indian affairs, and the power to purchase and sell new lands, raise troops for the common defense, and levy "such general duties, imposts, or taxes . . . as may be collected with the least inconvenience to the people."

Both the British government and the colonial assemblies opposed the Albany Plan as involving too large a grant of power. Britain was not prepared to give the colonies that much autonomy, while the assemblies were not ready to share their power to tax. "The different and contrary reasons of dislike to my plan made me suspect that it was really the true medium," Franklin later wrote, "and I am still of the opinion it would have been happy for both sides of the water if it had been adopted."[1]

As it was, the Albany Plan reflected a growing awareness of the need for a common approach to administration of the expanding American colonies. Rejection of the plan was a major landmark along the way to the Declaration of Independence in 1776 and the Constitutional Convention of 1787.

1. Quoted in Carl Van Doren, *Benjamin Franklin* (Westport, Conn.: Greenwood Press, 1973), 223.

COLONIAL WARS FROM 1689 TO 1763

Between 1689 and 1763 the American colonies were involved in four wars born of European conflicts and the imperial rivalries of England, France, and Spain.

At the outset, French Canada was only sparsely settled and Spanish Florida not at all, but the French had built a lucrative fur trade with the Indians throughout the Great Lakes region while La Salle had sailed down the Mississippi in 1682 and claimed Louisiana. Most of the fighting that ensued, however, involved New England and New York.

King William's War—1689–1697 (called the War of the League of Augsburg in Europe). When William of Orange became king of England, the English joined a continental alliance against Louis XIV of France. In America, French and Indian soldiers raided English settlements in New York, New Hampshire, and Maine. New Englanders captured the French base at Port Royal, Nova Scotia, but an English attempt to take Quebec failed. The Treaty of Ryswick restored Port Royal to the French.

Queen Anne's War—1702–1713 (War of the Spanish Succession). In America, the French and their Indian allies burned Deerfield and raided many other of the frontier settlements in Massachusetts and New Hampshire. The French captured the English post of St. John's, Newfoundland, while the English and colonials retook Port Royal. But expeditions against Quebec and Montreal again failed. In the Treaty of Utrecht the French accepted British sovereignty over Nova Scotia and Hudson's Bay, and the English inherited Spain's monopoly over the slave trade with its colonies.

King George's War—1745–1748 (War of the Austrian Succession). The major military event in America was the capture of Louisbourg, a French fortress on Cape Breton Island, by an army of four thousand colonial militiamen led by William Pepperell, a Maine merchant. By the Treaty of Aachen, England restored Louisbourg to France in exchange for Madras in India but paid the cost of the colonial campaign.

French and Indian War—1754–1763 (Seven Years War). In America this worldwide conflict focused on upper New York state and western Pennsylvania where the French built several forts. The English fared badly until William Pitt came to power in 1758 and reorganized the war effort under new and younger generals. The French were dislodged from Fort Duquesne (renamed Pittsburgh), Fort Niagara, and Fort Ticonderoga. The English took Quebec in 1759, and Montreal the next year. The English also defeated the French in India and the West Indies and, after Spain entered the war in 1762, took Havana and Manila.

The Peace of Paris (1763) left England the dominant power in North America. France ceded Canada and all claims east of the Mississippi to England; it gave Louisiana to Spain. England also got Spanish Florida in exchange for Havana. Manila reverted to Spanish rule.

---

colonies and to make the colonists pay a share of the costs of imperial overhead. The shift in English colonial policy began in 1763 when George Grenville became prime minister.

Grenville's first step was to set aside the claims of Virginia and other colonies to portions of the vast lands taken from the French. By the Proclamation of 1763, the entire region between the Appalachians and the Mississippi, south of Quebec and north of Florida, was reserved for the Indians. And the English adhered to this policy despite strong pressures from highly placed speculators (including Franklin) who promoted the settlement of such proposed inland colonies as Vandalia, Charlotiana, and Transylvania.

At the same time, Parliament began to strengthen enforcement of trade controls. Admiralty courts, which tried smuggling cases without juries, could now move such trials to Halifax in Nova Scotia at considerable cost to those whose goods and ships were detained. Colonial issues of paper money, which had been permitted during the war, were banned by the Currency Act of 1764. And to lighten the British tax load, Grenville pushed three other laws through Parliament.

The Revenue Act of 1764, designed to defray the expenses of defending, protecting, and securing the colonies, cut in half the widely evaded duty laid on foreign molasses in 1733 but placed new duties on such colonial imports as wine, silk, and linen. It also enumerated more colonial products, including hides and skins, that could be exported only to England.

The Quartering Act of 1765 required the colonies to contribute to the upkeep of the ten thousand troops England planned to station in America. The colonies were to supply them with barracks or other quarters and with some of their provisions.

The Stamp Act of 1765 required that revenue stamps costing up to twenty shillings be affixed to all licenses, legal documents, leases, notes and bonds, newspapers, pamphlets, almanacs, advertisements, and other documents issued in the colonies. Passed on March 22, the law was to take effect November 1 and was expected to yield £60,000 a year.

None of these measures sat well with the Americans, but opposition focused on the Stamp Act as the first direct tax ever laid on the colonies by Parliament. Americans felt they could be taxed only by their own assemblies and that the Stamp Act, which was taxation without representation, was unconstitutional. The Virginia House of Burgesses so resolved at the urging of Patrick Henry, while the Massachusetts House of Representatives called for the convening of an intercolonial conference.

The Stamp Act Congress, held in New York in October 1765, was attended by twenty-eight delegates from nine colonies. They affirmed their allegiance to the Crown, asserted their right as English subjects not to be taxed without their consent, noted that the colonists were not represented in the House of Commons, and concluded that "no taxes ever have been or can be constitutionally imposed on them, but by their respective legislatures." The delegates urged Parliament to repeal the Stamp Act and other recent laws that had "a manifest tendency to subvert the rights and liberties of the colonists."

Grenville insisted that Parliament represented and acted in behalf of all English subjects. But he could not ignore the sharp drop in exports that followed a colonial boycott of English goods or the attacks on royal officials by colonial mobs calling themselves "Sons of Liberty." When it became clear in 1766 that the Stamp Act could not be enforced, it was repealed. But Parliament, through a declaratory act, asserted its authority to legislate for the colonies "in all cases whatsoever" and declared colonial resolves to the contrary to be "utterly null and void."[2]

The Intolerable Acts

After repeal of the Stamp Act, Chancellor of the Exchequer Charles Townshend proposed an increase in customs receipts as a way of raising the needed revenue. Parliament passed laws in 1767 laying new duties on imports by the colonies of paper, lead, glass, paint, and tea; reorganizing the customs service in America; and authorizing broad use of general search warrants, known as Writs of Assistance, to ferret out violations. The Townshend Acts were greeted by a new outbreak of protests. Colonial merchants revived their nonimportation agreements, and the adverse effect on English business again persuaded Parliament to retreat. When Lord North came to power in 1770, all of the Townshend duties except the one on tea were repealed. Most of the colonists were appeased, trade revived, and for three years England and the colonies lived in relative harmony.

To American radicals such as Samuel Adams of Massachusetts, this period of calm foreshadowed a further attack on colonial liberties. The English had begun to pay the salaries of the royal governors and other officials from their increased customs receipts, thus freeing them from the hold of the assemblies. Adams, Patrick Henry, Thomas Jefferson, and many others, who now questioned the right of Parliament to legislate for the colonies in any respect, formed committees of correspondence that became the underground of the colonial resistance movement.

The quiet years ended abruptly in 1773 when the faltering East India Company was authorized to dump a surplus of tea on the American colonies by undercutting the price of tea smuggled in from Holland. Colonial merchants, foreseeing ruinous competition, joined the radicals in protesting the Tea Act, and virtual unanimity existed in the colonies in favor of boycotting the first shipments. In Boston, however, Adams and John Hancock urged direct action, and on December 16, 1773, a mob disguised as Indians boarded three tea ships and dumped their cargoes into the harbor.

The "Boston Tea Party" alarmed many Americans who opposed British policy, and it also provoked the English government into a series of coercive acts that drove the colonists together. On March 26, 1774, the House of Commons ordered the port of Boston closed until the city paid for the tea thrown into the harbor. That order was followed by laws revising the Massa-

Considered America's first political cartoon, this drawing by Benjamin Franklin presented two stark options to the colonies—join together and become a formidable force or perish separately.

chusetts charter to strengthen England's authority and transferring to England the trials of colonists charged with murder.

To these Intolerable Acts, as the colonists dubbed them, Parliament added one that alienated most of Protestant America by giving to the French-Canadian—and Catholic—royal province of Quebec all of the land west of the Appalachians lying north of the Ohio River and east of the Mississippi. The Quebec Act of June 22, 1774, was regarded as another punitive measure by most colonists and helped to muster broad support for a "general congress of all the colonies" proposed by the Virginia and Massachusetts assemblies.

First Continental Congress

Every colony except Georgia, whose governor blocked the selection of delegates, was represented at the First Continental Congress, which met in Philadelphia on September 5, 1774. Describing the Congress in a letter to his wife, John Adams wrote: "The business of the Congress is tedious beyond expression. This assembly is like no other that ever existed. . . . Every man upon every question must show his oratory, his criticism, and his political ability."[3] Conservative Joseph Galloway of Pennsylvania hoped to conciliate the English, while radical Samuel Adams wanted to defy all British controls. As the session continued, more and more delegates joined in the movement to protest and repudiate British policies toward the colonies.

The turning point came when Paul Revere arrived with the Suffolk Resolves, adopted by a convention of towns around Boston, which called on Massachusetts to arm itself against efforts to "enslave America" and urged the Congress to adopt economic sanctions against England. To Galloway, these "inflammatory resolves . . . contained a complete declaration of war against Great Britain." Others agreed with Galloway, but most delegates felt compelled to register their support of Massachusetts. By a vote of six colonies to five, they set aside Galloway's plan (based on the Albany Plan of Union of 1754) to give

Parliament and a colonial legislature joint control over American affairs and endorsed the Suffolk Resolves.

The Congress then adopted a Declaration of Rights and Grievances against all British acts to which "Americans cannot submit" and approved a wide-ranging nonimportation, non-consumption, and nonexportation agreement as "the most speedy, effectual, and peaceable" means of swaying England. Locally elected committees were directed to enforce this commercial boycott by publicizing violations so that "all such foes to the rights of British-America may be publicly known and universally condemned as the enemies of American liberty." On October 22, 1774, the Continental Congress adjourned, after agreeing to meet again the following May if necessary.

King George III declared that the colonies were "now in a state of rebellion; blows must decide whether they are to be subject to this country or independent." While the Earl of Chatham and Edmund Burke hoped conciliation was possible, they held firmly to "the view that the British Parliament was supreme over the colonies, that the authority of the empire could not be surrendered."[4] In the colonies patriot forces began to gather arms and supplies and to train militia. In Massachusetts, rebels soon controlled all of the colony except Boston, where the governor, Gen. Thomas Gage, was installed with five thousand English troops.

On April 19, 1775, Gage sent one thousand of his soldiers to destroy the patriots' stores in Lexington and Concord. They were met by Minutemen, and shooting broke out. British casualties were 247 dead and wounded before Gage's forces could get back to Boston. This encounter turned out to be the opening shots of the Revolutionary War, although more than a year would pass before the Americans were sufficiently united to declare their independence.

REVOLUTION AND CONFEDERATION

When the Second Continental Congress met on May 10, 1775, in Philadelphia, most of the delegates still hoped to avoid war with England and were reluctant to opt for independence. But faced with pleas for help from Massachusetts, the delegates agreed in mid-June to raise a Continental Army of twenty thousand men, to ask the colonies for $2 million (in proportion to their population) for the army's support, and to make George Washington, a delegate from Virginia, the army's commander in chief.

The Congress, however, also approved a petition to George III drafted by John Dickinson asking for "a happy and permanent reconciliation" between the colonies and England. The delegates also adopted a Declaration of the Causes of Necessity of Taking up Arms, drafted by Dickinson and Jefferson, in which they disavowed any desire for independence but resolved "to die free men rather than live slaves."

King George's response of August 23 was to proclaim a state of rebellion in America. The British began to hire mercenaries in Germany and to incite the Iroquois against the colonials, while Congress authorized an expedition against Canada and

efforts to contact other nations for aid. Yet the legislatures of five of the colonies took positions against independence that autumn. Pennsylvania's delegation to the Continental Congress was told to "utterly reject any proposition . . . that may cause or lead to a separation from our mother country or a change in the form of this government."

The British gave no signs of retreating, however, and the appearance in January 1776 of Thomas Paine's pamphlet "Common Sense" further spurred the rising demand for independence. Paine argued that it was time for Americans to stand on their own feet, for there was "something absurd in supporting a continent to be perpetually governed by an island," and "it is evident that they belong to different systems: England to Europe, America to itself." Paine also put the onus for the colonies' troubles on King George rather than Parliament.

Declaration of Independence

Pressure on the Congress to act reached a climax on June 7, 1776, when Richard Henry Lee of Virginia introduced a resolution stating that "these United Colonies are, and of right ought to be, free and independent States." Jefferson, Adams, Franklin, Roger Sherman, and Robert Livingston were named to draw up a declaration, but it was largely Jefferson's draft that was presented on June 28. Lee's resolution was adopted on July 2; Jefferson's Declaration then was debated and slightly amended (to strike out an indictment of the British slave trade, for example) before it was approved July 4 by all of the delegations to the Congress except New York's, which later voted for it after receiving new instructions.

The greater part of the Declaration—and the most important to Americans at that time—consisted of a recitation of every grievance against English colonial policy that had emerged since 1763. The grievances were presented as facts to prove that George III was seeking "the establishment of an absolute Tyranny over these States" and to justify the colonists' decision to dissolve "all political connection" with Britain. But the preamble was to exert the greatest influence on others as a statement of political philosophy with universal appeal. Rooted in the concept of natural rights as developed by such English philosophers as Thomas Hooker and John Locke, the preamble made these assertions:

We hold these truths to be self-evident, that all men are created equal, that they are endowed by their Creator with certain unalienable Rights, that among these are Life, Liberty, and the pursuit of Happiness. That to secure these rights, Governments are instituted among Men, deriving their just powers from the consent of the governed. That whenever any Form of Government becomes destructive of these ends it is the Right of the People to alter or to abolish it, and to institute new Government, laying its foundation on such principles and organizing its powers in such form, as to them shall seem most likely to effect their Safety and Happiness.

In conclusion, the signers, who styled themselves "the Representatives of the United States of America, in General Congress, Assembled," declared that "these United Colonies are, and of Right ought to be Free and Independent States," that as such

Those Americans who waged and won the Revolutionary War did so under severe handicaps. Many of the colonists—one-third of them, said John Adams; four-fifths, said Loyalist Joseph Galloway—were opposed to the cause of independence to the end, and more than a few collaborated openly with the British. Apathy was widespread and parochialism common; those not in the direct line of fire were often unwilling either to fight the war or to help pay for it.

As commander in chief, George Washington was plagued by problems of raising and maintaining an effective military force. At no time did he have more than about thirty thousand men under arms, less than half of whom had enlisted for three years. The balance were militia, signed up for as little as three months.

The Continental Congress assumed responsibility for prosecuting the war, but it had no power to tax or to compel actions by the states, and it was no more successful than the British in its requisitions for money and supplies for the colonial armies. The war was financed largely by paper money—some $240 million in national bills and $210 million in state bills—which depreciated to the point of being worthless. Without subsidies and loans of about $8 million from France, and French military intervention in 1778, the war might have been lost.

England also was sharply divided by the war, however, and the opposition increased in Parliament as time went on. The British were forced to hire thirty thousand mercenaries in Germany to supplement the fifteen thousand regulars sent to America. The transport, supply, and direction of such a force over a distance of three thousand miles was even more difficult after France entered the war. Major developments in the war were:

1775. Washington took command after the Battle of Bunker Hill (June 17); the British occupied Boston until they evacuated the city March 17, 1776. Meanwhile, Americans under Ethan Allen and Benedict Arnold took Montreal on November 13. But they were badly beaten at Quebec (December 31).

1776. After a buildup of forces at Halifax and in Quebec, the British launched three campaigns. General Clinton sailed for the Carolinas but was beaten off at Charleston June 28 and withdrew. Generals Carleton and Burgoyne marched for Albany but were stopped at Fort Ticonderoga in October. General Howe sailed for New York and inflicted heavy losses on Washington in several battles there; New York stayed in British hands from September 15 to the end of the war. Washington retreated across the Delaware, recrossing it the night of December 25 to surprise and capture one thousand Hessians at Trenton. He then set up winter quarters at Morristown with fewer than five thousand men.

1777. In August Howe sailed up the Chesapeake Bay with fifteen thousand men, defeated Washington at Brandywine Creek, and oc-

cupied Philadelphia September 25. Washington set up winter quarters at Valley Forge. Meanwhile, Burgoyne launched a two-pronged attack on Albany, suffered a series of reverses in August and September, and surrendered October 17 at Saratoga with five thousand men. His defeat led to a French-American treaty of alliance, signed February 6, 1778.

1778. The British offered wide concessions to end the war short of independence, but Congress rejected the offer June 17. Clinton evacuated Philadelphia, moving back to New York. No decisive battles were fought.

1779. The British captured Savannah December 29, 1778, and took control of Georgia, but Americans under Benjamin Lincoln successfully defended Charleston. However, Lincoln's attempt to retake Savannah, with the help of the French fleet, failed October 9. Spain joined the war against England June 21 but did not enter into alliance with the Americans.

1780. Long unpaid and underfed, American troops in Morristown, New Jersey, mutinied. On May 12 the British captured Charleston and five thousand troops—the worst American defeat of the war. Benedict Arnold defected to the British in September.

1781. The South was the major fighting arena. Americans under Nathanael Greene beat Lord Cornwallis at Cowpens, South Carolina, on January 17. In July Cornwallis moved north with seven thousand men to fortify Yorktown, Virginia. More than fifteen thousand American and French troops converged there in September and surrounded the town on land and sea; Cornwallis surrendered on October 17.

1782. The House of Commons resolved on March 4 to give up the struggle. Lord North resigned, and a new government asked for peace talks. Congress named John Adams, envoy to the Netherlands, John Jay, envoy to Spain, Benjamin Franklin, envoy to Paris, and Henry Laurens to negotiate jointly with the French. Jay, suspicious of the French, who supported Spanish claims in America, persuaded the others to enter separate negotiations with the British in September. On November 30, a preliminary treaty was signed pending an Anglo-French accord.

1783. The Treaty of Paris was signed September 3 and approved by Congress on January 14, 1784. It validated the former colonies' independence and claims to the West, fixed the boundary with Canada along the St. Lawrence and the Great Lakes, and retained American fishing rights around Newfoundland. It also validated private debts to England and stated that Congress would "earnestly recommend" to the states that they restore property confiscated from Tories. England then gave West and East Florida back to Spain. The last British troops left New York November 25. Washington resigned December 23 to take "leave of all the employments of public life."

John Trumbull's *Declaration of Independence* illustrates John Adams, Roger Sherman, Robert Livingston, Thomas Jefferson, and Benjamin Franklin presenting the document to Congress for signatures on July 4, 1776.

"they have full Power to levy War, conclude Peace, contract Alliances, establish Commerce, and to do all other Acts and Things which Independent States may of right do," and that in support of this stand "we mutually pledge to each other our Lives, our Fortunes, and our Sacred Honor."

Formation of State Governments

The Declaration of Independence committed the colonies to wage a war that was already under way and that would drag on for more than five years before England gave up the struggle. The Declaration also put an end to tolerance of the many Americans who remained loyal to the king. Tories who refused to sign an oath of allegiance to the United States suffered imprisonment and confiscation of property; as many as eighty thousand fled to Canada and England. At home, the Declaration put to immediate test the capacity of the patriots to govern.

As early as the fall of 1774 Massachusetts had set up a provisional government in response to the Intolerable Acts. As revolutionary sentiment grew, patriots took control of provincial as-

semblies and conventions, and the royal governors and judges began to leave. New Hampshire adopted a constitution in January 1776, South Carolina followed suit in March, and on May 10 the Continental Congress advised all of the colonies to form new governments. All except Massachusetts and the self-governing charter colonies of Connecticut and Rhode Island had done so by July 4, 1777, the first anniversary of the signing of the Declaration of Independence. Four days later, Vermont, not previously a separate colony, declared its independence and adopted a constitution. Connecticut and Rhode Island did not get around to replacing their colonial charters with state constitutions until 1818 and 1842, respectively.

The new state constitutions of the Revolutionary period emerged in various ways. Those of South Carolina, Virginia, and New Jersey were drafted by legislative bodies without explicit authorization and put into effect without popular consent. Those of New Hampshire, Georgia, Delaware, New York, and Vermont were authorized but were not submitted to the voters for approval. In Maryland, Pennsylvania, and North Carolina the constitutions were authorized and ratified by the voters. Only Massachusetts and New Hampshire (which wrote a new constitution in 1784 to replace the one adopted in 1776) employed what was to become the standard method of electing a constitutional convention and putting the product to a vote of the people.

Although they varied in detail, the new constitutions reflected a number of concepts held in common by Americans of the period. All were written, because the unwritten British constitution had become a source of such great contention between the colonists and England. All included or were accompanied by some kind of "Bill of Rights" to secure those English liberties that George III had violated, such as freedom of speech, press, and petition and the rights of habeas corpus and trial by jury. All paid tribute to the doctrine of separation of powers among the legislative, executive, and judiciary, as it had been developed in England after the revolution of 1688 and expounded by Montesquieu's *Spirit of Laws*, published in 1748.

Separation did not mean balance, however, and most of the constitutions betrayed the colonists' great fear of executive authority, born of their many conflicts with the Crown and the royal governors. Executive power was weakened in every state except New York, Massachusetts, and New Hampshire, and the governors of only two states were given the power of veto. In most cases the state legislature appointed the judiciary, although efforts were made to protect the independence of judges by preventing their arbitrary removal.

Power under most of the colonial constitutions was lodged in the state legislatures. Ten of these were bicameral (Pennsylvania, Georgia, and Vermont had one house), with the lower house predominant. Virginia's constitution provided, for example, that "All laws shall originate in the House of Delegates, to be approved of or rejected by the Senate, or to be amended, with consent of the House of Delegates; except money bills, which in no instance shall be altered by the Senate, but wholly approved or rejected."[5]

All of the constitutions recognized the people as sovereign, but few entrusted them with much power. The Pennsylvania constitution (copied by Vermont), written by radicals who came to power early in 1776 after a major reapportionment of the colonial assembly, was the most democratic. It replaced the governor and the upper chamber with an executive council, from whose ranks a president was chosen. Its members could serve no more than three years in seven while assemblymen were limited to four years in seven, to guard against establishing an aristocracy. There were no property qualifications for voting or for holding office.

Most other states adhered to prerevolutionary limits on suffrage. Ownership of some amount of property was generally required as a qualification to vote and more usually was required to hold office. The property qualification to become a state senator in New Jersey and Maryland was £1,000; in South Carolina, £2,000. Most states also imposed religious qualifications for public office.

FIRST STATE CONSTITUTIONS

State	Date Adopted
New Hampshire (1st)	January 6, 1776
South Carolina (1st)	March 26, 1776
Virginia	June 29, 1776
New Jersey	July 2, 1776
Delaware	August 22, 1776
Pennsylvania	September 28, 1776
Maryland	November 11, 1776
North Carolina	December 18, 1776
Georgia	February 5, 1777
New York	April 20, 1777
Vermont[1]	July 8, 1777
South Carolina (2nd)	March 19, 1778
Massachusetts	June 15, 1780
New Hampshire (2nd)	June 13, 1784

1. Vermont became a state in 1791.

Articles of Confederation

When Richard Henry Lee called for a declaration of independence on June 7, 1776, he proposed also that "a plan of confederation be prepared and transmitted to the respective Colonies for their consideration and approbation." On June 11 Congress agreed and named a committee of thirteen (one from each colony) to undertake the task. The plan that was recommended, based on a draft by John Dickinson of Delaware, was presented on July 12, but it was not until November 15, 1777, that Congress, after much debate and some revision, adopted the Articles of Confederation and Perpetual Union.

The Articles reflected the dominant motive of Americans who were rebelling against British rule: to preserve their freedoms from the encroachments of centralized power. Even as the Congress set up under the Articles was struggling with tenuous authority to prosecute the war (and it gave Washington dictatorial powers over the army in December 1776), few of the delegates or other American leaders were prepared to entrust a national government with any power that would diminish the sovereignty and independence of the states. Thus the scope of federal authority was not a central consideration in the design of the confederation.

What was at issue was the relative standing of thirteen rival and jealous states. Would they be represented equally in the national legislature, as they were in the Continental Congress and as the smaller states desired, or in proportion to their population, as the larger states wished? The cost of a national government would have to be shared, but on what basis—wealth, the total population of each state, or, as the southerners insisted, on the white population only? States without claims to lands west of the Appalachians thought Congress should control the area; those with claims were reluctant to give them up.

As finally adopted, the Articles conferred less authority on the national government than had the proposal envisioned by the Albany Plan of Union of 1754. The Articles did little more than legalize what Congress already was doing by sufferance of the states. The Congress remained the sole organ of government; the states retained their equality, each having one vote; and of the specific powers delegated to Congress, the most important could not be exercised without the assent of nine of the thirteen states.

The delegated authority included the power to declare war, enter treaties and alliances, raise an army and a navy, regulate coinage, and borrow money. Congress also was empowered to regulate Indian affairs, establish a postal service, and adjudicate disputes between the states. But it had no power to tax (other than to charge postage); the costs of government would be allocated to the states in proportion to the value of their land and improvements as determined by Congress. The states also were to be assigned quotas for troops in proportion to the number of white inhabitants. But Congress was not empowered to compel compliance.

The Articles provided that Congress was to be composed of from two to seven delegates from each of the states (and from Canada if it chose to join). The delegates were to be selected annually and paid by the states, but they could serve for no more than three years in any six. Members of Congress were barred from holding any federal post for pay and were immune from arrest while in attendance and from legal action for anything said in debate—provisions that later were incorporated in the Constitution. A Committee of the States (with one delegate from each) was authorized to act for Congress during a recess on matters that did not require the assent of nine states.

Congress was authorized to appoint committees and civil officers necessary for managing the affairs of the United States. After ratification of the Articles of Confederation, Livingston was named secretary of foreign affairs, Robert Morris became superintendent of finance, and Gen. Benjamin Lincoln was appointed secretary of war. But the Articles made no provision for a federal executive or judiciary, and they gave Congress no sanction by which to enforce any of its decisions. Control of taxation and tariffs was left to the states, and unanimous consent of the states was required for the adoption of amendments.

Final ratification was delayed by the reluctance of Maryland, New Jersey, and Delaware to act until the states with western claims agreed to cede them to the national government. Cession of state claims did not begin until 1784, but it was clear by the beginning of 1781 that the states would cede, and Maryland, the last holdout, ratified the Articles on March 1, 1781. Congress proclaimed them to be in effect the same day.

Defects of the Confederation

Adoption of the Articles of Confederation did nothing to relieve the chaotic state of federal finances. Of $10 million requisitioned by Congress in the first two years, the states paid in less than $1.5 million. From 1781 to 1786 federal collections averaged half a million dollars a year, which was barely enough to meet current expenses. After two years as superintendent of finance, Morris resigned in 1783, saying "our public credit is gone." The foreign debt of the United States increased from less than $8 million in 1783 to more than $10 million in 1789, plus almost $1.8 million in unpaid interest.

Congress recognized the need for some independent financial authority even before the Articles took effect. Early in 1781 it had asked the states for authority to levy a duty of 5 percent on all imports. But it took unanimous agreement to amend the Articles, and the proposal died in 1782 when Rhode Island rejected it. In 1783 Congress again asked for the power to levy import duties, and this time New York refused to give its approval.

Peace put an end to the destruction and drain of war, but it also underscored the weakness and disunity of the now sovereign and independent American states. As agreed in the peace treaty with England, Congress in 1783 recommended that the states restore the property confiscated from the Loyalists, but few of them took any steps to do so. And instead of helping British merchants to recover their prewar debts (as the treaty obligated them to do), many of the states enacted laws making recovery more difficult. The British, in turn, refused to evacuate several posts on the American side of the border with Canada.

The inability of Congress to force the states to comply with terms of the peace treaty contributed to the refusal of England, France, and Spain to enter commercial treaties with the Confederation. Lacking any authority over trade, Congress was unable to retaliate when the British in 1783 closed Canada and the British West Indies to American shipping; the attempts of the states to retaliate individually failed completely. The weakness of the Confederation also encouraged Spain to close the Mississippi River to American ships in 1784 and to intrigue for the secession of frontier areas north of the Floridas.

Congress was equally powerless to help resolve a postwar conflict between debtors and creditors that was aggravated by an economic depression and a shortage of currency. Most of the states stopped issuing paper money and set out to pay off their war debts by raising taxes. At the same time, merchants and other creditors began to press for the collection of private debts. Squeezed on all sides, debtors (who were mostly farmers) clamored for relief through state laws to put off the collection of debts and to provide cheap money.

In response to this pressure, seven of the states resorted to paper money issues in 1786, during the worst of the depression. Debtors put over their entire program in Rhode Island where creditors, compelled by law to accept repayment in highly depreciated paper money, fled the state to avoid doing so. But in Massachusetts, where the commercial class was in power, the state government refused to issue paper money and pressed forward with a deflationary program of high taxes; cattle and land were seized for debts, debtors crowded the jails, and all petitions for relief were ignored.

Out of this turmoil came Shays's Rebellion of 1786, an uprising of distressed farmers in central Massachusetts led by Daniel Shays. Although the rebellion was put down by state militia in fairly short order, a good deal of sympathy was evident for the rebels. Their leaders were treated leniently, and a newly elected legislature acted to meet some of their demands. But the rebellion aroused the fears of many Americans for the future, and it pointed up another weakness of the Confederation—Congress had been unable to give Massachusetts any help. The rebellion also gave a strong push to the growing movement for governmental reform.

The Constitution: Breaking the Bonds

The state of the Union under the Articles of Confederation had become a source of growing concern to leading Americans well before Shays's Rebellion shook the confidence of a wider public. In voluminous correspondence beginning as early as 1780, George Washington, John Jay, Thomas Jefferson, James Madison, James Monroe, and many others expressed their fears that the Union could not survive the strains of internal dissension and external weakness without some strengthening of central authority.

To Washington, writing in 1783, it was clear "that the honor, power, and true interest of this country must be measured by a Continental scale, and that every departure therefrom weakens the Union, and may ultimately break the band which holds us together. To avert these evils, to form a Constitution that will give consistency, stability, and dignity to the Union and sufficient powers to the great Council of the Nation for general purposes" was a challenge to every patriot.[6]

How to form such a constitution was not yet clear. Opinions varied widely as to what would be "sufficient powers . . . for general purposes." Alexander Hamilton, in 1780, thought Congress should be given "complete sovereignty" over all but a few matters. But Congress had ignored proposals of its committees in 1781 that it seek authority to use troops "to compel any delinquent State to fulfill its Federal engagement" and to seize "the property of a State delinquent in its assigned proportion of men and money." While general agreement existed on congressional authority to levy a federal import duty, the effort to amend the Articles foundered on the rule of unanimity.

At Hamilton's urging, the New York Assembly asked Congress in 1782 to call a general convention of the states to revise the Articles. The Massachusetts Legislature seconded the request in 1785. Congress studied the proposal but was unable to reach any agreement. Then, Virginia and Maryland in 1785 worked out a plan to resolve conflicts between the two states over navigation and commercial regulations. This gave Madison the idea of calling a general meeting on commercial problems. In January 1786 the Virginia Assembly issued the call for a meeting in Annapolis in September.

Nine states named delegates to the Annapolis convention, but the dozen persons who assembled represented only five states—New York, New Jersey, Pennsylvania, Delaware, and Virginia. Instead of seeking a commercial agreement from so small a group, Madison and Hamilton persuaded the delegates on

An organizer of the convention, James Madison was among those who felt that the fledgling nation needed a strong federal government to survive. Often called the "Father of the Constitution," Madison provided the "Virginia Plan" that served as the basis for debate on how to form the new government.

September 14 to adopt a report that described the state of the Union as "delicate and critical." The report recommended that the states appoint commissioners to meet the next May in Philadelphia "to devise such further provisions as shall appear to them necessary to render the constitution of the Federal Government adequate to the exigencies of the Union."

The proposal was deliberately vague. Madison and Hamilton knew strong opposition existed to giving the central government much more power. And some officials, they knew, preferred the alternative of dividing the Union into two or more confederations of states with closer economic and political ties. Southerners were convinced that this was the ultimate objective of John Jay's offer to Spain to give up free navigation of the Mississippi in return for trading concessions of interest to New England. Monroe, a Virginia delegate to Congress, saw it as part of a scheme "for dismembering the Confederacy and throwing the states eastward of the Hudson into one government."

The Virginia Assembly, prodded by Madison and Washington, agreed on October 16, 1786, to send delegates to Philadelphia, and six other states took similar action before Congress, on February 21, 1787, moved to retain control of the situation. It passed a resolution endorsing the proposed convention for the purpose of reporting to Congress and the several legislatures on its recommendations. Officially, therefore, the convention was to be no more than advisory to Congress.

THE CONVENTION ASSEMBLES

Soon after the Philadelphia convention opened on May 25, 1787, the delegates were asked to decide whether to try to patch up the Articles of Confederation or to ignore them and draw up a new plan of government.

Congress, the state legislatures, and many of the delegates expected the session in Philadelphia to do no more than draft proposals to revise the Articles in a way that would somehow strengthen the Confederation without altering the system of state sovereignty. But Madison and others who had worked to bring about the convention were convinced of the need for fundamental reform.

The Virginia Plan

These nationalists had come prepared, and on May 29 they seized the initiative. Edmund Randolph, acting for the Virginians, introduced fifteen resolutions that added up to a plan for a new "National Government" of broad powers. The Virginia Plan called for a "National Legislature" of two houses, one to be elected by the people and the other by members of the first; a "National Executive" to be chosen by the Legislature; and a "National Judiciary." The legislature would have power to legislate in all cases where the states were "incompetent" or would interrupt "the harmony of the United States" and to "negate" state laws contrary to the Articles of union. And the states would be represented in both chambers in proportion to their wealth or their white population.[7]

The convention moved at once into Committee of the Whole to consider the Randolph resolutions. The proposals clearly envisaged a central government that, unlike that of the Confederation, would operate directly upon the people and independently of the states. It was to be a "national government" in contrast to the "merely federal" system that had been tried and found wanting. What the Virginians had in mind, though, was a system in which national and state governments would exercise dual sovereignty over the people within separate and prescribed fields. Randolph said that his plan "only means to give the national government power to defend and protect itself—to take, therefore, from the respective legislatures of states no more sovereignty than is competent to this end."

Such a dual system was unknown in 1787. To many delegates the term "national government" implied a unitary or consolidated regime of potentially unlimited powers that would extinguish the independence of the states. However, on May 30, with only Connecticut opposed and New York divided, they adopted Randolph's proposition "that a National Government ought to be established consisting of a supreme Legislative, Executive, and Judiciary." This opening commitment by most of the delegates then present reflected the air of crisis in which they met.[8]

The next step of the Committee of the Whole was to take up and approve several of the specific proposals of the Virginia Plan. As the debate proceeded, some members from smaller states became alarmed by the insistence of the larger states on proportional representation in both houses of the proposed Legislature. Under one formula, this would have given Virginia, Pennsylvania, and Massachusetts—the three most populous states—thirteen of twenty-eight seats in the Senate as well as a similar share of seats in the House. This spelled domination to those accustomed to the equality of states that prevailed in the Congress of the Confederation and in the convention as well.

To Luther Martin of Maryland, such a plan meant "a system of slavery which bound hand and foot ten states of the Union and placed them at the mercy of the other three." Dickinson declared that "we would rather submit to a foreign power than submit to be deprived of an equality of suffrage in both branches of the Legislature, and thereby be thrown under the domination of the large states." New Jersey would "never confederate" on such a basis, said William Paterson, for "she would be swallowed up" and he would "rather submit to a monarch, to a despot, than to such a fate."

The New Jersey Plan

On June 11 the convention voted six states to five to constitute the Senate on the same proportional basis as the House. That decision led Paterson and others to draft a purely federal alternative to the Virginia Plan. The New Jersey Plan, presented June 15, proposed amending the Articles of Confederation to give Congress authority to levy import duties and to regulate trade. It also would have provided for a plural executive, to be chosen by Congress, and a federal judiciary. It proposed that treaties and acts of Congress "shall be the supreme law" and that the executive be authorized to "call forth the power of the Confederated States" to enforce the laws if necessary. But the plan would have left each state with an equal voice in Congress and most of the attributes of sovereignty.

Paterson argued that his plan "accorded first with the powers of the convention, and second with the sentiments of the people. . . . Our object is not such a Government as may be best in itself, but such a one as our constituents have authorized us to prepare and as they will approve."

The nationalists rejected this concept of their responsibility. As Hamilton put it, the Union was in peril and "to rely on and propose any plan not adequate to these exigencies, merely because it was not clearly within our powers, would be to sacrifice the means to the end."

Madison was the last to speak against the New Jersey Plan, pointing up serious problems of the Confederation for which it offered no solution. On June 19 the delegates were asked to decide whether the Randolph resolutions "should be adhered to as preferable to those of Mr. Paterson." Seven states voted yes and only three states no. That settled the issue of partial versus total reform; a clear majority of the delegates were now committed to abandoning the Articles and to drafting a new constitution.

The Great Compromise

The task was to take three months. Few points of unanimity existed among the fifty-five men participating. Delegates from

All of the states except Rhode Island (whose upper house balked) were represented at the Constitutional Convention of 1787. The states appointed a total of seventy-four delegates, but only fifty-five attended. On May 14, when the convention was scheduled to open at the State House in Philadelphia, only the delegates from Virginia and Pennsylvania were on hand. It was May 25 before delegates from a majority of the states (seven) had arrived and the twenty-nine delegates present could organize. From that time until the Constitutional Convention finished its work on September 17, the comings and goings of delegates held the average attendance to little more than thirty.

DELEGATES

The fifty-five delegates who took part included many of the most distinguished men in America. Eight had signed the Declaration of Independence, seven had been governors of their respective states, and thirty-nine had served in the Congress of the Confederation. More than half were college graduates and at least thirty-three were attorneys. Most of them had held prominent positions in the Revolutionary War and all were men of position and substance in their states. A majority were under the age of fifty (five were under thirty) and only four were sixty or older.

George Washington, then fifty-five, and Benjamin Franklin, the oldest delegate at eighty-one, were the most influential Americans of the time.

General Washington, who had not wanted to participate at the convention as a delegate but had yielded for fear that his absence might be construed as indifference to the outcome, was the unanimous choice to preside over the proceedings, in which role he took a limited but effective part in the deliberations.

Those credited with the greatest influence at the convention were Gouverneur Morris and James Wilson of Pennsylvania, James Madison of Virginia, and Roger Sherman of Connecticut, each of whom spoke over one hundred times. Others who took leading roles were George Mason and Edmund Randolph of Virginia, Oliver Ellsworth of Connecticut, Rufus King and Elbridge Gerry of Massachusetts, John Rutledge and Charles Pinckney of South Carolina, Alexander Hamilton of New York, John Dickinson of Delaware, and William Paterson of New Jersey.

Prominent men of the period who were not delegates included John Jay, who was serving as secretary of foreign affairs, and America's envoys to France and England—Thomas Jefferson and John Adams. Also missing were many leaders of the American Revolution: Samuel Adams, Patrick Henry, John Hancock, Christopher Gadsden, and Richard Henry Lee.

RULES

The convention adopted its rules of procedure on May 28 and 29. There was some talk of the larger states getting more votes than the smaller, but the convention followed the custom under the Articles of Confederation in giving one vote to each state. The rule provided that seven states would constitute a quorum and that "all questions should be decided by a majority of the states which shall be fully represented." This rule was amended to permit reconsideration of any vote—a step taken many times during the convention.

Reconsideration was made easier by a rule of secrecy providing that "nothing spoken in the House [was to] be printed or otherwise published or communicated without leave." Most delegates agreed with Madison, who had written to Jefferson that secrecy was needed "to secure unbiased discussion within doors and to prevent misconceptions and misconstructions without." The press was critical, but the delegates abided by the rule. The official journal, limited to a report of formal motions and votes, was closed until 1819. Madison's shorthand notes, withheld until 1840, provided the fullest account.

PROCEDURE

The convention began by moving into committee of the whole to debate the Virginia resolutions, a proposal that called for a national government with a bicameral legislature, an executive, and a judiciary. The smaller states then rallied behind the New Jersey Plan, which proposed only modest revisions in the Articles of Confederation. After that plan was defeated June 19, the members reverted to convention, and a threatened deadlock was broken by the "Great Compromise" of July 16 giving each state an equal vote in the Senate.

On July 24 a Committee of Detail (Nathaniel Gorham of Massachusetts, Ellsworth, Wilson, Randolph, and Rutledge) was appointed to draft a constitution based on agreements already reached. The convention took a ten-day recess during which Washington went fishing near Valley Forge. The draft presented August 6 included changes and additions that were discussed and refined through the following month. On September 8 another committee (composed of William S. Johnson of Connecticut, Hamilton, Gouverneur Morris, Madison, and King) was named to revise the style and arrange the articles that had been agreed to. The final document, published by Morris, was put before the convention on September 17.

THE SIGNING

At this point, Franklin said: "There are several parts of this Constitution which I do not at present approve, but I am not sure I shall never approve them." He would accept the Constitution, he said, "because I expect no better and because I am not sure that it is not the best." And he hoped that "every member of the Convention who may still have objections to it, would, with me, on this occasion doubt a little of his own infallibility, and to make manifest our unanimity, put his name to this instrument."

Franklin then moved that the Constitution be signed by the unanimous consent of the states present. The motion was approved as was one final change increasing representation in the House from one member for every forty thousand inhabitants to one for every thirty thousand—a change supported by Washington, in his only speech of the convention. The Constitution then was signed by all but three of the forty-two delegates still in attendance on the final day: Mason and Randolph of Virginia and Gerry of Massachusetts. After agreeing that the Constitution should be submitted to special conventions of the states for ratification, the convention adjourned.

the same state frequently were divided; as a result, states occasionally were unable to cast votes on constitutional proposals. The records of the convention also reveal that, although the nationalists won over a majority to their cause at an early stage, the original Virginia Plan was unacceptable in many of its details. The Constitution could not have been written without some degree of willingness on all sides to compromise in the interests of designing a workable and acceptable plan.

One student of the convention has described the sometimes haphazard way in which delegates finally reached an agreement in this way: "Drawing on their vast collective political experience, employing every weapon in the politician's arsenal, looking constantly over their shoulders at their constituents, the delegates put together a Constitution. It was a makeshift affair; some sticky issues they ducked entirely, others they mastered with that ancient instrument of political sagacity, studied ambiguity, and some they just overlooked."[9]

The need for compromise became evident soon after defeat of the New Jersey Plan when the small states continued to demand and the large states to oppose equal representation in the Senate. On July 1 the convention split five to five on this issue, with Georgia divided. Faced with a deadlock, the convention named a committee to seek a compromise. It proposed on July 5 that, in return for equality of state representation in the Senate, the House be given sole power to originate money bills, which the Senate could accept or reject but not modify. This formula was finally approved July 16, five states to four, with Massachusetts divided and New York not voting because two of its three delegates had departed, never to return. On July 24 a Committee of Detail was appointed to draft the Constitution according to the resolutions adopted by the convention.

Without the Great Compromise the convention would have collapsed. As Madison pointed out, however, "the great division of interests" in America was not between the large and small but between the northern and southern states, partly because of climate but "principally from the effects of having or not having slaves." Although the southerners were mostly supporters of a strong central government, they were determined to limit its power to discriminate against the South's special interests in slavery, agricultural exports, and western expansion. This stand necessitated other compromises that accounted for some of the key provisions of the new plan of government.

What finally emerged September 17 as the Constitution of the United States was a unique blend of national and federal systems based on republican principles of representative and limited government. It met the basic objective of the nationalists by providing for a central government of ample powers that could function independently of the states. It also met the concerns of states' rights supporters by surrounding that government with checks and balances to prevent the tyranny of any one branch.

The text of the Constitution does not follow the order in which the separate provisions were developed. The convention moved generally from decisions on broad principles to questions of detail and precision. But the interdependent nature of the various parts of the plan made for frequent reconsideration of decisions in one area to take account of subsequent decisions in another but related area. As a result, many of the provisions were altered or added in the final weeks of the convention.

THE STRUCTURE OF CONGRESS

The convention's early decision that a national government, if formed, should consist of three branches—legislative, executive, and judicial—was undisputed. This division of governmental functions had been recognized from early colonial times and was reflected in most of the state constitutions. The failure of the Articles of Confederation to separate the functions was generally recognized as a serious mistake. The decision by the convention in favor of three branches of government also implied broad acceptance of the principle of separation of powers, although most of the provisions of the Constitution that gave effect to this principle were adopted on practical, not theoretical, grounds.

The Virginia Plan had called for a National Legislature of two houses, according to the practice initiated by the English Parliament and followed by most of the colonial governments and retained by ten of the thirteen states. The Continental Congress and the Congress of the Articles of Confederation were unicameral, but once the convention had decided to abandon the Articles there was little question that the new Congress should be bicameral. As George Mason saw it, the minds of Americans were settled on two points—"an attachment to republican government [and] an attachment to more than one branch in the Legislature." Only Pennsylvania dissented when the Committee of the Whole voted for two houses, and the convention confirmed the committee's decision June 21 by a vote of seven states to three.

Election to the House

The nationalists insisted that the new government rest on the consent of the people instead of on the state legislatures. So they held it as essential that at least "the first branch," the House, be elected "by the people immediately," as Madison put it. The government "ought to possess . . . the mind or sense of the people at large," said James Wilson, and for that reason "the Legislature ought to be the most exact transcript of the whole society." The House "was to be the grand depository of the democratic principles of the government," said Mason.

Those who were suspicious of a national government preferred election of the House by the state legislatures. "The people immediately should have as little to do" with electing the government as possible, said Roger Sherman, because "they want information and are constantly liable to be misled." Elbridge Gerry was convinced that "the evils we experience flow from the excess of democracy," while Charles Pinckney thought "the people were less fit judges" than the legislatures to choose

The illustration is of Independence Hall in Philadelphia, where the fifty-five delegates drafted the Constitution from May to September 1787.

members of the House. The proposal for election by state legislatures twice was defeated, however, and popular election of the House was confirmed June 21 by a vote of nine states to one.

Election to the Senate

The Virginia Plan proposed that the House elect the "second branch" from persons nominated by the state legislatures. But this plan garnered little support because it would have made the Senate subservient to the House. Most delegates agreed with Gouverneur Morris that it was to be the Senate's role "to check the precipitation, changeableness, and excesses of the first branch." (The concept of the Senate's role as that of representing the states emerged later, after the decision in favor of equal representation.) Neither was there any support for the view of Madison and Wilson that the people should elect the Senate as well as the House. Election of senators by the state legislatures was carried unanimously in the Committee of the Whole on

June 7 and confirmed June 25 by a convention vote of nine states to two.

Basis of Representation

The Virginia Plan called for representation of the states in both the House and Senate in proportion to their wealth or free population. This proposal led to the revolt of the small states, which was resolved by a vote on July 16 for equal representation of the states in the Senate. But while the principle of proportional representation in the House was never seriously challenged, the idea of basing it on wealth or the free population raised questions that led to adoption of important qualifications.

To retain southern support for proportional representation in the Senate, Wilson had proposed on June 11 that the House be apportioned according to a count of the whole number of free citizens and three-fifths of all others (meaning slaves), excluding

Indians not paying taxes. This formula (first proposed in Congress in 1783) was adopted with only New Jersey and Delaware opposed. Then on July 9 the convention decided that the new Congress should have the power "to regulate the number of representatives upon the principles of wealth and number of inhabitants."[10] Because southerners regarded slaves as property, this led northerners who wanted representation in the House to be based on population alone to ask why slaves should be counted at all.

As a result, on July 11 the convention voted six states to four to exclude blacks from the formula proposed June 11. At this point Gouverneur Morris proposed that the power of Congress to apportion the House according to wealth and numbers be subject to a proviso "that direct taxation shall be in proportion to representation." The proviso was adopted without debate. The slave issue now appeared in a different light because the Morris proviso seemed to mean that the South would have to pay additional taxes for any increases in representation it gained by counting slaves. So the northerners dropped their opposition to the three-fifths count demanded by the southerners, and on July 13 the convention restored that provision.

Because it was agreed that representation was to be based solely on population (counting all whites and three-fifths of the blacks), the word "wealth" was deleted from the provision adopted July 9. This solution to the issue gave five free voters in a slave state a voice in the House equivalent to that of seven free voters in a nonslave state, according to Rufus King, but it was "a necessary sacrifice to the establishment of the Constitution."

Size of Congress

The convention committee that recommended equal representation in the Senate on July 5 also proposed that each state have one vote in the House for every forty thousand inhabitants. This proposal precipitated the debate on representation, during which it was decided to let Congress regulate the future size of the House so as to allow for population changes and the admission of new states. Upon reflection by the delegates, however, it was feared that under such an arrangement a majority in Congress would be able to block a reapportionment plan or change the basis of representation for slaves. Thus northerners and southerners now agreed that the periods between reapportionments and the rules for revising representation in the House ought to be fixed by the Constitution.

Randolph was the first to propose a regular census, and on July 13 the convention adopted the plan, finally incorporated in Article I, Section 2, linking the apportionment of representatives to an "enumeration" every ten years of the "whole number of free persons . . . and three fifths of all others." On August 8 it was decided that the number of representatives "shall not exceed one for every 40,000," a figure that was lowered to 30,000 on the last day of the convention. Until the first census was taken, the size of the House was fixed at sixty-five representatives, allotted as set forth in Article I.

The size of the Senate was fixed on July 23 when the Convention considered and adopted (with Maryland alone voting against it) a proposal that the body should "consist of two members from each state, who shall vote per capita." A proposal to allow each state three senators had been turned down on the ground that it would penalize poorer and more distant states and that "a small number was most convenient for deciding on peace and war," as Nathaniel Gorham put it.

The idea that senators should vote individually instead of as a delegation came from Elbridge Gerry, who wanted to "prevent the delays and inconveniences" that had occurred in Congress in voting under the unit rule. Although this provision was at odds with the decision that the states should be equally represented in the Senate, it was accepted with little objection and included in Article I, Section 3.

Terms of Office

The convention had a strong attachment to the tradition of annual elections—"the only defense of the people against tyranny," according to Gerry. But Madison argued that representatives would need more than one year to become informed about the office and the national interests, and his proposal of a three-year term for the House was adopted June 12. Many delegates continued to press for more frequent elections, however. "The Representatives ought to return home and mix with the people," said Sherman, adding that "by remaining at the seat of Government they would acquire the habits of the place, which might differ from those of their constituents." The convention reconsidered the question June 21 and compromised on biennial elections and a two-year term for representatives.

The delegates also changed their minds about the Senate, agreeing first to a term of seven years, although the terms of state senators varied from two years to a maximum of five. When this decision was reviewed, alternatives of four, six, and nine years were considered. Charles Pinckney opposed six years,

LEGISLATIVE NOMENCLATURE

The Constitutional Convention continued to speak of the "Legislature of the United States" and its "first branch" and "second branch" until those terms were changed in the August 6, 1787, report of the Committee of Detail, to the "Congress of the United States," the "House of Representatives," and the "Senate." The term "Congress" was taken from the Articles of Confederation. "House of Representatives" was the name of the first branch in five states (the others being called the Assembly, House of Delegates, and House of Commons). The second branch was called the "Senate" in all but two states.

Provisions of the Constitution relating to both the House and Senate referred to "each House" in keeping with English usage. But the terms "upper house" and "lower house" to denote the Senate and the House, which also were taken from English usage, were not included in the Constitution.

arguing that senators would be "too long separated from their constituents, and will imbibe attachments different from that of the state." But having decided on biennial elections for the House, the convention voted June 26 to make it a six-year term in the Senate, with one-third of the membership to be elected every two years.

Qualifications of Voters

The report of the convention's Committee of Detail on August 6 provided that the qualifications of electors for the House should be the same as those required by the states for "the most numerous branch" of their own legislatures. Because property and other voting qualifications varied widely from state to state, no uniform standard seemed feasible. When Gouverneur Morris proposed giving Congress power to alter the qualifications, Oliver Ellsworth replied: "The clause is safe as it is—the states have staked their liberties on the qualifications which we have proposed to confirm." A proposal by Morris and others to limit the franchise to those who owned land was rejected, and on August 8 the convention adopted the committee's proposal without dissent.

Regulation of Elections

The Committee of Detail also proposed that the states regulate the times and places of electing senators and representatives, but that Congress retain the power to change the regulations. The states should not have the last word in this regard, said Madison, because "it was impossible to foresee all the abuses that might be made of the discretionary power." The convention adopted this provision on August 9 but amended it September 14 by adding the qualification: "except as to the places of choosing Senators," who were to be elected by the state legislatures. The purpose of the change was to "exempt the seats of government in the states from the power of Congress."

Qualifications of Members

The convention decided in June on a minimum age of twenty-five for representatives and thirty for senators. The Committee of Detail added two more qualifications: United States citizenship (three years for the House, four for the Senate) and residence within the state to be represented. Fearful of making it too easy for foreigners to be elected, the convention lengthened the citizenship requirement to seven years for representatives and nine years for senators, after voting down fourteen years as likely, in Ellsworth's view, to discourage "meritorious aliens from emigrating to this country."

Some delegates wanted to require residence in a state for a minimum time—from one to seven years. Mason feared that "rich men of neighboring states may employ with success the means of corruption in some particular district and thereby get into the public councils after having failed in their own state." But these proposals were voted down, and it was left that "no person shall be a representative [or senator] who shall not, when elected, be an inhabitant of that state in which he shall be chosen."

The convention debated the desirability of a property qualification. Most of the state constitutions required members of their legislatures to own certain amounts of property. Dickinson doubted the wisdom of a "policy of interweaving into a Republican Constitution a veneration of wealth." But on July 26, by a vote of eight states to three, the convention instructed the Committee of Detail to draft a property qualification. As written, this would have given Congress authority to establish "uniform qualifications . . . with regard to property." But when the provision was debated on August 10 it was rejected, and no further efforts were made to include a property qualification.

Even less disposition existed to include a religious qualification, although all of the states except New York and Virginia imposed such a qualification on state representatives. The convention's outlook on this point was made clear when, in debating an oath of office on August 30, the delegates adopted without dissent Charles Pinckney's proviso (which became a part of Article VI) that "no religious test shall ever be required as a qualification to any office or public trust under the United States." Thus the only qualifications established by the Constitution for election to Congress were those of age, citizenship, and residence.

Pay of Members

The Virginia Plan wanted members of the National Legislature to be paid "liberal stipends" without saying who should pay them. To the nationalists, however, one of the weaknesses of the Confederation was that members of Congress were paid by their states. So on June 12, after submitting "fixt" for "liberal," the Committee of the Whole agreed that in the case of representatives "the wages should be paid out of the National Treasury." But on June 22 Ellsworth moved that the states pay their salaries. Randolph opposed the change, saying it would create a dependence that "would vitiate the whole system." Hamilton agreed, saying "those who pay are the masters of those who are paid." The motion was rejected, four states to five.

When the pay of senators was discussed on June 26, Ellsworth again moved that the states pay. Madison argued that this would make senators "the mere agents and advocates of state interests and views, instead of being the impartial umpires and guardians of justice and general good." Ellsworth's motion was again defeated, five states to six. Despite the vote, the August 6 report of the Committee of Detail provided that the pay of senators and representatives should be "ascertained and paid" by the states. But Ellsworth and others by now had changed their minds, and on August 14 the convention voted nine states to two to pay members out of the national treasury.

Whether the amount of pay should be fixed in the Constitution was another matter. To let Congress set its own wages, said Madison, "was an indecent thing and might, in time, prove a dangerous one." Ellsworth proposed five dollars a day. Others thought the decision should be left to Congress, although Sherman was afraid the members would pay themselves too little instead of too much, "so that men ever so fit could not serve unless they were at the same time rich." But on August 14 the convention voted to give Congress full authority to fix its own pay by law.

Length of Service

Because of the attachment of several states to the theory of rotation in office, the Articles of Confederation had provided that "no person shall be capable of being a delegate for more than three years in any term of six years."[11] This rule had forced out of Congress some of its better members and was widely criticized. The Virginia Plan proposed, nevertheless, that members ought not to be eligible for reelection indefinitely after the expiration of their initial term of service and that they should be subject to recall. But this provision was eliminated in the Committee of the Whole, without debate or dissent, and no further effort was made to restrict the eligibility of representatives or senators for reelection.

Whether members of Congress should be eligible to hold other offices was debated at much greater length. Under the Articles, a delegate was not "capable of holding any office under the United States for which he, or another for his benefit, receives any salary, fees or emolument of any kind." But the Congress had appointed many delegates to diplomatic and other jobs, and the practice had created much resentment.

General concern also existed over the office-seeking propensities of state legislators. So the Virginia Plan proposed making any member of Congress ineligible for any office established by a particular state, or under the authority of the United States, during his term of service and for an unspecified period after its expiration.

Although this provision, with a period of one year after expiration specified, was adopted in the Committee of the Whole on June 12, the convention reconsidered and modified it several times before the final form was approved on September 3. Delegates who wanted to shut the door on appointments saw them as a source of corruption. "What led to the appointment of this Convention?" asked John Mercer, who answered: "The corruption and mutability of the legislative councils of the states." Those opposed to too many strictures feared they would discourage good men from running for Congress. "The legislature would cease to be a magnet to the first talents and abilities," said Charles Pinckney.

The compromise that emerged was a twofold disqualification. A member could not be appointed during his term to a federal office created during his term or to a federal office for which the pay was increased during the member's term, and no one holding federal office could be a member of Congress at the same time. The provision, incorporated in Section 6 of Article I, made no reference to state office or to ineligibility following expiration of a member's term.

TWO-THIRDS RULE

To the men who drafted the Constitution, a major weakness of the Articles of Confederation was the rule that nine (or two-thirds) of the thirteen states had to concur in all important decisions. So there was broad agreement on the general principle embodied in Article I, Section 5, that in the two chambers of Congress "a Majority of each shall constitute a Quorum to do Business." With respect to certain powers, however, a requirement for something greater than a majority seemed essential to a balanced design of government.

As finally approved, the Constitution imposed a two-thirds requirement in six instances. No one was to be convicted on impeachment nor could a treaty be made without the concurrence of two-thirds of the senators "present." Neither chamber could expel a member without "the concurrence of two-thirds." A bill could be enacted over the president's veto by the votes of two-thirds of each chamber. Congress could propose amendments to the Constitution "whenever two-thirds of both Houses shall deem it necessary." And if the House was called upon to ballot for president, a quorum was to "consist of a Member or Members from two-thirds of the States."

Only the provisions relating to the Senate's role in trying impeachments and approving treaties made it clear that the decision rested with two-thirds of the members present and voting, rather than with two-thirds of the entire membership. Persuasive evidence exists that the latter interpretation was intended by the delegates for the provisions relating to vetoes, expulsion of members, and constitutional amendments. However, in the absence of an explicit requirement to that effect, Congress over the years established the precedent that two-thirds of members "present" and voting likewise was sufficient for a decision in those cases—an assumption sustained by the Supreme Court in 1919 (*Missouri Pac. R. R. Co. v. Kansas*) and 1920 (*Rhode Island v. Palmer*).

The convention also considered but rejected proposals to require the consent of two-thirds of both houses to admit new states and to enact laws to regulate foreign commerce (leaving these matters to be decided by majority vote) and to permit export taxes to be levied by a two-thirds vote of both houses (leaving a flat prohibition on such taxes).

Rules and Regulation of Congress

Article I included four provisions for the regulation of the House and Senate that originated with the Committee of Detail and were only slightly modified by the full convention. They were:

• The provision that "Each House shall be the Judge of the Elections, Returns and Qualifications of its own Members." This language was found in the constitutions of eight of the states and was agreed to without debate.

• The provision that "Each House may determine the Rules

of its Proceedings, punish its Members for disorderly Behaviour, and, with the Concurrence of two-thirds, expel a Member." This provision was amended by addition of the two-thirds vote requirement for expulsion. The change, proposed by Madison because "the right of expulsion was too important to be exercised by a bare majority of a quorum," was approved unanimously.

• The provision that "Each House shall keep a Journal, and from time to time publish the same." This language stemmed from a similar provision in the Articles of Confederation. When Madison proposed giving the Senate some discretion in the matter, Wilson objected that "the people have a right to know what their agents are doing or have done, and it should not be in the option of the legislature to conceal their proceedings." The convention voted to require publication of the journals of each house, but with the proviso "excepting such parts as may in their judgment require secrecy." The clause also provided for recording the "yea" and "nay" votes of members, although some delegates objected that "the reasons governing the votes never appear along with them."

• The provision that "Neither House, during the Session of Congress, shall, without the Consent of the other, adjourn for more than three days, nor to any other Place than that in which the two Houses shall be sitting." This was agreed to after brief debate. Most of the state constitutions had similar provisions, reflecting a common commitment to legislative independence born of the colonial experience with the right of royal governors to suspend and dissolve the state assemblies.

POWERS OF CONGRESS

The Virginia resolutions proposed that the National Legislature be empowered:

> to enjoy the Legislative Rights vested in Congress by the Confederation and moreover to legislate in all cases to which the separate States are incompetent, or in which the harmony of the United States may be interrupted by the exercise of individual Legislation;
>
> to negate all laws passed by the several States, contravening in the opinion of the National Legislature the articles of Union; and
>
> to call forth the force of the Union against any member of the Union failing in its duty under the articles thereof.

These proposals reflected the great concern of the nationalists with the powerlessness of Congress under the Articles of Confederation to protect the interests of the United States at large against the "prejudices, passions and improper views of the state legislatures," in the words of John Dickinson. Madison deplored "a constant tendency in the states to encroach on the federal authority, to violate national treaties, to infringe the rights and interests of each other, to oppress the weaker party within their respective jurisdiction." So it seemed essential that, in addition to adequate authority to legislate for the general interests of the Union, the new national government should possess the power to restrain the states and to compel their obedience.

When these proposals were first discussed May 31, some delegates wanted an exact enumeration of such powers before voting, but the first of the Virginia resolutions was approved after brief debate without dissent. The second, granting a power to negate state laws—which was akin to the royal disallowance of colonial laws—also was approved without debate or dissent. When the third resolution was called up, however, Madison moved to set it aside because he feared that "the use of force against a state would look more like a declaration of war than an infliction of punishment."[12] Although the New Jersey Plan contained a similar provision, this power was not considered further by the convention.

On June 8 Charles Pinckney proposed that the power to nullify state laws be extended to all such laws Congress should judge to be improper. Such an expansion would enslave the states, said Gerry, and the motion was rejected, seven states to three. Strong opposition now developed to any power to negate state laws. Madison continued to defend it as the most certain means of preserving the system, but Gouverneur Morris concluded that it would disgust all the states. On July 17 the convention reversed its earlier action by voting seven states to three against the power to veto. The problem of securing conformity of the states to national law finally was resolved by adoption of a "supremacy" clause and a specific prohibition on certain types of state laws.

The convention on July 17 also reconsidered the first of the Virginia resolutions. Sherman proposed as a substitute that Congress be empowered "to make laws binding on the people of the United States in all cases which may concern the common interests of the Union; but not to interfere with the Government of the individual States in any matters of internal police which respect the Government of such States only, and wherein the general welfare of the United States is not concerned." This formulation, in which the term "general welfare" made its first appearance in the convention, seemed too restrictive to most delegates and it was rejected, eight states to two. Then, by a vote of six states to four, the convention inserted in the resolution approved May 31 the additional power to legislate "in all cases for the general interests of the Union."

When this broad grant of legislative authority was examined by the Committee of Detail it seemed so vague and unlimited that the committee decided to replace it with an enumeration of specified powers. Eighteen of these powers were listed in the report of August 6, which also contained for the first time lists of powers to be denied to Congress and to the states. The various lists formed the basis for the powers and prohibitions that were finally incorporated in Sections 8, 9, and 10 of Article I of the Constitution, of which the major provisions were the following:

Power to Tax

The committee's first proposal—that Congress "shall have the power to lay and collect taxes, duties, imposts and excises"—was adopted August 16 without dissent. The convention then became embroiled in the issue of paying off the public debt and decided to amend the tax clause to provide that Congress "shall fulfill the engagements and discharge the debts of the United States and shall have the power to lay and collect taxes." Pierce Butler objected that this language would require Congress to redeem at face value all government paper, including that held by "bloodsuckers who had speculated on the distresses of others and bought up securities at heavy discounts." He thought Congress should be free to buy up such holdings at less than full value.

As a result, the convention dropped the language added to the tax clause and adopted in its place the declaration found in Article VI: "All debts contracted and engagements entered into before the adoption of this Constitution shall be as valid against the United States under this Constitution as under the Confederation." This declaration left open the question of full or partial redemption, which was to become a major issue in the First Congress.

But some delegates now thought that the power to tax should be linked explicitly to the purpose of paying that debt. Their position led to further amendment of the tax clause on September 4 to provide that Congress "shall have power to lay and collect taxes, duties, imposts and excises, to pay the debts and provide for the common defense and general welfare of the United States." A further proviso in the first clause of Section 8, Article I, that "all duties, imposts and excises shall be uniform throughout the United States," had been approved earlier to prevent Congress from discriminating against the commerce of any one state.

It was to be argued later that inclusion of the words "general welfare" was intended to confer an additional and unlimited power on Congress. The records of the convention indicate, however, that when it was decided to qualify the power to tax by adding the words "to pay the debts," it became necessary to make clear that this was not the only purpose for which taxes could be levied. "To provide for the common defense and general welfare" was taken from the Articles of Confederation and used to encompass all of the other specific and limited powers vested by the Constitution in Congress.

In settling the basis for representation in the House, the convention had linked the apportionment of "direct taxes" as well as representatives to a count of all whites and three-fifths of the blacks. When this provision was reconsidered August 20, King asked, "What was the precise meaning of direct taxation," but according to Madison "no one answered." The only direct taxes in use at that time were land taxes and capitation or poll taxes. Because southerners feared that Congress might seek to levy a special tax on slaves, the Committee of Detail recommended, and the convention later adopted, a further provision, incorporated in Section 9 of Article I, that "No Capitation, or other direct, Tax shall be laid, unless in Proportion" to the count required by Section 2. Another limitation on the power to tax—also adopted as a concession to the South—prohibited levies on exports.

Power to Regulate Commerce

Trade among the states and with other countries was severely handicapped under the Confederation by a lack of uniformity in duties and commercial regulations. The states commonly discriminated against the products of neighboring states, incurring retaliation in kind that added to the divisiveness and suspicions of the times. To Madison and many others, the new plan of government must provide that Congress have the power to regulate commerce as well as the power to tax. It soon became clear, however, that the southern states would not accept a Constitution that failed to protect their vested interest in slave labor and agricultural exports from the burdensome restrictions that a Congress controlled by northerners might seek to impose.

As a result, the Committee of Detail proposed that Congress be given the power to regulate commerce with foreign nations and among the several states, subject to two limitations: a ban on taxing exports and a prohibition on efforts to tax or outlaw the slave trade. The general power to regulate commerce was approved on August 16 without dissent. (The words "and with the Indian Tribes" were added September 4.) The proposed limitations met with considerable opposition, however.

In keeping with mercantilist doctrines, it was common practice at that time for governments to tax exports. The idea of prohibiting such action was novel. "To deny this power is to take from the common government half the regulation of trade," said Wilson. It also acted to deny Congress the power to menace the livelihood of the South by taxing exports of rice, tobacco, and indigo on which its economy was largely dependent. Other northerners considered this concession to the South as wise as it was necessary. Gerry said the convention already had given Congress "more power than we know how will be exercised." On August 21, by a vote of seven states to four, the convention agreed that "No Tax or Duty shall be laid on Articles exported from any State." This provision was placed in Section 9 of Article I in the final draft.

The second limitation on the power to regulate commerce provided that no tax or duty was to be laid on the migration or importation of persons, nor was such migration or importation to be prohibited. The limitation was designed to meet the South's objection to any interference with the slave trade, although those words were carefully avoided. Luther Martin thought it was "inconsistent with the principles of the Revolution and dishonorable to the American character to have such a feature in the Constitution." But most other delegates, including those opposed to slavery, argued that it was a political, not a moral, issue.

Some northerners, as well as southerners, agreed with Ellsworth that "the morality or wisdom of slavery" should be left to the states to determine. "Let us not intermeddle," he said, predicting that "slavery, in time will not be a speck in our country." Many others agreed with Mason that the "infernal traffic" in slaves was holding back the economic development of the country and that for this reason the national government

The delegates to the Constitutional Convention, unlike in this illustration, debated the particulars of the new government behind closed shutters—to guarantee the privacy of the deliberations.

"should have power to prevent the increase of slavery." Because the provision reported by the Committee of Detail was clearly unacceptable to many delegates, a committee was named to seek a compromise.

The panel now proposed that Congress be barred from prohibiting the slave trade until the year 1800, but that it have power to levy a duty on slaves as on other imports. Both provisions were approved August 25, the first by a vote of seven states to four after the year 1800 had been changed to 1808, and the second after limiting the duty to $10 per person. So the power of Congress to regulate commerce was further limited by these provisions respecting slaves, which became the first clause of Section 9 of Article I.

Still another limit on the commerce power sought by the South and recommended by the Committee of Detail would have required a two-thirds vote of both houses of Congress to pass a navigation act. England had used such laws to channel colonial imports and exports into British ships and ports, and southerners now feared that the North, where shipping was a major interest, might try to monopolize the transport of their exports by a law requiring them to be carried aboard American ships.

Northern delegates were strongly opposed to the two-thirds proposal, and in working out the compromise on the slave trade they succeeded in having it dropped. As a result, Charles Pinckney moved to require a two-thirds vote of both houses to enact any commercial regulation. This motion was rejected August 29 by seven states to four, and the convention confirmed the decision to drop the proposed two-thirds rule for navigation acts. Mason, one of three delegates who refused to sign the Constitution, later argued that a bare majority of Congress should not have the power to "enable a few rich merchants in Philadelphia, New York, and Boston to monopolize the staples of the Southern States."

A relatively minor limitation on the power to regulate commerce was adopted to allay the fear of Maryland that Congress might require ships traversing the Chesapeake Bay to enter or clear at Norfolk or another Virginia port to simplify the collection of duties. As approved August 31 and added to Section 9, Article I, the language provided that "No Preference shall be given by any Regulation of Commerce or Revenue to the Ports of one State over those of another; nor shall Vessels bound to or from one State be obliged to enter, clear or pay Duties in another."

War and Treaty Power

The Articles of Confederation had given Congress the exclusive right and power of deciding issues of peace and war. The Committee of Detail proposed giving to the new Congress as a whole the power to make war and giving to the Senate alone the power to approve treaties. The treaty power subsequently was divided between the president and the Senate. But in discussing the war-making power on August 17, Charles Pinckney also favored giving that authority exclusively to the Senate because "it would be singular for one authority to make war, and another peace." However, Butler thought the war power should rest with the president, "who will have all the requisite qualities and will not make war but when the Nation will support it." Neither view drew any support, and the convention voted to give Congress the power "to declare war." The word "declare" had been substituted for "make" to leave the president free to repel a sudden attack. Sherman said, "The Executive should be able to repel, and not commence, war."[13]

On August 18 the convention agreed to give Congress the power "to raise and support Armies," "to provide and maintain a Navy," and "to make Rules for the Government and Regulation of the land and naval Forces." All of these provisions were taken from the Articles of Confederation. Gerry, voicing the old colonial fears of a standing army, wanted a proviso that "in time of peace" the army should consist of no more than two thousand or three thousand men, but his motion was unanimously rejected.[14] On September 5, however, the convention added to the power to "raise and support Armies" the proviso that "no Appropriation of Money to that Use shall be for a longer Term than two Years."[15] This was intended to quiet fears similar to those that had led the British to require annual appropriations for the army.

The convention approved without dissent the power, proposed by the Committee of Detail and included in Section 8, Article I, "To provide for calling forth the Militia to execute the Laws of the Union, suppress Insurrections and repel Invasions." But a further proposal by Mason that Congress have the power to regulate the militia alarmed the defenders of state sovereignty. To Gerry this was the last point remaining to be surrendered. Others argued that the states would never allow control of the militia to get out of their hands.

The shortcomings of the militia during the Revolutionary War were a bitter memory to most of the delegates, however, and they shared the practical view of Madison that "as the greatest danger to liberty is from large standing armies, it is best to prevent them by an effectual provision for a good militia."[16] So on August 23 the convention adopted the provision, as later incorporated in Section 8, giving Congress power "To provide for organizing, arming, and disciplining the Militia, and for govern-

ing such Part of them as may be employed in the Service of the United States."

Special Status of Money Bills

The committee named to resolve the issue of equal or proportional representation in the Senate had proposed as a compromise that each state have one vote in the Senate, but that the House originate all bills to raise and appropriate money or pay government salaries and that the Senate be denied the right to amend such bills. Included in the proposal was the phrase, "No money shall be drawn from the public Treasury, but in pursuance of appropriations to be originated in the first branch." Seven states at this time required that money bills originate in the lower house, but only four of those states forbade amendment by the upper house. Some delegates objected that such a provision would be degrading to the Senate, but it was approved July 6 by a vote of five states to three.

The Committee of Detail phrased the provision as follows: "All bills for raising or appropriating money, and for fixing the salaries of the officers of Government, shall originate in the House of Representatives, and shall not be altered or amended by the Senate." Madison was for striking the entire provision as likely to promote "injurious altercations" between House and Senate; others insisted that it was necessary because the people "will not agree that any but their immediate representatives shall meddle with their purse." The convention's division on the question reflected contrasting concepts of the Senate as likely to be the most responsible branch or the most aristocratic one, to be strengthened or checked accordingly.

But on August 8 the convention reversed itself, voting seven states to four to drop the provision. However, further debate underscored the importance of reaching a compromise, and the one finally proposed was adopted September 8 by a vote of nine states to two. It provided that "All bills for raising revenue shall originate in the House of Representatives, and shall be subject to alterations and amendments by the Senate; no money shall be drawn from the Treasury but in consequence of appropriations made by law." The first sentence, slightly revised, was incorporated in the final draft as the first clause of Section 7, while the second sentence was made one of the limitations on the powers of Congress listed in Section 9, Article I.

The Constitution thus gave the House exclusive power to originate any bill involving taxes or tariffs of any kind, but it did not extend that power to appropriations bills. However, the House assumed that additional power, on the basis of the consideration it had received in the convention; it became the recognized prerogative of the House to originate spending as well as revenue bills.

Admission of New States

As early as 1780 the Continental Congress had resolved that lands ceded to the United States "shall be disposed of for the common benefit of the United States, and be settled and formed into distinct republican States, which shall become members of the Federal Union, and have the same rights of sovereignty, freedom and independence as the other States." By 1786 the Congress of the Confederation was in possession of all land south of Canada, north of the Ohio, west of the Allegheny Mountains, and east of the Mississippi. Guidelines for governing this great territory were laid down by Congress in the Northwest Ordinance of July 13, 1787.

The Ordinance provided that, upon attaining a population of five thousand free male inhabitants of voting age, the territory would be entitled to elect a legislature and send a nonvoting delegate to Congress. It provided also that no fewer than three and no more than five states were to be formed out of the territory. Each state was to have at least sixty thousand free inhabitants to qualify for admission to the Union "on an equal footing with the original States in all respects whatever." And the Ordinance declared that "there shall be neither slavery nor involuntary servitude in the said territory."

As this farsighted plan was being approved in New York by the Congress of the Confederation, Gouverneur Morris and other eastern delegates to the Constitutional Convention in Philadelphia were arguing strongly against equality for the new states. "The busy haunts of men, not the remote wilderness, are the proper school of political talents," said Morris. "If the western people get the power into their hands, they will ruin the Atlantic interests. The back members are always most adverse to the best measures."

Among those opposing this view were the delegates of Virginia and North Carolina, whose western lands were to become Kentucky and Tennessee. Mason argued that the western territories "will either not unite with or will speedily revolt from the Union, if they are not in all respects placed on an equal footing." In time, he thought they might well be "both more numerous and more wealthy" than the seaboard states. Madison was certain that "no unfavorable distinctions were admissible, either in point of justice or policy."

In the light of that debate, the Committee of Detail proposed on August 6 that Congress have the power to admit new states upon the consent of two-thirds of the members present of each house (the Articles of Confederation required the consent of nine states) and, in the case of a state formed from an existing state, upon the consent of the legislature of that state. New states were to be admitted on the same terms as the original states. But when this proposal was considered August 29, the convention adopted a motion by Morris to drop the provision for equality of admission.

Morris and Dickinson then offered a new draft, eliminating the condition of a two-thirds vote in favor of a simple majority, which was adopted and became the first clause of Section 3, Article IV. It provided simply that new states could be admitted by Congress. Although this provision of the Constitution was silent as to the status of the new states, Congress was to adhere to the principle of equality in admitting them.

The convention then adopted the provision governing territories set out in the second clause of Section 3, Article IV. Madison had first proposed adding such a provision to the Constitution to give a legal foundation to the Northwest Ordinance, because the Articles of Confederation had given Congress no explicit power to legislate for territories. A proviso ruling out prejudice to any claims of the United States or of a particular state was added because some delegates feared that, without it, the terms on which new states were admitted might favor the claims of a state to vacant lands ceded by Britain.

Power of Impeachment

It was decided early in the convention that the chief executive should be "removable on impeachment and conviction of malpractice or neglect of duty." Who should impeach and try him, however, depended on how he was to be chosen. So long as Congress was to elect the president—and that decision stood until September 4—few delegates were willing to give Congress the additional power to remove him. The final decision to have the president chosen by presidential electors helped to resolve the problem.

The Virginia Plan called for the national judiciary to try "impeachments of any National officers," without specifying which branch of government would impeach. Because all the state constitutions vested that power in the lower house of the assembly, the Committee of Detail proposed removal of the president on impeachment by the House and conviction by the Supreme Court "of treason, bribery, or corruption." No action was taken on this proposal until the special committee, in advancing the plan for presidential electors, suggested that the Senate try all impeachments and that conviction require the concurrence of two-thirds of the members present.

When this plan was debated September 8, Charles Pinckney opposed trial by the Senate on the ground that if the president "opposes a favorite law, the two Houses will combine against him, and under the influence of heat and faction throw him out of office." But the convention adopted the formula for impeachment by the House, trial by the Senate, and conviction by a two-thirds vote. It also extended the grounds for impeachment from treason and bribery to "other high crimes and misdemeanors" and made the vice president and other civil officers similarly impeachable and removable. These provisions were incorporated in Sections 2 and 3 of Article I and in Section 4 of Article II.

Miscellaneous Powers

The Committee of Detail proposed that Congress retain the power granted in the Articles "to borrow money and emit bills on the credit of the United States." But state emissions of paper money in 1786 had contributed greatly to the alarms that had led to the calling of the convention, and most delegates agreed with Ellsworth that this was a "favorable moment to shut and bar the door against paper money."[17] So the words "and emit bills" were struck out, with only two states dissenting, when this provision was approved August 16.

Most of the other powers of Congress specified in Section 8 of Article I were derived from the Articles of Confederation or included as appropriate to the new plan of government. Little debate or dissent was heard on these provisions. This was true of the language concerning naturalization and bankruptcy, coinage, counterfeiting, post offices, copyrights, inferior tribunals, piracies, and the seat of government. Also approved with little debate was the final provision of Section 8, proposed by the Committee of Detail and adopted August 20, which was to become the basis of one of the most sweeping grants of power in the entire Constitution.

That clause authorized Congress "To make all Laws which shall be necessary and proper for carrying into Execution the foregoing Powers, and all other Powers vested by this Constitution in the Government of the United States, or in any Department or Officer thereof." The intent of this grant was simply to enable Congress to enact legislation giving effect to the specified powers. No member of the convention suggested that it was meant to confer powers in addition to those previously specified in the article. But the meaning of the clause and of the words "necessary and proper" was to become the focus of the continuing controversy between broad and strict constructionists of the Constitution that began with the passage by the First Congress of a law creating a national bank.

Limits on Congressional Power

Section 9 of Article I as finally adopted imposed eight specific limitations on the powers of Congress. Five of the limitations—those relating to the slave trade, capitation taxes, export taxes, preference among ports, and appropriations—have been discussed in connection with the powers to tax, to regulate commerce, and to originate money bills. The others were adopted as follows:

• On August 28 Charles Pinckney moved to adopt a provision in the Massachusetts Constitution that barred suspension of the writ of habeas corpus except on the most urgent occasions and then for a period not to exceed one year. This was amended and adopted to provide that "The Privilege of the Writ of Habeas Corpus shall not be suspended, unless when in Cases of Rebellion or Invasion the public Safety may require it."

• On August 22 Gerry proposed a prohibition on the passage of bills of attainder and ex post facto laws. Some delegates objected that such a provision would imply an improper suspicion of Congress and that it was unnecessary. The convention agreed, however, that "No Bill of Attainder or ex post facto Law shall be passed." A subsequent motion by Mason to delete ex post facto laws on the ground that the ban might prevent Congress from redeeming the war debt at less than face value was rejected unanimously.

• On August 23 the convention adopted the two provisions that make up the final clause of Section 9, Article I, both of which were taken from the Articles of Confederation. The bar to titles of nobility was proposed by the Committee of Detail. The bar to acceptance of emolument, office, or title from foreign governments without the consent of Congress was urged by

Pinckney to help keep American officials independent of external influence.

Pinckney and others proposed adding to the Constitution a number of provisions similar to those contained in the Bills of Rights of the various states. On September 12 Gerry moved to appoint a committee to draft a Bill of Rights, but ten states voted no. Anxious to complete their work and return home, the delegates were in no mood to spend additional time on something most of them believed to be unnecessary because none of the powers to be vested in Congress seemed to countenance legislation that might violate individual rights.

The omission of a Bill of Rights later became a major issue in seeking the states' approval of the Constitution and led to assurances by those favoring ratification that guarantees would be added to the Constitution promptly once the new system of government was established.

THE EXECUTIVE BRANCH

No question troubled the convention more than the powers and structure to be given the executive in the new government. The office did not exist under the Articles of Confederation, which placed the executive function in Congress. A long-standing fear of executive authority had led Americans "to throw all power into the Legislative vortex," as Madison explained it. Under most of the state constitutions, the executives were "little more than cyphers, the Legislatures omnipotent." How much more authority and independence to give the national executive remained in dispute until the end of the convention.

The Virginia Plan had recommended a national executive chosen by the legislative branch for a fixed term. He would be ineligible for reappointment and empowered with "a general authority to execute the National laws" as well as "the Executive rights vested in Congress by the Confederation." Debate on these proposals disclosed a spectrum of views ranging from that of Sherman, who thought the executive should be "nothing more than an institution for carrying the will of the Legislative into effect," to that of Gouverneur Morris, who felt the chief executive should be "the guardian of the people" against legislative tyranny.

Until September, the convention favored a single executive, chosen by Congress for a single term of seven years, whose powers would be limited by Congress's ability to appoint judges and ambassadors and make treaties. This plan for legislative supremacy was then abandoned for the more balanced one that finally was adopted and incorporated in Article II of the Constitution. A president would be chosen by electors for a four-year term without limit as to reelection, and he would have the power to make all appointments subject to confirmation by the Senate and to make treaties subject to approval by a two-thirds vote of the Senate.

A Single Executive

Randolph, who presented the Virginia Plan, opposed a single

THE PRESIDENT'S CABINET

In 1787 eight states had a Privy Council to advise the governor, and the idea of providing for a similar body to advise the president was discussed at length at the Constitutional Convention. Elbridge Gerry and others thought it would "give weight and inspire confidence" in the executive. To Benjamin Franklin, "a Council would not only be a check on a bad President, but be a relief to a good one." But Gouverneur Morris saw it in a different light: "Give him an able Council and it will thwart him; a weak one, and he will shelter himself under their sanction."

On August 22 the Committee of Detail submitted the following proposal (first offered by Morris and Charles Pinckney) to the convention:

The President of the United States shall have a Privy Council which shall consist of the President of the Senate, the Speaker of the House of Representatives, the Chief Justice of the Supreme Court, and the principal officer in the respective departments of Foreign Affairs, Domestic Affairs, War, Marine, and Finance, as such departments of office shall from time to time be established, whose duty it shall be to advise him in matters respecting the execution of his office, which he shall think proper to lay before them; but their advice shall not conclude him, nor affect his responsibility for the measures which he shall adopt.

The convention did not vote on the foregoing proposal. The September 4 report of the special committee proposed only that the president "may require the Opinion in writing of the principal Officer in each of the executive Departments, upon any Subject relating to the Duties of their respective Offices." This provision, adopted September 7 after the convention had rejected, eight states to three, a proposal by George Mason for an executive council to be appointed by Congress, was included among the powers of the president set out in Section 2 of Article II.

The word "Cabinet" was not used in the convention or in the Constitution. But as that body developed under Washington and later presidents, it conformed to the limited role that had been envisioned in the Morris-Pinckney proposal for a Privy Council.

executive as "the foetus of monarchy" and proposed three persons, who, Mason thought, should be chosen from the northern, middle, and southern states. But Wilson foresaw "nothing but uncontrolled, continued, and violent animosities" among three persons. A single executive, he said, would give "most energy, dispatch and responsibility to the office." On June 4 the delegates voted for a single executive, seven states to four, and the convention confirmed the decision July 17 without dissent.

The Committee of Detail then proposed that "the Executive Power of the United States shall be vested in a single person" to be called the president and to have the title of "His Excellency." These provisions were adopted August 24 without debate, but in drafting the final document the Committee of Style dropped the title and provided simply that "the Executive Power shall be vested in a President of the United States of America." The omission from the Constitution of any title other than president helped to defeat a proposal in the First Congress that he be addressed as "His Highness."

Method of Election, Term of Office

The method of election and the term of office of the executive were closely related issues. If Congress were to choose the president, most delegates thought he should have a fairly long term and be ineligible for reappointment. For as Randolph put it, "if he should be reappointable by the Legislature, he will be no check on it." But if the president was to be chosen in some other manner, a shorter term with reeligibility was favored by most of the delegates. Thus the method of election was the key question.

The convention first decided that Congress should choose the president for a single seven-year term. On reflection, however, some delegates thought this would not leave him sufficiently independent. Wilson proposed election by electors chosen by the people, but Gerry considered the people "too little informed of personal characters" to choose electors, and the proposal was rejected, eight to two. Gerry proposed that the governors of the states pick the president to avoid the corruption he foresaw in having Congress choose, but this plan also was rejected.

Several other methods were proposed, and at one point the delegates agreed on selection by electors chosen by the state legislatures. But this decision then was reversed. However, when Morris on August 24 renewed Wilson's original proposal for electors chosen by the people only six states were opposed; five voted in favor of it. Three of the latter were smaller states that had opposed an earlier proposal to have the membership of the Senate and the House vote to elect the president, thereby giving the large states (having a greater number of representatives) a bigger voice in making the selection.

All of the questions concerning the presidency then were reconsidered by a special committee on postponed matters, whose report of September 4 recommended most of the provisions that were finally adopted. According to Morris, the committee rejected choice of the president by Congress because of "the danger of intrigue and faction" and "the opportunity for cabal." Instead, it proposed that he be chosen by electors equal in number to the senators and representatives from each state, who would be chosen as each state decided. They would vote by ballot for two persons, at least one of whom could not be an inhabitant of their state. The one receiving a majority of the electoral votes would become president; the one with the next largest vote would become vice president. In the event of a tie, or if no one received a majority, the Senate would decide.

The plan provided for a four-year term with no restriction as to reelection; shifted from the Senate to the president the power to appoint ambassadors and judges and to make treaties subject to Senate approval; and gave to the Senate, instead of the Supreme Court, the power to try impeachments. This realignment of powers between the president and the Senate appealed to the small states because it was generally assumed that the Senate (in which each state was to be represented equally) would have the final say in choosing the president in most cases.

For the same reason, however, some delegates now feared that the combination of powers to be vested in the Senate would, in Randolph's words, "convert that body into a real and dangerous aristocracy." Sherman thereupon proposed moving the final election of the president from the Senate to the House, with the proviso that each state have one vote. The change, which preserved the influence of the small states while easing the fears expressed about the Senate, was quickly adopted, as was the rest of the electoral plan and the four-year term without limit as to reeligibility.

Qualifications

The Committee of Detail first proposed that a president be at least thirty-five years of age, a citizen, and an inhabitant of the United States for twenty-one years, just as age, citizenship, and minimum period of residence were the only qualifications stipulated for senators and representatives. The committee added the qualification that the president had to be a natural-born citizen or a citizen at the time of the adoption of the Constitution, and it reduced the time of residence within the United States to at least fourteen years "in the whole." The phrase "in the whole" was dropped in drafting the final provision of Section 1, Article II, which also was adjusted to make it clear that the qualifications for president applied equally to the vice president.

The Vice President

The office of the vice president was not considered by the convention until September 4, when a special committee proposed that a vice president, chosen for the same term as the president, serve as ex officio president of the Senate. (A vice president or lieutenant governor served in a similar capacity in four of the thirteen states.) The proposal was designed to provide a position for the runner-up in the electoral vote and to give the Senate an impartial presiding officer without depriving any state of one of its two votes.

When this proposal was debated September 7, Mason objected that "it mixed too much the Legislative and the Executive." Gerry thought it tantamount to putting the president himself at the head of the Senate because of "the close intimacy that must subsist between the president and the vice president." But Sherman noted that "if the Vice President were not to be President of the Senate, he would be without employment."[18] The convention adopted the proposal of the special committee, with only Massachusetts opposed. The provision that the vice president "shall be president of the Senate, but shall have no Vote unless they be equally divided," was placed in Section 3 of Article I.

The convention never discussed the role of the vice president as the successor to the president in the event of a vacancy in the office of the presidency. The delegates seemed to have assumed that he would merely perform the duties of president until an-

Chosen to preside over the convention, George Washington's participation lent the gathering legitimacy and luster. When the delegates fashioned the presidency, their fears about giving the chief executive too much power were lessened by their certain belief that he would first hold the office.

other was elected. Thus the special committee proposed that in case of the president's removal by impeachment, "death, absence, resignation, or inability to discharge the powers or duties of his office, the Vice President shall exercise those powers and duties until another President be chosen, or until the inability of the President be removed."

This language was revised slightly to provide that "In case of the removal of the President from office, or of his death, resignation, or inability to discharge the powers and duties of the said office, the same shall devolve on the Vice President." The revised wording, incorporated in Article II, left it unclear as to whether it was the "said office" or the "powers and duties" that were to "devolve" on the vice president. The right of the vice president to assume the office of president was first asserted by John Tyler in 1841. He assumed the presidency on the death of William Henry Harrison and served for the remainder of Harrison's term, thus establishing the practice.

There remained the question of providing for the office in the event both men died or were removed. Randolph proposed that Congress designate an officer to "act accordingly until the time of electing a President shall arrive." Madison objected that this would prevent an earlier election, so it was agreed to substitute "until such disability be removed, or a President shall be elected." The Committee of Style ignored this change, so the convention voted on September 15 to restore it. The final provision, authorizing Congress to designate by law an officer to "act as President" until "a President shall be elected," was joined to the earlier provision in Article II relating to the vice president.

Presidential Powers

Initially, the convention conferred only three powers on the president: "to carry into effect the National laws," "to appoint to offices in cases not otherwise provided for," and to veto bills. The Committee of Detail proposed a number of additional powers drawn from the state constitutions, most of which were adopted with little discussion or change. This was true of provisions (placed in Section 3 of Article II) directing the president "from time to time" to inform Congress "of the State of the Union" and to recommend legislation, to convene and adjourn Congress under certain circumstances, to receive ambassadors, and to see "that the Laws be faithfully executed."

The convention also agreed without debate that "the President shall be Commander in Chief of the Army and Navy" and of the militia when called into national service. Almost all of the state constitutions vested a similar power in the state executives. The power of the president "to grant reprieves and pardons except in cases of impeachment" likewise was approved, although Mason argued that Congress should have this power and Randolph wanted to bar pardons for treason as "too great a trust" to place in the president. These two provisions were included in Section 2 of Article II.

Power to Appoint. The appointive powers of the president initially were limited by the convention to "cases not otherwise provided for." The Virginia Plan had proposed that judges be appointed by the National Legislature, a practice followed in all except three states, but the delegates voted to give the power to the Senate alone as the "less numerous and more select body." In July the delegates considered and rejected alternative proposals that judges be appointed by the president alone, by the president with the advice and consent of the Senate, and by the president unless two-thirds of the Senate disagreed.

But sentiment had changed by late summer. On September 7 the convention adopted the proposal of the special committee that the president appoint ambassadors and other public ministers, justices of the Supreme Court, and all other officers of the United States "by and with the Advice and Consent of the Senate." This power, incorporated in Section 2 of Article II, later was qualified by requiring that offices not otherwise provided for "be established by law" and by authorizing Congress to vest appointment of lower-level officers in the presidency, the courts, and the heads of departments. Nothing was said about a presidential power to remove executive branch officials from office once confirmed by the Senate—a power that was to become a much-argued issue.

Treaty Power. The proposal that the Senate alone be given the power to make treaties, a recommendation first put forward by the Committee of Detail, drew considerable opposition. Mason said it would enable the Senate to "sell the whole country by means of treaties." Madison thought the president, representing the whole people, should have the power. Morris argued for a provision that "no treaty shall be binding . . . which is not ratified by a law." Southern delegates were especially concerned about preventing abandonment by treaty of free navigation of the Mississippi River.

The issue was referred to the Special Committee on Postponed Matters, which recommended vesting the president with the power to make treaties, subject to the advice and consent of two-thirds of the senators present. The latter provision provoked extended debate. Motions were made and rejected to delete the two-thirds requirement, to require consent by two-thirds of the entire Senate membership, to require a simple majority vote of the Senate membership, and to provide that no treaty could be drafted without previous notice to the members.

On September 7 the convention voted to except peace treaties from the two-thirds rule. Madison then moved to allow two-thirds of the Senate alone to make peace treaties, arguing that the president "would necessarily derive so much power and importance from a state of war that he might be tempted, if authorized, to impede a treaty of peace." The motion was rejected, but after further debate on the advantages and disadvantages of permitting a majority of the Senate to approve a peace treaty, the convention reversed itself and made all treaties subject to the concurrence of a two-thirds vote of the senators present.

Veto Power. The Virginia Plan had proposed joining the judiciary with the executive in exercising the power to veto acts of the legislature, subject to a vote in Congress on overriding vetoes. Because the judiciary was expected to have to pass on the constitutionality of legislation, most delegates thought giving the judiciary a share of the veto power was improper; the proposal was rejected.

Wilson and Hamilton favored giving the executive an absolute veto, but on June 4 the delegates voted for Gerry's motion for a veto that could be overridden by two-thirds of each branch of the legislature.

When this provision was reconsidered on August 15, it was in the context of a plan to lodge in Congress the power to elect the president, to impeach him, and to appoint judges. Many delegates then agreed with Wilson that such an arrangement did not give "a sufficient self-defensive power either to the Executive or Judiciary Department," and the convention voted to require a vote of three-fourths of each chamber to override a veto. But on September 12, after having adopted the presidential elector plan and other changes proposed by the special committee, the convention restored the earlier two-thirds requirement.

The veto power was incorporated in Section 7 of Article I, setting out the procedure for the enactment of a bill with or without the president's signature. This section also made provision for the "pocket veto" of a bill when "the Congress by their Adjournment prevent its return, in which Case it shall not become Law." Although some delegates indicated a belief that the two-thirds provision was intended to apply to the entire membership of the House and Senate, a two-thirds vote of those present and voting came to be accepted in practice.

THE JUDICIARY

Article III of the Constitution, relating to "the judicial Power of the United States," was developed in the convention with relative ease. The Virginia Plan called for "one or more supreme tribunals" and inferior tribunals to be appointed by the National Legislature to try all cases involving crimes at sea, foreigners, and citizens of different states, "collection of the National revenue," impeachments, and "questions which may involve the national peace and harmony." The convention went on to spell out the jurisdiction of these courts in greater detail, but the only basic changes made in the plan were to vest initially in the Senate and then in the presidency the power to appoint judges, and to transfer the trial of impeachments from the Supreme Court to the Senate.

Lower Courts and Appointment of Judges

The delegates agreed to one Supreme Court without debate, but some objected to establishing any lower courts. John Rutledge thought the state courts should hear all cases in the first instance, "the right of appeal to the Supreme National Tribunal being sufficient to secure the National rights and uniformity of judgments." Sherman deplored the extra expense. But Madison argued that without lower courts "dispersed throughout the Republic, with final jurisdiction in many cases, appeals would be multiplied to an oppressive degree." Randolph said the state courts "cannot be trusted with the administration of the National laws." As a compromise, the convention agreed to permit Congress to decide whether to "ordain and establish" lower courts.

The proposal that the National Legislature appoint the judiciary was based on similar provisions in most of the state constitutions. Wilson, arguing that "intrigue, partiality and concealment" would result from such a method, proposed appointment by the president. Madison urged appointment by the Senate as "a less numerous and more select body," and this plan was approved on June 13. A proposal that the president appoint judges "by and with the advice and consent of the Senate" was defeated by a tie vote July 18, but that was the method finally adopted in September as part of the compromise that moved the trial of impeachments from the Supreme Court to the Senate.

Tenure and Jurisdiction

Both the Virginia Plan and the New Jersey Plan provided that judges would hold office "during good behaviour"—a rule long considered essential to maintaining the independence of the judiciary. When this provision was considered August 27, Dickinson proposed that judges "may be removed by the Executive on the application by the Senate and the House of Representatives." Others objected strongly; Wilson contended that "the Judges would be in a bad situation if made to depend on every gust of faction which might prevail in two branches of our Government."[19] Only Connecticut voted for the proposal. The convention also agreed to tenure during good behavior.

Most of the provisions embodied in Section 2 of Article III, specifying the cases to which "the judicial Power shall extend" and the cases in which the Supreme Court would have original or appellate jurisdiction, were set out in the August 6 report of the Committee of Detail and adopted by the convention on August 27 with little change or debate. The most important modification was in the committee's first provision—extending jurisdiction to "all cases arising under the laws" of the United States. Here, the convention voted to insert the words "the Constitution and" before "the laws." This made it clear that the Supreme Court ultimately was to decide all questions of constitutionality, whether arising in state or federal courts.

Article III did not explicitly authorize the Court to pass on the constitutionality of acts of Congress, but the convention clearly anticipated the exercise of that power as one of the acknowledged functions of the courts. Several delegates noted that state courts had "set aside" laws in conflict with the state constitutions. The convention debated at great length, and rejected four times, a proposal to link the Court with the president in the veto power. Wilson favored it because "laws may be unjust, may be unwise, may be dangerous, may be destructive, and yet may not be so unconstitutional as to justify the judges in refusing to give them effect."

Mason agreed that the Court "could declare an unconstitutional law void."

Supremacy Clause

The role of the judiciary in determining the constitutionality of the laws of the land also was implicit in the provision, incorporated in Article VI, that asserted that the Constitution, the laws, and the treaties of the United States "shall be the supreme Law of the Land." This provision first appeared on July 17 after the convention had reversed itself and voted to deny Congress the proposed power. Anxious to place some restraint on the freewheeling state legislatures, the convention adopted instead a substitute offered by Luther Martin and drawn directly from the New Jersey Plan of June 14.

The substitute provided that the laws and treaties of the United States "shall be the supreme law of the respective States, as far as those acts or treaties shall relate to the said States, or their citizens and inhabitants—and that the Judiciaries of the several States shall be bound thereby in their decisions, anything in the respective laws of the individual States to the contrary notwithstanding." In its report of August 6, the Committee of Detail dropped the qualifying phrase "as far as those acts or treaties shall relate to the said States," substituted the word

"Judges" for "Judiciaries" in the next clause and the words "Constitutions or laws" for "laws" in the final proviso, and made a few other language changes.

The convention agreed to these modifications August 23 and then prefaced the entire provision with the words, "This Constitution." Further revision by the Committee of Style changed "supreme law of the several States" to "supreme law of the land," in what became the final phrasing of the provision in Article VI. The effect of the various changes was to make it clear that all judges, state and federal, were bound to uphold the supremacy of the Constitution over all other acts.

The "supremacy" clause was reinforced by a further provision in Article VI stating that all members of Congress and of the state legislatures, as well as all executive and judicial officers of the national and state governments, "shall be bound by Oath or Affirmation to support this Constitution."

Limits on Powers of the States

The "supremacy" clause was designed to prevent the states from passing laws contrary to the Constitution. Because the Framers of the Constitution also intended to specify the powers granted to Congress, those powers by implication were denied to the states. By the same reasoning, however, any powers not specifically granted to Congress remained with the states.

To eliminate any doubt of their intention to put an end to ir-responsible acts of the individual states, the delegates decided to specify what the states could not do as well as what the states were required to do. Acts prohibited to the states were placed in Section 10 of Article I, while those required of them were placed in Sections 1 and 2 of Article IV.

Most of these provisions—many of which were taken from the Articles of Confederation—were proposed by the Committee of Detail and adopted by the convention on August 28 with little debate or revision. The committee had proposed that the states be required to use gold or silver as legal tender unless Congress gave its consent to another medium of exchange, but the convention voted for an absolute prohibition on other forms of legal tender. Sherman said the times presented "a favorable crisis for crushing paper money." The convention also added a provision, drawn from the Northwest Ordinance, aimed at the welter of state laws favoring debtors over creditors: No state was to pass any ex post facto law or law impairing the obligation of contracts.

The provisions of Article IV requiring each state to give "full faith and credit" to the acts of other states, to respect "all Privileges and Immunities" of all citizens, and to deliver up fugitives from justice were derived from the Articles of Confederation. To these the convention, at the suggestion of southerners, added a provision that became known as the "fugitive slave" clause; it required such persons to be "delivered up on Claim of the Party to

The signing of the Constitution on September 17, 1787.

whom such Service or Labour may be due." As with the rest of the Constitution, the enforcement of these provisions was assigned, by the "supremacy" clause, to the courts.

AMENDMENT PROCESS

A major reason for calling the Constitutional Convention had been that the method for amending the Articles of Confederation—requiring the unanimous consent of the states—had proved to be impractical. So there was general agreement that it was better to provide a process for amending the Constitution "in an easy, regular, and constitutional way, than to trust to chance and violence," as Mason put it. But the formula for doing so received little consideration until the final days of the convention.

The Committee of Detail first proposed that the legislatures of two-thirds of the states have the sole power to initiate amendments by petitioning Congress to call a convention for that purpose. This provision was adopted August 30 after a brief debate during which no one supported the argument of Gouverneur Morris that Congress also should have the power to call a convention. But when the convention reconsidered the issue September 10, Hamilton asserted that Congress "will be the first to perceive and will be the most sensible to the necessity of amendments." He proposed that two-thirds of the Senate and House also be given the power to call a convention.

Wilson moved that amendments to the Constitution be considered adopted when they had been ratified by two-thirds of the states. When that proposal was defeated, six states to five, Wilson moved to substitute ratification by three-fourths of the states, which was approved without dissent. The convention then adopted a new process, providing that Congress "shall" propose amendments "whenever two-thirds of both Houses shall deem necessary or on the application of two-thirds" of the state legislatures and that such amendments would become valid when ratified by either the legislatures or conventions of three-fourths of the states depending on which mode of ratification Congress directed.

Under this formula, any proposed constitutional amendment offered by two-thirds of the states would be submitted directly to the states for ratification. This was modified September 15 on a motion by Morris. His revision provided that on the application of two-thirds of the states, Congress "shall call a Convention for proposing Amendments." Thus, as finally drafted, Article V provided that, in proposing amendments, Congress would act directly while the states would act indirectly. In either case, however, amendments would take effect when approved by three-fourths of the states.

While working out these terms, the convention was forced to place some restrictions on the amending power. As a concession to the southern states, the convention (in Section 9 of Article I) already had barred Congress from outlawing the slave trade before 1808 and from levying any direct tax unless it was in proportion to a count of all whites and three-fifths of the black population. But Rutledge, a delegate from South Carolina, noted that nothing in the proposed article on the amending process would prevent adoption of a constitutional amendment altering the prohibition on outlawing the slave trade before 1808. He said the provisions "relating to slaves might be altered by the States not interested in that property and prejudiced against them" and that he could never agree to such an amending power. So on September 10 it was agreed without debate to add to Article V the proviso that no amendment adopted before 1808 "shall in any manner affect" those two provisions of Article I.

Sherman now worried that "three fourths of the States might be brought to do things fatal to particular States, as abolishing them altogether or depriving them of their equality in the Senate." He proposed, as a further proviso to the amending power, that "No state shall without its consent be affected in its internal police, or deprived of its equal suffrage in the Senate." The term "internal police" covered much more than most delegates were prepared to exclude, and only three states supported Sherman. But the more limited proviso that "no State, without its Consent, shall be deprived of its equal suffrage in the Senate" was accepted without debate and added at the end of Article V.

CAMPAIGN FOR RATIFICATION

According to the resolution of the Congress authorizing the Philadelphia convention, the delegates were expected to meet for the "sole and express purpose of revising the Articles of Confederation and reporting to Congress and the several legislatures" its recommendations. But the nationalists who organized the convention and persuaded it to ignore these narrow instructions were determined that the fate of the new Constitution not be entrusted to the state legislatures. They insisted that the Constitution should be considered "by the supreme authority of the people themselves," as Madison put it. The legislatures, he pointed out, were in any event without power to consent to changes that "would make essential inroads on the State Constitutions."

By "the people themselves" the nationalists meant special conventions elected for the purpose. Conventions would be more representative than the legislatures, which excluded "many of the ablest men," they argued. The people would be more likely than the state legislatures to favor the Constitution because, according to Rufus King, the legislatures, which would "lose power [under the Constitution,] will be most likely to raise objections." Opposing this view were Ellsworth and other delegates who thought conventions were "better fitted to pull down than to build up Constitutions," and Gerry, who said the people "would never agree on anything." But the convention rejected Ellsworth's motion for ratification by the legislatures and agreed July 23, by a vote of nine states to one, that the Constitution should be submitted to popularly elected state conventions.

After this decision was made, the convention on August 31 reached agreement on a crucial point: that the Constitution should enter into force when approved by the conventions of nine of the thirteen states. By this time only a few of the delegates still felt, as Martin did, that "unanimity was necessary to dissolve the existing Confederacy." Seven and ten states also were proposed as minimums for ratification, but nine was chosen as the more familiar figure, being the number required to act on important matters under the Articles. It also was clearly impractical to require (as the Committee of Detail had proposed) that the Constitution be submitted to the existing Congress "for their approbation," so it was agreed to delete that provision.

Randolph and Mason (two of the three delegates who refused to sign the final version of the Constitution) continued to argue that it should be submitted to another general convention, along with any amendments proposed by the state conventions, before being acted upon. Few others believed another such gathering could improve the product significantly, and the two Virginians' proposal was rejected on September 13. As finally drafted, Article VII provided simply that "The Ratification of the Conventions of nine States shall be sufficient for the Establishment of this Constitution between the States so ratifying the Same."

By a separate resolution adopted September 17, it was agreed by the convention that the Constitution should "be laid before the United States in Congress assembled" and that it should then be submitted to "a Convention of Delegates, chosen in each State by the People thereof." As soon as nine states had ratified, the resolution continued, Congress should set a day for the election of presidential electors, senators, and representatives and "the Time and Place for commencing Proceedings under this Constitution."

Ten days after the convention adjourned on September 17, 1787, the Congress of the Confederation submitted the Constitution to the states for their consideration, and the struggle for ratification began. In that contest, ironically, those who had argued successfully in the convention for a national instead of merely a federal system, and who now took the lead in urging ratification, called themselves Federalists, although no reference was made to anything federal in the Constitution. Those who opposed the Constitution became known as the Anti-Federalists, although the sentiments they espoused had been forming for several years before the fight over ratification.

These two factions, out of which the first political parties in the United States were formed, tended to reflect long-standing divisions among Americans between commercial and agrarian interests, creditors and debtors, men of great or little property, tidewater planters and the small farmers of the interior. But important and numerous exceptions existed to the tendency of Federalists and Anti-Federalists to divide along class, sectional, and economic lines. Among the Anti-Federalists were some of the wealthiest and most influential men of the times, including George Mason, Patrick Henry, Richard Henry Lee, George Clinton, James Winthrop, and many others.

As in initiating the constitutional convention, the Federalists seized the initiative in the ratification process. The ensuing cam-

THE

FEDERALIST:

ADDRESSED TO THE

PEOPLE OF THE STATE OF
NEW-YORK.

NUMBER I.

Introduction.

AFTER an unequivocal experience of the inefficacy of the subsisting federal government, you are called upon to deliberate on a new constitution for the United States of America. The subject speaks its own importance; comprehending in its consequences, nothing less than the existence of the UNION, the safety and welfare of the parts of which it is composed, the fate of an empire, in many respects, the most interesting in the world. It has been frequently remarked, that it seems to have been reserved to the people of this country, by their conduct and example, to decide the important question, whether societies of men are really capable or not, of establishing good government from reflection and choice, or whether they are forever destined to depend, for their political constitutions, on accident and force. If there be any truth in the remark, the crisis, at which we are arrived, may with propriety be regarded as the æra in which

The Federalist, a collection of eighty-five letters to the public signed with a pseudonym, Publius, appeared at short intervals in the newspapers of New York City beginning on October 27, 1787. The identity of Publius was a secret until several years after publication. In March 1788 the first thirty-six letters were issued in a collected edition. A second volume containing numbers 37–85 was published in May 1788.

The idea for *The Federalist* letters came from Alexander Hamilton, who wanted to wage a literary campaign to explain the proposed Constitution and build support for it. James Madison and John Jay agreed to work with him.

Of the eighty-five letters, Hamilton wrote fifty-six; Madison, twenty-one; and Jay, five. Hamilton and Madison collaborated on three. Jay's low productivity was attributed to a serious illness in the fall of 1787.

The essays probably had only a small impact on the ratification of the Constitution. Even the most widely circulated newspapers did not travel far in 1788. But they gained importance later as a classic exposition of the Constitution.

Clinton Rossiter wrote in a 1961 introduction to the papers: "*The Federalist* is the most important work in political science that has ever been written, or is likely ever to be written, in the United States. It is, indeed, the one product of the American mind that is rightly counted among the classics of political theory. . . . *The Federalist* stands third only to the Declaration of Independence and the Constitution itself among all the sacred writing of American political history."[1]

1. Alexander Hamilton, James Madison, and John Jay, *The Federalist Papers,* with an introduction by Clinton Rossiter (New York: New American Library, 1961), vii.

paign of political maneuver, persuasion, and propaganda was intense and bitter. Both sides questioned the motives of the other and exaggerated the dire consequences of one or the other course. All Anti-Federalists, wrote Ellsworth, were either "men who have lucrative and influential State offices" or "tories, debtors in desperate circumstances, or insurgents." To Luther Martin, the object of the Federalists was "the total abolition of all State Governments and the erection on their ruins of one great and extreme empire."

All of the newspapers of the day published extensive correspondence on the virtues and vices of the new plan of government. The fullest and strongest case for the Constitution was presented in a series of letters written by Madison, Hamilton, and Jay under the name of "Publius." Seventy-seven of the letters were published in New York City newspapers between October 27, 1787, and April 4, 1788, and in book form, along with eight additional letters, as *The Federalist,* on May 28, 1788. These letters probably had only a small influence on ratification, but *The Federalist* came to be regarded as the classic exposition of the Constitution as well as one of the most important works on political theory ever written.

Political maneuvers were common in both camps. In Pennsylvania, Federalists moved to call a convention before Congress had officially submitted the Constitution. Nineteen Anti-Federalists thereupon withdrew from the assembly, thus depriving it of a quorum, until a mob seized two of them and dragged them back. When the Massachusetts Convention met, the Anti-Federalists were in the majority until John Hancock, the president of that state's constitutional convention, was won over to the Federalist side by promises of support for the new post of vice president of the United States.

Among the major arguments advanced against the Constitution were the failure of the convention to include a Bill of Rights; the fear that an elected president, with no ban on the number of terms he could serve, would tend toward monarchy; and concern that the strong central government would lead to the consolidation and destruction of the separate states. Anti-Federalists accused supporters of the Constitution of deliberately trying to end state sovereignty. They also charged that in drafting the Constitution the Federalists hoped to establish a small ruling class that would protect their economic interests.

Federalists met the first argument by pledging early enactment of a Bill of Rights as the first amendments to the Constitution. Both Massachusetts and Virginia were particularly determined that they should be added.

The fear of monarchy was mitigated by a widespread assumption—held also in the convention—that George Washington would become the first president. This assumption, together with the fact that most Americans knew Washington and Benjamin Franklin supported the Constitution, contributed as much as anything to the success of the ratification campaign.

The Delaware convention on December 7, 1787, unanimously ratified the Constitution, the first state to do so. Then came

Pennsylvania, by a 46–23 vote, on December 12; New Jersey, unanimously, on December 18; Georgia, unanimously, on January 2, 1788; Connecticut, by a 128–40 vote, on January 9, 1788; Massachusetts, 187–168, on February 6; Maryland, 63–11, on April 28; South Carolina, 149–73, on May 23; and New Hampshire, 57–46, on June 21. This met the requirement for approval by nine states, but it was clear that without the approval of Virginia and New York the Constitution would stand on shaky ground.

In Virginia, according to Ellsworth, "the opposition wholly originated in two principles: the madness of Mason, and enmity of the Lee faction to Gen. Washington." But Randolph, who had refused with Mason and Gerry to sign the Constitution, eventually was persuaded to support it, and on June 25 the Federalists prevailed by a vote of 89–79.

New York, where Governor George Clinton led the Anti-Federalists, finally ratified on July 26 by an even narrower margin of 30–27, after Hamilton and Jay had threatened that otherwise New York City would secede and join the Union as a separate state.

North Carolina did not ratify the Constitution until November 21, 1789; the vote was 184–77. Rhode Island, which ratified by a vote of 34–32 on May 29, 1790, became the last of the thirteen original states to ratify.

In accordance with the request of the Constitutional Convention, the Congress of the Confederation on September 13, 1788, designated New York City as the seat of the new government, the first Wednesday of January 1789 as the day for choosing presidential electors, the first Wednesday of February for the meeting of electors, and the first Wednesday of March for the opening session of the first Congress under the new Constitution.

THE FIRST ELECTIONS

The Constitution empowered the state legislatures to prescribe the method of choosing their presidential electors as well as the time, place, and manner of electing their representatives and senators. Virginia and Maryland put the choice of electors directly to the people; in Massachusetts, two were chosen at large and the other eight were picked by the legislature from twenty-four names submitted by the voters of the eight congressional districts. In the other states, the electors were chosen by the legislature.

In New York, where the Federalists controlled the state Senate and the Anti-Federalists dominated the Assembly, the two houses became deadlocked on the question of acting by joint or concurrent vote, and the legislature adjourned without choosing electors.

Election to the House of Representatives also involved a number of spirited contests between Federalists and Anti-Federalists, although the total vote cast in these first elections, estimated to be between 75,000 and 125,000, was a small fraction of the free population of 3.2 million. In Massachusetts and Con-

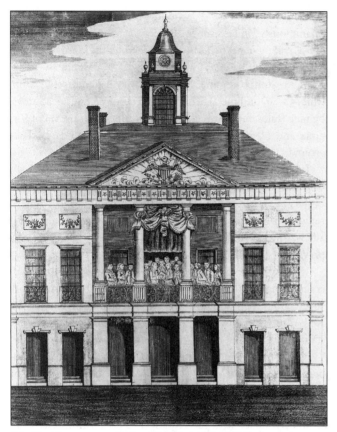

The First Congress met in New York City's Federal Hall on March 4, 1789. A quorum of members did not arrive for another month.

necticut, several elections were required in some districts before a candidate obtained a majority of the popular vote. (In the nineteenth century, five of the New England states required a majority vote to win election to the House; all such requirements had been phased out by the 1890s.[20]) Elbridge Gerry, who had refused to sign the Constitution, finally beat Nathaniel Gorham, also a delegate to the Philadelphia convention, after saying he no longer opposed it. In New Jersey the law did not fix a time for closing the polls, and they stayed open for three weeks. The elections of all four New Jersey representatives were contested when the House organized for the First Congress.

Although March 4, 1789, had been fixed as the day for commencing proceedings of the new government, only thirteen of the fifty-nine representatives and eight of the twenty-two senators had arrived in New York City by then. (Seats allotted to North Carolina and Rhode Island were not filled until 1790, after those states had ratified the Constitution.) It was not until April 1 that a thirtieth representative arrived to make a quorum of the House; the Senate attained its quorum of twelve on April 6. The two houses then met jointly for the first time to count the electoral vote.

Meanwhile, as everyone had assumed, the electors met on February 4 and each of those present—sixty-nine—cast his vote for George Washington, who thus became president by unani-

mous choice. (Four additional electors—two from Maryland and two from Virginia—failed to show up for the vote.) Of eleven men among whom the electors distributed their second vote, John Adams received the highest number—thirty-four—and was declared vice president.

Adams arrived in New York on April 21, Washington arrived on the 23rd, and the inaugural took place on the 30th. Washington took the oath of office prescribed by the Constitution on the balcony of Federal Hall, New York's former City Hall, which housed the president and both houses of Congress until the government moved to Philadelphia in 1790. The president then went to the Senate chamber to deliver a brief inaugural address, in the course of which he declined to accept whatever salary Congress might confer on the office.

Thus, by April 30, 1789, the long task of designing and installing a new government for the thirteen states had been completed.

NOTES

1. Jack P. Greene, ed., *Great Britain and the American Colonies, 1606–1763* (New York: Harper Paperbacks, 1970), xxxix.

2. Edmund S. Morgan, *The Birth of the Republic* (Chicago: University of Chicago Press, 1956), 31.

3. L. H. Butterfield, ed., *Adams Family Correspondence* (Cambridge, Mass.: Belknap Press, 1963), vol. 1, *December 1761–May 1776*, 166.

4. Edmund Cody Burnett, *The Continental Congress* (New York: Norton, 1964), 61.

5. Charles Ramsdell Lingley, *The Transition in Virginia from Colony to Commonwealth* (New York: Columbia University Press, 1910), 172.

6. Unless otherwise noted, the following account was drawn from Charles Warren, *The Making of the Constitution* (Boston: Little, Brown, 1928).

7. James Madison, *Notes of Debates in the Federal Convention of 1787* (Athens: Ohio University Press, 1966), 30.

8. Ibid., 36.

9. John P. Roche, "Constitutional Convention of 1787," in *Encyclopedia of the American Constitution*, ed. Leonard W. Levy, Kenneth L. Karst, and Dennis J. Mahoney (New York: Macmillan, 1986), 365.

10. Madison, *Notes of Debates in the Federal Convention*, 257.

11. Merrill Jensen, *The Articles of Confederation* (Madison: University of Wisconsin Press, 1940), 264.

12. Madison, *Notes of Debates in the Federal Convention*, 45.

13. Ibid., 475–477.

14. Ibid., 482.

15. Ibid., 580.

16. Ibid., 516.

17. Ibid., 471.

18. Ibid., 596.

19. Ibid., 536–537.

20. *Guide to U.S. Elections*, 3rd ed. (Washington, D.C.: Congressional Quarterly, 1994), 916.

SELECTED BIBLIOGRAPHY

American Political Science Association and the American Historical Association. *This Constitution: Our Enduring Legacy.* Washington, D.C.: CQ Press, 1986.

———. *This Constitution: From Ratification to the Bill of Rights.* Washington, D.C.: CQ Press, 1988.

Andrews, Charles M. *The Colonial Period of American History.* 4 vols. New Haven, Conn.: Yale University Press, 1934.

Bailyn, Bernard. *The Ideological Origin of the American Revolution.* Cambridge, Mass.: Harvard University Press, 1992.

Barbash, Fred. *The Founding: A Dramatic Account of the Writing of the Constitution.* New York: Linden Press/Simon and Schuster, 1987.

Beard, Charles A. *An Economic Interpretation of the Constitution of the United States.* New York: Macmillan, 1935.

Beard, Charles A., ed. *The Enduring Federalist.* Garden City, New York: Doubleday, 1948.

Bowen, Catherine Drinker. *Miracle at Philadelphia: The Story of the Constitutional Convention, May to September 1787.* Boston: Little, Brown, 1966.

Brant, Irving. *James Madison: Father of the Constitution, 1787–1800.* Indianapolis: Bobbs-Merrill, 1950.

Burnett, Edmund C. *The Continental Congress.* New York: Macmillan, 1941.

Butterfield, L. H., ed. *Adams Family Correspondence.* Vol. 1, *December 1761–May 1776.* Cambridge, Mass.: Belknap Press, 1963.

Collier, Christopher, and James Lincoln Collier. *Decision in Philadelphia: The Constitutional Convention of 1787.* New York: Ballantine, 1986.

Farrand, Max, ed. *The Records of the Federal Convention of 1787.* 4 vols. New Haven, Conn.: Yale University Press, 1973.

Greene, Jack P., ed. *Great Britain and the American Colonies, 1606–1763.* New York: Harper Paperbacks, 1970.

Hamilton, Alexander, James Madison, and John Jay. *The Federalist Papers.* Introduction by Clinton Rossiter. New York: New American Library, 1961.

Hutson, James H., ed. *Supplement to Max Farrand's The Records of the Federal Convention of 1787.* New Haven, Conn.: Yale University Press, 1987.

Jensen, Merrill. *The Articles of Confederation.* Madison: University of Wisconsin Press, 1940.

Kelly, Alfred H., and Winifred A. Harbison. *The American Constitution: Its Origins and Development.* 7th ed. New York: Norton, 1991.

Levy, Leonard W., ed. *Essays in the Making of the Constitution.* New York: Oxford University Press, 1969.

Levy, Leonard W., Kenneth L. Karst, and Dennis J. Mahoney, eds. *Encyclopedia of the American Constitution.* New York: Macmillan, 1986.

Lingley, Charles Ramsdell. *The Transition in Virginia from Colony to Commonwealth.* New York: Columbia University Press, 1910.

Loss, Richard, ed. *Corwin on the Constitution.* Ithaca, N.Y.: Cornell University Press, 1981.

Lutz, Donald. *Origins of American Constitutionalism.* Baton Rouge: Louisiana State University Press, 1988.

McLaughlin, Andrew C. *The Confederation and the Constitution, 1783–1789.* Foreword by Henry Steele Commager. New York: Collier Books, 1962.

Madison, James. *Notes of Debates in the Federal Convention of 1787.* Introduction by Adrienne Koch. Athens: Ohio University Press, 1966.

Nevins, Allan. *The American States During and After the Revolution, 1775–1789.* New York: Macmillan, 1924.

Peters, William. *A More Perfect Union: The Making of the United States Constitution.* New York: Crown, 1987.

Rakove, Jack N. *The Beginnings of National Politics: An Interpretive History of the Constitutional Congress.* New York: Knopf, 1979.

Rossiter, Clinton. *1787: The Grand Convention.* New York: Macmillan, 1966.

Smith, David G. *The Convention and the Constitution.* New York: St. Martin's Press, 1965.

Smith, Page. *A New Age Now Begins: A People's History of the American Revolution.* 2 vols. New York: McGraw-Hill, 1976.

Van Doren, Carl. *The Great Rehearsal: The Story of the Making and Ratifying of the Constitution of the United States.* New York: Viking, 1948.

Warren, Charles. *The Making of the Constitution.* Boston: Little, Brown, 1928.

Wilson, Woodrow. *Congressional Government: A Study in American Politics.* Boston: Houghton Mifflin, 1885. Reprint. Cleveland: Meridian Books, 1956.

Wood, Gordon S. *The Creation of the American Republic, 1776–1787.* New York: Norton, 1972.

Wright, Benjamin F. *Consensus and Continuity, 1776–1787.* Boston: Boston University Press, 1958.

CHAPTER 2

History of the House

WHEN THE THIRTIETH of the fifty-nine representatives elected to the First Congress reached New York on April 1, 1789, the assembled quorum promptly chose as Speaker of the House Frederick A. C. Muhlenberg of Pennsylvania. The next day Muhlenberg appointed a committee of eleven representatives to draw up the first rules of procedure, which the House adopted April 7. The first standing committee of the House—a seven-member Committee on Elections—was chosen April 13, and its report accepting the credentials of forty-nine members was approved April 18. By then the House already was debating its first piece of legislation, a tariff bill.

By contrast, it took five years of study and negotiation to produce agreement in 1970 on a limited revision of House rules. Long before 1970 the House of Representatives had become a highly structured institution governed by an elaborate set of rules, precedents, and customs, all closely guarded by its most senior, privileged, and influential members.

Since its founding the House often has adapted its procedures to the needs or pressures of the moment. Some changes, including the Legislative Reorganization Acts of 1946 and 1970, were products of lengthy House study and debate. Partisan groups were responsible for other changes, such as changes in Democratic Caucus rules in the mid-1970s that gave more influence to junior members.

From the beginning politics and personalities have played their part in influencing the timing and direction of changes in House procedure and organization. But the rapid increase in the size of its membership in the nineteenth century and of its workload in the twentieth century compelled development of what became the major features of the legislative process in the House—strict limitations on floor debate, a heavy reliance on the committee system, and techniques for channeling the flow of business.

It was Speaker Thomas Brackett Reed, R-Maine, who in 1890 told the House that "the object of a parliamentary body is action, and not stoppage of action."[1] But how to ensure the right of a majority to work its will has been a perennial challenge in the House, which was conceived by George Mason in 1787 as the governing body that would become "the grand depository of the democratic principles of the government."

The people, parties, and events that contributed to the evolution of the House of Representatives as a legislative body are the focus of this history.

The Formative Years: 1789–1809

Only thirteen representatives had arrived in New York by March 4, 1789, the date scheduled for the First Congress to convene. Nearly a month passed before a quorum of thirty members gathered on April 1. Rep. Fisher Ames of Massachusetts gave this early assessment of his colleagues in a letter to a friend: "Though I am rather less awed and terrified at the sight of the members than I expected to be, I assure you I like them very well. There are few shining geniuses; there are many who have experience, the virtues of the heart, and the habits of business. It will be quite a republican assembly. It looks like one."[2]

The great majority of the representatives elected to the First Congress had served in the Continental Congress or in their state legislatures, and the procedures followed in those bodies—derived in large part from English parliamentary practice—formed the basis for the first rules of the House. Those rules included provisions that:

• The Speaker was to preside over the House, preserve decorum and order, put questions to members, decide all points of order, announce the results of votes, and vote on all ballots taken by the House.

• Committees of three or fewer members were to be appointed by the Speaker, while larger ones were to be chosen by ballot.

• Members could not introduce bills or speak more than twice to the same question without leave of the House. They were required to vote if present, unless excused, and were barred from voting if not present or if they had a direct personal interest in the outcome.

The first rules also set forth legislative procedures. As in the Continental Congress, the principal forum for considering and perfecting legislation was to be the Committee of the Whole House on the State of the Union—the House itself under another name. When the House sat as the Committee of the Whole, a member other than the Speaker occupied the chair and certain parliamentary motions permitted in the House—such as the "previous question" and the motion to adjourn—were not in order, nor were roll-call votes taken. Amendments rejected in the Committee of the Whole could not be offered again in the House except as part of a motion to recommit the entire bill to the committee that reported the measure. As in the House, originally a majority of the House membership constituted a quorum in the Committee of the Whole.

The letters of Rep. Fisher Ames provided chatty accounts of the House in its first decade.

EARLY HOUSE PROCEDURE

In the early years of the House, it was the practice to begin discussion of all major legislative proposals in the Committee of the Whole. After broad agreement had been reached on the purposes of the measure, a select committee was named to draft a bill. After considering it, the panel reported the measure back to the House together with any amendments that may have been adopted. The legislation then was considered by the Committee of the Whole for section-by-section debate and approval or further amendment. Its work completed, the committee rose, the Speaker resumed the chair, and the House either accepted or rejected the amendments agreed to in the Committee of the Whole. This was followed by a third and final reading of the engrossed, or completed, version, and a vote on final passage by the House.

Originally no time limits were set on the right of members to speak; even the small membership of the First and Second Congresses found this procedure cumbersome and inefficient. Rep.

James Madison of Virginia blamed the "delays and perplexities" of the House on "the want of precedents." But Fisher Ames saw the problem as an excessive concern with detail in the "unwieldy" Committee of the Whole, for "a great, clumsy machine is applied to the slightest and most delicate operations—the hoof of an elephant to the strokes of mezzo-tinto."

A small time-saver was introduced in 1790, when the House amended its rules to permit the Speaker to appoint all committees unless otherwise specially directed by the House. Similarly, in 1794, the House empowered the Speaker to name the chairman of the Committee of the Whole, who previously had been elected. But the time-consuming practice of reaching a consensus on the broad terms of major legislative proposals in the Committee of the Whole before naming a select committee to draft a bill (more than 350 select committees were formed during the Third Congress) continued into the 1800s.

By entrusting each proposal to a special committee that ceased to exist once the measure was reported, the House kept effective control over all legislation. But as its business multiplied and its membership increased (to 106 after the census of 1790 and to 142 after that of 1800), the House began to delegate increasing responsibility for initiating legislation to standing, or permanent, committees. Four committees had been established by 1795; between 1802 and 1809, six more were added. Among the more important were Commerce and Manufactures, created in 1795; Ways and Means, a select committee made permanent in 1802; and Public Lands, whose establishment in 1805 was prompted by the Louisiana Purchase.

EMERGENCE OF PARTIES

Neither the Constitution nor the early rules of the House envisioned a role for political parties in the legislative process. The triumph of the Federalists over the Anti-Federalists in winning ratification of the Constitution, the unanimous and nonpartisan choice of George Washington as the first president, and the great preponderance of nominal Federalists elected to the First Congress tended to obscure the underlying economic, sectional, and philosophic differences existing at the time. But these differences were not long in surfacing once Alexander Hamilton took office as the first secretary of the Treasury. The statute creating the department required the Treasury "to digest and prepare plans for the improvement and management of the revenue and for the support of the public credit."

Hamilton, a skilled financier, administrator, and political organizer at thirty-four, quickly responded with proposals for paying off the national and state debts at par and for creating a bank of the United States. Designed to establish confidence in the new federal government, these proposals also appealed to the mercantile and moneyed interests to whom Hamilton looked for support in his desire to strengthen central authority. Because most of those elected to the First Congress shared his outlook, and some members stood to profit from his proposals, he soon emerged as the effective leader of a new Federalist Party, though it remained a loose alliance of interests. Even the Federalists never considered themselves a political party, although they met frequently in caucus to plan legislative strategy.

Madison was the first to take issue with the substance of Hamilton's program as well as with executive branch dominance in guiding the decisions of the House. He was joined by his close friend and fellow Virginian, Thomas Jefferson, who became secretary of state in 1790. Jefferson strongly opposed Hamilton from within the cabinet. In a letter to President Washington, Jefferson criticized his colleague for attempting to exert undue influence upon Congress. He wrote that Hamilton's "system flowed from principles adverse to liberty, and was calculated to undermine and demolish the republic, by creating an influence of his department over the members of the legislature."[3]

The cleavage was reinforced by the French Revolution and the wars that followed in its wake. Hamilton and the Federalists, with strong commercial and other ties to England, urged American neutrality, while Jefferson and his followers looked on the French as democratic allies to be helped.

By 1792 Madison and Jefferson were the recognized leaders of a nascent opposition party, rooted in southern fears of Federalist economic policies and rising agrarian antagonism to the aristocratic views of Hamilton, Vice President John Adams, and other prominent Federalists. In the Third through the Sixth Congresses, spanning Washington's second term and Adams's single term as president, the House was closely divided between the so-called Jeffersonians and the Federalists. But in 1800 Jefferson's party emerged with a clear majority, and during his two terms as president his party outnumbered the Federalists in the House by two- and three-to-one.

The Jeffersonians never acquired a nationally accepted name, though many referred to themselves as Republicans. Jeffersonians were labeled by their opponents as Anti-Federalists, disorganizers, Jacobins, and Democrats—the latter considered in the early years of the Republic to be an unflattering term. To many Americans in the late eighteenth century a Democrat was considered to be a supporter of mob rule and one identified ideologically with the French Revolution. In some states the designation Democrat-Republican was used by the Jeffersonians, but it was not widely accepted. Most historians eventually began to refer to them as Democratic-Republicans to avoid confusion with the unrelated Republican Party created in 1854.

Although politicians by the time of the Jefferson administration had acknowledged the existence of political parties, they did not foresee the development of a two-party system. Instead, they tended to justify the existence of their own party as a reaction to an unacceptable opposition. Jefferson himself justified his party involvement as a struggle between good and evil.

LEADERSHIP IN THE HOUSE

With the early emergence of two parties, the choice of a Speaker soon fell to the party with a majority in the House. Thus in 1799 Theodore Sedgwick of Massachusetts was elected Speaker over Nathaniel Macon of North Carolina by a vote of 44–38, a margin that approximated that of the Federalists over the Jeffersonians in the Sixth Congress. Two years later, in the Seventh Congress, Macon was elected Speaker by a wide margin over the Federalist candidate.

Backed by party support, the early Speakers were not unwilling to use their powers to promote party policies. In 1796, when Jeffersonians in the House mounted an attack on the Jay Treaty with Britain, Speaker Jonathan Dayton, a Federalist, twice voted to produce ties that resulted in the defeat of antitreaty motions. Jeffersonians in the Sixth Congress found the rulings of Sedgwick so partisan that they refused to join in the by-then customary vote of thanks to the Speaker at adjournment.

But the early Speakers were not the real political or legislative leaders of the House. Until he left the Treasury in 1795, Hamilton, operating through members of his own choice, dominated the Federalist majority. According to one Jeffersonian observer, Hamilton was an "all-powerful" leader, who "fails in nothing he attempts." As the leader of the Jeffersonians in the House until he left Congress in 1797, Madison was seen in much the same light by Federalist Fisher Ames, who wrote: "Virginia moves in a solid column and the discipline of the party is as severe as the Prussian. Deserters are not spared."

The Jeffersonians (or Democratic-Republicans) were opposed in principle to the concept of executive supremacy embraced by Hamilton and the early Federalists. When he became president in 1801, Jefferson promptly discarded a favored symbol of Federalist theory—the personal appearance of the president before a joint session of Congress to read his annual State of the Union message—and instituted the practice, followed by all presidents until Woodrow Wilson, of sending up the message to be read by a clerk. But Jefferson also took steps to assert his leadership over the new Democratic-Republican majority in the House.

Jefferson's secretary of the Treasury, Swiss-born Albert Gallatin, who had succeeded Madison as leader of the Jeffersonians, soon became as adept as Hamilton had been in guiding administration measures through the party caucus and the House. Moreover, Jefferson picked his own floor leader, who was named chairman of the Ways and Means Committee at the same time. The men who held the posts of floor leader and Ways and Means chairman during Jefferson's tenure were known as the president's spokesmen in establishing party policy. When one of these leaders, the tempestuous John Randolph, broke with Jefferson over a plan to acquire Florida, the president had him deposed as Ways and Means chairman.

Randolph, meanwhile, already had affronted some members of the House by his conduct as committee chairman. Rep. James Sloan of New Jersey complained in 1805 that Randolph had tied up committee business "by going to Baltimore or elsewhere, without leave of absence," and by keeping appropriations estimates "in his pockets or locked up in his drawer" and that he had rushed out important bills at the end of the session "when many members had gone home."

Sloan proposed that members of all standing committees be elected by ballot and that committees be allowed to choose their own chairmen. A rules change in the Eighth Congress gave committees the right to select their own chairmen if they so chose, but at the beginning of the 11th Congress selection of chairmen as well as committee members reverted to the Speaker.

In sum, the first twenty years of the House saw the beginnings of the standing committee system and the emergence of a floor leader and committee chairmen as key men in the legislative process. But that process was dominated, by and large, by the executive branch, and major decisions on legislative issues were reached behind the scenes in closed caucuses of the majority party. As Federalist Josiah Quincy of Massachusetts lamented in 1809, the House "acts and reasons and votes, and performs all the operations of an animated being, and yet, judging from my own perceptions, I cannot refrain from concluding that all great political questions are settled somewhere else than on this floor."

Rise of Congress: 1809–1829

The era of executive supremacy over Congress came to an end under Jefferson's successor, James Madison, whose strong leadership in the Constitutional Convention of 1787, in the House, and as secretary of state for eight years was not matched in his presidency. Although he was nominally backed by Demo-cratic-Republican majorities during his two terms in office, Madison soon lost control of his party to a group of young "war hawks" (as John Randolph called them) first elected to the 12th Congress. These men eventually pushed the president into the War of 1812 against England. Led in the House by Henry Clay and John C. Calhoun, these radicals within Madison's party capitalized on the president's weakness and a rising resistance to executive control to effect a shift of power to Congress that was not reversed until Andrew Jackson became president in 1829.

CLAY AS SPEAKER

Henry Clay first came to national attention while serving briefly as a senator from Kentucky in 1810–1811. He then spoke eloquently of the need for "a new race of heroes" to preserve the achievements of America's founders. He proposed the conquest of Canada, asserting that "the militia of Kentucky are alone competent to place Montreal and Upper Canada at your feet."[4] It was as spokesperson for a new nationalism, affronted by British interference with American trade and shipping, that Clay entered the House in 1811 and, although only thirty-four and a newcomer, promptly was elected Speaker by like-minded Democratic-Republicans. Using to the full his power to select committee chairmen and appoint members to committees, Clay put his fellow war hawks in all the key positions. Together they took control of the House.

The great chandelier is lighted as night falls in the old House chamber in this scene painted by Samuel F. B. Morse in the early 1820s. The House did not move into the chamber it occupies today until 1867.

Clay greatly enhanced the power and prestige of the Speaker. In addition to presiding over the House as his predecessors had done, he took over the leadership of the majority party. This made him the leader of the House in fact as well as name. A forceful presiding officer, Clay also was an accomplished debater who frequently participated in House legislative debates. Gifted with great charm and tact, Clay remained Speaker as long as he was in the House. Although he resigned his seat twice (in 1814, to help negotiate an end to the War of 1812, and in 1820), he was reelected Speaker as soon as he returned to the House in 1815 and again in 1823.

It was the job of the Speaker, Clay said in his 1823 inaugural speech, to be prompt and impartial in deciding questions of order, to display "patience, good temper, and courtesy" to every member, and to make "the best arrangement and distribution of the talent of the House" for the dispatch of public business. Above all, he said, the Speaker must "remain cool and unshaken amidst all the storms of debate, carefully guarding the preservation of the permanent laws and rules of the House from being sacrificed to temporary passions, prejudices or interests."

This was no easy job in Clay's time, when political passions were strong, the size of the House was increasing rapidly (to 186 members after the census of 1810 and to 213 after that of 1820), and the right of debate was essentially unlimited. It is true that the House, after becoming exasperated with the unyielding tactics of Rep. Barent Gardenier, a New Yorker who once held the floor for twenty-four hours, decided in 1811 that a majority could shut off further debate on an issue by employing a parliamentary tactic known as the previous question. In time this became the normal and accepted means of closing House debate, but in the early years many representatives, such as John Randolph, regarded this device as a gag rule, and it was not easily invoked. Under the rules then existing, moreover, those skilled in parliamentary tactics—as Randolph was—could and frequently did succeed in tying up House proceedings.

Clay once outwitted Randolph. It was after the House in 1820 finally had passed the hotly disputed Missouri Compromise bill admitting Missouri to the Union as a slave state but barring slavery in any future state north of 36°30′ north latitude. When Randolph, who opposed the bill, moved the next day to reconsider the vote, the Speaker held the motion to be out of order pending completion of the prescribed order of business. Clay then proceeded to sign the bill and send it to the Senate before Randolph could renew his motion. The Speaker's action was upheld, in effect, when the House refused, 61–71, to consider Randolph's subsequent motion to censure the clerk for having removed the bill.

GROWTH OF STANDING COMMITTEES

Efforts to refine House procedures continued in the period from 1809 to 1829. The first rule to establish a daily order of business was adopted in 1811. In 1812 the Committee on Enrolled Bills was given leave to report measures at any time—a privilege later granted to certain other committees to expedite considera-

tion of important legislation. A rule adopted in 1817 enabled the House to protect itself against business it did not wish to consider. In 1820 the House created through its rules the first legislative calendars of the Committee of the Whole. And in 1822 it was decided that no House rule could be suspended except by a two-thirds majority vote.

But the chief development in House procedures during this period was the proliferation of standing committees and their emergence as the principal forums for the initial, most detailed, consideration of proposed legislation—a practice recognized in 1822 by a rule giving standing committees the right to originate and report legislation directly to the House. The number of select (ad hoc) committees created to draft bills had dropped from 350 in the Third Congress (1793–1795) to seventy in the 13th Congress (1813–1815). And the number of standing (permanent) committees grew from ten in 1809 to twenty-eight in 1825.

Among the standing committees created in this period were the Judiciary Committee, made permanent in 1813, and the Military Affairs, Naval Affairs, and Foreign Affairs committees, all created in 1822. Six committees on Expenditures, one for each of the executive departments then in existence, were established by Clay in 1816 to check up on economy and efficiency in the executive branch. Between 1816 and 1826 these and other House committees conducted at least twenty major investigations. The inquiries included such matters as the conduct of General Andrew Jackson in the Seminole War, charges against Secretary of the Treasury William Crawford, and the conduct of John C. Calhoun as secretary of war.

DECLINE OF KING CAUCUS

During Clay's reign as Speaker, the party caucus still afforded the House majority, the Democratic-Republicans, an important means of reaching legislative decisions. It took Federalist Daniel Webster less than two weeks after being seated in 1813 to conclude that "the time for us to be put on the stage and moved by the wires has not yet come," because "before anything is attempted to be done here, it must be arranged elsewhere." Webster soon noted that the caucus worked "because it was attended with a severe and efficacious discipline, by which those who went astray were to be brought to repentance." But the extent of party unity had already started to decline under Jefferson as a result of sectional rivalries, and while the Federalists continued to lose ground as a national party, factionalism increased among the Democratic-Republicans in Congress.

The change was reflected also in the rise and fall of the congressional caucus as the vehicle for selecting party nominees for president and vice president. The practice began in 1800, when both Federalist and Democratic-Republican members of the House and Senate met secretly to pick running mates for Jefferson and Adams. In 1804 Jefferson was renominated unanimously and openly by a caucus of 108 Democratic-Republican senators and representatives. Four years later, a caucus of 94 party members nominated Madison for president over the protests of others who preferred James Monroe. But only 83 of the 133

Democratic-Republicans in Congress attended the caucus that renominated Madison in 1812, just before he asked Congress for the declaration of war against England that Clay and others had been urging.

The party's caucus of 1816 drew 119 of the party's 141 members in the House and Senate. Madison favored the nomination of Monroe, then secretary of state, for president, but there was rising opposition to continuation of the Virginia "dynasty" in the White House, and Monroe was nominated by only 65 votes to 54 for Secretary of War William Crawford of Georgia. By 1820, however, no real opposition arose in either party to Monroe, who was credited with bringing about an "Era of Good Feelings"—a phrase coined by a Boston paper to describe the brief period of virtual one-party rule in the United States. (During his administration, Monroe had kept clear of the controversy over the Missouri Compromise.) Fewer than fifty members showed up for the caucus given that Monroe's candidacy was not contested. The caucus voted unanimously to make no nomination and passed a resolution explaining that it was inexpedient to do so. Monroe subsequently was reelected with every electoral vote but one.

In 1824 there still was only one party, the Democratic-Republicans. Within that party, however, an abundance of candidates wished to succeed Monroe, including three members of the president's own cabinet (Crawford, Calhoun, and John Quincy Adams) as well as Henry Clay and Andrew Jackson, hero of the Battle of New Orleans during the War of 1812. When it appeared that Crawford would get a majority in the party caucus, supporters of the other candidates began to denounce the caucus system. As a result, only sixty-six of the 261 senators and representatives then seated in Congress attended the caucus that nominated Crawford in 1824. The election that fall gave Jackson a plurality but not a majority of the electoral, or popular, vote, and the choice went to the House, which picked Adams.

The presidential contest of 1824 marked the end of the old party system and the congressional nominating caucus. Helping to kill the caucus were changes in voting procedures and an expansion of the suffrage. Between 1800 and 1824 the number of states in which the electors were chosen by popular vote instead of by the legislature increased from five out of sixteen to eighteen out of twenty-four. Four years later, in 1828, the electors were popularly chosen in all except two of the twenty-four states in the Union, and the popular vote jumped from less than 400,000 in 1824 to more than 1.1 million. With the emergence of a mass electorate, aspirants for the presidency were forced to seek a much broader base of support than the congressional caucus.

A House Divided: 1829–1861

National politics entered a period of increasing turmoil, which lasted until the Civil War, during the presidency of Andrew Jackson from 1829 to 1837. Jackson made unprecedented use of the presidential veto and of the removal and patronage powers of the executive office to establish its primacy over Congress. Two new parties emerged during his presidency: the Jacksonian Democrats, heirs to the agrarian and states' rights philosophy of the Jeffersonian Democratic-Republicans, and the Whigs, spokespeople for the commercial and industrial interests once represented by the Federalists. But the Democrats now embraced the Federalist principle of strong executive leadership, while the Whigs extolled the Republican doctrine of legislative supremacy and tried thereafter to weaken the presidency.

The power and influence of the House began to decline under Jackson, while House membership increased to 242. Former luminaries of the House, including Henry Clay, Daniel Webster, and John C. Calhoun, moved to the Senate, which now became the major arena of debate on national policy. Party control of the presidency, the House, and the Senate fluctuated considerably after Jackson. Increasingly, however, both Democrats and Whigs found themselves divided by the issue of slavery and its extension to the new territories and states beyond the Mississippi River. The issue was reflected in the bitter election battles for the speakership that occurred in 1839, 1849, 1855, and 1859.

CONTESTS TO ELECT THE SPEAKER

Intraparty contests for Speaker were not new in the House. In 1805, when Democratic-Republicans outnumbered Federalists almost four-to-one, it took four ballots to reelect Nathaniel Macon, a southerner, over Joseph B. Varnum of Massachusetts, the northern candidate. Two years later, among five candidates, Varnum won on the second ballot after Macon withdrew. By 1820—the year of the Missouri Compromise—the issue of slavery was an explicit part of the sectional contest for Speaker. To replace Clay, who had resigned, the House cast twenty-two ballots before electing John W. Taylor of New York, the antislavery candidate, over William Lowndes of South Carolina, a compromiser.

Taylor was one of five candidates the next year in a contest that underscored the breakup of the Democratic-Republicans and foreshadowed the presidential race of 1824. Taylor lost on the twelfth ballot to Philip P. Barbour of Virginia, a Crawford supporter. And in 1834, when Andrew Stevenson resigned in his fourth term as Speaker (only to see the Senate reject his nomination as minister to Great Britain), it took ten ballots to elect John Bell over his fellow Tennessean, James K. Polk.

Contest of 1839

Democrat Martin Van Buren, Jackson's handpicked successor, was elected president in 1836, but the Democrats barely won control of the House in the 25th Congress (1837–1839). When it adjourned, Whigs deplored the "most partial and unjust rulings" of Speaker Polk, who had succeeded Bell in 1835. Polk then left the House to become governor of Tennessee. At the opening of the 26th Congress on December 2, 1839, the House found itself with 120 Democrats, 118 Whigs, and five contested seats in New Jersey. Control of the House rested on the decision of these contests, but the clerk (who presided under House practice pending election of a Speaker) refused to choose between the claimants or to bring up the question of the contested seats until the House was organized.

After four days of bitter debate, members elected a temporary chairman—the venerable John Quincy Adams, who had returned to the House in 1831. But it was December 14 before the House decided to elect a Speaker without the contested New Jersey votes. There were six candidates initially, and John W. Jones of Virginia led on the first five ballots. But Robert M. T. Hunter, also of Virginia, was elected December 16 on the eleventh ballot (when there were thirteen candidates) because he "finally united all the Whig votes and all the malcontents of the administration," according to Adams.

Contest of 1849

Control of the House passed to the Whigs in the 27th Congress (1841–1843), then to the Democrats in the 28th and 29th, then back to the Whigs in the 30th (1847–1849) during the last two years of the Polk administration. Zachary Taylor, the Whig candidate, was elected president in 1848. But neither party had a majority in the House when the 31st Congress met on December 3, 1849, because a number of Free-Soil Whigs and Democrats refused to support the leading candidates for Speaker: Robert C. Winthrop of Massachusetts, Whig Speaker in the previous Congress, or Howell Cobb, a Democrat from Georgia. The pending issue was what to do about slavery in the territory won in the war against Mexico, and the Free Soilers were determined to prevent the election of a Speaker who would appoint proslavery majorities to the committees on Territories and the District of Columbia.

Cobb led eleven candidates on the first ballot with 103 votes. But with five recognized factions in the House, neither Cobb nor Winthrop, who alternated in the lead for sixty ballots, could get a majority. Finally, on December 22 the House voted, 113–106, to elect a Speaker by a plurality, so long as it was a majority of a quorum. Cobb, the proslavery candidate, was elected on the sixty-third ballot when he received 102 votes to 100 for Winthrop, with twenty spread among eight other candidates. This decision then was confirmed by a majority vote.

Contest of 1855

Proslavery Democrats held firm control of the House in the 32nd and 33rd Congresses (1851–1855), when Linn Boyd of Kentucky was Speaker. But their attempt to extend slavery into the Kansas and Nebraska Territories produced a large turnout of antislavery forces in the election of 1854—the first in which a new Republican Party, successor to the Whigs, participated. When the 34th Congress convened on December 3, 1855, the House membership was divided among 108 Republicans or Whigs, 83 Democrats, and 43 members of minor parties that sprang up in the 1850s. Although the so-called Anti-Nebraska men were in the majority, they were unable to unite behind any candidate for Speaker; two months passed and 133 ballots were taken before a choice was made.

The twenty-one candidates on the first ballot were led by William A. Richardson of Illinois with seventy-four votes. As in previous contests, various motions to help resolve the deadlock—including one to drop the low man on each ballot until only two remained—were made and tabled as the voting continued. After a series of votes in which Nathaniel P. Banks of Massachusetts fell only a few votes short of a majority, the House finally agreed to follow the plurality rule of 1849. On February 2, 1856, Banks was declared Speaker. On the 133rd ballot he received 103 votes to 100 for William Aiken of South Carolina. Banks, who had been elected to the 33rd Congress as a Coalition Democrat and to the 34th as a candidate of the nativist American Party, or Know Nothings, fulfilled the expectations of the antislavery forces by his committee appointments.

Contest of 1859

Democrats won the presidency in 1856 with James Buchanan, last of the "northern men with southern principles." They also gained control of the House in the 35th Congress (1857–1859). But the 36th opened on December 5, 1859, with no party in control of the House, which was composed of 109 Republicans, 101 Democrats, and twenty-seven Know Nothings. Pro- and antislavery blocs were again deadlocked over the choice of a Speaker. With passions running high and debate unchecked by a presiding clerk who refused to decide any points of order, the struggle continued for two months.

John Sherman of Ohio, the Republican choice, led the early balloting, receiving 110 votes at one point, just six short of a majority. But Sherman had become anathema to the proslavery camp, and the Republicans finally concluded that he could not be elected. So Sherman withdrew on the thirty-ninth ballot, and the Republicans switched their support to William Pennington of New Jersey, a new member of the House and a political unknown. Pennington received 115 votes on the fortieth ballot (compared with one on the thirty-eighth) and was elected on the forty-fourth ballot, on February 1, 1860, by a bare majority of 117 votes out of 233. Pennington's distinction, shared with Clay, of being Speaker in his first term ended there, for he was defeated at the polls the next year and served only the one term in the House.

CHANGES IN HOUSE RULES

Agitation over the issue of slavery was not confined to the contests over the choice of a Speaker. In 1836 John Quincy Adams challenged a House practice, begun in 1792, of refusing to receive petitions and memorials on the subject of slavery. Adams offered a petition from citizens of Massachusetts for the abolition of slavery in the District of Columbia. His action led to protracted debate and the adoption of a resolution by a 117–68 vote directing that any papers dealing with slavery "shall, without being either printed or referred, be laid upon the table and that no further action whatever shall be had thereon."[5]

Adams, who considered adoption of the resolution to be a violation of the Constitution and of the rules of the House, re-

Former president John Quincy Adams served in the House for seventeen years until his death in 1848. Adams conducted an almost single-handed attack on rules that prevented discussion of antislavery proposals.

opened the issue in 1837 by asking the Speaker how to dispose of a petition he had received from twenty-two slaves. Southerners moved at once to censure Adams. The move failed, but the House agreed, 163–18, that "slaves do not possess the right of petition secured to the people of the United States by the Constitution." Further agitation led the House in 1840 to adopt, by a vote of 114–108, a rule that no papers "praying the abolition of slavery . . . shall be received by this House or entertained in any way whatever."[6] Four years later, however, the rule was rescinded by a vote of 108–80.

Other rules adopted in this period were more significant to the long-range development of House procedures. In 1837 precedence was given to floor consideration of revenue-raising and appropriations bills, and the inclusion of legislation in an appropriations bill (which had led the Senate to kill a number of such bills) was barred.

In 1841 the House finally agreed to limit to one hour the time allowed any member in a debate—a proposal first made in 1820 after John Randolph had spoken for more than four hours against the Missouri Compromise. At the same time, a rule was adopted to prevent indefinite debate in the Committee of the Whole. It provided that the House, by majority vote and without debate, could discharge the Committee of the Whole from consideration of a bill after pending amendments had been disposed of.

Objection to the latter provision led, in 1847, to adoption of the five-minute rule, giving any member that much time during floor debate to explain any amendment he had offered. But this rule encouraged the practice of offering but then withdrawing scores of amendments in an effort to delay action on controversial bills. So the rule was amended in 1850 to prohibit the withdrawal of any amendment without unanimous consent. But the House was still at the mercy of a determined minority. During debate on the Kansas-Nebraska bill of 1854, according to *Hinds' Precedents of the House of Representatives,* opponents engaged in "prolonged dilatory operations, such as the alternation of the motions to lay on the table, for a call of the House, to excuse individual members from voting, to adjourn, to reconsider votes whereby individual members were excused from voting, to adjourn, to fix the day to which the House should adjourn, and, after calls of the House had been ordered, to excuse individual absentees," all of which required 109 roll calls and consumed many days.

In 1858 the House agreed to set up a select committee to revise the accumulation of more than 150 rules. The committee included the Speaker—the first time that officer had served on any committee of the House. While its recommendations were not acted on at the time, most of the proposals were resubmitted in 1860 by another committee named the day Pennington was chosen Speaker. As approved by the House in March of that year, this first general revision of the rules was largely of a technical nature, although it included changes affecting important aspects of the parliamentary process: use of the previous question motion and the motion to strike (delete) the enacting clause. On balance, however, the revised rules of 1860 left ample opportunity for a resolute minority to keep a closely divided House tied up in parliamentary knots for days at a time.

Apart from the adoption of the first limitations on debate— the one-hour rule and the five-minute rule in the 1840s—few significant changes were made in House procedures in the period from 1829 to 1860. The committee system in place by 1825 was expanded by the addition of eight permanent committees, bringing the total to thirty-four. The Ways and Means Committee continued to handle both appropriations and revenue bills; and while its chairman was not always the designated floor leader of the majority party, he was always among the most influential members. The Speaker continued to appoint members to committees and to designate committee chairmen.

But none of the Speakers who followed Clay achieved his stature or influence. Of the fourteen who were elected between 1825 and 1860, only three—Stevenson, Polk, and Boyd—served for more than one Congress. In only one respect was the job of leading the House made, if not easier, at least no more difficult: the size of the House, after increasing to 242 in 1833, remained about the same for the next forty years. Otherwise, the rising passions in the country on the slavery issue doomed the House to increasing turmoil as America moved toward a mutually destructive conflict.

New Complexities: 1861–1901

The Civil War all but eliminated the South from national politics and representation in Congress for eight years. Most of the sixty-six House seats held by the eleven secessionist states in 1860 remained vacant from 1861 to 1869. The war also greatly weakened the Democratic Party outside the South. The situation was not dissimilar to that prevailing after the War of 1812 when the Federalists were on the defensive because of their pro-British sympathies. In 1865 the Democratic Party suffered from an identification with the southern cause. And Democratic weakness helped the Republicans to retain control of the presidency until 1885, the House until 1875, and the Senate until 1879.

At the same time, the war and its aftermath gave rise to bitter conflict between Congress and the White House and led to the House vote to impeach President Andrew Johnson in 1868 and to a prolonged period of legislative dominance thereafter. The years from 1860 to 1901 saw a further expansion of House membership, an intensification of House efforts to control government spending, an increase in the number and power of House committees, and a continuing struggle to adapt the rules of the House to that body's legislative goals.

CONGRESS IS PARAMOUNT

President Abraham Lincoln assumed unprecedented powers during the Civil War, at a time when the Republican majorities in Congress were dominated by Radicals committed to the Whig doctrine of legislative supremacy. The conflict between Lincoln and Congress was sharpest over the issue of Reconstruction. Lincoln, who held that the Confederate states had never left the Union, was prepared to restore their political rights as quickly as possible. But the Radicals were determined to reshape the power structure of the South before readmitting the secessionists and insisted that the final decision rested with Congress.

When President Lincoln set up new governments in Louisiana and Arkansas in 1863, the Radicals passed a bill placing all Reconstruction authority under the direct control of Congress. Lincoln pocket-vetoed the bill after Congress had adjourned in 1864, whereupon the Radicals issued the Wade-Davis Manifesto asserting that "the authority of Congress is paramount and must be respected." If the president wanted their support, said the Radicals, "he must confine himself to his executive duties— to obey and execute, not make the laws—to suppress by arms armed rebellion, and leave political reorganization to Congress."

The Radicals proceeded to put their views into effect with a vengeance under Andrew Johnson, the Tennessee Democrat who became president when Lincoln was assassinated in 1865. Johnson's views were openly sympathetic to the established order in the South. Passed over Johnson's veto were numerous bills, the effects of which were to give Congress full control over Reconstruction policy and to strip the president of much of his authority.

One of these measures was the Tenure of Office Act of 1867, passed on the suspicion that Johnson intended to fire Secretary of War Edwin Stanton. The law made it a high misdemeanor to remove without the Senate's approval any government official whose nomination had been confirmed by the Senate. The Radicals' intention was to protect incumbent Republican office-holders from executive retaliation if they did not support Johnson. After Johnson, holding the law to be unconstitutional, had removed Stanton, the House voted 126–47 to impeach him. Tried by the Senate, Johnson was acquitted May 16, 1868, when a vote of 35–19 for conviction fell one short of the two-thirds majority required by the Constitution.

POWER OF THE PURSE

The Civil War led the House to increase efforts to control government expenditures by exercising its power over appropriations more carefully. Federal spending had climbed from $63 million in 1860 to $1.3 billion in 1865. Until then, the Ways and Means Committee had handled all funding and revenue-raising bills as well as legislation relating to monetary matters. But in 1865 the House, with little opposition, agreed to transfer some of these responsibilities to two new standing committees—a Committee on Appropriations and a Committee on Banking and Currency. Speaking of the duties of members assigned to the Appropriations panel, the sponsor of the committee reorganization declared that "we require of this new committee their whole labor in the restraint of extravagant and illegal appropriations."[7]

Congress began to tighten controls on spending. Wartime authority to transfer funds from one account to another was repealed, agencies were required to return unexpended funds to the Treasury, and obligation of funds in excess of appropriations was prohibited. Although Congress continued to make lump-sum appropriations to the army and the navy, it specified in great detail the amounts and purposes for which money could be spent by the civilian departments and agencies. These efforts helped to keep federal expenditures below $300 million in every year except one from 1871 to 1890.

The House's "power of the purse" was exercised to another end during the administration of Rutherford B. Hayes, the Republican successor to Ulysses S. Grant. Democrats were again in the majority in the House in the 45th Congress (1877–1879) and won control of both chambers in the 46th, but by margins too small to be able to override a presidential veto. So in attempting to repeal certain Reconstruction laws, the Democrats revived the practice of adding legislative riders to appropriations bills in the hope of forcing the president to accept them. But Hayes vetoed a series of such bills, calling the tactic an attempt at coercive dictation by the House. When they were unable to override his vetoes, the Democrats relented and approved the appropriations bills without the riders.

During the height of the dispute in 1879, Hayes wrote in his diary:

This is a controversy which cannot and ought not to be compromised. The Revolutionists claim that a bare majority in the House of Representatives shall control all legislation, by tacking the measures they

The most treasured possession of the House of Representatives is the mace, a traditional symbol of legislative authority. The concept, which the House borrowed from the British House of Commons, had its origin in republican Rome, where the fasces—an ax bound in a bundle of rods—symbolized the power of the magistrates.

The House adopted the mace in its first session in 1789 as a symbol of office for the sergeant at arms, who is charged with preserving order on the House floor. The first mace was destroyed when the British burned the Capitol in 1814. A mace of painted wood was used until 1841, when a replica of the original mace of 1789 was made by William Adams, a New York silversmith, for the sum of $400. That mace consists of a bundle of thirteen ebony rods bound in silver, terminating in a silver globe topped by a silver eagle with outstretched wings. It is forty-six inches in length.

RESTORING ORDER

On a number of occasions in the history of the House, the sergeant at arms, on order of the Speaker, has lifted the mace from its pedestal and "presented" it before an unruly member. On each of these occasions, order is said to have been promptly restored. At other times the sergeant at arms, bearing the mace, has passed up and down the aisles to quell boisterous behavior in the chamber.

In recent years the mace more often has served as a signal. When the House is in regular session, the staff rests on a tall pedestal at the right of the Speaker's desk, but when the House is sitting as the Committee of the Whole, the mace is moved to a low pedestal nearby. Members entering the chamber can thus tell at a glance whether the House is meeting in regular session or as the Committee of the Whole.

THE SENATE GAVEL

The Senate has no mace, but it cherishes another symbol—a small silver-capped ivory gavel that Vice President John Adams is believed to have used in calling the first Senate to order in 1789. Evidence exists that it was in use by the presiding officer at least as early as 1831, and it remained in use until 1954 when it began to disintegrate beyond repair. It has no handle.

A replica of the old gavel, a gift of the government of India, was presented to the Senate on November 17, 1954. Since then a case carrying both the old and new gavels is carried into the Senate chamber and placed on the vice president's desk just before the opening of each Senate session. The new gavel is removed from the case for use by the presiding officer. The old gavel remains in its case, a symbol of the continuity of the Senate.

can't pass through the Senate, or over the President's objections, to the appropriation bills which are required to carry on the government. . . . It is idle to talk of compromises as to the particular measures which are used as riders on the appropriation bills. These measures may be wise or unwise. It is easy enough to say in regard to them, that used as they are to establish a doctrine which overthrows the Constitutional distribution of power between the different departments of the government, and consolidates in the House of Representatives, the whole lawmaking power of the government . . . we will not discuss or consider them when they are so presented. . . .

To tack political legislation to appropriations bills and to threaten that no appropriations will be made unless the political measures are approved is not in my judgment constitutional conduct.[8]

Meanwhile, House members of both parties were becoming concerned over the concentration of power in the Appropriations Committee itself. In 1877 the committee was deprived of its jurisdiction over appropriations for rivers and harbors—the "pork barrel" on which members relied to finance projects of interest to their districts. The agriculture appropriation was taken from the committee in 1880, and in 1885 the panel was stripped of authority over six other funding bills—Army, Navy, Military Academy, Consular and Diplomatic Affairs, Post Office and Post Roads, and Indian Affairs—all of which were transferred to the appropriate legislative committees.

In taking from the Appropriations Committee control over bills comprising almost one-half of the federal budget, the House was apparently moved by hostility to Chairman Samuel J. Randall, D-Pa., and what was considered to be the committee's excessive concern for economy under his leadership. The feeling was widespread and bipartisan; three-fourths of the Democrats and the Republicans joined in the 227–70 vote stripping the committee of a giant share of its jurisdiction. They were led, moreover, by the senior members of most of the other important committees, underscoring the rivalry that had developed among House committees.

The effect of this vote in 1885 was to reinforce the decentralization of power in the House and to give added weight to the criticism of Congress voiced by Woodrow Wilson that year in his book *Congressional Government*. According to Wilson, power in the House was scattered among "forty-seven seigniories, in each of which a standing committee is the court-baron and its chairman lord-proprietor."[9]

Wilson noted that, "by custom, seniority in congressional service determines the bestowal of the principal chairmanships" and that on the House floor "chairman fights against chairman for use of the time of the assembly."

Wilson attributed the lack of strong party control in the House to the fact that committees were not composed entirely of members of the majority, as he believed they should be. "The legislation of a session does not represent the policy of either [party]," he wrote; "it is simply an aggregate of the bills recommended by committees composed of members from both sides of the House, and it is known to be usually not the work of the majority men upon the committees, but compromise conclusions . . . of the committeemen of both parties."

INFLUENTIAL SPEAKERS

If power in the House was dispersed among the standing committees and their chairmen, it was also true, as Wilson noted, that "he who appoints those committees is an autocrat of the first magnitude." While Speakers had held that authority since the earliest days of the House, it had assumed new importance with the broadening legislative interests of the country and of Congress.

Schuyler Colfax of Indiana, first elected to the House in 1854, served as Republican Speaker from 1863 to 1869 and then left to become vice president in President Grant's first term. Although Colfax enjoyed as much personal popularity as had Henry Clay, he was not a forceful Speaker and was regarded as a figurehead in a House dominated by Republican Thaddeus Stevens of Pennsylvania, who became chairman of the Ways and Means Committee in 1861 and of the newly created Appropriations Committee in 1865.

Stevens, who engineered the impeachment of President Johnson, was described by George Boutwell, a fellow Republican, as "a tyrant" in his role as the real leader of the House who was "at once able, bold and unscrupulous."[10]

Colfax's successor as Speaker was James G. Blaine of Maine, one of the founders of the Republican Party, who entered the House in 1863. As Speaker from 1869 to 1875, Blaine was an avowed partisan of Republican principles and successfully manipulated committee assignments to produce majorities favorable to legislation he desired. Like Clay, Blaine aspired to the presidency. After losing the Republican nomination to Hayes in 1876 and to James A. Garfield in 1880, he won the party's nomination in 1884, only to lose in a close election to Democrat Grover Cleveland.

Democrats won control of the House in 1875. After the death in 1876 of their first choice for Speaker, Michael C. Kerr of Indiana, they elected Samuel J. Randall of Pennsylvania, who had entered the House with Blaine and Garfield in 1863.

Randall, who was Speaker until 1881, initiated a thorough revision of House rules in 1880 designed "to secure accuracy in business, economy in time, order, uniformity and impartiality." The net effect of these changes was to increase somewhat the ability of floor leaders and committee chairmen to expedite legislation on the floor.

The Rules Committee, which had been a select committee since 1789 and had been chaired by the Speaker since 1858, was made a standing committee. Soon thereafter it began to make systematic use of special orders, also called special rules, which, when adopted by the House, governed the amount of time to be allowed for debate on major bills and the extent to which members might offer amendments. Such special orders from the committee also were a convenience in that they could prohibit potential points of order against provisions of bills that violated a particular rule of the House.

The Democrats lost control of the House in the 47th Congress (1881–1883) but regained it in the 48th (1883–1885). They

Rep. Thaddeus Stevens controlled the House during the Civil War, unchecked by a weak Republican Speaker. Stevens is shown here closing House debate on the impeachment of President Andrew Johnson in 1868.

then passed over Randall, because he had opposed the party's low-tariff policy, and elected John G. Carlisle of Kentucky as Speaker. Carlisle, a member since 1877, remained Speaker from 1883 to 1889. He made notable use of his power of recognition to forestall motions he opposed. By the device of asking "For what purpose does the gentleman rise?" Carlisle was able to withhold recognition from any member whose purpose he did not share. But Carlisle did not lead a united party. In 1884, for example, the Democrats lost the fight for tariff reduction through the defection of Randall and forty other party members.

Blaine, Randall, and Carlisle all contributed importantly to the body of precedents by which subsequent Speakers have been guided under the rules of the House. But none was able or willing to prevent determined minorities from obstructing the business of the House. Under Carlisle, in particular, the House frequently was subjected to organized filibusters and such dilatory tactics as the "disappearing quorum," which usually resulted in endless roll calls to no purpose except delay. These displays, coupled with a disappointing legislative output, led to increasing public criticism of the House and to demands that the rules be modified "to permit the majority to control the business for which it is responsible," as the *New York Tribune* wrote.

THE REED RULES

The opportunity for further reform came when Republicans took control of the House in 1889 and picked Thomas Brackett Reed of Maine as Speaker. First elected in 1876, Reed had been a Republican leader in the House since 1882, when he became a member of the Rules Committee and an increasingly outspoken critic of the rules. He once said, "The only way to do business inside the rules is to suspend the rules."

When the 51st Congress convened on December 2, 1889, the House was composed of 330 members, with the Republicans commanding a small majority. Reed was elected Speaker, and in keeping with long-standing practice the rules of the 50th Congress were referred to the five-member Rules Committee, of which the Speaker was chairman, while the House proceeded temporarily under general parliamentary procedure. With the previous general election results for several House seats still being contested, the Republicans, before adopting new rules, were expected to settle the election disputes in their favor—as party majorities had always done—so as to increase their majority.

On January 29, 1890, the Republicans called up the West Virginia election case of *Smith v. Jackson*. Charles F. Crisp of Georgia, the Democratic leader, immediately raised objection to considering the Republican motion, which had to be decided by majority vote. The roll call produced 161 "yeas," two "nays," and 165 not voting—mostly Democrats who, although present, were using the device of the "disappearing quorum" to block action. But when the point of "no quorum" was made, because less than one-half of the members had voted, Speaker Reed ordered the clerk to enter the names of those present who had refused to vote. He then ruled that a quorum was present and that consideration of the question was in order.

In the ensuing uproar, Reed was denounced as a "tyrant" and a "czar," but he held to his position. An appeal from his ruling was tabled (killed) by a majority of the quorum. The next day, again to make a quorum, Reed once more counted nonvoting Democrats who were present, and he refused to allow another appeal of the ruling on the ground that the House had already decided the question. Reed went on to declare that he would refuse to recognize any member rising to make a dilatory motion, saying:

There is no possible way by which the orderly methods of parliamentary procedure can be used to stop legislation. The object of a parliamentary body is action, and not stoppage of action. Hence, if any member or set of members undertakes to oppose the orderly progress of business, even by the use of the ordinarily recognized parliamentary motions, it is the right of the majority to refuse to have those motions entertained.

Reed's rulings on dilatory motions and the counting of a quorum were incorporated in the revised rules reported by the Rules Committee on February 6, 1890, and adopted by the House after four days of debate by a vote of 161–144. Of the rule that "no dilatory motion shall be entertained by the Speaker," the committee report said:

There are no words which can be framed which will limit members to the proper use of proper motions. Any motion the most conducive to progress in the public business . . . may be used for purposes of unjust and oppressive delay. . . . Why should an assembly be kept from its work by motions made only to delay and to weary, even if the original design of the motion was salutary and sensible?

In addition to these changes in the rules, the revisions of 1890 reduced the size of the quorum required in the Committee of the Whole House from one-half of the membership of the House to 100 members—a change that facilitated floor action, particularly as the size of the House continued to grow. The revised rules also took account of the fact that the House had long since abandoned its original requirement that members obtain leave to introduce bills. The practice of introducing bills simply by filing them with the clerk was made a rule.

Coincidentally, the number of bills introduced, which had first passed the one thousand mark during the 24th Congress (1835–1837) and had not exceeded two thousand until the 40th Congress (1867–1869), reached a new peak of more than nineteen thousand in the 51st Congress (1889–1891). The fate of most of these bills, however, continued to be as described by Woodrow Wilson in 1885: "As a rule, a bill committed [to committee] is a bill doomed. When it goes from the clerk's desk to a committee room, it crosses a parliamentary bridge of sighs and dim dungeons of silence whence it will never return."

Under the Reed Rules of 1890, the Speaker was enabled to take effective command of the House. By his authority to name the members and chairmen of all committees he had the power to reward or to punish his fellow members. As chairman of the Rules Committee, which by now shared with Ways and Means and Appropriations the right to report legislation at any time and thereby get immediate access to the floor, he could control the timing and content of bills to be brought before the House. And with unlimited power of recognition, he could determine in large measure what business would be taken up on the floor.

CENTRALIZATION OF POWER

Although the Democrats dropped the rule against the "disappearing quorum" when they took control of the House in the 52nd Congress (1891–1893), they restored it in the 53rd (1893–1895). Crisp, the Democratic Speaker in both Congresses, used his powers as fully as Reed had done in the 51st Congress. Crisp, who persuaded two party rivals to withdraw from the contest for Speaker by promising them the chairmanships of Appropriations and Ways and Means, once refused to entertain an appeal by Reed from a ruling, refused to let Reed speak any further, and directed the sergeant at arms to see that he took his seat.

Reed, who served as minority leader during these four years and as Speaker again for the next two Congresses (1895–1899), was able by his forceful leadership of House Republicans to restore the concept of party responsibility in the House. His chief aides in the 51st Congress included William McKinley Jr., R-Ohio, chairman of the Ways and Means Committee, and Joseph G. Cannon, R-Ill., chairman of the Appropriations Committee.

McKinley left the House in 1891 to become governor of Ohio and then president in 1897. When Reed resumed the speakership in 1895 he named Nelson Dingley Jr., R-Maine, to head Ways and Means. Cannon again became chairman of the Appropriations Committee in 1897, when Reed also named James A. Tawney, R-Minn., as the first Republican whip, charged with keeping party members on the floor and voting in favor of the leadership's positions. Under Reed, House Republicans in the 1890s achieved an exceptional degree of party unity, occasionally voting solidly for measures on which they had been sharply divided in their caucus.

The centralization of power in the House during this period coincided with another, less visible change. Until the Civil War, few members had chosen—or had been enabled by the voters— to make a career of service in the House. As late as the 1870s, more than half of the 293 representatives then elected to the House were freshmen, and the mean length of service for all members was barely two terms. Thus, although Speakers for some time had followed seniority to a certain extent in appointing members to subcommittees and committees of their choice and in advancing them to chairmanships, it was not a matter of great importance to most members if the Speaker failed to do so.

By 1899, however, the proportion of newcomers among the 357 members entering the House had fallen to 30 percent, while the mean period of service had increased to more than three terms. As more members sought to stay in the House for longer periods, it became of increasing importance to them that they have the opportunity to gain political recognition through specialization and rising influence within the committee structure. A demand thus grew among members of both parties for assurance that their seniority would be respected in assigning them rank on committees of their choice. The resulting new expectations contributed to the reaction against centralization and against the strong leadership exercised by Speaker Cannon.

Tyranny and Reaction: 1901–1919

Speaker Reed resigned from the House in 1899, having broken with President McKinley over U.S. intervention in Cuba and the annexation of Hawaii. The Republican majority in the 56th Congress (1899–1901) replaced Reed with David B. Henderson, R-Iowa, who served two ineffective terms as Speaker (1899–1903) before retiring from the House. In 1903 Joseph G. Cannon was finally elected Speaker by the Republicans (having been an unsuccessful candidate in 1881, 1889, and 1899). At age sixty-seven he was the oldest representative and had the longest service record (twenty-eight years) of any member ever to have headed the House of Representatives.

Like Reed, Cannon set out to rule the House and its Republican majority through his control of the Rules Committee and the key committee chairmen. He kept Sereno E. Payne, R-N.Y., as majority leader and chairman of the Ways and Means Committee (positions to which Payne was first appointed by Henderson in 1899). He also retained Tawney as majority whip until 1905, when he named him chairman of the Appropriations panel. Cannon turned over the committee assignments of Democrats to their leader, John Sharp Williams, D-Miss., subject to his veto. But Williams used his authority to build party unity among the Democrats, and Cannon took back the privilege in 1908 when James Beauchamp "Champ" Clark, D-Mo., succeeded Williams as minority leader.

As a strong conservative, Cannon was out of sympathy with much of the progressive legislation sought by President Theodore Roosevelt and by a growing number of liberal Republicans and Democrats in the House. To maintain control, therefore, he made increasing use of his powers as Speaker to block legislation that he opposed and to thwart and punish members who opposed him. In a period of rising public interest in political re-

Autocratic Speaker Joseph G. Cannon lost much of his power in a 1910 House revolt, but he remained Speaker until his term ended in March 1911.

form, "Cannonism" came to be a synonym for the arbitrary use of the Speaker's powers to obstruct the legislative will, not of the majority party itself, but of a new majority of House members of both parties.

INITIAL EFFORTS

The movement to curb Cannon got under way during the last session of the 60th Congress (1907–1909) when, just before final adjournment on March 3, 1909, the House adopted the Calendar Wednesday rule. This rule set aside Wednesday of each week for calling the roll of committees, whose chairman or other authorized members then were permitted to call up bills that their committees had reported but that had not received clearance from the Rules Committee. At the time progressives considered this a major reform because it seemed to guarantee that the House would have an opportunity to act on measures favored in committee but opposed by the leadership. In practice, however, the procedure proved ineffective, and in later years the House routinely agreed to dispense with Calendar Wednesday by unanimous consent.

When the 61st Congress first met, in special session, on March 15, 1909, the House was composed of 219 Republicans and 172 Democrats. But the Republicans included about thirty insurgents led by George W. Norris, R-Neb., and John M. Nelson, R-Wis. After helping to elect Cannon to a fourth term as Speaker, the Republican insurgents joined with the Democrats to defeat the usually routine motion adopting the rules of the preceding Congress. Champ Clark, the Democratic leader, then offered a resolution to take away the Speaker's existing authority to appoint the members of all committees, to limit that authority to only five committees, of which the only important one was Ways and Means, to remove the Speaker from membership on the Rules Committee, and to triple the size of that body by adding ten new members.

Although twenty-eight Republicans joined in supporting the Clark resolution, twenty-two Democrats, led by John J. Fitzgerald, D-N.Y., voted with the majority of Republicans to defeat the maneuver. The House thereupon adopted a compromise solution, offered by Fitzgerald, that sidestepped the principal abuses complained of and only slightly curtailed the Speaker's authority. The main change was to establish a Consent Calendar for minor bills of particular interest to individual members and to set aside two days each month when bills on this Calendar could be called up without the prior approval of the Speaker; approval required unanimous consent. (Adoption of this rule led both parties to designate certain members as official "objectors," to prevent passage of bills opposed for any reason by party members. But the Consent Calendar became a useful device for processing minor bills.)

CANNON'S DEFEAT

Agitation against "Cannonism" continued, and the coalition of Democrats and progressive Republicans finally prevailed in 1910. Taking advantage of a parliamentary opening on March 16, Representative Norris asked for immediate consideration of a reform resolution modeled on Clark's previous proposal, which had been bottled up in the Rules Committee. When Cannon held the motion to be out of order, the House overruled him by a decisive vote. Debate then began on the Norris resolution, which stripped the Speaker of all authority to appoint committee members and their chairmen, removed him from the Rules Committee, and expanded that committee to ten members, who would choose their own chairman.

Representative Nelson expressed the feelings of the insurgents in these terms:

Have we not been punished by every means at the disposal of the powerful House organization? Members long chairmen of important committees, others holding high rank—all with records of faithful and efficient party service to their credit—have been ruthlessly removed, deposed and humiliated before their constituents and the country because, forsooth, they would not cringe or crawl before the arbitrary power of the Speaker and his House machine. . . . We are fighting with our Democratic brethren for the common right of equal representation in this House, and for the right of way of progressive legislation in Congress.

The House finally adopted the Norris resolution on March 19 by a vote of 191–156, after a continuous session of twenty-nine hours during which Cannon had done his best to round up absentees among his supporters. Recognizing the nature of his defeat, Cannon invited a motion to declare the chair vacant so that the House might elect a new Speaker. A. S. Burleson, D-Texas, made the motion, but it was quickly tabled. Cannon, known to the House as "Uncle Joe," was personally popular with many members, and the Republican insurgents were unwilling to help elect a Democrat. Cannon stayed on as Speaker until the end of the 61st Congress in March 1911 and remained a member of the House, except during the 63rd Congress, until 1923, by which time he had completed forty-six years of service.

The revolt against "Cannonism" was consolidated in 1911, when the Democrats took control of the House, elected Champ Clark as Speaker, and adopted a revised body of rules that incorporated most of the changes agreed to in 1909–1910. The new rules provided that all members of the standing committees, including the chairmen, would be "elected by the House, at the commencement of each Congress." The rules of 1911 included the Calendar Wednesday and Consent Calendar innovations of 1909 as well as a discharge rule, adopted in 1910, by which a petition signed by a majority of House members could be used to free a bill bottled up in a committee for one reason or another. Also established at this time was a special calendar for private bills that could be called up on two designated days of each month.

RETURN OF THE CAUCUS

No less important than the rules of 1911 were the procedures adopted by the Democratic majority to solidify their control of the House. At the party caucus of January 19 that nominated Clark for Speaker, it was agreed that Oscar W. Underwood, D-Ala., would be the majority leader and chairman of the Ways and Means Committee. And it was decided that the Democratic members of Ways and Means would constitute the party's Committee on Committees, whose task it was to draw up the committee assignments of all Democrats. It was left to the Republicans themselves—who established their own Committee on Committees in 1917—to select their own committee members.

The election of the members and chairmen of House committees, therefore, now took the form of a perfunctory vote approving the slates drawn up by key members of the majority and minority parties (the Ways and Means Committee Democrats for the Democratic Party) and endorsed by the party caucus.

Underwood instead of Speaker Clark became the recognized leader of House Democrats from 1911 to 1915, when he moved to the Senate. Underwood made frequent use of the party caucus to develop unity on legislative issues. Democratic Caucus rules at this time provided that "in deciding upon action in the House involving party policy or principle, a two-thirds vote of those present and voting at a caucus meeting shall bind all members of the caucus" so long as the vote represented a majority of the Democrats in the House. But no member could be bound "upon questions involving a construction of the Constitution of the United States or upon which he made contrary pledges to his constituents prior to his election or received contrary instructions by resolution or platform from his nominating authority."

A typical caucus resolution of 1911 bound members of the Democratic Party to vote on the House floor for certain bills reported by the Ways and Means Committee and "to vote against all amendments, except formal committee amendments, to said bills and [against] motions to recommit changing their text from the language agreed upon in this conference."

Underwood also used the caucus to develop legislative proposals, which then would be referred to committees for formal approval; to instruct committees as to which bills they might or might not report; and to instruct the Rules Committee on the terms to be included in its special orders governing floor consideration of major bills and proposed amendments.

Thus the power once concentrated in the hands of Speaker Cannon was transferred to the Democratic Caucus, which was dominated by Underwood as majority leader. House historian George B. Galloway described Underwood's power:

As floor leader, Underwood was supreme, the Speaker a figurehead. The main cogs in the machine were the caucus, the floor leadership, the Rules Committee, the standing committees, and special rules. Oscar Underwood became the real leader of the House. He dominated the party caucus, influenced the rules and, as chairman of Ways and Means, chose the membership of the committees. Clark was given the shadow, Underwood the substance, of power. As floor leader, he could ask and obtain recognition at any time to make motions, restrict debate or preclude amendments or both.[11]

WILSON AND CONGRESS

As president from 1913 to 1921, Wilson revived the custom initiated by Washington and Adams, but abandoned by Jeffer-

The first woman to serve in Congress, Jeannette Rankin entered Congress in 1917, four years before ratification of the Nineteenth Amendment guaranteeing women the right to vote.

son, of addressing Congress in person. He worked closely with the Democratic leaders in both houses and conferred frequently with committees and individual members to solicit support for his legislative program. With Wilson's help, Underwood and the Democrats were able to effect House passage of four major pieces of legislation in the 63rd Congress—the Underwood Tariff Act, the Federal Reserve Act, the Clayton Antitrust Act, and the Federal Trade Commission Act.

The Democrats were less united on foreign policy, however. Both Speaker Clark and Majority Leader Underwood disagreed with Wilson over repeal of the exemption from Panama Canal tolls originally accorded to American coastal shipping. Claude Kitchin, D-N.C., who had become second-ranking Democrat on Ways and Means in 1913 and who succeeded Underwood as committee chairman and majority leader in 1915, openly challenged the president on several issues, notably when Wilson asked for a declaration of war against Germany in 1917. Clark later denounced the president's military conscription program. Despite this, House Democrats supported Wilson's decision. The only vote against the war was cast by Jeannette Rankin, R-Mont., elected four years before the Nineteenth Amendment gave women the right to vote and the only member of Congress to vote against both world wars.

Reflecting these disagreements, the strong party unity displayed by House Democrats during Wilson's first term began to fracture in his second. By the time the party lost control of the House at the midterm elections of 1918, the binding party caucus had ceased to be an effective instrument in the hands of the leadership. The Republican minority, meanwhile, in 1911 had all but abandoned use of the binding caucus, erecting in its place a nonbinding "conference" used for little more than choosing the party's nominee for Speaker and ratifying committee slates. By 1919 the House no longer was willing to accept the centralization of power that had developed under Speakers Reed, Crisp, and Cannon and Majority Leader Underwood. Party leaders thus were faced with the task of finding new ways to build and maintain consensus.

Accompanying this change—and helping to account for it—was a hardening of the unwritten rule of seniority that virtually guaranteed succession to committee chairmanships, when such vacancies occurred, by the next-ranking majority members on the committees. Democrats violated the rule three times in 1911 and on a few occasions thereafter, as did the Republicans. But members could now be fairly confident of rising in the ranks of their committees—so long as they were reelected—upon the retirement or death of the more senior members of those committees. Such assurance gave chairmen and ranking members a degree of independence from dictation that put a new premium on the persuasive skills of party leaders.

Recognition of seniority as the way of advancement on committees still left each party's Committee on Committees with the job of assigning newcomers to committees, particularly important at the beginning of a new Congress when many slots usually had to be filled, and filling interim vacancies when members died or sought to switch from one committee to another.

The task of filling vacancies often was complicated by keen competition among individuals and among state and regional delegations for the right to spots on such choice committees as Ways and Means and Appropriations. (The popularity of many of the committees, and thus the competition for membership on them, varied to some extent with the issues dominating at the time.) In the inevitable bargaining, the political loyalties of the competitors weighed as much as their interests, capabilities, and experience. The filling of important committee vacancies was to remain a significant tool in the hands of party leaders.

Republican Years: 1919–1933

By 1918, the last year of World War I, a majority of American voters already appeared anxious for the return to "normalcy" promised them two years later by Warren G. Harding, the Republican nominee for president.

For the first six years of his administration, Wilson had Democratic majorities to work with. But in the midterm congressional elections of 1918 Republicans captured both houses. It was in the 66th Congress (1919–1921) that Wilson lost his historic battle with the Senate over the Treaty of Versailles. With the election of Harding in 1920 a decade began of undivided GOP control of the executive and legislative branches of the federal government, lasting until Democrats recaptured the House in 1931.

These were not years of presidential leadership or strong party government. Harding's administration was marked by widespread corruption, brought to light by Senate investigators after his death in 1923. As Harding's successor, Calvin Coolidge did little to push his legislative program through Congress. President Herbert Hoover was unable to deal effectively with the economic depression that began during his first year in office in 1929. Meanwhile, Republican control of the Senate was occasionally nominal, and a minority of progressives in the party often held the balance of power. Party conservatives were more successful in keeping control of the House during the 1920s, and legislative conflicts between the Senate and the House were common. A notable case in point involved the Senate-approved "lame-duck" amendment to the Constitution, which House leaders managed to block until 1932. (See "Lame-Duck Amendment," p. 58.)

Some important changes were made in the organization and procedures employed by the House in this period. Full authority over all money bills funding the operations of the federal departments and agencies was returned to the Appropriations Committee in 1920, and some minor committees were abolished in 1927. Republican leaders introduced, then abandoned, use of a party Steering Committee to guide their legislative program. Under pressure from Republican progressives, some House rules were modified in 1924, but the Rules Committee continued to exercise tight control over the legislative options of members. Meanwhile, the representative nature of the chamber was brought into question by the House's failure to reapportion its seats to reflect the results of the 1920 census. There was no reapportionment until 1931, after the census of 1930.

NEW BUDGET SYSTEM

Until 1920 there was no central system in the government for drawing up the federal budget and, therefore, no procedure for congressional consideration of a national budget covering all programs and expenditures. The secretary of the Treasury did no more than compile the estimates of the various departments. These then were referred to eight different House committees, each of which would report an appropriations bill for the departments and programs under its jurisdiction, with no reference to governmentwide expenditures or revenues.

Nor were all the requests of a single department necessarily considered by the same committee or funded in the same bill. The appropriations for some departments came from more than one bill and were considered by different committees that could work at cross-purposes. This process, which was repeated in the Senate, led to rising criticism. As Alvan T. Fuller, R-Mass., complained in 1918: "The president is asking our business men to economize and become more efficient while we continue to be the most inefficient and expensive barnacle that ever attached itself to the ship of state."[12]

To improve control over expenditures within the executive branch, President Wilson in 1919 proposed a new budget system. Wilson vetoed the first bill from Congress embodying his proposal because it placed the comptroller general beyond the president's power of removal, but a second bill, signed by President Harding, became the Budget and Accounting Act of 1921. This measure directed the president to prepare and transmit to Congress each year a budget showing federal revenues and expenditures for the previous and current years and the estimated levels for the ensuing year. It set up a Bureau of the Budget within the executive branch to undertake these tasks. The new law also created a General Accounting Office under the comptroller general to assist Congress in exercising oversight of the administration of federal funds.

Anticipating enactment of this bill, the House on June 1, 1920, voted to restore to the Appropriations Committee jurisdiction over all money bills originally given to it in 1865. Many senior Republicans and Democrats opposed that move, and the House barely agreed, 158–154, to a crucial parliamentary step allowing the recommendation to be brought to the floor. As finally passed, the reorganization of the committee's jurisdiction also increased the size of the panel from twenty-one to thirty-five members. At the same time, the House barred its conferees on appropriations bills from accepting Senate amendments that contravened the rules of the House—such as nongermane provisions, or riders—unless specifically authorized by a separate House vote on each such amendment.

Most of the responsibility for reviewing budget estimates now was lodged in ten five-member subcommittees of the House Appropriations Committee, each of which passed on the requests of one or more agencies. Parallel subcommittees were set up by the Senate Appropriations Committee, and in 1922 it, too, was given exclusive authority over money bills. These steps toward a more systematic approach to federal expenditures came at a time of general concern about economy in government. They helped to hold expenditures to little more than $3 billion a year from 1922 to 1930. With revenues of close to $4 billion each year, the public debt was reduced from $25 billion in 1919 to $16 billion in 1930.

OTHER HOUSE INNOVATIONS

When the Republicans regained control of the House in 1919, the leading contender for Speaker was Rep. James R. Mann, R-Ill., who had been minority leader since 1911. But Mann had offended some of his party colleagues by objecting to passage of their private bills, while others feared he would seek to centralize power once again in the Speaker's office. He had considered Cannon his mentor and close friend. So the Republican Conference, looking for someone who would be less forceful, nominated the respected Frederick H. Gillett, R-Mass. Mann refused the title of majority leader, which then was given to Frank W. Mondell, R-Wyo., and for the first time this position was separated from the chairmanship of the Ways and Means Committee.

In a further effort to decentralize power, the Republicans created a five-member Steering Committee chaired by the majority leader. Both the Speaker and the chairman of the Rules Committee were barred from sitting on it. Complaints about the narrow range of views and regions represented on the Steering Committee led, in the 67th Congress (1921–1923), to enlarging its membership to eight. Mondell also invited the Speaker, the chairman of the Rules Committee, and others to attend meetings of the Steering Committee, which met almost daily and served as the major organ of party leadership from 1919 to 1925.

With a Republican majority of three hundred in the 67th Congress, the party's leaders nevertheless came in for growing criticism for blocking action on measures with wide support in the House. Rules Chairman Philip P. Campbell, R-Kan., for example, simply refused to report a number of resolutions approved by a majority of his committee to authorize certain investigations. He once told the committee: "You can go to hell. It makes no difference what a majority of you decide. If it meets with my disapproval, it shall not be done. I am the committee. In me repose absolute obstructive powers."[13] Campbell's right to pocket resolutions reported by his committee was upheld by Speaker Gillett and, on appeal, by the House.

But Campbell and many other Republicans were defeated in the elections of 1922, and when the 68th Congress met in December 1923 the House consisted of 225 Republicans and 207 Democrats. Lack of a larger majority enabled the group of about twenty reform-minded Progressives to hold up the election of a Speaker in an effort to bring about some liberalization of the rules. For two days and eight ballots the two party nominees—Speaker Gillett and Minority Leader Finis J. Garrett, D-Tenn.—received about 195 votes each, while the members of the Progressive Party cast seventeen votes for Rep. Henry A. Cooper, R-Wis.

Then Nicholas Longworth, R-Ohio, who had succeeded Mondell as majority leader, persuaded the insurgents to support the election of Gillett in return for a promise to allow full debate on revision of the rules in January. Gillett was reelected Speaker on the ninth ballot. Democrat Henry T. Rainey, D-Ill., congratulated Longworth for having steered safely "between the Scylla of progressive Republicanism . . . and the Charybdis of conservative Republicanism. . . . There is not a scratch on the ship. The paint is absolutely intact."

The promised debate lasted five days and led to a number of changes in House rules. One, designed to outlaw the "pocket veto" exercised arbitrarily by Rules Chairman Campbell, required the committee to "present to the House reports concerning rules, joint rules, and order of business within three legislative days of the time when ordered reported by the Committee." The new rule provided also that if the member making the report failed to call it up within nine days, any other member designated by the committee could do so.

The House also agreed at this time to amend the discharge rule first adopted in 1910. The amended rule reduced from 218 (or a majority of the House membership) to 150 the number of members needed to bring to the floor a bill being bottled up in committee. Once a discharge petition was signed by the required number of members, however, the legislation could be called up for debate only on the first and third Monday of the month, and it was subject to other constraints. The single attempt, led by Democrats, to use the new rule in the 68th Congress (1923–1925) was successfully thwarted by the Republican Party leadership.

DISCIPLINING THE PROGRESSIVES

President Coolidge won an easy victory in the election of 1924, receiving 15.7 million votes to 8.4 million for Democrat John W. Davis and 4.8 million for the Progressive candidate, Sen. Robert M. La Follette Sr., R-Wis. In the same election, the Republican majority of 225 in the House was increased to 247. This gain in the 69th Congress wiped out the leverage that Republican Party progressives had been able to exert at the beginning of the 68th Congress and opened the way for party leaders to discipline those—including most of the Wisconsin delegation—who had supported La Follette in the 1924 campaign.

By the time the new Congress met on December 7, 1925, the Republican Conference had chosen Majority Leader Longworth for Speaker, Gillett having been elected to the Senate. It also decided to oust the progressive leaders, John M. Nelson and Florian Lampert, both R-Wis., from their positions as chairmen of the Committee of Elections and the Committee on Patents, respectively, and to let the other insurgents know that their committee assignments would depend on how they voted for Speak-er and for a harder discharge rule. The insurgents responded by again nominating and voting for Cooper. As Rep. James A. Frear, R-Wis., put it:

The Wisconsin delegation in Congress today finds itself challenged by those assuming to be in control of the Republican Party by threats and intimidation on the one hand and by the offer of party recognition with its favors and patronage on the other. We refuse to compromise, or to bargain with Mr. Longworth or with any other Member of the House on an issue affecting our rights as Representatives in Congress to vote our convictions. . . . Neither flattery nor suggestions concerning committee assignments nor threats will cause the Wisconsin delegation in the House to deviate.

Longworth was easily elected Speaker on the first ballot, receiving 229 votes to 173 for Democratic Leader Garrett and 13 for Cooper. By a vote of 210–192, the House then agreed to a new discharge rule in place of the 1924 version. It was described by Charles R. Crisp, D-Ga., the son of the one-time Speaker, as one that "hermetically seals the door against any bill ever coming out of a committee when the Steering Committee or the majority leaders desire to kill the bill without putting the members of this House on record on the measure."

To discharge a recalcitrant committee from a bill under its jurisdiction, the new rule required a majority of the House membership (218), instead of the old rule's 150, to sign the discharge petition. Once the bill was on the floor, the new rule also stipulated that a majority, established by means of a teller vote, was needed to second a motion to consider the measure, a difficult hurdle because members rarely showed up for teller votes. Moreover, the discharge procedure could be used in the House only on the third Monday of the month, and if it failed to be seconded as prescribed, the bill could not be brought up again in the same Congress. (Not surprisingly, the rule was never invoked during its life and was dropped when Democrats revived the old discharge rule in 1931.)

Soon after Longworth was installed as Speaker, the Republican slate of committee assignments was submitted to the House. Those Progressives who had voted for Cooper and against the new discharge rule found themselves demoted to the bottom of their committees, thus changing their committee seniority. (Senate Progressives who had supported La Follette also were dropped to the bottom of their committees.)

Some other Republicans were brought into line by threats of similar action, according to Minority Leader Garrett, who said: "It was demanded that seventy-one gentlemen who at the beginning of the 68th Congress thought a discharge rule was proper should change their votes" and be forced to "eat the bravest word that many of them ever spoke in order to maintain their standing with the party."

These developments at the beginning of the 69th Congress reflected Longworth's determination to play the role of party leader in the House. He had already stated his belief that it was the duty of the Speaker, "standing squarely on the platform of his party, to assist in so far as he properly can the enactment of legislation in accordance with the declared principles and policies of his party and by the same token resist the enactment of legislation in violation thereof." As Speaker, Longworth ignored the party Steering Committee and for six years (1925–1931) personally took charge of the House with the aid of Majority Leader John Q. Tilson, R-Conn., and Rules Committee Chairman Bertrand H. Snell, R-N.Y.

LAME-DUCK AMENDMENT

The power wielded by House Republican leaders during the 1920s was illustrated by their success in blocking a proposed amendment to the Constitution designed to abolish the regular "short" session of every Congress by advancing from March to January 3 the date when the life of the previous Congress expired and that of the new one began. House leaders liked the short session because its automatic termination on March 3 strengthened their ability to control the legislative output of the House.

The constitutional change was sponsored by Republican George W. Norris of Nebraska, the progressive who had helped to curb the power of Speaker Cannon in the House in 1910 before moving to the Senate in 1913. Norris's proposal to abolish the short session was approved six times by the Senate before the House in 1932 finally consented to what was to become the Twentieth Amendment.

The effort to adopt what was then called the "lame-duck" amendment began in the Senate in 1922. Sen. Thaddeus H. Caraway, D-Ark., offered a resolution stating "that all members defeated at the recent polls abstain from voting on any but routine legislation." Instead, the committee considering the resolution, the Agriculture Committee chaired by Norris, reported a joint resolution embodying the lame-duck amendment. The Senate endorsed it on February 13 by a 63–6 vote—well over the two-thirds majority needed to approve constitutional amendments.

A week later the Norris amendment was approved by the House Election Committee, and a special rule providing for its consideration by the House was approved by a majority of members on the Rules Committee. But Rules Chairman Campbell pocketed the rule. Then, while sitting in for the ailing Speaker during the last few days of the session, Campbell—himself a lame duck, having been defeated at the polls the previous November—refused to recognize members seeking a House vote to reverse Campbell's action.

On March 18, 1924, in the first session of the 68th Congress, the Senate again adopted the Norris proposal. Three days later, the amendment again was approved by the Election Committee. This time, however, it was blocked in the Rules Committee, leading Norris to accuse House leaders of "killing it, not directly but smothering it without giving the House of Representatives an opportunity to vote." Norris charged that his amendment was "being held up because machine politicians can get more out of this [legislative] jam than the people's representatives can get." The amendment died with the adjournment of the 68th Congress on March 3, 1925.

The Senate approved the proposed amendment a third time on February 15, 1926, in the first session of the 69th Congress. On February 24 it once more was reported to the House by a unanimous vote of its Election Committee. The committee's chairman, Hays B. White, R-Kan., then discussed the problem he faced under the rules: "Gentlemen, realize how meager is the chance to reach the resolution [proposed amendment] under the Calendar Wednesday rule. That is the logical and proper rule under which it should be considered. . . . I cannot get unanimous consent . . . nor can I hope to pass a measure as fundamental as this under a motion to suspend the rules. . . . The last alternative is for the Rules Committee to grant a special rule for its early consideration." But the rule was not forthcoming before final adjournment of the 69th Congress on March 3, 1927.

The proposed constitutional amendment was adopted by the Senate a fourth time on January 4, 1928, and this time its supporters in the House were able to bring it to the floor. Rep. Ole J. Kvale, a Farmer Laborite from Minnesota, said the leaders who had kept the House from voting on it for so long "did not dare block it any longer." Rules Committee Chairman Snell acknowledged that "if it had not been for the significant application of these two words, lame duck, the propaganda that has been spread throughout this country would never have been one-half as effective as it has been, and if it had not been for that propaganda I doubt whether this proposition would be on the floor at this time." The amendment was endorsed by a majority of the House on March 9, 1928, but the vote of 209–157 fell thirty-five short of the two-thirds required for approval.

The Senate approved the Norris amendment a fifth time on June 7, 1929, by a vote of 64–9. A slightly amended version was approved by the House committee on April 8, 1930, but was not taken up and debated until February 24, 1931, a week before adjournment. Speaker Longworth then offered a further amendment providing that the second session of each Congress must expire automatically on May 4. The Longworth amendment was adopted by a vote of 230–148 before the resolution itself was approved, 290–93. But the measure was locked in conference when Congress adjourned March 3.

When the 72nd Congress convened in December 1931, Democrats had taken control of the House, and after the Senate had adopted the resolution for a sixth time on January 6, 1932, the House on February 16 quickly passed it without amendment by a vote of 335–56. Within less than a year, the Twentieth Amendment had been ratified by three-fourths of the states.

STRUGGLE OVER REAPPORTIONMENT

By 1920 no state had lost a seat in the House through reapportionment since Maine and New Hampshire were deprived of one each after the census of 1880. The reason was that Congress regularly had agreed to increase the total membership by a sufficient number to prevent such a loss. Thus the House was increased to 357 members after the census of 1890, to 391 after that of 1900, and to 435 after the 1910 census.

The 1920 census showed that unless the size of the House was

TERMS AND SESSIONS OF CONGRESS

Under the Constitution, representatives were to be elected "every second year," and Congress was to meet at least once each year—"on the first Monday in December, unless they shall by law appoint a different day." But the Continental Congress, which had been asked by the Federal Convention in Philadelphia to fix "the time and place for commencing proceedings" of the new government, told the First Congress to meet on the first Wednesday of March 1789, which happened to be March 4. Soon afterward, Congress decided that the terms of office of the president, senators, and representatives would begin on March 4 of the year following their election and expire, in the case of representatives, exactly two years later.

Out of these early precedents developed the practice of long and short sessions. The Fourth Congress, for example, met for the first time on December 7, 1795, and remained in session until June 1, 1796. A second session, beginning December 5 of that year, lasted until March 3, 1797, when by law the terms of the representatives elected in 1794 expired. Congresses thereafter often were called into special session by the president, and on numerous occasions they fixed earlier dates for meeting.

For more than 140 years, however, Congress stuck closely to the basic pattern of two sessions: the first, a long one of six months or so that began in December of odd-numbered years—more than one year after the election; the second, a short one that met from December to March—a session that did not begin until after the next election had already taken place.

The political consequences of this schedule became apparent in short order. Presidents inaugurated on March 4 were generally free to make recess appointments and take other actions without consulting Congress until the following December. The short sessions became prey to filibusters and other delaying tactics by members determined to block legislation that would die upon the automatic adjournment of Congress on March 3. Moreover, the Congresses that met in short session always included a substantial number of "lame-duck" members who had been defeated at the polls, yet were able in many instances to determine or greatly influence the legislative outcome of the session.

Dissatisfaction with short sessions of Congress began to mount after 1900. During the Wilson administration, each of four second sessions of Congress ended with a Senate filibuster and the loss of important bills including one or more appropriations bills.

Sen. George W. Norris, R-Neb., became the leading advocate of a constitutional amendment to abolish the short session by starting the terms of Congress and the president in January instead of March. The Senate approved the Norris amendment five times during the 1920s, only to see it blocked by the House each time. It was finally approved by both chambers in 1932 and became the Twentieth Amendment upon ratification by the thirty-sixth state in 1933.

The amendment established January 3 of the year following the election as the day on which the terms of senators and representatives would begin and end, and January 20 as the day on which the president and vice president would take office.

The Twentieth Amendment provided also that Congress should meet annually on January 3 "unless they shall by law appoint a different day." The second session of the 73rd Congress was the first to convene on the new date, January 3, 1934, and Franklin D. Roosevelt was the first president to be inaugurated on January 20, when he began his second term in 1937.

The amendment was intended to permit Congress to extend its first session for as long as necessary and to complete the work of its second session before the next election, thereby obviating legislation by a lame duck body. Congress met in almost continuous session during World War II, however, and the lawmakers have held a number of postelection sessions since that time. *(See "Sessions of the U.S. Congress, 1789–1999," p. 1118; "Extraordinary Sessions of Congress since 1797," p. 1145; and "Special Sessions of the Senate, 1789–1933," p. 1144 in Reference Materials, Vol. II.)*

---

again increased, eleven states would lose seats through reapportionment while eight would gain seats. One argument against making such a shift in the House was that voiced by Rep. John E. Rankin, D-Miss., in 1921:

The census was taken at a time when we were just emerging from the World War, and when so many thousands of people had left the farms and the small towns temporarily and gone to the large cities of the North and East that a reapportionment under that census would necessarily take from Mississippi and other agricultural states their just representation and place it to the credit of the congested centers.

Limit on Size of House

To avoid reducing the representation of any state, the House Census Committee early in 1921 reported a bill to increase the membership to 483, with the additional seats going to twenty-five states whose population relative to that of the others had grown the most. But the House proceeded to reverse the committee's action, voting 267–76 to keep the membership at 435. Proponents of that limit argued that the great size of the membership already had resulted in serious limitations on the right to debate and an overconcentration of power in the hands of the leadership. Much also was made of the increased costs of a larger House.

The version of the reapportionment legislation passed by the House on January 19, 1921, thus provided for changes in the states' representation on the basis of the existing membership, taking twelve seats from eleven states and dividing them up among those states that had increased their populations by the largest percentage. But the Senate failed to act on the measure before the 66th Congress adjourned on March 3. When the 67th Congress was called into special session a month later, the House Census Committee approved a new bill fixing the membership at 460 and costing only two states—Maine and Missouri—one seat each. But in October the House voted 146–142 to recommit the bill to committee, and no further action was taken.

By 1925 it was clear that the wartime shift of population from rural to urban areas was not a temporary trend. Such rapidly growing cities as Los Angeles and Detroit began to clamor for the increased representation to which they were entitled. When the House Census Committee refused to report another reapportionment bill, Rep. Henry E. Barbour, R-Calif., on April 8, 1926, offered a motion to discharge the committee from a bill similar to that passed by the House in 1921. Barbour argued that the bill was privileged under the Constitution, while Rules Committee Chairman Snell, raising a point of order, denied that reapportionment was mandatory under the Constitution.

Speaker Longworth found that three of his predecessors—Joseph W. Keifer, R-Ohio, Thomas Brackett Reed, R-Maine, and David B. Henderson, R-Iowa—had ruled, to the contrary, that Congress was required to order a new apportionment after each census. But Longworth said he doubted that such a ruling was correct, and he put the question to the House for a final decision. As formulated the question was phrased: "Is the consideration of the bill called up by the motion of the gentleman from California in order as a question of constitutional privilege, the rule prescribing the order of business to the contrary notwithstanding?" By a vote of 87–265, the House decided the question in the negative.

Reapportionment Bill Enacted

In January 1927 President Coolidge made it known that he favored enactment of a reapportionment bill. When the House Census Committee refused to act, its chairman, E. Hart Fenn, R-Conn., tried on March 2, the day before adjournment, to suspend the rules and pass his own bill authorizing the secretary of commerce to reapportion the House on the basis of the 1930 census. With only forty minutes of debate allowed under the rule, which also required a two-thirds vote for passage, and with a filibuster under way in the Senate, the House rejected the Fenn motion, 183–197.

The Fenn bill was resubmitted in modified form early in the 70th Congress, but on May 18, 1928, the House voted 186–165 to recommit it to committee. After further revision the measure was passed by voice vote on January 11, 1929. Reported by a Senate committee four days later, it was eventually abandoned by its supporters on February 27—five days before the end of the session—in the face of a threatened filibuster by senators from states destined to lose seats in the House.

President Hoover called the 71st Congress into special session on April 15, 1929, and listed provision for the 1930 census and for a corresponding reapportionment as priority matters. On June 13, 1929, the Senate passed a combined census-reapportionment bill that had been approved by voice vote by the House two days earlier.

Automatic Reapportionment

The 1929 law established a permanent system for reapportioning the 435 seats in the House following each census. It provided that immediately after the convening of the regular session of the 71st Congress in December 1930, the president should transmit to Congress a statement providing for the apportionment of representatives to the House by each state according to the existing size of the House. Failing enactment of new apportionment legislation by Congress, that apportionment would go into effect for ensuing elections without further action and would remain in effect until another census had been taken. Reapportionment then would be effected in the same manner after each decennial count of the population.

The reapportionment based on the 1930 census resulted in a major reshuffling of House seats in the 73rd Congress, which was elected in 1932. Twenty-one states lost a total of twenty-seven seats. Missouri alone lost three seats, and Georgia, Iowa, Kentucky, and Pennsylvania lost two each. Among the eleven states to which these seats were transferred, California gained nine, increasing the size of its delegation from eleven to twenty. Other states gaining more than one additional seat were Michigan (four); Texas (three); and New Jersey, New York, and Ohio (two each).

Democratic Years: 1933–1947

The Great Depression that began in 1929 foreshadowed the end of Republican rule in Washington. The party's majority status in the House (267 members) in the 71st Congress (1929–1931) evaporated in the midterm elections of 1930. That election gave the Republicans 218 seats and the Democrats 216; there also was one independent. By the time the 72nd Congress met on December 7, 1931, however, fourteen representatives-elect, including Speaker Longworth, had died, and special elections to fill the vacancies had resulted in a net gain of four seats for the Democrats, giving them control of the House.

With twelve million Americans unemployed by 1932, Democrat Franklin D. Roosevelt was elected president along with commanding Democratic majorities in both houses of Congress.

A strong party leader, Roosevelt in his first term (1933–1937) won approval of a broad range of his "New Deal" economic and social measures. He was less successful in dealing with Congress in his second term (1937–1941), during which he came into conflict with a conservative coalition opposed to many of his domestic programs. Germany's attack on Poland in 1939, followed by the fall of France in 1940, helped to reelect Roosevelt to an unprecedented third term (1941–1945) that was largely devoted to waging and winning World War II. Legislative-executive relations deteriorated during the war, and when Roosevelt died in April 1945 at the beginning of his fourth term, Congress was in open rebellion against his plans for postwar reconstruction.

The Democrats who led the House during the Roosevelt years worked closely with the president to marshal support for the administration's requests. But their power to shape the legislative output of the House was sharply curtailed after 1937 when a coalition of southern Democrats and Republicans gained effective control of the Rules Committee, which had been a key arm of House leaders since 1880.

This situation, along with the unprecedented four-term presidency of Roosevelt and concern about the capacity of Congress to function effectively as a coequal branch of government, increased demands for government reforms. This led to substantial institutional changes in the way Congress operated that were embodied in the Legislative Reorganization Act of 1946.

PARTY LEADERS

The long period of southern Democratic influence, and even dominance, in the House began when the party took control of that chamber in 1931. John Nance Garner, D-Texas, who had become minority leader upon the retirement of Garrett in 1929, was elected Speaker. At the time Garner was the second-ranking Democrat in the House. Third-ranking Democrat Henry T. Rainey of Illinois was named majority leader. But southern Democrats became chairmen of twenty-eight of the forty-seven standing committees of the House. Among them were Edward W. Pou, D-N.C., Rules; Joseph W. Byrns, D-Tenn., Appropriations; James W. Collier, D-Miss., Ways and Means; and Sam Rayburn, D-Texas, Interstate and Foreign Commerce.

When Garner became vice president in 1933, House Democrats elevated Rainey to Speaker and made Byrns the new majority leader. Rainey died in 1934, and Byrns was elected Speaker at the beginning of the 74th Congress in 1935. He was succeeded as majority leader by William B. Bankhead, D-Ala., who had become chairman of the Rules Committee on the death of Pou in 1934. When Byrns died in 1936, Bankhead became Speaker and the Democrats chose Rayburn as majority leader.

Bankhead remained Speaker until his death in 1940, when he was succeeded by Rayburn; a northern Democrat—John W. McCormack, D-Mass.—became majority leader. Rayburn and McCormack remained in these posts until Republicans took control of the House in 1947.

While the Democrats had been in the minority during the 1920s, southerners had constituted more than half of their ranks and there was little occasion for complaint about an unwarranted influence in party councils. But when the party won control in 1931, northern and western Democrats pressed for a larger voice in committee assignments. They proposed entrusting this crucial authority to a new Committee on Committees, replacing the Democratic members of the Ways and Means Committee, who had performed this function since 1911. The new committee was to be made up of one member from each state having Democratic representation in the House. The committee also was to select a nine-member steering committee that would be in charge of the Democrats' legislative program.

STEERING COMMITTEE

These steps were not agreed to in 1931, although additions to the Ways and Means Committee, including McCormack, brought about a better balance of geographical representation. By 1933, however, the Democratic majority in the House had been increased to 313 members, nearly two-thirds of whom were from states outside the South. As a result, it was agreed to set up a Steering Committee composed of the Speaker, the majority leader, and the whip; the chairmen of the Appropriations, Ways and Means, and Rules committees, and of the party caucus; plus fifteen representatives from as many regions to be chosen by Democratic members within those areas. This Steering Committee operated with some success during the 73rd Congress (1933–1935) but fell into disuse thereafter.

GAG RULES

The Rules Committee itself was the major tool of House Democratic leaders during the 73rd Congress. It was this Congress that was called into special session by President Roosevelt on March 9, 1933, and asked to pass a series of emergency economic recovery measures almost sight unseen. Ten of the measures were brought to the House floor under special "closed" rules—drafted by the Rules Committee and adopted by majority vote in the House—that barred all except committee amendments, waived points of order against provisions or procedures violating rules of the House, and sharply limited debate.

Among the laws enacted with the help of these "gag" rules during the famous "Hundred Days" were the Emergency Banking Act, the Economy Act, the Emergency Relief Act, the first Agricultural Adjustment Act, the Tennessee Valley Authority Act, and the National Industrial Recovery Act.

Faced with mounting opposition to cuts in veterans' benefits and government salaries ordered under the Roosevelt recovery program, the Rules Committee at the opening of the second session on January 3, 1934, brought in a rule to bar amendments to any appropriations bill for the remainder of the session that would conflict with the economy program. The purpose, said Representative Bankhead, was to have the House "deliberately determine for today and hereafter . . . whether they are going to follow the president's recommendations or not."

Minority Leader Snell maintained that he had never been opposed to special rules so long as they were "fairly fair" and called the new proposal "the most vicious, the most far-reaching special rule" ever drafted. No majority, he said, had "ever dared bring in a rule that not only hog-tied and prohibited the members from expressing themselves on the legislation in hand but even extended through the entire session of Congress." The real purpose, said Snell, was that "you think it will be easier to hog-tie your own men today than it will [be] after we have been in session for five months." Snell was joined by all the Republican members, eighty-four Democrats, and five Farmer Laborite members in voting against the rule, but it was narrowly adopted by a 197–192 vote.

With members of Congress looking on, President Franklin D. Roosevelt signs the Serviceman's Readjustment Act of 1944. Roosevelt was nearing the end of his unprecedented third term.

The only major change in the standing rules of the House in this period involved the discharge rule. When the Democrats took control of the House in 1931 they replaced the unworkable rule of 1925 with that of 1924, which was altered slightly to reduce from 150 to 145 the number of signatures needed to place a discharge motion on the calendar. But that number was increased to 218 again (the number in force from 1910 to 1924) at the beginning of the 74th Congress in 1935, when Democrats in the House numbered 322 but the leadership was finding it difficult to maintain party unity.

THE CONSERVATIVE COALITION

Party unity was badly shaken at the beginning of the 75th Congress in 1937 when President Roosevelt submitted a plan to reorganize the Supreme Court and the lower courts. His plan, among other changes, would have allowed the president to appoint up to six additional Supreme Court justices whenever a sitting justice age seventy or over refused to retire. Its implied purpose was to increase the likelihood that the Supreme Court

could be counted on to uphold the constitutionality of New Deal economic measures, of which six of the most sweeping already had been overturned.

The plan to "pack" the Court—which eventually died in the Senate—created a furor in the country and led to a new alignment of conservative Democrats and Republicans in Congress generally and on the House Rules Committee in particular. In the long run, ironically, it was a conservative coalition in Congress, not the Supreme Court, that was the greater threat to New Deal programs.

The "conservative coalition" first appeared in August 1937, when the Rules Committee voted 10–4 against granting a special rule for floor consideration of an administration bill that eventually became the Fair Labor Standards Act. The committee was chaired by Rep. John J. O'Connor, D-N.Y., and was composed of five northern Democrats, five southern Democrats, and four Republicans. After the committee's refusal to grant the special rule, House leaders obtained 218 signatures on a discharge petition, but when they brought the bill to the floor in December the House voted 216–198 to recommit it to the Labor Committee.

When the Rules Committee in 1938 again refused to clear the wage-hour bill, House leaders once more resorted to the discharge rule to bring the bill to a vote, winning House approval this time by a margin of 314–97. (Although the House occasionally had passed a bill by use of the discharge rule, the Fair Labor Standards Act of 1938 was the first such measure to become law.)

Chairman O'Connor's defection on this bill made him one of the targets of President Roosevelt's attempted purge of anti–New Deal Democrats in the 1938 primaries. At a press conference on August 16, Roosevelt denounced the Rules chairman as "one of the most effective obstructionists in the lower house." O'Connor, unlike other prominent targets of the purge effort, lost his bid for renomination.

O'Connor was succeeded as chairman of the Rules Committee in 1939 by Adolph J. Sabath, D-Ill., the senior House Democrat at the time and an ardent New Dealer. But Sabath continued to be outvoted in the committee by a coalition of Republicans and southern Democrats led by E. E. Cox, D-Ga., and Howard W. Smith, D-Va. During the 76th Congress (1939–1940), the committee began the practice of demanding, as the price of sending administration bills to the floor, substantive changes to accord with the views of the conservatives.

Besides blocking or weakening administration measures, the coalition used its power on the Rules Committee to clear measures opposed by Roosevelt. The committee authorized an investigation of the National Labor Relations Board in 1939; an investigation of activities of executive agencies in 1943; and, in 1944, an investigation of the government's seizure of properties of Montgomery Ward & Co. All were intended to embarrass the administration. The panel in 1944 also approved a special rule bringing to the floor a price control bill that had been rejected by the Banking and Currency Committee and never reported by any legislative committee. Speaker Rayburn took the floor to denounce the rule, saying the Rules Committee "was never set up to be a legislative committee," and the House rejected it.[14]

At the beginning of the 79th Congress in 1945, the size of the Rules Committee was reduced from fourteen to twelve members, consisting of eight Democrats and four Republicans. Sabath was still chairman, but whenever Cox and Smith decided to vote with the Republicans they could produce a tie that would block committee action. In 1945, for example, the committee by a 6–6 vote refused a direct appeal from President Harry S. Truman for a rule permitting the House to vote on a bill to establish a permanent Fair Employment Practices Commission. The coalition also blocked a rule permitting consideration of an administration bill to raise the minimum wage from forty cents to sixty-five cents an hour.

In 1946, when the Rules Committee was asked to clear an administration-backed labor relations bill reported by the House Labor Committee, it reported instead a rule to permit substitution of a more drastic measure sponsored by Francis H. Case, R-

S.D., that had just been introduced. Chairman Sabath denounced the action as arbitrary and undemocratic, but in this case a majority of House members upheld the committee majority by adopting the rule and passing the Case substitute, which Truman later vetoed.

The Rules Committee thus ceased to be a dependable arm of the Democratic leadership after 1937, when the coalition of conservative Democrats and Republicans took control. While the views of members of the coalition on social and economic issues were in conflict with those of most Democrats, they frequently reflected the legislative preferences of a Republican-conservative Democratic majority in the House, and it was the support of this broader conservative coalition that enabled those who controlled the Rules Committee to make the most effective use of its powers.

1946 LEGISLATIVE REORGANIZATION ACT

Talk of the need for congressional reform mounted in World War II, during which the powers of the executive branch were vastly enlarged. A report of the American Political Science Association asserted in 1945 that Congress needed to "modernize its machinery and methods to fit modern conditions if it is to keep pace with a greatly enlarged and active executive branch. This is a better approach than that which seeks to meet the problem by reducing and hamstringing the executive. A strong and more representative legislature, in closer touch with and better informed about the administration, is the antidote to bureaucracy."[15]

Responding to such criticisms, the House and Senate agreed early in 1945 to establish a Joint Committee on the Organization of Congress composed of six members from each house equally divided among Democrats and Republicans. Sen. Robert M. La Follette Jr., a Wisconsin Progressive, was named chairman, with Rep. A. S. Mike Monroney, D-Okla., as vice chairman. From March 13 through June 29, 1945, the group took extensive testimony from more than one hundred witnesses, including many members of Congress.

In its final report issued March 4, 1946, the La Follette-Monroney committee made no recommendations on proposals to curb the House Rules Committee "because of a lack of agreement within the committee as to workable changes in existing practices." Nor did the committee recommend any of the numerous proposals it had received for appointing committee chairmen on some basis other than seniority, or to make it easier to limit debate in the Senate.

The report nevertheless included a broad range of proposals designed to streamline the committee structure, strengthen congressional control over the budget, reduce and redistribute the workload of Congress, and improve staff assistance. Most of these reforms were incorporated in the Legislative Reorganization Act enacted on August 2, 1946. The major provisions of the act dealt with committees, the federal budget, congressional workload, staff, and salaries.

Standing Committees

The reorganization reduced the number of standing committees from thirty-three to fifteen in the Senate and from forty-eight to nineteen in the House. Many inactive committees were dropped; some others having related functions were consolidated.

All standing committees, except Appropriations, were directed to fix regular days for meeting; to keep complete records of committee action, including votes; and to open all sessions to the public except when marking up bills or voting, or when the committee by a majority vote ordered a closed session to discuss national security or other sensitive subjects. The act made it the duty of each committee chairman to bring bills to a final vote and to see to it that any measure approved in committee was reported promptly to the House. But no measure was to be reported from any committee unless a majority of the members were present.

Control of the Federal Budget

The act directed the House Ways and Means and Senate Finance committees and the Appropriations committees of both houses, acting as a Joint Budget Committee, to prepare each year a governmentwide budget containing estimates of total receipts and expenditures. The Joint Budget Committee's report was to be accompanied by a concurrent resolution that would be the legislative vehicle for congressional approval of each year's budget and fixing the amount to be appropriated for each federal agency. Congress was prohibited from appropriating more than the estimated receipts without at the same time authorizing an increase in the public debt. The act did not include a proposal that the president be required to reduce all appropriations by a uniform percentage if expenditures later were found to have exceeded receipts.

Congressional Workload

The act prohibited private bills from being used for the payment of pensions or tort claims, the construction of bridges, or the correction of military records—categories of legislation that at one time consumed much of the lawmakers' time. But Congress did not accept the Joint Committee's proposal that the District of Columbia be given home rule, a step that would have eliminated the District of Columbia committees in both houses and a considerable amount of legislative work.

Committee Staff

The act authorized each standing committee to appoint four professional and six clerical staff members, although no limit was placed on the number that could be hired by the Appropriations committees. It also made the Legislative Reference Service (later renamed the Congressional Research Service), which as an arm of Congress provided information for committees and members upon request, a separate department of the Library of Congress.

The Joint Committee had recommended the appointment of a director of personnel, with authority to establish the equivalent of a Civil Service for legislative employees, but this proposal was eliminated in the Senate.

Salaries/Benefits

The act increased the salaries of senators and representatives from $10,000 to $12,500, effective in 1947, and retained an existing $2,500 nontaxable expense allowance for all members. The salaries of the vice president and the Speaker were raised to $20,000. The act also brought members of Congress under the Civil Service Retirement Act and made them eligible for benefits at age sixty-two after at least six years of service.

Regulation of Lobbying

The 1946 reorganization also included a section on lobbying (Title III—the Federal Regulation of Lobbying Act) that for the first time required lobbyists to register with and report their expenditures to the clerk of the House. But it did not include a provision, recommended by the La Follette-Monroney committee, that both parties establish seven-member policy committees in each chamber, with the majority policy committees serving as "a formal council to meet regularly with the executive, to facilitate the formulation and carrying out of national policy and to improve relationships between the executive and legislative branches of government." Republicans and Democrats in the Senate, but not in the House, agreed later in 1946 to set up party policy committees.

Inadequacies of 1946 Reforms

Although the 1946 act was regarded at the time as a major achievement, its provisions for budget control as a tool in controlling government spending soon proved to be unworkable and were dropped after three years. And the Regulation of Lobbying Act proved to be too weak to shed much light on the purposes and activities of pressure groups. In reducing the number of standing committees, one of the goals had been to limit representatives to membership on one committee (and on two committees for senators) to make more efficient use of their time. But in practice this broke down, as a result in part of the establishment in both chambers in later years of numerous subcommittees and several select committees.

The 1946 reorganization skirted the issue of the distribution of power within Congress and did not address the question of the balance of power between the legislative branch and the executive branch. These remained troublesome issues throughout the postwar years.

Postwar Era: 1947–1969

The Democrats lost control of the House and Senate in the 80th Congress (1947–1949) and in the 83rd (1953–1955) but won majorities in all other Congresses throughout the postwar period.

Meanwhile, the presidency passed from Democrat Harry S.

Truman to Republican Dwight D. Eisenhower in 1953, followed by Democrats John F. Kennedy in 1961 and Lyndon B. Johnson in 1963. Thus during two years of Truman's term and six of Eisenhower's, the president was faced with a Congress controlled by the other party.

These periods of divided government were characterized by partisan conflicts between the president and Congress over public policy. But none of the postwar presidents was in full command of his party in Congress, whether the president's party was in the majority or the minority. All of them were forced to varying degrees to seek bipartisan support to get their programs enacted. In the House the Democratic Party always included sixty or more southern conservatives who were opposed to much of their party's economic and social programs. And about twenty moderate to liberal Republicans frequently were at odds with their party's conservative majority.

Leadership in the House was relatively stable in this period. After World War II the control of federal expenditures became a central issue, as it had after the Civil War and World War I. Attempts by Congress in general and by the House Appropriations Committee in particular to exercise the power of the purse were matters of controversy. There was continuing agitation over the power of the House Rules Committee to block or reshape major legislation, leading once again to several attempts to restrict the panel's powers. Talk of the need for broad-scale congressional reform increased in the 1960s, and in 1970 the House finally approved a reorganization bill first passed by the Senate in 1967.

PARTY LEADERS

Sam Rayburn of Texas was the unrivaled leader of House Democrats from 1940 until his death in 1961, serving as Speaker in all but the Republican-controlled 80th and 83rd Congresses, during which he was minority leader. Rayburn was a strong Speaker, whose influence was enhanced by his veneration of the House of Representatives as an institution and his high personal standing with most of his colleagues. Faced with a divided party on many issues, he relied heavily on his personal friendships with key members on both sides of the aisle to attain his legislative objectives. And younger Democrats who followed his advice—"to get along, go along"—could expect to be rewarded with preferment of some kind, especially if they could demonstrate talent and a capacity for hard work.

Although he was in many ways a lonely individual with an unhappy personal life, Rayburn had a profound understanding of human nature as well as of House procedures. James M. Landis, a Harvard Law School professor who worked closely with Rayburn on key New Deal legislation when Rayburn was chairman of the Interstate Commerce Committee, described him this way: "Sam was an expert on the integrity of people. . . . He knew when a man . . . was telling the truth. . . . He had no patience for men who were not sincere and honest. . . . He was an expert on procedure, and sizing up the motives of what made human beings tick."[16]

Rayburn's preferences were controlling when it came to

Sam Rayburn holds the record for longest service as Speaker. He occupied the post from 1940 until his death in 1961, except for stints as minority leader in 1947–1949 and 1953–1955.

Democratic committee assignments. In 1948 he obtained the removal from the Un-American Activities Committee of three Democrats who had supported Dixiecrat Strom Thurmond in the 1948 presidential campaign. He saw to it that Democrats named to vacancies on the Ways and Means Committee were favorable to reciprocal trade bills and opposed to reductions in the oil depletion allowance. And he turned the predominantly conservative Education and Labor Committee into a liberal body during the 1950s by an infusion of younger Democrats. But Rayburn resisted pressure from party liberals to restructure the Rules Committee until 1961, when he reluctantly agreed to go along.

When Rayburn died late that year after forty-nine years in the House, he was replaced by John W. McCormack, D-Mass., who had served as majority leader during Rayburn's entire tenure as Speaker. Carl Albert, D-Okla., was named majority leader at the same time. McCormack's performance as Speaker suffered by comparison with that of Rayburn. Criticism of his weakness as a party leader culminated at the beginning of the 91st Congress in 1969 when fifty-eight Democrats voted for Morris K. Udall, D-Ariz., for Speaker in the party caucus. Although easily reelected as Speaker, McCormack decided in 1970 to retire at the end of his term, after forty-three years in the House. Albert was designated to succeed him as Speaker. Hale Boggs, D-La., became majority leader when Albert moved up. Albert was reelected Speaker for the 93rd and 94th Congresses (1973–1977). After Boggs was pronounced "missing and presumed dead" following an airplane accident in October 1972, Thomas P. O'Neill Jr., D-Mass., succeeded him as majority leader in January 1973 at the beginning of the 93rd Congress.

House Republicans were led from 1939 to 1959 by Joseph W. Martin Jr., R-Mass. Martin served as Speaker in the 80th and 83rd Congresses, during which Charles A. Halleck, R-Ind., held the post of majority leader. Martin, a close friend of Rayburn's, was considered by more conservative House Republicans to be too accommodating to the Democratic leadership during the 1950s, and in 1959 he lost his post as minority leader to Halleck, an outspoken partisan. Before long, however, Halleck began to incur the opposition of younger Republicans seeking a more forceful and positive style of leadership, and in January 1965 he himself was ousted when the Republican Conference (the party's caucus), chose Gerald R. Ford, R-Mich., as minority leader on a 73–67 vote.

EFFORTS TO CONTROL SPENDING

In 1947, as required by the Legislative Reorganization Act of 1946, the Republican-controlled 80th Congress formed a Joint Committee on the Legislative Budget, which quickly agreed to ceilings on governmentwide appropriations and expenditures that were substantially under the amounts projected in President Truman's federal budget. The House approved the ceilings, but the Senate raised them and insisted that any budget surplus be used to reduce the public debt instead of to provide a tax cut desired by House leaders. As a result, the resolution embodying the federal budget died in a House-Senate conference.

In 1948 both chambers reached quick agreement on a federal budget that projected a surplus of $10 billion—more than double President Truman's estimate—and paved the way for enactment, over the president's veto, of a tax cut. But Republican leaders expressed doubt about the efficacy of the budget procedure as a device for reducing expenditures. Rep. John Taber, R-N.Y., chairman of the House Appropriations Committee, called it "a stab in the dark." His Senate counterpart, H. Styles Bridges, R-N.H., said it was "a pre-game guess at the final score." In fact, the projected surplus vanished in fiscal 1949, which ended with a deficit of $1.8 billion.

Democrats took control of the 81st Congress in 1949, and the new chairman of the House Appropriations Committee, Clarence A. Cannon, D-Mo., proposed suspension of the budget provisions of the 1946 act, saying they were "unworkable and impracticable." He told the House: "We have tried it. We gave it every opportunity. It cannot be made effective. We can no more expect success . . . with this well-meant but hopeless proposal than we can expect a verdict from the jury before it has heard the evidence." Congress put off a decision by voting to postpone until May of that year the deadline for the Joint Committee's recommendations, but these were never forthcoming. The budget provisions of the 1946 act remained a part of the law, but Congress made no further effort to comply with them.

In 1950 Cannon tried another approach to expenditure control by having his committee draft a single omnibus appropriations bill that carried almost $37 billion in spending authority as finally enacted. But this bill was quickly outdated by the Korean War and the need for large supplemental appropriations. More significant, the omnibus approach had the effect of reducing the authority of the Appropriations Committee's subcommittees and their chairmen. Cannon asserted that "every predatory lobbyist, every pressure group seeking to get its hands into the U.S. Treasury, every bureaucrat seeking to extend his empire downtown is opposed to the consolidated bill." But in 1951 the committee voted 31–18 to return to the traditional method of separate appropriation bills for each government department.

Cannon and his committee were in full agreement, however, in opposing the concept of a Joint Budget Committee, to be composed of several members of the Senate and House Appropriations committees. Bills to create such a group were passed by the Senate eight times between 1952 and 1967, but they were never accepted by the House. George H. Mahon, D-Texas, who succeeded Cannon as chairman of the Appropriations Committee in 1964, summed up the prevailing House view in 1965 when he said that "every key provision of the [Senate's] bill . . . is, in my judgment, either unsound, unworkable, or unnecessary."

Behind Mahon's statement lay a long history of resentment over the Senate's claim to coequal status in the appropriations process, where the House had always asserted its primacy. The issue boiled over in 1962 when the House Appropriations Committee demanded that conference meetings, traditionally held on the Senate side, be rotated between the House and Senate wings of the Capitol. Senate Appropriations countered by proposing that it initiate one-half of all appropriation bills. The ensuing deadlock froze action for months.

The House committee complained at one point that "in the past ten years the Senate conferees have been able to retain $22 billion of the $32 billion in increases which the Senate added to House appropriations—a 2 to 1 ratio in favor of the body consistently advocating larger appropriations, increased spending, and corresponding deficits." Sen. A. Willis Robertson, D-Va., called the communication in which this complaint was voiced "the most insulting document that one body has ever sent to another." When the Senate adopted an emergency funding resolution allowing federal agencies to keep on spending at the old rate until appropriations for the new fiscal year had been approved (called a continuing resolution), the House went on record, in a 245–1 roll call, that the Senate action was "an infringement on the privileges" of the House. The Senate resolved, in turn, that "the acquiescence of the Senate in permitting the House to first consider appropriation bills cannot change the clear language of the Constitution nor affect the Senate's coequal power to originate any bill not expressly 'raising revenue.'"

The feud was allowed to die without resolution. While it was true that the Senate had consistently voted for larger expenditures than the House, it was also true that Congress had managed generally to authorize less spending than was proposed by the postwar presidents. Yet the amounts authorized grew more or less steadily after 1947, and it became increasingly apparent that the capacity of Congress to control expenditures through its power of the purse was limited. Congress did not pass any further legislation to reform its budget procedures until 1974.

CHECKING THE RULES COMMITTEE

The negative power of the Rules Committee was forcefully displayed during the Republican 80th Congress in connection with efforts to enact a major housing bill. The committee insisted that the Banking and Currency Committee delete provisions for public housing and slum clearance before it would agree to release the bill. The Rules panel also refused to allow the House to vote on a new universal military training bill reported by the Armed Services Committee, and it was only under strong pressure from Speaker Martin that the committee cleared a bill to revive the existing Selective Service System.

Liberals dominated the 263-member Democratic majority elected to the House in 1948, but they were again faced with the prospect that the twelve-member Rules Committee would be controlled by a conservative coalition of four Republicans and three southern Democrats—E. E. Cox of Georgia, Howard W. Smith of Virginia, and William M. Colmer of Mississippi. Thus, with the backing of Speaker Rayburn, the party caucus voted 176–48 for a "twenty-one-day rule" proposed by Rules Committee Chairman Adolph J. Sabath of Illinois. The rule authorized the chairman of any legislative committee that had reported a bill favorably, and requested a special rule from the Rules Committee, to bring the matter to the House floor if the committee failed to act within twenty-one calendar days of the request.

Adopted by the House on January 3, 1949, by a procedural vote of 275–143, the twenty-one-day rule was used eight times during the 81st Congress to obtain House passage of bills blocked in the Rules Committee. These included an anti–poll tax bill and statehood measures for Alaska and Hawaii. An effort to repeal the new rule in 1950, led by Representative Cox, was rejected by the House by a vote of 183–236.

The Democrats lost twenty-nine seats in the 1950 congressional elections, and when the 82nd Congress met on January 3, 1951, Cox again moved to drop the rule. It had been adopted in 1949, he said, because the Rules Committee had "refused to stampede under the lash of the whip applied by strong

unofficial minority groups." Halleck supported repeal because, he said, it was the job of the Rules Committee to screen "unwise, unsound, ill-timed, spendthrift, and socialistic measures." Sabath protested that repeal would permit an "unholy alliance" of southern Democrats and Republicans to "tear down the rights of every member of the House." But ninety-one Democrats joined 152 Republicans to repeal the twenty-one-day rule on a 243–180 vote.

Chairman Smith's Reign

Control of the Rules Committee by a conservative coalition virtually went unchallenged for the next decade. Smith, who became chairman in 1955, made the most of his power to censor the legislative program of the House. The committee had no regular meeting day and could be called together only by the chairman. It often was unable to clear any bills for floor action during the final days of a session, as Chairman Smith simply would disappear to his Virginia farm.

In 1958, 283 Democrats were elected to the House, their largest majority since 1936, and party liberals again talked of curbing the Rules Committee. They proposed changing the ratio of Democrats to Republicans on the committee from 8–4 to 9–3 and reinstituting the twenty-one-day rule. Speaker Rayburn was opposed to any changes, however, and the liberals called off their drive when he "offered his personal assurance" that housing, civil rights, labor, and other social welfare legislation "would not be bottled up in the committee."[17]

Enlargement of the Rules Committee

Rayburn was unable to fulfill his pledge during the 86th Congress (1959–1961). When Democrat John F. Kennedy was elected president in 1960, along with a reduced Democratic majority in the House of 263, it was clear that much of his program might be stymied unless administration Democrats gained control of the Rules Committee at the start of the 87th Congress. Rayburn decided to try to enlarge the committee from twelve to fifteen members to make room for the addition of two loyal Democrats and thus create an 8–7 majority that would be more likely to act favorably on administration bills. His plan was stoutly opposed by Chairman Smith and Republican leader Halleck, and it took Rayburn and his lieutenants a month of maneuvering and lobbying to round up enough votes to win.

The House finally adopted the plan increasing the size of the committee from twelve to fifteen members on January 31, 1961, by a vote of 217–212. Voting for the change were 195 Democrats, including forty-seven southerners led by Carl Vinson of Georgia, and twenty-two Republicans, including former Speaker Martin. Opposed were sixty-four Democrats, all except one of them southerners, and 148 Republicans. But the new balance thus achieved on the Rules Committee proved to be precarious. A major school aid bill was effectively killed by the committee in 1961 when James J. Delaney, D-N.Y., a Catholic from a heavily Catholic district, joined the conservative coalition in voting against the measure because no provision was made for aid to parochial schools. Two pro-administration southern Democrats on the committee in 1962 helped to kill a bill to create a cabinet-level urban affairs department after Robert C. Weaver, a black, was designated to become the new secretary.

The 1961 resolution enlarging the size of the committee was limited to the life of the 87th Congress. But the House on January 9, 1963, at the beginning of the 88th Congress, agreed by a vote of 235–196 to make the change permanent. Although party ratios had scarcely changed, the resolution was supported this time by 207 Democrats, fifty-nine of whom were southerners, and twenty-eight Republicans. Opposed were 148 Republicans and forty-eight Democrats, all but three of them southerners.

MEMBERSHIP TURNOVER

Democratic leaders nevertheless continued to have problems with the Rules Committee. But the election in 1964 of Lyndon B. Johnson as president, together with a Democratic majority of 295 in the House, paved the way for three further changes in the House rules at the beginning of the 89th Congress in 1965, again over the opposition of a conservative coalition.

The new rules were adopted January 4 by voice vote after a key procedural motion backed by proponents of the rules change had been adopted by a roll-call vote of 224–202. Only sixteen Republicans voted with 208 Democrats for the motion, while seventy-nine Democrats, all except four of them southerners, and 123 Republicans opposed the motion, which had the effect of ending further debate on the issue and bringing the rules changes to a final vote.

The first of the new rules revived, with one change, the twenty-one-day rule that had been in force during the 81st Congress. Under the 1949 rule the Speaker had been required to recognize the chairman or other member of any committee seeking to bring before the House a bill that had been denied a rule by the Rules Committee for twenty-one days. The 1965 version left the question of recognition to the discretion of the Speaker, thereby ensuring that no bill opposed by the leadership could be brought up under the rule.

The second change permitted the Speaker to recognize any member to offer a motion (which would be agreed to if approved by majority vote) allowing the House to send a bill to conference with the Senate, provided such action was approved by the committee with jurisdiction over the bill. Previously, it had been necessary to obtain unanimous consent, or approval of a special rule from the Rules Committee, or agreement by the House to suspend the rules (requiring a two-thirds vote) to send a bill to a conference committee.

The third change repealed a rule dating from 1789 that had permitted any member to demand the reading in full of the engrossed (final) copy of a House bill. Members opposed to legislation frequently had used this privilege to delay final passage of a bill until it could be printed.

The twenty-one-day rule was employed successfully eight times during the 89th Congress, and the threat of its use persuaded the Rules Committee to send several other controversial measures to the floor. As in 1951, however, Republican gains in the 1966 elections opened the way to repeal of the rule at the beginning of the 90th Congress; this was accomplished on January 10, 1967, by a vote of 233–185. The prevailing coalition included 157 Republicans and sixty-nine southern Democrats. The two other rules adopted in 1965 were retained.

Repeal of the twenty-one-day rule in 1967 proved to be of little consequence during the 90th Congress, largely because of two other developments affecting the Rules Committee. Chairman Smith had been defeated in a primary election in 1966, as had another committee Democrat, and these vacancies were filled by administration supporters. Smith's successor as chairman, Colmer of Mississippi, was no less strong a conservative, but he now was outvoted on the committee. This became apparent on February 28, 1967, when for the first time in its history the committee adopted a set of rules governing its procedures. These rules took away the chairman's exclusive power to set meeting dates, required the consent of a committee majority to table a bill, and set limits on proxy voting by members. The net effect of these changes was substantial cooperation with the Democratic leadership in 1967–1968 and the end of a decade of agitation for reform of the committee. Cooperation between Rules and the leadership continued in subsequent Congresses.

FURTHER PRESSURES FOR REFORM

Efforts to modify the organization and procedures of the House after 1946 were not confined to the protracted struggle for control of the Rules Committee. The leadership of the Senate as well as the House came under pressure in the 1950s to curb the freewheeling activities of their investigating committees. And in the 1960s the conduct of some senators and representatives raised concern about the personal and professional ethics of members, forcing both chambers to respond. Mounting criticism of the methods and operations of Congress as a whole led both chambers in 1965 to begin a reexamination of their operations, which produced a second reorganization act in 1970.

Fair Play for Committee Witnesses

The efforts of the House Un-American Activities Committee to expose alleged subversion and disloyalty through public hearings became a subject of great controversy in the early 1950s. The committee's access to television was cut off in 1952 when Speaker Rayburn effectively banned radio, television, or film coverage of any House committee hearing by holding that there was no authority for such coverage in the House rules.

Criticism of the committee's operations increased in the Republican-controlled 83rd Congress when Chairman Harold H. Velde, R-Ill., and Sen. Joseph R. McCarthy, R-Wis., head of the Senate Permanent Investigations Subcommittee, were accused of conducting one-man witch hunts and mistreating witnesses.

Criticism of the controversial operation of the House Un-American Activities Committee, which held public hearings to expose communist activity, led to reform of House committee procedures.

McCarthy eventually was censured by the Senate for contemptuous treatment of two Senate committees. *(See "Censure of McCarthy," p. 273.)*

The Rules committees of both chambers held hearings in 1954 on proposals to reform committee procedures. On March 23, 1955, the House adopted ten rules dealing with the conduct of committee hearings. They:

• Required a quorum of no fewer than two committee members to take testimony and receive evidence.

• Allowed witnesses at investigative hearings to be accompanied by counsel for the purpose of advising them on their constitutional rights.

• Stipulated that if a committee found that evidence might tend to defame, degrade, or incriminate any person, it would have to receive such evidence in executive (closed) session and allow such persons to appear before the committee as witnesses and request the subpoena of others.

• Barred the release or use in public sessions of evidence or testimony received in executive session without the consent of the committee.

The Senate Rules Committee recommended a similar set of standards in 1955, but the Senate left it to individual committees to draw up their own rules of conduct. Those adopted by the Permanent Investigations Subcommittee in 1955, when Sen. John L. McClellan, D-Ark., became chairman, incorporated provisions similar to those approved by the House. Although the investigative practices of congressional committees continued to vary considerably thereafter, concern about the fair treatment of witnesses declined in importance as a public issue.

Congressional Scandals

Although members of Congress were never immune to the temptations of using public office for private gain, the ethics of Congress as a whole did not begin to stir broad public interest until after World War II. Contributing to this interest were the rising costs of political campaigns and greater concern about conflicts of interest at all levels of government. The fact that some members continued to engage in private law practice or other business activities, and to hold a financial interest in such government-regulated businesses as banks and television stations, added to that concern.

Pressure to do something about congressional ethics was intensified in the 1960s by scandals in the Senate. One involved Robert G. "Bobby" Baker, secretary of the Senate majority; another focused on Sen. Thomas J. Dodd, D-Conn. *(See Chapter 35, Ethics and Criminal Prosecutions.)*

The House, meanwhile, had become embroiled in attempts to discipline one of its members—Adam Clayton Powell Jr., D-N.Y., chairman of the Education and Labor Committee since 1961. Powell, one of the few black members in the House, was indicted for tax evasion in 1958 and eventually paid $28,000 in back taxes and penalties. He was sued for libel in 1960 and held in contempt of court in the case on several occasions. He kept his wife on his congressional payroll at $20,000 a year although she lived in Puerto Rico. However, it was his extensive travels at public expense, his prolonged absences from Congress, and his high-handed actions as a committee chairman that eventually turned most of his colleagues against him.

At the beginning of the 90th Congress in 1967, the Democratic Caucus removed Powell from his chairmanship of the Education and Labor Committee, and the House by a vote of 365–65 decided to deny him his seat pending an investigation by a special committee. The committee later recommended that Powell be seated but that he be censured for "gross misconduct," stripped of his seniority, and fined $40,000 for misuse of public funds. But on March 1, 1967, the House rejected these proposals and voted instead to exclude Powell from the 90th Congress and declare his seat vacant.

Powell promptly filed suit in federal court to regain his seat on the grounds that he met all of the constitutional qualifications for membership and that the House had no authority to exclude him. A district court dismissed the case for lack of jurisdiction, and the court of appeals affirmed the district court's finding, noting that the case involved a political question that, if decided by the courts, would constitute a violation of the separation of powers. However, on June 16, 1969, the Supreme Court reversed the lower courts by a vote of 7–1. The majority opinion, written by Chief Justice Earl Warren, held that Powell had been improperly excluded by the House. The Constitution prescribes only three criteria for seating a person elected to the House, Warren noted, all of which Powell met.

Powell had been overwhelmingly reelected in a special election following his exclusion in 1967, but he had made no effort to take his seat during the 90th Congress. Reelected in 1968, he presented himself at the opening of the 91st Congress in 1969. By this time tempers had cooled. The House by a vote of 254–158 adopted a resolution that permitted Powell to take his seat but fined him $25,000 as punishment and "stripped him of his seniority." Powell accepted the judgment, but his career in the House was destroyed. In 1970 he was defeated for renomination in a primary election.

The Powell case, together with the Senate's actions, helped to persuade the House in 1967 to establish its own twelve-member, bipartisan Committee on Standards of Official Conduct (ethics committee). In 1968 the House adopted a Code of Official Conduct (Rule LXIII). The code included provisions that:

• Barred House members or employees from receiving compensation through improper use of their official position.

• Prohibited the acceptance of gifts of substantial value from an individual or group with a direct interest in legislation before Congress.

• Prohibited acceptance of honoraria of more than the usual and customary value for speeches and articles.

• Required representatives to keep campaign funds separate from personal funds and prohibited them from converting campaign funds to personal use.

• Required that, unless some other purpose was made clear in advance, all funds raised at testimonial events had to be treated as campaign contributions subject to the reporting requirements and spending limits of the Corrupt Practices Act of 1925.

• Required a member's staff employees to perform the work for which they were paid.

The House also adopted a rule (Rule LXIV) requiring members and officers of the House, their principal assistants, and professional staff members of committees to file annually with the ethics committee a report disclosing certain financial interests—which were to be made available to the public—and a sealed report on the amount of income received from those interests. As under the Senate rules, the sealed report could be opened by the committee only if it determined that such information was essential to an investigation, while the data that could be made public were extremely limited.

Institutional Changes: 1969–1981

The winds of reform that had begun to blow through the House in the 1960s reached hurricane force in the 1970s, as traumatic divisions in society as a whole and a new generation of members forced fundamental shifts in the way the chamber operated. Power, which had been concentrated among a handful of senior members, was far more widely dispersed, both to the growing array of committees, subcommittees, and their staffs, and to individual members determined to pursue their own issues and the interests of their districts.

The reforms of the period brought many positive changes to the House. No longer forced into the lock-step of "to get along, go along," even junior members became more able to influence policy. Decisions that had once been made behind closed doors were brought out into the "sunshine" of public scrutiny. Ethical standards and oversight were stiffened, and members were made more accountable to the public for the ways in which they raised campaign funds.

At the same time, however, the reforms had costs. Having lost their command of solid blocs of votes, House leaders were forced to negotiate for members' support for important legislation on an individual basis, often at considerable cost in time, money, and overall policy and political unity. The growth of the committee system greatly increased the cost of the House and, critics said, gave too much power to unelected staff members. Opening up the legislative process to the public seemed at times to make members more subject to the will of special interest lobbyists than to the voters as a whole.

By the end of the decade, the Democratic leadership's position of authority over the House had so eroded that many basic majority party functions had become heavy burdens rather than exercises of power.

WAR, INFLATION, AND SCANDAL

Major changes in the House probably were inevitable given the tremendous social and political pressures on government during this period. Three issues in particular—the Vietnam War, a troubled economy, and the Watergate scandal—formed much of the context within which the House reforms came about.

Congress's legislative and institutional problems, and the resulting calls for major reforms in congressional operations, were not new to the 1970s. However, the urgency of the demands for change cast them in a different light. The war in Indochina and the rising costs of operating the federal government were critical matters that compelled Congress to examine the way legislative business was conducted and power was distributed within its chambers. That examination, which was initiated in the 1960s by junior members, aided by some senior colleagues, led to major congressional changes in the decade of the 1970s.

In the case of the Vietnam War, many members of Congress had concluded by the early 1970s that they were institutionally unable to influence the policies of a president bent on engaging in an unpopular war. As a result, in 1973 they passed the War Powers act, which defined and limited the presidential authority to make war. In practice, however, the law did little to expand the House's traditionally secondary role in foreign and military policy.

The results of Congress's confrontation with President Richard Nixon over federal economic and fiscal policies proved to have a much more significant impact on the way the House was run. Nixon arrived in the White House committed to curbing spending for Great Society programs and facing a bout of inflation touched off by President Johnson's "guns and butter" policies. Nixon sought to challenge the congressional power of the purse by strengthening the Office of Management and Budget and impounding—refusing to spend—money appropriated by lawmakers.

In response to that challenge—and out of an acknowledgment that their fiscal mechanisms were disjointed and inadequate in the face of a massive and growing federal budget—members of Congress approved the Congressional Budget and Impoundment Control Act of 1974. By establishing Budget committees and an elaborate process for comprehensive consideration of spending and tax policies each year, the 1974 law was to have a profound impact on the distribution of power in the House.

Finally, the House was to play a key role in the agonizing scandal brought on by the June 17, 1972, burglary at the Democratic Party's national headquarters at the Watergate Hotel in Washington and the ensuing revelations of political misdeeds and a cover-up campaign by Nixon and his aides. The House's most electrifying moment on the national stage in years came during the spring and summer of 1974, as the Judiciary Committee investigated and debated the resulting impeachment charges against Nixon. The House was on the verge of approving the first impeachment charges brought against a president in more than a century when Nixon resigned on August 9, 1974.

In addition to dealing a serious blow to the strength and prestige of the presidency, the Watergate scandal led to heightened congressional attention to and influence over virtually every aspect of government activities. It greatly emboldened House reformers to take on the entrenched powers of the leadership and brought in a huge crop of young, liberal Democrats elected in 1974 who were eager to take on the established order.

CHANGING MEMBERSHIP

The crisis in Americans' confidence in their government, caused by Watergate and other events, and the growing pressure on Congress to change its way of doing business, came at a time of substantial turnover in the membership of the House. About one-half of the House membership at the beginning of the 1970s had been elected during the 1960s. By the start of the 94th Congress in 1975, 82 percent of the members had been elected since 1960 and almost two-thirds—61 percent—had entered Congress since 1967.

This meant that a substantial majority of the House in the first half of the decade was relatively new to the system and had less interest in maintaining the congressional status quo than the more senior members. A sizable number of the younger lawmakers—especially those elected in the late 1960s and early 1970s—had a personal interest in changing the way the House operated because they were excluded from exercising much influence by the rules and folkways that dominated the institution when they first became members. The principal custom that relegated junior members to the lowly status of backbenchers was the inflexible seniority system.

Underlying the junior members' discontent with the congressional power structure was that they were predominantly liberal in their political outlook, while the hierarchy of senior members who controlled the committee system was dominated by southern conservatives. The junior members' lack of power and influence, despite their greater numbers, made them look to structural changes as an alternative path to achieving positions of power and influence in Congress.

Thus, by 1970, the events, the people, and the internal conflicts were in place in the House to launch the most significant internal reforms in half a century.

NEW LEADERSHIP

House reformers hoped the retirement of seventy-nine-year-old Speaker McCormack would result in a new Democratic leadership team supportive of their cause. In Carl Albert, D-Okla., they found a helpful and cooperative friend, though hardly an outspoken champion of their interests. Albert, who had served as majority leader since 1962, was acceptable to most factions of the Democratic Party and was elected Speaker with only token, last-minute opposition.

Speaker Albert did little either to help the liberals or to impede their reform efforts. His passive manner soon drew criticism, especially after the 1974 elections in which House Democrats won a two-to-one majority through the election of seventy-five freshmen. That largely liberal class, disdaining the backbencher role expected of freshmen, was particularly vociferous in its outcry against the leadership's inability to muster the two-thirds majority needed to override President Ford's vetoes of numerous Democratic bills.

Albert retired from the House at the end of the 94th Congress in 1977. He was succeeded by O'Neill, who had served as majority leader since 1973. During his long career in the Massachusetts legislature and in the House, O'Neill had always been more interested in pure politics than in the content of legislation. His specialty had been to count votes, twist arms, and broker deals rather than to write bills or work out the fine points of legislative compromises. And his Boston origins instilled in him the importance of constituent service and party loyalty.

O'Neill reflected these same skills and biases as Speaker. He fought hard for the legislative programs advanced by the Carter administration, though he showed little enthusiasm for their specific content. While generally supportive of liberal Democrats' demands, he also emphasized that he was Speaker of all House Democrats.

In the final year of the Carter presidency and early in the Reagan administration, O'Neill was criticized by the younger and generally more liberal Democrats for failing to crack down on conservative members who voted against positions supported by a majority of the party. But O'Neill maintained that the party's diversity left him powerless to discipline or even threaten to discipline disloyal members.

Elected majority leader at the time O'Neill became Speaker was Jim Wright of Texas, who beat out three opponents by the margin of a single vote. Wright's Republican counterpart was John J. Rhodes of Arizona, who had taken over the minority leadership in December 1973, after Ford became Nixon's vice president. Rhodes, whose colorless style and passive approach to leadership frequently angered younger and more militant members of his party, gave up his post at the end of the 96th Congress. He was replaced by Robert H. Michel, R-Ill., a low-key but tireless leader who was to play a vital role in pushing President Reagan's economic program through the House in 1981.

DEMOCRATIC CAUCUS

Although the demands for changes in the House came from Republicans as well as Democrats, the key focus for reform was the House Democratic Caucus, the formal organization of all House Democrats. Changes in caucus rules often had the same impact on the House as changes in House rules because the Democrats' majority status in the House gave them procedural control of the chamber.

Once a powerful instrument in implementing Woodrow Wilson's domestic program, the caucus had fallen into disuse, meeting only at the beginning of a new Congress for the pro forma election of the Democratic leadership.

The move to revitalize the caucus was led by the House Democratic Study Group (DSG), an organization of moderate and liberal Democrats that comprised the largest reform bloc in the House. Eager to attack the power structure in the House, DSG members saw the caucus as a particularly advantageous arena in which to attack the seniority system and what they saw as antiquated House procedures.

The reform effort within the caucus was to direct most of its energy to altering the institutional structure that determined how Congress conducted its business. Occasionally, liberal members would try to use the body to affect legislative policy, as when the caucus in 1975 passed a resolution calling for an end to U.S. military aid to Indochina. But the controversy stirred up by those efforts—as well as an effort by conservatives to use the caucus to advance antibusing legislation—ultimately caused the leadership to back away from using the organization as a major force determining party policy on substantive issues.

TARGETS FOR CHANGE

The changes made in House operations were tied together by some common threads. Reformers attempted to link advancement in the House hierarchy to a member's party loyalty and job skills instead of to seniority alone. They tried to open to the public and the press the inner workings of Congress. And they sought to increase members' accountability for their official actions to their colleagues as well as to their constituents.

The rigid seniority system in Congress had guaranteed a member's rise to a position of authority, particularly as committee chairman, if he or she remained in Congress long enough and belonged to the majority party. Once having attained power, committee chairmen could carry out their official duties behind closed doors and without much regard for the wishes of the party leadership, their colleagues, or the voters outside their own districts.

The first major wave of reforms of the decade was brought about by enactment in 1970 of the first major congressional reorganization measure since 1946. The Legislative Reorganization Act of 1970 was designed to give both House and Senate more information on government finances, guarantee certain rights for minority party members, and maintain a continuing review

Massachusetts Democrat Thomas P. "Tip" O'Neill Jr. was a representative for twenty-four years before becoming Speaker of the House. O'Neill held the speakership from 1979 to 1987.

of the legislative machinery through a Joint Committee on Congressional Operations. That panel went out of business before the end of the decade, however.

The act required committees for the first time to have written rules, to make public all roll-call votes taken in closed committee sessions, and to make committee reports on bills available to the public and members at least three days before the bill was brought to the floor.

One of the act's most significant provisions was a change in the voting rule in the House that for the first time forced members to disclose their positions on all major legislative issues. Previously, nonrecorded "teller votes" enabled members to cast their votes on amendments without being recorded. The 1970 act authorized use of recorded teller votes upon the request of a sufficient number of members. These votes were similar to roll calls in that the individual members' positions would be record-

ed and published in the *Congressional Record.* This change put the House on a par with the Senate, where important floor votes almost always were taken by roll call.

In January 1973 another voting change replaced the recorded teller vote. The House installed an electronic tallying system, making it faster and easier to take recorded votes and quorum calls. Members were given fifteen minutes in which to cast their vote. As members voted, large lighted panels installed on the chamber's wall provided a running breakdown of the votes as they were cast and indicated how each individual member had voted.

ATTACKING THE COMMITTEE CITADEL

Although institutional changes were taking place at a rapid pace, committee chairmen continued to hold an iron grip on their panels. But the Democratic Caucus in 1974 approved a sweeping attack on the seniority system by requiring that each Democratic committee chairmanship be filled by secret ballot at the beginning of each new Congress.

Vote on Chairman

The new rule had little impact until the 94th Congress convened in January 1975, when the caucus included a large class of newly elected freshmen who owed no favors to the chamber's senior establishment. By the time the caucus had finished its work, three chairmen had been deposed: Wright Patman, D-Texas, of the Banking, Currency, and Housing Committee; F. Edward Hébert, D-La., of the Armed Services Committee; and W. R. Poage, D-Texas, of the Agriculture Committee.

Various reasons were given for the three men's ouster, but there was little doubt the trio had made a poor impression on the freshmen Democrats who interviewed all three before deciding whom to support in the caucus. Each of the three had been accused of dominating the operation of their committees and denying equitable treatment to their fellow committee members. Because of the freshmen's strong liberal bent, ideology also was thought to have played a role, though not a major one.

The removal of the three chairmen jarred the system that for decades had governed representatives' progression to power. The last time a chairman had been removed had been in 1967 when Adam Clayton Powell was relieved as head of the Education and Labor Committee following allegations of misconduct. Before that, the House had not ousted a chairman since 1925.

Other reform efforts adopted by the House or its Democratic Caucus at about the same time further eroded the authority of the House committee chairmen.

One of the principal targets of these efforts was Wilbur D. Mills, D-Ark., chairman of the powerful Ways and Means Committee. Mills for years had run his committee with an iron hand and had been successful in bringing his legislation to the floor under a closed rule, barring floor amendments. A skilled parliamentarian and an authoritarian chairman, Mills had argued successfully that tax legislation was so complex that amendments by individual members, offered from the floor without prior committee consideration, would twist the bills out of shape.

To curb Mills's power, the caucus adopted a new rule providing that if a minimum of fifty Democrats proposed an amendment to the caucus and a caucus majority approved the amendment, Democrats on the Rules Committee would be required to write a rule allowing the amendment to be offered on the floor.

A further assault on Mills's power occurred following disclosure in late 1974 of a series of bizarre incidents involving Mills's personal life. Sensing Mills's vulnerability after these incidents came to light, the caucus moved rapidly in the ensuing months to further diminish the power and authority of the Ways and Means chairmanship.

One of the most important changes made by the caucus involved Mills's dual role as Ways and Means chairman and chairman of the Democratic Committee on Committees. Since 1911 Ways and Means had served as the Democratic Party's body responsible for committee assignments of House Democrats. But in December 1974 the caucus transferred this authority to the party's Steering and Policy Committee, subject to confirmation by the caucus. The Steering and Policy Committee had been created by the caucus in 1973 to assist the Speaker in developing party and legislative priorities. The committee's membership was composed of House leaders, their appointees, and members elected by the caucus on a regional basis.

Subcommittees

Another caucus line of attack on the power of the full committee chairmen concentrated on increasing the autonomy of the House's numerous subcommittees. In changes adopted gradually during the 1971–1975 period, the caucus voted to limit the number of subcommittee chairmanships that a single member could hold, and to give these subcommittee chairmen their own staffs and budgets as well as significant freedom from the chairmen of the full committees.

In the House Appropriations Committee, caucus reformers faced a different sort of problem. There, senior conservative Democrats had dominated the important subcommittees handling the funding for defense, agriculture, and health, education, and welfare, leaving the less influential subcommittee slots to the junior members. In the Appropriations Committee, unlike the legislative committees, the subcommittees traditionally wielded great power. In a move designed to make the subcommittee chairmen more accountable, the caucus required that, starting in 1975, each of the Appropriations Committee's thirteen subcommittee chairmen had to be approved by the caucus at the beginning of each new Congress.

OTHER REFORM TARGETS

Reformers also sought during the 1970s to effect changes in other important aspects of House operations, including opening up the process to public view, restructuring committee jurisdictions, and curbing campaign finance abuses. Their efforts in those areas, however, met with mixed success in the eyes of most observers.

'Sunshine' Rules

Perhaps the most obvious changes were those brought about by new "sunshine" rules. The House by the mid-1970s had required all committees and subcommittees to open most of their bill-drafting, or markup, sessions and other business meetings to the public, unless a majority voted at an open session to close a particular hearing. House-Senate conference committee meetings, called to resolve differences in the two chambers' versions of a bill, also were opened up. Previously, hearings had been open, but conference meetings and the markup sessions where bills were considered and amended usually were closed.

Broadcast Coverage

Although the Senate had a long tradition of permitting television and radio coverage of its committee hearings, the House did not amend its rules to permit broadcast coverage of hearings until 1970. Even then, the House rules imposed severe restrictions on broadcasters, including a prohibition on coverage of markup sessions. But the public interest in the Judiciary Committee's 1974 televised broadcasts of impeachment proceedings against President Nixon went far toward making other House committees and the membership more receptive to the presence of TV cameras in their midst. To allow television into the Judiciary Committee sessions on impeachment, the House had to amend its rules once more because the proceedings were in fact markup sessions, during which discussion and votes on the articles of impeachment took place.

Gavel-to-gavel broadcast coverage of congressional floor proceedings had been proposed as early as 1944. It was not until 1977, however, that the House took its first steps toward broadcast coverage of its proceedings with a ninety-day experiment of closed-circuit black-and-white telecasts. In March 1979, a permanent, high-quality color broadcast system, operated by House employees, began providing full coverage. Tennessee representative Albert Gore Jr., who had led the campaign for televising floor action, delivered the chamber's first televised speech.

Broadcast of House proceedings by the Cable Satellite Public Affairs Network (C-SPAN) during the next decade was to make the House a living presence for millions of viewers. But critics were to charge that the presence of cameras led to lengthier speeches and encouraged members to offer amendments merely to appeal to their constituents back home. Moreover, the issue of control of the cameras was to become a subject of bitter partisan rancor in the 1980s.

Exposure to televised House debates not only made millions of viewers into fans of the chamber, but also convinced at least one future member to seek the job. Richard Armey, an economics professor at North Texas State University with no previous political experience, attributed his decision to challenge Rep. Tom Vandergriff, D-Texas, to his exposure to C-SPAN. "C-SPAN changed my life," he later recalled. "I watched everything I could. And I began to feel a more intimate relationship to the process. I began to understand that these folks weren't bigger than life, and that, in fact, most of them weren't bigger than me. I finally just said, the job's not being done right. I need to go do it myself. I wouldn't have known that if I hadn't been watching."[18] Armey would go on to become House majority leader in 1995.

Committee Reorganization

Attempts to reorganize the committee system met with far less success. Two major reorganization efforts bore little fruit. Committee jurisdictions in the 1970s were a jumble of contradictions, legislative conflicts, and outmoded and overlapping divisions. They were still based on the 1946 Legislative Reorganization Act—a plan drawn up when many of the problems experienced during the 1970s, such as energy use and environmental protection, were unknown. Yet attempts to modernize the committee structure seemed doomed to failure.

The most comprehensive reorganization effort occurred in 1974 when a special committee headed by Richard Bolling, D-Mo., suggested sweeping changes in the committee structure. But the plan failed largely because of its ambitious scope and sweeping nature. By proposing a wholesale realignment of committee jurisdictions and a limitation of one major committee per member, the select committee alienated younger members with ambitions that went beyond issues dealt with by just one committee, as well as chairmen and senior members whose power bases would have been diminished or eliminated.

In place of the comprehensive reorganization package drafted by the Bolling committee, the House adopted a far less drastic scheme that left committee jurisdictions largely unchanged. Some of the Bolling proposals were adopted, but generally they were toned down in redrafting carried out by the Democratic Committee on Organization, Study, and Review.

The second major reorganization attempt ended in total failure in early 1980 when the House Select Committee on Committees closed its doors with almost nothing to show for its year-long effort. The work of the panel, which had proposed creation of a single committee with jurisdiction over energy issues, had one major result: The House designated the Commerce Committee as the leading committee on energy matters and renamed it the Energy and Commerce Committee.

In an earlier change in the committee system, the Democratic Caucus in 1975 had voted to abolish the House Internal Security Committee, which before 1969 was known as the House Committee on Un-American Activities. The caucus decision ended thirty years of controversy during which the committee zealously pursued alleged subversives in every segment of American society.

Campaign Finance

Campaign finance laws passed by Congress in 1972, 1974, and 1976 brought about major changes in the way House members ran for office. Taken as a package, the three election measures approved during the period went a long way toward opening the election process to the press and public. But there were unintended consequences—notably, according to critics, an increasing dependence by members on funding from political action committees.

ETHICS ISSUES

After enactment of the new campaign laws, a series of congressional conflict-of-interest cases and other questionable activities in the mid-1970s prompted both the House and Senate to adopt new ethics codes.

The new House code of conduct, adopted in March 1977, was

drafted by a bipartisan fifteen-member Commission on Administrative Review, chaired by Democrat David R. Obey of Wisconsin. Though the commission's draft was toned down somewhat during House debate, it significantly toughened existing House rules governing financial disclosure and conflicts of interest. The new code required the disclosure of substantial data on the financial status of members and their top aides, imposed new restrictions on members' outside earned income, ended unofficial office accounts that many members had used to supplement their official allowances, and tightened the standards on use of Congress's free mailing privileges.

Perhaps the most controversial code provision limited House members' outside earnings to 15 percent per year of their official salaries. Because the code did not affect unearned income such as interest payments, dividends, and rent from properties, members with few holdings maintained that the code discriminated in favor of the rich. To partially remedy the disparity, the House in December 1981 doubled—to 30 percent of a member's salary—the amount allowed for outside earned income.

Despite the new code of conduct, the House's record on disciplinary matters in the 1970s was at best spotty. Only when pressed by the most serious circumstances did the House spend much time policing the ethical conduct of its members or staff.

From 1967 through 1975, the House Committee on Standards of Official Conduct, which had been created following the Powell scandal of the 1960s, made no formal investigations of any House member, although several representatives were convicted of crimes during the period. But in 1976 the ethics committee, as the panel was commonly called, was forced into action by several cases it could not ignore.

The most spectacular centered on a sex and payroll scandal that erupted after an employee of the House Administration Committee, Elizabeth Ray, asserted that she had been put on the payroll solely as the mistress of the committee's chairman, Wayne L. Hays, D-Ohio. Ray said she had done no work for the panel and possessed no office skills. Hays subsequently admitted a "relationship" with her but denied she was paid with public funds simply to be his mistress.

The resulting uproar forced Hays to resign as committee chairman and as head of the Democratic Congressional Campaign Committee, the group that raised and distributed campaign donations to the party's House candidates.

Hays had used his authority as chairman of the Administration Committee to enhance his own power and influence in the House. As a result, the scandal set in motion efforts to limit the power of the Administration Committee chairman as well as to revise many of the prerogatives benefiting members that had been handed out by the committee during Hays's chairmanship, such as additional stationery funds and mailing allowances and travel privileges.

Other ethics cases of note during the period included that of Robert L. Sikes, D-Fla., who was reprimanded by the House on conflict-of-interest charges in 1976 and ousted as chairman of the Appropriations Subcommittee on Military Construction the following year, and a lengthy investigation into alleged South Korean influence peddling, which resulted in 1978 in reprimands against three California Democrats.

An even more controversial scandal was that brought on by an undercover FBI corruption investigation known as "Abscam." The FBI probe employed agents who masqueraded as wealthy Arabs and businessmen to entice members of Congress and others into accepting bribes in return for promises of legislative help. Because the FBI appeared to rely heavily on government-created "crimes" in Abscam, the entire undercover operation was heavily criticized by civil libertarians and many members of Congress. But six House members were convicted as a result of the corruption probe, and by the end of 1981 all had left the House, either because of formal expulsion, resignation to avoid expulsion, or defeat for reelection.

Reagan and Bush Era: 1981–1992

The 1980 elections put Ronald Reagan in the White House and swept the Republicans to a majority in the Senate for the first time since the 83rd Congress (1953–1955). The House thus became the last bastion of Democratic power and the center of opposition to Reagan. Even after the Democrats regained control of the Senate in 1986, the presidency remained in Republican hands. In 1988 George Bush became the first sitting vice president since Martin Van Buren in 1836 to win the White House.

Not surprisingly, partisanship during this time was intense. While always present in the House, Democratic-Republican differences grew more frequent and more personally bitter. A generation of younger Republicans, unwilling to accept their party's seemingly permanent minority status, challenged their own leaders to take a more confrontational stance and used legislative tactics to frustrate, and at times enrage, the Democrats. Democratic leaders, as a result of the 1970s reforms, found they had few tools of discipline to hold their followers in line.

The three Speakers during this period were widely viewed as more able and vigorous than their immediate predecessors. Although his grasp on the details of policy debates was never comprehensive, O'Neill established himself as the first media celebrity to hold the speakership and a leading spokesman for his party's philosophy. Until his downfall, Jim Wright was a determined legislative strategist who was able to push through an extensive policy agenda in a short time. And while Wright's successor, Thomas S. Foley of Washington, was generally credited with restoring a measure of comity to a deeply divided chamber during his tenure, he would be swept out of office as a result of the 1994 elections, which also would bring GOP dominance to both the House and Senate.

REAGAN TRIUMPHANT

That the Democratic leadership and the party's liberal wing would soon return to a position of solid authority in the House seemed highly unlikely during the tumultuous days of 1981, when a Reagan-led coalition pushed a radical economic program through the House, shattering traditional procedures and the existing balance of power and leaving the nominal majority party in profound disarray.

The foundations of the Democratic leadership's humiliations that year were laid the previous November when, in addition to taking control of the Senate, the Republicans scored solid gains in the House. Their victories reduced the Democratic margin of control to 243–192 and brought in a corps of self-proclaimed "Reagan robots" eager to enact the president's economic program of tax and spending cuts and to provide funding for his massive defense buildup. Moreover, the elections led to the departure from the House of a number of senior Democrats, such as Ways and Means Committee Chairman Al Ullman, Ore., and left those who remained anxious that their party's decades-old dominance, and perhaps their own seats, were at risk.

The results of the elections also emboldened the Democratic Party's conservative wing. From the beginning of the 97th Congress in 1981, a group of some forty conservatives, mostly from the South and West, began pressing the leadership for more important assignments and a greater say in party councils. Organized formally into the Conservative Democratic Forum—but widely known as the "Boll Weevils"—the group was to provide the key margin for the Reagan economic proposals and a major point of evidence for the argument that a long-term realignment in the House was under way.

The most outspoken of the Boll Weevils was a former Texas A&M University professor named Phil Gramm, D-Texas, who had been sparring with the party leadership ever since he arrived in the House in 1979. Working with his former House ally, David A. Stockman, R-Mich., who had left the House to become Reagan's director of management and budget, Gramm was to play a key role in pushing Reagan's legislative program through Congress. By the end of 1981 the program was to provide for $35 billion in program reductions and $4 billion in appropriations cuts, while adding $18 billion to defense and cutting taxes a total of $749 billion over five years. Forty-eight Democrats defied their leaders to vote for Reagan's "supply-side" tax cut.

By the end of 1981, Reagan's conservative coalition in the House began to unravel, as enthusiasm for further cuts in social spending waned. And Democratic leaders were able to claim vindication for their opposition to the president's economic plan the following year, as the nation plunged into its deepest recession since World War II.

ELECTION CHANGES

The Democrats' views also found support among the voters, whose rejection of many of the Reagan supporters elected in 1980 contributed to a twenty-six-seat Republican loss in the November 1982 elections—the worst setback for a party at the two-year point in a presidential term since 1922.

The 1982 elections also offered conclusive evidence against the theory that demographic changes during the 1970s would enable Republicans to take control of the House. The movement of population away from the industrial Northeast and Midwest would cost votes in the Democratic heartland, the theory went, while adding seats in fast-growing, Republican-leaning areas in the South and West. The 1980 census resulted in the shift of seventeen seats to the Sun Belt.

One reason that reapportionment and redistricting did not produce a major advance for the GOP was that the Democrats still controlled the legislatures in most states. As a result, they were able to draw the new district lines to their favor—so favorably that critics accused them of engaging in partisan "gerrymanders." The results of the 1982 elections showed that Democrats had won ten of the seventeen new Sun Belt seats, while minimizing their losses in the North. The linchpin of Democratic success was California, where Rep. Phillip Burton designed a district map that gained his party five seats, even though the state as a whole had picked up only two, while strengthening the Democrats' hold on other districts.

PARTISAN WARFARE

The stronger hand dealt the Democratic leadership as a result of the 1982 elections led to a standoff with Reagan. For the next four years, House leaders were able to prevent Reagan from making further major spending cuts, while gaining only limited ability to push their own legislation.

Partisan warfare deepened, leading to turmoil and bitter confrontation between Democrats and Republicans. Throughout the mid-1980s, GOP "Young Turks" used long-dormant House rules to harass Democratic leaders and disrupt floor proceedings. They took advantage of the coverage of House proceedings on C-SPAN to reach out to a mass audience through "special order" speeches, which frequently focused on O'Neill as a symbol of Democratic corruption and bloated government. The Democrats responded in kind, attempting to use their numerical advantage to retaliate through rules changes and other tactics.

The feelings of many Republicans were perhaps best summarized by Minority Leader Michel, who himself was sometimes accused by more militant members of his party of being too accommodating to the Democrats. "The most important thing we have done is rid ourselves of that subservient, timid mentality of the permanent minority. The Republican Party in the House is no longer content to go along. We want to go for broke," he said.

The first sign of the new partisan antagonism came at the opening of the 97th Congress in 1981. Despite their losses in the previous elections, Democrats refused to alter the partisan ratios on key committees and offered rules changes aimed at strengthening the power of the Speaker. Republicans objected strongly, but their efforts to resist were turned back on a party-line vote.

In 1983 Democrats offered a controversial set of rules changes for the new Congress that, they said, merely represented a modest streamlining of operations. The changes made it harder for members to offer "limitation riders" on appropriations bills and sought to prevent "nuisance" votes on procedure. Republicans denounced the proposals as a trampling of minority rights but could not block them. However, a bipartisan majority earlier forced withdrawal of a proposal to make it harder to use a discharge petition to push proposed constitutional amendments out of the Judiciary Committee—a tactic that conservatives frequently sought to use to force floor votes on such controversial social issues as busing.

Democrats also counterattacked against Gramm, against whom many harbored deep resentments not only for leading the charge for the Reagan economic program but also, they charged, for giving away party secrets to the administration. Early in 1983, Democrats voted to strip Gramm of his Budget Committee membership. Unwilling to submit, Gramm resigned his House seat and campaigned in a special election to regain it, this time as a Republican. He won easily. In an effort to prevent further defections, however, Democratic leaders agreed to put more southern conservatives on the party's Steering and Policy Committee.

The partisan acrimony was strikingly evident in 1984, as junior Republicans used their special-order speeches to goad Democratic leaders into a fury. In one such speech, Newt Gingrich, R-Ga., attacked the foreign policy views of some Democrats so stridently that some accused him of McCarthyism. Enraged, O'Neill retaliated by ordering television cameras covering such speeches to pan the House chamber, showing the home audience that virtually no one was listening in person. In a floor speech O'Neill said that Gingrich was challenging the "Americanism of Democrats," adding, "It's the lowest thing I have ever seen in my thirty-two years of Congress." Even in the new atmosphere, that went too far beyond the bounds of whatever comity still remained in the chamber. The House officially chastised O'Neill for his remarks—the first time a Speaker had been so reprimanded since 1797.

In his autobiography, O'Neill recalled the incident—which was touched off when he ordered the House cameras to show Robert S. Walker, R-Pa., addressing an empty chamber—with a mixture of pride and regret:

Walker looked like a fool. The Republicans went wild when we did this, especially since I didn't consult them. They were right about that, I should have issued a warning before going ahead. But I wasn't going to tolerate members making charges in front of an empty hall when there was nobody around to refute what they were saying. I couldn't stop them from speaking, but I could certainly prevent the cameras from helping them stage their cynical charade.

Of his remarks that were later removed from the record, O'Neill said, "I had done my best to control my temper, but much harsher thoughts were on my mind."[19]

Relations got even worse, if that was possible, in the early months of 1985, when Republicans returned with a fifteen-seat pickup in Reagan's landslide reelection year. One of those new Republicans, however, Richard D. McIntyre of Indiana, was soon to lose his office. McIntyre arrived at the House bearing a certification from the Indiana secretary of state that he had defeated the Democratic incumbent, Frank McCloskey, by a few hundred votes.

But House Democrats refused to accept that result and ordered a recount overseen by a bipartisan House panel. The recount continued for several months, while Republicans seethed at McIntyre's ouster, and finally produced the result that McCloskey had won by four votes. Republican anger exploded at an outcome that their representative on the recount panel described as "nothing short of rape." GOP members staged a momentary walkout when McCloskey was sworn in but could do nothing to reverse the situation.

Bitterness over that issue gradually subsided. Meanwhile, both parties were struggling with their own internal divisions in the 99th Congress (1985–1987). In their first move against a committee chairman since 1975, Democrats voted to oust Melvin Price of Illinois as chairman of the Armed Services Committee, less out of differences over policy than from the belief that the octogenarian member was no longer up to the job. In an even more dramatic break with seniority, Democrats voted to skip over the next in line for the chairmanship, Charles E. Bennett of Florida, and select seventh-ranking Les Aspin of Wisconsin.

Also that year, Republicans revealed a deep split over tax policy and handed Reagan a stinging initial defeat. Angered that they had been left out of development of Reagan's tax-reform plan, all but fourteen Republicans voted against the rule providing for floor consideration of their president's chief legislative initiative for the year. Reagan made a rare trip to Capitol Hill to lobby for the proposal, however, and succeeded in turning around enough Republicans to enable the rule and the bill to pass.

WRIGHT'S RISE AND FALL

To a great extent the history of the House in the 100th Congress (1987–1989) and the first months of the 101st was dominated by one man, Jim Wright. During his two-and-a-half years as Speaker, he established himself as potentially one of the most powerful leaders ever to hold that office, and a prime mover in what was widely considered to be one of the most legislatively productive Congresses in years. At the same time he was found by a panel of his peers to have flouted ethical standards and became the first Speaker ever to resign his office in the middle of a term.

Wright came to power in 1987 with a specific legislative agenda and the know-how to push it through. Working with Sen. Robert C. Byrd of West Virginia, the leader of the newly restored Democratic majority in the Senate, he opened the year with an ambitious design to showcase Democratic priorities at a time when Reagan's power was seen as waning. Wright pushed confrontation on such issues as arms control, civil rights, and pork-barrel spending, flexing his new found power and putting the Republicans on the defensive.

On the controversial and divisive Nicaraguan contra issue, Wright moved to establish himself as the dominant player on Capitol Hill. In August 1987 the Reagan administration unveiled

Rep. Jim Wright gives an impassioned defense of his ethics before resigning as Speaker and leaving the house in 1989. Wright was the first Speaker in history to be forced from office at midterm. Majority Leader Thomas S. Foley, at left, succeeded him in the post.

a peace plan, drafted in large part by Wright, that helped spark an agreement two days later by Central American presidents. But Wright's subsequent intervention in the Nicaraguan peace talks stirred controversy, with the administration and some members of Congress accusing him of infringing on the president's diplomatic prerogatives.

But Wright's hardball pursuit of victory also involved liabilities that were to lead to his downfall. His efforts to put a strongly partisan imprint on policy and use the rules to his advantage infuriated Republicans and spurred Gingrich to begin an investigation of his ethics. Moreover, Wright's tendency to exclude other Democratic leaders from many of his decisions undermined his support in his own party.

A key turning point in the growing uneasiness over Wright's leadership methods came in 1987, when he scored a costly victory on a budget reconciliation bill cutting $14.5 billion from the deficit. Wright managed to push through the Democratic plan on a 206–205 vote, after delaying announcement of the vote's outcome—which would have gone against Wright—long enough to persuade a fellow Texas Democrat, Jim Chapman, to switch his vote in favor. Wright's biographer described the

mood of the House the following day this way: "Wright had stripped power bare and exposed truths, uncomfortable truths. . . . Members shied away from that nakedness. The truth was that the leadership would strong-arm people, and that some members were cowards."[20]

Gingrich and his allies continued to press for an investigation into alleged ethical violations by Wright. After the self-styled citizens' lobby Common Cause called for an investigation, there was no way to prevent a formal inquiry by the ethics committee. While the committee was to look into a number of alleged abuses by the Speaker, two main areas stood out. One charge involved the financial arrangements surrounding sales of Wright's book, *Reflections of a Public Man*, which was sold primarily at political rallies and in bulk purchases to lobbyists. Critics said the $55,000 Wright earned in royalties from the book amounted to a scheme to avoid limits on outside earned income. The other area of allegations concerned gifts, money, and other benefits Wright had received from Texas developer George Mallick.

The ethics panel's investigation stretched over ten months, spanning the end of the 100th and the beginning of the 101st

Congress. In the meantime Wright blundered in handling a pay raise for members of Congress that many said fatally weakened his base of support in the House. To add to Wright's problems at the outset of the new Congress, House Republicans chose Gingrich to be minority whip, replacing Dick Cheney of Wyoming, who had resigned to become President George Bush's secretary of defense.

On April 17, 1989, the ethics panel released a devastating report on Wright's activities. The committee cited sixty-nine instances in five broad categories where there was "reason to believe" Wright had violated House rules over the past ten years. The report agreed that Wright's book sales were an effort to evade earned-income limits, and it found that he and his wife had received benefits worth $145,000 from Mallick over a decade.

Wright resigned his office on June 6. Before leaving the House he gave a final speech in which he portrayed himself as a victim of a partisan vendetta and denounced the "mindless cannibalism" of attacks on politicians' personal ethics. To add to the turmoil, the Democratic whip, Tony Coelho of California, on May 26 announced his intention to resign from the House to head off an investigation into his personal finances in connection with his involvement with a "junk bond" deal.

SEARCH FOR STABILITY

Democrats moved quickly to restore order by picking as Wright's successor Majority Leader Foley, who was known for his steady leadership and ability to build bridges to members on both sides of the aisle. To replace Foley as floor leader, they chose Richard A. Gephardt of Missouri, who had sought unsuccessfully the Democratic presidential nomination in 1988. Chosen as whip was William H. Gray III of Pennsylvania, who became the highest-ranking black leader in House history. (Gray's tenure as whip was brief—he resigned his House seat in 1991. His successor as whip was David E. Bonior of Michigan.)

Foley made reestablishing a sense of bipartisan order and civility a major goal of his speakership. But he faced a continuing atmosphere of frustration and anger on both sides, as was illustrated on the day he took office by a blistering speech by Minority Leader Michel. "Thirty-five years of uninterrupted power can act like a corrosive acid upon the restraints of stability and comity," said Michel. "Those who have been kings of the Hill for so long may forget that majority status is not a divine right." By year's end, however, Foley could assert that he had achieved a "mood of comity and confidence" in the chamber.

1990 BUDGET DEBACLE

In 1990 the Democratic leadership joined with the Bush administration in an embarrassing debacle that raised questions about whether the leaders, or any force, could control the House and resolve the profound issues facing the nation. In the spring of that year, Democratic leaders agreed to work with administration officials in a "budget summit" aimed at producing a long-range attack on the huge federal deficit. Even after Bush

agreed to drop his 1988 campaign pledge of "no new taxes," it took many months of negotiations before all sides could come to accord on a plan to reduce the deficit by roughly $500 billion over five years.

But, in a devastating defeat for both the House leadership and Bush, House members rejected the budget accord by a wide margin when it came to the floor. The setback was especially irritating to administration officials because Gingrich, the second-ranking Republican leader, had been outspoken in opposing his president's plan. The collapse of the plan spurred an outburst of public rage and scorn at Congress and led some political analysts to predict that a tidal wave of voter unrest would bring down many incumbents in the November elections.

In the negotiations that followed the defeat of the initial plan, however, House Democrats were able to seize the initiative by stressing the need to raise taxes on upper-income taxpayers, while painting their Republican opponents as defenders of the rich. The result was that Congress, shortly before adjourning, finally approved a package that raised taxes more on the rich while reducing the amount of spending reductions in the Medicare program called for in the initial budget accord.

VOTER DISSATISFACTION

In the 1990 elections, Democrats scored an eight-seat gain in the House, solidifying their hold on the chamber. However, the returns provided compelling evidence of voter dissatisfaction with incumbent members of both parties. While only fifteen House members were defeated for reelection, fifty-three others scored their lowest winning percentage ever, and fifty-seven won with their lowest vote share since they were first elected. Combined, they constituted about one-fourth of the House membership in the 102nd Congress.

Voter dissatisfaction was further reflected in a spate of proposals to limit the number of years a senator or representative might serve in Congress. While the constitutionality of term limitation proposals was widely questioned, the warning to members seemed clear.

While the somber yet passionate January debate over whether to authorize the use of force against Iraq was Congress's finest hour in 1991, considerable competition existed for its lowest point. The leading contender in the House was the General Accounting Office disclosure that 325 sitting and former members for years had routinely overdrawn their accounts at the House members-only bank without penalty. The check-kiting scandal infuriated voters, who saw it as further proof that members of Congress refused to play by the rules that governed everybody else. Of the 269 sitting members with overdrafts, 77—more than one in four—retired or were defeated in 1992 primary or general election bids for the House or other offices. That was a far higher casualty rate than other members suffered. Only 28 of 166 members (about one in six) with clean bank records had their political careers cut short.

Another blow to the public's opinion of Congress came as a result of a federal investigation into charges of embezzlement and drug dealing among postal clerks at the House Post Office, which mushroomed in 1992 into a full-scale scandal that included allegations that members used the facility to convert campaign checks or House expense vouchers to cash through sham transactions made to look like stamp purchases. Implicated in the scandal were House Ways and Means Chairman Dan Rostenkowski, D-Ill., and Rep. Joe Kolter, D-Pa. By 1996, Rostenkowski, who lost his reelection bid in 1994, pleaded guilty to two counts of felony mail fraud stemming from his misuse of public funds to purchase gifts and to pay employees who did little or no official work and began serving a seventeen-month prison term. In addition to prison time, Rostenkowski was fined $100,000. Also in 1996, Kolter, who failed in his reelection attempt in 1992, pleaded guilty to one count of conspiring to steal thousands of dollars of taxpayers' money by converting government-purchased stamps at the House Post Office. He was sentenced to six months in prison, fined $20,000, and ordered to pay $9,300 in restitution.

The initial reporting of the scandals put House Speaker Foley on the defensive and led to speculation about whether he could hang on to his job after the 1992 election. Democratic critics were especially furious about Foley's handling of the bank affair, arguing that he should have moved more decisively after learning of the problem back in 1989. That complaint dovetailed with a broader critique of Foley—that he was not aggressive enough in advancing Democrats' legislative interests.

Foley struggled to quell the institutional crisis first by pushing in-house reforms: curbing perquisites, overhauling the way the House was administered, and endorsing a panel to propose reforms in legislative procedures. He leaned on committee chairmen to get major legislation to the floor, reasoning that the best way for the House to put the scandals behind it was to see to its legislative business. And Foley tried to reinforce his personal bond with fellow Democrats by inviting small groups of members to private dinners to discuss the House and its leadership. He also talked to almost every 1992 Democratic nominee for the House and contributed money to many of their campaigns.

By the end of the session, with Democratic presidential nominee Bill Clinton riding high in the polls and Democrats eager for unity, all talk of a challenge to Foley vanished. No one ran against him when Democrats met to organize for the 103rd Congress.

Clinton and the Republicans: 1993–1999

Voter discontent and redistricting took a toll on House members who sought reelection in 1992, but the much-discussed possibility of an election day cyclone of anti-incumbent sentiment failed to materialize: only twenty-four incumbents were defeated. Republicans, who began the campaign cycle with high hopes for substantially eroding the Democratic majority in the House, had to settle for a very modest nine-seat gain. A faltering economy and Bush's evaporating popularity proved to be

a drag to the GOP at the polls. Presidential victor Bill Clinton presented himself as an agent for change throughout the campaign.

The fanfare and calls for change that heralded the opening of the 103rd Congress turned sour by the end of 1994, however. Despite enormous amounts of time and effort, none of the changes that congressional Democrats and President Bill Clinton wanted to make in the way Congress operates had become law. Democrats were held accountable for that failure. The 1994 elections brought an end to forty years of one-party rule in the House. Republicans gained fifty-two seats, increasing their number in the House from 178 to 230. No Republican incumbent was defeated. The GOP takeover was attributed to a Democratic president held in disfavor, a Democratic-controlled Congress held in disrepute, a redistricting that strongly favored Republicans, and an infusion of money for some Republican challengers.

As a result of the election, Foley not only lost the speakership but also became the first sitting House Speaker to lose reelection since 1862. Newt Gingrich became the first Republican Speaker of the House from the South. Gingrich's ascendancy accompanied the long-anticipated realignment of the South. For the first time since the end of Reconstruction in the 1870s, Republicans won a majority of the congressional districts in the South. The Democrats' 83–54 majority vanished with a GOP pickup of nineteen seats, giving Republicans a 73–64 majority in the region.

GOP IN CHARGE

Republicans took charge believing that their mandate was to reduce the size, power, and involvement of the federal government.

On the opening day of the 104th Congress, the House adopted numerous rules changes drafted by the Republicans that gave the House majority leadership more power, made it easier to cut spending but harder to raise taxes, and increased public scrutiny of House actions. The most significant provisions ended funding for three House committees and twenty-eight legislative caucuses; cut the committee staff by one-third; limited members to three consecutive terms as committee or subcommittee chairs or four consecutive terms as Speaker; barred committees from meeting in private, with limited exceptions; required committees to allow radio and television coverage; required committee members to be present to establish a quorum or to vote; eliminated a procedural barrier to amendments that proposed to bar spending on a specific program—a technique used to block the administration from carrying out a disputed policy; required a three-fifths majority to pass any legislation containing an income tax increase; and prohibited the delegates and resident commissioner from voting in or presiding over the Committee of the Whole, which the House entered into when it amended a bill on the floor.

The House agenda for the first one hundred days of the 104th Congress was set in the Republicans' Contract with America, which had been signed September 27, 1994, by more than 350 GOP incumbents and challengers. By April 7, 1995, the House passed eight of the ten contract planks and the bulk of a ninth. The House failed to pass one plank that called for adopting a constitutional amendment to limit members' terms. Among the initiatives the House passed were a balanced budget constitutional amendment and a line-item veto, changes in the welfare and legal systems, tax cuts, and a curb on unfunded mandates.

The public generally seemed to support the efforts to enact the contract, but reservations emerged about the details of proposed policy changes and the speed with which House Republicans had moved the legislation. In some cases, committees took shortcuts to keep on schedule, cutting off debate when amendments were still pending, skipping hearings or subcommittee action, or moving a bill to the floor before the report was available. Also, because Gingrich insisted that the specifics were subject to revision, many members were willing to send through bills they conceded were flawed on the assumption that they would be fixed later.

In time, the momentum of the early days of the 104th Congress and the Republicans' good fortune began to slide. By the late summer of 1995, Democrats gained ground by defining the Republican agenda as one benefiting the rich. By the fall, Republicans also ran up against forces within their own party that were less enthusiastic about throwing out the old ways of Washington. Efforts to curb government payouts to cotton and rice farmers as part of an effort to dismantle costly farm-support programs, for example, ran into strong resistance from farm-state Republicans on the House Agriculture Committee.

A larger problem was posed by the revolutionary vanguard in the House. Gingrich had frequently used the intransigence of the highly conservative and assertive freshmen as leverage with the Senate and the White House. But when it came to enacting GOP bills, the freshmen's stubbornness became a liability. Many House Republicans were loath to soften their positions to accommodate their more moderate colleagues in the Senate, which they viewed as a bastion of status quo politics. Thus, bills that had sailed through the House suddenly bogged down in the Senate, where moderate Republicans held more sway and GOP leaders usually needed sixty votes—the supermajority to stop a filibuster—to pass anything. Often, it seemed the House preferred to do nothing rather than accept a watered-down version of what it sent the Senate. And by insisting for months on attaching policy riders to every measure that came along, House freshmen radically slowed the progress of the thirteen annual appropriations bills, opening Republicans to accusations from Democrats that they were failing at Congress's basic work.

The first year of the so-called Republican revolution closed with institutional Washington much the way the GOP majority found it: no federal departments were eliminated, and no long-standing social policies were reshaped. Only five of the twenty-one legislative priorities expressed in the Contract with America were enacted—and none of the full planks became law. The successful initiatives were relatively minor: applying workplace laws to members of Congress and their staff, limiting unfunded mandates on the states, reducing paperwork requirements, increasing penalties for sex crimes against children, and making it hard for investors to sue companies. Overall, Republicans were unable to turn quickly into reality their vision of a smaller government that lived within its means.

SPEAKER GINGRICH

With the historic Republican takeover of Congress, a lawmaker from Georgia known more for his aggressive tactics than his legislative acumen ascended unchallenged to become Speaker of the House. Gingrich, widely regarded as the mastermind of the GOP's 1994 upset victory, moved quickly to consolidate power and to elevate the role of Speaker as few before him had. However, he had always been a divisive figure, and he became a lightning rod for criticism.

Gingrich's ascendancy to the speakership was nothing short of phenomenal. Most Speakers had been patient institutionalists, lifted slowly to high office by the traditions of the House. Gingrich scrambled up the ladder with deliberateness and drive. He had never chaired a committee or even a subcommittee. The former college history professor instead perfected a boisterous, confrontational style of opposition politics that was a world apart from the low-key, deal-making politics practiced by more senior GOP leaders.

From the moment he entered Congress, Gingrich worked to reverse the GOP's permanent minority status in the House. He was one of the chief practitioners of a highly negative brand of politics aimed to wholly discredit the opposition. He led the attack on Speaker Wright, who resigned in 1989. Outside of Washington, Gingrich worked tirelessly to recruit and elect Republicans to Congress. In the late 1980s and early 1990s, he controlled a political action committee called GOPAC, which aimed to cultivate local and state politicians for eventual races for Congress. He took the lead in orchestrating the Contract with America, which was intended to give a national focus to House races and help invigorate Republican challengers in the 1994 election.

Maximizing both the formal and informal powers at his disposal, Gingrich used his position as Speaker to consolidate power like no one since Joseph Cannon in the early twentieth century. In part, he was capitalized on two previous decades of incremental change that had gradually centralized control in the Speaker's office.

Bolstered by wide support in the Republican Conference, a group of all House Republicans, Gingrich effectively named the new committee chairmen. Gingrich also imposed six-year term limits on committee chairmen and abolished the practice of proxy voting, which allowed chairmen to walk into legislative markups with fistfuls of votes. In a dramatic break with tradition, Gingrich appointed freshmen to subcommittee chairmanships and gave freshmen seats on the major committees, further cementing the already strong loyalty that the younger members felt for him. In addition, observed political scientist James A. Thurber in his 1995 book *Remaking Congress: Change and Stability in the 1990s,* Gingrich "appointed the chair of the Republican Congressional Campaign Committee, thus having a direct impact on the flow of campaign funds and political action committee dollars for future elections for Republican members of the House. This was another method of assuring loyalty and consolidation of power by controlling the 'mother's milk of politics,' campaign funds."

Gingrich's control of the House came at the expense of the committee chairmen, who no longer had the opportunity to build power bases in their committees. Gingrich stepped in and overruled chairmen whenever an issue was important to him or to the Republican Conference. In many cases, the committee chairmen subordinated their policy goals to the collective agenda as defined by Gingrich. Though Gingrich's involvement worked well for the Republicans as a whole, it raised questions about the ability of individual chairmen to exercise the policy expertise found only at the committee and subcommittee levels. It also made it difficult for chairmen to maintain discipline.

Gingrich also envisioned the speakership as a powerful pulpit from which he hoped to displace the president as the primary source of ideas and vision about where the country should be going. During his years in the minority, Gingrich developed his central philosophy, a conservative but futuristic creed that called for replacing the welfare state with an "opportunity society" in which the rising technological tide of the Information Age would help lift the poor to prosperity. In contrast to the antigovernment beliefs of some conservatives, Gingrich saw a role for government to solve social problems using conservative levers, such as changes in the tax code.

GINGRICH UNDER ATTACK

Gingrich may have been considered a savior to House Republicans, but Democrats had an entirely different view of the man. Many harbored deep resentment over Gingrich's treatment of Wright, and they saw his ethics as questionable. At the beginning of his speakership, Gingrich had signed a $4.5 million book deal. After receiving sharp criticism that a sitting Speaker should not receive so much money, Gingrich instead accepted only a $1 advance against royalties. House Democrats pressed their calls for an investigation of his ethics.

On December 6, 1995, the House Committee on Standards of Official Conduct announced that it had unanimously found Gingrich guilty of violating House rules in three instances but imposed no punishment. It dismissed two other complaints, including the one involving the book deal. The committee found that Gingrich violated rules governing the proper use of the House floor by touting his college course, by promoting a GOPAC seminar in floor speeches, and by allowing one of his political consultants to interview candidates for congressional staff jobs. The panel also named former prosecutor James M. Cole as an outside counsel to investigate the charges that Gingrich violated federal tax laws by raising funds for his college course through tax-exempt foundations.

The two partial government shutdowns during 1995–1996 added to Gingrich's declining national image. The staunchly conservative House Republicans led by Gingrich thought they could use the shutdowns to force Clinton to compromise on their balanced budget plan. But when it became clear that the Republicans were being blamed by the public for the lack of some government services, the Republicans reversed course and voted to fund the government, giving Clinton a major victory.

Gingrich was also prone to embarrassing public gaffes, as when he said women in the military could not fight in foxholes because they got "infections." But his most stunning public stumble came when he revealed that he had forced the first of two government shutdowns (in November 1995) in part because he felt that Clinton had snubbed him during an overseas diplomatic trip to attend the funeral of Israeli Prime Minister Yitzhak Rabin and later made Gingrich and Senate Majority Leader Bob Dole, R-Kan., exit by the rear of the plane.

Chastened by the government shutdown disaster, Gingrich also lowered himself in the eyes of some of his conservative allies by attempting to find grounds for a budget deal with the White House during the spring of 1996. The intense negotiations among Gingrich, Dole, and Clinton forced the Speaker into the unaccustomed role of dealbroker, which sometimes put him at odds with other House members. In addition, the ethics

Republican Speaker Newt Gingrich was credited with creating a new Republican era in Congress.

investigation opened in 1994 would come to fruition, resulting in the first reprimand of a sitting Speaker.

In a kind of plea bargaining arrangement with the House ethics committee, Gingrich on December 21, 1996, acknowledged that he had failed to properly manage the financing of his political activities through charitable foundations. He also conceded a more serious offense—that he had given the committee misleading information in the course of its investigation. In formal terms, Gingrich admitted that he had violated a House rule requiring that members act in a way that "shall reflect creditably on the House of Representatives."

The 105th Congress began with Gingrich in the midst of an all-out struggle to retain the speakership. A loosely aligned group of Republicans who had grown disillusioned with Gingrich's erratic style engaged in a silent revolt, refusing to publicly proclaim their support of him. Gingrich, Majority Leader Dick Armey, R-Texas, and the top Republican leader and their aides waged a remarkable lobbying effort, undertaking a one-on-one, members-only campaign to put down the rebellion. On January 7, 1997, joyless House Republicans reelected their Speaker, 216–205, by just three more votes than needed to attain a majority of those present and voting.

On the heels of the highly visible vote returning Gingrich to the top House job, the Republicans were put in the embarrassing position of having to vote on a punishment for him as a result of his admission of guilt regarding the ethics charges against him. On January 21, 1997, the House voted to reprimand Gingrich and to impose a $300,000 penalty. The tally was 395–28, with five members voting present.

A humbled Gingrich accepted the reprimand and then began a campaign in 1997 to reform his image. In April 1997, he stumbled again when he announced that he would pay the penalty with money borrowed under extremely favorable terms from former Senate majority leader Bob Dole. The arrangement kicked up a new round of criticism about Gingrich's judgment. Some Republicans thought he gave the appearance of accepting a special deal from Dole, who had gone to work for a major Washington lobbying and law firm.

As badly as 1997 started out for Gingrich, discontent with his leadership grew as the year progressed and began to infect the upper reaches of the GOP leadership. Ironically, even as reservations about Gingrich spread among the rank and file, he was able to lead Republicans to their crowning achievement, a deal with Clinton to balance the budget in five years.

The Speaker's tendency to be only intermittently involved in problems that arose and his penchant for unilateral decision making, however, began to grate. The breakdown of the leadership, which had mostly unfolded behind closed doors, exploded into public view with revelations in July 1997 that the leaders and GOP rebels had discussed ways of ousting Gingrich. The coup never got off the ground, but plotting behind the Speaker's back by the men he had brought to power was nonetheless shocking.

In the aftermath of the coup attempt, Gingrich began to stick closer to the House and involve himself in the day-to-day concerns of fellow Republicans. He generally maintained a low profile, and his control strengthened over the course of 1998. However, ill will blossomed again when lawmakers stitched together an unwieldy omnibus appropriations bill, and when GOP leaders made a failed, last-ditch attempt to improve their electoral standing with television commercials that focused on Clinton's affair with former White House intern Monica Lewinsky.

House Republicans forced Gingrich to step down from his leadership post after the party lost a net five House seats in the November 1998 elections. Gingrich's announcement that he intended to resign came just hours after he drew a challenge from a candidate with the stature and connections to beat him—Appropriations Committee Chairman Robert L. Livingston, R-La. Gingrich also said he would resign his House seat. Gingrich's move followed days of recrimination over who was to blame for the election results, which handed House Republicans the thinnest margin a majority would hold in forty-six years: The party breakdown was 223 Republicans, 211 Democrats, and 1 independent. It was only the second time since the Civil War that the party not in control of the White House lost seats in a midterm election. Gingrich acknowledged that Republicans had underestimated how quickly people tired of the Lewinsky scandal, though he said the media were preoccupied with it.

Gingrich had built a strong following within the party for having led Republicans to control of the House after forty years in the minority. But persistent, nagging doubts had existed about his ability to lead the GOP in the majority. A major frustration during Gingrich's career as Speaker was the extent to which President Clinton was able to take credit for the political successes of their shared time in power, while laying blame for many failures squarely at Gingrich's feet. Even if Republicans blame Democrats for "demonizing" their fallen leader, Gingrich himself was unable to restrain the habits of a political lifetime. He tried to soften his image but inevitably fell back on the rhetoric of confrontation. Gingrich was in effect a parliamentary leader who had to step down rather than take a bow for his achievement when his party did not know what to do for a second act. He may ultimately be seen as a transitional figure, someone whose divisiveness alienated many mainstream voters and who was unable to build a large and stable coalition.

In choosing Gingrich's successor, Republicans had to come to terms with the bitter splits within their ranks, primarily the fissure that divided conservatives and moderates—a division that reflected a broader struggle within the national party. House GOP members clearly wanted a shift in strategy, perhaps to something more pragmatic, but certainly to an agenda that could be better articulated to voters. Republicans thought they had a good chance of having found that in Speaker-designate Livingston. He was known to be able to work with Democrats, had legislative know-how, and was genuinely liked. However, on December 19 he said that he would not run for Speaker and that he intended to resign from the House within six months. His stunning announcement came only two days after he confessed that he had "on occasion" engaged in adulterous affairs.

J. Dennis Hastert, R-Ill., was elected Speaker on January 6, 1999, by 220–205. Hastert was a solid conservative known for his relaxed style and low profile. He was expected to be something of a throwback to the Speakers who preceded Gingrich, which, if proven true, would be ironic. The attack politics that led to his ascension were mostly of Gingrich's making.

CLINTON IMPEACHMENT AND AFTERMATH

The House on December 19, 1998, approved two articles of impeachment—one for perjury and one for obstruction of justice—related to Clinton's affair with Lewinsky and his subsequent attempts to cover it up. The House rejected two associated charges of perjury and violation of the oath of office.

The historic votes were a stunning victory for social conservatives, who dominated the House Republican caucus and controlled the top House leadership positions. Defying overwhelming odds, they united their fractious party to push an impeachment resolution through the House for only the second time in U.S. history. To Democrats, the votes were an egregious example of the political overreaching that characterized Republicans since they won control of Congress as a result of the 1994 elections.

Conservatives, led by Majority Whip Tom DeLay, R-Texas, drove forward despite polls showing that two-thirds of Americans opposed impeachment. They risked further public disapproval by proceeding with the vote while Clinton was overseeing military action against Iraq. The votes were a testament to the power of the conservative movement that dominated the Republican electoral base. The process was an illustration of the bitter partisan split that had all but paralyzed the House, as well as a sign of deep cultural divisions over standards of personal conduct for public officials.

Republicans argued that they had no choice but to act, calling the debate principled, not political. Based on evidence gathered by Independent Counsel Kenneth W. Starr that Clinton may have committed perjury and obstructed justice, they said they were forced to take the somber step of impeachment. In one sense, the GOP responded to the poll that, for them, mattered most—a clear demand from its conservative base for strong action against Clinton. Republicans hoped that they could drive the broader electorate their way, but this did not happen.

The ideological hardening of both parties diminished the middle ground in the House and made bipartisan compromise an endangered art. Moderates were often marginalized as Republican and Democratic leaders chose conflict and stalemate over negotiation. It was against this backdrop that impeachment was considered.

Activists on the right, the conservative-dominated Judiciary

Committee, and DeLay brought the party together. They painted Clinton's alleged perjury as not only a political or legal issue but also part of a pattern of lies and a sign of a moral decline in society that had to be checked. Republicans were helped in no small measure by a White House and Democratic Party that did not dispute basic facts and used terms such as "reprehensible" to describe the president's behavior. To ease the pressure on wavering Republicans, GOP leaders emphasized that a vote for impeachment was not a vote to remove the president from office but to send the case to the Senate for trial.

A middle group in each party sought a lesser censure resolution as a compromise and an alternative to impeachment. Citing concerns that such an effort was unconstitutional, DeLay and other House leaders refused to allow a vote on a censure resolution. Democrats called the move to block censure a baldfaced political tactic designed to increase the odds that impeachment would pass. GOP moderates generally voted for impeachment, in part because they grew increasingly angry about what they saw as Clinton's evasiveness and lies. Some also argued that, to the extent GOP moderates stuck with the House

leadership, they would gain more leverage on other issues in the 106th Congress.

The Senate on February 12, 1999, acquitted Clinton on both impeachment charges against him. Even though the impeachment effort seriously drove down the GOP's approval ratings and threatened to unseat Republicans in 2000, House GOP members made clear that they were still seething with anger at the president months after the trial ended, did not trust him, and were unwilling to endorse his actions as commander in chief. On April 28, the House rejected on a 213–213 vote a resolution endorsing the North Atlantic Treaty Organization (NATO) bombing mission, led by the United States, against Serbia's ethnic-cleansing campaign in its Kosovo province.

Minority Leader Gephardt publicly condemned the leadership style of Speaker Hastert, who endorsed and voted for the president's prosecution of the air campaign while he declined to exert any pressure for that position. Hastert's decision not to throw the weight of his office behind his views allowed DeLay to put his considerable influence as majority whip to work to engineer the symbolic rejection of Clinton's position. In the floor

Speaker J. Dennis Hastert swears in the 106th Congress in January 1999.

debate, DeLay urged Republicans not to "take ownership" of the air campaign, which in the past he had called "Clinton's war." DeLay maintained that the administration had been "incompetent" in carrying it out.

Gephardt called the congressional defeat for the president and DeLay's role in it a "low moment in American foreign policy" and a further indication that "the extreme right wing of the Republican Party remains in control of that party." For all of the customary pronouncements at the Capitol that partisanship on foreign affairs must cease at the water's edge, the bitterness left by impeachment—and fueled by a narrowly divided Congress operating in a divided government—was impossible to miss.

In early June, after ten weeks of sustained NATO air attacks, Serbia buckled and agreed to NATO's terms for peace, giving Clinton a foreign policy triumph and congressional Democrats vindication. In July 1999 Hastert faced another test of his speakership in passing a massive $792 billion tax-cut package supported by party conservatives. Exerting his leadership more forcibly than on the NATO vote, Hastert appealed to the party's caucus and engaged in eleventh-hour deal making to keep wavering Republican moderates in line. The tax cut, which passed by a slim 223–208 margin, was largely symbolic: as expected, President Clinton vetoed it once it reached his desk in September. But the close vote demonstrated how fragile the GOP eleven-seat House majority had become, and the difficult challenges that remained for Hastert in leading a fractious Republican Party in the House.

NOTES

1. The principal source for the history of the House from 1789 to 1919 was George B. Galloway, *History of the House of Representatives* (New York: Crowell, 1969).

2. Quoted in James T. Currie, *The United States House of Representatives* (Malabar, Fla.: Krieger, 1988), 113.

3. Paul Leicester Ford, ed., *The Writings of Thomas Jefferson* (New York: Putnam's, 1895), vol. 6, 102.

4. Bernard Mayo, *Henry Clay: Spokesman of the New West* (Boston: Houghton Mifflin, 1937), 346–347.

5. Marie B. Hecht, *John Quincy Adams: A Personal History of an Independent Man* (New York: Macmillan, 1972), 545.

6. Asher C. Hinds, *Hinds' Precedents of the House of Representatives* (Washington, D.C.: Government Printing Office, 1907), vol. 4, 278.

7. Richard F. Fenno Jr., *The Power of the Purse: Appropriations Politics in Congress* (Boston: Little, Brown, 1966), 8.

8. T. Harry Williams, *Hayes: The Diary of a President, 1875–1881* (New York: David McKay, 1964), 206.

9. Woodrow Wilson, *Congressional Government: A Study in American Politics* (Boston: Houghton Mifflin, 1885; Cleveland: Meridian Books, 1956), 76.

10. Neil MacNeil, *Forge of Democracy: The House of Representatives* (New York: McKay, 1963), 185.

11. Galloway, *History of the House of Representatives,* 140.

12. Paul DeWitt Hasbrouck, *Party Government in the House of Representatives* (New York: Macmillan, 1972), 15.

13. Quoted in Floyd M. Riddick, *The United States Congress: Organization and Procedure* (Manassas, Va.: National Capitol Publishers, 1949), 123.

14. Richard W. Bolling, *Power in the House: A History of the Leadership of the House of Representatives* (New York: Dutton, 1968), 164.

15. *The Reorganization of Congress,* A Report of the Committee of Congress of the American Political Science Association (Washington, D.C.: Public Affairs Press, 1945), 80–81.

16. Robert A. Caro, *The Years of Lyndon Johnson: The Path to Power* (New York: Knopf, 1982), 323.

17. James A. Robinson, *The House Rules Committee* (Indianapolis: Bobbs-Merrill, 1963), 72.

18. Brian Lamb and the staff of C-SPAN, *C-SPAN: America's Town Hall* (Washington, D.C.: Acropolis Books, 1988), 14.

19. Thomas P. O'Neill Jr., with William Novak, *Man of the House: The Life and Political Memoirs of Speaker Tip O'Neill* (New York: Random House, 1987), 354.

20. John M. Barry, *The Ambition and the Power* (New York: Viking Penguin, 1989), 479.

SELECTED BIBLIOGRAPHY

Barry, John M. *The Ambition and the Power.* New York: Viking Penguin, 1989.

Bolling, Richard W. *House Out of Order.* New York: Dutton, 1965.

———. *Power in the House: A History of the Leadership of the House of Representatives.* New York: Dutton, 1968.

Brown, George Rothwell. *The Leadership of Congress.* New York: Arno Press, 1974.

Burns, James MacGregor. *Congress on Trial.* New York: Harper and Brothers, 1949.

Carroll, Holbert N. *The House of Representatives and Foreign Affairs.* Pittsburgh: University of Pittsburgh Press, 1958.

Chiu, Chang-Wei. *The Speaker of the House of Representatives since 1896.* New York: Columbia University Press, 1928.

Clapp, Charles L. *The Congressman: His Work as He Sees It.* Washington, D.C.: Brookings Institution, 1963.

Davidson, Roger H., and Walter Oleszek. *Congress and Its Members.* 7th ed. Washington, D.C.: CQ Press, 2000.

Dodd, Lawrence C., and Bruce I. Oppenheimer, eds. *Congress Reconsidered.* 6th ed. Washington, D.C.: CQ Press, 1997.

Duncan, Philip, and Brian Nutting, eds. *Politics in America 2000: The 106th Congress.* Washington, D.C.: Congressional Quarterly, 1999.

Fenno, Richard F., Jr. *The Power of the Purse: Appropriations Politics in Congress.* Boston: Little, Brown, 1966.

Follett, Mary P. *The Speaker of the House of Representatives.* New York: Longmans, Green, 1896. Reprint. New York: Burt Franklin Reprints, 1974.

Ford, Paul Leicester, ed. *The Writings of Thomas Jefferson.* Vol. 6. New York: Putnam's, 1895.

Froman, Lewis A., Jr. *Congressmen and their Constituencies.* Chicago: Rand-McNally, 1963.

Galloway, George B. *Congress at the Crossroads.* New York: Thomas Y. Crowell, 1946.

———. *History of the House of Representatives.* 2nd ed. New York: Thomas Y. Crowell, 1976.

———. *The Legislative Process in Congress.* New York: Thomas Y. Crowell, 1953.

Griffith, Ernest S. *Congress: Its Contemporary Role.* New York: New York University Press, 1951.

Hasbrouck, Paul O. *Party Government in the House of Representatives.* New York: Macmillan, 1927.

Hecht, Marie B. *John Quincy Adams: A Personal History of an Independent Man.* New York: Macmillan, 1972.

Hinds, Asher C. *Hinds' Precedents of the House of Representatives of the United States.* 8 vols. Washington, D.C.: Government Printing Office, 1907.

Huitt, Ralph K., and Robert L. Peabody. *Congress: Two Decades of Analysis.* New York: Harper and Row, 1972.

MacNeil, Neil. *Forge of Democracy: The House of Representatives.* New York: David McKay, 1963.

McConachie, Lauros G. *Congressional Committees: A Study of the Origins and Development of Our National and Local Legislative Methods.* New York: Burt Franklin Reprints, 1973.

Mayo, Bernard. *Henry Clay: Spokesman of the New West.* Boston: Houghton Mifflin, 1937.

O'Neill, Thomas P., Jr., with William Novak. *Man of the House: The Life and Political Memoirs of Speaker Tip O'Neill.* New York: Random House, 1987.

Peabody, Robert L., and Nelson W. Polsby. *New Perspective on the House of Representatives.* 4th ed. Baltimore: Johns Hopkins University Press, 1992.

Polsby, Nelson W. "The Institutionalization of the House of Representatives." *American Political Science Reveiw* 62, no. 1 (March 1968): 144–168.

Riddick, Floyd M. *The United States Congress: Organization and Procedure.* Manassas, Va.: National Capitol Publishers, 1949.

Ripley, Randall B. *Party Leaders in the House of Representatives.* Washington, D.C.: Brookings Institution, 1967.

Robinson, James A. *The House Rules Committee.* Indianapolis: Bobbs-Merrill, 1963.

Sinclair, Barbara. *Majority Leadership in the U.S. House.* Baltimore: Johns Hopkins University Press, 1983.

Tacheron, Donald G., and Morris K. Udall. *The Job of the Congressman: An Introduction to Service in the U.S. House of Representatives.* 2nd ed. New York: Macmillan, 1970.

Williams, T. Harry. *Hayes: The Diary of a President, 1875–1881.* New York: McKay, 1964.

Wilson, Woodrow. *Congressional Government: A Study in American Politics.* Boston: Houghton Mifflin, 1885. Reprint. Cleveland: Meridian Books, 1956.

Young, Roland. *The American Congress.* New York: Harper and Brothers, 1958.

CHAPTER 3

History of the Senate

THE UNITED STATES SENATE ranks as the most powerful upper legislative chamber in the world. Its traditions of unlimited debate and collegiality and its constitutional powers over such executive functions as foreign policy and appointments have earned it a unique status among representative assemblies.

Even so, some people have been questioning whether the Senate was a good idea almost ever since it was created. Forged by a political "deal" at the Constitutional Convention of 1787, its very nature conflicts with the basic democratic principle that each citizen have an equal voice in government. It has been said that the Senate—where Wyoming has as much power as California, with more than fifty times the population—so clearly violates the "one person, one vote" principle that it would certainly be struck down by the Supreme Court as unconstitutional were it not already written into the founding document itself. For decades the fact that senators were selected by frequently corrupt state legislators and machine politicians lowered its prestige in the eyes of the public. More recently the rampant individualism and obstructionism in the chamber has led some experts to wonder whether the Senate was capable of grappling with the issues facing the nation.

Such problems were scarcely contemplated, though, by the Founding Fathers, who had two main goals in mind when they decided to add a Senate to the unicameral system of the Continental Congress. One was to provide an aristocratic bulwark against the potential excess of popular rule. Edmund Randolph said its purpose was to provide a cure for the "turbulence and follies of democracy,"[1] and James Madison asserted that "the use of the Senate is to consist in its proceeding with more coolness, with more system, and with more wisdom, than the popular branch." At the Constitutional Convention in Philadelphia, Madison maintained that the purpose of the Senate was, first, "to protect the people against their rulers" and, second, "to protect the people against the transient impressions into which they themselves might be led."[2]

The second goal of the Senate was to express the "federal principle," in contrast to the "national principle" embodied by the House of Representatives. Under the "Great Compromise" adopted by the Constitutional Convention, not only would each state have two votes in the Senate, but the election of senators by the state legislatures was also thought to be a means of making the states a component of the national governing system. However, although the basis of representation assured each state an equal voice, senators voted as individuals, their salaries were paid by the federal government instead of by the states, and the legislatures that elected them had no power to recall them. Thus it is not surprising that most senators, even in the early years, refused to consider themselves merely the agents of the state governments.

Efforts by various state legislatures in the nineteenth century to instruct their senators met with mixed success, although the practice did not die out entirely until 1913, when adoption of the Seventeenth Amendment to the Constitution took the election of senators out of state legislators' hands.

The Framers of the Constitution left unsettled many questions concerning the relationships among the three branches of government, and it remained for the Senate—born of compromise and fashioned after no serviceable model—to seek its own place in the governmental structure. In the unending competition for a meaningful share of power, the Senate for more than two centuries has been trying to define its role, and the history of the Senate is in large part the story of this quest.

It had been confidently predicted that the popularly elected House of Representatives would be the predominant chamber in the national legislature, with the Senate acting chiefly as a revisory body, checking and moderating actions taken by the House. At first the House did overshadow the Senate, both in power and prestige, but within a few decades the Senate, endowed with executive functions that the House did not share and blessed with a smaller and more stable membership, had achieved primacy over the directly elected chamber. In subsequent periods of American history the balance of power shifted from time to time, but the Senate never followed the British House of Lords into decline.

As the nation's population expanded, the size of the House mushroomed. But the Senate, in which the large and small states were equally represented, remained a comparatively small body. The growth of the House membership compelled it to impose stringent limitations on floor debate, to rely heavily on its committee system, and to develop elaborate techniques to channel the flow of legislation—all steps that diminished the power of individual representatives. Such restrictions were not considered necessary in the Senate, where members tended to view themselves as ambassadors of sovereign states even though they exhibited independence in casting their votes. And in the upper chamber the right of unlimited debate became the most cherished tradition. To the House, action was the primary object; in the Senate, deliberation was paramount.

It had also been expected that the Senate would serve as an

advisory council to the president, but natural friction between the two, aggravated by the rise of the party system, made such a relationship impracticable. As time passed the Senate was far more likely to try to manage the president than to advise him. In the nineteenth century the Senate often was the dominant force in Washington, but the rapid expansion of presidential power in the twentieth century was accompanied by a corresponding decline in the power of the legislative branch. As a result, the Senate felt from time to time that its existence as a viable legislative institution was threatened.

The Framers had expressed their distrust of democracy by providing for election of senators by the state legislatures instead of by the people directly. In "refining the popular appointment by successive filtrations," they hoped to ensure excellence, guard against "mutability," and, incidentally, protect the interests of the propertied classes.[3] Under this system, which Madison described in *The Federalist* as "probably the most congenial with public opinion," the Senate enjoyed its period of greatest prestige.[4] But as the trend toward democratization in government and expansion of the suffrage developed early in the twentieth century, public opinion increasingly favored popular election of senators. Eventually, the Senate was forced to participate in its own reform: in 1912 Congress approved a proposed constitutional amendment providing for direct election of the Senate.

The Seventeenth Amendment, ratified in 1913, curtailed the abuses that so frequently had been associated with election by the legislatures, but its other effects were difficult to measure. At any rate, no revolutionary change in the overall character of the institution was discerned.

So successful were the framers in insulating the Senate from popular pressure that the body often seemed to care more for what British statesman and historian James Bryce called its "collective self-esteem" than it did for public opinion. Sometimes it could be forced to act, as in the case of the Seventeenth Amendment and the adoption of the cloture rule (limitations on the filibuster) in 1917, but its resistance to impetuous action was for the most part all that its creators could have wished.

The Early Senate: 1789–1809

Only eight senators had reached New York City by March 4, 1789, the date fixed for the first meeting of Congress, and a quorum of the twenty-two-member Senate—two of the thirteen original states had not yet ratified the Constitution—did not appear until April 6, five days after the House had organized. Crucial questions concerning the nature of the Senate and its proper role in the new government remained to be worked out.

Was the upper chamber to be principally a council to revise and review House measures, or a fully coequal legislative body? And should it also serve in a quasi-executive capacity as an advisory council to the president, particularly with respect to appointments and treaties? Was the Senate primarily the bastion of state sovereignty, the defender of propertied interests, a necessary check on the popularly elected House, or was it, as its op-

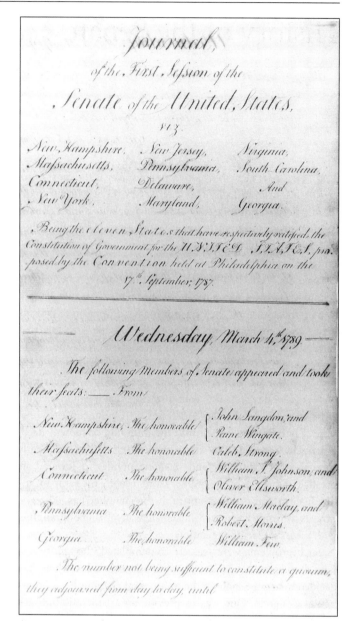

The Senate Journal recorded that only eight senators took their seats on March 4, 1789, the date fixed for the first meeting of Congress. A quorum did not appear until April 6.

ponents charged, a threat to republican principles and an incipient American House of Lords? Even the method of electing senators was in dispute: Were the members to be chosen by joint or concurrent vote in bicameral state legislatures? This issue, which was not resolved until 1866, cost New York its Senate representation during most of the first session of Congress.

The terms of individual senators also were in doubt. Under the Constitution, the first senators were to be divided into three classes—with terms of two, four, and six years, respectively—so that one-third of the Senate might be chosen every second year. To avoid charges of favoritism, the Senate chose to make the division by lot.

The first Senate, preoccupied with questions of form and

precedence, was quick to claim for itself superiority over the House, but the lower chamber initially was the more important legislative body. James Madison stated in a letter to Virginia governor Edmund Randolph that he would rather serve in the House than in the Senate. He wrote: "I prefer the House of Representatives, chiefly because, if I can render any service there, it can only be to the public, and, not even in imputation, to myself."[5] (Madison subsequently was elected to the House in the First Congress after being defeated for a Senate seat.)

In the earliest days of the first session, while the House was focusing on the financial problems of the infant nation, the Senate devoted three weeks to the consuming problem of an appropriate title for the president. The debate apparently was instigated by Vice President John Adams, whose penchant for ceremony—coupled with his physical appearance—earned him the mocking title of "His Rotundity."

The Senate's early insistence on form and its claim to deference from the House led to disputes over the method of transmitting communications between the two chambers, the wording of the enacting clause in proposed legislation, and proposals, which were agreed to for a brief period, for higher pay for senators. With a mixture of resentment and amusement, the House rebuffed most Senate efforts to enhance its prestige. The Senate soon abandoned its aristocratic claims, and relations between the two chambers became more cordial.

In the earliest years most laws originated in the House (78 percent from 1789 to 1809), with the Senate occupied primarily in reviewing and revising House-passed legislation. During the first session of the First Congress only five bills were introduced in the Senate, of which four—including the important Judiciary Act, which established the framework of the American judicial system—were passed. During the same period the House originated and passed twenty-six bills. Two of these were rejected by the Senate, one was turned down in conference, and the Senate modified at least twenty of the remaining twenty-three.[6]

EARLY RELATIONS WITH THE PRESIDENT

The concept of the Senate as an advisory council to the president never materialized. President George Washington took informal advice, but not formally from the Senate as a body. But he relied heavily for advice on Alexander Hamilton, and also on Madison, then a House member, and others. The constitutional role of the Senate in the appointment process also fell short of the consultative role that some framers of the Constitution had envisioned. Washington's exercise of the appointment power carefully stressed the separate natures of the nomination and confirmation processes, a point underscored by his decision to submit nominations to the Senate in writing instead of in person. The Senate's role as an advisory council was further restricted in the first session, when the Senate narrowly accepted House-passed language vesting in the president alone the power to remove executive officers. Under Washington's successors, members of Congress had greater influence over appointments,

but the principle of executive initiative remained firmly established.

In 1789 Washington attempted to put into practice his early view that "in all matters respecting treaties, oral communications [with the Senate] seem indispensably necessary." On August 22 and 24 he appeared in the Senate chamber to consult with the Senate concerning an Indian treaty. His presence during Senate proceedings, however, created a tense atmosphere that was uncomfortable for the senators and the president. As a result, Senate participation in the early stages of treaty making declined. This development made possible greater freedom of action when the time came for senators to vote on treaties. *(See box, Washington in the Senate, this page.)*

In 1795, when the treaty with Great Britain negotiated in 1794 by Chief Justice John Jay was brought before the Senate for its approval, a bitter dispute arose. The controversial treaty secured American frontier posts in the Northwest but permitted Britain to search American merchant ships and confiscate provisions destined for Britain's enemy, France. Ultimately, the treaty was

---

WASHINGTON IN THE SENATE

President George Washington's early view was that "in all matters respecting treaties, oral communications [with the Senate] seem indispensably necessary." Accordingly, on August 22, 1789, the president and his secretary of war, Gen. Henry Knox, appeared in the Senate chamber to consult with the Senate about a treaty with the Southern Indians. Sen. William Maclay of Pennsylvania gave an account of the proceedings in his *Journal*.

The vice president hurriedly read a paper containing the president's proposal to the Senate, but members were not able to hear because of the noise of carriages passing in the street outside. The windows were closed and the proposals read again. In the silence that followed, the vice president began to put the first question, but Maclay, fearing "that we should have these advices and consents ravished in a degree from us," rose and called for reading of the treaties and supporting documents alluded to in the president's paper. The president "wore an aspect of stern displeasure." Maclay "saw no chance of a fair investigation of subjects while the President of the United States sat there, with his Secretary of War, to support his opinions and over-awe the timid and neutral part of the Senate." Therefore, he backed a move to refer the entire subject to a committee. At this suggestion, the president "started up in a violent fret," exclaiming, "This defeats every purpose of my coming here." After he had "cooled down, by degrees," the president agreed to a two-day postponement, then withdrew from the chamber "with a discontented air."

On his return to the Senate two days later, Washington was "placid and serene, and manifested a spirit of accommodation," but the atmosphere was still tense, and "a shamefacedness, or I know not what, flowing from the presence of the President, kept everybody silent." At length, the treaties were agreed to and the president departed. The experience was not one that Washington cared to repeat.

approved by a bare two-thirds majority June 24, 1795, but not before the Senate deleted a clause restricting U.S. trading rights in the British West Indies.

The concept of senators as agents of state sovereignty led to repeated, but largely unsuccessful, efforts to make them accountable to their state legislatures. Some members of Congress felt an obligation to make periodic reports on their activities to the state governments, and a continuing controversy raged over the right of state legislatures to instruct their senators. Instruction was more general in the South than in the North, but opinion on the question was divided. However, with the emergence of political parties, party loyalty gradually took the place of allegiance to state legislatures even in those states where the concept received some acceptance.

EARLY SENATE PROCEDURES

Courtesy, dignity, and informality marked the proceedings of the Senate in the early days of the Republic. A body whose members on a chill morning might leave their seats to gather around the fireplace had no need for an elaborate system of procedure and rules. At the first session in 1789 the Senate adopted only twenty short rules, a number deemed sufficient to control the proceedings of a Senate no larger than some modern-day congressional committees. In 1806 the number of rules rose to forty, with most of the additions dealing with nominations and treaties. *(See box, Official Rules of the First Senate, p. 94.)*

The rules left a wide area of discretion to the Senate president (the vice president of the United States), particularly Rule XVI, which gave him sole authority to decide points of order. Vice President Adams presided over the Senate between 1789 and 1797 with no specific guidelines on procedures, but his successor as vice president, Thomas Jefferson (1797–1801), felt the need to refer "to some known system of rules, that he may neither leave himself free to indulge caprice or passion nor open to the imputation of them." The result was Jefferson's *Manual of Parliamentary Procedure*, which also was adopted by the House in 1837.

Closed Sessions

Following the practice of the Congress under the Confederation, the Senate originally met behind closed doors. Total secrecy was not maintained, however, because senators often freely discussed their activities outside the chamber, and the Senate Journal as well as sketchy reports of Senate action appeared in print from time to time. The principal result of the closed-door policy was to focus public attention on the widely reported debates of the House and to encourage suspicion of the aristocratic Senate. Beginning in 1790 various state legislatures determined to press for open sessions of the Senate, in part as a means of enforcing accountability of their senators.

The Senate rejected public meetings four times in four years but in 1794 finally agreed to open its sessions "after the end of the present session of Congress, and so soon as suitable galleries shall be provided for the Senate chamber." Almost two years went by before the galleries were erected and the rule put into

---

THE EARLY SENATE

This eyewitness description of the Senate in session about 1796 was offered by William McKoy in a series of articles in Poulson's *American Daily Advertiser* in 1828–1829:

Among the Thirty Senators of that day there was observed constantly during the debate the most delightful silence, the most beautiful order, gravity, and personal dignity of manner. They all appeared every morning full-powdered and dressed, as age or fancy might suggest, in the richest material. The very atmosphere of the place seemed to inspire wisdom, mildness, and condescension. Should any of them so far forget for a moment as to be the cause of a protracted whisper while another was addressing the Vice President, three gentle taps with his silver pencilcase upon the table by Mr. Adams immediately restored everything to repose and the most respectful attention, presenting in their courtesy a most striking contrast to the independent loquacity of the Representatives below stairs, some few of whom persisted in wearing, while in their seats and during the debate, their ample cocked hats, placed "fore and aft" upon their heads.

---

effect, but at the beginning of the Fourth Congress, in December 1795, the Senate's doors finally were opened to the public. The immediate effects of this action were not great, because the Senate sessions were too decorous to attract widespread attention and the more spirited House remained the center of public interest. Furthermore, the Senate had no official reporters of debates and made no accommodation for newspaper reporters until 1802, after the government had moved to Washington.

Light Workload

The demands upon senators in the early Congresses do not appear to have been unduly burdensome. Ordinarily, the Senate met at 11 a.m., except near the end of the session when the press of business was greater, and 3 p.m. adjournments were common. Sen. William Maclay of Pennsylvania, whose *Journal* provides a prejudiced but invaluable record of the Senate in the First Congress, frequently noted that the Senate adjourned its own tedious sessions so that members could go and listen to the livelier floor debates in the House. Absenteeism, a continuing problem, was only in part attributable to the difficulties of travel in this period. Accordingly, in 1798 the Senate finally added enforcement machinery to its rule prohibiting absence without leave.

Because most legislation initially originated in the House, the Senate had little to do early in a session. Under the so-called de novo rule of 1790, all bills died at the end of each session of Congress, so the Senate did not have House-passed bills from a previous session on which to work. The House scornfully rejected Senate proposals that the two chambers jointly prepare a legislative program for an entire session. However, joint committees often were appointed near the end of sessions to determine

Vice President John Adams presided over the Senate from 1789 to 1797. His penchant for ceremony earned him the mocking title of "His Rotundity."

what business had to be completed before adjournment. Much of the legislative output of each session was pushed through in the closing days. In the second session of the Sixth Congress, for example, the Senate passed thirty-five bills, one-third of them on the final day.

Presidential messages provided a partial agenda for each session. Washington and Adams delivered their messages in person annually, and each chamber prepared a reply that was delivered orally with great ceremony. Because these replies were carefully debated and amended, they provided a valuable opportunity for consideration of the overall legislative program. But Jefferson abandoned his predecessors' practice and delivered his messages in writing, and such messages were not thought by Congress to require a reply.

Rules on Debate

The absence of restrictions on debate in the Senate opened the door to delaying tactics as well as illuminating discussions. But dilatory actions appeared only occasionally in the early Senate and apparently did not present a serious problem. Only three of the rules in 1789 had any direct bearing on limitation of debate: Rule IV, providing that no member should speak more than twice in any one debate on the same day without permission of the Senate; Rule VI, providing that no motion should be debated until seconded; and Rule XVI, providing that every

question of order should be decided by the president of the Senate without debate. The so-called previous question motion, authorized under Rule IX, was not then used to close debate on a measure but to remove a question from further consideration by reverting to a previous one. This procedural motion was dropped when the rules were revised in 1806. At the same time, motions to adjourn were made nondebatable.

Although bills could be introduced by individual members with the permission of a Senate majority after one day's notice, the more common practice was to request the appointment of a committee to consider and report a bill. Thus only a limited number of bills were introduced, and most of those introduced were passed.

Committee System

Standing committees as they are known today did not exist in the early sessions of the Senate. Legislation was handled by ad hoc committees, which were appointed to consider a particular issue and disbanded once their work was finished, with the full Senate maintaining firm control over their activities. Membership was flexible, although the same senators frequently were assigned to committees dealing with a particular field of legislation. Following British precedent, opponents of a measure were excluded from membership on the committee that considered it, and the Federalist majority frequently excluded non-Federalists from committees appointed to consider legislation involving party issues.

MEMBERSHIP AND TURNOVER

In terms of previous experience, members of the early Senate were well qualified to serve in the national legislature. Of the ninety-four men who served in the Senate between 1789 and 1801, eighteen had participated in the Constitutional Convention of 1787, forty-two in the Continental Congress or the Congress of the Confederation, and eighty-four in their state or provincial legislatures. Only one or two were without some experience in government. A majority were men of wealth and social prominence, but they were a young "council of elders"—the average age in 1799 was only forty-five years.

Experience did not bear out the warnings of those who feared that senators would entrench themselves in office for life. Thirty-three of the senators who served between 1789 and 1801—nearly a third—resigned within that period before completing their terms, and only six did so to take other federal posts. Frequent resignations continued for many years—thirty-five in the period from 1801 to 1813—and the rate of reelection also was low.

EMERGENCE OF PARTIES

Political parties had no place in the constitutional framework, and early Senate voting reflected chiefly sectional or economic divisions within the chamber. But upon the presentation of Alexander Hamilton's financial measures, the Senate—and also the House—began to exhibit a spirit of partisanship. Supporters of a strong central government, chiefly representatives of mercantile and financial interests, banded together as Federalists under the leadership of Hamilton, while exponents of agrarian democracy, led by Madison and Jefferson, became known as Republicans (and here subsequently referred to as Democratic-Republicans to distinguish them from the Republican Party established in 1854).

Party alignments, still fluid in 1791, gradually hardened in the next two years in the face of the excesses of the French Revolution and troubled relations with Great Britain. By 1794 Sen. John Taylor of Virginia had observed: "The existence of two parties in Congress is apparent. The fact is disclosed almost upon every important question. Whether the subject be foreign or domestic—relative to war or peace—navigation or commerce—the magnetism of opposite views draws them wide as the poles asunder."

The Federalists held the Senate until 1801, but in 1794 the Democratic-Republicans came close to overturning that control. The Federalists succeeded in unseating Albert Gallatin on the charge that he had not been a citizen of the United States for the number of years required under the Constitution to be a senator. He was deprived of his seat on a 14–12 party-line vote, but on six other occasions during the session the Federalists needed the vote of Vice President Adams to sustain their program.

Approval of the Jay Treaty in 1795 united the Federalists and firmly identified the Senate in the public mind as being dominated by the Federalist Party. From that time on, both Federalists and Democratic-Republicans voted with a high degree of party regularity. During the Fourth, Fifth, and Sixth Congresses, the Federalists enjoyed roughly a two-to-one edge in the Senate over the backers of Jefferson. (The House during this time was closely divided between the two factions.) But the rapprochement with France, engineered by President John Adams, deprived the Federalists of their principal issue. This development, combined with the increased size of the chamber resulting from

---

OFFICIAL RULES OF THE FIRST SENATE

I. The President having taken the chair, and a quorum being present, the journal of the preceding day shall be read, to the end that any mistakes may be corrected that shall have been made in the entries.

II. No member shall speak to another, or otherwise interrupt the business of the Senate, or read any printed paper while the journals or public papers are reading, or when any member is speaking in any debate.

III. Every member, when he speaks shall address the chair, standing in his place, and when he has finished shall sit down.

IV. No member shall speak more than twice in any one debate on the same day, without leave of the Senate.

V. When two members shall rise at the same time, the President shall name the person to speak; but in all cases the person first rising shall speak first.

VI. No motion shall be debated until . . . seconded.

VII. When a motion shall be made and seconded, it shall be reduced to writing, if desired by the President, or any member, delivered in at the table, and read by the President before the same shall be debated.

VIII. While a question is before the Senate, no motion shall be received unless for an amendment, for the previous question, or for postponing the main question, or to commit, or to adjourn.

IX. The previous question being moved and seconded, the question for the chair shall be: "Shall the main question now be put?" and if the nays prevail, the main question shall not then be put.

X. If a question in a debate include several points, any member may have the same divided.

XI. When the yeas and nays shall be called for by one-fifth of the members present, each member called upon shall, unless for special reasons he be excused by the Senate, declare, openly and without debate, his assent or dissent to the question. In taking the yeas and nays, and upon the call of the House, the names of the members shall be taken alphabetically.

XII. One day's notice at least shall be given of an intended motion for leave to bring in a bill.

XIII. Every bill shall receive three readings previous to its being passed; and the President shall give notice at each, whether it be the first, second, or third; which readings shall be on three different days, unless the Senate unanimously direct otherwise.

XIV. No bill shall be committed or amended until it shall have been twice read, after which it may be referred to a committee.

XV. All committees shall be elected by ballot, and a plurality of votes shall make a choice.

XVI. When a member shall be called to order, he shall sit down until the President shall have determined whether he is in order or not; and every question or order shall be decided by the President, without debate; but, if there be a doubt in his mind, he may call for the sense of the Senate.

XVII. If a member be called to order for words spoken, the exceptionable words shall be immediately taken down in writing, that the President may be better enabled to judge the matter.

XVIII. When a blank is to be filled, and different sums shall be proposed, the question shall be taken on the highest sum first.

XIX. No member shall absent himself from the service of the Senate without leave of the Senate first obtained.

XX. Before any petition or memorial, addressed to the Senate, shall be received and read at the table, whether the same shall be introduced by the President or a member, a brief statement of the contents of the petition or memorial shall verbally be made by the introducer.

SOURCE: Roy Swanstrom, *The United States Senate, 1787–1801*, 100th Cong., 1st sess., 1988, S Doc 100-31, 317.

newly admitted southern and western states, broke the power of the Federalists in the Senate. In the elections of 1800, Jefferson's Democratic-Republicans won the presidency and both houses of Congress. When the Seventh Congress convened in December 1801, the Jeffersonians held a narrow Senate majority. Federalist strength in the Senate continued to decline throughout Jefferson's two terms in office.

LEADERSHIP IN THE SENATE

The drafters of the Constitution solved the problem of a job for the vice president by also making him president of the Senate, and they directed the Senate to choose a president pro tempore to act in the absence of the vice president. There were good reasons, however, why neither of these officers could supply effective legislative leadership.

The vice president was not chosen by the Senate but imposed upon it from outside, and there was no necessity for him to be sympathetic to its aims. Precedent was set by John Adams who, although clearly in general agreement with the majority of the Senate during his term as vice president, perceived his role as simply that of presiding officer and made little effort to guide Senate action. His successor, Thomas Jefferson, could not have steered the Federalist-controlled Senate even if he had wanted to, although Jefferson did maintain a watchful eye on the interests of the Democratic-Republicans in the upper chamber.

The Senate elected the president pro tempore from among its own members, but he could not supply legislative leadership because his term was too random and temporary. By custom a president pro tempore was elected only during the immediate absence of the vice president, and his duties as such ended with the reappearance of the vice president. From the First through the Sixth Congresses (1789–1801), fifteen senators served as president pro tempore.

Thus the mantle of legislative leadership soon fell upon individual senators—in the beginning these included Oliver Ellsworth and Rufus King, among others—and, more importantly, upon the executive branch. Presidents Washington and Adams shared a strong belief in the separation of powers. Neither was willing to take upon himself the role of legislative leader, but Alexander Hamilton had no such qualms. As secretary of the Treasury until 1795, and even after his retirement to private life, Hamilton not only developed a broad legislative program but also functioned, in the words of one historian, "as a sort of absentee floor leader," in almost daily contact with his friends in the Senate.

Under Jefferson and his secretary of the Treasury, Albert Gallatin, legislative leadership continued to emanate from the executive branch. Jefferson, wrote Sen. Timothy Pickering of Massachusetts, tried "to screen himself from all responsibility by calling upon Congress for advice and direction. . . . Yet with affected modesty and deference he secretly dictates every measure which is seriously proposed."[7]

By the end of Jefferson's administration, the Senate had established internal procedures and sampled many of the functions given it under the Constitution. It had both initiated and revised proposed legislation, given its advice and consent to treaties and nominations, conducted its first investigations, and held two impeachment trials—the first resulting in the removal from office of a federal judge and the second in the acquittal of Supreme Court Justice Samuel Chase. But the breadth of its powers was not yet clear; relations with the House, the executive branch, and the state governments still were only tentatively charted and awaited further tests.

Emerging Senate: 1809–1829

Two decades of legislative supremacy began with the administration of Jefferson's successor, James Madison. The "Father of the Constitution" proved himself incapable of presidential leadership. He lost control of his party to the young "war hawks" in the House, who succeeded in forcing him into the War of 1812, and for the remainder of his presidency Madison suffered defeats at the hands of Congress.

James Monroe was no more fortunate in his relations with Congress than Madison had been. At the time of Monroe's second inauguration Henry Clay of Kentucky commented that "Mr. Monroe has just been re-elected with apparent unanimity, but he had not the slightest influence on Congress."[8]

Neither Madison nor Monroe was temperamentally fit for legislative leadership, and both were further handicapped by their obligation to the congressional caucus that had nominated them for the presidency. The situation of John Quincy Adams was even more difficult, because he owed his election to the members of the House of Representatives.

RISING SENATE INFLUENCE

Under Clay's speakership, the House took a commanding role in government, but the influence of the Senate was on the rise. The trend toward Senate dictation of executive appointments, which had begun late in Jefferson's presidency, continued and increased under Madison. When he sought to make Gallatin secretary of state, the Senate blocked his choice and forced him to accept a secretary of its own choosing.

The importance of the Senate's treaty and appointment powers, in which the House had no share, was only one factor in the Senate's rise. The rapidly expanding size of the House soon suggested the advantages of serving in a smaller body (in 1820 there still were only forty-six senators). The Senate's longer term and more stable membership also made it seem a more desirable place in which to serve. Henry Clay moved from the Senate to the House in 1811, but by 1823 Martin Van Buren was able to claim that the Senate, more than any other branch, controlled all the important power of government. Clay later returned to the Senate.

The Senate's legislative importance increased gradually. In the early years, the great debates, such as those surrounding the War of 1812, occurred in the House. But the Senate took a leading role in the struggle over the Missouri Compromise of 1820 and succeeded in imposing upon the House an amendment barring slavery in any future state north of 36°30′ north latitude. Because that was the region in which the country's population was expanding most rapidly, proponents of slavery could no longer hope to uphold the cause of states' rights in the House indefinitely. The Senate—where the two sides on the issue were more evenly matched—inevitably became the forum for the great antislavery debates of the following decades.

CHANGES IN PARTY ALIGNMENT

Party alignments changed during the 1809–1829 period. The withering Federalist Party ceased to be a factor in national politics after the election of 1816, and Democratic-Republican supremacy was marred by increasing factionalism. The suffrage expanded, and the newly enfranchised small farmers of the South and West had little in common with the landed aristocracy that was the backbone of the party. Thus the democratic masses rejected the slaveholding planters and turned to Andrew Jackson of Tennessee, an exponent of their fiercely egalitarian philosophy, for leadership. In 1825 when the House made Adams president—although Jackson had led in the popular vote—the Democratic-Republican Party split, and a new Democratic Party was organized by Jackson's lieutenants. (All the presidential candidates in the 1824 election had represented factions of the Democratic-Republican Party.) In 1826 the Democratic Party won control of both houses of Congress, and in 1828 supporters of the new party elected Andrew Jackson as president—the office they thought he had been wrongly denied four years earlier.

GROWTH OF STANDING COMMITTEES

The Senate lagged behind the House in establishing a formal committee structure. In its first quarter century it created only four standing committees, all chiefly administrative in nature: the Joint Standing Committee on Enrolled Bills, the Senate Committee on Engrossed Bills, the Joint Standing Committee for the Library, and the Senate Committee to Audit and Control the Contingent Expenses of the Senate.

Most of the legislative committee work fell to ad hoc select committees, usually of three members, appointed as the occasion demanded. But eventually the need to appoint so many committees (nearly one hundred in the session of 1815–1816) exhausted the patience of the Senate, and in 1816 it established several standing committees, each with a legislative jurisdiction: Foreign Relations; Finance, Commerce and Manufactures; Military Affairs, the Militia; Naval Affairs; Public Lands; Claims; the Judiciary; the Post Office and Post Roads; and Pensions. Most of the new committees were parallel in function to previously created committees of the House. Their usual membership at this time was five, rising to seven by midcentury and to nine by 1900.

Membership on Senate committees were chosen by ballot until 1823. In that year the Senate adopted an amendment to its rules giving the presiding officer authority to appoint committee members, unless otherwise ordered by the Senate. At first this power was exercised by the president pro tempore, an officer of the Senate's own choosing, but in 1825–1827 Vice President John C. Calhoun assumed the appointment power and used it to place Jackson supporters in key committee positions. In the face of this patent effort to embarrass the administration of John Quincy Adams, the Senate quickly returned to the ballot as the method of filling committee slots. In 1828 the rule was changed again, this time to give appointment power to the president pro tempore, but in 1833 the Senate once more reverted to selection by ballot.

A general revision of the Senate rules in 1820, bringing the total number of rules to forty-five, was remarkable chiefly because it incorporated the provisions relating to standing committees that the Senate had adopted four years earlier. No great spirit of reform was involved. As in the case of other general revisions of Senate rules, the 1820 revision primarily represented an attempt to codify changes that had accumulated over a number of years.

'A SENATE OF EQUALS'

Sen. Daniel Webster described the upper chamber in 1830 as a "Senate of equals, of men of individual honor and personal character, and of absolute independence," who knew no master and acknowledged no dictation. In such a body it is not surprising that no single leader emerged to parallel the rise of Henry Clay in the House.

Statesmen of prominence served in the Senate during the 1809–1829 period. The roster included four future presidents—Andrew Jackson, Martin Van Buren, William Henry Harrison, and John Tyler—and a number of presidential hopefuls. And by the close of the period the great figures of the ensuing "Golden Age" were beginning to gather in the chamber: Thomas Hart Benton of Missouri arrived in 1821, Robert Y. Hayne of South Carolina in 1823, and Daniel Webster of Massachusetts in 1827. Clay, after serving briefly in the Senate in 1810–1811, went to the House, then returned to the Senate in 1831. Calhoun resigned as vice president in 1832 to succeed Hayne as senator from South Carolina.

Until Calhoun assumed office in 1825, the vice presidents of the period did not play influential roles. Madison's first vice president, George Clinton, was old and feeble and died in office, as did his successor, Elbridge Gerry. Monroe's vice president, Daniel D. Tompkins, hardly ever entered the Senate chamber.

Vice President Calhoun, hostile to the Adams administration and harboring presidential ambitions of his own, had no desire to alienate the Senate by exercising undue authority, but he was a commanding figure and his influence was felt. Sen. Hayne generally served as his spokesperson on the floor.

Calhoun took advantage of his position to make obviously biased committee appointments, but in other respects he assumed as little outward authority as possible. Although all of his predecessors in the chair had assumed direct authority to call

John C. Calhoun was one of the powerful voices in the Senate in the years leading up to the Civil War. Calhoun also presided over the Senate when he served as vice president for John Quincy Adams and Andrew Jackson.

senators to order for words used in debate, Calhoun contended that his power was appellate only and refused to act unless an offending senator first was called to order by another senator. He once declared that he would not "for ten thousand worlds look like a usurper."

Calhoun's refusal to act on his own initiative led the Senate in 1828 to amend its rules. Henceforth, the chair would have the power to call a senator to order, but for the first time in the upper chamber's history, the rule permitted an appeal from the chair's decision on a question of order.

During the 1809–1829 period, greater continuity of service developed in the office of president pro tempore. John Gaillard of South Carolina occupied the post for most of the period between 1814 and 1825 and presided over the Senate almost continuously during the eight years that Tompkins served as vice president. Elected by the Senate and thus considering himself enti-

tled to its support, Gaillard enforced the rules rigidly but did not exercise a true leadership role.

The Golden Age: 1829–1861

In the years leading up to the Civil War, the Senate became the chief forum for the discussion of national policy. The preeminent national issue in the period between the Missouri Compromise of 1820 and the outbreak of war in 1861 was the struggle between North and South over slavery. The Senate, where the two sides were equally matched because of the system of representation, inevitably became the principal battleground.

Sectional interests were more important than party loyalty during the years preceding the Civil War, and divisions between the major parties often were blurred. The Jacksonian Democrats had adopted the agrarian and states' rights philosophy of the Jeffersonians, but their concept of strong executive leadership was at odds with the Jeffersonian view. Meanwhile, the Whig Party was formed through a coalition of eastern financial and business interests that once had constituted the strength of the Federalists, but the Whigs were committed to a doctrine of legislative supremacy that was alien to Federalist thought.

The Democratic Party was split over the question of slavery, and many southern Democrats allied themselves with the Whigs in the hope of finding protection for states' rights and the institution of slavery under the Whig banner of legislative supremacy. However, the Whig Party had no answer to the slavery question, and in the 1850s it gave way to the new Republican Party—an alliance of northern interests dedicated to preventing the spread of slavery into the territories. Mounting southern defiance of northern opinion led to a North-South split in the Democratic Party, and secession and war soon followed.

In this age of national turmoil three men dominated the Senate chamber. All were former members of the House, and all had presidential aspirations that were to influence the shifting coalitions of a turbulent era. Daniel Webster of Massachusetts—Whig, spokesperson for eastern moneyed interests, sectionalist turned nationalist, supreme orator—entered the Senate in 1827 and remained there for most of the period until 1850. Henry Clay—Whig, westerner, brilliant tactician, and compromiser—returned to the Senate between 1831 and 1842 and again between 1849 and 1852. John C. Calhoun of South Carolina—outstanding logician, devoted son of the South, and champion of the right of secession—stepped down from the vice presidency in 1832 to defend his nullification doctrine on the Senate floor and remained a senator for most of the period until his death in 1850. (Nullification was the refusal of a state to recognize or enforce a federal law it regarded as an infringement on its rights.)

French historian and politician Alexis de Tocqueville in 1834 contrasted the "vulgarity" of the House with the nobility of the Senate, where "scarcely an individual is to be found . . . who does not recall the idea of an active and illustrious career." The Senate, he said, "is composed of eloquent advocates, distinguished generals, wise magistrates, and statesmen of note, whose language would, at all times, do honor to the most remarkable parliamentary debates of Europe."[9]

SENATE PREEMINENCE OVER THE HOUSE

Tocqueville could think of only one explanation for the Senate's superiority: its members were elected by elected bodies, whereas representatives were elected by the people directly. Thomas Hart Benton disputed that analysis. The Senate, he argued, enjoyed advantages of smaller membership, longer terms, and, collectively, greater experience on the part of its members, and it was composed of "the pick of the House of Representatives, and thereby gains doubly—by brilliant accession to itself and abstraction from the other."[10]

Undoubtedly the Senate's greater stability of membership contributed to its preeminence over the House. More significant, perhaps, was the introduction of the spoils system and the

Senate's increasing domination of the nomination and confirmation process. Finally, national expansion had strengthened the Senate by turning it from a small, intimate body into one large enough to showcase stirring oratory and the exercise of brilliant parliamentary skills. With the addition of two senators from every new state, the Senate increased from forty-eight members at the beginning of Jackson's administration to sixty-six in James Buchanan's. Its roster included such luminaries, in addition to Benton, as Lewis Cass of Michigan, Sam Houston of Texas, Jefferson Davis and Henry S. Foote of Mississippi, William H. Seward of New York, Stephen A. Douglas of Illinois, and Charles Sumner of Massachusetts.

SENATE QUARREL WITH JACKSON

The eclipse of presidential power that had begun under Madison came to an end when Andrew Jackson became president in 1829. Backed by strong popular majorities and skilled in the use of patronage, Jackson was able to dominate the House,

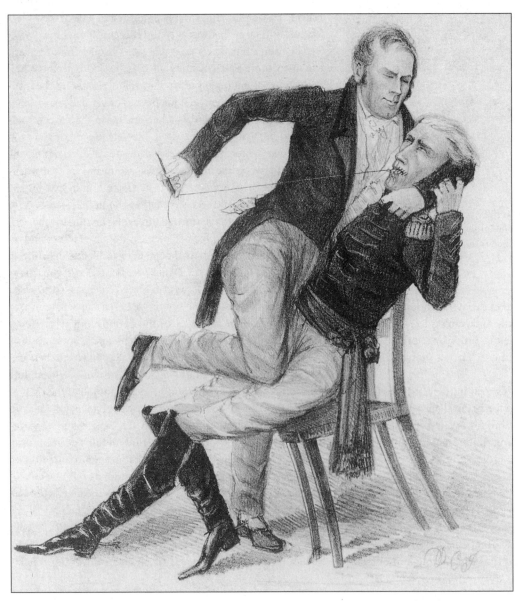

A contemporary cartoon, "Symptoms of a Locked Jaw," illustrates Henry Clay's censure of President Andrew Jackson in 1834. Jackson's supporters eventually had the censure expunged from the Senate Journal.

but in the Senate he met vigorous opposition from the new Whig Party. The Whigs were made up of commercial and industrial interests dedicated to the principle of legislative supremacy. They were quick to challenge the president on questions of policy and executive prerogative, and Jackson's term was marked by numerous acrimonious struggles with the Senate over legislation and executive appointments.

These disputes reached a peak in 1834 when Jackson removed deposits from the Bank of the United States and refused to hand over to the Senate communications to his cabinet relating to that issue. Outraged, the Senate adopted a resolution censuring the president for his actions. The resolution, pushed through by Clay, charged "that the President, in the late executive proceedings in relation to the public revenue, has assumed upon himself authority and power not conferred by the Constitution and laws and in derogation of both."

Jackson countered with a message, which the Senate refused to receive, declaring that so serious a charge as that contained in the censure resolution called for impeachment. Because impeachment had to originate in the House, he protested the Senate's action as a violation of the Constitution.

Benton, Jackson's leader in the Senate, promptly undertook a campaign to vindicate the president by expunging the censure resolution from the Senate Journal. Under pressure from Jackson, some state legislatures instructed their senators to support Benton's efforts, while others forced anti-Jackson senators into retirement. By the time Jackson's second term was drawing to a close in 1837, the Jacksonian Democrats had gained control of the Senate, and the expunging resolution finally was adopted by a 24–19 vote.

In one of the most dramatic scenes in Senate history, the terms of the resolution were carried out: "The Secretary of the Senate . . . shall bring the manuscript journal of the session of 1833–1834 into the Senate, and, in the presence of the Senate, draw black lines round the said resolve, and write across the face thereof, in strong letters, the following words: 'Expunged by order of the Senate, the 16th day of January, in the year of our Lord 1837.'"

WHIGS VERSUS PRESIDENT TYLER

Undeterred by their failure to dominate Jackson, the Whigs persisted in their efforts to establish the doctrine of legislative supremacy. With the election of Whig President William Henry Harrison, they thought their moment had come. Daniel Webster was named secretary of state, Clay supporters were put in other cabinet positions, and Harrison's inaugural address—revised by Webster—was a model statement of Whig doctrine. But Harrison died after only one month in office, to be succeeded by John Tyler, a states' rights Virginian and former Democrat who had been chosen as vice president to give the Whig ticket factional and geographic balance. Tyler also had been a friend of Clay's.

Clay, as the leading Whig member of Congress, at first thought he could assume effective leadership of the government, and he even introduced a set of resolutions designed to be the party's legislative program. But Tyler, it turned out, was determined to be president in fact as well as in name, and the two men soon clashed. Tyler's exercise of the veto power drove the Whigs to threats of impeachment and to abortive efforts to force his resignation, but Clay was unable to push through his own legislative program. Although all presidents had trouble with appointments during this period, Tyler, who lacked much support in either party, was more unfortunate than most. The Senate rejected many of his nominations, including four to the cabinet.

After Tyler's presidency the Whigs were never again able to muster a majority in the Senate that would permit them to put their doctrine of legislative supremacy to a test. Difficulties with nominations continued, for this period was the height of the spoils system, but a succession of strong presidents established a pattern of executive leadership that even the weak leadership of Presidents Franklin Pierce and James Buchanan could not entirely destroy.

THE DEBATES OVER SLAVERY

Oratory in the Senate reached its peak on the eve of the Civil War, and visitors often thronged the galleries to hear the great debates over slavery. Never had the Senate seemed so splendid as in this period when it served as the forum for the nation.

But the courtesy and decorum of the early Senate gradually began to crumble under the mounting pressures of the time. Although debates were for the most part still brief, passions often ran high and legislative obstruction became increasingly common. Filibusters were threatened and occasionally undertaken, but they were not yet fully exploited as a means of paralyzing the Senate. Senators in this period seldom admitted they were employing dilatory tactics.

The first notable Senate filibuster occurred in 1841, when dissident senators held the floor for ten days in opposition to a bill to remove the Senate printer. Later in the same year a Whig move to reestablish the Bank of the United States was subject to an unsuccessful two-week filibuster. Henry Clay said the tactics of the minority would "lead to the inference that the embarrassment and delay were the objects aimed at," and he threatened to introduce a rule to limit debate. Unabashed, the filibusterers invited Clay to "make his arrangements at his boarding house for the winter" and warned that they would resort to "any possible extremity" to prevent restriction of their debate. Unable to obtain majority support for his "gag rule," Clay never carried out his threat. The bank bill eventually was passed, only to be vetoed by President Tyler.[11]

In 1846 a bill providing for U.S.-British joint occupancy of Oregon was filibustered for two months. The measure was finally brought to a vote through use, apparently for the first time, of a unanimous consent agreement—a device still employed today to speed action in the Senate. Later in 1846 the Wilmot Proviso was talked to death in the closing hours of the session. That measure, which the House had attached as a rider to an appro-

South Carolina Rep. Preston S. Brooks attacked Sen. Charles Sumner of Massachusetts on the Senate floor in 1856. Seriously injured, Sumner did not return to the Senate until 1859.

priation bill in the early months of the Mexican War, stipulated that slavery was to be excluded from any territory acquired from Mexico.

Slavery was again the issue in the extended debates over the Compromise of 1850, Clay's valiant attempt to resolve the sectional controversies that were tearing the nation apart. In a crowded chamber, the great triumvirate—Webster, Clay, and Calhoun—made their last joint appearance in the Senate. The dying Calhoun dragged himself into the chamber to hear his final speech read by his colleague James Murray Mason of Virginia.

Violence threatened in April 1850 when Sen. Harry S. "Hangman" Foote of Mississippi brandished a pistol at Missouri's Benton, who was well known as a deadly duelist. Only the intervention of other senators prevented bloodshed. Greater violence marked the 1856 debate on the Kansas statehood bill. A House member from South Carolina attacked Charles Sumner while he sat at his desk in the Senate chamber and bludgeoned him so severely that the Massachusetts senator was unable to resume his seat until 1859. *(See box, Assault on Sumner, p. 936, Vol. II.)*

As the nation drifted toward war, debates continued to reflect the rancor of the period. Oratory had little place in a chamber where all members were said to carry arms, and by the time the Senate moved into its present quarters in the Capitol in 1859, the great epoch of Senate debate was at an end. Oratory had

flourished in the intimate grandeur of the old hall; in the new chamber—vast and acoustically poor—a new style of debate emerged.

THE COMMITTEE SYSTEM

The most important procedural development of the 1829–1861 period occurred in 1846 when the Senate transferred responsibility for making committee assignments to the party organizations in the chamber. As long as committee assignments were determined by Senate ballot, majority party control of the committees could not be assured, and, although by 1829 the majority usually controlled the working committees, the opposition party still held important chairmanships.

When the second session of the 29th Congress met in December 1846, the Senate rejected a proposal to let the vice president name the committees and then, in accordance with the existing rule, began balloting for chairmen. Midway through this process the balloting rule was suspended, and the Senate proceeded to elect on one ballot a list of candidates for all of the remaining committee vacancies. The list had been agreed on by the majority and minority. From that time on, the choice of committees usually has amounted to a routine acceptance by the Senate of lists drawn up by committees acting as representatives of the caucus, or conference, of each of the two major parties.

That party organizations did not become the standard instrument of committee selection until 1846 gives some indication of the limited extent of party discipline in the early years of the Senate. During that period, party authority was confined to organizational questions. When it came to substantive issues, senators voted as individuals rather than as Democrats or Whigs.

Party influence in the Senate was enhanced by the new method of committee selection, but rank within committees was thereafter increasingly determined by seniority, thus making chairmanships less subject to party control. Experience had always played a major role in making committee assignments, but as long as appointments to committees were made by ballot, rigid adherence to seniority was impossible. However, with the introduction of party lists in 1846 strict compliance with seniority began to be enforced. The bitter sectional disputes leading up to the Civil War may well have encouraged the use of seniority to avoid fierce interparty struggles for committee control.

The system was not impartial in distributing its favors. In 1859 a northern Democrat called the use of seniority "intolerably bad" and complained that it had "operated to give to senators from slave-holding states the chairmanship of every single committee that controls the public business of this government. There is not one exception."[12]

There had been one exception earlier that year: Stephen A. Douglas of Illinois was the chairman of the Committee on Territories; the Democratic Caucus took away his chairmanship, in spite of his seniority, because he refused to go along with President Buchanan and the southern wing of the party on the question of allowing slavery in the territories.

Party Government: 1861–1901

During the Civil War and Reconstruction periods, the Republicans controlled the presidency, the Senate, and the House throughout seven consecutive Congresses, ending in 1875. Not only did the Democrats lose their southern seats in Congress, most of which were vacant from 1861 to 1869, they also lost many northern Democrats, who defected to the Republicans rather than remain in a party so closely tied to the southern cause.

This period of Republican hegemony was marked by a power struggle between Congress and the White House. During the Civil War, Congress sought to assert its authority through such mechanisms as the Joint Committee on the Conduct of the War, consisting of three senators and four representatives, which exercised a wide range of authority. Yet President Abraham Lincoln managed to retain his independence from Congress as well as to increase the armed forces, call for volunteers, spend money on defense, issue a code of regulations for the military, suspend the writ of habeas corpus, and even emancipate the slaves in the rebellious states, all without waiting for authority from Congress.

When the president issued a proclamation on Reconstruction in December 1863, Congress passed the Wade-Davis bill transferring Reconstruction powers to itself. In response to the president's pocket veto of this measure, the Radical Republicans in Congress issued the Wade-Davis Manifesto, which declared that "the authority of Congress is paramount and must be respected; that the body of Union men in Congress will not submit to be impeached by him [Lincoln] of rash and unconstitutional legislation; and if he wishes our support he must confine himself to his executive duties—to obey and execute, not to make the laws—to suppress by arms any armed rebellion, and leave political reorganization to Congress."

RADICAL REPUBLICAN ERA

The Radical Republicans achieved their aims after Lincoln was assassinated. Under their domination, Congress passed its own Reconstruction Act, overrode President Andrew Johnson's veto of a civil rights bill, and set up Gen. Ulysses S. Grant as General of the Army in Washington, requiring all army orders to be issued through him—thus bypassing the president as commander in chief—and forbidding the president to remove or transfer the general without prior consent of the Senate. Over Johnson's veto, Congress passed the Tenure of Office Act requiring Senate assent before the president could remove any government official appointed through its advice and consent power. When Johnson dismissed his secretary of war to test the constitutionality of the act in the courts, the House voted to impeach him. The Senate subsequently came within one vote of removing him from office. Congress had broken the authority of the chief executive. Under a compliant President Grant, the Republican Congress governed.

In this period of one-party government, the House, led by Radical Republican Thaddeus Stevens of Pennsylvania, overshadowed the Senate. But after the failure of the Republicans' effort to impeach Johnson, and Stevens's death in August 1868, House prestige declined, and the Senate rapidly became the dominant arm of the national legislature. During the remainder of the nineteenth century, while control of the House shifted back and forth between the two parties, the Republicans managed to maintain control of the Senate in all but two Congresses, and in this era of stability, modern party government developed in the upper chamber.

Meanwhile, later presidents were able to recoup some of the power lost under Grant. With public support, Rutherford B. Hayes refused to let the Republican Senate dictate his cabinet and customs appointments, and Grover Cleveland's defense of the presidential appointment power led to repeal of the Tenure of Office Act, but on the whole the Senate remained the most powerful force in the government.

When William McKinley became president in 1897, Congress and the White House entered a period of almost unprecedented harmony. "We never had a president who had more influence with Congress than McKinley," said Sen. Shelby M. Cullom, R-Ill. "I have never heard of even the slightest friction between him and the party leaders in the Senate and House."[13]

POWER OF PARTY BOSSES

The character of the Senate underwent a marked change in the post–Civil War era. Senate membership grew from seventy-four in 1871 to ninety in 1901, and, as state politics became more centralized, a new breed of senator entered the chamber. The great constitutional orators of the prewar period were succeeded by "party bosses"—professional politicians who had risen through the ranks of their state party organizations and who came to Washington only after they had consolidated their power over the state party structure. As long as they maintained state control, they were immune from external political reprisal, but their dedication to party and their acceptance of the need for discipline made them good "party senators," willing to compromise their differences to maintain harmony within the party. To these men the Senate was a career, and a striking increase in average length of service occurred during this period.

The public viewed the Senate's changing character with suspicion, and the growing power of party organizations was widely attributed to the "trusts." In 1902 political analyst Moisei Ostrogorski charged that the economic interests "equipped and kept up political organizations for their own use, and ran them as they pleased, like their trains."[14] Other observers held that political centralization and business concentration were parallel developments, not directly related, but they agreed that the corporations contributed to the power of the party chiefs.

Lobbying by business groups became a vital element in government during the final decades of the nineteenth century, but business itself was not unified, and its efforts were too haphazard for it to attain great political control. Still, some of the lobbying practices of the period—ranging from wholesale distribution of railroad passes to loans and sales of stock at attractive prices to members of Congress—fostered concern about corruption in the Senate.

The Senate's "usurpation" of executive power, its failure to impose limitations on debate, and the undoubted incidence of corruption all contributed to a loss of public esteem. By the close of the century, the Senate was described derogatorily—and somewhat unfairly—as a "Millionaires' Club," and it was without question the most unpopular branch of the national government.

Dissatisfaction with the Senate led to demands for the direct election of senators, through which reformers hoped to curtail both the power of political parties and the political influence of the corporations. By 1900 it had become clear that a constitutional amendment providing for direct election eventually would be enacted.

DEVELOPMENT OF PARTY LEADERSHIP

Having assumed responsibility for organizational matters in the pre–Civil War Senate, political parties extended their authority during the war to substantive questions as well. However, the Senate had no strong tradition of leadership, and party discipline was expected to lapse after the war ended. The Republican and Democratic Parties themselves were expected to disintegrate, as other parties had done before them, once the issues that had brought them together faded or were resolved.

Although the parties failed to dissolve, party influence in the upper chamber did decline for a time. When Grant's administration began in 1869, political parties compelled unity only on organizational questions. Disputes over committee assignments were settled in the caucus, and pressing issues were discussed there, but caucus decisions could hardly be considered binding as long as there was no leader to enforce discipline or exact reprisals. The Republican caucus did remove Charles Sumner of Massachusetts from the chairmanship of the Foreign Relations Committee in 1871 when his differences with President Grant became so extreme that he refused to communicate with either the president or the secretary of state.

The possibilities of party leadership first became apparent in the Senate career of Roscoe Conkling of New York in the 1870s. Conkling gathered a loyal following, and after 1873 his faction usually controlled the Committee on Committees and thus was able to reward his supporters with valuable committee posts. But the Conkling forces stood together only on organizational questions. Their influence on substantive legislation was minimal. When Conkling resigned his Senate seat in 1881, following an altercation with President James A. Garfield over executive appointments, the Senate reverted to its old independent ways. "No one," wrote Woodrow Wilson in 1885, "is the Senator. No one may speak for his party as well as for himself; no one exercises the special trust of acknowledged leadership. The Senate is merely a body of individual critics."[15]

MODERN PARTY DISCIPLINE

Modern party discipline made its appearance in the Senate in the 1890s under the leadership of Sens. Nelson W. Aldrich of Rhode Island, William B. Allison of Iowa, and their fellow members of the School of Philosophy Club, an informal group that met regularly for poker at the home of Sen. James McMillan of Michigan. In March 1897 Allison, as the member of his party with the longest period of Senate service, was elected chairman of the Republican Caucus. The group soon assumed control of the Senate. Previous caucus chairmen had not viewed the office as a vehicle for consolidating party authority, but Allison was quick to see the possibilities of his new position. Holding that "both in the committees and in the offices, we should use the machinery for our own benefit and not let other men have it," Allison took advantage of his position to solidify the party's control.

A Republican Steering Committee had been appointed biennially since the mid-1880s to help schedule legislative business. Unlike previous caucus leaders, Allison determined to chair this committee himself, and he filled the committee with members of his group. Under Allison's guidance, the Steering Committee arranged the order of business in minute detail and also managed proceedings on the floor.

Allison likewise controlled the Committee on Committees, which made committee assignments. He had great leeway to appoint members who would be receptive to his wishes. Its chairman always was a member of the ruling faction, for example. Committee chairmanships were by this time invariably filled through seniority, and Allison and Aldrich made no attempt to overturn the seniority rule, to which they owed their own committee chairmanships (Allison on Appropriations and Aldrich on Finance). But seniority did not apply to the filling of committee vacancies, and here the party leaders found an opportunity to reward their supporters and punish dissidents.

Access to positions of influence soon depended on the favor and support of the party leaders. When Albert J. Beveridge of Indiana entered the Senate in 1899, he sought out Allison to make known his preferences for committee assignments, in recognition of the existing order. "I feel that the greatest single point is gained in the possession of your friendship," Beveridge told Allison. "I will labor very hard, strive very earnestly to deserve your consideration."

Caucus approval of the committee slates and order of business became a mere formality, but the caucus still met to consider important issues. Through the caucus mechanism divisive questions were compromised in privacy, and the party was enabled to speak with a unified voice on the Senate floor. Caucus decisions were not formally binding—"We can get along without that," Allison remarked—but once the party leadership was capable of enforcing discipline on those who broke ranks, party solidarity became the norm. "Senators willing to abandon the opportunity to increase their authority could act freely, following their own inclinations," historian David Rothman noted. "The country might honor their names, but the Senate barely felt their presence."

Under the leadership of Arthur P. Gorman of Maryland, Senate Democrats developed a power structure similar to that devised by the Republicans. As chairman of the Democratic Caucus in the 1890s, Gorman chaired not only the Steering Committee but also the Committee on Committees. In some ways his control over his party was greater than that of Allison and Aldrich over the Republicans. But the Democrats were in the

Four leaders held sway over the Senate at the turn of the century: Orville H. Platt, John C. Spooner, William B. Allison, and Nelson Aldrich. They are shown here in 1903 at Aldrich's estate in Newport, Rhode Island.

minority during most of this period, and they often split on substantive issues. Gorman never attained the power and influence wielded by his Republican counterpart.

The lack of harmony within Democratic ranks led, in 1903, to adoption of a rule making the decisions of the Democratic Caucus binding on members upon a two-thirds vote. Allison considered such a rule unnecessary for the Republicans, but Gorman enthusiastically supported it.

ATTITUDE TOWARD PARTY CONTROL

The growth of party government was viewed with grave misgivings by the general public and was by no means always popular in the Senate itself. As early as 1872 the Liberal Republicans—dissident Republicans opposed to the Grant administration—had protested efforts by "a few members of the Senate" to use the party organization to "seek to control first a majority of the members belonging to that organization and then of the Senate." Similar complaints came from the mugwumps—Republicans opposed to the party's leadership—in the 1880s and from the Populist Party in the 1890s.

The Senate in 1899 took one step to disperse authority within the chamber when it transferred responsibility for considering major appropriations bills from the Appropriations Committee to the various legislative committees. The change was promoted not in the party caucus but on the floor, where dissidents within both parties were able to prevail over the combined opposition of the Republican and Democratic leaders.

By the end of the nineteenth century, political parties had assumed a decisive role in the legislative process. The parties named the committees that made the initial decisions on proposed legislation, and they also determined what bills would be considered on the floor. When divisive issues arose, party members resolved their differences within the caucus and went forth in disciplined ranks to ratify caucus decisions on the floor, often acting without debate or the formality of a roll-call vote.

The Republicans had a plurality, but not a majority, in the Senate when a bill proposed by Rep. Nelson Dingley Jr., R-Maine, raising tariffs to a new high, was passed by the House in April 1897 and sent to the Senate. Allison, with the help of only the Republicans on the Finance Committee, drafted new tariff schedules, which all but three of the panel's Republicans had agreed in advance to support. After limited debate in the caucus, the bill went to the Senate, where united Republican support passed it over solid Democratic opposition. The Republicans, said Sen. Benjamin R. Tillman, Democrat of South Carolina, "under the stress of party orders, I suppose, given by the caucus, sit by quietly and vote. They say nothing . . . and every schedule prepared by the party caucus is voted by them unanimously." Tillman was wrong in only one particular: He credited the caucus with more influence than it actually had.

ELECTION LAW OF 1866

For more than seventy-five years after the adoption of the Constitution, Congress took no advantage of its power to regulate congressional elections. The method of electing senators was left to the states. At first, senators generally were chosen by concurrent vote of the two houses of the state's legislature. That is, a majority in each house had to agree on the candidates for them to be elected. Later, in about half the states the two houses, sitting together, elected senators by joint ballot.

The election system had serious flaws. Insistence on a majority vote in each house caused frequent deadlocks, which not only kept the legislature from considering other business, but also caused the state to lose its representation in the Senate. Irregular practices abounded, and the Senate itself was forced to decide many election contests because of the lack of a uniform election law.

Congress in 1866 enacted legislation designed to correct these problems. The new law provided that the first ballot for senator was to be taken by the two houses of a state's legislature voting separately. If no candidate received a majority of the vote in both houses, then the two houses were to meet and ballot jointly until a majority choice emerged. The law also contained provisions for roll-call votes in the state legislatures (secret ballots had been the custom in some states) and for an election timetable requiring a minimum of one ballot on every legislative day until someone was elected.

Senatorial elections were regulated by this law for almost half a century, but the measure was not a success. Deadlocks continued to occur, and irregularities increased. Historian George H. Haynes summarized some of the pitfalls of election by state legislatures that led to the direct election movement and adoption of the Seventeenth Amendment in 1913:

> Not a few, but nearly half the states of the Union suffered from serious deadlocks. These contests, the outcome of which was often as much a matter of chance as would be the throw of dice, aroused men's worst passions and gave rise now to insistent charges of bribery, now to riot, to assault and to threats of bloodshed, such that legislative sessions had to be held under protection of martial law.
>
> Fourteen contests lasted throughout an entire session of the legislature without affecting an election. Four states submitted to the heavy cost and inconvenience of special sessions to select senators. Six states preferred to accept vacancies, thus losing their "equal suffrage in the Senate" while the country was deprived of a Senate constituted as the fathers had intended. At times legislative election led to positive and flagrant misrepresentation of the state in the Senate. To the individual state it brought a domination of state and local politics by the fierce fight for a single federal office, and interference with the work of lawmaking, ranging all the way from the exaction of a few hours of the legislators' time to the virtual annihilation of the legislature, which had been constituted to care for the interests of the state.[16]

RISE OF THE FILIBUSTER

The oratorical splendor that had brought renown to the Senate in the years preceding the Civil War disappeared with the settlement of the slavery question. For the remainder of the century, Senate debate was not noted for its brilliance. Crucial legislative decisions came to be made in party councils, and few floor speeches were intended to sway votes. Attendance at formal sessions of the Senate became a tedious duty. "It would be a capital thing," wrote Republican Sen. George F. Hoar of Massachusetts in 1897, "to attend Unitarian conventions if there were not Unitarians there, so too it would be a delightful thing to be a United States Senator if you did not have to attend the sessions of the Senate."[17]

Filibusters, increasingly common as the century advanced, became a virtual epidemic in the 1880s and 1890s. And the Senate suffered a marked loss of public confidence because of its failure to impose stringent curbs on debate. Attempts to impose rules to limit filibusters were introduced from time to time, but the Senate held fast to its cherished tradition of unlimited speech.

Wartime pressures had produced two notable filibusters during the 1860s. In 1863 a measure to protect the president against loss in any action brought against him for having suspended the writ of habeas corpus touched off a filibuster in the closing hours of the session. But the talkathon failed when the presiding officer, in the face of obvious obstructionism, called for a vote and refused to entertain an appeal. In a floor speech, Sen. Lyman Trumbull, R-Ill., described the tactics of opponents of the legislation: "Motion after motion was made here last night to lay on the table, to postpone indefinitely, to adjourn, to adjourn, to adjourn and to adjourn again, and the yeas and nays called on each occasion." Similar tactics were employed by Senator Sumner in 1865 against a move to readmit Louisiana into the Union. He felt so strongly on the issue that he declared himself "justified in employing all the instruments that I find in the arsenal of parliamentary warfare."

Proposals by Democrats to suspend or repeal statutes authorizing the use of federal troops to supervise state elections were the subject of the next great filibusters, in 1876 and 1879. In the 1879 filibuster, Republicans relied on dilatory motions, roll-call votes, and refusal to answer quorum calls, whereupon the Senate's president pro tempore ruled that he could determine whether enough senators were present to constitute a quorum.

In a famous filibuster in 1881, the Democratic minority prevented the Republicans from organizing the Senate until the resignations of two senators—Roscoe Conkling and Thomas C. Platt of New York—had given the Democrats numerical control. The filibuster made it impossible for the upper chamber to take action on any legislation from March 24 to May 16 of that year.

In 1890 a bill to provide federal aid to education, sponsored by Sen. Henry W. Blair, R-N.H., was filibustered from February 26 to March 20 by Blair himself in an effort to get sufficient support for passage. Believing he had won the requisite strength, Blair permitted the bill to come to a vote, but two senators at the last minute decided to vote against it. The bill was defeated, 31–37. Blair voted nay to be eligible under Senate rules to move to reconsider the bill, but the measure was never revived.

A filibuster against the so-called Force Bill—authorizing federal supervision at polling places during national elections to prevent exclusion of black voters in southern states—lasted from December 2, 1890, to January 26, 1891. After seven weeks of debate, the bill's supporters tried to put through a Senate rule providing for majority cloture (allowing a majority of the Senate to end a filibuster). When that failed, the Senate was held in continuous session for four days and nights in an effort to exhaust the filibusterers. After thirty-three days of obstruction, the bill was dropped to permit the enactment of vital appropriation bills before the 51st Congress expired in March 1891. During the filibuster, West Virginia Democrat C. J. Faulkner nominally held the floor for eleven and a half hours, although for nearly eight hours of that time he was relieved of the necessity of speaking because a quorum was not present to conduct business.

In 1893 a filibuster against repeal of the 1890 Silver Purchase Act lasted from August 29 to October 24. After forty-six days of filibusters, including a period of thirteen continuous day-and-night sittings, the repeal was passed on October 30 and sent to the president. The minority made use of every weapon in the filibusterer's arsenal—dilatory motions, roll-call votes, and quorum calls, in addition to talk. A new record was set by Nebraska Populist William V. Allen, who held the floor with interruptions for fourteen hours.

That filibuster aroused widespread public concern over the conduct and viability of the Senate. "To vote without debating is perilous, but to debate and never vote is imbecile," wrote Sen. Henry Cabot Lodge, R-Mass., shortly after the struggle ended. "As it is, there must be a change, for the delays which now take place are discrediting the Senate. . . . A body which cannot govern itself will not long hold the respect of the people who have chosen it to govern the country."[18]

In 1897, during a mild filibuster on a naval appropriation bill, the chair ruled that a quorum call could not be ordered unless business had intervened since the last quorum call. However, since there was as yet no suggestion that debate was not business, this ruling had only limited effect in curbing the excesses of the filibuster.

In 1901 Montana Republican Thomas H. Carter, who was retiring from the Senate in a few hours, filibustered against a "pork-barrel" rivers and harbors bill from the night of March 3 until the Senate adjourned *sine die* at noon March 4. The bill was a raid on the Treasury, Carter said, and he was performing a "public service" in preventing it from becoming law. He readily yielded for other business but resumed his item-by-item denunciation of the bill whenever necessary. No determined attempt was made to stop him, and the bill died.

By the beginning of the twentieth century the filibuster had assumed scandalous proportions. This was, says historian Franklin Burdette, "the heyday of brazen and unblushing aggressors. The power of the Senate lay not in votes but in sturdy tongues and iron wills. The premium rested not upon ability and statesmanship but upon effrontery and audacity."[19]

Filibustering is the practice by which a minority of a legislative body employs extended debate and dilatory tactics to delay or block action favored by the majority.

The word filibuster is derived from the Dutch word *Vrijbuiter,* meaning freebooter. Passing into Spanish as *filibustero,* it was used to describe U.S. military adventurers who in the mid-1800s fomented insurrections against various Latin American governments.[1]

The first parliamentary use of the word is said to have occurred in the House in 1853, when a representative accused his opponents of "filibustering against the United States."[2] By 1863 *filibuster* had come to mean delaying action on the floor, but the term did not gain wide currency until the 1880s.

Although the word *filibuster* as applied to legislative obstruction is relatively new, the tactics it describes are as old as parliamentary government. What are now called filibusters occurred in the Colonial assemblies, and obstructive tactics were a feature of Congress from its earliest days. A bill to establish a "permanent residence" for the national government was subjected to a House filibuster early in the First Congress. When the same bill reached the Senate, Pennsylvania's Sen. William Maclay complained that "the design of the Virginians and the South Carolina gentlemen was to talk away the time so that we could not get the bill passed."[3]

OBSTRUCTION IN THE HOUSE

Legislative obstruction was characteristic of the House long before it became common in the Senate. But the unwieldy size of the lower chamber's membership soon led to various curbs on debate. A motion adopted by the House in 1789, known as the previous question, has been used since 1811 to close debate and bring a matter under consideration to an immediate vote.

Under a 1798 rule House members are permitted to speak only once during general debate, and for a specified period of time. Since 1847 debate on amendments has been limited to five minutes for each side, and since 1880 a rule of relevancy has been enforced by the Speaker. These limitations on debate curbed the practice of filibustering in the House, although delaying tactics continued to be used from time to time.

OBSTRUCTION IN THE SENATE

The Senate, with its cherished tradition of unlimited debate, offered a more favorable climate for obstruction. By the end of the nineteenth century the upper chamber had become notorious as the home of the filibuster.

The first notable Senate filibuster occurred in 1841, when dissident senators held the floor for ten days in opposition to a bill to shift the Senate's printing to new contractors. In the next forty years filibusters were undertaken with increasing frequency, but usually they were not successful. In the last two decades of the nineteenth century, the practice assumed almost epidemic proportions, and as filibusterers used more daring techniques their rate of success increased.

Efforts to curb obstruction in the twentieth century had only limited effectiveness. The filibuster came to be identified with southern efforts to block civil rights legislation, although northern liberals occasionally found it a useful device as well. Until 1964 the Senate had never been able to end a filibuster on civil rights legislation.

The most important tool of the filibusterer, once control of the floor proceedings is gained, is continued talk, for which a strong physical constitution is a prerequisite. Other techniques are dilatory motions, roll-call votes, quorum calls, points of order and appeals, and the interjection of other business. Successful use of these devices calls for in-depth knowledge of parliamentary procedure. Senators with less than expert knowledge are likely to rely on talk, because a parliamentary blunder could spell defeat for their cause.

FAMOUS FILIBUSTERS

The longest speech in the history of the Senate was made by Strom Thurmond, R-S.C. During a filibuster against passage of a civil rights bill in 1957, Thurmond spoke for 24 hours and 18 minutes in a round-the-clock session August 28–29. Second place goes to Wayne Morse, Ind.-Ore., who in April 1953 spoke for 22 hours and 26 minutes on the tidelands oil bill. The third longest individual filibuster was set by Robert M. La Follette Sr., R-Wis., who in 1908 held the floor for 18 hours and 23 minutes in a fight over the Aldrich-Vreeland currency bill. In fourth place is William Proxmire, D-Wis., whose 1981 speech in opposition to a bill to raise the public debt ceiling to more than a trillion dollars lasted 16 hours and 12 minutes. Huey P. Long, D-La., is next, for a June 1935 filibuster of 15 hours and 30 minutes in opposition to the extension of the National Industrial Recovery Act.

In this connection, special credit perhaps goes to Reed Smoot, R-Utah, who during a successful 1915 filibuster against President Woodrow Wilson's ship purchase bill spoke for 11 hours and 35 minutes without relief and without deviating from the subject.

Because the Senate has no germaneness rule, speakers do not always confine themselves to the subject under consideration. Senator Long in 1935 entertained his colleagues describing recipes for southern "potlikker," and Glen H. Taylor, D-Idaho, a former tent show performer, spent 8 hours and 30 minutes in 1947 expounding on fishing, baptism, Wall Street, and his children in an effort to delay a vote on overriding President Harry S. Truman's veto of the Taft-Hartley Act.

As a rule, a filibuster is more likely to be successful near the end of a session, when comparatively brief obstructionism can imperil all pending legislation. Before the adoption of the Twentieth (Lame-Duck) Amendment to the Constitution in 1933, Congress was required to meet annually in December. In an even-numbered year, following the election of its successor, Congress could remain in session until March 4 of the following year, when the term of the new Congress began. During this short, or lame duck, session—in which members who had been repudiated at the polls participated—filibusters were an almost routine occurrence. In midsession, a filibuster may be successful if urgent legislation is delayed or if the filibuster has a large number of senators participating.

A notable filibusterer in Senate history was Huey P. Long of Louisiana.

ANTIFILIBUSTER TECHNIQUES

Several techniques can be employed against the filibuster. The most spectacular, and probably least effective, is the use of prolonged sessions to break the strength of the obstructionists. A second technique is strict observance of Senate rules. A widely ignored rule provides that a speaker must stand, not sit or walk about. The rules also permit the presiding officer to take a senator "off his feet" for using unparliamentary language; require that business intervene between quorum calls; and prohibit the reading of speeches or other material by a clerk without Senate consent. Finally, a senator may be refused an opportunity to speak more than twice on a subject in any one day (a legislative day may spread over several calendar days if the Senate recesses instead of adjourns).

SENATE CLOTURE RULE

The Senate's ultimate check on the filibuster is the provision for cloture, or limitation on debate, contained in Rule XXII of its Standing Rules. The original Rule XXII was adopted in 1917 following a furor over the "talking to death" of a proposal by President Wilson for arming American merchant ships before the United States entered World War I. The new cloture rule required the votes of two-thirds of all of the senators present and voting to invoke cloture. In 1949, during a parliamentary skirmish preceding scheduled consid-

eration of a Fair Employment Practices Commission bill, the requirement was raised to two-thirds of the entire Senate membership.

A revision of the rule in 1959 provided for limitation of debate by a vote of two-thirds of the senators present and voting, two days after a cloture petition was submitted by sixteen senators. If cloture was adopted by the Senate, further debate was limited to one hour for each senator on the bill itself and on all amendments affecting it. No new amendments could be offered except by unanimous consent. Amendments that were not germane to the pending business and dilatory motions were out of order. The rule applied both to regular legislation and to motions to change the Standing Rules.

Rule XXII was revised significantly in 1975 by lowering the vote needed for cloture to three-fifths of the Senate membership (sixty, if there are no vacancies). That revision applied to any matter except proposed rules changes, for which the old requirement of a two-thirds majority of senators present and voting still applied. *(See box, Dilatory Tactics, p. 492; "Attempted and Successful Cloture Votes," p. 1116, in Reference Materials, Vol. II.)*

POSTCLOTURE CURBS

The 1975 revision succeeded in making it easier for a Senate majority to invoke cloture and thus cut off an extended debate mounted by a minority. But much of the revision's success relied on the willingness of the senators to abide by the spirit as well as the letter of the chamber's rules. When cloture was invoked on a particular measure, senators generally conceded defeat and proceeded to a vote without further delay.

But in 1976 James B. Allen, D-Ala., began violating this unwritten rule of conduct by using his mastery of parliamentary technique and the Senate's rules to eat up far more time than the one hour allotted him under the 1959 rules revision. He did so by capitalizing on a loophole that permitted unlimited postcloture quorum calls, parliamentary motions, and roll-call votes on amendments introduced before cloture was invoked.

The Senate closed this loophole in 1979 when it agreed to an absolute limit on postcloture delaying tactics. The rule provided that once cloture was invoked, a final vote had to be taken after no more than one hundred hours of debate. All time spent on quorum calls, roll-call votes, and other parliamentary procedures was to be included in that limit.

In 1986, as part of a resolution authorizing televising of floor proceedings, the Senate reduced from one hundred to thirty hours the time allowed for additional debate, procedural moves, and roll calls after cloture had been invoked.

1. Robert Luce, *Legislative Procedure: Parliamentary Practices and the Course of Business in the Framing of Statutes* (New York: Da Capo Press, 1972), 283.
2. George B. Galloway, *The Legislative Process in Congress* (New York: Crowell, 1953), 559–560.
3. Franklin L. Burdette, *Filibustering in the Senate* (New York: Russell & Russell, 1965), 14.

SENATE RULES ON DEBATE

The House must approve its rules at the beginning of each new Congress because its entire membership is elected anew every two years. But the Senate, which is considered a continuing body because only one-third of its membership is newly elected at a time, faces no such task. Its rules remain in force from Congress to Congress unless the Senate decides to change them. Many revisions of the Senate's rules have occurred since the first rules were adopted in 1789, but these revisions have been chiefly codifications of changes that had accumulated over a number of years.

Two such codifications occurred in the 1861–1901 period. The first, in 1868, increased the number of rules to an all-time high of fifty-three, reflecting the wartime strains. Another codification, in 1884, reduced the number of rules to forty. Although many changes were made in Senate's rules after 1884, another codification was not to take place for nearly one hundred years.

"Rules are never observed in this body; they are only made to be broken. We are a law unto ourselves," said Republican John J. Ingalls of Kansas in 1876.[20] His comment may help to explain why rules reform has not played as significant a role in the history of the Senate as it has in the House, though efforts to limit the Senate filibuster provide a notable exception. In the last half of the nineteenth century many proposals were introduced to curtail debate, either through use of the so-called previous question motion employed by the House or by some other means. Most of the proposals simply were ignored, but a few minor changes affecting debate were made.

In 1862 the Senate adopted a resolution stating that "in consideration in secret session of subjects relating to the rebellion, debate should be confined to the subject matter and limited to five minutes, except that five minutes be allowed any Member to explain or oppose a pertinent amendment." Adoption of this resolution was attributable to the exigencies of wartime. In later years it also became customary for the Senate, in the closing days of a session when the need for haste was great, to apply a five-minute limit on debate on appropriations bills.

In 1880 the Senate adopted the Anthony Rule named after its originator, Sen. Henry B. Anthony, R-R.I. The rule, which limited debate to five minutes for each senator unless objection was heard, was the most important limitation on debate the Senate had yet agreed to as a means of expediting business. The rule was so successful in speeding action on noncontroversial legislation that in 1880 it became part of the Standing Rules (Rule VIII). Any senator wishing fuller debate on an issue had only to object to consideration of the bill and it would be scheduled for debate.

Another change that helped to facilitate the business of the Senate was an 1875 decision that action on an amendment to an appropriation bill could be postponed without jeopardizing or affecting the status of the bill itself. This rule was so successful that its application later was extended to amendments to any bill being considered by the Senate.

Era of Reform: 1901–1921

The "Progressive Era" in American history began with movements in the 1880s and 1890s demanding economic reform. It gathered momentum and a radical democratic character after the turn of the century, but with the nation at war in 1914–1918, it gradually faded into the background.

The progressive program was foreshadowed in the platform of the Populist Party, which in 1892 polled more than a million votes for its presidential candidate, James B. Weaver. Though the party, centered in the agrarian Midwest and West, soon declined, the two major parties gradually adopted many of its programs. Under popular pressure, Congress enacted such early "progressive" legislation as civil service reform (1883), the Interstate Commerce Act (1887), the Sherman Antitrust Act (1890), conservation legislation (1891), and an income tax law (1894). But the income tax was invalidated by the Supreme Court, and the other measures were rendered ineffective by their vagueness, loopholes, court rulings, or unenthusiastic administration in the executive branch.

Finding themselves frustrated, and laying the blame on the alleged sinister influence of vested interests, reformers concluded that more democratic control of the government was necessary to secure the laws they sought. Accordingly, the reform movement increasingly concentrated on bringing about institutional changes such as direct election of senators, direct primaries, women's suffrage, and laws against corrupt election practices.

The power of the Senate declined during Theodore Roosevelt's presidency (1901–1909). Roosevelt was an aggressive national leader who took an active role in promoting progressive legislation. Though the House was under the highly centralized rule of Speaker Joseph G. Cannon, R-Ill., at this time, Roosevelt, through informal contacts with the House leadership, was able to advance his legislative program. Under Cannon the House often tried to exert its authority over the Senate. By 1910, however, House reformers were strong enough to break the power of the Speaker.

INSURGENT MOVEMENTS IN CONGRESS

Congress went along, though somewhat reluctantly, with Roosevelt's progressive program, passing such measures as the Hepburn Act, which strengthened the Interstate Commerce Commission, the pure food and drug laws, and a worker's compensation act. But Republican William Howard Taft, who was elected in 1908, failed to press Roosevelt's policies in the face of Old Guard opposition, and the defeat of major legislation sought by progressives in both parties led to the development of an insurgent movement among western Republicans in Congress.

In the House, Republican insurgents led the revolt against Speaker Cannon, while in the Senate the "Band of Six"—Robert M. La Follette of Wisconsin, Albert J. Beveridge of Indiana, Jonathan P. Dolliver and Albert B. Cummins of Iowa, Francis

Bristow of Kansas, and Edwin Clapp of Minnesota—challenged the Nelson W. Aldrich machine on a tariff bill that Aldrich sponsored. Though they failed to defeat the bill, enactment of this distinctly protectionist measure led to resounding Republican defeats in the congressional elections of 1910 and the formation of the Progressive (Bull Moose) Party, which nominated Roosevelt for president in 1912. The split between the Roosevelt and Taft wings of the Republican Party handed the Democrats an easy victory, and under President Woodrow Wilson the government entered a period of progressive rule that lasted through most of Wilson's first term.

PROGRESSIVE LEGISLATION UNDER WILSON

Wilson's early relations with Congress were harmonious. He returned to the pre-Jeffersonian practice of addressing Congress in person and frequently went to the president's room in the Capitol to confer with committees or individual members. Under his leadership a caucus of Democratic senators was proposed in 1913 to marshal party support for a tariff-cutting bill sponsored by Oscar W. Underwood of Alabama. Other legislative victories included the income tax (made valid by a constitutional amendment submitted to the states in 1909 and belatedly ratified on the eve of Wilson's inauguration), direct election of senators, the Clayton Antitrust Act, and the Federal Reserve and Federal Trade Commission acts.

This flow of progressive legislation ended when the United States entered World War I in 1917. During the war, Wilson assumed almost dictatorial powers, and criticism of his policies was silenced. But with the president's appeal for election of a Democratic Congress in the fall of 1918, the opposition surfaced. In the ensuing election, Republicans captured control of both houses of Congress, and the president went off to the Paris Peace Conference a rejected hero. Wilson's health broke in his futile efforts to enlist American support for the League of Nations, and the Republican Senate first emasculated and then rejected the Treaty of Versailles in which the League Covenant was embedded. A new period of congressional hegemony was at hand.

DIRECT ELECTION OF SENATORS

Direct election of senators was achieved in 1913 with the ratification of the Seventeenth Amendment to the Constitution. No longer would senators be elected by state legislators. The change was part of the Progressive era's movement toward more democratic control of government. Being less immediately dependent on popular sentiment than the House, the Senate did not move willingly to reform itself. Only strong pressure from the public, expressed through the House, the state governments, pressure groups, petitions, referenda, and other means, convinced the Senate that it must reform itself.

It was common in this period to attribute legislative disappointments to the dealings of vested interests operating behind the scenes. A Senate chosen by state legislatures, whose decisions often were made in closed-door party caucuses, could not easily escape suspicion. Moreover, the high-tariff views of the Senate served to link this body in the public mind with the great corporations that were widely accused of improper political influence.

Pressure for Reform

Andrew Johnson, who as president came within one vote of being removed from office at the hands of the Senate, was an early advocate of Senate election reform. Twice as a representative, once as a senator, and again as president in 1868, Johnson presented resolutions calling for direct election of senators. In the first eighty years of Congress, nine resolutions proposing a constitutional amendment to that effect were introduced in Congress. In the 1870s and 1880s the number increased significantly, but it was not until 1892 that a proposal for direct election of senators was approved in a House committee. In the next decade similar resolutions were passed five times by the House with only minor opposition. But the proposed amendment to the Constitution was not allowed to reach a vote in the Senate until 1911.

Petitions from farmers' associations and other organizations, particularly in the West, and party platforms in state elections pressured Congress until the national parties took up the issue. Direct election of senators was a plank in the Populist Party program at every election, beginning in 1892, and in the Democratic platform in each presidential election campaign from 1900 to 1912. Beginning with California and Iowa in 1894, state legislatures formally asked Congress to approve a constitutional amendment mandating direct election of the Senate. By 1905 the legislatures in thirty-one of the forty-five states had taken this step, many of them on several occasions. Referenda held in three states showed approval of the amendment by margins of 14–1 in California, 8–1 in Nevada, and 6–1 in Illinois. Support was strongest in the West and in north central states, where every legislature petitioned Congress at least once, and weakest in the Northeast, where only Pennsylvania's legislature voted to ask Congress in support of direct election.

In 1900 a majority of House members from every state except Maine and Connecticut voted for direct election of senators; the House approved the constitutional amendment by a vote of 240–15.

Still the Senate did not act. Because sitting senators were most reluctant to even consider a change in the method by which they were elected, supporters of direct elections turned to other tactics. Between 1902 and 1911 even the House did not vote on resolutions for direct election. But the states were finding ways to achieve the same results without a constitutional amendment.

The spread of direct primaries in many states in the 1890s led to voters expressing their choice for senator on the primary ballot. Although not legally binding on the legislatures, the popular choice was likely to be accepted. In the southern states, the primary winners soon were being "elected" by the one-party legislatures almost as a matter of course. But in states that did not

Before 1913 senators were selected by the legislatures of each state. Public disapproval of the role of party bosses and vested interests in this selection process ultimately lead to the passage of the Seventeenth Amendment, which mandated direct election of senators.

have a one-party system, and especially those states lacking clearly defined party lines, primaries were less effective in guaranteeing that the legislature would ratify the popular choice.

Oregon led the way in devising a system to guarantee popular choice of senators despite the Constitution's assignment of this function exclusively to the legislatures. In 1901 an Oregon law was enacted enabling voters to express their choice for senator in the same manner as they voted for governor, except that the vote for senator had no legal force. But the law specified that when the legislature assembled to elect a senator, "it shall be the duty of each house to count the votes and announce the candidate having the highest number, and thereupon the houses shall proceed to the election of a senator." In the first test of this system, the man who led the field with 37 percent of the popular vote for senator secured scant support from the legislators, who

scattered their votes among fourteen candidates. After a five-week deadlock, the legislature chose a man who had not received a single vote in the popular election.

Far from being discouraged at this mockery of "the people's choice," the people of Oregon in 1904 used their new initiative and referendum powers to petition for and approve a new law. Henceforth, each candidate for senator was to be nominated by petition and allowed to include on the petition a one-hundred-word statement of principles and on the ballot a twelve-word statement to be printed after the candidate's name. The legislators, who could not be denied their constitutional power to name senators, were permitted to include in their nomination petitions their signatures on either "Statement No. 1" or "Statement No. 2." The former pledged the signer always to vote "for that candidate for United States Senator in Congress who has received the highest number of the people's votes . . . without regard to my individual preference." The second statement was a pledge to regard the popular vote "as nothing more than a recommendation, which I shall be at liberty to wholly disregard." Meanwhile, citizen groups circulated pledges, which were widely subscribed to, that the signer would not support or vote for any candidate to the legislature who did not endorse "Statement No. 1."

The first legislature elected after enactment of this law promptly ratified "the people's choice" for senator. And two years later, when eighty-three of the ninety members of the legislature were Republicans, the popular choice—a Democrat—was elected. He received fifty-three votes, including the votes of all fifty-two legislators who had endorsed "Statement No. 1."

The "Oregon System" was adopted in other states in modified form. By December 1910 it was estimated that fourteen of the thirty senators about to be selected by state legislatures already had been designated by popular vote.

Constitutional Amendment

Gradually the mounting pressure for direct Senate elections began to be felt in the Senate. Some of the senators themselves were products of the new form of popular election. The leader in the fight for the Seventeenth Amendment, Sen. William E. Borah, R-Idaho, had entered the Senate through a popular mandate after an earlier defeat by the Idaho legislature.

By 1901 some state legislatures no longer were content simply to request Congress to submit a constitutional amendment to the states. They called for a convention to amend the Constitution, a method as yet untried in American history but obligatory once two-thirds of the states so petition Congress. Some senators, though they opposed popular election, feared that such a convention, like the original Constitutional Convention, might exceed its original mandate. Therefore, they agreed to vote for a specific amendment for direct election of senators that would be submitted to the states for ratification.

A resolution embodying the constitutional amendment was referred to the Senate Judiciary Committee, instead of to the more hostile Committee on Privileges and Elections that had considered it on previous occasions, and a favorable vote was at last obtained on January 1, 1911. However, as reported, the resolution contained a committee amendment, supported by southern senators, modifying Congress's power under Article I, Section 4, of the Constitution to control the states' regulation of Senate and House elections.

The committee amendment provoked such a storm of controversy that at times it overshadowed the popular election issue itself. The amendment would have transferred to the states exclusive power to regulate the election of senators, while leaving unchanged Congress's power to regulate House elections. Once on the floor, northern opposition prevailed, and the committee amendment was dropped on a vote of 50–37. But on February 28, 1911, the constitutional amendment itself failed, 54–33, to secure the necessary two-thirds majority support.

In a special session later that year, the House passed the direct election resolution again, by a 296–16 vote. But the House version was the same as that reported by the Senate committee, giving the states exclusive power to regulate Senate elections. The Senate, on a 45–44 roll call decided by Vice President James S. Sherman's tie-breaking vote, again rejected the committee amendment and this time adopted the original resolution by the required two-thirds majority, 64–24. A deadlock between the two houses was broken in the next session, and on May 13, 1912, the House, concurred in the Senate version, 238–39. By May 31, 1913, three-fourths of the states had ratified the amendment.

The immediate effects of the Seventeenth Amendment were difficult to assess. Even before its adoption, the direct primary movement had diminished the power of the legislatures. By 1913 three-fourths of the candidates for the Senate were being nominated in direct primaries. The terms of the senators in office at the time the amendment was ratified ended variously in 1915, 1917, and 1919, so the 66th Congress (1919–1921) was the first in which all members of the Senate were the products of direct election. "By that time," Senate historian George B. Galloway pointed out, "56 of the senators who owed their togas originally to state legislatures had been re-elected by the people, three had died, and 37 had disappeared from the scene either voluntarily or by popular verdict. In other words, more than half of those last chosen by legislative caucus were subsequently approved by the people."[21]

RESTRAINING THE FILIBUSTER

Senate filibusters continued apace in the early 1900s, and with a high degree of success. But mounting opposition to the practice led, in 1908, to efforts to curb obstructionism through new interpretations of the rules and, in 1917, to the Senate's first cloture rule.

Meanwhile, 1903 proved to be a vintage year for the filibuster. Democratic Senator Tillman of South Carolina, known as "Pitchfork Ben," filibustered against an appropriations bill until an item for payment of war claims to his state was restored. The item was put back in the bill after Tillman threatened to read Byron's "Childe Harold" and other poems into the record until his colleagues surrendered from boredom.

While Tillman resorted to "legislative blackmail," in the words of House Speaker Cannon, Republican Sen. Beveridge chose a different method. Beveridge, chairman of the Territories Committee and an opponent of statehood for Arizona and New Mexico, initially led a filibuster against an omnibus statehood bill. Then, taking advantage of a custom that no votes were taken on a measure in the absence of the chairman of the committee that had handled it, Beveridge hid for days in Washington and finally slipped away to Atlantic City. The bill ultimately was dropped.

In 1908 a bitter two-day filibuster against an emergency currency measure sponsored by Sen. Aldrich and Rep. Edward B. Vreeland, R-N.Y., brought the first significant steps to curb dilatory tactics. Wisconsin Republican Robert M. La Follette Sr., had held the floor for eighteen hours and twenty-three minutes, although he was interrupted by twenty-nine quorum calls and three roll calls on questions of order. La Follette fortified himself periodically with eggnogs from the Senate restaurant. According to one account, he rejected one of the eggnogs as doped, and it later was found to contain a fatal dose of ptomaine. However, no charge of deliberate poisoning was ever made. La Follette's filibuster was not matched until 1938, when Allen J. Ellender, D-La., mounted a filibuster against an antilynching bill that lasted off and on for twenty-nine days.

The filibusterers' cause finally was lost when Sen. Thomas P. Gore, D-Okla., who was blind, yielded the floor believing that Sen. William J. Stone, D-Mo., who was scheduled to relieve him, was in the chamber. But Stone had been called to the cloakroom, and Gore surrendered the floor. The bill then was approved on a hastily demanded roll call.

Three important curbs on obstructionism resulted from the 1908 filibuster. First, the chair could count a quorum if enough senators were present, even for a vote, whether or not they answered to a quorum call; second, debate did not count as intervening business for the purpose of deciding if another quorum call was in order; and third, senators could by enforcement of existing rules be prevented from speaking more than twice on the same subject in one day.

During a 1914 Republican filibuster against a rivers and harbors bill, the chair ruled that senators holding the floor could not yield for any purpose, even for a question, without unanimous consent. The Senate first tabled an appeal of this ruling on a 28–24 vote but reversed itself the next day. Thus the rule remained unchanged.

In 1915 a successful filibuster was organized against President Wilson's ship purchase bill. Republican Sen. Reed Smoot of Utah spoke for eleven hours and thirty-five minutes without relief and without deviating from the subject. After almost a month of delay, seven Democrats who thought the filibuster should give way to other important legislation joined the Republicans in moving that the bill be recommitted. But other Democrats supporting the bill then staged a five-day reverse fili-

A 1908 filibuster by insurgent Republican Robert M. La Follette of Wisconsin led to the first significant curbs on obstruction in the Senate.

buster until they regained control of the chamber. The Republican filibuster then was renewed. A Democratic motion to end debate was blocked, and the bill finally was dropped. As a result of the filibuster three important appropriation bills failed.

ELEVEN WILLFUL MEN

That episode produced expressions of public disgust, but it took one more great filibuster to force the Senate into action. The occasion came in 1917 when the Wilson administration's armed neutrality bill was talked to death by an eleven-man bloc in the closing days of the 64th Congress. Seventy-five senators who signed a statement supporting the bill asked that it be entered in the record "to establish that the Senate favors the legislation and would pass it, if a vote could be had." Not all of the obstruction came from the Republican side of the aisle. On the last day of the session, when it was clear that the bill was doomed, the Democrats staged their own filibuster to keep an outraged La Follette from being able to speak against the measure before crowded Senate galleries.

No sooner had the session ended than Wilson issued an angry statement: "The Senate of the United States is the only legislative body in the world which cannot act when its majority is ready for action. A little group of willful men, representing no opinion but their own, have rendered the great government of the United States helpless and contemptible." Wilson immediately called the Senate into special session and demanded that it amend its rules so that it could act and "save the country from disaster."[22]

The Senate yielded, and a conference of Republican and Democratic leaders hastily drew up the Senate's first cloture rule. After only six hours of debate, Rule XXII was adopted by the chamber March 8, 1917, by a vote of 76–3.

RULE XXII'S LIMITS ON DEBATE

The new rule provided for restricting further debate on any pending measure once a debate-limiting resolution was approved by two-thirds of senators present and voting (the vote on the resolution was to be held two days after a cloture motion had been signed by sixteen senators). After such a resolution was agreed to, further debate was limited to one hour for each senator on the bill itself and on all amendments and motions affecting it. No new amendments could be offered except by unanimous consent. Amendments that were not germane to the pending business, and amendments and motions clearly designed to delay action, were out of order.

During Senate debate on the proposed Rule XXII, an amendment was offered to authorize cloture by majority vote instead of a two-thirds vote. But opponents attacked the amendment as a breach of faith, and it was withdrawn before a vote could be taken. In 1918 the Senate rejected, 34–41, a proposal to allow use of the so-called previous question motion to limit debate during the war period.

For a time it looked as if the Senate would never make use of its new tool against obstructionism, but the interminable debates on the Treaty of Versailles in 1919 finally provided an occasion. The Senate adopted its first cloture motion November 15, 1919, on a 78–16 roll call, and four days later the treaty itself was brought to a vote after fifty-five days of debate.

PARTY LEADERSHIP

The system of party leadership that had evolved in the Senate at the end of the nineteenth century became institutionalized in the early years of the twentieth.

Both Republicans and Democrats for many years had elected chairmen of their party caucuses, but each party's caucus chairman was not necessarily the actual leader of his party in the Senate. Senators Allison and Gorman served as chairmen of their respective caucuses, but the position was not essential to their control. Aldrich, the most powerful member of the Senate until his retirement in 1911, never held any official position other than the chairmanship of the Senate Finance Committee.

With the departure of these dynamic leaders from the chamber, power was fragmented within the parties. It became common for both Republicans and Democrats to elect a different floor leader in each session, and the floor leadership did not necessarily correspond with the caucus chairmanship. Under these conditions party unity was hard to maintain.

Although historians quibble over when the Senate first formally designated majority and minority leaders, the positions were readily identifiable beginning in 1911. Party whips (assistant floor leaders) were added to the leadership structure in 1913 by the Democrats and in 1915 by the Republicans. From this period forward, the majority and minority leaders usually were the acknowledged spokespeople for their parties in the Senate. (*See Chapter 14, Party Leadership in Congress.*)

The importance of the leadership role was underscored in 1913 when progressive Democrats deposed conservative leader Sen. Thomas S. Martin (Va.) and engineered the election of Sen. John W. Kern (Ind.) as majority leader, even though Kern had served in the Senate only two years. The Steering Committee, appointed by Kern and dominated by progressives, made committee assignments to ensure that major committees would be sympathetic to the incoming Wilson administration's programs. Even seniority was ignored when necessary. The Steering Committee also recommended rules, later adopted by the caucus, that permitted a majority of committee members to call meetings, elect subcommittees, and appoint conferees. Thus party authority was augmented, and the power of committee chairmen curbed in a movement that somewhat paralleled the revolt against Cannonism in the House.

Both Senate parties at the turn of the century had replaced the title "caucus" with "conference," in formal recognition of the nonbinding nature of these party meetings. The Democratic Caucus in 1903 adopted a binding caucus rule, although there is no evidence that it ever was enforced. When Kern in 1913 proposed holding a binding caucus on the tariff bill, opposition was so vigorous that the idea had to be dropped. Nonetheless, Democratic senators during this period were under such strong pressure to support caucus decisions that the effect of a binding caucus was maintained.

Republican Stalemate: 1921–1933

After its victory over Woodrow Wilson on the League of Nations, the Senate was in no mood to submit to presidential leadership. The Republican majority expected to assume control of the government in the Republican administrations that followed Wilson, but after the House revamped its appropriations procedures in 1920, the lower chamber increasingly challenged Senate primacy.

Wilson's three Republican successors, faithful to the GOP doctrine of congressional independence, made little effort to direct Congress in legislative matters. Wilson's immediate successor, Warren G. Harding, promised before his election that he would take a hands-off approach with respect to lawmaking and that the Senate would "have something to say about the foreign relations, as the Constitution contemplates." Harding added

that he would "rather have the counsel of the Senate than all the political bosses in any party."[23]

Harding, who was an ex-senator, appeared before his former colleagues on several occasions. In an unprecedented move in 1921, he personally delivered his nominations for cabinet positions to the Senate. But he came to regret his promise not to intervene in legislative matters. When he appeared before the Senate in 1921 to urge a balanced budget, the Senate berated him for interfering in its business, and the House was offended that the issue had not been raised in that chamber, where money bills had to originate. Harding's subsequent halfhearted efforts to exert leadership were rebuffed by Congress, and his administration was tarnished by scandals that were exposed by Senate investigators after his death in 1923.

Harding's successor, Calvin Coolidge, was even less inclined to leadership than Harding had been. "I have never felt that it was my duty to attempt to coerce senators or representatives, or to make reprisals," Coolidge wrote. "The people sent them to Washington. I felt I had discharged my duty when I had done the best I could with them."[24] The Senate rejected Coolidge's nomination of Charles Beecher Warren as attorney general, the first rejection of a cabinet nomination since 1868, but in other respects it largely ignored the passive president.

More aggressive leadership was expected of Herbert Hoover, but he lacked political experience and, as a recent convert to Republicanism, was distrusted by many members of his party. Friction between the executive branch and the legislative branch thwarted his efforts to deal with the economic depression that engulfed the nation early in his one term in office.

If the presidents of the 1920s were unable to lead the nation, Congress itself was not much more successful. Although Republicans controlled the White House from 1921 to 1933, the House from 1919 to 1931, and the Senate from 1919 to 1933, the party solidarity that had characterized the McKinley-Roosevelt presidencies no longer existed. Throughout the 1920s a "progressive" farm bloc dominated by western Republicans held the balance of power in Congress, and the decade was marked by persistent deadlocks on major issues.

Meanwhile, significant internal changes took place in the Senate. A major consolidation of the committee system occurred in 1921, and exclusive authority over spending was returned to the Appropriations Committee in 1922. Ten years later in 1932 the Senate finally succeeded in winning House concurrence to the so-called lame-duck amendment, which altered the terms and sessions of Congress. But experience did not bear out the hope of Sen. George W. Norris, R-Neb., sponsor of the amendment, that it would end the filibusters that had plagued the Senate in the 1920s. Of the nine cloture votes taken during that decade, only three succeeded, and opponents of the filibuster continued to seek new ways to halt obstructionism.

REPUBLICAN INSURGENCY

Agriculture did not share in the prosperity of the 1920s, and efforts to relieve the farmers' plight led to a breakdown of party government and the development of legislative blocs representing sectional and economic interests. Efforts to enact agricultural relief legislation caused a split between eastern and western Republicans and the establishment of a powerful bipartisan farm bloc within Congress.

Insurgent Republicans, mostly from the Great Plains and Rocky Mountain areas, while usually keeping their formal ties to the Republican Party, cooperated with the Democrats on sectional economic legislation. Republican regulars in the House kept the upper hand for the most part. However, Republican control in the Senate often was only nominal. Insurgents frequently succeeded in blocking administration legislation but lacked the strength to carry their own alternatives. The divisions during the period extended to internal Senate matters.

The congressional elections of 1922 were a disaster for the regular Republicans. Though they retained control of both houses, the Republican margin declined from 169 to 15 in the House and from 22 to 6 in the Senate; there were 51 Republican senators, 43 Democrats, and 2 Farmer-Laborites.

And throughout the farm states progressive Republicans won over the regular party-backed candidates. When the 68th Congress convened in December 1923, the insurgents challenged the regulars' control.

The insurgent Republicans and the two Farmer-Labor senators from Minnesota accepted committee assignments from the Republicans but did not caucus with them. When the committee lists came to the floor, Senator La Follette led an effort to remove Sen. Albert B. Cummins of Iowa from the chairmanship of the Interstate Commerce Committee. A month-long deadlock ensued. La Follette was the second-ranking Republican member of the committee, but the regular Republicans, unable to elect Cummins, had no intention of letting La Follette succeed to the chairmanship. Finally, on the 32nd ballot the regulars threw their support to the committee's ranking Democrat, Ellison D. Smith, S.C., and Smith was elected chairman although he was of the minority party. Cummins continued as a member of the committee and also remained president pro tempore.

In 1924 La Follette ran for president under the Progressive banner, polling 16 percent of the popular vote but carrying only his state of Wisconsin. The Republicans gained five seats in the Senate, and party leaders felt strong enough to retaliate against the irregulars who had supported the Progressive ticket. The Republican Conference adopted a resolution stating that the disloyal senators "be not invited to future Republican conferences and be not named to fill any Republican vacancies on Senate committees." The irregulars were permitted to keep the committee assignments they then held, but in many instances they were placed at the bottom of the membership in seniority. In the Senate reorganization two years later, however, they were welcomed back into the Republican fold.

The Progressives continued to be a thorn in the side of the regular Republicans. In his last two years in office, President Hoover had to contend with a Democratic House in which the Republican Progressives regularly sided with the opposition.

The situation in the Senate was not much better. The Senate in the 72nd Congress consisted of forty-eight Republicans, forty-seven Democrats, and one Farmer-Labor member. Because some Progressive Republicans regularly voted with the Democrats, President Hoover advised Sen. James E. Watson of Indiana, the Republican leader, to let the Democrats organize the Senate "to convert their sabotage into responsibility." Hoover said he "could deal more constructively with the Democratic leaders if they held full responsibility in both houses, than with an opposition in the Senate conspiring in the cloakrooms to use every proposal of his for demagoguery."[25] But Watson, who wanted to be majority leader, and his Republican colleagues, many of whom wanted to retain their committee chairmanships, rejected Hoover's proposal.

CLOTURE IN PRACTICE

Early experience with the Senate cloture rule (Rule XXII) bore out the predictions of those who expected it to be used only sparingly. Between 1917, when the rule was adopted, and the end of the Hoover administration in 1933, the Senate took only eleven cloture votes, of which five occurred in one two-week period in 1927.

Four of the eleven votes were successful. In addition to ending a filibuster on the Treaty of Versailles in 1919, the Senate in 1926 ended a ten-day talkathon against the World Court Protocol by adopting cloture on a 68–26 vote, and in 1927 it voted cloture twice: on a branch banking bill, 65–18, and on a Prohibition reorganization measure, 55–27. The seven measures on which cloture failed included two tariff bills, a bill for development of the Lower Colorado River Basin, and a banking bill against which Huey P. Long, D-La., staged his first filibuster early in 1933. On this occasion cloture failed by a single vote. *(See "Attempted and Successful Cloture Votes," p. 1116, in Reference Materials, Vol. II.)*

Some issues were too sensitive for a cloture vote even to be attempted. In 1922 a group of southern senators mounted a filibuster against an antilynching bill. On behalf of the obstructionists, Senator Underwood of Alabama said:

It is perfectly apparent that you are not going to get an agreement to vote on this bill. . . . I want to say right now to the Senate that if the majority party insist on this procedure, they are not going to pass the bill and they are not going to do any other business. . . . We are going to transact no other business until we have an understanding about this bill. . . . We are willing to take the responsibility, and we are going to do it.[26]

The obstructionists were as good as their word: The Senate was unable to transact any legislative business until the antilynching bill was formally put aside on the last day of the session, but cloture was not attempted.

Similarly, in 1927 no attempt was made to end a filibuster against extending the life of a special political campaign investigating committee headed by Sen. James A. Reed, D-Mo. Although a majority of the Senate clearly favored its extension, a small group of senators succeeded in killing the committee,

CLOSED SESSIONS OF THE U.S. SENATE

Even after the Senate in 1795 opened its doors for regular legislative sessions, it continued to hold executive (closed to the public) sessions for the consideration of treaties and nominations. Under a rule adopted in 1800, all confidential documents sent by the president and all treaties laid before the Senate were to be kept secret until the injunction of secrecy was removed. In 1820 a similar restriction was adopted for nominations, and in 1844 penalties were provided for violations of these rules.

In practice, however, secrecy was difficult to maintain, and repeated efforts to abolish closed sessions finally bore fruit. In 1888 the Senate for the first time kept its doors open during the consideration of a treaty, and thereafter treaties increasingly came to be considered in open sessions. With few exceptions, nominations were considered in executive session until 1929, when the Senate, by a vote of 69–5, amended its rules to provide for open sessions for the consideration of all Senate business, including treaties and nominations, unless the Senate decides by majority vote to consider a particular matter in closed session.

Although treaties and nominations are no longer considered in secret sessions, the Senate goes into closed session occasionally, usually for the discussion of classified information. In such sessions, the public, the press, and most Senate aides are required to leave the chamber and galleries. Frequently, a censored transcript of the discussion is released later.

POSTWAR SECRET SESSIONS

From the end of World War II to the close of the 101st Congress in 1990, the Senate held thirty secret sessions:[1] April 11, 1963, to discuss classified information concerning missile defenses; July 14, 1966, to consider establishment of a special committee to oversee the activities of the Central Intelligence Agency; October 2, 1968, and again July 17, 1969, to consider classified material connected with the antiballistic missile program; December 15, 1969, to discuss U.S. military actions in Laos and Thailand; September 10 and December 18, 1970, to discuss legislative impasses; June 7, 1971, to discuss a report on American military and related activities in Laos; twice on May 2, 1972,[2] and once on May 4, 1972, to consider a request to print classified National Security Council documents in the *Congressional Record;* September 25, 1973, to debate the need for an accelerated Trident submarine program; June 10, 1974, to consider development of a new strategic missile system; June 4, 1975, again to discuss strategic missiles; November 20, 1975, to consider releasing a study on the Central Intelligence Agency and political assassinations; December 17 and 18, 1975, to consider U.S. activities in Angola; July 1, 1977, to consider sensitive information about the so-called neutron bomb; February 21 and 22, 1978, during debate on the then-pending Panama Canal treaties; May 15, 1978, to discuss the Carter administration's request to sell $4.8 billion worth of jet fighters to Israel, Egypt, and Saudi Arabia; September 21, 1979, to discuss classified data on a U.S. military exercise called "Nifty Nugget" that tested the military's readiness to mobilize for war; February 1, 1980, during debate on a military pay and benefits bill, to discuss personnel retention and recruitment problems in the military; May 4, 1982, on the defense capabilities of the United States and the Soviet Union; February 16, 1983, on the nominations of Richard R. Burt and Richard T. McCormack; February 1, 1984, on Soviet compliance with arms control agreements; April 26, 1984, on Nicaragua; June 12, 1984, on defense appropriations; October 7, 1988, on the impeachment of federal Judge Harry Claiborne; and March 29, 1988, on the Intermediate Nuclear Forces treaty.

1. *Source for dates:* United States Senate, Office of the Secretary, Historical Office.
2. Technically there were two separate secret meetings of the Senate on May 2, 1972, although the period of time between them was less than a minute.

---

which had exposed corruption in the 1926 election victories of Republicans Frank L. Smith, Ill., and William S. Vare, Pa., both former House members. Neither senator-elect was ever sworn in.

As it became apparent that Rule XXII was not an effective weapon against the filibuster, new curbs on obstruction were proposed. During the 1922 filibuster on the antilynching bill, Republican Whip Charles Curtis, R-Kan., asked the chair to follow the precedent of House Speaker Thomas Brackett Reed that, notwithstanding the absence of a specific rule on the question, dilatory motions could be ruled out of order under general parliamentary law. Such a precedent would have established a significant tool against obstruction, but Vice President Coolidge declined to make a ruling.

The next vice president, however, showed more resolve. When Charles G. Dawes made his inaugural address to the Senate in 1925, as president of the Senate, he coupled a scathing denunciation of the existing Senate rules with a call for new curbs on debate. Not content with attacking the Senate on its own turf, Dawes took his campaign to the country, where he encountered the rather surprising opposition of the American Federation of Labor (AFL). The Dawes scheme, said the AFL ominously, "emanates from the secret chambers of the predatory interests." Although Dawes aroused widespread public interest in the problem, the Senate in this period took no action on rules reform proposals.

THE LAME-DUCK AMENDMENT

One member of the Senate thought he saw a way to end the filibuster. Senator Norris, the progressive who earlier had led the House revolt against Speaker Cannon, proposed a constitutional amendment to eliminate the short, postelection sessions of Congress in which so many filibusters occurred.

Under the Constitution and existing law, a new Congress that was elected in November of an even-numbered year did not take office until March 4 of the following year and did not meet in its first regular session until December of that year, thirteen months after its election. Meanwhile, the old Congress regularly met in December following the election of its successor and remained in session until the new Congress began in March. This was known as the short session, in which "lame-duck" members who had been repudiated at the polls often determined the course of legislation. The fixed adjournment date was an invitation to filibuster because merely by talking long enough members could block action until the old Congress expired. It was hardly surprising that the short sessions seldom were productive.

Accordingly, Norris proposed a constitutional amendment abolishing the short session by starting the legislative and executive terms of office in January instead of March and providing that Congress should meet annually in January instead of December. The Senate approved the change six times before the House agreed to it in 1932.

The first Senate vote on the Norris amendment came early in 1923, during the short session of the 67th Congress. Approved by the Senate Agriculture Committee, of which Norris was chairman, the amendment was approved by the Senate February 13 by a vote of 63–6. In the House the amendment was reported by the Election Committee and approved by a majority of the Rules Committee, but the chairman of the Rules Committee, himself a lame duck, managed to keep the legislation from coming to the floor.

In 1924 the Norris amendment again was approved by the Senate, by a 63–7 vote, and again it was reported by the House Election Committee, but this time it was blocked in the Rules Committee. The same thing happened in 1926, when the Senate approved the amendment by a vote of 73–2.

The Norris amendment finally reached the House floor in 1928, after the Senate had approved it for a fourth time, 65–6. However, the House vote of 209–157 fell thirty-five short of the two-thirds required for approval under the Constitution. In the next Congress, the 71st, the Senate approved the Norris resolution for a fifth time, 64–9. The House adopted a different version, 290–93, and the measure died in a House-Senate conference committee.

Final action came in the 72nd Congress, with the Democrats now in control of the House. Early in 1932 the Senate adopted the Norris resolution for a sixth time, 63–7, and the House quickly approved it without amendment, 335–56. It became the Twentieth Amendment upon ratification early in 1933.

The amendment established January 3 of the year following a national election as the day on which the terms of senators and representative would begin and end, and January 20 as the day on which the president and vice president would take office. It provided also that Congress should meet annually on January 3 "unless they shall by law appoint a different day."

The second session of the 73rd Congress was the first to convene on the new date, January 3, 1934. And the first president to take office on January 20 was Franklin D. Roosevelt at the beginning of his second term in 1937. It quickly became apparent, however, that the amendment would not eliminate the filibuster, as Norris had hoped. The final sessions of the 73rd and 74th Congresses, the first to function under it, both ended in filibusters.

COMMITTEE REORGANIZATION

The Senate's standing committee system had expanded dramatically in the late nineteenth century, and by 1921 it was ripe for pruning. The twenty-five standing committees existing in 1853 had increased to forty-two by 1889, and in the next quarter-century this number almost doubled. Five select committees graduated to standing committee status in 1884, three more did so in 1896, and all of the remaining select committees were made standing committees in 1909. At the same time, nine new standing committees were created, followed by three more in 1913, bringing the total number on the eve of World War I to an all-time high of seventy-four.

The expansion of the committee system was in part a reflection of the increasing complexity of Senate business. But committees also provided welcome clerical services and office space for their chairmen in the days before such assistance was available to all members. Thus "sinecure committees" had a way of surviving long after any need for them had disappeared. Benefits did not go only to the party in power. In 1907 the Republican Party took sixty-one chairmanships but assigned ten others to the Democrats, who were in the minority, and several committees were established solely for the purpose of creating chairmanships.

When the 67th Congress convened in April 1921, the Senate effected a major consolidation of its committee system. The number of committees was cut to thirty-four, and a number of long-defunct bodies, such as the Committee on Revolutionary Claims, were abolished.

The committee system revision was initiated by the GOP Committee on Committees, which also proposed to increase the Republican margin on each of the major committees to reflect the 1920 gains in the Senate. To Democratic charges of "steamroller" tactics, committee chairman Frank B. Brandegee, R-Conn., replied: "Criticisms are purely professional. The Republicans are responsible to the country for legislation and must have control of committees. That's not tyranny; that's representative government—the rule of the majority."[27] The Republican proposal was adopted, 45–25, without substantial change.

A further modification of the committee structure occurred in 1922 when the Senate, following the lead of the House, restored exclusive spending power to the Appropriations Committee. (This authority had been taken away from the committee in 1899.) When each of the eight appropriation bills previously considered by a Senate legislative committee was taken up, three ad hoc members from the panel that previously considered the bill were allowed to serve on the Appropriations Committee. At the same time, Appropriations was deprived of its power to report amendments proposing new legislation.

The change in appropriations procedure was part of a larger

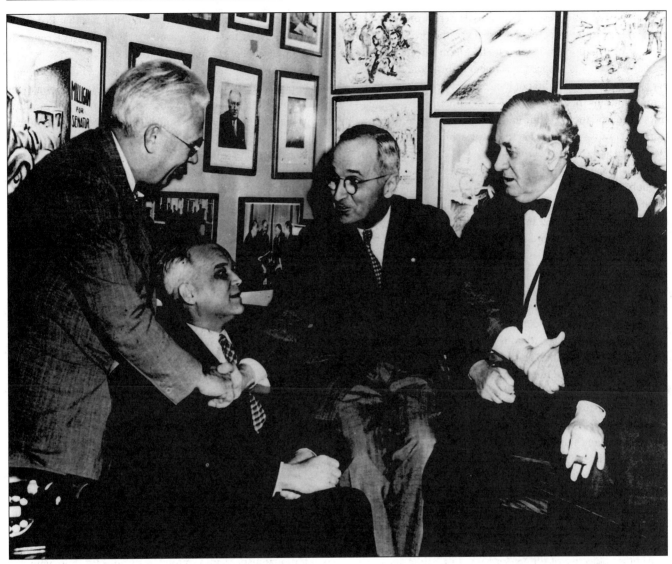

Harry S. Truman meets with Senate colleagues in the early 1940s.

effort to develop a more systematic approach to federal expenditures in both the executive and legislative branches. The 1921 Budget and Accounting Act set up the Bureau of the Budget (now the Office of Management and Budget) to assist the president in preparing an annual federal budget, including projections of surpluses or deficits. It also created the General Accounting Office to strengthen congressional surveillance over federal government spending.

Democratic Leaders: 1933–1945

The United States was in the depths of its greatest economic depression when Franklin D. Roosevelt entered the White House in 1933 with an overwhelming popular mandate. Along with the presidency, Democrats commanded large majorities in both houses of Congress.

Asked before his election what authority he would seek from Congress, Roosevelt had answered, "Plenty," which hardly con-

veyed the extent of the special powers Congress subsequently would give FDR to deal with the economic emergency.

Called into special session March 9, 1933, Congress in the next "hundred days" embarked on a whirlwind legislative course dictated by the president. On the first day of the special session, the House passed in thirty-eight minutes an emergency banking bill, the provisions of which at that point had not even been printed. The Senate took a little longer, two hours and fifteen minutes, but the measure was ready for the president's signature before the day ended.

In time, the pace slackened somewhat, but the pattern of action remained the same. The president would send a brief message to Congress, accompanied by a detailed draft of the legislation he proposed. Congress had been outraged when Lincoln dared to submit his own draft bills, but it readily accepted such action from Roosevelt.

Given the president's popularity and the prevailing economic conditions, opposition in Congress was futile and often nonexistent, and the president's proposals were promptly enacted. Along with the extensive powers given the president, Congress at the beginning of Roosevelt's first term agreed to various legislative shortcuts to speed enactment of his economic recovery program. Congress did not long remain a rubber stamp, but throughout his first term (1933–1937) Roosevelt was able—through negotiation, compromise, and the exercise of his patronage powers—to win enactment of a broad range of New Deal social and economic programs.

In his second term (1937–1941), a conservative coalition of Republicans and southern Democrats frequently opposed Roosevelt on domestic issues. The coalition thwarted his plan to enlarge the Supreme Court and blocked him on some legislative measures. During the president's unprecedented third term (1941–1945), wartime issues were paramount. As in previous wars, the executive branch assumed extraordinary powers, and Congress became increasingly restive under executive domination. As the war drew to a close, opposition to administration policies became more strident, and by the time Roosevelt died in April 1945—just three months into his fourth term—Congress was in open revolt. His successor, Harry S. Truman, won broad congressional support for his foreign policy measures, but his domestic programs were largely ignored.

In the mid-1940s, even before the war ended, Congress, in response to new international and domestic problems demanding attention and the corresponding increase in the volume of work before it, began to consider ways to modernize its machinery. The resulting Legislative Reorganization Act of 1946 was only partially successful in meeting those goals. For example, in the Senate no action was taken to strengthen the cloture rule, and filibusters were used repeatedly to defeat civil rights legislation.

Another objective of the 1946 act was to regain some of the initiative the legislative branch had lost to the White House under Roosevelt. Here, too, the results were mixed at best.

EXECUTIVE-SENATE RELATIONS

President Roosevelt, at times assisted by Vice President John Nance Garner (a former Speaker of the House), was his own legislative leader in the Senate during his first term. Senate Democratic leaders viewed themselves for the most part as the loyal lieutenants of the president. Senate rules and procedures precluded the close control exercised by party leaders in the House, but the Senate leadership was more experienced than its House counterpart, and it often was more successful in advancing the administration's legislative programs.

When Sen. Joseph T. Robinson, D-Ark., became Senate majority leader in 1933, he revived the Democratic Caucus and won from Democratic senators an agreement, adopted by a vote of 50–3, to make caucus decisions on administration bills binding by majority vote. A Democratic senator could vote against a binding caucus decision only if he told the caucus that a vote in favor of the caucus position would violate his conscience or campaign pledges. Although there is no evidence that Robinson ever made use of the binding caucus rule, nonbinding caucuses frequently were held to mobilize party support.

The Senate leadership had to contend with a higher percentage of potential dissidents than did House leaders, among them many southern Democrats who had risen to key committee chairmanships through the seniority system, but Roosevelt was remarkably successful at keeping them in line. Senate Agriculture Chairman Ellison D. Smith of South Carolina was not sympathetic to the proposed Agricultural Adjustment Act of 1933, but after the entire committee met with Roosevelt at the White House it reported the measure with this comment: "This bill . . . was drafted by the Department of Agriculture and is practically unchanged from the bill as presented to Congress. Considerable hearings were had by the Senate committee, but on account of the desire of the administration that no change be made the bill is presented to the Senate in practically an unchanged form."

As long as the Democrats maintained their tremendous margins in Congress and were able to curb the dissidents within their own party, the leadership could afford to ignore the minority, especially because many moderate and progressive Republicans supported early New Deal proposals. But by the beginning of Roosevelt's second term in 1937 these conditions no longer prevailed, and a conservative coalition of Republicans and southern Democrats emerged to oppose much of the New Deal.

FAILURE OF COURT PACKING PLAN

Stung by the Supreme Court's invalidation of major New Deal acts, Roosevelt sent to the Senate on February 5, 1937, a proposal to enlarge the Court by providing for the appointment of additional justices, up to a total of six, to assist those who did not retire within six months of reaching the age of seventy. For once, public opinion was not with the president, and Senate Republicans sat on their hands while conservative and New Deal Democrats fought over the issue. A series of Court decisions favorable to New Deal programs weakened support for the plan, as did the sudden death of Majority Leader Robinson on July 13.

In the leadership contest that followed, Alben W. Barkley, D-Ky., with perceived support from Roosevelt, defeated Pat Harrison, D-Miss., in a fight that brought to the surface the deep split in the Democrats' ranks. The fight also cost Roosevelt his Court plan, which was rejected shortly thereafter.

Struggling to reassert his party's leadership, Roosevelt decided to intervene in Democratic primaries in 1938 in an effort to block the renomination of conservative Democrats in Congress. The "purge" was notably unsuccessful. Senators on the purge list were triumphantly returned to office, and the president's only definite victory in the House was the unseating of Rep. John J. O'Connor, D-N.Y., chairman of the House Rules Committee. As a further embarrassment, Republicans gained seven Senate seats in the November election.

OPPOSITION TO ROOSEVELT

With the onset of World War II, opposition to Roosevelt was muted. Wartime expenditures and programs were freely voted. And the Senate's Special Committee to Investigate the National Defense Program, set up in 1941 under Truman's chairmanship, earned the president's gratitude by serving as a "friendly watchdog" over defense spending without embarrassing the administration. As the war went on, however, it became apparent that opposition to Roosevelt on domestic issues was rising.

The antagonism between Roosevelt and Congress broke into the open in February 1944 when the president, against the advice of party leaders, vetoed a revenue bill, the first veto of that type of measure by any president. Barkley denounced the action on the floor of the Senate as "a calculated and deliberate assault upon the legislative integrity of every member of Congress." Barkley said: "Other members of Congress may do as they please, but as for me I do not propose to take this unjustifiable assault lying down. . . . I dare say that, during the last seven years of tenure as majority leader, I have carried the flag over rougher territory than ever traversed by any previous majority leader. Sometimes I have carried it with little help from the other end of Pennsylvania Avenue." The following day Barkley resigned as floor leader, but he was immediately reelected by unanimous vote of the Democratic Caucus, and the bill was passed over Roosevelt's veto.

Roosevelt's problems with Congress increased after his election to a fourth term in 1944. His proposals for postwar economic and social legislation were ignored, and his nomination of Henry A. Wallace as secretary of commerce was confirmed only after the Reconstruction Finance Corporation had been removed from Commerce Department control. By the time of his death in April 1945, Roosevelt's support in Congress had disintegrated.

When Truman succeeded Roosevelt, many observers predicted a renewal of the happy relationship between Congress and the executive branch that had prevailed in the McKinley administration. Like McKinley, Truman was a former member of Congress who enjoyed the goodwill of his colleagues, but his honeymoon with Congress did not last long. Although he was markedly successful in pushing his foreign policy programs, the conservative coalition stood ready to oppose him on domestic issues. With the election of a Republican House and Senate in 1946, the Democrats' fourteen-year reign in Congress came to an end.

FILIBUSTERS AND CIVIL RIGHTS

Parliamentary obstruction continued to plague the Senate in the latter stages of the New Deal era, but no concerted efforts were made to put new curbs on the filibuster. The Senate took no cloture votes in the 73rd and 74th Congresses, but in the years 1938 through 1946 eight votes were taken to shut off debate on various issues—six of them on civil rights bills. None of the votes came close to the two-thirds majority needed to end a debate, and on four of the votes, all on civil rights, cloture did not win even a simple majority.

The most notorious filibusterer of the early New Deal period was Sen. Huey Long, who was at odds with the Roosevelt administration over patronage in Louisiana and other matters. Long staged his most famous filibuster in 1935, during debate on the proposed extension of the National Industrial Recovery Act. The "Kingfish," as he was called, spoke for fifteen and a half hours, filling eighty-five pages of the *Congressional Record* with remarks that ranged from commentaries on the Constitution to recipes for southern "potlikker," turnip greens, and corn bread. He said his intent in delaying action on the bill was "to save to the sovereign states their rights and prerogatives" and "to preserve the right and prerogative of the Senate as to the qualifications of important officers." Long conducted his last filibuster, against an emergency appropriation bill, less than two weeks before his assassination in the summer of 1935.

By the mid-1930s, the use of the filibuster had come to be associated with attempts to frustrate civil rights legislation. Southern senators might lack the votes to defeat civil rights measures outright, but they found they could accomplish the same objective through obstruction. Proponents of civil rights legislation could not muster the requisite majority to invoke cloture on these filibusters, even though they often apparently had the support of a Senate majority. Accordingly, the southerners used the filibuster to keep civil rights bills from coming to a vote. Anti-lynching bills were filibustered in 1935 and 1938 and anti–poll-tax measures in 1942, 1944, and 1946. Fair employment practices legislation was filibustered in 1946.

It was hard to keep senators in the chamber during these exhibitions. At one point during the 1942 anti–poll-tax debate a quorum could not be mustered, and the business of the Senate had to be halted. The sergeant at arms was directed to "request the attendance" of absent senators, and after a long delay forty-four senators, five short of a quorum, appeared. The sergeant at arms then was directed to "compel the attendance" of absent members. After more delay, he reported that forty-three senators were out of town and eight others were in Washington but could not be located. The exasperated Senate leadership then ordered him to "execute warrants of arrest" upon absent senators. The sergeant at arms was saved from this embarrassing duty by the timely appearance of five senators to complete a quorum. (The sergeant at arms had not always been so fortunate. During debate on the Lower Colorado River project in 1927, several infuriated senators were brought into the chamber under arrest warrants. And in 1988 deputies physically carried a senator, previously arrested in his office, onto the Senate floor.)

Although Rule XXII proved totally ineffectual against these southern filibusters, two minor curbs on delaying tactics were imposed during the period. The first dealt with the quorum call, a favorite obstructionist tool. During a 1935 filibuster by Huey Long, the chair ruled that a quorum call constituted business and that senators who yielded for a quorum call would lose the floor. Under this ruling a senator who yields twice for a quorum call while the same question is before the Senate can be denied the right to speak again on that question during the same legislative day. The second curb, contained in reorganization measures passed in 1939 and 1945, limited debate on government reorganization recommendations submitted by the executive branch.

REORGANIZATION ACT OF 1946

The tremendous expansion of the size and authority of the federal government under Roosevelt, especially through the plethora of New Deal programs and the wartime mobilization of the nation, led to a debate on reforming Congress. Proposals ranged from granting the president constitutional power to dissolve Congress to minor administrative changes in the way the legislative branch was run.

But two themes dominated the debate: the relationship between the organization of Congress and its increased workload, and relations between Congress and the executive branch. The feeling of many members was expressed by Rep. Jerry Voorhis, D-Calif. In urging the creation of a Joint Committee on the Organization of Congress, he said in January 1945, "In the midst of this war we have to grant executive power . . . of the most sweeping nature." But he wanted the groundwork laid so "that this Congress may perform its functions efficiently, effectively, and in accord with the needs of the people of this nation and so that it will become not merely an agency that says yes or no to executive proposals, but an agency capable of, and actually performing the function of, bringing forth its own constructive program [to benefit Americans]. Thus it will take its place and keep its place as an altogether coequal branch of our government."

In February 1945 Congress set up the Joint Committee on the Organization of Congress with Sen. Robert M. La Follette Jr., Prog.-Wis., as chairman, and Rep. A. S. Mike Monroney, D-Okla., as vice chairman. After extensive hearings the committee submitted a detailed report that formed the basis of the Legislative Reorganization Act of 1946. Passed with bipartisan support in both houses, the most important provisions of the act dealt with standing committees, committee staffs, and congressional review of the federal budget. *(See "1946 Legislative Reorganization Act," p. 63.)*

Postwar Era: 1947–1969

The election of a Republican Congress in 1946 marked the beginning of a period of divided government in which the White House and Congress often were in the hands of opposing political parties. From 1947 to 2001 Congress was controlled for twenty-eight of these years by the party in opposition to the president. For another six years control of the two chambers was divided between the parties.

Democratic President Truman faced a Republican House and Senate in the 80th Congress (1947–1949). His successor, Republican Dwight D. Eisenhower (1953–1961), dealt with a Republican Congress only in his first two years in office (1953–1955). The Democrats controlled Congress throughout the terms of Democrats John F. Kennedy (1961–1963) and Lyndon B. Johnson (1963–1969). In 1968 Republican Richard M. Nixon became the first president since Zachary Taylor to fail to win control of at least one house of the new Congress in his initial election. The House and Senate remained in Democratic hands for the duration of the Nixon and Ford presidencies (1969–1977). Democrats controlled Congress and the White House during the four years of Jimmy Carter's presidency (1977–1981). Republican Ronald Reagan had a Republican Senate for his first six years in office, although the House remained solidly Democratic. Democrats regained control of the Senate in 1986 and retained its grip on both chambers of Congress throughout Republican President George Bush's single term. President Bill Clinton enjoyed a Democratic Congress for only the first two years of his two-term tenure, which began in 1993.[28]

In only two postwar Congresses before 1980 did Republicans organize the Senate. In the 80th Congress (1947–1949) they enjoyed a 51–45 margin, but in the 83rd (1953–1955) their margin was so narrow that the death of Majority Leader Robert A. Taft, R-Ohio, gave a numerical majority to the Democrats. In the 82nd, 84th, and 85th Congresses, the Democratic margin of control was also razor-thin, but after the Democratic sweep in the 1958 elections the party had comfortable majorities in both houses.

The elections of 1958 proved to be a crucial turning point both for the Senate as an institution and for the Democratic majority. In addition to dramatically shifting the Democrat-Republican balance of power—from 49–47 to 64–34—the "class of 1958," as it was known, included a number of ambitious, mostly liberal, young Democrats who were to play key roles in the chamber for the next three decades. They included Robert C. Byrd of West Virginia, a future majority leader; Edmund S. Muskie of Maine, a future Democratic vice presidential candidate and secretary of state; Eugene McCarthy of Minnesota, whose 1968 presidential campaign helped force President Johnson out of office; and Philip A. Hart of Michigan, who was to earn the title of "conscience of the Senate." "They left their mark on this institution and on the nation," wrote Byrd, the last member of the class still in the Senate four decades later.[29]

BIPARTISAN FOREIGN POLICY

Throughout the postwar period the parties were often badly divided, and both Republican and Democratic presidents were forced to seek bipartisan support to win enactment of their programs. This proved to be easier on foreign than on domestic issues. Although Truman and the Republicans often were at loggerheads on domestic legislation, Sen. Arthur H. Vandenberg, R-Mich., led his once-isolationist party colleagues into a new bipartisan foreign policy in cooperation with the Democratic administration.

President Eisenhower often received more support from

Democrats than from members of his own party, particularly in the early years of his administration on foreign policy issues. Partisanship increased as the 1960 elections approached, and many domestic bills were not enacted.

President Kennedy's relations with Congress were far from ideal, although the Senate generally was more responsive to his proposals than was the House. Much of Kennedy's program was enacted after Johnson succeeded him in November 1963. Johnson won spectacular legislative victories in 1965–1966, but with the escalation of the war in Vietnam and increasing civil and economic disorders at home he lost his influence over Congress and was forced into retirement in 1969. During the Nixon administration, Congress and the White House usually were in conflict.

In the years following World War II, the Senate—and Congress as a whole—was preoccupied with the problem of preserving for itself a viable role in the American system of government. The rapid expansion of the power of the executive branch in the mid-twentieth century had seriously weakened legislative authority, but at the same time the volume and complexity of legislative business continued to mount. Congress as an institution suffered more and more public disfavor. In an effort to improve their public image, both chambers in 1968 adopted codes of ethics and rules requiring limited financial disclosures. But sensitive internal matters, such as the seniority system and limiting Senate debates, remained vexing problems.

DEMOCRATIC LEADERS

After World War II Democratic leadership in the Senate was relatively stable. Barkley remained majority leader from 1937 to 1947; he then served as minority leader until his resignation in 1949 to become Truman's vice president. The Democrats then had two majority leaders in as many Congresses: Scott W. Lucas of Illinois in the 81st and Ernest W. McFarland of Arizona in the 82nd, both of whom lost their Senate seats after two years in the leadership post.

When the 83rd Congress met in January 1953, with the Republicans in control, the Democrats chose as their minority leader Lyndon B. Johnson of Texas, who had served only four years in the Senate. Johnson, a member of the House from 1937 to 1949, was close to House Speaker Sam Rayburn, D-Texas, and had the backing of powerful Senate conservatives, notably Robert S. Kerr, D-Okla., and Richard B. Russell, D-Ga., but he promptly built bridges to the liberal Democrats in the Senate in an effort to heal the deep liberal-conservative split within the party. Johnson soon became one of the most powerful leaders in Senate history, serving as minority leader in 1953–1954 and as majority leader from 1955 until his resignation to become Kennedy's vice president in 1961.

As a leader, Johnson was noted for his powers of persuasion and his manipulative skills. He revitalized the Senate Democratic Policy Committee, saw to it that liberals won seats on both that panel and on the Steering Committee (the party's

President Lyndon B. Johnson meets with Senate Minority Leader Everett Dirksen in the Oval Office. Johnson also served as majority leader in the Senate from 1955 to 1961.

Committee on Committees), and modified the seniority system to assure freshman senators at least one major committee assignment, a practice later adopted by the Republicans as well. On the floor, efficiency was promoted through the use of such devices as unanimous consent agreements, simplified quorum calls, and night sessions. Through an active intelligence operation headed by Robert G. "Bobby" Baker, secretary to the Senate Democrats, Johnson kept himself informed about the views and positions of the Senate membership. He also was adept at rounding up votes for compromises acceptable to both parties. A system of rewards and punishments supplemented the famous "Johnson Treatment."

Russell B. Long, D-La., himself no mean practitioner of the Senate's inner ways, many years later described Johnson this way: "He was a tremendous salesman. He had a way of putting his attention and his warm smile, and his persuasive ways on the person that he chose to persuade, and he could be the most effective person I have ever seen in that respect, in selling his point of view and selling himself. Sometimes, perhaps, he got so enthused in what he was selling that he oversold himself on what he was trying to do."[30]

An apostle of "moderation" and "consensus government," Johnson supported the Eisenhower administration on many major policies and frequently solicited Republican support in the Senate. Such was his skill that in 1957 he was able to bring about passage of the first civil rights bill since Reconstruction without a filibuster and without splitting the Democratic Party.

Johnson's successor as majority leader was Mike Mansfield, D-Mont. Mansfield had served as party whip under Johnson, but his permissive style of leadership was in sharp contrast to the Johnson method. Mansfield held the respect of his colleagues, but he shied away from the aggressive approach, and under him the Johnson style gave way to a collegial leadership pattern in which the Policy Committee and the legislative committees played commanding roles.

Mansfield was called "the gentle persuader" because he felt that each senator should conduct his affairs with minimal pressure from the leadership. Despite his reticence on the national stage, Mansfield was a strong defender of Senate prerogatives during the Johnson and Nixon administrations, and he differed openly with Democrat Johnson on the Vietnam War.

Mansfield retired at the end of his term in January 1977. As of 1999, his sixteen-year tenure (1961–1977) as majority leader was the longest in Senate history.

REPUBLICAN LEADERS

Party authority on the Republican side was less concentrated than in the Democratic Party during the postwar period. Robert Taft had been the de facto Republican power in the Senate since the early 1940s. He had been the chairman of the Policy Committee since it was created in 1947, but he did not feel it necessary to assume the floor leadership of his party until the Eisenhower administration took office in 1953.

After Taft's death in July 1953, the majority leadership went to William F. Knowland of California, a conservative who frequently split with the Eisenhower administration, for the remainder of the 83rd Congress. During the 1950s H. Styles Bridges of New Hampshire also spoke for Senate Republicans as chairman of the Policy Committee.

Knowland, who became minority leader after Democrats regained control of the Senate in the 84th Congress, was succeeded in 1959 by Everett McKinley Dirksen of Illinois, one of the most colorful party leaders in recent history. His style, noted one observer, was "one of remaining vague on an issue, or taking an initial position from which he could negotiate: bargaining with the majority party, the president and his own colleagues, and eventually accepting a compromise."[31]

When Dirksen died in 1969, he was succeeded as minority leader by Hugh Scott of Pennsylvania, a liberal Republican who sometimes found it difficult to serve as spokesperson for the Nixon and Ford administrations.

EFFORTS TO CHANGE RULE XXII

With demands increasing in the 1950s and 1960s for enactment of civil rights legislation, liberals in the Senate made persistent, but largely unsuccessful, efforts to revise the cloture rule to make it easier to cut off filibusters. A change in Rule XXII in effect between 1949 and 1959 made it more difficult to invoke cloture.

Originally, Rule XXII required a vote of two-thirds of the senators present and voting to invoke cloture. However, a series of rulings and precedents over the years rendered Rule XXII virtually inoperative by holding that it could not be applied to debate on procedural questions. Because of this, President Pro Tempore Vandenberg ruled in 1948, during a filibuster against an attempt to bring up an anti–poll-tax bill, that cloture could not be used against debate on a motion to proceed to consideration of a bill. In making his ruling, Vandenberg conceded that "in the final analysis, the Senate has no effective cloture rule at all."

Rule Tightened in 1950s

In 1949 the Truman administration, desiring to clear the way for a broad civil rights program, backed a change in the cloture rule. After a long and bitter floor fight, the Senate adopted a proposal, backed by conservative Republicans and southern Democrats, that was more restrictive than the rule it replaced. The new rule required the votes of two-thirds of the entire Senate membership (instead of two-thirds of those present and voting) to invoke cloture, but the modification allowed cloture to operate on any pending business or motion with the exception of debate on motions to change the Senate rules themselves, on which Rule XXII previously had applied.

Given that under the new interpretation cloture could not be used to cut off a filibuster against a change in the rules, and because any attempt to change Rule XXII while operating under this rule appeared hopeless, Senate liberals devised a new approach. Senate rules always had continued from one Congress to the next in accordance with the theory that the Senate was a continuing body, but liberals now challenged this concept, arguing that the Senate had a right to adopt new rules by a simple majority vote at the beginning of a new Congress.

Nixon Ruling

Accordingly, in 1953 and 1957, at the opening of the 83rd and 85th Congresses, respectively, Sen. Clinton P. Anderson, D-N.M., made a motion that the Senate consider the adoption of new rules. On both occasions his motion was tabled, but during the 1957 debate Vice President Nixon offered a significant "advisory opinion" on how the Senate could proceed to change its rules. Citing the section of the Constitution providing that "each house may determine the rules of its proceedings," Nixon said he thought the Senate could adopt new rules "under whatever procedures the majority of the Senate approves."

Although each incoming Senate traditionally had operated under the existing rules, Nixon said it was his opinion that the Senate could not be bound by any previous rule "which denies the membership of the Senate the power to exercise its constitutional right to make its own rules." In this context, he said he regarded as unconstitutional the section in Rule XXII banning any limitation of debate on proposals to change the Senate's rules. The vice president explained that he was stating his personal opinion and that the question of constitutionality of the rule could be decided only by the Senate itself. The Senate did not vote on the question.

1959 Modification

A modest revision of Rule XXII was accomplished in 1959. Senate liberals hoped to make it possible to invoke cloture by a simple majority or by a three-fifths vote, but they were defeated in their efforts to bring about such a substantial change. Instead, a bipartisan leadership group engineered a slight revision of the rule that the southern bloc opposed but did not fight. The change, adopted by a 72–22 roll call, basically was drafted and put through by Lyndon Johnson, who seized the initiative from the liberals.

The revision permitted cloture to be invoked by two-thirds of those present and voting (instead of requiring two-thirds of the full membership as the 1949 rule had required), and it also applied to debate on motions to change the Senate's rules. But at the same time the Senate added a new provision to Rule XXXII (currently, section two of Rule V), dealing with the continuation of Senate business from one session of Congress to another. The new language stated: "The rules of the Senate shall continue from one Congress to the next unless they are changed as provided in these rules." That language buttressed the position of those who maintained that the Senate was a continuing body, but liberal opponents of the filibuster never conceded the point.

Passage of Civil Rights Acts

During the 1960s cloture votes were taken with increasing frequency. Four of twenty-three votes taken in this period were successful. In 1962 the Senate voted 63–27 to shut off a liberal fil-

Strom Thurmond of South Carolina set a record for the longest speech in Senate history during a 1957 filibuster on civil rights legislation.

ibuster against the administration's communications satellite bill. This was the first successful cloture vote since 1927 and only the fifth since the adoption of Rule XXII in 1917. In 1964 the Senate for the first time in its history invoked cloture, by a 71–29 vote, on a southern filibuster against a civil rights bill. This was followed by successful cloture votes on two other civil rights measures: the Voting Rights Act of 1965 and, on the fourth try, the historic open housing bill of 1968.

The defeat of the southern filibuster against the 1964 measure was a historic moment both in the movement for civil rights and in the development of the Senate. But the victory came only after a prodigious, seventy-five-day battle that riveted the attention of the nation. Civil rights forces were divided on strategy when the struggle began. President Johnson, seeking to push through a measure his slain predecessor had been unable to achieve, wanted to try to wear out his southern opponents by enforcing rules limiting each senator to two speeches a day and keeping the Senate in session continuously. But Mansfield and Hubert H. Humphrey, D-Minn., the floor manager of the bill, decided to focus their efforts on getting a two-thirds majority for cloture. With Dirksen's aid, they finally did. A dramatic incident during the crucial vote came when Clair Engle, D-Calif., who was terminally ill with cancer, entered the chamber. Too weak to speak, he managed to raise his left arm and nod his head to indicate an "aye" vote, thus adding to the thin margin of victory. A month later, he was dead.

Humphrey Ruling Reversed

The discovery that it was possible to impose cloture on civil rights bills under the existing rule took some of the steam out of the liberals' efforts to reform Rule XXII. In 1969 the liberals' strategy focused on obtaining a ruling from Humphrey, by then the vice president and near the end of his term of office, that at the start of a new Congress a simple majority could invoke cloture against filibusters on proposed changes in the Senate rules. After a cloture motion was filed on a liberal proposal to reduce the requirement for cloture from two-thirds to three-fifths of those present and voting, Humphrey announced, in answer to a parliamentary inquiry, that if a majority, but less than two-thirds, of those present and voting voted for cloture he would rule that the majority prevailed. He said that such a ruling, because it could be appealed by the Senate, would enable the Senate to decide the constitutional issue by a simple majority vote, without debate. Humphrey added that if he held that the cloture motion had failed because of the lack of a two-thirds vote, he would be inhibiting the Senate from deciding the constitutional question.

In explaining the ruling he proposed to make, Humphrey said: "On a par with the right of the Senate to determine its rules, though perhaps not set forth so specifically in the Constitution, is the right of the Senate, a simple majority of the Senate, to decide constitutional questions."

When the cloture motion came to a vote January 16, 1969, a slim majority (51–47) voted for it, and Humphrey ruled that debate would proceed under the limitations in Rule XXII. Opponents of the rules change immediately appealed his decision, and Humphrey's ruling was overturned, 53–45. The vote on the appeal meant that cloture was not invoked, thus leaving Senate opponents of changing Rule XXII free to continue their filibuster. Proponents of the change did not have enough support to limit debate through a two-thirds vote, so they ended their efforts in that Congress. (The real breakthrough for senators seeking a change in Rule XXII would not come until 1975.)

INTEGRITY OF THE SENATE

To much of the American public the Senate did not present a favorable image in the years following World War II. It often seemed unable, by virtue of its antiquated procedures, to do the work the public expected it to do, and the integrity of its personnel frequently came under attack. The Senate approached its image problem in its own way and in its own time.

The McCarthy Investigations

From 1950 until 1954 Sen. Joseph R. McCarthy, R-Wis., was by all odds the most controversial member of the Senate. McCarthy's career as a communist-hunter began with a speech in Wheeling, West Virginia, in February 1950 in which he charged that 205 communists were working in the State Department with the knowledge of the secretary of state. From that time until his formal censure by the Senate in 1954, McCarthy and his freewheeling accusations of communist sympathies among high- and low-placed government officials, former officials, and private citizens absorbed much of the public's attention.

The phenomenon of "McCarthyism" had a major impact on the psychological climate of the early 1950s. Taking over the chairmanship of the Senate Government Operations Committee in 1953, McCarthy investigated the State Department, the Voice of America, the Department of the Army, and other agencies. An opinion-stifling climate of fear throughout the country was said to be one of the results of his probes.

The first Republican to attack McCarthy's tactics was Sen. Margaret Chase Smith, R-Maine. In June 1950 she startled her colleagues with these words: "I do not like the way the Senate has been made a rendezvous for vilification, for selfish political gain at the sacrifice of individual reputations and national unity. I am not proud of the way we smear outsiders from the floor of the Senate. . . . I do not want to see the Party ride to political victory on the Four Horsemen of Calumny—fear, ignorance, bigotry and smear." For several years McCarthy's colleagues showed no disposition to tangle with him. But the Army-McCarthy hearings, televised in the spring of 1954, led finally to his censure by the Senate in a special session held after the midterm election of 1954.

McCarthy was censured, by a vote of 67–22, not for his "habitual contempt of people," as Sen. Ralph E. Flanders, R-Vt., originally had proposed, but for contemptuous treatment of the Senate itself—for his failure to cooperate with the Subcommittee on Privileges and Elections in 1952 and for his abuse of the select committee that had considered the censure charges against him. The censure resolution asserted that McCarthy had "acted contrary to senatorial ethics and tended to bring the Senate into dishonor and disrepute, to obstruct the constitutional processes of the Senate, and to impair its dignity. And such conduct is hereby condemned."

McCarthy remained in the Senate until his death in 1957, but he lost his committee and subcommittee chairmanships when the Democrats took control of Congress in 1955, and his activities no longer attracted much attention in the Senate, the press, or elsewhere.

Meanwhile, alleged excesses in treatment of witnesses by congressional committees led in 1954 to an extensive search for a "fair-play" rule to govern congressional investigations. Most of the criticism was directed at McCarthy's Permanent Investigations Subcommittee and at the House Un-American Activities Committee. In 1955 the House amended its rules to provide a minimum standard of conduct for House committees. The Senate adopted no general rules on the subject, but the Permanent Investigations Subcommittee, under its new chairman, John L. McClellan, D-Ark., adopted new safeguards for the protection of witnesses.

Bobby Baker Scandal

In 1963 the Senate was shaken by charges that Robert G. "Bobby" Baker had used his position as secretary to the Senate majority to promote outside business interests. Baker, who served as secretary from 1955 until his resignation under fire in August 1963, was no ordinary Senate functionary. Exposure of his numerous "improprieties" led to criticism of the Senate as a whole and prompted a review of congressional ethics.

A protégé of Lyndon B. Johnson, to whom the case was particularly embarrassing, Baker had access to leadership councils and was known as the Senate's "most powerful employee." He headed Johnson's intelligence network in the Senate and was celebrated for his ability to forecast the outcome of close votes. Johnson once hailed Baker's "tremendous fund of knowledge about the Senate, which is almost appalling in one so young."

In the wake of disclosures about Baker's wide-ranging business ventures, the Senate instructed its Rules and Administration Committee to investigate his activities from the standpoint of congressional ethics. The committee's Democratic majority, in reports issued in 1964 and 1965, accused Baker of "many gross improprieties" but cited no violations of law. Committee Republicans charged that the investigation was incomplete and a "whitewash." Both Republicans and Democrats called for rules requiring financial disclosure statements by members of Congress and their employees.

Baker ultimately was convicted in court and imprisoned for income tax evasion, theft, and conspiracy to defraud the government. Meanwhile, largely because of embarrassments caused by the Baker scandal, the Senate in 1964 created a Select Committee on Standards and Conduct to investigate allegations of improper conduct by senators and Senate staff, to recommend disciplinary action where relevant, and to draw up a code of ethical conduct. The House established a similar committee in 1967.

Dodd Investigation

The select committee's first investigation was implemented in 1966. It involved charges by syndicated columnists Drew Pearson and Jack Anderson that Sen. Thomas J. Dodd, D-Conn., had misused political campaign contributions and had committed other offenses. The committee in April 1967 recommended that the Senate censure Dodd for misuse of political funds and for double-billing for official and private travel. The Senate on June 23 censured Dodd on the first charge by a 92–5 roll-call vote but refused, on a 45–51 vote, to censure him on the second charge. The action marked the seventh time in its history that the Senate had censured one of its members. After the vote, the issue was closed, and Dodd continued to serve in the Senate until he was defeated for reelection in 1970.

ADOPTION OF ETHICS CODE

Concern over conflicts of interest at all levels of government had been rising since World War II, but Congress showed no inclination to adopt self-policing measures. Pressure generated by the Baker and Dodd cases in the Senate and by investigations of the activities of Rep. Adam Clayton Powell Jr., D-N.Y., in the House were largely responsible for the adoption of limited financial disclosure rules in both chambers in 1968.

In the Senate, a code of conduct proposed by the Select Committee on Standards and Conduct was adopted without substantial change on March 22, 1968, by a 67–1 vote. Included were provisions to regulate the outside employment of Senate employees, to require a full accounting of campaign contributions and restrict the uses to which they could be put, and to require senators and top employees to file detailed financial reports each year. However, these reports were to be made available only to the select committee. The only public accounting required was of campaign contributions of $50 or more and honoraria of $300 or more. The Senate rejected, 40–44, a proposal for full public disclosure of members' finances. The proposal had been pressed by Sen. Joseph S. Clark, D-Pa., who was a persistent advocate of congressional reform.

The code of conduct was embodied in four additions to the Senate Rules:

Outside Employment

Senate officers and employees were prohibited from engaging in any other employment or paid activity that was inconsistent with their official Senate duties. Employees were required to report any outside employment to their supervisors, who were required to monitor their employees' outside activities to prevent any conflicts of interest.

Campaign Contributions

Senators and declared candidates for the Senate were required to maintain a full accounting of the sources and amounts of all contributions to their campaigns. Senators and candidates were required to give their express approval to all fund-raising efforts conducted on their behalf, and campaign funds were to be limited to a candidate's nomination and election expenses and to pay for "the reasonable expenses," past or future, of the candidate's Senate office.

Political Fund-Raising

Senate staff members generally were prohibited from receiving, soliciting, or distributing funds collected in connection with any election campaign for the Senate or any other federal office. Exempted from the rule was any aide specifically designated by a senator to help raise campaign funds. The rule required senators to file the names of such designated aides with the secretary of the Senate, and such information was to be available to the public.

Financial Disclosure

Senators, declared candidates for the Senate, and Senate employees earning more than $15,000 a year were required to file by May 15 each year two financial disclosure reports, one to remain sealed and the other to be available for public inspection.

The sealed report was to contain a copy of the filer's U.S. income tax returns and a detailed disclosure of his financial interests, including major business interests, holdings, liabilities, legal fees of $1,000 or more, and gifts exceeding $50 in value. This report was to remain sealed in the custody of the U.S. comptroller general for a period of seven years, after which it was to be returned. The Select Committee on Standards and Conduct could examine the contents of the sealed report only if a majority of the committee's members voted to do so as part of an investigation.

The public report, to be filed with the secretary of the Senate, was to list all campaign contributions received in the previous year and the amount, value, and source of any honorarium of $300 or more.

The adoption of the 1968 code of conduct quieted for a time the public's uneasiness over ethical standards in the Senate. But in the following decade, the Watergate scandal was to cause the 1968 rules to be superseded by a more restrictive ethics code, more detailed public financial disclosure requirements, and more rigorous reporting of campaign finances.

SENATE-EXECUTIVE RIVALRY

One of the principal purposes of the Legislative Reorganization Act of 1946 was to help Congress hold its own against the rapidly expanding power of the executive branch. In this it was only partly successful. By the end of World War II the legislative initiative had shifted, apparently irretrievably, from Congress to the president, and during the postwar era Congress was for the most part concerned with preserving its powers to approve, revise, or reject presidential programs.

In those years the Senate's sense of itself was frequently offended by what it viewed as presidential encroachments on its constitutional functions. In 1954 the Senate came within one vote of approving a proposed constitutional amendment—the so-called Bricker Amendment—to restrict the president's power to negotiate treaties and other international agreements. Other conflicts arose over the spending power, the war power, and to a lesser extent, the appointment power. Frequently the Senate was in contention with the House as well as with the executive branch.

DISPUTES OVER THE SPENDING POWER

In the 1946 Legislative Reorganization Act Congress tried to assert new and meaningful control over the budget process through the creation of a congressionally drafted budget for the federal government that would be separate from the funding recommendations submitted by the executive branch. After three unsuccessful attempts to use this device, it was abandoned as an unqualified failure.

In 1947 the Joint Committee on the Legislative Budget, composed of members of the House Ways and Means and Appropriations committees and the Senate Finance and Appropriations committees, approved a resolution setting ceilings on federal appropriations and expenditures that were substantially lower than the amounts projected in President Truman's budget. The House approved the ceilings, but the Senate raised them and insisted that an expected budget surplus be applied to debt retirement rather than to a reduction in taxes as House leaders proposed. A stalemate resulted, and that year's congressional budget initiative died in conference.

In 1948 both houses reached agreement on a budget resolution, but Congress then went on to appropriate $6 billion more than the agreed-upon ceiling in the resolution. In 1949 the process broke down entirely when the deadline for adoption of a budget resolution was moved from February 15 to May 1. By that date eleven of the annual appropriation bills for government departments had been passed by the House and nine by the Senate, and the budget resolution never was approved.

Failure of the budget concept in the reorganization act prompted a serious effort in Congress in 1950 to combine the numerous separate appropriation bills into one omnibus measure. That year, Congress approved an omnibus measure about two months earlier than it had passed the last of the separate funding measures in 1949. In addition, the appropriations total was about $2.3 billion below President Truman's combined budget requests. Clarence A. Cannon, D-Mo., chairman of the House Appropriations Committee hailed the omnibus approach as "the most practical and efficient method of handling the annual budget."

Despite Cannon's support for the new approach, the House Appropriations Committee in 1951 voted 31–18 to return to the traditional method of considering in separate bills the appropriation for each government department. One reason was that the omnibus approach had undercut the authority of the full committee's subcommittees and their chairmen. (Under the traditional procedure, each subcommittee considered a different appropriation bill and was responsible for most of the funding decisions for an entire department or departments.) After the vote, Cannon charged that "every predatory lobbyist, every pressure group seeking to get its hands into the U.S. Treasury, every bureaucrat seeking to extend his empire downtown is opposed to the consolidated bill."[32]

The Senate in 1953 decided again to try the omnibus appropriation bill approach, but the House, which by long-standing precedent initiates funding measures, did not act on the Senate proposal. Another Senate proposal, to create a Joint Budget Committee to provide Congress with meaningful fiscal information, was approved by the Senate eight times between 1952 and 1967 but never accepted by the House.

Congress by the 1950s belatedly discovered that the world war and the expansion of government under the New Deal had diluted its "power of the purse," long considered one of the lawmakers' principal sources of power over the executive branch. Congress generally managed to authorize less spending than was proposed by the postwar presidents, but it proved unable to consider the budget as a whole or enforce funding priorities as a means of controlling expenditures. This point was underscored repeatedly by congressional conflicts with the White House over "backdoor spending" by Congress and executive branch impoundment of appropriated funds. Congressional frustration frequently found expression in mandatory spending ceilings imposed on executive branch agencies and written into program authorizations.

Meanwhile, long-standing disagreements between the Senate and House over their respective roles in the appropriations process caused new rifts between the two chambers. In 1962 this feud delayed final action on appropriation bills and kept Congress in turmoil through much of the session. It began as a disagreement over the physical location of conference committee meetings but soon engulfed the larger issues of whether the Senate could initiate its own appropriation bills and whether it could add to the House-passed money bills funds for items not previously considered, or considered and rejected, by the House.

When the Senate drafted and passed a resolution to provide emergency financing for federal agencies pending final congressional action on their regular appropriations, the House called the action an infringement on its "immemorial" right to initiate appropriation bills. In retaliation, the Senate adopted a resolution stating that "the acquiescence of the Senate in permitting the House to first consider appropriation bills cannot change the clear language of the Constitution nor affect the Senate's co-equal power to originate any bill not expressly 'raising revenue.'" Although the two chambers eventually reached a truce, the basic issues were not resolved. It was not until a decade later that the House and Senate agreed on new procedures for handling the federal budget. (See "Congress and the Budget," p. 166.)

EXERCISE OF THE WAR POWER

Events in the postwar era frequently reminded Congress that its constitutional power to declare war counted for little in the modern world. But in the late 1960s the Senate began to mount a substantial challenge to the president's authority over military involvement.

Congress did not seriously challenge President Truman's war powers until long after the start of the Korean War and the cold war in Europe. At issue in the early 1950s was the president's authority to dispatch troops to South Korea and Western Europe. Republican Senator Taft opened a three-month-long debate on January 5, 1951, by asserting that Truman had "no authority whatever to commit American troops to Korea without consulting Congress and without congressional approval." Moreover, he said, the president had "no power to agree to send American troops to fight in Europe in a war between members of the Atlantic Pact and Soviet Russia."

The debate revolved principally around the troops-to-Europe issue. It came to an end on April 4 when the Senate adopted two resolutions approving the dispatch of four divisions to Europe. One of the resolutions stated that it was the sense of the Senate that "no ground troops in addition to such four divisions should be sent to Western Europe . . . without further congressional approval." But neither resolution had the force of law because the House took no action.

Truman never asked Congress for a declaration of war in Korea, and he waited until December 16, 1950—six months after the outbreak of hostilities there—to proclaim the existence of a national emergency. In defense of this course, it was argued that the Russians or the Chinese or both had violated post–World War II agreements on Korea and that emergency powers authorized during World War II still could be applied.

The Korean conflict provided two further tests of presidential power. In 1951 the nation was split when Truman dismissed Gen. Douglas A. MacArthur from his post as commander of U.N. and U.S. forces in the Far East because of a dispute over policy. The Senate Foreign Relations and Armed Services committees reviewed the ouster, and their joint hearings were credited with cooling the atmosphere throughout the country. So bitter was the controversy that the committees refrained from making any formal report, but the president's right to remove MacArthur was conceded, and the principle of civilian control over the military upheld.

In 1952 Congress ignored Truman's request for approval of his seizure of the nation's steel mills, an action taken under his war powers, and the Supreme Court later ruled that the seizure was without statutory authority and constituted a usurpation of the powers of Congress.

Presidents who followed Truman made frequent use of their war powers, sometimes unilaterally, at other times in cooperation with Congress. President Eisenhower, for example, asked Congress in 1955 for advance approval to use American armed force in the event of a Chinese communist attack on Formosa or the Pescadores Islands. A resolution to that effect was adopted within a week. Eisenhower, however, landed troops in Lebanon in July 1958 strictly on his own authority.

President Kennedy, responding to Soviet threats to Allied rights in West Berlin, asked Congress on July 16, 1961, for authority to call up ready reservists and to extend the enlistments of men already on active duty. Such authority was granted in a joint resolution signed by the president August 1. But Kennedy did not wait for congressional approval of his actions in the Cuban missile crisis of October 1962. Confronted with a buildup of Soviet missile bases in Cuba, he ordered an immediate "naval quarantine" of Cuba to prevent delivery of additional Russian missiles. More than any other crisis of the postwar period, the Cuba episode illustrated the vast sweep of presidential power in times of great emergency.

Congress virtually abdicated its power to declare war in Vietnam when it adopted, in August 1964, the Gulf of Tonkin resolution authorizing the president to "take all necessary measures" to stop aggression in Southeast Asia. The resolution was requested by President Johnson and adopted by a vote of 88–2 in the Senate and 414–0 in the House. The president considered

Mike Mansfield's sixteen-year tenure as majority leader was the longest in Senate history. He is shown here (left) with colleague Hugh Scott.

the resolution adequate authority for expanding U.S. involvement in the Vietnam War, but in later years, as public support for the war deteriorated, Congress was to have second thoughts about its 1964 action. The Tonkin Gulf resolution was repealed in January 1971.

Liberal Advances: 1970–1981

The Senate power structure during the 1960s had been dominated by conservative southern Democrats who, through the seniority system, had slowly gained and tenaciously held onto many of the chamber's most prestigious leadership positions and committee chairmanships.

But by the late 1950s and early 1960s, big election victories by the Democrats had pushed into the seniority pipeline a predominance of northern liberals. By the 1970s many of these senators had worked their way to the top positions in the leadership structure, displacing their more conservative colleagues. The liberals' ascendancy led to important changes in the Senate's procedures as well as its legislative product.

The legislative output in the decade of the 1970s stressed the role of government in answering society's diverse needs and curing its ills. Lyndon Johnson's Great Society programs of the mid-1960s, created to bring the poor into the mainstream of

American life, were expanded to include aid to individuals and communities of greater means. State and local governments, themselves strapped for cash, eagerly accepted federal funding.

In the Senate, institutional reforms were adopted that paralleled this democratic surge, making the chamber more open and egalitarian. Organizational and procedural changes enabled less senior members to gain power at the expense of older and more experienced legislators. With more staff, more money, and more power, individual senators were able to maintain their independence from party leaders and more easily pursue their interests and legislative goals.

Senate reforms were not as broad as those in the House, mainly because the one-hundred-member Senate already was more accessible and less structured than the 435-member House. The Senate, unlike the House, did not use a closed rule to restrict its members' legislative prerogatives, leaving individual senators free to propose floor amendments even if opposed by the Senate leadership or committee chairmen. Similarly, the Senate did not rely on nonrecorded votes in acting upon major bills and controversial amendments, as did the House until its age-old floor procedures were modernized in 1970. Thus each senator could be held more closely accountable for his positions on legislation. And the Senate had admitted television and radio coverage of Senate committees, sanctioned in the Legislative Reorganization Act of 1946, long before the House generally ended its broadcast ban on committee hearings through enactment of the Legislative Reorganization Act of 1970.

But the reforms had a major impact on the way the Senate operated.

Several of the most important reforms centered on the filibuster. Many reformers felt the principal obstacle to a more democratic and responsible Senate was unlimited debate, which enabled a minority to use the filibuster to obstruct the majority. After years of trying, the reformers succeeded in 1975 in reducing the number of votes needed to invoke cloture. The modification to Rule XXII did not totally prevent a minority from talking legislation to death, but it diminished that power by reducing the number of senators needed to end debate from two-thirds of those members present and voting to three-fifths of the full Senate.

A second major filibuster reform occurred in 1979 when the Senate agreed to curb so-called postcloture filibusters, a delaying tactic that had been employed by a handful of senators to get around the 1975 rules change.

Reforms occurred in other areas, as well. In 1977 the Senate conducted a major overhaul of its committee system. And in the wake of the revelations of the Watergate years, the Senate adopted a new ethics code and took the lead role in strengthening federal election laws.

The events of Watergate also led to important changes in the relationship between the Senate and the executive branch. As public respect for the presidency waned, the Senate took the lead in Congress in reasserting many of the powers of the legislative branch that slowly had been ceded to the president since World War II.

Members of Congress began taking a more active role in reviewing the federal budget, were more willing to challenge the content and form of legislation drafted by the president, showed greater awareness of the need to strengthen congressional oversight of executive agencies, and assumed a higher profile in the formulation of defense and foreign policy.

PARTY LEADERS

The decade saw new Senate leadership on both sides of the aisle. Both Majority Leader Mike Mansfield and Minority Leader Hugh Scott announced their retirement from Congress effective at the conclusion of the 94th Congress in January 1977. Their departure coincided with the change in administrations in the White House from Gerald R. Ford to Jimmy Carter.

Mansfield, who had been the Democratic leader in the Senate since 1961, had capitalized during his final years as majority leader on his early opposition to the Vietnam War and his party's differences with the Nixon administration during Watergate. Despite his low-key approach to the job, he ended his career as a respected party leader.

But Scott finished out his Senate career under more difficult circumstances. He defended U.S. actions in Indochina long after much of his Pennsylvania constituency had turned against the war. Then he promised that White House tapes would exonerate President Nixon and suffered embarrassment when the Watergate evidence indicated Nixon's involvement.

Succeeding Mansfield as majority leader was Robert Byrd of West Virginia, who as whip had already assumed much of the responsibility for the day-to-day operations of the Senate while Mansfield still was leader. Other Senate Democrats—particularly Hubert Humphrey and Edward M. Kennedy, D-Mass., Byrd's defeated opponents for Senate leadership posts in the 1970s—had built their careers on national issues and oratorical flair. But Byrd built his by working quietly behind the scenes constructing a power base on a foundation of favors and parliamentary skills.

A conservative by ideology, Byrd let his own views play almost no role in carrying out his leadership functions. Instead, he viewed his task as one of sounding out his colleagues and then carrying out their wishes. Byrd's superb knowledge of Senate rules and procedures strengthened his hand in the Senate.

An aloof individual, Byrd confined his relationships with fellow Democrats purely to Senate business. His pompous manner also made him a somewhat stilted spokesperson for the Democratic party. But that did not prevent him from keeping a tight personal rein on the party apparatus in the chamber. The Senate Democratic Conference met rarely during his tenure as majority leader, and party staffers reported solely to him.

Succeeding Scott as minority leader in January 1977 was Howard H. Baker Jr., R-Tenn. Baker had mounted a last-minute campaign for the post and ended up defeating Minority Whip Robert P. Griffin, R-Mich., by one vote. Baker's principal leadership tools were his relaxed manner and personal friendships with his Republican colleagues. Like Byrd, he downplayed his own personal political views in favor of bringing his colleagues to a common view through gentle persuasion. Though some conservatives held against him a handful of votes he took on such key conservative issues as Senate approval of the Panama Canal treaties, he enjoyed great popularity with most Republicans as well as with Democrats. As a result, a bipartisan spirit prevailed during his tenure as minority leader, and the majority of Republicans were able to cooperate with Democrats in fashioning legislation.

LEGISLATIVE REORGANIZATION

The first significant changes in Senate procedures since the major overhaul of the legislative branch in 1946 were the result of the Legislative Reorganization Act of 1970. The act was intended to improve Congress's deliberative process in the House and Senate chambers as well as in the committees. It did so by authorizing additional congressional staff, beefing up Congress's research and information resources, and requiring the administration to provide Congress with more information about the federal budget. A separate section, consisting of rules changes applying only to the Senate, focused primarily on improving the accountability, openness, and efficiency of Senate committees.

Among the Senate rules changes were provisions allowing a committee majority to call a meeting when the chairman refused to do so, guaranteeing a committee's minority members the right to call witnesses, and requiring committees to adopt and publish their rules of procedure.

Other rules changes made the committee assignment process more egalitarian by limiting the ability of the most senior senators to snap up all the choice seats. Under the new regulations senators could be members of only two major committees and one minor, select, or joint committee; no senator could serve on more than one of the most prestigious committees; and no senator could hold the chairmanship of more than one full committee and one subcommittee of a major committee.

To provide senators with more information on which to base their votes, the new rules prohibited Senate consideration of a bill—exceptions included declarations of war and other emergencies—unless the committee report on the measure was available three days before it was brought to the floor. In addition, conference committees were required to explain the actions taken on bills during House-Senate conferences.

SENIORITY SYSTEM

In 1971 Sens. Fred R. Harris, D-Okla., and Charles McC. Mathias Jr., R-Md., led an unsuccessful move to scrap the seniority system for selecting committee chairmen, a custom practiced since the mid-nineteenth century, in favor of what they called "a standard of merit" in making the top choices.

Their plan called for amending Rule XXIV to require that committee chairmen and ranking minority members be nominated individually by a majority vote of the party caucuses and elected individually by majority vote of the full Senate at the beginning of each new Congress. But the Senate Rules and Administration Committee reported the proposal adversely. (Rule XXIV as then written merely stated that the Senate "shall proceed by ballot to appoint severally the chairmen of each committee, and then, by one ballot, the other members necessary to complete the same.")

Democratic reformers were more successful in January 1975 when they revised party rules to establish a method by which committee chairmen would have to face an election every two years, but a vote was not mandatory, as it was in the House. The Democratic Conference voted to require selection of chairmen by secret ballot whenever one-fifth of the caucus requested it. The modification did not affect chairmen in the 94th Congress.

The rules change was intended to make it easier for senators to depose a chairman without fear of retribution. Under the procedure, a list of proposed committee chairmen nominated by the Democratic Steering Committee would be distributed to all Democrats. Party members then would check off the names of the nominees they wished to subject to a secret ballot and would submit the list without signing it. If at least 20 percent of

the caucus members wanted a secret vote on any nominee, it would be held automatically two days later.

OPEN COMMITTEES AND STAFFING

Almost three years after the House in March 1973 voted to open up its committee bill-drafting sessions to the public and the press, the Senate in November 1975 adopted a similar rule, requiring most of its committees to work in public. At the same time, the Senate approved open conference committee sessions, as the House had done in January, thereby opening up one of the last bastions of congressional committee secrecy.

The new rules required all meetings to be public unless a majority of a committee voted in open session to close a meeting or series of meetings on the same subject for up to fourteen days. Meetings could be closed only if they concerned national security; committee personnel or internal staff management matters; charges against a person that might harm a person professionally or otherwise represent an invasion of privacy; disclosure of the identity of an informer or undercover agent or of the existence of a criminal investigation that should be kept secret; disclosure of trade secrets or other confidential business information; or disclosure of "matters required to be kept confidential under other provisions of law or government regulation."

The new Senate rules also required committees to prepare transcripts or electronic recordings of each of their sessions, including conference committee meetings, unless a majority of the committee voted not to comply with this rule.

In another 1975 reform, junior senators obtained committee staff assistance to aid them on legislative issues. Previously, committee staff members were controlled by chairmen and other senior members. Few junior members had regular and dependable access to staff personnel.

FILIBUSTER REFORM

After years of effort, Senate reformers succeeded in March 1975 in modifying Rule XXII to make it easier for the Senate to terminate filibusters mounted by a minority of its members. The existing rule had required two-thirds of senators present and voting—sixty-seven senators if all one hundred senators voted—to invoke cloture and thus bring a controversial bill or amendment to a vote. The 1975 change set the number of votes required to invoke cloture at three-fifths of the full Senate—sixty if there were no vacancies.

Before 1975 Senate liberals had attempted to modify the cloture rule every two years since 1959, with the exception of 1973. In 1971, the last time a concerted effort was made before the successful attempt in 1975, reformers failed on a series of four votes to amend Rule XXII. In the last few months of 1970 the Senate became embroiled in a confusion of filibusters on a variety of major questions. Although this spectacle led to soul-searching within the Senate and to calls from President Nixon for procedural reforms, the Senate refused to make any change when the 92nd Congress convened in 1971.

The change in the cloture rule finally was adopted in March 1975 after a bitter three-week struggle on the Senate floor. One reason for the reformers' success was that many of the younger senators gave a lower priority to a struggle to preserve the old rule than had their predecessors in previous Congresses. Historically, the filibuster had been most important to southern senators interested in blocking civil rights legislation. But by 1975 the big battles over civil rights already had taken place.

The reformers initially had sought to permit a simple majority or a three-fifths majority of senators present and voting to end a filibuster, but they subsequently settled for a compromise that set the number at three-fifths of the Senate membership, called "a constitutional majority." The new rule applied to any matter except a proposed change in the Standing Rules of the Senate—including Rule XXII—for which the old two-thirds majority rule for ending debate still held.

Based on historical voting patterns, the change in the filibuster rule appeared to make it only marginally easier for a Senate faction to invoke cloture. The record showed that the three-fifths "constitutional majority" rule would have made little difference in the outcome of legislation on which filibusters and cloture votes had occurred since Rule XXII was adopted in 1917. During the twenty years preceding the 1975 change, for example, sixty votes or more, but not a two-thirds majority, were obtained on only five of seventy-nine cloture attempts. However,

reformers saw the new rule speeding up the Senate's work as well as enhancing the chances of success for senators wanting to end filibusters on controversial legislation. *(See "Attempted and Successful Cloture Votes," p. 1116, in Reference Materials, Vol. II.)*

A second, less publicized change in the filibuster rule was approved by a coalition of Senate liberals and conservatives in April 1976. The change allowed the introduction of amendments to a bill being filibustered up until the announcement of the outcome of a cloture vote. Under the previous version of the rule, no amendment was to be considered after cloture was invoked that had not been formally read or considered prior to the cloture vote. In practice, the Senate routinely agreed by unanimous consent to consider all amendments at the Senate desk at the time of a cloture vote, so supporters said the change merely formalized the existing informal practice. But opponents argued that the change made it possible to delay bringing an amendment or bill to a final vote after cloture had been invoked.

POSTCLOTURE FILIBUSTERS

Over the next couple of years, the Senate was to pay increasing attention to the period following a cloture vote on a bill or amendment. The so-called postcloture filibuster was to become a new form of delay and the new focus of reform efforts in the Senate.

Rule XXII already allowed each senator just one hour to talk

Democratic floor leader Robert C. Byrd of West Virginia, left, performed his duties with old-fashioned courtesy and consummate parliamentary skills. His Republican counterpart, Howard H. Baker Jr., of Tennessee, had a more relaxed leadership style.

on a bill after cloture was invoked. For years that limit was enough to restrain debate because the minority conducting a filibuster abided by the spirit of the rule as well as the letter and acknowledged defeat once cloture was invoked.

But technically, the hour-per-senator limit did not include such parliamentary maneuvers as quorum calls and votes on amendments submitted before the cloture vote. In 1976 Sen. James B. Allen, D-Ala., began capitalizing on these loopholes by making frequent quorum calls and bringing up amendment after amendment for a vote, even after cloture had been invoked on bills he opposed. These parliamentary tactics soon made Allen a hero to conservatives but earned him the scorn of colleagues forced to accept compromises they otherwise would have opposed once a filibuster had been broken.

Majority Leader Byrd attempted to put an end to such tactics in early 1977, but his effort never gained momentum, and in the ensuing Congress use of the postcloture filibuster mushroomed. Most of the time, use of that technique was confined to conservatives. However, during a highly charged debate on legislation proposing to deregulate natural gas prices, two liberal Democrats mounted a postcloture filibuster that tied up the chamber for nine days before Senate leaders managed to end it.

The natural gas debate provided Byrd with one more reason to try again to curb the practice, and his second effort, begun in January 1979, met with greater success. Byrd initially proposed a package of seven changes in the filibuster rule, including an absolute time limit on postcloture filibusters, a limit on debate on motions to bring up a bill, a procedure to limit nongermane amendments to bills being filibustered, and a method to speed up consideration of cloture petitions.

Byrd pressed for adoption of the package for six weeks before a group of senators working behind the scenes agreed to a compromise. As adopted by the full Senate in February, the change included only the absolute time limit on postcloture filibusters. It required that after the Senate voted to invoke cloture on a bill, a final vote had to occur after no more than one hundred hours of postcloture debate. The new limitation appeared to put an end to the practice of postcloture filibusters, but Senate leaders warned that the rules still could be abused by a senator who was skillful enough and willing to incur the wrath of his colleagues.

COMMITTEE SYSTEM OVERHAUL

The Senate opened the 95th Congress in 1977 by reorganizing its committee structure. The committee overhaul was the first since the 1946 reorganization.

The reorganization was the product of the temporary Select Committee to Study the Senate Committee System, chaired by Sen. Adlai E. Stevenson III, D-Ill., although the overhaul as approved by the Senate was more modest in scope than that originally proposed by the Stevenson committee. For example, the Veterans' Affairs and Select Small Business committees were saved, as were the Joint Economic and Joint Taxation committees, although all of them would have been abolished under the Stevenson plan. But the reorganization did reduce the overall

number of Senate committees to twenty-five, from thirty-one, and substantially revised the remaining panels' jurisdictions. The overhaul also limited the number of committees and subcommittees a senator could belong to and authorized staff members to be assigned to work for the minority members of the committee.

WATERGATE

The Senate launched its inquiry into the Watergate scandal on February 7, 1973, when it approved by a 77–0 vote a resolution creating a Select Committee on Presidential Campaign Activities (known as the Senate Watergate Committee), to investigate and study "the extent . . . to which illegal, improper, or unethical activities" occurred in the 1972 presidential campaign and election. The nationally televised committee hearings were the major focus of Watergate developments during the summer of 1973.

Numerous former employees of the Committee to Re-Elect the President, which directed Nixon's 1972 campaign for reelection, as well as former White House aides appeared—some to admit perjury during earlier investigations. They drew a picture of political sabotage that went far beyond the break-in and attempted burglary of the headquarters of the Democratic National Committee in the Watergate Hotel complex.

The hearings brought forth details of a special White House investigative unit, known as the "plumbers," that had been responsible for "plugging leaks" in the administration through such tactics as harassment of Daniel Ellsberg, who had released the classified Pentagon Papers on the Vietnam War to the press. During a four-day appearance before the panel, former White House counsel John Dean turned over approximately fifty documents to the Senate committee, including a memorandum Dean had written on the subject of "dealing with our political enemies." White House lists subsequently made public named about two hundred important "enemies." Dean was the only witness to implicate the president directly in the Watergate cover-up.

Another important revelation to come out of the committee hearings resulted from questioning of Federal Aviation Administration chief Alexander P. Butterfield, a former White House aide. Butterfield testified publicly in July that the president's offices were equipped with a special voice-activated system that secretly recorded all conversations. The subsequent emergence of the taped evidence completely changed the course of the Watergate investigation and ultimately led to President Nixon's dramatic resignation.

In the next few years, investigations into the activities of the Central Intelligence Agency (CIA) and the Federal Bureau of Investigation (FBI) earned the Senate a reputation as a tough overseer of executive agencies.

In the post–World War II era, the CIA and the FBI routinely were excluded from congressional oversight, even during Congress's annual consideration of those agencies' budgets. But in a series of hearings in 1975, the Senate Select Committee to Study

Government Operations with Respect to Intelligence Activities revealed that the CIA had illegally kept deadly poisons, snooped into Americans' mail, and conducted extensive domestic spying operations, in violation of the agency's charter.

The committee in the spring of 1976 issued reports stating that since World War II Republican and Democratic administrations alike had used the FBI for secret surveillance of citizens. That year the Senate also established a permanent intelligence oversight committee.

NEW ETHICS CODE

In the wake of revelations of political wrongdoing that became public during the Watergate years, the Senate in 1977 adopted a new code of conduct. The new ethics code required substantial additional public disclosure of the financial activities of both senators and highly paid Senate employees, imposed tight restrictions on senators' outside employment activities, ended unofficial office accounts, and strengthened rules governing the use of the frank. The code also restructured the Senate's Ethics Committee. To sweeten the reform package, legislators got a 29 percent pay raise.

Drafted by a special committee headed by Sen. Gaylord Nelson, D-Wis., the code was weakened slightly before the Senate approved it after a spirited debate. A major concern of some senators during the debate on the code was a provision to take effect in 1979 limiting to 15 percent of a senator's official salary the amount of money a senator could earn each year in outside income. Senators relying to a significant extent on their official salaries alone argued bitterly that the rule favored their wealthier colleagues, who could continue to live on unearned income —in the form of rent, dividends, and interest payments—which was not affected by the code's restrictions. Despite the opposition, the 15 percent limit was upheld on the Senate floor. But in January 1979 senators reversed themselves and voted to delay the limit's effective date until 1983.

The adoption of the ethics code and other rules changes brought the total number of Senate rules to fifty. So the Senate in November 1979 and again in March 1980 revised, consolidated, and renumbered certain rules without changing either their substance or interpretation. These two recodifications brought the total number of Senate rules back down to forty-two.

Before the end of the decade, the Senate was to be shaken by a major misconduct cases against one of its most powerful members, Sen. Herman E. Talmadge, D-Ga. The action against Talmadge was taken after press reports surfaced that the senior Georgia Democrat had collected reimbursements from the Senate for expenses that he had never incurred or were not reimbursable under Senate rules, that he had accepted reimbursements from his campaign funds that were not reported to the Federal Election Commission, and that he lived for years off unreported gifts of cash, food, lodging, and even clothes from friends and constituents. After a lengthy investigation, a divided Senate Ethics Committee recommended that Talmadge be "denounced" by his colleagues instead of "censured"—the more

traditional punishment—apparently to enable Talmadge's Senate supporters to claim the punishment was less severe than censure. The denunciation was voted in October 1979 amidst lengthy testimonials to Talmadge's character. Talmadge was defeated for reelection in November 1980.

FOREIGN POLICY DEBATE

Concerted Senate efforts to reassert its voice in the conduct of foreign affairs dated back to the late 1960s and the opposition to the Vietnam War. The result was passage in 1973 of the War Powers Resolution, the first law ever passed by Congress defining and limiting presidential war powers. The legislation was approved after Congress overrode President Nixon's veto of the bill.

The war powers law proved to have only a limited impact, as presidents routinely ignored its demands that they obtain congressional approval before launching military actions. The Senate did play a major role in foreign policy during the late 1970s, however, through exercise of its power to approve or reject treaties. The most dramatic case came in 1978, when the Senate narrowly ratified two treaties with Panama relinquishing American control over the Panama Canal. The Carter administration argued that the treaties were in the best long-term interests of the nation, but conservatives mounted a fierce campaign to convince Americans and their legislators that the treaties would compromise U.S. national security. The treaties ultimately were approved, but only after thirty-eight days of Senate debate. Up to that time no other single foreign policy issue since the Vietnam War had attracted as much attention, aroused as many emotions, and consumed as much of an administration's time and effort. Senators' votes on the treaties remained a key issue in their reelection campaigns for years afterward.

The following year, a similarly intense executive-legislative struggle developed in the Senate over approval of a new U.S.-Soviet arms limitation treaty (SALT II). But on the eve of what observers expected to be a protracted Senate debate on the matter, the Soviet Union invaded Afghanistan. After that, President Carter withdrew the treaty from Senate consideration, explaining that the Soviet action had convinced him the treaty no longer served the nation's best interests. But both SALT II supporters and opponents agreed that Carter's decision simply reflected the political reality that the pact would not have come even close to winning the necessary two-thirds Senate majority had it come up for a vote.

Shifting Power: 1981–1992

The contentious debates over the Panama Canal and SALT II treaties hinted that the liberals' domination of the Senate was waning. The November 1980 general election confirmed this supposition.

The GOP gained control of the White House as well as the Senate. Adding to the election's impact was the defeat of many of the Senate's most senior Democrats, several of them liberals.

SENATE VOTES CAST BY VICE PRESIDENTS

From the beginning of the American republic, the executive branch has put to good use the constitutional authority granted the vice president to vote in the Senate in the event of a tie. Through October 1999, vice presidents had cast votes on more than two hundred occasions. Some of those votes were recorded against questions that would have failed even if the vice president had not voted, because a question on which the Senate is evenly divided automatically dies. In such cases the vice president's negative vote is superfluous. Its only purpose is to make known his opposition to the proposal. There are no records available showing how many of the votes cast by vice presidents were in the affirmative and thus decisive.

The first roll call cast by a vice president was a negative vote by John Adams on July 18, 1789, the effect of which was to support George Washington's right to remove an appointed official without consulting the chamber of Congress that had given original consent to the appointment. The House had included in a bill establishing the Department of Foreign Affairs language that implied recognition of the president's sole power of removal. When the bill reached the Senate, that body first rejected a motion to delete the House language on a 10–10 vote.

This action is not recorded in the Senate Journal, but Sen. William Maclay's *Journal* for July 16, 1789, describes the scene: "After all the arguments were ended and the question taken, the Senate was ten to ten, and the vice president with joy cried out, 'It is not a vote,' without giving himself time to declare the division of the House and give his vote in order." Two days later, when the bill came up for final action, a roll call was demanded on the same question. One senator was absent and another senator on the opposing side withheld his vote, so the Senate was divided 9–9 when the Senate secretary called for the vice president's vote. Adams voted nay.

Although the Adams vote had no effect on the issue, he considered his stand in support of the president's removal power one of his most important acts in public life. The vote was one of twenty-nine cast by Adams—a record approached only by John C. Calhoun, who cast twenty-eight votes as vice president.

One crucial vote by a vice president was cast in 1846 when George M. Dallas broke a tie in favor of the administration's tariff reform bill. Among other important vice presidential votes were two cast by Thomas R. Marshall on foreign policy issues. In 1916 his vote carried an amendment on a Philippines bill pledging full independence to the islands by March 4, 1921. (The amendment later was modified in conference.) In 1919 Marshall cast the deciding vote to table (kill) a resolution calling for withdrawal of U.S. troops from Russia.

The most active wielder of the tie-breaking power in recent decades has been George Bush, who cast a total of seven Senate votes during his vice presidency. Most of the votes were aimed at saving controversial weapons systems backed by the Reagan administration, including the MX missile, chemical weapons, and the Strategic Defense Initiative. In addition, Bush cast the deciding vote in favor of a GOP budget plan in a dramatic late-night session in 1985, after Sen. Pete Wilson, R-Calif., was brought to the Senate chamber from the hospital to force a tie.

Following is a list of the number of votes cast by each vice president since 1789:

Period	Vice President	Votes Cast
1789–1797	John Adams	29
1797–1801	Thomas Jefferson	3
1801–1805	Aaron Burr	3
1805–1812	George Clinton	11
1813–1814	Elbridge Gerry	8
1817–1825	Daniel D. Tompkins	5
1825–1832	John C. Calhoun	28
1833–1837	Martin Van Buren	4
1837–1841	Richard M. Johnson	14
1841	John Tyler	0
1845–1849	George M. Dallas	19
1849–1850	Millard Fillmore	3
1853	William R. King	0
1857–1861	John C. Breckinridge	10
1861–1865	Hannibal Hamlin	7
1865	Andrew Johnson	0
1869–1873	Schuyler Colfax	13
1873–1875	Henry Wilson	1
1877–1881	William A. Wheeler	5
1881	Chester A. Arthur	3
1885	Thomas A. Hendricks	0
1889–1893	Levi P. Morton	4
1893–1897	Adlai E. Stevenson	2
1897–1899	Garret A. Hobart	1
1901	Theodore Roosevelt	0
1905–1909	Charles W. Fairbanks	0
1909–1912	James S. Sherman	4
1913–1921	Thomas R. Marshall	4
1921–1923	Calvin Coolidge	0
1925–1929	Charles G. Dawes	2
1929–1933	Charles Curtis	3
1933–1941	John N. Garner	3
1941–1945	Henry A. Wallace	4
1945	Harry S. Truman	1
1949–1953	Alben W. Barkley	7
1953–1961	Richard M. Nixon	8
1961–1963	Lyndon B. Johnson	0
1965–1969	Hubert H. Humphrey	4
1969–1973	Spiro T. Agnew	2
1973–1974	Gerald R. Ford	0
1974–1977	Nelson A. Rockefeller	0
1977–1981	Walter F. Mondale	1
1981–1989	George Bush	7
1989–1993	Dan Quayle	0
1993–1999[a]	Al Gore	4
Total		227

a. Through September 1999.

SOURCE: Congressional Research Service, Library of Congress.

And though the House remained in Democratic hands, Republicans discovered they could in effect control that chamber too by luring to their side the votes of many conservative southern Democrats. This change in the congressional power balance signaled a reversal of two and a half decades of uninterrupted Democratic rule on Capitol Hill, and it put a halt to a decade of liberal domination in Congress.

Republican hegemony in the Senate lasted only six years, as the Democrats regained control of the chamber as a result of the 1986 elections. For many observers, however, the issue of whether Democrats or Republicans held nominal power was less important than whether any party or individual could exercise real power and leadership. The increasing use of obstructionist tactics, the rise of individualism, the decline of the tradition of courtesy, and the seeming ineffectiveness of those in leadership positions suggested to many that the Senate had changed in profound ways that made it less able to deal constructively with the issues facing the nation. The institution itself had been transformed, some analysts argued, from a closely knit body into a loose collection of individuals in which the defense of one's views was equated with lawmaking.

REPUBLICANS TAKE OVER

As the 97th Congress began the Senate's committees were taken over by Republican chairmen who were in many instances dramatically more conservative, younger, and less experienced than the Democrats they replaced. In the ensuing months even liberals began to act more like conservatives, out of fear that the 1980 election reflected a fundamental realignment of the political spectrum instead of a single instance of conservative success at the polls.

The Republicans elected to the 97th Congress were proud to follow the conservative president who had led their national ticket, Ronald Reagan. This attitude was in marked contrast to the Democrats' independence of Jimmy Carter during his administration. Rather than assert their own independence, most congressional Republicans quickly fell in line behind Reagan and his free market economic policies, even though it meant clipping their own wings.

During its first year, at least, the Reagan presidency appeared to prove that the era of the strong executive and the submissive legislature had not ended. With the aid of a nearly unanimous bloc of Republicans, the administration was able to push its program of social spending cuts and tax cuts through the Senate with relative ease. The year also seemed to augur a dramatically different Senate stance on social issues, as the large group of "New Right" freshmen used their committee posts to push their conservative views on such issues as abortion, teenage pregnancy, and prayer in schools.

The year also closed with radically different assessments of Baker and Byrd, who had changed places as majority and minority leaders after the elections. Baker, who had guided the package of tax and spending cuts through with relatively little difficulty, was already being hailed as one of the most effective

majority leaders in many years. But Byrd, whose mastery of Senate procedures was less significant in the minority, was widely seen as lacking both zest for his job and the ability to be an effective spokesperson for his party. Dispirited Democrats were divided between conservatives, who generally supported the Reagan proposals, and a shrunken band of liberals, who could do little more than warn that the budget measures would produce huge federal deficits and major social and economic problems in the future.

Republican unity proved to be short-lived, however. Already by 1982 Baker faced revolts by moderate Republicans, who were unwilling to agree to further deep cuts in social programs sought by Reagan and who thought that the massive budget deficits created by the 1981 tax cuts should be attacked at least in part through tax increases and loophole-closing "revenue enhancements." By the time Reagan's fiscal 1983 budget plan reached the Senate floor in the spring of 1982, moderate Republicans were rebellious enough to force removal of $40 billion in Social Security savings sought by the administration.

The 1982 elections proved to be a key turning point in undermining GOP unity over budget issues. Although the Republicans managed to avoid a net loss of seats—unlike their House counterparts, who suffered a major setback—several Republican moderates in the Senate narrowly won reelection only because they had distanced themselves from Reagan. The results helped further divide the GOP into two camps: those willing to consider tax increases and those wanting to counter the deficit only through spending cuts.

Those divisions led to a significant setback for the administration and the Republican leadership on budget issues in 1983. First, the Senate Budget Committee defied Reagan and passed a Democratic-inspired budget plan calling for $30 billion in new taxes. On the floor, another budget package opposed by Reagan passed by a 50–49 vote. But that occurred only after a three-week ordeal during which the Senate rejected a series of budget plans offered both by the GOP leadership and moderates. At one point, the Budget Committee itself was unable to agree on a proposal, leading its chairman, Pete V. Domenici, R-N.M., to complain, "It's insanity for the U.S. Senate not to vote in a budget resolution."

SEARCH FOR LEADERSHIP

As the budget debacle that year proved, the Senate during the early 1980s was an increasingly difficult place in which to exercise leadership or to make rapid progress on any legislation. Baker's early success in getting Reagan's economic program through in 1981 was followed by a period of growing frustration and futility as Baker frequently was unable to persuade his colleagues to display the understanding, courtesy, and willingness to compromise that are essential for smooth Senate operations.

In 1982 and throughout 1983–1984, Baker had difficulty in obtaining approval from his colleagues for unanimous consent agreements governing debate. Democrats were unwilling to agree to debate schedules that limited their flexibility, while conservative Republicans often were more concerned about advancing their legislative issues, even if they conflicted with the needs of the administration and the leadership. During 1982, for example, conservatives waged a nine-month struggle over antibusing legislation and engaged in a protracted battle over antiabortion and school prayer amendments. In the last four months of the year, the Senate took fifteen cloture votes on filibusters—a record for that length of time.

Matters came to a head in a postelection session that year. Conservatives organized to block a proposed gasoline-tax increase, waging a filibuster that brought them into direct conflict with the leadership. Republicans battled among themselves, with Baker unable to establish control over the leader of the conservative forces, Jesse Helms, R-N.C. Tensions ran so high that at one point the assistant majority leader, Alan K. Simpson, R-Wyo., said of Helms, "Seldom have I seen a more obdurate, more obnoxious performance."

Although Helms lost on that and most of his other battles during that year, many observers argued that he was less interested in victory than in focusing attention on his New Right agenda. At the head of a massive direct-mail organization known as the Congressional Club, he sought to force votes on controversial social issues both to help raise money from supporters and to create campaign issues against his liberal Democratic opponents. "It was not that he expected to win on them, especially with proponents split over both substance and procedure. It was that he wanted to put his colleagues on the spot, to get record votes to be churned out of the Congressional Club's computers and direct-mail machinery," wrote an unfriendly biographer. Helms himself seemed to confirm that that was his goal: "[Opponents of my proposals] have served a useful purpose because they have raised the adrenaline level of the people."[33]

Analysts pointed to several reasons for the problems Baker and other Senate leaders experienced in exercising some measure of authority in the Senate. A key factor was the development of rampant individualism within the chamber, where it might be said that virtually every member was a leader—89 percent of senators were chairmen or ranking members of a committee or subcommittee in the 100th Congress. Junior members no longer felt that it was their obligation to maintain a low profile for the first few years in the Senate before assuming a more prominent public role or gaining a powerful spot on a committee.

The pull of presidential ambitions also continued to affect members, leading some members to neglect legislative work in favor of activities that would draw national attention. During this period, however, the Senate did not prove a particularly effective launching pad for presidential hopefuls Edward Kennedy and Howard Baker in 1980; John Glenn, D-Ohio, the former astronaut, in 1984; and Bob Dole in 1988. Moreover, a growing number of members seemed willing to paralyze action on the floor over relatively small matters, leading some observers to deplore the "trivialization" of the Senate. In a body where informal agreements and extended debates were the tradition, even junior members were able to exert considerable pressure on behalf of their particular interest.

In response to those pressures Baker generally tried to accommodate members, particularly on such matters as scheduling. Rather than broker a deal to settle the question, he was more likely to allow the contending parties in a dispute to fight out the issue at length. This approach produced prolonged deadlocks over bills and conveyed to many the image that the Senate had fallen into anarchy. His efforts to persuade the Senate to approve televising its sessions were unsuccessful, and he decided not to push procedural reforms advocated in 1981 and 1984 studies, apparently for fear they would not be adopted. Baker also struggled to unify his party colleagues, despite White House reluctance to agree to compromises with the substantial group of Republican moderates.

A former Baker aide summed up his leadership this way: "Widely praised as one of the most effective Senate leaders of this century, Baker nevertheless does not enjoy the control over the membership that many of his predecessors did; senators are younger and bolder now, and more independent, and, perhaps most significantly, both media-wise and media-mad. They are thus less susceptible to blandishments from the party leadership. Indeed, an increasing number are virtually immune."[34]

To replace Baker after he retired in 1985, Republicans chose Bob Dole, whose approach to leadership was markedly different. As chairman of the Finance Committee, Dole had played a leading role on tax legislation under Reagan and was widely viewed as a crafty lawmaker with a pointed wit. In the race for the majority leadership, he faced four opponents, including Ted Stevens, R-Alaska, the assistant leader, who had earned the gratitude of his colleagues for his determined advocacy of higher pay and benefits for senators. Dole won in the final round, 28–25 over Stevens, in the first majority leader election since 1937 to come down to a vote.

Dole quickly sought to establish his authority on the budget debate in the spring of 1985. Forced to bring a budget plan to the floor without majority support, he faced a potentially crippling debate. But he managed to put together a plan to cut the deficit by $50 billion, after pressuring the White House to accept defense reductions and moderate Republicans to allow cuts in domestic programs. The climactic moment came during a late-night session when Dole got Sen. Pete Wilson, R-Calif., to come on a stretcher from the hospital, where he had recently had major surgery. Wilson provided the crucial vote that gave Dole the victory.

Dole oversaw passage of key legislation, such as the 1985 farm bill and the long-term deficit reduction measure authored by Phil Gramm, R-Texas, Warren Rudman, R-N.H., and Ernest Hollings, D-S.C. But perhaps Dole's chief accomplishment was his success in undermining the ability of small groups of senators to stop action. He used a combination of negotiation, compromise, arm-twisting, verbal whiplashing, and humor to bring competing interests into line.

A powerful Republican leader in the 1980s and 1990s, Sen. Robert Dole of Kansas served several terms as majority leader before resigning in 1996 to run unsuccessfully for the presidency.

Dole also helped shepherd through a measure authorizing Senate television, which Baker had sought without success. The 1986 drive for television was led by Minority Leader Byrd, an ardent advocate of the institutional Senate who was convinced that the Senate was losing public prestige because it was not televised while the House was. Byrd was assisted by Sen. Al Gore, who had recently arrived in the Senate in 1985 and who had led the drive to televise House proceedings in the late 1970s while he was a member of that body. The television resolution also called for procedural changes aimed at weakening obstructionism to make the Senate more telegenic and efficient. The proposals faced opposition, however, and the final version included only one significant change: reducing from one hundred to thirty hours the time allowed for additional debate, procedural moves, and roll calls after the Senate had voted to invoke cloture.

'QUALITY OF LIFE'

Pressures for changes in Senate procedures also came from a group focused on what its members called the "quality of life" issue. This bipartisan group vented its frustration with the Senate's endless delays, draining and unpredictable schedule, and extended battles over seemingly minor issues. Those particularly concerned about the situation pointed to the retirements relatively early in the careers of several respected members during the 1980s, at least in part because of frustration over both the demands and the results of their work. Late in 1985, some seventy senators held a closed meeting in which they agreed to four changes in the Senate's informal rules, covering such questions as the length of time for roll-call votes, quorums, "holds" placed by senators on bills, and the scheduling of votes. The Senate also agreed to slight reductions in the number of committee assignments, as a panel headed by Sen. Dan Quayle, R-Ind., had recommended.

Those steps did not end concerns over scheduling and procedures, however. In 1987 Byrd and Dole reconstituted the "quality of life" group in the face of growing frustration over the unpredictability of the Senate schedule. While some of the frustration reflected members' concerns over the effect of the schedule on their family life, an equally important source of anger was the conflict between evening sessions and the need for senators to be able to schedule campaign fund-raising events. As a result Senate leaders experimented with different schedules, including barring roll-call votes on Mondays and giving senators one week off a month to attend campaign or fund-raising events in their home states. Though these moves by no means resolved all complaints, they did make the Senate a bit more predictable and eased pressures on the members.

DEMOCRATS RETURN

Despite his numerous successes as a leader, Dole was not able to protect his fellow Republicans who were up for reelection in 1986 from issues that their opponents could use against them— for example, budget cuts in social programs. Although observers had speculated that the Democrats might be able to regain control of the Senate in the 1986 elections, few predicted the major sweep that allowed them to capture nine GOP seats, while losing only one, and jump to a 55–45 majority. The election was particularly important because it shored up Democratic strength in the South and showed that Democrats could win a number of close contests despite the Republicans' substantial advantage in money and technology.

Restored to the majority, Democrats again selected Byrd as their leader. In that position, Byrd was most active during the 100th Congress in protecting the prestige and internal customs of the Senate—for example, by delivering a daily series of speeches on the history of the Senate. While Byrd saw himself as the guardian of Senate tradition, some of the new minority Republicans complained that he was using his vast knowledge of Senate rules to frustrate their legitimate rights. Other Democrats wondered whether his rather pompous and old-fashioned manner made him an effective national spokesperson for the party in the media.

Under the new Democratic majority, the Senate was sometimes torn by sharp partisan divisions. The 1987 nomination of Robert H. Bork to the Supreme Court, for example, led to a bitter three-month fight over Bork's judicial philosophy and the right of the Senate to play an equal role with the president in appointing a judge. On other matters, both parties showed a greater willingness to cooperate.

The Democratic takeover also created strains within the GOP, as Republicans were forced to give up their committee and subcommittee chairmanships. A major battle developed in 1987 when Helms, who had been chairman of the Agriculture Committee, decided to use his seniority to become ranking member on Foreign Relations. To do that, however, he had to oust Richard Lugar, R-Ind., who had been seen as an effective chairman of Foreign Relations. The ensuing fight was in part ideological, with some moderate Republicans backing the more centrist Lugar over the conservative Helms. But other senators who had frequently clashed with Helms voted for him, to uphold the principle of seniority, where Helms had the advantage. As ranking member of the powerful committee, Helms was able to exercise what some observers described as a strong influence at times over State Department nominations in the Reagan and Bush administrations, using his access to a private information network in the department and his ability to block approval of appointments.

Byrd served only one Congress as majority leader before giving up the post to take the chairmanship of the Appropriations Committee, where he was better able to obtain help for his state's struggling economy. (Byrd also became president pro tempore.) In his place, Democrats chose George J. Mitchell of Maine, a former federal judge, first appointed to the Senate in 1980, when Sen. Edmund S. Muskie resigned to become secretary of state. Mitchell had earned the gratitude of his colleagues by serving as Democratic campaign chairman going into the 1986 elections, when the party scored a resounding victory, and in the 100th Congress he was given the prestigious but rarely filled position of deputy president pro tempore.

Mitchell was a cautious leader, mindful that he owed his election in part to reform-minded Democrats who had opposed power-hungry autocratic leaders in the past. He also was pragmatic. He created goodwill by living up to his promise to improve senators' working conditions through more predictable hours. Few late-night sessions were held, and no roll-call votes were scheduled after 7 p.m. except on Thursdays. Most roll-call votes were taken in the middle of the week, allowing members to visit their districts and take care of other responsibilities over long weekends. Mitchell continued a popular innovation begun by Byrd: holding the Senate in session for three weeks, then having a week off for senators to tend to home-state business.

Most senators found Mitchell's style open and consultative. And he earned good marks for his fairness and serious intent. He was also known, however, as a devoted partisan. Mitchell assumed a prominent role as a national media spokesperson for the Democrats and as a combative floor leader frequently at odds with the Bush administration. Mitchell led the fight against Bush's proposed cut in the capital gains tax, for example,

and managed to hold off the plan despite initially broad support.

However, Mitchell was one of the handful of Democratic leaders during 1990 who worked closely with administration officials trying to develop a long-range agreement to cut the federal deficit. By working to keep together a bipartisan, centrist coalition in support of a budget agreement, Mitchell and others were able to avoid an embarrassing defeat such as the one that befell Bush and the House leadership. The 1990 budget fiasco generated widespread predictions of a strongly anti-incumbent feeling among the electorate, but senators running for reelection in 1990 enjoyed almost total success, with only one—Rudy Boschwitz, R-Minn.—going down to defeat.

WAR POWERS DEBATE CONTINUED

In October 1983, Congress passed and President Ronald Reagan signed a resolution authorizing U.S. Marines to serve in a Beirut "peacekeeping" force for eighteen months. It was the first time since its enactment in 1973 that the War Powers Resolution had been invoked. Reagan had refused to invoke the War Powers act, but Senate Democrats ultimately forced his hand when they voted 29–0 in caucus to introduce a resolution triggering the clause of the act that required congressional authorization to station troops in hostile areas for more than sixty days.

No president had ever acknowledged the constitutionality of the War Powers act, and Reagan held to that tradition. While signing the bill invoking the War Powers Resolution, Reagan questioned its constitutionality and said he would not be bound by its terms.

Talk of invoking the War Powers act arose again when Reagan sent American troops into Grenada late in 1983, overturning the Marxist government that had recently seized control of the Caribbean island, and when he ordered a bombardment of Libyan military targets in 1986 for that country's alleged backing of terrorism. Some members of Congress also questioned President George Bush's invasion of Panama in December 1989 to oust dictator Manuel Noriega, but these actions did not last long, cost comparatively few American lives, and were supported by a majority of Americans. Congress did not force the issue.

On January 12, 1991, Congress for the first time since World War II directly confronted the issue of committing large numbers of troops to combat, voting to authorize the president to use U.S. troops to enforce the January 15 deadline set by the United Nations for Iraq to withdraw from Kuwait. Senate Majority Leader Mitchell and other top Democratic leaders in the House and Senate opposed the authorization, arguing that economic sanctions on Iraq should be given more time to work. Iraq's invasion of its neighbor on August 2, 1990, had been followed by an intensive buildup of U.S. and allied forces in Saudi Arabia.

Constitutional scholars disagreed about whether Bush's request for congressional backing was in effect an acknowledgment that he lacked the authority to wage war without such legislative action. Some said it was, while others said Bush was simply seeking political, not constitutional, support.

ETHICS DEBATES

Concerns over ethics issues also played a major role in the Senate during the 1980s and early 1990s. Several senators were the targets of ethics investigations. In addition, members continued to debate the whole complex of moral quandaries surrounding such issues as campaign finance, honoraria, and congressional pay. Disputes over those matters frequently divided senators, whose ranks included a number of independently wealthy people, from House members, who were more likely to want a pay raise. Conversely, senators usually were more reluctant to agree to restrictions on their honoraria for speaking and writing engagements, where they had considerably more opportunity to earn money than did a rank-and-file House member.

The first formal investigation of the period was the result of the FBI "Abscam" investigation, which also led to the downfall of several House members. Its target was Sen. Harrison A. Williams Jr., D-N.J., a member of the class of 1959 and chairman of the Labor and Human Resources Committee. Williams's expulsion was debated by the Senate after a federal jury in Brooklyn, N.Y., found him guilty of bribery and conspiracy in May 1981. Williams resigned on March 11, 1982, only hours before the Senate was expected to vote on his expulsion—a vote that seemed certain to go against the Senate veteran. By resigning, Williams avoided becoming the first senator to be expelled since the Civil War and the first in history on grounds other than treason or disloyalty.

The next senator to be disciplined was Dave Durenberger, R-Minn., a respected member of the moderate wing of his party who had established himself as a leader on health legislation. That reputation ultimately led to his undoing, however. A favorite speaker for health care organizations, he found himself during the mid-1980s running up against the new Senate limits on honoraria. Under heavy personal financial pressure, he participated in a scheme under which honoraria funds in excess of the limit were passed through a small publisher, nominally as promotional fees for a book of speeches the senator had written. After investigating the arrangement, the Ethics Committee concluded in 1990 that the arrangement was merely a cover for receiving improper amounts of honoraria. The Senate then voted to "denounce" Durenberger—a term previously used only with Talmadge—and ordered him to pay more than $120,000 in restitution.

Durenberger's case was overshadowed in 1990, however, by the "Keating Five"—five senators who allegedly had used improper influence in behalf of Charles H. Keating Jr., an Arizona savings and loan executive. According to charges before the Senate Ethics Committee, the senators—Democrats Alan Cranston of California, Dennis DeConcini of Arizona, John Glenn of Ohio, and Donald W. Riegle Jr. of Michigan, and Republican John McCain of Arizona—attempted to intervene with federal

thrift regulators in Keating's behalf after receiving a total of $1.3 million in campaign contributions from Keating and his associates.

After lengthy public hearings, the Ethics Committee in 1991 essentially exonerated DeConcini, Glenn, Riegle, and McCain, finding them guilty only of poor judgment and, in the cases of DeConcini and Riegle, the appearance of acting improperly. Finding it likely that Cranston had violated the Senate's general standard against improper behavior, the committee reprimanded him—marking the Senate's first use of a reprimand as a form of punishment halfway between a committee rebuke and a full-Senate censure. The committee also recommended that the Senate create two task forces, one to write rules clarifying how far senators can go in helping constituents and the other to recommend campaign finance reforms.

Sen. Brock Adams, D-Wash., abruptly gave up his bid for re-election in March 1992, when the Seattle Times detailed the stories of eight unidentified women who accused him of serious sexual misbehavior. The Ethics Committee in August 1992 rebuked Mark O. Hatfield, R-Ore., for misreporting gifts. And after the 1992 session ended, the Washington Post published a long article detailing allegations that Bob Packwood, R-Ore., made unwanted sexual advances toward a number of women. The disclosure began a three-year saga of allegations and investigations that ended with Packwood resigning in October 1995 in the face of almost certain expulsion. The ethics panel assembled evidence, including pages from Packwood's personal diaries, showing that he tampered with evidence, made unwanted sexual advances to at least seventeen women, and abused his office in trying to arrange job offers for his estranged wife.

The Senate scandals and the continuing public concern over congressional ethics led to efforts to gain control over the volatile mixture of questions involving honoraria, campaign finance, and pay that some observers warned was undermining the integrity of representative government. While those issues involved the House as well, the special nature of the Senate created a difference in approach to ethics matters and divergence in the provisions of law governing members' income. Those issues also created deep splits within the Senate itself that did not follow the customary partisan or ideological lines. Instead, they pitted the large number of senators who were independently wealthy—who could afford to back curbs on pay or honoraria to shore up their ethical images—against those for whom pay raises and outside income were important.

Honoraria, or cash gifts from interests in return for a speech or article, were a major issue to senators because almost all had the opportunity to earn sizable amounts of income from them. Unlike in the House, where many obscure members rarely received speaking invitations, even junior senators were quickly able to gain positions that made them of interest to generous lobbying groups. So, while limits on honoraria were backed by those who said the payments were little more than bribes, a substantial number of senators strongly resisted such curbs. In 1983 senators agreed to limit honoraria income to 30 percent of their salary, in return for a pay raise in 1984. In 1985, however, the Senate voted to raise the cap to 40 percent, allowing a jump in income from about $22,500 to about $30,000.

The issue of congressional pay also roiled the Senate, but generally less so than in the House, where the official salary was more frequently the only major source of income for members. By positioning themselves as more reluctant to accept pay raises, senators were able to earn credit with the voters, even at the price of infuriating House members, who deeply resented being denied a raise by a chamber of millionaires.

The split culminated in 1989 ethics legislation, which created a two-tier system of congressional pay. As a result, House members at the beginning of 1991 got a 25 percent raise plus a cost-of-living increase, while senators got only the inflation hike. However, the bill—considered the most sweeping change in congressional rules of conduct since 1977—allowed senators to continue receiving honoraria, while barring House members from doing so. The ceiling on honoraria was dropped from 40 percent to 27 percent of Senate salaries and was set to decline in subsequent years. In 1991 the Senate voted to ban honoraria and accept the same salary as House members, ending the two-tier pay system.

The issue of campaign finance also provoked a sharp split in the Senate, this time of a partisan nature. Throughout the late 1980s the Senate Democratic leadership tried to push legislation to overhaul the way money is raised and spent in congressional elections. But while many agreed that changes were needed in the existing system, Republicans argued that the bills put forward by the Democrats would put the GOP at a disadvantage in efforts to win a majority of seats in Congress. In the 100th Congress, for example, the Democratic bill called for state-by-state limits on campaign spending, which backers said was the key to curbing skyrocketing election costs. But such limits were anathema to Republicans, who thought a spending cap would institutionalize the Democrats' majorities in Congress. Republicans also opposed a provision to provide public financing for Senate candidates who agreed to abide by the spending limits, arguing that it represented a government intrusion into the private realm.

Efforts by Byrd and other key Democrats to pass that bill touched off a bitter and prolonged floor battle. Republicans filibustered the Democratic bill, forcing Byrd to attempt a record eight cloture motions—all of them unsuccessful. The climactic moment came in early 1988, when Byrd sought to break the filibuster by staging round-the-clock Senate sessions. Republicans responded in kind, moving repeatedly for quorum calls and then leaving, thus forcing Democrats to keep their members near the floor to provide the quorum needed to continue business.

At one point, the Senate even used its little-known power, last used in 1942, to call for the arrest of absent members to bring them to the floor. In the middle of the night, Sen. Packwood was arrested by the sergeant at arms and physically carried onto the Senate floor. Byrd's final cloture attempt failed, however. In 1990 Senate Democrats were able to force through a campaign finance bill that also would have dismantled political action committees. The bill died in conference, however, and undoubtedly would have been vetoed by President Bush as unfair to Republicans. Bush vetoed a similar campaign finance reform bill that reached his desk in 1992.

THOMAS CONFIRMATION

The Senate on October 15, 1991, confirmed Clarence Thomas as an associate justice of the Supreme Court by 52–48, the closest vote in favor of a Supreme Court nominee in more than a century. Eleventh-hour hearings on a former employee's allegations that Thomas had sexually harassed her in the early 1980s constituted one of the wildest spectacles in modern congressional history, prompting an outpouring of public anger and scorn that rocked the Senate.

The harassment charges by Anita F. Hill, a professor of law at the University of Oklahoma, had received only a cursory behind-the-scenes examination before the Senate Judiciary Committee deadlocked 7–7 on the Thomas nomination on September 27. The weekend before the full Senate's scheduled October 8 vote on the nomination, word of the allegations leaked to the Long Island, N.Y., newspaper *Newsday* and to a National Public Radio reporter. The latter obtained an interview with Hill confirming that she had submitted an affidavit to the Judiciary Committee outlining Thomas's unwelcome sexual advances to her when she worked with him at the Department of Education and the Equal Employment Opportunity Commission. The day of the originally scheduled vote, the Senate agreed to postpone its decision until the Judiciary Committee could take testimony from Thomas, Hill, and witnesses supporting each.

The disclosure of the allegations—and the fact that the committee had failed to investigate them thoroughly—touched off a storm of criticism. Women were particularly outraged, and they let senators know it. Senators were barraged with accusations that they were insensitive to women and out of touch with America. Angry women asked whether the male-dominated institution recognized the seriousness of Hill's charge, why the committee had not pursued it until it became public, and why the full Senate had been left in the dark. "What disturbs me as much as the allegations themselves," said Sen. Barbara A. Mikulski, D-Md., "is that the Senate appears not to take the charge of sexual harassment seriously."

As the committee girded for a new round of hearings, senators were stunned by the public response to Hill's allegations. Their offices reported dozens of calls from women wanting them to get to the bottom of the charges. In their defense, Senate leaders said Hill originally sought confidentiality and that they acted properly. In the end, most senators said Hill's charges and Thomas's defense—a categorical denial—were inconclusive. Senators fell back on their previous positions based on Thomas's judicial philosophy or his determined character and rise from poverty.

The episode was not long forgotten, however. Some attributed the strong showing of women in the 1992 election in part to it. The new Senate convened in January 1993 with a record number of women, six; the first black woman senator, Carol Moseley-Braun; and the first pair of women to represent a state, Democrats Dianne Feinstein and Barbara Boxer of California.

Clinton Years: 1993–1999

After eight years in the minority, Republicans reversed their fortunes in dramatic fashion in 1994, capturing 52–48 control of the Senate by sweeping all nine open-seat races and ousting two Democratic incumbents. Adding insult to the Democrats' injury, the day after the election one of their own, Sen. Richard C. Shelby of Alabama, announced that he was switching parties, giving the GOP a 53-seat majority to start the 104th Congress. The incoming Senate freshman class had eleven Republicans and no Democrats. Since 1914, when the popular election of senators began, there had never been an all-Republican Senate freshman class.

While the House Republicans forged ahead with their "Contract with America" agenda during the first one hundred days of the 104th Congress, the slower, more deliberate pace of the Senate reflected that chamber's rules, which allowed virtually limitless amendments. It also was a product of the role played by GOP moderates, who did not share the House freshmen's enthusiasm for such planks as a middle-class tax cut and a balanced budget constitutional amendment.

Although Republican freshmen on both sides of the Capitol felt frustrated, almost everyone agreed that Congress was functioning in a way that was entirely consistent with what the drafters of the Constitution had in mind when they created the House and Senate. With its six-year terms and unlimited debate, the Senate played a role of cooling legislative passions. A determined minority often was enough to block any bill. Measures that lacked a broad, bipartisan base had trouble moving. Few of the contract items enjoyed that kind of support, and a number of them were opposed even by Republicans in the Senate. GOP senators had never endorsed the contract.

Majority Leader Bob Dole—a centrist and a pragmatist with a style that differed markedly from that of House Speaker Newt Gingrich, R-Ga., and his House allies—at first declined to embrace the new mood and the policy prescriptions in the contract, saying he had not thought much about it. But soon, under pressure from conservatives not to compromise away the House victories, he found himself attempting to win Senate approval for many of the contract-related bills sent over by the House. The result was a series of defeats for Dole. Democratic opponents, sometimes joined by Republicans, blocked several key elements of the contract, including a proposed constitutional amendment to balance the federal budget. The pattern was repeated on other House initiatives. Time and again the Senate took positions that were less aggressive and far-reaching than those in the House. And when the House tried to insist on its position in negotiations over a final version of a bill, the legislation stalled. It was, as one GOP senator put it, a clash of cultures.

In 1996 Dole, who was vying for the Republican presidential nomination, was under conflicting pressures. He did not want to appear ineffective as the Senate majority leader, yet he did not want President Bill Clinton—who was up for reelection—to be able to claim credit for a host of legislative accomplishments. Meanwhile, Senate Democrats were busily trying to embarrass Dole by filibustering Republican bills and demanding a decidedly un-Republican increase in the minimum wage. By the time Dole left the Senate in June, the Senate was in a partisan funk. Although a few major bills had cleared, most notably a farm bill and telecommunications reform, little else had gotten past the gridlock on the Senate floor. Dole had hoped to use his Senate position to define issues and demonstrate his leadership. Instead, he became a part-time leader absorbed by the presidential race and hobbled by Senate Democrats determined to keep the GOP leader and his agenda off-balance.

After his resignation from the Senate, Dole and his allies urged the GOP leadership to use the legislative process as a political tool against Clinton, to put him in awkward positions and to play up the divisions in the Democratic ranks. But the instinct for self-preservation led Dole's former colleagues to strike deal after deal with the administration, piling up a legislative record that would help their reelection campaigns.

For example, Dole urged the leadership to combine the politically popular welfare overhaul with a bill curbing the growth of Medicaid, the health insurance program for the poor and disabled. Clinton was strongly opposed to cuts in the growth of Medicaid, so such a combination would probably had stopped Clinton from signing the bill and fulfilling his campaign pledge to "end welfare as we know it." House and Senate committees followed through on Dole's recommendation, drawing a veto threat. But rank-and-file lawmakers, thinking that a successful bill would do more for their reelection prospects than another veto, pressured the leadership to abandon the Medicaid provisions. They did, and Clinton later signed the welfare bill.

Dole's replacement as Senate majority leader, Trent Lott of Mississippi, proved particularly adept at sealing deals and freeing bills stuck in partisan logjams. Although a conservative, Lott was also a pragmatist who understood the art of compromise.

Dole won his party's nomination but lost the election to Clinton in November 1996. Republicans, however, gained two seats in the Senate, giving the GOP a solid 55–45 majority in the 105th Congress. That was the party's high-water mark in the Senate following an election since 1928.

In 1997 Lott proved he had a strong practical side. He helped shepherd through the Senate legislation protecting people from losing health insurance and improving the nation's drinking water systems. Despite his willingness to deal with the Democrats, Lott suffered some high-profile defeats in 1997, including the Senate's failure by one vote to enact a constitutional amendment requiring a balanced federal budget.

Shortly after the 1996 congressional elections, newly elected senators Robert Torricelli, D-N.J., and Susan Collins, R-Maine, shake hands as Senate Majority Leader Trent Lott, R-Miss, center, and Minority Leader Tom Daschle, D-S.D., right, look on.

Even without the constitutional amendment, Lott went out of his way to negotiate a balanced budget with President Bill Clinton. His letter to Clinton pleading for cooperation reportedly assuaged the president's fears about negotiating in good faith with the Republicans. The majority leader's willingness to deal culminated in the balanced budget agreement Clinton and Congress announced in May 1997. The Republicans retained their 55–45 seat edge in the Senate as a result of the 1998 elections.

CLINTON IMPEACHMENT TRIAL

For only the second time in U.S. history, the Senate in 1999 sat in judgment of a president to determine whether he should be removed from office. In a similar fashion to the progress of Contract with America items, which the Senate was almost forced to deal with once they passed the House, senators were drawn into the political ordeal of President Clinton by rabidly anti-Clinton forces in the House, who had impeached him in December 1998. Unlike the first president to face an impeachment trial—Andrew Johnson, who in 1868 escaped removal by a single Senate vote—the outcome of Clinton's fate was never seriously in doubt.

In a solemn ceremony on January 7, 1999, Supreme Court Chief Justice William Rehnquist swore the Senate to an oath of impartiality. The Constitution mandates that the chief justice preside over the impeachment trial of a president. Unlike the hostile partisanship that characterized the proceedings in the House, the Senate conducted a short, but decorous, five-week trial.

From February 10 to 12, senators deliberated behind their chamber's closed doors on the two articles of impeachment that alleged that Clinton committed perjury and obstruction of justice in trying to conceal his relationship with a former White House intern, Monica Lewinsky. In a lopsided verdict February 12, 1999, the Senate acquitted Clinton. The verdict was not a surprise. It was clear for weeks that the Senate would not even approach the two-thirds majority the Constitution requires for conviction on impeachment articles and removal from office.

While some scholars maintained that the Senate made every effort to follow Senate precedent, others pointed to the obvious reluctance of Senate leaders to conduct a full trial, the start-and-stop pacing of the proceedings, the abbreviated House prosecution, and the lack of defense witnesses as evidence that perhaps new precedents had been set. Regardless, agreement existed that the Senate in effect felt its way through something that had never been contemplated: an impeachment that did not pose a full national crisis and that did not command full attention from the public.

NOTES

1. James Madison, *Notes on Debates in the Federal Convention of 1787*, with an introduction by Adrienne Koch (Athens: Ohio University Press, 1966), 42.

2. Charles Warren, *The Making of the Constitution* (Boston: Little, Brown, 1929), 195.

3. George H. Haynes, *The Senate of the United States: Its History and Practice* (Boston: Houghton Mifflin, 1938), vol. 1, 11.

4. James Madison, Alexander Hamilton, and John Jay, *The Federalist Papers*, with an introduction by Clinton Rossiter (New York: New American Library, 1961), 377.

5. Gaillard Hunt, ed., *The Writings of James Madison, 1787–1790* (New York: Putnam's Sons, 1904), vol. 5, 276.

6. Roy Swanstrom, *The United States Senate, 1787–1801*, 100th Cong., 1st sess., 1988, S Doc 100-31, 86. Unless otherwise indicated, Swanstrom is the primary source for the remainder of the section on the early Senate.

7. W. E. Binkley, *The Powers of the President* (New York: Russell & Russell, 1973), 52.

8. Binkley, *The Powers of the President*, 60–61.

9. Alexis de Tocqueville, *Democracy in America* (New York: Shocken Books, 1967), vol. 1, 233–234.

10. Haynes, *The Senate of the United States*, vol. 2, 1002.

11. Franklin L. Burdette, *Filibustering in the Senate* (New York: Russell & Russell, 1965), 22–25.

12. Haynes, *The Senate of the United States*, vol. 1, 298.

13. Binkley, *The Powers of the President*, 207.

14. David J. Rothman, *Politics and Power: The United States Senate 1869–1901* (Cambridge, Mass.: Harvard University Press, 1966), 188. Unless otherwise noted, Rothman is the primary source for the discussions of party bosses, modern party discipline, and attitudes toward party control.

15. Woodrow Wilson, *Congressional Government: A Study in American Politics* (Boston: Houghton Mifflin, 1885; Cleveland: Meridian Books, 1956), 147.

16. Haynes, *The Senate of the United States*, vol. 1, 95.

17. Rothman, *Politics and Power*, 146.

18. Haynes, *The Senate of the United States*, vol. 1, 398–399.

19. Burdette, *Filibustering in the Senate*, 80.

20. George B. Galloway, *The Legislative Process in Congress* (New York: Crowell, 1953), 542.

21. George B. Galloway, *Congress at the Crossroads* (New York: Crowell, 1946), 38.

22. Haynes, *The Senate of the United States*, vol. 1, 402–403.

23. Ibid., vol. 2, 973.

24. Binkley, *The Powers of the President*, 243.

25. Charles O. Jones, *The Minority Party in Congress* (Boston, Little, Brown, 1970), 144.

26. Haynes, *The Senate of the United States*, vol. 1, 411.

27. Ibid., 286.

28. Unless otherwise indicated, the primary sources for the remainder of this chapter are the *Congressional Quarterly Weekly Report* and *Congressional Quarterly Almanac* for various years, and *Congress and the Nation* (Washington, D.C.: Congressional Quarterly, various years), vols. 1–9.

29. Robert C. Byrd, *The Senate 1789–1989: Addresses on the History of the United States Senate* (Washington, D.C.: Government Printing Office, 1988), vol. 1, 643.

30. Byrd, *The Senate 1789–1989*, vol. 1, 610.

31. Jones, *The Minority Party in Congress*, 168.

32. Galloway, *The Legislative Process in Congress*, 659.

33. Ernest B. Furguson, *Hard Right: The Rise of Jesse Helms* (New York: Norton, 1988), 161.

34. James A. Miller, *Running in Place: Inside the Senate* (New York: Simon and Schuster, 1986), 28.

SELECTED BIBLIOGRAPHY

Asbell, Bernard. *The Senate Nobody Knows*. Garden City, N.Y.: Doubleday, 1978.

Bailey, Christopher J. *The Republican Party in the U.S. Senate, 1974–84*. Manchester, England: Manchester University Press, 1988.

Baker, Richard A., and Roger H. Davidson, eds. *First Among Equals: Senate Leaders of the 20th Century*. Washington, D.C.: Congressional Quarterly, 1991.

Baker, Ross K. *Friend and Foe in the U.S. Senate*. New York: Free Press, 1980.

———. *House and Senate*. 2nd ed. New York: Norton, 1995.

Benton, Thomas Hart. *Thirty Years' View*. 2 vols. New York: Greenwood Press, 1968.

Bickford, Charlene Bangs, and Kenneth R. Bowling. *Birth of the Nation: The First Federal Congress, 1789–1791*. Washington, D.C.: First Federal Congress Project, George Washington University; New York: Second Circuit Committee on the Bicentennial of the United States Constitution, 1989.

Binder, Sarah A., and Steven S. Smith. *Politics or Principle? Filibustering in the U.S. Senate*. Washington, D.C.: Brookings Institution, 1997.

Binkley, Wilfred E. *Presidents and Congress*. New York: Knopf. 1947.

———. *The Powers of the President*. New York: Russell & Russell, 1973.

Burdette, Franklin L. *Filibustering in the Senate*. New York: Russell & Russell, 1965.

Byrd, Robert C. *The Senate 1789–1989: Addresses on the History of the United States Senate*. Washington, D.C.: Government Printing Office, 1988.

Clark, Joseph S. *Congress: The Sapless Branch*. New York: Harper and Row, 1964.

———. *The Senate Establishment*. New York: Hill & Wang, 1963.

Cotton, Norris. *In the Senate: Amidst the Conflict and the Turmoil*. New York: Dodd, Mead, 1978.

Davidson, Roger H., and Walter J. Oleszek. *Congress and Its Members*. 7th ed. Washington, D.C.: CQ Press, 2000.

Dodd, Lawrence C., and Bruce I. Oppenheimer, eds. *Congress Reconsidered*. 6th ed. Washington, D.C.: CQ Press, 1997.

Dole, Bob. *Historical Almanac of the United States Senate*. Washington, D.C.: Government Printing Office, 1989.

Drew, Elizabeth. *Senator*. New York: Simon and Schuster, 1979.

Evans, Rowland, and Robert Novak. *Lyndon B. Johnson: The Exercise of Power*. New York: New American Library, 1966.

Fenno, Richard F., Jr., *Congressmen in Committees*. Boston: Little, Brown, 1974.

Fiorina, Morris P. *Congress: Keystone of the Washington Establishment*. 2nd ed. New Haven, Conn.: Yale University Press, 1989.

Foley, Michael. *The New Senate: Liberal Influence on a Conservative Institution, 1959–1972*. New Haven: Conn.: Yale University Press, 1980.

Galloway, George B. *Congress at the Crossroads*. New York: Crowell, 1946.

———. *The Legislative Process in Congress*. New York: Crowell, 1953.

Harris, Fred R. *Deadlock or Decision: The U.S. Senate and the Rise of National Politics*. New York: Oxford University Press, 1993.

Harris, Joseph P. *The Advice and Consent of the Senate*. New York: Greenwood Press, 1968.

Haynes, George H. *The Senate of the United States: Its History and Practice*. 2 vols. Boston: Houghton Mifflin, 1938.

Huitt, Ralph K., and Robert L. Peabody. *Congress: Two Decades of Analysis*. New York: Harper and Row, 1972.

Jones, Charles O. *The Minority Party in Congress*. Boston: Little, Brown, 1970.

Josephy, Alvin M., Jr. *On the Hill: A History of the American Congress*. New York: Simon and Schuster, 1980.

Kornacki, John J., ed. *Leading Congress: New Styles, New Strategies*. Washington, D.C.: CQ Press, 1990.

Loomis, Burdett A. *The New American Politician.* New York: Basic Books, 1988.

Mackaman, Frank H., ed. *Understanding Congressional Leadership.* Washington, D.C.: CQ Press, 1981.

MacNeil, Neil. *Dirksen: Portrait of a Public Man.* New York: World Publishing, 1970.

Madison, James. *Notes of Debates in the Federal Convention of 1787.* Introduction by Adrienne Koch. Athens: Ohio University Press, 1966.

Madison, James, Alexander Hamilton, and John Jay. *The Federalist.* Introduction by Clinton Rossiter. New York: New American Library, 1961.

Matthews, Donald R. *U.S. Senators and Their World.* New York: Norton, 1973.

Miller, James A. *Running in Place: Inside the Senate.* New York: Simon and Schuster, 1986.

Oleszek, Walter J. *Majority and Minority Whips of the Senate: History and Development of the Party Whip System in the United States Senate.* Washington, D.C.: Government Printing Office, 1973.

Price, David E. *Who Makes the Laws: Creativity and Power in Senate Committees.* Cambridge, Mass.: Schenkman, 1972.

Reedy, George E. *The U.S. Senate.* New York: Crown, 1986.

Reid, T. R. *Congressional Odyssey: The Saga of a Senate Bill.* San Francisco: Freeman, 1980.

Riddick, Floyd M. *Majority and Minority Leaders of the Senate: History and Development of the Offices of the Floor Leaders.* 100th Cong., 2nd sess., 1988. S Doc. Y1.1/3:100-29.

Ripley, Randall B. *Majority Party Leadership in Congress.* Boston: Little, Brown, 1969.

———. *Power in the Senate.* New York: St. Martin's, 1969.

Rothman, David J. *Politics and Power: The United States Senate, 1869–1901.* Cambridge, Mass.: Harvard University Press, 1966.

Sinclair, Barbara. *The Transformation of the U.S. Senate.* Baltimore: Johns Hopkins University Press, 1989.

Sundquist, James L. *The Decline and Resurgence of Congress.* Washington, D.C.: Brookings Institution, 1981.

Swanstrom, Roy. *The United States Senate, 1787–1801.* 100th Cong., 1st sess., 1988. S Doc 100-31.

Tocqueville, Alexis de. *Democracy in America.* 2 vols. New York: Schocken Books, 1967.

Warren, Charles. *The Making of the Constitution.* Boston: Little, Brown, 1928.

White, William S. *The Citadel: The Story of the United States Senate.* New York: Harper and Row, 1956.

Wilson, Woodrow. *Congressional Government: A Study in American Politics.* Boston: Houghton Mifflin, 1885. Reprint. Cleveland: Meridian Books, 1956.

Young, James S. *The Washington Community, 1800–1828.* New York: Columbia University Press, 1966.

Powers of Congress

CHAPTER 4

Power of the Purse

O F THE NUMEROUS POWERS of Congress, the "power of the purse" is perhaps the most important. For more than two hundred years, the constitutional grant of the powers to tax, spend, and borrow has given the legislative branch paramount authority to command national resources and direct them to federal purposes. Directly or indirectly, congressional historian George B. Galloway wrote, "perhaps nine-tenths of the work of Congress is concerned . . . with the spending of public money."[1] No other congressional prerogative confers so much control over the policies and goals of government or has such an impact on the nation's well-being.

Since the 1930s Congress has made broad use of its taxing, spending, and borrowing powers to vastly enlarge the government and expand its influence over the U.S. economy. Federal spending mounted to $1.653 trillion in fiscal 1998, accounting for about one-fifth of the gross domestic product.[2] The way the government spends its money—and raises it through taxes or borrowing—carries enormous consequences for the nation's economic performance and its political and social balance.

Through the years the House and Senate have jealously guarded their congressional powers to finance the machinery of government. But for decades Congress had trouble using its tax and spending powers to shape a coherent federal budget policy. The result was runaway budget deficits as well as constant battling between Congress and successive presidents for final authority to set federal fiscal policy.

In passing the Congressional Budget and Impoundment Act of 1974, Congress tried to provide a structure for tying together separate revenue and spending decisions into a cohesive plan for the nation's budget. Previously, it had left to the executive branch the task of drawing up a yearly federal budget proposing fiscal policy and setting forth revenue, outlay, and deficit or surplus targets. The new process compelled Congress to set overall revenue and spending targets before considering individual tax and appropriations measures. That in turn forced the House and Senate to make budget choices and go on record with regard to decisions on taxes, spending, and deficits. But it also allowed Congress to choose between sticking to those overall budget targets or bending them to encompass other objectives. All too often the other objectives won out, and Congress backed away from politically tough decisions to bring the budget closer to balance by cutting spending or raising taxes.

By 1985 budget deficits exceeded $200 billion annually and the total federal debt had reached more than $2 trillion. In a drastic move to reduce federal spending, Congress passed the Gramm-Rudman-Hollings deficit-cutting law. The legislation created a mechanism for automatic budget cuts if Congress lacked the political will to make cuts on its own. Only once, in fiscal 1986, did the automatic ax of Gramm-Rudman do its job. After that, Congress chose for the most part to use accounting practices to avoid the hard choices. There was some real deficit reduction in the late 1980s, but the budget deficit still remained high.

By 1990 budget deficits were again on the rise and Congress and the White House were at a crossroads. President George Bush had made "no new taxes" the cornerstone of his 1988 election campaign, but the slow economy was pushing the deficit to record heights. Bush in 1990 reluctantly backed down on his tax pledge, and after intense negotiations Congress and the White House agreed on a $500 billion, five-year package of tax increases and spending reductions. The new package backed away from the strict budget targets of the past and played down the size of the deficit.

With unemployment on the rise, personal income growth stagnant, and the American public unconvinced that the 1990–1991 recession had passed, Bush succumbed in his reelection bid in 1992. Bill Clinton entered office in 1993 with forecasts of significantly steeper deficits than expected. As a result, he abandoned his campaign promise of a middle-class tax cut and pushed for a deficit reduction bill that relied on a whopping tax increase targeted on the wealthy. According to budget experts, the effects of the 1990 and 1993 deficit reduction bills allowed the federal government to officially post a surplus at the end of fiscal 1998, the first since 1969.

The Power to Tax: Broad Congressional Authority

Without sufficient revenues no government could function effectively. The Constitution, along with the Sixteenth Amendment, grants Congress the right to enact virtually any tax, except for duties on exports. Article I, Section 8, clause 1 gives Congress the power "to lay and collect taxes, duties, imposts, and excises, to pay the debts and provide for the common defense and general welfare of the United States."

This authority was broad enough to encompass nearly all known forms of taxation, including tariffs on imported goods and excise taxes on the manufacture, sale, use, or transfer of property within the United States. And, in general, both Congress and the courts have construed the taxing power liberally to

DEVELOPMENT OF FEDERAL-STATE TAX IMMUNITIES

"The power to tax involves the power to destroy," declared Chief Justice John Marshall in 1819. This statement, in *McCulloch v. Maryland*, became the basis for a long, involved series of rulings in which the Supreme Court—for a time—granted to federal and state governments and their officials immunity from taxation by each other.

The first of these rulings came in 1842 in *Dobbins v. Erie County*, when the Court ruled that the states could not tax the incomes of federal officers. In 1871 the Court granted a corresponding immunity to state officials, with its ruling in *Collector v. Day*, striking down a federal tax on the salary of a federal judge.

The immunity cut both ways: if the states could not threaten the sovereignty of the federal government by taxing its officers, instrumentalities, and property, then neither could the national government use the taxing power to threaten the sovereignty of the states. In 1895 the Court granted state and municipal bonds—and the interest they generated—immunity from federal taxation similar to that already enjoyed by national securities from states. This was part of the Court's income tax ruling in *Pollock v. Farmers' Loan and Trust Co.*

But gradually the Court began to limit immunities granted to both the federal and state governments. In 1905 state immunity from federal taxation was restricted to activities of a "strictly governmental nature" *(South Carolina v. United States)*. In decisions handed down in 1937 and 1939, the Court sustained, respectively, the levying of a federal income tax on the salary of an employee of the Port of New York Authority *(Helvering v. Gerhardt)* and the levying of the New York state income tax on the salary of a federal employee *(Graves v. O'Keefe)*. A week after the second Court decision,

Congress completed action on the Public Salary Tax Act of 1939, which provided for federal taxation of state and local governmental salaries and gave the federal government's consent to state taxation of federal salaries.

As the doctrine of immunity stood in the early 1990s, the federal government was prohibited from taxing traditional state governmental activities or functions. The most significant of these prohibitions continued to bar federal taxation of most state and municipal bonds. The Tax Reform Act of 1986 made interest on industrial development bonds subject to the individual and corporate minimum income tax, though it effectively remained tax-exempt for all but high-income taxpayers.

The most recent challenge to the federal taxing power on state government was brought by South Carolina against a 1982 provision of the federal tax code that required that state and local bond-issuing authorities issue their bonds in registered form, as opposed to bearer form, to qualify for a federal tax exemption on interest earned. The Supreme Court upheld the registration requirement in *South Carolina v. Baker*.

Conversely, federally owned property generally was immune from state taxation. States were forbidden to tax congressionally chartered fiscal institutions without the consent of Congress, but state property taxes could be levied on other federally chartered corporations. Income from federal securities and tax-exempt bonds was not taxable by the states, although the Supreme Court has ruled that a state may tax the interest accrued on government bonds and estates that included U.S. bonds.

---

generate additional sources of revenue for the federal government.

Constitutional historian C. Herman Pritchett, in his book *The American Constitution*, noted that adequate sources of funds and broad authority to use them are "essential conditions for carrying on an effective government." "Consequently," he observed, "the first rule for judicial review of tax statutes is that a heavy burden of proof lies on anyone who would challenge any congressional exercise of fiscal power. In almost every decision touching the constitutionality of federal taxation, the Supreme Court has stressed the breadth of congressional power and the limits of its own reviewing powers."[3]

The Constitution did set some limits. Article I, Section 9, clause 5 forbade export duties. Section 9, clause 4 prohibited direct taxes unless each state paid a share in proportion to its population. And Section 8, clause 1 directed that "all duties, imposts, and excises" be imposed uniformly throughout the nation. The Sixteenth Amendment, however, removed the limitation on income taxes posed by clause 4. Implied limitations, as interpreted by the Supreme Court in 1819 *(McCulloch v. Maryland*, exempted state and local governments—and income from most state

and local bonds—from federal taxes. *(See box, Development of Federal-State Tax Immunities, this page.)*

SOURCES OF REVENUE

In the course of the nation's history, the primary source of revenue has shifted from tariffs on imported goods to individual and corporate income taxes. In the 1990s the main sources of revenue are individual income taxes, corporate income taxes, and social insurance taxes and contributions. Excise taxes, estate and gift taxes, and customs duties and fees contribute a smaller share of revenues.

Tariffs

The first congressional measure to raise revenue was a tariff act approved on July 4, 1789. Until the Civil War, customs duties produced sufficient revenue to meet most of the government's needs, accounting for more than 90 percent of total federal receipts. Tariffs, in addition to supplying funds for government operations, protected the nation's fledgling industries against competition from foreign imports. Through most of the nation's history, until the early years of the Great Depression in the

1930s, regions and economic interests often fought over tariff policy.

During the first half of the nineteenth century, the tariff laws offered protection mainly to manufactured goods. Western and northern farmers supported a protectionist policy for manufacturers on the assumption that industrial development, aided by high tariffs, would create a profitable home market for their products.

The Republican Party, founded in the West in 1854, lined up behind the protectionist principle on the eve of the Civil War, thereby availing itself of a policy that was to ensure it the enduring adherence of northern and eastern industrialists after the slavery issue was settled. The Democratic Party, however, generally favored a moderate- or low-tariff policy that helped it to retain the solid support of the agricultural South for years.

After the Civil War, tariff policy was the major issue in many presidential and congressional elections. Before World War I, a change in administrations often led to passage of new tariff laws. Congress devoted an inordinate amount of time to tariff making, not only because the customs duties were made and remade so frequently but also because tariffs potentially affected the interests of many segments of American commercial life.

Congress finally delegated virtually all of its tariff-making power to the president, beginning with the Fordney-McCumber Act of 1922 and the Reciprocal Trade Agreements Act of 1934. By then individual and corporate income taxes had begun replacing customs receipts as the main source of government revenue. In 1910 customs duties still brought in more than 49 percent of federal revenues; by fiscal 1998 they contributed 1.1 percent, even though customs receipts had passed the $18 billion level.[4]

Individual Income Taxes

Since the adoption of the Sixteenth Amendment, federal taxes on individual incomes and corporate profits have become the principal revenue sources. That amendment, ratified in 1913, removed an obstacle to income taxes posed by the constitutional prohibition on direct taxes unless apportioned among the states according to population.

Congress in 1862 levied a tax on individual incomes to help finance the Civil War. That tax brought in a total of $376 million, and at its peak in 1866 it accounted for 25 percent of the year's internal revenue collections. It expired in 1872. The levy was challenged as violative of the constitutional requirement that direct taxes be apportioned among the states, but the Supreme Court ruled that it was not a direct tax (*Springer v. United States*, 1881).

During the 1870s and 1880s little interest was shown in enactment of a new income tax law. But the country's growth and the accumulation of large fortunes began in the 1890s to generate pressure for a return to income taxation. After the depression of 1893 had reduced federal revenues, Congress yielded and in 1894 levied a tax of 2 percent on personal incomes in excess of $3,000. Before the new tax law became operative, however, it was challenged, and this time the Supreme Court held that an income tax was a direct tax and therefore unconstitutional without apportionment (*Pollock v. Farmers' Loan and Trust Co.*, 1895).

Although the Court had blocked the road to this attempted expansion of the tax system, a solution was afforded by the power of Congress and the states to revise the Constitution. A campaign to do so was begun immediately, and on February 23, 1913, the Sixteenth Amendment was officially declared ratified. The one-sentence amendment stated tersely: "The Congress shall have power to lay and collect taxes on incomes from whatever source derived, without apportionment among the several states, and without regard to any census or enumeration."

Thus the problem of apportioning income taxes was swept away, and Congress was left free to do what it had tried to do two decades earlier. The new grant of power came at a providential time, as the great expansion of federal revenues made necessary by America's entry into World War I would have been difficult, if not impossible, to achieve by any other means.

Congress imposed a federal income tax the same year the amendment was ratified, applying the tax to wages, salaries, interest, dividends, rents, entrepreneurial income, and capital gains from the sale of assets. It set the initial rate at 1 percent, plus a surtax of 1 to 6 percent on larger incomes. The 1913 law exempted income up to $3,000 ($4,000 for a married couple). It allowed deductions for personal interest, tax payments, and business expenses.

In the years following passage of the 1913 law, Congress complicated the federal income tax code with numerous changes that granted tax advantages to encourage specific types of activities. It also frequently changed tax rates and the level of exempted income. Maximum marginal rates—the tax rate imposed on the last dollar of income—reached as high as 94 percent during World War II.

In 1981 Congress cut the maximum rate on investment income from 70 percent to 50 percent. In 1986 a major overhaul of the tax code lowered income tax rates to 15 and 28 percent, with a 33 percent rate for certain taxpayers in the so-called income "bubble." In 1990 the "bubble" was eliminated and rates were changed to 15, 28, and 31 percent. The 1993 budget reconciliation bill imposed a fourth tax bracket, increasing the top marginal rate to 36 percent for individuals with taxable income above $115,000, joint filers with taxable income above $140,000, and heads of households with taxable income above $127,000. A 10 percent surtax was imposed on taxable income above $250,000, creating an effective top rate of 39.6 percent for these taxpayers. These provisions took effect retroactively, beginning January 1, 1993.

Corporate Taxes

Congress did not have the constitutional difficulty with a corporate income tax that it had experienced with the tax on individual income. A corporate income tax was levied in 1909 in the guise of "a special excise tax" at a rate of 1 percent of net income in excess of $5,000. That tax, like the 1894 individual income tax, was challenged in the courts, but the Supreme Court let it stand as an excise on the privilege of doing business as a corporation (*Flint v. Stone Tracy Co.*, 1911).

After ratification of the Sixteenth Amendment, an outright corporate income tax at the same rate was made a part of the Revenue Act of 1913, alongside the individual income tax. The two taxes together, broadened and modified through the years as circumstances required, became the basic elements of the nation's revenue system.

In most years corporate taxes have produced less revenue than individual income taxes. But during World War I, World War II, and the Korean War, Congress raised additional revenues by imposing an excess profits tax to supplement corporate income taxes.

Social Insurance Taxes and Contributions

Since passage of the Social Security Act of 1935, one of the most important sources of revenue has been social insurance taxes and contributions: old-age and survivor insurance, disability insurance, Medicare Part A, the railroad retirement pension fund and railroad social security equivalent fund, and unemployment insurance. Revenues for these programs go to separate trust funds that meet the current benefit obligations of the programs. The Social Security programs are financed through the payroll tax (and a matching percentage paid by employers) and from income taxes paid on Social Security benefits. Unemployment compensation programs are funded by a tax on the first $7,000 paid annually by covered employers to each employee.

Social insurance taxes have increased steadily over time, with a rapid expansion in recent years. With more people living longer, the money needed to fund the programs has increased dramatically. In fiscal year 1935 the revenue from social insurance taxes was $31 million, or less than 1 percent of total federal revenues. By fiscal year 1950 it had reached more than $4 billion, or 11 percent of federal revenues. The rapid growth began in the mid-1970s, when social insurance tax revenue reached more than $84 billion in fiscal 1975. By fiscal 1998 this revenue tallied $571.8 billion, or 33.2 percent of federal revenues, and was projected to reach more than $600 billion by 1999.[5]

The escalating Social Security tax, which does not apply to income from assets such as interest and dividends, is now larger than income taxes for most U.S. taxpayers if both employee and employer contributions are counted.

As of 1970, the individual worker paid 4.8 percent on the first $7,800 of annual income for the tax. Before the decade ended, the rate was 6.13 percent and the taxable maximum had almost tripled to $22,900. In 1998 the rate was 6.2 percent (plus a matching percentage paid by the employer) on a taxable maximum of $68,400.[6]

Excise and Other Taxes

Excise taxes have always been a part of the federal tax system. They were mentioned specifically in Article I, Section 8 of the Constitution among the various levies that Congress was authorized to impose. The excises levied upon ratification of the Constitution included taxes on carriages, liquor, snuff, sugar, and auction sales. These and similar taxes have been controversial throughout the Republic's history, in part because they were considered unfair and burdensome to the poor. Over the years excises have been imposed and repealed or lowered. During every major war the perennial liquor and tobacco taxes were supplemented by taxes on manufactured goods, licenses, financial transactions, services, luxury articles, and dozens of other items that lent themselves to this form of taxation.

The power of Congress to tax in other areas has become well established over time. Estate taxes date from the Civil War period and have been a permanent part of the national tax structure since 1916. The gift tax, levied to check avoidance of the estate tax, has been permanent since 1932.

GROWTH OF FEDERAL REVENUES

Since passage of the Revenue Act of 1913, the federal tax system has steadily produced huge increases in government revenues. Even though Congress periodically cut taxes, individual and corporate income tax revenues rose almost without interruption as a growing population and an expanding economy enlarged the base on which they were levied.

Low rates kept revenues from federal income taxes at modest levels until the United States entered World War I. Then Congress sharply increased the tax rates, raising the revenue yield to $2.3 billion in fiscal 1918 from $360 million in fiscal 1917. Since then federal individual and corporate income taxes have produced more revenue annually than all excise and other internal revenue taxes combined—except for the nine fiscal years from 1933 through 1941 when the government levied numerous excise taxes to replace revenues as incomes sagged during the Depression.

During World War II in the early to mid-1940s, high rates and a broadened tax base doubled and redoubled receipts from income and profits taxes. Those revenues fell off after the war, rose again during the Korean conflict during the early 1950s, and fell once more after hostilities ended and wartime tax rates were reduced. In the following three decades, federal income tax revenues climbed year after year even as Congress reduced rates and introduced new benefits.

By fiscal 1998 individual income taxes provided $828.6 billion in revenues. Corporate taxes were $188.7 billion. Together, they accounted for more than 59 percent of the $1.72 trillion in federal revenues for that fiscal year.

For the same year, social insurance payroll taxes and contributions of $571.8 billion accounted for more than 33 percent of revenues. Other federal receipts included $57.7 billion from excise taxes, $24.1 billion from estate and gift taxes, $18.3 billion in customs duties and fees, and more than $32 billion in receipts from miscellaneous government activities and services.[7]

TAXES AND ECONOMIC POLICY

In the 1960s Congress and the president began to use the federal tax power as a means to promote certain economic policies.

Based on Keynesian economics, the theory for using the tax power in this way, simply put, held that a slow economy could be stimulated by cutting taxes or increasing spending while an inflation-ridden economy could be defused by raising taxes or cutting spending.

Congress in 1964 approved an $11.6 billion tax cut designed to stimulate a lagging economy. Congress temporarily raised taxes in 1968 by imposing a 10 percent surcharge on personal and corporate income tax liabilities. President Lyndon B. Johnson had requested the surcharge to help finance the Vietnam War. But in 1971, with the economy in recession, Congress agreed to President Richard Nixon's proposal for an $8.6-billion-a-year tax cut to renew growth. After the economy went into a deep recession in late 1974, Congress in 1975 approved an emergency $22.8 billion tax cut. Those reductions were extended through the end of the decade.

By the 1980 presidential election it was clear that the economy was not responding to tax stimulation in the manner predicted. Inflation remained extraordinarily high at the same time that productivity decreased and joblessness was on the rise. Republican presidential candidate Ronald Reagan campaigned successfully on a new "supply-side" theory, which held that high taxes were a disincentive to work, save, and invest. This theory advocated broad tax cuts, particularly at the high end of the rate scale, to encourage more productivity and greater investment.

Congress in 1981 went along with President Reagan's request for massive tax reductions that slashed individual tax rates 25 percent over thirty-three months and then, for the first time ever, indexed the tax system to keep inflation from forcing taxpayers into higher brackets as their incomes kept pace with prices. The 1981 bill also included the biggest package of tax breaks for business in history.

By 1982 it became clear that Reagan's unorthodox economic policies were not working. Interest rates and inflation dropped during 1982, but unemployment reached a post–World War II high of 10.8 percent. The Reagan administration retreated from its supply-side tax policy and reluctantly agreed to a $98.3 billion tax increase over three years to close the budget deficit gap. As it emerged from Congress, the tax-increase measure met its target by closing tax loopholes and focusing on taxpayer compliance but did not touch individual income tax rates.

President George Bush, elected in 1988, assumed Reagan's economic mantle of low taxes, limited government, and reduced regulation, but that inheritance became a liability when the

Members of Congress gather around President Ronald Reagan in the Oval Office after the signing of his massive 1981 tax cut. Republicans and conservative Democrats banded together to win passage of the bill.

economy faltered. Economic growth began to slide in the first quarter of 1989 and, though it recovered slightly in early 1990, the economy was plainly headed for a contraction. At the outset of the Bush administration, unemployment reached its low point following the 1981–1982 recession, before starting a significant upturn in mid-1990 that continued through the end of Bush's term. Inflation jumped in 1990, though it subsided during the 1990–1991 recession. And interest rates—instead of falling—stayed relatively flat until pressure from the economic slowdown forced them into a steep downward path at the end of 1990. Furthermore, personal income at the end of 1992 was at the same level as the day Bush took office.

In 1990 administration officials, concerned that a soaring deficit could severely damage the economy and hurt Bush's 1992 reelection chances, sought to work out a deficit reduction package. Democrats refused to negotiate on reducing the deficit until Bush abandoned his "no new taxes" campaign pledge, which he subsequently did. The 1990 budget deal promised to raise a net of $137 billion in new taxes over five years. Nevertheless, instead of declining, the deficit attained its four highest levels in history in fiscal 1990–1993.

By the time Bill Clinton took office in 1993, the federal budget deficit—predicted to balloon to $304 billion in fiscal 1997—had begun to crowd out other budget issues. According to the administration, the 1993 deficit reduction bill, which passed without one Republican vote, was expected to cut the deficit by $496 billion over five years—$240 billion of it coming from net tax increases.

TAX FAIRNESS

The issue of tax fairness was the basis of a major overhaul of the federal tax code, the Tax Reform Act of 1986. Tax experts generally agree that the tax code was made more fair, if not more simple, in 1986. In the 1990s tax fairness continued to be the buzzword used by Democrats and Republicans alike in shaping tax policy.

Tax reform was President Reagan's number one domestic priority of his second term. The Tax Reform Act of 1986 reduced marginal tax rates in exchange for "broadening the base" through trimming tax breaks and making more of a household's income subject to tax in the first place. Rates were lowered to 15 percent and 28 percent, with a top marginal rate of 33 percent for some taxpayers. Six million of the working poor were freed from the burden of paying taxes. Deductions for sales tax, consumer interest, as well as miscellaneous deductions were limited or phased out. The deduction for home mortgage interest was one of the few tax breaks to survive tax reform. Although the bill was designed to be revenue neutral over the long term to meet budget deficit requirements, economists disagreed over the law's ultimate impact on the economy.

The issue of tax fairness reappeared in 1990. President Bush reluctantly backed down on his 1988 campaign pledge of "no new taxes." The policy reversal was seen as the only way to ad-dress the critical budget deficit issue. In this case the fairness question revolved around consumption taxes versus progressive taxes. Democrats skillfully painted the issue in terms of poor versus rich.

The argument for consumption taxes, such as excise or sales taxes, is that they are levied equally on all buyers and leave savings and investments alone. Opponents of consumption taxes argue that they are regressive taxes, levied without regard to one's ability to pay, and therefore hit the poor harder than the wealthy.

Progressivity in taxes, or basing tax rates on relative ability to pay, is the basis of the federal income tax. The argument for progressive taxes is that they fall more heavily on those more able to bear them and they address the income inequities associated with a market economy. The argument against high marginal tax rates is that they slow investment and job creation and create disincentives to work.

In 1990, after prolonged negotiations and the defeat of an initial plan, a package of tax changes raised the top rate on individuals from 28 percent to 31 percent, added a luxury tax on certain goods, and imposed a number of other changes designed to shift the tax burden to the wealthy.

Most of the tax revenue raised by the 1993 deficit reduction measure came from the wealthiest taxpayers.

WRITING TAX LEGISLATION

In both the House and Senate, powerful and prestigious committees control the complicated process of putting tax legislation together. Those committees—Ways and Means in the House and Finance in the Senate—accumulated vast power to shape the federal tax system and to influence the varied economic interests at stake in the tax laws.

The Constitution requires that revenue measures originate in the House, and the Ways and Means Committee writes the first draft of nearly all tax measures. The House often passes Ways and Means measures with few, if any, changes and then sends them to the Senate.

The Finance Committee may rework the House provisions—and in some cases it may write entirely new legislation. The full Senate as a rule approves even more far-reaching amendments before passing the measure. As with all legislation, the House and Senate must resolve their differences on the bill before sending it to the White House for the president's signature.

In the decades after World War II, the tax committees worked closely with the executive branch in drawing up tax legislation. Before the 1970s Treasury officials usually offered tax proposals and Congress acted on their recommendations. Congress itself initiated major tax-revision measures in 1948, 1952, and again in 1975. The tax cut enacted in 1981 was largely designed by the Reagan administration; the tax increase bills in 1982 and 1984 were congressional ideas. But committee members, congressional staffs, and Treasury officials continued to consult throughout the process to ensure agreement on tax-code changes. Starting in the late 1980s, Democratic-controlled Congresses became reluctant to initiate taxes without the support of Republican presidents for fear of negative political repercussions. The struggle in the mid- to late 1990s was between a Republican majority in Congress that advocated across-the-board tax cuts and a Democratic president who sought targeted tax relief for specific segments of the population.

In the 1980s taxes frequently were enacted in omnibus budget reconciliation bills that packaged together spending cuts and revenue increases necessary to meet the targets mandated by the annual congressional budget resolution. Reconciliation bills frequently have served as legislative catch-all bills with the addition of "sweeteners," such as members' pet projects, to balance the spending cuts and revenue increases. Because members generally vote on the entire package, the bill can provide political cover for difficult votes. Changes in the congressional budget process in 1990 led to a decline in the use of reconciliation bills.

In both the House and Senate, the chairs of the influential tax committees have dominated congressional revenue deliberations. Carefully balancing competing interests during committee action, these committee chairs usually receive strong backing from their panel's members in fending off floor amendments that would change the basic shape of the legislation.

Both committees are assisted by the Joint Taxation Committee, which exists largely to provide the staff expertise needed in dealing with complex tax bills. In addition to serving as technical advisers, the committee staff prepares revenue estimates for the use of the tax committees and Congress.

The collection of federal revenues affects virtually all Americans, and a growing band of labor, industry, and public interest organizations has sought to win special treatment for particular interests. Although often successful, the special interest lobbyists on tax legislation find it difficult to combat legislation that is seen as a "tax fairness" issue. In the Tax Reform Act of 1986, the special interest victories were few when compared with the closing of billions of dollars of special interest tax loopholes.

Ways and Means Role

The House created Ways and Means in 1802 and gave it responsibility for spending as well as taxes. In subsequent years the House gradually reduced the panel's control over spending legislation, and in 1865 it set up a separate Appropriations Committee.

The key to success and power for Ways and Means has often been linked to the skill of its chairman. Congressional analyst Allen Schick notes that "the committee is successful when it controls the House and when the chairman controls the committee. The chairman is the critical link."[8]

Of the ten members who chaired Ways and Means from the late 1940s to the end of the twentieth century, none matched the extraordinary authority over tax legislation exercised by Wilbur D. Mills, D-Ark., during the sixteen years he led the committee (1957–1974). His long tenure and command of complex tax laws

won him wide respect from House members. Mills also kept control over all tax measures by bringing them before the whole committee and refusing to establish permanent subcommittees to consider different issues.

Mills solidified his power by accurately sensing what the House would support and drafting legislation accordingly. House leaders sent Ways and Means measures to the floor under so-called closed rules—which barred amendments—and the full House regularly passed the panel's bills by large margins.

By the 1970s, however, the House was changing. Democratic supporters of sweeping tax-law "reforms" grew restless with the power Mills held over revenue legislation. In 1974 Mills's self-confessed alcoholism and erratic personal behavior forced him to resign as chairman. House Democrats took the opportunity in October and December of that year to make the committee more liberal and to break the chairman's grip over tax deliberations.

The reforms required that the committee set up subcommittees, add both members and staff, open its meetings to the public—although by the mid-1980s some meetings were once again closed—and give up its power to make Democratic committee assignments. The committee also had to give up a slice of its legislative jurisdiction.

Al Ullman, D-Ore., succeeded Mills, chairing Ways and Means from 1975 through 1980. But Ullman, for several reasons, was a weaker leader than Mills, and the expanded committee proved too fragmented and contentious for Ullman to forge the consensus that Mills had constructed on behalf of the panel's tax bills. As a result, Ways and Means suffered some embarrassing defeats during House debate on its measures. And unlike Mills, Ullman was unable to match Finance Committee Chairman Russell B. Long's, D-La., experience and expertise in House-Senate negotiations on tax legislation.

When Ullman was defeated for reelection in 1980, House Democrats named Dan Rostenkowski, D-Ill., to chair the committee. After two early losses on tax issues in 1981 and 1982, Rostenkowski reevaluated his strategy. Rather than focus on compromise with Republicans on his committee, he decided that the key to success was to work with Republican leaders who could deliver the votes. Thus he worked with Senate Republican leaders when they controlled the Senate and with the White House. Rostenkowski could not control Ways and Means the way Mills once did, but he restored the committee to its preeminent role in the House.[9]

As a result of rules changes by the GOP-led House in 1995, the Ways and Means chairman—like most other committee chairmen—could hold his position for no more than three consecutive terms, beginning with the 104th Congress. The move was expected to keep the chairman from creating a powerful fiefdom as in the past.

As of 1999, Ways and Means had jurisdiction over revenue, debt, customs, trade, Social Security, and Medicare legislation. Five subcommittees have jurisdiction over health, human resources, oversight, Social Security, and trade legislation. But the full committee still considers basic tax law proposals, conducting lengthy hearings with testimony from the secretary of the Treasury and other expert witnesses.

After hearings, the committee normally begins markup sessions to draft the bill. The Treasury Department may have submitted its own proposals, but preparation of legal language often is left to congressional and Treasury experts working together after the hearings have delineated the general scope of the provisions to be included in the bill. Despite the 1973 House rule limiting closed committee meetings, many Ways and Means markups are closed.

House Action on Tax Measures

Changing House procedures have loosened Ways and Means control over the bills it writes and reports to the House. Before 1973 the House took up tax measures under special procedures that had become traditional for Ways and Means legislation and all but guaranteed acceptance of the committee's work without change. Technically, under House rules in effect until 1975, revenue legislation was "privileged" business, which meant that it could be brought up for consideration on the floor ahead of other measures and without a special rule from the Rules Committee. In practice, Ways and Means usually obtained a closed rule before sending its bills to the floor. Under that procedure the bill was not open to amendment in the course of House debate; essentially, the House had to accept or reject the bill as a whole. Opponents of the bills had one opportunity, at the end of the debate, to try to make changes in the legislation, but significant revisions seldom resulted.

One exception existed to the prohibition against floor amendments. Any amendments that were approved by the Ways and Means Committee could be offered by a committee member and put to a vote. This gave the committee an opportunity to backtrack on any provision that appeared to be in danger of drawing unusual House opposition.

Use of a closed rule was justified on the ground that tax, trade, and other Ways and Means bills were too complicated to be revised on the floor, particularly because many of the proposed changes probably would be special interest provisions designed to favor a small number of persons or groups. Floor amendments, it was argued, might upset the carefully balanced legislation considered and approved by the committee.

Nonetheless, the closed rule tradition came under attack as members of the House began to challenge the power of the Ways and Means Committee. Finally, in 1973, Democrats modified the closed rule by adopting a proposal that allowed fifty or more Democrats to bring up proposed amendments to Ways and Means bills at the party caucus. If the caucus voted to approve them, the Rules Committee was instructed to write a special rule permitting the amendments to be offered on the floor. In 1975 the House went a step further by changing its rules to require that all Ways and Means revenue bills receive a rule before

they were brought to the floor; their "privileged" status was eliminated.

The full impact of the House reforms was not evident until 1981 when the Democratic-controlled Ways and Means Committee brought a tax-cut bill to the House floor that differed significantly from the large, three-year tax reduction proposal offered by President Reagan. Even though committee Democrats had added sweeteners to the committee bill in an effort to win support, enough Democrats voted with Republicans to defeat the committee bill and replace it with a Reagan-endorsed version. The vote was 238–195. The prevailing substitute was sponsored by two Republican members of Ways and Means, including the ranking minority member, Barber B. Conable Jr., N.Y.

The full House continued to challenge the power of the Ways and Means Committee during the 1980s. In 1985 House Republicans opposed the major tax-reform legislation that was supported by both Rostenkowski and President Reagan. To block the legislation, Republicans and a core group of Democrats defeated the rule that allowed consideration of the bill on the House floor. It took a presidential visit to Capitol Hill to reverse rank-and-file House Republican opposition and save the legislation. In 1983 the same tactic had been used by Republicans to defeat another Rostenkowski tax package. The 1983 legislation passed only after a new, less restrictive rule was adopted by the House.

Senate Finance Committee

The Senate Finance Committee, created in 1816, shares almost the same jurisdiction as Ways and Means. Historically, its power and influence on revenue matters have been more limited. Because of the constitutional directive that tax legislation originate in the House, the Finance panel usually has taken on a review or appellate role for interests trying to change House-approved provisions.

Despite the constitutional stricture, in recent years the Senate's role in shaping the final package of tax legislation has become much more important. On occasion the Senate has done all but originate tax legislation. In 1982, under the chairmanship of Bob Dole, R-Kan., the Finance Committee initiated a politically sensitive tax increase; the Ways and Means Committee voted to forgo writing its own bill and go directly to conference on the Senate measure. The Tax Reform Act of 1986 also was largely shaped by the Finance Committee. After initial House passage of the bill in late 1985, the Finance Committee put together a no-frills, low-tax-rate alternative plan that went on to become law.

Through the years the Finance Committee acquired a reputation for being receptive to special interest tax schemes. That impression may trace to the second part of Article I, Section 7 of the Constitution, which declares that "the Senate may propose . . . amendments" to revenue legislation. At times, the Finance panel has had little to do except tinker with the House-passed bills and add provisions in which individual senators have a spe-

The chairman of the Senate Finance Committee is one of the most influential figures in the Senate. Here Finance Chairman William V. Roth Jr., R-Del., left, and Sen. John H. Chafee, R-R.I., discuss welfare and Medicaid legislation.

cial interest. Today, the Finance Committee subscribes to a broad interpretation of its authority to amend tax legislation. On occasion, it attaches a major revenue-affecting amendment to a minor House-passed tax bill awaiting Senate action.

Under Russell Long's chairmanship, from 1965 to 1981, the committee became known for its practice of tucking a variety of special interest amendments into unrelated revenue measures. Long claimed fatherhood of the "Christmas tree bill"—so called because it is adorned with amendments like baubles on a holiday tree. The prototype was a 1966 international payments measure, which Long's committee transformed into a gem of legislative vote trading and congressional accommodation that aided, among others, presidential candidates, the mineral ore industry, large investors, hearse owners, and Scotch whiskey importers.

Long's extended tenure as chairman would not be possible today. The Republican Senate in 1995 imposed a six-year term limit on committee chairmanships beginning in 1997. The new rule would apply even if Republicans were in the minority. A member who had served six years as chairman could continue another six years as ranking minority member.

Senate Handling of Tax Bills

Senate floor action on tax legislation often radically departs from the careful consideration that the House and the Finance Committee give revenue proposals. The Senate has no procedures or rules to ward off amendments to tax bills. And at times senators have used their prerogative to offer amendments

to rewrite House bills or load them with unrelated provisions.

Senate tax-bill debates often have evolved into legislative logrolling and mutual accommodation, particularly late in congressional sessions when members try to push through favorite proposals before adjournment. Senate amendments, germane to tax legislation only because they would amend some Internal Revenue Code provision, have turned many tax measures into Christmas tree bills bestowing benefits on varied economic interests. Tight budget constraints in the 1980s and 1990s somewhat limited this practice.

The Senate sometimes approves popular amendments in full knowledge that House conferees will insist that they be dropped. Finance Committee leaders sometimes accept amendments out of courtesy to a sponsoring senator. As chairman, Long frequently agreed to take amendments to conference with the House as bargaining chips that could be discarded in trade-offs for other provisions that senators considered essential. Senate floor maneuvering on tax bills often lasts several weeks.

Conference Negotiations

Like other acts of Congress, most tax legislation is put in final form by a House-Senate conference committee. But because the economic stakes are high, tax-bill conferences have produced intense and dramatic bargaining. Conferees from each side vote as a unit, with the majority view determining the position of each side on every issue.

The conference may last from a day or two to several weeks

At a conference meeting on the federal budget, House Budget Chairman John R. Kasich, R-Ohio, right, presents the gavel to House Ways and Means Chairman Bill Archer, R-Texas, center.

on controversial bills. Congressional and Treasury tax experts are present to assist the conferees. Once all differences are resolved, the bill is sent back to each chamber for approval of the conference agreement. The House files a conference report (usually for both chambers, although the Senate may file an identical report) listing the differences and how they were resolved. If the conference agreement is approved by both, the bill is sent to the president.

House and Senate action on tax legislation often is not completed until late in a congressional session, and conferees have had to negotiate their differences under tight deadlines to finish by adjournment. Astute conference leaders have used the pressures of time to strengthen the case for their positions. The final products, sometimes negotiated in all-night sessions, usually represent careful compromises that take account of House and Senate politics. The legislation that conferees fashion also may determine how much money the government collects for years to come.

During conference negotiations, Treasury officials and Joint Taxation Committee staff aides help members keep track of the revenue impact of their decisions. With the strict controls on revenues mandated by the Budget Enforcement Act of 1990, House and Senate tax negotiators must consider the budgetary impact of tax changes and must find offsetting tax receipts for any tax cuts. *(See "Congress and the Budget," p. 166.)*

The Power to Spend: Twentieth Century Growth

The Constitution gives Congress the basic authority to decide how the government should spend the money it collects. That power is protected by Article I, Section 9, clause 7, which stipulates that the federal government may spend its revenues only in such amounts and for such purposes as Congress specifically has approved.

The Constitution sets few other limits on the spending power. Section 9, clause 7 requires that "a regular statement and account of the receipts and expenditures of all public money shall be published from time to time." Elsewhere, Article I, Section 8, clause 12 prohibits appropriating money "to raise and support armies" for longer than two years. *(See box, Control of the Nation's Currency, p. 412.)*

FEDERAL SPENDING: WHERE THE MONEY GOES

An analysis of federal spending from the early 1960s to the late 1990s shows striking changes in federal priorities. Increases in spending can be seen across the board, but growth in "entitlement" spending is the most dramatic.

Entitlement spending is often called uncontrollable spending. These federal programs—such as Social Security, Medicare, Supplemental Security Income, and child nutrition programs—provide benefits to which the recipients have a legally enforceable right. As long as a person meets the program criteria, the government must pay these programs' bills and appropriate more if money runs out during a fiscal year. Some of the programs, such as Social Security and Medicare, have permanent funding and do not have to go through the annual appropriations process.

The charts provide information on changing budget priorities from fiscal 1962 to fiscal 1998.

Defense: Despite President Ronald Reagan's massive military buildup in the 1980s, defense spending as a percent of total federal outlays declined from 49 percent of outlays in fiscal 1962 to 26.5 percent in fiscal 1989. By fiscal 1998, defense spending accounted for 16.2 percent of total outlays.

Direct Benefits to Individuals: An increase in "Great Society" social programs during President Lyndon B. Johnson's administration and an ever-expanding population of older Americans made direct benefit payments to individuals—or entitlements—the fastest growing part of federal spending. In fiscal year 1962 direct benefits to individuals accounted for only 24.3 percent of federal spending; the fiscal 1998 figure was 49.4 percent. Medicare, which was added to the Social Security program in 1965, accounted for a large part of the growth in direct benefits, while spending on veterans benefits significantly declined.

Net Interest: As the federal debt soared because of massive budget deficits, interest on the debt as a percent of federal spending more than doubled from fiscal 1962 (6.4 percent) to fiscal 1998 (14.7 percent).

Grants to State and Local Governments: At first glance, the federal government seems to have been generous with the states over the years. Grants to state and local governments were 7.4 percent of outlays in fiscal 1962 and more than doubled to 14.9 percent in fiscal 1998. A closer look, however, reveals that most of the increase has been in federal payments to states for social programs, such as Medicaid. Federal grants for capital investment have remained steady. (During the late 1970s federal spending for capital investment was significantly increased, but funding was discontinued during the Reagan administration.)

All Other Federal Spending: Out of the remaining funds, the federal government must run all government programs related to agriculture, education, foreign aid and diplomacy, the environment, the judiciary, and hundreds more.

Fiscal Year 1962

Fiscal Year 1998

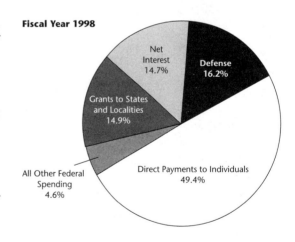

Note: Figures may not add to 100% because of rounding.

The Constitution explicitly directs the government to perform various functions—establish post offices, roads, armed forces, and courts, pay debts, and take a decennial census—that can be accomplished only by spending money. But by authorizing Congress to "provide for the common defense and general welfare of the United States," the Constitution by implication grants broad authority to spend. It was this implied spending power that opened the way for expansive interpretation of the congressional power to make outlays to address a growing nation's changing problems and challenges.

When the Republic was founded, political leaders differed over what spending for the general welfare meant. One strict interpretation, voiced by James Madison in *The Federalist* (No. 41), insisted that such outlays were limited to the purposes connected with the powers specifically mentioned by the Constitution.[10] A looser construction, advocated by Alexander Hamilton, contended that the general welfare clause conferred on the government powers separate and different from those specifically enumerated in the Constitution. Under the latter interpretation the federal government was potentially far more powerful than the strict constructionists intended.

Deep disagreement about the extent of congressional spending powers continued well into the twentieth century. The broad interpretation came to be the generally accepted view, but it was not until 1936 that the Supreme Court found it necessary to give its opinion on the meaning of the controversial wording. In a decision that year *(United States v. Butler)*, the Court invalidated the Agricultural Adjustment Act of 1933, which had provided federal payments to farmers who participated in a program of production control for the purposes of price stabilization. Although this law was held unconstitutional, the Court construed the general welfare clause to mean that the congressional power to spend was not limited by the direct grants of legislative power found in the Constitution.

Rather, an expenditure was constitutional "so long as the welfare at which it is aimed can be plausibly represented as national rather than local." The 1933 law was overturned on other grounds but was later reenacted on a different constitutional basis and was upheld by the Court. Decisions in the years immediately following upheld the tax provisions of the Social Security Act, thus confirming the broad authority of Congress to use its taxing and spending powers to provide for the general welfare of the nation *(Steward Machine Co. v. Davis,* 1937; *Helvering v. Davis,* 1937).

EXPANSION OF FEDERAL SPENDING

Before the Great Depression of the 1930s, government spending was limited by a consensus that outlays should not exceed revenues except in times of war. In their study, *Democracy in Deficit,* James M. Buchanan and Richard E. Wagner maintained that the unwritten "fiscal constitution" in the past constrained the federal government's impulse to launch new spending programs. "Barring extraordinary circumstances," they wrote, "public expenditures were supposed to be financed by taxation, just as private spending was supposed to be financed from income."[11]

Furthermore, the federal government's role in the economic affairs of the country was minimal. "The original role of the federal government was limited both by the precise language of the Constitution and by the prevailing social consensus that powerful central governments should be avoided," Donald G. Ogilvie, associate dean of the Yale University School of Organization and Management, wrote in 1979. "As a result, federal activities were restricted to those traditional 'public good' functions such as the maintenance of national security forces, management of the monetary system, and the operation of the executive, congressional, and judicial branches of the government."[12]

Annual federal outlays reached the $1 billion level only in 1865, the last year of the Civil War, then subsided below that mark until the nation entered World War I. The government spent $18.4 billion in fiscal 1919, incurring a $13.4 billion deficit. But as in the decades after the Civil War, outlays again fell off in peacetime, holding steady between $2 billion and $3 billion a year during the 1920s.

Between the end of the Civil War and the 1920s the nation experienced rapid change. Its population soared, and its economy grew vastly larger and more complex. People crowded into fast-sprawling metropolitan regions and moved from place to place more frequently. Life expectancies lengthened, while families grew apart. Those changes "combined to produce new requirements for federal programs," Ogilvie suggested, and "complicated and expanded the role of the public sector in social, economic, and political affairs."[13]

The nation's federal system reached a turning point in the 1930s during the Great Depression. President Franklin D. Roosevelt and Congress launched massive federal programs to pull the economy out of the worst downturn in U.S. history. Spending for domestic assistance programs jumped to $7 billion by 1939 as outlays for civilian needs surpassed spending on the military, veterans, and war-incurred debt. During the Depression strict adherence to balanced budgets was impossible. At the same time economists advising the government gave theoretical support to deficit spending during peacetime years to stimulate production. The old link between taxes and spending gradually gave way.

According to Ogilvie, ending the balanced-budget consensus in the 1930s "stimulated spending by allowing the federal government to avoid the pain of directly imposing the cost of new programs on the people through higher taxes." In the process, Ogilvie added, "government lost its only yardstick by which to determine how many worthy federal programs the country could afford."[14]

Government's Expanding Role

Roosevelt's New Deal programs marked a fundamental shift away from the limited role that the federal government had previously filled in the nation's economic and social life. During the 1930s the government first took on responsibility for managing an economy that previous *laissez-faire* policy assumed to be self-regulating. The New Deal also produced a host of programs that redistributed the nation's wealth from one group to another and from some regions to others.

"Over the next forty years," Ogilvie observed, "this income redistribution function dramatically changed the structure of the federal budget and increased its share of the national wealth. For the first time, federal officials and elected legislators began to influence the distribution of wealth significantly, initially through the tax system and then increasingly through direct spending programs of the federal government."[15]

Most New Deal initiatives were implemented as countercyclical programs to be phased out as economic conditions improved. Some were terminated within a few years. Others—such as the Social Security system and federal credit assistance for housing, small business, and farmers—remained major func-

The Great Society was the most ambitious social agenda advanced by any president since the New Deal era. Here President Lyndon B. Johnson signs legislation establishing the Medicare program as former president Harry S. Truman looks on.

tions of the government into the 1990s. More significantly, the New Deal set precedents for federal efforts to provide for the poor and assure economic security for all Americans when times were hard.

The Depression ended when the nation began to mobilize for war, but the federal government continued to expand income transfer programs and take over more and more functions that states, local governments, and individuals previously had performed. "In essence, almost without knowing it, we decided to tax ourselves at the federal level and to commission the federal government to provide goods and services that we had historically provided for ourselves," Ogilvie wrote.[16]

Those programs, including many that provided federal grants to state and local governments to finance specific projects, grew gradually from the late 1930s to the mid-1960s. Then, starting in 1965, with a forceful Lyndon B. Johnson as president prodding a heavily Democratic 89th Congress, the government launched a stream of "Great Society" programs that extended its role in providing medical care, education assistance, regional development, nutrition, urban renewal, job training, and other services for people and localities. During the 1970s Congress kept enlarging most of these programs—and adding a few new ones—despite the opposition of Republican presidents.

These new programs translated into increased federal spending. A government that spent less than 4 percent of the nation's gross national product in calendar 1930 was spending more than

19 percent in 1998. Outlays rose from $3.6 billion in fiscal 1931 to $9.5 billion in fiscal 1940. In fiscal 1998 federal outlays reached $1.653 trillion.

During World War II federal spending multiplied almost tenfold, reaching $92.7 billion in fiscal 1945. Postwar spending declined but stayed well above previous peacetime levels. The Korean War buildup more than doubled outlays from less than $30 billion in fiscal 1948 to $76.1 billion in fiscal 1953. Spending fell below $70 billion in fiscal 1955, but from fiscal 1956 through fiscal 1998 the budget increased in every year except fiscal 1965.[17]

Ogilvie noted that it took 186 years for federal spending to exceed $100 billion; it took only nine more years to reach $200 billion; four more to exceed $300 billion; two more to reach $400 billion; and an additional two years to go to $500 billion.[18] It took only eight more years for federal spending to double, to more than $1 trillion, in 1987.

Changing Budget Priorities

Shifting national priorities resulted not only in increased spending but also in changed spending patterns. Federal outlays grew rapidly for tasks, notably national defense, that the federal government traditionally had performed. But as new social programs came along, they absorbed more and more of the government's resources.

Annual U.S. military spending peaked at $83 billion during World War II and again at $53 billion during the Korean War.

Defense outlays fell off in the mid-1950s but climbed back above $50 billion in fiscal 1962. Defense spending then climbed steadily to a Vietnam War peak of $82.5 billion. After declining slightly in the early 1970s, defense outlays accelerated as the country sought to upgrade its military capabilities, reaching a peak of $303.6 billion for fiscal 1989. In fiscal 1998, defense spending tallied $268.5 billion.[19]

Spending for national defense declined as a percent of federal spending each year from 1954, when it accounted for 69.5 percent of spending, until 1965, when it fell to 42.8 percent of spending. The national defense share rose a small amount during the next three years and then began a decline that continued until the late 1970s. By 1980 national defense accounted for only 22.7 percent of federal spending. The military buildup during President Reagan's administration led to a small increase in the defense share, which reached 28.1 percent of spending in fiscal 1987. In the 1990s defense spending fell below 20 percent of total federal spending, hitting 16.2 percent in fiscal 1998.[20]

At the same time federal government direct payments to individuals—the poor, the sick, the elderly, retired government workers—jumped. From $21.7 billion in the fiscal 1960 budget, such payments rose to $817.1 billion in fiscal 1998, accounting for 50 percent of total outlays. And federal grants to state and local governments—for purposes such as highway construction, mass transit, sewage treatment plants, job training, revenue sharing, community development, education, and welfare services—escalated from 5 percent of total federal outlays in fiscal 1955 to 15 percent in fiscal 1998.[21]

Although most of the post-Depression social programs were intended to assist the poor and to improve public services in parts of the nation with hard-pressed regional or local economies, many of them also benefited middle-income Americans, and even the wealthy. Moreover, state and local governments had grown dependent on federal grants for operating funds. "We have, in effect, created a special interest group that includes a majority of the population," Ogilvie contended.[22]

Congress, as a political institution, is attuned to the broad appeal that its benefit programs carry. Beneficiaries of federal programs—particularly older Americans, state and local officials, teachers and students, social workers and welfare recipients, and entrepreneurs who win government contracts—have become adept at lobbying for ever-higher funding. Such lobbying organizations often work with the agency officials who run the programs and with congressional committees that authorize them.

Some changes may be in the offing, however. In 1992, on the campaign trail, Bill Clinton vowed to "end welfare as we know it"; in 1996, as president, he signed into law a bill ending the federal government's sixty-one-year-old entitlement of cash aid to poor women and children. Federal funding would be provided to states, which would determine eligibility. In addition, the new law cut the federal food stamp program, denied various federal benefits—including Supplemental Security Income (SSI)—to legal immigrants, made it harder for disabled children to qualify

for federal aid, reorganized federal child care assistance programs, and toughened enforcement of child support orders.

Backdoor Spending

In political reality, broad-based and determined support makes any program tough to cut. Congress in some cases has made budget cutting even harder by insulating programs against budget restraint. Through various legislative routes, Congress has exempted from the annual appropriations process about three-quarters of the money the government spends each year.

Congress deliberately authorized some so-called uncontrollable, or "backdoor," spending simply because the government must shield certain obligations from political controversy. An example of that kind of spending is the permanent appropriation, passed in 1847, to pay interest as it comes due on the national debt. The government must meet that obligation to retain its borrowing credibility. For many other programs Congress set up backdoor financing arrangements to shield their budgets from annual scrutiny by the Appropriations committees.

Backdoor spending obligations take several forms. For some programs Congress authorizes agencies to enter into contracts, borrow money, or guarantee loans that eventually obligate the government to make payments. And Congress excludes some quasi-government agencies—such as the Post Office—from the annual federal budget, effectively exempting them from overall fiscal controls.

But by far the largest backdoor outlays result from the tremendous growth of federal entitlement programs—so-called because Congress by law entitles their recipients to the benefits the government programs provide. Entitlement programs include Social Security, Medicare, and veterans' pensions. In 1990 Congress made an attempt to slow the expansion of entitlement programs by putting them on a "pay-as-you-go" basis, requiring that any expansion be paid for by a corresponding entitlement cut or revenue increase. Pay-as-you-go restrictions do not affect increases in entitlement spending that result when more people meet eligibility requirements, however.

TWO-STEP FUNDING PROCESS

Congress's appropriation of funds is part of a two-step authorization-appropriations process that must take place in most cases before money from the U.S. Treasury can be spent. Authorization bills set up or continue a federal program or agency, either indefinitely or for a specific period of time, and generally provide a ceiling on the amount of funding for the program. Appropriations bills then permit federal agencies to incur obligations and make payments out of the Treasury.

The Constitution gives the House power to originate tax bills, but it contains no specific provision to that effect concerning appropriations bills. However, the House traditionally has assumed the responsibility for initiating all appropriations bills and has jealously guarded this self-assumed prerogative whenever the Senate from time to time has attempted to encroach upon it. The practical result, as far as appropriations are concerned, is that traditionally the House Appropriations Committee has been more powerful than its counterpart on the Senate side because the bulk of basic appropriations decisions were made in the House committee.

Early Funding Procedures

Before World War I, neither the expenditures nor the revenues of the federal government exceeded $800 million a year. No comprehensive system of budgeting had been developed, although the method of handling funds had undergone various changes in Congress. During the pre–Civil War period, both taxing and spending bills were handled in the House by the Ways and Means Committee. That eventually proved too difficult a task for a single committee, and in 1865 the House established an Appropriations Committee. A similar situation existed in the Senate, where an Appropriations Committee was created in 1867.

In subsequent years both the House of Representatives and Senate dispersed appropriations functions to other committees as well. Between 1877 and 1885 the House transferred jurisdiction over eight of fourteen annual appropriations bills from the Appropriations Committee to various authorizing panels. The Senate eventually followed the House lead in reducing what members considered the excessive authority of the appropriations panels. Such actions gave the committees most familiar with a government agency and its programs the power to control that agency's appropriations. But that divided responsibility also frustrated any unified control over government budget policy.

After World War I Congress again consolidated the appropriations function while giving the executive branch stronger budgeting capabilities. The House in 1920 restored to the Appropriations Committee exclusive appropriations authority, and the Senate in 1922 similarly concentrated power over spending measures in its Appropriations panel. What evolved from those steps was the two-stage authorization-appropriations process.

Authorizations

By its own rules, Congress cannot consider appropriations for a federal program until the president has signed legislation authorizing its functions during a fiscal year. The House has had a rule since 1837 that "no appropriation shall be reported in any general appropriations bill, or be in order as an amendment thereto, for any expenditure not previously authorized by law." The Senate has a similar rule but, because appropriations bills originate in the House, the House rule is governing in any case. There are some exceptions. For example, a portion of the annual appropriations for the military is authorized by the Constitution, and occasionally Congress turns a blind eye to its rule. Generally, however, appropriations must await congressional action on the authorizations.

This requirement has led to conflict in Congress on numerous occasions. Since the 1950s Congress increasingly has re-

quired annual authorizations of programs that previously had permanent or multiyear authorizations. The trend toward annual authorizations represented a victory for the legislative committees—such as Agriculture, Armed Services, and Education and Labor—which felt that they had lost effective control over their programs to the Appropriations committees. The Appropriations committees, particularly in the House, took a dim view of annual authorizations, in part because they felt the procedure tended to diminish their power.

Annual authorizations also have added one more roadblock to the slow funding process. With government programs growing in number and becoming more complex, congressional committees needed more time to review agency operations and financing needs. In its 1974 budget law Congress set a deadline of May 15 for legislative committees to report authorization bills; the deadline was eliminated in the mid-1980s when Congress consistently missed the target date.

Appropriations

The House and Senate fund federal government programs through thirteen annual appropriations bills and often one or two supplemental appropriations measures. In recent years a continuing appropriations resolution has been used to fund programs that have not received their annual appropriation by the beginning of a fiscal year on October 1.

In the House, the Appropriations Committee rivals Ways and Means in power and prestige. Traditionally composed largely of senior members elected from safe congressional districts, the Appropriations Committee for the most part has been a fiscally conservative body. Since the mid-1970s, however, House rules have worked to give younger, more liberal members a voice on the committee.

Its thirteen subcommittees have functioned largely as independent kingdoms. The subcommittees, organized along functional lines, divide up total budget authority and outlays allocated to the full Appropriations Committee by the budget resolution. Each subcommittee—like its counterparts in the Senate—has responsibility for one of the thirteen annual appropriations bills. Generally, members of the subcommittees become expert in their assigned areas. The subcommittees, and particularly their chairmen, consequently wield substantial power over spending.

After each House and Senate Appropriations subcommittee receives spending allocations from the full Appropriations Committee, it begins shaping its individual bill. Legislation enacted in 1990 stipulated that appropriations bills could not break overall spending caps for domestic, defense, and international programs during fiscal 1991–1993 and single caps for all discretionary spending in fiscal 1994–1995. These spending caps, to be adjusted for economic conditions, were put in place as part of the 1990 budget reconciliation package.

Until the 1970s House Appropriations subcommittee hearings usually were closed, with testimony almost always restricted to that given by agency officials. A voluminous record of the

APPROPRIATIONS BILLS

Each year, Congress must pass thirteen general appropriations bills to fund various parts of the federal government. About one-half of federal spending each year is funded through this process. The other half is funded automatically, by the authority granted by laws governing entitlement and other mandatory programs.

The thirteen general appropriations bills are:

- Agriculture
- Commerce, Justice, State, Judiciary
- Defense
- District of Columbia
- Energy and Water Development
- Foreign Operations
- Interior
- Labor, Health and Human Services, Education
- Legislative Branch
- Military Construction
- Transportation
- Treasury, Postal Service, General Government
- Veterans Affairs, Housing and Urban Development, Independent Agencies

hearings, along with the parent committee's report, usually was not made public until shortly before House floor action on the appropriations bill. As a result, few if any members not on the subcommittee were prepared to challenge the bill. The Legislative Reorganization Act of 1970 provided that all House committee and subcommittee hearings must be open unless a majority determines otherwise. By the mid-1980s, however, approximately half of all appropriations subcommittee markups —where new language is inserted into a bill—remained behind closed doors.

The House procedure used for appropriations bills permits amendments from the floor. However, the prestige of the Appropriations Committee is such that relatively few major changes are made. In the 1980s floor amendments that cut 1 or 2 percent across the board sometimes were used to reduce spending without targeting individual programs. Efforts to increase funding for various programs were rarely successful, particularly after passage of the Gramm-Rudman-Hollings deficit reduction law in 1985. (See "Gramm-Rudman-Hollings," p. 175.)

Once an appropriations bill has been passed by the House, it is sent to the Senate and referred to that chamber's Appropriations Committee, where a parallel system of subcommittees exists. During the 1980s, as protracted budget battles pushed enactment of appropriations later and later into the year, the Senate Appropriations Committee acted on some spending bills before its House counterpart. However, the Senate did not take up the bills on the floor before the House acted. The Senate sub-

committees review the work of the House at hearings that are open to the public. The Senate usually does not attempt to perform the same amount of work on a bill that the House already has gone over thoroughly. The time required and the heavy workload of most senators preclude the same detailed consideration that is given in the House.

Until the mid-1970s most Senate-passed appropriations bills were larger than the House-approved versions. Since the congressional budget process has been in use, the House-passed figures are frequently higher than the Senate appropriations. House-Senate disputes over funding are resolved in conference, generally by splitting the differences.

Since the late 1950s, the House and Senate seldom have had all appropriations bills in place before the fiscal year began. To keep government agencies from a cutoff of operating funds, Congress has adopted the practice of passing emergency funding bills—called continuing appropriations resolutions or "CRs"—that allow agencies to keep spending money for a specified period. Funding is generally continued at the level of the previous year, or either the House-passed or Senate-passed level for the current year. Use of continuing resolutions has grown in recent years. Controversy over spending levels for some programs, such as foreign aid, became so great at times during the 1980s that those programs had to operate for entire fiscal years under continuing resolutions.

Continuing resolutions, like debt limit bills, became politicized in recent years. On the assumption that the president will have to sign a continuing resolution or face the political consequences of closing down entire federal departments, Congress frequently has attached controversial legislative riders to these measures. Such riders, or nongermane amendments, have included pay raises for members, prohibitions on federal funding of abortions, and revisions of the criminal code, to cite a few.

In recent years both President Ronald Reagan and President George Bush vetoed continuing resolutions. In November 1981, when Congress had enacted only one of the regular appropriations bills for fiscal 1982, it had to approve a continuing resolution to fund virtually the entire federal government. But the spending levels were higher than Reagan wanted and he vetoed the "budget-busting" bill in November. The veto left government agencies without legal authority to operate, except for essential activities such as defense and law enforcement. Thousands of government workers left their jobs for part of the day. Congress quickly passed a new continuing resolution acceptable to the president, and most government workers returned to work the following day. Reagan vetoed continuing resolutions twice more during his presidency, shutting down the government for a few hours each time.

In October 1990, after the House defeated a budget package negotiated by congressional leaders and the White House, President Bush vetoed a continuing resolution that continued funding for the entire government, temporarily extended the federal debt limit, and suspended the Gramm-Rudman automatic cuts.

The veto shut down the government over the Columbus Day holiday weekend, closing Washington tourist sites such as the Washington Monument and Smithsonian Institution. After further negotiations, Congress went on to pass a revised budget package and all thirteen of its regular appropriations bills for fiscal 1991. *(See box, Budget Timetable, p. 173.)*

A protracted battle between the newly Republican-led 104th Congress and the Clinton White House over GOP efforts to shrink the size and power of the federal government began in 1995 and finally concluded seven months later in April 1996, after fourteen continuing resolutions and an omnibus spending bill were enacted. Two politically debilitating government shutdowns—November 14–19, 1995, and December 16, 1995–January 2, 1996—took much of the starch out of the so-called Republican revolution and, by the end of the process, President Clinton had won at least partial funding for all of his priorities.

The Power to Borrow: Mounting Federal Deficits

The Constitution gives Congress the authority to borrow funds in any amounts for any purposes. The debt incurred by this borrowing is the most explicit and legally binding obligation of the federal government. In recent years the federal debt had grown at such an alarming rate and become such a large dollar amount that economists feared it would take its toll on the nation's economic health for decades to come. Large budget deficits emerged during the 1970s, but it was in the 1980s that debt grew at an unprecedented rate. Federal debt more than tripled in the 1980s, to $3.207 trillion in fiscal 1990. It reached $5.479 trillion in fiscal 1998, and the net annual interest on the debt was $243.4 billion, or more than 14 percent of all government spending for that year. *(See Table 4-1, this page.)*

Debt is incurred when it becomes necessary to spend more than the Treasury collects in taxes and other forms of revenue. When expenditures outstrip revenues, the deficit must be made up by borrowing. Through the first 150 years of the nation's history, a surplus resulting from an excess of revenues over expenditures was used, at least in part, to reduce outstanding debt. In the long string of federal budget deficits that began in fiscal 1931 and ended in fiscal 1998, there were budget surpluses in only eight years.

During the 1980s Congress made numerous attempts to slow the growth of the federal debt by holding down annual budget deficits. Because the political will to curtail deficits was often lacking, Congress in 1985 passed legislation designed to automatically cut the budget to meet deficit targets each year and completely eliminate deficits over a five-year period. Ironically, the Balanced Budget and Emergency Deficit Control Act of 1985 (commonly known as Gramm-Rudman-Hollings) was an amendment to legislation that raised the statutory limit on federal borrowing to more than $2 trillion. The Gramm-Rudman deficit targets were revised upward in 1987 and 1990.

TABLE 4-1 Debt of U.S. Government *(Billions of dollars)*

Fiscal year	Gross debt[a]	Debt held by the public	Net interest paid
1940	$ 50.7	$ 43.0	$ 0.9
1945	260.1	235.2	3.1
1950	256.9	219.0	4.8
1955	274.4	226.6	4.9
1960	290.5	236.8	6.9
1961	292.6	238.4	6.7
1962	302.9	248.0	6.9
1963	310.3	254.0	7.7
1964	316.1	256.8	8.2
1965	322.3	260.8	8.6
1966	328.5	263.7	9.4
1967	340.4	266.6	10.3
1968	368.7	289.5	11.1
1969	365.8	278.1	12.7
1970	380.9	283.2	14.4
1971	408.2	303.0	14.8
1972	435.9	322.4	15.5
1973	466.3	340.9	17.3
1974	483.9	343.7	21.4
1975	541.9	394.7	23.2
1976	629.0	477.4	26.7
1976[b]	643.6	495.5	6.9
1977	706.4	549.1	29.9
1978	776.6	607.1	35.4
1979	829.5	640.3	42.6
1980	909.0	709.8	52.5
1981	994.8	785.3	68.8
1982	1,137.3	919.8	85.0
1983	1,371.7	1,131.6	89.8
1984	1,564.7	1,300.5	111.1
1985	1,817.5	1,499.9	129.5
1986	2,120.6	1,736.7	136.0
1987	2,346.1	1,888.7	138.7
1988	2,601.3	2,050.8	151.8
1989	2,868.0	2,189.9	169.3
1990	3,206.6	2,410.7	184.2
1991	3,598.5	2,688.1	194.5
1992	4,002.1	2,998.8	199.4
1993	4,351.4	3,247.5	198.8
1994	4,643.7	3,432.1	203.0
1995	4,921.0	3,603.4	232.2
1996	5,181.9	3,733.0	241.1
1997	5,369.7	3,771.1	244.0
1998	5,478.7	3,719.9	243.4
1999[c]	5,614.9	3,669.7	227.2
2000[c]	5,711.4	3,571.8	215.2

NOTES: a. The gross debt includes the amount held by trust funds and other government accounts. Debt ceiling limits are calculated using the gross debt. Debt held by the public includes only funds owed to people outside of the government.   b. The figures represent 1976 plus transition quarter when the U.S. government moved the beginning of the fiscal year from July 1 to October 1.   c. Estimates as of February 1999.

SOURCE: Executive Office of the President, Office of Management and Budget, *Budget of the United States Government, Fiscal Year 2000, Historical Tables* (Washington, D.C.: Government Printing Office, 1999), Tables 3.1, 7.1.

By the end of the 1990s the pendulum appeared to be swinging back as a result of deficit control agreements between Congress and the White House, plus a long-blooming economy that was pouring revenues into the Treasury. The projected federal surpluses were so large that the primary Washington political battle in 1999 focused on how to spend the surplus: by deeply slashing taxes or by paying off a sizable portion of the national debt.

CONSTITUTIONAL AUTHORITY

Article I, Section 8, clause 2 of the Constitution gives Congress the power "to borrow money on the credit of the United States." This borrowing power is extensive. In their *Introduction to American Government*, Frederic A. Ogg and P. Orman Ray noted that the "power to borrow not only is expressly conferred in the Constitution, but is one of the very few federal powers entirely unencumbered by restrictions—with the result that Con-

gress may borrow from any lenders, for any purposes, in any amounts, on any terms, and with or without provision for the repayment of loans, with or without interest."[23]

Ogg and Ray noted also that the United States has no constitutional debt limit, whereas many state constitutions and state charters for counties and local governments impose debt ceilings. The United States has had a statutory debt ceiling for many decades. During the years of the ballooning national debt, the ceiling had to be raised repeatedly by Congress—usually at least once a year—generally with an intense political fight in Congress. (See box, Raising the Federal Debt Limit, this page.)

FEDERAL DEBT COMPONENTS

The debt consists of various types of obligations. David J. Ott and Attiat F. Ott in *Federal Budget Policy* gave the following definitions:

RAISING THE FEDERAL DEBT LIMIT

Although it holds the power to borrow, Congress generally has sidestepped responsibility for the mounting federal debt. By permanently appropriating funds for interest owed by the government, Congress has spared members the pain of voting each year to set funds aside for that purpose. Only since 1975 have the House and Senate gone on record on the level of the deficit projected by the annual budget resolutions.

The federal government, unlike some states, does not have a constitutional restriction on budget deficits. Since World War I Congress from time to time has set statutory limits through legislation. But as the federal debt rose—because Congress continued to approve spending without adequately increasing revenues—the House and Senate have had no choice but to raise the ceiling, while members lamented deficit spending.

Congress frequently has used debt limit extensions to shield controversial, often nongermane amendments that might have been vetoed if enacted separately. Although debt ceiling measures are not completely veto-proof, the debt bill is considered must-pass legislation to authorize the government to meet its financial obligations.

DEBT CEILING

Congress established the first overall debt ceiling in 1917, when the Second Liberty Bond Act fixed the limit at $11.5 billion. By 1945 Congress had amended that act sixteen times, lifting the ceiling to $300 billion to accommodate World War II borrowing. In 1946 Congress reduced the limit to a "permanent" $275 billion level. In 1972 the permanent level rose to $400 billion, but by 1982 the $890.2 billion temporary portion of the ceiling was more than double the permanent ceiling. (The total debt limit was the sum of the permanent and temporary limits.) In 1983 the distinction between permanent and temporary debt limits was ended with the enactment of a single permanent limit.

Although Congress had little choice but to increase the statutory debt limit, the heated debates—primarily in the House—suggested that the events were milestones in public financial affairs. The con-

troversy over increasing the debt ceiling flowed essentially from the broader issue of government spending. Congressional conservatives thought that a firm commitment by Congress not to increase the debt limit would force a cut in spending, especially spending that exceeded the tax revenues.

Officials in the executive branch responsible for paying the government's bills, as well as a majority of members of Congress, were convinced that a debt ceiling could not control expenditures. Throughout the postwar period, secretaries of the Treasury expressed their opposition to using the debt ceiling for that purpose.

Practice proved them right. When it came down to the final vote, Congress always has raised the debt limit enough to allow the government to keep borrowing funds to finance daily operations. As a result of this politicization of the issue, the government on several occasions nearly ran out of money.

DEBT LIMIT STRATEGY

In 1980 the House began experimenting with new shortcut procedures to make debt battles unnecessary. Under that plan, known as the "Gephardt Rule" (for its author, Rep. Richard A. Gephardt, D-Mo.) and adopted in 1979, the House agreed to set the debt limit at whatever level was projected by the most recently approved congressional budget resolution. After the House gave final approval to the budget resolution, the debt limit would be incorporated in a joint resolution that would be deemed approved by the House and sent—without a separate House vote—to the Senate for consideration.

That strategy presumed that budget resolutions would be enacted on time. In 1980, however, action on the budget resolution fell behind schedule, forcing Congress to consider a stopgap resolution increasing the debt ceiling. Seizing the opportunity, lawmakers added to that measure a provision overturning President Jimmy Carter's highly unpopular oil import fee. Carter vetoed the debt limit resolution, but Congress promptly overrode the veto. The House plan also did not apply to the Senate and thus did not prevent that chamber from turning debt limit extensions into political footballs.

The federal debt consists of direct obligations or debts of the U.S. Treasury and obligations of federal government enterprises or agencies. It is broken down into "public debt"—that part issued by the Treasury—and "agency debt"—that part issued by federal agencies. The public debt consists of issues (that is, bonds, notes, and bills), which are generally sold to the public (some are held by federal agencies and trust funds), and "special issues," which are held only by government agencies and trust funds. Of the issues sold to the public, some are "marketable," that is, they are traded on securities markets, and some are "non-marketable" and cannot be traded (for example, U.S. savings bonds). The latter may, however, be redeemed in cash or converted into another issue.[24]

Agency debt traditionally has made up less than 1 percent of the total federal debt.

GROWTH OF THE FEDERAL DEBT

The explosive growth in federal spending since the 1930s has affected significantly the nation's perception of the borrowing power and the national debt. Throughout most of the nation's history, the principal concern of government budget policy was to ensure that revenues were sufficient to meet expenditures. That philosophy, which in application meant an approximate balance between receipts and outlays, was generally accepted during most of the nation's history.

Writing in *Federal Budget and Fiscal Policy, 1789–1958*, Lewis H. Kimmel pointed out that three key ideas generally were accepted by federal officials and economists alike in the period leading up to the Civil War: a low level of public expenditures was desirable; the federal budget should be balanced in peacetime; and the federal debt should be reduced and eventually extinguished. "These ideas," he observed, "were a reflection of views that were deeply rooted in the social fabric."[25]

The Civil War, like the major wars of modern times, resulted in a much enlarged national debt. The reported debt in 1866 amounted to almost $2.8 billion, in contrast to less than $90.6

CONTINUING PROBLEMS

Congress continued to fall behind on passage of the budget resolution in the 1980s, and it had to pass two to four debt limit acts every year except 1988. In 1990 Congress passed seven such acts, the most ever enacted in a single year.

Also in 1990, President George Bush vetoed a continuing appropriations resolution that contained a short-term debt limit extension, but a new version was passed before the debt ceiling was reached. The debt extension had been added to the continuing resolution because the budget resolution had once again been mired in political turmoil.

Because of these legislative delays, several times in the 1980s the debt was virtually at the statutory limit for a number of days. In 1985 the Treasury ran out of money during the extended consideration of the Gramm-Rudman-Hollings amendment to debt limit legislation. Treasury had to resort to survival tactics that included trading securities with the off-budget Federal Financing Bank and disinvestment of Social Security and other retirement funds, which were later restored.

The Gramm-Rudman-Hollings amendment, which led to these emergency measures, created a mechanism to automatically cut the budget and reduce the deficit over a five-year period. When part of the process was ruled unconstitutional by the Supreme Court, debt limit legislation again was used to "fix" the process in 1987.

CONFRONTATION WITH WHITE HOUSE

House GOP leaders took steps in early 1995 to hold the debt limit increase in reserve as a potential weapon in the coming budget fight with President Bill Clinton. They hoped to force Clinton to accede to their plan for balancing the budget in seven years without having to make major concessions to the White House. But they had not counted on Clinton's determined resistance.

The Republicans included a provision in the House budget resolution that waived the Gephardt Rule. While the cancellation of the Gephardt Rule applied only to 1995, the House budget resolution recommended that it be repealed permanently.

By late September, Republicans were aggressively threatening to provoke the nation's first-ever default on its Treasury obligations. House Speaker Newt Gingrich, R-Ga., said he would block any action to raise the government's credit limit until Clinton accepted tax and spending cuts along the lines Republicans were proposing. He said, "I don't care what the price is. I don't care if we have no executive offices, no bonds for 60 days. What we are saying to Clinton is: Do not assume that we will flinch, because we won't."

The last debt limit increase had been enacted in 1993 as part of Clinton's budget reconciliation bill. Treasury officials said that ceiling—$4.9 trillion—would last until September or October 1995, although Republicans expected them to use various debt management strategies to stretch that deadline until mid-November. And mid-November was about the point when Republicans expected to send their seven-year balanced budget plan to Clinton. By including the critical debt limit increase in their budget reconciliation bill, GOP leaders believed they would make it all but impossible for Clinton to reject the centerpiece of their 1995 legislative agenda.

The Clinton administration thwarted the GOP plan, however. Treasury Secretary Robert E. Rubin, saying he would do "everything in my power" to avert a first-ever default on U.S. government obligations, took extraordinary (but legal) actions to keep the government solvent through the end of the year and beyond. Frustrated, House Republicans made a futile effort at legislation to roll back the Treasury secretary's authority to juggle the books.

Furthermore, the GOP strategy resulted in two politically unpopular government shutdowns. According to opinion polls, the American public overwhelmingly disapproved of the Republicans' actions. Republicans subsequently backed down in 1996 and voted to raise the accumulated federal debt to $5.5 trillion. The debt limit would be raised again in 1997 to $5.95 trillion.

TABLE 4-2 Deficit History, 1929–2000 *(Current billion dollars)*

Fiscal year	Receipts	Outlays	Surplus or deficit(−)
1929	3.9	3.1	0.7
1933	2.0	4.6	−2.6
1939	6.3	9.1	−2.8
1940	6.5	9.5	−2.9
1945	45.2	92.7	−47.6
1950	39.4	42.6	−3.1
1955	65.5	68.4	−3.0
1960	92.5	92.2	0.3
1965	116.8	118.2	−1.4
1969	186.9	183.6	3.2
1970	192.8	195.6	−2.8
1975	279.1	332.3	−53.2
1980	517.1	590.9	−73.8
1981	599.3	678.2	−79.0
1982	617.8	745.8	−128.0
1983	600.6	808.4	−207.8
1984	666.5	851.9	−185.4
1985	734.1	946.4	−212.3
1986	769.2	990.5	−221.2
1987	854.4	1,004.1	−149.8
1988	909.3	1,064.5	−155.2
1989	991.2	1,143.7	−152.5
1990	1,032.0	1,253.2	−221.2
1991	1,055.0	1,324.4	−269.4
1992	1,091.3	1,381.7	−290.4
1993	1,154.4	1,409.4	−255.0
1994	1,258.6	1,461.7	−203.1
1995	1,351.8	1,515.7	−163.9
1996	1,453.1	1,560.5	−107.4
1997	1,579.3	1,601.2	−21.9
1998	1,721.8	1,652.6	69.2
1999[a]	1,806.3	1,727.1	79.3
2000[a]	1,883.0	1,765.7	117.3

NOTE: a. Estimates as of February 1999.

SOURCE: Executive Office of the President, Office of Management and Budget, *Budget of the United States Government, Fiscal Year 2000, Historical Tables* (Washington, D.C.: Government Printing Office, 1999), Table 1.1.

million in 1861. The debt was gradually reduced after the war to a low of $961 million in 1893. However, after the Civil War less concern existed about eliminating the outstanding debt. Increasingly, the emphasis was on servicing the debt in an orderly manner. Proposals to liquidate it became fewer and fewer.

From the post–Civil War low point in 1893, the debt increased very slowly for half a dozen years and then hovered between $1.1 billion and $1.2 billion until 1917, when the United States entered World War I. The debt jumped from just under $3 billion in fiscal 1917 to a peak of $25.5 billion at the end of fiscal 1919. In the 1920s the debt receded steadily, year by year, to $16.2 billion at the end of fiscal 1930.

In the 1930s the government turned away from its former insistence on balancing revenues and outlays, gradually adopting in its place an economic philosophy developed by British economist John Maynard Keynes that justified peacetime deficits when needed to ensure stable economic growth. Discussing the early years of the Depression, Kimmel noted:

A concerted effort was made by the President and the leadership of both parties in Congress to adhere to the balanced budget philosophy. Yet a balanced federal budget was almost impossible to attain—the annually balanced budget dogma in effect gave way to necessity. Alternatives were soon suggested, and within a few years what came to be known as compensatory fiscal theory gained numerous adherents.[26]

The practice of using the federal budget to help solve national economic problems became acceptable. Budget deficits and a rapidly increasing national debt were the result. The debt rose to nearly $58 billion—more than twice the World War I peak—at the end of fiscal 1941. After America's entry in World War II, the debt passed the $100 billion mark in fiscal 1943 and was $271 billion in fiscal 1946. There was no steady reduction after World War II. The debt total fluctuated for a few years but then began a new rise that took it past the World War II peak in fiscal 1955, past $300 billion in fiscal 1962, and to $484 billion at the end of fiscal 1974.

The debt grew quickly during the 1980s. In 1982 federal debt passed the $1 trillion mark. It took only four more years for it to reach $2 trillion. By 1990 the debt exceeded $3 trillion; by 1992, $4 trillion; and by 1996, $5 trillion. With the return of budget surpluses in 1998, the debt began to level off at $5.6 trillion in 1999. *(See Table 4-2, this page.)*

Congress and the Budget: Struggling for Control

The formulation of a comprehensive federal budget is a relatively recent development in the nation's history. The federal government has operated under a budget only since 1921. Perhaps ironically, Congress at that time granted the president power to shape the budget by giving the executive branch the tools to view federal fiscal policy as a whole and by requiring the chief executive to recommend to Congress how federal funds should be raised and spent.

Congress exercised its powers to tax, spend, and borrow, but until 1975 it never successfully integrated those individual decisions into any sort of comprehensive review of the budget. The diffusion of fiscal power among congressional committees was perhaps a political necessity for a smoothly running Congress, but it did not permit the centralization of decision making needed for a coherent budget system. That institutional dispersion of power, combined with economic forces, made it increasingly difficult for Congress to take responsibility for a federal budget that by the late 1970s appeared to be racing out of control.

In the 1980s federal budget action centered on how to control the growing federal deficit. By 1981 the federal debt passed the trillion-dollar mark and Congress became increasingly anxious to slow the growth of the nation's debt. Year after year, however, lawmakers lacked the political will to make the hard spending and revenue choices required. In 1985 Congress took drastic action by passing a law that forced members either to make the difficult budget decisions or live with automatic, across-the-

---

BUDGET TERMINOLOGY

The federal budget is the financial plan for the federal government. It accounts for how government funds have been raised and spent, and it proposes financial policies. It covers the *fiscal year*, which begins on October 1 and ends the following September 30.

The budget discusses *revenues*, amounts the government expects to raise in taxes; *budget authority*, amounts agencies are allowed to obligate or lend; and *outlays*, amounts paid out by the government in cash or checks during the year. Examples of outlays are funds spent to buy equipment or property, to meet the government's liability under a contract, or to pay employees' salaries. Outlays also include net lending—the differences between disbursements and repayments under government lending programs.

The purpose of the budget is to establish priorities and to chart the government's *fiscal policy*, which is the coordinated use of taxes and expenditures to affect the economy.

Congress adopts its own budget in the form of a *budget resolution*, due April 15, which sets overall goals for taxing and spending, broken down among major budget categories, called *functions*.

An *authorization* is an act of Congress that establishes government programs. It defines the scope of programs and sets a ceiling for how much can be spent on them. Authorizations do not provide the money. In the case of authority to enter contractual obligations, though, Congress authorizes the administration to make firm commitments for which funds must later be provided. Congress also occasionally includes mandatory spending requirements in an authorization to ensure spending at a certain level. Some authorizations, such as Medicare, are structured so that anyone who meets the eligibility requirements of the program may participate and enough funding must be made available to cover all participants; such authorizations are known as *entitlements*.

An *appropriation* provides money for programs within the limits established in authorizations. An appropriation may be for a single year, a specified period of years (multiyear appropriations), or an indefinite number of years (no-year appropriations). Most appropriations are for a single year. Appropriations generally take the form of budget authority, which often differs from actual outlays. That is because, in practice, funds spent or obligated during a year may be drawn partly from the budget authority conferred in the year in question and partly from budget authority conferred in previous years.

When Congress wants to revise program authorizations to achieve savings required by the budget resolution, it uses a *reconciliation bill*. The bill, formulated from instructions in the budget resolution, consolidates program changes and revenue increases from all pertinent committees into a single legislative measure.

Sequestration is an automatic procedure for making spending cuts required by the Gramm-Rudman-Hollings law if Congress and the president fail to make them legislatively. Shortly after Congress adjourns for the year, separate sequestration procedures are used for *discretionary spending* and *mandatory spending* programs. If necessary, there is a last sequestration for all nonexempt programs.

---

board spending cuts. Events such as the stock market crash in 1987 and the failure of hundreds of savings and loan institutions later in the decade intensified the budget crisis.

The deficit remained out of control, and by 1990 the federal debt had tripled to more than $3 trillion. Congress responded in 1990 by passing a five-year, $500 billion deficit reduction plan that also included significant changes to the budget system. However, that measure alone proved unable to stem the tide of rising deficits or to uplift a faltering economy.

In November 1992, Democrat Bill Clinton rode a wave of recession-induced mistrust and disappointment into the White House over an incumbent president, George Bush. In 1993, with no help from the GOP, he got enacted into law a reconciliation bill that, along with the 1990 legislation, allowed him by his re-election campaign in 1996 to point to a budget deficit that had declined in every year of his presidency and an economy that was generating jobs without apparent risk of inflation. Clinton struck a balanced budget agreement with the Republican Congress in 1997, and by the end of fiscal 1998 the federal government was in the black for the first time in almost thirty years.

DEVELOPING A BUDGET SYSTEM

Although the federal government did not operate under a budget for its first 130 years, Lewis Kimmel noted, "The budget idea . . . was clearly in the minds of leading political and financial leaders as early as the Revolutionary and formative periods. The absence of logical or systematic budget methods during the early years and throughout the nineteenth century should not be construed as a lack of appreciation of the role of public finance."[27]

Ratification of the Constitution cleared the way for establishment of a government financial system. In September 1789 Congress enacted a law establishing the Treasury Department and requiring the secretary of the Treasury "to prepare and report estimates of the public revenues, and the public expenditures." However, Kimmel wrote, "Alexander Hamilton's efforts in the direction of an executive budget were unsuccessful, mainly because of congressional jealousy and existing party divisions."[28]

Because the federal government relied on customs duties for the bulk of its revenues throughout the nineteenth century—and there was an abundance of such revenues—no need existed to weigh expenditures against revenues. Consequently, the budget-making process suffered a progressive deterioration.

According to Kimmel, the first important step toward establishing a federal executive budget was taken in 1910, when President William Howard Taft appointed a Commission on Economy and Efficiency to study the need for a federal budget. The commission concluded that a restructuring of the system for determining and meeting the financial needs of the government was of paramount importance. But Congress resented the commission's proposed system, and the panel's report was not even considered by the House Appropriations Committee, to which it was referred.

The 1921 Budget Act

After World War I the diffuse appropriations system that had grown up in place of a budget procedure could no longer meet the needs of an increasingly complex government. Federal receipts exceeded $4 billion in all but two years in the 1920s, and expenditures dropped to only about $3 billion at the lowest point (fiscal 1927) in the decade. Having seen the government spend $18.5 billion in fiscal 1919 (which included the last four and a half months of the war) and having appropriated $6.5 billion for fiscal 1920 (the first full postwar year), Congress decided it must reorganize its financial machinery, both to retrench on expenditures and to tighten control over the administration of fiscal policy.

The reorganization was accomplished through enactment of the Budget and Accounting Act of 1921. First, however, the House on June 1, 1920, restored exclusive spending powers to its Appropriations Committee and enlarged the committee to thirty-five members, from twenty-one. (By 1999 the membership was sixty.) The Senate on March 6, 1922, similarly concentrated spending powers in its Appropriations Committee but left the membership at sixteen. (By 1999 it was twenty-eight.)

In the Budget and Accounting Act, Congress sought to reform the financial machinery of the executive branch. The 1921 act established two important offices—the Bureau of the Budget and the General Accounting Office. The former was created to centralize fiscal management of the executive branch directly under the president; the latter was designed to strengthen congressional oversight of spending.

Bureau of the Budget. With passage of the 1921 act, Congress ended the right of federal agencies to decide for themselves what appropriations levels to request from Congress. The Budget Bureau, serving under the president's direction, was to act as a central clearinghouse for budget requests.

Budget Circular 49, approved by President Warren G. Harding on December 19, 1921, required all agency proposals for appropriations to be submitted to the president before they were presented to Congress. Agency proposals were to be studied for their relationship to "the president's financial program" and were to be sent to Capitol Hill only if approved by the president. The bureau, though placed in the Treasury, was kept under the supervision of the president.[29]

In 1935 President Franklin D. Roosevelt broadened the clearance function to include legislative as well as appropriation requests. According to political scientist Richard E. Neustadt, Roosevelt's new clearance system was not a mere extension of the budget process. "On the contrary . . . this was Roosevelt's creation, intended to protect not just his budget, but his prerogatives, his freedom of action, and his choice of policies in an era

of fast-growing government and of determined presidential leadership."[30]

Roosevelt in 1939 issued, and Congress approved, Reorganization Plan No. 1, creating the Executive Office of the President and transferring the Budget Bureau from the Treasury to the new office. The bureau's legislative clearance procedures were further strengthened by Roosevelt and later presidents.

In 1970 President Richard Nixon streamlined the budget process by restructuring the Bureau of the Budget. The new office, called the Office of Management and Budget (OMB), was given sweeping authority to coordinate the execution of government programs as well as the Budget Bureau's old role of advising the president on agency funding requests. In 1974 Congress approved legislation making future OMB directors and deputy directors subject to Senate confirmation.

General Accounting Office. In setting up the General Accounting Office (GAO), Congress attempted to strengthen its surveillance of government spending. The GAO is headed by the comptroller general and an assistant comptroller general, appointed by the president with the advice and consent of the Senate, for a period of fifteen years. They can be removed only by joint resolution of Congress, thus making the agency responsible to Congress instead of the administration. The comptroller general was granted wide powers to investigate all matters relating to the use of public funds and was required to report annually to Congress and to include in his report recommendations for greater economy and efficiency.

Many of the auditing powers and duties of the comptroller general already had been established by the Dockery Act of 1894, which assigned them to the then new office of the comptroller of the Treasury. But under that act the comptroller and his staff remained executive branch officers, and Congress lacked its own agency for independent review of executive expenditures.

The results of GAO audits are transmitted to Congress by the comptroller general. The results of special investigations of particular agencies and the annual report are referred to the House and Senate Government Operations committees. *(See "General Accounting Office," p. 755, Vol. II.)*

Early Budget Experiments

Although Congress saw the need to centralize budget making in the executive branch, authority for its fiscal decisions remained dispersed among its committees. As a deliberative body representing different regions and economic interests, Congress always has been ambivalent about budget control.

In the few instances where the House and Senate did vote for overall budget restraints, they were unable or unwilling to cut enough from individual programs to meet those goals. Throughout the thirty years following World War II, the momentum of those separate spending decisions sooner or later overwhelmed whatever devices Congress used to try to keep the budget in check.

Immediately after World War II, Congress attempted to draw

up its budget priorities to relate appropriations to overall fiscal objectives. In three years of trying, the House and Senate never fully implemented a legislative budget process created by the Legislative Reorganization Act of 1946. After unsuccessful attempts in 1947, 1948, and 1949, Congress abandoned the experiment as an unqualified failure.

Similar in some respects to the reform procedures later adopted by Congress in 1974, the 1946 act required Congress to approve a concurrent resolution setting a ceiling on the amount to be appropriated in each fiscal year. The ceiling was to be part of a budget drawn up by Congress based on revenue and spending estimates prepared by a massive Joint Budget Committee composed of all members of the House and Senate Appropriations committees and of the tax-writing House Ways and Means and Senate Finance committees.

In 1947 House-Senate conferees were deadlocked over Senate amendments to the budget resolution directing an expected federal surplus to be used for tax reductions and debt retirement. In 1948 Congress appropriated $6 billion more than its budget ceiling allowed. In 1949 the process broke down completely and the legislative budget never was produced.

One of the principal reasons the legislative budget failed was the inability of the Joint Budget Committee to make accurate estimates of spending early in the congressional session, before individual agency requests had been considered in detail. In addition, the committee was said to be inadequately staffed and, with more than one hundred members, much too unwieldy for effective operation.

Failure of the legislative budget prompted a serious effort in Congress in 1950 to combine the numerous separate appropriations bills into one omnibus measure. The traditional practice of acting on the separate bills one by one made it difficult to hold total outlays in check.

In 1950 the House Appropriations Committee agreed to give the omnibus-bill plan a trial. The omnibus appropriations bill was passed by Congress about two months earlier than the last of the separate bills had been passed in 1949. The overall appropriations in that measure were about $2.3 billion less than the president's budget request. The omnibus approach was praised by many observers and was particularly well received by those seeking reductions in federal spending.

Nevertheless, the House Appropriations Committee in January 1951 voted 31–18 to go back to the traditional method of handling appropriations bills separately. Two years later, in 1953, the Senate proposed a return to the omnibus plan, but the House did not go along. The plan was dead. Opponents said the omnibus bill required more time and effort than separate bills. Equally important was the opposition from the chairs of the House Appropriations subcommittees, who feared their power would be eroded under the omnibus approach.

With the failure of those efforts, Congress's only means of budget restraint was to write into appropriations bills specific restrictions on how funds could be spent. Those provisions provided little overall control on spending, and for the remainder of the 1950s and 1960s Congress discussed several other plans for restraining outlays, but no steps were taken.

Seven times between 1952 and 1965 the Senate approved creation of a Joint Budget Committee, but the House never acted on the Senate measures. Other spending control measures proposed during that time included a mandatory balanced budget, statutory spending ceilings, and a separate congressional budget session to handle only appropriations bills.

Spending Ceilings

The spending issue came to a head in the late 1960s and early 1970s, when spending for Great Society programs combined with military outlays for the Vietnam War to accelerate the budget deficit. Distressed by ever-increasing levels of federal spending growth, House Republicans launched an economy drive in 1966. Their first efforts—to cut several annual appropriations bills by 5 percent—were unsuccessful.

Fiscal conservatives were more successful in the next four years. Four times between 1967 and 1970 Congress wrote federal spending limits into law. But those limits proved ineffective. In 1967 Congress cut controllable spending by $4 billion, but uncontrollable spending rose $5 billion for a net spending increase of $1 billion. In 1968, 1969, and 1970, Congress simply raised or ignored the limits when they proved too low to accommodate spending required by existing programs.

No spending ceiling was enacted in 1971, but Nixon's request for a fiscal 1973 spending ceiling provoked a dispute with Congress that was thrashed out in the 1972 presidential election campaign. In what Democrats conceded was a masterful political stroke, Nixon in July 1972 asked Congress for authority to trim federal spending as he saw fit to meet a $250 billion ceiling on fiscal 1973 outlays. If such power were denied, Nixon warned, Congress would be responsible for tax increases in 1973.

The House complied by writing the ceiling into a debt limit extension bill. But the Senate balked at giving the president unlimited discretion to cut federal outlays; it added strict guidelines on the size and nature of the spending reductions. The ceiling was dropped altogether after the Senate turned down a White House-backed compromise that limited presidential authority to dictate where reductions could be made. Controversy in 1973 and 1974 also killed enactment of any spending ceiling in those years.

Conflict over Impoundments

Nixon's campaign to curb federal spending brought to a head long-simmering differences over whether the government must spend all the money that Congress appropriates. Continuing a practice that many presidents had followed, Nixon in the early 1970s impounded billions of dollars Congress had provided—despite the president's objections—for certain government programs. By withholding the funds, Nixon set off a legal and political struggle over the issue of whether the executive or the legislature held final authority over how the government spent its money.

President Richard Nixon set off a legal and political struggle in the 1970s by refusing to spend all the money Congress appropriated.

Nixon's extensive use of the power to withhold funds intensified the conflict between a Republican administration pledged to hold down domestic spending and a Democratic Congress determined to preserve the health, welfare, environment, public works, and other programs it had put in place during the preceding decade. "The Nixon administration treated the president's budget as a ceiling on Congress," Louis Fisher, a Congressional Research Service specialist, recalled in 1979. "Any funds that Congress added to the president's budget could be set aside and left unobligated."[31]

Nixon argued that he was withholding funds only as a financial management technique, primarily to slow inflation through temporary reductions in federal spending. House and Senate Democratic leaders contended that Nixon used impoundments to impose his own priorities in defiance of laws passed by Congress. The Nixon impoundments suggested, according to Fisher, that "whatever Congress did during the appropriations phase to fix budget priorities was easily undone by officials during the budget execution phase."[32]

THE 1974 BUDGET LAW

Frustrated by the impoundment battle and acknowledging that it had forfeited control of the budget through the haphaz-

ard way it dealt with presidential spending requests, Congress in 1974 set up a new process, significantly changing the way it handled the federal budget. Under the Congressional Budget and Impoundment Control Act of 1974, Congress had to vote each year to set specific spending, tax, and deficit limits. Perhaps more important in the long run for the U.S. economy, Congress also gave itself the machinery necessary to tailor its individual taxing and spending decisions to the government's fiscal policy objectives.

For the first time since the legislative budget experiments of the post–World War II years, lawmakers were forced to consider thoroughly the president's fiscal policy goals as they acted on the annual appropriations measures. And—by requiring Congress to set initial budget targets and subsequently to adhere to them or make adjustments—the budget law compelled the House and Senate to go on record for each fiscal year on how much the government should spend, how much revenue it should raise, and how much money it should borrow to make up for any deficit.

The budget law steered a careful course through the cross-currents of congressional politics. It left the jurisdictions of the existing tax and appropriations committees intact and it left legislative committees free to push new and additional spending proposals. The 1974 measure did not require a balanced budget or impose specific spending ceilings (later added by the Budget Enforcement Act of 1990) but instead superimposed an annual budget review process on top of the yearly procedure of appropriating funds for government agencies.

Genesis of the Process

In revising its budgetary procedures, Congress once again undertook a task that had been tried and abandoned in the budget experiments nearly twenty-five years earlier. But in the early 1970s, in the midst of angry spending fights with Nixon, congressional leaders finally concluded that the House and Senate had to put their fiscal procedures in order if they were to hold their own in future budget policy battles.

After a lively political sparring match completed a month before the 1972 presidential election, Congress denied Nixon's request to set a $250 billion ceiling on fiscal 1973 spending and give him authority to enforce it. But it did enact a little-noticed provision setting up a joint House-Senate study committee to review the way Congress acted on the budget.

The thirty-two-member panel, composed almost entirely of members from the House and Senate tax-writing and Appropriations committees, proposed major changes in congressional procedures in April 1973. Their recommendations included establishment of House and Senate Budget Committees. The panel urged enactment of a concurrent resolution early in each session to set limits on spending and appropriations for the coming fiscal year, followed by a second resolution later in the session to adjust ceilings and subceilings as necessary to meet unanticipated budget requirements.

The joint committee plan called for instituting procedures requiring that amendments to budget resolutions raising outlays for one program category be accompanied by equivalent cuts from another category or by tax increases to provide the additional funding. It also proposed that all future backdoor spending programs, including entitlements, be subject to spending ceilings set through the annual appropriations process. Other proposals included binding limits on outlays written into appropriations measures and a general appropriations bill to reconcile spending totals at the end of each congressional session.

Congressional Deliberations

What followed during the rest of 1973 and first six months of 1974 turned into a complex exercise in congressional power brokering. Although "impoundment was a powerful spur to budget reform," wrote budget specialist Allen Schick, "when it wrote the Budget Act, Congress was much more concerned about the distribution of power within its own ranks than between it and the executive branch."[33] Powerful committee chairmen jockeyed behind the scenes to preserve their panels' existing authority to shape tax and spending decisions. Conservative members sought budget procedures that would restrict congressional spending habits as much as possible, while liberals resisted proposals that they felt would squeeze funding for domestic programs.

In a significant departure from the joint committee's proposals, the House bill made the initial budget resolution a flexible guideline that would set targets but not restrict subsequent decisions on separate appropriations and spending measures. The Rules Committee report argued that the change would "preserve and enhance the appropriations process, which has consistently demonstrated its effectiveness."

The initial Senate version of the budget control legislation was more rigid than the House proposal. But tight budget ceilings, along with provisions making backdoor spending programs subject to the regular appropriations process, aroused concern among the powerful members of the legislative committees. If committees were subject to a firm initial ceiling that would be difficult to adjust, their power to initiate new programs or step up federal efforts through existing programs would be severely limited. The upshot was a Senate bill with procedures and timetables less stringent than those in the House version.

The House passed its version of the bill in December 1973. The Senate passed its compromise version without dissent in March 1974. Conferees negotiated some further refinements, particularly on impoundment controls, and the conference report won easy approval in both houses in June. President Nixon signed the final measure into law on July 12, 1974.

New Impoundment Procedures

The 1974 budget law set up two procedures—rescissions and deferrals—whereby presidents could delay or cancel the expenditure of congressionally appropriated funds. Both were subject to congressional review, but only one—rescissions—stood the test of time and the Constitution. The act's impoundment provisions were included in Title X of the 1974 law.

If the president felt that money should not be spent at all, he must propose that Congress rescind the appropriation making the funds available. In that case, both the House and Senate must approve the rescission within forty-five days. If the two houses did not act, the president must release the funds at the end of the forty-five-day period.

To simply delay spending temporarily, the law provided a way for the president to defer outlays. Under the budget act, the deferral stood unless either the House or Senate passed a resolution directing that the money be spent. Congress could act on a deferral at any time.

From the beginning, criticisms and concerns arose about both rescissions and deferrals. Some members of Congress complained about the rescission provision because the president, by asking that appropriations be canceled, could block spending for nearly seven weeks. Even if Congress refused to approve a rescission measure, the law provided no opportunity for the House and Senate to force the administration to spend the funds before the forty-five-day period was up.

The concerns, though, went far beyond that. A basic issue

was whether Title X gave the president new powers to withhold funds and cancel or greatly delay previously approved spending. During 1974 debate on the provisions, the House asserted that Title X created new authority for the withholding of funds and allowed the president to propose deferrals for reasons other than administrative housekeeping. (Deferring spending for purely managerial reasons was allowed under the old government budgeting procedures that the budget control act replaced.)

The Senate argued that Title X did not allow the president to defer spending for policy reasons. After studying this dispute, Comptroller General Elmer B. Staats in late 1974 supported the House view of the matter. The Senate, however, was unconvinced and the dispute remained unresolved.

Criticisms aside, the congressional authors of the 1974 law predicted that impoundment proposals for policy reasons would amount to only a few dozen each year. But after the law went into effect, Presidents Gerald R. Ford and Ronald Reagan, both Republicans, requested numerous policy impoundments. President Jimmy Carter, a Democrat, proposed far fewer policy deferrals. The main source of consternation, however, was not the number of rescissions and deferrals requested but the belief among some members of Congress that the executive branch was circumventing the process and impounding funds without telling Congress what it had done.

Two court cases clarified the matter of deferrals for policy reasons. In an unrelated case in June 1983, *Immigration and Naturalization Service v. Chadha*, the Supreme Court struck down the procedure for overruling deferrals. The one-house legislative veto by which either chamber could reject an executive branch action was declared unconstitutional.

In 1986 the National League of Cities and four House members sued the Reagan administration over its use of deferrals effectively to rescind funds by deferring the money over and over again. A federal district court decision, upheld in January 1987 by the Court of Appeals for the District of Columbia Circuit, threw out the concept of deferrals for policy reasons. The courts argued that when the legislative veto was struck down, so was the deferral authority granted a president because the two procedures were inseparable. Deferrals henceforth could be used only for management reasons. The Gramm-Rudman amendments to the 1987 debt limit bill later clarified the original 1974 impoundment language and limited the deferral authority to contingencies, efficiency, or other management reasons.

Presidents Reagan, Bush, and Clinton called for increased rescission authority, and "enhanced rescission" and "expedited rescission" proposals were introduced in Congress. Enhanced rescission authority would allow a request by the president to remain in effect unless Congress rejected it. Expedited rescission authority would ensure timely congressional action on rescission requests.

Under Title X the president must keep Congress informed of impoundments by sending deferral and rescission requests to Capitol Hill. The General Accounting Office may review defer-

ral and rescission messages for accuracy, and the comptroller general has authority to report to Congress any executive branch action that impounds funds without proper notification of Congress. Such a report triggers rescission or deferral proceedings as though the president had made a request to Congress. The comptroller general also may reclassify deferrals as rescissions, or vice versa, and may go to federal court to enforce the law's impoundment requirements.

Testing the New Procedure: 1975–1980

Between 1975 and 1980, the budget process scored some notable successes and survived some near-disasters. Through the first six years the new budget process was used, the House and Senate moved through a series of political mine fields. At times conflicting political pressures raised doubts that the beleaguered system could continue to work. Yet, even though the House and Senate often slipped badly behind the timetable that the budget law established, the process functioned more or less intact.

The budget law mandated that Congress start using the process for fiscal 1977, beginning October 1, 1976. The law allowed Congress to use the 1975 session as a trial run to get the feel of the procedures, if it chose, by putting the fiscal 1976 budget through a preliminary test of the process. But House and Senate Democratic leaders, determined to rework President Ford's budget that year, agreed instead to implement key parts of the process for the fiscal 1976 budget.

In the first year some budget deadlines were waived and potentially controversial budget targets for certain program categories were left out. But in December 1975 legislators approved a budget resolution in which Congress for the first time specified the total size of the federal budget.

The budget law went into full effect in 1976. That year's debates on the budget resolution produced sharp liberal and conservative differences over the recommendations of the House Budget Committee. House leaders, unable to count on backing from a disgruntled Republican minority, were forced to barter with liberal Democrats and southern fiscal conservatives for support. The Senate, with its tradition of legislating by consensus, was able to use the budget procedures much more smoothly than the deeply divided House.

The 1976 elections brought Democrat Jimmy Carter to the presidency in 1977. Carter's election, with comfortable Democratic majorities in the House and Senate, promised to end nearly a decade of budget battles between Congress and the executive. That never developed. Carter wavered during his four-year term between spending restraints to curb inflation and stimulative measures to fight unemployment. House Democrats remained badly divided over federal budget priorities, while a defense-minded Senate pushed hard to boost military spending to counter a Soviet arms buildup. The fiscal policy turmoil of the Carter years severely tested the congressional budget process.

Throughout the Ford and Carter years, congressional use of the budget mechanism was largely a matter of accommodation.

BUDGET TIMETABLE

January 21: President must notify Congress before exercising any option to adjust the maximum deficit amounts for future fiscal years.

First Monday in February: President submits budget request and economic forecast to Congress for the fiscal year beginning October 1. Budget also includes Office of Management and Budget (OMB) sequester preview. Congressional Budget Office (CBO) sequester preview due five days earlier.

Six weeks after president submits the executive branch's budget: All legislative committees submit their "views and estimates" of spending under their jurisdiction for the coming fiscal year to the Budget committees.

April 1: Senate Budget Committee reports its budget resolution to the Senate floor (no comparable deadline for the House Budget Committee).

April 15: Congress completes action on its budget resolution.

May 15: Annual appropriations may be considered on the House floor, even if there is no adopted budget resolution.

June 10: House Appropriations Committee reports the last annual appropriations bill to the floor.

June 30: House completes action on last annual appropriations bill.

Prior to July 1: Supplemental appropriations for the current fiscal year that exceed discretionary spending targets and are enacted before this date trigger a sequester fifteen days after enactment; after July 1, if appropriations are enacted that exceed the spending caps for the current fiscal year, the spending caps for the next fiscal year are lowered.

July 15: President submits executive branch's midsession review of the budget to Congress.

August 10: President must notify Congress of any intention to exempt military personnel from sequestration or sequester such accounts at a lower percentage rate.

August 15: CBO updates sequester preview.

August 20: OMB updates sequester preview.

October 1: Fiscal year begins.

Ten days after adjournment: CBO final sequester report.

Fifteen days after adjournment: OMB final sequester report. President issues sequester order.

Thirty days after sequester report: General Accounting Office compliance report.

House and Senate leaders, anxious to keep the process going, steered away from proposing budget resolutions that would force legislative and Appropriations committees to compete openly for budget resources. The House and Senate Budget committees considered the spending needs for each of nineteen budget categories before setting an overall total, instead of first establishing the size of the overall budget.

As long as Congress remained in an expansive mood, the House and Senate were able to construct budgets in a piecemeal fashion that satisfied the particular interests of various commit-

tees and groups. When Congress tried to shift toward fiscal austerity in mid-1979, it encountered much rougher going. The budget process sputtered—and at times nearly foundered—when changing economic conditions forced Congress to shift to a policy of fiscal restraint requiring politically difficult spending reductions.

By 1980 critics were charging that the budget process had turned into a meaningless exercise of adding up separate spending proposals rather than disciplining them to meet overall budget goals. As Schick pointed out, "At no time during the first five years of budgeting did either committee vote explicitly to take from one function in order to give more to another."[34]

At the end of 1980, the fight to put teeth into budget goals paid off. Congress for the first time put together a reconciliation bill incorporating spending cuts and revenue increases that the first fiscal 1981 budget resolution had ordered congressional committees to prepare. By putting the reconciliation mechanism to use—at the end of a year in which budget balancing efforts had collapsed—Congress salvaged some hope for the process. By following through on reconciliation, Congress set a precedent for a sweeping 1981 budget-cutting feat that gave the budget process unexpected, and to some observers unintended, power to change the whole course of government in the administration of President Reagan.

REAGAN REVOLUTION

President Reagan, after taking office in 1981, asked Congress to cut Carter's proposed fiscal 1982 budget by more than $40 billion through spending reductions in more than eighty federal programs. With former representative David A. Stockman, R-Mich., Reagan's Office of Management and Budget (OMB) director, masterminding the campaign, Republican leaders who had just taken control of the Senate agreed early in the 1981 session to consolidate the budget reductions in one reconciliation measure. By packaging the budget cuts and forcing the House and Senate to vote on a single measure, Republicans hoped to prevent congressional committees and interest groups from chipping away at the president's budget plan through piecemeal changes.

The strategy worked, far better than many dismayed Democrats could have imagined. The Senate, with its Republican majority, had moved smoothly to rubber-stamp the president's requests. In the House after momentous floor battles, Democratic fiscal conservatives from southern states, labeled "Boll Weevils," joined with a united Republican minority to pass the administration-backed measures. On August 13, 1981, Reagan signed into law the deepest and farthest-reaching package of budget cuts that Congress had ever approved. The final reconciliation measure, curbing outlays for scores of federal programs, was designed to reduce fiscal 1982 spending by nearly $35.2 billion. In all, the package sought to trim estimated outlays in fiscal years 1981–1984 by $130.6 billion.

Reagan's success startled the Democrats' confidence in their House leaders and suggested that the drive to cut spending was encouraging fundamental realignments of power in a chamber no longer dominated by liberal, pro-spending sentiments.

In 1982, however, a recession sent budget deficits spiraling, and thereafter deficit control would be the key element driving budget decisions on Capitol Hill in the 1980s. The subsequent recovery, although as strong as the recession was devastating, did little to curb the growing deficits.

By early 1982 a majority in Congress became convinced that the Reagan tax cut of the previous year had to be corrected to hold down the deficit. By mid-year, a revenue-raising tax bill had been enacted. Congress's concern about Reagan's economic plan (termed "Reaganomics") carried over to the president's

proposed fiscal 1983 budget request. Congressional reaction to this budget was a sharp reversal from the previous year. Although Republicans continued to dominate the budget debate, there was increasing dissension among the ranks. In mid-June the House and Senate adopted a compromise budget that projected a budget deficit of more than $103 billion. Congress's attempts to tackle the deficit using procedures set forth in the 1974 budget law clearly were not working.

In 1983 political power and momentum shifted back to the Democrats after they picked up twenty-six seats after the 1982 congressional elections. The 1983 budget resolutions called for new taxes, a rollback in defense, and the restoration of some so-

LINE-ITEM VETO, BALANCED BUDGET AMENDMENT

The Republican-led 104th Congress in 1996 cleared a bill giving the president the functional equivalent of a line-item veto. The new law—one of the few Contract with America bills that Democratic president Bill Clinton had eagerly signed—took effect on January 1, 1997. However, the Supreme Court in 1998 declared the law unconstitutional, a violation of the separation of powers doctrine.

Technically, the legislation did not provide for a true line-item veto, which would allow the president to strike individual lines from an appropriations bill before signing it. A constitutional amendment—extremely difficult to achieve—would have been required to give the president line-item veto power. Instead, lawmakers gave the White House what was termed a legislative line-item veto, significantly strengthening the president's existing power to rescind, or cancel, individual items within already signed bills.

The bill created a complex and untested process under which the president could send Congress a rescissions message proposing to cancel specific items in any appropriations act, new entitlement spending, or targeted tax benefit that met certain criteria. The proposal would take effect automatically unless it was blocked by a special "disapproval bill" passed in identical form by both chambers. The president could then veto that bill, requiring a two-thirds vote in each chamber to override him.

Under previous law, the president could propose rescission only in certain enacted appropriations bills, and the proposals expired after forty-five days unless Congress chose to enact them. Congress was free to ignore a proposed rescission.

Presidents since Ulysses S. Grant had sought the line-item veto. Supporters of the veto said it would curb the practice of slipping "pork barrel" spending into huge appropriations bills that presidents have little choice but to accept. Opponents said it gave away too much of Congress's power of the purse and handed the executive branch a club with which to beat Congress on other issues.

As used by Clinton, however, the veto did not become a club, nor did it curb Congress's appetite for parochial pet projects. He first used it in 1997 against three obscure spending provisions, which generated the successful constitutional challenge.

When the first of the fiscal 1998 spending bills was sent to the White House, Clinton provoked outrage with his vetoes of numer-

ous military construction projects. (His actions subsequently were overridden.) Later, he used the new tool more delicately, taking care not to alienate powerful allies or enemies and limiting his vetoes to projects that were parochial or downright silly. He never tried to use veto threats to win votes on unrelated issues.

The Supreme Court's 6–3 decision on June 25, 1998, striking down the law capped years of debate over whether Congress could, by statute, transfer such potentially sweeping power over the lawmaking process to the president. The Court declared the law unconstitutional because it permitted the president to rewrite bills that he had already signed. Under the Constitution, the president must accept or reject bills in their entirety.

Congress has shown some support for another budget restraint mechanism—a constitutional amendment to balance the budget. The balanced budget amendment would mandate that each year revenues be equal to or exceed outlays.

The drive to adopt a balanced budget amendment first gained momentum in the states in the mid-1970s. By 1984, legislatures of thirty-two states—just two short of the two-thirds needed to force a convention—had adopted resolutions calling for a constitutional convention to draft an amendment. Shortly thereafter, however, a number of states began rescinding their resolutions and the balanced budget movement lost steam in the states.

Congress came close to adopting a resolution calling for such an amendment to the U.S. Constitution in 1982. That year the Senate passed a balanced budget amendment by slightly more than the two-thirds majority needed for passage, but the measure failed to garner enough votes in the House. In 1986 the Senate rejected a balanced budget proposal. Efforts in the House were defeated in 1990 and 1992. Both houses of Congress rejected an amendment in 1994.

When the GOP took control of Congress in 1995, the centerpiece of the House Republicans' ambitious agenda was passage of a balanced budget amendment. The House passed such a measure in 1995, but the Senate failed to in both 1995 and 1996. In the 105th Congress, in 1997, the Senate again rejected an amendment to balance the budget. The House declined to push for a floor vote, expecting certain defeat.

cial spending cutbacks of the previous years. With the Reagan White House adamantly opposed, legislative action on the reconciliation bills ground to a halt by the end of 1983 and Congress went home without completing action on the bills.

In 1984 the House wanted to follow the regular order of procedures and passed a budget resolution in early April. But the White House and the Senate, led by Republicans, insisted on using the reconciliation bills left over from the previous year as the central points of legislative activity. Only after passing the deficit reduction legislation did the Senate adopt its own budget resolution in mid-May. Final adoption of the House-Senate budget resolution conference agreement was not completed until October 1, the day the new fiscal year began.

GRAMM-RUDMAN-HOLLINGS

The biggest change in the congressional budget process and in budget politics since enactment of the Congressional Budget and Impoundment Act of 1974 was the enactment of a new anti-deficit law in 1985. The legislation, properly called the Balanced Budget and Emergency Deficit Control Act of 1985, was the handiwork of Senators Phil Gramm, Warren B. Rudman, and Ernest Hollings and is often referred to as Gramm-Rudman-Hollings, or just Gramm-Rudman.

By 1985 Congress was stalemated over Reagan's opposition to more tax increases, his demands for additional domestic spending cuts, and pressure for a larger defense budget. And nearly everyone thought the deficit was getting out of hand. Lawmak-

ers struggled to adopt a budget, but in the end politics and legislative inertia were more powerful than Congress's desire to cut the deficit in a meaningful way. Once again the budget process had failed to provide a structure for deficit reduction.

Several budget-control mechanisms were discussed in 1985, including the line-item veto for the president and a constitutional amendment to balance the budget. In the end, though, the idea of mandatory spending targets and an enforcement tool that provided automatic spending cuts was the only serious plan. *(See box, Line-Item Veto, Balanced Budget Amendment, p. 174.)*

A Rapid Legislative Journey

The legislation originated in the Senate in 1985. Throughout the year, Senators Bob Dole, R-Kan., and Pete V. Domenici, R-N.M., tried to craft deficit reduction legislation that would be acceptable to both the White House and Democrats in Congress. Finally a Senate budget resolution was adopted on May 10 by just one vote—a tie-breaker by Vice President Bush. The controversial plan called for a freeze in Social Security cost-of-living increases, a cap in military spending increases at the rate of inflation, and the termination of thirteen small programs.

Two months after the Senate adopted the plan, President Reagan abandoned Dole and Domenici by cutting a deal with House Speaker Thomas P. O'Neill Jr., D-Mass., that effectively killed the original Senate resolution. Senate Republicans felt be-

In 1985 this threesome gave their names to a new measure to rein in the federal deficit: from left, Sens. Warren B. Rudman, R-N.H., Phil Gramm, R-Texas; and Ernest F. Hollings, D-S.C.

trayed by their president. Although a House-Senate budget compromise was finally worked out, the tough work was still ahead. The budget required reconciliation legislation to bring about more than $75 billion in savings over three years, and the reconciliation battle was so fierce that little hope existed for a successful agreement.

In the meantime, with the fiscal 1986 deficit headed for a record high, Congress began searching for new ways to control the budget. Texas Senator Phil Gramm, a key player in the esoteric world of budget politics, first formulated the idea of a budget-cutting plan when he was a member of the House in the early 1980s. The basic framework called for mandatory deficit targets that Congress would have to meet each year until a balanced budget was reached, plus a mechanism that would automatically cut federal spending across the board if Congress could not reach the deficit target.

In late September 1985, Gramm focused on the pending debt limit legislation as his means of enacting the budget-cutting plan. Majority Leader Dole offered the Gramm plan as an amendment to the debt limit bill, which was passed by the Senate in October. After a number of stops and starts in the House, Congress passed the compromise budget-cutting plan in De-

---

CONGRESSIONAL BUDGETING IN BRIEF: PROCESS AS REVAMPED BY 1990 LAW

The Congressional Budget and Impoundment Control Act of 1974 provides the framework for congressional action on the budget. Congress has made numerous changes in the original process, primarily through the Balanced Budget and Emergency Deficit Control Act of 1985 (Gramm-Rudman-Hollings) and the Budget Enforcement Act of 1990. Also, in recent years, Congress has missed many of the deadlines listed below.

FISCAL YEAR

To keep track of its revenues and expenditures in an orderly way, the federal government has established a twelve-month period known as the fiscal year. For many years the government's fiscal year ran from July 1 through June 30. To give Congress more time to consider the budget during its annual sessions, which start in January, the 1974 budget law pushed back the start of the fiscal year to October 1.

BUDGET SUBMISSION

The president is required to submit an annual budget request and economic forecast to Congress by the first Monday in February. The president's budget sets out a spending and revenue plan for the coming fiscal year. The budget figures must be presented in terms of national needs, agency missions, and basic programs and must include five-year projections of expected spending for federal programs. *(See box, Budget Timetable, p. 173.)*

BUDGET COMMITTEES

To give Congress a more expert perspective on budget totals and on fiscal policy requirements, the 1974 budget act established House and Senate committees to study and recommend changes in the president's budget.

House Budget Committee members are prohibited from serving for more than four two-year terms during any six Congresses. No rotation of members is required for the Senate Budget Committee.

CONGRESSIONAL BUDGET OFFICE

The 1974 act established an office within Congress to provide the experts and the computer support services needed to absorb and analyze information that accompanies the president's budget. The act requires the Congressional Budget Office (CBO) to make its staff and resources available to all congressional committees and members,

but with priority given to the House and Senate Budget committees. The office is run by a director appointed for a four-year term by the Speaker of the House and the president pro tempore of the Senate. *(See "Congressional Budget Office," p. 757, Vol. II.)*

BUDGET RESOLUTION

After reviewing the president's budget proposals, and considering the advice of CBO and other committees, the House and Senate Budget committees draw up a concurrent resolution outlining a tentative alternative federal budget. A budget resolution requires approval by both houses in identical form, but it does not go to the president for his signature. Under the law's timetable, Congress must complete action on the budget resolution by April 15. If Congress does not adopt a budget resolution by April 15, the House Budget Committee must report spending limits to the House Appropriations Committee based on discretionary spending in the president's budget, and the House Appropriations Committee must make suballocations to its subcommittees as soon after that as is practical.

The budget resolution sets budget target totals for budget authority (or appropriations), outlays, revenues, the deficit, and the federal debt. Within those overall targets, the resolution breaks down appropriations and spending among the functional categories—defense, health, income security, and so forth—used in the president's budget document. The resolution also includes caps for three broad categories of discretionary spending—defense, foreign, and domestic programs. Provisions for mandatory spending (or entitlement) programs that are budgeted as "pay-as-you-go" programs may be spelled out in the resolution. Finally, reconciliation instructions, used to guide authorizing committees on the savings cuts required to meet the deficit target, may be included. Budget resolutions must project spending, revenues, and deficits for five years.

Once finally approved, the budget resolution guides Congress as it acts on the separate appropriations bills and other measures providing budget authority for spending on federal programs.

The law directs that the budget resolution must be adopted before consideration in either chamber of any measure appropriating funds, changing taxes or the public debt level, or creating a new entitlement program committing the government to pay certain benefits. If a budget resolution is not adopted by May 15, however, annual appropriations bills may be considered anytime thereafter on the

cember. When the dust settled, Democratic House negotiators were successful in fine-tuning the procedure to their liking. The deal exempted Social Security and many social programs for the poor from the automatic cuts, limited cuts in the Medicare and Guaranteed Student Loan programs, and required that half of the cuts come from defense.

How the Process Worked

The original plan called for balancing the budget in five years beginning in 1986, set annual maximum deficit targets, and mandated across-the-board cuts (or "sequestration") if the deficit goals were not achieved through regular budget action. Half of the cuts would come from defense and half from nondefense programs, with a uniform percentage cut in each program, project, and activity of the government. Some programs, such as Social Security, interest on the public debt, veterans' compensation and pensions, Medicaid, and food stamps, were exempt from the cuts.

As enacted, the law called for OMB, led by the president's budget director, and the Congressional Budget Office (CBO) to review progress toward meeting the law's deficit target each year. The OMB and CBO projections of necessary automatic

House floor. In the Senate a majority vote can permit the consideration of appropriations bills anytime prior to passage of a budget resolution.

APPROPRIATIONS

Once the budget resolution is in place, Congress begins processing the thirteen regular appropriations bills for the coming fiscal year through its regular appropriations process. The law requires that the House must complete action on all appropriations bills by June 30. Within five days after passage of any appropriations bill, OMB must send the House and Senate a report containing CBO and OMB estimates of budget authority and outlays for the bill, and an explanation of differences between the two estimates.

Supplemental appropriations are used to provide funds in addition to a regular appropriation. If a supplemental bill is enacted prior to July 1 and provides funds for the current fiscal year that exceed a spending cap, it will trigger automatic cuts fifteen days after enactment within the spending category—defense, domestic, or foreign aid—in which the excess occurs. If a supplemental bill providing funds for the current fiscal year is enacted after June 30 and it exceeds a spending cap, the cap for that category for the next fiscal year must be reduced by the amount of the excess. The president alone may determine that a particular supplemental appropriations bill qualifies as an emergency measure exempt from automatic spending cuts.

Continuing appropriations resolutions provide Congress with a way to fund the government if regular appropriations bills have not been passed by October 1. A continuing resolution, or CR, generally continues funding for a specified period of time at the level of the previous year or the level of an appropriation passed by either or both houses of Congress for the current year.

MANDATORY SPENDING

Spending on entitlement and other mandatory programs is allowed to grow to accommodate the needs of additional people who become eligible for the programs. The deficit is adjusted for this program growth. For any new entitlements or changes that expand a program, Congress mandates that offsetting revenues or cuts must be made in other programs. If this pay-as-you-go procedure is not followed, automatic cuts across a wide range of nonexempt entitlement programs may be triggered.

RECONCILIATION

The budget resolution uses reconciliation instructions to direct committees to change existing law to bring spending, revenues, or the debt limit into conformity with the budget resolution and to report these program changes to the Budget committees. If the changes involve two committees—program changes by the House Education and Labor and Senate Labor and Human Resources committees and tax changes by the House Ways and Means and Senate Finance committees, for example—those committees would submit recommendations to the Budget committees. The Budget committees then would combine the recommendations without substantial change and send them to the floor as a reconciliation bill. Reconciliation bills are required to project spending, revenues, and deficits for five years.

AUTOMATIC SPENDING CUTS

Automatic spending cuts, or sequesters, go into effect if the federal deficit exceeds the deficit target after Congress completes its work for the year. On August 15 and August 20 CBO and OMB update the sequester previews that they issued when the president presented his budget request. Ten days after Congress adjourns, CBO issues its final sequester report.

When OMB issues its final sequester report fifteen days after Congress adjourns, a set of three sequesters go into effect if cuts are needed to meet the deficit target. The first sequester offsets discretionary appropriations for the coming fiscal year that exceed statutory limits. It affects only discretionary spending in the category—such as defense, foreign aid, or domestic programs—where an excess exists. The second sequester is triggered if Congress enacts entitlement spending increases or revenue decreases during the year without compensating for the program changes. It affects only nonexempt entitlements. The third sequester will offset an increase in the deficit above the limit set in the law if the first two sequesters have not eliminated the excess deficit. It covers all nonexempt spending, with 50 percent of the outlay reductions from nonexempt defense accounts and 50 percent from nonexempt nondefense accounts.

A declaration of war cancels the sequester process. Also, Congress can vote to cancel the sequester process in a recession or if economic growth is below 1 percent for two consecutive quarters.

cuts would be averaged and then reviewed by the General Accounting Office (GAO), which would instruct the president as to whether automatic cuts would be necessary. In late August each year, the president was to issue an initial sequestration order temporarily making the necessary cuts by putting a hold on spending. In mid-October, a second order would be issued and the spending cuts would become final. *(See box, Congressional Budgeting in Brief, p. 176.)*

Reagan, Bush, and Budget Summits

Budget deficits dipped only slightly in the late 1980s before resuming their rapid climb. During this time there were mixed results from the Gramm-Rudman law. To reach the deficit targets, Congress resorted to a number of accounting techniques, such as sales of assets and manipulation of the government pay calendar. Deficit reduction (or reconciliation) legislation became known as much for the "pork barrel" proposals attached by members as for the deficit reduction. Senators Gramm and Rudman argued that the law drastically reduced the federal spending growth rate and led to the decline of government spending as a percentage of the gross national product.[35] In a paraphrase of Winston Churchill, Gramm acknowledged that it is the "worst way of doing budgets except for all the other ways we've tried."[36]

In early 1986 Gramm-Rudman was put into effect for the first time, using special rules to make cuts for fiscal 1986, the year in progress. On February 1, $11.7 billion in automatic cuts were ordered and on March 1 they became permanent; Gramm-Rudman seemed to be working. But a special three-judge panel of the federal district court in Washington, D.C., ruled that GAO's role in ratifying the amount of the across-the-board cuts was unconstitutional. The argument was that GAO was an arm of the legislative branch of government, and under the separation of powers doctrine it could not direct the president to make the spending cuts.

On July 7 the Supreme Court upheld the lower court ruling. Late in July both the House and Senate voted to ratify the $11.7 billion in fiscal 1986 spending cuts that had been struck down by the Court to retain the progress that had been made on deficit reduction.

Congress was determined to fix the automatic-cut provision of Gramm-Rudman, and it did so as part of another must-pass debt limit bill in September 1987. The "fix," as it was known, gave all authority for ordering automatic cuts to OMB. The sequestration procedure was back on track and was scheduled to cut $23 billion from the deficit in October. Then on October 19 the Dow Jones Industrial Average fell 508 points, the largest one-day drop in the history of the stock index. Financial markets around the world panicked, and President Reagan and Congress had little choice but to work together on a deficit-cutting deal.

Budget summits became a new way for Congress and the president to reach agreement on deficit reduction. Only a handful of congressional and administration officials participated in the 1987 summit, virtually shutting most members of Congress out of the process. Reached after four weeks of negotiations, the two-year package gave members a way to avoid a debilitating budget fight in 1988. To implement the summit agreement, a government-wide continuing appropriations resolution and a reconciliation bill enacted $76 billion in cuts over the two-year period. For the first time the agreement put in place a two-year commitment to specified levels of defense and nondefense program spending. It allowed members of Congress to avoid a budget battle in 1988 because most of the big decisions on defense and domestic spending had already been made, and there was no need for Gramm-Rudman cuts or a reconciliation bill.

President Bush's first budget plan, presented to Congress in February 1989, was criticized for failing even to identify the specific spending cuts necessary to reach the fiscal 1990 Gramm-Rudman deficit target of $100 billion. By the spring, Congress and the president were able to put aside their differences and hold a budget summit to reach an April bipartisan pact. The summit agreement was hailed for its cooperative spirit but was criticized for its failure to take bold steps such as proposing major tax increases or entitlement program cuts. Even the savings were considered to be mostly accounting gimmicks.

Implementation of the 1989 pact proved to be more difficult than the summit negotiations. The reconciliation bill became bogged down over Bush's proposed cut in the capital gains tax, and agreement finally was reached in late November. The bill contained $14.7 billion in "deficit reduction," although close to $5 billion in savings resulted from controversial accounting maneuvers. The bill did break a decade-long pattern of using reconciliation bills as vehicles for lawmakers' unrelated pet proposals.

1990: SEARCH FOR BUDGET CONTROL

By the time Bush began his second year as president, it was apparent that the budget deficit was rapidly growing out of control. A slowdown in the economy coupled with the huge cost of bailing out hundreds of savings and loan thrifts—which had failed due to the recession, bad real estate loans, and fraud—led OMB to estimate that the deficit would exceed $169 billion in fiscal 1991. The Gramm-Rudman target for the year was $64 billion.

Budgeting in 1990 was a painful process for both the White House and Congress. When Congress finally adjourned on October 28, it had changed the face of federal budgeting once again through passage of the Budget Enforcement Act of 1990. The act rescinded many provisions of the 1985 Gramm-Rudman law. New, higher deficit targets were set for fiscal 1991–1995, with automatic adjustments in fiscal 1992–1993 and optional adjustments in 1994–1995 to account for changes in the economy and technical estimates of the cost of entitlements. In short, the deficit would be allowed to grow with the economy. The new law limited the role of the Budget committees because the major spending and taxing decisions for Congress had already been set forth until the mid-1990s. Congress was perhaps most pleased that the deal meant that no more summits needed to be held between Congress and the White House, at least for a while.

White House and congressional negotiators stand by as President George Bush announces a budget package drafted in the 1990 summit meeting. The negotiators' grim faces point to the plan's subsequent defeat.

Developing the Five-Year Plan

The House more or less adhered to the budget process timetable and passed its version of the budget resolution on May 1, 1990. It soon became clear, however, that serious negotiations between the White House and Congress would be necessary to reach an agreement. President Bush called for a bipartisan budget summit in late spring; negotiations began on May 15. The goal was to cut the deficit by $50 billion in fiscal 1991 and $500 billion over five years.

Four months passed with little progress made on a plan to reduce the deficit. After Labor Day, negotiators reconvened their talks at Andrews Air Force Base, just outside Washington, in a ploy to keep lobbyists and the news media away from the talks. But on September 17, negotiations broke down. To keep the lines of communication open between Congress and the White House, a "hyper-summit" of eight White House and congressional leaders convened in the office of House Speaker Thomas S. Foley, D-Wash., on September 18. Talks continued as the October 1 beginning of the fiscal year drew near. Congress had yet to clear a single appropriations bill needed to run the government or to provide the necessary increase in the public debt limit to allow the sale of government securities in the nation's financial markets. And a massive $105.7 billion Gramm-Rudman sequester loomed on the horizon. The chaos of federal budgeting was far worse than in any other year in memory.

Finally, on September 30, a budget deal was announced. The announcement was followed by passage of a stopgap continuing appropriations resolution to avoid a government-wide shut-down. The budget package and the summit that produced it, however, led to widespread rank-and-file dissatisfaction. Members questioned whether they had delegated too much authority to the few negotiators. The $500 billion package called for some distasteful elements, including an enormous increase in cost to Medicare beneficiaries and higher taxes for the middle class primarily through energy taxes and the "sin" taxes on tobacco and alcoholic beverages.

On October 5 the rank and file had their say. The budget package was soundly defeated in the House by an unusual coalition of liberal Democrats and conservative Republicans, led by Newt Gingrich, R-Ga. President Bush had made a rare, prime-time television address to the nation calling for support of the package, but it turned into an embarrassing political disaster for him. In a show of anger with Congress, the president refused to sign a second continuing appropriations resolution, and the "nonessential" parts of the government shut down over the Columbus Day weekend, October 6–8.

After the defeat of the budget package, House Democrats reasserted their power. On October 8 they passed a new "stripped down" budget resolution that would allow them to make the real decisions through the reconciliation bill. The Senate passed its budget resolution in the early morning hours of October 9. President Bush signed a new continuing appropriations resolution shortly thereafter, and government workers returned to work on the morning of October 9.

At this point, White House credibility eroded because of a curious period of mixed signals and indecision. Congressional

Republicans searched for unity after a period of infighting over the original budget package. Led by Ways and Means Chairman Dan Rostenkowski, the House on October 16 passed a "soak the rich" reconciliation bill that was vehemently opposed by the White House. Several days later, on October 19, the Senate passed a bipartisan reconciliation package that had been framed by the Senate Finance Committee.

The last week of negotiations between House and Senate conferees was a delicate process of bringing the two groups together at a time when most members were tired and anxious to go home to campaign for reelection. The long struggle ended with a $500 billion compromise package that made no one completely happy. The largest deficit reduction bill in the nation's history was cleared by both chambers of Congress on October 27.

Controlling the Deficit in the 1990s

The Budget Enforcement Act of 1990, which was part of the 1990 deficit reduction law, once again changed Congress's budget-making procedures. In a major budget policy change, the 1990 law played down the sheer size of the deficit. The law set revised deficit targets, but the targets were designed to be adjusted in the future for economic conditions or errors in technical forecasts.

The law retained use of the budget resolution, but the Budget committees had little real power to influence major spending decisions. Appropriations were capped in three separate categories—domestic, defense, and international programs—for fiscal years 1991–1993. Under a new "minisequester" mechanism, only spending within the specific spending cap that had exceeded its limit would be subject to cuts. A single overall appropriations cap was set forth for each of fiscal years 1994 and 1995.

In case of war or natural disaster, the president could authorize supplemental spending above the appropriations caps that would not be subject to sequester. In 1991 President Bush authorized two such measures to finance the military and home-front costs of Operation Desert Shield/Storm—the war to liberate Kuwait, which had been invaded and occupied by Iraq in August 1990.

Entitlement programs were allowed to grow as more people became eligible for benefits. Increases in benefits or expansions of entitlement programs, however, were put on a "pay-as-you-go" plan that required either a revenue increase or a cut in another entitlement program.

REACHING A BALANCED BUDGET

Following the 1990 summit, and the enactment of new budget rules, little action was seen on the budget front. Battles over tax cuts and tax increases, or proposals to spend more money on favored domestic programs, were almost nonexistent. Even in the case of the 1990–1991 recession, little agreement existed about what the government could, or should, do. In part, the lack of consensus stemmed from a real fear of adverse consequences from a policy misstep. In part, it resulted as lawmakers

engaged in high-stakes political poker with the White House, which was up for grabs in 1992.

As the election approached, louder calls for middle-class tax cuts came from both ends of the political spectrum. But economists poured cold water on the idea, and opinion polls showed that even the public seemed uneasy with it. Despite opposition from most Republicans, congressional Democrats exercised their majority will to send two tax bills in 1992 to Bush for his signature—one a middle-class tax cut, the other a package of tax cuts to aid businesses in urban areas, with a little middle-class tax relief on the side. Bush vetoed both.

While the two political parties policed each other for strict adherence to the 1990 budget rules, neither paid much attention to the overall size of the deficit. Bush in his 1992 State of the Union address announced that he was immediately reducing the amount of income tax withheld from employee paychecks to give consumers more spending money. The move would reduce tax receipts by $15 billion in fiscal 1992—and increase the deficit by a like amount. A boost to the deficit of that size would have been unthinkable under the old Gramm-Rudman rules, but the new rules imposed no penalty on a deficit increase that did not result from legislation, and this plan did not require congressional approval.

Some in Congress chafed at the limits imposed by the new budget laws. Democrats in 1992 launched an effort to remove the "walls" that barred using extra large cuts in defense spending to finance domestic initiatives. But that plan failed, in part because many lawmakers believed that junking the budget rules would remove the insulation that protected them from charges that they were ignoring the deficit. And the alternative would have been to make another stab at deficit reduction, which few wanted to try in a presidential election year.

In his 1992 presidential campaign, Clinton was criticized for promising a middle-class tax cut while promoting new "investment" spending. Deficit reduction, Clinton claimed, would come via strong economic growth and tax increases on the wealthy. His plan was severely weakened when the Congressional Budget Office forecast a fiscal 1996 deficit $76 billion larger than the previous estimate. Then, just before Clinton took office, the Office of Management and Budget announced that the fiscal 1997 deficit was expected to balloon to $305 billion. All of a sudden, the deficit, on which Clinton had barely focused during the campaign, was front and center.

President Clinton had campaigned on the promise to cut the 1997 deficit roughly in half—to $145 billion. To accomplish that goal, Clinton's 1993 deficit reduction bill, crafted to appeal to Democrats, featured taxes on the wealthy, plus spending restraint from cuts in defense, caps on appropriations, and reductions in the growth of Medicare payments to doctors and hospitals. Getting the measure passed required a full court press from Clinton and his supporters on Capitol Hill. Republicans and their allies, such as the Christian Coalition, mounted a ferocious campaign against the bill, calling it the biggest tax hike of all time—which was technically true, although it was smaller than

As congressional leaders and White House officials watch, President Bill Clinton signs the balanced budget agreement of 1997.

Reagan's 1992 tax increase after adjusting for inflation. The bill ultimately passed both houses of Congress by the narrowest of margins and with no Republican votes in favor.

The Clinton plan proved the Republicans wrong. As the economy recovered from the 1990–1991 recession, the resulting deficit reduction was impressive. The potential of chronic $300 billion-a-year deficits that faced Clinton had disappeared; the fiscal 1996 deficit shrank to $107.3 billion.

Clinton and GOP Congress

While ultimately successful in its goal of halving the deficit by the end of Clinton's first term, the deficit-cutting drive of the president's first year in office contributed to a devastating political loss: the 1994 elections produced the first GOP Congress in forty years.

In the early days of Republican rule in 1995, the hard-charging conservatism of the House dominated. The House conservatives set their sights on wholesale spending cuts, tax cuts, and elimination of entire departments of government—Energy, Education, and Commerce. House Republicans were first determined to pass the elements of the Contract with America—the national political platform used by Republicans in the 1994 congressional elections. One of its most important planks was a constitutional amendment to balance the federal budget by 2002. The House passed the measure easily, but the Senate killed it. The defeat of the amendment was devastating for Republicans, and it could have given them an excuse to adopt a more cautious approach to budget policy. But House Republican leaders declared that they wanted to balance the budget outright. *(See box, "Contract with America," p. 441.)*

Adopting a budget resolution and then passing a budget reconciliation bill to implement the GOP's balanced budget plan took almost all of 1995. Republicans devised early plans to try to force Clinton into signing their budget bill—knowing he was prepared to veto it. The government's authority to borrow money was slated to expire near the end of the year, and Republicans would use the threat of the first-ever default on the national debt, which could have devastating effects on financial markets and send interest rates soaring, as leverage to get the president to negotiate. The thirteen annual appropriations bill might also be withheld, threatening a government shutdown.

Republicans produced a reconciliation bill that would reduce Medicare spending by $270 billion, turn Medicaid into a block grant program for the states, dramatically overhaul welfare, squeeze $12 billion from farm programs, cut the earned-income tax credit for low-income workers by $32 billion, reduce capital gains taxes, end the corporate alternative minimum tax, lower taxes on estates, provide new reductions for individual retirement accounts, and install an array of tax breaks for small businesses. Democrats began their attack: Republicans were slashing Medicare to give tax breaks to the rich.

Meanwhile, the GOP revolution was taking hold in the Appropriations committees, especially in the House, where back-slapping bipartisanship was replaced with budget-cutting fervor and a desire to use the must-pass spending bills as locomotives for policy "riders," such as blocking the Environmental Protection Agency from implementing antipollution laws. This not only led to a standoff with Clinton, but also led to intraparty battles that took months to sort out and delayed all but two of the thirteen regular appropriations bills past the October 1 start of fiscal 1996.

All of this built toward a massive collision November 13, when a stopgap spending bill expired. With their work behind schedule and the White House refusing to yield, Republicans seized on the need for both a new interim spending bill and a stopgap debt limit increase to force Clinton to bend on their budget demands. They attached to the legislation a GOP plan to cut Medicare spending and provisions that would sharply limit the Treasury Department's ability to use creative methods to stave off default. Contrary to GOP expectations, Clinton did not blink. He vetoed the measure, calling it blackmail, and a week-long partial shutdown of the government began, sending 800,000 federal workers home. Treasury Secretary Robert E. Rubin found accounting ways to skirt a default on the federal debt.

The situation was a disaster for the Republicans, but the shutdown ended when Clinton met a key GOP demand to produce a plan to balance the budget in seven years. Another stopgap bill provided time for talks between congressional Republicans and the White House. However, those talks quickly collapsed amid bitter recriminations. When the temporary spending bill expired December 15, angry Republicans refused to immediately pass another one. A second government shutdown began. Clinton had vetoed the GOP budget reconciliation bill on December 7.

Budget talks between the two parties proved futile. The Republican "train wreck" strategy had backfired badly. Public opinion polls ran 2–1 against the GOP Congress. A series of stopgap spending bills financed the government until Republicans and the president agreed in April 1996 on an omnibus bill to cover the balance of the fiscal year. The frontal attack on the budget by the new Republican majority had been repelled.

Congressional Republicans scored no big victories on the fiscal policy front in 1996—no balanced budget deal, no sweeping tax cuts. Such actions eluded the majority in part because the GOP did not want to repeat the knock-down, drag-out budget fight that had consumed much of the 1995 session. Lawmakers did not want to spend the time or the political capital needed to wage such a battle, let alone win it.

Balanced Budget Agreement

While Republicans were unsuccessful in forcing Clinton to sign their budget bills, the budget fights drew Clinton in their direction and forced him to embrace their budget-balancing goal if not their policies. Ultimately, negotiations spanning the first several months of Clinton's second term led to a historic agreement in 1997 to balance the federal budget in five years, while cutting taxes and increasing spending on selected administration priorities in areas such as children's health care. It was almost immediately translated into a congressional budget resolution that formally set Congress's budget guidelines.

Angry Democrats denounced the closed-door negotiations and objected to their second-class status as Clinton and the Republicans made their final compromise. In the end, pro-business, conservative, and moderate Democrats were pleased with the budget agreement, while liberal and blue-collar Democrats viewed the package as tilted against the poor and the tax cuts as stacked in favor of the rich.

Regardless, the deficit juggernaut had been stalled. The government recorded a surplus of $69 billion in fiscal 1998, the first time the federal budget had been in the black since fiscal 1969. In September 1999 the federal budget surplus for 1999 was expected to reach $115 billion. The Democratic White House and Republican members of the 106th Congress spent a good portion of 1999 arguing not about how to cut the budget but about how to spend the surplus.

NOTES

1. George B. Galloway, *The Legislative Process in Congress* (New York: Crowell, 1955), 91.

2. Executive Office of the President, Office of Management and Budget (OMB), *Budget of the United States Government, Fiscal Year 2000, Historical Tables* (Washington, D.C.: Government Printing Office, 1999), Table 1.3.

3. C. Herman Pritchett, *The American Constitution*, 3rd ed. (New York: McGraw-Hill, 1977), 167.

4. OMB, *Fiscal 2000 Budget, Historical Tables*, Table 2.5.

5. Ibid., Tables 2.1, 2.2.

6. House Committee on Ways and Means, *Overview of the Federal Tax System* (Washington, D.C.: Government Printing Office, 1990), 151; Internal Revenue Service.

7. OMB, *Fiscal 2000 Budget, Historical Tables*, Tables 2.1, 2.2, 2.5.

8. Allen Schick, "The Ways and Means of Leading Ways and Means," *The Brookings Review*, Fall 1989: 17.

9. Ibid., 22.

10. *The Federalist Papers*, with an introduction by Clinton Rossiter (New York: New American Library, 1961), 263.

11. James M. Buchanan and Richard E. Wagner, *Democracy in Deficit: The Political Legacy of Lord Keynes* (New York: Academic Press, 1977), 21.

12. Donald G. Ogilvie, "Constitutional Limits and the Federal Budget," in *The Congressional Budget Process after Five Years*, ed. Rudolph G. Penner (Washington, D.C.: American Enterprise Institute, 1981), 103–104.

13. Ibid.

14. Ibid., 109.

15. Ibid.

16. Ibid., 110.

17. OMB, *Fiscal 2000 Budget, Historical Tables*, Tables 1.1, 1.2.

18. Ogilvie, "Constitutional Limits," 106.

19. OMB, *Fiscal 2000 Budget, Historical Tables*, Table 3.1.

20. Ibid.

21. Ibid., Tables 6.1, 12.1.

22. Ogilvie, "Constitutional Limits," 115.

23. Frederic A. Ogg and P. Orman Ray, *Introduction to American Government*, 10th ed. (New York: Appleton-Century-Crofts, 1951), 527.

24. David J. Ott and Attiat F. Ott, *Federal Budget Policy*, rev. ed. (Washington, D.C.: Brookings Institution, 1969), 110.

25. Lewis H. Kimmel, *Federal Budget and Fiscal Policy, 1789–1958* (Washington, D.C.: Brookings Institution, 1959), 55.

26. Ibid., 306.

27. Ibid., 2.

28. Ibid., 3.

29. Louis Fisher, *Presidential Spending Power* (Princeton, N.J.: Princeton University Press, 1975), 39.

30. Richard E. Neustadt, "Presidency and Legislation: The Growth of Central Clearance," *American Political Science Review,* 48 (1954): 641ff.

31. Louis Fisher, "Effect of the Budget Act of 1974 on Agency Operations," in *The Congressional Budget Process after Five Years,* ed. Rudolph G. Penner (Washington, D.C.: American Enterprise Institute, 1981), 150.

32. Ibid., 149.

33. Allen Schick, "The Three-Ring Budget Process: The Appropriations, Tax, and Budget Committees in Congress," in *The New Congress,* ed. Thomas E. Mann and Norman J. Ornstein (Washington, D.C.: American Enterprise Institute, 1981), 289.

34. Allen Schick, *Congress and Money: Budgeting, Spending, and Taxing* (Washington, D.C.: Urban Institute, 1980), 333.

35. Helen Dewar, "Five Years of Gramm-Rudman-Hollings," *Washington Post,* Oct. 15, 1990, A13.

36. Quoted in Dewar, "Five Years of Gramm-Rudman-Hollings," A13.

SELECTED BIBLIOGRAPHY

Aaron, Henry J., and Michael J. Boskin, eds. *The Economics of Taxation.* Washington, D.C.: Brookings Institution, 1980.

Aaron, Henry J., Barry P. Bosworth, and Gary Burtless. *Can America Afford to Grow Old? Paying for Social Security.* Washington, D.C.: Brookings Institution, 1989.

Aaron, Henry J., and John B. Shoven. *Should the United States Privatize Social Security?* Cambridge, Mass.: MIT Press, 1999.

Ball, Robert M. *Social Security: Today and Tomorrow.* New York: Columbia University Press, 1978.

Bell, Daniel, and Lester Thurow. *The Deficits: How Big? How Long? How Dangerous?* New York: New York University Press, 1985.

Berman, Larry. *The Office of Management and Budget and the Presidency, 1921–1979.* Princeton, N.J.: Princeton University Press, 1979.

Birnbaum, Jeffrey H., and Alan S. Murray. *Showdown at Gucci Gulch: Lawmakers, Lobbyists, and the Unlikely Triumph of Tax Reform.* New York: Random House, 1987.

Eisner, Robert. *How Real Is the Federal Deficit?* New York: Free Press, 1986.

Fenno, Richard F., Jr. *The Power of the Purse: Appropriation Politics in Congress.* Boston: Little, Brown, 1973.

Findley, William. *Review of the Revenue System Adopted by the First Congress.* Philadelphia: T. Dobson, 1794. Reprint. New York: Kelley, 1971.

Fisher, Louis. *Presidential Spending Power.* Princeton, N.J.: Princeton University Press, 1975.

Galloway, George B. *The Legislative Process in Congress.* New York: Crowell, 1955.

Gilmour, John B. *Reconciliable Differences? Congress, the Budget Process, and the Deficit.* Berkeley: University of California Press, 1990.

Gramlich, Edward M. *Is It Time to Reform Social Security?* Ann Arbor: University of Michigan Press, 1998.

Harriss, C. Lowell, ed. *Control of Federal Spending.* New York: Academy of Political Science, 1985.

Horn, Stephen. *Unused Power: The Work of the Senate Committee on Appropriations.* Washington, D.C.: Brookings Institution, 1970.

Ippolito, Dennis S. *The Budget and National Politics.* San Francisco: Freeman, 1978.

Kimmel, Lewis H. *Federal Budget and Fiscal Policy, 1789–1958.* Washington, D.C.: Brookings Institution, 1959.

LeLoup, Lance. *The Fiscal Congress: Legislative Control of the Budget.* Westport, Conn.: Greenwood Press, 1980.

Manley, John F. *The Politics of Finance: The House Committee on Ways and Means.* Boston: Little, Brown, 1970.

McAllister, Eugene J., ed., *Agenda for Progress: Examining Federal Spending.* Washington, D.C.: Heritage Foundation, 1981.

———. *Congress and the Budget, Evaluating the Process.* Washington, D.C.: Heritage Foundation, 1979.

Mills, Gregory B., and John L. Palmer. *The Deficit Dilemma: Budget Policy in the Reagan Era.* Washington, D.C.: Urban Institute Press, 1984.

Pechman, Joseph A. *Federal Tax Policy.* 5th ed. Washington, D.C.: Brookings Institution, 1987.

Penner, Rudolph G., ed. *The Congressional Budget Process after Five Years.* Washington, D.C.: American Enterprise Institute, 1981.

Phillips, Kevin. *The Politics of Rich and Poor: Wealth in the American Electorate in the Reagan Aftermath.* New York: Random House, 1990.

Pressman, Jeffrey L. *House vs. Senate: Conflict in the Appropriation Process.* New Haven, Conn.: Yale University Press, 1966.

Pritchett, C. Herman. *The American Constitution.* 3rd ed. New York: McGraw-Hill, 1977.

Savage, James D. *Balanced Budgets and American Politics.* Ithaca, N.Y.: Cornell University Press, 1988.

Schick, Allen. *Congress and Money: Budgeting, Spending, and Taxing.* Washington, D.C.: Urban Institute, 1980.

———. *Crisis in the Budget Process: Exercising Political Choice.* Washington, D.C.: American Enterprise Institute, 1986.

———. *The Federal Budget: Politics, Policy, Process.* Washington, D.C.: Brookings Institution, 1995.

———. "The Three-Ring Budget Process: The Appropriations, Tax, and Budget Committees in Congress." In *The New Congress,* edited by Thomas E. Mann and Norman J. Ornstein, 288–328. Washington, D.C.: American Enterprise Institute, 1981.

———, ed. *Making Economic Policy in Congress.* Washington, D.C.: American Enterprise Institute, 1983.

Selko, Daniel T. *The Federal Financial System.* Washington, D.C.: Brookings Institution, 1940.

Stockman, David A. *The Triumph of Politics: Why the Reagan Revolution Failed.* New York: Harper and Row, 1986.

Weidenbaum, Murray L. *Federal Budgeting, The Choice of Government Programs.* Washington, D.C.: American Enterprise Institute, 1964.

West, Darrell M. *Congress and Economic Policymaking.* Pittsburgh: University of Pittsburgh Press, 1987.

White, Joseph, and Aaron Wildavsky. *The Deficit and the Public Interest: The Search for Responsible Budgeting in the 1980s.* Berkeley: University of California Press, 1989.

Wildavsky, Aaron, and Naomi Caiden. *The New Politics of the Budgetary Process.* 3rd ed. New York: Longman, 1997.

Williams, Walter. *The Congressional Budget Office: A Critical Link in Budget Reform.* Seattle: Institute of Government Research, University of Washington, 1974.

Wilmerding, Lucius, Jr. *The Spending Power: A History of the Efforts of Congress to Control Expenditures.* New Haven, Conn.: Yale University Press, 1943.

CHAPTER 5

Foreign Policy Powers

THE BLUEPRINT THE FOUNDERS established for the conduct of foreign policy was not detailed. It was obvious that certain powers were the exclusive domain of the executive or the legislative branch. But when it came to other powers, either the Constitution was not clear about which branch was foremost or it gave the two branches overlapping authority.

How the roles of the president and Congress would mesh in the conduct of foreign affairs was left to history—and the two branches—to resolve. The Constitution was, in the oft-quoted words of Edward S. Corwin, "an invitation to struggle for the privilege of directing American foreign policy."[1]

The struggle over roles and prerogatives began in George Washington's presidency and continues today. From the beginning it was apparent that the presidency had decided advantages over Congress, including, as John Jay pointed out in *Federalist* No. 64, its unity of office, capacity for secrecy and dispatch, and superior sources of information. Moreover, the president was readily available for decision making, at a time when Congress was often not in session. It was the verdict of history, Corwin continued, that the "lion's share" of the power to determine the substantive content of American foreign policy fell "usually, though by no means always," to the president.

Congress contributed to the steady growth of presidential power. It generally acquiesced in the president's deployment of forces and negotiation of executive agreements. It was willing to accept informal consultations with the executive branch, instead of demanding formal participation in the decision making. It quickly ratified or confirmed actions the president had already taken and delegated its own huge powers in broad terms so that the president could later claim to have acted under Congress's authority as well as his own. The president's accumulation of power happened gradually and not without resistance and occasional retreat, Louis Henkin wrote. Congress "never formally adopted or approved the large conception of the presidential office as it developed, though it generally acquiesced in that conception."[2]

But when Congress does choose to assert itself, it has an impressive array of powers to use, including its war, treaty, and foreign commerce powers, as well as general legislative powers. The effect is such, in the words of scholars Roger H. Davidson and Walter J. Oleszek, that "[e]ven the most decisive chief executives can find themselves constrained by active, informed, and determined policy makers on Capitol Hill."[3]

Occupants of the White House in recent decades have experienced this first hand. Congress had been generally acquiescent during the critical post–World War II period when, with the cold war gripping the globe, the United States had emerged as a world leader and made vast overseas commitments. But by the late 1960s Congress was becoming increasingly dissatisfied with its supporting role and far less pliable. Members started to question commitments the executive had made and the secrecy surrounding them. An intense struggle between the executive and legislative branches over foreign policy prerogatives erupted in the wake of U.S. military involvement in Southeast Asia.

Throughout the 1970s a resurgent Congress hurled challenge upon challenge at a presidency weakened by the Vietnam ordeal and the Watergate scandal. The clash of the two branches was only intensified by the election of a new generation of members of Congress to whom not much was sacrosanct. Procedural reforms on Capitol Hill gave members the power to challenge the old ways of doing business with the executive branch.

The combative congressional attitude deepened during the 1980s. The Reagan years produced almost perpetual crisis in executive-legislative relations over a myriad of issues—from aid to Central America to observance of arms control agreements, to use of force abroad, to the Iran-contra affair. And, although the tone was less strident, the debate over prerogatives carried over into the Bush administration and was perhaps best illustrated by Congress's struggle both with itself and the executive branch to have a say in the decision to go to war in the Persian Gulf. The stridency returned in the foreign policy debates between Congress and the Clinton administration over the increased U.S. involvement in the policing of global trouble spots.

The Constitution: Division of Powers

Article I, Section 8 of the Constitution assigned to Congress the powers "to . . . Provide for the common Defence and general Welfare of the United States; . . . To regulate Commerce with foreign Nations, and among the several States, and with the Indian Tribes; . . . To define and punish Piracies and Felonies committed on the high Seas, and Offences against the Law of Nations; To declare War, grant Letters Of Marque and Reprisal, and make Rules concerning Captures on Land and Water; To raise and support Armies . . . ; To provide and maintain a Navy; . . . And To make all Laws which shall be necessary and proper for carrying into Execution the foregoing Powers, and all other Powers vested by this Constitution in the Government of the United States, or in any Department or Officer thereof."

The Constitution also provided that "the President shall be Commander in Chief of the Army and Navy. . . . He shall have Power, by and with the Advice and Consent of the Senate, to make Treaties, provided two-thirds of the Senators present concur; and he shall nominate, and by and with the Advice and Consent of the Senate, shall appoint Ambassadors, other public Ministers, and Consuls. . . . He shall receive Ambassadors and other public Ministers; he shall take Care that the Laws be faithfully executed" (Article II, Sections 2 and 3).

PRESIDENT'S AUTHORITY

Throughout American history, constitutional scholars have analyzed and debated this division of foreign policy powers. The courts for the most part have left this debate to the political arena and have sought to avoid definitive rulings in such matters. However, in the 1936 case *United States v. Curtiss-Wright Export Corp.*, the Supreme Court's opinion included sweeping language about the president's authority in foreign affairs:

It is important to bear in mind that we are here dealing not alone with an authority vested in the President by an exertion of legislative power, but with such an authority plus the very delicate, plenary and exclusive power of the President as the sole organ of the federal government in the field of international relations—a power which does not require as a basis for its exercise an act of Congress, but which . . . must be exercised in subordination to the applicable provisions of the Constitution.

Whatever the Founders' intent, two outstanding facts have emerged from the resulting picture of alternate tension and cooperation: first, the overwhelming importance of presidential initiative in this area; second, the ever-increasing dependence of American foreign policies on congressional cooperation and support.

Issuance of the Proclamation of Neutrality by President Washington in 1793, upon the outbreak of war between France and Great Britain, marked the start of the continuing struggle between the president and Congress for control of the nation's foreign policy. The proclamation was attacked by the pro-French Jeffersonian Democratic-Republicans as a usurpation by the president of authority granted to Congress under the Constitution.

In a series of articles published in a Philadelphia newspaper under the pseudonym "Pacificus," Alexander Hamilton defended Washington's action. He argued that the conduct of foreign relations was by nature an executive function and therefore, except where the Constitution provided otherwise, belonged to the president, upon whom was bestowed "the executive power." Possession by Congress of the power to declare war, as well as other powers affecting foreign relations, did not diminish the discretion of the president in the exercise of his constitutional powers, Hamilton said. He wrote: "The division of the executive power in the Constitution creates a *concurrent* authority in the cases to which it relates."[4]

This view was disputed by James Madison, writing as "Helvidius." Emphasizing that the vital power to declare war was vested in Congress, Madison took the position that the powers of the executive in foreign relations were to be strictly construed. Any doubt regarding a power in this field was to be resolved in favor of the legislature. Madison attempted to bolster his argument by pointing to the confusion likely to ensue if concurrent discretionary powers were exercised by different branches of the new government.

Over time, however, Hamilton's view has prevailed.

CONGRESS'S POWERS

Despite the widely recognized prerogatives of the president in foreign relations, Congress has enormous powers that are indispensable to the support of any administration's foreign policy. Congress's specific foreign policy powers include the power to declare war and the Senate's powers to give advice and consent to treaties and to the appointment of ambassadors, public ministers, and other diplomatic officers.

Beyond those, Congress has general powers it can use to influence foreign policy. The most potent, but least utilized, of these has been the power of the purse—the power to raise revenues and authorize and appropriate funds for national defense, war, foreign aid, and the general execution of foreign policy. Congress can also use its regular legislative powers to express its view, set limits, or promote policies it favors.

The commerce power has given Congress authority in a number of areas, including international trade, shipping, aviation, and communications. Other powers with international applications include Congress's powers over U.S. territory, marine law, the postal system, regulation of patents and copyrights, and the District of Columbia, the center of U.S. diplomatic activity.

Primacy of the President

The early presidents—Washington, Adams, Jefferson, Madison, and Monroe—exercised commanding influence in the young country's relations with other nations. Washington's Neutrality Proclamation, his Farewell Address, and Monroe's warning against foreign intervention in the Western Hemisphere laid the basis for American foreign policy.

Most of the nineteenth century was dominated by the twin domestic issues of slavery and the development of the American West, which shifted national attention away from foreign affairs. But a major turn in foreign policy, strongly supported by Congress, occurred in 1898: the country dropped its traditional policy of nonintervention, went to war to rid Cuba of Spanish rule, and emerged from the conflict with overseas outposts as far distant as the Philippines in the western Pacific.

In the twentieth century two world wars and other foreign threats to the nation's security of necessity made the chief executive the dominant figure in American foreign policy. During this period legislation enacted by Congress enhanced presidential power much more often than it curtailed that power. One important exception was the fifteen-year period of congression-

Secretary of State John Foster Dulles confers with senators Arthur H. Vandenberg, left, and Tom Connally, right, during Foreign Relations Committee hearings on the Marshall Plan.

al dominance following the Senate's rejection of the Treaty of Versailles after World War I. But on the eve of the next great conflict, the country's overseas interests as interpreted by the president once again became the controlling factor in U.S. foreign policy.

Changing Congressional Role

During and after World War II, the role of Congress in foreign affairs shifted. It was a time of great new commitments, responsibilities, and risks for the United States, all of which contributed to a consensus on the need for strong presidential leadership. Because an aggressor nation with nuclear weapons would benefit from a tactical surprise attack, quick action on the part of the United States could be of paramount importance. It was frequently argued that the new generation of weapons made Congress's power to declare war too slow a process to be meaningful.

The Senate was left on the sidelines as the number of executive agreements with other countries, which do not require Senate approval, increased dramatically during the 1940s.

But as Congress's power was eroded in some areas, its influence over other aspects of foreign affairs greatly expanded in the postwar years. Massive military and economic aid programs for Greece and Turkey and for Western Europe (the Truman Doctrine and the Marshall Plan) evolved into broad foreign aid programs funded by Congress. This gave the legislative branch an unprecedented role in international relations. And for the first time the House had equal power over and impact on the shape of U.S. foreign policies.

Era of Bipartisanship

The postwar period spanning the late 1940s and early 1950s is usually cited as the high-water mark for bipartisanship in foreign policy. The Senate approved, by overwhelming votes, the United Nations Charter, the peace treaty with Italy, and a whole network of regional security treaties—the Rio Treaty, NATO (North Atlantic Treaty Organization), SEATO (Southeast Asia Treaty Organization), and other collective and mutual security arrangements. Congress approved the Marshall Plan, aid to Greece and Turkey, and U.S. participation in a wide variety of UN specialized agencies.

In describing the executive-legislative consensus on formation of the United Nations, Sen. Arthur H. Vandenberg, R-Mich., whose name is synonymous with bipartisanship in foreign policy, commented that "partisan politics, for most of us, stopped at the water's edge. I hope they stay stopped, for the sake of America, regardless of what party is in power." But even during this period President Harry S. Truman faced bitter Republican criticism of his China policy and had to compromise his plans for U.S. aid to the European recovery.

The era of bipartisanship was followed by another period of presidential ascendancy in foreign affairs:

For nearly twenty years, from 1950 to the mid-1960s, there was a national consensus on the main lines of foreign policy associated with the cold war; with strong executive leadership there developed a mystique of the president and State Department being absolutely in control, and of Congress, with rare exceptions, going along.[5]

During this period Congress passed five policy resolutions authorizing the president to use force if necessary to repel armed attacks or threats against certain nations or geographic areas. They were the Formosa resolution, 1955; Middle East resolution, 1957; Cuban resolution, 1962; Berlin resolution, 1962; and Tonkin Gulf resolution, 1964.

Congressional Disillusionment

By the late 1960s, however, Congress had become increasingly troubled by what many members considered the aggrandizement of presidential power over foreign policy. Critics cited the costly undeclared wars in Korea and Vietnam, the overseas deployment of troops without prior congressional consent, and the array of international commitments negotiated through executive agreements.

Congressional discontent surfaced as early as 1951. During the "great debate" on Truman's authority to send troops to Europe, two resolutions were introduced to require congressional authorization for sending military forces abroad. Neither measure was approved by Congress, however. A constitutional amendment intended to restrain the president's power to make executive agreements was rejected in 1954 by one vote in the Senate.

Disillusionment with the Vietnam War in the 1960s prompted Congress to make new efforts to regain influence in foreign affairs. In June 1969, by an overwhelming 70–16 vote, the Senate adopted a "national commitments" resolution that declared the sense of the Senate that a national commitment could be made only through a treaty, statute, or concurrent resolution approved by both houses of Congress.

Beginning in 1969 there were repeated, though unsuccessful, attempts in Congress to terminate funding to continue U.S. military action in Indochina. Congress also became increasingly concerned about the executive branch's failure to keep Congress informed of foreign policy decisions. During this period, an investigation by a Senate Foreign Relations subcommittee chaired by Stuart Symington, D-Mo., revealed for the first time the full extent of major U.S. commitments to other nations. Congress also learned that the White House had not been candid about the extensive U.S. bombing of Laos and Cambodia.

A Resurgent Congress

In 1972 legislation to require that Congress be informed of executive agreements was enacted. In June 1973, six months after the signing of a cease-fire in Vietnam, Congress voted to cut off funding of future U.S. combat activities in or over Cambodia and Laos after August 15, 1973. And in July of that year Congress passed over President Richard Nixon's veto the War Powers Resolution, which set a sixty-day limit on any presidential commitment of U.S. troops abroad where there was fighting, or where hostilities might be imminent, without specific congressional approval.

Procedural and substantive disputes between the two branches continued to mount as Congress sought a more influential role in foreign affairs. In 1974 Congress passed a major trade bill only after approving an amendment linking trade concessions for communist countries to Soviet-bloc emigration policies. The Soviet Union refused to accept such terms for trade and repudiated a U.S.-Soviet trade agreement. In a move made in reaction to the Turkish invasion of Cyprus, Congress imposed a ban on military aid and arms shipments to Turkey.

Also in 1974 Congress passed legislation requiring that it be notified of covert CIA operations. And it gave itself veto power over large-scale arms sales abroad; within a few years, Congress was using its new authority effectively to block arms sales to the Middle East.

In 1975 committees in both chambers conducted a major probe of the intelligence community—the first such investigation since establishment of the Central Intelligence Agency in 1947. The investigations brought to light serious abuses of power by intelligence and law enforcement agencies and resulted in recommendations for structural changes in both Congress and the agencies, including better congressional oversight.

In 1976, fearing that U.S. involvement in Angola could draw the United States into another Vietnam, Congress banned aid to anti-Marxist guerrillas in that African country.

Congressional involvement in the treaty process reached an unprecedented level in the late 1970s during negotiation of the U.S.-Soviet strategic arms limitation talks (SALT II) treaty and during consideration of the Panama Canal treaties and related legislation to carry out the accords.

The struggle between the two branches intensified during the 1980s. Almost from the start, Congress and President Ronald Reagan squared off repeatedly over foreign policy. The root of nearly every dispute was Reagan's use of military muscle to address foreign policy questions, particularly whether Reagan had the right to do so on his own initiative.

The 1983 invasion of Grenada and a bomb strike against Libya in 1986 won broad congressional approval and demonstrated the president's continued flexibility in the case of quick strikes that had few long-term implications for U.S. military involvement. But on more extended ventures—particularly where the goals seemed unclear or where the threat to the United States was not easy to portray—Congress insisted on involving itself in ways that often set limits on executive action.

Questions about Congress's ability to limit the president's war powers arose in debates over actions taken in Lebanon and the Persian Gulf. A key provision of the war powers act was invoked for the first time when Congress and Reagan in 1983 reached a compromise on keeping U.S. troops in Lebanon. Congressional action on Reagan's use of U.S. ships to escort Kuwaiti oil tankers in the Persian Gulf ended in a stalemate: members were unhappy that Reagan had committed U.S. forces to a risky

ARMS SALES ABROAD

Burgeoning sales of American-made weapons to other nations attracted the attention of a resurgent Congress in the 1970s and 1980s. Legislators—fearful that the sales could spark an international arms race and involve the United States in overseas military encounters—demanded a role in arms sales decisions.

Of particular concern on Capitol Hill were sales to Arab countries. Members of Congress feared that sophisticated weapons might be used against Israel, might fall into unfriendly hands, or might embroil the United States in a military conflict.

Legislation giving Congress the authority to reject arms sales was enacted in 1974. By mid-1999 Congress had never formally blocked an arms sale, but it had forced administrations to withdraw, defer, and modify arms sales proposals. The mere threat of rejection had led to concerted lobbying campaigns on the most controversial sales packages. These were clear indications of what a potent weapon the congressional review had become.

The 1974 legislation permitted Congress to reject government-to-government weapons contracts amounting to $25 million or more by using a legislative veto procedure. To kill an arms deal, both houses of Congress had to pass a concurrent resolution of disapproval, which did not have to be sent to the president and therefore could not be vetoed.

In 1976 Congress extended its legislative veto authority to government sales of a single piece of military equipment costing $7 million or more. Congress also was given authority to review certain commercial arms sales.

Legislation enacted in 1981 modified the congressional role in reviewing arms sales:

First, the thresholds for reporting individual contracts to Congress were doubled: sales made through U.S. government channels had to be reported to Congress if they exceeded $14 million for a single item (instead of $7 million) or $50 million for a package of items (instead of $25 million).

Second, the length of time Congress had to review and vote on whether to veto arms sales to close allies (NATO and its members, Japan, New Zealand, and Australia) was reduced from thirty to fifteen days. The review period remained thirty days for all other purchasers. (In practice Congress still had longer than thirty days because of an agreement to give informal notice of a sale twenty days before the formal notice was sent to Congress.)

Legislative veto by concurrent resolution was declared unconstitutional by the Supreme Court in 1983 because it did not permit the president to participate in the process. Congress revised its procedures in 1986 by passing legislation requiring a joint resolution to block an arms sale. Such a resolution would have to be presented to the president for signature or veto. *(See "Separation of Powers," p. 680.)*

mission without consulting Congress, but there was not enough opposition to the escort policy to support a change.

Congress scored important political victories in 1987 when it stymied administration efforts to dismantle two legacies of the arms control negotiations of the 1970s—the 1972 U.S.-Soviet treaty limiting antiballistic missile (ABM) weapons and the unratified SALT II treaty negotiated by President Jimmy Carter.

U.S. aid to Central America prompted repeated battles. Fear of a Vietnam-type commitment spurred Congress to impose rigid conditions on U.S. arms aid to the government of El Salvador in the early 1980s. In the case of Nicaragua, President Reagan's determination to support the contra rebels fighting against the leftist government forced more than a dozen major political battles on Capitol Hill. Making it clear that the president would not have a free hand to pursue his goals in the region, Congress set limits on both the types and goals of aid to the guerrillas. Reagan won approval for his aid requests only twice. In every other case, Congress rejected the request or reduced or changed the nature of the aid to be given. Not only was Reagan forced to regularly seek renewed approval for assistance, but Congress also got deeply involved in the details of contra aid, writing lengthy documents that outlined policy, defined what was military and nonmilitary aid, and gave detailed prescriptions for what items could and could not be delivered.

Revelations in late 1986 that the administration had contradicted its own publicly declared policy by selling arms to Iran and also had secretly armed the Nicaraguan contras in possible violation of law forced Reagan onto the defensive for his remaining two years in office.

George Bush came into the White House in 1989 determined not only to protect the executive branch from congressional intrusion but also to reclaim lost ground. Bush and members of his administration criticized Congress for what they saw as encroachments on executive prerogatives and a tendency to "micromanage" the conduct of foreign policy. In his first year as president Bush backed up his words with several vetoes of foreign policy legislation. The following year he indicated that he might ignore provisions in a State Department authorization bill that he claimed were unconstitutional intrusions into his right, as president, to conduct foreign policy.

But Bush also indicated a willingness to work with Congress. Early in 1989 he and the State Department struck an agreement with congressional Democrats to keep money flowing to the Nicaraguan contras. A side deal left Democrats with the option of an informal veto. In 1991, after months of all but ignoring Congress, Bush asked for congressional approval of the use of force to end Iraq's occupation of Kuwait. Congress obliged with what was, for all intents and purposes, a declaration of war.

The Bush administration presided over the transition to a new era. The breakup of the Soviet Union produced the most profound changes in the global landscape in half a century. Yet it soon became clear that the post–cold war period would be no less prone to violence and instability than the previous one. From Europe to Asia, the United States faced new threats and

Secretary of State Madeleine K. Albright testifies before the Senate Foreign Relations Committee on the expansion of NATO.

unfamiliar challenges to its interests. And there was no consensus between the White House and Congress on how to meet those challenges.

Bill Clinton came into office confident of smooth relations with his fellow Democrats who were in control on Capitol Hill. But the honeymoon was short, and he soon found himself in battles with Congress reminiscent of those waged by his Republican predecessors.

When a onetime humanitarian mission in Somalia got caught up in that country's internal strife and resulted in the loss of American lives in 1993, Congress pressured Clinton to set a deadline for the removal of U.S. forces and then proceeded to write into law a cutoff of funds after that date. This marked the first such cutoff since the end of the Vietnam War.

Clinton's performance gradually improved after the Somalia debacle, although Republican critics continued to lambaste him for taking an overly reactive approach to overseas crises. For example, despite widespread opposition on Capitol Hill and among the American people, Clinton dispatched U.S. forces to Haiti in 1994 to oversee the return of democracy to that troubled nation. Congressional efforts to force Clinton to seek authorization before deploying troops failed and, when the operation went smoothly, Congress backed off from proposals to set a deadline for withdrawal.

When the GOP took control of Congress in 1995, relations between the White House and Capitol Hill became predictably tense. Republicans challenged the president's policies on a wide range of issues, from the relations between the United States and China to the U.S. role in the United Nations. Congress also forced significant reductions in the administration's requests for international spending and pushed Clinton to reform the foreign policy bureaucracy. But on the major questions—particularly those involving the deployment of troops—the president prevailed.

Neither branch had easy answers for how to deal with the tinderbox produced by the breakup of Yugoslavia. Well-armed Serbs were accused of carrying out a genocidal campaign of "ethnic cleansing" against Muslims, first in Bosnia, which had declared its independence from Yugoslavia, and then in Kosovo, which was a province in Serbia, the main component of what was left of Yugoslavia. Congress failed in its attempts to force Clinton to lift a UN arms embargo in order to arm the outgunned Muslims. Many in Congress had hoped that supplying arms would be a way of avoiding direct involvement in the conflict, but Clinton opposed unilateral action. NATO air strikes finally pushed the warring parties to the negotiating table, and an agreement was reached in 1995. But then Congress was confronted with Clinton's pledge to provide U.S. ground troops to help maintain the peace. Determined efforts were made in the House and Senate to cut off funds for the deployment, but in the end Congress grudgingly acquiesced in the commander in chief's decision.

Peace in the Balkans was short-lived. When civil war broke out in Kosovo in 1998, the Clinton administration, encouraged by Congress, moved quickly on the diplomatic front in hopes of containing the fighting, preventing the massacre of thousands of ethnic Albanians, and forestalling a massive refugee crisis in Europe. But the talks broke down and the United States joined with its NATO allies in waging an air campaign to force the Serbian-dominated Yugoslav military and police out of the region and help the displaced ethnic Albanian population to return. The Kosovo crisis produced a rancorous debate on Capitol Hill, and no consensus on how to respond to it emerged in the votes cast in Congress. Yet even some of the most vigorous Republican critics of Clinton's handling of the crisis conceded that the onset of combat had foreclosed any option other than seeing the air campaign to a successful conclusion. Congressional fears of a wider conflict involving U.S. ground troops were put to rest when the NATO strikes succeeded in forcing a Serb pullout. However, U.S. and allied peacekeeping troops were once again dispatched to the Balkans to maintain the peace.

Legislative Process: Opportunities to Influence Policy

Great attention is given to Congress's constitutional powers in the areas of war and treaties and commerce, and rightfully so. But Congress is confronted with major decisions in those areas only infrequently. Much of its influence over foreign and defense policies comes from the tools of the everyday legislative process.[6]

The power of the purse gives Congress a significant role in advancing, restricting, and shaping policies and programs. Through the adoption of resolutions and policy statements, Congress can express its views. And through regular legislation Congress can require that its views be followed. Congress can mandate procedural changes to enhance its influence and oversight of the executive branch. Congressional hearings, investigations, and reporting requirements also give members substantial opportunities for oversight. Members can sometimes maneuver the White House into trade-offs by blocking one proposal in order to advance another.

Other ways for members to influence policy include advising and consulting with the executive branch. They also join with colleagues to send letters to the White House expressing their views in hopes that the names or numbers of those who have signed the letter will influence the direction of policy. Members have ample opportunities for making public appeals and speeches and meeting with the press. Occasionally members file lawsuits aimed at forcing or halting some action by the executive branch.

Members meet with representatives of foreign governments, take official trips abroad, and are sometimes involved in negotiations with foreign entities, not always with the blessing of the White House.

POWER OF THE PURSE

The power of the purse—the power to raise revenue and to approve expenditures—has given Congress a way to directly affect U.S. foreign and defense policies.

The authorization and appropriations processes provide Congress with avenues through which it can affect foreign policy and national security decisions and check on how these policies are being implemented. Congress may increase funds above the White House request; refuse funds for programs and policies; place conditions on the use of funds; terminate existing programs; or exercise legislative oversight of programs. Political scientist Cecil V. Crabb Jr. described Congress's power of the purse as "by many criteria . . . the most potent weapon available to Congress for determining public policy."

The use of money to influence foreign and defense policy has been a modern phenomenon. Although in Congress's possession since 1789, the power has been used regularly to influence such matters only since the closing stage of the Vietnam War. But it has been underutilized, according to Crabb. Resourceful presidents have been able to find their way around congressional roadblocks, at least in the short run, through various devices such as emergency funds at their disposal. Moreover, Congress has at times been reluctant to cut off funds for fear that it would be held responsible for the adverse consequences of doing so.

"Nevertheless, in the long run," Crabb wrote, "all chief executives are aware that nearly every worthwhile program in foreign affairs requires funds for its implementation; and if Congress does not provide those funds, the program has no future."[7]

It may mean accepting some provisions the president would prefer not to. As Davidson and Oleszek put it, "To get the 95 percent of the budget they need, presidents may have to swallow the 5 percent they oppose."[8] But Congress knows as well that if there are too many strings attached there is a good chance the president will veto the bill. Compromises and trade-offs are usually inevitable.

Foreign Policy Spending

The initiation of massive spending on foreign aid—starting with the World War II lend-lease program—gave Congress a power in foreign affairs not anticipated by the nation's founders. In almost every instance, proposals to aid other nations require the consent of Congress to the expenditures; thus the House of Representatives has become involved in foreign policy.

Foreign economic and military aid programs necessarily are undertaken at the initiative of the executive branch. In the early post–World War II period Congress for the most part supported expensive assistance programs, particularly to aid Europe's recovery and to contain Soviet expansionism.

In the late 1960s, however, disenchantment began to set in. Congress repeatedly slashed administration requests for foreign assistance and, in response to the way the executive branch had prosecuted the Vietnam War and made other foreign commitments, began to load the annual foreign aid authorization and appropriation bills with policy directives and restrictions on the president's use of aid to set foreign policy. Despite administration protests, Congress banned or placed restrictions on military aid and arms sales to certain countries. Among the most controversial in the 1970s were the ban on aid to Turkey in 1974 (modified in 1975, lifted in 1978) and Angola in 1976 (lifted in 1985).

Assistance to Central America was the dominant aid issue in the next decade. Congress's concern with administration policies resulted in the early 1980s in the drafting of restrictions on El Salvador's aid that were more detailed than any in the prior history of the U.S. foreign aid program.

As the controversy over aid to El Salvador subsided, Nicaragua became the key point of contention between Ronald Reagan and Congress. Indeed, U.S. aid to the contra rebels fighting the leftist Nicaraguan government proved to be the single most contentious foreign policy question for Reagan throughout his two terms in office. Between 1983 and 1988, the president and his congressional opponents fought more than a dozen battles over providing aid to the contras. Through a series of "Boland amendments," named for Intelligence Committee Chairman Edward P. Boland, D-Mass., Congress first limited and finally cut off military aid to the contras. Aid was renewed in 1986 but ultimately doomed by the Iran-contra affair. *(See "Iran-contra," p. 275.)*

Cutting off aid to some countries and placing restrictions on aid to others are two ways in which Congress has influenced the foreign aid program. Another potent weapon has been the practice of earmarking—that is, specifying minimum or maximum amounts the administration must give to certain countries and programs. By the late 1980s Congress was earmarking spending on more than 90 percent of key foreign aid accounts. Some of these earmarks were added at the administration's request, others not. However, in the 1990s, many of the earmarks were dropped, reflecting House Democrats' determination to give the Clinton administration broad latitude in allocating foreign aid. But politically popular earmarks for aid to such countries as Israel and Egypt were continued.

The foreign aid authorization bill became so laden with divisive foreign policy issues in the 1980s that Congress increasingly found itself unable to agree on one. The bill lost further support when the end of the cold war had many members questioning the necessity of foreign aid. As of mid-1999, Congress had not passed a foreign aid authorization bill since 1985.

The foreign aid program was continued through the foreign operations appropriations bill, albeit at drastically reduced levels by the late 1990s. Restrictions on the use of aid were continued as well. Action on the fiscal 1999 funding bill was fairly typical. Congress granted Clinton's request for additional credit for the International Monetary Fund after more than a year of wrangling over it, but Congress made release of the funds contingent on IMF changes demanded by members. The bill continued existing sanctions against Azerbaijan even though the White House had wanted them lifted, and it set some restrictions on the use of money appropriated for a program aimed at halting North Korea's development of a nuclear capability. A familiar battle over abortion-related restrictions on international family planning funds was fought, but the restrictions ultimately were dropped to avoid a veto.

The biennial authorization of the State Department and related agencies also became an important barometer of congressional sentiment on controversial issues—and an increasingly difficult bill to clear as well. In 1996, for example, Congress cleared a bill after a bitter yearlong battle, only to have it vetoed by Clinton. The president objected to provisions that would have reorganized the foreign policy bureaucracy and reversed a number of administration policies on Asia. (It would take a few more years before Congress was able to pressure the White House into realigning foreign policy agencies. *See "'Hostages' and Trade-offs," p. 195.*)

Defense Spending

The congressional decision in 1973 to cut off funds for further U.S. combat activities in Indochina was largely a symbolic gesture because the Vietnam War already was winding down. But it was a significant step in congressional-executive relations because, as Crabb pointed out, it marked a beginning of greater willingness by Congress to use its appropriating power to affect U.S. defense policy.

Numerous attempts early in the 1970s to cut off funds for U.S. combat activities in Indochina had proved to be ineffective. Opponents of the war had tried to attach riders to various military and foreign policy bills, including the annual defense authorization and appropriations measures and foreign aid bills, but they were unable to gain approval for any legislative measures cutting off funds for the war or setting a date for a U.S. military withdrawal from Southeast Asia.

Congress in 1969 had approved an amendment to a defense appropriations bill prohibiting use of any funds in the bill to finance the *introduction* of U.S. ground combat troops into Laos or Thailand. A similar prohibition on introducing U.S. ground troops into Cambodia was passed in 1970 (but air activity was not barred). But it was not until 1973 that Congress passed legislation prohibiting all U.S. combat activities in Indochina as of August 15, 1973. Six other bills enacted that year contained similar prohibitions.

Congress did not again use its power to cut off funding for an overseas deployment until 1993, when the mission in Somalia turned violent and cost American lives. An outraged Congress pressured the White House to set a date for withdrawal and then included in a defense appropriations bill a provision cutting off funding after that date. The following year Congress attached a provision to an appropriations bill that cut off funding for a U.S. military role in Rwanda, a country wracked by tribal warfare.

Sometimes Congress will use funding bills for overseas deployments to force the president to accept provisions he would have rejected under other circumstances. For example, although Clinton objected to a number of costly add-ons (for such items as the B-2 bomber and antimissile defense) in a fiscal 1996 funding bill, he needed money in it to pay for U.S. peacekeeping troops in Bosnia and therefore allowed the bill to become law without his signature. Similarly, when he needed funds for the NATO air campaign over Yugoslavia, he signed a fiscal 1999 supplemental spending bill that included environmental riders to which he objected.

That a more activist Congress had emerged from the Vietnam experience was apparent in other actions as well. Congress increasingly used its power of the purse to help shape defense budgets, advance or hinder specific weapons and policies, affect troop levels overseas, and influence administration arms control positions and strategic policies.

Congress traditionally has gone along with the defense budget guidelines proposed by the executive. However, in the 1980s, with the onslaught of a serious budget crunch and its squeeze on domestic spending, Congress routinely cut large amounts out of Reagan's defense budget. Some members had hoped to do the reverse in the 1990s. Already suspicious of Clinton for his avoidance of military service during the Vietnam War and his early attempt to eliminate the ban on homosexuals' serving in the military, defense hawks pushed for spending levels higher than Clinton's requests. Some money was added but—with military leaders apparently satisfied and no consensus among Republicans on a post–cold war defense policy—the increases during much of the 1990s were not at the levels critics had wanted. By the late 1990s, however, the Pentagon was voicing concern over a decline in military readiness and was pressing for increases in future defense budgets.

Congress occasionally has used its power over the defense budget to mandate decisions on individual weapons systems and military programs. In some cases, Congress has denied or reduced funds for specific programs. At other times, Congress has appropriated funds for weapons the president did not request or had even actively opposed.

For example, during the Carter administration, congressional insistence on building another *Nimitz*-class nuclear aircraft carrier, costing about $2.1 billion, caused the president to veto a defense procurement authorization bill. But an undaunted Congress pushed it through the next year. The Bush administration decided in 1989 to cancel the V-22 Osprey, a hybrid airplane/helicopter intended for Marine Corps use as a troop carrier. But its supporters on Capitol Hill interceded, the Pentagon backed down, and the plane was still being funded a decade later.

Lawmakers are not always so successful. Congress and the Bush administration reached an agreement in 1992 to limit to twenty the number of radar-evading B-2 stealth bombers. With a price tag of several hundred million dollars per plane, the B-2 was difficult to justify in the post-Soviet era. The plane's supporters in Congress, however, did not give up easily. They pushed Congress to add B-2 funds to defense bills for several years in the mid-1990s in hopes that it would lead to the resumption of production. But in the end the decision on whether the money would be used to buy new planes or upgrade existing ones was left to the Clinton administration, and no one doubted that Clinton would choose the latter.

The House in 1999 sent shock waves through the defense community when it omitted from an appropriations bill funding to begin production of the F-22 fighter plane, the air force's top priority. The Senate had not acted on the bill by August 1999, but there appeared to be little chance it would agree to halt the F-22 program. The action was seen as a maneuver by the House Defense Appropriations Subcommittee to goad the Clinton administration and Congress into resolving what it insisted were fundamental problems in the Pentagon's long-term plans—problems, subcommittee members said, that were typified by the stealth fighter plane. They contended that the plane was too costly ($120 million each) and unnecessarily complex and that it was shortchanging personnel programs and equipment more relevant to the post–cold war world.

For much of the 1980s and 1990s, defense bills served as a battleground for fights over the issue of whether or not to build a nationwide antimissile defense system. Depending on who was in the White House and which party controlled Congress, funding bills became the vehicles for members' attempts to curtail, expand, and/or refocus administration proposals.

Congress in 1987 repudiated Reagan's attempt to reinterpret the 1972 antiballistic missile (ABM) treaty with the Soviet Union—so that tests of his proposed antimissile system could go forward—by denying funding for such tests. Over Reagan's objections, Congress also required the retirement of missile-launching submarines so that the United States would continue to observe weapons limits set by the unratified 1979 SALT II treaty. *(See "SALT II Treaty," p. 211.)*

LEGISLATION

Congress uses bills other than authorizations and appropriations to affect foreign policy. If the president opposes the bill, it will very likely be vetoed unless political circumstances demand otherwise or Congress gives the president an escape clause. Laws imposing sanctions on foreign countries provide some good examples.

Congress in 1986 enacted into law over Reagan's veto legislation imposing economic sanctions against the white minority regime in South Africa in hopes of pressuring it to end apartheid, its system of racial discrimination. The episode was a major foreign policy defeat for the president. Reagan had headed off final action on similar legislation in 1985 by signing an executive order imposing limited sanctions against South Africa. But Reagan's actions did not go far enough for most members of Congress, inspiring them to take matters into their own hands the following year.

Congress in 1996 cleared a bill to tighten a long-standing U.S. trade embargo against Cuba. U.S. trading partners denounced the bill and Clinton opposed it as well, but his opposition faded away after Cuba downed two U.S. civilian planes. He did win a key concession allowing him to delay one of the bill's provisions indefinitely. Of equal interest was a provision in the bill that put into law all existing sanctions against Cuba. Previously, the embargo had been imposed by executive orders and regulations, which meant the president could lift or ease it without congressional approval. The new law took that decision, a jealously guarded presidential prerogative, out of the hands of the White House and gave it to Congress.

Congress sometimes legislates structural or procedural changes to enhance its influence, such as the 1974 and 1988 trade laws which required greater consultation with Congress and set up congressional approval procedures.

POLICY DECLARATIONS

Adoption of resolutions and "sense of Congress" declarations is another of the ways Congress has of indicating its views on controversial issues and influencing policy decisions. Congress uses these tools to voice support or opposition to presidential policies and, on rare occasions, to attempt to initiate a policy. They sometimes represent fallback positions when Congress is unable or unwilling to take substantive action on an issue.

Several avenues are available to Congress. Among these are House and Senate resolutions and concurrent resolutions, which are not signed by the president, do not have the force of law, and thus cannot force the president to act, yet are still good indicators of congressional sentiment. Congress can also express its views through a joint resolution, which must be presented to the president for signature or veto. "Sense of Congress" provisions, which state an opinion but do not compel specific action, can also be attached to regular legislation.

Views on Key Issues

Congress expresses its views on a wide variety of issues. Some are almost routine, while others are timely pronouncements on policy hot spots.

Over the years Congress has used policy resolutions to support the use of U.S. forces abroad. The most controversial of these was the 1964 Gulf of Tonkin resolution, which years later supporters of U.S. involvement in Vietnam claimed was evidence of congressional concurrence in America's military commitment. (See box, Resolutions Authorizing Use of U.S. Forces, p. 238.)

Congress and the White House worked closely on developing U.S. policy toward the Ferdinand Marcos government in the Philippines in the mid-1980s. Congressional disenchantment with Marcos, expressed in various resolutions, was a significant factor in the Reagan administration's decision to pressure Marcos to step down. Members also urged the White House to turn up the heat on the Manuel Noriega government in Panama. For several years prior to the U.S. invasion of Panama and ousting of Noriega in 1989, the House and Senate had adopted a series of resolutions and amendments relating to his removal from office. (See "Panama," p. 237.)

After the deaths of the U.S. soldiers in Somalia in 1993, congressional apprehension over U.S. involvement in UN peacekeeping operations was high, as evidenced by the policy declarations attached to various foreign policy bills. They included provisions urging the administration to notify Congress before deployments and to obtain prior approval before placing U.S. troops under foreign command.

Policy statements also documented the mounting concern on Capitol Hill in the 1990s over U.S. involvement in Bosnia. They included statements urging that a UN arms embargo be lifted and that any deployment of troops be authorized by Congress.

Congress gave the Clinton administration the political cover it needed in 1994 to lift a trade embargo against Vietnam. Clinton took the action a week after the Senate adopted a nonbinding amendment—written by senators John Kerry, D-Mass., a decorated Vietnam veteran, and John McCain, R-Ariz., a prisoner of war in Vietnam for nearly six years—urging him to do so. With the support of Kerry and McCain, Clinton normalized diplomatic relations in 1995.

A Long History

In 1836 President Andrew Jackson received resolutions from the House and Senate calling on the United States to acknowledge the independence of Texas. The preamble of the House resolution intimated that recognition of Texas's independence

should be left to Congress. On December 21, 1838, Jackson replied: "In this view, on the ground of expediency, I am disposed to concur, and do not, therefore, consider it necessary to express my opinion as to the strict constitutional right of the executive, either apart from or in conjunction with the Senate, over the subject."

While the Civil War was in progress, there was congressional resentment of French interference in Mexico. Numerous resolutions were introduced in the Senate condemning the French action, but all were tabled. The House, however, by unanimous vote adopted a resolution April 4, 1864, declaring: "It does not accord with the policy of the United States to acknowledge a monarchical government erected on the ruins of any republican government in America, under the auspices of any European power."

Lincoln's secretary of state, William H. Seward, responded by instructing the U.S. minister to France to inform the French government that "the decision of such questions of policy constitutionally belongs, not to the House of Representatives nor even to Congress, but to the president." When the House learned of this, it passed a resolution "that Congress has the constitutional right to an authoritative voice in declaring and prescribing the foreign policy of the United States as well as the recognizing of new powers as in other matters; and it is the constitutional duty of the President to respect that policy."[9]

The Civil War period also saw repeated attempts by the Senate to control, by resolution, U.S. relations with Mexico.

CONGRESSIONAL OVERSIGHT

Through its oversight power Congress can influence executive branch policies and uncover areas where legislation is needed. Congress's power of the purse provides the most effective tool for oversight, but there are others as well, ranging from well-publicized hearings and investigations to routine reports to Congress.

There are examples throughout history of the potency of hearings but the Senate Foreign Relations Committee hearings on the Vietnam War was one of the standouts. Committee Chairman J. William Fulbright was an outspoken critic of President Lyndon B. Johnson's policy of expanding the U.S. role in the Vietnam War. To dramatize his opposition Fulbright held nationally televised hearings on the war in the middle and late 1960s. The hearings commanded public attention and helped organize widespread opposition to Johnson's policies.

Investigations can also highlight problems and lead to calls for change. Senate and House probes in the 1970s unveiled abuses by the CIA and resulted in the creation of congressional committees to oversee the intelligence community. After the 1987 congressional investigation into the Iran-contra affair revealed that Congress had been kept in the dark about controversial U.S. activities abroad, members pushed, albeit with limited success, for ways to be kept better informed of covert activities.

But much of Congress's oversight is far less dramatic and

Sen. Jesse Helms, R-N.C., an influential chairman of the Senate Foreign Relations Committee, brought about a major reorganization of the foreign policy bureaucracy in the late 1990s.

colorful. Routine hearings are held throughout the year at which members can question executive branch witnesses on how policies and programs are being implemented—and tell them in turn what members would like to see done. Reports from agencies and the White House also provide members with much needed information. Some six hundred foreign policy reporting requirements were said to be embedded in legislation in the late 1990s.[10]

"HOSTAGES" AND TRADE-OFFS

Sometimes members put executive business on hold in order to win approval of their own proposals. Senate Foreign Relations Committee Chairman Jesse Helms's campaign in the 1990s to reorganize the foreign policy bureaucracy provided a good illustration of "hostage taking" and trade-offs.

The North Carolina Republican embarked in 1995 on his crusade to eliminate a trio of cold war–era foreign affairs agencies—the Agency for International Development, the Arms Control and Disarmament Agency, and the United States Information Agency—and merge them into the State Department. Helms held up action on eighteen ambassadorial appointments and a pair of important arms control treaties in 1996 until a scaled-down version of his plan was included in a State Department authorization bill. But Clinton vetoed the bill, partly, he said, because the proposal would infringe on his prerogatives. The following year Clinton agreed to restructure the foreign policy bureaucracy as part of a deal to get Helms and GOP leaders to put the 1993 Chemical Weapons Convention on the Senate agenda. A reorganization plan was finally included in an omnibus appropriations bill that was enacted in 1998.

CONGRESSIONAL DIPLOMACY

Although diplomacy is largely an executive branch function, Congress can be involved in a variety of ways. Members meet with embassy personnel and visiting foreign leaders. In 1999, for example, Egyptian President Hosni Mubarak made an impromptu appearance on the Senate floor during debate on a foreign aid bill that included funding to buttress the Middle East peace process. Mubarak was escorted by Helms.

Occasionally foreign dignitaries will be invited to address joint meetings of Congress. Speakers have included the Marquis de Lafayette, Winston Churchill, Nelson Mandela, Queen Elizabeth II, Boris Yeltsin, King Hussein, and Yitzhak Rabin. *(See "Joint Meetings, Joint Sessions," in Reference Materials, p. 1132, Vol. II.)*

Members frequently make fact-finding trips abroad. Although these trips are sometimes criticized if they include a great deal of entertainment and sightseeing, they do give members the opportunity to meet with officials of foreign governments and to evaluate programs or trouble spots firsthand. Most of these trips are coordinated with the various executive departments and pose no problem for the administration. But the White House remains on the watch for any activity that might interfere in the diplomatic activities of the executive branch.

Although negotiations with foreign governments have been considered an executive prerogative since the earliest days of the Republic, and Congress in 1799 even passed legislation (the Logan Act) barring private citizens from unauthorized contact with foreign governments, members of Congress frequently are involved in the conduct of diplomacy. Besides their meetings

House Speaker Jim Wright and Secretary of State George Shultz read a joint statement in 1987 pledging to work together for peace in Central America, after patching up their differences over Wright's role in negotiations.

with foreign dignitaries, members sometimes sit in on treaty negotiations, observe foreign elections, and serve as personal emissaries of the president. For example, Senate Armed Services Committee Chairman Sam Nunn, D-Ga., was a member—along with former president Jimmy Carter and former Joint Chiefs of Staff chairman Colin L. Powell Jr.—of the high-level U.S. delegation that President Clinton sent to Haiti in 1994 to negotiate with Haitian military leaders to avert a full-scale military invasion.

But sometimes Congress pursues diplomacy without being invited to do so by the president. Crabb and Pat M. Holt wrote: "The novel feature of Congress's involvement in diplomatic negotiations today is the tendency of legislators to engage in them independently—without White House approval, and sometimes in the face of presidential opposition."[11]

Take, for example, the role played by Speaker Jim Wright, D-Texas, in Central American peace negotiations in the 1980s. Although Wright had been deeply involved in the peace process and had been invited by Reagan to cosign a Nicaraguan peace plan, he set off a round of controversy in Congress and throughout Washington in 1987 when he met with Nicaraguan president

Daniel Ortega and then with contra rebel leaders to urge them to begin talks aimed at producing a cease-fire in that country's civil war. Wright insisted that he was acting as a "friend" of all sides, not as a negotiator, but his highly unusual role raised questions about whether he had overstepped his position as a member of Congress. Some Republicans and administration officials insisted that Wright was inserting himself into a diplomatic process normally reserved for the executive branch. Even Wright conceded to a group of reporters later that he might have unintentionally overstepped his role.

Some members' activities at the time of the NATO air campaign against Yugoslavia in 1999 came under criticism. For example, a bipartisan group of House members met with members of Russia's parliament in Vienna to develop a diplomatic framework for bringing peace to Kosovo and thus reducing tensions between Moscow and Washington. Although members of the U.S. delegation insisted that they had coordinated with the State Department throughout the process and been accompanied by a State Department official, they were still criticized by some of their colleagues and were asked by the State Department not to press for congressional support of the deal they had worked out. Under Secretary of State Thomas Pickering told a House International Relations Committee hearing, "Our efforts are not helped—indeed, they are hurt—by uncoordinated, freelance efforts at negotiating with [Yugoslavian President Slobodan] Milosevic." But both the delegation and Republicans on the committee repeatedly expressed frustration at having no say in the administration's policy.

The Treaty Power: Constitutional Role

The whole of the treaty-making power is contained in a single clause of the Constitution. Spelling out presidential authority, Article II, Section 2, Clause 2 declares: "He shall have Power, by and with the Advice and Consent of the Senate, to make Treaties, provided two-thirds of the Senators present concur."

Contrary to a widespread misconception, the Senate does not have the power under the Constitution to ratify treaties. Ratification—formal acceptance of a treaty by the government—is a power of the president. But the Constitution provides that the president can take this step only with the approval of two-thirds of the senators present and voting. Technically speaking, what the Senate actually votes on is not the text of a treaty but rather a resolution approving ratification by the president.

No provision is made in the Constitution for a congressional role in ending a treaty. Congressional conservatives in 1979 challenged President Carter's plans to terminate, on January 1, 1980, a 1955 mutual defense treaty with Taiwan without Senate approval. A lower court ruled that the president should seek approval of a majority of both houses of Congress or of two-thirds of the Senate, but the decision was reversed on appeal. The Supreme Court sidestepped the issue, and cleared the way for

INTERNATIONAL AGREEMENTS

American constitutional law recognizes three basic types of international agreements and leaves it up to the executive branch to determine which type to use in particular international situations.

A treaty is an international—bilateral or multilateral—compact that requires consent by a two-thirds vote of the Senate to take effect. Presidents on a few occasions have called for an agreement to be submitted to Congress as a joint resolution—which must be signed by the president to take effect and have the same force of law as bills—when there was fear that a treaty would not command a two-thirds majority in the Senate. A joint resolution requires only a simple majority for approval, but it must be adopted by both houses in identical form.

A congressional-executive international agreement is an agreement made by presidents to carry out legislation or treaty obligations. Examples of this type include presidential agreements with foreign countries on the distribution of U.S. assistance, based upon the foreign aid laws; and the 1946 executive agreement providing for the establishment of the United Nations Headquarters District in New York, after Congress gave its approval to the arrangement.

A "pure" or "true" executive agreement is one negotiated by presidents entirely on their constitutional authority as (1) commander in chief, (2) chief executive, a function that the courts have interpreted to include foreign relations, and (3) their other roles as delineated in Article II of the Constitution. It is implemented without congressional approval. Only a small percentage of executive agreements fall into this category, but they are often the most important and controversial pacts.

Carter to terminate the treaty, when it dismissed the suit on technical grounds.

For years the treaty clause served as a major tool of American foreign policy. It brought peace with other nations, supported American territorial expansion, established national boundaries, protected U.S. commerce, and regulated government affairs with Native Americans.

But the treaty clause is ambiguous on some points. This ambiguity has caused problems and misunderstandings, including conflicts between the executive and legislative branches, from the very beginning of the Republic. Neither the Senate procedure for advising the president nor the stage in the treaty-making process at which the Senate was to act in an advisory capacity was spelled out. And the Constitution ignored the role of the House of Representatives in treaty making, even in cases where legislation or appropriations are needed to make a treaty effective.

It is generally agreed that the main purpose of the advice and consent formula is to provide for democratic control of foreign policy. In the early years of the nation, the executive branch sought to incorporate Senate advice into the process of treaty negotiations by such means as presidential meetings with senators, Senate confirmation of negotiators, and special presidential messages. But as international relations became more complicated, presidents abandoned, one after another, the various devices by which the Senate's advice had been obtained.

Feeling deprived of adequate opportunities to make its influence felt in treaty negotiations, the Senate resorted to "advising" the president by attaching drastic amendments to some treaties and rejecting others outright. The classic display of senatorial dissatisfaction came in 1919 and 1920 with the prolonged debate on, and ultimate rejection of, the Treaty of Versailles, which embodied not only the World War I treaty of peace with Germany but also U.S. membership in the League of Nations.

Subsequent presidential reaction to the rejection of the Treaty of Versailles took two forms. On the one hand, presidents made renewed efforts to court Senate support of proposed treaties by reinstituting some of the old methods, and developing some new ones, for associating senators with the treaty-making process. On the other hand, there was a growing tendency to rely on the executive agreement as a vehicle for U.S. relations with other countries and for international accords, thus eliminating altogether the need for Senate approval. There was adverse reaction also in Congress, where a number of constitutional amendments were introduced to curtail the power of the Senate over treaties. But the Senate's rejection of a major arms control treaty in 1999 served as a reminder of just how potent its treaty power could be.

SENATE'S RATIFICATION RECORD

The Senate's voting record on treaty ratification has been overwhelmingly favorable, despite the occasional shock. Between 1789 and 1999, only twenty-one treaties were rejected outright. The most recent was a comprehensive nuclear test ban treaty in 1999. (See Table 5-1, p. 203).

The Senate has ways of thwarting treaties short of outright rejection. It can leave a treaty languishing in the committee and thus delay it to death. In early 1999 there were about fifty treaties and other international agreements awaiting action, including one that dated back to 1949. (But the Senate's approval in 1986 of a treaty on genocide nearly thirty-seven years after it had been submitted did offer some hope to advocates of stalled treaties.) The Senate can also make changes in the treaty that the president or other signatories may refuse to accept.

MODERN USE OF TREATY POWER

After World War II the treaty-making power took on added importance. Membership in the United Nations was accomplished by Senate consent to the ratification of the UN Charter, while membership in an expanding number of international organizations was brought about either by treaty or by House and Senate approval of appropriate implementing legislation. Treaties were used to conclude the widening circle of U.S. mutual security agreements designed to provide collective defense against communist aggression. Other agreements were intended to restrict the military use of atomic energy or curtail the spread and production of nuclear armaments. And, as new frontiers in space and under the oceans opened up, additional treaties were concluded or proposed to govern their use.

Old conflicts over treaty making were renewed. The early post–World War II period was a time of strong executive branch leadership, producing congressional reaction that came to a head in 1953–1954 with debate on a proposed constitutional amendment to curtail the executive's powers to make treaties and other international agreements.

Although the amendment was never adopted, Congress found other means of making its influence felt in the negotiation, ratification, and implementation of treaties. Members of the Senate participated directly in negotiating with Panama over conditions attached to the Panama Canal treaties in 1978. They attached numerous conditions and stipulations during committee consideration of the 1979 strategic arms limitation talks treaty (SALT II). They held up approval in 1988 of a treaty banning intermediate-range nuclear-force (INF) missiles until negotiators clarified several issues. In the late 1980s the House joined with the Senate in mandating continued U.S. compliance with two earlier arms agreements with the Soviet Union. To win Senate approval in 1997 of a treaty banning chemical weapons, the White House, among other things, had to promise that it would submit to the Senate for its approval revisions of several other major treaties.

DEBATE OVER TREATY POWER

The recurring conflict between the president and Congress over the treaty-making power is rooted in the doctrine of separation of powers, which is basic to the governmental structure of the United States.

During the Constitutional Convention, the treaty power came up for discussion repeatedly.[12] At first, it was assumed that the existing power of Congress under the Articles of Confederation to approve treaties by a two-thirds majority vote would be transferred intact to the legislative branch of the new government. Continued legislative control of treaty making was taken for granted despite the fact that it was the exclusive prerogative of the executive in all other governments at that time.

The first suggestion that the treaty power should be divided between the legislative and executive branches seems to have been made at the convention session of June 18, 1787. Hamilton proposed the establishment of an executive elected for life, who, along with other powers, would have "with the advice and approbation of the Senate, the power of making all treaties." There was no discussion of Hamilton's suggestion, and it appeared to be dead when the August 6 report of the Committee of Detail proposed that "the Senate shall have power to make treaties." Debate on the committee's report failed to resolve the issue of who was to exercise the treaty power. The section was referred back to the committee.

On September 4 the report of the Committee of Eleven recommended that "the president, by and with the advice and consent of the Senate," would have the power to make treaties, and that no treaty could be approved "without the consent of two-thirds of the members present." Several attempts were made to alter the proportion of the Senate whose consent would be required and to add House participation in treaty making, but on September 8 the provision as proposed in the report was finally agreed to.

There was nearly unanimous support in the convention for some means of enabling the new government to require the states to honor treaty provisions. Although the Articles of Confederation entrusted the treaty-making power to Congress, fulfillment of Congress's promises to other nations was dependent on each state legislature. Inaction, or adverse action, by certain states had led to violation of some articles of the Peace Treaty of 1783 with Great Britain. A solution was provided in the declaration of Article VI, Clause 2 of the Constitution, which states that "all Treaties made, or which shall be made, under the Authority of the United States, shall be the supreme Law of the Land."

Exclusion of the House from the treaty-making process was defended by Hamilton and Jay in *The Federalist Papers*. Using similar arguments, they contended that the legislative role in treaty making should be limited to the Senate because decisions on treaties would thus be placed in the hands of persons chosen by the "select assemblies" of the states instead of the rank and file. The longer and overlapping Senate terms would provide relatively greater continuity, they said, while the smaller size of the Senate would aid "secrecy and dispatch." On the other hand, the agreement of the president, the Senate, and the House would be much more difficult to obtain.

Final adoption of the two-thirds rule reflected the special concern of certain states over fishing rights off Newfoundland and the right of navigation on the Mississippi River. Historian Charles Warren noted that the provision for a two-thirds rather than a majority vote of the Senate was inserted to calm the fears of Virginia, North Carolina, and the West lest the North and East should relinquish navigation rights on the Mississippi.

The first treaties to be laid before the Senate under the Constitution were submitted on May 25, 1789. They were a pair of treaties with Indian tribes negotiated and signed under the authority of the Continental Congress. The two treaties were not referred to committee for study until June 12 of that year. In the meantime, the president had submitted another treaty, a consular convention with France, concluded under the Articles of Confederation. After a series of meetings with Jay, secretary of foreign affairs (an office held over from the confederation), the Senate on July 29 unanimously consented to ratification of the consular treaty. This was the first time the Senate had given its advice and consent to ratification of a treaty.

The committee studying the two Indian treaties finally reported on August 12. Instead of recommending that the Senate advise and consent to ratification (as it had with the consular treaty with France), the committee recommended that the president "be advised to execute and enjoin an observance" of the agreements. The Senate on September 8 approved the committee recommendation for one of the treaties (that with the Wyandot, Delaware, Ottawa, Chippewa, Pattawattima, and Sacs nations) but took no action on the other (that with the Six Nations, except the Mohawks).

The Senate action confused President Washington. He was not certain whether the Senate meant that he should merely see that the approved treaty went into operation or that he should proceed with a formal ratification. In a message to the Senate September 17, the president asked for a clarification. His own opinion, he said, was that treaties with Indian tribes should be ratified in the same way as treaties with European nations. The Senate disagreed. A committee that studied the president's message reported September 18 that since past Indian treaties never had been solemnly ratified, it was not "expedient or necessary" to ratify the present treaties. The committee proposed a resolution to advise the president "to enjoin a due observance" of the Wyandot treaty, passing over the treaty with the Six Nations. But on September 22 the Senate substituted a resolution of advice and consent to the Wyandot treaty. No action was taken on the other agreement.

Senate consent to ratification of the Wyandot treaty set a precedent that endured until 1871, when a rider to that year's Indian Appropriations Act provided that, in the future, no American Indian nation or tribe was to be considered an independent nation with which the United States could conclude a treaty. Indian affairs were handled subsequently by statute.

ADVICE OF THE SENATE

The first treaties considered by the Senate had been negotiated under instructions from the Continental Congress because there was no executive in the confederation government. Although the new Constitution established an executive and authorized him to make treaties, with advice from the Senate, it failed to explain what kind of advice was appropriate or how and when it was to be offered. To be effective the advice would have to be given before negotiations ended.

In practice, procedures developed by Washington and the first Senate established precedents that exerted varying degrees of influence. After an abortive attempt at personal consultation with the Senate as an executive council, Washington's usual practice, until the Jay Treaty negotiations with Great Britain in 1794, was to ask for advice about opening negotiations; transmit the full instructions to be given to the negotiators; submit their names for confirmation; and keep the Senate fully informed of the progress of negotiations. If matters came up that were not covered in the original instructions, Washington again would call for the Senate's advice. When treaties required appropriations, he reported the proceedings to the House as well as to the Senate.

Additional procedures adopted by early administrations included requesting advance appropriations to cover the cost of the negotiations, appointing senators and representatives to the negotiating team, and consulting personally with key members of the Senate, and, after its establishment in 1816, with the Foreign Relations Committee. At times Congress took the initiative by considering resolutions proposing or opposing negotiations.

Consultation with the Senate

The Senate on August 3, 1789, named a committee to meet with the president to establish ground rules for consultation on the making of future treaties. Washington favored oral communications rather than written exchanges, and, following a committee recommendation, the Senate on August 21 adopted a rule providing for meetings with the president either in the Senate chamber or elsewhere. Later the same day, the Senate received a message announcing that Washington was coming to the Senate chamber the next day "at half past 11 o'clock" to discuss proposed terms for a treaty.

Unfamiliar with the background of the situation or with the proposed treaty terms, the Senate sought to refer the papers to a committee for study. Washington, who had hoped for prompt action, objected strenuously. He finally agreed to defer action to August 24. The second meeting went more smoothly. The Senate agreed to vote its advice on each of the points raised by the president. However, Washington never again went before the Senate to consult on treaty terms or discuss foreign policy, nor did any other president, until Woodrow Wilson appeared on January 22, 1917, to call for "peace without victory" and propose a League for Peace.

President Washington, after his initial venture in direct consultation, relied on special messages in seeking the advice of the Senate. According to tradition, the chilly reception he had received in the Senate chamber led him to swear he would never go there again.

Although Washington's general position was that he considered it advisable to postpone negotiations until he had received the advice of the Senate on the terms to be offered, he did not follow this course in the case of the Jay Treaty. He named Jay as the negotiator of the treaty and submitted his name to the Senate for confirmation, but he withheld the instructions to be given him. The same procedure was adopted by Washington's successors John Adams and James Madison, and by some other presidents.

James K. Polk returned to the earlier practice in 1846 when he asked for the Senate's advice on whether negotiations should be undertaken with Great Britain on proposals submitted by London for the settlement of the Oregon boundary question. Similar requests for preliminary advice were sent to the Senate by James Buchanan, Abraham Lincoln, Andrew Johnson, Ulysses S. Grant, and Grover Cleveland. Warren G. Harding, in 1922, asked the Senate's advice on reinstating a patents treaty with Germany.

The right of the Senate to initiate treaty making by proposing negotiations has been vigorously debated by the Senate. Proponents have defended such initiatives as the right and duty of the Senate under the Constitution and as a demonstration of national unity. Opponents have contended that for the Senate to make the first move was "officious and disrespectful," and that it

THE HOUSE AND THE TREATY POWER

The Constitutional Convention deprived the House of a share in the treaty-making power, thus relegating the House to a position subordinate to the Senate in treaty affairs. However, through its normal legislative powers, most especially the power of the purse, the House can at times exercise considerable—albeit indirect—influence on treaty matters. Often this comes at the stage where legislation is needed to implement a treaty. The House also becomes an equal partner with the Senate when an international agreement is submitted as legislation requiring simple majorities in both chambers instead of as a treaty requiring a two-thirds majority in the Senate.

In the administration of George Washington, when the Senate agreed to a treaty with the dey of Algiers for release of American captives, "provided the expense do not exceed $40,000," President George Washington announced that he would wait to conclude negotiations until the money had been appropriated by Congress. The Senate objected, urging that the money be taken from the Treasury or raised by borrowing. As reported in *Jefferson's Writings*, the senators feared that "to consult the representatives on one occasion would give them a handle always to claim it." The House in 1792 then passed a bill appropriating a stated sum to cover the expenses involved, and the Senate consented to ratification of a treaty specifying the sum appropriated.

In considering appropriations for the Jay Treaty, the House called for all documents in the case. Washington refused this request on the ground that "the assent of the House of Representatives is not necessary to the validity of a treaty." The House made the necessary appropriation in 1796 after a long debate, but at the same time it adopted a resolution that said "it is the constitutional right and duty of the House of Representatives in all such cases to deliberate on the expediency or inexpediency of carrying such treaty into effect and to determine and act thereon as in their judgment may be most conducive to the public good."

Submission of commercial and reciprocity treaties has led to repeated assertions of authority by the House, frequently with support from the Senate. The reciprocity treaty with Great Britain in 1854 made its effectiveness dependent upon passage of the laws necessary to put it into operation. In 1883 the Senate amended a reciprocity convention with Mexico to provide that it should not come into force until the legislation called for had been passed by Congress, and the treaty never took effect because the House never acted on the implementing legislation.

The House participated in the annexation of Texas and Hawaii, which was accomplished by joint resolution—in the first case after a treaty of annexation had been defeated in the Senate, and in the second case when a two-thirds vote in the Senate seemed doubtful.

In at least one case, House opposition prevented ratification of a treaty that would have required Congress to approve an appropriation. Shortly before the original treaty for the purchase of the Danish West Indies was submitted in 1867, the House resolved that "in the present financial condition of the country, any further purchases of territory were inexpedient, and this House will hold itself under no obligation to vote money for any such purpose unless there is greater necessity than now exists." In the debate it was said that this resolution was intended to serve notice on the king of Denmark that "this House will not pay for that purchase." When the treaty was sent to the Senate, no action was taken. When the islands finally were acquired fifty years later, the price had risen from $7,500,000 to $25,000,000.

Attempts in the House to influence the treaty process have continued in modern times. In 1979 the House's appropriations powers gave that chamber an important voice in shaping legislation to implement the Panama Canal treaties. Angered that they had had no role in approving the treaties in 1978, many House members insisted on legislation giving Congress more control over canal operations than President Jimmy Carter had been willing to grant. *(See "Panama Canal Treaties," p. 212.)*

The House in the mid-1980s led the way on the issue of continued compliance with the unratified 1979 strategic arms limitations talks (SALT II) treaty between the United States and the Soviet Union. But the final provision that, in effect, required the United States to continue to observe SALT II weapons limits was carefully worded so as not to tread on the Senate's jealously guarded prerogatives in the treaty area. *(See "SALT II Treaty," p. 211.)*

The House held up for a year and a half a bill to implement a treaty banning chemical weapons when it attempted to use it to win White House approval of unrelated legislation. The ploy failed and the implementing legislation was finally approved in 1998, amid warnings from one nonpartisan arms control group that failure to act soon could set off an international crisis.

Neither the Senate nor the House were called on to approve major trade agreements concluded in the early 1990s—the 1992 North American Free Trade Agreement (NAFTA) and the 1994 General Agreement on Tariffs and Trade (GATT). But both played important roles in approving implementing legislation.

SOURCES: George H. Haynes, *The Senate of the United States* (Boston: Houghton Mifflin, 1938), vol. 2, 686–691; Congressional Quarterly *Almanacs*.

tended to "shelter" the president from responsibility in treaty making. In a 1902 report the Foreign Relations Committee stated: "The initiative lies with the president. . . . Whether he will negotiate a treaty, and when, and what its terms shall be are matters committed by the Constitution to the discretion of the president."[13]

Today the right of either house of Congress to offer advice about negotiations is not questioned, but the advice of the legislative branch is merely persuasive, not compelling. In its landmark decision in the *Curtiss-Wright* case in 1936, the Supreme Court ruled: "The President . . . alone negotiates. Into the field of negotiation the Senate cannot intrude; and Congress itself is powerless to invade it."

The reaction of presidents to the Senate's power to advise presidents on the negotiation of treaties has varied. President Andrew Jackson acted on a Senate resolution in opening negotiations with Central American governments for an interoceanic canal. Cleveland replied with some asperity to a Senate suggestion for negotiations on a treaty to limit the importation of Chinese labor. Harding refused to recognize that a Senate resolution calling for an agreement with Great Britain and Japan on reduction of naval expenditures was responsible for the calling of the Washington Conference on the Limitation of Armament. Sponsored by Sen. William E. Borah, R-Idaho, the resolution was adopted by the Senate May 26, 1921, and by the House on June 29. Formal invitations to the conference were issued August 11, 1921.

Confirmation of Negotiators

Through the Madison administration, the names of treaty negotiators were referred to the Senate for confirmation. This gave the Senate an important power, which was recognized early by both the Senate and the executive branch. Subsequent neglect of the practice was repeatedly protested in the Senate.[14] In 1883 the Senate attempted to revive the earlier practice by adopting a resolution stipulating that, in approving a treaty with Korea, the consent given to ratification did not "admit or acquiesce in any right or constitutional power in the president to employ any person to negotiate treaties . . . unless such person shall have been appointed . . . with the advice and consent of the Senate."

Cleveland's appointment of a special commissioner with "paramount authority" to negotiate with Hawaii was declared by the Republican members of the Foreign Relations Committee to be "an unconstitutional act, in that such appointee . . . was never nominated to the Senate."

The practice of having the Senate confirm the appointment of negotiators was largely abandoned, apparently as a response to the need for secrecy. Special agents were appointed by the executive; their use was recognized as within the president's constitutional powers. This change also reflected acceptance of the principle—in Thomas Jefferson's words to Citizen Genet, envoy to the United States from the first French Republic—that the president is "the only channel of communication between the United States and foreign nations."[15]

In later years the executive occasionally sought Senate confirmation of treaty negotiators. Polk submitted the names of his appointees to negotiate a treaty with Mexico. Grant submitted to the Senate the names of the commissioners who were to negotiate the Treaty of Washington with Great Britain. Harding submitted the names of his appointees to the World War Foreign Debt Commission in 1922, but in this case the submission was required by a provision of the act creating the commission.

The United Nations Participation Act of 1945 provided for Senate confirmation of the United States representatives to the United Nations, of members of the U.S. delegation to the General Assembly, and of delegates to various UN agencies.

Negotiators' Instructions

While Washington was president, submission of the negotiators' instructions along with the names of negotiators amount-

ed to a chance for the Senate to advise on treaty proposals. Subsequent administrations did not provide the Senate with the opportunity to consider the terms of treaties not yet agreed upon until President Polk in 1846 submitted the skeleton of a treaty ending the war with Mexico.

Preliminary drafts of treaties were sent to the Senate by four other presidents—Buchanan, Lincoln, Andrew Johnson, and Grant. In 1919 the Senate requested a copy of the Treaty of Versailles as presented to the representatives of Germany. The secretary of state replied that the president felt it would not be in the public interest to communicate to the Senate a provisional text and found no precedent for such a procedure.

In several instances, the Senate (with the concurrence of the House) "advised" the executive by specifying the limits within which negotiators of international agreements were to operate. In legislation creating the Foreign Debt Commission, enacted February 9, 1922, it was provided that "nothing contained in this act shall be construed to authorize . . . the commission to extend the time of maturity of . . . obligations due the United States . . . beyond June 15, 1947, or to fix the rate of interest at less than 4¼ per centum per annum." In a joint resolution making funds available to send a delegation to the Opium Conference of 1924, Congress specified certain results it wanted the negotiators to obtain.

Legislators as Negotiators

The first members of Congress selected to negotiate a treaty were Sen. James A. Bayard of Delaware and House Speaker Henry Clay. Madison named them to help negotiate a treaty of peace with Great Britain in 1814. Both resigned their places in Congress on the ground that the two offices were not compatible.

On at least three occasions resolutions were introduced in the Senate to prohibit members of that body from serving as treaty negotiators. The first resolution, introduced in 1870, was defeated after a heated all-night debate when it was turned into a question of confidence in President Grant. The second was occasioned by President William McKinley's appointment of three members of the Foreign Relations Committee to a commission to negotiate the Treaty of Paris in 1898. The Senate committee, to which a resolution of protest was referred, hesitated to make a report that might have appeared to censure some of its own members, but it directed its chairman to visit the president and express the Senate's strong disapproval.

Theodore Roosevelt's selection of Sen. Henry Cabot Lodge, R-Mass., to serve on the Alaskan boundary tribunal led to the third attempt of the Senate to prohibit such service by senators. But a resolution opposing the selection was never acted upon.

The Senate's resentment of Wilson's failure to include any senators on the 1919 peace commission was a new reaction. To compensate for lack of representation on the commission, a resolution was introduced calling for the appointment of a bipartisan committee of eight senators to visit Paris during the sessions of the Peace Conference to "make itself familiar with all facts" and report to the Senate "as often as it deemed desirable." The resolution was never acted upon, however. Senate attempts to offer advice on the negotiations through debate on the floor and through a round-robin warning against inclusion of provisions for a League of Nations in the peace treaty proved to be ineffective.

After Wilson's experience, the appointment of senators to important international conferences subsequently became more common. President Harding in 1921 chose Lodge, then chairman of the Foreign Relations Committee, and Minority Leader Oscar W. Underwood, D-Ala., as delegates to the Conference on the Limitation of Armament. Members of both houses were appointed by President Herbert Hoover to the American delegation to the London Naval Conference in 1930. President Franklin D. Roosevelt recognized Congress in his selection of commissioners to the World Monetary and Economic Conference in 1933 and to the International Refugee Conference in 1943.

During World War II, Roosevelt included members of Congress in a foreign policy advisory committee that discussed the creation of an international peace organization. In 1945 the eight-member U.S. delegation to the San Francisco conference that established the United Nations included four members of Congress: Foreign Relations Committee Chairman Tom Connally, D-Texas, and committee Republican Arthur H. Vandenberg of Michigan, as well as Sol Bloom, D-N.Y., and Charles A. Eaton, R-N.J., chairman and ranking minority member, respectively, of the House Foreign Affairs Committee. Since the founding of the United Nations, two senators and two representatives have alternated as members of the U.S. delegation.

Successive administrations have followed the practice of including members of Congress on delegations to international conferences and involving members in negotiations. President Carter, for example, appointed a diverse group of fourteen representatives and thirty senators as advisers to the SALT delegation in 1977. That same year Senate members became involved to an unprecedented degree in negotiating reservations with Panamanian officials after the signing of the Panama Canal treaties. The Reagan administration consulted closely with Senate leaders in 1988 when questions raised on Capitol Hill forced the negotiation of addenda to the INF treaty with the Soviet Union. During negotiation of the North American Free Trade Agreement (NAFTA), which was not a treaty but did require implementing legislation, the U.S. trade representative and others held more than forty consultations with members of Congress and nearly two hundred staff consultations in 1991 and 1992.

CONSENT OF THE SENATE

Through the years, Senate action on treaties has repeatedly led to controversy. Generally, the dispute has centered on rival claims of the president and the Senate over the treaty power. On the vast majority of treaties submitted to it, the Senate has adopted a simple resolution of consent to ratification. But the importance of some of the rejected treaties has prompted criticism of the Senate's treaty-making role—as well as the two-thirds requirement for approval—and has spawned a variety of proposed constitutional amendments designed to modify the Senate's power. *(See Table 5-1, p. 203.)*

Senate Procedures

Treaties are transmitted to the Senate by the president under an injunction of secrecy, which normally is removed shortly after the Senate receives the treaty. Once a treaty is submitted, it remains before the Senate until it is approved or rejected, or until the president requests its return and the Senate agrees to withdraw it. The Senate also may take the initiative to return a treaty to the president.

Senate consideration of a treaty is open to presidential discretion at a number of points. The president may refuse to submit a treaty, may withdraw it after it is submitted, or may refuse to ratify it even after the Senate has given its consent.

The Senate Foreign Relations Committee has jurisdiction over all treaties, no matter what the subject. The committee considers a treaty in much the same way it considers proposed legislation. It may hold open or closed hearings and may recommend Senate approval or rejection, with or without modifications. Committee decisions require a majority vote of the members present and no measure or recommendation can be reported unless a majority of the committee's members are physically present.

After treaties are reported by Foreign Relations, they are considered by the full Senate. Senators used to debate treaties in closed executive session, preserving the cloak of secrecy. By the late nineteenth century, however, there were increasing demands to open treaty debates to the public. In 1888 a fisheries treaty with Great Britain was considered—and rejected—in the first open executive session. Other public treaty debates followed, and the Senate on June 18, 1929, amended its rules to provide that all Senate business, including action on treaties, was to be conducted in open session unless a majority of the Senate decided to hold a closed session to consider a particularly sensitive matter.

After a brief experiment in 1801–1803 with a rule requiring a two-thirds vote on all floor action on treaties, the Senate limited the two-thirds rule to two votes: the final vote on whether to give its advice and consent and a vote on a motion for indefinite postponement. All other questions are decided by majority vote.

A separate roll call vote normally is taken on each treaty. But the Senate sometimes departs from that procedure when a large number of similar treaties, or a variety of noncontroversial treaties, are considered. It has become the practice in these cases to consider the group of treaties en bloc, taking one vote on several resolutions of consent, or taking a single vote, which by unanimous consent is shown separately in the *Congressional Record* as the vote on each of the treaty resolutions.

Although Senate rules do not require roll call votes on treaties, that practice has become customary. It grew out of a 1952 incident in which three noncontroversial consular conven-

TABLE 5-1 Treaties Killed by the Senate (through September 1999)

Date of vote	Country	Vote Yea–Nay	Subject
March 9, 1825	Colombia	0–40	Suppression of African Slave Trade
June 11, 1836	Switzerland	14–23	Personal and Property Rights
June 8, 1844	Texas	16–35	Annexation
June 15, 1844	German Zollverein	26–18	Reciprocity
May 31, 1860	Mexico	18–27	Transit and Commercial Rights
June 27, 1860	Spain	26–17	Cuban Claims Commission
April 13, 1869	Great Britain	1–54	Arbitration of Claims
June 1, 1870	Hawaii	20–19	Reciprocity
June 30, 1870	Dominican Republic	28–28	Annexation
Jan. 29, 1885	Nicaragua	32–23	Interoceanic Canal
April 20, 1886	Mexico	32–26	Mining Claims
Aug. 21, 1888	Great Britain	27–30	Fishing Rights
Feb. 1, 1889	Great Britain	15–38	Extradition
May 5, 1897	Great Britain	43–26	Arbitration
March 19, 1920	Multilateral	49–35	Treaty of Versailles
Jan. 18, 1927	Turkey	50–34	Commercial Rights
March 14, 1934	Canada	46–42	St. Lawrence Seaway
Jan. 29, 1935	Multilateral	52–36	World Court
May 26, 1960	Multilateral	49–30	Law of the Sea Convention
March 8, 1983	Multilateral	50–42	Montreal Aviation Protocol
Oct. 13, 1999	Multilateral	48–51	Comprehensive Nuclear Test Ban

NOTE: A two-thirds majority vote is required for Senate consent to the ratification of treaties. In many cases, treaties were blocked in committee or withdrawn before ever coming to a vote in the Senate.

SOURCE: Compiled by Senate Historical Office from W. Stull Holt, *Treaties Defeated by the Senate* (Baltimore: Johns Hopkins University Press, 1933) and from *Senate Executive Journal*.

tions were approved on June 13 when only two senators were present in the chamber. On July 20, 1953, acting Majority Leader William F. Knowland, R-Calif., announced that it would be standard procedure in the future to have a roll call vote on all treaties. The requirement for a recorded vote had also been adopted as a de facto practice of the Senate in order to weaken support for the so-called Bricker constitutional amendment proposal that would have limited the executive's treaty power.[16]

Amendments to Treaties

The Constitution sets forth no procedures for, or restrictions on, amending treaties. But since the time of the Jay Treaty with Great Britain, the Senate has claimed authority to modify treaties after the completion of negotiations. The Senate on June 24, 1795, by a 20–10 vote, consented to ratification of the Jay Treaty on condition that an additional article be negotiated to suspend portions of the treaty's twelfth article, relating to trade between the United States and the British West Indies. Scores of treaties since then have been subjected to amendments, reservations, conditions, and qualifications, some of which have been added at the request of the president.

The wisdom of the Senate practice of amending treaties was questioned as early as 1805 by John Quincy Adams, who was then a senator from Massachusetts. "I think amendments to treaties imprudent," Adams said in Senate debate. "By making them you agree to all the treaty except the particular you amend, and at the same time you leave it optional with the other party to reject the whole."[17]

On two occasions the Supreme Court has sustained the power of the Senate to amend treaties. In 1869 the Court stated in *Haver v. Yaker:*

In this country, a treaty is something more than a contract, for the Federal Constitution declares it to be the law of the land. If so, before it can become a law, the Senate, in whom rests the authority to ratify it, must agree to it. But the Senate are not required to adopt or reject it as a whole, but may modify or amend it.

And in a 1901 opinion the Court said the Senate "may refuse its ratification, or make such ratification conditional upon the adoption of amendments to the treaty." *(Fourteen Diamond Rings v. United States)*

One of the best known U.S. qualifications to an international agreement is the so-called Connally reservation to the compulsory jurisdiction clause of the statute of the International Court of Justice.

In adhering to the UN Charter in 1945, the United States accepted membership in the International Court. President Truman contended that the country should also accept compulsory jurisdiction under terms of the court's statute, which excluded matters deemed to be within the domestic jurisdiction of any nation. On July 31, 1946, the Senate considered a resolution to that effect. But some senators, recalling fears that had led to Senate refusal in 1935, after a decade of discussion, to approve U.S. membership in the World Court, objected to letting the International Court of Justice determine what matters might or might not be within U.S. jurisdiction. To obviate this possibility, Senator Connally proposed adding to the resolution's clause excluding "matters which are essentially within the domestic jurisdiction of the United States" the words "as determined by the

United States." The Senate, before approving the resolution on August 2, 1946, agreed to the Connally reservation by a 51–12 vote, in effect negating the U.S. commitment in principle. Subsequent attempts to repeal the reservation were unsuccessful.

When the Senate amends a treaty, the amendment, if it is accepted by the president and the other parties to the treaty, changes the treaty for all parties. A Senate reservation limits only the treaty obligation of the United States, although the reservation may be so significant that the other treaty parties may file similar reservations or refuse to ratify the treaty.

The Senate Foreign Relations Committee has identified four types of conditions the Senate may use to qualify its consent to a treaty. The Senate may:

- Require "amendments" to the text of the treaty itself.
- Attach "reservations," which are presumed to be deliberate changes in the legal effect of treaty provisions, particularly as they affect the country entering the reservation.
- Add "understandings," which are statements of interpretation intended to clarify the legal effect of the agreement without necessarily changing it.
- Attach "declarations," statements of intent or policy which accompany ratification, but which are not directly related to provisions of the treaty itself.[18]

Reservations, understandings, and declarations are used more frequently than amendments. But the differences among these various conditions have become less distinct over the years. Amendments to a treaty automatically require the concurrence of the other parties to the accord. Reservations and understandings are different from amendments in that their substance dictates whether the conditions must be formally communicated to the other parties and whether they must be agreed to before the treaty can go into effect.

The Senate's substitution of reservations for amendments in recent years has not lessened the difficulty faced by the executive branch. From the administration's point of view, the Senate's alteration of treaties has become an increasingly serious problem because of the growing tendency to modify U.S. foreign relations through multilateral treaties. Resubmission of an amended treaty to foreign governments—any one of which may wish to alter other provisions of the treaty in view of U.S. changes—presents almost insuperable obstacles to final agreement.

EFFORTS TO ALTER TREATY POWER

Attempts have been made to alter the treaty-making provisions of the Constitution. Most of the proposals have sought to eliminate the two-thirds requirement for Senate approval of treaties, or to require consent to ratification by the House as well as the Senate. The Bricker amendment of the 1950s, which sought to curtail the president's treaty power, was a marked exception to the pattern.

Ratification Changes

Following the war with Spain, two resolutions were introduced in the House proposing a constitutional amendment giving the power of consent to a majority of the whole Senate. In 1920 amendments were offered in both houses stipulating that consent to ratification should be by majority vote of members present in the Senate.

Between 1919 and 1928, five resolutions were introduced in the House to let that body participate in giving "advice and consent" on treaties. As Democratic candidate for president in 1924, John W. Davis endorsed the plan to substitute a majority for a two-thirds vote. William Jennings Bryan, in a 1920 address, advocated associating the House with the Senate. An even more fundamental change was proposed in Congress in 1921 whereby certain treaties would have to be approved by popular vote.

Mindful of the Senate's rejection of the Treaty of Versailles and the League of Nations, Congress considered a number of proposals during World War II to change the treaty ratification provisions. The intent of this legislation was to reduce the possibility that new postwar arrangements for world peace would be rejected.

Josephus Daniels, Navy secretary under Wilson, suggested in a 1942 speech that the Constitution be amended to provide for consent to ratification by majority vote of both chambers. Proposed amendments to carry out his suggestion were introduced the following year in the House. In the Senate, a proposed amendment was introduced in 1943 to allow Senate consent by a simple majority.

In 1945, while the San Francisco conference was debating the charter of the United Nations—destined for consideration by the Senate alone—the House in May took up a resolution by Hatton Sumners, D-Texas, to amend the Constitution to require that "treaties shall be made by the president by and with the advice and consent of both houses of Congress." Despite general agreement that the Senate never would agree to share its treaty power, the House adopted the resolution by a 288–88 vote. The Senate never acted on the resolution.

Bricker Amendment

Congress engaged in an historic debate in the 1950s on an amendment to the Constitution proposed by Sen. John W. Bricker, R-Ohio, that would have curbed the executive's powers to make treaties and other international agreements.

The amendment reflected fears that American adherence to various United Nations covenants and conventions, such as the genocide convention submitted by President Truman in 1949 (which was not approved by the Senate until 1986), would greatly expand the powers of the federal government and jeopardize enforcement of state laws by reason of the constitutional provision making treaties the "supreme law of the land." The proposed amendment stemmed also from congressional resentment of the White House tendency to substitute executive agreements, not subject to ratification, for treaties.

The Bricker amendment had forceful supporters in Congress, and the controversy between the two branches of government turned a highly technical legal question into a wide-ranging debate between "isolationists" and "one-worlders." Bricker's amendment has been described as "among the most controversial proposals considered by Congress during the early years of the Cold War."[19]

Section 1 of the amendment stated that a provision of a treaty which conflicted with any provision of the Constitution should not be of any force or effect. Section 2 provided that a treaty would become effective as internal law in the United States "only through legislation which would be valid in the absence of a treaty." Section 3 made executive agreements subject to regulation by Congress and to the limitations imposed on treaties in Section 2.

The Judiciary Committee's majority report on the proposed amendment stated that in view of recent efforts to "use the treaty-making power as an instrument for the alteration of purely domestic policy," it was important to "establish once and for all, by unequivocal language, that the treaty power cannot be used for purposes in conflict with the Constitution." The report also said that the power of Congress to regulate the making of executive agreements "must be firmly established" because the president's authority in this regard "has been exploited to the point where the treaty procedure may ultimately become an historical relic." The report held that the amendment would "prevent the reduction of the states' power . . . through ratification of treaties."

No great objection was voiced to the first provision, which simply affirmed the power of courts to pass on the constitutionality of treaties as well as statutes. The heart of the controversy lay in the second and third sections of S J Res 1. There was little agreement as to the precise meaning of the "which" clause in Section 2, but, in the Eisenhower administration's view, it clearly subordinated the treaty power of the president to the powers of Congress and the states. Section 3 was scarcely less objectionable to the administration because it would sharply curtail the president's use of agreements other than treaties. The idea of giving Congress a say on agreements other than treaties enjoyed wider support than did the highly disputed intent of Section 2.

The controversial Section 2 was dropped when several substitute versions were offered. In a showdown on the Bricker amendment and its various revisions, the Senate rejected a substitute amendment stating that any provision of a treaty or international agreement that conflicted with the Constitution was invalid; nontreaty agreements could not take effect as internal law unless implemented by congressional action; and Senate consent to ratification of treaties must be by roll call vote. The February 26, 1954, vote fell one short (60–31) of the two-thirds majority required for Senate approval of a proposed amendment to the Constitution.

MAJOR TREATIES SINCE 1919: HIGHLIGHTS OF ACTION

League of Nations

Senate opposition to the Treaty of Versailles was directed principally at the League Covenant, which formed an integral

As chairman of the Senate Foreign Relations Committee, Sen. Henry Cabot Lodge was the most powerful congressional opponent of the League of Nations.

part of the treaty, although other provisions, especially the Shantung settlement—which favored Japan at the expense of China—also aroused strong objections. It was upon the League issue, however, that ratification hinged.

The treaty was lost in the conflict that developed between a large group of Republicans led by Henry Cabot Lodge, chairman of the Foreign Relations Committee, who refused to accept the treaty without major reservations, and a group of loyal Democratic supporters of President Woodrow Wilson, who in turn would not accept any compromise involving the Lodge reservations.

On more than one occasion during World War I, Lodge publicly had advocated an international league for the maintenance of world peace, but his final position was that it should be postponed to allow time for adequate study and that to attempt to make it part of the treaty of peace with Germany would lead only to prolonged discussion.

Focus of Disagreement. The Lodge viewpoint was supported by thirty-nine Republican senators and senators-elect, who signed a proposal drafted by Philander C. Knox, R-Pa., which was offered by Lodge in the form of a Senate resolution on March 3, 1919, the closing day of the 65th Congress. The resolution declared that "the constitution of the League of Nations in the form now proposed to the Peace Conference should not be accepted by the United States" and "that the negotiations on the part of the United States should immediately be directed to the utmost expedition of the urgent business of negotiating peace terms with Germany, . . . and that the proposal for a League of Nations to insure the permanent peace of the world should be then taken up for careful and serious consideration."

President Wilson lost no time in responding. On the evening of March 4, the day before he sailed a second time for France, he told a large audience in the Metropolitan Opera House in New York City that when he returned with a final treaty it would contain not only the League Covenant but would have so many threads "tied to the covenant that you cannot dissect the covenant from the treaty without destroying the whole vital structure."[20]

The Foreign Relations Committee, composed of ten Republicans and seven Democrats, held public hearings on the treaty from July 31 to September 12, 1919. The majority report, written by Lodge, recommended ratification but proposed forty-five amendments and four reservations. The minority report, signed by Gilbert M. Hitchcock of Nebraska and five other Democrats, argued against any amendments and reservations. A third report, submitted by Porter J. McCumber, R-N.D., referred to the League Covenant as "a mighty step in the right direction" and pointed out that "it still leaves to each nation the right of withdrawal, and depends to a great extent upon the moral sentiment of each nation to comply with its own obligations or the enforcement of such obligations upon a recalcitrant member."

Senate Factions. Even before the Foreign Relations Committee submitted its reports, the Senate was dividing into a number of factions. At one extreme stood the group of "irreconcilables" or "bitter-enders," led by William E. Borah, R-Idaho, Hiram W. Johnson, R-Calif., and James A. Reed, D-Mo. They were opposed to the treaty with or without reservations. Borah contended that "it really incorporates a scheme which, either directly or indirectly, greatly modifies our governmental powers." At the other extreme were the administration Democrats led by Hitchcock, who lined up with the president in favoring unconditional ratification. Between these two extremes was the important group of "reservationists," which included Lodge. There were also the "mild reservationists," who wanted the treaty accepted with slight alterations.

During the Senate debate, the friends of the treaty, represented by the Democrats and mild reservationists, had succeeded by the end of October in defeating all amendments proposed by the Foreign Relations Committee. Amendments were opposed not only for their content but also because they would have required approval by all other signatories of the treaty—a virtual impossibility—whereas reservations applied only to the country that made them. It was after defeat of the amendments that the struggle over the Lodge reservations began. But the inability of Congress and the president to reach a compromise killed the treaty.

Opposition to the League Covenant centered on Article X, of which Wilson himself was the author. This article read as follows:

The members of the League undertake to respect and preserve as against external aggression the territorial integrity and existing political independence of all members of the League. In case of any such aggression or in case of any threat or danger of such aggression the Council shall advise upon the means by which this obligation shall be fulfilled.

The irreconcilables feared that Article X would draw the United States into foreign wars at the bidding of the League of Nations. Another fear was that the League proposal would deprive the United States of full liberty of action under the Monroe Doctrine's ban on the extension of European influence and power to the American continents.

Lodge Reservations. The apprehension aroused by the League Covenant and the objections to that instrument and to other parts of the treaty were reflected in the fourteen reservations finally incorporated in the Lodge resolution. The resolution stipulated that ratification by the United States would not become effective until the reservations had been accepted, through an exchange of notes, by three of the four following powers: Great Britain, France, Italy, and Japan.

The reservations disclosed a determination on the part of their authors to prevent any encroachment on the powers of Congress as well as any encroachment on the sovereignty of the United States. In carrying out that purpose, in the view of proponents of American membership in the League, the reservations went far beyond any necessary precautions. They were so distasteful to President Wilson that he wrote to Senator Hitchcock on November 18, 1919, that in his opinion the Lodge resolution "does not provide for ratification but rather for nullification of the treaty."

The Lodge resolution finally was brought to a vote on November 19 and was twice defeated. On the first vote there were 39 yeas and 55 nays. On a procedural vote the resolution again failed, 41–51. Without further debate the Senate then proceeded to vote on a resolution of approval of the treaty without reservations of any kind. But the treaty did not win even a simple majority. The vote was 38–53. Thirteen Republican irreconcilables, who on the two previous votes had opposed ratification even with the Lodge reservations, were joined by the whole body of reservationists. McCumber was the sole Republican to favor unconditional consent to ratification.

Another Round. The treaty issue was revived in the second session of the 66th Congress, and another vote was taken on March 19, 1920. On this occasion there was no question of unconditional approval. The resolution before the Senate contained the original Lodge reservations, slightly revised but with no essential change. President Wilson still characterized them as amounting to a "sweeping nullification of the terms of the treaty"; but shortly before the vote was taken, Thomas J. Walsh, D-Mont., who had opposed the Lodge resolution the previous November, appealed to his colleagues to accept the reservations since the treaty was too important to be lost. Although twenty-one Democrats and twenty-eight Republicans consented to the ratification resolution, the 49–35 vote was seven short of the two-thirds majority required for approval.

Many believe the defeat could have been avoided. I. M. Destler wrote: "Wilson's treaty went down to defeat because he would not make the concessions necessary for ratification. Historians generally have concluded that the practical impact of the Lodge reservations would have been minor and that Wilson's stubbornness was therefore 'an error of tragic magnitude.'"[21]

United Nations

With Senate rejection of the League of Nations in mind, the Roosevelt administration had begun to court bipartisan support for the United Nations long before the Dumbarton Oaks meetings of August–October 1944, at which a draft charter was drawn up. Secretary of State Cordell Hull had assured congressional leaders of both parties in 1943 that Congress would have the final say on U.S. participation in any world security organization.

The eight-member delegation to the San Francisco conference, announced February 13, 1945, was picked with an eye to the widest public support. Headed by Secretary of State Edward R. Stettinius Jr. (who had succeeded Hull December 1, 1944), it included Hull; Senators Connally and Vandenberg; Representatives Bloom and Eaton; Republican former governor Harold E. Stassen of Minnesota; and Virginia Gildersleeve, dean of Barnard College. John Foster Dulles, foreign policy adviser to Governor Thomas E. Dewey of New York during the 1944 presidential campaign, was named a principal adviser to the delegation.

Public discussion of the charter was intense and widespread before and during the two-month conference, at which Vandenberg and Dulles played leading roles. Speaking on June 26, the day the conference ended, President Truman acclaimed the charter as a declaration of "faith that war is not inevitable." In a personal appearance before the Senate July 2, he called for prompt ratification of the charter and the annexed statute of the International Court of Justice. Said Truman: "The choice before the Senate is now clear. The choice is not between this charter and something else. It is between this charter and no charter at all."

Following a week of hearings, the Foreign Relations Committee on July 13 voted 21–1 to approve the charter. The lone dissenter was Hiram W. Johnson of California, the highest-ranking Republican on the committee. During Senate debate July 23–28, most of the discussion focused on Article 43, pledging members to "make available to the security council, on its call and in accordance with a special agreement or agreements, armed forces, assistance and facilities, including rights of passage, necessary for the purpose of maintaining international peace and security."

Burton K. Wheeler, D-Mont., and others feared this would give the U.S. delegate "the war-making power," but the president assured the Senate on July 27 that any agreements under Article 43 would be sent to Congress for "appropriate legislation to approve them." Next day, the Senate overwhelmingly approved, 89–2, the charter establishing the United Nations. Opposed were Republicans William Langer, N.D., and Henrik Shipstead, Minn. Johnson (who was unable to vote and died August 6) had announced his opposition.

North Atlantic Treaty Organization

After Congress in 1948 passed the so-called Vandenberg Resolution, which affirmed the U.S. determination to exercise the right of individual or collective self-defense, President Truman directed the State Department to explore the question of regional security with Canada, Britain, France, Belgium, the Netherlands, and Luxembourg. In October, the seven countries reached tentative agreement on a collective defense arrangement and had invited Norway, Denmark, Iceland, Italy, and Portugal to join them. Negotiations were concluded April 4, 1949, when representatives of the twelve nations signed the North Atlantic Treaty in Washington "to unite their efforts for collective defense and for the preservation of peace and security."

The text reaffirmed support for the United Nations and for the peaceful settlement of disputes. It also pledged the signatories to work jointly for political, economic, and social stability within the North Atlantic area, defined to extend from Alaska through the North Atlantic to the three French departments in Algeria. But its key provisions called for intensified self-help and mutual aid measures to defend the area and pledged that, in the event of an armed attack against one of the members, each of the others would come to its aid by taking "such action as it deems necessary, including the use of armed forces, to restore and maintain the security of the North Atlantic area." The treaty also provided for a North Atlantic Council to draw up plans for concerted actions and policies, for the admission of other nations by unanimous invitation, and for the right of members to withdraw after twenty years.

President Truman sent the treaty to the Senate April 12, 1949, and urged prompt approval. The key question that arose at once was the relationship between the treaty and the not-yet submitted military assistance program for Europe. Would approval of the treaty commit Congress to vote for the latter? To clarify the matter, several senators called for consideration of the two together. But the administration refused, withholding its military aid proposals until action on the treaty had been completed.

Hearings by the Foreign Relations Committee began April 27. Secretary of State Dean Acheson and other administration officials gave strong backing to the treaty. Former vice president Henry A. Wallace denounced the pact, saying it would destroy the chances for European recovery and entail costs of $20 billion for military aid. On June 6 the committee voted unanimously to approve the treaty. Its report asserted that approval would not commit the Senate to approve military aid requests and that the treaty did not give the president any powers "to take any action, without specific congressional authorization," that he could not already take.

The Senate debated the treaty July 5–20, with Senators Connally and Vandenberg carrying the burden of the defense. Robert A. Taft, R-Ohio, announced that he would oppose ratification without a reservation disclaiming any obligation to arm Western Europe—a step he said would "promote war." Answering Taft was Sen. John Foster Dulles, R-N.Y., sworn in July 8 as the appointed successor to Sen. Robert F. Wagner, D-N.Y.: "If the impression became prevalent that this country was turning its back on international cooperation, the results would be disastrous. Other free countries . . . would almost certainly fall. We would be encircled and, eventually, strangled ourselves."

On July 21 the Senate voted, rejecting three reservations by large margins before approving the treaty. The first reservation—sponsored by Kenneth S. Wherry, R-Neb., Taft, and Arthur V. Watkins, R-Utah—stated that nothing in the treaty would commit the signatories "morally or legally to furnish or supply arms" to the others. It was rejected, 21–74. Watkins then proposed two other reservations, both of which disclaimed any intention to employ U.S. armed forces without the express approval of Congress. These were rejected, 11–84 and 8–87. The Senate then approved the North Atlantic Treaty, 82–13 (Democrats, 50–2; Republicans, 32–11). The only senator not present was Allen J. Ellender, D-La., who supported the treaty.

Congress later approved massive amounts of military and economic aid for postwar Western Europe, Greece, and Turkey, which faced threats from Soviet expansionist policies and internal communist subversion.

Nuclear Test Ban Accord

The world's brush with nuclear war in the 1962 Cuban missile crisis gave a new urgency to the search for an agreement to stop nuclear testing. Such a step, it was hoped, would help to stabilize the nuclear balance between the United States and the Soviet Union, discourage the proliferation of nuclear arsenals among other countries, and provide a critical turning point in the arms race. Through four years of negotiations the same stumbling blocks had prevented an agreement: America's insistence on the right of on-site inspection to guard against undetected violations of any prohibitions on underground nuclear testing, and the Soviet Union's refusal to accept inspection on Russian soil by foreign observers. Late in 1962, however, the Soviets said they might accept two or three inspections a year, in addition to several unmanned "black-box" seismic detection stations.

The Americans, British, and Soviets resumed private talks in January 1963 but soon reached an impasse on the number of on-site inspections to be permitted. The Soviets refused to accept more than three a year, while the United States insisted on a minimum of seven. Attention then shifted to the broader seventeen-nation disarmament negotiations under way in Geneva. There, on April 5, American and Soviet delegates agreed to establish a direct telegraphic "hot line" between the White House and the Kremlin as a precaution against the kind of accident or miscalculation that might have touched off a nuclear exchange during the Cuban missile crisis. Symbolizing a mutual concern for the prevention of nuclear war, the "hot-line" agreement was formally signed June 20.

In Washington, meanwhile, Senators Hubert H. Humphrey, D-Minn., and Thomas J. Dodd, D-Conn., with thirty-two cosponsors, had introduced a resolution urging the United States to seek agreement on a treaty banning atmospheric and underwater tests but not those conducted underground. Their proposal sidestepped the inspection issue, since it was generally believed that any clandestine tests in the other environments could be detected by national systems without the need for on-site verification. Two weeks later, in a June 10 speech at American University calling for reexamination of attitudes toward the Soviet Union and the cold war, President John F. Kennedy announced that "high-level discussions will shortly begin in Moscow looking toward early agreement on a comprehensive test ban treaty."

Under Secretary of State W. Averell Harriman represented the United States in the negotiations, which began July 15 and led, with surprising swiftness, to the initialing on July 25 of a treaty banning all except underground tests. The treaty was signed in Moscow August 5, 1963, by the United States, Great Britain, and the Soviet Union.

President Kennedy sent the treaty to the Senate August 8, with a message designed to answer the various arguments being voiced by certain political and military leaders against the treaty. On September 3 the Foreign Relations Committee reported the treaty favorably, having found "the balance of risks weighted in favor" of the pact. But as Senate debate began September 9, the Preparedness Investigating Subcommittee of the Senate Armed Services Committee issued a separate report. The subcommittee's report was based on secret hearings at which Dr. Edward Teller, the physicist credited with development of the hydrogen bomb, and Gen. Thomas S. Power, chief of the Strategic Air Command, had persuaded the panel that the treaty involved "serious—perhaps formidable—military and technical disadvantages to the United States."

Senate debate focused on a series of proposed reservations, all of which came to a vote September 23. By heavy bipartisan majorities, the Senate rejected several moves to add restrictions and qualifications. There was little opposition to adding a preamble to the resolution of approval reasserting the Senate's right to pass on any future amendments to the treaty. On September 24 the Senate consented to ratification by a vote of 80–19 (Democrats, 55–11; Republicans, 25–8), or fourteen more than the required two-thirds majority.

The Soviet Union ratified the pact the next day, and it went into effect October 10, 1963. In short order, more than a hundred nations signed the treaty. But two major powers refused to do so: France, which had opposed any test ban because of its determination to achieve full status as an independent nuclear power, and the People's Republic of China, which was bent on the same goal and coincidentally locked in conflict with the Soviets over Premier Nikita Khrushchev's policy of "peaceful coexistence" with the West. On October 16, 1964, the Chinese entered the nuclear "club" by setting off their first fission explosion just as Khrushchev was being ousted from power in Moscow.

Nuclear Nonproliferation Treaty

The Soviet occupation of Czechoslovakia in August 1968 dealt a mortal blow to President Lyndon B. Johnson's hope of ratifying a nuclear nonproliferation treaty before leaving office. Johnson continued to press vigorously for Senate action on the treaty, but to no avail. Senate approval came during the Nixon administration.

On June 12, 1968, the United Nations General Assembly had voted 95–4, with twenty-one abstentions, to approve a draft treaty banning the spread of nuclear weapons to states that did not already have them. The product of more than four years of negotiations at the eighteen-nation disarmament conference in Geneva, the treaty was signed July 1 by the United States, the Soviet Union, and sixty other nations. Shortly thereafter, on July 9, Johnson submitted the treaty to the Senate.

The treaty consisted of a preamble and eleven articles, the most important of which were those banning the spread of nuclear weapons, providing for safeguards against violations of the treaty, and ensuring nondiscriminatory access to the peaceful uses of nuclear energy.

The Foreign Relations Committee took the unprecedented step of beginning its consideration of the treaty less than twenty-four hours after it was submitted to the Senate. Members of the Joint Committee on Atomic Energy joined with the Foreign Relations Committee in questioning administration witnesses about the treaty. A principal concern was whether the treaty would impose any new obligation on the United States to defend a nonnuclear nation threatened with or actually experiencing a nuclear attack. While the testimony of Secretary of State Dean Rusk and U.S. Arms Control and Disarmament Director William C. Foster contained no direct reference to this point, Rusk said repeatedly under questioning that the treaty would in no way add to existing U.S. military commitments abroad.

The committee approved the treaty September 17 by a 13–3 vote, with three abstentions. In its report the committee recommended that after the Senate acted, the president delay formal ratification (that is, depositing the actual instruments of ratification) until a majority of nations "nearest to a nuclear weapons capability" promised to honor the agreement.

On October 11 Majority Leader Mike Mansfield, D-Mont., said he would not call up the treaty because "the leadership will not be a party to a partisan treatment of a matter which by its very nature is and must remain nonpartisan." The treaty had become involved in the presidential election campaign. Vice President Hubert Humphrey, the Democratic candidate, urged quick ratification of the agreement. Nixon, the Republican candidate, said that going ahead with the treaty might appear to be "condoning" the Soviet invasion of Czechoslovakia, which he said could have "a tremendously bad moral effect, detrimental moral effect, all over the world." He said he supported the treaty but believed it desirable to delay ratification until a later date.

After Nixon won the election, his views favoring delay took on increased importance. There was no further action in 1968, but on February 5, 1969, President Nixon called for the Senate's "prompt consideration and positive action" on the treaty. Approval of the treaty at that time, he said, "would advance this administration's policy of negotiation rather than confrontation

with the U.S.S.R." On March 13 the Senate, by an 83–15 vote (Republicans, 34–8; Democrats, 49–7), consented to the ratification of the treaty.

SALT Agreements

After ratification of the nuclear nonproliferation treaty, the two superpowers initiated a series of strategic arms limitation talks on November 17, 1969. The first round of talks eventually culminated in the signing of two agreements in Moscow on May 26, 1972 (known as SALT I and SALT II). The first pact limited strategic missile defense systems; the other, a five-year interim agreement, restricted offensive nuclear weapons.

Almost as soon as SALT I was signed, negotiations began on SALT II, to take effect when the interim agreement expired in October 1977. Those negotiations took a hopeful turn on November 24, 1974, when President Gerald R. Ford and Soviet Communist Party General Secretary Leonid I. Brezhnev, meeting in Vladivostok, reached tentative agreement on guidelines for an arms pact. But a final agreement was delayed until 1979 when President Jimmy Carter and Brezhnev signed the SALT II treaty in Vienna on June 18. The treaty was never approved by the Senate, however.

SALT I Agreements. The first arms agreement was a treaty limiting the United States and the Soviet Union to two antiballistic missile (ABM) sites: one for the defense of each nation's capital and another for the defense of an intercontinental ballistic missile (ICBM) installation in each country. (In 1973 Congress stopped the Defense Department from beginning work on the ABM site to defend Washington. A 1974 protocol between the two nations restricting each nation to just one site was approved by the Senate November 10, 1975.)

The second pact was a five-year interim agreement limiting offensive missile launchers—land-based silos and submarine missile tubes—to those under construction or deployed at the time of the signing.

President Nixon presented the two pacts to Congress June 1, 1972, less than half an hour after returning from an eight-day trip to the Soviet Union, where he and Brezhnev had signed the SALT accords. Nixon urged the assembled lawmakers to "seize the moment so that our children and the world's children live free of the fears and free of the hatreds that have been the lot of mankind through the centuries."

The ABM treaty had to be approved by a two-thirds majority of the Senate, the offensive arms agreement by simple majorities of both houses. Theoretically, the president did not have to submit the offensive arms agreement to Congress since it was an executive agreement. However, because of the importance of the issue, a legal challenge might have arisen if the president had not requested formal approval from Congress. A provision of the 1961 law establishing the Arms Control and Disarmament Agency, which negotiated the pacts, stated that any agreement to "limit" U.S. armed forces or armaments had to be approved by legislation or treaty.

Nixon had several advantages as the congressional hearings

Members of Congress look on as President Richard Nixon signs the resolution authorizing approval of the SALT I interim agreement in 1972.

on the nuclear arms pacts got under way: the agreements had been reached by a president with a long record of militant anti-communism; had been approved early on by the Joint Chiefs of Staff; were supported by a secretary of defense (Melvin R. Laird) with a congressional record of backing a strong military posture; and had been negotiated in a period of relaxed tensions between the United States and the Soviet Union.

The Senate August 3 gave its approval to ratification of the ABM treaty by a vote of 88–2, after the Foreign Relations Committee unanimously approved both the treaty and the interim agreements. In urging Senate support for the accords, however, the committee made clear that a majority of its members questioned the need for an ABM site to protect Washington, D.C., or for accelerated development of offensive weapons as requested by the administration.

James B. Allen, D-Ala., and James L. Buckley, C-N.Y., cast the only votes against the ABM treaty. Both argued that the treaty, by limiting each nation to two ABM sites, would expose their civilian populations to destruction in the event of nuclear war.

Despite the Senate's quick approval of the ABM treaty, the debate was far from over. The treaty became the focus of pro-

tracted arms control battles between the White House and Congress in the 1980s and 1990s. *(See box, Institutional Prerogatives in Arms Control Debate, p. 212.)*

The interim agreement had some difficult moments on Capitol Hill before it was approved September 25. The House gave routine consideration to the resolution authorizing approval of the five-year U.S.-Soviet pact. The resolution was passed August 18 by a 329–7 vote after about an hour of debate. No changes were made on the floor.

But when the measure reached the Senate, the going was rougher. Breaking a six-week deadlock, the Senate September 14 approved it, 88–2, after insisting on a stiff U.S. bargaining stance in subsequent nuclear arms talks with the Soviet Union. The hard-line instructions for the SALT negotiators were contained in an amendment, sponsored by Henry M. Jackson, D-Wash., which requested that any future permanent treaty on offensive nuclear arms "not limit the United States to levels of intercontinental strategic forces inferior to" those of the Soviet Union, but rather be based on "the principle of equality." The amendment stipulated that failure to negotiate a permanent treaty limiting offensive arms would be grounds for abrogating the U.S.-Soviet

ABM agreement. It also endorsed the maintenance of a vigorous research, development, and modernization program. The Jackson amendment was adopted, 56–35, after its supporters had beaten back several attempts to weaken it.

The White House August 7 endorsed Jackson's effort after he modified his proposal by dropping a stipulation that any Soviet action or deployment that threatened U.S. deterrent capability would be grounds for repudiating the interim agreement. In its place, Jackson and the White House agreed on a statement that failure to negotiate an offensive arms treaty by 1977 would be grounds for repudiating the ABM treaty—a position already taken by the administration.

The Jackson and other amendments added to the measure had no effect on the accord itself. But they served to emphasize the disquiet of many members of Congress concerning the terms of the interim agreement.

Final action came September 25 when the House, by a 308–4 vote, approved a resolution accepting the Senate amendments.

SALT II Treaty. The proposed SALT II treaty set basic numerical limits on intercontinental missiles and bombers that were to be in effect until 1985.

Through nearly six months of Senate committee action on the treaty, beginning July 8, 1979, the Carter administration argued that restrictions on the arms race were of such vital importance that they should be considered on their own merits, regardless of various ongoing U.S.-Soviet conflicts. The administration insisted that the treaty would be militarily advantageous to the United States since it would halt some Soviet arms programs and at the same time not interfere with planned U.S. weapons programs. To win the support of key Senate conservatives, the administration and Senate backers of the treaty had to agree to substantially higher defense spending.

Treaty opponents maintained that SALT II would not prevent a substantial Soviet strategic arms buildup and thus would leave Moscow capable, theoretically, of destroying the entire U.S. ICBM force by 1982. On broader, political grounds they argued that the treaty would be dangerous to the United States by anesthetizing Congress and the public to the need for increases in U.S. defense efforts at home and for resistance to Soviet adventurism around the world.

The Foreign Relations Committee approved the treaty by a 9–6 vote November 9, 1979, after adopting several reservations. However, the Armed Services Committee, which had no formal jurisdiction over the treaty, held separate hearings and issued its own report in which it concluded that the treaty, as submitted to Congress, was not in the national security interests of the United States. The report was approved by a 10–0 vote, with seven committee members voting "present."

Senate approval of the SALT II treaty was foreclosed by the Soviet invasion of Afghanistan December 27, 1979. President Carter January 3, 1980, asked the Senate majority leader to defer action on the treaty. Treaty supporters and opponents agreed that Carter's decision simply reflected the political reality that the pact would not have come even close to winning the neces-

sary two-thirds majority in the wake of the Soviet invasion and other adverse international developments.

Even before the Soviet invasion, it was questionable whether the treaty could win Senate approval, despite Congress's extensive role in the SALT II process under Carter. The administration had consulted with Senator Jackson and other hard-liners on negotiating positions and had appointed fourteen representatives and thirty senators as advisers to the SALT delegation. One observer described the congressional involvement as "a marked departure from the earlier SALT period and . . . unprecedented in the modern history of treaty negotiations."[22]

But Carter was unable to win support from two quarters. First, the administration's insistence that SALT II was militarily advantageous to the United States never was endorsed by some of the Senate Democrats who had strong reputations as defense specialists. Jackson kept up an unremitting drumfire of attack, and Sam Nunn of Georgia, a key Armed Services Committee member, withheld his endorsement, even after Carter met Nunn's demand for a commitment to increased defense spending.

Second, GOP support had been crucial to Carter's other foreign and defense policy victories—most notably the 1978 battle over the Panama Canal treaties. But Minority Leader Howard H. Baker Jr., R-Tenn., opposed the SALT treaty, and the administration was unable to find any other conservative Republican to give the treaty a bipartisan flavor.

Given the treaty's uncertain backing, developments in the 1980s seemed somewhat ironic. Not only did the United States comply with the unratified pact, Congress demanded that it do so. Both the United States and the Soviet Union informally observed the agreement's numerical limits on certain weapons, on a reciprocal basis.

President Ronald Reagan, who had denounced SALT II for years as being advantageous to the Soviet Union, delighted liberals and confounded some of his staunchest conservative allies when he decided in 1985 that he would "go the extra mile" to maintain SALT II by dismantling an older missile-launching submarine as a new one went into service.

But the following year Reagan announced that the United States would no longer observe the SALT II agreement because the Soviets had repeatedly violated the terms of the treaty. Congress responded by approving nonbinding language urging the president to continue to observe the limits. A House attempt to make the requirement binding had been abandoned on the eve of a U.S.-Soviet summit meeting, largely because members were loath to undercut Reagan's negotiating position.

The move by the House to continue observance of SALT II was attacked by the administration as an attempt to bypass the treaty ratification process and to micromanage strategic arms negotiations in Geneva. But Dante B. Fascell, D-Fla., chairman of the House Foreign Affairs Committee, defended the House action: "If a congressional mandate happens to coincide with a former presidential policy expressed in the unratified treaty, then that is certainly not unconstitutional and it has nothing to

INSTITUTIONAL PREROGATIVES IN ARMS CONTROL DEBATE

The quick approval the Senate gave the 1972 antiballistic missile (ABM) treaty between the United States and the Soviet Union belied the contentious battles that lay ahead. At issue in the 1980s and 1990s was how the provisions of the treaty would mesh with proposals to develop a national antimissile defense system.

Congress and the White House repeatedly fought over how to interpret the treaty and whether to comply with it, amend it, or withdraw from it. The debate encompassed not only substantive defense issues but also questions of legislative and executive prerogatives under the constitutional treaty power.

REAGAN ADMINISTRATION

The ABM pact codified a relationship of "mutually assured destruction," which assumed that each country would be deterred from attacking by their fear of the other's retaliation. Though the treaty was signed by Republican President Richard M. Nixon and approved by an overwhelming majority in the Senate, conservatives rejected its logic from the outset, insisting that the United States should base its security on its own defensive efforts. *(See "SALT I Agreements," p. 209.)*

President Ronald Reagan ignited controversy in 1983 when he announced plans to develop a nationwide antimissile defense known as the strategic defense initiative (SDI). The traditional interpretation of the ABM treaty was that it covered all existing and future antimissile systems. Critics of Reagan's proposal argued, among other things, that the 1972 ABM treaty ruled out many of the exotic antimissile weapons envisioned for SDI. The Reagan administration at first assured its critics that, for years to come, the program would be conducted in accord with the limits of the treaty.

But the issue came to the forefront in the mid-1980s, when some officials within the administration began pressing Reagan to accelerate the timetable for SDI deployment, which would require tests that would violate the traditional interpretation. The administration subsequently announced a new, broader interpretation that held that the negotiating record showed that the treaty had barred only 1972-style equipment and not future space-based ABM testing. The White House insisted that the interpretation of the treaty was its prerogative.

The issue was argued on several levels on Capitol Hill. For some it was a question of being for or against SDI. But for others the constitutional issue was paramount. Political scientist Thomas E. Mann wrote: "The administration's tactic, by challenging so directly the Senate's authority as ratifier and thus ultimate arbiter of treaties, forced a more process-based opposition led by Senate Armed Services Committee Chairman Sam Nunn, D-Ga. Nunn's opposition to the president's reinterpretation of the ABM treaty attracted support from a wide range of senators precisely because it was based on issues of process, not substance."[1]

Nunn battled for nearly a year to win access for selected members of Congress to the secret negotiating record that was the basis for the administration's revised reading of the treaty. In a letter to Reagan in February 1987, Nunn demanded that the administration consult with Congress and warned that, without a consensus, Congress would make "much deeper SDI cuts than would otherwise occur." In addition, Nunn declared that if the president unilaterally disregarded the interpretation of the treaty that had been presented to the Senate in 1972, he "would provoke a constitutional confrontation of profound dimensions."

And in March 1987 Nunn weighed in with his long-awaited analysis of the negotiating record, the record of committee hearings and

do with the president's treaty-making power. The House determined a benchmark for weapons production, and in this case it conformed with the sub-limits set forth in the SALT II treaty."[23]

Congress soon added teeth to its wishes. Despite strong opposition from the Reagan White House, the 100th Congress in 1987 and again in 1988 approved provisions requiring the retirement of U.S. missile-launching submarines in order to reduce the extent to which new weapons deployments would outstrip the SALT II numerical limits.

The net effect of the congressional action was to continue de facto observance of the treaty, although there was no explicit mention of the SALT II agreement. An obvious reason for not mentioning the treaty was the White House threat to veto any bill containing SALT II limits. A more subtle reason was Senate vigilance against any House inroads on its treaty power. As Barry M. Blechman wrote:

The compromises that emerged from House-Senate conferences made no mention of the treaty itself, so as to assuage Senate sensibilities about its unique role as arbiter of treaties. For the Senate to grant the House any explicit role concerning a treaty would be like the House permitting the Senate to initiate a tax bill. Few things are guarded more jealously in the Congress than the respective prerogatives of the two chambers.[24]

Panama Canal Treaties

Aside from the Vietnam War backlash of the late 1960s, there had been few foreign policy battles in the preceding thirty years to match the national emotions roused by the Panama Canal treaties. The product of negotiations that formally began in 1964 but had in fact gone on intermittently ever since the original pact was signed in 1903, the basic treaty proposed to turn over the U.S.-constructed, -owned, and -operated Panama Canal to the government of Panama by the year 2000.

A second treaty, a neutrality treaty, guaranteed the United States and Panama the right to defend the canal after December 31, 1999.

The two treaties were signed by President Carter and Panamanian leader Brig. Gen. Omar Torrijos Herrera on September 7, 1977, but it was not until the spring of 1978 that the Senate approved them with just one vote more than the two-thirds ma-

floor debate in 1972, and the Reagan administration position. Nunn told the Senate in a speech that extended over three days (March 11, 12, and 13) that the preponderance of evidence in the negotiating record supported the Senate's original understanding of the treaty.

Nunn's views were backed by a majority of his colleagues on Capitol Hill. By considerable margins, the Senate and House in 1987 added amendments to the defense authorization bill in effect barring SDI tests in space that would violate the traditional interpretation of the ABM treaty. The ban was enacted again in 1988 and 1989.

The Senate revisited the treaty interpretation issue in 1988 when it considered the U.S.-Soviet treaty banning intermediate-range nuclear-force (INF) missiles. To prevent a replay of the confrontation over the ABM treaty, the Senate adopted an amendment to the resolution of approval of the INF treaty stipulating that neither the current nor any future president could depart from any interpretation of the treaty that had been officially presented to the Senate. *(See "INF Treaty," p. 215.)*

BUSH ADMINISTRATION

With the Soviet empire crumbling in the early 1990s, President George Bush proposed to refocus the antimissile defense program to protect against a more limited attack, but the proposals still ran counter to the ABM treaty. Congress for its part came up with a compromise that was consistent with the treaty but also called on the president to negotiate changes in the treaty to allow more extensive tests and deployments. The Bush administration negotiated with Russia but reached no conclusions.

CLINTON ADMINISTRATION

The Clinton administration in 1993 ended efforts to broaden the ABM treaty and reduced the national defense program to an effort to develop relevant technologies, with no commitment to deploy a defense.

But the issue came to the forefront once again when the Republicans won control of Congress in the 1994 elections. Republicans tried to run over or around the treaty and force Clinton to build a national antimissile defense system no matter what the Russians thought. But the administration argued that only with the 1972 treaty in place would Moscow have the confidence to reduce the size of its missile force. Clinton vetoed a defense authorization bill in 1995 in large part because it mandated a system that would have violated the treaty.

Clinton, however, shifted gears in 1996 and decided to recast the effort into a program aimed at developing a system within three years that could be fielded in another three. The administration acknowledged the possibility of choosing a system that would require amendments to the treaty.

The Republican crusade for a national defense shield against ballistic missiles lost much of its steam in light of Clinton's new proposal and a general lack of public interest in the issue. But Republicans insisted on a role in amending the treaty. One of the concessions Clinton made to win approval of a chemical weapons treaty in 1997 was his commitment to submit to the Senate as treaty amendments changes that U.S. and Russian negotiators had agreed to in 1996. Since these amendments would require a two-thirds Senate majority for approval, this would give conservative critics another chance to affect the direction of the antimissile defense program.

1. Thomas E. Mann, ed., *A Question of Balance: The President, the Congress, and Foreign Policy* (Washington, D.C.: Brookings Institution, 1990), 24.

---

jority needed for ratification. All told, the debate had lasted thirty-eight days—the longest on a treaty since the Treaty of Versailles. In all, eighty-eight proposed changes were voted on during Senate debate on the two treaties.

At the heart of the debate over the future of the canal—long a symbol of American power and engineering ability—lay basic foreign policy and national security issues. Supporters argued that the practical advantage of the treaties for the United States was that the canal would be open, neutral, secure, and efficiently operated without cost to U.S. taxpayers. For Panama, there would be economic benefits from toll revenues and, most important, full jurisdiction over its own territory.

The degree of involvement of senators in direct negotiations with Panamanian officials after the signing of the treaties was unprecedented. From the signing of the treaties in September 1977 until the opening of floor debate in February 1978, nearly half the Senate toured the fifty-one mile waterway, met with Panamanian officials, including General Torrijos, and received political and military briefings from U.S. officials stationed in the country. In addition to providing information, these trips, according to one detailed account, "also served a rather unique and innovative function in the treaty-making process. In some instances, such as with the group led by [Senate Republican Leader] Howard Baker, the senators worked out deals and compromises with General Torrijos in order to improve the chances the Senate would pass the treaties."[25]

At the start of Senate debate on the treaties the leadership counted sixty-two members favoring the agreements, twenty-eight opposed, and ten undecided. Sixty-seven votes were needed for Senate approval if all senators voted.

In contrast to the streamlined approach of considering the treaties as a whole—the practice followed since 1922, partially as a result of the defeat of the Treaty of Versailles—the Senate debated the Panama treaties article by article.

Taking up the neutrality treaty first, the Senate deleted a number of amendments dubbed "killer" amendments by treaty backers, because they would have required new negotiations between the United States and Panama and thus would have jeopardized the treaty. However, the outcome was still in doubt March 16, the day set for the vote on the neutrality pact.

President Jimmy Carter and Panamanian leader Brig. Gen. Omar Torrijos Herrera sign the Panama Canal Treaty in 1977. After a lengthy, emotional debate in 1978, the Senate ratified the treaty, which provided for transfer of control of the canal from the U.S. to Panama in 2000.

The administration agreed to accept two understandings to the treaty. Based on an agreement reached between Carter and Torrijos, these alterations (1) gave the United States the right to defend the canal if it were threatened, and (2) granted "head of the line" passage privileges for U.S. ships during emergencies.

Besides these changes, the administration accepted two reservations (technically called conditions) as the price for winning crucial last-minute votes. One stated that provisions of the treaty did not prevent the United States and Panama from working out an agreement for stationing U.S. forces in Panama after 1999. The other, authored by Dennis DeConcini, D-Ariz., allowed the United States to "use military forces in the Republic of Panama" after the year 1999 to reopen the canal should it be closed for any reason.

On March 16, the twenty-second day of debate, the Senate approved the neutrality treaty, 68–32.

The Senate then turned to the basic treaty. In the days following approval of the neutrality treaty, little seemed to stand in the way of a second success. But the outlook was less optimistic in early April after Panama circulated a letter at the United Nations complaining that the DeConcini reservation would give the United States the right to intervene in Panama's internal affairs, contrary to an October 14, 1977, agreement between Carter and Torrijos.

The problem facing the Senate leadership was to find a way

to assure Panama that the DeConcini reservation did not violate U.S. nonintervention principles while maintaining DeConcini's wording giving the United States the right to use military force to reopen the canal if it were closed. Negotiations with DeConcini were handled by the Democratic leadership after the Carter administration failed to come up with language preserving the thrust of the senator's reservation. The leadership's compromise was to offer a reservation to the basic treaty stating that any action the United States might take to keep the canal "open, neutral, secure, and accessible" did not give the United States the right to intervene in Panama's internal affairs.

On April 16 Senate Majority Leader Robert C. Byrd, D-W.Va., and the floor managers of the treaties met with representatives of the Panamanian government and the Carter administration to present the compromise text. Senate leaders were informed later that day that Panama had accepted the compromise. The Senate adopted several other reservations and understandings, before approving the second of the two treaties on April 18 by the same 68–32 vote cast on the neutrality pact.

Hoping to involve the House in the canal controversy, and thus weaken support for the treaties, opponents had maintained that the House as well as the Senate had to approve all agreements turning the canal over to the Panamanians. They based their claim on numerous arguments, including alleged constitutional grounds. The United States owned the waterway, they contended, because the Canal Zone was conveyed to the United States in perpetuity by the 1903 treaty. Therefore, to dispose of U.S. land both the House and Senate needed to give their consent, as required by Article IV, Section 3, Clause 2 of the Constitution.

Using this argument, sixty members of the House filed suit in federal court challenging the president's authority to sign the Panama Canal treaties. The U.S. Circuit Court of Appeals for the District of Columbia turned back the challenge on April 6, 1978, just days before the final vote on the treaty. The court ruled that Congress's power to dispose of U.S. property was not exclusive and, therefore, did not preclude the president from using his treaty power to convey U.S. property in the Canal Zone to the Panamanian government. On May 15, 1978, the Supreme Court declined to review the lower court's decision.

Legislation to implement the treaty prolonged the canal debate into 1979 and 1980. The implementing bill was first rejected by the House before a slightly altered version was passed just five days before the treaties were to take effect. As enacted, the measure permitted much greater congressional control than the Carter administration had envisaged.

INF Treaty

The Senate in 1988 gave its approval to a landmark U.S.-Soviet treaty banning intermediate-range nuclear-force (INF) missiles. The INF agreement, the first arms accord between the two powers to be ratified since 1972, was the most important arms control achievement of the Reagan presidency.

The treaty required the destruction within three years of all missiles with ranges of between 500 and 5,500 kilometers (roughly 300 to 3,400 miles), together with their associated launchers and support facilities. To verify compliance, the pact established an unprecedented system for each country's inspectors to visit, on very short notice, facilities in the other country where the banned missiles had been deployed, stored, or serviced.

In calling for the destruction of an entire class of nuclear weapons, the INF treaty embodied the so-called zero-option, which had been widely dismissed as unrealistic when President Reagan first proposed it in November 1981. The pact had been viewed with profound misgivings by centrist national security experts in both parties, such as Senate Armed Services Committee Chairman Nunn and former Secretary of State Henry A. Kissinger, who feared that removal of the missiles would erode the nuclear threat on which NATO historically had relied to offset the more numerous conventional forces of the Soviet-led Warsaw Pact.

But once the treaty was signed in December 1987, most of the centrists, including Nunn and Kissinger, reluctantly supported Senate approval for fear that public opinion in some Western European countries would be outraged if the agreement fell apart.

Politically, the INF treaty offered something for everyone. It gave Reagan a major arms accord in the final year of his presidency, when his sights were trained on his place in history. It gave Republicans a popular election-year defense vote and helped them argue that events had vindicated their past support for Reagan's peace-through-strength defense budgets. And for Democratic arms control advocates, having the INF treaty negotiated by a hard-liner such as Reagan lent the force of bipartisanship to their cause. About the only opponents of the INF treaty were conservatives who argued that the treaty was flawed in detail and in its basic assumption that the Soviets could be trusted. But the band of conservatives was too small to pose a significant threat to the pact: in the end only five senators voted against approving the agreement.

The treaty was reported by the Foreign Relations Committee March 30 by a lopsided vote of 17–2. The Senate Armed Services Committee on March 28 had urged approval of the treaty 18–2.

Even though Senate approval was a foregone conclusion, several disputes prolonged consideration of the treaty. Before the treaty came to the floor in May 1988, Senate demands for clarification of two issues sent treaty negotiators back to the bargaining table in Geneva. At issue were questions about whether futuristic weapons were banned by the treaty and about the scope of the treaty's detailed inspection provisions. Majority Leader Byrd announced that the Senate would not take up the treaty until the loose ends had been tied up. The way was cleared for Senate action only after negotiators signed two addenda to the treaty settling the disagreements.

Another dispute reflected the long power struggle between Senate Democrats and the White House over the making and interpretation of treaties and, more specifically, Reagan's attempt to reinterpret the 1972 ABM treaty to permit certain tests of the strategic defense initiative (SDI), Reagan's proposed antimissile defense. Senate Democrats rejected his approach and argued that the traditional reading of the 1972 treaty barred testing of the SDI. (*See box, Institutional Prerogatives in Arms Control Debate, p. 212.*)

With the ABM treaty dispute fresh in their minds, senators adopted by a 72–27 vote an amendment to the INF treaty's resolution of ratification stating that no president could later repudiate, without Senate approval, treaty interpretations presented by administration aides during the ratification process.

The Senate cast its 93–5 vote in favor of ratification on May 27, in time for ratification at a summit meeting in Moscow on June 1.

CFE, START Treaties

Two major arms control treaties were signed in the early 1990s, amid enormous uncertainty as to how the agreements would play out. One treaty required the destruction of tens of thousands of conventional forces in Europe (CFE). The other, a strategic arms reduction talks (START) treaty, was intended to cut by about one-third the U.S. and Soviet arsenals of long-range, nuclear-armed missiles and bombers.

But world events were moving so quickly and dramatically that these traditional arms control agreements—arrived at through laborious superpower negotiations and loaded down with intricate trade-offs and safeguards—were effectively eclipsed by the crumbling of the Soviet Union.

In early 1993, the United States signed a second START treaty with Russia, the ultimate heir to the Soviet Union's nuclear force.

Conventional Forces. The Senate closed a chapter from the era of superpower military competition by overwhelmingly endorsing the CFE treaty just over a year after its November 19, 1990, signing in Paris by President George Bush, Soviet President Mikhail S. Gorbachev, and the leaders of twenty other nations.

The treaty imposed ceilings on military equipment deployed by NATO states and the former members of the Warsaw Pact in an area between the Atlantic Ocean and the Ural Mountains. The goal of the treaty from the outset had been sharp reductions in weapons that were seen as particularly useful in a blitzkrieg, a tactic NATO had feared for twenty years from the tank-heavy forces of the Soviet Union and its Warsaw Pact allies. Once-major provisions, such as a limit on troop levels in Europe, were dropped from the final accord, having become moot in light of the dramatic military retrenchment that already had taken place in the Soviet Union.

Most senators agreed that the pact was "demonstrably and overwhelmingly favorable to the United States and its NATO allies," as Senate Armed Services Committee Chairman Nunn put it. But a handful of Republicans opposed the resolution of ratification, charging that the Soviets had violated the treaty's provisions even before its ratification.

The Senate vote on the resolution, taken on November 25, 1991, was 90–4. The Senate Foreign Relations Committee had approved the treaty unanimously on November 19, after attaching five conditions to which the administration did not object. A sixth was added on the floor.

The Senate committee also had added four declarations. To avoid a repeat of the battle over the White House's attempt to reinterpret the ABM treaty, the Senate stipulated that its approval of the CFE treaty was based on the assumption that the administration had provided "authoritative" testimony about the interpretation of the pact. *(See box, Institutional Prerogatives in Arms Control Debate, p. 212.)*

The CFE treaty was amended in 1997 to meet some of the problems that had risen in its implementation in the post-Soviet era. The resolution of approval of the amendment, adopted 100–0 on May 14, included a controversial condition requiring the president to obtain Senate approval for a proposed agreement to make four former Soviet republics parties to the separate 1972 ABM treaty. The White House had maintained that the president had the power to decide which republics would inherit the Soviet obligations under the ABM pact. But conservatives insisted that "multilateralizing" the pact to include the former Soviet states, instead of just Russia, would make it harder to negotiate a more liberal limit on antimissile systems and was therefore a significant change in the treaty requiring

approval by a two-thirds Senate majority. The Clinton administration and leading Senate Democrats opposed the provision but accepted it at the last minute.

START. Signed July 31, 1991, by Bush and Gorbachev, the START treaty provided for a reduction in the U.S. inventory of intercontinental nuclear bombs and missile warheads from more than 12,000 to fewer than 9,000. It provided for reducing the Soviet stock of such weapons from about 11,000 to 6,000. The treaty had been nearly a decade in the making, the talks having begun in 1982.

With the demise of the Soviet Union at the end of 1991, the treaty in some ways seemed to be a cold war anachronism. However, in a treaty amendment (or "protocol") signed May 23, 1992, the four republics that assumed control of the former Soviet nuclear arsenal agreed to take on the obligations the treaty would have imposed on the Soviet government. Under the protocol, only Russia was allowed to maintain nuclear weapons. The agreement bound the other republics—Ukraine, Belarus, and Kazakhstan—to forswear all nuclear weapons by signing the 1968 nuclear nonproliferation treaty. The three also signed letters in which they promised to dispose of all deployed strategic weapons within seven years.

The Senate Foreign Relations Committee on July 2, 1992, unanimously approved a resolution to ratify the treaty, after adding to the resolution several conditions. Blocking attempts by a few conservatives to amend the treaty and strengthening one of the conditions, the Senate easily approved ratification by a vote of 93–6 on October 1.

START II. A second START treaty was signed by Bush and Russian President Boris N. Yeltsin on January 3, 1993. START II called for slashing U.S. and Russian nuclear weapons deployed to no more than 6,500 weapons—3,500 for the United States and 3,000 for Russia. The agreement would eliminate all land-based intercontinental ballistic missiles equipped with multiple warheads—the backbone of the Russian nuclear arsenal—and make deep cuts in the number of warheads on submarine-launched missiles, which made up the largest part of the U.S. force.

A resolution of ratification was unanimously approved by the Senate Foreign Relations Committee on December 12, 1995. The Senate on January 26, 1996, approved the pact by a vote of 87–4. To answer some conservative GOP members' concerns about the administration's nuclear reduction policy, the Senate by voice vote attached to the resolution of ratification a package of eight declarations and one condition.

By mid-1999 Russia still had not ratified the treaty.

Chemical Weapons Treaty

On January 13, 1993, the United States, Russia, China, and more than 120 other countries signed a treaty that sought to eliminate chemical weapons within twenty years. The far-reaching treaty banned the use of chemical weapons in combat, as well as the development, production, purchase, or stockpiling of chemical weapons for battlefield use. Negotiated by the Reagan and Bush administrations, it was signed shortly before Bush left office and had the strong backing of the Clinton administration.

The Senate approved the treaty's ratification in 1997 after a costly battle with conservative Republicans who saw the treaty as fatally flawed. Treaty opponents contended that the few nations that posed the most plausible chemical-weapons threat were unlikely to submit to the treaty. They were also highly critical of the treaty's verification procedures, arguing that they would put onerous reporting burdens on chemical companies, were intrusive enough to put trade secrets of U.S. companies at risk, and were unlikely to catch violators.

The Senate Foreign Relations Committee approved a resolution ratifying the treaty by a vote of 13–5 on April 25, 1996, after attaching seven conditions and eleven declarations. The panel voted to eliminate language authored by committee chairman Jesse Helms, R-N.C., that would have effectively ruled out U.S. assent to the pact by holding U.S. ratification in abeyance until the treaty had been ratified by rogue nations, such as Libya, Iraq, Syria, and North Korea.

Floor action was scheduled for later in 1996 but the Clinton administration asked for a deferral after a vigorous campaign by Helms and other GOP conservatives made it doubtful that the resolution would pass by the two-thirds majority needed. The biggest factor in derailing the treaty was the last-minute opposition of GOP presidential candidate and former Senate majority leader Bob Dole of Kansas.

The treaty was finally approved by the Senate on April 24, 1997, by a vote of 74–26. It was a big win for President Bill Clinton, but the victory came at a hefty price. The Senate added to the resolution twenty-eight understandings—negotiated between Helms and ranking Foreign Relations Democrat Joseph R. Biden of Delaware, and agreed to by the White House—limiting the treaty's reach. Biden and other treaty supporters managed to defeat five additional provisions backed by Helms that they said would have rendered the treaty useless.

Clinton made significant concessions on collateral issues. The White House agreed to restructure the nation's foreign policy agencies, a top Helms goal. Clinton also agreed to submit to the Senate as treaty amendments the changes he had negotiated with Russia to the 1972 ABM treaty and the 1990 CFE treaty.

On the morning of the treaty vote, Senate Majority Leader Trent Lott, R-Miss., won a final concession from Clinton—a letter in which the president promised that the United States would withdraw from the treaty if two contentious sections of the pact—dealing with the right to obtain antichemical defense technology and to conduct international trade in chemicals—ever allowed unfriendly nations to acquire chemical weapons or compromised U.S. security.

Congress also added restrictions to 1998 legislation implementing the treaty.

Comprehensive Nuclear Test Ban

The Senate in 1999 handed the Clinton administration a humiliating defeat, when it rejected the 1996 Comprehensive Test Ban Treaty. It was the first time the Senate had rejected an international security agreement since the Treaty of Versailles in 1920. *(See Table 5-1, p. 203.)*

The controversial test ban treaty became entangled in a series of partisan political skirmishes and in the end fell nineteen votes short of the two-thirds majority needed for Senate approval.

The treaty had been a long-sought prize for President Clinton and arms control advocates, who touted it as the most effective means of halting a global arms race. But critics insisted that the treaty was dangerously flawed, questioning the impact of a test ban on the long-term effectiveness of the U.S. nuclear arsenal and whether the treaty was enforceable.

A partial test ban accord halting all but underground tests had been reached in 1963 but it was not until 1994 that serious talks on a comprehensive ban had begun. A treaty was concluded in 1996. On September 24, 1996, Clinton became the first world leader to sign it. *(See "Nuclear Test Ban Accord," p. 208.)*

The 1996 treaty was intended to ban all nuclear explosions, including those for peaceful purposes and those underground. An international network of monitoring stations was to verify compliance. The treaty allowed tests of nuclear weapons components, including the high explosives used to trigger the weapons, as long as no radioactivity was released. It also allowed on-site inspections—on short notice, in some cases—where testing was suspected.

The treaty could not take effect until it had been approved by forty-four nations that had either nuclear power plants or nuclear research reactors. Although 154 countries had signed the treaty, only twenty-six of the forty-four nations with nuclear capabilities had ratified it by the time the Senate took it up.

Administration officials had lobbied sporadically for the treaty after Clinton submitted it to the Senate in September 1997. They stepped up their efforts in advance of an October 1999 conference of treaty signatories to determine what might be done to get nonratifying members to join.

The Senate Republican leadership, which staunchly opposed the treaty, startled Democrats when on October 1, 1999, it abruptly yielded to Democratic demands and proposed to schedule a vote after twenty-two hours of debate. Democrats complained that the amount of time was inadequate but reluctantly accepted. Within days, however, they realized they could not attract enough GOP votes to approve the treaty and a bipartisan group of senators began struggling to craft a graceful exit strategy. They said they feared the treaty's defeat would send an alarming and unwelcome signal to other nations—mainly India, Pakistan, and North Korea—that either had developed or were interested in developing nuclear weapons of their own.

Protracted haggling over delaying the vote produced a turbulent week of public statements, rampant rumor, and backroom arm-twisting over the treaty's fate. Senate Foreign Relations Chairman Helms, one of the treaty's most ardent opponents, insisted that Clinton promise in writing that the pact would not come up again for the remainder of his presidency. Clinton did ask that the vote be postponed but refused to forswear the treaty for the rest of the 106th Congress.

Twenty-four Republicans and thirty-eight Democrats signed a letter to Senate Majority Leader Lott and Senate Minority Leader Tom Daschle, D-S.D., asking that consideration of the treaty be postponed. Lott and Daschle seemed at one point to reach a compromise, but Lott could not bring around a handful of key conservatives who vowed to block any attempt to postpone the vote.

Prior to the final vote on Oct. 13, Daschle forced a crucial test vote on a motion to move to executive session. But the vote was seen as a test of party loyalty, and lawmakers cast a party-line vote of 55–45. The 48–51 vote to defeat the treaty also fell largely along party lines. Four Republicans joined forty-four Democrats in support of the treaty. (Robert C. Byrd, D-W. Va., voted present.)

Lott said the Senate rejected the treaty on its merits because it "is ineffectual, even dangerous, in my judgment." But Clinton called the Senate vote "politics, pure and simple." Both Clinton and Senate Democrats vowed to continue to fight for ratification and said they would make the treaty an election issue.

Executive Agreements: Congressional Concerns

International agreements other than treaties are called executive agreements. They are understandings between heads of state or their designees that do not require the approval of the Senate. These agreements may be oral or written and have the force of law, although, unlike treaties, they do not supersede U.S. laws with which they conflict.

The vast majority of international pacts are executive agreements. Most of those deal with routine matters, such as the regulation of fishing rights, private claims against another government, and postal agreements. But in a few cases major U.S. foreign policies have been carried out by executive agreements, sometimes with far-reaching results. Among the more controversial agreements in modern times were the 1940 deal with Great Britain to trade U.S. destroyers for bases in British territories in the Western Hemisphere, the Yalta and Potsdam agreements of 1945, the Vietnam peace agreement of 1973, the Sinai agreement of 1975, and agreements for military base rights in Spain, Diego Garcia, and Bahrain. Major trade policies have also been set by executive agreements, including the 1992 North American Free Trade Agreement (NAFTA) and the 1994 General Agreement on Tariffs and Trade (GATT).

The executive branch's right to conclude executive agreements with foreign powers has been accepted since the early days of the Republic and has been repeatedly upheld by the courts. Most executive agreements are sanctioned by Congress, either through advance authorization in statutes or treaty provisions or through such vehicles as joint resolutions expressing support or legislation implementing the agreements. But a small percentage are negotiated and implemented without congressional approval, resting instead on the president's powers in foreign relations or as commander in chief. According to scholar Louis Fisher, presidents have cited four sources of constitutional authority under which they may enter into executive agreements: (1) duty as chief executive to represent the nation in foreign affairs; (2) authority to receive ambassadors and other public ministers; (3) authority as commander in chief; and (4) duty to "take care that the laws be faithfully executed."[26]

INCREASED USE IN WORLD WAR II

The number of executive agreements skyrocketed during and after World War II, as the United States greatly increased its foreign policy activities. During the eighteenth and nineteenth centuries presidents concluded an average of only one executive agreement per year. But by the 1930s executive agreements were as common as treaties. In 1946–1998 less than 6 percent of all international agreements were treaties. (See Table 5-2, p. 219.)

Modern presidents have viewed executive agreements as essential instruments for the conduct of diplomacy in a world of rapid communications and the threat of nuclear war. Executive agreements have the advantage of speed, flexibility, and secrecy, in contrast to treaties, which are subject to a complex, cumbersome, and public process.

But the use of executive agreements in the post–World War II years alarmed a growing number of lawmakers, who charged that some of the agreements had resulted in major commitments of American resources or had implemented significant policy decisions without the input of Congress. They saw the greater use of executive agreements as presidential usurpation of the treaty power.

Political scientist Lawrence Margolis expressed a contrary view:

It is very difficult to estimate what percentage of executive agreements are attempts by the president to avoid having to pass a treaty through the Senate. The State Department has stated that at least 90 percent of all executive agreements follow the will of Congress. . . . I would guess that their estimate is a pretty good one. The overwhelming majority of executive agreements would receive little opposition from Congress.[27]

But it was the relatively rare instances when presidents concluded controversial agreements abroad that troubled members of Congress. The executive branch argued on constitutional, foreign policy, and pragmatic grounds against placing any curbs on such agreements, suggesting instead a more informal and cooperative relationship between the legislative and executive branches. But that approach failed to satisfy Congress.

CONGRESSIONAL RESPONSE

Under a law enacted in 1950, the secretary of state was directed to compile and publish annually the contents of all treaties and executive agreements entered into during the previous year. In practice, however, agreements considered sensitive to national security were withheld from Congress as a whole and even

TABLE 5-2 Agreements and Treaties, 1789–1998

The following table lists the number of published treaties and executive agreements entered into by the United States.

Varying definitions of what comprises an executive agreement and their entry-into-force dates make all numbers approximate. State Department compilations for international agreements, other than treaties, include agreements concluded on the basis of prior or subsequent legislation, existing treaties, and the constitutional authority of the president.

Year	Treaties	Executive agreements	Year	Treaties	Executive agreements
1789–1839	60	27	1964	3	222
1839–1889	215	238	1965	14	204
1889–1929	382	763	1966	14	237
1930	25	11	1967	18	223
1931	13	14	1968	18	197
1932	11	16	1969	6	162
1933	9	11	1970	20	183
1934	14	16	1971	17	214
1935	25	10	1972	20	287
1936	8	16	1973	17	241
1937	15	10	1974	13	230
1938	12	24	1975	13	264
1939	10	26	1976	13	402[b]
1940	12	20	1977	17	424
1941	15	39	1978	15	417
1942	6	52	1979	28	378
1943	4	71	1980	26	321
1944	1	74	1981	12	322
1945	6[a]	54	1982	17	343
1946	19	139	1983	23	282
1947	15	144	1984	15	336
1948	16	178	1985	8	336
1949	22	148	1986	17	400
1950	11	157	1987	12	434
1951	21	213	1988	21	387
1952	22	291	1989	15	363
1953	14	163	1990	20	398
1954	17	206	1991	11	286
1955	7	297	1992	21	303
1956	15	233	1993	17	257
1957	9	222	1994	24	338
1958	10	197	1995	17	300
1959	12	250	1996	48	253
1960	5	266	1997	37	253
1961	9	260	1998	24	249
1962	10	319			
1963	17	234	Total	1,725	15,855

NOTES: a. Includes unpublished water treaty with Mexico, in force since November 18, 1945.   b. The sharp increase in agreements in 1976 reflected a large number of interagency-level agreements not previously included. The subsequent decline reflected in part the decision in October 1978 not to include aid agreements below a certain dollar level.

SOURCES: 1789–1929: Rep. Emanuel Celler, D-N.Y., *Congressional Record*, May 2, 1945, 4049; 1930–1945: Edwin M. Borchard, "Treaties and Executive Agreements," *American Political Science Review* 40 (August 1946): 735; 1946–1998: U.S. Department of State, Office of the Legal Adviser, Treaty Affairs.

from the committees with jurisdiction over the subject of the agreements.

Two years after rejecting the Bricker amendment, which would have curbed the president's powers to make treaties and executive agreements, the Senate unanimously passed, over the objections of the Eisenhower administration, a bill requiring all executive agreements to be submitted to the Senate within sixty days. The House never acted on the bill. *(See "Bricker Amendment," p. 204.)*

The issue was rekindled in the 1960s and 1970s because, according to Thomas E. Cronin, "while the Senate was asked to ratify international accords on trivial matters, the White House arranged critically important mutual aid and military-base agreements without even informing Congress."[28]

In 1972 secret agreements were uncovered by the Senate Foreign Relations Subcommittee on Security Agreements and Commitments Abroad. The subcommittee, chaired by Stuart Symington, D-Mo., found that commitments and secret conditions had been made throughout the 1960s to such countries as Ethiopia, Laos, Thailand, South Korea, and Spain.

Causing particular controversy was an agreement permitting the United States to use Spanish bases in return for American grants, loans, and other assistance. Sen. J. W. Fulbright, D-Ark., summed up the growing congressional sentiment: "We get many treaties dealing with postal affairs and so on. Recently, we had an extraordinary treaty dealing with the protection of stolen art objects. These are treaties. But when we put troops and take on commitments in Spain, it is an executive agreement."[29]

Adding to congressional frustrations were agreements made by the Nixon administration in 1971 with Portugal, on the use of an air base in the Azores, and with Bahrain, for naval base facilities in the Persian Gulf. The two agreements raised important foreign policy questions and should have been submitted as treaties, argued members of the Foreign Relations Committee. The Senate passed a sense of the Senate resolution to that effect.

Another legislative result of that controversy was congressional approval, initially over Nixon administration opposition, of a measure requiring the secretary of state to submit to Congress within sixty days the final text of any international agreement made by the executive branch. Those having national security implications were to be submitted on a classified basis to the House and Senate foreign policy committees. Sen. Clifford P. Case, R-N.J., the author of the legislation, argued that Congress could not adequately perform its duties without knowledge of commitments made by the executive branch. Both the Senate and House passed the bill unanimously.

Congress tightened reporting deadlines under the Case Act in 1977 and amended the act again in 1978 to make clear that oral agreements were to be submitted to Congress, to designate the secretary of state as the judge within the executive branch of what constitutes an international agreement, and to require a

British Prime Minister Winston Churchill addressed this joint session of Congress in the House chamber on May 19, 1943. He also had addressed a joint meeting in December 1941, shortly after the United States entered World War II. Churchill was one of many foreign leaders who have appeared before Congress over the years.

formal explanation from the president when agreements were not transmitted before the sixty-day deadline.

Although the Case Act dealt with the problem of secrecy, it did not provide for any formal congressional response to executive agreements. The Senate in 1974 passed a bill to establish congressional procedures for disapproving executive agreements, but the House did not act on it.

Congress does have other tools at its disposal for dealing with executive agreements. It can conduct investigations. It can adopt resolutions and pass legislation. It controls appropriations, a power seen by some as the principal safeguard for Congress's role in the area of executive agreements. But Fisher has questioned the effectiveness of Congress's power of the purse. Theoretically, Congress could withhold funds needed to implement an agreement, Fisher wrote, but "Congress finds it difficult to exercise its power of the purse if doing so means diplomatic embarrassment for the nation and humiliation to the president."[30]

The War Power: Continuing Controversy

The war power—like the treaty power—is split between Congress and the president. And, no less than the treaty power, it has been the subject of recurring controversy and debate involving rival claims by the executive and legislative branches.

Article II, Section 2, of the Constitution provides: "The President shall be Commander in Chief of the Army and Navy of the United States, and of the Militia of the several States, when called into the actual Service of the United States."

Article I, Section 8, provides: "The Congress shall have Power . . . To declare War, grant Letters of Marque and Reprisal, and make Rules concerning Captures on Land and Water; To raise and support Armies . . . ; To provide and maintain a Navy; To make Rules for the Government and Regulation of the land and naval Forces; To provide for calling forth the Militia to execute the Laws of the Union, suppress Insurrections and repel Invasions; To provide for organizing, arming, and disciplining the Militia, and for governing such Part of them as may be employed in the Service of the United States, reserving to the States respectively, the Appointment of the Officers, and the Authority of training the Militia according to the discipline prescribed by Congress."

ONGOING CONSTITUTIONAL DEBATE

At the time the American Constitution was framed, the war-making power in all other countries was vested in the executive. When the Constitutional Convention at Philadelphia took up this question, at the session of August 17, 1787, Pierce Butler, a delegate of South Carolina, proposed that the power to make war be granted to the president, "who will have all the requisite qualities and will not make war but when the nation will support it." Elbridge Gerry of Massachusetts thereupon objected that he "never expected to hear in a republic a motion to empower the executive alone to declare war." George Mason of Virginia also opposed "giving the power of war to the executive, because he is not safely to be trusted with it." He was "for clogging rather than facilitating war."[31]

Charles Pinckney of South Carolina contended that the proceedings of the House of Representatives were too slow and that it would be "too numerous for such deliberations." He suggested that the war power be placed in the Senate, which would be "more acquainted with foreign affairs and most capable of proper resolutions." The convention nevertheless conferred the power on Congress as a whole. It changed the phrase "to make war," as reported by the Committee of Detail, to "to declare war," so as to leave the president the power to repel sudden attacks but not to commence war.

The innovation of placing the war power in the legislative rather than the executive branch was hailed by Thomas Jefferson as a valuable restraint upon exercise of the power. He wrote to James Madison on September 6, 1789: "We have already given, in example, one effectual check to the dog of war, by transferring the power of letting him loose from the executive to the legislative body, from those who are to spend to those who are to pay." Madison himself wrote: "The Constitution supposes what the history of all governments demonstrates, that the executive is the branch of power most interested in war and most prone to it. It has accordingly, with studied care, vested the question of war in the legislature."

Writing in *Federalist* No. 69 against giving the war power to Congress, Alexander Hamilton noted that the power of the president as commander in chief would be "much inferior" to that of the British king; "it would amount to nothing more than the supreme command and direction of the military and naval forces, as first general and admiral . . . while that of the British King extends to the declaring of war and to the raising and regulating of fleets and armies—all of which, by the Constitution . . . would appertain to the legislature."

"Those who are to conduct a war cannot in the nature of things be proper or safe judges whether a war ought to be commenced, continued, or concluded," wrote Madison. "They are barred from the latter functions by a great principle in free government, analogous to that which separates the sword from the purse, or the power of executing from the power of enacting laws."

The debate over the division of the war powers between the executive and legislative branches was far from settled with the signing of the Constitution.

Shift to Executive Branch

"As with other constitutional issues," political scientist Cecil V. Crabb Jr. pointed out, "the precise balance or allocation of the war powers . . . has been determined more by experience, precedents, and circumstances than by the intentions of the founders or by contending legal theories." And the verdict of history has not been on Congress's side. "In this case, the overall tendency has been for legislative prerogatives to be eclipsed by executive initiative and leadership."[32]

Similarly, constitutional historian C. Herman Pritchett concluded that presidential powers are of "tremendous impact—so great in fact that to a considerable degree they cancel out the most important grant of external authority to Congress, the power to declare war."[33]

American government scholar Louis Fisher attributed this shift of power to three major developments:

First, the president acquired the responsibility to protect American life and property abroad. He has invoked that vague prerogative on numerous occasions to satisfy much larger objectives of the executive branch. Second, the time boundaries of the "war period" have become increasingly elastic. The president may initiate military operations before congressional action, and he retains wartime powers long after hostilities have ceased. Third, the postwar period, which has been marked by nuclear weapons, the cold war, intercontinental missiles, military alliances, and greater U.S. world responsibilities, has accelerated the growth of presidential power.[34]

Declared and Undeclared Wars

Estimates of the number of instances in which the United States has used its armed forces abroad vary depending on definitions and criteria. A 1999 Library of Congress study listed a total of 277 instances over two centuries, beginning with a naval conflict with France in 1798 and continuing through U.S. participation with NATO in extensive air strikes against Yugoslavia in 1999. The engagements ranged from the dispatching of a few soldiers or Marines to protect American lives and property abroad to the deployment of hundreds of thousands in Korea and Vietnam and millions in World War II.[35]

Congress has formally declared war in only five conflicts: the War of 1812, the Mexican War, the Spanish-American War, World War I, and World War II. (Congress has approved eleven separate formal declarations of war in all: against Great Britain in 1812, Mexico in 1846, Spain in 1898, Germany in 1917, Austria-Hungary in 1917, Japan in 1941, Germany in 1941, Italy in 1941, Bulgaria in 1942, Hungary in 1942, and Rumania in 1942.)[36]

No declaration of war was made or requested in the Naval War with France (1798–1800), the First Barbary War (1801–1805), the Second Barbary War (1815), or the various Mexican-American clashes of 1914–1917.

There have been no formal declarations of war since World War II, although U.S. combat troops were involved in wars in Korea (1950–1953), Vietnam (1963–1973), and the Persian Gulf (1991). Congress did pass resolutions supporting the presidential decision to use force in the latter two conflicts. The Persian Gulf resolution of 1991, in which Congress supported the use of force if needed to oust Iraqi invading forces from Kuwait, was regarded by many as the functional equivalent of a declaration of war. But there was no such consensus on Johnson administration claims that the 1964 Tonkin Gulf resolution authorized the executive to wage full-scale war in Vietnam.

The Vietnam War provoked extensive debate in the 1960s and 1970s over war powers. Some authorities contended that declarations of war were outmoded, given the existence of nuclear weapons and the need to commit troops overseas in emergencies on a limited war basis. So where did that leave Congress? Testifying before the Foreign Relations Committee in 1971, Alpheus T. Mason counseled:

The Framers, with deliberate care, made war making a joint enterprise. Congress is authorized to "declare war"; the president is designated "commander in chief." Technology has expanded the president's role and correspondingly curtailed the power of the Congress. Unchanged are the joint responsibilities of the president and Congress. The fact that a congressional declaration of war is no longer practical does not deprive Congress of constitutionally imposed authority in war making. On the contrary, it is under obligation to readjust its power position.[37]

Congress attempted to do just that in 1973 by passing the War Powers Resolution and in 1991 by insisting on a voice in the decision to go to war in the Persian Gulf. But clashes over the two branches' respective prerogatives continued, as administration after administration denied the constitutionality of the War Powers Resolution and gave cursory notice to Congress before committing U.S. forces overseas. Despite the disgruntlement—outrage, in some cases—voiced by some members, Congress declined to undercut its commander in chief.

THE DECLARED WARS

The early presidents made little use of their war powers. In 1798, during the undeclared naval war with France, John Adams went so far as to divest himself of the title of commander in chief and confer it upon George Washington. The Senate approved that action unanimously. Three years later President Jefferson forbade the Navy to attack the Tripoli pirates on the ground that Congress had not declared war. Alexander Hamilton ridiculed Jefferson for his inaction. Hamilton said the Constitution meant that it was "the peculiar and exclusive province of Congress, when the nation is at peace, to change that state into a state of war." But "when a foreign nation declares or openly and avowedly makes war upon the United States, they are then by the very fact already at war and any declaration on the part of Congress is nugatory; it is at least unnecessary."[38]

War of 1812

Congress's first declaration of war came in 1812. President James Madison's annual message of 1811 listed the familiar trade grievances against Great Britain and called upon Congress to "put the United States into an armor and an attitude demanded by the crisis." Congress in January 1812 approved legislation raising twenty-five thousand regular soldiers, but debate on a militia bill, authorizing the president to train and equip fifty thousand volunteers, bogged down on constitutional issues. Under the Constitution the president may call men into service for any of three purposes: to execute the laws, to put down insurrection, or to repel invasion.

In the situation that prevailed in 1812, however, it was well understood that the proposed volunteers were to accompany the regulars on an invasion of Canada, and most members of Congress felt it would be unconstitutional to use them outside the United States. The question was never settled, and the militia bill, as signed by Madison, said nothing about use of the volunteers beyond the nation's boundaries, an omission that subsequently had disastrous consequences.

Although twenty-five thousand regular troops probably could not have been trained and made available for at least a year—and the fifty thousand volunteers probably could not have been used in Canada—legislation to raise a provisional army of twenty thousand men for immediate service was voted down in the House.

The nation remained apathetic to the idea of actual hostilities. By June 1, 1812, when Madison asked for a declaration of war, less than half of the hoped-for twenty-five thousand regulars had enlisted, and adequate equipment was available for only ten thousand soldiers. Nevertheless, on June 4 the House voted 79–49 for war. The Senate concurred on June 17 by a vote of 19–13, after debating and rejecting proposals that would have limited the war to the high seas.

In accordance with the law, the secretary of war issued a call for the militia, but the governors of Massachusetts, Rhode Island, and Connecticut refused to authorize use of their troops. On July 6, 1812, Congress adjourned. Federalist members openly denounced the war as being against the wishes of the people. Within a month the American army under Gen. William Hull had surrendered at Detroit, almost without firing a shot. The garrison at Fort Dearborn had been massacred by Indians. A large part of Gen. Stephen Van Rensselaer's force of New York militia had been slaughtered on the Canadian side of the Niagara River, within sight of other militiamen who remained on the U.S. side and refused to move into foreign territory.

The 13th Congress met in special session in May 1813, and opposition to the administration was immediately evident in the Senate. Daniel Webster offered a series of resolutions designed to embarrass Madison. Numerous appointments by the president were rejected by Congress, and a resolution of the Massachusetts legislature reportedly characterized the war as one "waged without justifiable cause."

Once Congress declares war and votes the necessary funds, presidents enjoy vastly enlarged authority in both domestic and foreign affairs.

During the Civil War, Congress delegated sweeping power to President Abraham Lincoln to enable him to prosecute the war. Several months after he issued proclamations calling up the state militias and ordering a naval blockade of the South, Congress passed an act on August 6, 1861, approving and making valid "all the acts, proclamations, and orders of the presidents . . . as if they had been issued and done under the previous express authority and direction of the Congress of the United States."

By the turn of the century, the federal government had become increasingly active in regulating the economy, and when the United States entered World War I Congress delegated to President Woodrow Wilson extensive and far-reaching powers over the economy and domestic affairs.

The foreign policy and domestic powers exercised by President Franklin D. Roosevelt in World War II were even greater, as the concept of a national emergency expanded with the necessity of placing the entire country on a war footing. Edward S. Corwin wrote:

In the First World War, as in the Civil War, the emergency that constitutional interpretation set itself to meet was a *war* emergency in the narrow, palpable sense. In the Second World War the emergency preceded the war and continued beyond it—a fact of special significance when it is considered in relation to the effect of wartime practices on the constitutional law of peacetime.[1]

Both world wars, as well as the Civil War, highlighted the problems of ending a national emergency. Delegations of duties and new responsibilities to the president remained in the president's hands long after hostilities ended and national emergencies were over. On July 25, 1947, Congress terminated certain temporary emergency and war powers involving about 175 statutory provisions, some of which dated back to World War I. Nonetheless, 103 war or emergency statutes remained in effect.[2]

Congressional concern with the continuing existence of national emergencies and concomitant delegation of power to the president led to the creation in 1973 of a Senate Special Committee on the Termination of the National Emergency. At the outset of the study it was thought that the state of national emergency then existing dated back to President Harry S. Truman's December 1950 proclamation of an emergency in response to China's decision to come to the aid of North Korea during the Korean War. However, research by the committee showed that the United States had been living in a state of declared national emergency since March 1933, when Congress ratified Roosevelt's declaration of an emergency because of the Depression.

The discovery pointed up Congress's lack of knowledge in the area of emergency powers. The committee reported: "Because Congress and the public are unaware of the extent of emergency powers, there has never been any notable congressional or public objection made to this state of affairs. Nor have the courts imposed significant limitations." The committee listed four existing states of national emergency that it said should be ended. It released a catalog of some 470 provisions of law that, according to the panel, "delegate to the president extraordinary powers, ordinarily exercised by the Congress, which affect the lives of American citizens in a host of all-encompassing manners. This vast range of powers, taken together, confer enough authority to rule the country without reference to normal constitutional processes."[3]

As a result, Congress in 1976 approved legislation ending the four emergency conditions. They were:

- Roosevelt's 1933 declaration.
- Truman's declaration in 1950 at the time of China's intervention in the Korean War.
- Richard M. Nixon's declaration in response to a national postal strike in 1970.
- Nixon's 1971 declaration in response to the international monetary situation.

The 1976 measure also provided for congressional oversight and review of future declarations of emergency. Taking as a model the 1973 War Powers Resolution, the bill provided that any future national emergency proclaimed by the president could be terminated by Congress through a concurrent resolution—not subject to presidential veto—or by presidential proclamation. The use of a concurrent resolution to veto a presidential action, the so-called legislative veto, was declared unconstitutional in 1983. (See "Separation of Powers," p. 680.)

In 1977 Congress approved a bill restricting the authority of the chief executive to impose economic controls during presidentially declared national emergencies. The legislation did not weaken the wartime powers of the president.

1. Edward S. Corwin, *The President: Office and Powers, 1787–1984*, 5th rev. ed. (New York: New York University Press, 1984), 272.

2. Louis Fisher, *President and Congress: Power and Policy* (New York: Free Press, 1972), 193.

3. Senate Special Committee on the Termination of the National Emergency, *Emergency Powers Statutes: Provisions of the Federal Law Now in Effect Delegating to the Executive Extraordinary Authority in Time of National Emergency*, 93rd Cong., 1st sess., 1973, S Rept 93-549, iii, 6.

Congress reassembled in temporary quarters in the burned city of Washington in September 1814. Little hope was held that success would attend the negotiations then being carried on by peace commissioners in London. Yet, with the Army still at only about half its paper strength and enlistments falling off, Congress failed to agree to a conscription bill proposed by James Monroe, then secretary of war as well as secretary of state. Fortunately for the administration, the Treaty of Ghent was signed by the American commissioners on December 24, 1814, and won unanimous consent of the Senate on February 16, 1815.

War with Mexico, 1846

The war with Mexico was distinctly unpopular among large numbers of Americans, particularly in the North. Recurring expressions in Congress of opposition to the prosecution of the war were in part a reflection of that antiwar sentiment.

President John Tyler had long desired to annex Texas but was blocked by the Senate until after the 1844 presidential election, in which Henry Clay, who opposed annexation without the consent of Mexico, was defeated by James Polk, an ardent expansionist. On March 1, 1845, three days before Polk was inaugurated, annexation was accomplished by adoption of a joint resolution by the 28th Congress.

In the spring of 1846 Gen. Zachary Taylor led his army into a disputed strip of territory claimed by Texas but occupied exclusively by Mexicans. A clash between Mexican soldiers and a reconnoitering party of Americans occurred on April 25. It was unclear whether the skirmish was on Texan or Mexican soil. A few American soldiers were killed. On May 11, two days after the news of the fighting reached Polk, he sent a war message to Congress declaring that Mexico had passed the boundary of the United States, had invaded American territory, and had shed American blood upon American soil. "War exists," he said, "and notwithstanding all our efforts to avoid it, exists by the act of Mexico herself."

The House at once passed legislation declaring that a state of war existed with Mexico. The vote was 174–14. The House also appropriated $10 million and authorized a call for fifty thousand volunteers. Some opposition to the war, in part sincere and in part partisan, was offered by northern Whigs. Somewhat stronger opposition was voiced in the Senate, but senators approved the bill by a 40–2 vote the next day.

In the congressional elections of 1846, the Democrats retained control of the Senate, but the House was lost to the Whigs. Moreover, as General Taylor marched victoriously through Mexico, the war was being widely denounced in the North and was proving far from universally popular in the South. By the time Congress met in December 1846 members had gathered new courage to question the war's justification and purpose. Polk's annual message, devoted almost wholly to a defense of the war, was deeply resented by the Whigs, for in it the president charged that those opposing his policies were giving aid and comfort to the enemy. Thereafter, although the necessary military measures were passed as they came up, debate focused less on the merits of particular measures than on the causes, justice, and necessity of the war itself.

The House was especially sensitive to the growing discontent. Rep. Abraham Lincoln, W-Ill., offered his "Spot Resolutions," all of which ignored the current status of the war and were intended to probe the original causes of the conflict. A resolution presented in the House late in 1847 stated that the war should not be further prosecuted for any purpose. Another proposed the creation of a joint House and Senate committee to consult with the president on how to quickly end the war. Other resolutions of similar purport were introduced, though most of them did not come to a vote. However, a resolution offered in January 1848 by George Ashmun, W-Mass., which declared the war to have been "unnecessarily and unconstitutionally begun by the president of the United States," was adopted in the House by a margin of four votes. The House also adopted a resolution calling on the president to supply information on the objectives of the war and the exact nature of the proposed terms of peace. This request was refused by Polk.

On February 23 the president sent a peace treaty with Mexico to the Senate, which consented to ratification on March 10, 1848, by a vote of 38–14—three more than the required two-thirds majority.

Neither the opposition of a considerable section of the population, nor various "obstructionist tactics" of certain members of Congress hampered the administration's war effort. The enemy forces were so inconsiderable that no extraordinary requests had to be made of Congress. If the United States had suffered military reverses comparable to those in the War of 1812, thus requiring the passage of drastic measures by Congress, it is possible that the Whig opposition might have forced far-reaching alterations in the war plans of the expansionists led by Polk.

War with Spain, 1898

War with Spain over the independence of Cuba was forced on President William McKinley in 1898 by strong expansionist sentiment in Congress and in the press. Two years earlier, McKinley's predecessor, Grover Cleveland, had succeeded in averting a similar result only by defying Congress: in 1896 a resolution according belligerent rights to the Cuban insurgents had been adopted in both houses by large majorities.

Soon after the presidential election in November of that year, won by McKinley on a platform calling for the independence of Cuba, a resolution granting recognition to the island was offered in Congress. Cleveland's secretary of state, Richard Olney, at once declared to the press that the resolution, if adopted, could "probably be regarded only as an expression of opinion by the eminent gentlemen who vote for it." He added:

The power to recognize the so-called Republic of Cuba as an independent state rests exclusively with the executive. A resolution on the subject . . . is inoperative as legislation, and is important only as advice of great weight voluntarily tendered to the executive regarding the manner in which he shall exercise his constitutional functions. . . . The resolution will be without effect and will leave unaltered the attitude of this government toward the two contending parties in Cuba.

A few days later the lame-duck president, Grover Cleveland, reportedly told a congressional delegation that if Congress declared war on Spain he would refuse to mobilize the army. In view of Cleveland's intransigent attitude, Congress took no action on the resolution recognizing Cuba's independence.

After McKinley's inauguration in March 1897, relations with Spain steadily worsened, in spite of a series of diplomatic concessions by that country. After the sinking of the battleship *Maine* in Havana harbor in February 1898, it became clear that nothing short of war would satisfy congressional belligerence. On April 11 McKinley submitted a message to Congress proposing forcible intervention in Cuba. Although Spain already had capitulated to American demands for Cuban autonomy, on April 19 a resolution declaring that the people of the island "are, and of right ought to be, free and independent," and authorizing the president to employ the land and naval forces of the United States to expel Spain from Cuba, was adopted in the Senate by a vote of 42–35 and in the House by 310–6. A declaration of war, retroactive to April 21, was approved by voice votes on April 25. McKinley immediately ordered a blockade of Havana, and the war had begun.

The brevity of the war, the ease with which it was won, and the relatively popular nature of the conflict, among members of Congress and the public, worked to ensure a satisfied and wholly cooperative attitude by Congress toward the executive branch. However, opposition to the acquisition of the Philippines led to a month's debate on the treaty of peace, to which the Senate consented February 6, 1899, by 57–27, only one vote more than the necessary two-thirds majority.

World War I

When World War I began in 1914, Woodrow Wilson announced that the United States would stay out of the conflict. But by 1917 the United States had been drawn in. After Wilson's efforts to mediate an end to the war in Europe failed and Germany mounted a submarine offensive through a wide zone of the Atlantic, the president on April 2, 1917, asked Congress for a declaration of war. The Senate adopted a joint resolution declaring war on Germany by an 82–6 vote on April 4, and the House approved it two days later by a 373–50 vote. Wilson asked for a declaration of war against Austria-Hungary on December 4, 1917. The House adopted the resolution on December 7 by a 365–1 vote, and the Senate approved it that same day by a 74–0 vote.

During the war Wilson amassed greater powers than those employed by any previous war president. Many of the extraordinary powers exercised by Wilson were delegated to him by Congress. However, Wilson also drew upon his constitutional powers to implement policies Congress opposed or delayed.

A week after war was declared, the president used his authority as commander in chief to create by executive order the Com-

mittee on Public Information, under whose direction a system of voluntary news censorship was established and various government publicity services were organized. On April 28, 1917, again acting as commander in chief, Wilson imposed stringent cable censorship, which later was extended to other forms of communication with foreign countries under authority of the Trading with the Enemy Act of October 6, 1917.

Wilson on May 19, 1917, appointed Herbert Hoover as food administrator. Then, on June 12, two months before passage of the Food and Fuel Control Act, the president gave Hoover "full authority to undertake any steps necessary" for the conservation of food resources. The functions of the War Industries Board, created originally by the Council of National Defense, were expanded and vested almost exclusively in its chairman, Bernard M. Baruch, by a letter from the president to Baruch on March 4, 1918. By an executive order of May 28, 1918, Wilson formally established the War Industries Board "as a separate administrative agency to act for me and under my direction." Although created without statutory authority, the board was able to exert wide control over industry. Behind its "requests" stood the president's power to commandeer factories or withhold fuel and establish transportation priorities.

The sweeping control of the economy acquired by Wilson during the war constituted, in the opinion of Rexford G. Tugwell, a member of the Roosevelt "braintrust" in the New Deal and under secretary of agriculture (1934–1937), "the most fantastic expansion of the executive known to American experience."[39]

The wide authorities conferred upon the president by Congress included powers to:

- Take over and operate enemy vessels for use in war.
- Regulate and prohibit exports.
- Take over and operate the railroads.
- Regulate priorities in transportation.
- Regulate by a licensing system the importation, manufacture, storage, mining, or distribution of all goods necessary for the war effort.
- Requisition foods, fuels, and other supplies necessary for any public use connected with national defense.
- Fix a reasonable guaranteed price for wheat based upon a statutory minimum.
- Fix the price of coal and regulate the method of its production, sale, shipment, distribution, and storage.
- Prohibit or license transactions in the United States by foreign insurance companies.

Congress delegated these powers to the president because it recognized that modern warfare required singleness of direction, unity of command, and coordination of vital resources. After the war ended, Republican majorities in Congress reasserted the prerogatives of the legislative branch. Feelings on Capitol Hill were ruffled by Wilson's failure to include senators in the American delegation to the Paris Peace Conference. The Senate twice refused, in 1919 and again in 1920, to approve the

Treaty of Versailles, which included the establishment of the League of Nations. *(See "League of Nations," p. 205.)*

World War II

The prevailing mood of isolationism in Congress and the country during the 1930s sharply limited President Franklin D. Roosevelt's freedom of action in foreign affairs. This mood found expression in such laws as the Neutrality Acts of 1935 and 1937, which prohibited shipments of arms, ammunition, or implements of war to belligerent nations. A resolution introduced by Rep. Louis L. Ludlow, D-Ind., in 1935 and again in 1937 would have restricted the war powers of Congress as well as those of the president. The resolution proposed a constitutional amendment to require submission of a declaration of war to a popular referendum. Although the Ludlow resolution was pried from committee by a discharge petition on December 14, 1937, a motion to bring it to the House floor for a vote failed to carry.

After Roosevelt's proclamation of a limited national emergency on September 8, 1939, a week after the outbreak of war in Europe, the United States began to drift from neutrality to active support of the Allied cause. At a special session from September 21 to November 3, 1939, called by the president, Congress revised the Neutrality Act to repeal the arms embargo and allow sales of munitions to belligerents on a cash-and-carry basis. An act of June 15, 1940, authorized military assistance to any Latin American republic that requested it.

On September 3, 1940, the president announced that the United States had entered into an executive agreement under which Great Britain would receive fifty "over-age" (but reconditioned and recommissioned) destroyers in return for U.S. rights to lease certain sites on British territory in the western Atlantic for U.S. naval and air bases. There had been no consultation with Congress. The attorney general defended the constitutionality of the "lend-lease" transaction on the ground that the president's power as commander in chief enabled him to "dispose" the armed forces of the United States. It was also argued that he was responsible for securing adequate bases for national defense.

On March 11, 1941, Congress passed the Lend-Lease Act, authorizing the president to manufacture any defense article and to "sell, transfer title to, exchange, lease, lend, or otherwise dispose of" defense articles to any country whose defense he deemed vital to the defense of the United States. Corwin called it the most "sweeping delegation of legislative power" ever made to an American president.[40] It gave Roosevelt authority to aid the Allied cause by all means short of using armed forces.

But later that year Roosevelt, again citing his power as commander in chief and again not consulting with Congress, ordered American troops to Greenland and Iceland. In a special message to Congress July 7, 1941, the president asserted that the occupation of Iceland by Nazi Germany would constitute a serious threat to Greenland and North America, to North Atlantic shipping, and to the steady flow of munitions to Britain. While the establishment of bases in Greenland and Iceland was not an act of war, it reflected this nation's hostility toward Germany.

Existence of a state of war with Japan was formally declared

Sen. Tom Connally shows his relief upon passage of the Lend-Lease bill in 1941.

President Franklin D. Roosevelt signs the declaration of war in 1941. Congress delegated sweeping powers to Roosevelt during World War II—contributing substantially to the concentration of virtually all war powers in his hands.

by Congress on December 8, 1941, the day after Japan's attack on Pearl Harbor. Existence of a state of war with Germany and Italy was declared on December 11. The resolution declaring war against Japan was adopted by the Senate 82–0 and by the House 388–1. (The one negative vote was cast by Jeannette Rankin, R-Mont., who had cast a similar vote on the declaration of war against Germany in 1917.) The declaration of war against Germany was adopted by the Senate 88–0 and by the House 393–0; the declaration of war against Italy, by 90–0 in the Senate and 399–0 in the House.

On June 2, 1942, Roosevelt requested three additional declarations of war. Resolutions declaring war on Bulgaria, Hungary, and Rumania were adopted by the House on June 3 by votes of 357–0, 360–0, and 361–0, respectively. The Senate approved the three declarations on June 4 by 73–0 votes.

Entry of the country into World War II was accompanied by the concentration of virtually all war powers in the president's hands. The president's war mobilization authority included sweeping powers over the economy, specifically authority to regulate industry needed in the war effort and the power to reopen and operate plants closed by strikes.

Under his power as commander in chief and using powers delegated by Congress, Roosevelt created many new emergency agencies and made them responsible to him rather than to existing departments or independent regulatory agencies. According to Corwin, by April 1942 some forty-two new agencies had been created to oversee the war effort; thirty-five were of "purely presidential creation," an origin that provoked controversy over their constitutional and legal status.[41]

THE UNDECLARED WARS

The president's warmaking powers, Louis Fisher has written, were derived originally from: (1) his responsibilities as commander in chief; (2) his oath to preserve, protect, and defend the Constitution; (3) his duty to protect the nation from sudden attack; and (4) the inherent powers derived from the general heading "executive power." The definition of inherent and implied powers has become increasingly generous in modern times because of treaty commitments, vaguely worded congressional resolutions, and an accumulation of emergency statutes. Moreover, the president's constitutional responsibility for repelling sudden attacks and waging defensive war has expanded in scope until it is now used to justify involvement in full-scale wars without legislative approval.[42]

The Korean Conflict

The war in Korea began with an attack on South Korea by North Koreans on June 25, 1950, and continued for three years at a cost of more than 150,000 U.S. casualties. On June 26 President Truman ordered American air and sea forces in the Far East to aid South Korea. The next day the United Nations Security Council called on UN members for help in repelling the attack.

CONGRESSIONAL POWER TO RAISE AN ARMY

Congress's constitutional power to "raise and support Armies" has served as a basis for the enactment of laws to draft men into the armed forces.

Conscription was first used in the United States during the Civil War. The 1863 Enrollment Act set up a draft system run by the War Department and administered by military officers.

A compulsory draft was instituted again in World War I, when Congress passed the Selective Service Act of 1917 setting up a decentralized system for registering and drafting men. The draft was conducted by local and state boards composed entirely of civilians.

The 1917 act was challenged in the courts, but the Supreme Court in 1918 unanimously upheld the law in a series of cases known collectively as the *Selective Draft Law Cases.* The Court held that Congress had the authority to institute the draft under its express war powers as well as through its mandate to make laws "necessary and proper" to carry out its constitutional powers. Moreover, the Court held that military service was one of a citizen's duties in a "just government."

WORLD WAR II DRAFT

World War II prompted Congress to reinstate conscription in 1940, before the United States had entered the war. The first peacetime draft law in U.S. history, the Selective Training and Service Act, took administration of the draft out of the War Department and established an independent Selective Service System, headed by a presidential appointee. The law required one year of military service. As with the 1917 law, the 1940 act created civilian-run local and district draft boards.

The draft law was amended by Congress in 1941 to lower the minimum draft age to eighteen from twenty and extend compulsory service to eighteen months. The nation still was at peace in mid-1941 and isolationist sentiment in Congress remained strong. The administration of Franklin D. Roosevelt had a difficult fight before winning enactment of the draft amendments. In the House, the measure was passed on August 12 by a one-vote margin, 203–202. But after the Japanese attack on Pearl Harbor, sentiment quickly changed, and Congress froze all enlistments in the armed forces for the duration of the war.

On April 18, 1942, Roosevelt established the War Manpower Commission to determine the manpower needs of the military, industry, and agriculture during the war. On December 5, 1942, Roosevelt, under authority granted by the 1940 act, transferred the functions of the Selective Service System to his manpower commission. The president's action was opposed in Congress, and exactly one year later, on December 5, 1943, Congress amended the draft law to restore the Selective Service System's independent status.

The draft law was extended in 1945 and 1946 before Congress allowed it to expire in 1947. Congress during this period had refused to act on President Harry S. Truman's call for a new universal military training law, subjecting all eighteen-year-old males to one year of training and six years in the reserves. However, in 1948 Congress voted to reinstate the Selective Service Act, which was still in effect at the beginning of the Korean War. Draft eligibility was broadened somewhat by 1951 amendments to include eighteen-and-a-half-year-olds, once all men nineteen and older had been called. The draft law then was amended five times between 1955 and 1971.

In 1969 President Richard Nixon ordered a lottery set up to draft men for the Vietnam War. In 1971 Congress abolished the local board quota system at Nixon's request. Inductees thereafter were selected on a nationwide basis, determined by their lottery number, instead of making induction dependent on both the lottery number and the quotas of their local boards. Congress also prohibited any person from serving more than twenty years on a local board and required the boards to reflect proportionately the racial and religious makeup of the community in which the board was located.

DRAFT REPLACED BY VOLUNTEER FORCE

The 1971 extension of the draft was allowed to expire July 1, 1973. Eighteen-year-old males still had to register until President Gerald R. Ford suspended that obligation April 1, 1975.

Congressional acquiescence in the draft's expiration in 1973, which had the backing of Nixon, paved the way for the administration to establish the all-volunteer armed services concept, which had been under study since 1970. Although the plan was established administratively and did not need the approval of Congress, it would not have been feasible without congressional backing, including the support needed to provide the appropriations to run the volunteer system, promote enlistments, and realize the higher pay incentives that were crucial to the success of the all-volunteer plan.

Peacetime draft registration resumed in 1980, at the urging of President Jimmy Carter, with the enactment in June of that year of legislation requiring nineteen- and twenty-year-old men to register. Registration of eighteen-year-olds began in 1981.

The House in 1993 attempted to end the Selective Service System by slashing its funding, but the proposal died in conference with the Senate. Opponents had argued that registration and the Selective Service System were wasteful in light of the breakup of the Soviet Union and the Warsaw Pact.

The president on June 30 ordered ground troops into South Korea and sent the Seventh Fleet to act as a buffer between China and Taiwan.

Secretary of State Dean Acheson recommended to Truman that he "should not ask [Congress] for a resolution of approval, but rest on his constitutional authority as commander in chief."[43] Truman never did ask Congress for a declaration of war in Korea, and he waited until December 16, 1950—six months after the outbreak of hostilities—to proclaim the existence of a national emergency. In defense of this course, it was argued that the Russians or Chinese, or both, had violated post–World War II agreements on Korea and that emergency powers authorized during World War II still could be applied.

Provisions in the UN Charter also were used to justify Truman's action. A legal memorandum by the State Department in 1950 offered this defense: "Both traditional international law and Article 39 of the UN Charter and the resolution pursuant thereto authorize the United States to repel the armed aggression against the Republic of Korea."[44] However, the legality of that argument was questioned on the grounds that U.S. armed forces were ordered to South Korea before the UN Security Council authorized the action.

Although there was never a formal declaration of war or congressional resolution supporting Truman's decision, Congress implicitly ratified the action by consistently appropriating the requested funds for the war.

There was no serious challenge in Congress to Truman's war powers until 1951, when some members questioned whether the president had the authority to dispatch troops to Korea and to Western Europe. Republican Senator Robert Taft of Ohio opened a three-month-long "great debate" on January 5, 1951, by charging that Truman had involved the United States in the Korean War without authority and was planning to substantially increase U.S. forces in Europe, again without congressional approval. But on April 4 the Senate adopted two resolutions approving the dispatch of four divisions to Europe. One of the resolutions stated that it was the sense of the Senate that "no ground troops in addition to such four divisions should be sent to Western Europe . . . without further congressional approval."

Truman hailed the action as a "clear endorsement" of his troop plans, saying "there has never been any real question" about the United States doing its part in the defense of Europe. But he ignored the Senate's claim to a voice in future troop commitments. Neither resolution had the force of law. In essence, the "great debate" had confirmed both the president's power to commit U.S. forces without prior congressional approval and the decision to defend Western Europe.

Testifying in 1951 on the plan to station American soldiers in Europe, Acheson asserted: "Not only has the president the authority to use the armed forces in carrying out the broad foreign policy of the United States and implementing treaties, but it is equally clear that this authority may not be interfered with by Congress in the exercise of powers which it has under the Constitution."[45]

Truman on April 8, 1952, overstepped use of his powers as commander in chief when he took possession and control of all facilities, plants, and properties of eighty-six steel companies involved in a dispute with the United Steelworkers. Congress ignored the president's request to approve the seizure order. Then, on June 2, the Supreme Court ruled in *Youngstown Sheet and Tube Co. v. Sawyer* that his action was without statutory authority and that it violated the concept of separation of powers by usurping functions of Congress.

War in Vietnam

U.S. military aid to Vietnam was initiated by the Truman administration. In 1951 military aid to that country amounted to more than $500 million. Although President Dwight D. Eisenhower barred a U.S. combat role in Vietnam, in 1954 the United States sent two hundred air force technicians to aid the French in their fight against the Viet Minh. The Senate Foreign Relations Committee subsequently expressed concern at the lack of congressional consultation in that decision, and the State Department pledged to consult with Congress before making any other moves in Vietnam.

In March 1954, at the beginning of the fifty-six-day battle at Dien Bien Phu that ended with France's defeat, the White House tentatively approved a plan for immediate U.S. air intervention, but Senate Minority Leader Lyndon B. Johnson, D-Texas, and Richard B. Russell, D-Ga., the senior Democrat on the Armed Services Committee, and other members rejected the proposal.

American involvement in Indochina increased during the Kennedy administration—there were about fifteen thousand U.S. advisers in Vietnam by early 1964—and criticism intensified. On March 10, 1964, Senators Wayne Morse, D-Ore., and Ernest Gruening, D-Alaska, demanded total U.S. withdrawal. But a military incident in the summer of 1964 between U.S. and North Vietnamese forces led to much deeper American military involvement in Vietnam.

Tonkin Gulf Resolution. Following reports that North Vietnamese PT boats had attacked American destroyers patrolling the Gulf of Tonkin on August 2 and August 4, 1964, President Johnson ordered a retaliatory air strike on Hanoi's naval base, destroying or damaging twenty-five boats. On August 5 the president asked Congress to adopt a resolution to "give convincing evidence to the aggressive Communist nations, and to the world as a whole, that our policy in Southeast Asia will be carried forward, and that the peace and security of the area will be preserved."

On August 7 both chambers adopted the resolution by overwhelming majorities—416–0 in the House and 88–2 in the Senate, with only Gruening and Morse voting against it. The resolution (Joint Resolution to Promote the Maintenance of International Peace and Security in Southeast Asia) expressed support for the "determination of the president . . . to take all necessary measures to repel any armed attack against the forces of the United States and to prevent further aggression."

The resolution went on to say:

Consonant with the Constitution and the Charter of the United Nations and in accordance with its obligations under the Southeast Asia Collective Defense Treaty, the United States is, therefore, prepared, as the president determines, to take all necessary steps, including the use of armed force, to assist any member or protocol state of . . . [SEATO] requesting assistance in defense of its freedom.

The implications of the Tonkin Gulf resolution became a source of intense debate as the war grew in scope and members who had supported the resolution became increasingly disillusioned with America's involvement. Some lawmakers maintained the resolution did not commit the United States to massive participation in the war. Sen. John C. Stennis, D-Miss., rejected Secretary of State Dean Rusk's 1966 characterization of the resolution as a grant of authority for U.S. action in the war.

During hearings before the Preparedness Investigating Subcommittee, Stennis said: "You stand on mighty thin ice if you rely on the Tonkin Gulf resolution as a constitutional basis for this war."

The resolution's meaning was debated again in 1967 during hearings by the Foreign Relations Committee on U.S. foreign commitments. Under Secretary of State Nicholas deB. Katzenbach described it as the "functional equivalent" of a declaration of war. "What could a declaration of war have done that would have given the president more authority and a clearer voice of the Congress than that did?" Katzenbach asked rhetorically. Katzenbach also maintained that, in "limited wars" such as Vietnam, a declaration of war was "inappropriate."

Sen. Albert Gore Sr., D-Tenn., rejected Katzenbach's view. "I did not vote for the resolution with any understanding that it was tantamount to a declaration of war," he said. Senators Charles H. Percy, R-Ill., and Bourke B. Hickenlooper, R-Iowa, expressed doubt that the resolution would have been adopted had it been known that it would lead to large-scale U.S. military action.

But President Johnson said at an April 1967 news conference:

We stated then, and we repeat now, we did not think the resolution was necessary to do what we did and what we're doing. . . . But we thought it was desirable, and we thought if we are going to ask them [Congress] to stay the whole route and if we expected them to be there on the landing, we ought to ask them to be there on the takeoff.

In a Foreign Relations Committee report released in 1967, Chairman Fulbright said that "in adopting the [Tonkin Gulf] resolution Congress was closer to believing that it was helping to prevent a large-scale war by taking a firm stand than that it was laying down the legal basis for the conduct of such a war."

Congress on December 31, 1970, approved legislation that repealed the Tonkin Gulf resolution. The repeal provision was added to a foreign military sales bill, which was signed by President Nixon January 12, 1971. The Nixon administration initially objected to the repeal, but in early 1970 it modified its opposition and maintained that the authority for pursuing the war rested on the president's constitutional power as commander in chief.

The Tonkin issue was revisited in June 1971 with the unauthorized publication by the *New York Times* of the Defense Department's secret history of the Vietnam War (the so-called Pentagon Papers) and the public reading of it by Sen. Mike Gravel, D-Alaska, during a subcommittee meeting on June 29. The study, which had been denied to the Foreign Relations Committee two years earlier, raised questions about the scope of the 1964 destroyer attack and strongly suggested that Congress had been manipulated into granting the authorization.

Commenting on the revelations concerning U.S. Vietnam policy, Raoul Berger wrote: "We can only conjecture whether the course of events would have been changed had the . . . facts [disclosed in the papers] been spread before Congress and the people. But undeniably they were deprived of the choice which was theirs to make."[46]

Antiwar Votes. After adoption of the Tonkin Gulf resolution,

Hearings by the Senate Foreign Relations Committee under Chairman J. W. Fulbright helped build opposition to U.S. involvement in the Vietnam War.

neither the Johnson nor Nixon administrations returned to Congress to seek specific legislative consent or additional authority for stepped-up military activity. Nixon ordered U.S. troops into Cambodia in 1970, provided air support for South Vietnam's invasion of Laos in 1971, ordered the mining of Haiphong harbor in North Vietnam in 1972, and launched the heaviest bombing of North Vietnam in December 1972—all without seeking specific congressional consent.

As the war dragged on in the period spanning the Tonkin resolution and the 1973 Vietnam cease-fire, complaints about aggrandizement of presidential war powers began to surface. Increasing criticism of U.S. involvement was followed by outright disaffection in Congress. But once Congress committed itself to the war it was unable to bring itself to force an end to the conflict.

At the peak of antiwar strength in Congress, there was considerable support in the Senate for proposals to limit or end the war but only one out of every three House members voted to back end-the-war proposals. On the few bills to reach House-Senate conference deliberations, House conferees almost invariably were responsible for deleting or weakening Senate-passed antiwar amendments. The few restrictions that survived conference committee rewriting and became law were largely moot since they affected military activity the executive branch no longer intended to pursue.

President Nixon's 1970 decision to send U.S. forces into Cambodia to clean out communist sanctuaries provoked a six-week Senate debate in May and June on an amendment sponsored by

Senators John Sherman Cooper, R-Ky., and Frank Church, D-Idaho, to bar use of U.S. funds for military operations in Cambodia. A weakened version of the amendment—barring use of ground forces but not aircraft—was passed in December, months after Nixon had removed the U.S. troops from Cambodia.

Other action on antiwar proposals in 1970 included defeat in the Senate of two "end-the-war" amendments sponsored by Senators Mark O. Hatfield, R-Ore., and George McGovern, D-S.D. On three occasions in 1971 the Senate adopted amendments introduced by Mansfield calling for withdrawal of troops from Indochina by a certain date. Two of these survived a House-Senate conference (with the withdrawal deadline deleted), the first time the House had gone on record urging an end to the war. The president, however, said the provision was not binding and that he would not be bound by it. A new Cooper-Church amendment, limiting use of U.S. military funds in Indochina to troop withdrawals, was defeated in the Senate in a series of close votes.

The Senate on August 2, 1972, posed its most serious challenge to the president's policies by adopting on a 49–47 vote an amendment cutting off funds for U.S. participation in the war. The amendment barred use of funds for U.S. participation beginning four months after enactment. All U.S. ground, naval, and air forces were to be out of Indochina by that date if North Vietnam and its allies released all American prisoners of war. But House conferees refused to accept the amendment.

The picture of the Johnson and Nixon administrations carrying on military activities in Indochina without congressional consent often was overdrawn by critics of the war. They tended to overlook the frequent votes in Congress in favor of military appropriations. While they spoke of a constitutional crisis over war powers, there never was a constitutional confrontation between the president and Congress because Congress always was willing to appropriate the necessary funds. Once a president had committed men and materiel to battle, it became much harder for lawmakers to deny the forces the money they needed to wage the war.

Shortly before the January 27, 1973, signing of the Vietnam peace agreement, Senate Majority Leader Mansfield insisted that Congress "can't end the war." "It's really up to the president," Mansfield said. "We shouldn't fool ourselves in that respect."

Yet, from another viewpoint, the increasing number of antiwar votes in Congress—from five in 1969 to thirty-five in 1972—may well have served to reinforce President Nixon's decision to continue troop withdrawals from Indochina, a policy Nixon had announced in June 1969. The votes were a constant signal that slowing down, or reversing, the troop withdrawals would involve heavy political costs.

In the spring of 1973 there was a postscript to Congress's response to the Vietnam War. Although it had pulled out of Vietnam two months after the January peace agreement, the Nixon administration continued its bombing of Cambodia and Laos.

In action on a supplemental appropriations bill, the House for the first time voted to cut off funds for U.S. military activity in Southeast Asia. Final provisions of that measure, signed by Nixon, barred the use of any past or existing funds for financing directly or indirectly U.S. combat activities in, over, or off the shores of North Vietnam, South Vietnam, Laos, or Cambodia.

Congress did not stop with a bombing ban in finally challenging presidential power. In July 1973 it followed up with a tough measure to limit the president's powers to commit troops abroad without the approval of Congress. But its sponsors' hopes for a new partnership with the executive branch in decisions on committing troops abroad have never been realized. (See "1973 War Powers Resolution," p. 233.)

Persian Gulf War

The lessons of Vietnam and the track record of the War Powers Resolution provided the backdrop for the 1990–1991 debate over the U.S. decision to go to war to end Iraq's occupation of Kuwait.

After several months of voicing concerns over congressional prerogatives but doing little about it, Congress voted to back a presidential decision to go to war if necessary to oust the Iraqi army from Kuwait. While not a formal declaration of war, it was the closest Congress had come to that step since World War II. Most legal experts agreed that the vote by Congress authorizing President George Bush to use force qualified as an exercise of its constitutional authority to "declare war."

In a somber and historic debate, member after member came to the podium to speak his or her conscience on the issues at hand. The vote reflected the divisions within the country over whether to go to war, but once it was taken, Congress closed ranks with the chief executive and remained supportive throughout the brief and highly successful conflict.

The crisis had begun in the early morning hours of August 2, 1990, when Iraqi leader Saddam Hussein ordered more than one hundred thousand troops and several hundred tanks to attack the lightly armed Arab emirate of Kuwait. Administration officials and members of Congress alike were surprised by the intensity and machinelike efficiency of the Iraqi invasion. Within a few hours Iraq controlled the neighboring country.

President Bush immediately imposed what amounted to a total ban on economic relations with Iraq. Congress also responded quickly, as the House passed an economic sanctions bill and the Senate adopted a resolution condemning Iraq. On August 7 Bush dispatched troops to Saudi Arabia to prevent an Iraqi invasion of that country. Two days later Bush officially notified Congress of the deployment of troops but said he did not believe involvement in hostilities was imminent, thus sidestepping a triggering of the War Powers Resolution.

A number of reasons for U.S. actions were put forward by the administration at various times, including the need to protect American lives, to restore the territorial integrity of Kuwait, and to stop Saddam Hussein's advancement of nuclear and chemical warfare capabilities. But for many the main goal was to

Gen. Colin L. Powell Jr., chairman of the Joint Chiefs of Staff, gives a press briefing on the progress of the Persian Gulf War in 1991.

secure a steady flow of oil from the Middle East to the industrialized world. As Sen. John McCain, R-Ariz., put it: "Let's have no illusions; if this were another part of the world, we would not see this kind of response."

Iraq's occupation of Kuwait increased its control over the world's oil reserves from 10 percent to almost 20 percent. If Iraq managed to take over Saudi Arabia's oil fields—either by military force or intimidation—its control would jump to 45 percent. Bush attempted to instill a fear of this danger in the nation in August when he declared: "Our jobs, our way of life, our own freedom, and the freedom of friendly countries around the world would all suffer if control of the world's greatest oil reserves fell into the hands of Saddam Hussein."

In the ensuing weeks and months Bush courted support for a tough stance against Saddam Hussein among U.S. allies, Arab states, and the United Nations, while building up a U.S. force in Saudi Arabia and the surrounding area that would eventually number more than five hundred thousand. Bush activated the reserves under a law initially passed in 1976 and revised in 1986 that allowed him to order to active duty as many as two hundred thousand reservists for up to ninety days. Other nations joined with the United States to form a multinational force opposing Iraq.

With the largest deployment of U.S. forces since the Vietnam War under way, Congress was slow, cautious, even reluctant, to respond to it. Nearly two months went by before Congress acted. Then, during the first week of October, both chambers overwhelmingly passed carefully circumscribed resolutions designed to offer support for the actions Bush had taken but not to authorize any future military operations against Iraq.

Despite administration pledges to consult with Congress over the Persian Gulf crisis, Secretary of State James A. Baker III made the administration's position clear when he told the House Foreign Affairs Committee in mid-October that prior congressional approval for military action in the gulf would be "self-defeating." Senate Majority Leader George J. Mitchell, D-Maine, was equally emphatic: "The president has no legal authority—none whatsoever—to commit the United States to war. Only Congress can make that grave decision." Fearful that military action might be taken after Congress's election-year adjournment, Senate and House leaders designated a group of lawmakers who would be available for consultation while Congress was not in session.

Congressional sentiment for a role in approving military action against Iraq intensified in November, when Bush announced a massive new buildup of U.S. forces in the Persian Gulf with the intent of developing an "adequate offensive military option" against Iraq. In a letter to congressional leaders, the president said that this was a continuation of the deployment already reported to Congress, and he reiterated his belief that involvement in hostilities was not imminent.

In ordering a deployment intended to shock Iraq into retreat, Bush also sent shock waves across Capitol Hill and galvanized members into realizing that they had to take some kind of action on the issue, although there was still no consensus as to what that should be. Many members feared they might appear to be undermining their president if they questioned his policy in a public forum. The complexities of the gulf crisis, combined with the omnipresence of television, placed Congress in a peculiar situation. Members were fearful of what type of signal might be sent to Saddam by a drawn-out debate.

Forty-five House Democrats (later joined by eight more House members and one senator) filed a lawsuit asserting that the president needed congressional authorization to go to war, but a federal judge the following month declined to rule on it because the full Congress had not taken a stand on the issue.

After Secretary of Defense Dick Cheney stated that the president could launch a military strike without prior congressional authorization, the House Democratic Caucus in early December approved a resolution explicitly stating that the president should first seek such authorization, unless American lives were in danger.

Congress finally acted on the issue January 12, 1991, just three days before the expiration of a UN deadline after which member nations were allowed to "use all necessary means" to force Iraq to withdraw from Kuwait. Both chambers passed a joint resolution authorizing the president "to use United States Armed Forces" to enforce the ultimatum set by the UN Security Council. Bush had requested the congressional resolution in a letter January 8, after refusing for months to acknowledge that Congress had a formal role in deciding whether to use force against Iraq. It was the first such request by a president since the 1964 Tonkin Gulf resolution that authorized force in Vietnam. Yet, despite his request, Bush told reporters that he still believed he had the authority to act without such a vote.

Passage of the Persian Gulf resolution put the political and constitutional weight of the legislative branch behind Bush as he prepared the nation for potential battle. But the divided vote revealed deep fissures in Congress over the wisdom of going to war. The Senate adopted the resolution, 52–47, and the House, 250–183. Underscoring much of the debate was a sense that the legislative branch had acted too late to have any real choice except to back Bush in his showdown with Iraq.

Hostilities began four days later, on January 16. The resolution authorizing the use of force had required that before exercising that authority the president notify Congress of his determination that diplomatic and other peaceful means had failed. But Bush's calls to Capitol Hill were merely protocol—designed to notify, not consult. By the time the first member of Congress was notified, bombers had been in the air for thirty minutes.

Congress rushed to support the president, with the Senate voting 98–0 on January 17 and the House voting 399–6 (with six

members voting "present") the next day for a resolution backing the president. But having already authorized Bush to begin a war, members were well aware that they were reduced—politically and even constitutionally—to the role of bystanders. Congress continued to play a peripheral role as the war widened. It passed resolutions denouncing the Iraqis for launching missile attacks against Israel and for mistreating the allied prisoners of war, and considered legislation to benefit U.S. troops and their families.

The United States conducted an aerial blitz that pulverized Iraq's military machine for more than a month, but still Saddam refused to withdraw from Kuwait. The U.S.-led coalition then launched a ground offensive, sending troops and tanks into Kuwait and adjacent parts of Iraq. The six-week war officially came to an end just days later, on February 27, after coalition forces recaptured Kuwait.

1973 WAR POWERS RESOLUTION

Increasingly frustrated with its ineffectual influence on American involvement in Indochina and on the scope of U.S. military commitments abroad, Congress in 1973 responded by passing—over President Nixon's veto—legislation designed to limit the president's powers to commit U.S. forces abroad without congressional approval.

Known as the War Powers Resolution, the measure was the product of three years of effort in Congress.

National Commitments Resolution

The Senate in 1969 had taken the first step toward reasserting a congressional role in decisions committing the United States to the defense of foreign nations by passing a "national commitments" resolution. The resolution stated it to be the sense of the Senate that a national commitment "results only from affirmative action taken by the legislative and executive branches . . . by means of a treaty, statute, or concurrent resolution of both houses of Congress specifically providing for such commitment."

The measure did not have the force of law, nor was a similar resolution ever passed by the House. It was only an admonition to the president to consult with Congress—one Nixon did not heed. April 30, 1970, the date Nixon told the nation about the "incursion" of American forces into Cambodia, marked a turning point in the debate over war powers and prerogatives. Congress had not been consulted about the Cambodian incursion, and reaction on Capitol Hill was swift though not certain. Legislative initiatives sprang up, culminating three years later in passage of the war powers legislation with the support of members across the political spectrum.

War Powers Compromise

In response to the Nixon administration's military actions against Cambodia, the House between 1970 and 1972 passed several war powers measures but would not agree to a tougher bill the Senate passed in 1972. In 1973, however, the House approved a war powers bill much stronger than its earlier versions. The Senate again passed its bill, and a compromise was worked out.

Passage of the measure was heralded by its supporters as a major step in reasserting Congress's warmaking powers. Said Jacob K. Javits, R-N.Y., chief architect of the Senate's bill:

With the war powers resolution's passage, after 200 years, at last something will have been done about codifying the implementation of the most awesome power in the possession of any sovereignty and giving the broad representation of the people in Congress a voice in it. This is critically important, for we have just learned the hard lesson that wars cannot be successfully fought except with the consent of the people and with their support.

Provisions. The final version of the resolution stated that the president could commit U.S. forces to hostilities or imminent hostilities pursuant only to a declaration of war, specific statutory authority, or a national emergency created by an attack on the United States, its territories, or its armed forces. It required the president to consult with Congress "in every possible instance" before introducing U.S. forces into hostilities and to report any such commitment to Congress within forty-eight hours. The president was required to terminate any troop commitment within sixty to ninety days unless Congress specifically authorized its continuation or was unable to meet because of an attack on the United States. *(See box, War Powers Provisions, this page.)*

The measure permitted Congress at any time by concurrent resolution to direct the president to disengage troops involved in an undeclared or unauthorized war. Opponents had argued that the use of a concurrent resolution was unconstitutional and would not be binding on the president. However, others insisted that there were precedents for its use and that it would eliminate the possibility of a presidential veto. The so-called legislative veto was, indeed, declared unconstitutional by the Supreme Court in 1983. Although the circumstances in the court case were slightly different, the decision in *Immigration and Naturalization Service v. Chadha* made the constitutionality of the war powers veto provision suspect. The War Powers Resolution, however, contained a "separability clause" that said if one provision were declared invalid, the remainder would stand. *(See "Separation of Powers," p. 680.)*

The Senate attempted later in 1983 to amend the War Powers Resolution to allow Congress to force the withdrawal of troops by passing a joint resolution, which would require a presidential signature. But House conferees on the bill in question refused to go along; the final bill contained a provision setting priority procedures for Senate consideration of a bill or joint resolution to force withdrawal of U.S. forces from overseas combat.

Veto Override. In vetoing the legislation, President Nixon declared that the resolution would impose restrictions on the authority of the president that would be "both unconstitutional and dangerous to the best interests of our nation." The major provisions of the bill, he contended, would "purport to take away, by a mere legislative act, authorities which the president

WAR POWERS PROVISIONS

The 1973 War Powers Resolution:

• Stated that the president could commit U.S. armed forces to hostilities or situations where hostilities might be imminent only pursuant to a declaration of war, specific statutory authorization, or a national emergency created by an attack upon the United States, its territories or possessions, or its armed forces.

• Urged the president "in every possible instance" to consult with Congress before committing U.S. forces to hostilities or to situations where hostilities might be imminent, and to consult Congress regularly after such a commitment.

• Required the president to report in writing within forty-eight hours to the Speaker of the House and president pro tempore of the Senate when, in the absence of a declaration of war, U.S. forces were introduced: into hostilities or into situations where hostilities might be imminent; into foreign territory while equipped for combat, except for deployments related solely to supply, replacement, repair, or training of such forces; in numbers that substantially enlarged U.S. forces equipped for combat already located in a foreign country. Required supplementary reports at least every six months while the forces continued to be engaged in such hostilities or situation.

• Authorized the Speaker of the House and the president pro tempore of the Senate to reconvene Congress, if it was not in session, to consider the president's report.

• Required the termination of a troop commitment within sixty days after the president's initial report was submitted, unless Congress declared war, specifically authorized continuation of the commitment, or was physically unable to convene as a result of an armed attack upon the United States; allowed the sixty-day period to be extended for up to thirty days if the president determined and certified to Congress that unavoidable military necessity respecting the safety of U.S. forces required their continued use in bringing about a prompt disengagement.

• Allowed Congress at any time U.S. forces were engaged in hostilities without a declaration of war or specific congressional authorization to pass a concurrent resolution directing the president to disengage such troops. (This use of a concurrent resolution, which does not require the signature of the president, became constitutionally suspect in 1983 when the Supreme Court in *Immigration and Naturalization Service v. Chadha* declared the so-called legislative veto unconstitutional.) *(See "Separation of Powers," p. 680.)*

• Set up congressional procedures for consideration of any resolution or bill introduced pursuant to the provisions of the War Powers Resolution.

• Provided that if any provision of the War Powers Resolution was declared invalid, the remainder of the resolution would not be affected.

has properly exercised under the Constitution for almost two hundred years." Many of the act's provisions were unconstitutional, he asserted, because "the only way in which the constitutional powers of a branch of the government can be altered is by amending the Constitution—and any attempt to make such alterations by legislation alone is clearly without force."

The president's position was argued by some conservatives and administration supporters during debate on the bill. In their assertions that the bill was unconstitutional they were joined by a small group of liberals who feared that the legislation gave the president too much authority to commit troops.

But a commanding majority supported the resolution. After the president, as expected, vetoed the bill on October 24, the House on November 7 overrode the veto by a vote of 284–135—four votes more than the two-thirds majority needed to override. Four hours later, the Senate completed the process with a 75–18 vote to override.

Ongoing Controversy

The War Powers Resolution was controversial when it was adopted and it has remained so. Presidents have refused to invoke the law—or even concede its constitutionality—while Congress has been reluctant to challenge the president directly. As Robert A. Katzmann described it:

As a matter of strategy, the executive has been careful not to do anything that might be construed as an acknowledgment of the constitutionality of the War Powers Resolution. Moreover, presidents have proceeded in ways that test congressional tolerance for their military initiatives, generally calculating that the legislature will ultimately acquiesce to the decisions of the commander in chief. At the same time, they have skillfully avoided constitutional confrontations with Congress.[47]

Executives argued that the War Powers Resolution was unconstitutional because of the concurrent resolution provision, as well as the provision that forced the president to withdraw troops if Congress failed to give its approval to the troop commitment. The latter, they claimed, violated the "presentment clause" (Article I, Section 7, Clause 2), which holds that every bill passed by Congress must be presented to the president before it becomes law. Presidents also have argued that Congress could not impede their ability to carry out their constitutional duties as chief executive and commander in chief to deal promptly with threats to the national security.

On practical grounds, presidents have alleged that the deadlines set by the resolution could interfere with the completion of initiatives and that the very existence of limits could signal to the enemy that the United States was divided, so that the enemy might be emboldened to wait out the sixty-day deadline. Executives also have maintained that the deadlines could pose risks for troops, if they had to be withdrawn under fire, and could make allies less willing to commit their forces if they thought the U.S. commitment could be terminated by Congress. Moreover, they have insisted that Congress already has at its disposal the means—authorizations and appropriations—to constrain an executive.

The Vietnam Veterans Memorial in Washington, D.C. Congressional dissatisfaction with its ineffectual influence during the Vietnam War led to passage of the 1973 War Powers Resolution. The act attempted to limit the president's power to commit U.S. forces to hostilities abroad without the approval of Congress.

Views of members of Congress vary. A 1996 Congressional Research Service (CRS) report stated:

Some Members of Congress believe the Resolution has on some occasions served as a restraint on the use of armed forces by Presidents, provided a mode of communication, and given Congress a vehicle for asserting its war powers. Others have sought to amend the Resolution because they believe it has failed to assure a congressional voice in committing U.S. troops to potential conflicts abroad. Others in Congress, along with executive branch officials, contend that the President needs more flexibility in the conduct of foreign policy and that the time limitation in the War Powers Resolution is unconstitutional and impractical. Some have argued for its repeal.[48]

While fierce defenders of the resolution are few in number, Congress still has turned back efforts to repeal it.

There was enough dissatisfaction with the War Powers Resolution after a contentious 1987–1988 debate over Reagan administration policy in the Persian Gulf to spur a reexamination of the law by a specially created subcommittee of the Senate Foreign Relations Committee and by the House Foreign Affairs Committee. No changes were enacted.

In 1995 the House, anxious over the prospects that U.S. ground troops might be deployed to Bosnia, rejected a Republican-led effort to repeal the War Powers Resolution. The House voted 201–217 to defeat the repeal amendment, which would have retained only the resolution's consulting and reporting requirements. Amendment sponsor Henry J. Hyde, R-Ill., called the War Powers Resolution "a useless anachronism" and said that Congress could still stop a military operation in its tracks by exerting its power of the purse. But Lee H. Hamilton, D-Ind., disagreed: "The power of the purse is not equivalent to Congress sharing the critical threshold decision, up front, about whether to send troops at all." He went on to say that the power of the purse was usually exercised after the fact, at which point it was very difficult to cut off funding.

Opponents of Hyde's proposal conceded that the law's automatic cutoff of hostilities was essentially unworkable. But they argued that its mere existence forced presidents to recognize the need to involve Congress in decisions involving the use of force.

Consulting with Congress

The executive branch's "consultation" with Congress under the War Powers Resolution has, in the view of some members of Congress, basically meant presenting Congress with a fait accompli. As Davidson and Oleszek put it: "Often when executive decision makers fear congressional opposition, they simply neglect to inform Capitol Hill until the planned action is under way."[49]

The lack of a clear definition of "consultation" has exacerbated the problem. Katzmann wrote: "For the most part, the executive branch has interpreted 'consultation' to mean 'inform,' whereas Congress had hoped that the term would require the president to seek the advice of and even in 'appropriate circumstances' the 'approval of action contemplated.'"[50]

For example, congressional leaders in 1983 were informed of the planned invasion of Grenada two hours after President Reagan had signed the directive ordering the landing but before it actually took place. Reagan and congressional leaders discussed plans for the bombing of Libya in 1986 while the aircraft were on their way. President Bush informed key congressional leaders of his not unexpected decision to send forces into Panama in 1989 after the operation had been set in motion and only a few hours before the shooting started.

There was considerable executive-legislative consultation on the Reagan administration's 1987–1988 policy of reflagging and providing U.S. Navy escorts for Kuwaiti-owned oil tankers in the Persian Gulf once it was under way but not at the outset. In a report to Congress, Secretary of Defense Caspar W. Weinberger provided a telling commentary on the process: "As soon as Kuwait indicated its acceptance of our offer, we began consultations with Congress."[51]

Reporting to Congress

By June 1999, more than seventy reports had been submitted under the War Powers Resolution, although not all reports specifically mentioned the act. President Ford submitted four reports, President Carter one, President Reagan fourteen, President Bush six, and President Bill Clinton fifty. From 1974 to 1992, there were seventeen other deployments of U.S. forces in potentially hostile situations that were not reported to Congress.[52]

In most reports the presidents cited their authority under the Constitution for the actions they had taken and usually indicated that the reports were being submitted "consistent with" the War Powers Resolution. To have said the report was being filed "pursuant to" or "under" the War Powers Resolution would have been interpreted as acknowledgment of the act's constitutionality, and no president has been willing to do that.

Only one of these reports cited section 4(a)(1), the section that required the president to report to Congress any introduction of U.S. forces into hostilities or imminent hostilities. It was this section that would trigger the requirement that the forces be withdrawn within sixty to ninety days if Congress did not authorize them to remain. And in the one case when section 4(a)(1) was cited—President Ford's use of troops in 1975 to free the American ship *Mayaguez* and its crew, seized by Cambodian communist troops—the operation was essentially over when the report was submitted to Congress.

Under the War Powers Resolution, Congress also was empowered to trigger the sixty-day clock for troop commitments, which it did in 1983 when it authorized U.S. participation in a multinational peacekeeping force in Lebanon. Congress extended the deadline for withdrawal to eighteen months, and in return President Reagan signed a resolution invoking the War Powers Resolution while denying its constitutionality.

MAJOR DEPLOYMENTS SINCE 1973

Since the enactment of the War Powers Resolution in 1973, the United States has deployed its armed forces on a number of occasions with varying degrees of congressional involvement. As pointed out in the 1996 CRS report, the issues raised in the debates on these deployments have changed over the years.[53]

Defining "Consultation"

In the 1970s Congress's main concern was the level of consultation.

Vietnam, Mayaguez Rescue. In reporting to Congress on evacuations from Vietnam and on the *Mayaguez* rescue, President Ford set a pattern for executive consultation that has largely been followed by his successors. Ford opted for notification of Congress prior to the actual introduction of forces. Congress had hoped to be consulted prior to the making of the decision to deploy the forces.

As noted earlier, when Ford reported to Congress on the *Mayaguez* rescue operation, he became the only president to cite section 4(a)(1) of the war powers act and thus trigger a time limit. But the operation was over and the troops had been withdrawn when the timetable was set in motion.

Iran. President Carter sent one war powers report to Congress—on the failed military attempt to rescue Americans being held hostage in Iran. The White House had not informed Congress prior to the operation, arguing that because this was a surprise rescue mission and not a military offensive, consultation was not only unnecessary but unwise.

Challenging the President

By the 1980s members focused on presidential compliance and whether they could use the War Powers Resolution to restrain the executive.

Early in the Reagan administration some members of Congress challenged the White House decision not to report under the War Powers Resolution its 1981 increase in the number of U.S. military advisers in El Salvador. But neither a lawsuit nor various legislative proposals succeeded in pressuring the administration to report. Some members also questioned the administration's decision not to report U.S. participation in military exercises in Honduras in 1983 and subsequent years.

Lebanon. A major test of the War Powers Resolution began to unfold in 1982 when Reagan dispatched a contingent of Marines to Lebanon to take part in a multinational peacekeeping force. The operation evolved into a far larger commitment and a major foreign policy dilemma for Congress. Reagan sent several reports to Congress on the deployment but did not invoke section 4(a)(1), even after U.S. troops came under fire and two soldiers were killed. House Foreign Affairs Committee Chairman Clement J. Zablocki, D-Wis., said Reagan was "unnecessarily risking a confrontation with Congress."

Lengthy negotiations between the two branches resulted in a compromise setting an eighteen-month limit on the U.S. deployment in Lebanon. In essence, the compromise required Reagan to sign a joint resolution invoking the War Powers Resolution and imposing the eighteen-month limit. In return, the president could declare in writing that he did not recognize the constitutionality of the resolution and that he retained his constitutional authority as commander in chief to deploy U.S. forces.

The compromise was hailed by some as a historic step toward giving the War Powers Resolution more political validity than it had acquired during its first ten years of existence. Zablocki insisted it was a victory for Congress: "This will be the first administration that has acknowledged the war powers act." But critics of the agreement said Congress gave away too much: instead of a sixty-day or ninety-day limit, Reagan was given eighteen months, basically so neither side would have to deal with the issue during the 1984 national election.

Grenada. Reagan's decision in 1983 to send U.S. troops to Grenada to restore order and protect Americans from the civil strife on the Caribbean island prompted the House and Senate to each pass measures declaring that section 4(a)(1) had gone into effect on the day of the invasion. But neither measure cleared Congress, and all troops were withdrawn in less than sixty days. A lawsuit filed by several members challenging Reagan's action was turned down by the courts.

Libya. U.S. air strikes against Libya in 1986 for its support of terrorists renewed debate about the role of Congress in initiating armed conflict. But lawmakers took no action on proposals to alter existing war powers restrictions.

Persian Gulf. The Reagan administration's 1987 decision to fly American flags on Kuwaiti-owned oil tankers and provide them with U.S. Navy escorts in the Persian Gulf during the Iran-Iraq war triggered another struggle with Congress. The proposal had drawn scant attention on Capitol Hill until Iraqi missiles struck a U.S. ship and killed thirty-seven U.S. sailors. Both the House and Senate cast largely symbolic votes in favor of delaying Reagan's policy but a Republican filibuster blocked Senate passage of even a nonbinding resolution calling for delay. Efforts in the Senate to invoke the War Powers Resolution also were stymied, and a lawsuit brought by more than one hundred members of the House asking that Reagan be required to initiate war powers procedures was dismissed by a federal court on the ground that it was a political question on which the courts could not rule.

Panama. Citing a growing threat to U.S. personnel in Panama, President Bush in 1989 ordered a massive invasion of that country, resulting in the removal from power of Panamanian dictator Gen. Manuel Antonio Noriega. Bush did not seek prior approval for the deployment, notified leaders a few hours before it began, and refused to put a time limit on the operation once it was under way. Yet there was little talk of the War Powers Resolution. For one thing, Congress was not in session; in addition, the deployment had broad support on Capitol Hill and among the American people. Noriega's nullification of elections, brutal treatment of opposition leaders, and indictment on drug trafficking charges made his ouster widely popular. Earlier Congress had called on the president to consult with other nations on ways to remove Noriega from power and to intensify unilateral, bilateral, and multinational efforts on measures directed at his removal. The Senate had defeated an amendment authorizing the president to use the armed forces to remove Noriega and accepted instead an alternative expressing its support for the president's efforts to remove Noriega and to utilize the full range of appropriate diplomatic, economic, and military options in Panama.

Multilateral Deployments

In the post–cold war era of the 1990s, Congress was confronted with a new issue: how to respond to U.S. participation in military actions authorized or supported by multilateral organizations such as the United Nations and NATO.

Persian Gulf War. After Iraq invaded Kuwait in 1990, President Bush sent the first of what would be more than a half-million military personnel to the Persian Gulf region and marshaled international support. With war looming, a divided Congress voted to authorize the use of force against Iraq if it did not meet a United Nations deadline to withdraw from Kuwait. The authorizing resolution stated that it was intended to constitute specific statutory authorization within the meaning of the War Powers Resolution. But even as he signed the resolution, Bush insisted that he could have acted without it:

RESOLUTIONS AUTHORIZING USE OF U.S. FORCES

Between 1955 and mid-1999 Congress on six occasions passed joint resolutions authorizing or approving the president's determination to use such armed forces as he deemed necessary to repeal armed attacks or threats against certain nations or geographical areas.

Two of these resolutions, the Tonkin Gulf resolution of 1964 and the Persian Gulf resolution of 1991, were used, in part, to justify U.S. participation in full-scale wars.

FORMOSA RESOLUTION, 1955

Mounting tensions in the Taiwan Strait in 1954 prompted the United States to sign a mutual defense treaty with Taiwan (which was also called Formosa until the 1960s and later the Republic of China or Nationalist China). While the treaty was pending before the Senate, Communist, or mainland, China stepped up pressure against Taiwan in January 1955 by seizing the island of Ichiang, just off the mainland, 210 miles north of Taiwan, and at the same time increasing its pressure on two other offshore islands, Quemoy and Matsu.

The situation led President Dwight D. Eisenhower to ask Congress, in a special message January 24, 1955, for explicit authority to use American armed forces to protect Taiwan, the Pescadores Islands, and "related positions and territories." But what was not clear was the administration's intent regarding Quemoy, Matsu, and the other offshore islands. The president's statement implied that he might commit American forces to repel an invasion of Quemoy—the message, essentially, that the administration wished to give mainland China.

To a number of Democrats, however, the offshore islands, unlike Taiwan, clearly belonged to mainland China; the question of the islands' disposition, they felt, was beyond the scope of legitimate U.S. security interests. They feared that the Nationalists, in their efforts to regain the mainland, would use this "fatal ambiguity" over the offshore islands to maneuver the United States into war.

Nevertheless, despite their misgivings, Democratic leaders in Congress hastened to comply with the president's request. The resolution authorizing the president to "employ the armed forces of the United States as he deems necessary" was adopted by the House January 25, 1955, by a 410–3 vote, after Speaker Sam Rayburn, D-Texas, said the resolution added nothing to the constitutional powers of the president and should not be taken as a precedent. The Senate passed it, 85–3, without amendment on January 28 and it was signed into law the next day. The Senate approved the mutual defense pact with Taiwan less than two weeks later.

Both the Eisenhower and Kennedy administrations reaffirmed the U.S. commitment to defend Taiwan when tensions flared up again in 1958 and 1962. In the late 1960s and early 1970s, however, the Nixon administration, supported by a majority in Congress, dropped America's two-decade-old policy of isolating Communist China. The Formosa resolution, which came to be regarded as outdated by the Nixon administration and many in Congress, was repealed in 1974.

MIDDLE EAST RESOLUTION, 1957

Concerned that the 1956 Suez crisis had left a power vacuum in the Middle East into which the Soviets would move unless deterred by the United States, the Eisenhower administration asked Congress for an expression of congressional support for presidential discretion in the Middle East similar to the 1955 Formosa resolution. In a January 5, 1957, appearance before a joint session of Congress, the president asked Congress for authority to extend economic and military aid to friendly nations and to "employ the armed forces of the United States" as deemed necessary to protect the area against "overt armed aggression from any nation controlled by international communism."

Promptly dubbed the Eisenhower Doctrine, the policy proposal was greeted with little enthusiasm by Republicans and with some asperity by Democrats, who decried the president's request for a "blank check" and complained that it skirted the basic issues of Arab-Israeli hostility and control of the Suez Canal.

But Secretary of State John Foster Dulles warned Congress that unless the United States acted promptly, the area would very likely be lost. When Majority Leader Lyndon B. Johnson, D-Texas, and others complained that his case rested on generalities, with little information, Dulles replied: "If we have to pinpoint everything we propose to do, this program will not serve its purpose. If Congress is not willing to trust the president to the extent he asks, we can't win this battle."

Faced with this argument, most members were unwilling to withhold a vote of confidence. The House passed the resolution by a 355–61 vote. The Senate approved it, 72–19, after rejecting amendments that would have made substantive changes. The resolution proclaiming U.S. policy to defend Middle East countries "against aggression from any country controlled by international communism" was signed into law March 9, 1957.

The first test of the Eisenhower Doctrine came in 1958 following a coup in Iraq, which overthrew the pro-Western government and replaced it with a regime favorable to the Soviet Union and the United Arab Republic. The United States refrained from military action in this case. But when the government of Lebanon came under similar pressure in 1958 and U.S. assistance was requested, U.S. Marines

---

As I made clear to congressional leaders at the outset, my request for congressional support did not, and my signing this resolution does not, constitute any change in the long-standing positions of the executive branch on either the President's constitutional authority to use the Armed Forces to defend vital U.S. interests or the constitutionality of the War Powers Resolution.

Some questioned the effectiveness of the War Powers Resolution, given how close the United States was to war by the time Congress gave its approval. But many members came away from the debate confident that Congress had asserted its authority and performed its duty. Richard Grimmett of the Congressional Research Service noted that House Foreign Affairs Committee Chairman Fascell saw the War Powers Resolution as "alive and well. . . . In his view, the strength and wisdom of the War Powers Resolution was that it established a process by which Congress could authorize the use of force in specific settings for limited purposes, short of a total state of war."[54]

The allies began a bombing campaign in mid-January 1991; a

were sent in. Eisenhower justified his action on the ground that American lives were endangered, and, indirectly, on the application of the Eisenhower Doctrine.

CUBAN RESOLUTION, 1962

Cuban leader Fidel Castro's open avowal of his attachment to communism late in 1961 triggered an ever increasing flow of Soviet-bloc military and economic aid to Cuba.

President John F. Kennedy on September 13, 1962, declared that, at that time, the Soviet arms shipments did not constitute a serious threat to the rest of the hemisphere and did not warrant unilateral military intervention. But he warned that if they did become a threat "this country will do whatever must be done to protect its own security and that of its allies."

As the issue heated up in the midterm election campaign, Kennedy asked for and received authority to call up reservists if needed. To head off any congressional initiatives to commit the United States to some specific course of action against Cuba, the administration endorsed a joint resolution modeled on the president's September 13 statement.

The resolution declared that the United States was determined to prevent Cuba—with arms if necessary—from extending its subversive activities to any part of the hemisphere, and that it also would prevent the creation there of an externally supported military capability endangering U.S. security. The Senate adopted the resolution September 20 by an 86–1 vote. The House passed it September 26, 384–7. It was signed into law October 3.

Within weeks aerial intelligence showed that the Soviets were building offensive missile sites in Cuba. On October 22 Kennedy announced that he was imposing a U.S. naval quarantine on Cuba. He used the congressional resolution to justify his actions but also invoked his constitutional authority as commander in chief. A head-on clash was avoided when the Soviets diverted ships moving toward Cuba and subsequently dismantled the offensive missile sites.

Congress in 1982 adopted a resolution reaffirming its 1962 threat to use force to stop Cuban subversion or the use of Cuba by the Soviet Union as a base for nuclear weapons. But the bill provided that this was not to be interpreted as authorization for the president to use U.S. troops outside the limits of the 1973 War Powers Resolution.

BERLIN RESOLUTION, 1962

Congress took the initiative in 1962 to pass a resolution reaffirming U.S. determination to use armed force, if necessary, to defend West Berlin. The resolution, which merely expressed the sense of Congress and did not have the force of law, was an outgrowth of the 1961 Berlin crisis in which East Germany cut off its sector of Berlin from the rest of the city and led President Kennedy to call up reservists.

The resolution was adopted by the House October 5 by a 312–0 vote. During the debate Clement J. Zablocki, D-Wis., sponsor of the resolution, said the executive branch had stood up firmly to the Soviet Union on Berlin, and "the only voice that has not been officially heard on this issue is the voice of the U.S. Congress."

The Senate approved the resolution without change on October 10.

TONKIN GULF RESOLUTION, 1964

A revealing picture of the congressional role in foreign policy decisions leading up to the Vietnam War was provided by the adoption in 1964 of the Tonkin Gulf resolution, the most controversial of the post–World War II resolutions. The resolution, signed into law August 10, 1964, authorized the president to use U.S. armed forces to repel attacks against U.S. forces and affirmed U.S. determination to defend any Southeast Asia Treaty Organization (SEATO) member or protocol state (this included Vietnam) requesting assistance.

Initially approved overwhelmingly by Congress on the basis of what later emerged as a distorted account of a minor naval engagement, the resolution became the primary legal justification of the Johnson administration's prosecution of the war. Years later it came to represent one of the most vivid examples of congressional willingness to hand the president a blank check in foreign policy, even in the area of war making and U.S. military commitments abroad.

Congress voted to repeal the Tonkin resolution in 1970. (See "Tonkin Gulf Resolution," p. 229.)

PERSIAN GULF RESOLUTION, 1991

The issue of Congress's war-making powers was thrust back into the limelight after the August 1990 invasion of Kuwait by Iraq and President George Bush's massive deployment of troops to the area. For months Bush refused to acknowledge that Congress had a formal role to play in deciding whether to use force against Iraq, while Congress insisted that it did.

Finally, in January 1991, with war imminent, Bush requested and received a congressional resolution authorizing the use of force if necessary to enforce a U.N. mandate that Iraq withdraw from Kuwait. Just four days later hostilities began. (See "Persian Gulf War," p. 231.)

little more than a month later, a four-day ground war ousted Iraqi forces from Kuwait. (See "Persian Gulf War," p. 231.)

Somalia. Bush's successor in the White House, Bill Clinton, assumed office in 1993 confident that he could avoid the clashes with Congress over war powers that had bedeviled his Republican predecessors. Indeed, the Clinton administration briefed Congress so regularly and solicited guidance so deferentially on intervention abroad that in some cases lawmakers questioned whether the administration had a position of its own.

But before the end of his first year in office, Clinton was replicating battles with Congress that President Reagan had waged a decade earlier. Having initially appeared to support the war powers law, he by then had adopted the same linguistic straddle used by his predecessors, describing his reports on the use of U.S. armed forces abroad as "consistent with" the law.

Clinton's first clash with Congress over war powers came early in his administration, when a once peaceful U.S. humanitarian effort in famine- and civil war–torn Somalia turned into an increasingly violent operation under United Nations command. Following the deaths of eighteen U.S. soldiers in a battle with a local warlord in 1993, an outraged Congress pressured Clinton to agree to withdraw most U.S. forces from Somalia by March 31, 1994. Congress followed up the agreement with a cut-off of funds for the Somalia mission after that date. A House GOP proposal to advance the withdrawal date was defeated; interestingly, Republicans had invoked provisions of the War Powers Resolution, which they had long rejected as unconstitutional, to force expedited House action on their Somalia resolution.

Mindful of the Somalia experience, Congress subsequently attempted to restrict the president's authority to place U.S. troops in peacekeeping operations under UN command. The Somalia contingent had been the first combat-capable unit to serve outside the U.S. chain of command. Temporary restrictions were included in appropriations bills enacted in the 104th Congress (1995–1996), but House Republicans' attempts to push through permanent limits either died in the Senate or fell to a Clinton veto.

Haiti. The war powers debate was reignited the following year, when Clinton dispatched twenty thousand U.S. soldiers to oversee the return of democracy to Haiti. The refusal of a military junta to step down in the face of international sanctions, along with U.S. concern about a flood of Haitian refugees, had triggered the deployment. Eleventh-hour negotiations between Haitian military leaders and a U.S. delegation led by former president Carter averted a full-scale military invasion. Prior to the operation Congress had gone on record urging the White House to seek congressional approval before launching any military action in Haiti. Senate attempts to force Clinton to obtain prior authorization failed, a reflection of senators' reluctance to tie the hands of the commander in chief, not enthusiasm for military action in Haiti. Clinton had requested and received UN authorization for an invasion.

Once the troops had been dispatched, Congress passed resolutions supporting the troops and urging a prompt withdrawal. Then, after an exhaustive and at times rancorous debate, Congress did little more than require the president to provide detailed reports on the mission. This lowest-common-denominator approach attracted broad, if not enthusiastic, support. But it outraged longtime defenders of Congress's foreign policy prerogatives. "We have not approved of the policy, we have not disapproved of the policy," said House Foreign Affairs Committee Chairman Hamilton: "We simply default." On the Senate side, Appropriations Committee Chairman Byrd characterized congressional action as a "shrug of the shoulders in terms of any real assertion of the constitutional role of Congress."

Bosnia-Herzegovina. A bloody civil war in the former Yugoslav republic of Bosnia-Herzegovina led to concern over atrocities being committed by the Serbian military against the Muslims and the possibility of a wider conflict. The Clinton administration began in 1993 to report to Congress on U.S. participation in various activities, including airlifts of relief supplies, enforcement of a military "no-fly zone" over Bosnia, and aerial

protection of safe havens. But the president and Congress alike were in a quandary over how to find a long-term solution to the centuries-old enmity that existed among the warring factions.

The one option a majority on Capitol Hill could agree on was a partial lifting of a UN arms embargo that had benefited the already well armed Serbs while putting the besieged Muslim-led government forces at a serious disadvantage. Ending the embargo against the Muslims was seen by many members as the best way of stopping Serbian aggression without involving U.S. troops in the war. But the Clinton administration opposed unilateral action by the United States, and congressional attempts to require him to lift the embargo failed. In the end Congress managed only to cut U.S. funding for enforcement of the ban, not adherence to it.

The controversy over Bosnia policy intensified in late 1995 when U.S.-brokered peace talks produced an agreement. Clinton previously had pledged to police a peace with twenty thousand U.S. ground troops as part of a NATO force. The House had voted to block any such deployment unless Congress approved funds for it. But once the peace agreement was reached, efforts to keep U.S. troops out of Bosnia quickly collapsed. This episode once again demonstrated that the president enjoys wide discretion in deciding whether to deploy U.S. forces on missions abroad, no matter how vehement his opponents in Congress are.

Clinton had presented Congress with a fait accompli. He had staked the U.S. government's credibility abroad on the peace deal. Moreover, given that Congress had no practical way to bar Clinton from sending the troops, members faced the possibility that any effort to compel a withdrawal by cutting off funds would put the troops at greater risk. The Senate rejected the House position and the House later defeated a second attempt to deny funds for the mission, albeit by a surprisingly close vote.

In 1997 Congress allowed Clinton to extend the mission as long as he told Congress why and for how long. In 1998 the House rejected an attempt to make the Bosnia deployment a test case of the constitutionality of the War Powers Resolution.

Kosovo. When civil war broke out in the Serbian province of Kosovo in 1998, the Clinton administration, encouraged by Congress, moved quickly on the diplomatic front to bring the warring parties to the negotiating table in hopes of containing the fighting, preventing the massacre of thousands of ethnic Albanians, and forestalling a massive refugee crisis in Europe. After Serbia failed to agree to the peace accord, the United States and its NATO allies launched air strikes on Serbia in March 1999 with the goal of forcing Slobodan Milosevic, president of Serbia and the larger Yugoslavia, into signing.

A number of votes on Kosovo were taken on Capitol Hill over a period of several months but no clear strategy emerged. Congressional ambivalence on Kosovo was fueled by divisions in both parties on such questions as to whether the United States should have entered the conflict at all, whether ground troops should be considered, and whether NATO was too reliant on U.S. financing.

Prior to the air strikes the House had voted to support U.S. participation in a NATO peacekeeping operation. The administration was grateful for the support, although it had asked the House not to debate the issue while delicate peace talks were under way. But House Speaker Dennis Hastert, R-Ill., rebuffed the entreaties, saying that he did not want to repeat the pattern of recent years, when Congress had expressed its opinion only after troops had been deployed, making it difficult to oppose a mission without harming morale in the military.

On the eve of the first air strikes the Senate adopted a bipartisan resolution in support of them. A month later the House took a series of votes on Kosovo in which it refused to either support or disown Clinton's policy. The House rejected a resolution ordering a withdrawal of U.S. forces and another that would have declared war on Yugoslavia, as well as the Senate resolution supporting the air strikes, which lost on a tie vote. The only measure that passed the House that day was a bill requiring authorization for any ground troops. But the following week the House declined to put teeth in that position when it rejected an amendment barring the use of any funds in a defense supplemental appropriations bill for an invasion of Yugoslavia. That same week the Senate killed a resolution that would have authorized Clinton to use "all necessary force" to prevail in the Kosovo conflict. But on one point Congress was clear: its support of U.S. armed forces. Clinton's $5.5 billion request to pay for the U.S. role in the NATO campaign was nearly doubled in the bill Congress cleared.

In the meantime, eighteen members of Congress filed a lawsuit against Clinton in federal district court, asserting that his commitment of forces to the NATO campaign violated the War Powers Resolution. They wanted to force Clinton to either withdraw forces from the NATO mission or seek congressional authorization. The case was dismissed on the grounds that the plaintiffs lacked legal standing to bring the suit.

After eleven weeks of bombing, Yugoslav forces began pulling out of Kosovo, allowing U.S. and allied peacekeeping troops to pave the way for the return of more than 750,000 ethnic Albanian refugees.

Intelligence Oversight: Congress Asserts Itself

"No more dramatic example of the new congressional assertiveness with respect to foreign policy is to be found than that of the changed relationship between Congress and the intelligence community," wrote former Senate Foreign Relations staff director Pat M. Holt in 1989.[55]

Congressional oversight of the intelligence community had been a long time in coming. Although the modern intelligence apparatus was established after World War II, it was not until the mid-1970s, after revelations of abuses by the executive branch, that Congress insisted on a role in supervising the U.S. government's intelligence agencies and its covert activities.

That there were limits to the new system became apparent in the 1980s in the pitched executive-legislative battles over U.S. policy toward the leftist government of Nicaragua. The revelations of the Iran-contra affair dramatized how difficult it was for Congress to influence the conduct of covert operations and an intelligence process that was structured to serve the president. The Iran-contra affair "left both the intelligence community and the oversight mechanism in such disarray as had rarely been seen," Holt observed. "A system that had been carefully and laboriously constructed had failed, and thoughtful people at both ends of Pennsylvania Avenue were asking themselves what had gone wrong and how it could be put right."[56]

In the wake of the Iran-contra scandal, Congress sought ways to enhance its oversight role. It also was preoccupied in the 1990s with the issue of overhauling the intelligence community to meet the challenges of the post–cold war era. Several major security and intelligence failures in the 1990s rocked the intelligence community and added urgency to Congress's oversight efforts.

SLOW START FOR OVERSIGHT

Congress was deeply involved in intelligence activities at the beginning of the Republic, but that role lapsed for a century and a half. For most of that period America was disengaged and had little need for foreign intelligence. But in the post–World War II era, the situation changed dramatically. The United States emerged as a world leader, and an elaborate intelligence system evolved to meet the needs of its vastly expanded international role. In this period, according to Gregory F. Treverton, "the preeminence of the president and the imminence of the cold war induced Congress to leave intelligence to the executive, for better or worse."[57]

Holt described the years of congressional neglect:

For more than twenty-five years following the passage of the National Security Act, which created the Central Intelligence Agency in 1947, Congress largely ignored the intelligence community. It allowed the National Security Agency and the Defense Intelligence Agency to be created by executive order. It voted for untold billions of dollars in hidden appropriations for intelligence activities with very few, if any, of its members knowing either the amounts or the purposes of the funds. Members of Congress who were actively concerned . . . were rebuffed by large majorities on the few occasions when they tried to ask questions or to establish procedures for doing so.[58]

Oversight in that period was conducted through a kind of "buddy system," which consisted of informal conversations between the director of intelligence and a few senior members of Congress. And that appeared to be fine with most members of Congress. Leverett Saltonstall, R-Mass., a senior member of the Senate Armed Services Committee, probably expressed a widely held view when he once told a congressional hearing that there was some intelligence information he would rather not have.[59]

Senator Mansfield, who later became majority leader, made several unsuccessful attempts in the 1950s to win support for creation of a "watchdog" committee to keep an eye on the CIA.

The one time his proposal came to a vote, in 1956, it was defeated by a 27–59 margin in the face of strong administration opposition and arguments that Congress was adequately apprised of CIA activities through established subcommittees of the Armed Services and Appropriations committees. Although the meetings of the Armed Services subcommittees were secret, they reportedly rarely met—sometimes not even once a year.[60]

Two intelligence operations in the early 1960s set off controversies over the activities of the U.S. intelligence community. In May 1960, on the eve of a U.S.-Soviet summit meeting, the Soviets shot down over their territory a U.S. reconnaissance plane. When President Eisenhower admitted that the U-2 plane was on an espionage mission, the Soviets canceled the summit. In April 1961 a CIA-sponsored invasion of Cuba by Cuban exiles with the goal of overthrowing the Castro regime ended in disastrous defeat, as well as acute embarrassment for the Kennedy administration, which had taken office in January.

After both foreign policy catastrophes, the Senate Foreign Relations Committee held extensive hearings that helped to heighten some senators' skepticism of the intelligence community.

In 1966 another attempt was made to broaden congressional oversight but it, too, was unsuccessful. A resolution was drafted by the Foreign Relations Committee, and largely backed by Vietnam War critics, that would have permitted members of the committee to participate directly in Senate oversight of U.S. intelligence operations. This was rejected by a 61–28 vote after a bitter debate. The resolution was referred to the Armed Services Committee, which did not act on it. But that committee's chairman, Georgia Democrat Richard B. Russell, announced in January 1967 that he would ask three members of the Foreign Relations Committee to attend CIA oversight committee meetings during the 90th Congress.

Russell's arrangement did not last long. As Holt described it, "The members of Foreign Relations found it generally unsatisfactory. They participated by sufferance and not by right; the group met infrequently and was inadequately staffed."[61]

MOVES TOWARD REAL OVERSIGHT

In the 1970s Congress moved toward real oversight of the intelligence community. Several factors accounted for the changed attitude on Capitol Hill. Watergate had a profound effect on members of Congress, as did revelations of CIA involvement in a clandestine war in Laos, CIA interference in Chilean politics, U.S. activities in the war in Angola, and improper and illegal activities within the United States by the CIA and other government intelligence groups. (See "1975 CIA Investigation," p. 274.)

In addition, Congress itself changed. Senior members of Congress who had made up the CIA's constituency on Capitol Hill retired. Reforms were adopted that dispersed power previously held by committee chairs. A new generation was voted into Congress. Treverton described the results: "Congress's disinclination to ask about secret operations was the first change.

Neither reticence nor deference were hallmarks of the congressional class of 1974, elected as Watergate played out on the nation's television screens."[62]

In 1974 Congress approved legislation requiring the executive branch to notify the appropriate congressional committees "in a timely fashion" of any covert CIA operation. The amendment, sponsored by Sen. Harold E. Hughes, D-Iowa, and Rep. Leo J. Ryan, D-Calif., was attached to a foreign aid authorization bill.

Initially, six committees were notified: Senate Foreign Relations and House Foreign Affairs, and the Appropriations and Armed Services committees in each chamber. The number of committees increased to eight with the creation of the Senate Select Intelligence Committee in 1976 and the House Select Intelligence Committee in 1977.

The Hughes-Ryan amendment subsequently came under much criticism. The CIA and its supporters said the reporting requirements discouraged covert operations by allowing too many persons in Congress—members as well as staff—to have access to such information. Those who favored greater congressional oversight were concerned that the requirement that activities be reported "in a timely fashion" opened a potential loophole allowing the president to inform Congress of covert operations after the fact.

As a result, Congress passed legislation in 1980 to repeal Hughes-Ryan, reduce the number of committees to be notified of covert actions from eight to two—the House and Senate Intelligence committees—and set more definitive reporting requirements spelling out under what conditions Congress had to be notified in advance of covert actions. The act permitted the president, under "extraordinary circumstances," to restrict prior notification to the chairs and ranking minority members of the Intelligence committees, the Speaker and minority leader of the House, and the majority and minority leaders of the Senate (a group that was to become known to some as the "gang of eight"). If Congress was not given advance notice, the president was to report the operation "in a timely fashion."

Intelligence Committees

After its investigation of the CIA in 1975, the Senate on May 19, 1976, had voted 72–22 to establish a Select Intelligence Committee to monitor the activities of the CIA and other intelligence agencies.

The committee was given exclusive legislative and budget authorization authority over the CIA, but jurisdiction over the intelligence components of the FBI, the Defense Department, the National Security Agency, the State Department, and other intelligence units had to be shared with other committees, such as Judiciary and Armed Services.

The House on July 14, 1977, by a 227–171 vote, created its Select Intelligence Committee. The powers and responsibilities of the panel essentially paralleled those of the Senate panel.

With the creation of the new committees, Congress began to receive a greatly improved flow of information from the intelli-

The Iran-contra affair raised important questions as to the limits of congressional oversight of intelligence. A bipartisan majority of the House and Senate special committees that investigated the affair in 1987 found that the failures of Iran-contra stemmed from White House "secrecy, deception, and disdain for the rule of law."

gence community, which, according to Holt, "put Congress on a much more nearly equal footing in dealing with other government agencies concerned with the making of foreign policy."[63]

And in 1978 Congress—for the first time in its history—authorized funds for the operation of the intelligence agencies. The actual amounts authorized were classified but were made available to members of Congress (but not to their staffs) in a secret annex to the conference report on the bill. As in previous years, the actual appropriations approved for these agencies were not revealed but instead were scattered throughout the budgets of various federal agencies and were not identified in any of the regular legislative documents.

The intelligence budget remained classified until the late 1990s, when the CIA twice revealed the overall budget total. *(See "Changes in the 1990s," p. 245.)*

The Iran-Contra Affair

The centralizing of reporting in the two intelligence panels did not fully resolve the tension existing between Congress and

the intelligence agencies. Critics still claimed that Congress was not careful enough about keeping classified information secret, and the intelligence agencies continued to withhold information from Congress. The Iran-contra affair, which shook the Reagan administration in the 1980s, illustrated the magnitude of the problem.

President Reagan came into office in 1981 eager to transform his broad philosophy of anticommunism into concrete foreign policy. One of the devices he chose to use was extending covert aid to a broad range of guerrilla groups that were attempting to overthrow Soviet-backed governments in the third world. In agreeing to the expansion of covert action, the Intelligence committees reflected the mood of Congress and probably the American people, Treverton concluded.[64] But at some point the consultation and communication between the White House and Capitol Hill broke down and the resultant Iran-contra affair raised important questions as to the limits of congressional oversight of intelligence.

U.S. involvement with the Nicaraguan contra rebels began in

the early 1980s when the Reagan administration authorized the CIA to form a paramilitary force to harass the Sandinista government. Aid to the contras grew, but in late 1982 a skeptical Congress began to restrict and ultimately cut off U.S. aid through a series of amendments named after Rep. Edward P. Boland, D-Mass., who was then chairman of the House Intelligence Committee. Particularly galling for some members had been the administration's failure to fully brief them on the CIA's mining of Nicaraguan harbors in early 1984. Political support for aid to the contras dissipated rapidly.

As it became clear in 1984 that Congress would block further contra assistance, an alternative network of aid was developed, under the direction of an aide to the president's National Security Council (NSC), Lt. Col. Oliver L. North. North raised funds for the contras from wealthy Americans, while other members of the administration solicited money from foreign allies. The NSC aide, apparently working closely with CIA director William J. Casey, provided the contras with intelligence information and advice on military tactics and arranged for the contras to buy covert shipments of arms. Although regular CIA aid was illegal, CIA agents cooperated unofficially with North's private aid network. When questions were raised on Capitol Hill about North's activities, the administration insisted that it was complying with the Boland amendment. Several key NSC officials took the position that the Boland amendment barred involvement with the contras by the U.S. intelligence agencies, not by the NSC staff.

In early 1986 the contra operation crossed paths with another covert operation, arms sales to Iran, when some profits from the Iranian sales were used to help finance the contra-aid network. Despite a U.S. policy against arms sales to Iran and deep enmity between the United States and the militant Iranian government, the Reagan administration in 1985 had approved Israeli sales of U.S. arms to Iran and in 1986 had begun selling directly to Iran. The sales had been aimed at winning through Iranian intercession the release of U.S. hostages held in Lebanon. Reagan in December 1985 had signed a "finding" retroactively authorizing CIA participation in a November 1985 arms sale. Another finding had been signed in January 1986 authorizing direct arms sales and containing an important and unusual provision directing that Congress not be told about it. Reagan allowed ten months to pass before he formally notified Congress, and he did so only after his secret was published in a Beirut magazine.

When the Iran-contra story broke in November 1986, it triggered multiple investigations within the administration and on Capitol Hill. An independent investigator was appointed to determine whether there had been criminal wrongdoing. (See "Iran-contra," p. 275.)

Many questions were raised about the Iran-contra affair, not the least of which were why executive-legislative relations had broken down and what the episode meant for the newly established congressional oversight system. Reagan's own review board, known as the Tower Commission after its chairman, former senator John Tower, R-Texas, served up a damning indictment of failures by Reagan and his aides throughout the events of the Iran-contra affair. The commission produced no major recommendations for legal or institutional changes but said Reagan's administration and future ones should adhere to existing structures and procedures instead of creating ad hoc means of carrying out foreign policy. It said the White House should be more responsive to congressional concerns.

The bipartisan majority of House and Senate special investigating committees found that the failures of the Iran-contra affair stemmed from White House "secrecy, deception, and disdain for the rule of law." The committees found a pervasive willingness by administration officials to use any means, legal or otherwise, to accomplish the president's policy objectives. The panels decided that the fault lay with the people who ran the government, not with the laws or institutions of government, and recommended only modest changes in law and procedure.

Procedural Changes

Reagan in the meantime had ordered changes in the way covert operations were handled. In August 1987 he signed a national security decision directive ordering, among other things, that all covert-action findings be made in writing and be reviewed annually by the White House. Reagan also ordered that covert findings be reported to Congress within two working days except in "rare, extraordinary" cases. Reagan's aides insisted that the order solved all the problems the Iran-contra hearings had exposed.

But the Intelligence committees continued to press for legislation aimed at preventing a similar scandal in the future. Congress closed several legal loopholes that had become apparent and created an independent inspector general at the CIA who would be subject to Senate confirmation and whose reports would be available to the Intelligence committees.

But the issue of when the president would notify Congress of a covert operation remained a thorny one. Congressional attempts to draft new rules triggered a veto by President Bush in 1990, but compromise legislation was enacted the following year. After eight months of negotiations, Intelligence committee leaders in effect agreed to disagree with the administration on the notification issue. The final bill generally called for prior notification, but it maintained the existing provision of law allowing the president to inform Congress "in a timely fashion" if prior notice was not given. Conferees wrote that they believed notification should be within a few days, but they realized the president might assert constitutional authority to withhold notice for a longer period.

Under the new law, the president generally would have to authorize all covert acts in advance with a written finding that the action was needed to achieve a specific foreign policy objective and was important for national security. If immediate action was required, the president had up to forty-eight hours to put his decision into a written finding. The legislation expanded to the entire federal government prohibitions—which previously had applied only to the CIA—against conducting covert actions without a finding and notification of Congress. The bill also required that Congress be informed of any significant involvement of third-party nations or individuals in a covert operation but, to meet Bush's objections, did not require that they be identified.

CHANGES IN THE 1990S

The dissolution of the Soviet Union obviously meant enormous change for the intelligence community. In Holt's words, "The end of the cold war left a big part of the intelligence community a bureaucracy searching for a mission."[65] Congress and the intelligence agencies focused in the 1990s on what that new mission should be—a task made more difficult by revelations of damaging security breaches and intelligence failures, as well as by some budget cuts.

The Intelligence committees in 1992 launched a high-profile attempt to restructure the nation's multiagency intelligence apparatus for the post–cold war era. But the Bush administration, on guard against congressional attempts to restructure executive agencies, was cool to the proposals and announced its own overhaul of the CIA and other intelligence operations. The more sweeping congressional proposals were set aside and provisions reflecting the administration's changes enacted instead.

Congress in 1994 approved changes with potentially significant consequences for the intelligence community. The policy changes came after what was perhaps the worst U.S. espionage case up to that time. In early 1994 a longtime CIA official, Aldrich H. Ames, and his wife were arrested for having sold top-secret information to the Soviet Union, and later Russia, from 1985 until their arrest. Their actions had resulted in the execution of ten CIA and FBI sources in the Soviet Union and the imprisonment of others.

Congressional criticism—which grew increasingly harsh as details of the scandal emerged—focused on three issues: the CIA's failure to detect and stop the massive security breach; the lack of an aggressive response to the scandal by the CIA director; and the discovery that the CIA had failed repeatedly to notify lawmakers of intelligence compromises in the mid-1980s, which were later linked to Ames. The Senate and House Intelligence committees each produced reports on the case. Over the objections of the Clinton administration, Congress passed legislation that effectively put the FBI in charge of counterintelligence and established a blue-ribbon commission to carry out a wholesale review of the mission and conduct of the CIA and other intelligence agencies. Clinton signed the bill into law.

But when the commission reported in 1996, it rejected radical changes that had been proposed by members of Congress over the years and made modest recommendations instead, such as giving the director of central intelligence more help in managing the intelligence community. This and several other minor changes were enacted into law. Some critics believed that Congress missed a golden opportunity to take a bureaucracy still largely oriented to deal with cold war military threats and refocus it to address such pressing challenges as terrorism, crime, and drug trafficking.

Congress had cut and then frozen intelligence funding in the early 1990s, in response to the end of the cold war and growing demands for the government to do more to address domestic needs. But with the GOP takeover in the mid-1990s, much of the overall spending for intelligence was protected from the budget ax, reflecting the new Republican majority's desire for robust spending on national security–related operations. By the late 1990s some members were calling for increased spending after several shocking intelligence and security lapses made them fearful that resources had been stretched too thin. In May 1999, during the NATO air campaign against Yugoslavia, the Chinese embassy in Belgrade had been mistakenly bombed and three Chinese journalists killed because an outdated CIA map had incorrectly identified the building as belonging to the Yugoslav government. A few weeks later a bipartisan House select committee report confirmed a stream of earlier newspaper revelations that China had used a network of spies, front companies, and visitors to the United States to obtain nuclear secrets and other military technology over several decades. The report found that security at nuclear weapons laboratories did not meet even minimal standards. A number of procedural and legislative changes were recommended.

The actual amount spent annually on intelligence-related activities has traditionally been classified. Despite support for disclosing the overall budget figure from some members of Congress, the Clinton administration, and various study commissions, Congress had refused. However, in 1997 Director of Central Intelligence George J. Tenet, prompted by a lawsuit, ended the years of secrecy by making public the total amount spent on intelligence—$26.6 billion in fiscal 1997. The lawsuit, filed in the U.S. District Court in Washington, D.C., by the Federation of American Scientists, claimed the CIA was violating the Freedom of Information Act by refusing to disclose the overall budget figure. In 1998 Tenet again revealed the overall figure—$26.7 billion for the fiscal 1998 budget—but added that the CIA continued to reserve the right to withhold budget numbers and would not release the proposed budget for the next year.

NOTES

1. Edward S. Corwin, *The President: Office and Powers, 1787–1984*, 5th rev. ed. (New York: New York University Press, 1984), 201.

2. Louis Henkin, "Foreign Affairs and the Constitution," *Foreign Affairs* 66 (Winter 1987–1988): 292–293.

3. Roger H. Davidson and Walter J. Oleszek, *Congress and Its Members*, 7th ed. (Washington, D.C.: CQ Press, 2000), 381.

4. Quoted in Corwin, *The President*, 209.

5. Lee H. Hamilton and Michael H. Van Dusen, "Making the Separation of Powers Work," *Foreign Affairs* 57 (Fall 1978): 17.

6. The sources for this discussion are: Davidson and Oleszek, *Congress and Its Members*, 387–393; Eileen Burgin, "Assessing Congress's Role in the Making of Foreign Policy," in *Congress Reconsidered*, 6th ed., ed. Lawrence C. Dodd and Bruce I. Oppenheimer (Washington, D.C.: CQ Press, 1997), 296–302; *CQ Weekly* and Congressional Quarterly reference books.

7. Cecil V. Crabb Jr. and Pat M. Holt, *Invitation to Struggle: Congress, the President, and Foreign Policy*, 3rd ed. (Washington, D.C.: CQ Press, 1989), 47, 50–51, 253.

8. Davidson and Oleszek, *Congress and Its Members*, 388.

9. George H. Haynes, *The Senate of the United States* (Boston: Houghton Mifflin, 1938), vol. 2, 673–675.

10. Davidson and Oleszek, *Congress and Its Members*, 392.

11. Crabb and Holt, *Invitation to Struggle*, 235.

12. The sources for this discussion are Haynes, *The Senate of the United States*, vol. 2, 573–575; and Charles Warren, *The Making of the Constitution* (Boston: Little, Brown, 1928), 651–658.

13. Quoted in Haynes, *The Senate of the United States*, vol. 2, 581.

14. Unless otherwise noted, the source for this discussion is Haynes, *The Senate of the United States*, vol. 2, 593, 595.

15. Jefferson to Genet, November 22, 1793; quoted in Corwin, *The President*, 208.

16. Senate Foreign Relations Committee, *Background Information on the Committee on Foreign Relations, United States Senate*, 99th Cong., 2nd sess., 1986, S Doc 99-21, 14.

17. Haynes, *The Senate of the United States*, vol. 2, 608.

18. Senate Foreign Relations Committee, *Background Information*, 13.

19. Loch K. Johnson, *The Making of International Agreements: Congress Confronts the Executive* (New York: New York University Press, 1984), 86.

20. Quoted in Haynes, *The Senate of the United States*, vol. 2, 698.

21. I. M. Destler, "Treaty Troubles: Versailles in Reverse," *Foreign Policy* 33 (Winter 1978–1979): 46, with quote from Arthur Link, *Wilson the Diplomatist: A Look at His Major Policies* (Baltimore: Johns Hopkins University Press, 1957), 154.

22. Stephen J. Flanagan, "The Domestic Politics of SALT II: Implications for the Foreign Policy Process," in *Congress, the Presidency, and American Foreign Policy*, ed. John Spanier and Joseph Nogee (Elmsford, N.Y.: Pergamon, 1981), 53.

23. Dante B. Fascell, "Congress and Arms Control," *Foreign Affairs* 65 (Spring 1987): 744–745.

24. Barry M. Blechman, "The New Congressional Role in Arms Control," in *A Question of Balance: The President, the Congress, and Foreign Policy*, ed. Thomas E. Mann (Washington, D.C.: Brookings Institution, 1990), 134.

25. William L. Furlong and Margaret E. Scranton, *The Dynamics of Foreign Policymaking: The President, the Congress, and the Panama Canal Treaties* (Boulder, Colo.: Westview Press, 1984), 140.

26. Louis Fisher, *Constitutional Conflicts between Congress and the President* (Princeton, N.J.: Princeton University Press, 1985), 273.

27. Lawrence Margolis, *Executive Agreements and Presidential Power in Foreign Policy* (Westport, Conn.: Greenwood Press, 1986), 97.

28. Thomas E. Cronin, "A Resurgent Congress and the Imperial Presidency," *Political Science Quarterly* (Summer 1980): 213.

29. Quoted in Arthur M. Schlesinger Jr., "Congress and the Making of American Foreign Policy," in *The Presidency Reappraised*, 2nd ed., ed. Thomas E. Cronin and Rexford G. Tugwell (New York: Praeger, 1977), 216.

30. Fisher, *Constitutional Conflicts*, 80.

31. Unless otherwise noted, the sources for this discussion are Raoul Berger, *Executive Privilege* (Cambridge, Mass.: Harvard University Press, 1974), 63 ff.; and Corwin, *The President*, 263 ff.

32. Crabb and Holt, *Invitation to Struggle*, 53.

33. C. Herman Pritchett, *The American Constitution* (New York: McGraw-Hill, 1959), 357–358.

34. Louis Fisher, *President and Congress: Power and Policy* (New York: Free Press, 1972), 175.

35. Richard F. Grimmett, "Instances of Use of United States Armed Forces Abroad, 1798–1999," Library of Congress, Congressional Research Service, May 17, 1999.

36. David M. Ackerman and Richard F. Grimmett, "Declaration of War Against Yugoslavia: Implications for the United States," Library of Congress, Congressional Research Service, Rept. No. RL30146, April 30, 1999, 1.

37. Senate Foreign Relations Committee, *Hearings on War Powers Legislation*, 91st Cong., 1st sess., 1971, 254.

38. Quoted in Berger, *Executive Privilege*, 69.

39. Rexford G. Tugwell, *The Enlargement of the Presidency* (Garden City, N.Y.: Doubleday, 1960), 194.

40. Corwin, *The President*, 272.

41. Ibid., 277–278.

42. Fisher, *President and Congress*, 193.

43. Berger, *Executive Privilege*, 76.

44. Fisher, *President and Congress*, 194.

45. Quoted in Berger, *Executive Privilege*, 111.

46. Ibid., 279–280.

47. Robert A. Katzmann, "War Powers: Toward a New Accommodation," in *A Question of Balance: The President, the Congress, and Foreign Policy*, ed. Thomas E. Mann (Washington, D.C.: Brookings Institution, 1990), 35.

48. Richard F. Grimmett, "The War Powers Resolution: Twenty-Two Years of Experience," Library of Congress, Congressional Research Service, May 24, 1996, 1.

49. Davidson and Oleszek, *Congress and Its Members*, 393.

50. Katzmann, "War Powers: Toward a New Accommodation," 61.

51. Quoted in Grimmett, "The War Powers Resolution: Twenty-Two Years of Experience," 22.

52. Ibid.; Richard F. Grimmett, "War Powers Resolution: Presidential Compliance," Library of Congress, Congressional Research Service, June 15, 1999; with update from Congressional Research Service.

53. The primary source for this discussion is Grimmett, "The War Powers Resolution: Twenty-Two Years of Experience." Other sources include Grimmett, "War Powers Resolution: Presidential Compliance" and Congressional Quarterly *Almanacs*.

54. Grimmett, "The War Powers Resolution: Twenty-Two Years of Experience," 29.

55. Crabb and Holt, *Invitation to Struggle*, 190.

56. Ibid., 169.

57. Gregory F. Treverton, "Intelligence: Welcome to the American Government," in *A Question of Balance: The President, the Congress, and Foreign Policy*, ed. Thomas E. Mann (Washington, D.C.: Brookings Institution, 1990), 70.

58. Crabb and Holt, *Invitation to Struggle*, 163–164.

59. Treverton, "Intelligence: Welcome to the American Government," 72–74.

60. Crabb and Holt, *Invitation to Struggle*, 170.

61. Pat M. Holt, *Secret Intelligence and Public Policy: A Dilemma of Democracy* (Washington, D.C.: CQ Press, 1995), 214.

62. Treverton, "Intelligence: Welcome to the American Government," 75–76.

63. Crabb and Holt, *Invitation to Struggle*, 182.

64. Treverton, "Intelligence: Welcome to the American Government," 91.

65. Holt, *Secret Intelligence and Public Policy*, 240.

SELECTED BIBLIOGRAPHY

Abshire, David M. *Foreign Policy Makers: President vs. Congress.* Beverly Hills, Calif.: Sage Publications, 1979.

Barnhart, Michael, ed. *Congress and United States Foreign Policy: Controlling the Use of Force in the Nuclear Age.* Albany: State University of New York Press, 1987.

Berger, Raoul. *Executive Privilege: A Constitutional Myth.* Cambridge, Mass.: Harvard University Press, 1974.

Blechman, Barry M. *The Politics of National Security: Congress and U.S. Defense Policy.* New York: Oxford University Press, 1990.

Blechman, Barry M., and Stephen S. Kaplan. *Force Without War: U.S. Armed Forces as a Political Instrument.* Washington, D.C.: Brookings Institution, 1978.

Cheever, Daniel S., and H. Field Haviland Jr. *American Foreign Policy and the Separation of Powers.* Cambridge, Mass.: Harvard University Press, 1952.

Corwin, Edward S. *The President: Office and Powers, 1787–1984.* 5th rev. ed. New York: New York University Press, 1984.

Crabb, Cecil V., Jr., and Pat M. Holt. *Invitation to Struggle: Congress, the President, and Foreign Policy.* 4th ed. Washington, D.C.: CQ Press, 1992.

Cronin, Thomas E., and Rexford G. Tugwell, eds. *The Presidency Reappraised.* 2nd ed. New York: Praeger, 1977.

Dahl, Robert A. *Congress and Foreign Policy.* New York: Harcourt, Brace, 1950.

Eagleton, Thomas J. *War and Presidential Power.* New York: Liveright, 1974.

Fisher, Louis. *Constitutional Conflicts between Congress and the President.* 4th ed. Lawrence: University Press of Kansas, 1997.

———. *The Politics of Shared Power: Congress and the Executive.* 4th ed. College Station: Texas A&M University Press, 1998.

———. *President and Congress: Power and Policy.* New York: Free Press, 1972.

———. *Presidential War Power.* Lawrence: University Press of Kansas, 1995.

Franck, Thomas M., ed. *The Tethered Presidency: Congressional Restraints on Executive Power.* New York: New York University Press, 1981.

Franck, Thomas M., and Edward Weisband. *Foreign Policy by Congress.* New York: Oxford University Press, 1979.

Furlong, William L., and Margaret E. Scranton. *The Dynamics of Foreign Policymaking: The President, the Congress, and the Panama Canal Treaties.* Boulder, Colo.: Westview Press, 1984.

Garthoff, Raymond L. *Policy versus Law: The Reinterpretation of the ABM Treaty.* Washington, D.C.: Brookings Institution, 1987.

Goldwin, Robert A., and Art Kaufman, eds. *Separation of Powers: Does It Still Work?* Washington, D.C.: American Enterprise Institute, 1986.

Goldwin, Robert A., and Robert A. Licht, eds. *Foreign Policy and the Constitution.* Washington, D.C.: American Enterprise Institute, 1990.

Haass, Richard N. *Intervention: The Use of American Military Force in the Post–Cold War World.* Washington, D.C.: Brookings Institution, 1998.

Harris, Joseph P. *The Advice and Consent of the Senate.* Westport, Conn.: Greenwood Press, 1968.

Haynes, George H. *The Senate of the United States: Its History and Practice.* 2 vols. Boston: Houghton Mifflin, 1938.

Henkin, Louis. *Foreign Affairs and the Constitution.* New York: Norton, 1972.

Hinckley, Barbara. *Less Than Meets the Eye: Foreign Policy Making and the Myth of the Assertive Congress.* Chicago: University of Chicago Press, 1994.

Holt, Pat M. *Secret Intelligence and Public Policy: A Dilemma of Democracy.* Washington, D.C.: CQ Press, 1995.

———. *The War Powers Resolution: The Role of Congress in U.S. Armed Intervention.* Washington, D.C.: American Enterprise Institute, 1978.

Jentleson, Bruce W. *American Foreign Policy: The Dynamics of Choice in the 21st Century.* New York: Norton, 1999.

Johnson, Loch K. *The Making of International Agreements: Congress Confronts the Executive.* New York: New York University Press, 1984.

———. *A Season of Inquiry: Congress and Intelligence.* Lexington: University Press of Kentucky, 1985.

Koh, Harold Hongju. *The National Security Constitution: Sharing Power after the Iran-Contra Affair.* New Haven, Conn.: Yale University Press, 1990.

Lindsay, James M. *Congress and the Politics of U.S. Foreign Policy.* Baltimore: Johns Hopkins University Press, 1994.

Mann, Thomas E., ed. *A Question of Balance: The President, the Congress, and Foreign Policy.* Washington, D.C.: Brookings Institution, 1990.

Margolis, Lawrence. *Executive Agreements and Presidential Power in Foreign Policy.* New York: Praeger, 1985.

Muskie, Edmund S., Kenneth Rush, and Kenneth W. Thompson, eds. *The President, the Congress and Foreign Policy.* Lanham, Md.: University Press of America, 1986.

Paul, Roland A. *American Military Commitments Abroad.* New Brunswick, N.J.: Rutgers University Press, 1973.

Peterson, Paul E., ed. *The President, the Congress, and the Making of Foreign Policy.* Norman: University of Oklahoma Press, 1994.

Pritchett, C. Herman. *The American Constitution.* 3rd ed. New York: McGraw-Hill, 1977.

Reveley, W. Taylor, III. *War Powers of the President and Congress: Who Holds the Arrows and Olive Branch?* Charlottesville: University Press of Virginia, 1981.

Ripley, Randall B., and James M. Lindsay. *Congress Resurgent: Foreign and Defense Policy on Capitol Hill.* Ann Arbor: University of Michigan Press, 1993.

Robinson, James A. *Congress and Foreign Policy Making.* Homewood, Ill.: Dorsey, 1967.

Rosati, Jerel A. *Readings in the Politics of U.S. Foreign Policy.* New York: Harcourt Brace, 1998.

Rosner, Jeremy D. *The New Tug-of-War: Congress, the Executive Branch, and National Security.* Washington, D.C.: Carnegie Endowment for International Peace, 1995.

Rourke, John. *Congress and the Presidency in U.S. Foreign Policymaking: A Study of Interaction and Influence, 1945–1982.* Boulder, Colo.: Westview Press, 1983.

Schlesinger, Arthur M., Jr. *The Imperial Presidency.* Boston: Houghton Mifflin, 1989.

Smyrl, Marc E. *Conflict or Codetermination? Congress, the President, and the Power to Make War.* Cambridge, Mass.: Ballinger, 1988.

Sofaer, Abraham D. *War, Foreign Affairs, and Constitutional Power: The Origins.* Cambridge, Mass.: Ballinger, 1976.

Spanier, John, and Joseph Nogee, eds. *Congress, the Presidency, and American Foreign Policy.* Elmsford, N.Y.: Pergamon, 1981.

Sundquist, James L. *The Decline and Resurgence of Congress.* Washington, D.C.: Brookings Institution, 1981.

Thurber, James A., ed. *Rivals for Power: Presidential-Congressional Relations.* Washington, D.C.: CQ Press, 1996.

Treverton, Gregory F. *Covert Action: The Limits of Intervention in the Postwar World.* New York: Basic Books, 1987.

Tugwell, Rexford G. *The Enlargement of the Presidency.* Garden City, N.Y.: Doubleday, 1960.

Warren, Charles. *The Making of the Constitution.* Boston: Little, Brown, 1928.

Wilcox, Francis O. *Congress, the Executive, and Foreign Policy.* New York: Harper and Row, 1971.

Wormuth, Francis D., and Edwin B. Firmage. *To Chain the Dog of War: The War Power of Congress in History and Law.* 2nd ed. Urbana: University of Illinois Press, 1989.

CHAPTER 6

Congressional Investigations

OVER THE COURSE of two centuries Congress has investigated scandals, wars, national security concerns, and any number of other topics that captivated inquiring minds on Capitol Hill. Investigations serve as the eyes and ears of the legislative branch. They test the effectiveness of existing laws and gather information on the need for further legislation. They inquire into the performance of government officials, including members of Congress themselves. They expose waste and corruption in government. They educate the public on great issues of the day.

All those purposes have been served at one time or another. Investigations have given Congress some of its finest—and some of its most deplorable—hours. They have transformed minor politicians into household names and broken the careers of important officials. Televised investigative hearings have permitted millions of Americans to witness an important function of Congress from the comfort of their homes and receive a civics lesson no textbook can match.

Harry S. Truman and Richard Nixon both gained national fame for their work in congressional investigations and ultimately attained the presidency. Truman, a Democratic senator from Missouri, won distinction during World War II for his committee's investigations of the nation's defense program. Nixon, a first-term Republican representative from California, drew wide attention in 1948 for his zealous pursuit of anticommunist investigations.

Soon afterward, Sen. Joseph R. McCarthy, R-Wis., captured the investigatory spotlight. He skillfully used speeches, press releases, and congressional hearings to accuse—often falsely accuse—many prominent Americans of being communists or communist sympathizers and disloyal to their nation. McCarthy was feared for his reckless attacks and popular backing, but gradually public sentiment shifted as television cameras displayed his antics to a viewing nation during investigative hearings in 1953–1954. A Senate inquiry into the senator's misconduct led to a vote of censure by his colleagues in 1954, draining him of political power.

Twenty years later, President Nixon was forced from office by the threat of impeachment arising from investigations into the Watergate scandal. The House Judiciary Committee had recommended his impeachment for obstruction of justice, abuse of power, and contempt of Congress. The committee's work, concluding with a dramatic televised debate, helped prepare the nation to accept the resignation of a president it had overwhelmingly reelected less than two years earlier. The Senate Select Committee on Presidential Campaign Activities, better known as the Watergate Committee, had meanwhile exposed efforts by the Nixon administration to cover up political sabotage in the Watergate scandal. Sen. Sam J. Ervin Jr., D-N.C., chairman of that committee, once observed that the power to investigate is a double-edged sword. He said:

The congressional investigation can be an instrument of freedom. Or it can be freedom's scourge. A legislative inquiry can serve as the tool to pry open the barriers that hide governmental corruption. It can be the catalyst that spurs Congress and the public to support vital reforms in our nation's laws. Or it can debase our principles, invade the privacy of our citizens, and afford a platform for demagogues and the rankest partisans.[1]

The Investigative Process: Exercise of Implied Power

Many reasons may cause a senator or representative to propose an investigation: gathering facts on widely known public occurrences such as an airplane crash; probing reports of improper conduct in the government, labor unions, or business; or pursuing a personal interest, such as government monetary policy or fees charged ranchers for grazing cattle on federal rangeland. A study of nine major investigations of foreign affairs between 1919 and 1940 indicated that "five . . . grew out of the personal predilections of certain congressmen." For example, Sen. Key Pittman, D-Nev., reflected his state's silver mining interests when he conducted an investigation in 1930 of the reduced trade between the United States and China, believing that it resulted from the depreciated price of silver in relation to gold.[2]

Although the legislative power to investigate is only implied in the Constitution—never expressly stated—Congress has asserted it since 1792, when the House inquired into the massacre of U.S. soldiers in Indian territory. No period of American history since then has been without a major congressional investigation.

Most of the earliest congressional inquiries concerned the military or civil activities of the executive branch. Of all the major U.S. military engagements through the Vietnam War, only the Spanish-American War of 1898 escaped congressional scrutiny. President William McKinley, himself a former member of the House, forestalled a legislative inquiry by naming a commission to conduct that investigation.

From 1880 until America's entry into World War I, a time of great expansion and growth, the nation's economic and social

Sen. Harry S. Truman won distinction during World War II for his committee's investigation of the nation's defense program. The committee is shown here on a visit to the Ford Motor Company in April 1942.

problems joined government operations as the principal fields of investigation. Inquiries were made into black migration from South to North (1880), strikebreaking by the railroads (1892), and concentration of wealth in the "money trust" (1912–1913).

Between the two world wars (1918–1939), subversive activities aimed at overthrowing the government emerged as an investigative concern. They became the dominant interest for the first decade or so after World War II. These hearings often resulted in intrusions into the thoughts, actions, and associations of all manner of persons and institutions, and they raised legal and moral questions about the power and procedures of congressional inquiry.

The spectacular growth of the executive branch during the New Deal and World War II years led to a proliferation of congressional investigating committees as Congress struggled to fulfill its traditional function of overseeing the administration of laws and the spending of appropriations. The expanded use of investigations in the 1930s made Congress's investigating power a political issue. To some, the threat to national security posed by communist subversion was so great as to justify exceptional procedures. To others, the threat to individual liberties from the behavior and authority of some committees appeared a more real danger than that of communism. The conflict over the powers of the committees and the rights of witnesses con-

tinued, with shifting results and varying intensity, into the 1990s. It was waged in Congress, in the courts, in the executive branch, in the councils of the Democratic and Republican parties, and in public debates and election campaigns.

THE COURSE OF AN INVESTIGATION

Whatever the reason for an inquiry, it must be approved in advance by the House or Senate—by both in case of a joint inquiry. A sponsor introduces a resolution setting out the need for the inquiry and its scope. In the Senate such a resolution is considered by the Rules and Administration Committee and by the standing legislative committee having jurisdiction over the subject to be studied. The House Oversight Committee considers the funding of investigations in that chamber. Prior to January 1975, House resolutions for investigations also had to be considered by the Rules Committee before being sent to the floor. In 1975 all standing committees were given direct authority to conduct investigations. After being reported by the committees, a resolution is voted on by the full chamber. Joint House-Senate investigating committees are authorized by a concurrent resolution adopted by both chambers.

As a matter of courtesy in both the House and Senate, the sponsor presides over the inquiry. When the study is to be made by a standing committee, a subcommittee generally is appointed by the chairman of the full committee, with the sponsor being named the subcommittee chairman. When a select committee is authorized, the members are chosen by consultation among the vice president (as presiding officer of the Senate) or the Speaker of the House and the majority and minority leaders of that chamber. The life of a special House investigation committee expires with a Congress, but that of a Senate committee depends upon its authorization.

Staff Preparation

Public hearings are the most visible and controversial element of investigations, but as a rule they bring forth little material not already uncovered or suggested by staff work. Investigating committee staffs first came into use in the late 1800s and by the 1920s and 1930s the practice of relying on staff members to gather information was firmly established. However, the staffs remained relatively small. The staff of the Nye Committee, in its investigation of the munitions industry in the 1930s, usually consisted of about twenty persons.[3] In contrast, the Senate Watergate Committee at its peak strength in 1973 had a staff of sixty-four, including seventeen attorneys; the House Judiciary Committee's impeachment inquiry staff in 1974 numbered close to one hundred and included forty-three attorneys. In addition, investigating committees frequently borrow personnel from the administrative agencies.

The staff's activities in a major inquiry are indicated by the volume of its work. The Truman Committee, active from 1941 to 1948, issued 51 reports totaling 1,946 pages and held 432 public hearings at which 1,798 witnesses appeared, filing 27,568 pages of testimony. The transcripts of about three hundred private sessions held by the committee covered 25,000 pages.[4] From 1957 to 1959 the Senate Select Committee on Improper Activities in the Labor or Management Field heard 1,726 witnesses whose testimony filled 46,150 pages. Staff members traveled nearly 2.5 million miles, forwarded 128,204 documents to the committee, conducted 253 investigations, served more than 8,000 subpoenas, and filed more than 19,000 investigative field reports.

Committee Hearings, Report

Following the staff inquiry, the committee holds formal hearings, at which witnesses appear. These may become dramatic public spectacles intended to educate and influence the public through the media. For example, the House Judiciary Committee's televised hearings on impeachment charges in 1974 helped pave the way for President Richard Nixon's departure from office.

At the conclusion of the investigation, the committee issues a report summarizing its findings and offering recommendations for future action. Many investigations have partisan overtones, and votes on the final committee recommendation—like earlier votes on areas to be investigated and witnesses to be heard—may divide along party lines. Partisanship may be the reason that an investigation is undertaken in the first place, and this can influence how it is conducted.

SOURCES OF INVESTIGATIVE POWER

The power of Congress to investigate, one of the most controversial and highly publicized powers of the national legislature, is implied constitutionally in the opening declaration of Article I that "all legislative Powers herein granted shall be vested in a Congress of the United States." The authors of the Constitution were familiar with two centuries of British precedents for legislative investigations. The House of Commons had asserted its investigative power as early as the sixteenth century. That practice had been adopted in America by colonial legislative bodies, the Continental Congress, and the new state legislatures.

At first Commons asserted an investigative power to determine its own membership but later invoked it for purposes of making laws and seeing that they were carried out. Parliamentary committees could summon witnesses, demand documents, and punish persons who refused to comply. The investigative power of Parliament was amply demonstrated at the very time the Constitution was being drafted at Philadelphia, in 1787. The famous impeachment of Warren Hastings was being carried forward in London by a Parliament that investigated, tried, and ultimately acquitted him on charges of misconduct as governor-general of India.

Despite a general acceptance of Congress's power to investigate, disagreement arose over its scope. Strict constructionists argued that, because the Constitution assigned to Congress "all legislative powers herein granted," the authority of Congress was limited to specifically granted powers. Thus they insisted that its investigations be confined to such clearly defined areas as election disputes, impeachments, and cases involving congressional privileges. Broad constructionists argued that ample precedents supported an inherent investigative power as broad as the legislative function. They prevailed and won approval of the military investigation in 1792.

That first investigation served as a precedent for others. Since then, the basic authority of Congress to investigate has not been seriously challenged. However, specific investigations have been challenged, with mixed results; opposition has arisen mainly in inquiries that have pried into private affairs, infringed on personal liberties, or conflicted with executive branch prerogatives. Moreover, challenges have been brought to the contempt power of Congress since it was first invoked by the House in 1795 to jail a nonmember named Robert Randall. He was confined for one week for attempting to bribe a representative. In the following years both chambers relied on that precedent to punish other nonmembers for contemptuous acts.

CONTEMPT CASES AND JUDICIAL REVIEW

Like the investigative power it reinforces, the congressional power to punish for contempt is based on parliamentary precedents dating from Elizabethan times. No express power to punish for contempt, except in the case of a member, was granted

CONTEMPT OF CONGRESS

Congress in 1857 enacted a statute that allowed it to turn over congressional contempt cases to the federal courts for indictment and trial. Under this statute, as it has been amended and interpreted, the courts are obligated to provide the defendant all the protections guaranteed defendants in other criminal actions.

The statute, now known as Section 192, states:

Every person who having been summoned as a witness by the authority of either House of Congress to give testimony or to produce papers upon any matter under inquiry before either House, or any joint committee established by a joint or concurrent resolution of the two Houses of Congress, or any committee of either House of Congress, willfully makes default, or who having appeared, refuses to answer any question pertinent to the question under inquiry, shall be deemed guilty of a misdemeanor, punishable by a fine of not more than $1,000 nor less than $100 and imprisonment in a common jail for not less than one month nor more than twelve months.

Congress in the Constitution. But Congress assumed that it had inherent power to send persons in contempt to jail without a court order because it regarded such power as necessary for its own protection and for the integrity of its proceedings.

The use of this contempt power has fallen into two general classes: (1) those involving positive acts, such as bribery or libel, which directly or indirectly obstruct the legislature in carrying out its function, and (2) those involving refusal to perform acts that the legislature claims authority to compel, such as testifying or producing documents. Few cases of the first type have occurred in recent years, and the courts have had little opportunity to define positive acts of contempt. The second type, while giving rise to much more extensive judicial interpretation, continues to raise many legal questions because of its greater complexity.

In 1821 the Supreme Court upheld the congressional use of the contempt power by declaring that it was assumed to be inherent. The case, *Anderson v. Dunn*, grew out of an attempt by a man named John Anderson to bribe a member of the House of Representatives to help push a land claim through Congress. Anderson was given a summary trial at the bar of the House and received a reprimand. He then brought charges against Thomas Dunn, the House sergeant at arms, for assault and battery and for false arrest.

In ruling against Anderson, the Supreme Court said Congress required the power of contempt. Without it, the Court said, Congress could be "exposed to every indignity and interruption that rudeness, caprice, and even conspiracy may meditate against it." This would lead to "the total annihilation of the power" of Congress. However, the Court ruled that the contempt power was limited "to the least power adequate to the ends proposed," and imprisonment for contempt could not extend beyond the adjournment of Congress.

Considering imprisonment only to the end of the legislative session inadequate, Congress in 1857 passed a law making it a criminal offense to refuse information demanded by either chamber. The law enabled contempt citations to be turned over to federal prosecutors for court action. However, for a long time afterward, Congress still preferred to deal out its own punishment. The lawmakers reasoned that, by retaining control of the punishment, they might induce a balky witness to cooperate by agreeing to reduce the time of his confinement.

Judicial Review

For sixty years, the *Anderson* case shielded congressional investigations from legal challenges. But in 1881 the Supreme Court's decision in another contempt case, *Kilbourn v. Thompson*, brought congressional investigations within the scope of judicial review. In subsequent decisions the Supreme Court has applied varying standards to such cases, but on the major point established by *Kilbourn*, that these congressional investigations are subject to review by the federal courts, the Supreme Court has not wavered.

Hallet Kilbourn, manager of a real estate pool involved in the failure of the banking firm of Jay Cooke, was subpoenaed to appear and produce certain papers sought by a select House committee investigating the firm's failure. He refused, challenging the subpoena as exceeding the scope of the committee's investigation and representing nothing more than an attempt to exercise "the naked, arbitrary power of the House to investigate private business in which nobody but me and my customers have concern."

Kilbourn was arrested and held by the House in contempt. He subsequently sued the Speaker, members of the committee, and the sergeant at arms, John G. Thompson, for false arrest. When his case reached the Supreme Court, the justices agreed with Kilbourn's challenge. The Court ruled that Congress did not have a general power to punish for contempt. A recalcitrant committee witness could be punished for contempt, the Court held, only if the inquiry for which he had been called was within the "legitimate cognizance" of Congress. Neither chamber "possesses the general power of making inquiry into the private affairs of the citizen."

The decision appeared to restrict congressional investigations to subjects clearly related to specifically granted powers, such as the impeachment power, the commerce power, and so on. Later rulings by the Court blurred this restriction considerably.

In 1897, for instance, the Supreme Court held in *In re Chapman* that investigations were "legitimate" inquiries within the meaning of the *Kilbourn* decision so long as they involved the conduct of members of Congress. Committees investigating the involvement of senators in sugar speculation could compel testimony about matters that would be considered outside the scope of congressional investigations were it not for senatorial involvement.

Expansion of Contempt

In 1927 the Court issued a decision in the case of *McGrain v. Daugherty* that swept away nearly all the restrictions on the investigating power of Congress that *Kilbourn* had seemed to impose. In *McGrain,* the Court upheld the power of Congress to conduct broad-ranging investigations.

Mally S. Daugherty, brother of Attorney General Harry M. Daugherty (1921–1924), was subpoenaed to testify before a select committee created by the Senate to investigate an oil-leasing scandal known as Teapot Dome. He refused, and the Senate issued a warrant ordering its deputy sergeant at arms to arrest him. Daugherty, in turn, challenged the Senate's power to compel him to testify. The Court held that the Senate and the House had the power to compel private citizens to appear before their committees and to answer pertinent questions to aid the legislative function:

The power of inquiry—with process to enforce it—is an essential and appropriate auxiliary to the legislative function. A legislative body cannot legislate wisely or effectively in the absence of information respecting the conditions which the legislation is intended to affect or change; and where the legislative body does not itself possess the requisite information. . . . [R]ecourse must be had to others who do possess it. Experience has taught that mere requests for information often are unavailing, and also that information which is volunteered is not always accurate or complete; so some means of compulsion are essential to obtain what is needed.

The Court indicated further that it would presume a legislative purpose to lie behind a congressional investigation, whether that was the purpose of the inquiry or not. "The only legitimate object the Senate could have in ordering the investigation was to aid it in legislating, and we think the subject matter was such that the presumption should be indulged that this was the real object," the Court said. "An express avowal of the object would have been better; but in view of the particular subject matter was not indispensable," the Court added.

After giving this broad sanction to congressional investigations, the Court appended two reservations. It cautioned, first, that "neither house is invested with 'general' power to inquire into private affairs and compel disclosures" and, second, that "a witness rightfully may refuse to answer where the bounds of the power are exceeded or the questions are not pertinent to the matter under inquiry."

In 1929 the Supreme Court held that a witness who refused to answer questions asked by a congressional committee could be punished if he were mistaken as to the law on which he based his refusal. The fact that the witness acted in good faith on the advice of counsel was no defense, the Court held.

This case, *Sinclair v. United States,* also grew out of an investigation of the Teapot Dome scandal. The Interior Department had leased public lands, containing oil, to the Mammoth Oil Co., of which the president and sole stockholder was Harry F. Sinclair. Sinclair had refused to answer questions of a Senate investigating committee on the ground that the matter was of exclusively judicial concern and therefore beyond the Senate's le-

gitimate range of inquiry. He was convicted of contempt. In upholding the conviction, the Supreme Court declared that the naval oil reserves and their disposition were clearly a proper matter for congressional scrutiny.

Some three decades later, Supreme Court Chief Justice Earl Warren would write more expansively on the power of Congress to conduct investigations. It "is inherent in the legislative process," he said in the 1957 case of *Watkins v. United States.* "That power is broad. It encompasses inquiries concerning the administration of existing laws as well as proposed or possibly needed statutes. It includes surveys of defects in our social, economic, or political system for the purpose of enabling the Congress to remedy them. It comprehends probes into departments of the Federal Government to expose corruption, inefficiency, or waste."

However, this investigative power has its limits. In *Watkins* the Court ruled that a witness, John T. Watkins, was not guilty of contempt for refusing to answer certain questions before the House Committee on Un-American Activities. The Court said

---

CBS CONTEMPT CITATION

One exception to the modern rule that the House and Senate normally support a committee's contempt citation resolution occurred in 1971. On July 13 the House, by a 226–181 roll-call vote, recommitted—and thus killed—a House Interstate and Foreign Commerce Committee resolution recommending that the Columbia Broadcasting System (CBS) and its president, Frank Stanton, be cited for contempt of Congress.

Stanton had refused to comply with a subpoena issued by the committee's investigations subcommittee for film and sound recordings prepared for but not used in the network's controversial documentary "The Selling of the Pentagon."

Appearing before the subcommittee, Stanton invoked the First Amendment guarantee of freedom of the press when he refused to supply the requested material. "If broadcast journalism must comply with subpoenas such as this," he argued, "it can never perform the independent role in preserving those freedoms which the Constitution intended for American journalism." Rep. Harley O. Staggers, D-W.Va., chairman of both the full committee and the subcommittee, replied: "The issue here today is not the First Amendment. It is the willful deception of the public." Critics of the program had asserted that CBS's editing of film had distorted the meaning of statements made by persons who were interviewed.

The subcommittee recommended that CBS and Stanton be cited for contempt, and the full committee endorsed the proposal.

Although most members of Congress usually support a committee's contempt recommendation, in this case the House leadership of both parties backed away from Staggers's request and supported the move to recommit the resolution to the committee.

the committee had failed to show that its questions were pertinent to the ostensible subject of the inquiry, communist infiltration of labor unions. Warren asserted that there is "no congressional power to expose for the sake of exposure." If a witness objects to a question, Warren said, the committee must "state for the record the subject under inquiry at that time and the manner in which the propounded question is pertinent thereto."

The vote in Watkins was 8 to 1, but two years later the Court softened the decision in a 5–4 ruling upholding a contempt citation against a witness for refusing to answer questions in another investigation by the House Committee on Un-American Activities, this one examining communist infiltration of higher education. Writing for the majority in *Barenblatt v. United States,* Justice John Marshall Harlan said the panel's legislative mandate was not excessively vague and that the witness, a university professor, understood the pertinence of the questions. In that light, Harlan said, the witness's claimed First Amendment right to avoid testifying had to be balanced against "the governmental interests at stake," which he defined as "the right of self-preservation."

The Court has continued to use this balancing approach, with mixed results. It upheld contempt citations in two cases in 1961 after determining that an Un-American Activities subcommittee had shown the pertinence of its questions. Four months later, however, the Court reversed a contempt citation in another case where it said the government had failed to prove the relevance of the questions put to the witness. In later decisions, the Court has also insisted that congressional committees follow their own procedures. In one case, *Yellin v. United States* (1963), the Court reversed the conviction of a witness for contempt on the ground that the Committee on Un-American Activities violated its own rules by failing to consider his request for an executive session before he was questioned.

Contempt Prosecution

In matters of contempt, neither chamber has imposed punishment since 1932. Since then all contempt-of-Congress citations have been prosecuted by the Justice Department in the courts—primarily under an 1857 law, variously amended but still in effect, that makes it a crime to withhold legitimate information demanded by Congress. When a committee wishes to institute criminal proceedings against a rebellious witness, it introduces a resolution in the parent body citing the witness for contempt. Only a simple majority vote is necessary for approval; there seldom is opposition to such a resolution. The matter is then referred to a U.S. attorney for presentation to a grand jury.

For instance, in 1972 the House cited Watergate conspirator G. Gordon Liddy for contempt of Congress. The case was turned over to the U.S. attorney in the District of Columbia for presentation to a grand jury. Liddy was cited for his refusal to be sworn in to testify before the House Armed Services Committee's Special Intelligence Subcommittee. In 1974 Liddy was found guilty of contempt by U.S. District Court Judge John H.

Pratt, who heard the case without a jury in Washington, D.C. He gave Liddy a suspended six-month sentence.

THE RIGHTS OF WITNESSES

Congress issued only 108 contempt citations from 1796 until 1945, but 226 during the next twelve years.[5] In 1950 the House alone issued fifty-nine contempt citations. The great flurry of citations in those later years reflected a proliferation of investigations into national security threats, real or imagined, by panels such as the House Committee on Un-American Activities. Many witnesses refused to testify and challenged the questioning on constitutional grounds. *(See box, Investigations of 'Un-Americanism,' p. 272.)*

By the late 1930s committee investigations into "un-American" activities of individuals frequently attained the decorum of street carnivals. In that era of headline-making accusations in front of massed newsreel (later television) cameras and flash-bulbs, witnesses typically faced relentless questioning and bullying tactics by committee and staff members. In search of protection for a refusal to answer questions, witnesses turned to the Constitution, frequently citing the First, Fourth, and Fifth Amendments. They asserted, with mixed results, that the First Amendment protected their private convictions, political views, and propaganda activities. The Fourth Amendment guarantee against unreasonable search and seizure likewise offered uncertain protection; the power of committees to demand documents continued to be widely used. The Fifth Amendment's protection against self-incrimination proved to be a better defense, but it was not firmly established as a protection until the 1950s, when the Supreme Court started addressing the constitutional issues. In the preceding years the Court attempted to rule on narrow points of law and thus avert a potential showdown between the congressional and judicial branches of government.

"It would be an unwarranted act of judicial usurpation . . . to assume for the courts the function of supervising congressional committees," Justice Robert Jackson wrote on behalf of the Supreme Court in the 1949 case of *Eisner v. United States.* From the beginning, Congress had delegated its power to investigate to committees, and the conservative-minded Supreme Court of that era was reluctant to invade an area of authority long held exclusively by Congress. But after World War II, the legal community and the public generally showed more concern for the rights of witnesses in congressional hearings. Television coverage of hearings, first used spectacularly during House committee investigations of communism in 1948, exposed witnesses to vast viewing audiences, jeopardizing their privacy, their reputations, and sometimes their careers.

'Few Safeguards'

A 1954 study of congressional investigative power by the Legislative Reference Service (now the Congressional Research Service) of the Library of Congress concluded: "There are few safeguards for the protection of a witness before a congressional committee. . . . In committee, his treatment usually depends upon the skill and attitude of the chairman and the members."[6] That conclusion was underscored by an earlier comment by J. Parnell Thomas, R-N.J., chairman of the House Un-American Activities Committee in 1947–1949: "The rights you have are the rights given you by this committee," he said. "We will determine what rights you have and what rights you have not got before the committee."[7]

It was not until 1955 that the Supreme Court considered any contempt-of-Congress cases against witnesses who had invoked the Fifth Amendment in not answering questions. But it had previously handed down two important rulings dealing with witnesses who refused to testify before grand juries on that ground. In the first case, *Blau v. United States* (1950), the Court acknowledged that the admission of communist activity might be incriminating. In the second, *Rogers v. United States* (1951), it held that a witness who had already answered questions about materially incriminating facts could not then invoke the Fifth Amendment.

Once the courts upheld the right of congressional committee witnesses to invoke the Fifth Amendment's protection against self-incrimination, use of the amendment to avoid answering questions became highly controversial. The Fifth Amendment generally stood up as a defense against prosecution for contempt of Congress. However, witnesses could not invoke it partially, answering a question and then refusing further explana-

tion. For this reason some witnesses repeatedly pleaded the Fifth Amendment, refusing to answer apparently innocuous questions.

All the while, pressure mounted for reform of committee procedures to protect the rights of witnesses and to give greater assurance that the purposes for which the investigations were instituted would be accomplished. "In order to investigate effectively, a congressional committee must have within the field of inquiry assigned to it a virtually unrestrained delegation of this vast congressional power," Sen. J. W. Fulbright, D-Ark., observed in 1951. "As a practical matter, this means that the power to investigate is wielded by individuals, not by institutions. . . . This is . . . at once both the weakness and the strength of our legislative processes."[8]

Rule Reforms

The House in 1955 amended its rules to establish a minimum standard of conduct for House committees. It permitted witnesses at investigations to be accompanied by counsel; required that a committee finding evidence that might "tend to defame, degrade, or incriminate any person" receive the evidence in secret session and allow the person to appear as a witness and request supporting witnesses; and required committee consent for release of evidence taken in secret session.

The Senate prescribed no "fair play" code for its committees,

Sen. Joseph R. McCarthy was Congress's most notorious anti-communist investigator of the post–World War II period. McCarthy's abuse of committee power led to his censure by the Senate in 1954 and reform in congressional committee procedures.

although it received several proposals. The Senate left investigative procedures to the discretion of individual committees, whose practices varied considerably. Not only did rules vary from one Senate committee to another; the committees also did not apply their own rules uniformly. However, some improvement was noted.

For example, after Sen. John L. McClellan, D-Ark., replaced Joseph R. McCarthy in 1955 as chairman of the Permanent Investigations Subcommittee of the Senate Government Operations Committee, the panel adopted rules requiring the presence of two committee members when testimony was being taken, permitting anyone who was the subject of an investigation to submit questions in writing for cross-examination of other witnesses, and allowing any person harmed by testimony to request an appearance or file a statement. In earlier years power was concentrated in a handful of leaders, and junior members did not expect to share it.

USES OF SUBPOENA POWERS

The Legislative Reorganization Act of 1946 extended permanent subpoena power to all standing committees of the Senate. General subpoena power for House committees was blocked for many years by Speaker Sam Rayburn, D-Texas, and Minority Leader Joseph W. Martin Jr., R-Mass., for fear that it would lead to sensational inquiries motivated by political ambitions. It was not granted until 1974, after both leaders had left Congress. Until 1973, a time of Watergate investigations, only the Committee on Expenditures in the Executive Departments and the Committee on Un-American Activities were regularly authorized to issue subpoenas. When the latter was reorganized in 1969 as the House Committee on Internal Security, it retained that authority.

Other committees had to seek specific House approval for authority to compel testimony and documents. In such cases the House normally authorized broad committee investigatory power and use of the subpoena. Although the 1974 change gave all House committees and subcommittees general subpoena power, approval by a majority of a panel's members was required before a subpoena could be issued. Compliance could be enforced only with the approval of the House.

When the 93rd Congress opened in 1973, for example, the House on one day adopted resolutions authorizing eight standing committees to investigate subjects within their legislative jurisdictions and to issue subpoenas. One of those committees was Banking and Currency, which issued more than three hundred subpoenas between 1965 and 1974. All requests specified how the documents or testimony related to the committee's work.

This "conservative view" of the manner in which a committee should use its subpoena power was based on a 1966 Supreme Court decision, *Gojack v. United States.* John T. Gojack was convicted of contempt of Congress for refusing to answer certain questions during testimony before a subcommittee of the House Committee on Un-American Activities in 1955. The Court reversed his conviction, saying that the committee had not specified the subject of the inquiry or authorized the subcommittee to conduct it.

The Senate Select Committee on Presidential Campaign Activities (Watergate Committee) construed its subpoena power broadly when it sought a large but unspecified number of White House tapes and documents on December 18, 1973. (The committee had issued earlier subpoenas in July.) The House Judiciary Committee, responsible for conducting the inquiry into charges against President Nixon, was one of the standing committees granted general subpoena power by resolution at the beginning of the 93rd Congress in 1973. At that time, however, the official list of subjects under the committee's jurisdiction did not include impeachment.

But on February 6, 1974, with only four members voting "nay," the House formally granted the committee power to investigate the conduct of President Nixon to determine whether grounds existed for his impeachment. The resolution gave explicit authorization for the committee to conduct the investigation, which was already under way, and granted it special subpoena power during the inquiry.

The committee's issuance of subpoenas to Nixon in the spring and summer of 1974 was a singular action. In neither the impeachment proceedings against Andrew Johnson in 1867–1868 nor those against Bill Clinton in 1998–1999 was the president himself subpoenaed. *(See Chapter 9, Impeachment Power.)*

Before Nixon was served with subpoenas for tapes and documents July 23, 1973 (two from the Senate Watergate Committee and one from the Watergate special prosecutor), the only president ever to be subpoenaed while in office was Thomas Jefferson. That occurred in 1807 when Supreme Court Chief Justice John Marshall, presiding in the treason trial of Vice President Aaron Burr, subpoenaed a letter from the president that Burr said he needed for his defense. Jefferson produced the letter but did not testify in person.

IMMUNITY

To obtain testimony from individuals who would otherwise claim their constitutional right to remain silent to avoid incriminating themselves, Congress has authorized grants of immunity from prosecution to such witnesses.

When it approved the federal statute providing for punishment of recalcitrant witnesses before congressional committees, Congress in 1857 added a second section that contained an automatic and sweeping grant of immunity to witnesses testifying under the compulsion of congressional power. As enacted, the law provided that

no person examined and testifying before either House of Congress or any committee of either House, shall be held to answer criminally in any court of justice, or subject to any penalty or forfeiture, for any fact or act touching which he shall be required to testify before either House of Congress, or any committee of either House, as to which he shall have testified, whether before or after this act. . . . Provided, that nothing in this act shall be construed to exempt any witness from prosecution and punishment for perjury committed by him in testifying as aforesaid.

The disadvantages of this sort of immunity "bath" became evident in 1862 when it was revealed that embezzlers of millions in Indian trust bonds would escape prosecution because they had testified about their crime to a congressional committee and so, under the 1857 law, could not be prosecuted for it.

Congress replaced the 1857 law in 1862 with one narrowing the basis for immunity. It stated: "No testimony given by a witness before either House, or before any committee of either House . . . shall be used as evidence in any criminal proceedings against him in any court, except in a prosecution for perjury committed in giving such testimony." Thus, a witness's own testimony could not be used as evidence to convict him, but nothing could prevent its being used as a lead in discovering other evidence of crime.

An 1892 Supreme Court ruling raised questions about the adequacy of the 1862 immunity law, but that law remained unchanged until the Eisenhower administration proposed, and Congress passed, the Immunity Act of 1954. The 1954 law permitted either chamber of Congress by majority vote, or a congressional committee by two-thirds vote, to grant immunity to witnesses in national security investigations, provided that an order was first obtained from a U.S. district court judge and the attorney general was given an opportunity to offer objections in advance.

The law also permitted the U.S. district courts to grant immunity to witnesses before the courts and before grand juries. The act granted immunity from prosecution for criminal activity revealed during compelled testimony. In a 1956 decision, *Ullmann v. United States*, the Supreme Court upheld the 1954 immunity statute as it applied to grand jury witnesses but clearly proffered no opinion on its provisions granting immunity to congressional witnesses.

In 1970 Congress wrote a whole new immunity law as a part of the Organized Crime Control Act. It set out the rules for granting immunity to witnesses before congressional committees, courts, grand juries, and administrative agencies. Under the new law, witnesses who received immunity to waive their Fifth Amendment rights and testify were guaranteed that their testimony and the information it contained would not be used against them in any criminal prosecution unless they lied in their testimony. However, they could still be prosecuted on evidence that had been obtained from sources other than their testimony. *(See box, Witness Immunity Statute, this page.)*

Witnesses under oath may be prosecuted for perjury if they do not tell the truth in their testimony. Even unsworn witnesses are subject to prosecution for false statements.

A federal law makes it a felony to make false statements or representations regarding "any matter within the jurisdiction of any department or agency of the United States."

WITNESS IMMUNITY STATUTE

In 1970 Congress enacted a comprehensive immunity statute. The following sections are those dealing with witnesses before committees of Congress:

(a) In the case of any individual who has been or may be called to testify or provide other information at any proceeding before either House of Congress, or any committee, or any subcommittee of either House, or any joint committee of the two Houses, a United States district court shall issue, in accordance with subsection (b) of this section, upon the request of a duly authorized representative of the House of Congress or the committee concerned, an order requiring such individual to give testimony or provide other information which he refuses to give or provide on the basis of his privilege against self-incrimination, such order to become effective as provided in section 6002 of this part.

(b) Before issuing an order under subsection (a) of this section, a United States district court shall find that—

(1) in the case of a proceeding before either House of Congress, the request for such an order has been approved by an affirmative vote of a majority of the Members present of that House;

(2) in the case of a proceeding before a committee or a subcommittee of either House of Congress or a joint committee of both Houses, the request for such an order has been approved by an affirmative vote of two-thirds of the members of the full committee; and

(3) ten days or more prior to the day on which the request for such an order was made, the Attorney General was served with notice of an intention to request the order.

(c) Upon application of the Attorney General, the United States district court shall defer the issuance of any order under subsection (a) of this section for such period, not longer than twenty days from the date of the request for such order, as the Attorney General may specify.

Watergate Witnesses

Congressional grants of immunity became an issue during the hearings of the Senate Select Committee on Presidential Campaign Activities (the Watergate Committee). In one of his first moves as Watergate special prosecutor, Archibald Cox urged the committee on June 4, 1973, to delay its public hearings. One of his arguments for postponement was that a grant of immunity for certain witnesses before the committee might prevent them from being convicted later.

U.S. District Judge John J. Sirica denied Cox's request that he order the committee to delay its hearings. Sirica then approved grants of limited immunity—under the 1970 law—to White House Counsel John W. Dean III and Jeb Stuart Magruder, a former White House aide who was serving as deputy director of the Committee for the Re-Election of the President. Both were known to be under consideration for indictment in connection with the Watergate scandal and were reportedly prepared to offer evidence of the involvement of top White House officials, including the president. Both later served prison terms after pleading guilty to Watergate-related charges.

Oliver North Case

The peril of granting a congressional witness limited immunity was pointed out in 1990 when a federal appellate court set aside the convictions of Oliver L. North for wrongdoing in the Iran-contra scandal. A three-judge panel of the U.S. Court of Appeals for the District of Columbia Circuit on July 20 struck down one conviction outright and ordered the trial court to conduct an elaborate inquiry to determine if the other two guilty verdicts had been tainted by testimony North gave Congress during nationally televised hearings in July 1987. North, a former Marine Corps lieutenant colonel who served on the National Security Council staff, was implicated in an alleged White House cover-up of selling U.S. arms to Iran to win the release of American hostages in Lebanon and illegally funneling profits from the sales to guerrilla fighters (contras) in Nicaragua.

North had been convicted by a U.S. district court jury in Washington, D.C., on May 4, 1989, of three felonies: deceiving Congress about the arms sales, illegally accepting a home security system as a gift, and altering and destroying government documents. The trial judge, Gerhard A. Gesell, fined North $150,000 and ordered him to perform 1,200 hours of community service in lieu of a jail sentence. The appellate panel, splitting 2–1 in its rulings, vacated the first two convictions and struck down the third one.

In its Iran-contra investigations, Congress granted more than twenty witnesses—including North—partial immunity from prosecution to obtain their testimony. Nothing they said before Congress could be used against them in court. In its prosecution of North, the legal team led by independent counsel (special prosecutor) Lawrence E. Walsh was compelled to introduce into court only evidence that could be obtained elsewhere. In overturning one of North's convictions, the appellate panel ruled that the trial judge had failed to instruct the jury properly. On the other two convictions, which were set aside and subject to retrial, the panel said the judge did not ensure that the trial witnesses had not made use of the defendant's congressional testimony to refresh their memories or otherwise influence their courtroom testimony.

Walsh petitioned the Supreme Court to overturn the appeals court's decision. But he later concluded that it would be nearly impossible to demonstrate that witnesses who testified in North's 1989 trial had not been influenced by his televised testimony to Congress. In September 1991 Gesell dropped all charges against North at Walsh's request.

EXECUTIVE PRIVILEGE

Congressional investigations have often sparked conflict with the executive branch, most frequently because a president has refused to comply with congressional demands for information.

Practically every administration since 1792 has clashed with Congress over the question of "executive privilege" to withhold information, and the issue has yet to be resolved. An argument can be made that executive departments, established by Congress and maintained by its appropriations, are the creatures of the legislature and cannot deny it information regarding their activities. Congress may back up its demands by arousing public support for disclosure, especially if there is suspicion that an administration is seeking to protect its political reputation by hiding mistakes or wrongdoing. However, presidents have defied congressional demands for information on many occasions. Those precedents tend to support arguments that the constitutional separation of powers permits the president, at his discretion, to withhold information sought by Congress.

Presidents have used a variety of reasons to justify denying information to Congress. Perhaps the most common has been the need for secrecy in military and diplomatic activities. Presidents have also sought to avoid unwarranted exposure of individuals to unfavorable publicity, especially when documents or files requested contain incomplete, inaccurate, misleading, or unsubstantiated information. The need for confidential exchange of ideas between members of an administration has been cited as justifying refusal to provide records or describe conversations in the executive branch. Fears that disclosures would interfere with criminal or security investigations sometimes have prompted administrative secrecy. Critics of an administration have frequently charged that its real motive for refusing to divulge information was to escape criticism or scandal.

"Clearly, the president cannot turn over documents to Congress so that Congress can then decide whether or not they should have been turned over," the lawyer-author Telford Taylor wrote in 1955. "If there is an executive privilege to withhold information when disclosures would not be 'in the public interest,' then the president must be the one to determine in any particular case whether the public interest permits disclosure or requires nondisclosure. Just as clearly, this leaves open the possibility that the president may abuse his prerogative, especially in instances where the information would reflect unfavorably on him or his administration of the nation's affairs."[9]

Taylor was writing during the McCarthy era, when criticism of congressional investigating power ran high. Twenty years later, the weight of opinion had shifted—after clashes between President Lyndon B. Johnson and Congress over Vietnam War information and between President Nixon and Congress over Watergate documents and testimony. Law professor Raoul Berger, writing in 1974, described "executive privilege" as a "constitutional myth"—"a product of the nineteenth century, fashioned by a succession of presidents who created 'precedents' to suit the occasion."[10]

The list of presidents who refused to provide information to congressional committees goes back beyond the nineteenth century, to George Washington, although the term "executive privilege" did not come into use until much later. In some instances the rebuffed committees accepted the president's refusal without comment. At other times, the refusals led to constitutional confrontations. Summaries of selected cases follow.

Early Refusals to Give Information

George Washington. In 1792 the first president was first confronted with the question of whether to turn over documents requested by Congress. A select House committee, conducting the first congressional inquiry, wanted information on the circumstances that resulted in an Indian victory over Maj. Gen. Arthur St. Clair and his men in the Northwest Territory. The committee asked Secretary of War Henry Knox to turn over all the documents relating to the St. Clair expedition. Knox asked President George Washington for advice; the president raised the subject at a cabinet meeting.

The cabinet agreed that the House could conduct such an investigation and could call for such papers. It decided, according to the report of Secretary of State Thomas Jefferson, "that the executive ought to communicate such papers as the public good would permit, and ought to refuse those, the disclosure of which would endanger the public." As it developed, none of the St. Clair papers was regarded as confidential, and the president directed Knox to make them available to the committee.

Four years later, however, Washington did not yield to a House request for correspondence relating to the intensely controversial Jay Treaty with Great Britain. The House was debating a bill to implement portions of the treaty; the bill eventually was passed.

Andrew Jackson. A House committee appointed "to examine into the conditions of the executive departments" adopted a series of resolutions in 1837 that directed President Andrew Jackson and members of his cabinet to furnish lists of federal appointments made without the concurrence of the Senate, the amounts of their pay, and whether they were paid before they took office. Jackson, backed by a large Democratic majority in the House, categorically refused. His defiance has been called the most successful effort of any president to resist the demands of congressional investigators.[11]

"According to the established rules of law," Jackson wrote, "you request myself and the heads of departments to become our own accusers, and to furnish the evidence to convict ourselves." The president continued: "If you either will not make specific accusations, or if, when made, you attempt to establish them by making free men their own accusers, you will not expect me to countenance your proceedings." He then invoked "the principles of justice" as well as the Constitution in refusing the congressional request.

After three months of fruitless questioning of some cabinet officers and others, the committee concluded that it had overstepped its authority in submitting a blanket request for documents and dropped the inquiry. The Jackson majority on the committee explained that it had gone along with the requests of Rep. Henry A. Wise, D-Va., the committee chairman, to avoid charges of protecting the administration. In a report on March 3, 1837, the committee said: "The condition of the various executive departments is prosperous, and . . . they have been conducted with ability and industry."

John Tyler. The House in 1842 passed a resolution requesting that Secretary of War J. C. Spencer give the Indian Affairs Committee reports on the Cherokee Indians and alleged frauds committed against them. After consulting with President John Tyler, Spencer refused, asserting that negotiations to settle claims with the Indians still were in progress. The committee persisted in its request, and the House twice approved committee resolutions requesting that Tyler provide the information that Spencer had withheld. Tyler responded only to the second resolution.

Tyler replied, January 31, 1843, that the claims negotiations had been concluded, and he would submit information dealing with the alleged frauds. However, the president withheld portions of the reports containing personal comments about Indian negotiators and about recommendations for future action.

In doing so, the president argued that the House could not demand information, even if relevant to a House debate, if the information would interfere with the discretion of the executive branch. "It cannot be that the only test is whether the information relates to a legitimate subject of deliberation," Tyler said. Also to be considered, he added, were the protection of confidential sources of information and the protection of officials from malicious publicity. The president's message was referred to the Indian Affairs Committee, which criticized the president's position but did not pursue the matter.[12]

Grover Cleveland. President Grover Cleveland in 1885 was the first Democrat in the White House since James Buchanan departed in 1861. Democrats controlled the House, but Republicans had a majority in the Senate. As the new president began replacing holdover Republican officeholders with Democrats, Senate committees to which the nominations were referred repeatedly requested information as to why the incumbents had been replaced. The standard reply from the various departments was that they were refusing the information at the direction of the president because the public interest would not be served by releasing it or that the removals had been a purely executive action.[13]

Some 650 Republican officeholders were replaced. Finally, on December 26, 1885, the Senate Judiciary Committee, receiving no reply from Attorney General A. H. Garland on the dismissal of George N. Durskin as a U.S. district attorney in Alabama, prevailed on the Senate to approve a resolution January 26, 1886, directing the attorney general to furnish the papers. In reply, Garland said the president had directed him to report that "the public interest would not be promoted by compliance with the resolution." The Senate responded by promptly approving another resolution—this one refusing to concur in the removal of officeholders when the documents on which the removal was based were withheld.

Cleveland sent the Senate a message on March 1, disclaiming any intent to withhold official papers. He asserted that the letters and reports leading to the dismissals were inherently private and confidential. "I do not suppose that the public offices of the United States are regulated or controlled in their relations to either house of Congress by the fact that they were created by laws enacted by" Congress, he wrote.

Cleveland's argument raised the recurring question of whether government departments are creatures of the executive branch, because they carry out executive functions, or creatures of the legislative branch, because they are established and financed through congressional action. From March 9 to March 26 the Senate debated the issue. It concluded by passing a resolution citing the attorney general for being "in violation of his official duty and subversive of the fundamental principles of the government." President Cleveland stood his ground, however, and the Senate ultimately confirmed his nominee to replace Durskin, John D. Burnett.

Continued Insistence on Privilege

Hebert Hoover. During Senate consideration of the London Naval Treaty of 1930, the Foreign Relations Committee asked for the papers relating to the London Conference at which the treaty had been negotiated. Secretary of State Henry L. Stimson submitted some of the papers but withheld others, explaining June 6, 1930, that he had been "directed by the president to say" that their production "would not in his opinion be compatible with the public interest." The committee formally asserted that the documents were "relevant and pertinent when the Senate is considering a treaty for the purpose of ratification."

The full Senate followed with a resolution requesting the president to submit the material, "if not incompatible with the public interest." Pleading the next day that the papers were confidential, Hoover again declined to produce them. The Senate on July 21 consented to ratification of the treaty, with "the distinct and explicit understanding" that it contained no secret agreements.[14]

Harry S. Truman. President Truman in 1948 became involved in a head-on clash between the executive branch and an investigating committee of Congress. On March 1 a special subcommittee of the House Committee on Un-American Activities issued a report that called Dr. Edward U. Condon, director of the Bureau of Standards, "one of the weakest links in our national security." The subcommittee promptly subpoenaed Commerce Department records of loyalty investigations of Condon, but Secretary of Commerce W. Averell Harriman refused to release them on the ground that their publication would be "prejudicial to the public interest."

Truman took a direct hand in the controversy on March 13 when he issued a directive barring disclosure of any loyalty files to Congress. The president said:

Any subpoena or demand or request for information, reports, or files of the nature described, received from sources other than those persons in the executive branch . . . who are entitled thereto by reason of their special duties, shall be respectfully declined on the basis of this directive, and the subpoena or demand or other request shall be referred to the office of the president for such response as the president may determine to be in the public interest in the particular case. There shall be no relaxation of this directive except with my express authority.[15]

On April 22 the House by a 302–29 vote adopted a resolution demanding that Harriman surrender a Federal Bureau of Investigation (FBI) report on Condon. The disputed documents were transferred to the White House, and the president refused to release them—despite Condon's request that they be made public. The House on May 12 passed by a 219–152 vote a bill "directing all executive departments and agencies of the federal government to make available to any and all standing, special, or select committees of the House of Representatives and the Senate, information which may be deemed necessary to enable them to properly perform the duties delegated to them by Congress." Refusal to comply was to be considered a misdemeanor, punishable by a fine of up to $1,000 or imprisonment for up to one year, or both. In the Senate, the bill was referred to the Committee on Expenditures in the Executive Departments (now Governmental Affairs), where it died upon expiration of the 80th Congress.

Dwight D. Eisenhower. During the Army-McCarthy hearings, President Dwight D. Eisenhower on May 17, 1954, forbade testimony about a meeting between Attorney General Herbert Brownell Jr. and Army Counsel John Adams. Developments in the aggressively anticommunist hearings being conducted by Senator McCarthy had been discussed at the meeting. In a letter to Secretary of Defense Charles E. Wilson imposing the ban on testimony about the meeting, Eisenhower stressed the importance of candid, private communication within the executive branch and the "proper separation of power between the executive and legislative branches." When Adams cited the president's order in refusing to answer a question in congressional hearings on May 24, McCarthy accused Adams of using "a type of Fifth Amendment privilege."

McCarthy said three days later that he wanted all federal workers to know "that I feel it's their duty to give us any information which they have about graft, corruption, Communists, treason, and that there is no loyalty to a superior officer which can tower above and beyond their loyalty to their country." The senator promised to shield the identity of informants. The Democrats on the subcommittee protested McCarthy's call for informers, and Brownell on May 28, with the president's approval, issued a statement: "The executive branch . . . has the sole and fundamental responsibility under the Constitution for the enforcement of our laws and presidential orders. . . . That responsibility cannot be usurped by an individual who may seek to set himself above the laws of our land or to override orders of the president of the United States to federal employees of the executive branch."

President Eisenhower's position soon became the basis for an extension of the claim of executive privilege far down the administrative line from the president. After that time, according to a 1973 report prepared by the Government and General Research Division of the Library of Congress, "the executive branch answer to nearly every question about the authority to withhold information from the Congress was 'yes,' they had the authority."[16]

PRESIDENTIAL PRIVILEGES CURTAILED

In the course of Independent Counsel Kenneth W. Starr's investigation into President Bill Clinton's alleged extramarital affair, courts adjudicated questions of "executive privilege," attorney-client privilege, and the "protective function" privilege involving the president's Secret Service detail. The loser in almost all the rulings was the White House. Legal scholars speculated that the effect might be a shifting of power from the presidency to Congress.

U.S. District Court Judge Norma Holloway Johnson ruled May 4, 1998, that Clinton could not invoke executive privilege to keep his aides from testifying before Starr's grand jury. While Johnson recognized claims of executive privilege, she found that the needs of the prosecutors outweighed the privilege in this case. Clinton dropped his executive privilege bid on June 1.

A federal appeals panel July 7, 1998, upheld Johnson's May 22 ruling that the Secret Service agents were obligated to testify about what they witnessed while protecting the president. The Justice Department sought to create a protective function privilege because it feared that a president would not trust having Secret Service agents close enough to protect him. Johnson had written that such a privilege would have to be established by Congress, not the courts.

On July 27, 1998, a three-judge panel of the U.S. Circuit Court of Appeals for the District of Columbia also upheld Johnson's May 4 ruling rejecting the administration's claim of attorney-client privilege in Clinton's effort to keep White House deputy counsel Bruce Lindsay from testifying before Starr's grand jury. White House attorneys were not seen by the panel as any different from other government lawyers who were called on to give evidence about possible criminal wrongdoing.

The new precedents removed flexibility and discouraged negotiated agreements between Congress and the White House, legal experts said. The rulings created ambiguities, rigidity, and the potential for further rulings. They also eroded something known as the "political question doctrine," a body of jurisprudence that says courts should stay out of political disputes. The new rulings also offered Congress new avenues for challenging the president. Future Congresses would be emboldened to issue subpoenas to future administrations. Some predicted that Congress would dig deeper into the inner workings of the White House, demanding to know of events on an hour-by-hour, even minute-by-minute, basis.

Along a similar vein in 1982, the Reagan administration in *United States v. The House of Representatives of the United States* had sought to clarify and bolster the doctrine of executive privilege in light of a congressional subpoena of environmental policy documents. U.S. District Court Judge John Lewis Smith Jr. would have none of it. The case, he concluded, demanded a political accommodation instead of a new body of case law. "Courts have a duty to avoid unnecessarily deciding constitutional issues," said Smith. The Starr investigation, however, forced the courts to do what Smith was trying to avoid: rule on what privileges (exemptions from subpoenas) the president and White House aides are entitled to.

Although legal scholars found the Clinton rulings persuasive, they noted that, if presidents could not count on candid advice from their advisers, they likely would have a difficult time asserting control over the vast executive branch. Presidents routinely use their most trusted White House aides to imbue the federal bureaucracy with their policy objectives. They do this through centralization of the decision-making process and control of the flow of information, among other things. A hamstrung White House would presumably mean more decisions being made further down the chain of command, sometimes by bureaucrats or officers less sympathetic to the goals of the administration. If presidential advisers know they could be forced to testify—either as a result of a court order or because a president does not have the power to stand up to a congressional subpoena—they might be more inhibited in what they say.

The question arises as to whether the country is better off with such court rulings. Most legal experts argue that presidential privileges are a separation-of-powers issue. As such, it is best if they are left undefined and constantly argued over by the legislative and executive branches as they try to advance their policy and political agendas. In hindsight, President Clinton could have avoided the legal downside of the court rulings on future presidential privileges by not challenging Starr's subpoenas.

John F. Kennedy. The pattern of invoking the privilege by executive branch officials was altered, but not broken, by President John F. Kennedy in 1962. The previous year a special Senate subcommittee had opened hearings on the Pentagon's system for editing speeches of military leaders. When the panel asked the identity of the editors, the president directed the secretary of defense "not to give any testimony or produce any documents which would disclose such information."

Kennedy added, however: "The principle which is at stake here cannot be automatically applied to every request for information. Each case must be judged on its own merits." Soon afterward the president wrote, "Executive privilege can be invoked only by the president and will not be used without specific presidential approval." Nonetheless, after the Kennedy directive, executive branch officials in his administration refused to provide information to congressional committees at least three times, apparently without presidential authorization.

Lyndon Johnson. President Lyndon Johnson similarly stated in a letter of April 2, 1965, that "the claim of 'executive privilege' will continue to be made only by the president." Although he did not personally invoke the privilege, at least two appointees in his administration refused to provide information to congressional committees.

Richard Nixon. In addition to Watergate-related information, Nixon personally and formally invoked the claim of executive privilege against congressional committees four times. In a memorandum issued on March 24, 1969, Nixon stated that the privilege would not be used without presidential approval.

Between 1969 and 1973, however, there were at least fifteen other instances (most of them related to defense or foreign policy) in which documents or testimony were refused to congressional committees without direct presidential approval. "In fact, the presidential statements [on executive privilege] have been limitations in name only," said the Library of Congress report.

Congress in 1973 and 1974 considered but did not enact legislation to set out procedures for Congress to use in considering and overriding such claims. The Senate in 1973 approved a bill requiring that all information requested by Congress be provided by the executive unless the president in writing ordered the material withheld. A divided House committee sent the measure on to the House, but the bill never came to a vote.

Bill Clinton. Republicans in Congress, upon assuming the majority as a result of the 1994 elections, opened numerous investigations into the activities of the Clinton administration, which evoked several claims of executive privilege. In 1996 Republican leaders launched a high-profile investigation of reports that Clinton in April 1994 had approved secret Iranian arms shipments to Bosnia through Croatia. The White House had not notified Congress about the secret policy, which occurred at a time when the administration was lobbying Congress against unilaterally lifting the international arms embargo on Bosnia.

The Intelligence Oversight Board, a small, presidentially appointed panel responsible for investigating wrongdoing in the intelligence community, reviewed the administration's actions and concluded that the shipments did not meet the legal definition of a covert action and thus did not require that Congress be notified. The White House subsequently denied a request—which amounted to a claim of executive privilege—by Senate Intelligence Committee Chairman Arlen Specter, R-Pa., for access to the board's secret report on the grounds that it needed to protect confidential policy discussions.

The House Government Reform and Oversight Committee on May 9, 1996, voted to cite three White House lawyers for contempt of Congress for refusing to surrender documents related to the 1993 firing of White House travel office employees. One of the lawyers, Jack Quinn, sent a letter to the committee saying that Clinton invoked executive privilege in declining to give additional files on the case to the panel. The committee later expanded its request to include documents related to the White House possession of FBI files on hundreds of Republican officials from former administrations. Further action on the contempt resolution was forestalled when an agreement was reached that allowed members of Congress and their staffs access to papers regarding the travel office and the FBI files. *(See "White House Travel Office," p. 279; "FBI Files," p. 279.)*

President Clinton on September 23, 1996, invoked executive privilege, declining to release forty-seven of fifty-one documents on Haiti policy that had been subpoenaed by the House International Relations Committee. Republicans alleged that the administration was trying to cover up embarrassing information showing the complicity of the U.S.-backed Haitian government in political murders. The White House said the documents being withheld included confidential memoranda on conversations with foreign leaders and deliberations by the president's national security advisers.

The White House September 27, 1996, refused a request from the House Government Reform and Oversight Committee for a memo by FBI Director Louis J. Freeh and Drug Enforcement Administration Administrator Thomas A. Constantine, which the Republicans contended was critical of the way the Clinton administration had run the war against drugs. The committee then subpoenaed the document. White House Counsel Quinn responded October 1 with a letter to the panel in which he denied the request by invoking executive privilege.

A federal court in 1998 denied a claim of executive privilege made by President Clinton. The ruling was triggered by subpoenas of administration officials from Independent Counsel Kenneth W. Starr's grand jury, not a congressional committee. Starr subsequently asserted in his September 1998 report to Congress that a possible ground for impeaching Clinton was that he abused his constitutional authority by invoking executive privilege in "an effort to hinder, impede, and deflect possible inquiry" into his alleged extramarital affair. *(See box, Presidential Privileges Curtailed, p. 261.)*

Watergate and Beyond

The most dramatic clash between Congress and the White House over executive privilege came during the inquiry into the Watergate scandal. It pitted Nixon against two congressional committees, two special prosecutors—Archibald Cox and his successor, Leon Jaworski—and a grand jury.

The confrontation began when the Senate Watergate Committee was created in February 1973. At first Nixon pleaded executive privilege, refusing to allow his aides to appear before the panel. But in April he reversed himself, stating that government employees and particularly White House employees "are expected fully to cooperate in this matter. I condemn any attempts to cover up in this case, no matter who is involved."

On May 3 the White House issued a new guideline on the privilege, stating: "The President desires that the invocation of executive privilege be held to a minimum." The privilege should be invoked only in connection with conversations with the president, conversations among aides involving communications with the president, and with regard to presidential papers and national security.

On May 29 Nixon said he would not provide information through oral or written testimony to the Watergate grand jury or to the Senate committee. For him to do so would be "constitutionally inappropriate" and a violation of the separation of powers.

Nixon repeated his refusal to appear before the committee or to hand over presidential papers in a letter to Sen. Sam J. Ervin Jr., the committee chairman, dated July 6. "No president could function if the private papers of his office, prepared by his personal staff, were open to public scrutiny," he wrote. "Formulation of sound public policy requires that the president and his

Now where ?

EXECUTIVE PRIVILEGE

SUPREME COURT

The Supreme Court in July 1974 rejected President Richard Nixon's claim of executive privilege, ruling unanimously that Oval Office tape recordings had to be turned over to Congress.

personal staff be able to communicate among themselves in complete candor. . . . If he were to testify before the committee irreparable damage would be done to the constitutional principle of separation of powers."

Nixon's declaration assumed new dimensions later in July, however, when it was revealed that tape recordings had been made of many presidential conversations in the White House during the period under investigation. Immediately, a struggle for the tapes began. The legal battle lasted almost exactly a year, from July 23, 1973, when the Senate committee and the Watergate grand jury subpoenaed the first group of tapes, to July 24, 1974, when the Supreme Court ruled against Nixon and ordered that he hand over the tapes sought by the special prosecutor. But the Senate investigating committee never obtained the tapes it sought. The administration's argument prevailed in that case.

U.S. District Court Judge John J. Sirica ruled, August 29,

1973, that the president should give him the tapes subpoenaed by Special Prosecutor Cox so that he could review them. On October 12 the U.S. Court of Appeals for the District of Columbia upheld Sirica's decision. Five days later Sirica ruled against the Watergate Committee's request for the same tapes. He said he had no authority to hand them over. Moving quickly to rectify the situation, Congress on December 3 sent to the White House legislation specifically granting the court jurisdiction over suits brought by the committee to enforce subpoenas. The bill became law without Nixon's signature, and the committee promptly approved new subpoenas for nearly five hundred presidential tapes and documents; Nixon refused to comply.

Deciding to seek enforcement of the original subpoenas before litigating Nixon's refusal to comply with the more recent demands, the committee on January 7, 1974, renewed its original suit and asked Sirica to reconsider it in light of the new law. Sirica referred the case to U.S. District Court Judge Gerhard A.

Gesell. Again, the White House asked the court to dismiss the suit.

On January 25 Gesell issued his ruling, quashing the subpoena for documents but directing Nixon to respond to a subpoena for five tapes. The judge asked Nixon to provide a detailed statement explaining what parts of the subpoenaed tapes he considered covered by executive privilege. "This statement must be signed by the president," Gesell wrote, "for only he can invoke the [executive] privilege at issue." On February 6, Nixon sent Gesell a letter saying that disclosure of the tapes "would not be in the public interest."

Gesell refused to require the White House to turn over the tapes to the Senate panel, citing the risk that the committee's use of the tapes might make it difficult to obtain an unbiased jury for the trials arising out of the Watergate scandal. "The committee's role as a 'grand inquest' into governmental misconduct is limited," wrote Gesell. "It may only proceed in aid of Congress's legislative function. . . . The time has come to question whether it is in the public interest for the criminal investigative aspects of its work to go forward in the blazing atmosphere of . . . publicity." The Senate Watergate Committee agreed February 19 to end its public hearings. It also appealed Gesell's ruling, but the appeal was rejected by a federal appellate court on May 23.

Meanwhile, Jaworski and the House Judiciary Committee, which had begun an impeachment inquiry, issued their subpoenas for tapes and documents. Again, Nixon and his lawyers, arguing presidential confidentiality, refused to comply. However, Nixon announced April 29, 1974, the day before the deadline set by the Judiciary Committee subpoena, that he would make public the transcripts of forty-six tapes the next day. The committee was not satisfied. It voted May 1 to inform the president that "you have failed to comply with the committee's subpoena." Jaworski, whose subpoena for evidence Nixon had also rejected, took his case to the Supreme Court.

Nixon's lawyer, James D. St. Clair, argued before the Court that "inherent in the executive power vested in the president under Article II of the Constitution is executive privilege, generally recognized as a derivative of the separation of powers doctrine." Jaworski, in contrast, argued that "the qualified executive privilege for confidential intra-governmental deliberations" was intended "to promote the candid interchange between officials and their aides," and "exists only to protect the legitimate functioning of the government."

"The privilege must give way where, as here, it has been abused," Jaworski continued. "There has been a *prima facie* showing that each of the participants in the subpoenaed conversations, including the president, was a member of the conspiracy to defraud the United States and to obstruct justice. . . . The public purpose underlying the executive privilege for governmental deliberations precludes its application to shield alleged criminality."

On July 24, hours before the Judiciary Committee began public debate on impeachment, the Supreme Court ruled unanimously against the president and ordered him to give up the tapes. Within a week the Judiciary Committee adopted three articles of impeachment, among them one citing Nixon for contempt of Congress for failing to comply with the panel's subpoenas.

Nixon began surrendering the tapes to Sirica on July 30. On August 2 the president made public the transcript of some of the tapes. They showed his participation in a cover-up after the Watergate break-in and his approval of the use of the Central Intelligence Agency to block an FBI investigation of the Watergate scandal. Those revelations led directly to his resignation on August 9.

Citing Cabinet Members, 1975–1998

Another aspect of the executive privilege issue surfaced in November 1975 when the House Intelligence Committee issued three subpoenas for State Department documents. Secretary of State Henry A. Kissinger refused to turn over the documents on orders of President Gerald R. Ford, who cited executive privilege. In a letter to Kissinger ordering the material be withheld, the president said it contained "highly sensitive military and foreign affairs assessments and evaluations," and consultations and advice to former presidents Kennedy, Johnson, and Nixon.

Rep. Otis G. Pike, D-N.Y., the committee chairman, contended that Ford could not invoke executive privilege to withhold documents of previous administrations. The committee voted to cite Kissinger for contempt of Congress—the first such action against a cabinet member—but did not move forward with the contempt proceeding after it received "substantial compliance" from the White House.

President Jimmy Carter invoked executive privilege against Congress only once, in 1980, to withhold documents concerning his unsuccessful effort to impose an oil import fee. But it resulted in the second instance of a House panel voting to hold a cabinet member, Secretary of Energy Charles Duncan, in contempt. After the vote the White House agreed to let the panel—the Government Operations Subcommittee on Environment, Energy, and Natural Resources—see the documents. It took no further action against Duncan.

Two years later another House committee, Energy and Commerce, started contempt proceedings against Secretary of the Interior James G. Watt. President Ronald Reagan had invoked executive privilege and instructed Watt not to give the panel documents concerning the administration's consideration of the impact of Canadian energy policies on American companies. The White House contended that the papers related to sensitive foreign policy matters. But once again, after the committee vote the White House yielded—agreeing to turn over the documents temporarily for examination by the committee members. In return the committee dropped the contempt citation it had voted.

Later the same year—1982—a contempt citation against Anne M. Gorsuch (later Burford), head of the Environmental Protection Agency (EPA), went further. It was voted December 16 by the entire House, 259–105, marking the first time a full chamber had used its contempt power against an official who had invoked executive privilege. On Reagan's orders Burford refused to turn over EPA documents to two House committees investigating the agency's enforcement of a 1980 "superfund" law for cleaning up hazardous wastes. The Justice Department refused to prosecute her and instead filed a lawsuit to block action on the contempt citation.

The constitutional test of wills between the White House and Congress was short-lived, however. On February 3, 1983, a federal district court in Washington, D.C., granted a motion filed by lawyers for the House of Representatives to dismiss the Justice suit. Shortly afterward Burford resigned as EPA director, and both sides to the dispute worked out a compromise arrangement whereby committee members gained access to some of the EPA documents. The House on August 3 voted to drop its contempt citation against Burford. The following day, Rita M. Lavelle, the former EPA assistant administrator, was indicted by a federal grand jury on charges of perjury and obstructing a federal investigation. She was later convicted on four of five counts and sentenced to six months' imprisonment.

The House Government Reform and Oversight Committee on August 6, 1998, voted along party lines, 24–19, to cite Attorney General Janet Reno for contempt of Congress for refusing to hand over internal Justice Department memos making the case for the appointment of an independent counsel to investigate alleged campaign fund-raising abuses by the Democrats in 1996. The committee sought a twenty-seven-page document written in November 1997 by FBI Director Louis J. Freeh and a ninety-four-page report by Charles G. LaBella, the former head of the Justice Department's campaign finance task force. Neither Freeh nor LaBella thought that the memos should be made public.

Committee Chairman Dan Burton, R-Ind., had subpoenaed the two memos in July. On September 2, Reno shared heavily redacted versions of the memos with lawmakers. Not satisfied, Burton announced September 17 that he had filed a contempt-of-Congress resolution against Reno. But the full House did not take up the matter.

Reno was only the second attorney general cited for contempt of Congress by a congressional committee. President Reagan's attorney general, William French Smith, was cited by a Senate subcommittee for failing to produce documents in 1981 pertaining to a probe of defense contractor General Dynamics Corp., but the matter was also dropped by the full House.

Major Investigations: History in Brief

Following are summaries of selected major congressional investigations conducted since 1789:

ST. CLAIR INQUIRY

The House approved the first congressional investigation in American history when it adopted on March 27, 1792, by a 44–10 vote, a resolution authorizing a select committee to investigate an Indian victory the previous year over troops commanded by Maj. Gen. Arthur St. Clair. The action came after the House, also on March 27, had rejected, 21–35, a resolution calling on President Washington to carry out the investigation.

Setting precedents along the way, the committee under the chairmanship of Thomas Fitzsimmons, a Pennsylvania Federalist, asked for and received War Department papers on the expedition that had sent St. Clair and about fifteen hundred soldiers on a road- and fort-building trip through the Northwest Territory. An Indian attack had killed about six hundred men and wounded some three hundred. Witnesses called by the committee included St. Clair, Secretary of War Henry Knox, and Secretary of the Treasury Alexander Hamilton.

The report of the committee, filed May 8, 1792, completely absolved St. Clair, a former president of the Continental Congress. Blame for the disaster was placed on the War Department, particularly the quartermaster and supply contractors, who were accused of mismanagement, neglect, and delay in supplying necessary equipment, clothing, and munitions. The House took no action on the report, and Federalists prevented its publication because of its reflections on Knox and Hamilton. Early in 1818 Congress approved a $60 monthly pension for the elderly and impoverished St. Clair, who died a few months later. Nearly forty years later, in 1857, Congress appropriated a substantial sum to be paid to his heirs.

CIVIL WAR STUDY

The Joint Committee on the Conduct of the [Civil] War compiled what was widely considered—at least until the McCarthy era of the 1950s—the worst record of any congressional investigating unit. It was a political vehicle for Radical Republicans opposed to President Abraham Lincoln, and its far-ranging inquiries were used for intensely partisan purposes.

The Senate on a 33–0 vote December 9, 1861, and the House by a voice vote the next day, authorized appointment of the joint committee simply "to inquire into the conduct of the present war." It was the first time a joint House-Senate panel had been created to carry out a congressional inquiry. The committee was set up in the aftermath of the Union defeats at Manassas (Bull Run) in July and Ball's Bluff in October. At first it was thought the panel would investigate those defeats, but the Radical majority on the committee, with Sen. Benjamin F. Wade, R-Ohio, as chairman, had more ambitious ideas.

In hearings that began December 24, 1861, and continued until early 1865, the committee examined past and future battle plans, disloyal employees, navy installations, naval engagements, war supplies, and war contracts. It filed its final report May 22, 1865.

In a sense the committee took over partial control of Union operations. It harassed conservative and Democratic generals, particularly Gen. George B. McClellan. Typically, when investigating a general, the committee first would interrogate his subordinate officers, searching for adverse information. With such

POLITICS OF CONGRESSIONAL INVESTIGATIONS

The three most intensive periods of congressional investigative activities—the last years of the Grant administration and the periods immediately following World Wars I and II—coincided with shifts of congressional majorities that transferred power to a party long in the minority.

Ulysses S. Grant, a Republican, was president from 1869 to 1877; when the Democrats in the 1874 election recaptured control of the House for the first time since 1859, the number of investigations soared. In the 1918 election, Republicans gained control of the House and set off on a series of studies of World War I mobilization under President Woodrow Wilson, a Democrat. In similar fashion, World War II mobilization and reported infiltration of the government by communists during the administrations of Democratic Presidents Franklin D. Roosevelt and Harry S. Truman were studied closely by committees of the Republican 80th Congress, elected in 1946.

A subtler form of investigation politics takes place in the maneuvering for control of a particular inquiry. The conduct of investigations depends substantially on the attitude of the investigating committees and of their chairmen. Thus Radical Republicans, gaining control of the joint committee investigating the conduct of the Civil War, used the committee as a forum for criticizing the moderate policies of President Abraham Lincoln and to force more vigorous prosecution of the war.

Another example, after World War II, had different results. President Truman's release in August 1945 of army and navy reports on the Pearl Harbor disaster brought numerous Republican demands for a congressional investigation. Through quick maneuvering, the Democrats initiated action, establishing a joint House-Senate committee, which, with the Democrats in control of Congress, would have a Democratic majority. The resolution was adopted by both chambers without opposition.

The committee's final report, filed July 20, 1946, absolved President Roosevelt of blame for the Pearl Harbor disaster but held the chief of naval operations and the army commander in Hawaii primarily responsible. A Republican minority report laid the primary blame on Roosevelt, suggesting what might have been the majority view if Republicans had been in command of the inquiry.

information in hand, the committee would summon the general for questioning, frequently without informing him of the accusations against him or the disclosures made by his subordinates. The committee's next step would be a meeting with President Lincoln at which the general's resignation or reassignment would be demanded.

Committee sessions were supposed to be closed to the press, but information often would be made public if it suited the purpose of the Radicals. As a result, Confederate Gen. Robert E. Lee was moved to observe that the committee was worth about two divisions of Confederate troops.

CRÉDIT MOBILIER

The number of congressional investigations soared during Ulysses S. Grant's eight years as president. According to Joseph Harris, author of *Congressional Control of Administration*, between 1869 and 1877 Congress undertook thirty-seven inquiries into charges of maladministration. Although the investigations were a response to well-founded dissatisfaction with the practices of the executive branch, the Crédit Mobilier scandal touched some outstanding members of Congress and tarnished the legislative branch as well.

Two committees in the House and one in the Senate investigated charges that arose during the 1872 presidential campaign of wholesale corruption in connection with construction by Crédit Mobilier of America of the last 667 miles of the Union Pacific Railroad, which had been completed three years earlier. The inquiries disclosed perhaps the most serious legislative scandal in the country's history.

The charges first appeared when the New York *Sun* of September 4, 1872, reported that Rep. Oakes Ames, R-Mass., a principal stockholder in both the Union Pacific and the Crédit Mobilier construction company, had used Crédit Mobilier stock to bribe Vice President Schuyler Colfax, Sen. Henry Wilson, R-Mass., Speaker James G. Blaine, R-Maine, Sen. James W. Patterson, R-N.H., Rep. James Brooks, D-N.Y., and Rep. James A. Garfield, R-Ohio. The reported bribes represented an attempt to head off a congressional investigation of railroad transportation rates.

Blaine proposed the first inquiry, and the House on December 2, 1872, appointed a select committee headed by Rep. Luke P. Poland, R-Vt., "to investigate and ascertain whether any member of this House was bribed by Oakes Ames, or any other person or corporation, in any manner touching his legislative duty." A month later, January 6, 1873, the House appointed another select committee, headed by Rep. Jeremiah M. Wilson, R-Ind., to investigate the financial arrangement between Union Pacific and Crédit Mobilier.

As the House investigations proceeded simultaneously, the Poland committee discovered evidence implicating members of the Senate. Upon receiving the information, the Senate on February 4, 1873, established a select committee of its own to look into the alleged bribery. The committee was headed by Sen. Lot M. Morrill, R-Maine.

The Poland committee filed a report February 18, 1873, clearing Blaine but recommending that Ames and Brooks be expelled from the House. The committee said Ames had been "guilty of selling to members of Congress shares of stock in the Crédit Mobilier of America, for prices much below the true value of such stock, with intent thereby to influence the votes and decisions of such members in matters to be brought before Congress for action." Brooks had purchased stock in his son-in-law's name but for his own benefit, the committee added. The House ultimately censured the two representatives but did not expel them.

The Wilson committee issued its report March 3, saying that Crédit Mobilier had been making exorbitant profits and that some persons connected with it were holding bonds illegally. In addition, the committee recommended that court action be undertaken to eliminate the financial irregularities.

The Senate's committee had meanwhile come out with its report on March 1, saying that Patterson had bought Crédit Mobilier stock from Ames at below-market prices. The committee recommended Patterson's expulsion, but his retirement upon the expiration of his term on March 3 precluded Senate action to expel him.

Colfax, whose involvement was not satisfactorily explained, had fallen from favor with the regular Republicans before the scandal broke and was not renominated in June 1872 for a second term on the Grant ticket. Henry Wilson, who replaced Colfax as vice president, and Garfield, elected president in 1880, never explained away their connection with the affair.

STUDY OF THE MONEY TRUST

The House on February 24, 1912, authorized its Banking and Currency Committee to investigate the concentration of money and credit in the nation. Conducted at a time when the national interest already was turned to such industrial concentrations as the sugar trust, the meat trust, and the steel trust, the new inquiry soon became known as the money trust investigation.

Conducted by a Banking and Currency subcommittee headed by committee chairman Arsène P. Pujo, D-La., the inquiry brought to light previously unknown interlocking directorates among two sets of New York banks, controlled by Morgan and Rockefeller interests, and 112 of the country's largest corporations in banking, public utilities, transportation, insurance, manufacturing, and trading.

Witnesses called by committee counsel Samuel Untermyer, the real director and principal actor in the hearings, included such financial giants as J. P. Morgan Sr., George F. Baker of the First National Bank of New York, James Stillman of the National City Bank of New York, Jacob H. Schiff of Kuhn, Loeb & Co., and James J. Hill, the railroad magnate. The range of activities investigated by the subcommittee turned the hearings into the most ambitious inquiry to date.

The subcommittee filed its report February 28, 1913, summarizing its findings and calling for corrective legislation. Within two years Congress, prodded by President Woodrow Wilson, enacted the Federal Reserve Act of 1913, creating a central banking system, and the Clayton Antitrust and the Federal Trade Commission acts of 1914, strengthening federal regulation of commerce.

TEAPOT DOME

Teapot Dome is the enduring legacy of Warren G. Harding's presidency (1921–1923), a code name for scandal in government. After the disclosures of a long congressional investigation, one member of the president's cabinet, Secretary of the Interior Albert B. Fall, went to prison for accepting bribes to lease government-owned oil land to favored persons. Teapot Dome was the most prominent of several shady activities going on in Washington at that time, leaving a taint of corruption on the Harding administration.

The name Teapot Dome comes from a sandstone formation, faintly resembling a teapot, that rises above the sagebrush plains of north-central Wyoming. Deep below the rock outcropping is a reservoir of oil that nature had formed vaguely in the shape of a dome. This underground oil and the land above it made up a tiny portion of the vast federal holdings in the West. In 1915 President Wilson assigned control of Teapot Dome to the Navy Department as a reserve source of fuel for American warships. Two other oil fields, Elk Hills and Buena Vista in California, had already been selected. But none had to be tapped during World War I because the U.S. petroleum supply turned out to be bigger than geologists had expected.

Harding transferred jurisdiction over naval oil reserves to the Interior Department in May 1921. Early the next year Interior leased the Elk Hills reserve in California to Edward L. Doheny of the Pan-American Petroleum and Transport Co. and the Teapot Dome reserve in Wyoming to Harry F. Sinclair's Mammoth Oil Co.

Pressure mounted for a congressional investigation of the transactions. Tight Republican control blocked action in the House. But Senate Democrats and insurgent Republicans succeeded in pushing through a resolution that authorized the Senate Committee on Public Lands and Surveys "to investigate this entire subject of leases upon naval oil reserves." The committee was headed by a series of Republican chairmen, but a Democrat on the panel, Thomas J. Walsh of Montana, took charge of the inquiry.

When the hearings opened on October 25, 1923, they concentrated at first on the legality of the two leases. Then Walsh developed information that Fall had accepted bribes from Doheny and Sinclair. Doheny had given Fall at least $100,000, and Sinclair had given the interior secretary at least $300,000. Fall, who had meanwhile resigned his cabinet post for reasons that were not entirely clear, protested that he had received only "gifts and loans." He was later convicted of accepting a bribe from Doheny in connection with the Elk Hills lease. However, in a separate trial Doheny was acquitted on charges of making the bribe. After Fall exhausted his court appeals, he entered prison in June 1931 and served eleven months.

Harding, at Congress's request, initiated court action to cancel the oil leases. The courts did so and also invalidated the president's executive order transferring jurisdiction over the oil reserves from the navy to the Interior Department.

Acting on information developed in the Teapot Dome inquiry, the Senate on March 4, 1924, created a Select Committee to Investigate the Justice Department, which had appeared reluctant to investigate and prosecute the scandal. Calvin Coolidge, who had become president in 1923 after Harding's death, demanded Attorney General Harry M. Daugherty's resignation. Daugherty, who had been Harding's campaign manager

Who Says a Watched Pot Never Boils?

A Senate investigating committee uncovered much of the evidence in the Teapot Dome Scandal of the 1920s. The scandal shattered the administration of President Warren G. Harding and shook public faith in government officials generally.

in the 1920 presidential election, was prosecuted for conspiracy to defraud the government, but at two trials the juries failed to reach a verdict.

Sinclair went to jail twice, first for three months for contempt of Congress over his refusal to answer questions and then for six months for contempt of court for attempting to bribe a juror at his trial on bribery charges arising from the Teapot Dome investigation. He was ultimately acquitted of those charges.

PECORA STOCK EXCHANGE PROBE

The Senate Banking and Currency Committee from 1932 to 1934 conducted an important investigation of the stock exchange and Wall Street financial manipulations, reminiscent of the earlier money trust hearings.

Authorized March 4, 1932, while Sen. Peter Norbeck, R-S.D.,

was chairman of the committee, the hearings concentrated initially on stock exchange practices. The 1929 stock market collapse had plunged the nation into a severe depression and a congressional examination of exchange operations became a political necessity. The hearings began inconspicuously, and some observers expected them to become a "whitewash."

Then, in January 1933, the committee hired Ferdinand Pecora as chief counsel. As the country's banking system headed for collapse, the committee broadened its investigation to include a study of the financial dealings of New York's major banking houses. When the Democrats took over control of the Senate, Sen. Duncan U. Fletcher, D-Fla., became chairman of the committee.

Chief Counsel Pecora demanded careful research and thorough investigation by the committee staff. Pecora, in turn, relied on evidence gathered by the staff as he conducted the interrogation of committee witnesses. Committee members normally listened in silence, asking few questions of their own. Pecora came to dominate the hearings, far overshadowing Fletcher, to the extent that the inquiry was to become known as the Pecora investigation.

As the 1933 hearings progressed under Pecora, they produced spectacular accounts of dubious financial actions. The salary of Charles E. Mitchell, president of the National City Bank of New York, had doubled from $100,000 to $200,000 as the bread lines of the unemployed had lengthened. Albert H. Wiggin, president of the Chase National Bank of New York, had sold short the stock of his own bank. J. P. Morgan Jr. had paid no income tax for several years because his losses offset his gains. Other witnesses recounted the operation of security flotation syndicates and stock market polls. It developed that friends of Morgan, including cabinet officers, former president Coolidge, and top Republican and Democratic Party officials, had been let in on some profitable security transactions.

The hearing disclosures paved the way for such New Deal regulatory measures as the Banking Acts of 1933 and 1935, the Securities Act of 1933, and the Securities Exchange Act of 1934. The committee filed its final report on June 16, 1934.

NYE MUNITIONS INQUIRY

Riding a wave of public sentiment for a congressional investigation of the munitions industry, the Senate on April 12, 1934, established the Senate Special Committee Investigating the Munitions Industry. Despite Democratic control of the Senate and a Democratic majority on the committee, Sen. Gerald P. Nye, R-N.D., was picked as chairman. A Progressive Republican, he had earned a measure of public prominence as chairman of a special Senate committee that scrutinized spending in the 1930 election contests.

The munitions inquiry made Nye a national figure, a leader of the movement to curb the arms traffic, and the nation's most eloquent isolationist. The Nye Committee, as it soon was called, opened hearings on September 4, 1934. It investigated business profits during World War I, particularly in munitions making and shipbuilding. Witnesses included leading businessmen, financiers, and their associates.

Committee investigators gathered documents from government and diplomatic files and from private corporations. Worldwide attention, carefully cultivated by Nye, focused on the committee's efforts to prove that arms makers were "merchants of death," linked together in a global ring, opposed to disarmament, promoting armed conflicts, and reaping enormous profits along the way. However, the evidence was thin and failed to support such general conclusions.

Public sentiment, which strongly favored the investigation at its onset, appeared to shift. The Senate in 1936 refused to provide additional funds for the investigation, and the committee filed its final report April 20, 1936. It recommended a definition of armed merchant ships and placement of ceilings on wartime exports and loans to belligerent nations. The committee members agreed on a need for strictly controlling the munitions industry but divided on how the control could best be exercised.

TRUMAN COMMITTEE

The World War II Senate Special Committee to Investigate the National Defense Program came to be widely regarded as the most effective investigating group in the history of Congress. Created March 1, 1941, nine months before the Japanese attack on Pearl Harbor plunged the United States into the war, the committee sought to uncover and to halt wasteful practices in war preparations. Its studies were broadened to cover the entire war mobilization effort once the country entered the conflict.

Closely identified with its first chairman, Sen. Harry S. Truman, D-Mo., the committee had the broadest possible investigating authority. The Truman Committee was "to make a full and complete study and investigation of the operation of the program for the procurement and construction of supplies, materials, vessels, plants, camps, and other articles and facilities in connection with the national defense." The group was mostly composed of freshman senators, able to devote much of their time to the inquiry.

Confusion in the program for constructing training camps, and concentration of war contracts in a few areas of the country and among a few businesses, had led Truman to propose the investigating committee. But the committee's first hearings, which began April 15, 1941, were devoted to a general investigation of the status of the national defense program. Later the committee examined camp construction and other problems of war mobilization; shortages of critical war materials, such as aluminum, rubber, petroleum products, housing, and steel; the quality of materials supplied under defense contracts and the distribution of the contracts; and war frauds among contractors, lobbyists, and government officials.

Aware of the excesses of the Civil War investigating committee, Truman scrupulously avoided any attempt to judge military policy or operations. Hearings of the Truman Committee were conducted in a restrained, thoughtful manner, after careful and thorough preparation. Frequently, private meetings or correspondence with contractors or federal officials led to corrective action, and no public hearings were held.

The committee worked closely with executive branch departments and agencies. Special liaison officers were assigned to it in the War Department, the Navy Department, the War Production Board, the Maritime Commission, and the War Shipping Administration. Reports and recommendations were supported unanimously by committee members, and most recommendations were put into effect before the findings were published.

The Truman Committee was not the only congressional group studying national mobilization, but it was the only one to make a systematic effort to survey the entire war program on a continuing basis. Its work continued beyond the war, until 1948, under three successive chairmen after Truman resigned August 3, 1944, after receiving the Democratic vice presidential nomination. They were James M. Mead, D-N.Y., who was succeeded in 1946 by Harley M. Kilgore, D-W.Va., and Owen Brewster, R-Maine, who took over when Republicans gained control of the Senate in 1947. They led investigations into charges of wartime profiteering. The committee submitted its final report April 28, 1948, and went out of business.

KEFAUVER CRIME HEARINGS

At the urging of Sen. Estes Kefauver, D-Tenn., the Senate in May 1950 created the Special Committee to Investigate Organized Crime in Interstate Commerce. As its chairman for the next twelve months, he conducted headline-making hearings in city after city across the country to the rapt attention of millions of television viewers. The Kefauver Committee, as it quickly became known, put its work and the chairman's name in the nation's consciousness. The fame Kefauver won in that role made him a leading but ultimately unsuccessful contender for the Democratic presidential nomination in 1952.

The creation of a special committee represented a compromise in a jurisdictional dispute between the Judiciary Committee and the Interstate and Foreign Commerce Committee over which one should conduct an investigation of organized crime. The committee's work was continued for a few months beyond the end of Kefauver's chairmanship, in May 1951, but by then the hearings had already turned much of the nation's attention to a network of organized crime the hearings had publicized.

The committee questioned governors, mayors, sheriffs, and police officers and turned the spotlight on gangsters, gamblers, racketeers, and narcotics peddlers. The hearings were full of names of prominent racketeers, including reputed heirs of the Chicago Capone gang and leaders of the Mafia. Many of them proved difficult to locate. Hearings were followed by scores of citations for contempt of Congress and many local indictments for criminal activities.

One of the highlights of the hearings was the appearance before the committee of Frank Costello, the reputed underworld

Sen. Estes Kefauver, second from right, used televised hearings by his special investigation committee to spotlight organized crime in 1950–1951. After the widely viewed hearings, Kefauver became a leading, though ultimately unsuccessful, contender for the presidency.

king. He refused to have his face televised, so TV audiences saw only his hands. Many other witnesses likewise complained about testifying before television cameras. Some who refused were cited for contempt. The U.S. District Court for the District of Columbia ruled on October 6, 1952, that two of the contemptuous witnesses, Morris Kleinman and Louis Rothkopf, were "justified" in refusing to testify while television and newsreel cameras were in operation. They were freed of the contempt-of-Congress charges.

In a series of reports, the committee said that crime syndicates were operating with the connivance and protection of law enforcement officials and that the two major syndicates were centered in Chicago and New York. "Shocking" corruption existed, according to one report, "at all levels of government." The committee recommended creation of a privately financed National Crime Coordinating Committee, a thorough overhaul of state and local crime laws, a stronger attack on narcotics trafficking, legalization of wiretapping, and the adoption by Congress of a code or procedure for the broadcasting or televising of committee hearings.

MCCARTHY'S INVESTIGATIONS

Under the chairmanship of Sen. Joseph R. McCarthy, the Permanent Investigations Subcommittee of the Senate Government Operations Committee conducted a series of wide-ranging and controversial hearings in 1953 and 1954. The hearings were the highwater mark of the "McCarthy era" and were carried out in keeping with the senator's abrasive and aggressive character. He investigated such varied subjects as Korean War atrocities and a Greek shipping deal, but his main focus was on a purported communist subversion of the U.S. government, including the armed forces, and the United Nations.

McCarthy tangled with the press, Harvard University, and other senators. The three Democratic members of the subcommittee—Senators Henry M. Jackson of Washington, John L. McClellan of Arkansas, and Stuart Symington of Missouri—resigned from the subcommittee on July 10, 1953, in protest against the chairman's handling of the staff. But the following January McCarthy announced changes in subcommittee procedure, and the three Democrats returned.

Long before the stormy McCarthy hearings got under way, the senator had become a controversial public figure. On February 9, 1950, he delivered a speech before the Ohio County Women's Republican Club in Wheeling, West Virginia. According to the Wheeling *News Register* and the Wheeling *Intelligencer*, the senator said at one point: "While I cannot take the time to name all the men in the State Department who have been named as members of the Communist Party and members of a spy ring, I have here in my hand a list of 205 that were known to the secretary of state as being members of the Communist Party and who, nevertheless, are still working and shaping policy in the State Department." The number varied in later versions of the speech, and the text that was read into the *Con-gressional Record* omitted the paragraph referring to the list of 205 communists.

A special subcommittee of the Senate Foreign Relations Committee was set up under the chairmanship of Millard E. Tydings, D-Md., to investigate McCarthy's charges. The subcommittee, in one of the most bitterly controversial investigations in the history of Congress, held thirty-one days of hearings between March 8 and June 28, 1950. During the course of the hearings McCarthy charged ten individuals by name with varying degrees of communist activity. One was Professor Owen J. Lattimore of Johns Hopkins University, who in the summer of 1950 published a book, *Ordeal by Slander,* defending his record against McCarthy's accusations of disloyalty.

The investigation was a major issue in the 1950 elections. Charges of "softness" toward communism were widely credited with the defeat of Tydings in the Maryland senatorial contest. On August 6, 1951, after a Senate Rules and Administration Committee report had criticized McCarthy's part in the Maryland election, Sen. William Benton, D-Conn., demanded his expulsion from the Senate. The following April McCarthy demanded an investigation of Benton. The result was a simultaneous investigation of both men by the Privileges and Elections Subcommittee of the Senate Rules and Administration Committee.

The subcommittee's report on January 2, 1953, asserted that McCarthy had "deliberately set out to thwart" the investigation. Although it did not accuse him of any specific wrongdoing, the report raised a number of questions, such as whether McCarthy had diverted to his "personal advantage" funds collected to fight communism. Benton was criticized for accepting a campaign contribution from a former director of the Reconstruction Finance Corporation. By the time the subcommittee reported, Benton had been defeated in the 1952 election; his defeat was widely attributed to his feud with McCarthy.

The 1952 elections gave Republicans a majority in both chambers of the 83rd Congress, and McCarthy became chairman of the Senate Government Operations Committee and its Permanent Investigations Subcommittee.

After the first year of McCarthy's chairmanship, the subcommittee claimed in its annual report that its exposures had caused the removal of "Fifth Amendment Communists" from federal jobs and defense plants, the removal of incompetent and undesirable persons from federal employment, and indictment of several witnesses. The report was not signed by the three Democratic members of the subcommittee who had resigned in July.

Army-McCarthy Dispute

In the continuation of the subcommittee's investigation of the armed forces that began in 1953, McCarthy became involved during the first half of 1954 in a controversy with high officials of the army and, by extension, with the Eisenhower administration itself.

At issue was the question of whether or not McCarthy and

INVESTIGATIONS OF 'UN-AMERICANISM'

One of the most significant expansions of congressional investigative powers beyond direct legislative matters was the study of subversive movements after World War II. Instead of pursuing traditional lines of congressional inquiry—government operations and national social and economic problems—committees probed into the thoughts, actions, and associations of persons and institutions.

The House Committee on Un-American Activities was the premier example of these investigative panels. The committee was abolished in January 1975, ending thirty years of controversy over its zealous pursuit of subversives. Its long survival surprised many observers. From the outset the panel, renamed the Internal Security Committee in 1969, was attacked by liberals and civil libertarians. Throughout the 1960s it withstood court suits challenging the constitutionality of its mandate and attempts in the House to end its funding. The death blow finally came when the House Democratic Caucus, by voice vote in January 1975, transferred its functions to the House Judiciary Committee.

EARLY HISTORY

The first congressional investigation of un-American activities was authorized September 19, 1918, toward the close of World War I. That original mandate was to investigate the activities of German brewing interests. The investigation, conducted by the Senate Judiciary Committee, was expanded in 1919 to cover "any efforts . . . to propagate in this country the principles of any party exercising . . . authority in Russia . . . and . . . to incite the overthrow" of the U.S. government.

The House on May 12, 1930, set up a Special Committee to Investigate Communist Activities in the United States—the Fish Committee, so called after its chairman, Rep. Hamilton Fish Jr., R-N.Y. On March 20, 1934, the House created a Special Committee on Un-American Activities, under Chairman John W. McCormack, D-Mass. On May 26, 1938, three years after the McCormack Committee submitted its report, which covered Nazi as well as communist activities in the United States, the House set up another Special Committee on Un-American Activities, under Chairman Martin Dies Jr., D-Texas. The committee, whose chairman was avowedly anticommunist and anti–New Deal, was given a broad mandate to investigate subversion.

Dies focused his early investigations on organized labor groups, especially the Congress of Industrial Organizations, and set a tactical pattern that would guide the permanent Un-American Activities Committee, which was created in 1945. Friendly witnesses, who often met in secret with Dies as a one-man subcommittee, accused hundreds of persons of supporting communist activities, but few of the accused were permitted to testify in rebuttal. The press treated Dies's charges sensationally, a practice that was to continue after World War II.

The Dies Committee was reconstituted in succeeding Congresses until 1945. That January, at the beginning of the 79th Congress, it was renamed the House Committee on Un-American Activities and made a standing committee.

The next five years marked the peak of the committee's influence. In 1947 it investigated communism in the motion picture industry, with repercussions that lasted almost a decade. Its hearings resulted in the Hollywood blacklist that kept many writers and actors suspected of communist leanings out of work.

The committee's investigation in 1948 of State Department official Alger Hiss, and Hiss's subsequent conviction for perjury, established communism as a leading political issue and the committee as an important political force. The case against Hiss was vigorously developed by a young member of the committee, Richard Nixon, R-Calif.

The committee's tactics during this period included extensive use of contempt citations against unfriendly witnesses, some of whom pleaded their Fifth Amendment right against self-incrimination. In 1950, for instance, the House voted fifty-nine contempt citations, of which fifty-six had been recommended by the committee.

SENATE INVESTIGATIONS

In the early 1950s the Un-American Activities Committee was overshadowed by Senate investigations conducted by Joseph R. McCarthy, R-Wis., chairman (1953–1954) of the Senate Government Operations Committee's Permanent Investigations Subcommittee. McCarthy's investigation into alleged subversion in the U.S. army—televised nationwide in 1954—intensified concern over the use by Congress of its investigating powers and led to his censure by the Senate in 1954. (See "McCarthy's Investigations," p. 271.)

During the same period, the Senate Judiciary Committee's Internal Security Subcommittee, established in 1951, also investigated subversive influences in various fields, including government, education, labor unions, the United Nations, and the press.

his staff had used improper means to secure preferential treatment for a former subcommittee consultant, G. David Schine, who had been drafted into the army. Also involved was a charge that the army had tried to pressure McCarthy into calling off his investigation of alleged Communists in the army.

The army on April 14, 1954, filed a formal "bill of particulars" detailing charges against McCarthy, subcommittee chief counsel Roy M. Cohn, and subcommittee staff director Francis P. Carr. The subcommittee reciprocated April 20 by filing charges against Secretary of the Army Robert T. Stevens, army counsel John G. Adams, and Assistant Secretary of Defense H. Struve Hensel. To investigate the charges, the subcommittee held hearings, with Sen. Karl E. Mundt, R-S.D., as acting chairman. McCarthy resigned temporarily from subcommittee membership. The subcommittee in effect began an investigation of its own activities.

The thirty-five days of hearings from April 22 to June 17 attracted, during 187 hours of television coverage, as many as twenty million viewers at peak periods. In addition to the principals charged in the case and the subcommittee members, the drama featured, as the main interrogators, special army counsel Joseph N. Welch and special subcommittee counsel Ray H. Jenkins. In a report the subcommittee issued August 31, the Republican majority concluded that the charge of "improper influence" by McCarthy on behalf of Schine "was not established," but that Cohn had been "unduly aggressive and persistent" on Schine's behalf.

The Republicans said also that Stevens and Adams had tried "to terminate or influence" investigations of the army. The Democratic minority asserted that McCarthy had "fully acquiesced in and condoned" the "improper actions" of Cohn, who in turn had "misused and abused the powers of his office and brought disrepute to the committee." The minority report said also that Stevens "merits severe criticism" for "an inexcusable indecisiveness and lack of sound administrative judgment."

Censure of McCarthy

On June 11, 1954, while the Army-McCarthy hearings were in progress, Sen. Ralph E. Flanders, R-Vt., initiated a six-month controversy over the Senate's official attitude toward McCarthy's actions.

Flanders introduced a resolution to remove McCarthy from the chairmanship of the Government Operations Committee and any of its subcommittees and to prohibit him from reassuming such posts unless he answered questions raised in 1952 by the Privileges and Elections Subcommittee of the Senate Rules and Administration Committee.

After Senate Majority Leader William F. Knowland, R-Calif., voiced opposition, Flanders on July 30 introduced a substitute resolution, charging McCarthy with "personal contempt" of the Senate. These resolutions were referred to a Select Committee to Study Censure Charges. After nearly two weeks of hearings, the committee on September 27 unanimously recommended that the Senate censure McCarthy for his conduct in the Benton-McCarthy investigation in 1952 and toward Army Brig. Gen. Ralph W. Zwicker. At a Permanent Investigations Subcommittee hearing in 1954, McCarthy had told Zwicker that he was "not fit to wear that uniform" and implied that Zwicker did not have "the brains of a five-year-old."

The Senate adopted a substitute resolution, 67–22, on December 1, 1954, that "condemned" McCarthy's abuse of the Privilege and Elections Subcommittee in 1952 and several of his statements about the Select Censure Committee and the special postelection Senate session that had been called to consider the committee's recommendations. Condemnation of McCarthy's comments on the censure move itself had been substituted, during preliminary action on the final resolution, for condemnation of McCarthy's abuse of Zwicker. McCarthy lost his committee and subcommittee chairmanships when control of Congress passed to the Democrats in January 1955. His activities no longer attracted any notable attention. He died May 2, 1957.

WATERGATE

"Watergate" is the descriptive word for political scandals in the Nixon presidency. They dwarfed all others in American history. The evidence of lawbreaking led directly to the White House and even into its Oval Office. Facing impeachment charges in Congress, Richard Nixon became the first president ever to resign from office. His departure from the White House on August 9, 1974, ended a constitutional crisis that was marked by the president's defiance of Congress and the courts through spurious claims to executive privilege and obstruction of justice on the false grounds of national security. *(See box, Nixon Resigns in Face of Impeachment, p. 351.)*

Nixon was spared the likelihood of criminal prosecution when he received a pardon from his successor, President Gerald R. Ford, on September 8, 1974. But nearly a score of others in his 1972 reelection campaign, including several close associates, drew prison sentences. Still others, including some prominent people, paid fines or—in a few instances—went to prison for Watergate-related activities. Those activities included illegal contributions to Nixon's reelection campaign and such "dirty tricks" as spying and sabotage to undermine his Democratic foes and cause trouble for "enemies" of various political stripes.

When the 93rd Congress met in January 1973, the Senate promptly approved a resolution by Majority Leader Mike Mansfield, D-Mont., to create a seven-member, bipartisan committee to investigate rumors and allegations that arose from a break-in the previous June 17 at Democratic National Committee offices in a posh Washington apartment-office complex called the Watergate. District of Columbia police arrested five men at the scene; one of them, James W. McCord Jr. was director of security for the Committee for the Re-Election of the President. Republican officials and the White House denied any knowledge about or responsibility for the break-in. Those arrested remained quiet for several months. A number of publications, notably the *Washington Post*, had developed information that cast doubt on the denials.

The Watergate Committee, formally named the Senate Select Committee on Presidential Campaign Activities, was provided subpoena powers and authorized $500,000 (ultimately $2 million) for its work. On May 17 it opened hearings in the ornate Caucus Room of the Old Senate Office Building, where many of the McCarthy and Kefauver hearings had been conducted. There, in the glare of television lights, the Watergate Committee held forth from May until August. (Later hearings in September, October, and November were not televised.)

Sam J. Ervin Jr., an elderly North Carolina Democrat serving out his last Senate term, was chairman of the seven-member committee. His courtly manner, jowly appearance, and propensity for quoting the Bible made him briefly a cult hero—and disguised his skill as a former judge and trial lawyer. The Watergate Committee hearings had their moments of high drama as men near the top of the White House hierarchy gave their de-

Televised hearings of the Senate Watergate Committee exposed a web of political scandals in the Nixon administration—and made a cult hero of Sam J. Ervin, D-N.C., center, the committee's chairman.

tailed versions of the byzantine workings of Nixon's executive branch and reelection committee.

The viewing public would not soon forget this most extensive look at a congressional hearing. The personal qualities and interrogation techniques of the seven senators left their lasting impressions. So did the style and mannerisms of the nearly three dozen men and women who testified.

Even before the Watergate Committee hearings began, Senate Judiciary Committee confirmation hearings on the nomination of L. Patrick Gray as FBI director implicated several officials in the Nixon administration in an effort to thwart the agency's investigation of Watergate. Other parts of the Watergate puzzle were being pieced together in a Washington federal courtroom. McCord and G. Gordon Liddy, two break-in defendants who had not already pleaded guilty, were convicted by a jury on January 30, 1973.

The trial judge, John J. Sirica, provisionally imposed maximum sentences of up to forty years in prison but suggested they could obtain leniency if they told what they knew about the break-in. When formal sentencing came due on March 23, Sirica stunned the court by reading a letter from McCord saying that he and the other defendants had been under political pressure not to identify others who were also involved in the break-in.

Another startling disclosure came a few weeks later in a Watergate Committee hearing. Alexander Butterfield, a former White House aide, mentioned almost casually that Oval Office conversations were routinely taped. From that time on, the Watergate struggle focused on the investigators' attempts to gain control of certain tapes that would verify or disprove the presi-

dent's direct involvement. Several witnesses before the Watergate Committee, including former White House counsel John Dean, had implicated Nixon.

Citing executive privilege, Nixon at first refused to obey subpoenas from the committee and a special prosecutor to produce the tapes, but gradually he yielded them under public pressure and the threat of impeachment. In October 1973 the House Judiciary Committee began an impeachment investigation. The following spring a Watergate grand jury indicted John N. Mitchell, Nixon's former law partner and attorney general, and three former White House staff advisers—H. R. Haldeman, John D. Ehrlichman, and Charles Colson—on charges of conspiring to cover up unlawful activities. They were later convicted and sent to prison. The same grand jury named Nixon a co-conspirator but, at the prosecutor's request, did not indict him. The president chose resignation, which came on August 9 in a tearful, televised farewell at the White House.

The Watergate Committee released its 2,217-page final report on July 13, 1974. The report included thirty-five recommendations for preventing abuses of government power. Some were contained in an election reform bill passed later that year.

1975 CIA INVESTIGATION

Early in 1975 both the House and Senate set in motion the first major investigation and review of the Central Intelligence Agency (CIA) since its creation in 1947. (Between 1947 and 1975, Congress had either rejected or ignored nearly two hundred legislative proposals to strengthen its oversight of the agency.)

The first step was taken by the Senate on January 27, 1975,

when it voted 82–4 to establish a Select Committee to Study Government Operations with Respect to Intelligence Activities. The eleven-member panel was given broad authority to conduct a comprehensive examination of all fifty-eight federal agencies having responsibility for federal law enforcement of intelligence activities.

The committee was given instructions to determine: (1) whether existing laws governing intelligence and law enforcement operations were adequate; (2) whether existing congressional oversight of the agencies was satisfactory; and (3) the extent to which overt and covert intelligence activities in the United States and abroad were necessary. The Senate's decision to establish a select committee was prompted by newspaper reports that the CIA had violated its charter and spied on U.S. citizens during the Vietnam War and that the FBI maintained derogatory files on members of Congress.

Appointed chairman of the panel was Sen. Frank Church, D-Idaho. He was also chairman of the Foreign Relations Subcommittee on Multinational Corporations, which in 1973 conducted widely publicized hearings into the role of the CIA in efforts to block the 1970 election of Marxist candidate Salvador Allende Gossens as president of Chile.

Throughout the year, in both closed and open hearings, the special committee probed alleged CIA involvement in foreign assassination plots. It issued its final report April 26, 1976.

Meanwhile, the Rockefeller Commission reported that the CIA had engaged in widespread illegal activities in the United States. The eight-man commission, established January 5, 1975, had compiled 2,900 pages of sworn testimony from fifty-one witnesses and took depositions and affidavits from many others. In its report, which President Ford released June 10, the commission noted that, although "the great majority of the CIA's domestic activities comply with its statutory authority," some were "plainly unlawful and constituted improper invasions upon the rights of Americans." Among the activities that "should be criticized and not permitted to happen again," the report said, were some "initiated or ordered by presidents, either directly or indirectly."

The report disclosed that the CIA had intercepted mail between the United States and Soviet Union, infiltrated dissident groups, set up a computerized index with the names of more than three hundred thousand persons and organizations, compiled files on 7,200 American citizens, conducted unlawful bugging and wiretaps, and monitored overseas telephone calls.

While the Senate committee was conducting its investigation, a similar House panel was beset with internal wrangling and a successor House committee locked horns with the Ford administration over secret information and suffered the indignity of having its report blocked by the House.

The Senate Select Intelligence Committee April 26, 1976, recommended that Congress enact new charters for the CIA and other intelligence agencies to prevent the "abuses that have occurred in the past from occurring again." A second report, issued April 28, pinpointed domestic spying abuses by the FBI,

the Internal Revenue Service, and other agencies over a forty-year period. "Intelligence agencies have served the political and personal objectives of presidents and other high officials," the report said.

Two months earlier, President Ford had issued his own intelligence reorganization plan. By executive order, instead of through legislation, Ford had spelled out the missions of the CIA and related agencies. The select committee insisted that this should be written into law to prevent alteration by a future president.

But Senators John G. Tower, R-Texas, and Barry Goldwater, R-Ariz., the two members who refused to sign the final report, disagreed. Tower called the recommendations an "overreaction" by the majority and said they were "potentially dangerous" to the nation's security.

Eighteen of the committee's eighty-seven recommendations dealt with the CIA. To clear up ambiguities in the 1947 act establishing the agency, the committee proposed that a new charter be established "which makes clear that CIA activities must be related to foreign intelligence." As the centerpiece of its recommendations, the committee proposed that a new congressional oversight panel be given authority to consider and approve a "national intelligence budget" each year. The total amount then would be made public. Acting quickly, the Senate on May 19 voted to establish a permanent Select Committee on Intelligence with legislative and budgetary authority over the CIA and other federal intelligence agencies.

IRAN-CONTRA

The administration of Ronald Reagan was shaken by disclosures in November 1986 of secret U.S. arms sales to Iran and the illegal diversion of some of the profits from these sales to U.S.-backed contra rebels fighting the Sandinista government in Nicaragua. The revelations triggered multiple investigations and curtailed the political effectiveness of an otherwise popular president. Several participants, including key White House aides, were indicted by a federal grand jury and two drew prison sentences.

When the story broke, investigators scrambled to find out what happened. Their job was complicated by conflicting recollections, contradictory statements from the White House, sloppy record keeping, a misleading chronology prepared by key participants, destruction and alteration of documents, and the illness and death of former CIA director William J. Casey. Attorney General Edwin Meese III conducted the first inquiry, on behalf of the administration. Although it was much criticized for its investigative techniques, the inquiry did uncover a memo from Lt. Col. Oliver North, a member of the National Security Council staff based in the White House, that mentioned the diversion of funds to the contras. In the aftermath of that disclosure, North was fired and his boss, Vice Adm. John M. Poindexter, resigned.

Reagan then appointed a blue-ribbon board of inquiry, headed by former senator John Tower, a Texas Republican, and

Senate and House committees held joint hearings on the Iran-contra affair in 1987. Marine Lt. Col. Oliver North is shown here being sworn in by Sen. Daniel K. Inouye, D-Hawaii, before giving testimony.

including Edmund S. Muskie, a Maine Democrat who had served as senator and secretary of state, and former national security adviser Brent Scowcroft.

Congress began its own investigations. The House and Senate intelligence committees and the House Foreign Affairs Committee held hearings. Each chamber also appointed a special investigating committee. After a partisan battle, the Senate Intelligence Committee in January 1987 released a report chronicling the affair. A much more complete picture was provided the next month when the Tower Commission released its report. While

cautiously worded, the Tower report served up a damning indictment of failures by Reagan and his aides. The commission criticized the president's inattention to detail—which was gingerly described as his "management style"—and the White House staff's failure to take compensating steps.

After the Tower report, Reagan fired his White House chief of staff, Donald T. Regan, and in a televised speech accepted responsibility for any failures. For the first time he acknowledged that the United States had traded arms to Iran, a bitter enemy, in the hope of gaining the release of Americans being held hostage in Lebanon. The House and Senate intelligence committees, during twelve weeks of hearings, filled in many details of what had happened. For the American public, the focal point of the hearings was the combative and articulate North, in his beribboned Marine Corps uniform. He portrayed himself as a loyal military man who had done only what he had been authorized to do.

North was followed to the witness table by Poindexter, who testified that he had never told the president about the diversion of funds to the contras. Congress had cut off U.S. support for the contras over Reagan's objections. To fill the void, North apparently worked closely with Casey to provide the contras intelligence information and advice on military tactics. The administration solicited conservative fund-raisers to obtain money for the contras from wealthy Americans. Then through private agents, including retired Air Force major general Richard V. Secord and his partner Albert Hakim, North secretly arranged to supply them. By early 1986 the contra operation crossed paths with another covert operation, arms sales to Iran. Profits from the sales were funneled into the contra-aid network.

In a strongly worded report released in November 1987, the bipartisan majority of the select committees castigated the White House for "secrecy, deception, and disdain for the rule of law." Reagan himself was held responsible for setting loose a "cabal of zealots" and for failing to instill a respect for the law among his subordinates. The majority devoted a chapter in the report to the proposition that Congress and the executive branch have shared power over foreign policy. North and Poindexter bluntly told Congress that it should stay out of foreign policy. A Republican minority on the joint committees agreed that Reagan had made mistakes but said most of the fault lay with Congress for interfering with the president's policies.

In March 1988 a federal grand jury indicted North, Poindexter, Secord, and Hakim on various charges related to Iran-contra. Robert C. McFarlane, Poindexter's predecessor as national security adviser, had already pleaded guilty to misdemeanor charges arising from the same investigations. Secord and Hakim later pleaded guilty to a single felony count after the others were dropped. North and Poindexter were tried and convicted on felony charges but appealed their sentences. The charges against North were dropped in 1991.

CLINTON INVESTIGATIONS

Beginning with the 104th Congress in 1995, attack politics targeting the Democratic administration of President Bill Clinton permeated Republican-controlled investigatory and oversight committees. Congressional hearings were held on the Clintons' personal financial involvement in a failed Arkansas land deal known as Whitewater, the firing of White House travel office employees, the request for FBI background files on former Republican administration officials, and 1996 Democratic campaign fund-raising.

The congressional investigations regarding Whitewater, the travel office, and the FBI files were separate from the probe into

these matters conducted by Independent Counsel Kenneth W. Starr, which led to President Clinton's impeachment in 1999. (See "President Bill Clinton," p. 343.)

Whitewater

"Whitewater" became shorthand for investigations into the land deal in which the Clintons had invested in the 1980s; the dissolution of Madison Guaranty Savings and Loan, an Arkansas thrift at the center of Whitewater; and the suicide of Deputy White House Counsel Vincent W. Foster Jr., who had handled legal work for the Clintons related to Whitewater.

Beginning the week of July 25, 1994, the House and Senate Banking committees held separate hearings on the narrow "Washington" sliver of the controversy, exploring potentially improper contacts between White House staff aides and bank regulators. Although no evidence was produced to indicate that any Clinton administration official tried to derail the probe by the regulators, the hearings uncovered details of a number of improper contacts, evasive testimony before Congress by administration officials, and a widespread Whitewater political damage control effort within the White House. Two top Treasury officials resigned as a result of the hearings: Deputy Treasury Secretary Roger C. Altman, who had been acting head of the Resolution Trust Corporation (RTC), which conducted the original investigation into the Whitewater-Madison link, and White House Counsel Bernard Nussbaum, who participated in briefings with Altman and advised the Clintons on Whitewater. In the final report issued January 3, 1995, Senate Banking Committee Democrats said no laws or ethical standards were breached as a result of the contacts between White House aides and Treasury officials.

The Republicans in 1995 used their newfound control of Congress to launch fresh inquiries into the Whitewater affair. The Senate created a special committee to handle the probe, while the House gave the task to its Banking Committee.

Over the course of nearly a year, the Senate Special Committee to Investigate Whitewater Development Corporation and Related Matters held fifty-two sessions, heard from more than 260 witnesses, and took more than 35,000 pages of depositions. The work of the committee, which was headed by Sen. Alfonse M. D'Amato, R-N.Y., was tinged with partisanship from the beginning.

The first round of Senate hearings, held in July 1995, started with an inquiry into the events surrounding Foster's death and the subsequent removal of documents from his office. The panel heard occasionally conflicting accounts about how White House aides searched for and handled Foster's papers in the immediate aftermath of his death. The second round of hearings, held in November and December 1995, continued to examine the communications among White House officials and confidants about Foster's papers, the RTC's findings regarding Whitewater, and other aspects of the affair.

Averting a court showdown, the White House December 22 turned over notes taken by White House Associate Counsel

William Kennedy III during a November 5, 1993, meeting in which administration aides had discussed Whitewater. The White House had refused to release the subpoenaed notes, contending that they were protected by attorney-client privilege.

In 1996 the special committee turned its attention to events in Arkansas during Clinton's tenure as governor. Among other issues, it focused on the legal work done for Madison Guaranty by Hillary Rodham Clinton, who was a lawyer at the Rose Law Firm in Little Rock before becoming first lady. On June 11, committee Democrats blocked GOP efforts to give former Arkansas banker and municipal judge David L. Hale special immunity to testify before the panel. Hale had directly linked Clinton to misdeeds regarding Whitewater, accusations the first lady denied under oath.

In their final report issued June 18, 1996, committee Republicans portrayed a fledging Clinton administration that feared the legal and political fallout from investigations into Whitewater and that used the power of the executive branch to undermine the probes. Crossing the line of propriety, the report said, senior administration officials obtained confidential information about the RTC inquiry into Madison. The Republicans said the White House's misuse of power was clearly evident in the hours and days following Foster's suicide. White House officials mis-

handled documents in Foster's office and thwarted law enforcement authorities in their investigation of Foster's death, the report said. The GOP report alleged that Mrs. Clinton in 1988 ordered the destruction of records related to her representation of Madison Guaranty at the same time federal regulators were investigating the savings and loan. But the Republicans stopped short of charging her with criminal behavior. In their questioning of Mrs. Clinton's actions, Republicans also pointed out the discovery in August 1995 of missing billing records from the Rose Law Firm in the White House private quarters. The Republicans contended that she likely placed the records in the White House book room.

The Democrats on the committee issued a dissenting report, which drew sharply different conclusions. They said Clinton did not misuse his office as either president or governor of Arkansas. The Democrats expressed surprise at the Republican "venom" directed toward Mrs. Clinton. The Democrats concluded that the White House did not interfere with ongoing investigations into Whitewater and related matters by the RTC and other agencies. The evidence presented to the committee showed no unethical or unlawful conduct by any White House official in the days after Foster's suicide, Democrats said. As for the billing records, Democrats pointed out that the documents supported

During the mid- to late 1990s, the Republican-led Congress conducted numerous investigations into the activities of President Bill Clinton and his administration. Here, former associate attorney general Webster Hubbell testifies before the Senate committee investigating Whitewater.

Mrs. Clinton's claim that she did minor work for Madison Guaranty during the time she was with the Rose Law Firm.

White House Travel Office

Seven White House travel office employees were fired on May 19, 1993, amid allegations of mismanagement and possible financial wrongdoing. In a report issued July 2, 1993, White House chief of staff Thomas F. McLarty III acknowledged that poor judgment led to the firings. Five fired employees were offered new jobs, and Congress provided funds to cover their legal expenses.

Office director Billy Dale was indicted on charges of embezzling $68,000 from the travel office; he was acquitted in November 1995. Dale admitted moving more than $50,000 to his personal checking account from office funds, but he said the money went back into arranging accommodations for reporters traveling with the president, the office's main function. He was the only one of the seven to be indicted.

The House Judiciary Committee on July 20, 1993, adversely reported a resolution to force a congressional inquiry into allegations of misconduct at the travel office. However, when the GOP assumed the majority in the 104th Congress, the House Government Reform and Oversight Committee opened an investigation.

In the committee report issued Sept. 18, 1996, Republicans said the president and first lady fired the employees so they could hire their own supporters and then falsely accused the employees of corruption. It said the White House "politicized" the FBI and the Internal Revenue Service by inappropriately bringing them into the White House travel office investigation. The report also said that the White House obstructed the review of documents belonging to deputy counsel Foster after his suicide, in part because of concerns about the travel office matter. Democrats said the president acted within his authority to fire the employees for running an office with questionable financial practices, and they accused Republicans of using smear tactics.

FBI Files

The House and Senate opened inquiries in June 1996 after the administration acknowledged that it had obtained the confidential FBI files of almost five hundred former White House passholders, mainly Republican officials from the Reagan and Bush administrations. Like other GOP-led congressional probes of the Clinton administration, the hearings sparked bitter partisan debate.

The House Government Reform and Oversight Committee held three hearings on the file controversy; the Senate Judiciary Committee, four. At a June hearing before the House panel, low-level White House officials contended that the files on former Reagan and Bush officials were obtained because the Secret Service provided an outdated list of those needing background checks. However, Secret Service officials denied providing such a list. The House panel in September approved an interim report that concluded that the White House improperly requested the files "seemingly without justification." At a September hearing of the Senate panel, Chairman Orrin G. Hatch, R-Utah, said a White House log on the files contained unexplained gaps and the committee had discovered that pages had been deliberately removed.

Campaign Fund-Raising

Congressional Republicans in 1997 sought to showcase what they saw as egregious abuses of campaign finance laws by the Democrats during the 1996 elections. Beyond the numerous stories of bent or broken campaign regulations, Republicans believed they had a particularly explosive mix that included conspiracy by the Chinese communist government to try to influence U.S. elections; the virtual sale of the White House and high-level access to President Clinton, Vice President Al Gore, and the Democratic National Committee (DNC); and the spectacle of a variety of Asian and Asian American fund-raisers contravening U.S. laws by funneling foreign cash into Democratic campaigns.

A year-long probe by the Senate Governmental Affairs Committee, chaired by Fred Thompson, R-Tenn., turned up many incidents of fund-raising excesses but found no smoking gun. Moreover, Senate Democrats managed to reveal that Republicans in some cases had been just as lax about letting foreign money infiltrate GOP political organizations. A parallel investigation by the House Government Reform and Oversight Committee, chaired by Dan Burton, was criticized for covering the same ground as the Thompson committee while spending a considerable amount of money. In addition, the panel's credibility was whittled away by nonstop partisan sniping. Both chambers' investigations did little more than bolster the public's preexisting belief that both parties were conducting business as usual.

Thompson claimed from the outset that he would expose a plot by the Chinese government to influence foreign policy with large and illegal political donations. However, the committee could turn up no direct proof of a Chinese conspiracy, no proof that the White House ever knowingly accepted foreign money, and no proof that the Clinton administration ever changed policy in exchange for campaign contributions.

Thompson and the Republicans further alleged that Clinton approved a scheme by the DNC to help the Teamsters raise money for the 1996 reelection campaign of union president Ron Carey in exchange for Teamster contributions to the DNC. They were unable to prove that the president knew of the arrangement, though the fund-raising irregularities were highly embarrassing for the Democrats.

More eye-opening testimony came from a group of Buddhist nuns, who each gave $5,000 to the DNC after a speech by Gore at a Buddhist temple in California. The event was organized by John Huang, a former Commerce Department official suspected of raising money from foreign sources. Although Thompson was attempting to show that the nuns and the temple were used as conduits for donations made by others, the committee was unable to say where the money came from. The committee also showed that the DNC accepted tainted donations from people acting as conduits for Asian American businessmen and for the Lippo Group, an Indonesian conglomerate run by the Riady family, which had ties to the Clintons. What, if anything, Lippo or the Riadys received in exchange remained an unanswered question.

House Speaker Newt Gingrich in April 1998 proposed having the House Oversight Committee take over major portions of the campaign fund-raising investigation because the House Government Reform Committee had stalled. Democrats on the panel, enraged at Burton's description of Clinton as a "scumbag," for months refused to go along with the chairman's request for immunity for four witnesses. In a controversial move, Burton released edited transcripts of telephone conversations former associate attorney general Webster L. Hubbell had while serving a federal prison term for tax evasion and mail fraud. Burton's committee looked into whether the Lippo Group made payments to Hubbell to keep him from cooperating with Independent Counsel Starr's probe into the Clintons' involvement in Whitewater. In August 1998, along party lines, the committee voted to cite Attorney General Janet Reno for contempt of Congress for refusing to make available to the panel two memos written by Justice Department personnel that argued for the appointment of an independent counsel to investigate Democratic fund-raising. The full House did not pursue the matter, however.

NOTES

1. Quoted in James Hamilton, *The Power to Probe: A Study of Congressional Investigations* (New York: Random House, 1976), xii.

2. James A. Perkins, "Congressional Investigation of Matters of International Import," *American Political Science Review* 39 (1940): 285–287.

3. John E. Wiltz, *In Search of Peace* (Baton Rouge: Louisiana State University Press, 1963), 48.

4. Donald H. Riddle, *The Truman Committee: A Study in Congressional Responsibility* (New Brunswick, N.J.: Rutgers University Press, 1964), 142.

5. Ronald L. Goldfarb, *The Contempt Power* (New York: Columbia University Press, 1963), 196.

6. Legislative Reference Service, Library of Congress, "Congressional Power of Investigation" (Washington, D.C.: Government Printing Office, 1954), 15.

7. Quoted in Telford Taylor, *Grand Inquest* (New York: Simon and Schuster, 1955), 240.

8. J. W. Fulbright, "Congressional Investigations: Significance for the Legislative Processes," *University of Chicago Law Review* (1951), 442.

9. Taylor, *Grand Inquest*, 101.

10. Raoul Berger, *Executive Privilege* (Cambridge, Mass.: Harvard University Press, 1974), 1.

11. Legislative Reference Service, "Congressional Power of Investigation," 51.

12. Asher C. Hinds, *Hinds' Precedents of the House of Representatives of the United States*, vol. 3 (Washington, D.C.: Government Printing Office, 1907), 181–186.

13. Hinds, *Precedents*, vol. 3, 190–192.

14. Clarence Cannon, *Cannon's Precedents of the House of Representa-*

tives of the United States, vol. 6 (Washington, D.C.: Government Printing Office, 1935), 597–599.

15. *Federal Register*, March 16, 1948.

16. Cited in Berger, *Executive Privilege*, 373–386.

SELECTED BIBLIOGRAPHY

Barth, Alan. *Government by Investigation.* New York: Viking, 1955.

Beck, Carl. *Contempt of Congress: A Study of the Prosecutions Initiated by the Committee on Un-American Activities, 1945–1957.* New Orleans: Hauser Press, 1959.

Bentley, Eric, ed. *Thirty Years of Treason: Excerpts from Hearings before the House Un-American Activities Committee, 1938–1968.* New York: Viking, 1971.

Berger, Raoul. *Executive Privilege.* Cambridge, Mass.: Harvard University Press, 1974.

Congressional Quarterly. *The Iran-Contra Puzzle.* Washington, D.C.: Congressional Quarterly, 1987.

———. *Watergate: Chronology of a Crisis.* 1974. Reprint. Washington, D.C.: Congressional Quarterly, 1999.

Eberling, Ernest J. *Congressional Investigations: A Study of the Origin and Development of the Power of Congress to Investigate and Punish for Contempt.* New York: Columbia University Press, 1928.

Galloway, George B. *History of the House of Representatives.* 2nd ed. Rev. by Sidney Wise. New York: Crowell, 1976.

Ginsberg, Benjamin, and Martin Shefter. *Politics by Other Means: Politicians, Prosecutors, and the Press from Watergate to Whitewater.* Rev. ed. New York: Norton, 1999.

Goldfarb, Ronald L. *The Contempt Power.* New York: Columbia University Press, 1963.

Goodman, Walter. *The Committee: The Extraordinary Career of the House Committee on Un-American Activities.* New York: Farrar, Straus and Giroux, 1968.

Hamilton, James. *The Power to Probe: A Study of Congressional Investigations.* New York: Random House, 1976.

Harris, Joseph P. *Congressional Control of Administration.* Washington, D.C.: Brookings Institution, 1964.

Johnson, Lock K. *A Season of Inquiry: The Senate Intelligence Investigation.* Lexington: University Press of Kentucky, 1985.

McDougal, Jim, and Curtis Wilkie. *Arkansas Mischief: The Birth of a National Scandal.* New York: Holt, 1998.

McGeary, M. Nelson. *The Development of Congressional Investigative Power.* New York: Octagon Books, 1973.

Ogden, August R. *The Dies Committee: A Study of the Special House Committees for Investigation of Un-American Activities, 1938–1944.* Washington, D.C.: Catholic University of America Press, 1945.

Riddle, Donald H. *The Truman Committee: A Study in Congressional Responsibility.* New Brunswick, N.J.: Rutgers University Press, 1964.

Rovere, Richard H. *Senator Joe McCarthy.* Cleveland: World Publishing, 1968.

Schlesinger, Arthur M., Jr., and Roger Burns, eds. *Congress Investigates: A Documented History, 1792–1974.* 5 vols. New York: Bowker, 1975.

Stewart, James B. *Blood Sport: The President and His Adversaries.* New York: Simon and Schuster, 1996.

Taylor, Telford. *Grand Inquest: The Story of Congressional Investigations.* New York: Ballantine Books, 1961.

Wiltz, John E. *In Search of Peace: The Senate Munitions Inquiry, 1934–1936.* Baton Rouge: Louisiana State University Press, 1963.

Woodward, Bob. *The Final Days.* New York: Touchstone Books, 1989.

Woodward, Bob, and Carl Bernstein. *All the President's Men.* New York: Touchstone Books, 1987.

CHAPTER 7

The Senate's Confirmation Power

THE SENATE SHARES with the president the responsibility for filling many high-level government positions. Through its power to give "advice and consent" to presidential appointments, the Senate participates in the selection of Supreme Court justices, cabinet and subcabinet officers, members of independent boards and commissions, ambassadors, and other top government officials. The Senate also uses its confirmation power as a tool to help shape public policy.

Under a compromise forged at the Constitutional Convention in 1787, only the president has the formal right to nominate someone to fill top-level positions. But the Senate may use its confirmation power to turn down presidential nominees or pressure the president into selecting people more to the liking of the senators. In some cases, such as certain federal judgeships, senators traditionally have dictated the selection of nominees.

Most nominations are approved by the Senate with little debate or objection. The effect of the Senate's power is seen most clearly in the small number of cases in which a nominee encounters substantial opposition. Often such nominations are rejected or bottled up in committee and never reach a Senate floor vote. In many instances presidents or the nominees themselves will withdraw an appointment when it becomes clear that a large number of senators are prepared to vote against it. Less often presidents will continue to press for approval of an appointment even though it clearly faces possible defeat on the Senate floor. Outright rejection of an important nomination represents a major political setback for a president.

The Senate's use of its confirmation power has evolved into something more than simply saying "aye" or "nay" to a presidential nominee. It has become, in the words of political scientist G. Calvin Mackenzie, "a versatile tool for the Senate in its efforts to enlarge its influence on public policy decisions." Nominations become, in effect, bargaining chips. Instead of defeating a nomination, the Senate more commonly will use its power of rejection as a threat. It may withhold action until the nominee or the White House agrees to pursue certain courses of action or policies, or it may use its position to negotiate a policy issue completely unrelated to the nomination.[1]

However senators choose to use their confirmation power, the Constitution has given them an effective weapon to wield in the give-and-take relationship between the executive and legislative branches.

Senate's Power to Confirm

Virtually every president has faced difficult confirmation battles with the Senate. Presidents with solid political support have generally fared better than those who had to contend with a hostile Senate. Even strong chief executives sometimes have been subjected to embarrassing defeats of their nominees.

Such battles will dominate newspaper headlines and broadcast news, galvanize interest groups, and strain relations between the parties and the branches of government. But they are the exception.

In the vast majority of cases the Senate's power over appointments is little more than a bureaucratic chore. In 1993, the first year of President Bill Clinton's presidency, the Senate received more than 42,000 nominations, but only about 700 involved high-level positions that might invite Senate scrutiny. Action on most of the remaining nominations was perfunctory. The vast majority—nearly 39,500—consisted of routine military commissions and promotions. Lists of routine civilian nominations—to the Foreign Service and Public Health Service, for example—accounted for approximately 2,000. Similarly, in 1997, the first year of Clinton's second term, all but 500 of the nearly 26,000 nominations fell in the routine category.

PATRONAGE, COURTESY RULE DECLINE

Postmasters of the first, second, and third classes at one time constituted the largest group of civilian employees requiring Senate confirmation. Although it was the Senate that gave its advice and consent, custom decreed that members of the House, if they were of the president's party, made the actual selection of appointees in their districts. That patronage system survived until 1970, when Congress created the independent U.S. Postal Service to take over operations of the Post Office Department. In relinquishing control over postal employment, Congress continued a gradual withdrawal from patronage that began with its creation of the civil service in 1883.

The decline in patronage appointments has been accompanied by a decline in the practice of senatorial courtesy. Under this unwritten custom, first seen as early as 1789, the Senate would refuse to confirm a nomination within a particular state unless the nominee had been approved by the senators of the president's party from that state. A senator typically invoked the rule of courtesy by stating that the nominee was "personally obnoxious" to him. This might mean that the senator and the nominee were personal or political foes, or simply that the senator had another candidate for the post.

In practice senators usually were allowed to select many officeholders directly—a power they used to add to their political strength within their state. When neither of the senators from a state was of the president's party, that right was often given to party members in the House or to local party officials.

The tradition of senatorial courtesy declined in importance as positions once filled by patronage were brought into the civil service. It now primarily affects nominations of judges to federal district courts and certain other courts, U.S. attorneys, federal marshals, and other federal officials based locally.

Another aspect of senatorial courtesy, still widely observed, often enables a single senator to delay action on a nomination by placing a "hold" on it. *(See "Holds," p. 304.)*

SENATE SCRUTINY

The scrutiny to which nominees are subjected has increased dramatically since the 1970s. In the wake of the Vietnam War and the Watergate scandal, there was a general push for greater accountability, as well as congressional vigilance and involvement. At the same time the confirmation process itself came under fire.

Critics charged in 1977 that the Senate's probe of the finances of Bert Lance, President Jimmy Carter's director of the Office of Management and Budget, had been inadequate during his confirmation hearings. But they said that the Lance episode, which ended with his resignation after eight months in the job, was a blatant example of generally slipshod Senate confirmation practices. Later that year, Common Cause, the self-styled citizens' lobby, issued a report in which it labeled Senate confirmation proceedings a "rubber-stamp machine." The group accused the Senate of failing to develop a full record on all nominees, of devoting insufficient time to reviewing nominations, and of lacking standards by which nominees could be judged.

Soon committee after committee began revising the way presidential nominations were handled and by the 1980s nominees were being subjected to vigorous review. Some observers question whether the Senate may have gone too far. A 1996 study by the Twentieth Century Fund found much to criticize in the current system:

There are too many questions, too many forms, too many clearances and investigations and hearings. The appointment process is too slow because it is too cumbersome and redundant. It is repellent to potential appointees and abusive to those nominated because it is so often unnecessarily intrusive and humiliating. Simplicity, clarity, and a focused sense of the public interest have vanished from the appointment process.[2]

Confirmation debates increasingly go beyond basic questions of competence and conflict of interest to explore the political beliefs and personal ethics of nominees, particularly candidates for positions on the Supreme Court and in the cabinet. At the same time top-level nominations are being subjected to greater scrutiny by the media and controversial ones often become the target of ideological interest groups. Disagreements over nominees sometimes become entangled in larger struggles between the executive and legislative branches.

Robert H. Bork, nominated to the Court by President Ronald Reagan, lost his confirmation battle in 1987 at least in part because a majority of senators believed that his judicial views on subjects such as civil rights and privacy were so conservative as to be outside the "mainstream" of American legal philosophy. The fight over Bork's nomination even gave rise to a new slang word—*borking*—to describe the rough treatment a nominee sometimes receives.

The Bork battle set the tone for the confirmation struggle of Clarence Thomas, President George Bush's Supreme Court nominee in 1991. Thomas ultimately won a seat on the Court but only after a bitter fight over allegations of sexual harassment that had been leveled against him. The nomination was also troubled by the belief of many Democrats that Thomas was too conservative in his judicial philosophy.

Reagan adviser Edwin Meese III was confirmed as attorney general in 1985 after a bitter thirteen-month battle that turned on his ethical conduct and fitness for office. Confirmation came only after a special prosecutor appointed to review the matter found "no basis" for criminal prosecution.

In 1989 the Senate rejected Bush's nomination of former senator John Tower, R-Texas, to be secretary of defense—the first rejection of a cabinet nominee since 1959. Democratic opponents of the nomination questioned Tower's fitness for the position, raising allegations of alcohol abuse and womanizing. They also expressed concern over potential conflicts of interest. Republicans blasted the rejection of Tower, a longtime member and former chairman of the Senate Armed Services Committee, as a Democratic power grab. The action marked only the ninth time that the Senate had turned down a cabinet nominee, the second time it had rejected a former senator nominated to the cabinet, and the first time it had denied a president a cabinet nominee at the start of his first term. *(See Table 7-1, p. 286.)*

President Clinton had to drop two candidates for attorney general when controversy erupted over their hiring of illegal immigrants as domestic workers. Other Clinton nominees were blocked in the Senate because of their views on such topics as minority rights, affirmative action, and abortion.

In 1997 Clinton's choice to head the Central Intelligence Agency, former national security adviser Tony Lake, abruptly asked that his name be withdrawn. Lake issued a scathing condemnation of the Senate confirmation process after his nomination encountered a series of delays and got caught up in a partisan controversy over White House and Democratic fund-raising practices. "I have gone through the past three months or more with patience and, I hope, dignity," Lake wrote to Clinton. "But I have lost the former and could lose the latter as this political circus continues indefinitely."[3]

The Lake nomination provided a good illustration of the debate on the confirmation process. For his opponents, the system worked exactly as it was supposed to. "The process worked. In

The Senate Judiciary Committee listens to testimony given by Clarence Thomas at his Supreme Court confirmation hearing in 1991. The Senate must confirm the president's selection of Supreme Court justices, cabinet officers, ambassadors, and other high-level government officials.

the end he didn't stand up," said Sen. Phil Gramm, R-Texas. "He was the wrong person for the wrong job." Added Sen. Jon Kyl, R-Ariz., "This is a tough job. I don't think the hearings were that tough at all."[4] And former CIA director Robert Gates stated: "If you can't fight your way through the process, you might not just do a hot job as director."[5]

But for others the process had gone too far. Congressional Democrats and White House officials accused Senate Republicans of politicizing the confirmation process and waging personal attacks against Lake's integrity. White House Press Secretary Mike McCurry said the confirmation process Lake went through was "inexcusably flawed." Clinton declared that "the cycle of political destruction must end." Senate Minority Leader Tom Daschle, D-S.D., said the hearings on Lake amounted to "character assassination." Even some Republicans criticized the way in which Lake's nomination was handled.[6]

Presidents have one way to get around the Senate confirmation process, although it works only temporarily. The Constitution allows the president to fill vacant positions between sessions of Congress, when the Senate is not meeting. These "recess appointments" are allowed to stand until the completion of the Senate's next session. But the Senate takes a dim view of the use of this power for anything other than a routine appointment. (See "Recess Appointments," p. 305.)

History of Appointments: The Senate's Role

The president "shall nominate, and by and with the Advice and Consent of the Senate, shall appoint. . . ." (Article II, Section 2).

The constitutional language governing the appointment power, drafted and agreed to in the final weeks of the Constitutional Convention of 1787, represented a compromise between delegates who favored vesting in the Senate sole authority for appointing principal officers of the government and those who held that the president alone should control appointments as an executive function.

As finally adopted, the Constitution required Senate confirmation of principal officers of the government—"Ambassadors, other public Ministers and Consuls, Judges of the Supreme Court" were mentioned specifically—but provided that Congress could "by Law vest the Appointment of such inferior Officers, as they think proper, in the President alone, in the Courts of Law, or in the Heads of Departments."

Approval of that compromise language did not settle the controversy over the Senate's role in the appointment process. To Alexander Hamilton, writing in *The Federalist Papers* (No. 66), the Senate's function did not appear significant: "It will be

CONSTITUTIONAL MANDATE

ARTICLE II, SECTION 2

The President . . . shall nominate, and by and with the Advice and Consent of the Senate, shall appoint Ambassadors, other public Ministers and Consuls, Judges of the supreme Court, and all other Officers of the United States, whose Appointments are not herein otherwise provided for, and which shall be established by Law; but the Congress may by Law vest the Appointment of such inferior Officers, as they think proper, in the President alone, in the Courts of Law, or in the Heads of Departments.

The President shall have Power to fill up all Vacancies that may happen during the Recess of the Senate, by granting Commissions which shall expire at the End of their next Session.

the office of the President to *nominate,* and with the advice and consent of the Senate to *appoint.* There will, of course, be no exertion of *choice* on the part of the Senate. They may defeat one choice of the Executive and oblige him to make another; but they cannot themselves *choose*—they can only ratify or reject the choice he may have made."

John Adams saw it differently. "Faction and distraction," he wrote, "are the sure and certain consequences of giving to the Senate a vote on the distribution of offices."[7] Looking ahead to the emergence of political parties, Adams foresaw the rise of the spoils system and the use of the appointive power as a senatorial patronage tool.

George Washington regarded the appointment power as "the most irksome part of the executive trust."[8] But his exercise of the power was widely acclaimed; the Senate withheld its consent only five times during his tenure.

EARLY PRACTICES

Methods of handling presidential nominations had to be instituted early in the new government. Washington established the precedent of submitting nominations to the Senate in writing, and the Senate after debate on the propriety of the secret ballot determined to take voice votes on nominations. The president rejected suggestions that he be present during Senate consideration of appointments: "It could be no pleasing thing, I conceive, for the President, on the one hand to be present and hear the propriety of his nominations questioned; nor for the Senate on the other hand to be under the smallest restraint from his presence from the fullest and freest inquiry into the character of the person nominated."

Uncertainty over the extent of the Senate's role in executive appointments surfaced early in Washington's administration. Could the Senate decide only whether or not to give its consent to the person named, or could it also rule on the necessity of the post and the grade of the appointee? Washington's nominations of ministers to Paris, London, and The Hague in December 1791

were blocked for weeks by Senate debate on a resolution opposing the appointment of "ministers plenipotentiary to reside permanently at foreign courts." Washington's nominations finally were approved, by narrow votes, on the ground of special need for representation at those three capitals.

Washington maintained high standards for selection of appointees, and although he consulted widely both with members of Congress and other persons, he rebuffed all attempts at encroachment on his prerogatives. Thus he refused to appoint Aaron Burr as minister to France in 1794, despite such a recommendation by a caucus of Democratic-Republican senators and representatives, because he questioned Burr's integrity.

Washington was not always able to resist senatorial pressure. Early in the First Congress, the Senate rejected his nomination of Benjamin Fishbourn to the post of naval officer (a customs official handling manifests, clearances, and similar documents) for the Port of Savannah out of courtesy to the two Georgia senators, who had a candidate of their own. Washington yielded, nominating the senators' choice, and senatorial courtesy was born.

The practice of inquiring into the political views of a presidential nominee also began in the Washington administration. John Rutledge of South Carolina, nominated in 1795 to succeed John Jay as chief justice of the United States, was rejected by the Senate on a 10–14 vote, primarily because of his opposition to the Jay Treaty with Great Britain. Rutledge, one of the original six Supreme Court justices (1789–1791), was already serving as chief justice on a recess appointment. (*See "Recess Appointments," p. 305.*)

Injection of Politics

John Adams, that vigorous critic of the appointment provisions of the Constitution, found nothing in his experience as president to make him change his view. The Federalist Senate cleared his appointments with Federalist leader Alexander Hamilton, at the time a private citizen, and Adams later complained that he "soon found that if I had not the previous consent of the heads of departments, and the approbation of Mr. Hamilton, I ran the utmost risk of a dead negative in the Senate."

During Adams's tenure, appointments became increasingly determined by political considerations. The practice of consulting and bowing to the wishes of state delegations in Congress in making appointments from a member's state also was solidified.

One of the most famous decisions in Supreme Court history—*Marbury v. Madison,* which established the principle of judicial review—stemmed from a controversy over judicial appointments by Adams following his defeat for reelection in 1800. Adams's successor, Thomas Jefferson, blocked several of Adams's appointees by refusing to deliver their commissions. William Marbury sought delivery of his commission of appointment as a justice of the peace. In a historic 1803 decision Chief Justice John Marshall held that Marbury should have re-

President John Adams is shown here signing judicial appointments two days before he left office in 1801. Although the appointees were confirmed by the Senate the following day, the Supreme Court ruled in *Marbury v. Madison* that the succeeding president, Thomas Jefferson, could not be forced to deliver the commissions.

ceived his commission, but the Court lacked the power to enforce its delivery. The effect of the *Marbury* decision was that, even after a nominee was confirmed by the Senate, the president was under no enforceable obligation to deliver a commission.

Jefferson had far less trouble with appointments than his predecessor. He was the acknowledged leader of his party, and for most of his term that party was in control of Congress. Perhaps his most embarrassing failure was the unanimous rejection of his final nomination, that of William Short as minister to Russia. However, the opposition apparently was directed more against the establishment of the mission than against Short himself.

Unlike Jefferson, James Madison soon found that he had to submit to Senate dictation in the matter of appointments. A small clique of senators was able to force the appointment of Robert Smith as secretary of state, although Madison had wanted to give the post to his secretary of the Treasury, Albert Gallatin.

Gallatin's subsequent appointment as envoy to negotiate a peace treaty with Great Britain also met with difficulty in the Senate. Gallatin was already in Europe when the Senate adopted a resolution declaring that the duties of envoy and secretary of the Treasury were incompatible. Subsequently Gallatin resigned his Treasury post and was confirmed as envoy.

That nomination led to a controversy over the propriety of consultation between the president and a Senate committee on pending nominations. Although previous presidents had agreed to consult with committees appointed by the party caucus or by the Senate itself, Madison decided to put an end to the practice. In a message to the Senate, he insisted that if the Senate wanted information on nominations, the correct procedure was to confer with appropriate department heads, not the president. "The appointment of a committee of the Senate to confer immediately with the executive himself," he said, "appears to lose sight of the coordinate relation between the executive and the Senate, which the Constitution has established, and which ought therefore to be maintained." In spite of this message, Madison received a special committee appointed by the Senate to confer with him about the Gallatin nomination, but the president refused to discuss the nomination with them.

Madison in 1811 suffered the second outright rejection of a Supreme Court nomination. Alexander Wolcott was opposed by

TABLE 7-1 Supreme Court Nominations Not Confirmed by the Senate

In the more than two centuries from 1789 to 1999, the Senate has rejected Supreme Court nominees twenty-eight times. One nominee, Edward King, twice failed to win Senate confirmation. A dozen have been rejected outright, and the remainder have been withdrawn or allowed to lapse when Senate rejection seemed imminent. Three were renominated later and confirmed. Following is the complete list of nominees failing to receive confirmation:

Nominee	President	Date of nomination	Senate action	Date of Senate action
William Paterson	Washington	February 27, 1793	Withdrawn[a]	
John Rutledge[b]	Washington	July 1, 1795	Rejected (10–14)	December 15, 1795
Alexander Wolcott	Madison	February 4, 1811	Rejected (9–24)	February 13, 1811
John J. Crittenden	John Quincy Adams	December 17, 1828	Postponed	February 12, 1829
Roger Brooke Taney	Jackson	January 15, 1835	Postponed (24–21)[c]	March 3, 1835
John C. Spencer	Tyler	January 9, 1844	Rejected (21–26)	January 31, 1844
Reuben H. Walworth	Tyler	March 13, 1844	Withdrawn	
Edward King	Tyler	June 5, 1844	Postponed	June 15, 1844
Edward King	Tyler	December 4, 1844	Withdrawn	
John M. Read	Tyler	February 7, 1845	Not acted upon	
George W. Woodward	Polk	December 23, 1845	Rejected (20–29)	January 22, 1846
Edward A. Bradford	Fillmore	August 16, 1852	Not acted upon	
George E. Badger	Fillmore	January 10, 1853	Postponed	February 11, 1853
William C. Micou	Fillmore	February 24, 1853	Not acted upon	
Jeremiah S. Black	Buchanan	February 5, 1861	Rejected (25–26)	February 21, 1861
Henry Stanbery	Andrew Johnson	April 16, 1866	Not acted upon	
Ebenezer R. Hoar	Grant	December 15, 1869	Rejected (24–33)	February 3, 1870
George H. Williams[b]	Grant	December 1, 1873	Withdrawn	
Caleb Cushing[b]	Grant	January 9, 1874	Withdrawn	
Stanley Matthews	Hayes	January 26, 1881	Not acted upon[a]	
William B. Hornblower	Cleveland	September 19, 1893	Rejected (24–30)	January 15, 1894
Wheeler H. Peckham	Cleveland	January 22, 1894	Rejected (32–41)	February 16, 1894
John J. Parker	Hoover	March 21, 1930	Rejected (39–41)	May 7, 1930
Abe Fortas[b]	Lyndon Johnson	June 26, 1968	Withdrawn	
Homer Thornberry	Lyndon Johnson	June 26, 1968	Not acted upon	
Clement F. Haynsworth Jr.	Nixon	August 18, 1969	Rejected (45–55)	November 21, 1969
G. Harrold Carswell	Nixon	January 19, 1970	Rejected (45–51)	April 8, 1970
Robert H. Bork	Reagan	July 1, 1987	Rejected (42–58)	October 23, 1987

NOTES: a. Later nominated and confirmed.   b. Nominated for chief justice.   c. Later nominated for chief justice and confirmed.

SOURCES: Library of Congress, Congressional Research Service.

the Federalists because as collector of customs in Connecticut he had vigorously enforced the unpopular embargo acts passed prior to the War of 1812. He was rejected, 9–24, following charges by the press that he lacked the requisite legal qualifications for service on the Court.

The "Spoils System"

The administrations of James Monroe and John Quincy Adams were marked by the growth of the so-called spoils system, as members of the Senate increasingly insisted on control of federal appointments in their states.

Legislation known as the Four Years Law, enacted in 1820, greatly increased the number of appointments available. This law provided fixed, four-year terms for many federal officers who previously had served at the pleasure of the president. Although its ostensible purpose was to ensure the accountability of appointees, its value as a patronage tool soon became clear. Commented Adams: "The Senate was conciliated by the permanent increase of their power, which was the principal ultimate effect of the act, and every senator was flattered by the power conferred upon himself of multiplying chances to provide for his friends and dependents."

Both Monroe and John Quincy Adams resisted pressure to use the Four Years Law as a means of introducing rotation in office. They followed the policy of renominating officers upon expiration of their terms unless they had been guilty of misconduct. Upon taking office as president in 1825, Adams resubmitted all of Monroe's nominations on which the Senate had failed to act. President Andrew Jackson did not follow that policy, however, and withdrew all of Adams's nominations.

One of Adams's Supreme Court nominations was blocked by the Senate. The name of John J. Crittenden, a Kentucky Whig, had been sent up shortly before the Adams administration ended in 1829. Jacksonians, who wished to allow the newly elected Democratic president to make the appointment, voted 23–17 to block Senate action on confirming Crittenden. Jackson later filled the seat with his own nominee.

Jackson, to whom rotation in office was a leading principle, made full use of the Four Years law to find places for his supporters. Although he was in constant conflict with the Senate over appointments, such was his popularity in the country that relatively few were rejected.

One significant rejection was that of Martin Van Buren as minister to England. Van Buren in 1831 had resigned as secretary of state in a cabinet reorganization, and President Jackson then gave him a recess appointment to the Court of St. James. He was already in London when the Senate met in December. Henry Clay, Daniel Webster, and John C. Calhoun, all aspirants for the presidency, looked on Van Buren as a likely opponent and led the opposition to his appointment. When the nomination came to a vote in January 1832, a tie was contrived so that Vice President Calhoun could vote against Van Buren. Although his opponents thought a Senate rejection would end Van Buren's political career, he returned home as a martyr and was soon elected vice president.

The Senate twice rejected Jackson's renomination of four incumbent directors of the Bank of the United States. Senate opposition stemmed from reports critical of the bank that the directors had submitted to the president. After efforts to recommit the nominations failed, the Senate rejected them by a 20–24 vote. Jackson renominated the same persons, only to have them rejected once again.

The Bank of the United States also figured in controversy over the nomination of Roger B. Taney as secretary of the Treasury in 1834. Taney was rejected on an 18–28 vote after he had served for nine months under a recess appointment. Opposition rested on his withdrawal of federal funds from the bank, an action he had recommended as attorney general. In fact, it was to carry out that policy that he had been appointed Treasury secretary.

Taney's nomination was the first outright Senate rejection of a cabinet appointee in U.S. history, although James Madison had been prevented from appointing Gallatin as secretary of state in 1809 because he feared Gallatin would be rejected.

Early in 1835 Jackson nominated Taney to the Supreme Court. The Senate did not take up that nomination until the closing days of its session, when it voted 24–21 for an indefinite postponement. Undaunted, the president in December 1835 named Taney to be chief justice, a position made vacant by the death of John Marshall. Notwithstanding charges that the selection was an insult to the Senate, because it had twice rejected the nominee, Taney's appointment was confirmed in March 1836 by a vote of 29–15.

PATRONAGE AND REFORM

The forty-year period from 1837 to 1877 marked the high point of Senate efforts to control executive appointments. During this period the spoils system reached its peak and all presidents were subject to intense pressure for patronage appointments. Senatorial courtesy was firmly entrenched.

President John Tyler, a dissident Democrat who had accepted the Whig nomination for vice president in 1840 and then repudiated the Whigs upon succeeding William Henry Harrison as president, was peculiarly unfortunate in his relations with the Senate. Since he was without a following in either party, Whigs and Democrats alike were anxious to embarrass him, and many of his nominees—including four to the cabinet and four to the Supreme Court—were rejected. In 1843 his nomination of Caleb Cushing as secretary of the Treasury was rejected three times in one day.

Tyler's first Supreme Court rejection came in 1844, when the Senate turned down John C. Spencer, 21–26. Two subsequent Court nominations, of Reuben H. Walworth and Edward King, were postponed and later withdrawn. On a final effort to fill the two Court vacancies, Tyler won approval of one nominee, Samuel Nelson, but the Senate adjourned without acting on the second nominee, John Meredith Read.

Nine months after succeeding Tyler in 1845, President James K. Polk offered the still vacant Supreme Court seat to Secretary of State James Buchanan. Buchanan declined, and Polk then named to the Court an obscure but able Pennsylvania judge, George W. Woodward. Polk interpreted the Senate's 20–29 rejection of the nomination as an attempt to weaken his administration.

In the tension-filled decade of the 1850s, President Millard Fillmore was unable to persuade the Senate to approve his southern nominees to the Court. In 1852 the Senate refused to act upon the nomination of Edward A. Bradford of Louisiana. In 1853 Democratic opposition forced the postponement, on a 26–25 vote, of Senate action on the nomination of Sen. George E. Badger of North Carolina. The Democratic Senate that year also did not act on Fillmore's nomination to the Court of William C. Micou of Louisiana.

Weakened by resignations of senators from seceding states, the Senate in 1861 rejected, 25–26, President James Buchanan's nomination of Jeremiah S. Black of Pennsylvania to the Supreme Court. Black, former attorney general and secretary of state, was opposed by the Republicans, who wished the newly elected President Abraham Lincoln to fill the Court seat with his own choice.

Lincoln made masterful use of the appointment power to hold the divided factions of his party together and to advance his legislative goals. Early in his administration he devoted much of his time to patronage. Most officers subject to presidential appointment had been removed after the 1860 election, and Lincoln tried to distribute these offices equitably among his various supporters. Only for major posts was a high standard of qualification deemed essential.

Andrew Johnson's bitter struggle with the Senate over appointments, a by-product of the fight over the post–Civil War Reconstruction policy, led to curbs on the president's removal powers in the Tenure of Office Act of 1867 and to Johnson's impeachment trial. *(See Chapter 9, Impeachment Power.)*

Senate hostility to Johnson blocked the elevation of Attorney General Henry Stanbery of Ohio to the Supreme Court in 1866. The Senate never acted directly on the nomination but instead passed a bill to reduce the size of the Court from ten to eight justices. The purpose of the bill was to kill the Stanbery nomination by abolishing the seat to which he was named. Stanbery resigned as attorney general in 1868 to serve as Johnson's chief counsel during the impeachment proceedings. When Johnson subsequently renominated him to the post of attorney general, the Senate refused, 11–29, to confirm the appointment.

Civil Service Act

Senatorial ascendancy over the presidency in the matter of appointments and the excesses of the spoils system led, under President Ulysses S. Grant, to public pressure for civil service reform. In response to that pressure, Congress in 1871 enacted a civil service law but did not appropriate funds to implement it.

Three of Grant's appointments to the Supreme Court failed to win Senate approval. The first was his attorney general, Ebenezer Rockwood Hoar, who had earned the enmity of the Senate by refusing to bow to political pressure in the filling of new judgeships created under an 1869 law. After Hoar's rejection, 24–33, Sen. Simon Cameron of Pennsylvania exclaimed: "What could you expect for a man who has snubbed seventy senators!" In 1874 Grant was forced to withdraw two successive nominations for chief justice, Attorney General George H. Williams and former attorney general Caleb Cushing. Cushing had been rejected also for the post of secretary of the Treasury in the Tyler administration.

The accession to the presidency of Rutherford B. Hayes in 1877 marked the beginning of presidential efforts to curb senatorial control over nominations. Hayes's selection of his own cabinet members without consulting Senate leaders was viewed as presumptuous by them, and they countered with an unprecedented delay in acting upon his nominations. However, when public opinion came to the aid of the president, the nominations were confirmed quickly.

Unable to obtain from Congress the civil service reform legislation he recommended, Hayes nevertheless attempted throughout his one term of office to curb patronage abuses.

The Senate did not consider Hayes's nomination in 1881 of former Republican senator Stanley Matthews of Ohio to the Supreme Court. There was some feeling that Hayes was rewarding Matthews for his support in the Hayes-Tilden presidential election contest in 1876 and for his service as counsel before the commission that dealt with disputed returns from that election. President James A. Garfield, who succeeded Hayes, later resubmitted Matthews's name, and he was then confirmed by a one-vote margin.

A protracted conflict over the corruption-ridden New York customhouse led to a showdown between Hayes and Republican senator Roscoe Conkling of New York over the right of senators to control nominations. When two Conkling protégés—Chester A. Arthur, the customs collector, and Alonzo B. Cornell, the naval officer of the customhouse—refused to comply with a presidential order prohibiting federal employees from actively

Sen. Roscoe Conkling resigned from the Senate in 1881 as a result of a patronage dispute with President James A. Garfield.

engaging in partisan politics, Hayes asked for their resignations. When they refused to resign, he nominated two other persons to replace them. Conkling appealed to senatorial courtesy, and the president's nominees were rejected, 25–31. After Congress adjourned, Hayes suspended Arthur and Cornell and made two more nominations to the posts. Despite Conkling's opposition, the Senate in the next session confirmed the president's choices by wide margins.

Conkling was the loser in another showdown with President Garfield. Garfield's nomination in 1881 of one of his own supporters, Judge W. H. Robertson, as collector of the New York port, infuriated the senator, who wanted to maintain control of all New York patronage. Conkling invoked the rule of courtesy in his effort to block Robertson's confirmation, and the Republican caucus supported him. However, the Democrats would not agree to vote against the nominee, and Conkling feared a rebuff on the floor.

Asserting that they had been humiliated, Conkling and his New York colleague, Sen. Thomas C. Platt, also a Republican, took the extraordinary step of resigning from the Senate as a rebuke to the president for his presumption in making his own appointment. They expected to be reelected by the state legislature as a vindication of their position, but they were turned down. Conkling's political career was at an end, but Platt later returned to the Senate and to leadership of the Republican Party in New York.

Meanwhile the heyday of the spoils system was drawing to a close. Previous efforts at meaningful civil service reform had ended in failure, but public revulsion over Garfield's assassination by a disappointed office seeker in 1881 provided new impetus for change. With the rather surprising endorsement of President Chester A. Arthur, who had been Garfield's vice president, a civil service system was established by the Pendleton Act of 1883.

Resistance to Patronage

A key test of the president's right to suspend federal officers, which occurred during President Grover Cleveland's first term, was followed by repeal of the Tenure of Office Act. After that, few Cleveland nominations were rejected. In his second term, however, two conservative appointees to the Supreme Court were rejected upon appeal to the rule of courtesy by Sen. David B. Hill, D-N.Y. William B. Hornblower and Wheeler H. Peckham, respected New York attorneys but of a political faction opposed to Hill, were rejected by votes of 24–30 and 32–41, respectively. Cleveland then nominated Sen. Edward Douglas White, D-La., who was confirmed immediately—an example of the courtesy traditionally accorded by the Senate to one of its own members.

President Theodore Roosevelt, like William McKinley before him, tried to avoid patronage fights with Congress. However, Roosevelt, an advocate of civil service reform, insisted on high qualification for federal office. Members of Congress, he said, "may ordinarily name the man, but I shall name the standard, and the men have got to come up to it." His care in the matter of judicial appointments twice led him to refuse to nominate candidates recommended by Senator Platt of New York. On one of these occasions he wrote to Platt, "It is, I trust, needless to say that I fully appreciate the right and duty of the Senate to reject or to confirm any appointment according to what its members conscientiously deem their duty to be; just as it is my business to make an appointment which I conscientiously think is a good one."

President William Howard Taft recommended a dramatic extension of the civil service system that would have included postmasters and other field officers then subject to Senate confirmation, but Congress did not enact the necessary legislation.

WILSON TO TRUMAN

President Woodrow Wilson accepted Treasury Secretary William G. McAdoo's suggestion that he let his department heads handle distribution of patronage, a chore that traditionally had been undertaken by the president himself. Wilson generally tried to get along with the Senate and on occasion yielded to it in the interests of party harmony, but he suffered several notable rejections in contests over local offices.

Two nomination controversies of national significance during Wilson's administration were those of George Rublee to head the Federal Trade Commission (FTC) and Louis D. Brandeis to fill a vacancy on the Supreme Court.

Rublee was rejected in 1916 following a two-year fight led by Sen. Jacob H. Gallinger, R-N.H., who opposed the nomination on the ground that it was "personally obnoxious" to him. Sen. Robert M. La Follette, R-Wis., deplored Gallinger's use of the "personally obnoxious" formula against a national appointment. It was the first such application of the rule, he said, since he had been in the Senate. Meanwhile, Rublee served on the FTC for a year and a half on a recess appointment made when the Senate was not in session.

The nomination and subsequent confirmation of Brandeis in 1916 ended one of the most bitter appointment struggles in the nation's history. The opposition to Brandeis was led by New England business groups that considered him a radical and a crusader because of his unpaid public activities. Industrial interests charged that he was antibusiness and guilty of unethical conduct, but four months of unusual open hearings by a Senate judiciary subcommittee—hearings that were reopened twice—failed to turn up any valid grounds for rejection. One of his supporters, Arthur Hill of the Harvard Law School, attributed the opposition to the fact that "Mr. Brandeis is an outsider, successful, and a Jew." The committee procrastinated, despite the fact that both the adjournment of Congress and the national political conventions were fast approaching. Finally, following personal appeals by Brandeis and the president to wavering senators, the committee cleared the nomination by a 10–8 party-line vote. When the Senate voted June 1, Brandeis was confirmed, 47–22, the vote again following party lines.

Harding, Coolidge, Hoover

Few of President Warren G. Harding's nominees were rejected. Early in his administration the White House announced that Republican senators would select nominees for local offices and that the president "will hold Republican senators to account for appointments made by him on their recommendations." Should the appointees prove unworthy or incompetent, he said, the senators would bear "the responsibility for whatever trouble arises through this means."

Trouble did indeed arise from Harding's appointments. One member of his cabinet, Interior Secretary Albert B. Fall, went to prison for his role in the Teapot Dome affair. Several other high-level appointees also became involved in scandals, leaving a taint of corruption on Harding's administration.

Although President Calvin Coolidge had few clashes with the Senate over appointments, he became the first president since 1868 to have a cabinet nominee rejected. Coolidge in 1925 nominated Charles Beecher Warren, a prominent Michigan attorney, to be his attorney general. Little opposition was expected. But when the nomination reached the Senate floor, where it was considered in unusual open session (until 1929 most nominations were considered in closed session), opponents attacked

The confirmation of Supreme Court Justice Louis D. Brandeis in 1916 ended one of the most bitter appointment struggles in the nation's history.

Warren for his association with the "Sugar Trust." Such a man, they said, could not be relied upon to enforce the antitrust laws.

The Senate vote on Warren ended in a 40–40 tie, rejecting the nominee. Vice President Charles G. Dawes, napping at his hotel, was not present to cast the deciding vote. While efforts were being made to get Dawes to the floor, a Republican senator changed his vote so he could offer a motion to reconsider the nomination. His motion then was tabled 41–39, effectively killing the nomination. A furious Coolidge promptly renominated Warren, who was again defeated, 39–46. A contributing factor to the second defeat was the president's announcement as debate was in progress that if Warren was not confirmed, he would be given a recess appointment. Warren declined that honor.

President Herbert Hoover took a firm line on patronage abuses and refused to nominate candidates simply because they were recommended by GOP organizations. He also instituted the practice of making public the endorsers of judicial nominees.

Hoover met one notable nomination defeat: the rejection of Judge John J. Parker to the Supreme Court in 1930—the first such rejection in thirty-six years. The Parker case marked the third effort in five years by Senate liberals to block appointments to the Court of persons they thought to be too conservative. They had failed to block the confirmation of Harlan Fiske Stone in 1925 and of Charles Evans Hughes as chief justice earlier in 1930. But, with the aid of a campaign mounted by organized labor and the National Association for the Advancement of Colored People, they were able to defeat Parker, 39–41.

Controversial Roosevelt Appointments

President Franklin D. Roosevelt had few problems with appointments in his first years in office, but difficulties increased following the defeat of his 1937 Court-packing plan and his unsuccessful effort to purge Democratic opponents in the 1938 primaries.

The only major appointment controversy of his first term involved Rexford G. Tugwell, a member of the president's "brain trust" who was nominated in 1934 to the newly created post of under secretary of agriculture. Despite opposition based on his liberal views, Tugwell was confirmed, 53–24. In Roosevelt's second term many more appointees came under attack because of their allegedly radical positions. Perhaps the most notable of the second-term controversies involved Harry Hopkins, who won confirmation as secretary of commerce in 1939 only after a fight in which politics in the Works Progress Administration was the central issue. Hopkins was confirmed, 58–27, but a number of Democrats abstained.

Roosevelt's efforts to cut off patronage of Democratic senators who opposed his program had mixed success. He succeeded in disciplining senators Huey P. Long, La., and Rush D. Holt, W.Va., but failed with Harry F. Byrd and Carter Glass, both of Virginia, Pat McCarran, Nev., and W. Lee O'Daniel, Texas—all of whom successfully invoked senatorial courtesy to defeat nominations they had opposed.

Of Roosevelt's eight nominees to the Supreme Court, only one—Sen. Hugo L. Black, D-Ala.—faced serious opposition. Roosevelt appointed Black, who had vigorously supported New Deal programs, in 1937 after defeat of the president's Court-packing plan. Although it was traditional for the Senate to confirm one of its own members immediately without reference to committee, the Black nomination was sent to the Judiciary Committee—the first such action in fifty years. The nomination was cleared by the committee, 13–4, and by the Senate, 63–16, after a debate punctuated by charges that Black had been a member of the Ku Klux Klan and had received Klan support in his 1926 election campaign. Black's confirmation did not end this controversy, and he finally made a public statement that he had once been a member of the Klan but had resigned and severed all ties with the organization.

Partisanship declined during World War II, and the president in the interests of national unity tried to avoid controversial nominations. Most of the emergency agencies were created by executive order, and their heads did not require Senate confirmation.

Controversy erupted anew in 1945 with the appointment of Henry A. Wallace as secretary of commerce to succeed Jesse Jones. Wallace, vice president in Roosevelt's third term, had been dumped from the Democratic ticket in 1944 because of conservative opposition to his "radical" economic views, but he had participated vigorously in the fall campaign and was expected to be rewarded with a cabinet post. On Inauguration Day 1945, Roosevelt wrote to Jones asking him to step aside for Wallace. "Henry Wallace deserves almost any service which he believes he can satisfactorily perform," the letter said.

Wallace's chief reason for wanting the commerce post was that it would give him control of the vast lending powers of the Reconstruction Finance Corporation (RFC). But before acting on the Wallace nomination, Congress passed legislation removing the RFC from the Commerce Department and giving it independent status. Jones, testifying on the bill, said the RFC should not be directed by a man who was "willing to jeopardize the country's future with untried ideas and idealistic schemes." Wallace, replying to charges that he was not qualified to supervise the RFC, said, "It is not a question of my lack of experience. Rather, it is a case of not liking the experience I have."

After enactment of the RFC removal bill, the Senate on March 1, 1945, confirmed Wallace as secretary of commerce by a 56–32 vote. Ten Republicans joined forty-five Democrats and one independent in voting for confirmation; five Democrats and twenty-seven Republicans voted against him.

Three weeks later the Senate rejected another Roosevelt appointee charged with radical views. Aubrey W. Williams, nominated to be Rural Electrification administrator, had a background as a social worker, administrator of the National Youth Administration, and organization director of the National Farmers Union. Opposition was based on his racial positions and on charges that he was an atheist and a Communist sympathizer. Nineteen Democrats joined thirty-three Republicans to defeat Williams, 36–52.

Truman's Battles with the Senate

President Harry S. Truman tangled repeatedly with the Senate over appointments. Early in his administration he was widely criticized for appointing "cronies" to important offices.

In 1946 Truman was forced, after a two-month fight, to withdraw the nomination of Edwin W. Pauley to be under secretary of the navy. Pauley was a California oil man and former treasurer of the Democratic National Committee. In hearings before the Senate Naval Affairs Committee the opponents, led by Sen. Charles W. Tobey, R-N.H., presented witnesses who accused Pauley of having used political influence to protect his oil interests. Secretary of the Interior Harold L. Ickes said Pauley had told him during the 1944 presidential campaign that $300,000 in campaign contributions from California oil interests could be raised if the government would drop its suit to establish federal title to the tidewater oil lands. When Truman said at a press conference that Ickes might be mistaken, Ickes resigned, accusing

the president of wanting him to commit perjury for the sake of the Democratic Party. Pauley denied categorically all the charges made against him and then asked the president to withdraw his nomination. The committee was reported to be divided, 8–10, against him.

After the 1946 midterm election, in which the Republicans won control of Congress, Truman tried to avoid controversy by nominating persons who would be acceptable to the Senate. The Republican 80th Congress did not reject any of Truman's nominees, although 153 names were withdrawn. In 1948 the Senate did not act on 11,122 nominations—apparently in the expectation that Truman would lose his bid for reelection, enabling a Republican president to fill the vacancies with Republicans in 1949. Truman won.

The two most explosive contests that occurred in the 80th Congress concerned nominees who had been named before the 1946 election, David E. Lilienthal and Gordon R. Clapp. In the autumn of 1946, Truman gave Lilienthal, chairman of the Tennessee Valley Authority (TVA), a recess appointment to the chairmanship of the newly created Atomic Energy Commission. Truman appointed Clapp, who had served under Lilienthal, to replace him as TVA chairman.

The opposition to both nominations was led by Sen. Kenneth McKellar, D-Tenn., who for years had been engaged in a patronage dispute with the TVA management. Although he was not a member of the committees that considered the two nominations, McKellar conducted lengthy interrogations of witnesses and accused both Lilienthal and Clapp of having Communist sympathies. When the nominations finally reached the floor in April 1947, Lilienthal was confirmed, 50–31, and Clapp, 36–31. During the debate on Clapp, McKellar complained that the president had appointed him "without saying beans to me" and declared that he was "hurt beyond expression" that his colleagues should vote for nominees he opposed.

In 1949 President Truman met two outright defeats at the hands of the Senate. Leland Olds, nominated to a third term as member of the Federal Power Commission (FPC), was rejected, 15–53, in the face of opposition by oil and natural gas interests. Opponents, led by Sen. Lyndon B. Johnson, D-Texas, cited articles Olds had written in the 1920s for the labor press as evidence of Communist leanings. As a member of the FPC, Olds had played a key role in the development of federal regulation of the natural gas industry.

The other 1949 rejection was that of Carl A. Ilgenfritz, who refused to take the chairmanship of the Munitions Board (at a salary of $14,000) unless he could retain his $70,000 annual salary as a steel executive. The Senate vote was 28–40.

Senatorial courtesy played a role in several of Truman's defeats. In 1950 the Senate rejected, 14–59, the nomination of Martin A. Hutchinson to be a member of the Federal Trade Commission. Hutchinson, a foe of Senator Byrd's Virginia political machine, was opposed by Senators Byrd and A. Willis Robertson, D-Va. In 1951 Sen. Paul H. Douglas, D-Ill., successfully

TABLE 7-2 Senate Rejections of Cabinet Nominations

Nominee	Position	President	Date	Vote
Roger B. Taney	Secretary of Treasury	Jackson	June 23, 1834	18–28
Caleb Cushing	Secretary of Treasury	Tyler	March 3, 1843	19–27
Caleb Cushing	Secretary of Treasury	Tyler	March 3, 1843	10–27
Caleb Cushing	Secretary of Treasury	Tyler	March 3, 1843	2–29
David Henshaw	Secretary of Navy	Tyler	Jan. 15, 1844	6–34
James M. Porter	Secretary of War	Tyler	Jan. 30, 1844	3–38
James S. Green	Secretary of Treasury	Tyler	June 15, 1844	Not recorded
Henry Stanbery	Attorney General	Johnson	June 2, 1868	11–29
Charles B. Warren	Attorney General	Coolidge	March 10, 1925	39–41
Charles B. Warren	Attorney General	Coolidge	March 16, 1925	39–46
Lewis L. Strauss	Secretary of Commerce	Eisenhower	June 19, 1959	46–49
John Tower	Secretary of Defense	Bush	March 9, 1989	47–53

SOURCES: Adapted from George H. Haynes, *The Senate of the United States: Its History and Practice,* 2 vols. (Boston: Houghton Mifflin, 1938); *Congressional Quarterly Almanac,* various years.

appealed to the courtesy tradition to defeat two of Truman's choices for federal district judgeships in Illinois. Douglas said the president should have nominated two candidates recommended by him.

One of the plums of congressional patronage came to an end in 1952. President Truman proposed, and Congress accepted, a reorganization plan putting all Internal Revenue Bureau (later renamed the Internal Revenue Service) jobs except that of commissioner under civil service. The action followed congressional hearings in 1951 on scandals in the agency. The Senate, however, defeated other reorganization plans to put postmasters, customs officials, and U.S. marshals under civil service.

EISENHOWER TO JOHNSON

At the outset of his administration in 1953, President Dwight D. Eisenhower was criticized by conservative Republicans who contended that his cabinet selections failed to give appropriate recognition to the wing of the Republican Party led by Sen. Robert A. Taft of Ohio. The president also gave his department and agency heads free rein to select their own subordinates, but when Republican leaders in the Senate complained that their suggestions were being ignored and that even the customary clearances were not being obtained, the senators were invited to take their recommendations directly to the department heads. Subsequently, more appointments went to conservative Republicans.

Several of Eisenhower's early nominations were opposed on conflict-of-interest grounds. The most celebrated was that of Charles E. Wilson as secretary of defense. Wilson, former president of General Motors (GM), was required to divest himself of all GM stock before the Senate Armed Services Committee consented to recommend his confirmation. Similar issues arose with the nominations of Harold E. Talbott as secretary of the air force and Robert T. Stevens as secretary of the army. From this time on, the Senate showed a greater interest in conflict-of-interest questions in the consideration of presidential nominations.

One of Eisenhower's subsequent cabinet nominations was rejected—the first such rejection since 1925. Lewis L. Strauss already was serving under a recess appointment when, after months of hearings, the Senate rejected his nomination as secretary of commerce by a 46–49 vote. Opponents accused Strauss of a lack of integrity and criticized his conservative approach to government. Specific issues raised against him included his role in the Dixon-Yates power contract, viewed by public power advocates as an attempt to undermine the Tennessee Valley Authority; his actions in the J. Robert Oppenheimer security case; and his alleged withholding of information from Congress and the public while chairman of the Atomic Energy Commission.

Of Eisenhower's five appointees to the Supreme Court, three took their seats on the Court under recess appointments before they had been confirmed by the Senate. Chief Justice Earl Warren was unanimously confirmed in 1954 despite publication of a ten-point summary of charges against him, including allegations that he was at one time connected with a liquor lobbyist and that he lacked judicial experience. William J. Brennan Jr. was confirmed in 1957 by voice vote, although Sen. Joseph R. McCarthy, R-Wis., had protested Brennan's comparison of congressional investigations of communism to Salem witch hunts. Potter Stewart was confirmed in 1959 by a 70–17 vote; the opposition came entirely from southern Democrats who criticized his concurrence in the Supreme Court's 1954 school desegregation decision.

In 1960 the Senate adopted a Democratic-sponsored resolution expressing the sense of the Senate that the president should not make recess appointments to the Supreme Court except to prevent or end a breakdown in the administration of the Court's business, and that recess appointees should not take their seats on the Court until the Senate had "advised and consented" to their nomination. Proponents claimed it was difficult to investigate the qualifications of a person already sitting on the Court. Opponents charged that the Democrats hoped for a victory in the 1960 presidential election and feared that a vacancy might occur on the Court in time for Eisenhower to give a recess appointment to a Republican.

Efforts of the Democratic-controlled Congress to keep judicial appointments out of the hands of the Republican president also led to a four-year delay in enacting legislation to create seventy-three new circuit and district court judgeships. Proposed by Eisenhower in 1957, the bill did not become law until after President John F. Kennedy took office in 1961.

Kennedy Appointments

Kennedy participated far more actively than had Eisenhower in the selection of appointees. Although recruitment of candidates for federal office was carried out by a well-publicized talent hunt, some care was taken to clear appointments with appropriate members of Congress.

None of Kennedy's nominations was rejected by the Senate, and few were contested. His two nominees to the Supreme Court—Byron R. White and Arthur J. Goldberg in 1962—were confirmed without difficulty.

Racial issues figured in several of Kennedy's nominations. Kennedy's nomination of Thurgood Marshall, a black civil rights lawyer, to the Second Circuit Court of Appeals was held up by the Senate Judiciary Committee for a year. Marshall was confirmed in 1962, 54–16, with the dissenting votes again coming from southern Democrats.

Johnson: Fight over Fortas

President Lyndon B. Johnson, with one dramatic exception, had little trouble with the Senate over nominations. His cabinet appointees were confirmed without difficulty, and his first two Supreme Court appointments encountered only routine opposition. The Senate confirmed his nomination of Abe Fortas to be an associate justice of the Supreme Court by voice vote in 1965. In 1967 the Senate confirmed the nomination of Thurgood Marshall, by then solicitor general, as the first black member of the Supreme Court; the vote was 69–11, with ten southern Democrats and one northern Democrat voting against him.

In 1968 Johnson was unsuccessful in his effort to elevate Fortas to chief justice of the United States as the replacement for Warren, who sought to retire. The Fortas nomination finally was withdrawn in the face of a Senate filibuster led by Republicans. Warren agreed to remain on the Court through the 1968–1969 term, thus ensuring that his successor would be appointed by the incoming president. There was no action on Johnson's nomination of Judge Homer Thornberry of the Fifth Circuit Court of Appeals to replace Fortas as associate justice, since there was no vacancy for Thornberry, a former member of the House (D-Texas), to fill.

The fight against Fortas was led by Sen. Robert P. Griffin, R-Mich. He charged that the appointment was based on "cronyism" and that Warren had timed his retirement to ensure appointment of his successor by a Democratic president. The "lame-duck" charge gave way to more serious questions of pro-

The Senate in 1968 rebuffed Supreme Court Justice Abe Fortas's bid to become chief justice of the Court. Fortas resigned from the Court in 1969, becoming the first justice in history to step down under threat of impeachment.

priety in the course of Senate Judiciary Committee hearings. One was the question of Fortas's continued involvement in White House affairs after he went to the Court in 1965, an involvement that Fortas admitted but played down in his testimony before the committee. Toward the end of the hearings, it was disclosed that Fortas had received $15,000 for conducting a nine-week law seminar at American University in the summer of 1968. The money for the fee and other seminar expenses had come from five former business associates, one of whom had a son who was involved in a federal criminal case.

On September 17, 1968, the Judiciary Committee approved the Fortas nomination by an 11–6 vote. The majority, made up of eight Democrats and three Republicans, described Fortas as "extraordinarily well qualified for the post" of chief justice. His acceptance of a fee for teaching at American University and his participation in White House discussions, the report said, were within his rights and in line with what other justices had done over the years. Three dissenting Democrats contended that Fortas had shown poor judgment in advising the president on legislative matters and in accepting the $15,000 teaching fee, and that the positions he had taken in Court decisions on crime, obscenity, and other matters had been too liberal.

Griffin pressed the attack relentlessly during Senate debate. Majority Leader Mike Mansfield, D-Mont., moved to end what was plainly a filibuster, but a cloture motion was rejected October 1, 1968, by a 45–43 vote, fourteen votes short of the two-thirds majority needed to cut off debate. The next day Fortas asked the president to withdraw his name. Terming the action of the Senate "tragic," Johnson consented. Renewed controversy over Fortas's extrajudicial activities led to his resignation from the Court in 1969. He was the first justice in history to step down under threat of impeachment.

NIXON, FORD, AND CARTER

President Richard Nixon's early appointments to major policy posts were confirmed without difficulty, but two of his nominations to the Supreme Court led to epic struggles with the Senate. His first nomination, of Warren E. Burger to replace Chief Justice Earl Warren, was confirmed quickly by a 74–3 vote in 1969. Burger, a judge of the Court of Appeals for the District of Columbia Circuit, was little known outside legal circles at the time of his nomination.

Nixon's next opportunity to nominate a justice came when Justice Fortas resigned under fire in May 1969 for accepting an outside fee from the family foundation of a convicted stock manipulator. To fill the vacancy Nixon nominated Clement F. Haynsworth Jr. of South Carolina, chief judge of the Fourth Circuit Court of Appeals.

As in the Fortas case the debate centered on judicial ethics. Opponents of the nomination said they did not question Haynsworth's honesty or integrity but, rather, his sensitivity to the appearance of ethical impropriety and his judgment regarding participation in cases in which his financial interests could be said to be involved, if only indirectly.

During committee hearings, Haynsworth's financial affairs and judicial record were scrutinized more thoroughly and extensively than those of any other Court nominee. The Judiciary Committee approved the nomination October 9 by a 10–7 vote. The ten-man majority asserted that Haynsworth was "extraordinarily well qualified" for the Court post. But after a week's debate, the Democratic-controlled Senate on November 21, 1969, rejected the nomination by a 45–55 vote. Seventeen Republicans, including the three top GOP leaders in the Senate, joined thirty-eight Democrats in voting against confirmation. Twenty-six Republicans and nineteen Democrats voted to confirm.

In 1970 Nixon nominated another southerner, G. Harrold Carswell of Florida, a judge of the Fifth Circuit Court of Appeals, to fill the Fortas seat. Few senators wanted a repetition of the Haynsworth fight, but opposition to Carswell began to build when charges of racism were raised against him. Other critics, including many within his own profession, contended that Car-

swell was a man of mediocre abilities who lacked the judicial competence requisite for service on the High Court.

Carswell won the Judiciary Committee's approval February 16 by a vote of 13–4. But when the nomination moved to the Senate in March 1970, opponents succeeded in delaying the final vote until after the Easter recess. When the Senate returned to consider the nomination, the outcome was in doubt. In this atmosphere Nixon wrote a letter to a pro-Carswell Republican senator declaring that rejection of the nomination would impair his legal responsibility and the constitutional relationship of the president to Congress.

"What is centrally at issue in this nomination," Nixon said, "is the constitutional responsibility of the president to appoint members of the Court—and whether this responsibility can be frustrated by those who wish to substitute their own philosophy or their own subjective judgment for that of the one person entrusted by the Constitution with the power of appointment. The question arises whether I, as president of the United States, shall be accorded the same right of choice in naming Supreme Court Justices which has been freely accorded to my predecessors of both parties."

Nixon said he respected the right of any senator to differ with his selection. However, he continued: "The fact remains, under the Constitution, it is the duty of the president to appoint and of the Senate to advise and consent. But if the Senate attempts to substitute its judgment as to who should be appointed, the traditional constitutional balance is in jeopardy and the duty of the president under the Constitution impaired."

When the final vote on Carswell was taken April 8, 1970, the nomination was rejected 45–51. Thirteen Republicans joined thirty-eight Democrats, five of them from the South, in opposition to Carswell. Not since 1894 had a president suffered consecutive rejections of two nominees for the same Court seat. Nixon responded to the Senate's action with an angry statement to the effect that he had "reluctantly" decided that the Senate "as presently constituted" would not confirm a judicial conservative from the South.

Nixon then nominated Harry A. Blackmun of Minnesota, a judge of the Eighth Circuit Court of Appeals, to fill the Supreme Court vacancy. Blackmun had a reputation as a moderate and scholarly judge, and both liberals and conservatives praised the president's selection. The Senate Judiciary Committee unanimously reported the nomination, and the Senate confirmed it May 12, 1970, by a 94–0 vote.

In 1971 Nixon nominated and the Senate confirmed Lewis F. Powell Jr. and William H. Rehnquist as justices of the Supreme Court. Not since Harding had one president, in his first term, had the opportunity to appoint so many members of the Court.

Ford's Appointments

The Senate approved all the top-level appointments of Gerald R. Ford, who assumed the presidency when Nixon resigned in 1974. Only one of Ford's cabinet nominations was highly controversial. Stanley K. Hathaway, his choice as secretary of the interior, was attacked by liberal senators and environmental groups for what they considered a prodevelopment and anti-conservation record as governor of Wyoming. Hathaway was confirmed in June 1975 by a 60–36 vote but resigned the following month "for reasons of personal health."

Ford's selection of federal appeals judge John Paul Stevens to fill the Supreme Court seat left vacant by the retirement of William O. Douglas was confirmed without difficulty in 1975.

Senate committees rejected a number of Ford's nominations to regulatory agencies, however, including that of former representative Ben B. Blackburn, R-Ga., to be chairman of the Federal Home Loan Bank Board. Foes of the nomination objected to Blackburn's attitude toward blacks and public housing tenants and his opposition to civil rights legislation during his years in the House.

The Senate Judiciary Committee blocked the nomination of William B. Poff to a U.S. district court judgeship for the western district of Virginia. Poff fell victim to the tradition of senatorial courtesy: His nomination was opposed by Sen. William Lloyd Scott, R-Va. Scott's preferred candidate, Glen M. Williams, subsequently was nominated and confirmed.

Carter Nominations

Although none of President Jimmy Carter's nominations was rejected by the full Senate, several were killed in committee, either by vote or inaction. Opposition to some nominees was strong enough to force Carter to withdraw their names. Included in this category was Theodore C. Sorensen, a former Kennedy aide whom Carter nominated in 1977 to be director of central intelligence. Faced with strong conservative opposition, Sorensen asked that his name be withdrawn. Carter subsequently nominated Adm. Stansfield Turner, who easily won Senate confirmation to the CIA post.

The nomination of Paul C. Warnke as chief U.S. delegate to the strategic arms limitation talks (SALT) with the Soviet Union and as director of the U.S. Arms Control and Disarmament Agency drew fire from defense hard-liners who objected to his so-called soft views on arms control. After personal lobbying by Carter, the Senate confirmed Warnke by a 58–40 vote.

Carter's nomination in 1977 of Samuel D. Zagoria to the bipartisan Federal Election Commission (FEC) showed how the rules of the appointments game were expected to be played. A former aide to Republican senator Clifford P. Case of New Jersey, Zagoria had not been recommended for the Republican vacancy on the FEC by either the Senate or the House Republican leadership. They immediately charged that Carter had reneged on his pledge to pick Republican nominees from a leadership-approved list and refused to accept it. Carter resubmitted Zagoria's nomination early in 1978, but Republicans still refused to accept a nominee who had not been recommended by them. Carter eventually withdrew Zagoria's name. (Zagoria later won confirmation for a position on the Consumer Product Safety Commission.)

TABLE 7-3 Senate Action on Nominations, 1929–1998

Congress	Received	Confirmed	Withdrawn	Rejected[a]	Unconfirmed[b]
71st (1929–1931)	17,508	16,905	68	5	530
72nd (1931–1933)	12,716	10,909	19	1	1,787
73rd (1933–1935)	9,094	9,027	17	3	47
74th (1935–1937)	22,487	22,286	51	15	135
75th (1937–1939)	15,330	15,193	20	27	90
76th (1939–1941)	29,072	28,939	16	21	96
77th (1941–1943)	24,344	24,137	33	5	169
78th (1943–1945)	21,775	21,371	31	6	367
79th (1945–1947)	37,022	36,550	17	3	452
80th (1947–1949)	66,641	54,796	153	0	11,692
81st (1949–1951)	87,266	86,562	45	6	653
82nd (1951–1953)	46,920	46,504	45	2	369
83rd (1953–1955)	69,458	68,563	43	0	852
84th (1955–1957)	84,173	82,694	38	3	1,438
85th (1957–1959)	104,193	103,311	54	0	828
86th (1959–1961)	91,476	89,900	30	1	1,545
87th (1961–1963)	102,849	100,741	1,279	0	829
88th (1963–1965)	122,190	120,201	36	0	1,953
89th (1965–1967)	123,019	120,865	173	0	1,981
90th (1967–1969)	120,231	118,231	34	0	1,966
91st (1969–1971)	134,464	133,797	487	2	178
92nd (1971–1973)	117,053	114,909	11	0	2,133
93rd (1973–1975)	134,384	131,254	15	0	3,115
94th (1975–1977)	135,302	131,378	21	0	3,903
95th (1977–1979)	137,509	124,730	66	0	12,713
96th (1979–1981)	156,141	154,665	18	0	1,458
97th (1981–1983)	186,264	184,856	55	0	1,353
98th (1983–1985)	97,893	97,262	4	0	627
99th (1985–1987)	99,614	95,811	16	0	3,787
100th (1987–1989)	94,687	88,721	23	1	5,942
101st (1989–1991)	96,130	88,078	48	1	8,003
102nd (1991–1993)	76,628	75,802	24	0	802
103rd (1993–1995)	79,956	76,122	1,080	0	2,754
104th (1995–1997)	82,214	73,711	22	0	8,481
105th (1997–1999)	46,290	45,878	40	0	372

NOTES: a. Category includes only those nominations rejected outright by a vote of the Senate. Most nominations that fail to win approval of the Senate are unfavorably reported by committees and never reach the Senate floor, having been withdrawn. In some cases, the full Senate may vote to recommit a nomination to committee, in effect killing it.   b. Nominations must be returned to the president unless confirmed or rejected during the session in which they are made. If the Senate adjourns or recesses for more than thirty days within a session, all pending nominations must be returned. (*Senate Rule XXI*)

SOURCES: 71st to 80th Congresses: Floyd M. Riddick, *The United States Congress: Organization and Procedures;* 81st to 105th Congresses: "Résumé of Congressional Activity," *Congressional Record.*

For the first time since 1938 the Senate Judiciary Committee in 1980 rejected outright a federal judgeship nominee. By a 9–6 vote, the panel refused to approve Charles B. Winberry, Carter's nominee for a district judgeship in North Carolina's eastern district. The state's Democratic senator, Robert Morgan, had recommended Winberry, who was the senator's longtime friend and former campaign manager. Opponents, led by Democrat Patrick J. Leahy of Vermont and Republican Orrin G. Hatch of Utah, contended that Winberry was not qualified because of alleged ethical indiscretions and lack of experience.

Carter was the first full-term president who did not have an opportunity to make an appointment to the Supreme Court.

REAGAN AND BUSH

Several of President Ronald Reagan's cabinet nominations sparked considerable controversy, but only two faced serious Senate challenges. In 1981 the Republican-dominated Senate held up confirmation of one of Reagan's original nominees—Labor Secretary–designate Raymond J. Donovan—because of allegations that Donovan had links to organized crime and labor racketeers. He finally was confirmed February 3, 80–17. A special prosecutor subsequently found "insufficient evidence" to support the allegations. Donovan resigned his cabinet post in 1985 after he was indicted on larceny and fraud charges in connection with his New Jersey construction firm; he was acquitted of the charges.

The confirmation of Edwin Meese to be attorney general was delayed for thirteen months after Senate Judiciary Committee hearings raised questions about his ethical conduct and fitness for office. Meese, a close friend of the president, was confirmed in February 1985 after an independent counsel reported that he found "no basis" for criminal prosecution. The vote for confirmation was 63–31; all the nays were cast by Democrats. Meese resigned in July 1988 after another independent counsel concluded that in some instances he had "probably violated" the law but decided not to indict him for wrongdoing.

The Meese controversy also reflected an ongoing ideological dispute over the Reagan administration's conservative social goals. The principal battleground in Congress was the Senate Judiciary Committee, where the administration fought repeatedly with liberal Democrats and moderate Republicans. Many of these fights were over judicial and Justice Department nominations. In a noteworthy failure for the president, the Senate in 1985 decisively rejected the nomination of William Bradford Reynolds to be associate attorney general. Reynolds was head of the department's civil rights division and remained in that job. In 1986 the Senate narrowly confirmed, 48–46, the nomination of Daniel A. Manion to the Seventh U.S. Circuit Court of Appeals. Judiciary Committee Democrats had argued that Manion was unqualified for the post, but Republicans charged that much of the opposition to Manion was based on his reputation as a conservative.

Other Reagan nominees encountered opposition from conservatives in his party, led by Sen. Jesse Helms of North Carolina. The conservatives' tactics often resulted in infighting between Senate factions over issues that had little to do with the nominees' qualifications. Helms opposed diplomatic nominees whose positions did not square with his own conservative views—and held hostage dozens of other nominations until those he opposed were dispensed with in a way that satisfied him.

Reagan Supreme Court Nominations

President Reagan used his appointment power to move the Supreme Court toward his own philosophy of judicial restraint. He appointed three Supreme Court justices during his two terms in office. He also elevated a sitting member to chief justice.

Reagan named one member of the Court in 1981; Sandra Day O'Connor, the first woman justice, was confirmed 99–0. Reagan had to wait five years for his next opportunity. When Chief Justice Burger resigned in 1986, Reagan nominated Associate Justice Rehnquist to succeed him. Although civil rights groups mounted an all-out effort to defeat the nomination, Rehnquist was confirmed by a 65–33 vote after a six-week fight. The nomination of Antonin Scalia, Reagan's choice to fill the seat vacated by Rehnquist, cleared the Senate with ease.

Reagan's final exercise in Supreme Court appointments was one of the most embarrassing episodes of his presidency. In 1987 he nominated Robert Bork, a judge of the Circuit Court of Appeals for the District of Columbia, to succeed Justice Powell, who retired. Civil rights groups mobilized against the nomination, citing Bork's criticism of major civil rights legislation. His supporters portrayed him as a scholar who favored judicial restraint. Bork was questioned extensively during Judiciary Committee hearings that were unprecedented in their scope and detail. After a battle lasting more than three months the Senate rejected Bork's nomination on a 42–58 vote. He was the first Supreme Court nominee to be rejected since 1970.

The Bork episode reopened an informal debate over the Senate role in the confirmation process. Republicans argued that the president was entitled to his choice unless the candidate was unqualified. But Democrats said the Senate should be an equal partner and they insisted that it was proper to examine a nominee's judicial philosophy as well as his qualifications.

Following Bork's defeat Reagan selected Douglas H. Ginsburg, one of Bork's colleagues on the Court of Appeals, to fill Powell's seat. But within days questions were raised about Ginsburg's background. After acknowledging that he had used marijuana during the 1960s and 1970s, Ginsburg asked that his nomination, which had not been formally submitted to the Senate, not go forward. Reagan then nominated another appeals court judge, Anthony M. Kennedy of California, who was confirmed early in 1988, 97–0.

Bush Appointments

All but one of the initial nominations of President George Bush sailed through the Senate in 1989. The exception was the nomination of John Tower, a former Republican senator from Texas and chairman of the Senate Armed Services Committee, to be secretary of defense. Democratic opponents of the nomination cited secret files of interviews conducted by the FBI, which alleged that Tower had a long record of alcohol abuse. He would be an unreliable link between the president and the armed services, the critics said. Concerns were also raised about potential conflicts of interest because of Tower's work for clients in the defense industry. Republicans angrily insisted that Democrats feared Tower would be too tough for them to browbeat. The nomination was rejected by a party-line 11–9 vote of the

In 1989 the Senate rejected the nomination of former senator John Tower to be secretary of defense. Tower was the first cabinet nominee to be rejected since 1959.

Armed Services panel, but Republicans vowed to take the fight to the Senate floor. After a bruising debate with strong partisan overtones, the Senate rejected the nomination by a 47–53 vote. Bush then nominated Rep. Dick Cheney, R-Wyo., who was confirmed unanimously.

David H. Souter, Bush's first nominee to the Supreme Court, won confirmation in 1990 despite vigorous opposition from abortion rights activists and civil rights groups. Souter, who was confirmed 90–9, replaced William J. Brennan Jr., the Court's leading liberal. Souter had been a New Hampshire state judge for twelve years but had served only a few months on a federal appeals court before his nomination. He lacked an extensive record of opinions and writings, but Souter impressed senators with his knowledge of constitutional issues and his ability to finesse controversial subjects.

Bush's second nomination to the Court touched off a bitter fight between the White House and the Senate. The debate split along political lines, with a divided government heightening the tensions. A Democratic Senate had been reviewing the nominations of Republican presidents since 1987, and Senate Democrats had become increasingly frustrated by nominees' refusal to discuss politically contentious issues.

The conflict came to a head in 1991, when Bush nominated federal appeals court judge Clarence Thomas to succeed Justice Thurgood Marshall, who retired. Marshall was the first African American to serve on the Court; Thomas also was black. Before joining the Court of Appeals for the District of Columbia in March 1990, he had served as assistant secretary of education for civil rights and chairman of the Equal Employment Opportunity Commission (EEOC).

Following five days of hearings, the Senate Judiciary Committee split 7–7 on whether to recommend Thomas to the full Senate, then voted 13–1 to send his nomination on for a floor vote. Thomas's critics on the committee faulted him for refusing to give direct answers to committee members' questions. They also criticized him for disavowing statements he had made as chairman of the EEOC. Civil rights and abortion rights groups, among others, fought the conservative nominee, largely because of his stand on affirmative action and hints that he opposed abortion.

Despite strong opposition to Thomas, confirmation seemed assured. But two days before the scheduled Senate floor vote, the Judiciary Committee reopened its hearings to consider charges of sexual harassment raised by Anita F. Hill, an attorney who had worked for Thomas at the Education Department and EEOC in 1981–1983. Thomas's Republican backers were outraged at what they called last-minute character assassination and mudslinging. After three days of dramatic—though inconclusive—testimony before the committee, the nomination moved to a Senate floor vote. Thomas won confirmation on a 52–48 roll call, one of the narrowest margins in history.

CLINTON

Bill Clinton came into office with both houses of Congress under Democratic control and few of his initial appointments ran into serious opposition in the Senate. One major exception was his selection of an attorney general. The first nominee for the post, corporate lawyer Zoë Baird, ran into strong opposition and withdrew because she had hired illegal immigrants as domestic help and at the time had not paid Social Security or unemployment taxes on their wages. Clinton's apparent second choice, U.S. District Court Judge Kimba M. Wood, also withdrew her name from consideration because she had hired an illegal immigrant, although she had broken no laws. After the two false starts, Clinton selected Florida prosecutor Janet Reno to head the Justice Department; her nomination proceeded smoothly through the Senate.

Clinton also ran into trouble with his nomination of law professor and former Justice Department lawyer Lani Guinier to be assistant attorney general and head the Justice Department's civil rights division. Conservatives accused her of holding dangerously radical views on minority rights and even some moderate Democrats expressed doubts and urged Clinton not to send her before an uneasy Senate for confirmation. But Guinier's allies turned up the heat on Clinton to stand by his nominee. In the end Clinton withdrew the nomination, saying that he had not read Guinier's legal writings prior to selecting her and would not have nominated her if he had. Some observers saw the criticisms of Guinier as payback for the failed 1987 Supreme Court nomination of Bork, who sank in the

Democrat-led Judiciary Committee in part because of his extensive and controversial academic writings.

Later in his presidency the civil rights slot in the Justice Department proved troublesome once again for Clinton. This time he sought to nominate civil rights lawyer Bill Lann Lee to the post. When Lee's nomination stalled because of GOP opposition to his views on affirmative action, Clinton considered giving him a recess appointment. But to avoid a confrontation with Congress, Clinton opted instead to make Lee "acting" assistant attorney general. *(See "Recess Appointments," p. 305.)*

Clinton suffered a major setback in his second term appointments when former national security adviser Tony Lake in 1997 asked the president to withdraw his nomination to be director of central intelligence. Lake complained that the nomination process had become a "political football in a game with constantly moving goal posts," after his nomination got caught up in a partisan controversy over White House and Democratic fund-raising practices.[9]

Clinton had nothing but headaches from his attempts to appoint—and keep—a surgeon general of the United States. His first surgeon general, Joycelyn Elders, was approved in 1993 after two months of acrimonious opposition from conservatives. Critics attacked Elders for her fiery rhetoric and firm views on politically charged issues such as abortion and teenage sex. Her outspokenness ultimately proved to be her downfall, when Clinton fired her in 1994 because of controversial remarks she made on sex education. Clinton's nomination of Henry W. Foster Jr. to succeed Elders got caught up in controversy over the abortion issue as well and was ultimately blocked by a threatened filibuster. The job of surgeon general remained open until 1998, when the nomination of David Satcher survived a conservative GOP filibuster—launched in part because of his views on a controversial abortion procedure—and was confirmed by the Senate.

Clinton Judicial Appointments

In selecting the first Democratic-appointed Supreme Court justices since Lyndon Johnson's administration, Clinton avoided a repeat of the fierce battles over Court nominees waged in the recent past. His choices, Ruth Bader Ginsburg and Stephen G. Breyer, two moderately liberal veteran federal appellate judges, won Senate confirmation easily with bipartisan support in 1993 and 1994, respectively. Journalist Robert Shogan speculated that Clinton's caution in making his Court selections may in part have been the result of his harsh experience with executive nominations but also because conservatives were "raring for a fight over the Court—in fact they have been gearing up for one since Clinton was elected."[10]

Clinton did not fare as well in his attempts to fill lower court vacancies. Initially Clinton shared in the blame because of his slow pace in sending nominations to Capitol Hill. "The Senate cannot confirm judges that the president does not nominate," said Senate Judiciary Committee Chairman Hatch.[11] But, more importantly, Republicans began a concerted campaign to challenge Clinton's judicial nominees after resuming control of the Senate in 1995. When the Senate Republican Conference called on the Senate to reject judicial nominees with "activist" philosophies, Democrats insisted that there was nothing particularly activist about Clinton's nominees and charged that Republicans hoped to slow the process until they could retake the White House and, thus, the power to nominate judges. Chief Justice Rehnquist in 1998 used his annual report on the state of the judiciary to deliver some tough criticism of Congress. He warned that the high level of vacancies could not continue without "eroding the quality of justice" on the federal bench.[12] While suggesting that the White House could have acted more quickly to nominate judges, Rehnquist emphasized the Senate's sluggish pace.

In October 1999 Senate Democrats dropped their filibuster of a judicial nominee favored by the GOP—Ted Stewart—in return for action on several other nominations. Stewart was confirmed, but another U.S. District Court nominee, Ronnie White, was rejected. This was the first outright rejection of a nomination since Tower in 1989 and the first of a judicial nominee since Bork in 1987. GOP critics said White was too much of an "activist" jurist, but Democrats questioned whether the defeat was racially motivated because White was an African American. Republicans angrily denied the charge.

The Power of Removal: Long-Term Controversy

Controversy over the role of the Senate in the removal of government officers began in the early days of the Republic and continued intermittently in the twentieth century.[13]

The Constitution contained no language governing removals except for the impeachment provisions of Article II, Section 4. Alexander Hamilton, writing in *Federalist* No. 77, contended that the consent of the Senate "would be necessary to displace as well as to appoint," but this view soon was challenged.

Debate over the power of removal began in the First Congress, during consideration of a bill to establish the Department of Foreign Affairs. Two principal theories were advanced. One group insisted that since the Constitution gave the Senate a share in the appointment power, the Senate must also give its advice and consent to removals. The other group, led by James Madison, maintained that the power of removal was an executive function, necessarily implied in the power to nominate, and that Senate participation would violate the principle of separation of powers.

Madison's view prevailed in the House, which passed the bill by a 29–22 vote after deleting language specifically vesting removal power in the president and substituting a provision that implied recognition of the president's exclusive power of removal under the Constitution.

After a lengthy and spirited debate in closed session, the Senate narrowly acceded to the House interpretation. A motion to drop the House language recognizing the president's sole power

Supreme Court nominee Stephen G. Breyer meets with the Senate Judiciary Committee members at the start of his confirmation hearing. From left are Strom Thurmond, R-S.C.; Orrin Hatch, R-Utah; Breyer; and Joseph Biden, D-Del.

of removal was rejected on a tie vote, with Vice President John Adams, voting for the first time, recorded in opposition. The fact that the Senate agreed to limit its own powers was widely attributed to senatorial respect for President Washington.

Early presidents exercised great restraint in use of the removal power, even after the enactment in 1820 of a statute known as the Four Years Law. This law established a fixed, four-year term for district attorneys, customs collectors, and many other officers who previously had served at the pleasure of the president.

Presidents James Monroe and John Quincy Adams followed a policy of renominating all such persons when their terms expired unless they had been guilty of misconduct. However, senatorial pressure for patronage was on the rise, and Adams's self-restraint was met by Senate demands for a broader role in appointments and removals.

JACKSON'S CLASHES WITH SENATE

Andrew Jackson's sweeping and partisan use of the removal power soon brought fresh Senate demands for a larger share in the patronage pie. Controversy over the issue led to a series of Senate resolutions requesting the president to inform the Senate of his reasons for removing various officials. Jackson complied

with several of these requests, but by 1835 he had had enough. A Senate resolution, adopted by a 23–22 vote, requesting information on the "charges, if any," against the recently removed surveyor general of south Tennessee brought the following response:

It is . . . my solemn conviction that I ought no longer, from any motive, nor in any degree, to yield to these unconstitutional demands. Their continued repetition imposes on me, as the representative and trustee of the American people, the painful but imperious duty of resisting to the utmost any further encroachment on the rights of the Executive. . . . The President in cases of this nature possesses the exclusive power of removal from office; and under the sanctions of his official oath, and of his liability to impeachment, he is bound to exercise it whenever the public welfare shall require. On no principle known to our institutions can he be required to account for the manner in which he discharges this portion of his public duties, save only in the mode and under the forms prescribed by the Constitution.

Meanwhile, the Senate had appointed a committee "to inquire into the extent of Executive patronage; the circumstances which contributed to its increase of late; the expediency and practicability of reducing the same, and the means of such reduction." The committee reported a bill to repeal the first two sections of the Four Years Law and to require the president to submit to the Senate the reasons for each removal. John Quincy

Adams called this an effort "to cut down the Executive power of the President and to grasp it for the Senate."

Supported by John C. Calhoun, Daniel Webster, and Henry Clay, the measure won Senate approval, 31–16, but was never taken up in the House. Webster and Clay disputed the interpretation of the removal power established by the First Congress. Attributing that interpretation largely to congressional confidence in President Washington, Clay said it had not been reconsidered only because it had not been abused prior to the Jackson administration.

OPPOSITION TO TENURE ACTS

The next great clash between the Senate and the chief executive over the removal power occurred in the administration of Andrew Johnson. Among its consequences were the Tenure of Office Act of 1867 and Johnson's impeachment trial.

The conflict grew out of Johnson's fight with the Radical Republican leaders of Congress over Reconstruction policy and his use of the removal power to provide jobs for his own followers.

As passed by the Senate, the Tenure of Office bill enabled civil officers—excluding members of the cabinet—who were appointed by and with the advice and consent of the Senate, to remain in office until their successors were appointed by the president and confirmed by the Senate. It permitted the president to suspend an officer during a recess of the Senate and appoint a temporary successor, but it provided that the suspended officer should resume his post if the Senate failed to approve the suspension. The Senate rejected an amendment to delete the clause excluding cabinet members as well as one to require Senate confirmation of the appointment of all officers with salaries exceeding $1,000. However, the House deleted the exclusion of cabinet members from the bill, and in conference it was agreed that cabinet members should hold office for the term of the president who appointed them and for one month thereafter, subject to removal by and with the advice and consent of the Senate.

President Johnson vetoed the bill on the ground that it was unconstitutional to restrict the president's power of removal, but Congress enacted the measure over the veto by a 35–11 vote in the Senate and a 133–37 vote in the House.

Johnson promptly put the Tenure of Office Act to the test. First, he suspended Secretary of War Edwin M. Stanton, but the Senate refused to concur in the suspension. Johnson then attempted to dismiss Stanton and make another appointment to the post. The House immediately initiated impeachment proceedings and on February 24, 1868, adopted eleven articles of impeachment. The House vote was 126–47. The principal charge against President Johnson was that he had violated the new law by dismissing Stanton. On this charge, the Senate May 26, 1868, failed to convict by only one vote; seven Republicans and twelve Democrats voted for acquittal, while thirty-five Republicans voted for conviction. A two-thirds majority was required to convict. (See Chapter 9, Impeachment Power.)

Early in President Ulysses S. Grant's administration, Congress repealed certain provisions of the Tenure of Office Act that regulated suspensions. As partially repealed in 1869, the law provided that the president might suspend officers "in his discretion" without, as before, reporting to the Senate the reasons for his action, but it required prompt nomination of successors. A subsequent dispute between President Grover Cleveland and the Republican-controlled Senate finally led to repeal of what was left of the Tenure of Office Act.

While Congress was in recess in the summer of 1885, Cleveland suspended 643 government officers whose positions were subject to senatorial confirmation. When Congress reconvened, he submitted to the Senate the names of their replacements, to whom he had given recess appointments. The committees handling these nominations then called upon the executive departments for information on the reasons for the suspensions, information the departments refused to give. The dispute stalled action on the nominations.

The climax to the controversy came over the nomination of a U.S. attorney in Alabama. The Justice Department refused demands by the Senate Judiciary Committee to provide the reasons for removal of his predecessor. The Senate responded with a resolution, adopted on a party-line vote, censuring the attorney general for his refusal to transmit the desired papers. A second resolution, adopted by a one-vote margin, said it was "the duty of the Senate to refuse its advice and consent to proposed removals of officers" in cases where information requested by the Senate was withheld.

The Senate debated the resolutions heatedly over a two-week period. While they were pending, Cleveland sent a special message to the Senate reasserting the president's authority:

The requests and demands which by the score have for nearly three months been presented to the different departments of the government, whatever their form, have but one complexion. They assume the right of the Senate to sit in judgment upon the exercise of my exclusive function, for which I am solely responsible to the people from whom I have so lately received the sacred trust of office. . . .

The pledges I have made were made to the people, and to them I am responsible. I am not responsible to the Senate, and I am unwilling to submit my actions and official conduct to them for judgment. . . .

Public opinion responded to the president's message, and the nomination logjam was broken. The following year Sen. George F. Hoar, R-Mass., introduced legislation to repeal the Tenure of Office Acts, and the bill was speedily enacted into law.

CONTROVERSIES UNDER WILSON AND COOLIDGE

Another major controversy over the removal power occurred in 1920 when President Woodrow Wilson vetoed the forerunner of the Budget and Accounting Act of 1921. That measure, as transmitted to Wilson, provided that the comptroller general and assistant comptroller general were to be appointed by the president subject to Senate confirmation but were to be subject to removal by concurrent resolution of Congress. A concurrent resolution does not require the president's approval to take effect and thus the president would have had no control over the removal of these officers. Wilson's veto message was emphatic: "I am convinced that the Congress is without constitutional power to limit the appointing power and its incident power of removal derived from the Constitution."

The following year the Budget and Accounting Act of 1921 became law with the signature of President Warren G. Harding. The enacted legislation differed from the 1920 version in providing for removal of the comptroller general and assistant comptroller general by joint resolution, which, like a bill, requires the signature of the president, or passage over his veto, to take effect.

SENATE REMOVAL EFFORTS

The Senate also has attempted to force the removal of officials, although without notable success. President Abraham Lincoln was able to head off efforts by a group of Republican senators to force the resignation of Secretary of State William H. Seward in 1862.

In 1924 the Senate adopted a resolution "that it is the sense of the United States Senate that the president of the United States immediately request the resignation of Edwin Denby as secretary of the Navy." Denby had been implicated in the naval oil lease scandals, and Senate Democrats hoped to press similar resolutions against other members of President Coolidge's cabinet. The Denby resolution was adopted on a 47–34 roll call and a copy sent to the president. Coolidge promptly issued a statement:

No official recognition can be given to the passage of the Senate resolution relative to their opinion concerning members of the cabinet or other officers under executive control. . . . The dismissal of an officer lof the government, such as is involved in this case, other than by impeachment, is exclusively an executive function.

A few days later Denby resigned.

Another Senate removal effort, with a different twist, occurred during the 71st Congress and involved appointees to the newly created Federal Power Commission (FPC). Dissatisfied with the actions of FPC members it had confirmed shortly before the Christmas recess in 1930, the Senate in January 1931 tried to recall the nominations for reconsideration. President Hoover refused, saying: "I am advised that these appointments were constitutionally made, with the consent of the Senate, formally communicated to me, and that the return of the documents by me and reconsideration by the Senate would be ineffective to disturb the appointees in their offices."

In the last year of the Carter administration, the removal power surfaced as an issue during consideration of the nomination of air force Gen. David C. Jones to a second two-year term as chairman of the Joint Chiefs of Staff. Jones's first term expired June 20, 1980. Although the Senate Armed Services Committee approved Jones's reappointment, Republican senators Gordon J. Humphrey of New Hampshire and Jesse Helms of North Carolina opposed Jones because of his support for President Carter's Panama Canal and the strategic arms limitation talks (SALT II) treaties.

However, Helms said he would not "raise any ruckus" about the nomination because "General Jones has agreed to tender his resignation if Governor Reagan is elected."

At the hearing on his renomination, Jones denied striking any such bargain, although he acknowledged that he and Sen. John W. Warner, R-Va., had discussed the law, which said the chairman of the Joint Chiefs served "at the pleasure of the president." He also agreed with Warner when the Virginia senator recalled that Jones pledged to go "gracefully" if asked by the president to resign. But he added that he had no intention of submitting his resignation to a new president—as political appointees routinely do when an administration changes—because it would politicize his office and set a bad precedent. (After he was elected president, Reagan retained Jones as chairman of the Joint Chiefs of Staff.)

COURT DECISIONS

The courts have upheld the president's right to unilaterally remove government officials. After nearly 140 years of controversy over the issue, the Supreme Court met the issue head on in 1926. In the words of Chief Justice William Howard Taft, the Court had "studiously avoided deciding the issue until it was presented in such a way that it could not be avoided."

The case involved a postmaster who had been removed from office by President Wilson in 1920, without consultation with the Senate, although the 1876 law under which the man had been appointed stipulated: "Postmasters of the first, second and third classes shall be appointed and may be removed by the president, by and with the advice and consent of the Senate, and shall hold their offices for four years, unless sooner removed or suspended according to law."

In a 6–3 decision the Court upheld the president's unrestricted power of removal as inherent in the executive power invested in the office by the Constitution. The Court concluded:

It therefore follows that the Tenure of Office Act of 1867, in so far as it attempted to prevent the president from removing executive officers who had been appointed by him by and with the consent of the Senate was invalid, and that subsequent legislation of the same effect was equally so. . . . The provision of the law of 1876, by which the unrestricted power of removal of first-class postmasters is denied to the president, is in violation of the Constitution and invalid. (*Myers v. United States,* 1926)

In a unanimous 1935 decision, the Court modified this position. The 1935 case involved a federal trade commissioner whom President Franklin D. Roosevelt had tried to remove because, he told the commissioner, "I do not feel that your mind and my mind go along together on either the policies or the administration" of the FTC. The Court held that the FTC was "an administrative body created by Congress to carry into effect legislative policies" and thus could not "in any proper sense be characterized as an arm or an eye of the Executive."

The Court continued:

Whether the power of the president to remove an officer shall prevail over the authority of Congress to condition the power by fixing a definite term and precluding a removal except for cause will depend upon the character of the office; the *Myers* decision, affirming the power of the president alone to make the removal, is confined to purely executive officers, and as to officers of the kind here under consideration, we hold that no removal can be made during the prescribed term for which the officer is appointed, except for one or more of the causes named in the applicable statute. *(Humphrey's Executor v. United States)*

In ruling that Roosevelt had exceeded his authority in removing the commissioner, the Court indicated that except for officials immediately responsible to the president and those exercising nondiscretionary or ministerial functions, Congress could apply such limitations on removal as it saw fit.

In a later decision *(Wiener v. United States,* 1958), the Court built on the *Humphrey's* decision. The *Wiener* case involved the refusal of a member of the War Claims Commission appointed by President Truman to resign when the Eisenhower administration came to power. Congress created the commission with "jurisdiction to receive and adjudicate according to law" certain damage claims resulting from World War II. The law made no provision for removal of commissioners.

The commission member was removed by Eisenhower and sought his pay in court. The Supreme Court agreed with him. It noted the similarity between the *Wiener* and *Humphrey's* cases: In both situations, presidents had removed persons from quasi-judicial agencies without showing cause for the sole purpose of naming persons of their own choosing. The Court said it understood the *Humphrey's* decision to draw "a sharp line of cleavage between officials who were part of the executive establishment and were thus removable by virtue of the president's constitutional powers, and those who are members of a body 'to exercise its judgment without the leave or hindrance of any other official or any department of the government,' . . . as to whom a power of removal exists only if Congress may fairly be said to have conferred it." This sharp differentiation derives from the difference in functions between those who are part of the executive establishment and those whose tasks require absolute freedom from executive interference." The Court also noted the "intrinsic judicial character" of the commission.

As a result of the case and of the *Myers* and *Humphrey's* cases, the rule has developed that a president can remove a member of a quasi-judicial agency only for cause, even if Congress has not so provided.

Two major modern rulings concerning the separation of powers turned in large part on the power to appoint and remove officials. In a 1986 decision *(Bowsher v. Synar)* declaring provisions of a 1985 deficit control act unconstitutional, much of the Court's reasoning turned on the question of who could remove the nation's comptroller general. The law in question allowed the comptroller general to dictate to the president where the executive branch had to reduce its spending. However, the comptroller general, who headed the General Accounting Office, the investigatory and auditing arm of Congress, was appointed by the president but could be removed only by Congress. Therefore, the Court held, the comptroller general was

part of the legislative branch and could not participate in the execution of laws. Chief Justice Warren E. Burger wrote: "The structure of the Constitution does not permit Congress to execute the laws; it follows that Congress cannot grant to an officer under its control what it does not possess."

In another separation of powers case *(Morrison v. Olson)* in 1988, the Court upheld the 1978 Ethics in Government Act's complex process for appointing an independent counsel to investigate high-level wrongdoing. Under the law, the counsel was appointed by a three-judge court but could be removed by the attorney general for good cause. In its decision, the Court dismissed the argument that the law interfered with the president's exercise of his constitutional functions. By requiring that there must be good cause to remove a special prosecutor, the Court held, the law guaranteed the counsel a necessary measure of independence. At the same time, this requirement did not interfere with the president's ability to ensure the faithful execution of the laws.

Nomination Procedures: The Senate's Role

Before submitting a nomination, the president normally consults with key members of Congress, political organizations, and special interest groups in an effort to obtain informal clearance for a candidate. Because the president prefers to avoid a confirmation fight, serious opposition at this stage may lead to the selection of another person for the post.

"Senatorial courtesy"—the custom of senators refusing to confirm a nominee for an office in the state of a senator of the president's party if that senator disapproves of the candidate—provides additional incentive for the president to consult before making appointments to certain federal positions in the states. *(See "Patronage, Courtesy Rule Decline," p. 281.)*

If the candidate's prospects look good, the president submits the person's name to the Senate. It has been customary since the time of George Washington for the chief executive to submit nominations in written form, although President Harding in 1921 proceeded directly from his inaugural ceremonies to the Senate chamber to present his cabinet nominations in person.

When a nomination is formally submitted to the Senate, the president's message transmitting the nomination is read on the chamber floor. The nomination is received by the parliamentarian and assigned a number by the executive clerk. It is then referred to the appropriate committee for consideration. The review process that follows may be brief or may last for months.

COMMITTEE CONSIDERATION

Since 1868 most nominations have been referred to committee. The basic purpose of the congressional confirmation proceedings is to determine the character and competence of the nominee: whether there is any conflict of interest—particularly

Gentlemen of the Senate,

I nominate for the Department of the Treasury of the United States—

Alexander Hamilton (of New York) Secretary.

Nicholas Eveleigh (of S.º Carolina) Comptroller.

Samuel Meridith (of Pensylvania) Treasurer.

Oliver Wolcott Jun.ʳ (of Connecticut) Auditor.

Joseph Nourse (in office) Register.

For the Department of war—

Henry Knox.

For Judge in the Western Territory, in place of William Barton who declines the appointment

George Turner.

President George Washington established the precedent of submitting nominations to the Senate in writing.

financial—and whether his or her qualifications are deemed appropriate for the job. Senators also use confirmation hearings to voice their constituents' concerns and, when relevant, to find out what the nominee may do for their states or regions.

Senators also try to extract promises from nominees that they will be responsive and cooperative once they are on the job. According to congressional scholars Roger H. Davidson and Walter J. Oleszek, "Senate committees usually elicit the following promise from nominees they have confirmed: 'The nomination was approved subject to the nominee's commitment to respond to any requests to appear and testify before any duly constituted committee of the Senate.'"[14]

There is considerable variation in the way committees handle nominations. A committee may require nominees to fill out lengthy questionnaires and respond to written questions from members; conduct its own background investigations, in addition to those already performed by the executive branch; impose financial disclosure requirements more stringent than those re-

quired by federal ethics laws; and hold hearings that may focus more on a nominee's political convictions than on his or her professional credentials.

Most nomination hearings are routine, although some have turned into grueling inquisitions. Nominees have been known to ask the president to withdraw their names rather than face such an ordeal.

"The Senate's review of executive appointees has become more thorough, independent, and procedurally consistent during the last two decades," political scientist Christopher J. Deering concluded in a 1987 study of the appointment process. "Unfortunately, the process has also become more tedious, time-consuming, and intrusive for the nominees. For some, this price is too high."[15]

For many years it was unusual for Supreme Court nominees to be invited to appear before the Senate Judiciary Committee. Felix Frankfurter, who received such an invitation in 1939, noted that on only one previous occasion had a Supreme Court nominee testified before the committee. Frankfurter originally declined the committee's invitation but later appeared at the committee's request. Ten years later the committee, by a 5–4 vote, invited Court nominee Sherman Minton, a former senator, to appear before it. But when Minton questioned the propriety of such an appearance, the committee reversed itself and reported the nomination favorably to the Senate.

These precedents notwithstanding, in recent years Supreme Court nominees have been expected to testify at hearings on their nominations. Justice Abe Fortas in 1968 became the first nominee for chief justice ever to appear before the committee and the first sitting justice, except for recess appointees, ever to do so.

When hearings on a nomination have been completed, the full committee may report the nomination favorably, unfavorably, or without recommendation, or it may simply take no action at all.

The confirmation burden is unevenly distributed among Senate committees. Judiciary (judges, U.S. attorneys, and U.S. marshals), Commerce (regulatory agencies), Foreign Relations (ambassadors), and Armed Services (primarily military) are among those committees with major confirmation duties. Most committees have some confirmation responsibility, the most prominent being to review the nominees to head the executive departments and agencies within their jurisdiction.

FLOOR ACTION

Once a nomination is reported out of committee, the report is filed with the legislative clerk and then placed on the executive calendar by the executive clerk. Nominations that reach the floor frequently are called up en bloc and usually approved without objection. The question takes the following form: "Will the Senate advise and consent to this nomination?" Controversial nominations may be debated at length, but few of them are brought to the floor unless sufficient votes for confirmation can be mustered.

In 1987 the Senate denied confirmation to Appeals Court Judge Robert H. Bork, center, who had been nominated to the Supreme Court by President Ronald Reagan. Bork is shown here as he arrived for hearings of the Senate Judiciary Committee.

Since 1929 Senate rules (Rule XXXI) have provided that nominations shall be considered in open session unless the Senate, by a majority vote in open session, decides to go into closed session to consider a nomination. Before 1929 the customary practice was to consider nominations in closed session (also called executive session), and votes taken in executive session were not supposed to be made public. Today senators may make public the votes they cast in closed session.

Pending nominations may not be put to a Senate vote on the day they are received or on the day they are reported from committee, except by unanimous consent. They may be approved, rejected, or returned (recommitted) to the committee that considered the nominee. Confirmation requires the approval of a majority of the senators present and voting. Once the Senate votes to confirm or reject a nomination, a motion to reconsider the vote may be made on the day the vote is taken or on either of the next two days the Senate is in session.

Pending nominations expire at the end of each congressional session.

HOLDS

While the number of nominations effectively controlled by senators in their home states has declined, another aspect of senatorial courtesy—the power to place a "hold" on a nomination to delay floor action—has increased dramatically. Usually the leadership of a senator's party will honor the hold; to do otherwise would be self-defeating since a hold request usually carries an implicit threat of a filibuster. A senator simply may be waiting for more information or want to be present when the nomination is brought to the floor. But he or she also could be using the nominee as leverage on the administration or other senators. Holds on nominations, as well as legislative matters, can be especially potent tools in the waning days of a session when a delay of just a day or two can prove devastating.

Sometimes a hold can turn a noncontroversial nomination into a political football. In the 1980s and 1990s, for example, Sen. Jesse Helms stalled dozens of diplomatic nominations of presidents of both parties, sometimes because he opposed the nominee but frequently because he wanted to extract concessions from the White House.

The increased use of holds in the past few decades has had its critics. Political scientist Deering found that holds were being used for political gains that had nothing to do with the quality or integrity of nominees and that "the use of nominees as, in effect, hostages has undermined the integrity of the system."[16]

In the past holds could be placed anonymously. Attempts to

remove the cloak of secrecy failed until early 1999, when the bipartisan leadership of the Senate announced that in the future a senator placing a hold on a matter would have to inform its sponsors and the committee with jurisdiction over it. The senator also would have to provide written notification to party leaders. The change would make it easier for members to push for consideration of a stalled nomination or measure, without wasting time trying to discover who had placed the hold.

But the change did not end the controversy over the larger issue of members' ability to place holds on nominations to block floor action. In early October 1999, for example, Democratic attempts to break holds on two nominees to the 9th U.S. Circuit Court of appeals—Richard A. Paez and Marsha Berzon—were defeated on the Senate floor in party-line votes. Paez had been first nominated in January 1996 and Berzon in January 1998. Both had been approved by the Judiciary Committee.

RECESS APPOINTMENTS

The Constitution provides in Article II, Section 2, that "the President shall have Power to fill up all Vacancies that may happen during the Recess of the Senate, by granting Commissions which shall expire at the End of their next Session." A recess is held to mean periods longer than a holiday observance or a brief and temporary adjournment.[17] Such appointments are a remnant of the days when senators could be out of touch with Washington for months, as they traveled to and from their states on horseback.

The ambiguities of the constitutional language have produced repeated controversies between the president and the Senate. One point of contention has been the constitutional meaning of the word *happen*. If it means "happen to occur," then the president can only fill offices that become vacant after the Senate adjourns. If it means "happen to exist," the president can fill any vacancy existing while the Senate is in recess, whatever the cause.

President Washington, taking a strict view of his powers, sought specific Senate authorization to make recess appointments of military officers created by a bill enacted near the end of a session. Madison opted for a broad construction. His recess appointment of envoys to negotiate a peace treaty with Great Britain brought outcries from the Senate that a recess appointment could not be made to an office never before filled. However, resolutions protesting Madison's action never came to a vote, and the appointments ultimately were confirmed.[18]

Although the recess appointment debate continued for years, it gradually became accepted practice that the president could make recess appointments to fill any vacancies, no matter how they arose. However, their use has in effect been restrained by a federal law that prohibits payment of salary to any person appointed during a recess of the Senate if the vacancy existed while the Senate was in session, until the appointee has been confirmed by the Senate. This prohibition does not apply if the vacancy occurred during the last thirty days of a congressional session or if the Senate failed to act on a nomination the president had submitted to it before adjournment.

Disputes over recess appointments continue to erupt from time to time. In 1985, for example, Senate Majority Leader Robert C. Byrd, D-W.Va., placed a two-month hold on virtually all executive nominees to protest the large number of recess appointments made by President Ronald Reagan. Byrd was particularly angered that Reagan made recess appointments during the Senate's five-week August recess. He and other senators felt the president was misusing his authority to make temporary appointments during congressional recesses. Byrd finally withdrew his hold on 5,871 nominations after the White House agreed to notify the Senate in advance of all future recess appointments.

Tempers flared in 1997 when it appeared that the Clinton administration might use a recess appointment to install a nominee for a high-ranking Justice Department post. Clinton's choice for assistant attorney general for civil rights, former NAACP Legal Defense and Education Fund lawyer Bill Lann Lee, had become the embodiment of a fight between Congress and the White House over affirmative action and racial quotas. When Lee's nomination was blocked in the Senate Judiciary Committee, some of Lee's supporters urged Clinton to give him a recess appointment. But recess appointments traditionally had been used to fill noncontroversial positions, and senators from both parties, including Byrd, warned against such a move. Clinton avoided a fight over the Senate's confirmation powers by opting instead to make Lee "acting" assistant attorney general.

The battle over Lee was reignited in early 1999 when Senate Judiciary Committee Chairman Orrin Hatch called on the White House to come up with "a confirmable candidate" for the civil rights post and Clinton formally resubmitted Lee's nomination. Hatch had insisted that Lee was covered by language in a 1998 omnibus spending law—PL 105–277—that had limited most "acting" appointments to 210 days. The Justice Department, however, maintained that the provision was not retroactive and Lee could stay in his post indefinitely.

NOTES

1. G. Calvin Mackenzie, *The Politics of Presidential Appointments* (New York: Free Press, 1981), 134.

2. *Obstacle Course: The Report of the Twentieth Century Fund Task Force on the Presidential Appointment Process* (New York: Twentieth Century Fund Press, 1996), 7.

3. Quoted in *Congressional Quarterly Almanac, 1997*, vol. 53 (Washington, D.C.: Congressional Quarterly, 1998), 8–51.

4. Ibid.

5. Quoted in Roger H. Davidson and Walter J. Oleszek, *Congress and Its Members*, 7th ed. (Washington, D.C.: CQ Press, 2000), 315.

6. Quoted in *Congressional Quarterly Almanac, 1997*, 8–51.

7. Quoted in Joseph P. Harris, *The Advice and Consent of the Senate: A Study of the Confirmation of Appointments by the United States Senate* (Westport, Conn.: Greenwood Press, 1968), 29. Unless otherwise noted, this book was the principal source for the account of presidential appointments through the Truman administration. For the Eisenhower administration and subsequent periods the principal sources were the *Congressional Record*

and other official documents, and Congressional Quarterly's *Almanac* and *Weekly Report* for various years.

8. Quoted in George H. Haynes, *The Senate of the United States: Its History and Practice* (Boston: Houghton Mifflin, 1938), vol. 2, 724.

9. Quoted in *Congressional Quarterly Almanac, 1997*, 8–50.

10. *Obstacle Course*, 148.

11. Quoted in *Congressional Quarterly Almanac, 1997*, 5–20.

12. Ibid., 5–19.

13. The following discussion of the removal power is drawn from Haynes, *The Senate of the United States*, vol. 2, 785–837.

14. Davidson and Oleszek, *Congress and Its Members*, 314.

15. Christopher J. Deering, "Damned If You Do and Damned If You Don't: The Senate's Role in the Appointment Process," in *The In-and-Outers: Presidential Appointees and Transient Government in Washington*, ed. G. Calvin Mackenzie (Baltimore: Johns Hopkins University Press, 1987), 119.

16. Ibid., 117.

17. Joan Biskupic and Elder Witt. *Congressional Quarterly's Guide to the U.S. Supreme Court*, 3rd ed. (Washington, D.C.: Congressional Quarterly, 1997), 220.

18. Harris, *The Advice and Consent of the Senate*, 255–257.

SELECTED BIBLIOGRAPHY

Abraham, Henry Julian. *Justices, Presidents, and Senators: A History of the U.S. Supreme Court Appointments from Washington to Clinton*. New York: Roman and Littlefield, 1999.

Arnold, R. Douglas. *Congress and the Bureaucracy: A Theory of Influence*. New Haven, Conn.: Yale University Press, 1979.

Bork, Robert H. *The Tempting of America: The Political Seduction of the Law*. New York: Free Press, 1990.

Bronner, Ethan. *Battle for Justice: How the Bork Nomination Shook America*. New York: Norton, 1989.

Carter, Stephen L. *The Confirmation Mess: Cleaning up the Federal Appointment Process*. New York: Basic Books, 1994.

Corson, John J., and R. Shale Paul. *Men Near the Top: Filling Key Posts in the Federal Service*. Baltimore: Johns Hopkins University Press, 1966.

Corwin, Edward S. *The President's Removal Power under the Constitution*. New York: National Municipal League, 1927.

Fenno, Richard F. *The President's Cabinet: An Analysis of the Period from Wilson to Eisenhower*. Cambridge, Mass.: Harvard University Press, 1959.

Fisher, Louis. *Constitutional Conflicts between Congress and the President*. 4th ed. Lawrence: University Press of Kansas, 1997.

———. *The Politics of Shared Power: Congress and the Executive*. 4th ed. College Station: Texas A&M University Press, 1998.

Harris, Joseph P. *The Advice and Consent of the Senate: A Study of the Confirmation of Appointments by the United States Senate*. Westport, Conn.: Greenwood Press, 1968.

Haynes, George H. *The Senate of the United States: Its History and Practice*. 2 vols. Boston: Houghton Mifflin, 1938.

Heclo, Hugh. *A Government of Strangers: Executive Politics in Washington*. Washington, D.C.: Brookings Institution, 1977.

Mackenzie, G. Calvin. *The Politics of Presidential Appointments*. New York: Free Press, 1981.

———, ed. *The In-and-Outers: Presidential Appointees and Transient Government in Washington*. Baltimore: Johns Hopkins University Press, 1987.

Maltese, John A. *The Selling of Supreme Court Nominees*. Baltimore: Johns Hopkins University Press, 1995.

Riddick, Floyd M. *The United States Congress: Organization and Procedure*. Manassas, Va.: National Capitol Publishers, 1949.

Rogers, Lindsay. *The American Senate*. New York: Knopf, 1926.

Rothman, David J. *Politics and Power: The United States Senate, 1869–1901*. New York: Atheneum, 1969.

Simon, Paul. *Advice and Consent: Clarence Thomas, Robert Bork, and the Intriguing History of the Supreme Court's Nomination Battles*. Washington, D.C.: National Press Books, 1992.

Thurber, James A. *Divided Democracy: Cooperation and Conflict Between the President and Congress*. Washington, D.C.: CQ Press, 1991.

Tribe, Laurence H. *God Save This Honorable Court: How the Choice of Justices Can Change our Lives*. New York: Random House, 1985.

Twentieth Century Fund. *Obstacle Course: The Report of the Twentieth Century Fund Task Force on the Presidential Appointment Process*. New York: Twentieth Century Fund Press, 1996.

Warren, Charles. *The Supreme Court in United States History*. Boston: Little, Brown, 1926.

CHAPTER 8

Regulation of Commerce

"The Congress shall have Power . . . To regulate Commerce with foreign Nations, and among the several States, and with the Indian Tribes."—U.S. Constitution: Article I, Section 8, clause 3

WITH THIS simple grant of authority the Founding Fathers attempted to remedy one of the basic weaknesses of the federal government under the Articles of Confederation. Each state had the right to regulate its own trade, effectively preventing the national government from settling trade disputes or retaliating against Britain for closing the West Indies to American shipping after the Revolutionary War.

To rectify that situation, the drafters of the new federal Constitution wrote a broad and general "commerce clause," without an accompanying statement of the powers reserved to the states or a definition of terms. Only a few limitations could be applied from other parts of the Constitution, and only one—a provision forbidding Congress to lay a tax or duty on articles exported from any state—has had much practical significance.

Broad as the grant of power seemed to be, it nevertheless remained for judicial decisions to determine the full scope of the commerce clause. The evolution of the commerce clause has not been an easy one. "Of all the powers granted to government, perhaps none has resulted in more controversies and litigation than the power to regulate commerce," political scientists Lee Epstein and Thomas G. Walker have written. "Concern over the exercise of this power was present at the Constitution's birth and continues today."[1]

Chief Justice John Marshall gave the commerce power an expansive interpretation in the landmark case *Gibbons v. Ogden* in 1824. On behalf of the Supreme Court, he emphatically asserted the supremacy of federal control over commerce with foreign countries and between the states.

With that declaration, Marshall laid the basis for the Court's subsequent interpretations of the commerce clause. This view has afforded Congress virtually unrestricted authority to regulate all commerce crossing state lines (interstate) and any commerce within a state (intrastate) that in any way affects interstate commerce.

More than a century passed before the Supreme Court gave full approval to Marshall's expansive interpretation. For several decades after *Gibbons v. Ogden,* most cases before the Court involved the question of state power to regulate commerce in the absence of federal controls. Only in the last decades of the nineteenth century did Congress begin actively to regulate interstate commerce. With the Interstate Commerce Act of 1887 and the Sherman Antitrust Act of 1890, Congress responded to a changing economic scene in which post–Civil War industrial growth produced interstate railroads and large national corporations

and trusts. Industrial concentration often meant less competition and higher prices. The laissez-faire doctrine of little or no government regulation of business became less acceptable to farmers, laborers, and consumers.

However, the conservative Court of that era often took a far narrower view of the commerce clause than Marshall had. For years the Supreme Court held to the view that manufacturing and production were not a part of interstate commerce and that the commerce power extended only to activities that affected such commerce directly. That view from the bench was altered only after President Franklin D. Roosevelt, disturbed by its rejections of key blocks of New Deal legislation, threatened the Supreme Court's very independence with a plan to enlarge its membership.

Roosevelt's "Court-packing" plan failed, but the Court's subsequent rulings were more favorable to him. A majority of the justices came around to the view in 1937 that the commerce power embraced activities that had an "effect upon commerce," however indirectly, thereby upholding the federal regulation of labor-management relations. Four years later the Court upheld a federal minimum wage law, acceding to the congressional opinion that substandard labor conditions unconstitutionally burdened interstate commerce.

Those rulings and subsequent ones over the ensuing decades repeatedly reaffirmed Congress's domination over commerce. In addition to its use for ever more detailed supervision of the commercial life of the nation by Congress and the executive branch, the power was extended further to accomplish such goals as prohibiting racial discrimination in public accommodations and regulating environmental pollutants.

The Court's modern interpretation of the commerce power was widely viewed as "settled law."[2] Typical were the views of constitutional scholar Charles A. Lofgren, who wrote in the mid-1980s that the commerce clause "stands dramatically revealed as a fountain of vast federal power. . . . The clause's text provides only an inkling of its present meaning and potential."[3]

A decision a decade later had some questioning whether the era of a seemingly boundless federal commerce power was coming to a close. In a 1996 decision striking down a federal law that prohibited people from carrying guns near local schools, the Court held that lawmakers had overstepped their authority to intervene in local affairs. It was only the second time in nearly sixty years that the Court had found unconstitutional a congressional exercise of the commerce power.

The Commerce Clause
Enacted and Defined

The necessity for national control over interstate and foreign commerce was the immediate occasion for the calling of the Constitutional Convention in 1787. "Most of our political evils," James Madison had written to Thomas Jefferson the previous year, "may be traced to our commercial ones." Under the Articles of Confederation, adopted during the Revolutionary War, Congress had power to regulate trade only with the Indians; the control of interstate and foreign commerce was left to the states.

But commercial regulation by the several states proved increasingly chaotic after the Revolutionary War. Each state attempted to build up its own prosperity at the expense of its neighbors. Justice William Johnson, in a concurring opinion in *Gibbons v. Ogden*, described the situation that had developed:

For a century the states had submitted, with murmurs, to the commercial restrictions imposed by the parent state; and now, finding themselves in the unlimited possession of those powers over their own commerce, which they had so long been deprived of and so earnestly coveted, that selfish principle which, well controlled, is so salutary, and which, unrestricted, is so unjust and tyrannical, guided by inexperience and jealousy, began to show itself in iniquitous laws and impolitic measures, from which grew up a conflict of commercial regulations, destructive to the harmony of the states, and fatal to their commercial interests abroad.

State legislatures imposed tariffs on goods from other states as well as from foreign countries. Thus, New York levied duties on firewood from Connecticut and cabbages from New Jersey. "The commerce which Massachusetts found it to her interest to encourage," wrote John Bach McMaster, "Virginia found it to hers to restrict. New York would not protect the trade in indigo and pitch. South Carolina cared nothing for the success of the fur interests."[4]

Seaport states financed their governments through duties on European goods passing through their harbors but destined for consumption in neighboring states. Madison described the plight of those states not having seaports: "New Jersey placed between Philadelphia and New York was likened to a cask tapped at both ends; and North Carolina, between Virginia and South Carolina, to a patient bleeding at both arms."

Different currencies in each of the thirteen states likewise hampered commerce. If merchants were able to carry on an interstate business in spite of tariff and currency difficulties, they often had trouble collecting their bills. Local courts and juries were less zealous in protecting the rights of distant creditors than those of their neighbors and friends.

The chaotic condition of interstate trade prompted the General Assembly of Virginia, in 1786, to adopt a resolution proposing a joint meeting of commissioners appointed by each of the states "to take into consideration the trade of the United States; to examine the relative situations and trade of the said states; [and] to consider how far a uniform system in their commercial regulations may be necessary to their common interest and

their permanent harmony." The action of the Virginia Assembly led to a meeting at Annapolis later in the year of commissioners from five states: Delaware, New Jersey, New York, Pennsylvania, and Virginia.

However, the members of the Annapolis convention thought it inadvisable to act with so few of the colonies represented and instead recommended a general meeting of all the colonies at Philadelphia in 1787.

ADOPTION OF THE COMMERCE CLAUSE

The desirability of uniform regulation of interstate and foreign commerce was so generally recognized that the proposal to give Congress blanket authority in this field occasioned comparatively little discussion at the Philadelphia convention. Some controversy arose over an attempt by the South to limit the power of a congressional majority to regulate commerce. The southern states feared that the North might seek to dominate their commerce. Charles Pinckney of South Carolina proposed, therefore, that "all laws regulating commerce shall require the assent of two-thirds of the members present in each house," but this proposal was defeated.

"Had Pinckney's proposal been adopted," wrote historian Charles Warren, "the course of American history would have been vitally changed. Enactment of protective tariffs might have been practically impossible. The whole political relations between the South and North growing out of commercial legislation would have been changed. The Nullification movement in the 1830s, which arose out of opposition to a northern tariff, might not have occurred."[5]

In return for the South's acceptance of the unlimited power of a majority in Congress to regulate commerce, the northern states agreed to a ban on export taxes and agreed not to prohibit the importation of slaves before the year 1808. Many persons consider it remarkable that so important a part of the Constitution as the commerce clause should be so briefly expressed and should leave so much to future determination. Warren observed that "at that time . . . there seems to have been no doubt as to its meaning." The great differences of opinion as to what the term *commerce* included arose later.

Scholars generally agree that nothing more was immediately intended than that Congress should be empowered to prevent commercial wars among the states. Yet it is not to be doubted that the Framers were aware of the scope of the power granted to Congress. James Monroe pointed out that the commerce clause involved "a radical change in the whole system of our government."

GIBBONS V. OGDEN

Although the federal government's power over interstate commerce was to become one of the most important and conspicuous it possesses, it was so little exercised in the first years of the nation's history that there was no need to define precisely what was meant by commerce "among the several States." Not until thirty-five years after the adoption of the Constitution did a case involving the scope of this power come before the Supreme Court.

The circumstances leading to the Court's decision in the case of *Gibbons v. Ogden* involved precisely the sort of commercial warfare that had prompted the drafting of the Constitution in the first place. New York in 1798 granted to Robert R. Livingston, chancellor of the state, a monopoly over all steamboat operations in New York waters. In partnership with the inventor Robert Fulton, Livingston turned the monopoly into a viable transportation system and in 1811 was granted similar exclusive rights to operate in the waters of the territory of New Orleans.

Those grants prompted the other states to fight back. Connecticut, New Jersey, and Ohio enacted retaliatory measures, closing their waters to ships licensed by the New York monopoly, while five other states granted steamship monopolies of their own. The result was navigational chaos.

The case that broke the monopoly involved Aaron Ogden, a former New Jersey governor (1812–1813), and his partner Thomas Gibbons. They ran a steam-driven ferry between Elizabethtown, New Jersey, and New York City. Ogden in 1815 had acquired a license from the Livingston-Fulton monopoly and Gibbons held a permit under the federal coastal licensing act of 1793 for his two boats. Despite their partnership, Gibbons ran his boats to New York in defiance of the monopoly rights that Ogden held, and in 1819 Ogden sued for an injunction to stop Gibbons's infringement of his rights under the monopoly. New York courts ordered Gibbons to halt his ferry service. Gibbons appealed to the Supreme Court, arguing that his federal license took precedence over the state-granted monopoly license and that he should be allowed to continue his ferrying in New York waters.

The questions before the Supreme Court were: Did Congress have power under the commerce clause to regulate navigation and, if so, was that power exclusive? Could federal regulation of commerce leave room for the states to act?

Delivering the Court's opinion on March 2, 1824, Chief Justice Marshall refused to construe the federal commerce power narrowly or to omit navigation from its scope:

The subject to be regulated is commerce; and . . . to ascertain the extent of the power, it becomes necessary to settle the meaning of the word. . . . Commerce undoubtedly is traffic, but it is something more; it is intercourse. It describes the commercial intercourse between nations, and parts of nations, in all its branches, and is regulated by prescribing rules for carrying on that intercourse. The mind can scarcely conceive a system for regulating commerce between nations, which shall exclude all laws concerning navigation. . . . All America understands, and has uniformly understood, the word 'commerce' to comprehend navigation. . . . The power over commerce, including navigation, was one of the primary objects for which the people . . . adopted their government and must have been contemplated in forming it.

The second question, Marshall said, was to what commerce did congressional power apply? Certainly it applied to commerce with foreign nations, and, Marshall said, it also applied to

In a landmark 1824 decision, Chief Justice John Marshall emphatically asserted the supremacy of federal control over commerce with foreign countries and between the states.

" 'commerce among the several states.' The word 'among' means intermingled with. A thing which is among others, is intermingled with them. Commerce among the states cannot stop at the external boundary line of each state, but may be introduced into the interior."

But Marshall did not find that the commerce power foreclosed all state regulation: "It is not intended to say that these words comprehend that commerce which is completely internal, which is carried on between man and man in a state, or between different parts of the same state, and which does not extend to or affect other states. Such a power would be inconvenient or unnecessary." With regard to the supremacy of the federal power, Marshall said: "This power, like all others vested in Congress, is complete in itself, may be exercised to its utmost extent, and acknowledges no limitations, other than are prescribed in the Constitution."

Marshall did not address the question whether states could regulate areas Congress had not regulated. Nor did he answer the question of whether the states could regulate commerce simultaneously with Congress. His opinion settled only two points—first, that navigation was commerce and, second, that where state exercise of its power conflicts with federal exercise of the commerce power, the state must give way. In making the second point, Marshall laid the groundwork for extending the

From the beginning, the congressional power to regulate foreign commerce has been complete. The constitutional grant encompasses "every species of commercial intercourse between the United States and foreign nations. No sort of trade can be carried on between this country and any other, to which this power does not extend," wrote Chief Justice John Marshall in *Gibbons v. Ogden* (1824), in the classic interpretation of the commerce clause.

The power to regulate commerce is inextricably tied to the powers over foreign relations and fiscal policies. Using these powers, Congress may pass legislation to set tariffs; regulate international shipping, aviation, and communications; and establish embargoes against unfriendly countries. In conjunction with its powers to coin money, regulate its value, and borrow funds for government activities, Congress may authorize U.S. participation in and appropriate contributions for international financing, banking, and monetary systems such as the International Development Association and the World Bank.

The commerce power may be used to promote, inhibit, or simply make rules for trade with other nations. It may be implemented by treaty or executive agreement as well as by acts of Congress.

PROMOTION OF TRADE

Policies to encourage trade may take the form of opening up new markets for U.S. goods in other countries or securing favorable conditions for American traders abroad. The earliest actions in this field were efforts to replace markets lost when the nation won its independence from England. Modern laws have ranged from antitrust exemptions for exporters to the use of tariff reductions to stimulate trade.

Efforts to encourage American shipping have ranged from legislation providing preferential duties for goods imported in U.S. vessels (first enacted in 1789) to federal subsidies (since 1936) for merchant ships that sailed under the U.S. flag.

TARIFFS

Historically, the predominant mechanism to restrict foreign trade has been the protective tariff. The first major business of the House of Representatives in 1789 was to devise a tariff schedule. Unlike many later tariff laws, this one had as its chief objective the raising of revenue to finance the new government.

Between the end of the Civil War and the Great Depression, Congress devoted an inordinate amount of time to tariff making. Affecting actually or potentially the varied interests of many segments of commercial life, a general revision of the tariff inevitably involved a great amount of political maneuvering. Moreover, members of Congress hardly could hope to master the intricacies of complicated tariff schedules. A measure of flexibility was introduced in 1922, when the Fordney-McCumber Tariff Act gave the president authority to adjust tariff rates based on the recommendations of the U.S. Tariff Commission, which previously had only investigative powers.

The Roosevelt administration's economic recovery program in 1934 included expansion of American exports, and the president proposed that Congress delegate some of its constitutional powers by authorizing him to negotiate U.S. trade agreements with other nations. The administration asked authority to cut tariffs by as much as 50 percent in return for equivalent concessions from other nations. Prodded by Secretary of State Cordell Hull, the Democratic-controlled 73rd Congress, over nearly unanimous Republican opposition, made this grant of authority in the Trade Agreements Act of 1934. Since then, no serious efforts have been made to restore congressional tariff making in place of executive branch negotiation of bilateral and, after World War II, multilateral trade agreements.

NONTARIFF BARRIERS

Nontariff barriers to the free flow of trade range from import quotas to embargoes. Although export taxes are forbidden under the Constitution, Congress can control export trade through licensing or other means. Thus it may bar shipment of strategic materials to hostile countries or restrict exports that would deplete essential domestic supplies. Congress has curbed imports that would interfere with domestic regulatory programs (such as agricultural commodities under production-control and price-support programs). It also has enacted "Antidumping," "Buy American," and "Ship American" legislation.

The ultimate restraint on foreign commerce is the embargo, which suspends commerce completely with specified countries. Examples include the embargo President Jimmy Carter imposed on the Soviet Union in 1980 after that country invaded Afghanistan, and the one President George Bush imposed on Iraq in 1990 after it invaded Kuwait. President Bill Clinton in 1995 tightened sanctions against Iran that had originally been imposed by President Ronald Reagan in response to Iran's involvement in the 1983 bombing of a U.S. Marine barracks in Beirut.

Congress pushed through legislation during the Bush and Clinton administrations to tighten the long-standing trade embargo against Cuba—in effect since 1962—in the hope of finally toppling the communist regime of Fidel Castro, which lost its lifeline after the fall of communism in Eastern Europe and the Soviet Union. Congress even went so far as to codify the 1962 Cuba embargo in 1996 legislation. Previously, the embargo had been imposed by executive orders and regulations, which meant the president could lift or ease it without congressional approval. The new law took that decision, a jealously guarded presidential prerogative, out of the hands of the White House and gave it to Congress.

commerce power to forms of transportation and communications not yet contemplated. By leaving the power to regulate wholly internal commerce to the states only so long as that commerce did not "extend to or affect" other states, he planted the seeds that eventually would allow Congress to regulate the manufacture of goods and matters that themselves were not in commerce but were deemed to affect interstate commerce.

GIBBONS AND THE STATES

Congress did not make much use of the power claimed for it by Marshall until later in the century. Between 1824, when *Gibbons v. Ogden* was decided, and the 1880s, when the need for federal regulation of the nation's railroads and interstate corporations became apparent, the Court's rulings on the commerce power focused primarily on determining when state actions impinged unconstitutionally on the federal commerce power.

The decision was politically popular except with staunch Republicans, including Thomas Jefferson. He wrote a friend in 1825 that he viewed "with the deepest affliction, the rapid strides with which the federal branch of our government is advancing towards the usurpation of all the rights reserved to the states." It was also disturbing the slave owners, who feared that Congress might invoke the commerce power to wrest control over slavery from the states and abolish it.

Before Marshall's death in 1835 the Supreme Court handed down two more decisions defining the range of state power to affect commerce. In *Brown v. Maryland* (1827), it forbade states to tax imports so long as they remained in their original package. In *Willson v. Blackbird Creek Marsh Co.* (1829), it held that a state could exercise its police power over matters affecting interstate commerce in the absence of conflicting federal legislation.

Under Marshall's successor, Roger B. Taney, the Court showed uncertainty as to the proper line between state and federal regulation of commerce. Taney maintained that Congress and the states held the commerce power concurrently; Justice John McLean held that it was exclusive to Congress. Rarely did any one doctrine win a majority. If it did, the majority dissolved when the next case was heard.

The conflict was temporarily resolved in *Cooley v. Board of Wardens of the Port of Philadelphia* (1852) when the Court upheld state regulation of city harbor pilots and adopted the so-called selective exclusiveness doctrine. In his majority opinion, Justice Benjamin R. Curtis shifted the focus of judicial scrutiny from the power itself to the nature of the subject to be regulated. Some fields of commerce were of necessity national in nature and demanded a uniform regulation provided by Congress, he said. Others demanded local regulation to accommodate local circumstances and needs. This doctrine left it up to the Court to determine on a case-by-case basis which matters were reserved to Congress and which to the states. Although the justifications for it varied, this case-by-case review of Congress's exercise of the commerce power continued for nearly a century.

EARLY EXERCISE OF THE COMMERCE POWER

For much of the nation's young life, most commerce was carried by water and so congressional regulation of interstate commerce primarily concerned navigation. Although *Gibbons v. Ogden* held that navigation was a form of commerce, the decision did not settle the question of whether the federal power over navigation was exclusive. In the 1829 *Willson* decision, the Marshall Court sustained Delaware's right to build a dam across a small but navigable tidal creek as an exercise of its police power. Marshall conveniently ignored the fact that the owner of the ship protesting the dam as an obstruction to interstate com-

---

COASTAL LICENSING ACT

In one of the earliest exercises of its commerce power, the First Congress in 1789 enacted a statute establishing a system for registering and regulating ships or vessels engaged in coastal trade and fishing activities. This act was soon replaced by a 1792 vessel registration law and a 1793 law licensing and regulating coastal trade and fishing vessels. These early laws, although periodically revised, remained the basis for documentation laws until 1980, when a new law streamlining the process was enacted.

Because the major commercial transportation system in the country for the first fifty years was water-based and partly because Congress seldom exercised its commerce power until late in the nineteenth century, the federal coastal licensing act played a key role in several major Supreme Court cases interpreting the commerce power. Among them were:

• *Gibbons v. Ogden* (1824), holding that Congress's power to regulate navigation between two states preempted a state's power.

• *Willson v. Blackbird Creek Marsh Co.* (1829), declaring that states may regulate interstate commerce in the absence of conflicting federal legislation.

• *Pennsylvania v. Wheeling and Belmont Bridge Co.* (1852), ruling that a bridge obstructing the passage of ships interfered with the congressional power to regulate commerce through the coastal licensing act. (Congress later nullified the ruling by declaring the bridge was not an obstruction.)

• *Veazie v. Moor* (1852), deciding that the federal law did not automatically entitle licensed vessels to operate on wholly intrastate waters.

In modern times, the Court ruled in the 1977 case of *Douglas v. Seacoast Products, Inc.* that a Virginia law denying certain fishing rights to federally licensed noncitizens was in conflict with the federal law. In the 1978 case of *Ray v. Atlantic Richfield Co.*, the Court struck down a Washington state law requiring state licensing of pilots on tankers entering and leaving the Puget Sound. The Court said the law was in conflict with federal power to regulate pilots on tankers licensed under the coastal act.

Sen. George W. Norris, right, waged a long campaign for federal development of public power plants on the Tennessee River. President Franklin D. Roosevelt signed legislation establishing the Tennessee Valley Authority in 1933.

merce was licensed under the same federal law that figured so prominently in the chief justice's reasoning in the *Gibbons* case. *(See box, Coastal Licensing Act, p. 311.)*

But in 1852 the Court ruled in *Pennsylvania v. Wheeling and Belmont Bridge Co.* that a bridge on the Ohio River had to be raised, so that ships could pass under it, or taken down. The Court held that the bridge not only obstructed interstate commerce but violated a congressionally sanctioned compact between Virginia and Kentucky in which the two states agreed to keep the river free of such obstructions. However, Congress immediately passed legislation declaring that the bridge was not an obstruction and requiring instead that ships be refitted so they could pass under it. The Supreme Court upheld that law in 1856. *(Pennsylvania v. Wheeling and Belmont Bridge Co.)*

In 1866 the Court reaffirmed Congress's complete control over navigable waters "which are accessible from a State other than those in which they lie." *(Gilman v. City of Philadelphia)* In 1871 congressional authority over navigation was further extended to permit federal regulation of a boat that transported goods in interstate commerce even though the boat operated solely on waters entirely within one state. *(The Daniel Ball)* In an opinion that was clearly a precursor of the "stream of commerce" doctrine, the Court said: "So far as [the ship] was

employed in transporting goods destined for other States, or goods brought from without the limits of Michigan and destined to places within that State, she was engaged in commerce between the States, and however limited that commerce may have been, she was . . . subject to the legislation of Congress. She was employed as an instrument of that commerce; for whenever a commodity has begun to move as an article of trade from one State to another, commerce in that commodity between the States has commenced." *(See "The 'Stream of Commerce,'" p. 316.)*

HYDROELECTRIC POWER

Control over the nation's waterways eventually led to disputes over who controlled, and thus benefited from the sale of, the hydroelectric power generated by those waterways. In 1913 the Supreme Court sustained an act of Congress allowing the federal government to sell excess electricity generated as a result of the improved navigability of a stream. *(United States v. Chandler-Dunbar Water Co.)* The Court reaffirmed that opinion in 1931, ruling in *Arizona v. California* that it would not inquire into the motives behind congressional waterways projects, in this case the Boulder Canyon Project Act, so long as the waterway concerned was navigable and the project not unrelated to the control of navigation.

Congress in 1933 created the Tennessee Valley Authority (TVA) to bring about a comprehensive development program in the Tennessee Valley that included flood control, power generation, and recreational, agricultural, and industrial development. Although the law establishing the TVA invoked no extension of federal authority over navigation, the TVA represented a major source of government-sponsored competition for the private power companies in the region. Its constitutionality was challenged immediately, but the Court upheld the TVA. (*Ashwander v. Tennessee Valley Authority*, 1936; *Tennessee Electric Power Co. v. Tennessee Valley Authority*, 1939)

NONNAVIGABLE WATERS

Congressional power over the nation's waterways was made virtually complete in 1940 when the Court held that federal authority even extended to some waters that were not at the time navigable. In *United States v. Appalachian Electric Power Co.*, the Court said the Federal Power Commission had the authority to regulate dam construction on a portion of Virginia's New River that might be made navigable after construction of the dam.

RAILROADS AND COMMERCE

The federal commerce power was extended to railroads less directly than to navigation, but ultimately it became just as complete. Initially the federal government's role toward the railroads was one of promotion, not regulation. Because the railroads were essential to military and postal operations, Congress aided their development through charters, rights-of-way, land grants, loans, and subsidies. But the first railway lines were operated locally, and therefore most early rail regulation essentially was left to the states. As late as 1877, the Supreme Court upheld the authority of the states to set rates for hauling freight and passengers within their boundaries. (*Munn v. Illinois*)

Business "panics" in the 1870s and 1880s, and the steadily expanding western frontier, led to the consolidation of the railroads into vast interstate networks. State regulation became increasingly less effective in the face of public demands for an end to price-fixing practices. Western and southern farmers complained that unfair rates drove up the price of manufactured goods they bought from the East and drove down the price of grain they shipped to that region.

Beginning in 1878, Congress for several years debated but was unable to pass legislation to regulate interstate rail commerce. Then, in 1886, the Supreme Court essentially ended state authority over interstate railroads by holding that the states could not set intrastate freight rates for goods if they were destined to cross state lines. Basing its decision in part on the selective exclusiveness doctrine accepted in the 1852 *Cooley* decision, the Court in the case of *Wabash, St. Louis & Pacific Railway Co. v. Illinois* found that "this species of regulation is one which must be, if established at all, of a general and national character, and cannot be safely and wisely remitted to local rules and local regulations."

Creation of the ICC

The decision virtually forced Congress to provide for federal regulation of interstate railroads. The Interstate Commerce Act of 1887 stipulated that all rates should be reasonable and just, and it prohibited rebate and price-fixing practices. To enforce the law, the act set up the Interstate Commerce Commission (ICC), which was given authority to issue cease-and-desist orders to halt any railroad found in violation of the act's provisions. The ICC was not given specific power to set rates or adjust those it found to be unreasonable, and it was unclear whether Congress intended the commission to have those powers. That determination fell to the Supreme Court.

At the time the ICC was created and for several years thereafter, a majority of justices on the Supreme Court opposed most government regulation, federal or state, that would impinge on the free development of business and industry. Moreover, many of the justices had been corporation lawyers before coming to the Court; interstate railroads had been former clients of three of the justices, including Chief Justice Melville W. Fuller. The Court viewed the ICC with little pleasure and in 1897 stripped the fledgling commission of its essential regulatory authority, holding that Congress had granted it no rate-fixing powers. The Court majority also thought that the power to establish rates was a legislative function that constitutionally could not be delegated to an executive branch agency without violating the separation of powers. (*Interstate Commerce Commission v. Brimson*, 1894; *Interstate Commerce Commission v. Cincinnati, New Orleans and Texas Pacific Railway Co.*, 1897; *Interstate Commerce Commission v. Alabama-Midland Railway Co.*, 1897)

The ICC was left toothless and the practices that led to its formation resumed with full force. Renewed demands from the public as well as from some of the rail companies encouraged Congress, in 1906, to revive the ICC and authorize it to adjust rates it deemed to be unreasonable and unfair. The Court upheld that law in 1910 (*Interstate Commerce Commission v. Chicago, Rock Island & Pacific Railway Co.*), and the same year Congress passed the Mann-Elkins Act, giving the commission authority to set a rate structure for the entire railroad system. The railroads challenged the act as an unconstitutional delegation of legislative authority, but the Court in 1914 called the contention "without merit" (*United States v. Atchison, Topeka & Santa Fe Railroad Co.*). The Court had now sanctioned what it had forbidden only seventeen years before. As one commentator noted, "the Court, which had long accepted the principle of rate regulation by the states, could find no constitutional reason to refuse to accept the same power when exercised unambiguously by the national government."[6]

Intrastate Rates

With federal control established over interstate rail rates, the next question was whether the federal government could exert any control over intrastate rates and, if so, under what circumstances. The Supreme Court answered that question in 1914 in the *Shreveport Rate Case*. A railroad based in Shreveport,

Louisiana, carried freight and passengers into East Texas in competition with two Texas-based railroads. The rail rates set by Texas officials for the state lines were substantially lower than those set by the ICC for the interstate Shreveport line, giving the Texas railroads a decisive competitive edge. To equalize the competition, the ICC required the intrastate lines to charge the same rates as the interstate rail company. They protested, but the Court upheld the ICC order.

"Wherever the interstate and intrastate transactions of carriers are so related that the government of the one involves the control of the other," the Court wrote, "it is Congress, and not the States, that is entitled to prescribe the final and dominant rule, for otherwise Congress would be denied the exercise of its constitutional authority and the States, and not the Nation, would be supreme in the national field."

With that decision, federal authority to regulate interstate and intrastate rail rates was fully acknowledged, and the Court thereafter endorsed even wider use of the authority. In 1922 it upheld the section of the 1920 Transportation Act that authorized the ICC to set intrastate rates high enough to guarantee the railroads a fair income based on the value of their railway property. (*Railroad Commissioner of Wisconsin v. Chicago, Burlington & Quincy Railroad Co.*) The 1920 law had been passed to return the railroads to private control; they had been run by the government during World War I. (*See box, "Extraordinary Powers during Wartime," p. 315.*)

OTHER COMMON CARRIERS

Having determined that Congress had broad authority to regulate the railroads, the Supreme Court showed little hesitancy in permitting Congress to regulate other common carriers. The *Pipe Line Cases* (1914) upheld Congress's inclusion of oil pipelines under the coverage of the Interstate Commerce Act. In 1927 the Court ruled that transmission of electric power from one state to another was interstate commerce and that rate regulation of that power by the state in which it was produced was an interference with and a burden on interstate commerce. (*Public Utilities Commission of Rhode Island v. Attleboro Steam & Electric Co.*) The Court in 1942 upheld the right of the Federal Power Commission, which had been created by Congress in 1920, to set the price of natural gas extracted in one state and sold wholesale to a distributor in another state. (*Federal Power Commission v. Natural Gas Pipeline Co.*)

Forms of communication across state borders also were held to be interstate commerce. In 1878 the Court ruled in *Pensacola Telegraph Co. v. Western Union Telegraph Co.* that an attempt by Florida to exclude out-of-state telegraph companies by granting a monopoly to a Florida company was a burden on interstate commerce. In 1933 the Court upheld federal regulation of radio transmissions in *Federal Radio Commission v. Nelson Bros.* "No state lines divide the radio waves, and national regulation is not only appropriate but essential to the efficient use of radio facilities," the Court said.

ANTITRUST AND COMMERCE

Simultaneous with the development of railroads into interstate networks was the growth of business combinations or trusts. The trusts were spurred during a depression ("panic") in the mid-1870s when bigger companies bought up smaller, economically troubled ones. With the return of prosperity the trusts grew even bigger, and they often used unsavory methods to drive smaller competitors out of business. By 1900 trusts dominated the steel, oil, sugar, meatpacking, leather, electrical, and tobacco industries.

This threat to the traditional concept of a competitive free-enterprise system was not popular. The public outcry led political party platforms to call on the federal government to control the trusts, and before the congressional elections of 1888 several antitrust bills were offered in Congress. But it was not until 1890 that Congress approved an antitrust measure, sponsored by Sen. John Sherman, R-Ohio.

Even as they worked on the measure, the lawmakers expressed concern about its constitutionality. The law was based on congressional authority to regulate interstate commerce. But many of the trusts involved only the manufacturing phase of commerce, an aspect that was not considered by many to be part of interstate commerce. In its final form, the Sherman Antitrust Act made illegal "every contract, combination in the form of trust or otherwise, or conspiracy, in the restraint of trade or commerce among the several states, or with foreign nations. . . . With that vague language Congress again left it to the courts to determine whether the law reached manufacturing trusts.

The Sugar Trust Case

The Supreme Court gave its first answer to that question in the 1895 case of *United States v. E. C. Knight Co.* Defendants in the suit were the American Sugar Refining Co. and four smaller Philadelphia processors. Through stockholder agreements the larger company had purchased stock in the smaller ones, and the resulting trust controlled more than 90 percent of all the sugar processed in the United States. The federal government's case was prosecuted less than vigorously by Attorney General Richard Olney, who had opposed passage of the Sherman Antitrust Act and later worked to repeal the act. Nevertheless Olney challenged the sugar combination as an illegal restraint of trade in interstate commerce designed to raise sugar prices.

Speaking through Chief Justice Fuller, the Court ruled that the combination in question related solely to the acquisition of refineries in Pennsylvania and to sugar processing in that state and was therefore not in interstate commerce and not touchable by the Sherman Act.

"Doubtless, the power to control the manufacture of a given thing involves in a certain sense the control of its disposition, but this is a secondary and not the primary sense; and although

Congress, mostly at the president's behest, approved during wartime legislation placing extraordinary controls and regulations on all phases of the economy, including matters over which the federal government might not have authority in peacetime.

Relatively few of the emergency statutes were challenged, and in all but a handful of cases the extraordinary exercise of power was upheld by the courts.

CIVIL WAR

Desperately in need of money to pay the armed forces and to finance the war effort, Congress in 1862 and 1863 passed laws making Treasury notes legal tender. This meant that creditors, including soldiers, had to accept paper money rather than gold or silver in payment of debts.

Challenged in court, the statutes were defended by the government as necessary and proper means of exercising the federal powers over war, commerce, and the borrowing of money.

Five years after the war ended, the Supreme Court disagreed. In the 1870 case of *Hepburn v. Griswold*, it struck down the Legal Tender Acts, maintaining that they carried "the doctrine of implied powers very far beyond any extent hitherto given to it." Little more than a year later, however, the Supreme Court in 1871 reversed itself and upheld the Legal Tender Acts as an appropriate exercise of congressional war powers. *(Knox v. Lee, Parker v. Davis)*

WORLD WAR I

War-related measures enacted during World War I authorized the federal government to force compliance with war contracts, to operate factories producing war goods, and to regulate the foreign-language press.

In conjunction with other express powers, the federal government also ran the nation's railroads, censored mail, and controlled radio and cable communications.

Among the more important war measures—and the one that most significantly impinged on traditional state authorities—was the Lever Act of 1917, which authorized the federal government to regulate all phases of food and fuel production, including importation, manufacturing, and distribution.

In 1921 the Supreme Court held unconstitutional a section of the Lever Act that provided penalties for anyone who sold basic food items at an unreasonable price. The section was so vague as to violate the accused's right to due process under the Fifth Amendment and the right to be informed of the nature and cause of the accusation guaranteed by the Sixth Amendment, the Court said. However, the decision, *United States v. L. Cohen Grocery Co.*, was of relatively little significance to the war effort since it came three years after the war had ended and involved language that could have been corrected by Congress.

In another World War I case, the Court firmly upheld the federal takeover of the railroads against a challenge that it violated states' rights. The specific challenge was to the authority of the Interstate Commerce Commission to set intrastate rail rates. In *Northern Pacific Railway Co. v. North Dakota ex rel Langer* (1919), the Court wrote that if a conflict occurs in a sphere that both the federal government and the states have authority to regulate, federal power is paramount.

WORLD WAR II

Mobilization of private industry and congressional delegation of authority to the president to conduct the war were even more extensive during World War II.

Among the more important measures passed by Congress were the Selective Service Act of 1940; the Lend-Lease Act of 1941, which allowed the president to ship supplies to U.S. allies; the First War Powers Act of 1941, which gave the president power to reorganize executive and independent agencies when, in his discretion, reorganization seemed necessary for more effective prosecution of the war; and the Second War Powers Act of 1942, which gave the president authority to requisition plants and to control overseas communications, alien property, and defense contracts. *(See box, Congressional Power to Raise an Army, p. 228.)*

Other acts included the Emergency Price Control Act of 1942, which established the Office of Price Administration (OPA) to control the prices of rent and commodities; the War Labor Disputes Act of 1943, authorizing seizure of plants threatened by strikes or other labor disputes; and the Renegotiation Act, which gave the executive branch authority to require compulsory renegotiation to recapture excessive profits made on war contracts.

During the war itself, the Supreme Court agreed to hear only one major case involving these enormous grants of power. *Yakus v. United States* (1944) challenged the Emergency Price Control Act as an unconstitutional delegation of legislative power to the executive branch. But the Court upheld the power of Congress to delegate to the OPA the authority to set maximum prices.

As in World War I, the Court avoided answering whether Congress had the authority under its war powers to empower the executive branch to fix prices. But in the postwar case of *Lichter v. United States* (1948), the Court gave some indication of how extensive it believed congressional wartime powers over commerce to be: "Congress, in time of war, unquestionably has the fundamental power . . . to conscript men and to requisition the properties necessary and proper to enable it to raise and support its Armies. Congress furthermore has a primary obligation to bring about whatever production of war equipment and supplies shall be necessary to win a war."

the exercise of that power may result in bringing the operation of commerce into play, it does not control it, and affects it only incidentally and indirectly. Commerce succeeds to manufacture, and is not a part of it," Fuller said. The fact that the sugar was manufactured for eventual sale, possibly in another state, also had only an indirect effect on interstate commerce, according to the Court.

That ruling narrowed the definition of interstate commerce to encompass only transportation. "Slight reflection will show," Fuller wrote, that if the federal antitrust law covers all manufacturing combines "whose ultimate result may effect external commerce, comparatively little of business operations and affairs would be left for state control." Ignoring the inability of the states to regulate gigantic trusts, he insisted that they should do so. Justice John Marshall Harlan wrote in a vigorous dissent that, consequently, the public was left "entirely at the mercy" of the trusts.

Fuller's distinction between the direct and the indirect effects of manufacturing on interstate commerce was a significant qualification of *Gibbons v. Ogden*, which sanctioned congressional regulation of intrastate matters that "affect" other states. The sugar trust ruling provided a handy tool for future courts that looked unkindly on congressional regulation of intrastate matters.

"The *Knight* decision made the [antitrust] statute a dead letter for more than a decade," Justice Wiley B. Rutledge wrote in 1948. Had its full force remained unmodified, he went on to say, "the Act today would be a weak instrument, as would also the power of Congress, to reach evils in all the vast operations of our gigantic national industrial system antecedent to interstate sale and transportation of manufactured products." *(Mandeville Island Farms v. American Crystal Sugar Co.)*

The Sherman Act Applied

Although the *Knight* ruling limited the scope of the Sherman Act, it did not declare it unconstitutional. Moreover, the Court almost immediately began to move away from its narrow ruling. In 1899, for the first time, it applied the antitrust act to an industrial combine, holding that a regional marketing agreement drawn up by six iron-pipe manufacturers that sold their products interstate was an illegal restraint of trade in violation of the act. The situation in this case, the Court said, was unlike the sugar trust case because the pipe combine "was clearly involved in selling as well as manufacturing." *(Addystone Pipe & Steel Co. v. United States)*

In 1904 the Court moved further away from its narrow ruling in the sugar case. A result of President Theodore Roosevelt's trust-busting campaign, the case of *Northern Securities Co. v. United States* involved the government's challenge to a holding company set up by the major stockholders of two competing railroads to buy the controlling interest of the roads. By a 5–4 vote, the Court ruled that the holding company clearly was intended to eliminate competition between the two rail lines.

"This combination is, within the meaning of the act, a 'trust'; but if not, it is a *combination in restraint of interstate and international commerce* and that is enough to bring it under the condemnation of the act," Justice Harlan wrote for the majority.

The "Stream of Commerce"

The next year the Supreme Court virtually abandoned the distinction it had drawn between direct and indirect effects on commerce. In that case, *Swift & Co. v. United States*, meatpacking houses had agreed to control livestock and meat prices in many of the nation's stockyards and slaughtering houses. One of them, Swift, contended that its livestock had been bought and sold locally and therefore it was not engaged in interstate commerce. The unanimous opinion rejecting Swift's claim was written by Justice Oliver Wendell Holmes Jr. "Although the combination alleged embraces restraint and monopoly of trade within a single State, its effect upon commerce among the States is not accidental, secondary, remote or merely probable," Holmes wrote.

He then enunciated what became known as the "stream-of-commerce" doctrine:

When cattle are sent for sale from a place in one state, with the expectation that they will end their transit, after purchase, in another, and when in effect they do so, with only the interruption necessary to find a purchaser at the stock yards, and when this is a typical constantly recurring course, the current thus existing is a current of commerce among the states, and the purchase of the cattle is a part and incident of such commerce.

This doctrine eventually would be used to rationalize federal regulation of actual production. Chief Justice William Howard Taft wrote in a 1923 decision that the *Swift* case "was a milestone in the interpretation of the commerce clause" because it "refused to permit local incidents of great interstate movement, which, taken alone, were intrastate, to characterize the movement as such. The *Swift* case merely fitted the commerce clause to the real and practical essence of modern business growth" *(Board of Trade of Chicago v. Olsen)*.

Federal Police Power

Without an explicit constitutional mandate to protect public health, welfare, and morals, Congress traditionally left such responsibility to the states to act through their police powers. But by the 1890s Congress was beset by social and economic problems that were no longer local. It looked to other sources of constitutional authority, primarily the commerce clause, to deal with a wave of national outrage arising from the exploitation of farmers and wage laborers, including women and children; the crowding of immigrants into urban slums; and widespread local political corruption.

"Where the commerce power had previously been used primarily to regulate, foster or promote commerce for its own sake, . . . it now seemed that Congress might seek to regulate so-

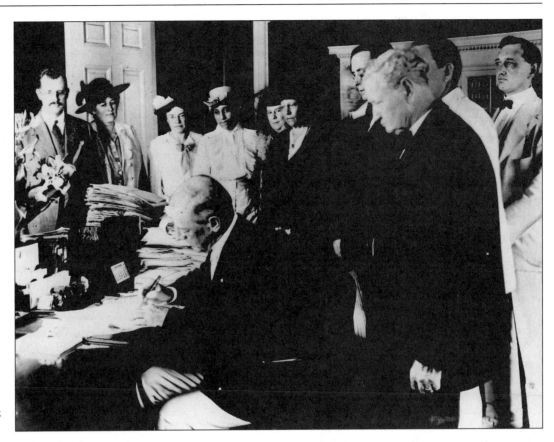

President Woodrow Wilson signing legislation in 1916 intended to discourage the use of child labor. The Supreme Court struck down the law in 1918.

cial and economic practices within the states, provided only that at some point they involved a crossing of state lines," wrote constitutional historian Robert K. Carr.[7]

Lottery Tickets

The Supreme Court initially ruled that such police power regulations as Congress sought could apply only in federal jurisdictions, such as the District of Columbia. In 1902, however, the Court upheld a federal statute prohibiting the transportation of diseased cattle in interstate commerce. *(Reid v. Colorado)* The following year it sanctioned the federal police power in *Champion v. Ames*, better known as "the Lottery Case." In 1895 Congress made it illegal to transport lottery tickets from a state or foreign country into another state. The law was challenged on the ground that lottery tickets were not commerce and that regulation of them was reserved to the states. It also was argued that Congress could only regulate commerce and not prohibit it altogether.

Rejecting those arguments, a five-justice majority of the Court declared that lottery tickets were commerce and that their shipment across state lines made them subject to regulation by Congress. Federal regulation in this case did not interfere with the commerce of lottery tickets within the states and so did not infringe on their right to regulate that traffic, the majority said. Furthermore, the Court said, the power to regulate commerce included the authority to prohibit that commerce. "We know of

no authority in the Courts to hold that the means thus devised [prohibition of shipment] are not appropriate and necessary to protect the country . . . against a species of interstate commerce which . . . has become offensive to the entire people of the nation."

This decision, historian Charles Warren wrote, "disclosed the existence of a hitherto unsuspected field of national power," and Congress was quick to take advantage of it.[8] Between 1903 and 1917 Congress enacted laws to prohibit the interstate movement of explosives, diseased livestock, insect pests, bogus articles of gold and silver, narcotics, adulterated or misbranded foods and drugs, and prostitutes.

The Supreme Court sustained all those acts, and the federal police power appeared well entrenched. Then, in 1918, the Court handed down a decision that left further expansion of the police power temporarily in doubt.

Child Labor

In that case, *Hammer v. Dagenhart*, the Court struck down a 1916 act of Congress that sought to discourage employment of children by banning the shipment across state lines of any product made in factories or mines that employed children under fourteen or permitted those fourteen to sixteen to work more than a limited number of hours a week. By a 5–4 vote, the Court declared that Congress had exceeded its authority. The power to regulate commerce is the authority "to control the means by

CONGRESS USES ITS POWER TO TAX AS A TOOL TO REGULATE COMMERCE

Since the inception of the nation Congress has used the taxing power as a tool of regulation as well as a source of revenue. The protective tariff was an early example of a regulatory tax.

The second statute passed by the First Congress provided that "it is necessary for the support of government, for the discharge of the debts of the United States and the encouragement and protection of manufacturers, that duties be laid on goods, wares and merchandise imported." The validity of such tariffs was much debated but not conclusively settled until 1928, when the Supreme Court wrote: "Whatever we may think of the wisdom of a protection policy, we cannot hold it unconstitutional. So long as the motive of Congress and the effect of its legislative action are to secure revenue for the benefit of the general government, the existence of other motives in the selection of the subject of taxes cannot invalidate congressional action." (*J. W. Hampton Jr. & Co. v. United States*)

The taxing power has been upheld as an auxiliary to the commerce power. In 1940, for example, the Supreme Court upheld the Bituminous Coal Conservation Act of 1937, which imposed a stiff tax on sales of coal in interstate commerce but exempted those producers who agreed to abide by industry price and competition regulations. The Court acknowledged that the exemption was intended to force compliance with the code but said that Congress "may impose penalties in aid of the exercise of any of its enumerated powers," in this case the commerce clause. (*Sunshine Anthracite Coal Co. v. Adkins*)

This ruling effectively overturned the Court's decision in *Carter v. Carter Coal Co.* (1936), which held a similar tax in the 1935 Bituminous Coal Conservation Act to be an unconstitutional penalty for noncompliance with industry regulations rather than a tax designed to raise revenues. (*See "Coal Codes," p. 321.*)

COLORED OLEO

Where Congress used the taxing power on its own to achieve a desired social or economic goal, the Court developed two distinct lines of precedents, just as it had in its early review of the commerce power as a policing mechanism. The first line essentially held that so long as the tax produced some revenue, the Court would not examine the motives behind its imposition.

Thus, just one year after the Court sustained use of the commerce power as a police tool to prohibit interstate shipment of lottery tickets, it upheld use of the taxing power to attain similar objectives. *McCray v. United States* (1904) involved a federal statute that placed a tax of ten cents per pound on oleo colored yellow to resemble butter, but taxed uncolored oleo only one-fourth of a cent per pound. The tax clearly was intended to remove the competition to butter by making it too expensive to manufacture colored oleo. The Court upheld that law, ruling that the tax was on its face an excise tax and therefore permissible. The judiciary, the Court said, may not "restrain the exercise of a lawful power on the assumption that a wrongful purpose or motive has caused the power to be exerted."

Similar reasoning was used by the Court to uphold the Harrison Anti-Narcotics Act of 1914. This statute required persons dealing in narcotics to pay a small annual registration fee and to keep certain records. It also made manufacture, sale, and shipment of narcotics illegal.

Declaring the law valid in 1919, the Court said in *United States v. Doremus*: "The Act may not be declared unconstitutional because its effect may be to accomplish another purpose as well as the raising of revenue." The four dissenters contended that the tax was an exercise of the police power, which they believed was reserved to the states.

CHILD LABOR

The dissenting view in the 1919 narcotics case was to become the majority position on the Court in the next major tax regulation case, beginning the second line of precedents. This reasoning held a tax to be unconstitutional if its primary purpose was the punishment of a certain action, not the raising of revenue.

Bailey v. Drexel Furniture Co. (1922) concerned Congress's second attempt to end child labor. After the Court ruled in 1918 that the

which commerce is carried on," and not the "right to forbid commerce from moving," Justice William R. Day wrote for the majority.

To reconcile his ruling with the previous commerce-clause decisions, Day declared that such things as diseased livestock and misbranded foods were harmful in themselves. Their regulation "could only be accomplished by prohibiting the use of the facilities of interstate commerce to effect the evil intended." That "element is wanting in the present case," he added; the goods manufactured by children "are of themselves harmless."

Day did not stop at this point but went on to examine the reasons why Congress enacted the law. "The act in its effect does not regulate transportation among the states," Day said, "but aims to standardize the ages at which children may be employed in mining and manufacturing within the states." Retreating to the earlier distinction the Court made between commerce and manufacture, Day said mining and manufacture were subject only to state regulation.

Justice Holmes's dissenting opinion left little doubt that the four minority justices believed the majority's ruling had been motivated largely by personal views. The act was indisputably within the federal commerce power, he wrote, and that being the case, "it seems to me that it is not made any less constitutional because of the indirect effects it may have (that is, the discouragement of child labor), however obvious it may be that it will have those effects."

Nor was it important that the evil was not itself in interstate transportation, Holmes continued. "It does not matter whether

commerce power could not be used to reach what many considered a despicable practice, Congress turned to the taxing power, imposing a 10 percent tax on the net profits of any company that employed children under a certain age. Although this tax was similar to statutory tax schemes the Court had approved before, the Court nonetheless declared it unconstitutional.

Chief Justice William Howard Taft, for the eight-justice majority, said the child labor tax was a penalty intended to coerce employers to end their use of child labor:

Taxes are occasionally imposed . . . on proper subjects with the primary motive of obtaining revenue from them and with the incidental motive of discouraging them by making their continuation onerous. They do not lose their character as taxes because of the incidental motive. But there comes a time in the extension of the penalizing features of the so-called tax when it loses its character as such and becomes a mere penalty with the characteristics of regulation and punishment. Such is the case in the law before us.

Commentators questioned the logic of Taft's reasoning. If it was clear that Congress wanted to stop child labor, it was just as clear that Congress intended to terminate the colored oleo industry and closely regulate the manufacture and sale of narcotics. But the significant factor was Taft's implicit claim that the Court would determine when a tax became a penalty; the Court would be the final authority in determining the primary motive of Congress in imposing a tax.

The *Bailey* precedent was applied in a second case decided the same day. *(Hill v. Wallace)* In an attempt to stop some unethical practices by some of the commodity exchanges, the Futures Trading Act of 1921 imposed a twenty-cents-a-bushel tax on all contracts for sales of grain for future delivery, but it exempted those sales arranged through boards of trade that met certain requirements set out in the act. The Court struck down the statute, claiming that its primary motive was not the raising of revenue.

This line of precedent culminated in two 1936 New Deal cases involving the taxing power. In *Carter v. Carter Coal Co.,* the Court struck down the Bituminous Coal Conservation Act of 1935 partly because of a provision providing for a lower coal tax on coal producers who complied with labor regulations set out in the statute. The Court found this provision to be a penalty on producers who refused to comply. In *United States v. Butler,* the Court invalidated a tax on certain food processors, the revenue from which was used to pay farmers to cut their production of certain crops. The Court said the tax was part of an unconstitutional regulatory scheme.

REGULATORY TAX UPHELD

A few months later, following the announcement of Roosevelt's "Court-packing" plan, the Court in 1937 abandoned this line of reasoning and retreated to that set out in the oleo case. The Court upheld the National Firearms Act of 1934, which imposed an annual license tax on manufacturers of and dealers in certain classes of firearms likely to be used by criminals, such as sawed-off shotguns and machine guns. The act, which also required identification of purchasers, clearly was intended to discourage sales of such weapons.

Upholding the validity of the tax, the Court in *Sonzinsky v. United States* struck directly at Taft's opinion in the *Bailey* child labor tax case. Noting that the license tax produced some revenue, the Court added:

Every tax is in some measure regulatory. . . . But a tax is not any the less a tax because it has a regulatory effect, . . . and it has long been established that an Act of Congress which on its face purports to be an exercise of the taxing power is not any the less so because the tax is burdensome or tends to restrict or suppress the thing taxed.

Inquiry into the hidden motive which may move Congress to exercise a power constitutionally conferred upon it is beyond the competency of the courts. . . . They will not undertake . . . to ascribe to Congress an attempt, under the guise of taxation, to exercise another power denied by the Federal Constitution.

Taxes on marijuana and on gamblers were upheld with similar reasoning in the 1950s. *(United States v. Sanchez,* 1950; *United States v. Kahriger,* 1953)

the supposed evil precedes or follows the transportation," Holmes said. "It is enough that in the opinion of Congress the transportation encourages the evil." Furthermore, the federal commerce power could not be limited by its potential to interfere with intrastate regulation of commerce. The states, Holmes wrote, "may regulate their internal affairs and their domestic commerce as they like. But when they seek to send their products across the State line they are no longer within their rights. . . . Under the Constitution such commerce belongs not to the States but to Congress to regulate. It may carry out its views of public policy whatever indirect effect they may have upon the activities of the States."

Congress in 1919 sought to use its tax power to discourage the use of child labor by placing a high tax on goods manufactured in factories employing children, but the Court declared the tax unconstitutional. The lawmakers then approved a constitutional amendment forbidding the employment of children, but the states had not ratified it by the time the Supreme Court itself in *United States v. Darby Lumber Co.* (1941) overturned its own ruling.

Effect of Dagenhart

Except for the child labor tax law, the Court did not rely on *Dagenhart* as a precedent. In fact, the justices continued to sanction use of the commerce power as a police tool when it was applied to universally recognized social evils. A few weeks after the child labor case decision, the Court unanimously upheld the constitutionality of the Meat Inspection Act of 1906, which required local inspection of meat products and banned from interstate commerce meat that had been rejected or not inspected. *(Pittsburgh Melting Co. v. Totten)*

Subsequent Supreme Court decisions let stand federal statutes prohibiting the interstate transportation of stolen automobiles, making transportation of kidnapped persons in interstate commerce a federal crime, and preventing the interstate shipment of convict-made goods to those states that prohibited them. *(Brooks v. United States, 1925; Gooch v. United States, 1936; Kentucky Whip and Collar Co. v. Illinois Central Railroad Co., 1937)*

Like child labor, the goods involved in those cases were not in themselves harmful. Yet the Court upheld their regulation. In upholding the stolen-car statute, the Court said in *Brooks v. United States:*

Congress can certainly regulate interstate commerce to the extent of forbidding and punishing the use of such commerce as an agency to promote immorality, dishonesty or the spread of any evil or harm to the people of other states from the state of origin. In doing this, it is merely exercising the police power, for the benefit of the public, within the field of interstate commerce.

The Court again sanctioned the use of the police power as recently as 1971 in *Perez v. United States* when it sustained provisions of the 1968 Consumer Credit Protection Act to prohibit loan sharking. Although individual loan-sharking activities might be wholly intrastate, the Court said that it was in a "class of activity" that affected intrastate commerce and thus could be regulated under the commerce power.

Labor and Commerce

The decision in the child labor case was but one example of the way the Supreme Court frustrated congressional attempts to use the commerce power to better the conditions of laborers. For the first thirty-five years of the twentieth century the Court declared unconstitutional most congressional efforts to regulate labor-management relations, and it used the Sherman Antitrust Act against striking labor unions, considering them to be combinations in restraint of trade.

One of the first labor laws to be declared unconstitutional was an 1898 statute aimed at ensuring collective bargaining rights for railway laborers. A provision of that law prohibited employers from making contracts that required, as a condition of employment, that employees not join a union. These so-called "yellow-dog contracts" had been effective in management's fight against the railway brotherhoods, and the statute barring them was challenged as exceeding Congress's power over interstate commerce and as a violation of the Fifth Amendment, which the Court then viewed as guaranteeing freedom of contract.

In 1908 the Supreme Court in *Adair v. United States* sustained the challenge. The majority indicated that the prohibition of yellow-dog contracts was particularly offensive to the Fifth Amendment guarantees, and it also said that there was no sufficient "connection between interstate commerce and membership in a labor organization" to justify the prohibition. Justice Holmes disagreed, saying that some labor relations in the railroad industry were closely enough related to interstate commerce to justify federal regulation.

The same year the Court, by a 5–4 vote, declared unconstitutional a second effort to regulate labor-management relations in the rail industry. The 1906 Employers' Liability Act made every common carrier liable for on-the-job deaths of employees. Declaring the law invalid, the Court in 1908 said the statute was an infringement of states' rights because it covered railway employees not directly involved in interstate commerce as well as those who were. Congress shortly thereafter enacted a second liability act that covered only railway workers in interstate commerce. The Court upheld the modified law in 1912. *(First Employers' Liability Case, 1908; Second Employers' Liability Case, 1912)*

Danbury Hatters

At the same time it was ruling that the federal commerce power was not broad enough to encompass labor relations, the Supreme Court held that the Sherman Act, which was based on the commerce power, forbade certain labor activities as illegal restraints of trade. The first of these decisions was handed down in 1908, the same year as the *Adair* decision. It was in the Danbury Hatters Case *(Loewe v. Lawlor)*, involving a union that attempted to organize workers at a hat factory in Danbury, Connecticut. In support of the union, the American Federation of Labor set up boycotts of stores in several states where the hats were sold.

The Court asserted that, because the antitrust act covered "any combination whatever" in restraint of trade, it extended to labor unions whose activities—as in this case—were "aimed at compelling third parties and strangers involuntarily not to engage in the course of trade except on conditions that the combination imposes." The Court also employed the stream-of-commerce doctrine to show that the boycotts, although intrastate, had a direct effect on interstate commerce. "If the purposes of the combination were, as alleged, to prevent any interstate transportation [of the hats] at all, the fact that the means operated at one end before the physical transportation ended was immaterial," the majority wrote.

The Clayton Act

In the Clayton Antitrust Act of 1914, Congress sought to exempt labor unions from antitrust actions. Section 6 of that act stipulated that labor was "not a commodity or article of commerce." Section 20 provided that "no restraining order or injunction shall be granted by a court of the United States . . . in any case between an employer and employees . . . unless necessary to prevent irreparable injury to property, or to a property right."

The Supreme Court did not consider the validity of these sections until 1921 when it held that the Clayton Act exemptions pertained only to legal and normal operations of labor unions. There was nothing in the act, the Court said, "to exempt such an organization or its members from accountability where it or they depart from its normal and legitimate objects and engage in an actual combination or conspiracy in restraint of trade." Such restraints included secondary boycotts, the Court said. (*Duplex Printing Press Co. v. Deering*)

The Court held in 1925 that an intrastate strike against a coal company directly affected commerce and violated federal antitrust laws, and in 1927 the Court overruled two lower federal courts to grant an injunction against a stonecutters union that had organized a secondary boycott of stone cut by non-union workers. (*Coronado Coal Co. v. United Mine Workers*, 1925; *Bedford Cut Stone Co. v. Journeymen Stone Cutters' Assn.*, 1927)

To overcome the narrow interpretations of the Clayton Act's labor exemption, Congress in 1932 passed the Norris-LaGuardia Act, which prohibited the issuance of injunctions by federal courts in labor disputes except when unlawful acts were threatened or committed. The Court in the 1938 case of *Lauf v. E. G. Shinner & Co.* upheld the act on the ground that it was within congressional power to determine the jurisdiction of the lower federal courts.

The Clayton Act gained new vigor when the Supreme Court in 1941 sustained a provision of section 20 declaring that strikes and secondary boycotts would not be considered violations of any federal law. (*United States v. Hutcheson*) The 1938 and 1941 decisions reflected a remarkable turnabout in the Court's view of the commerce clause, not only in labor relations but in business matters generally.

New Deal Enlargement of Federal Authority

Congress made little use of the commerce power to regulate business between the Court's 1918 ruling in the *Dagenhart* child labor case and the economic crisis of the Great Depression. Then, under President Roosevelt's forceful guidance, Congress in the 1930s attempted to use its commerce and fiscal powers to stimulate recovery. But the Supreme Court, still dominated by a small majority strongly disposed toward protection of private property rights and states' rights, resisted.

The resulting collision, dramatized by Roosevelt's threat to increase the size of the Court and fill the new seats with judges who would approve New Deal legislation, ultimately led to the birth of the modern commerce power. In 1937 the Court accepted Justice Benjamin Cardozo's view that the commerce power could properly be used to fight the nation's economic and social problems.

BLACK MONDAY

The centerpiece of Roosevelt's recovery program was the National Industrial Recovery Act (NIRA) of 1933. It declared a "national emergency productive of widespread unemployment and disorganization of industry, which burdens interstate and foreign commerce, affects the public welfare, and undermines the standards of living of the American people." To speed industrial recovery, the NIRA authorized the president to approve codes of fair competition. Each of those codes, among other conditions, had to contain hours and wage standards for workers in the particular industry.

In May 1935, on what came to be known as "Black Monday," the Supreme Court declared the entire NIRA invalid. *Schechter Poultry Corp. v. United States* was a test case brought by the Roosevelt administration in hope that a favorable response from the Court would encourage industry's compliance, which had been flagging. The circumstances involved, however, made it less than an ideal test.

The Schechter brothers bought live poultry that had been shipped into New York City largely from out of state, then slaughtered and sold it locally. They were accused of violating several provisions of the New York City live poultry industry code, including the wage and hours standards and the prohibition against "straight killing"—allowing a customer to select a bird for slaughter. They also were charged with selling an "unfit chicken" to a local butcher. Wags quickly dubbed the suit the "Sick Chicken Case."

The Supreme Court held that the Schechter operation was a local concern that did not directly affect interstate commerce. Instituting federal regulation through the fair competition codes was, therefore, an abridgment of states' rights and thus unconstitutional. The Court noted that the provisions of the code that the Schechters were charged with violating applied to the slaughtering operation and subsequent sale in local markets—activities, the Court said, that were not in interstate commerce. The Court also denied that these activities were part of the "stream of commerce."

The Court acknowledged that Congress had power not only to regulate interstate commerce but also to protect interstate commerce from burden or injury imposed by those engaged in intrastate activities. The effect of the burden must be direct, however, the Court said, recalling its distinction between direct and indirect effects first outlined in the 1895 sugar trust case. While the "precise line can be drawn only as individual cases arise," the Court said, the distinction was essential to maintenance of the federal system. Without it the federal government would have complete power over domestic affairs of the states.

COAL CODES

The opinion in *Schechter* was unanimous, but no such unanimity marked the next New Deal decision. In *Carter v. Carter Coal Co.* (1936) the Court declared the 1935 Bituminous Coal Conservation Act unconstitutional. That act said the production and distribution of coal so closely affected interstate commerce that federal regulation was necessary to stabilize the industry. Passed by Congress despite the adverse ruling in *Schechter*, the act authorized fixed prices for coal, provided for collective bargaining rights for coal miners, allowed a two-thirds majority of the industry to establish wage and hours standards for the entire industry, and established a tax scheme to ensure compliance with the regulations.

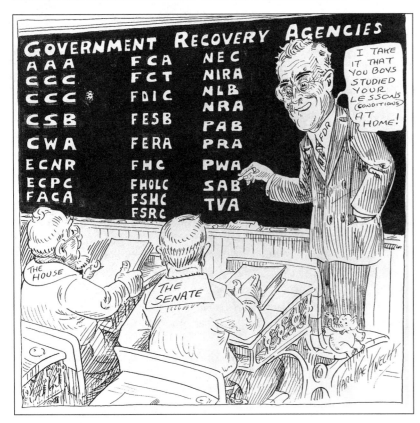

Under pressure from President Franklin D. Roosevelt, Congress created various "alphabet" agencies aimed at stimulating recovery from the Depression.

Speaking for the majority, Justice George Sutherland focused first on the labor relations provisions. He declared that mining was production, not commerce, and that the relationship between a mine operator and mine workers was purely local in character. Since mining itself was not in interstate commerce, Sutherland contended, the next step was to determine if its effect on that commerce was direct. Sutherland then set forth a definition of direct effect that turned not on the degree to which a thing affected interstate commerce but on the manner in which the effect occurred. It made no difference whether one man or several men mined coal for sale in interstate commerce. Labor problems were local controversies affecting local production. "Such effect as they have upon commerce, however extensive it may be, is secondary and indirect," Sutherland said.

Having declared the labor provisions an invalid exercise of federal power under the commerce clause, Sutherland proceeded to hold the price-fixing provisions invalid on the ground they were so dependent on the labor provisions that they could not stand on their own—this despite a clause in the legislation that said the price-fixing provisions could stand even if other provisions were found unconstitutional.

In fact, Sutherland never discussed whether the price-fixing provisions were in interstate commerce or directly affected it. If he had, he would have had to reconcile his opinion with the precedent in the *Shreveport Rate Case,* which permitted federal regulation of intrastate matters that were inextricably mingled with interstate commerce. It was this precedent that Justice Cardozo, in dissent, used to argue the validity of the price-fixing

precedents. Restating his thesis that the distinction between direct and indirect effect was one of degree rather than kind, Cardozo maintained that the federal commerce power was "as broad as the need that evokes it."

In this instance, the need was great, Cardozo said: "Congress was not condemned to inaction in the face of price wars. . . . Commerce had been choked and burdened; its normal flow had been diverted from one state to another; there had been bankruptcy and waste and ruin alike for capital and for labor. . . . After making every allowance for difference of opinion as to the most efficient cure, the student of the subject is confronted with the indisputable truth that there were ills to be corrected, and ills that had a direct relation to the maintenance of commerce among the states without friction or diversion. An evil existing, and also the power to correct it, the lawmakers were at liberty to use their own discretion in the selection of the means."

Cardozo's opinion recognized what the majority failed to acknowledge—that the many thousands of local economic problems of the Depression, taken together, were national in scope. In protecting state sovereignty and private property rights, the majority between January 1935 and June 1936 found unconstitutional eight of ten major New Deal laws. In those cases, the majority time and again rejected the concept of national supremacy and the theory that Congress might act to protect the general welfare. In reaction, Roosevelt introduced his plan to add as many as six justices to the nine-member Court.

Congress rejected his plan, but not before one of the justices who generally voted with the conservative majority, Owen J.

Roberts, did an about-face to convert the more liberal minority into a majority. In April 1937 Cardozo's reasoning in the *Carter* dissent became the majority opinion in a case upholding the 1935 National Labor Relations Act (NLRA).

NATIONAL LABOR LAW

Passed in 1935, the NLRA declared that the denial of the rights of workers to organize and bargain collectively caused strikes and other labor problems that directly burdened and obstructed interstate commerce.

To eliminate the obstruction and guarantee workers' rights, Congress prohibited both employees and employers from engaging in certain unfair labor practices. The act also established a National Labor Relations Board (NLRB) to administer the law and hear charges of violations.

In view of the *Schechter* and *Carter* decisions, it seemed likely that the Supreme Court also would invalidate the NLRA's application to employers and employees engaged in manufacturing and production. The question was put to the Court in 1937, in the midst of public and congressional debate over the so-called Court-packing plan, in the case of *National Labor Relations Board v. Jones & Laughlin Steel Corp.* Ten union employees whom the company had fired claimed they had been dismissed solely because they were members of a union. The NLRB agreed and ordered the company to stop discriminating against its union workers. When the company failed to comply, the NLRB asked a federal appellate court to enforce its orders. Relying on the *Carter* decision, that court refused the petition, saying Congress did not have the power to regulate local labor relations.

Arguing the case before the Supreme Court, attorneys for the NLRB contended that Jones & Laughlin was in a stream of commerce, receiving raw materials at its Pennsylvania mills from other states and moving its products back across state lines. The steel company argued that the NLRA was regulating labor relations, a local concern unrelated to interstate commerce and thus not subject to federal regulation.

By a 5–4 vote, the Supreme Court reversed the lower court, sustaining the National Labor Relations Act. Affirming that Congress had the authority to regulate intrastate matters that directly burdened or obstructed interstate commerce, Chief Justice Charles Evans Hughes said the fact that the employees were engaged in the local activity of manufacturing was not "determinative." The question was what effect a labor strike of the factory would have on interstate commerce.

Hughes answered:

In view of respondent's far-flung activities, it is idle to say that the effect would be indirect or remote. It is obvious that it would be immediate and might be catastrophic. We are asked to shut our eyes to the plainest facts of our national life and to deal with the question of direct and indirect effects in an intellectual vacuum. . . . When industries organize themselves on a national scale, making their relation to interstate commerce the dominant factor in their activities, how can it be maintained that their industrial labor relations constitute a forbidden field into which Congress may not enter when it is necessary to protect interstate commerce from the paralyzing consequences of industrial war? We have often said that interstate commerce itself is a practical conception. It is equally true that interferences with that commerce must be appraised by a judgment that does not ignore actual experience.

The Court upheld the NLRB in four other cases decided the same day. Two of the cases involved a large trailer manufacturing company and a men's clothing manufacturer. (*National Labor Relations Board v. Fruehauf Trailer Co.; National Labor Relations Board v. Friedman-Harry Marks Clothing Co.*) Although these businesses sold a large portion of their products interstate, a labor strike against either one would not have had devastating effects on the national economy. The third case involved the Associated Press; the Court held that interstate communication of any kind was interstate commerce subject to regulation by Congress. (*Associated Press v. National Labor Relations Board*) In the fourth case the Court held that a small company running buses between Virginia and the District of Columbia was an instrumentality of interstate commerce subject to the labor relations act. (*Washington, Virginia & Maryland Coach Co. v. National Labor Relations Board*)

With those decisions, the Court declared that labor problems in almost any industry that depended in any way on interstate commerce for a portion of its business might sufficiently injure or burden interstate commerce as to demand compliance with the national labor relations law.

WAGES AND HOURS

Given the new willingness of the Court to construe the commerce power broadly, Congress decided to try again to set federal minimum wage and maximum hours standards. Since the Court in 1918 had held that national hours limitations for child workers were an unwarranted federal intrusion into intrastate matters, reform attempts had been restricted to the individual states. Although the Supreme Court consistently upheld state laws setting maximum hours, it did not approve a state minimum wage law until 1937.

Taking that as a signal, Congress passed the Fair Labor Standards Act of 1938, which set a forty-hour workweek and an eventual minimum wage of forty cents an hour, with time and a half for overtime. The act covered most workers "engaged in commerce or in the production of goods for commerce." In a provision almost identical to that which was struck down in the child labor case (*Hammer v. Dagenhart*), it barred the shipment in interstate commerce of any products made in violation of the standards.

A test of the 1938 statute came to the Court in 1941 after the government charged Fred W. Darby with violations of the standards. Darby ran a lumber company in Georgia, processing logs into finished lumber and selling a large part of it in other states. The Court unanimously upheld the federal minimum wage statute in the case, reversing its *Dagenhart* decision. Addressing the power of Congress to prohibit the shipment of goods manufactured in violation of the wage-hours standards, the Court

As corporations, cartels, and trusts grew in the late nineteenth century, so did the public's distrust of them. Although revisionist history has challenged some of the charges laid to them, they were at the time despised for involvement in various abuses, including customer fraud and bribery of public officials.

In 1872 the Grangers, an activist farmers' association, issued the first real call for antimonopoly laws, specifically demanding regulation of railroads. By 1888 both the Democratic and Republican Parties had come out in favor of action to break up monopolies and trusts. The first trusts had only recently come into being, creating virtual monopolies in cotton, oil, sugar, and whiskey. Typically stockholders of formerly competitive companies would exchange their shares and voting rights for certificates of ownership in the new monolithic trust.

By 1890 opposition pressure resulted in the Sherman Antitrust Act, whose first section stated: "Every contract, combination in the form of trust or otherwise, or conspiracy in restraint of trade or commerce among the several states or with foreign nations is hereby declared to be illegal." The act did not rely just on government enforcement; it stipulated that individuals could sue and, if successful, receive treble damages.

The law's second section made it unlawful for any person to "discriminate in price between different purchasers of commodities . . . where the effect of such discrimination may be to substantially lessen competition or tend to create a monopoly in any line of commerce." Another section forbade corporations from acquiring "directly or indirectly . . . stock or other share capital of another corporation . . . where the effect of such acquisition may be to substantially lessen competition . . . or create a monopoly in any line of commerce."

Though bold and sweeping, the language was also vague, repeatedly requiring judicial interpretation and clarifying legislation. The Clayton Antitrust Act of 1914 was an attempt to specify what kinds of business behavior could be punished. But it fell short of the goal in some critical instances and it, too, became subject to a long spell of judicial interpretation.

Congress, however, did not cease trying to curb monopolies of commerce. The same year it passed the Clayton Antitrust Act, the lawmakers at President Woodrow Wilson's urging also passed the Federal Trade Commission (FTC) Act, creating the agency of that name to monitor business conduct and mergers. It was empowered to seek civil penalties against wrongdoers; the Justice Department had authority to seek civil or criminal penalties—in effect, fines or jail sentences.

The next major piece of antitrust legislation came twenty-two years later, in 1936, with passage of the Robinson-Patman Act. It amended the Clayton Act to make it illegal for any company to provide "any discount, rebate, allowance, or advertising service charge" to any purchaser unless the same offer was made to all other purchasers of the same products. While the apparent intent was to prevent a seller from unfairly favoring certain customers, the bill's drafters had a less exalted aim. It was promoted by wholesale grocers upset by discount deals being made directly between producers and retail chains. A number of economists contend that the provision has hindered legitimate price competition.

Mergers, in contrast to price competition, were the focus of antitrust legislation in 1950 and 1976. The Clayton Act prohibited mergers that would have anticompetitive effects, but some companies soon discovered that there was nothing to stop them from acquiring the *assets* of competitive companies. The Celler-Kefauver Act of 1950 sought to close that loophole. Another weakness in the Clayton Act prompted the passage of the Hart-Scott-Rodino Act of 1976. While Clayton stopped anticompetitive mergers, it could not break up one once it had occurred. The Hart-Scott-Rodino law required that the Justice Department and the FTC be notified of mergers and acquisitions that would exceed a certain size, either in terms of corporate assets or market sales.

Despite a sharply rising number of mergers in the ten years after that provision became fully effective in 1979, Justice Department statistics showed the number of merger investigations holding steady and in some years actually falling. Critics of the department's record contended that it reflected the Reagan administration's outspoken opposition to rigid antitrust enforcement. Key administration officials and a sizable number of economists argued that antitrust laws often obstructed rather than encouraged competition and put American companies at a disadvantage with Japanese and other foreign competitors that did not operate under similar constraints.

The legislative direction during the 1980s was also toward loosening rather than tightening antitrust laws. Congress enacted two antitrust-weakening bills. One was the Export Trading Act of 1982, to let exporting companies apply to the Commerce Department for exemption from the Sherman Antitrust Act. The other was the National Cooperative Research Act of 1984, allowing companies to engage in joint research and development projects without facing civil antitrust suits. The protections provided in the 1984 law were expanded by a 1993 statute.

Antitrust issues returned to the forefront in the late 1990s. The country was experiencing another wave of corporate mergers, leading some to question their impact on consumer choices and wallets. A Justice Department lawsuit against software giant Microsoft for "a broad pattern of anticompetitive conduct" was expected to trigger a broader debate on Capitol Hill on antitrust enforcement and legislation.

said: "The motive and purpose of a regulation of interstate commerce are matters for the legislative judgment upon the exercise of which the Constitution places no restriction and over which the courts are given no control." *(United States v. Darby Lumber Co.)*

Several legal scholars noted that the *Darby* decision brought back to prominence the broad interpretation of the commerce power first outlined in *Gibbons v. Ogden*. One scholar, Robert K. Carr, said that after the *Darby* decision, "about the only further step the Court might take in its general reasoning concerning the commerce power would be to cease denying that manufacture is not of itself commerce and conclude that where goods are produced for, or affect, interstate trade, the act of production is a phase of the total process of commerce."[9] The Court would take that step in 1942.

POWER EXTENDED TO PRODUCTION

After the Supreme Court in 1936 declared the Agricultural Adjustment Act of 1933—a key piece of Roosevelt's New Deal legislation—unconstitutional *(United States v. Butler)*, Congress passed a similar law two years later. Rather than paying farmers to reduce their production of certain commodities, as the 1933 law provided, the revised act established marketing quotas for the various commodities and penalized producers who exceeded them. The Court upheld the act against a challenge that, like the original measure, it infringed on the reserved powers of the states by attempting to regulate production. The 1938 law did not regulate production, the Court said, but, rather, marketing, which was at the "throat" of interstate commerce. *(Mulford v. Smith, 1939)*

The same broad interpretation was given to the 1937 Agricultural Marketing Act, which established milk marketing agreements to control milk prices. With regard to that act, Chief Justice Harlan Fiske Stone wrote for the Court in a 1942 case, *United States v. Wrightwood Dairy Co.*:

The power of Congress over interstate commerce is plenary and complete in itself, may be exercised to its utmost extent, and acknowledges no limitations other than are prescribed in the Constitution. . . . It follows that no form of a State activity can constitutionally thwart the regulatory power granted by the commerce clause to Congress. Hence the reach of that power extends to those intrastate activities which in a substantial way interfere with or obstruct the exercise of the granted power.

Just how "substantial" the intrastate activity had to be was tested later that year in the case of *Wickard v. Filburn*. Under terms of the revised Agricultural Adjustment Act, which sought to limit output and raise prices, Roscoe C. Filburn was permitted in 1941 to grow twelve acres of winter wheat on his small farm near Dayton, Ohio. He actually planted twenty-three acres and harvested 269 bushels more than his quota permitted. Filburn intended to sell what he was allowed and use the excess for feed and seed. Although he did not sell the excess, he was penalized nevertheless for raising more than his quota. He challenged the penalty.

The Court reasoned that farmers like Filburn who consumed their wheat still affected commerce: that they would not need to buy wheat, reducing the market demand and undermining the law's attempt to raise prices. Thus the Court found a rationale to uphold regulation by Congress of production that was not in commerce.

Constitutional historian C. Herman Pritchett called this case the "high-water mark of commerce clause expansionism."[10]

The Modern Commerce Power: Decades of Expansion

Not only has the commerce clause become the foundation for ever more detailed supervision of the commercial life of the nation by Congress and executive agencies, it also has been used to prohibit racial discrimination in public accommodations, remove restrictions on interstate travel, and justify federal regulation of environmental pollutants.

RACIAL DISCRIMINATION

After the Civil War, Congress attacked racial discrimination in public accommodations through several different means, all with little success. The most important tool was the Fourteenth Amendment, but the Court held in the 1883 *Civil Rights Cases* that the amendment applied only to discriminatory acts by states, not individuals, and thus the amendment could not be used to reach discrimination on railroads and other privately owned public carriers and accommodations.

Attempts during that era to use the commerce power to redress discriminatory practices were also thwarted. The Interstate Commerce Commission (ICC) dismissed a challenge to segregated railroad facilities based on a section of the Interstate Commerce Act that prohibited "undue or unreasonable prejudice or disadvantage" in such facilities. "The disposition of a delicate and important question of this character, weighted with embarrassments arising from antecedent legal and social conditions, should aim at a result most likely to conduce to peace and order," said the commission, in effect ruling that it would not enforce the prohibition.[11]

In the 1878 case of *Hall v. DeCuir*, the Court voided a Louisiana law to outlaw racial segregation on public carriers. Calling the law a burden on interstate commerce, the Court said prohibition of segregation was a matter on which there should be national uniformity and thus only Congress could act. Congress had acted in passing the Civil Rights Act of 1875, but the Court struck it down in the 1883 *Civil Rights Cases*.

Although there were subsequent sporadic attempts to end segregation through the commerce clause, congressional concern as well as public interest in resolving the problem waned in the first decades of the twentieth century. Then in 1946 the Supreme Court ruled in *Morgan v. Virginia* that segregation on a public carrier burdened interstate commerce. The case involved an African American woman who traveled on a bus from

The federal government in its first hundred years established numerous offices that performed regulatory functions as part of their overall duties. But it was not until after the Civil War, when the government began more fully to exercise its constitutional authority to regulate commerce, that Congress created regulatory agencies specifically to police an industry or some aspect of trade. The Interstate Commerce Commission (ICC), established by Congress in 1887 to regulate the railroads, was the first. The agency would survive for more than a century, until 1995, when deregulation led to its demise.

The ICC served as a prototype for regulation by "independent" commissions. However, the notion of an agency independent of the legislative and executive branches did not develop immediately—and for a long time regulatory independence often seemed stronger in theory than in actuality. ICC commissioners were appointed by the president, subject to Senate concurrence, and its appropriations came from Congress.

That arrangement has been the pattern for all independent agencies that have come into existence during the past hundred years, but it has left unsettled the question of whether such independent regulatory commissions are executive agencies in disguise or are really an arm of Congress because they operate under delegated legislative powers.

Congress placed the ICC in the Interior Department until 1889, when House Democrats persuaded their colleagues to give the commission more autonomy—in an apparent attempt to insulate it from the influences of a Republican-controlled White House. But seventeen more years passed before Congress, in the 1906 Hepburn Act, granted the ICC final authority to set railroad rates and enforce its rulings. Court challenges to the rulings did not cease, but gradually the courts looked more favorably toward regulatory action.

At first it appeared that the commission might handle all federal regulation of commerce. When this proved impracticable, Congress created more agencies patterned on the ICC, beginning with the Federal Reserve System in 1913 to regulate banking and the nation's money supply, and the Federal Trade Commission in 1914 to prevent or stop unfair trade practices, including monopolies, false advertising, and price discrimination.

Between 1915 and the beginning of the New Deal, Congress set up seven more agencies to regulate aspects of the nation's commercial and financial systems. They were the U.S. Coast Guard, 1915; the U.S. Tariff Commission, 1916 (later the U.S. International Trade Commission); the Federal Power Commission (FPC), 1920 (abolished in 1977, when many of its functions were transferred to the Federal Energy Regulatory Commission); the Grain Futures Administration, 1922 (later the Commodity Futures Trading Commission); the Bureau of Customs, 1927 (later the U.S. Customs Service); the Federal Radio Commission, 1927 (later the Federal Communications Commission); and the Food, Drug, and Insecticide Administration, 1927 (later the Food and Drug Administration). Of the seven, only the FPC, with authority over power projects on navigable waters and natural gas transmission, was created in the ICC's independent-agency mold. But while the other six were placed in the executive branch, they were given considerable autonomy. (Three of the six—the U.S. International Trade Commission, Commodity Futures Trading Commission, and Federal Communications Commission—are now independent agencies.)

FROM THE NEW DEAL THROUGH THE 1970S

The New Deal's response to the 1930s Great Depression resulted in a surge of administrative regulation. Among the most prominent of the agencies created between 1932 and 1938 were the Federal Home Loan Bank Board, to regulate federally chartered savings and loan associations (abolished in 1989, when its functions were transferred to other agencies, including the new Office of Thrift Supervision and the Federal Housing Finance Board); the Federal Deposit Insurance Corporation, to insure bank deposits and to supervise state-chartered banks outside of the Federal Reserve System; the Farm Credit Administration, to provide credit and other services for farmers and ranchers; the Securities and Exchange Commission, to protect the public against fraud and deception in securities and financial markets; the National Labor Relations Board, to prevent unfair labor practices and protect the right of employees to bargain collectively; the U.S. Maritime Commission (later the Federal Maritime Commission), to oversee merchant shipping and shipbuilding; and the Civil Aeronautics Authority (renamed the Civil Aeronautics Board in 1940 and abolished in 1984), to regulate the airlines.

Of the few regulatory agencies born in the two decades following the New Deal, the major ones were the Atomic Energy Commission, created in 1946 to supervise peaceful uses of atomic energy (and abolished in 1974, with some of its functions taken over by the new Nuclear Regulatory Commission); the Small Business Administration, created in 1953 to aid qualifying small enterprises with loans and services; and the Federal Aviation Agency, created in 1958 to enforce safety in civil aviation (it became the Federal Aviation Administration in the new Department of Transportation in 1967).

In the 1960s the federal government greatly expanded its efforts to solve many social problems as it carried out President Lyndon B. Johnson's Great Society programs. New agencies included the Equal Employment Opportunity Commission, which was created to enforce the 1964 Civil Rights Act's provisions against discrimination in the workplace.

In the 1970s environmental, safety, and consumer concerns came to the forefront. More than one hundred regulatory statutes were enacted, and many new regulatory entities were created, including the Environmental Protection Agency (1970), the Occupational Safety and Health Administration (1970), and the Consumer Product Safety Commission (1972).

DEREGULATION AND ITS AFTERMATH

By the late 1970s, however, the regulatory system was under widespread attack. Many agencies had been created in response to crises that had passed, and economic problems were focusing attention on inefficiencies in the haphazardly developed regulatory apparatus.

The public, politicians, and regulators themselves were demanding that regulatory benefits outweigh costs. Much of the attention was directed at trying to reform regulatory activities rather than eliminate them entirely. But reform efforts collapsed into controversy, ushering in what has been called the Age of Deregulation.

Some observers attribute the first big push toward deregulation to Democratic president Jimmy Carter. Others see the awakening of the deregulatory movement earlier, in the Republican Ford and Nixon presidencies. Regardless of the origin, the principal legislative activity occurred during the Carter presidency.

Soon after he was elected to the White House in 1976, Carter promised to "free the American people from the burden of overregulation" by looking "industry by industry" for harmful effects of stifled competition. Alfred E. Kahn, Civil Aeronautics Board chairman in 1977–1978, became the leading advocate for deregulating transportation. A bipartisan consensus emerged in Congress to deregulate airlines, railroads, trucking, and some aspects of telecommunications, and to ease control over financial institutions. All that had been done or was well under way before Carter left office in 1981.

His successor, Republican Ronald Reagan, seemed even more zealous in pursuit of what he considered unnecessary and meddlesome government regulations. In 1982 Congress extended deregulation to buses, and the nation's telephone system was transformed with a consent agreement that broke up the American Telephone & Telegraph Company in 1984. Moreover, Reagan's appointees to regulatory boards often were critical of the rules that remained in effect, and in several agencies enforcement suffered from staff reductions.

Republican George Bush, who succeeded Reagan, was also critical of federal regulations and set up a special council to review proposed regulations to see how they affected business and economic competitiveness in general.

But not all Americans were pleased with deregulation. Phone users grumbled that the once simple act of making long distance calls had often become cumbersome. Airline fares generally dipped in the new competitive atmosphere but in some instances climbed higher than ever as a number of airlines stopped serving less-traveled routes or went out of business altogether. Some small cities were left without airline service, and many small towns no longer had any kind of public transportation. Deregulation also brought concerns that truckers and airline operators were no longer devoting adequate attention to safety.

The deregulation of financial institutions caused the most sobering second thoughts. Inflation had been the driving force behind congressional action in 1980 to ease federal controls on banks and on savings and loan associations, the so-called thrifts or S&Ls. Of the changes enacted, the most far-reaching one allowed the thrifts to make consumer and business loans. In the past they had been limited to mortgage lending.

S&L officials and their critics alike trace the industry's subsequent difficulties—difficulties that would lead to the biggest federally financed bailout in U.S. history—to the 1980 deregulatory legislation. Saddled with low-interest mortgages when interest rates took off in the late 1970s, many S&Ls compounded their problems by making risky loans in real estate and oil enterprises. World oil prices collapsed in 1986–1987, creating economic havoc in the oil-producing American Southwest, and soon afterward the nation's real estate market began to sag. With one S&L after another facing bankruptcy, bailout legislation was enacted in 1989. The thrift cleanup, which cost taxpayers an estimated $150 billion or more by 1996, dramatically restructured federal regulation of thrifts. Several new entities were created, including the Office of Thrift Supervision and the Federal Housing Finance Board.

1990S COMPROMISES

When Democrat Bill Clinton came into the White House in 1993, one of his first acts as president was to disband Bush's regulatory council. But Clinton also advocated easing the regulatory burden on industry with less red tape and costly federal mandates.

When the Republican Party took control of Congress in 1995, the push for more deregulation gained momentum. Although sweeping proposals to change the way federal agencies developed regulations and to make it harder to impose new regulations on business and property owners failed, Republicans scored some notable victories when they scaled back their deregulatory ambitions enough to forge a consensus with the Democrats. Laws enacted, such as an overhaul of the New Deal–era Communications Act and revisions of pesticide and safe drinking water acts, required new approaches to regulation. The legislation called for increased flexibility, more analysis of the costs and benefits of regulations, and more information for consumers.

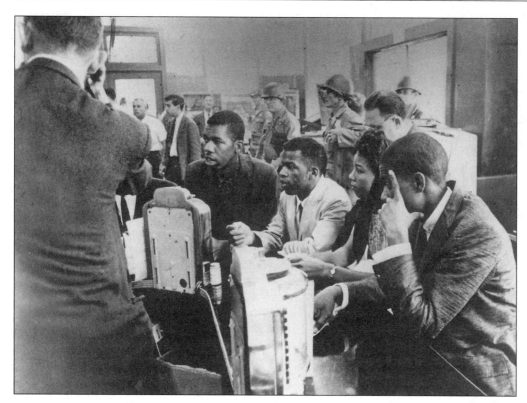

In the early 1960s blacks used lunch counter "sit-ins" to protest their exclusion from public accommodations in southern states. The Civil Rights Act of 1964, rooted in the commerce clause, barred discrimination in restaurants, hotels, and other public accommodations.

Virginia to Maryland. She refused to move to the back of the bus to make her seat available to a white person; the Court upheld her refusal.

In 1950 the Court ruled in *Henderson v. United States* that separate dining facilities on interstate trains were a violation of the Interstate Commerce Act provision that had gone unenforced for so long. In 1955 the ICC announced that it was prohibiting racial discrimination on all trains and buses that crossed state lines.

But it was not until its passage of the 1964 Civil Rights Act that Congress again tried to prohibit racial discrimination in all public accommodations. Title II of the 1964 law barred discrimination on grounds of race, color, religion, or national origin in public accommodations if the discrimination was supported by state law or official action, if lodgings were provided to transient guests, if interstate travelers were served, or if a substantial portion of the goods sold or entertainment provided moved in interstate commerce.

That portion of the act was immediately challenged as unconstitutional by Heart of Atlanta, a Georgia motel that served out-of-state travelers. The motel argued that Congress had exceeded its power to regulate interstate commerce. In a unanimous ruling in 1964 the Court upheld the validity of Title II, explaining that the power of Congress to regulate interstate commerce gave it the authority to regulate local enterprise that "might have a substantial and harmful effect" on that commerce. (*Heart of Atlanta Motel v. United States*)

It did not matter that the congressional intent was to correct a moral and social evil. The moral implications of the discrimi-

nation did "not detract from the overwhelming evidence of the disruptive effect" that discrimination had on interstate commerce, the Court said. In a companion case decided the same day, *Katzenbach v. McClung*, the Court upheld Title II as applied to Ollie's Barbeque, a restaurant in Birmingham, Alabama. Ollie's Barbeque did not cater to an interstate clientele, but 46 percent of the food it served was meat supplied through interstate commerce.

INSURANCE

In one instance the Supreme Court used the commerce clause to give Congress control of a field of trade it did not want. Ever since its 1869 decision in *Paul v. Virginia*, the Supreme Court had held consistently that purely financial or contractual transactions such as insurance were not in commerce, even if the transactions involved parties in different states. This left to the states full authority to regulate the insurance business.

In 1944 the Justice Department sought to use the Sherman Act to break up a conspiracy of insurance companies that sought to monopolize fire insurance sales in six southern states. Using the precedent established by *Paul v. Virginia*, the companies, all members of the South-Eastern Underwriters Association, contended that they could not be reached by the antitrust act since their business was not in commerce.

Overturning *Paul v. Virginia*, the Court ruled against the companies in *United States v. South-Eastern Underwriters Assn.* "No commercial enterprise of any kind which conducts its activities across state lines has been held to be wholly beyond the regulatory power of Congress under the Commerce Clause," wrote the Court. "We cannot make an exception for the business of insurance." Congress, not the Court, must make the exceptions to the antitrust act.

Because the decision called into question the validity of all state insurance regulations, Congress in 1945 passed the McCarran Act, which stated that "no Act of Congress shall be construed to invalidate, impair, or supersede" a state law regulating or taxing insurance unless the federal act specifically related to insurance. In 1946 the Court upheld the McCarran Act. *(Prudential Insurance Co. v. Benjamin)*

ENVIRONMENTAL LAW

Congress's police power to protect the public health and welfare, derived primarily from its commerce power, has become the constitutional basis for federal legislation regulating air and water pollution. The Water Quality Improvement Act of 1970, the primary federal vehicle for water pollution prevention and control programs, states in its declaration of policy that Congress stepped into the environmental area "in connection with its jurisdiction over the waterways of the Nation and in consequence of the benefits resulting to the public health and welfare by the prevention and control of water pollution." Likewise, the primary purpose given for passage of the Air Quality Act of 1967 is "to promote health and welfare and the productive capability of [the nation's] population." While various regulations promulgated under these statutes have been challenged in the courts, the Supreme Court has heard no case disputing the authority of Congress to act in these areas.

Restrictive Rulings on Commerce Power

After decades of decisions affirming Congress's steadily expanding commerce power, the Court issued a pair of restrictive rulings. The first of these decisions, in 1976, was subsequently overruled. The second decision, handed down in 1995, left a great deal of uncertainty in its wake.

STATE SOVEREIGNTY

A divided Supreme Court in 1976 placed the first restrictions in forty years on Congress's exercise of the commerce power when it struck down a portion of a 1974 act extending minimum wage and overtime requirements to state and local government employees. Congress was delving too far into the essential functions of state and local governments, the five-justice majority held in *National League of Cities v. Usery.*

Justice William H. Rehnquist, writing for the majority, said: "One undoubted attribute of state sovereignty is the state's power to determine the wages which shall be paid to those whom they employ in order to carry out their government functions, what hours those persons will work, and what compensation will be provided where these employees may be called upon to work overtime." Justice William J. Brennan Jr., in his minority

opinion, charged that the majority's reasoning was not far different from the pre-1937 Court's "overly restrictive construction of the commerce power."

Justice Harry A. Blackmun, in a concurring opinion in *Usery,* said he thought the Court's "balancing approach" in the case "does not outlaw federal power in areas such as environmental protection where the federal interest is demonstrably greater and where state facility compliance with imposed federal standards would be essential." In fact, in 1981 the Court unanimously upheld a federal strip-mining regulation act against a challenge from strip-mine operators, landowners, mining industry groups, and the states of Indiana and Virginia. They argued that Congress had overstepped its authority to regulate interstate commerce. Holding that Congress was well within its authority in enacting the Surface Mining Control and Reclamation Act of 1977, the Court said that once Congress has determined that some activity affects interstate commerce, "courts need only inquire whether the finding is rational." *(Hodel v. Indiana, Hodel v. Virginia Surface Mining and Reclamation Assn.)*

Nine years after the *Usery* ruling, after refusing several state invitations to expand the principle and further curtail federal interference in state matters, the Court reversed itself. Blackmun cast the swing vote, moving from support of *Usery* to opposition in the 1985 case of *Garcia v. San Antonio Metropolitan Transit Authority.* The issue was virtually the same as in *Usery;* this time the Court upheld the power of Congress to require that a city pay a federal minimum wage and overtime pay to its transit system employees. Blackmun explained that in *Usery,* the Court "attempted to articulate affirmative limits on the Commerce Clause power in terms of . . . state sovereignty. . . . Attempts by other courts since then to draw guidance from this model have proved it both impracticable and doctrinally barren. In sum . . . the Court tried to repair what did not need repair."

COMMERCE DEFINITION NARROWED

A more significant—and unsettling—ruling on Congress's exercise of its commerce power came in 1995. The Court, by a 5–4 vote, held that Congress had overstepped its constitutional powers to regulate interstate commerce when its passed a 1990 law designed to create gun-free zones near elementary and secondary schools. *(United States v. Lopez)* Chief Justice William H. Rehnquist, writing for the majority, said Congress had failed to prove that gun possession at or near schools had enough bearing on interstate commerce to justify federal involvement. The majority held that the law in question was "a criminal statute that by its terms has nothing to do with 'commerce' or any sort of economic enterprise, however broadly one might define those terms." If the Court were to accept such laws, Rehnquist wrote, "there never will be a distinction between what is truly national and what is truly local."

Justice Stephen G. Breyer, who wrote the main dissent, argued that the statute fell "well within the scope of the commerce power as this Court has understood that power over the last half-century." He said courts should give Congress more leeway in this area because the Constitution delegates commerce power directly to federal lawmakers, who are in a better position than judges to assess social needs in this area. Breyer said the legal test should be, not whether the regulated activity sufficiently affects interstate commerce, but rather whether Congress could have had a rational basis for concluding that it did so.

The *Lopez* decision was a surprising one and produced vastly different reactions. Political scientists Epstein and Walker said that some interpreted the decision "quite narrowly, as a simple warning to Congress that it must justify its legislation by showing the relationship between the activities regulated and interstate commerce." According to this viewpoint, if Congress had made a better case for the negative impact of school violence on commerce, the Court would have affirmed the law. The case, in any event, was seen as a narrow one and not a full-scale retreat from the Court's long-standing interpretation of the commerce clause. But other observers, according to Epstein and Walker, saw the *Lopez* decision "as much more significant, a signal that the Court will no longer allow Congress to regulate whatever it wishes on the ground that all activities somehow affect interstate commerce." Epstein and Walker themselves thought it was doubtful that the decision would mean a return to pre–New Deal notions about the commerce power, but still "Commerce Clause cases clearly merit close watching in the future."[12]

As scholars debated the effects of *Lopez*, new commerce clause cases began moving through the judicial system. The *Lopez* ruling spurred challenges to such federal laws as those making carjacking a federal crime, allowing victims of domestic violence to sue in federal court, and making it a crime to cross state lines to avoid child support.

NOTES

1. Lee Epstein and Thomas G. Walker, *Constitutional Law for a Changing America: Institutional Powers and Constraints,* 3rd ed. (Washington, D.C.: CQ Press, 1998), 359.

2. Ibid., 401.

3. Charles A. Lofgren, "'To Regulate Commerce': Federal Power under the Constitution," in *This Constitution: Our Enduring Legacy* (Washington, D.C.: CQ Press, 1986), 109.

4. John Bach McMaster, *A History of the People of the United States from the Revolution to the Civil War,* 8 vols. (New York: D. Appleton and Co., 1893), 206.

5. Charles Warren, *The Making of the Constitution* (Boston: Little, Brown, 1928), 16.

6. Loren P. Beth, *The Development of the American Constitution, 1877–1917* (New York: Harper and Row, Harper Torchbooks, 1971), 151.

7. Robert K. Carr, *The Supreme Court and Judicial Review* (New York: Farrar and Rinehart, 1942), 108.

8. Charles Warren, *The Supreme Court in United States History,* rev. ed. (Boston: Little, Brown, 1926), vol. 2, 736.

9. Carr, *The Supreme Court and Judicial Review,* 135.

10. C. Herman Pritchett, *The American Constitution,* 3rd ed. (New York: McGraw Hill, 1977), 198.

11. Quoted in C. Herman Pritchett, *The American Constitution,* 1st ed. (New York: McGraw-Hill, 1959), 604.

12. Epstein and Walker, *Constitutional Law for a Changing America,* 407–408.

SELECTED BIBLIOGRAPHY

Beard, Charles A. *Economic Interpretation of the Constitution of the United States.* New York: Macmillan, 1935.

Benson, Paul R., Jr. *Supreme Court and the Commerce Clause, 1937–1970.* Port Washington, N.Y.: Dunellen Publishing, 1970.

Beth, Loren P. *The Development of the American Constitution, 1877–1917.* New York: Harper and Row, 1971.

Beveridge, Albert J. *The Life of John Marshall.* 4 vols. Boston: Houghton Mifflin, 1919.

Biskupic, Joan, and Elder Witt. *Guide to the U.S. Supreme Court.* 3rd ed. Washington, D.C.: Congressional Quarterly, 1997.

Bork, Robert H. *The Antitrust Paradox.* New York: Basic Books, 1978.

Carr, Robert K. *The Supreme Court and Judicial Review.* New York: Farrar and Rinehart, 1942.

Conant, Michael. *The Constitution and the Economy: Objective Theory and Critical Commentary.* Norman: University of Oklahoma Press, 1991.

Corwin, Edward S. *The Commerce Power vs. States Rights.* Princeton, N.J.: Princeton University Press, 1936.

Crosskey, William W. *Politics and the Constitution in the History of the United States.* Chicago: University of Chicago Press, 1953.

Derthick, Martha, and Paul J. Quirk. *The Politics of Deregulation.* Washington, D.C.: Brookings Institution, 1985.

Epstein, Lee, and Thomas G. Walker. *Constitutional Law for a Changing America: Institutional Powers and Constraints.* 3rd ed. Washington, D.C.: CQ Press, 1998.

Frankfurter, Felix. *The Commerce Clause under Marshall, Taney, and Waite.* Chapel Hill: University of North Carolina Press, 1937.

Gavit, Bernard C. *Commerce Clause of the United States Constitution.* New York: AMS Press, 1970.

Harris, Richard A., and Sidney M. Milkis. *The Politics of Regulatory Change: A Tale of Two Agencies.* 2nd ed. New York: Oxford University Press, 1996.

Kallenbach, Joseph E. *Federal Cooperation with the States under the Commerce Clause.* Ann Arbor: University of Michigan Press, 1942.

Letwin, William. *Law and Economic Policy in America: The Evolution of the Sherman Antitrust Act.* Chicago: University of Chicago Press, 1959.

Leuchtenburg, William E. *The Supreme Court Reborn: The Constitutional Revolution in the Age of Roosevelt.* New York: Oxford University Press, 1995.

Levy, Leonard W., Kenneth L. Karst, and Dennis J. Mahoney, eds. *Encyclopedia of the American Constitution.* New York: Macmillan, 1986.

Liebhafsky, H. H. *American Government and Business.* New York: John Wiley & Sons, 1971.

Maxey, Margaret N., and Robert L. Kuhn. *Regulatory Reform: New Vision and Old Curse.* New York: Praeger, 1985.

Pritchett, C. Herman. *The American Constitution.* 3rd ed. New York: McGraw-Hill, 1977.

———. *The Roosevelt Court: A Study in Judicial Politics and Values, 1937–1947.* New York: Macmillan, 1948.

Reynolds, George G. *Distribution of Power to Regulate Interstate Carriers between the Nation and the States.* New York: AMS Press, 1928.

Swisher, Carl Brent. *American Constitutional Development.* 2nd ed. Cambridge, Mass.: Houghton Mifflin, 1954.

Tolchin, Susan, and Martin Tolchin. *Dismantling America: The Rush to Deregulate.* Boston: Houghton Mifflin, 1983.

Warren, Charles. *The Making of the Constitution.* Boston: Little, Brown, 1928.

———. *The Supreme Court in United States History.* Rev. ed. 2 vols. Boston: Little, Brown, 1926.

Witte, John. *The Politics and Development of the Federal Income Tax.* Madison: University of Wisconsin Press, 1985.

CHAPTER 9

Impeachment Power

IMPEACHMENT IS PERHAPS the greatest though least used power of Congress. In essence, it is a political action, couched in legal terminology, directed against a high official of the federal government. The Constitution lists impeachable offenses as treason, bribery, and other "high Crimes and Misdemeanors." The House of Representatives is the prosecutor. The Senate chamber is the courtroom, and the Senate is judge and jury. The penalty for conviction is removal from office and, if senators so decide, disqualification from holding further government office.

There is no appeal of a conviction. The Constitution states that the presidential power to grant reprieves and pardons does not include cases of impeachment. And officials convicted and removed from office remain subject to prosecution in the regular courts.

Impeachment proceedings have been initiated in the House on numerous occasions in the nation's history, but only seventeen government officials have been impeached: two presidents, one cabinet officer, one senator, and thirteen federal judges. Of the seventeen impeached, sixteen were sent to the Senate for trial (the other resigned before impeachment articles were drafted and sent to the Senate), but only seven ended in conviction. In two cases impeachment articles were dismissed before the trial began because the officials had left office. The seven other cases ended in acquittal. Through 1999, all of those convicted have been lower court judges.

Three of the impeachment cases stand out from all the rest—those of Supreme Court Justice Samuel Chase in 1804–1805, President Andrew Johnson in 1867–1868, and President Bill Clinton in 1998–1999. Chase was charged with partisan activity on the bench; Johnson for violating the Tenure of Office Act, which was devised by the Radical Republicans in Congress as a way to extend their control over the Johnson administration; and Clinton for perjury and obstruction of justice in trying to conceal an extramarital affair with a former White House intern.

All three men were acquitted by the Senate after sensational trials in which intense partisan politics was the major factor. Chase, a Federalist, was a victim of attacks on the Supreme Court by Jeffersonian Democrats, who planned to impeach Chief Justice John Marshall, also a Federalist, if Chase had been convicted. President Johnson was a victim of the Radical Republicans' opposition to his moderate reconstruction policies after the Civil War. Fervently anti-Clinton forces, particularly

conservatives in the House who considered him morally unfit, did not want to recognize the legitimacy of the Clinton presidency.

The power of the impeachment process was dramatically demonstrated in 1974 when the House initiated an inquiry into President Richard Nixon's involvement in the Watergate scandal, which began as a June 1972 break-in at Democratic National Headquarters in the Watergate office building in Washington, D.C., and White House efforts to cover up the burglary. In July 1974 the House Judiciary Committee, in sessions covered by nationwide television, approved three articles of impeachment. The articles charged Nixon with abuse of his presidential powers, obstruction of justice, and contempt of Congress. (See box, Nixon Resigns in Face of Impeachment, p. 351.)

Shortly after the committee's action, Republican leaders in both the House and Senate informed Nixon that the evidence against him virtually ensured that he would be impeached, convicted, and removed from office. Before the full House was scheduled to vote on the three articles, Nixon resigned on August 9. The House nevertheless formally acknowledged the committee's action. On August 20, 1974, by a 412–3 vote, it accepted the panel's report and recommendations and noted the president's resignation.[1]

Impeachment is just one of several means Congress can bring to bear against federal officers, including its own members, deemed to have committed criminal offenses or lesser acts of wrongdoing. Impeachment is the most drastic congressional remedy, and such proceedings—along with the related Senate trial—are very time consuming, requiring a major commitment of staff and other resources.

Alternatives Congress often uses include committee hearings on government scandals and oversight hearings of executive branch operations. Probes into some of the nation's most notorious scandals, including Crédit Mobilier, Teapot Dome, Watergate, and Iran-contra, did not result in any impeachments of federal officials. But many of those implicated were forced to resign from their government positions, and a number were later tried and convicted of criminal offenses. Often, the officials involved had left office before charges were brought against them. In the Iran-contra scandal, many of the key figures had already resigned, been fired, or retired from the government before the congressional hearings were held. (See Chapter 6, Congressional Investigations.)

In one unusual case, the second highest officer of the land

A rare sight in the Senate: the impeachment trial of a president. Here on January 7, 1999, the one hundred members of the body take an oath of impartiality at the start of President Bill Clinton's trial.

sought to begin impeachment proceedings against himself. In September 1973 President Nixon's vice president, Spiro T. Agnew, asked House Speaker Carl Albert, D-Okla., to initiate an impeachment investigation. This request came after Agnew learned the Justice Department was ready to seek an indictment against him for bribery, corruption, and income tax evasion. Agnew apparently believed the congressional impeachment proceeding would preempt the criminal investigation, while impeachment and conviction would result only in his removal from office. The House leadership, already facing a possible impeachment proceeding against President Nixon, denied his request.[2] Agnew resigned in October 1973 and pleaded "no contest" to a single charge of income tax evasion.

For members of Congress accused of wrongdoing or ethical violations while in office, the preferred type of sanction has been expulsion or, for lesser offenses, a formal rebuke, such as censure, condemnation, denunciation, reprimand, or other forms of disciplining. Between 1789 and 1999, four representatives and fifteen senators were expelled instead of being removed through the impeachment process. And many others resigned before the issue of their expulsion came to a vote. (*See Chapter 34, Seating and Disciplining; Chapter 35, Ethics and Criminal Prosecutions.*)

As outlined in the Constitution, the impeachment process was designed "as a method of national inquest into the conduct of public men," Alexander Hamilton wrote in *The Federalist* (No. 65).[3] The Constitution provides that impeachment proceedings may be brought against "the President, Vice President and all civil officers of the United States," but it does not explain who is a "civil officer." Impeachment is the only method Congress has to force a president to leave office. It was designed to deal with questions of high crimes and misdemeanors, and until ratification of the Twenty-fifth Amendment in 1967 no mechanism existed for dealing with situations in which a president was unfit to continue in office because of poor health but refused to resign or was mentally incapable of making a decision to resign. (*See "Presidential Disability," p. 371.*)

The overwhelming majority of impeachment proceedings since 1789 have been directed against federal judges, who hold lifetime appointments "during good behavior" and cannot be removed by any other method. Nor can their salary be taken away while in office except by impeachment. In addition to the twelve impeachments of judges that reached the Senate, judges also have been the target of most of the resolutions and investigations in the House that failed to result in impeachment.[4]

Others whose impeachment has been sought include presidents, cabinet members, diplomats, customs collectors, a senator, and a U.S. district attorney. In 1963 and again in 1970, attempts were made to impeach Supreme Court Justice William O. Douglas. The first occurred after he granted a stay of execution to convicted spies Julius and Ethel Rosenberg, the second after the Senate had rejected two of President Nixon's nominations to the Supreme Court. Neither attempt moved beyond the committee inquiry stage.

Proceedings against the only senator to be impeached, William Blount of Tennessee, were dismissed in 1799 after Blount had been expelled from the Senate instead. Secretary of War William W. Belknap, the only cabinet member to be impeached and tried by the Senate, was acquitted in 1876 largely because a number of senators questioned their authority to try Belknap after he had resigned from the Senate.

The House Judiciary Committee twice has ruled that certain federal officials were not subject to impeachment. In 1833 the committee determined that a territorial judge was not a civil officer within the meaning of the Constitution because he held office for only four years and the president could remove him at any time. In 1926 the committee said that a commissioner of the District of Columbia was immune from impeachment because he was an officer of the city of Washington, D.C., and not a civil officer of the United States.

History: Curbing Monarchs and Presidents

Impeachment as a constitutional process dates from fourteenth century England when the fledgling Parliament sought to make the king's advisers accountable. The monarch, who was considered incapable of wrongdoing, was immune. Impeachment was used against ministers and judges whom the legislature believed guilty of breaking the law or carrying out the unpopular orders of the king. The system was based on the common law, and the House of Lords could inflict the death penalty on those it found guilty.

Grounds for impeachment included both criminal and noncriminal activity. Joseph Story, in his *Commentaries on the Constitution of the United States,* wrote: "Lord chancellors and judges and other magistrates have not only been impeached for bribery and acting grossly contrary to the duties of their office, but for misleading their sovereign by unconstitutional opinions and for attempts to subvert the fundamental laws and introduce arbitrary power."[5]

In the mid-fifteenth century, impeachment fell into disuse, largely because the Tudor monarchs could force Parliament to

remove unwanted officials by bills of attainder and other penalties. But in the early seventeenth century the excesses and absolutist tendencies of the Stuart kings prompted Parliament to revive its impeachment power to curb the monarch by removing his favorite aides.

The struggle between the king and the Commons came to a head with the impeachment in 1642 of the earl of Strafford, a minister of Charles I. The House of Commons impeached the earl for subverting the fundamental law and introducing an arbitrary and tyrannical government. While the charge was changed to a bill of attainder in the House of Lords, an authority on English and U.S. constitutional law writes that "Strafford's impeachment may be regarded as the opening gun in the struggle whereby the Long Parliament 'prevented the English monarchy from hardening into an absolutism of the type then becoming general in Europe.'"[6]

More than fifty impeachments were brought to the House of Lords for trial between 1620 and 1787, when the American Constitution was being written. As the Framers toiled in Philadelphia, the long impeachment and trial of Warren Hastings was in progress in London. Hastings was charged with oppression, cruelty, bribery, and fraud as colonial administrator and first governor general in India. The trial before the House of Lords lasted from February 13, 1788, to April 23, 1795. Hastings was acquitted but by that time impeachment was widely regarded as unnecessary because of ministerial accountability to Parliament. The last impeachment trial in Britain occurred in 1806.

CONSTITUTIONAL CONVENTION DEBATE

Under the English system, an impeachment (indictment) was preferred by the House of Commons and decided by the House of Lords. In America, colonial governments and early state constitutions followed the British pattern of trial before the upper legislative body on charges brought by the lower house.

Despite these precedents, a major controversy arose over the impeachment process in the Constitutional Convention. The issue was whether the Senate should try impeachments. Opposing that role for the Senate, James Madison and Charles Pinckney asserted that it would make the president too dependent on the legislative branch. Suggested alternative trial bodies included the "national judiciary," the Supreme Court, or the assembled chief justices of state supreme courts. It was argued, however, that such bodies would be too small and perhaps even susceptible to corruption. In the end, the Senate was selected as the trial forum. Alexander Hamilton (a Senate opponent during the Convention) asked later in *The Federalist:* "Where else than in the Senate could have been found a tribunal sufficiently dignified, or sufficiently independent?"[7]

A lesser issue was the definition of impeachable crimes. In the original proposals, the president was to be removed on impeachment and conviction "for mal or corrupt conduct," or for "malpractice or neglect of duty." Later, the wording was changed to "treason, bribery or corruption," and then to "treason or bribery" alone. Contending that "treason or bribery" was too narrow, George Mason proposed adding "mal-administration" but then substituted "other high crimes and misdemeanors against the state" when Madison said that "mal-administration" was too vague. A final revision made impeachable crimes "treason, bribery or other high crimes and misdemeanors."[8] Debate over the meaning of this phrase has been reviewed during every serious impeachment inquiry.

The provisions of the Constitution on impeachment are scattered through the first three articles. The House of Representatives is given the "sole power of impeachment." The Senate is given "the sole power to try all impeachments." Impeachments may be brought against "the President, Vice President and all civil officers of the United States" for "treason, bribery or other high crimes or misdemeanors." Conviction is automatically followed by "removal from office" and possibly by "disqualification to hold" further public office. (See box, Constitutional Mandate, this page.)

The first attempt to use the impeachment power was made in 1796. A petition from residents of the Northwest Territory, submitted to the House on April 25, accused Judge George Turner of the territorial supreme court of arbitrary conduct. The petition was referred briefly to a special House committee

and then was referred to Attorney General Charles Lee. Impeachment proceedings were dropped after Lee assured residents the territorial government would prosecute Turner in the territorial courts.

CONTROVERSIAL QUESTIONS

Three major questions have dominated the history of impeachment in the United States:

• What is an impeachable offense?
• Can senators serve as impartial "jurors"?
• Are there ways other than impeachment to remove a federal judge from office?

Impeachable Offenses

"Treason" and "bribery," as constitutionally designated impeachable crimes, have caused little debate, for treason is defined elsewhere in the Constitution and bribery is well defined in statutory law. "High Crimes and Misdemeanors," however, have been anything that the prosecution has wanted to make them. In the 1970 attempt to impeach Supreme Court Justice Douglas, Rep. Gerald R. Ford, R-Mich., declared: "An impeachable offense is whatever a majority of the House of Representatives considers it to be at a given moment in history." The phrase is the subject of continuing debate pitting broad constructionists, who have viewed impeachment as a political weapon, against narrow constructionists, who have regarded impeachment as being limited to offenses indictable at common law.

The constitutional debates seem to indicate that impeachment is to be regarded as a political weapon. Narrow constructionists quickly won a major victory, though, when Supreme Court Justice Samuel Chase was acquitted, using as his defense the argument that the charges against him were not based on any indictable offense. President Andrew Johnson also won acquittal using a similar defense. His lawyers argued that conviction could result only from commission of high criminal offenses against the United States.

Impeachment trials in the twentieth century suggest that the arguments of the broad constructionists still carry considerable weight. Robert W. Archbald, associate judge of the U.S. Commerce Court, was convicted and removed from office in 1913, and Halsted L. Ritter, U.S. judge for the southern district of Florida, in 1936. Archbald was convicted of soliciting for himself and for friends valuable favors from railroad companies, some of which were litigants in his court. It was conceded, however, that he had committed no indictable offense. Ritter was convicted for conduct in a receivership case that raised serious doubts about his integrity.

This debate resumed in 1974 with the impeachment inquiry into the conduct of President Nixon. The impeachment inquiry staff of the House Judiciary Committee argued for a broad view of "high crimes and misdemeanors" while Nixon's defense attorneys argued for a narrow view. (See box, Constitutional Grounds for Impeachment, p. 336).

As adopted by the House Judiciary Committee, Article I

This ticket allowed admittance to the Senate galleries for the impeachment trial of President Andrew Johnson in 1868.

charged the president with obstruction of justice, a charge falling within the narrow view of impeachable offenses. Articles II and III reflected the broader interpretation, charging Nixon with abuse of his presidential powers and contempt of Congress.

The issue arose again in 1998 when the House Judiciary Committee considered impeachment charges against President Clinton. Republicans argued that Clinton had committed perjury and obstructed justice in dereliction of his duty as president to take care that the laws be faithfully executed. Democrats countered that Clinton's actions to cover up his extramarital affair were the natural reactions of a man trying to avoid personal and public embarrassment and that they did not rise to the level of impeachable "high crimes and misdemeanors." Republicans said the distinction between personal actions and official conduct was a false one; perjury was legally wrong under either circumstance, and no one, including the president of the United States, was above the law. These constitutional arguments were overshadowed, however, by the political animosity that many House Republicans harbored toward Clinton, and the impeachment of the president proceeded.

Conflicts of Interest

An equally controversial issue, particularly in earlier impeachment trials, concerned the partisan interests of senators, which raised serious doubt about their ability to sit as impartial jurors.

Had Andrew Johnson been convicted, and thus removed from office, his successor as president would have been Benjamin F. Wade, R-Ohio, the Senate's president pro tempore. Because the vice presidency was vacant, Wade would have become president under the constitutional line of succession then in effect. Wade took part in the Senate trial and voted for conviction. Fortunately for Johnson, the president's son-in-law, David T. Patterson, D-Tenn., also took part in the trial and voted acquittal.

In the Johnson trial and in others, senators have been outspoken critics or supporters of the defendant, yet have participated in the trial and have voted on the articles. Some senators who had held seats in the House when the articles of impeachment first came up, and had voted on them as representatives, have not disqualified themselves during the trial.

Intense outside lobbying for and against the defendant has been aimed at senators. Senators have testified as witnesses at some trials and then voted on the articles.

Senators may request to be excused from the trial, and in recent cases some senators have disqualified themselves when possible conflicts of interest arose.

Removal of Judges

For most of the twentieth century, Congress has been engaged in a continuing search for an alternative to impeachment as a method of removing federal judges. This search has been spurred by concern to free the Senate, faced by an enormous legislative workload, from the time-consuming process of sitting as a court of impeachment, and by the desire of some members to restrict judicial power by providing a simpler and swifter means of removal than the cumbersome and unwieldy impeachment process.

In three impeachment trials in 1986 and 1989, the Senate for the first time used a streamlined procedure to save time. Instead of convening the Senate to hear the entire trial, a special bipartisan twelve-member committee was appointed to hear witnesses and gather evidence. Once this process was completed, the full Senate then convened to hear final arguments and vote on the impeachment articles. This procedure had been authorized by a 1935 amendment to the Senate's impeachment trial rules. (*See box, Senate Rules of Procedure and Practice for Impeachment Trials, p. 338.*)

All other efforts to revise and accelerate the impeachment process have been unsuccessful. So, too, have attempts to amend the Constitution to limit the tenure of federal judges to a definite term of office. Also unsuccessful have been legislative efforts to provide a judicial trial and judgment for removal of federal judges who violate so-called good behavior standards.

Impeachment Procedure: No Uniform Practice

The first impeachment proceedings, against Judge George Turner, provided no precedents for later impeachments. The process has been used so infrequently and under such widely varying circumstances that no uniform practice has emerged.

HOUSE PROCEEDINGS

The House has no standing rules dealing with its role in the impeachment process, a role the Constitution describes in fewer than a dozen words. (*See box, Constitutional Mandate, p. 334.*)

At various times impeachment proceedings have been initiated by the introduction of a resolution by a member, by a letter or message from the president, by a grand jury action forwarded to the House from a territorial legislature, by a memorial setting

CONSTITUTIONAL GROUNDS FOR IMPEACHMENT

When Congress prepared for impeachment proceedings against President Richard Nixon in 1974, the long-standing controversy over the meaning of "high crimes and misdemeanors" among impeachable offenses listed in Article II, Section 4 of the Constitution surfaced anew. Members of the House Judiciary Committee offered a broad interpretation, while the president's defense team presented a narrow view.

OFFICIAL MISCONDUCT

The House inquiry staff argued:[1]

"The framers intended impeachment to be a constitutional safeguard of the public trust, the powers of government conferred upon the president. . . .

"Each of the 13 American impeachments involved charges of misconduct incompatible with the official position of the officeholder. This conduct falls into three broad categories: (1) exceeding the constitutional bounds of the powers of the office in derogation of the powers of another branch of government; (2) behaving in a manner grossly incompatible with the proper function and purpose of the office; and (3) employing the power of the office for an improper purpose or for personal gain. . . .

"In drawing up articles of impeachment, the House has placed little emphasis on criminal conduct. . . .

"All have involved charges of conduct incompatible with continued performance of the office; some have explicitly rested upon a 'course of conduct'. . . . Some of the individual articles seem to have alleged conduct that, taken alone, would not have been considered serious. . . .

"Impeachment and the criminal law serve fundamentally different purposes. Impeachment is the first step in a remedial process. . . . The purpose . . . is not personal punishment; its function is primarily to maintain constitutional government. . . .

"The general applicability of the criminal law also makes it inappropriate as the standard. . . . In an impeachment proceeding a president is called to account for abusing powers which only a president possesses.

"Impeachable conduct . . . may include the serious failure to discharge the affirmative duties imposed on the president by the Constitution. Unlike a criminal case, the cause for removal . . . may be based on his entire course of conduct in office. . . . It may be a course of conduct more than individual acts that has a tendency to subvert constitutional government.

"To confine impeachable conduct to indictable offenses may well be to set a standard so restrictive as not to reach conduct that might adversely affect the system of government. . . .

"In the English practice and in several of the American impeachments, the criminality issue was not raised at all. The emphasis has been on the significant effect of the conduct. . . . Impeachment was evolved . . . to cope with both the inadequacy of criminal standards and the impotence of the courts to deal with the conduct of great public figures. It would be anomalous if the framers, having barred criminal sanctions from the impeachment remedy . . . intended to restrict the grounds for impeachment to conduct that was criminal."

CRIMES AGAINST THE STATE

The president's lawyers argued:[2]

"To argue that the president may be impeached for something less than a criminal offense, with all the safeguards that definition implies, would be a monumental step backwards into all those old English practices that our Constitution sought to eliminate. American impeachment was not designed to force a president into surrendering executive authority . . . but to check overtly criminal actions as they are defined by law. . . .

"The terminology 'high crimes and misdemeanors' should create no confusion or ambiguity. . . . It was a unitary phrase meaning crimes against the state, as opposed to those against individuals. . . .

"The acquittal of President Johnson over a century ago strongly indicates that the Senate has refused to adopt a broad view of 'other high crimes and misdemeanors'. . . . Impeachment of a president should be resorted to only for cases of the gravest kind—the commission of a crime named in the Constitution or a criminal offense against the laws of the United States. If there is any doubt as to the gravity of an offense or as to a president's conduct or motives, the doubt should be resolved in his favor. This is the necessary price for having an independent executive. . . .

"Any analysis that broadly construes the power to impeach and convict can be reached only . . . by placing a subjective gloss on the history of impeachment that results in permitting the Congress to do whatever it deems most politic. The intent of the framers . . . was to restrict the *political* reach of the impeachment power.

"Those who seek to broaden the impeachment power invite the use of power 'as a means of crushing political adversaries or ejecting them from office'. . . . The acceptance of such an invitation would be destructive to our system of government and to the fundamental principle of separation of powers."

1. House Judiciary Committee, *Constitutional Grounds for Presidential Impeachment*, 93rd Cong., 2nd sess., 1974.

2. "An Analysis of the Constitutional Standards for Presidential Impeachment," February 1974, prepared by James D. St. Clair, John J. Chester, Michael A. Sterlacci, Jerome J. Murphy, and Loren A. Smith, attorneys for President Nixon.

forth charges, by a resolution authorizing a general investigation, or by a resolution reported by the House Judiciary Committee. The eight cases to reach the Senate between 1900 and 1991 were based initially on Judiciary Committee resolutions. In Bill Clinton's case in 1998–1999, the impetus for impeachment came—for the first time—from the investigation of a court-appointed independent counsel.

Before creation of the Judiciary Committee in 1813, such matters were referred to a special committee created for that purpose. This was the case in the first three impeachments that moved to the Senate, those of Sen. William Blount, Judge John Pickering, and Justice Samuel Chase. The impeachment of Judge James H. Peck in 1830 was the first referred to the Judiciary Committee.

After submission of the charges, a committee investigation is begun. The committee decides in each case whether the subject of the inquiry has the right to be present at committee proceedings, to be represented by counsel, to present and question witnesses.

If the charges are supported by the investigation, the committee reports an impeachment resolution. Since 1912, articles of impeachment have been reported by the committee simultaneously with the resolution. Before that time, the articles were drawn up after the House had approved the resolution of impeachment.

The House is no more bound by a committee's recommendation on impeachment than it is by a committee's recommendation and action on any legislative matter. In 1933 the House Judiciary Committee found insufficient grounds to recommend impeachment of Judge Harold Louderback, but the House impeached the judge anyway.

The target of an impeachment resolution is impeached if the House adopts a resolution of impeachment by majority vote. The articles of impeachment may be approved by a simple majority and may be amended on the House floor. When the articles of impeachment against President Andrew Johnson were considered by the full House in 1868, two additional articles were adopted along with those recommended by the committee.

After the resolution and the articles have been approved by the House, the House managers are selected to present the case for impeachment to the Senate, acting as prosecutors in the Senate trial. An odd number—ranging from five to eleven—has traditionally been selected, including members from both parties who voted in favor of impeachment. They have been selected in various ways: by ballot, with a majority vote necessary for election; by resolution naming the slate; or by the Speaker. Any House member may attend the trial, but the House managers are the official representatives in the Senate proceedings.

SENATE TRIAL

In 1868, for the impeachment trial of President Johnson, the Senate adopted a set of twenty-five rules. One new rule was added in 1935. *(See box, Senate Rules of Procedure and Practice for Impeachment Trials, p. 338.)*

The trial is conducted in a fashion similar to a criminal trial.

The Constitution mandates that the chief justice of the Supreme Court preside over the impeachment trial of a president. Here Chief Justice William H. Rehnquist, who presided over the 1999 trial of President Bill Clinton, is sworn in by president pro tempore Strom Thurmond, R-S.C.

SENATE RULES OF PROCEDURE AND PRACTICE FOR IMPEACHMENT TRIALS

Following are the major provisions of rules used by the Senate during impeachment trials. The Senate's impeachment trial rules are, by turns, excruciatingly precise and frustratingly vague. These rules were first written for the trial of President Andrew Johnson in 1868. Rule XI was adopted on May 28, 1935. The rules were modified slightly in 1986.

I. Whensoever the Senate shall receive notice from the House of Representatives that managers are appointed on their part to conduct an impeachment against any person and are directed to carry articles of impeachment to the Senate, the Secretary of the Senate shall immediately inform the House of Representatives that the Senate is ready to receive the managers, for purpose of exhibiting such articles of impeachment, agreeably to such notice.

II. When the managers of an impeachment shall be introduced at the bar of the Senate and shall signify that they are ready to exhibit articles of impeachment against any person, the Presiding Officer of the Senate shall direct the Sergeant at Arms to make proclamation, who shall, after making proclamation, repeat the following words, viz: 'All persons are commanded to keep silence, on pain of imprisonment, while the House of Representatives is exhibiting to the Senate articles of impeachment' . . . after which articles shall be exhibited, and then the Presiding Officer of the Senate shall inform the managers that the Senate will take proper order on the subject of the impeachment, of which due notice shall be given to the House of Representatives.

III. Upon such articles being presented to the Senate, the Senate shall, at 1 o'clock afternoon of the day (Sunday excepted) following such presentation, or sooner if ordered by the Senate, proceed to the consideration of such articles and shall continue in session from day to day (Sundays excepted) after the trial shall commence (unless otherwise ordered by the Senate) until final judgment shall be rendered . . .

IV. When the President of the United States or the Vice President of the United States . . . shall be impeached, the Chief Justice of the United States shall preside; and in a case requiring the said Chief Justice to preside notice shall be given to him by the Presiding Officer of the Senate of the time and place fixed for the consideration of articles of impeachment, as aforesaid, with a request to attend. . . .

V. The Presiding Officer shall have power to make and issue, by himself or by the Secretary of the Senate, all orders, mandates, writs, and precepts authorized by these rules or by the Senate, and to make and enforce such other regulations and orders in the premises as the Senate may authorize or provide.

VI. The Senate shall have power to compel the attendance of witnesses, to enforce obedience to its orders, mandates, writs, precepts, and judgments, to preserve order, and to punish in a summary way contempts of, and disobedience to, its authority. . . .

VII. The Presiding Officer of the Senate shall direct all necessary preparations in the Senate Chamber, and the Presiding Officer on the trial shall direct all the forms of proceedings while the Senate is sitting for the purpose of trying an impeachment . . . And the Presiding Officer on the trial may rule on all questions of evidence including, but not limited to, questions of relevancy, materiality, and redundancy of evidence and incidental questions, which ruling shall stand as the judgment of the Senate, unless some Member of the Senate shall ask that a formal vote be taken thereon. . . .

VIII. Upon presentation of articles of impeachment and the organization of the Senate as hereinbefore provided, a writ of summons shall issue to the person impeached, reciting said articles, and notifying him to appear before the Senate upon a day and at a place to be fixed by the Senate and named in such writ, and file his answer to said articles of impeachment and to stand to and abide the orders and judgments of the Senate thereon. . . .

IX. At 12:30 o'clock afternoon of the day appointed for the return of the summons against the person impeached, the legislative and executive business of the Senate shall be suspended, and the Secretary of the Senate shall administer an oath to the returning officer. . . .

X. The person impeached shall then be called to appear and answer the articles of impeachment against him. If he appears, or any person for him, the appearance shall be recorded. . . .

XI. That in the trial of any impeachment the Presiding Officer of the Senate, if the Senate so orders, shall appoint a committee of senators to receive evidence and take testimony at such times as the committee may determine . . .

XII. At 12:30 o'clock afternoon, or at such other hour as the Senate may order, of the day appointed for the trial of an impeachment, the legislative and executive business of the Senate shall be suspended, and the Secretary shall give notice to the House of Representatives that the Senate is ready to proceed to the impeachment of [the president] in the Senate chamber.

XIII. The hour of the day at which the Senate shall sit upon the tri-

Both sides may present witnesses and evidence, and the defendant is allowed counsel, the right to testify in his own behalf, and the right of cross-examination. If the president or the vice president is on trial, the Constitution requires the chief justice of the United States to preside. The Constitution is silent on a presiding officer for lesser defendants, but Senate practice has been for the vice president or the president pro tempore to preside.

The presiding officer can issue all orders needed to compel witnesses to appear or to enforce obedience to Senate orders.

The presiding officer administers the oath to all the senators before they take part in the trial. The presiding officer rules on all questions of evidence and the ruling stands unless the presider decides to submit the question to a vote of the Senate or unless a senator requests such a vote. Custom dictates that most questions concerning the admissibility of evidence are submitted to the Senate for decision. The presiding officer questions witnesses and asks questions submitted in writing by senators, who do not directly question witnesses themselves.

al of an impeachment shall be (unless otherwise ordered) 12 o'clock [noon]; and when the hour shall arrive, the Presiding Officer upon such trial shall cause proclamation to be made, and the business of the trial shall proceed. The adjournment of the Senate sitting in said trial shall not operate as an adjournment of the Senate; but on such adjournment the Senate shall resume the consideration of its legislative and executive business.

XIV. The Secretary of the Senate shall record the proceedings in cases of impeachment as in the case of legislative proceedings, and the same shall be reported in the same manner as the legislative proceedings of the Senate.

XV. Counsel for the parties shall be admitted to appear and be heard upon an impeachment.

XVI. All motions, objections, requests, or applications whether relating to the procedure of the Senate or relating immediately to the trial (including questions with respect to admission of evidence or other questions arising during the trial) made by the parties or their counsel shall be addressed to the Presiding Officer only, and if he, or any Senator, require it, they shall be committed to writing and read at the Secretary's table.

XVII. Witnesses shall be examined by one person on behalf of the party producing them, and then cross-examined by one person on the other side.

XVIII. If a Senator is called as a witness, he shall be sworn, and give his testimony standing in his place.

XIX. If a Senator wishes a question to be put to a witness, or a manager, or to counsel of the person impeached, or to offer a motion or order (except a motion to adjourn), it shall be reduced to writing, and put to the Presiding Officer. The parties or their counsel may interpose objections to witnesses answering questions propounded at the request of any Senator and the merits of any such objection may be argued by the parties or their counsel. Ruling on any such objection shall be made as provided in Rule VII. It shall not be in order for any Senator to engage in a colloquy.

XX. At all times while the Senate is sitting upon the trial of an impeachment the doors of the Senate shall be kept open, unless the Senate shall direct the doors to be closed while deliberating upon its decisions. A motion to close the doors may be acted upon without objection, or, if objection is heard, the motion shall be voted on without debate by the yeas and nays, which shall be entered on the record.

XXI. All preliminary and interlocutory questions, and all motions, shall be argued for not exceeding one hour (unless the Senate otherwise orders) on each side.

XXII. The case, on each side, shall be opened by one person. The final argument on the merits may be made by two persons on each side (unless otherwise ordered by the Senate upon application for that purpose), and the argument shall be opened and closed on the part of the House of Representatives.

XXIII. An article of impeachment shall not be divisible for the purpose of voting thereon at any time during the trial. Once voting has commenced on an article of impeachment, voting shall be continued until voting has been completed on all articles of impeachment unless the Senate adjourns for a period not to exceed one day or adjourns sine die. On the final question whether the impeachment is sustained, the yeas and nays shall be taken on each article of impeachment separately; and if the impeachment shall not, upon any of the articles presented, be sustained by the votes of two-thirds of the Members present, a judgment of acquittal shall be entered; but if the person impeached shall be convicted upon any such article by the votes of two-thirds of the Members present, the Senate shall proceed to the consideration of such other matters as may be determined to be appropriate prior to pronouncing judgment . . . the Presiding Officer shall first state the question; thereafter each Senator, as his name is called, shall rise in his place and answer: guilty or not guilty.

XXIV. All the orders and decisions may be acted upon without objection, or, if objection is heard, the orders and decisions shall be voted on without debate by yeas and nays, which shall be entered on the record, subject, however, to the operation of Rule VII, except that when the doors shall be closed for deliberation, and in that case no member shall speak more than once on one question, and for not more than 10 minutes on an interlocutory question, and for not more than 15 minutes on the final question, unless by consent of the Senate, to be had without debate. . . .

XXV. Witnesses shall be sworn. . . . Which oath shall be administered by the Secretary, or any other duly authorized person. . . .

XXVI. If the Senate shall at any time fail to sit for the consideration of articles of impeachment on the day or hour fixed therefor, the Senate may, by an order to be adopted without debate, fix a day and hour for resuming such consideration.

All of the Senate's orders and decisions during an impeachment trial are made by roll-call vote, and without debate unless in secret session. On the final question, guilt or innocence, each senator is limited to fifteen minutes of debate in secret session. The Senate votes separately on each article of impeachment; the Constitution requires a two-thirds vote for conviction. If no article is approved by two-thirds of the senators present, the impeached official is acquitted. If any article receives two-thirds approval, the person is convicted. The Senate may vote separately to remove the person from office. But this is not required. Article II, Section 4 of the Constitution states that federal officials shall be removed from office upon impeachment and conviction. The Senate also may vote to disqualify the person from holding future federal office. Disqualification is not mandatory. Only two of the seven convictions have been accompanied by disqualification, which is decided by majority vote instead of the two-thirds needed for conviction.

RECORDS, RESIGNATIONS, RECESSES

The shortest time from House impeachment to a Senate verdict was one month, in the impeachment of federal Judge Halsted Ritter in 1936. The longest was fourteen and a half months for the impeachment and conviction of federal Judge Alcee L. Hastings in 1988–1989. The impeachment of President Johnson took three months from the House vote to Senate judgment; President Clinton, less than two months.

The shortest Senate trial on record was that for Judge West H. Humphreys in 1862; it lasted only one day. The longest was the two months consumed in the Senate trial of President Johnson. The 1980s trials of federal judges Harry E. Claiborne, Walter L. Nixon Jr., and Hastings were special cases in that evidence was gathered by special committees instead of by the full Senate. In Hastings's case there was a time span of three and a half months between appointment of the twelve-member committee and the Senate vote.

In some instances, officials about to be impeached have resigned first, ending the proceedings because the objective of impeachment—removal from office—had been accomplished. This was the case in the impeachment proceedings against President Richard Nixon in 1974. Two federal judges, Mark H. Delahay, impeached in 1873, and George V. English, impeached in 1926, resigned before their Senate trials could begin.

Resignation, however, is not a foolproof way to escape impeachment. Secretary of War William Belknap, aware of the findings of a congressional committee implicating him in the acceptance of bribes, resigned at 10 o'clock on the morning of March 2, 1876. Some time after 3 o'clock that afternoon, the House impeached him by voice vote. The Senate debated the question of its jurisdiction, in light of his resignation, and decided by a vote of 37–29 that he could be impeached and tried despite his no longer being in office. He was found not guilty of the charges.

Historical precedent indicates that an impeachment proceeding does not die with adjournment. In 1890–1891 the House Judiciary Committee investigated the conduct of a federal judge and decided that he should be impeached; a resolution to that effect was reported in 1891 and the House began debate but did not conclude it before adjournment. In the new 52nd Congress in 1892, the evidence taken in the first investigation was referred to the committee again, a second investigation was conducted, and the committee decided against impeachment.

In the impeachment of Judge John Pickering, the House impeached him in 1803 but adjourned before drawing up articles of impeachment, which the next Congress completed.

The question of whether impeachment would have to begin again if the House impeached an official in one Congress but the Senate trial could not begin until the next was answered in the case of President Clinton. The lame-duck House voted articles of impeachment against him in the 105th Congress. The Senate proceeded with the trial in the 106th Congress without the House reconsidering the matter. The view of the Senate as a continuing body according to custom had indicated that a trial could take place in a new Congress without a repetition of the House impeachment proceedings. The Senate decided in 1876 that a trial of impeachment could proceed only when Congress was in session.

Officials Impeached: Two Presidents, Few Others

By far the largest category of government officials impeached has been federal judges. Through 1999, the House had impeached seventeen federal officials, thirteen of whom were judges (including one Supreme Court justice, Samuel Chase). Twelve impeached judges subsequently were tried by the Senate, but only seven were convicted and removed from office. Chase was acquitted. The other impeached officials—none of whom was convicted by the Senate—were President Andrew Johnson (1868), Sen. William Blount (1797), Secretary of War William Belknap (1876), and President Bill Clinton (1999).

Johnson, Belknap, and Clinton were acquitted, and charges against Blount were dismissed after the Senate decided to expel him. Johnson and Clinton underwent the entire House and Senate impeachment process; President Nixon faced certain impeachment and conviction by the Senate had he not resigned.

Besides Johnson and Clinton, campaigns to impeach two other chief executives progressed as far as a House vote. Both efforts were then decisively rejected.

PRESIDENT ANDREW JOHNSON

Impeachment is the ultimate limitation on the power of the president. The first presidential impeachment occurred in 1868. President Johnson was charged with violating a federal statute, the Tenure of Office Act. But, more importantly, the event represented a profoundly political struggle. Questions such as control of the Republican Party, dealing with the South in a state of chaos following the Civil War, and monetary and economic policy were all weighed heavily in the proceedings.[9]

Johnson had been the only member of the U.S. Senate from a seceding southern state (Tennessee) to remain loyal to the Union in 1861. Abraham Lincoln later made him military governor of Tennessee and chose him as his running mate in 1864. Johnson was a lifelong Democrat, but he and Lincoln ran on the Union Ticket in 1864 in an attempt to bridge the divisions within the war-torn nation.

On Lincoln's death in 1865, this outsider without allies or connections in the Republican Party succeeded to the presidency. Johnson's ideas on what should have been done to reconstruct and readmit the southern states to representation clashed with the wishes of a majority of Congress, overwhelmingly controlled by the Republicans.

Johnson as president was an anomaly. He was a southerner at a time when the South was out of the Union—a Jacksonian Democrat who believed in states' rights, hard money, and mini-

This photo taken in 1868 shows the managers of the House in the impeachment proceedings against President Andrew Johnson. Standing, from the left, are James F. Wilson, R-Iowa, George S. Boutwell, R-Mass., John A. Logan, R-Ill.; seated, from the left, Benjamin F. Butler, R-Mass., Thaddeus Stevens, R-Pa., Thomas Williams, R-Pa., John A. Bingham, R-Ohio.

mal federal government activity, running with an incumbent president who was pursuing a policy of expansion both in the money supply and the role of government.

Congress was divided into roughly three groups. The small minority of Democrats supported the president. About half the Republicans were known as "Radicals" because they favored strong action to revolutionize southern society, by harsh military means if necessary. The other half of the Republicans were more conservative; while unwilling to go so far as the Radicals, they wanted to make sure the South did not return to the unquestioned control of those who had ruled it before the Civil War.

Upon taking office, Johnson began to pursue Lincoln's mild and tolerant reconstruction plans. The new president felt that a few basics were all that needed to be secured: abolition of slavery; ratification of the Thirteenth Amendment, which abolished slavery in all states; repudiation of all state debts contracted by the Confederate governments; and nullification of secession. When the southern states had done these things, Johnson felt, they should be readmitted.

But Republicans wanted more: a Freedmen's Bureau, to protect and provide services for the ex-slaves, a civil rights bill guaranteeing blacks their rights, and an overall plan of reconstruction providing for temporary military governments in the South. Throughout 1866, Johnson and Congress battled over these issues.

The Tenure of Office Act, the violation of which was to be the legal basis for Johnson's impeachment, was passed over his veto March 2, 1867. The act forbade the president to remove civil officers (appointed with the consent of the Senate) without the approval of the Senate. Its purpose was to protect incumbent Republican officeholders from executive retaliation if they did not support the president.

Impeachment in the House

About the time the Tenure of Office Act was being debated, the first moves toward impeachment began. On January 7, 1867, Rep. James M. Ashley, R-Ohio, rose and formally charged the president with high crimes and misdemeanors. Ashley made

Article XI — May 16, 1868

YEAS.		NAYS.
Guilty	Anthony	
	Bayard	not guilty
	Buckalew	not guilty
Guilty	Cameron	
Guilty	Cattell	
Guilty	Chandler	
Guilty	Cole	
Guilty	Conkling	
Guilty	Conness	
Guilty	Corbett	
Guilty	Cragin	
	Davis	not guilty
	Dixon	not guilty
	Doolittle	not guilty
Guilty	Drake	
Guilty	Edmunds	
Guilty	Ferry	
	Fessenden	not guilty
	Fowler	not guilty
Guilty	Frelinghuysen	
	Grimes	not guilty
Guilty	Harlan	
	Henderson	not guilty
	Hendricks	not guilty
Guilty	Howard	
Guilty	Howe	
	Johnson	not guilty
	McCreery	not guilty
Guilty	Morgan	
Guilty	Morrill, of Maine	
Guilty	Morrill, of Vt.	
Guilty	Morton	
	Norton	not guilty
Guilty	Nye	
Guilty	Patterson, of N. H.	
	Patterson, of Tenn.	not guilty
Guilty	Pomeroy	
Guilty	Ramsey	
	Ross	not guilty
	Saulsbury	not guilty
Guilty	Sherman	
Guilty	Sprague	
Guilty	Stewart	
Guilty	Sumner	
Guilty	Thayer	
Guilty	Tipton	
	Trumbull	not guilty
	Van Winkle	not guilty
	Vickers	not guilty
Guilty	Wade	
Guilty	Willey	
Guilty	Williams	
Guilty	Wilson	
Guilty	Yates	
35		**19**

MAY 11, 1868.

Article II

YEAS.		NAYS.
1 Guilty	Anthony	
	Bayard	Not guilty 1
	Buckalew	Not guilty 2
2 Guilty	Cameron	
3 Guilty	Cattell	
Guilty	Chandler	
Guilty	Cole	
Guilty	Conkling	
Guilty	Conness	
Guilty	Corbett	
Guilty	Cragin	
	Davis	Not guilty 3
	Dixon	Not guilty 4
	Doolittle	Not guilty 5
Guilty	Drake	
Guilty	Edmunds	
Guilty	Ferry	
	Fessenden	Not guilty 6
	Fowler	Not guilty 7
Guilty	Frelinghuysen	
	Grimes	Not guilty 8
Guilty	Harlan	
	Henderson	Not guilty 9
	Hendricks	Not guilty 10
Guilty	Howard	
Guilty	Howe	
	Johnson	Not guilty 11
	McCreery	Not guilty 12
Guilty	Morgan	
Guilty	Morrill, of Maine	
Guilty	Morrill, of Vt.	
Guilty	Morton	
	Norton	Not guilty 13
Guilty	Nye	
Guilty	Patterson, of N. H.	
	Patterson, of Tenn.	Not guilty 14
Guilty	Pomeroy	
Guilty	Ramsey	
	Ross	Not guilty 15
	Saulsbury	Not guilty 16
Guilty	Sherman	
Guilty	Sprague	
Guilty	Stewart	
Guilty	Sumner	
Guilty	Thayer	
Guilty	Tipton	
	Trumbull	Not guilty 17
	Van Winkle	Not guilty 18
	Vickers	Not guilty 19
Guilty	Wade	
Guilty	Willey	
Guilty	Williams	
Guilty	Wilson	
Guilty	Yates	
35		**19**

MAY 11, 1868.

Article III

YEAS.		NAYS.
1 Guilty	Anthony	
	Bayard	not guilty 1
	Buckalew	not guilty 2
2 Guilty	Cameron	
3 Guilty	Cattell	
4 Guilty	Chandler	
5 Guilty	Cole	
6 Guilty	Conkling	
7 Guilty	Conness	
8 Guilty	Corbett	
9 Guilty	Cragin	
	Davis	not guilty 3
	Dixon	not guilty 4
	Doolittle	not guilty 5
10 Guilty	Drake	
11 Guilty	Edmunds	
12 Guilty	Ferry	
	Fessenden	not guilty 6
	Fowler	not guilty 7
13 Guilty	Frelinghuysen	
	Grimes	not guilty 8
14 Guilty	Harlan	
	Henderson	not guilty 9
	Hendricks	not guilty 10
15 Guilty	Howard	
16 Guilty	Howe	
	Johnson	not guilty 11
	McCreery	not guilty 12
17 Guilty	Morgan	
18 Guilty	Morrill, of Maine	
19 Guilty	Morrill, of Vt.	
20 Guilty	Morton	
	Norton	not guilty 13
21 Guilty	Nye	
22 Guilty	Patterson, of N. H.	
	Patterson, of Tenn.	not guilty 14
23 Guilty	Pomeroy	
24 Guilty	Ramsey	
	Ross	not guilty 15
	Saulsbury	not guilty 16
25 Guilty	Sherman	
26 Guilty	Sprague	
27 Guilty	Stewart	
28 Guilty	Sumner	
29 Guilty	Thayer	
30 Guilty	Tipton	
	Trumbull	not guilty 17
	Van Winkle	not guilty 18
	Vickers	not guilty 19
31 Guilty	Wade	
32 Guilty	Willey	
33 Guilty	Williams	
34 Guilty	Wilson	
35 Guilty	Yates	
35		**19**

MAY 11, 1868.

President Andrew Johnson came within one vote of removal from office in 1868. Senate tally sheets on Articles XI, II, and III record the outcome. Thirty-six votes were required for conviction.

only general charges, mentioning no specific violations of law. The matter was referred to the House Judiciary Committee, which reported on March 2, 1867, two days before the end of the 39th Congress, that it had reached no conclusion.

On March 7, 1867, the third day of the 40th Congress, Ashley again introduced his resolution, which was referred to the Judiciary Committee for further investigation. The committee studied the matter throughout the year and on November 25, 1867, reported an impeachment resolution. Johnson was charged with high crimes and misdemeanors, but the committee cited no specific violations of law. When the House voted on the matter December 6, most members saw the charges as political grievances instead of illegal acts. The impeachment resolution was easily rejected by a vote of 57–108, a crushing defeat for the Radicals.

Johnson had long wanted to rid himself of Secretary of War Edwin M. Stanton. Stanton was a close ally of the Radical Republicans, who had passed the Tenure of Office Act with an eye toward ensuring that he kept control of the army. After repeatedly trying to get Stanton to resign, Johnson suspended him on December 12, 1867. On January 13, 1868, the Senate refused to concur, thus, under the terms of the act, reinstating Stanton.

Apparently flushed by his victory on the impeachment issue, Johnson decided to force the issue. He unilaterally fired Stanton on February 21, citing the power and authority vested in him by the Constitution.

This action enraged Congress, driving conservative Republicans into alliance with the Radicals on impeachment. A House resolution on impeachment was immediately offered and was referred to the Committee on Reconstruction, headed by Rep. Thaddeus Stevens of Pennsylvania, one of the Radical Republican leaders. The next day, February 22, the committee reported a resolution favoring impeachment. The House two days later voted for impeachment, 126–47, on a strict party-line basis.

Trial in the Senate

The House March 2–3 approved specific articles of impeachment and appointed managers to argue the charges before the Senate. There were eleven articles in all, the main one directed at Johnson's removal of Stanton in contravention of the Tenure of Office Act. Articles IX, X, and XI were unrelated to Stanton and broader in scope.

The impeachment trial opened March 30, 1868. House managers, all Republicans, were John A. Bingham of Ohio; George S. Boutwell and Benjamin F. Butler, both of Massachusetts; James F. Wilson of Iowa; John A. Logan of Illinois; and Thomas Williams and Thaddeus Stevens, both of Pennsylvania. The president did not appear at the trial. He was represented by a team of lawyers headed by Henry Stanbery, who had resigned as attorney general to lead the defense.

After weeks of argument and testimony, the Senate on May 16 took a test vote on Article XI, a general, catch-all charge, thought by the House managers most likely to produce a vote for conviction. The drama of the vote has become legendary.

With thirty-six votes needed for conviction, the final tally was 35–19, one vote shy of the two-thirds present and voting required to convict.

Seven Republicans joined the twelve Democrats in supporting Johnson. Stunned by the setback, Senate opponents of the president postponed further voting until May 26. Votes were taken then on Article II and Article III. By identical 35–19 votes Johnson was acquitted. To head off further defeats for Johnson opponents, Sen. George H. Williams, Union Republican-Ore., moved to adjourn *sine die*, and the motion was adopted 34–16, abruptly ending the trial.

Why was Johnson acquitted? Between his impeachment in the House and the final votes in the Senate, conservative Republicans had time to reflect on the outcome. One of the main objects of their reflection was fiery Benjamin F. Wade of Ohio, president pro tempore of the Senate and, under the succession law then in effect, next in line for the presidency. He was also one of the most radical of the Radical Republicans, a hard-liner on southern reconstruction and a monetary expansionist. Wade had many enemies who did not want to see him elevated to the White House.

Another reason might have been the impending end of Johnson's term. With less than a year to go in his term, Johnson was hamstrung by a veto-proof Republican majority and was politically crippled throughout most of the nation. The Republicans who voted against conviction wanted General Ulysses S. Grant to be their party's presidential candidate. If Wade succeeded Johnson, this might not happen. Thus, the political considerations that brought on Johnson's impeachment also saved his presidency.

Some in the Senate also felt that the Tenure of Office Act was unconstitutional. The act was virtually repealed early in Grant's administration, once the Republicans had control of the appointing power, and was entirely repealed in 1887. In 1926 the Supreme Court declared in its decision in *Myers v. United States*: "The power to remove . . . executive officers . . . is an incident of the power to appoint them, and is in its nature an executive power."

The opinion, written by Chief Justice William Howard Taft, himself a former president, referred to the Tenure of Office Act and declared that it had been unconstitutional.

PRESIDENT BILL CLINTON

For only the second time in U.S. history, the Senate in 1999 sat in judgment of a president—Bill Clinton. Unlike the trial of President Johnson who escaped removal from office in 1868 by a single vote, the outcome of Clinton's impeachment trial was never seriously in doubt.

When the impeachment proceedings began in 1998, Clinton had been under scrutiny in two legal investigations for four years. Since August 1994, Independent Counsel Kenneth W. Starr had been investigating Clinton and his wife in connection with their involvement in the failed Arkansas land deal called Whitewater. (Independent Counsel Robert B. Fiske Jr. had in-

Independent Counsel Kenneth W. Starr, standing lower left, takes oath before testifying before the House Judiciary Committee, which was investigating possible impeachable conduct of President Bill Clinton.

vestigated the same matter for a year prior to the appointment of Starr.) The Starr probe was expanded to look into the firing of the White House travel office staff and the possible illegal misuse of confidential FBI files.

Clinton also was the defendant in a sexual harassment suit brought against him in February 1994 by Paula Corbin Jones, a former Arkansas state employee. In May 1997, the Supreme Court in *Clinton v. Jones* ruled that a sitting president was not immune to a civil suit for a personal action alleged to have occurred before he took office. Hoping to show that Clinton's alleged conduct with Jones was part of a broader pattern of sexual harassment, Jones's attorneys compiled a list of women whose names had been linked with Clinton's. The name of Monica S. Lewinsky, a Pentagon employee who had been a White House intern, was on that list.

Arguing that she had no information relevant to the Jones case, Lewinsky filed a sworn affidavit on January 7, 1998, in which she denied ever having sexual relations with Clinton. Lewinsky, however, had told several friends about having an involvement with Clinton, including Linda R. Tripp, who taped conversations in which Lewinsky described her intimate relationship with Clinton and said that Clinton had urged her to lie about it.

The two investigations were linked, according to Starr, when Tripp turned over the tape recordings to the independent counsel's office. Starr officially expanded his investigation into the Lewinsky matter on January 16.

On January 17 Clinton in a sworn deposition told Jones's attorneys that he had never had sexual relations with Lewinsky—a denial he repeated publicly on January 21 after news of the alleged affair broke. On April 1, U.S. District Judge Susan Webber Wright threw out the Jones case, ruling that "no genuine issues for trial" existed.

Appearing before the grand jury August 6, Lewinsky acknowledged that she and Clinton had had an affair but insisted that he never told her to lie about it. Clinton testified before the grand jury August 17 from the White House, through a remote television arrangement. That evening, in a national broadcast, he admitted to an "inappropriate" relationship with Lewinsky and to making "misleading" statements under oath, but he denied that he had done anything illegal. On September 9, Starr delivered a report to the House charging that Clinton had committed eleven potentially impeachable offenses in connection with his efforts to conceal his illicit affair.

House Proceedings

The House Judiciary Committee on largely party-line votes December 11 and 12 approved four articles of impeachment against Clinton. The committee in essence rubber-stamped the Starr report. During its rancorous, bitterly partisan inquiry, the panel uncovered no new evidence and called no witnesses with firsthand information on the events. The only significant witnesses were Starr and a team of Clinton's lawyers who rebutted Starr's charges.

Speaker Newt Gingrich immediately called the full House back into a lame-duck session to consider the impeachment articles. On the eve of the scheduled debate, President Clinton went on national television to inform the public that he had ordered a series of military strikes against Iraq in retaliation for its refusal to cooperate with United Nations weapons inspectors. Congressional Democrats advocated postponing the impeachment vote until the cessation of military activity. The Republican leadership, skeptical of the administration's timing of the strikes, put off the debate for only one day.

The House was further shaken when Republican Speaker-designate Robert L. Livingston, admitting that he had had several extramarital affairs, announced that he would not run for Speaker and would resign his seat in Congress. On December 19, with U.S. military forces engaged overseas and Livingston having just announced that he would resign, debate began on the four articles of impeachment. During the debate members spoke, almost reverently at times, of their constitutional duty and the solemnity of the occasion. However, political partisanship drove the proceedings, propelled by conservative Republicans who deeply disapproved of and mistrusted the president.

Some members of the Republican leadership were so intent on impeaching Clinton that they refused to allow a vote on censure, which was defeated on a procedural vote, 230–204. Censure was favored by Democrats and some Republicans as a punishment more fitting the president's alleged misdeeds. These legislators argued that deceptions, while deplorable, were the understandable actions of a man trying to hide an illicit affair and did not rise to the level of "high crimes and misdemeanors" required by the Constitution for impeachment. Republicans, led by Judiciary Committee Chairman Henry J. Hyde, countered that the president had lied under oath and that impeachment was the only constitutional punishment to demonstrate that no one, not even the president of the United States, was above the law. After losing the censure vote, Democrats responded with a brief, staged walkout in protest. When they returned voting began on each of the four articles of impeachment.

Then, by 228–206, the House adopted the first article, which accused Clinton of having committed perjury in his grand jury testimony. By 205–119, the House rejected the second article, which charged the president with committing perjury in his deposition in the Jones case. By 221–212, the House adopted the third article, which charged Clinton with obstruction of justice for "using the powers of his high office" to "delay, impede, cover up and conceal" his involvement with Lewinsky. By 148–285, the House rejected the fourth article, which accused the president of abuse of power.

The thirteen Republican House Judiciary members chosen to prosecute the case were Chairman Henry J. Hyde of Illinois, F. James Sensenbrenner Jr. of Wisconsin, Charles T. Canaday and Bill McCollum of Florida, George W. Gekas of Pennsylvania, Ed Bryant of Tennessee, Steve Buyer of Indiana, Steve Chabot of Ohio, Bob Barr of Georgia, Asa Hutchinson of Arkansas, Christopher B. Cannon of Utah, James E. Rogan of California,

and Lindsay Graham of South Carolina. President Clinton never appeared at any of the proceedings and was represented by his team of White House and private lawyers led by White House Council Charles F. C. Ruff and his personal attorney, David E. Kendall.

Senate Trial

The Senate on January 7, 1999, opened the second presidential impeachment trial in American history. In a solemn ceremony Chief Justice William Rehnquist swore the full Senate to an oath of impartiality. Dire predictions of a lengthy, tumultuous trial did not turn out to be true. Devoid of the hostile partisanship that characterized the proceedings in the House, the Senate conducted an abbreviated and decorous trial.

Led by Hyde, the thirteen House managers presented their arguments of Clinton wrongdoing in exhaustive detail. In rebuttal, Clinton's lawyer's methodically poked enough factual holes in the prosecution's case to raise doubts about the strength of the managers' conclusions.

The heart of the first article was the allegation that the president lied in saying he had not engaged in "sexual relations" with Lewinsky as defined in the Jones case. Clinton's lawyers asserted that the president's continual denial was factually accurate because the activities he and Lewinsky had engaged in did not meet that specific definition as given to him during his deposition.

Of the several allegations in the obstruction article, the one receiving the most attention pertained to gifts that Clinton gave Lewinsky, which were later retrieved by Clinton's secretary, Betty Currie. The House managers asserted that Clinton conspired to hide these gifts, which were subpoenaed by Jones's lawyers. The allegation centered on a December 28, 1997, meeting between Clinton and Lewinsky, in which Lewinsky asked if she should hide the gifts. Lewinsky never testified that Clinton told her to hide them. Deputy Counsel Cheryl D. Mills noted that the main purpose of the meeting was to exchange more gifts, so Clinton could not have been concerned about this evidence. The House managers said that Currie had retrieved the gifts at the urging of Clinton. Mills argued that it was Lewinsky who wanted the gifts hidden, pointing to Currie's testimony to that effect.

On an allegation that Clinton conspired to find Lewinsky a job in return for her silence, the defense team focused on chronology. The decision to have Lewinsky testify was made on December 11, 1997, by Judge Wright. On that same day, the prosecutor argued, Clinton confidant Vernon E. Jordan stepped up his long-moribund efforts to find Lewinsky a job. However, White House lawyers pointed out that Wright's ruling did not come down until late in the day, well after Jordan contacted two potential employers by telephone and met directly with Lewinsky.

Two allegations were based on Clinton's discussions with Lewinsky about the Jones case—first, that Clinton tried to get her to fill out a false affidavit, and second, that he tried to get her

House Judiciary Chairman Henry Hyde, right, leads the procession of the thirteen House trial managers to the Senate to read the two impeachment articles against President Bill Clinton in January 1999.

to lie in the deposition if called to testify. The managers argued that Clinton and Lewinsky had a tacit understanding that she would lie, in the affidavit and in testimony. The evidence, they asserted, was that Clinton remained silent about the topic and that she knew that he could not want her to testify truthfully. White House Counsel Ruff countered this by saying that the Senate could not remove the president from office because the House managers chose to ascribe sinister motives to his silence. Both Clinton and Lewinsky denied these allegations under oath.

The 56–44 vote on January 27 defeating a motion to end the trial clearly demonstrated that not enough votes existed to convict Clinton. Republicans won a motion, 56–44, to take depositions from Lewinsky, Jordan, and White House aide Sidney Blumenthal. Despite the managers' claims of the importance of the witnesses' testimony, the trio, sticking generally to previous testimony, offered no new bombshells.

For three days senators conducted their final deliberations in private. A few moderate Republicans came forward to announce that they would not vote to convict. Republican James M. Jeffords of Vermont said that although Clinton committed

shameful acts and "misled the American people. . . . his actions in this case do not reach the high standard of impeachment."

On February 12, Article I, alleging Clinton committed perjury before a federal grand jury, was defeated, 45–55, with ten Republicans joining all forty-five Democrats. Article II, which alleged a scheme by the president to obstruct justice, was defeated also, 50–50. The House prosecutors failed to achieve even the modest goal of garnering a simple majority of Senate support. The Senate then effectively postponed indefinitely, 43–56, a censure resolution.

On the day of his acquittal Clinton appeared in the White House's Rose Garden to issue his most humble apology yet for "what I said and did to trigger these events and the great burden they have imposed on the Congress and on the American people."

In the aftermath of the trial, bitterness over the impeachment was likely to remain in Congress for a long time. Democrats, while readily admitting that the president had committed moral misdeeds, saw the whole affair as a partisan witch hunt intent on the acute embarrassment of Clinton. But Republicans blamed it on the president himself, saying it was his character flaws, not politics, that brought about the national ordeal.

CABINET IMPEACHMENT

William W. Belknap, President Ulysses S. Grant's fourth secretary of war, was one of many high officials tainted by widespread corruption and incompetence in the Grant administration. In 1876 the House began a general investigation of government departments, and on March 2 it approved a resolution by the Committee on Expenditures in the War Department impeaching Belknap. He was charged with receiving bribes from traders at an Indian post. Although the secretary of war resigned immediately, the Judiciary Committee went ahead and drafted five impeachment articles, which the House approved April 3.

As pretrial maneuvering proceeded, the Senate by a 37–29 vote on May 29 affirmed that it had jurisdiction over Belknap despite his resignation. The trial ran from July 6 to August 1, 1876, and ended with Belknap's acquittal. While a majority of the Senate voted for conviction on each one, none of the five articles received the required two-thirds majority. A substantial number of senators indicated they voted against conviction on the ground that the Senate no longer had jurisdiction over Belknap.

CONGRESSIONAL IMPEACHMENT

Senator William Blount of Tennessee was impeached by the House July 7, 1797, for conspiring with the British to launch a military expedition for the purpose of seizing Spanish territory for Great Britain. The Senate quickly voted to expel him, and the charges brought by the House were dropped.

On July 3 President John Adams had sent to the House and Senate a letter written by Blount to James Carey, a U.S. interpreter to the Cherokee Nation of Indians. In his letter, Blount discussed his plan to launch an attack by Indians and frontiersmen, aided by the British fleet, to take control of Louisiana and Spanish Florida. President Adams's action initiated the first proceedings in U.S. history to result in impeachment. The House July 7 adopted a committee resolution impeaching Blount and on the same day appointed a committee to prepare impeachment articles. Seven months later, on January 29, 1798, the House approved five articles accusing the senator of attempting to influence the Indians for the benefit of the British.

In the Senate, meanwhile, Blount's letter was referred to a select committee, which recommended Blount's expulsion for "a high misdemeanor, entirely inconsistent with his public trust and duty as a Senator." The Senate expelled him July 8, 1797, by a 25–1 vote. Although he had been expelled more than a year earlier, the Senate opened proceedings in Blount's impeachment trial on December 11, 1798. Blount challenged the proceedings, contending they violated his right to a trial by jury, that he was not a civil officer within the meaning of the Constitution, that he was not charged with a crime committed while a civil servant, and that courts of common law were competent to try him on the charges. On January 11, 1799, the Senate by a 14–11 vote dismissed the charges for lack of jurisdiction. Citing the vote,

Vice President Thomas Jefferson ruled January 14 that the Senate was without jurisdiction, ending the proceedings.

JUDICIAL IMPEACHMENTS

Pickering

Judge John Pickering in 1803 was caught in a partisan congressional impeachment campaign. The House voted on March 2 of that year to impeach Pickering for misconduct during a trial and for being intoxicated. He was subsequently convicted by the Senate and removed from office.

Pickering was a Federalist. President Jefferson, a Democratic-Republican, on February 4, 1803, sent a complaint to the House citing Pickering, a U.S. judge for the district of New Hampshire. The complaint was referred to a special committee, and on March 2 the House supported the committee's recommendation, voting to impeach the judge by a 45–8 vote. On December 30 the House approved four impeachment articles, charging Pickering with irregular judicial procedures, loose morals, and drunkenness. Pickering was said to be insane at the time and did not attend the Senate trial of March 4–12, 1804. The Senate voted 19–7 to convict him on each of the four articles and then voted 20–6 to remove the judge from office. It declined to consider disqualifying him for further federal office.

Chase

In an equally partisan attack the same year against another Federalist figure, the House impeached Samuel Chase, an associate justice of the Supreme Court, for misconduct that allegedly impaired respect for the Court. The Senate acquitted him.

On January 7, 1804, the House by an 81–40 vote approved a resolution authorizing an investigation of Chase, and also of Richard Peters, a U.S. district judge from Pennsylvania. Ostensibly, the investigation was to study their conduct during a recent treason trial. On March 12 the House dropped the probe of Peters but voted 73–32 to approve a committee resolution calling for Chase's impeachment. In a series of votes December 4 the House approved eight articles, charging Chase with harsh and partisan conduct on the bench and with unfairness to litigants.

The trial began February 9, 1805, with Chase in attendance. The Senate voted March 1 but did not convict him on any of the articles. A majority voted for three of the counts, but the closest to the two-thirds vote (19–15) needed for conviction fell four short.

Peck

In 1830 James H. Peck became the next federal judge to be impeached. The charge against him also was misconduct in office, specifically misuse of the contempt power. He was subsequently acquitted in the Senate.

The House on January 7, 1830, authorized an investigation of Peck's conduct. The Judiciary Committee recommended his impeachment, and the House on April 24 voted 123–49 to impeach Peck. A single impeachment article was approved by voice vote

TABLE 9–1 Senate Impeachment Trials

Between 1789 and 1999 the Senate sat as a court of impeachment sixteen times, as follows:

Year	Official	Position	Outcome
1798–1799	William Blount	U.S. senator	charges dismissed
1804	John Pickering	district court judge	removed from office
1805	Samuel Chase	Supreme Court justice	acquitted
1830–1831	James H. Peck	district court judge	acquitted
1862	West H. Humphreys	district court judge	removed from office
1868	Andrew Johnson	president	acquitted
1876	William Belknap	secretary of war	acquitted
1905	Charles Swayne	district court judge	acquitted
1912–1913	Robert W. Archbald	commerce court judge	removed from office
1926	George W. English	district court judge	charges dismissed
1933	Harold Louderback	district court judge	acquitted
1936	Halsted L. Ritter	district court judge	removed from office
1986	Harry E. Claiborne	district court judge	removed from office
1989	Alcee L. Hastings	district court judge	removed from office
1989	Walter L. Nixon Jr.	district court judge	removed from office
1999	Bill Clinton	president	acquitted

NOTE: The House in 1873 adopted a resolution of impeachment against District Judge Mark H. Delahay, but Delahay resigned before articles of impeachment were prepared, so the Senate took no action.

May 1. It charged the judge with setting an unreasonable and oppressive penalty for contempt of court. The Senate trial stretched from December 20, 1830, to January 31 the following year, when the effort to convict Peck failed, 21–22.

Humphreys

The next impeachment proceeding took place during the Civil War. It involved another federal judge, West H. Humphreys, who was charged by the House with supporting secession in the South and holding an office in the Confederacy. The Senate subsequently removed him from office.

During the Civil War Humphreys, a federal judge for the east, middle, and west districts of Tennessee, accepted an appointment as a Confederate judge without resigning from his Union judicial assignment. Informed of the situation, the House on January 8, 1862, authorized an inquiry. Following an investigation, the Judiciary Committee recommended his impeachment, and the House on May 6 unanimously voted to impeach Humphreys. On May 19 it adopted seven impeachment articles.

Humphreys could not be served personally with the impeachment articles because he had fled Union territory. He neither appeared at his Senate trial nor contested the charges. In a one-day trial June 26 the Senate convicted Humphreys on six of the seven counts, on votes ranging from 28–10 to 39–0. By unan-

imous votes it then removed him from office and barred him from holding future office in the U.S. government.

Delahay

Another U.S. district judge, Mark H. Delahay, was impeached in 1873 for misconduct in office and unsuitable personal habits, including intoxication. Delahay resigned before articles of impeachment were drawn up and sent to the Senate.

In 1872 the House had authorized an investigation of Judge Delahay's behavior. This resulted the next year in approval of an impeachment resolution by the House Judiciary Committee. The House on February 28, 1873, agreed with the recommendation and by voice vote impeached the judge, but because of Delahay's resignation the Senate took no action in the case.

Swayne

The first federal official to be impeached in the twentieth century was Judge Charles Swayne in 1904. He was charged with padding expense accounts, using railroad property in receivership for his own benefit, and misusing the contempt power.

On December 10, 1903, the House authorized an investigation of Swayne, who was a judge for the northern district of Florida. After lengthy deliberations the Judiciary Committee recommended that he be impeached. The House unanimously voted to impeach him on December 13, 1904. Early the next year the House approved thirteen articles of impeachment.

The Senate subsequently considered twelve of the articles at Swayne's trial, which commenced February 10, 1905. On February 27 the Senate acquitted Swayne on all twelve articles. On none of the articles did even a majority of senators vote for conviction.

Archbald

In 1912 the House impeached an associate judge of the U.S. Commerce Court, Robert W. Archbald. He was charged with misconduct in office, including the acceptance of gifts and free trips to Europe as well as the improper appointment of a jury commissioner.

On May 4, 1912, the House authorized an investigation of Archbald, and on July 11 of that year, at the recommendation of the Judiciary Committee, the House voted 223–1 to impeach Archbald. The Senate considered twelve House articles of impeachment at Archbald's trial, which began December 3. On January 13, 1913, senators voted to convict Archbald on five of the articles. After unanimously voting to remove him from office, the Senate disqualified him from further office. That vote was 39–25, with only a simple majority needed.

English

The next impeachment proceeding occurred in 1925, when the House impeached Judge George W. English, charging him with tyranny, oppression, and partiality in some of his rulings. English resigned before the Senate considered the charges.

An investigation of English, a judge for the eastern district of

Illinois, had been authorized January 13. The Judiciary Committee recommended his impeachment and drafted five articles, and the House April 1, 1926, voted 306–72 to impeach him. English's trial was scheduled to begin on November 10, but six days earlier English resigned. At the request of the House managers the Senate December 13 voted 70–9 to dismiss the charges, ending the impeachment proceedings.

Louderback

In 1933 the House voted to impeach Harold Louderback, a judge for the northern district of California, despite a committee recommendation that he be censured instead. He was charged with appointing incompetent bankruptcy receivers and allowing them to take excessive fees.

In June 1932 the House authorized an investigation of Louderback's record by the Judiciary Committee. But the committee was split on impeachment. A majority opted for censuring Louderback instead of impeaching him. The House, however, backed an impeachment resolution favored by a minority on the committee. On February 24, 1933, the House voted 183–152 to impeach the judge. Five impeachment articles were approved, charging Louderback with favoritism in his rulings and with conspiracy in the appointment of bankruptcy receivers. The Senate trial of May 15–24 ended in the judge's acquittal, with the "not guilty" votes outnumbering the "guilty" ones on all but one of the five articles. The closest vote for conviction was 45–34, eight short of the required two-thirds.

Ritter

Judge Halsted L. Ritter of the southern district of Florida was impeached in 1936 after a protracted House proceeding lasting three years. His offenses included a variety of judicial improprieties, such as receiving illegal payments, practicing law while serving as a federal judge, and preparing and filing false income tax returns. The Senate removed him from office.

The House authorized an investigation of charges against Ritter on June 1, 1933. A long delay followed. On March 2, 1936, the House by a vote of 181–146 approved an impeachment resolution containing four articles recommended by the Judiciary Committee. The House added three more articles before the Senate trial commenced April 6. Voting took place April 17, with the Senate mustering a two-thirds majority (56–28) for conviction on only the last article. The Senate removed him from office but on a 0–76 vote refused to disqualify Ritter from further federal office.

Claiborne

Judge Harry E. Claiborne of Nevada, who was convicted of tax fraud in 1984 and was serving a prison sentence when the House considered his case, was impeached July 22, 1986, by a vote of 406–0. The House approved four articles of impeachment recommended by the Judiciary Committee. Appointed to the bench by President Jimmy Carter in 1978, Claiborne was the first sitting federal judge ever to be imprisoned.

For the first time the Senate used a 1935 amendment to its impeachment rules authorizing a special twelve-member committee, instead of the full Senate, to collect and hear evidence, which took place September 15–23. Claiborne tried unsuccessfully in court to block a Senate vote on grounds that use of the special committee deprived him of his constitutional rights. The Senate October 9 convicted the U.S. district court judge on three of the four articles. The votes were 87–10, 90–7, and 89–8. Because federal judges can be removed from office only through impeachment and are immune from a pay cut, Claiborne continued to receive his $78,700 annual salary even after his 1984 conviction and incarceration. Had the Senate not convicted and removed him from office, Claiborne could have returned to the bench after his release from prison and retired later with a full pension.

Hastings

Judge Alcee L. Hastings of Florida became the first federal official to be impeached after having been tried and acquitted by a jury. Despite his 1983 acquittal, a special judicial investigating committee of the Eleventh U.S. Circuit Court of Appeals concluded that Hastings had lied and fabricated evidence at his trial. Under procedures of a 1980 judicial discipline law, the judges recommended he be impeached, and the U.S. Judicial Conference—the policy-making arm of the federal judiciary—sent the recommendation to the House.

The Judiciary Committee unanimously backed his impeachment. The House by a 413–3 vote August 3, 1988, impeached Hastings, approving seventeen articles of impeachment stemming from his involvement in a 1981 bribery scheme in which he allegedly conspired to obtain $150,000 from two defendants in a racketeering case in return for sentences that would not require imprisonment. The impeachment counts included a charge of conspiracy to accept a bribe and one alleging the judge had perjured himself during his 1983 trial. He also was charged with leaking information about a wiretap he was supervising that forced the cancellation of a major federal undercover operation in the Miami area.

After the Senate in March 1989 refused to dismiss any of the charges against Hastings, a special committee took evidence between July 10 and August 3, 1989. Proceedings were delayed while the Senate approved a civil action to enforce a subpoena against a witness who refused to testify. The full Senate heard final arguments on October 18 and two days later convicted Hastings. It found him guilty on eight of eleven impeachment articles on which senators voted. Senators chose not to vote on six of the seventeen articles. On the first article, which alleged conspiracy to obtain a bribe and formed the basis for most of the other counts, the vote was 69–26—five more than the two-thirds needed for conviction.

Hastings's earlier acquittal by a federal jury troubled many of the senators who voted against conviction. This "feels like double jeopardy," Hastings said. The African American judge also claimed that the investigation was racially motivated.

Federal Judge Alcee L. Hastings, removed from office in 1989, returned in 1993 as a representative from Florida to the very body that impeached him.

The Senate did not vote to disqualify Hastings from holding federal office in the future. Three years after Congress impeached and removed Hastings from his office as federal judge, he returned to Washington to take his seat in the House as a representative from Florida. He would later join in offering an impeachment resolution of his own, calling for the removal of Whitewater independent counsel Kenneth Starr for "gross prosecutorial misconduct."

Nixon

Judge Walter L. Nixon Jr. became the third federal jurist in four years, and the thirteenth overall, to be impeached by the House. On May 10, 1989, following a unanimous committee recommendation, the House impeached Nixon by a 417–0 vote. Three articles of impeachment were approved. The first two alleged that he lied to a grand jury in 1984 about his role in trying to win leniency for the indicted son of a business associate. Prosecutors said Nixon, the chief judge of the southern district of Mississippi, had accepted a sweetheart deal on oil and gas royalties from a Mississippi businessman and then tried to win a lenient sentence for the businessman's son. The son had been indicted on drug trafficking charges.

Nixon was serving a five-year prison sentence at the time of his impeachment. In 1986 he had been convicted of perjury. The U.S. Judicial Conference at the urging of the Fifth U.S. Circuit Court of Appeals subsequently forwarded to the House a recommendation that he be impeached and removed from office.

A special twelve-member Senate committee took evidence in Nixon's impeachment trial September 7–13, 1989. After hearing final arguments, the full Senate on November 3 convicted Nixon on the two impeachment articles charging him with perjury by votes of 89–8 and 78–10. By a 57–40 vote, Nixon was acquitted on the third count, which accused him of undermining the confidence of the federal judiciary. Nixon became the seventh federal judge to be removed from office.

Nixon appealed his removal to the courts, contending that he was denied a fair trial by the Senate's shortcut procedure of delegating evidence to a committee. The Supreme Court in *Nixon v. United States* (1993) upheld his conviction, ruling that impeachment is a "political question" that is explicitly given to the legislative branch to decide, and that the judiciary is given no authority by the Constitution to review any aspect of the Congress's handling of impeachment cases. Although concurring on Nixon's removal, three justices disputed the majority opinion that the Court could not review the Senate's actions in an impeachment case.

CALLS FOR IMPEACHMENT: FREQUENTLY UNSUCCESSFUL

While relatively few federal officials have been impeached in the nation's two-hundred-year history, calls for impeachment of federal officials are frequently made by disgruntled and disaffected members of Congress. Seldom do such calls advance beyond rhetoric, however.

Formal impeachment proceedings have been initiated on more than sixty occasions. Campaigns that did not result in impeachment have been mounted against three presidents, a vice president, at least two cabinet secretaries, and a Supreme Court justice. In few of these cases, however, was impeachment a serious threat. In none of them did an impeachment resolution come to an up-or-down vote in the House. Nevertheless, the mere threat of impeachment has led to the dismissal or resignation of numerous federal officials or their transfer to other government posts. In the most famous case, President Richard Nixon resigned before the full House could vote on impeachment articles.

In some cases the timing of the alleged impropriety or criminal act—such as near the end of the official's term of office—helped the person to escape impeachment. For example, Vice President Aaron Burr on July 11, 1804, shot and killed former Treasury secretary Alexander Hamilton in a duel. Because Burr's term was set to expire less than eight months later, the House never launched impeachment proceedings against him, even

In the case of President Richard Nixon, the process of impeachment did not move beyond its first stage—and yet it realized its purpose. Ten days after the House Judiciary Committee recommended that Nixon be impeached for obstruction of justice, abuse of power, and contempt of Congress, Nixon resigned. In the face of certain impeachment by the House and removal by the Senate, he chose to leave the White House voluntarily.

The impeachment inquiry was but one in the chain of events that brought about Nixon's premature departure from the presidency—a chain that began on June 17, 1972, with a burglary at Democratic National Headquarters in the Watergate office building in Washington, D.C.

But the work of the House Judiciary Committee and its dramatic conclusion, a televised debate involving all thirty-eight members, were crucial in preparing the nation to accept the resignation of the man elected president by an overwhelming vote less than two years earlier.

Nixon precipitated the inquiry with the "Saturday night massacre"—his firing on October 20, 1973, of the first Watergate special prosecutor, Archibald Cox. Cox had been persisting in his effort to force Nixon to release tapes of certain of his conversations in the White House that, Cox suspected, concerned the Watergate break-in.

On the Monday following the Cox firing a number of impeachment resolutions were introduced in the House and referred to the House Judiciary Committee. On February 6, 1974, the House formally authorized the committee "to investigate fully and completely whether sufficient grounds exist for the House of Representatives to exercise its constitutional power to impeach Richard M. Nixon, President." The vote was 410–4.

Aware of the import of their task, the committee approached it deliberately. From February to May, the staff, led by former assistant attorney general John M. Doar, assembled evidence related to the various charges against the president, which ranged from Watergate-related matters to questions of his personal finances. The committee subpoenaed the president for additional material. Nixon refused to comply, although he did release edited transcripts of a number of the tapes of the conversations the committee sought.

On May 9, the committee began considering the evidence in executive session, a process that continued until mid-July. President Nixon was represented at the proceedings by James D. St. Clair, his chief defense counsel and a noted Boston trial attorney.

On July 18–19, the committee heard Doar and St. Clair summarize the arguments. Doar advocated impeachment, telling the committee that "reasonable men acting reasonably would find the pres-

ident guilty" of abusing his presidential powers. Defending the president, St. Clair argued that there was a "complete absence of any conclusive evidence demonstrating presidential wrongdoing sufficient to justify the grave action of impeachment."

On July 24 a unanimous Supreme Court rejected Nixon's claim of executive privilege to withhold evidence sought by the Watergate special prosecutor. Nixon, the Court ruled, must comply with subpoenas for the tapes of certain of his conversations.

That evening, on nationwide television, the Judiciary Committee began the final phase of its inquiry. For the first time, all thirty-eight members spoke publicly on the evidence.

By the end of the evening the outcome was clear. Seven of the seventeen Republicans indicated that they would support impeachment. All of the Democrats spoke in favor of impeachment. The vote would be bipartisan.

Four days later, July 27, the decisive roll call came. The committee approved, 27–11, the first article of impeachment, charging Nixon with obstructing justice, primarily in the Watergate investigation. Six Republicans joined all twenty-one Democrats.

The second article, charging abuse of power, was approved July 29 by the even wider margin of 28–10. The third, charging contempt of Congress, was approved July 30, 21–17. Two other proposed articles were rejected.

House floor debate on impeachment was to begin August 19; the outcome was considered a certainty. The Senate began preparing for a trial. Public opinion swung heavily in favor of impeachment and, for the first time, polls showed most of the American people favoring conviction and removal from office.

On August 5 Nixon released transcripts of three of the taped conversations that the Supreme Court ruling forced him to turn over to the special prosecutor. These made clear his knowing participation in the cover-up of White House involvement in the Watergate burglary.

Faced with this new evidence, even the members of the Judiciary Committee who had continued to defend Nixon called for his resignation or impeachment. On August 7 Republican leaders told him he had no more than ten supporters in the House and fifteen in the Senate. On August 8 Nixon told the nation he would resign. He made no mention of impeachment. On August 9, his resignation effective, he left the White House. The House August 20 accepted the report of the committee inquiry, 412–3, formally concluding the matter.

SOURCES: Congressional Quarterly, *Watergate: Chronology of a Crisis* (Washington, D.C.: Congressional Quarterly, 1974; Reprint 1999); and House Judiciary Committee, *Hearing Pursuant to H. Res. 803*, 93rd Cong., 2nd sess., 1974.

through he was indicted for murder in New York and New Jersey. Burr was never arrested and prosecuted.

In a few other cases, the target of an impeachment died before action was taken.

Descriptions of some of the many unsuccessful impeachment attempts follow:

Tyler

The House on January 10, 1843, rejected 84–127 a resolution to investigate whether there was cause to initiate impeachment proceedings against John Tyler, who had succeeded to the presidency upon the death of William Henry Harrison. Tyler had become a political outcast, ostracized by the Democrats and his own Whig Party. While still president he was excommunicated from the Whig Party. But a majority of the House apparently felt that impeachment was too drastic a measure to use against him and he was able to serve out his term.

Colfax

In 1872 a campaign was launched to impeach Schuyler Colfax, President Ulysses Grant's first vice president, because of his involvement in the Crédit Mobilier scandal. Crédit Mobilier was a dummy corporation set up by several members of Congress to pocket public funds intended to be used for the building of the Union Pacific Railroad, and Colfax was an owner of some of the company's stock. The House Judiciary Committee recommended that he not be impeached on the ground that he obtained his Crédit Mobilier stock before becoming vice president. Colfax had been a prominent member of Congress from Indiana (1855–1869). Despite the committee's decision Grant dumped him from the ticket before running for reelection in 1872.

Daugherty

A similar attempt was made in 1922 to impeach Harry M. Daugherty, President Warren G. Harding's second attorney general. Daugherty was severely criticized for failing to prosecute Interior Secretary Albert B. Fall (subsequently convicted and sent to prison) and others implicated in the Teapot Dome scandal. Fall had accepted bribes from individuals who were given leases to two federally owned naval oil reserves supervised by Fall's Interior Department. The impeachment probe of Daugherty was dropped in 1923 as Congress focused its attention on the scandal itself. In 1924, acting on the evidence gathered in the Teapot Dome inquiry, the Senate authorized a separate probe of the Justice Department. Daugherty's inaction during the scandal led Calvin Coolidge, who had assumed the presidency upon Harding's death, to demand the attorney general's resignation on March 28, 1924.

Mellon

A running fight between Rep. Wright Patman, D-Texas, and Secretary of the Treasury Andrew W. Mellon over the federal government's economic policy during the Great Depression came to a head in 1932. In January that year Patman demanded Mellon's impeachment on the ground of financial conflict of interest. To put an end to that threat, President Herbert C. Hoover

These four members, along with others of the House Judiciary Committee, voted three articles of impeachment against President Richard Nixon for his role in the Watergate scandal. Nixon resigned before the full House could vote on the articles.

in February 1932 nominated Mellon to be ambassador to Great Britain. The Senate confirmed his nomination February 6, and Mellon resigned from the Treasury post soon thereafter to assume his ambassadorship.

Hoover

Two other unsuccessful impeachment moves launched during the depression by an individual member of Congress occurred in 1932–1933. Rep. Louis T. McFadden, R-Pa., tried to impeach President Hoover on general grounds of usurping legislative powers and violating constitutional and statutory laws. The first attempt was tabled overwhelmingly by the House on December 13, 1932. The vote was 361–8. The second, on January 17, 1933, also was tabled, this time by a 344–11 vote.

Douglas

Associate Justice William Douglas was the target of several impeachment campaigns during his career on the Supreme Court. The day after Douglas granted a stay of execution for convicted spies Julius and Ethel Rosenberg in June 1953, Rep. W. M. Wheeler, D-Ga., introduced a resolution to impeach him. The resolution was unanimously tabled a month later after a one-day hearing in which Wheeler was the sole witness.

In April 1970 two resolutions for Douglas's impeachment were introduced in the midst of a bitter conflict between President Nixon and the Senate over the latter's rejection of two Supreme Court nominations. The campaign was initiated by House minority leader Gerald R. Ford. Among the charges were possible financial conflicts of interest similar to those that had led to the Senate's rejection of the Nixon nominees—Clement F. Haynsworth Jr. and G. Harrold Carswell. A special House Judiciary subcommittee on December 3, 1970, voted 3–1 that no grounds existed for impeachment.

NOTES

1. Lewis Deschler, *Deschler's Procedure in the U.S. House of Representatives,* 2nd ed. (Washington, D.C.: Government Printing Office, 1977), 127. For further details see Congressional Quarterly, *Watergate: Chronology of a Crisis* (Washington, D.C.: Congressional Quarterly, 1974; Reprint 1999), particularly part 3.

2. Michael Nelson, ed., *Congressional Quarterly's Guide to the Presidency,* 2nd ed. (Washington, D.C.: Congressional Quarterly, 1996), 463. See also Congressional Quarterly, *Watergate: Chronology of a Crisis,* 329; and *Deschler's Procedure in the U.S. House of Representatives,* 127.

3. Alexander Hamilton, James Madison, and John Jay, *The Federalist Papers,* with an introduction by Clinton Rossiter (New York: New American Library, 1961), no. 65, 397.

4. Unless otherwise noted, the basic historical source for the remainder of this chapter was House Judiciary Committee, *Impeachment: Selected Materials on Procedure,* 93rd Cong., 2nd sess., January 1974.

5. Joseph Story, *Commentaries on the Constitution of the United States* (Boston: Hilliard Gray, 1833), vol. 2, section 798.

6. Raoul Berger, *Impeachment: The Constitutional Problems* (Cambridge, Mass.: Harvard University Press, 1973), 31, quoting G. M. Trevelyan's *Illustrated History of England* (London: Longmans, Green, 1956), 391.

7. Hamilton, *The Federalist Papers,* no. 65, 398.

8. Max Farrand, ed., *The Records of the Federal Convention of 1787* (New Haven, Conn.: Yale University Press, 1911), vol. 1, 78; vol. 2, 116, 185–186, 292, 495, 545, 550–552.

9. The sources for this history of the Johnson impeachment are Michael Les Benedict, *The Impeachment and Trial of Andrew Johnson* (New York: Norton, 1973); Berger, *Impeachment: The Constitutional Problems;* and James G. Blaine, *Twenty Years of Congress, 1861–1881* (Norwich, Conn.: Henry Hill, 1886).

SUGGESTED BIBLIOGRAPHY

Benedict, Michael L. *The Impeachment and Trial of Andrew Johnson.* New York: Norton, 1973.

Berger, Raoul. *Impeachment: The Constitutional Problems.* Cambridge, Mass.: Harvard University Press, 1973.

Brant, Irving. *Impeachment: Trials and Errors.* New York: Knopf, 1972.

Congressional Quarterly. *Watergate: Chronology of a Crisis.* 1974. Reprint. Washington, D.C.: Congressional Quarterly, 1999.

Deschler, Lewis. *Deschler's Procedure in the U.S. House of Representatives.* 3rd ed. Washington, D.C.: Government Printing Office, 1979.

Dewitt, David M. *Impeachment and Trial of Andrew Johnson.* New York: Russell & Russell, 1967.

Farrand, Max, ed. *The Records of the Federal Convention of 1787.* Rev. ed. 4 vols. New Haven, Conn.: Yale University Press, 1966–1987.

Fisher, Louis. *Constitutional Conflicts between Congress and the President.* 4th ed. Lawrence: University Press of Kansas, 1997.

Gerhardt, Michael J. *The Federal Impeachment Process: A Constitutional and Historical Analysis.* Princeton, N.J.: Princeton University Press, 1996.

Hamilton, Alexander, James Madison, and John Jay. *The Federalist Papers.* Introduction by Clinton Rossiter. New York: New American Library, 1961.

Haynes, George H. *The Senate of the United States: Its History and Practice.* 2 vols. Boston: Houghton Mifflin, 1938.

Kurland, Philip B. *Watergate and the Constitution.* Chicago: University of Chicago Press, 1978.

McLoughlin, Merrill, ed. *The Impeachment and Trial of President Clinton: The Official Transcripts, from the House Judiciary Committee Hearings to the Senate Trial.* New York: Time Books, 1999.

Rehnquist, William H. *Grand Inquests: The Historic Impeachments of Justice Samuel Chase and President Andrew Johnson.* New York: Morrow, 1992.

U.S. Congress. House of Representatives. Committee on the Judiciary. *Constitutional Grounds for Presidential Impeachment: Report by the Staff of the Impeachment Inquiry.* 93rd Cong., 2nd sess., 1984.

Van Tassel, Emily Field, and Paul Finkelman. *Impeachable Offenses: A Documentary History from 1787 to Present.* Washington, D.C.: Congressional Quarterly, 1999.

White, Theodore H. *Breach of Faith: The Fall of Richard Nixon.* New York: Dell, 1975.

CHAPTER 10

Constitutional Amendments

THE CONSTITUTION never would have been written if amending the Articles of Confederation had been easy. To make any change in that first charter required the consent of both the Continental Congress and every state.

In drafting a better amending procedure, delegates to the Constitutional Convention in 1787 had little guidance. Six of the thirteen state constitutions had been written as "perpetual charters" without provision for amendment. Only three state legislatures were empowered to propose changes. In four, the amending power was vested solely in popular conventions.

The unwritten British constitution could be altered by Parliament. Although governmental principles did exist to contain and guide Britain's governing institutions, there was neither a document to define nor an agency to declare what was "unconstitutional." Acts of Parliament were the supreme law of the land.

America's Founders were unwilling to rely on so flexible a base. The thirteen independent states would not surrender part of their newly won sovereignty without a clear, written understanding of the Union they were joining. Furthermore, they would need guarantees that the new national government would not unilaterally alter the terms of the agreement, particularly to reduce the sovereignty retained by the states.

The reliance on separation of powers and on checks and balances for protection against capricious government required that the arrangement not be subject to easy alteration, lest the separation and the balance be destroyed. Arbitrary acts of Parliament persuaded the former colonists that certain rights must be inviolable and must be protected by a law that no one government agency could change.

Consequently, the Constitutional Convention sought to write a document to embody the fundamental law of the land. And yet the delegates assembled in Philadelphia realized that they could not anticipate all future needs of the new nation. They devised a Constitution that would be easier to amend than the Articles of Confederation but more difficult to revise than the British "constitution." They built into the amendment process the principle of checks and balances basic to the Constitution itself, and they reserved to the states the ultimate power to alter the agreement into which the states had entered.

Thus the task of amending the Constitution under Article V, while certainly easier than under the Articles of Confederation, still is a difficult undertaking. One-third plus one of the members voting in either chamber can block Congress from proposing an amendment. And if an amendment does receive congressional approval, the legislatures of only thirteen of the fifty states—or just one house of thirteen state legislatures—can block ratification. (The Constitution requires the consent of the entire legislature of three-fourths of the states to approve amendments.)

In their book *Government by the People,* James MacGregor Burns, Jack W. Peltason, and Thomas E. Cronin observed that

the entire amending procedure has been criticized because neither a majority of the voters at large nor even a majority of the voters in a majority of the states can formally alter the Constitution. But when a majority of the people are serious in their desire to bring about changes in our constitutional system, their wishes are usually implemented either by formal amendment or by the more subtle methods of interpretation and adaptation.[1]

C. Herman Pritchett in 1977 commented:

The adoption of four . . . amendments since 1961 is evidence that the amending machinery is not hard to operate if there is a genuine consensus on the need, and may even lead to some concern that amendments are too easy to achieve. . . . It is of prime importance that the Constitution retain its brevity and be limited to basic structural arrangements and the protection of individual liberties. It would be disastrous if it became, through the amending power, a vehicle by which pressure groups and crackpots could impose their nostrums on the nation.[2]

Constitutional Convention: Need for Amendments Foreseen

The plan for a national government presented by Edmund Randolph of Virginia on May 29, 1787, the fourth day of the Convention, said that "provision ought to be made for the amendment of the Articles of Union whensoever it shall seem necessary" and that "the assent of the National Legislature ought not to be required thereto." A plan proposed by Charles Pinckney of South Carolina on the same day provided that amendments "to invest future additional Powers in the United States" should be proposed by conventions and ratified by an unspecified percentage of the state legislatures.

When Randolph's proposal was raised in the Convention on June 5, Pinckney said he doubted its "propriety or necessity." But Elbridge Gerry of Massachusetts favored it: "The novelty and difficulty of the experiment requires periodical revision. The prospect of such a revision would also give intermediate stability to the Government."

George Mason of Virginia, supporting the Randolph proposal, said:

The plan now to be formed will certainly be defective, as the Confederation has been found, on trial, to be. Amendments, therefore, will be necessary and it will be better to provide for them in an easy, regular and constitutional way, than to trust to chance and violence. It would be improper to require the consent of the National Legislature, because they may abuse their power and refuse their consent on that very account.

On June 20, Mason said that "the Convention, though comprising so many distinguished characters, could not be expected to make a faultless government" and that he would prefer "trusting to posterity the amendment of its defects, rather than to push the experiment too far."

The Convention agreed on July 23 that "provisions ought to be made for future amendments . . . whensoever it shall seem necessary" and referred the matter to the Committee of Detail. In its report of August 6, the committee recommended: "On the application of the legislatures of two-thirds of the states in the Union, for an amendment of this Constitution, the Legislature of the United States shall call a convention for that purpose." The Convention adopted this recommendation on August 30 in spite of the contention of Gouverneur Morris of Pennsylvania that "the Legislature should be left at liberty to call a convention, whenever they please."

On the motion of Gerry, the Convention on September 10 voted to reconsider the amendment provision. Gerry argued that, because the Constitution was to be paramount to the state constitutions, "two-thirds of the states can bind the Union to innovations that may subvert the state constitutions altogether."

Alexander Hamilton of New York also favored reconsideration, but not for Gerry's reason. Hamilton said:

There was no greater evil in subjecting the people of the United States to the major voice than the people of a particular state. It had been wished by many and was much to have been desired that an easier mode for introducing amendments had been provided by the Articles of Confederation. It was equally desirable now that an easy mode should be established for supplying defects which will probably appear in the new system. The mode proposed was not adequate. The state legislatures will not apply for alterations but with a view to increase their own powers. The national Legislature will be most sensible to the necessity of amendments, and ought also to be empowered, whenever two-thirds of each branch should concur, to call a convention.

This was one of the few Hamilton suggestions that found a place in the Constitution.

Roger Sherman of Connecticut moved to add this language: "Or the Legislature may propose amendments to the several states for their approbation, but no amendments shall be binding until consented to by the several states." James Wilson of Pennsylvania moved to reduce the requirement of unanimous consent of the states to a two-thirds majority. Six states—Connecticut, Georgia, Massachusetts, New Jersey, North Carolina, and South Carolina—voted against this motion, and five states—Delaware, Maryland, New Hampshire, Pennsylvania,

Suffragists and their supporters march in Washington, D.C., for women's right to vote. American women did not win full voting rights until the Nineteenth Amendment was ratified in 1920.

and Virginia—voted in favor. But a later motion by Wilson to permit three-fourths of the states to make an amendment effective was adopted without dissent.

James Madison then proposed a substitute for the entire article, which was adopted with only one state dissenting. Madison's plan provided that amendments should be proposed by Congress when two-thirds of both houses considered it necessary or when two-thirds of the state legislatures made application and would be ratified by three-fourths of the state legislatures or three-fourths of the state conventions, as Congress might designate.

When this provision was reported by the Committee on Style on September 15, Morris and Gerry objected that both methods of amendment depended upon Congress. They urged a provision requiring Congress, when requested by two-thirds of the states, to call a convention to propose amendments. This provision was accepted without dissent.

John Rutledge of South Carolina protested that he "could never agree to give a power by which the articles relating to slaves might be altered by the states not interested in that property and prejudiced against it." The Convention consequently agreed to a provision prohibiting amendment before 1808 of the clauses concerned with slavery (the counting of slaves as three-fifths of the population for assessment of direct taxes and authorization of the slave trade). At the last minute, Sherman said he feared that "three-fourths of the states might be brought to do things fatal to particular states, as abolishing them altogether or depriving them of their equality in the Senate." He sought another proviso prohibiting any amendment by which any state would "be affected in its internal policy, or deprived of its equal suffrage in the Senate." Madison warned against adding special provisos restricting the amending power, lest every state insist on protecting its boundaries or exports. However, "the circulating murmurs of the small states" prompted Morris to propose protecting equal representation in the Senate from amendment, a proviso adopted unanimously. The Convention approved only these two limitations on the substance of amendments.

AMENDMENT PROCEDURE

As finally agreed upon, Article V of the Constitution provided that:

The Congress, whenever two thirds of both Houses shall deem it necessary, shall propose Amendments to this Constitution, or, on the Application of the Legislatures of two thirds of the several States, shall call a Convention for proposing Amendments, which, in either Case, shall be valid to all Intents and Purposes, as Part of this Constitution, when ratified by the legislatures of three fourths of the several States, or by Conventions in three fourths thereof, as the one or the other Mode of Ratification may be proposed by the Congress; Provided that no Amendment which may be made prior to the Year One thousand eight hundred and eight shall in any Manner affect the first and fourth Clauses in the Ninth Section of the first Article; and that no State, without its Consent, shall be deprived of its equal Suffrage in the Senate.

The article as adopted allowed either Congress or the state legislatures to initiate the amending process, either Congress or a general convention to propose amendments, and either state legislatures or state conventions to ratify amendments. Congress determines which method of ratification will be employed and what form a general convention would take if requested by the state legislatures.

The president has no formal authority over constitutional amendments; presidential veto power does not extend to them. Nor can governors veto amendments approved by their legislatures.

Notification of state ratification is transmitted by the states to the head of the General Services Administration. (Until 1950, the secretary of state performed this function.) The administrator's action in proclaiming the adoption of an amendment on receipt is purely ministerial; the amendment is brought into effect by the ratifying action of the necessary number of states on the day when the required number of ratifications is reached. (The Eighteenth Amendment had an unusual provision postponing its effectiveness for one year after ratification was completed.)

RATIFICATION OF THE CONSTITUTION

Omission of a Bill of Rights was the principal source of dissatisfaction with the new Constitution in the state ratifying conventions held in 1788. The demand for amendments to establish these rights, and to effect various other changes in the Constitution, made Article V an issue in the struggle for ratification. In the Virginia convention, Patrick Henry and George Mason raised vehement objections to the amending process.

"When I come to contemplate this part," Henry said,

I suppose that I am mad or that my countrymen are so. The way to amendments is, in my conception, shut. . . . Two-thirds of Congress or of the state legislatures are necessary even to propose amendments. If one-third of these be unworthy men, they may prevent the application for amendments; but what is destructive and mischievous is that three-fourths of the state legislatures, or of the state conventions, must concur in the amendments when proposed. . . . A bare majority in four small states may hinder the adoption of amendments. . . . Is this an easy mode of securing the public liberty? It is, sir, a most fearful situation, when the most contemptible minority could prevent the alteration of the most oppressive government, for it may in many respects prove to be such.[3]

George Washington, who presided over the Convention, admitted that defects existed in the Constitution it drafted, but he observed,

As a constitutional door is opened for future amendments and alterations, I think it would be wise in the people to accept what is offered to them and I wish it may be by as great a majority of them as it was by that of the Convention; but this is hardly to be expected. . . . Go matters, however, as they may, I shall have the consolation to reflect that no objects but the public good and that peace and harmony which I wished to see prevail in the Convention, obtruded even for a moment in my bosom during the whole session, long as it was.[4]

Madison, in *The Federalist* (No. 43), expressed the view that

the mode [of amendment] preferred by the convention seems to be stamped with every mark of propriety. It guards equally against that extreme facility, which would render the Constitution too mutable; and that extreme difficulty which might perpetuate its discovered faults. It moreover equally enables the general and the state governments to originate the amendment of errors, as they may be pointed out by the experience on one side or the other.[5]

CHANGE WITHOUT AMENDMENT

Not counting the first ten amendments, which are considered practically a part of the original document, the Constitution has been amended only seventeen times in more than two hundred years. Yet, since the Constitution was drafted in 1787, the federal government has been transformed almost beyond recognition. This document remains the fundamental law of the land because it has allowed necessary changes to be made outside the Constitution's arduous amendment process. Each of the three branches of government has modified the original arrangement of power created at the Constitutional Convention.

The U.S. Constitution, therefore, is a "living" document. Thanks to its flexibility, the Constitution has been able to evolve over the years in response to changing conditions at home and internationally. The Constitution makes no mention, for example, of political or government bodies that are basic today, such as parties, the president's cabinet, and the congressional committee system.

Even more dramatic have been the changes in the presidency, which has been transformed in ways that could not have been imagined by the Founders. The original Constitution did not envisage a president who intervenes in congressional affairs and molds the legislative agenda; a president with wide latitude to act unilaterally without consulting Congress, even in domestic affairs; a president with a vast bureaucracy ready to implement his initiatives; and a president who dominates the day-to-day affairs of government, overshadowing both the legislative and judicial branches.[6]

The Constitution's brevity and generality have allowed these and other changes to be incorporated in the U.S. governing system without destroying the basic ideas and principles set forth in 1787.

Judicial Review

The interpretation of the Constitution by the Supreme Court has been a major source of change. Early acceptance of the principle of judicial review established the Court as the authoritative interpreter of the Constitution.

LENGTH OF TIME FOR RATIFICATION

The time elapsing between the submission by Congress of a constitutional amendment and its ratification by the requisite number of states has ranged from one hundred days (Twenty-sixth Amendment) to more than two hundred years (Twenty-seventh Amendment). The first ten amendments were proposed and ratified as a group. The detailed record regarding time for ratification follows:

Amendment	Passed Congress	Ratified	Time elapsed	
			years	days
1–10 (Bill of Rights)	Sept. 25, 1789	Dec. 15, 1791	2	81
11 (Suits against states)	March 4, 1794	Feb. 7, 1795		340
12 (Presidential electors)	Dec. 9, 1803	June 15, 1804		189
13 (Abolition of slavery)	Jan. 31, 1865	Dec. 6, 1865		309
14 (Civil rights: due process)	June 13, 1866	July 9, 1868	2[a]	26
15 (Black suffrage)	Feb. 26, 1869	Feb. 3, 1870		342
16 (Income tax)	July 12, 1909	Feb. 3, 1913	3[a]	206
17 (Direct election of senators)	May 13, 1912	April 8, 1913		330
18 (Prohibition)	Dec. 18, 1917	Jan. 16, 1919	1	29
19 (Women's suffrage)	June 4, 1919	Aug. 18, 1920	1[a]	75
20 ("Lame-duck")	March 2, 1932	Jan. 23, 1933		327
21 (Prohibition repeal)	Feb. 20, 1933	Dec. 5, 1933		288
22 (Presidential tenure)	March 24, 1947	Feb. 27, 1951	3[a]	340
23 (D.C. vote)	June 16, 1960	March 29, 1961		286
24 (Poll tax)	Sept. 14, 1962	Jan. 23, 1964	1	131
25 (Presidential disability)	July 6, 1965	Feb. 10, 1967	1	219
26 (18-year-old vote)	March 23, 1971	July 1, 1971		100
27 (Congressional pay raise)	Sept. 25, 1789	May 7, 1992	202[a]	225

a. Includes leap year(s).

SOURCES: Congressional Research Service, Library of Congress, *The Constitution of the United States of America: Analysis and Interpretation* (Washington D.C.: Government Printing Office, 1973); and *Congressional Quarterly Almanac: 102nd Congress, 2nd Session, 1992*, vol. 48 (Washington, D.C.: Congressional Quarterly, 1993), 58–59.

The Supreme Court's power to declare acts of Congress unconstitutional was first asserted in 1803 by Chief Justice John Marshall, in *Marbury v. Madison.* Marshall said:

> The powers of the Legislature are defined and limited; and that those limits may not be mistaken, or forgotten, the Constitution is written. To what purpose are powers limited, and to what purpose is that limitation committed to writing, if these limits may at any time be passed by those intended to be restrained?
>
> It is a proposition too plain to be contested, that the Constitution controls any legislative act repugnant to it, or that the Legislature may alter the Constitution by an ordinary act. Between these alternatives there is no middle ground. The Constitution is either a superior paramount law, unchangeable by ordinary means, or it is on a level with ordinary legislative acts, and, like other acts, is alterable when the Legislature shall please to alter it. . . . If an act of the Legislature, repugnant to the Constitution, is void, does it, notwithstanding its invalidity, bind the courts, and oblige them to give it effect? . . . It is emphatically the province and duty of the judicial department to say what the law is. . . . So if a law be in opposition to the Constitution; if both the law and the Constitution apply to a particular case, so that the Court must either decide that case conformably to the law, disregarding the Constitution; or conformably to the Constitution, disregarding the law, the Court must determine which of these conflicting rules governs the case. This is the very essence of judicial duty.

New Needs, National Emergencies

The Constitution also has been modified in effect as Congress and the executive branch were forced to address urgent national needs with far-reaching programs and policies for a country of more than two hundred million people.

The most obvious changes in and expansion of government powers have come in the twentieth century as a result of two world wars, the Great Depression, and the role of superpower the United States assumed after World War II. *(See Chapter 5, Foreign Policy Powers; Chapter 8, Regulation of Commerce.)*

The Amending Process: Arduous but Workable

The Constitution has been amended twenty-seven times. Some of the amendments, such as the Eleventh and Sixteenth, reversed judicial interpretations of the Constitution, but a number of others made only technical adjustments in the mechanisms of government. For example, the Twelfth Amendment provided for separate balloting for president and vice president in the electoral college, and the Twentieth Amendment revised the dates for the beginning of presidential terms and the convening of Congress.

Other amendments advanced the course of democracy by extending the vote to blacks (Fifteenth) and women (Nineteenth), lowering the voting age from twenty-one to eighteen (Twenty-sixth), and providing for the direct election of senators (Seventeenth). The economy was profoundly affected by the Income Tax Amendment (Sixteenth) and social mores by the Prohibition Amendment outlawing intoxicating liquors (Eighteenth, repealed by the Twenty-first). The relationship between the national and state governments was altered by the Fourteenth Amendment, the most fundamental formal revision of the Constitution. Its consequences are still unfolding in Supreme Court decisions based on the amendment. *(See box, Versatile Fourteenth Amendment, p. 366.)*

The constitutional amendments have come in clusters. The first ten, the Bill of Rights, were practically a part of the original Constitution, having been ratified in 1791. The next two, the Eleventh and especially the Twelfth, corrected some obvious flaws in the Constitution. They were ratified in 1795 and 1804, respectively.

The Civil War, the nation's gravest crisis, prompted the Thirteenth (1865), Fourteenth (1868), and Fifteenth (1870) amendments. The next group of amendments did not come until early in the twentieth century. From 1913 to 1920, largely as the culmination of the Progressive movement, four amendments of fundamental importance were ratified. They established the income tax, direct election of senators, Prohibition, and women's suffrage.

The Twentieth Amendment rescinded Prohibition; the Twenty-first Amendment altered the dates for the beginning of presidential terms (January 20) and each two-year Congress (January 3). Both amendments took effect in 1933.

Most of the recent amendments were ratified during a twenty-year period after World War II. They made important modifications in presidential powers and succession (the Twenty-second and Twenty-fifth) and further broadened suffrage (Twenty-third, Twenty-fourth, and Twenty-sixth).

The Twenty-second Amendment was ratified largely in reaction to the four-term presidency of Franklin D. Roosevelt, which critics said went contrary to the two-term precedent set by George Washington. The dominance of the executive branch during the New Deal and World War II led to calls for other amendments curtailing presidential power. One proposal that Congress came close to approving was the so-called Bricker amendment. It would have restricted the president's flexibility in arranging treaties and his implied power to enter into executive agreements with other countries. In 1950 the amendment came within one vote in the Senate of securing the necessary two-thirds majority. *(See "Bricker Amendment," p. 204.)*

In 1992, as congressional pay raises became the target of vocal public hostility, the Madison Amendment became part of the Constitution as the Twenty-seventh Amendment. Named for James Madison, who proposed and wrote the amendment in 1789, it prohibited midterm changes in congressional salaries.

CONGRESSIONAL DOMINATION

Although the Constitutional Convention envisioned a substantial role for the states in the amendment process, Congress has dominated that procedure. The states never have been successful in calling for a convention to propose an amendment, as they are authorized to do, by petitions to Congress from two-thirds of the legislatures. During the first hundred years of its existence, Congress received only ten such petitions from state

AMENDMENTS NOT RATIFIED BY THE STATES

By the nation's two-hundredth birthday, well over 9,100 proposed amendments to the Constitution had been introduced in Congress. And of these, one-third had been introduced since 1960. Many were identical or similar in content, and some were introduced repeatedly. The unsuccessful Equal Rights Amendment (ERA), for example, was introduced in every Congress between 1923 and 1972. *(See box, Equal Rights Amendment, p. 369.)*

Congress has acted on proposals to amend the Constitution only when there was persistent and widespread public support. Only thirty-three proposals have been approved and sent to the states for ratification. Of these, twenty-seven were ratified and only six did not win the required three-fourths majority of the states—an indication of how well Congress usually reflects public sentiment.

Of the six congressionally approved amendments that were not ratified by the states, one was proposed in September 1789, along with the Bill of Rights. Concerned with the apportionment of representatives, it was ratified by ten states, one fewer than the number then required.

In 1810 an amendment providing for revocation of the citizenship of any American accepting a gift or title of nobility from any foreign power, without the consent of Congress, was submitted to the states for ratification. The amendment was ratified by twelve states and by the senate of the South Carolina Legislature; had it been approved by that legislature's other chamber, it would have become a part of the Constitution. The impression prevailed for nearly a generation that the amendment had been adopted.

A proposed amendment to prohibit interference by Congress with the institution of slavery in the states, offered in 1861 as a last effort to ward off the impending conflict between North and South, was ratified by the legislatures of only two states—Ohio and Maryland. A convention called in Illinois in 1862 to revise the state constitution also ratified the amendment, but because Congress had designated state legislatures as the ratifying bodies, this ratification was manifestly invalid.

The Child Labor Amendment would have empowered Congress to "limit, regulate, and prohibit the labor of persons under 18 years of age." The amendment sought to reverse rulings by the Supreme Court in 1918 in *Hammer v. Dagenhart* and in 1922 in *Bailey v. Drexel Furniture Co.* that had struck down child labor laws enacted by Congress. Submitted to the states June 4, 1924, without any deadline, the amendment had been ratified by twenty-eight of the forty-eight states by 1938. In that year Congress enacted a child labor law by exercising its constitutional power to regulate interstate commerce. In 1941 the Supreme Court in *United States v. Darby Lumber Co.* upheld the law, specifically reversing its 1918 decision. No further ratifications of the proposed amendment have been made since the 1930s.

The Equal Rights Amendment, approved by Congress in 1972, failed to win ratification by the deadline of June 30, 1982. Only thirty-five states approved it, three short of the necessary thirty-eight.

The proposed constitutional amendment providing for voting representation in Congress for Washington, D.C., was approved by Congress in 1978. It won ratification from only sixteen states by the August 22, 1985, deadline and thus did not become a part of the Constitution. It was the most recent proposed amendment to be approved by Congress.

legislatures. But between 1893 and 1974, more than three hundred such petitions were received.[7] The states, while approving twenty-seven amendments proposed by Congress, had refused to ratify only six. *(See boxes, Amendments Not Ratified by the States, this page; Unsuccessful Amendments in Congress, p. 373.)*

Undoubtedly, the need to obtain the approval of three-fourths of the states has deterred Congress from proposing amendments. On at least one occasion, the prospect that the states might take the initiative prompted Congress to act. The Seventeenth Amendment, providing for direct election of senators, was continually blocked in the Senate until the state legislatures were on the verge of requiring a convention. Even in this case, however, Congress had for years provided the principal public arena for debate on the issue.

Congress has the power to determine by which of the two procedures the states shall ratify a proposed amendment. In every case except one, approval by the state legislatures has been prescribed. Only for the Twenty-first Amendment, the repeal of Prohibition, did Congress call for ratification by state conventions. The exception occurred for three principal reasons: (1) a desire for speedy ratification; (2) the contention of repeal advocates that state legislatures ratifying the Eighteenth Amendment had yielded to pressure from Prohibition forces, had overrepresented rural areas favoring Prohibition, and had not represented the views of the majority of the people; and (3) the desire to remove permanently from the political arena a question that had divided states, regions, and political parties. The Twenty-first Amendment, submitted to the states in February 1933, was ratified by conventions in thirty-six of the then-existing forty-eight states by December of that year.

The Supreme Court has spoken infrequently about the amending power of Congress. Most of the Court's decisions came in the wake of the controversial Prohibition amendments *(National Prohibition Cases, 1920; Dillon v. Gloss, 1921)*. The Court held that liquor was a proper subject for a constitutional amendment, that two-thirds of the members of the House or Senate present must approve a proposed amendment (not two-thirds of the entire membership), and that Congress has the power to set a time limit for ratification. *(See "Time for Ratification," p. 362.)*

UNRESOLVED QUESTIONS

Of the two methods of proposing amendments—by a two-thirds majority of each house of Congress or by a convention called by Congress at the request of the legislatures of two-thirds of the states—only the former has been employed.

Convention Formula

In the 1960s the Council of State Governments mounted a campaign to secure a constitutional amendment that would allow one house of a state legislature to be apportioned on some basis other than population. In the early 1980s a similar drive for a convention to approve a balanced budget amendment high-lighted the many uncertainties about use of the convention formula, questions that have not yet been resolved. One major concern is whether a constitutional convention called by the states would be limited to proposing amendments mentioned in the petitions calling for a convention. Or would the entire Constitution be open to amendment, possibly threatening the foundation of the federal government? *(See box, Uncertainties about Convention Method, this page.)*

UNCERTAINTIES ABOUT CONVENTION METHOD

The states have never required Congress to call a convention to consider amendments to the Constitution. As a result, important questions about the procedures for holding a second constitutional convention have never been answered.

The close call in the 1960s, when thirty-three states (only one short of the two-thirds needed) petitioned for a convention to propose a reapportionment amendment, prompted constitutional law experts to urge Congress to draw up guidelines to avoid chaos should a convention ever be held. Many authorities as well as members of Congress feared that unless procedures were established a convention might become a "runaway" session that would expose the entire Constitution to revision.

In 1971 and 1973 the Senate passed bills establishing convention procedures. The legislation gave each state as many convention delegates as the state had members of the House and Senate, specified delegate election procedures, prohibited conventions from considering any matters except those amendments referred to it by the state resolutions, allowed Congress to determine the method of ratification, and set a seven-year time limit on the validity of state petitions for a convention. Neither bill was ever considered by the House.

The Senate Judiciary Committee approved similar bills in 1982, 1984, and 1985 after thirty-two states had called for a convention to consider a balanced budget constitutional amendment. None of these bills was considered by the full Senate. The states' campaign followed Congress's refusal to approve a proposed amendment to require a balanced budget.

The major concerns about convening a constitutional convention center on a number of uncertainties.

Valid Convention Call. What constitutes a valid call of two-thirds of the legislatures? Must the resolutions to Congress be identical in all details or simply relate to one general subject? Is it a valid convention call if thirty-four states wish to consider different amendment proposals?

Length of Time to Call. In what time span must the required two-thirds of the states submit their resolutions? The Constitution is silent on this point. In resolutions submitting proposed amendments to the states throughout most of the twentieth century, Congress has stipulated a seven-year maximum period for ratification.

Rescinding a Call. Can a state rescind a previous call for a convention? The Constitution says nothing about the legality of a rescinding action. In 1868, when New Jersey and Ohio attempted to withdraw their ratifications of the Fourteenth Amendment, Congress refused to accept the withdrawals. The issue has never been resolved by the Supreme Court.

Forcing Congress to Act. If the required two-thirds of the legislatures issue a convention call, is Congress obligated to call the convention? By the letter of the Constitution, it would appear to have no choice. But Congress might find pretexts to invalidate individual state petitions and the Supreme Court might consider Congress the final judge of those petitions.

Procedures for a Call. How would Congress act to call a convention? If there were no dispute, the Senate and House Judiciary committees probably would report appropriate resolutions that the two houses would approve.

But what would happen if one of the Judiciary committees refused to report such a resolution? The resolution might be considered a privileged proposition that could be referred to committee or considered directly without committee action or recommendation. But what if Senate opponents blocked the resolution with a filibuster?

Restricting a Convention. How should a congressional resolution calling a convention be worded? A convention might decide to consider a whole range of changes that could threaten the very foundations of the Constitution.

Should, or could, Congress limit the convention to the subject named in the states' petitions? Could it narrowly define that subject? The performance of state constitutional conventions raises serious doubts that a national convention to amend the Constitution could be bound in advance. The convention that wrote the U.S. Constitution ignored its original mandate merely to amend the Articles of Confederation. But if amendments were submitted on subjects not specified in the summoning of a convention, they might be subject to political attack on the ground that the convention had not been authorized, or its members elected, to act in other areas.

Apportionment of Delegates. What would be the apportionment of a constitutional convention? Here again, the Constitution is silent. The Constitutional Convention of 1787 had different numbers of delegates representing their states but each state was accorded only one vote.

Congress presumably could require that a new constitutional convention be apportioned on the same basis as the existing U.S. House, or the House and Senate combined, as proposed in the unsuccessful Senate bills in the 1980s.

Selecting Delegates. How would delegates be chosen? That question could be left to the discretion of the state legislatures, or Congress might try to lay down ground rules requiring election either by congressional districts or by statewide balloting, or by a combination of the two.

Ratification Procedures

Unresolved questions also exist about ratification of amendments. Constitutional authorities have disagreed about whether Congress or the state legislatures should determine the procedures for ratification by state conventions.

Bills have been introduced in Congress to spell out procedures, but none has passed. State legislatures have been divided on this question. At least twenty-one legislatures provided by statute that state officials were to follow the procedures specified in a federal law if Congress should enact one. Sixteen legislatures, assuming that the procedural question was within their jurisdiction, passed laws applicable not merely to the convention summoned for the Twenty-first Amendment, but for all future conventions called to ratify amendments to the U.S. Constitution. One state, New Mexico, claimed exclusive authority on the matter and directed its officials to resist any attempt at congressional encroachment on that authority.

Time for Ratification

Another uncertainty concerns the definition of a "reasonable" time period for ratification, a question that the Supreme Court has left to Congress.

The Eighteenth Amendment (Prohibition) was the first to specify a period of years, seven, to complete ratification. In 1921 the Court held in *Dillon v. Gloss* that Congress had the power to fix a definite ratification period "within reasonable limits." In 1939 the Court held in *Coleman v. Miller* that the definition of a "reasonable" period was essentially political and should be answered by Congress, rather than by the Court.

Congress got an opportunity to address the issue in 1992, when the Twenty-seventh Amendment (Madison Amendment) reached the three-quarters threshold for ratification by the states more than two hundred years after the measure was approved by the First Congress. The final ratification was controversial, with lawmakers at first hesitant to accept the drawn-out process as legal. Scholars had for decades considered the amendment dead because it had been around too long. Supporters, however, noted that the measure had been sent to the states without a deadline and, therefore, extensive gaps between state ratification did not invalidate the proposal. After the archivist of the United States certified ratification of the amendment, opposition melted. Lawmakers also proved unwilling to oppose such a popular measure during an election year and thus embraced the new amendment.

Like the Madison Amendment, the Child Labor Amendment was proposed, in 1924, with no time limit. Only twenty-eight states had ratified the amendment between 1924 and 1938. If ten more states were to ratify (the three-fourths requirement applies to the number of states currently in the Union, not the number at the time the amendment was proposed), Congress will have to consider the "reasonable" time period issue again. *(See box, Amendments Not Ratified by the States, p. 360.)*

In March 1976 Kentucky ratified the Thirteenth, Fourteenth, and Fifteenth amendments—more than a hundred years after they became part of the Constitution.

Two major questions concerning the amending power were reviewed by the Supreme Court in 1982 in a pair of cases involving the proposed Equal Rights Amendment (ERA), then being considered by the states. The cases were *National Organization for Women v. Idaho* and *Carmen v. Idaho*. The first question was whether Congress had the power to extend the period for ratification of an amendment beyond the deadline originally proposed. The issue arose after Congress in 1978 extended the ratification period for the ERA for thirty-nine months, to June 30, 1982.

The second question was whether a state that had ratified a proposed constitutional amendment could later rescind its approval. Five states that had ratified the ERA subsequently moved to nullify that action. The Supreme Court previously had recognized the power of a state to change its mind and ratify a proposed amendment after initially refusing to do so. But it had never addressed the opposite situation.

In its decision of October 4, 1982, the Court sidestepped both questions by dismissing the cases as moot. However, proponents of an expansive congressional power in the amending process and of a narrowly defined state power were encouraged by the Court's decision. Besides ruling the cases moot, the Court vacated a federal district court ruling that said (1) Congress had exceeded its power when it extended the ERA ratification period, and (2) states could rescind their approval of a proposed amendment if they acted within the period allowed for ratification. The High Court's action thus eliminated the lower court's decision from the law books, rendering it useless as a precedent. *(See box, Equal Rights Amendment, p. 369.)*

The Amendments: From Basic to Technical

Important guarantees of civil liberties were written into the Constitution. Ex post facto laws and bills of attainder were forbidden, as was suspension of the writ of habeas corpus. A religious test as a qualification for office was prohibited and trial by jury for criminal offenses was guaranteed. But other basic rights, such as free speech, were not spelled out and pressure soon rose to rectify this omission.

THE BILL OF RIGHTS

Little had been said at the Constitutional Convention in favor of a bill of rights. Most delegates were satisfied that the fundamental liberties they cherished would be safe because the federal government was limited to powers explicitly granted in the Constitution and thus was denied the authority to curtail citizens' rights.[8]

But during the campaign for ratification it became clear that many were not content to leave basic rights protected from government power by inference only. The colonists had long claimed the rights guaranteed Englishmen by precedents going back as far as the Magna Carta (1215), and civil liberties had been guaranteed in colonial charters. Since independence, six states had adopted bills of rights and others had incorporated similar guarantees into their state constitutions.

When Massachusetts ratified the new Constitution of the United States, its convention recommended amending the document to protect basic rights. The Virginia ratifying convention chose a committee to report on amendments for submission in the First Congress. New York attached a bill of rights to its ratification. There was little doubt that quick action was required to add explicit guarantees of fundamental liberties.

Madison yielded in his view that the grant of only specified powers to the federal government was sufficient protection of civil liberties. He proposed amendments to be fitted into the Constitution at appropriate points within the document. But the House of Representatives, after a committee had considered and revised Madison's proposals, decided to append the amendments as a supplement to the Constitution. Twelve amendments were finally approved by Congress and submitted to the states. The first two, which dealt with apportionment of representatives and compensation of members of Congress, were not ratified with the others. The remainder became the first ten amendments to the Constitution when Virginia, the eleventh state to ratify, approved them on December 15, 1791. (There were at the time fourteen states in the Union.)

Five of these ten provisions of the Bill of Rights are among the most frequently cited and most hotly debated provisions in the Constitution. The other five are rarely mentioned.

The First Amendment protects the freedom of thought and belief. It forbids Congress to restrict the freedom of religion, speech, the press, peaceable assembly, or petition.

The Second Amendment ensures the right of the states to maintain a militia and, in connection with that state right, the right of the people to keep and bear arms.

The Third Amendment restricts government power to quarter soldiers in private homes.

The Fourth Amendment forbids the government to conduct unreasonable searches of an individual's person, house, papers, or effects.

The Fifth Amendment requires indictment of all persons charged with serious crimes in civilian proceedings. It also forbids trying a person twice for the same offense or compelling a person to incriminate himself. It protects individuals against being deprived of life, liberty, or property without due process of law and protects private property against being taken for public use without just compensation to the owner.

The Sixth Amendment guarantees a speedy and public trial by jury for all persons accused of a crime. The defendant is also assured of the right to be notified of the charge against him, to confront those who testify against him, to compel witnesses to appear to testify for him, and to have the aid of a lawyer in his defense.

The Seventh Amendment provides for a jury trial in all common-law suits involving more than $20.

The Eighth Amendment forbids excessive bail, excessive fines, and cruel and unusual punishment.

The Ninth Amendment states that the Constitution's explicit mention of certain rights does not deny or disparage other rights not mentioned.

The Tenth Amendment declares that all powers that the Constitution does not give to the federal government or does not deny to the states are reserved to the states or the people.

In 1833 the Supreme Court ruled in *Barron v. Baltimore* that the Bill of Rights protected individuals against action by the federal government only; it was not applicable to the states. In a line of rulings beginning in 1925, however, the Court held that the Fourteenth Amendment's due process clause requires the states to conform to most of the guarantees in the Bill of Rights.[9]

OTHER EARLY AMENDMENTS

The experience of operating the new government quickly disclosed a couple of other problem areas in the original Constitution, and the next two amendments addressed those. One dealt with states' rights and the other with presidential elections.

States and Federal Courts

The principle that a sovereign state could not be sued by a private individual, except with its consent, was complicated by the establishment of a federal union. While state governments might refuse to entertain such suits in their own courts, the Constitution did not indicate whether they could similarly refuse to be sued in a federal court. Article III of the Constitution gave jurisdiction to federal courts in cases "between a state and citizens of another state."

Although no one doubted that a state could bring a suit against an individual, Article III had not been interpreted in state ratifying conventions as permitting an individual to sue a state without its consent. But the Supreme Court in 1793 in *Chisholm v. Georgia* upheld the suit of a British creditor against the state of Georgia, which refused to participate in the case.

The ruling angered individuals who opposed a strong federal government. The Massachusetts Legislature declared that the power exercised by the Supreme Court was "dangerous to the peace, safety, and independence of the several states and repugnant to the first principles of a federal government." The Georgia House of Representatives passed a bill providing that any official who attempted to enforce the Court's decision should be declared guilty of a felony and be hanged, without benefit of clergy. Congress quickly proposed an amendment providing that the power of the federal judiciary did not extend to private suits against states. Ratification was completed in February 1795.

Separate Ballot for Vice President

The Constitution provided that presidential electors chosen in each state were to cast two votes, with no distinction between the votes for president and vice president. The candidate receiving the highest number of votes, provided they constituted a majority, would be named president. In the absence of a majority, the House of Representatives would choose among the five candidates with the highest number of electoral votes. After selection of the president, the candidate with the next highest number of electoral votes would, in any case, be named vice president.[10]

The Constitutional Convention had not anticipated the development of political parties, whose candidates in the electoral college would be pledged to register the party choice for president.

In 1800 the Republican Party won a clear majority, with seventy-three electors as against sixty-five Federalist electors. But a deadlock resulted because all of the Republicans cast one vote for Jefferson and one vote for Aaron Burr. They had intended that Jefferson would be president and Burr vice president, but there was no way of distinguishing the votes cast. Because no candidate had a majority, the election was thrown into the House of Representatives. There many of the Federalists voted for Burr and a deadlock persisted until the thirty-sixth ballot. (*See "Election of 1800," p. 380.*)

A proposed amendment, providing that separate votes be cast by the electors for president and vice president, was rejected by the Senate in 1802 after having received the necessary two-thirds majority in the House. In 1803, however, both houses approved the proposed amendment.

Ratification probably was completed on June 15, 1804, when the legislature of the thirteenth state (New Hampshire) approved the amendment. However, the governor of New Hampshire vetoed the act on June 20, and the amendment failed to pass again by the two-thirds vote of the legislature required by the state constitution. But because Article V provides for ratification by state legislatures or conventions, it has generally been thought that approval or veto by a governor is without significance. If the ratification by New Hampshire was ineffective, then the amendment became part of the Constitution when Tennessee ratified it on July 27, 1804.

In any event, ratification was completed in time for the elections of 1804. Once this adjustment in electoral machinery was made, the two-party system kept election of the president out of the House of Representatives in every election except that of 1824.

The revised method of choosing the vice president reduced the prestige of that office. When filled by the person with next to the strongest support for the presidency, the post of vice president could serve as a platform for national leadership. After the election of 1796, Jefferson, the head of the opposition Republicans, had held the office under President John Adams, a Federalist. With ratification of the Twelfth Amendment, the vice presidency became a singularly powerless position. Men and women of presidential caliber often decline to run for the office, while political leaders may seek to get rid of an embarrassing party figure by placing the person in the obscurity of the vice presidency, as President William McKinley tried to do when he made the controversial Progressive Theodore Roosevelt his vice president. McKinley's assassination, however, put Roosevelt in the White House.

CIVIL WAR AMENDMENTS

The next round of constitutional amendments came sixty years after ratification of the Twelfth Amendment, with three revisions that addressed slavery and other issues of the Civil War period.

Abolition of Slavery

Anxious to preserve the Union, most northerners were not demanding abolition of slavery when the South seceded. As the Civil War progressed, however, abolition increasingly became part of the program of the federal government. President Abraham Lincoln and many members of Congress at first favored proposals to compensate slave owners for their property loss. In 1862 Congress provided for release of slaves in the District of Columbia, and owners loyal to the government received up to $300 for each slave freed. Later in the same year, the president recommended a constitutional amendment to authorize federal aid to states that abolished slavery.[11]

On January 1, 1863, Lincoln issued his Emancipation Proclamation, which stated that "all persons held as slaves within any state or designated part of a state, the people whereof shall be in rebellion against the United States, shall be then, thenceforward, and forever free."

The proclamation was issued without authorization by Congress, and it had no constitutional basis other than the war powers of the president. Although the legality of the action has been much disputed, subsequent constitutional sanction was provided by the Thirteenth Amendment. The resolution proposing this amendment, which was to abolish slavery throughout the United States, was approved by the Senate on April 8, 1864, but failed to receive a two-thirds vote in the House. The proposed amendment was an issue in the 1864 election. A Republican victory led in January 1865 to House approval by a vote of 119–56; a switch of only three votes would have prevented approval. The amendment was ratified December 6, 1865.

Due Process and Equal Protection

As southern state legislatures moved at the end of the war to limit the civil rights of freed slaves, more than the Thirteenth Amendment clearly was needed to protect those rights. The Freedmen's Bureau Act and the Civil Rights Act of 1866 sought to protect basic rights, and the latter attempted to void by legislation the famous *Dred Scott* decision of 1857 by which the Supreme Court had denied that a free black, let alone a slave,

CELEBRATION AT BALTIMORE ON MAY 19th 1870.

The Fifteenth Amendment, ratified in 1870, prohibited denial of the right to vote on the basis of race, color, or previous condition of servitude.

could be considered a citizen of the United States. Although the Civil Rights Act was passed by two-thirds votes in both houses to override President Andrew Johnson's veto, its constitutionality remained in doubt. And so the Fourteenth Amendment was adopted, among other things, to give the act constitutional support and accord permanence to the basic rights the act was intended to guarantee.

The Fourteenth Amendment was submitted to the states in June 1866. Ratification was refused by nine of the former Confederate states until after Congress had enacted a law making such ratification a condition of their restoration to the Union. In announcing adoption of the amendment in July 1868, Secretary of State William H. Seward declared it had been ratified by the legislatures of twenty-three states and "by newly constituted and newly established bodies . . . acting as the legislatures" of six southern states.

The first section of the Fourteenth Amendment declares that all persons born or naturalized in the United States (except those, such as diplomats, not subject to U.S. jurisdiction) are citizens of the United States and of the state in which they re-

side, thereby nullifying the *Dred Scott* decision. More important, it forbids states to deprive any person of life, liberty, or property without due process of law, or to deny anyone equal protection of the laws.

The second section of the amendment eliminated in effect the clause of Article I, Section 2, of the Constitution, which directed that three-fourths of the slave population of a state was to be counted in apportioning the House of Representatives. This provision had been rendered obsolete by the Thirteenth Amendment, but the Fourteenth did not stop at basing apportionment on total population (exclusive of Indians not taxed). It further provided that if any state abridged the right of its citizens to vote for federal or state offices, the number of its representatives in the House should be decreased in proportion to the number of adult male citizens denied the vote. Thaddeus Stevens, leader of the Radicals in the House of Representatives, expected this provision to be the most effective instrument for securing black rights, but its inadequacy in guaranteeing the right to vote led later to the Fifteenth Amendment.

The third and fourth sections of the amendment had tempo-

VERSATILE FOURTEENTH AMENDMENT

Of all twenty-seven amendments to the Constitution, none has a story more amazing than the Fourteenth Amendment. For the better part of the century after its ratification in 1868, this amendment was little used to protect individual rights. It was more effective, until the mid-1930s, in protecting property rights from government regulations.

But in the years following World War II the Supreme Court stopped using the amendment as a restriction on government regulation of property and business. The Court, for the most part, left Congress free to determine the boundaries of federal economic and social power. The Court began using the Fourteenth Amendment to restrict state action in civil and political rights.

Relying largely on the Fourteenth Amendment's guarantee of "equal protection of the laws," the Court forced fundamental reforms in state policies of racial segregation and legislative malapportionment. Under the amendment's due process clause, the Court extended to the states the protection of most of the Bill of Rights guarantees.

Undoubtedly the most controversial of the Supreme Court's postwar Fourteenth Amendment rulings was its unanimous 1954 decision in the case of *Brown v. Board of Education of Topeka*. The Court declared that racial segregation of students by the state in public schools denied black students the equal protection of the laws. That ruling set off a civil rights revolution.

A decade later, the Court launched another revolution when it held in *Baker v. Carr* (1962), *Gray v. Sanders* (1963), and *Reynolds v. Sims* (1964) that malapportionment of state legislatures violated the equal protection guarantee. Many populous urban areas of states were underrepresented in the legislatures, and rural areas were overrepresented. Because the legislatures made apportionment de-

cisions, there appeared to be no political way to force the legislators from rural areas to surrender their power to urban areas. The effect of the Court's one-person, one-vote decisions was a profound alteration in the character and policies of the legislatures of every state.

In 1833 the Supreme Court held that the guarantees of the first ten amendments—the Bill of Rights—were effective only against the actions of the federal government and not against state governments. Some of the men who drafted the Fourteenth Amendment thought they were extending those guarantees against state action, but the Court did not apply the amendment in that fashion until more than fifty years after its adoption.

Beginning with a 1925 ruling in the case of *Gitlow v. New York*, the Court held that the Fourteenth Amendment's guarantee of due process did in fact extend certain of the guarantees of the Bill of Rights to include actions by the states.

In *Gitlow*, the Court assumed that the First Amendment guarantee of free speech was applicable against the states. In the next few years the Court extended that assumption to prohibit state actions that violated First Amendment protections of freedom of the press, religious belief, assembly, and association. Following World War II, the Court extended this thinking to the remainder of the Bill of Rights. The justices said that other guarantees of those ten amendments were carried by the Fourteenth Amendment into the realm of state action. These included the Fourth Amendment's guarantee of security against unreasonable search and seizure, the Fifth Amendment's protection against compulsory self-incrimination, the Sixth Amendment's ensurance of the right to counsel, and the Eighth Amendment's prohibition of cruel and unusual punishment.

---

rary significance. They prohibited anyone from holding state or federal office (unless authorized by Congress) who had participated in rebellion after taking an oath to support the U.S. Constitution, and they denied the responsibility of federal or state governments for debts incurred in aid of rebellion.

The due process and equal protection clauses, both open to wide differences of interpretation, have served as the basis of controversial shifts in the role of American government. The Supreme Court at first frustrated the hopes of those backers of the Fourteenth Amendment who expected to see the federal government assume large responsibilities for civil rights. Next, the Court employed the due process clause to frustrate state interference with the principles of laissez faire economics, an approach not abandoned until the New Deal era. Gradually, freedoms guaranteed by the Bill of Rights were extended, by invoking the due process clause, to cover actions by state governments. After World War II, the Supreme Court ruled that the equal protection clause prohibited racial segregation in schools, and Congress enacted civil rights legislation sanctioned in part by this section of the Fourteenth Amendment.

Voting Rights

When it became apparent that the Fourteenth Amendment's threat of reduced representation in the House had failed to prompt southern states to extend the franchise to blacks, Congress proposed a more direct approach.

The Fifteenth Amendment, submitted to the states in February 1869, prohibited denial of the right to vote on the basis of race, color, or previous condition of servitude. Ratification was completed in February 1870.[12]

Congress in the same year passed an "Enforcement Act" designed to make the amendment effective. This statute sought to prevent the use of technicalities of registration and voting procedures to confuse and intimidate black voters. Heavy penalties were prescribed for state officials convicted of violating the act. Interference with voting rights by bribery or by threats of violence or economic discrimination was outlawed. Enforcement was to be in federal courts, and the president was authorized to use military force as necessary to support the judicial process. The Supreme Court in 1876 held portions of this act unconstitutional and in so doing limited the effectiveness of the Fifteenth

Amendment. The authority of Congress to enact "appropriate legislation" to enforce the amendment was construed as limited to legislation to combat outright discrimination on the basis of race; the authority, it was ruled, did not extend to the whole field of obstructions of the right to vote (*United States v. Reese*). Nearly a century passed before Congress, in the sweeping Voting Rights Act of 1965, finally provided effective means for federal enforcement of the Fifteenth Amendment's bar against racial discrimination affecting the right to vote.

TWENTIETH-CENTURY AMENDMENTS

The last three decades of the nineteenth century and the first decade of the twentieth century were a time of relative stability for the Constitution as amended through the Civil War era. Following ratification of the Fifteenth Amendment in 1870, no other amendments became law until 1913 when the states gave final approval to the Sixteenth Amendment, which empowered Congress to levy and collect taxes on incomes. Eleven other amendments were successful between then and 1992—five of them dealing with electoral rights, three with congressional or presidential terms and succession, two with liquor sales, and one with congressional salaries.

Federal Income Tax

Although the federal government had levied an income tax during the Civil War, a similar tax imposed in 1894 was held unconstitutional by the Supreme Court in 1895 in *Pollock v. Farmers' Loan and Trust Co.* Congress's neglect to submit a remedial amendment during subsequent years resulted in part from a belief that such an amendment was unnecessary and that it would be possible to draft an income tax law that would be held constitutional.[13]

Pressure to impose another income tax grew, but President William Howard Taft and others opposed action without an authorizing amendment. They feared that to enact a statute similar to one previously declared unconstitutional, in the expectation that the Supreme Court would reverse its earlier decision, would undermine confidence in the Constitution and would subject the Court to the pressures of a public campaign. The amendment to empower Congress to levy taxes on incomes "from whatever source derived" was approved by both houses in 1909, but ratification of the Sixteenth Amendment was not completed until early in 1913. At a special session that year, Congress enacted a graduated personal income tax and converted into a direct income tax a levy on corporation income imposed since 1909 in the guise of an excise tax. (*See Chapter 4, Power of the Purse.*)

Popular Election of Senators

The Seventeenth Amendment is of particular interest because it clearly was forced on Congress—specifically on the Senate—by popular pressure. The Constitution provided for the election of senators by the state legislatures. But the Seventeenth Amendment, ratified in 1913, changed the Constitution to provide for direct election of senators. The change was a part of the Progressive Era's movement toward more democratic control of government. Being less immediately dependent on popular sentiment than the House, the Senate did not seek to reform itself. Only persistent pressure from the public—expressed through the House of Representatives, the state governments, special interest groups, petitions, referendums, and other means—persuaded the Senate that it must participate in its own reform.[14]

In the first eighty years of Congress, only nine resolutions proposing a constitutional amendment for direct election of senators were introduced in Congress. In the 1870s and 1880s the number increased, and by 1912 no fewer than 287 such joint resolutions had been introduced. Not until 1892 was a resolution reported favorably from committee in the House. In the next decade such a resolution was carried five times in the House.

Petitions from farmers' associations and other organizations, particularly in the West, and party platforms in state elections pressed the issue until the national parties took it up. Direct election of senators was a plank in the Populist program at every election, beginning in 1892, and in the Democratic platform in each presidential election year from 1900 to 1912. Beginning with California and Iowa in 1894, state legislatures addressed Congress in favor of a direct election amendment; by 1905 the legislatures of thirty-one of the forty-five states had taken this step, many of them repeatedly. In 1900, when the House voted 240–15 to submit such an amendment to the states, the resolution was supported by a majority of the representatives from every state except Maine and Connecticut. Still the Senate would not act.

The spread of direct primaries in the 1890s led in many states to expressions of a popular choice for senator on the primary ballot. One-party legislatures in the South generally ratified the popular choice, though the primary was less effective in putting over the popular choice in other states. Oregon in 1901 adopted a plan under which voters could express their preferences for senator, though their expression of a preference carried no binding legal force. When the Oregon Legislature ignored the popular preference in its next election of a senator, voters used their new powers of initiative and referendum to approve a new law. Henceforth candidates for the legislature could indicate on the ballot whether they would vote for the Senate candidate with the highest popular vote total. This "Oregon system" proved effective and was adopted in other states in modified forms. By December 1910 it was estimated that fourteen of the thirty senators about to be named by state legislatures had already been designated by popular vote.

In 1901 some legislatures, no longer content to ask Congress to submit a constitutional amendment to the states, began calling for a convention to amend the Constitution. Some senators, though they opposed a popular election, feared that such a convention, like the original Constitutional Convention, might exceed its mandate; they preferred to submit to the states a specific amendment for direct election of senators.

A resolution was finally brought to the Senate floor in 1911, but its supporters failed, 54–33, to gain the two-thirds support required. In a special session later that year, the House passed, 296–16, a different version of the resolution. The Senate this time approved its original resolution, 64–24. A deadlock was broken at the next session when the House on May 13, 1912, concurred in the Senate version. By April 1913, three-fourths of the states had ratified the Seventeenth Amendment.

Prohibition

Prohibition and women's suffrage amendments were first proposed in the platform of the Prohibition Party in 1872. Favorable Senate action on the Prohibition (Eighteenth) Amendment was taken in the special session called in 1917 to declare war on Germany; House approval followed in December 1917. The vigorous campaign carried on by the Anti-Saloon League had already resulted in the enactment of prohibition laws in about half of the states. The war gave impetus to the movement by identifying the attack on alcoholic beverages with patriotism. The effectiveness of the armed forces and the defense industries, it was argued, would be impaired by drunkenness, and the production of alcoholic drinks would divert resources from the war effort. Exercising the war powers granted it by the Constitution, Congress enacted legislation to restrict production of liquor and its sale to members of the armed forces.

While the Eighteenth Amendment was awaiting ratification by the states, the Wartime Prohibition Act, approved ten days after the armistice was signed, prohibited sale of distilled spirits, wine, or beer in the United States from June 30, 1919, until the end of the war.

The Eighteenth Amendment was ratified in January 1919, only thirteen months after its approval by Congress. Power to enforce the amendment's prohibition of the manufacture, sale, or transportation of intoxicating liquors was granted concurrently to Congress and the states, a duality that hindered enforcement by dividing responsibility.

The Volstead Act, which Congress passed on October 28, 1919, over President Woodrow Wilson's veto, was intended not only to enforce the amendment but also to strengthen the Wartime Prohibition Act (which continued in effect because the country was still technically at war) until the amendment went into force January 16, 1920, one year after its ratification.

Before Prohibition was abandoned in 1933, it profoundly affected the mores of the American people in ways not anticipated by its advocates. Widespread violation of the amendment and the Volstead Act seriously undermined respect for the law and buttressed the foundations of organized crime.

Women's Suffrage

Because the Constitution left it to the states to set the qualifications for voting in federal elections, early attempts to grant women's suffrage focused on the state legislatures. When the Fourteenth and Fifteenth amendments were considered, efforts were made to extend their guarantees of voting rights for blacks to women as well. After these efforts proved unsuccessful, a resolution proposing an additional amendment granting the vote

to women was introduced in the Senate in 1878. The resolution was reintroduced regularly thereafter until it was finally adopted more than forty years later.[15]

Meanwhile, some of the states went ahead and gave the vote to women within their jurisdiction. Wyoming, which became a state in 1890, had begun blazing the trail toward women's suffrage by according women the right to vote for territorial officials in 1869. By 1914 equal suffrage had been granted in eleven states; New York, considered a center of opposition, joined the procession in 1917.

World War I added impetus to the suffrage movement because it was viewed as a crusade for democracy. President Wilson, who had previously favored attainment of women's suffrage by state action, explained his conversion to the amendment route in terms of the war. The House adopted the resolution proposing the Women's Suffrage Amendment in 1918 by a vote of 174–136, a bare two-thirds majority. Wilson, in a surprise visit to the Senate on September 30, urged approval as "vitally essential to the successful prosecution of the great war of humanity in which we are engaged." The next day, however, Senate supporters failed, in a 62–34 vote, to obtain the necessary margin.

When the Republicans won the November election, Wilson pleaded for approval by the "lame-duck" Democratic Congress, but a Senate vote of 55–29 in February again fell short of the required two-thirds majority. Within three weeks, however, the proposed Nineteenth Amendment was approved at a special session of the new Congress. Submitted to the states in June 1919, it was ratified in August 1920.

An amendment to guarantee equal rights to women, proposed in every Congress since 1923, was finally passed and sent to the states in 1972. By the June 30, 1982, deadline, however, the Equal Rights Amendment fell three states short of ratification, and the amendment died.

Lame-Duck Amendment

Like the Twelfth Amendment, the Twentieth Amendment effected a mechanical change in the Constitution. It abolished lame-duck sessions of Congress and advanced the date of the inauguration of the president and vice president from March 4 to January 20. Under the terms of the amendment, Congress was to convene annually at noon on January 3 unless it "shall by law appoint a different day."[16]

Before this change, the Constitution provided that the terms of representatives and outgoing senators were not to end until March 4, four months after the election of a new Congress. While members of the new Congress began their terms on March 4, the first regular session did not commence until the first Monday of the following December, thirteen months after the election.

Although the president often called Congress into special session in the interim, the long wait between the election and the first regular session of a new Congress, and the potential inequity inherent in actions of a lame-duck Congress at the "short

EQUAL RIGHTS AMENDMENT

The proposed Equal Rights Amendment (ERA) to the Constitution, approved by Congress in March 1972 after a forty-nine-year campaign by ERA proponents, died June 30, 1982. In all, thirty-five states voted for ratification, three short of the required three-fourths majority.

The proposed amendment originally required ratification within seven years, but Congress in 1978 extended the deadline by thirty-nine months. But despite a massive lobbying campaign by women's groups and other supporters, not a single additional state voted to ratify the amendment during the extension. The amendment's fate was sealed in June 1982 when the legislatures of North Carolina, Florida, and Illinois voted against ratification. They were among fifteen states that rejected the amendment during the ten-year ratification period.

The proposal was brief and to the point, stating that:

Equality of rights under the law shall not be denied or abridged by the United States or by any state on account of sex.

The amendment authorized Congress to enforce the provision by "appropriate legislation." The amendment would take effect two years after ratification.

A resolution proposing such an amendment had been introduced in every Congress since 1923. In 1950 and 1953, the Senate had approved the proposed amendment but the House took no action.

Less than two hours after the Senate acted on March 22, 1972, Hawaii became the first state to ratify the measure. In the six months following congressional passage, twenty other states followed suit. Nine states endorsed the amendment in 1973, three in 1974, and only one—North Dakota—in 1975.

By early 1978, thirty-five states had ratified the amendment, but several state legislatures had either shelved or flatly rejected it. Moreover, several states that had ratified it tried to rescind their approval. The validity of this action was challenged in the federal courts, but the Supreme Court never made a definitive ruling. (See "Time for Ratification," p. 362.)

Despite official endorsements from a wide spectrum of women's groups, labor unions, and political and civic organizations of every stripe, the drive for passage of the Equal Rights Amendment encountered vigorous opposition. It was argued that passage would subject women to the draft, abolish protections women had from dangerous and unpleasant jobs, wipe out women's rights to privacy in public facilities (hospital facilities, rest rooms, and so forth), and adversely affect marriage laws and property and divorce rights.

Supporters responded that the ERA would not have affected constitutional privacy rights but would have ended unlawful discrimination, ensuring equal treatment for men as well as women in areas such as employment, pay, benefits, and criminal trials and sentences.

Identical constitutional amendments were introduced in the mid-1980s, but by then support for the ERA had waned and none was approved by Congress. The House in November 1983 came close to approving another ERA attempt, voting 278–147 for a new constitutional amendment, but this was six votes short of the necessary two-thirds majority.

---

session" (December–March), had drawn criticism for at least a century. Finally, in 1922, the Senate took up a proposed corrective amendment, which it approved no fewer than six times between 1923 and 1932, when the House at last took favorable action.

The Twentieth Amendment also gives Congress power to act if a president-elect or a vice president–elect dies or fails to qualify for office by the date their terms are to commence.

Ratification was completed on January 23, 1933, and under its terms the amendment became effective the following October 15.

Repeal of Prohibition

Between 1921 and 1933 more than 130 amendments were proposed in Congress to repeal or modify the Eighteenth Amendment. Prohibition had become so discredited by 1932 that the platforms of both parties favored constitutional revision. The Democrats proposed repeal; the Republicans favored retaining some authority for the federal government to control liquor traffic and to protect those states that chose to continue Prohibition.[17]

The landslide victory at the polls of Franklin D. Roosevelt, who unequivocally supported repeal, probably contributed to the decision of the lame-duck Congress at the session convened in December 1932 to take action. A joint resolution proposing an amendment to repeal the Eighteenth Amendment was submitted to the states in February 1933 and, following ratification by the necessary thirty-six states, went into effect on December 5 of the same year.

The Twenty-first Amendment was the only one ratified by state conventions instead of by legislatures. Because delegates to these conventions were identified as favoring or opposing repeal of Prohibition, they did not meet to debate the issues but simply to execute the will of the voters. The elections to the conventions amounted to a national referendum on Prohibition. The result justified the expectations of advocates of ratification by conventions; they sought to remove the issue from partisan politics and from organized pressures on rural-dominated legislatures, and to obtain speedy action.

Presidential Tenure

The first Republican Congress after Franklin Roosevelt's election to his fourth term quickly approved and sent to the states a proposed amendment to limit presidential tenure to two terms.

The Twenty-second Amendment provided that no one might

The Eighteenth Amendment, which launched the Prohibition Era by prohibiting the manufacture and sale of liquor, was repealed by the Twenty-first Amendment.

be elected president more than twice; and no one who had served as president for more than two years of a term for which someone else had been elected president was to be elected more than once. The president serving when the amendment was proposed (Harry S. Truman) was exempted from its provisions, and the president serving on the effective date of ratification was to be allowed to complete that term.

During House debate, Republicans insisted that the proposal had nothing to do with politics. The purpose, they said, was merely to incorporate in the Constitution the two-term tradition set by George Washington and maintained until 1940, when Roosevelt was elected to a third term. They urged limitation of tenure to ward off any tendency toward dictatorship.

Democrats contended that the resolution would impose "a limitation upon the people," who had a right to make their own choice of president. Rep. John W. McCormack, D-Mass., declared that Washington, Jefferson, and Theodore Roosevelt had stated that an emergency—such as the war situations in 1940 and 1944—might make it advisable for a person to accept more than two terms as president.

The Twenty-second Amendment, submitted to the states March 24, 1947, was not ratified by the required three-fourths of the state legislatures until February 27, 1951, nearly four years af-

ter its submission by Congress. In 1959 a Senate subcommittee approved a proposal to repeal the amendment, but no further action was taken. At that time, former president Truman said he "never thought well" of the Twenty-second Amendment. His successor, Dwight D. Eisenhower, initially called it "unwise," but he later opposed repeal efforts, saying Congress should "see how it works" for a few years.

District of Columbia Vote

The Twenty-third Amendment, giving residents of Washington, D.C., the right to vote in presidential elections, was approved by Congress June 16, 1960. The last time that residents of the District had voted for president was in 1800. The D.C. Suffrage Amendment, as originally introduced, would have allowed residents of Washington to vote for president and vice president by giving them three representatives in the electoral college and also would have given the District a nonvoting delegate in the House of Representatives. To ensure House approval and to expedite ratification of the amendment, however, Congress agreed to drop the latter provision, limiting the amendment to national suffrage.

As approved by Congress, the proposed amendment authorized the District of Columbia to appoint a number of electors for president and vice president equal to the number of senators and representatives to which the District would have been entitled if it had been a state (in effect, three electors). It also authorized Congress to prescribe the qualifications of the District's electors and voters. The proposed amendment was submitted to the states in June; it was ratified in less than a year, on March 29, 1961.

Most of the opposition to the D.C. Suffrage Amendment came from the South and apparently was motivated by the race issue. (The District's population was then more than 50 percent black.) Not a single state of the Deep South was among the ratifying states. Some Republican state legislatures were reluctant to ratify the amendment because they feared the District would automatically vote Democratic. District Republican leaders sought to allay these fears, however, and it was a Republican-controlled legislature (Kansas) that gave the amendment its needed thirty-eighth ratification.

In 1961 Congress implemented the Twenty-third Amendment by enacting legislation spelling out the regulations under which District residents might participate in presidential elections. Principal discussion on the bill centered on voting age and residence requirements. President John F. Kennedy submitted draft legislation that provided for a ninety-day residence requirement and a minimum voting age of eighteen in the District, but the bill as enacted established a one-year residence requirement and a minimum voting age of twenty-one.

Poll Tax Ban

Poll taxes were introduced in some states during the early days of the Republic as a substitute for property qualifications for voting. The intent of the early levies was to enlarge the electorate. These taxes had been eliminated in most states before the Civil War, but between 1889 and 1908 poll taxes were instituted in eleven southern states. Although ostensibly adopted to "cleanse" elections of mass abuse, the taxes were approved in the South to keep blacks and poor whites from the polls. By 1953, however, only five southern states still required payment of a poll tax as a prerequisite for voting.

Bills to ban poll taxes by statute, rather than by constitutional amendment, were approved five times between 1942 and 1949 by the House, but they died each time in the Senate with filibusters in 1942, 1944, and 1946. Beginning in 1949, Sen. Spessard L. Holland, D-Fla., introduced a proposed anti–poll tax amendment in every Congress, but it was never reported by the Senate Judiciary Committee. Those who preferred action by legislation feared that reliance on amendment of the Constitution to make the desired reform would set a precedent that would hinder approval of other civil rights measures.

On the theory that poll taxes were not specifically designed to keep blacks from voting, Holland and most of his supporters argued that no language in the Constitution barred a poll tax and therefore such a ban had to be achieved by the amendment process. To do otherwise, they said, would open the states' control over election machinery to attack by federal legislation. (Language in Article I, Section 2, and in the Seventeenth Amendment to the Constitution set the "qualifications" for voters in federal elections as those "requisite" for the electors of the most numerous branch of the state legislature.)

Offered by Holland as a substitute for a minor measure in 1962, the joint resolution proposing the poll tax amendment was approved by the Senate in a 77–16 roll call. The House adopted the resolution, 295–86, on August 27, 1962, and ratification was completed January 23, 1964.

The Twenty-fourth Amendment outlawed payment of "any poll tax or other tax" as a voter qualification in federal elections. A move to extend the ban to state and local elections as part of the Voting Rights Act of 1965 was not successful, but the final compromise version of the act contained a finding that poll taxes in certain states denied or abridged the right to vote. The act directed the attorney general to challenge those taxes in the courts "forthwith."

The Supreme Court in two 1966 cases, *Harper v. Virginia State Board of Elections* and *Butts v. Harrison*, struck down Virginia's poll tax requirement for state elections as a violation of the equal protection clause of the Fourteenth Amendment.[18]

Presidential Disability, Succession

The Twenty-fifth Amendment deals with two separate constitutional questions: presidential disability and vice presidential succession.

The Constitution had no mechanism for filling the office of vice president after a vice president succeeded to the presidency or otherwise caused the office to become vacant by death, resignation, or removal by impeachment. Between 1789 and the mid-1960s, when the Twenty-fifth Amendment was drafted, the vice presidency became vacant sixteen times, sometimes for long periods.

UNUSED ALTERNATIVE: STATE-CALLED CONVENTION

The procedure for amending the Constitution requires Congress to call a constitutional convention whenever the legislatures of two-thirds of the states approve such a request. This alternative method for proposing amendments has never been used, although several attempts since the 1940s have come close.

A proposal to limit the maximum rate of federal income, death, and gift taxes to 25 percent was actively promoted among state legislatures before and after World War II. More than a score of legislatures petitioned Congress to call a convention that would propose such an amendment, but a number of the states subsequently rescinded the resolutions and the movement died out.

By 1969, thirty-three state legislatures, one short of the required number, had petitioned Congress for a convention to propose an amendment that would authorize states to apportion one house of a bicameral legislature on a basis of geography or political subdivisions, as well as population. This movement was prompted by the Supreme Court decision in 1964 in *Reynolds v. Sims* holding that representation in both chambers of a state legislature must be based on substantial equality of population. That decision struck both at states with malapportioned legislatures and at those with apportionment schemes, sometimes written in the state constitution, that allowed special senatorial representation, such as one senator for each city, town, or county.

Led by Sen. Everett McKinley Dirksen, R-Ill., many members of Congress vigorously attacked the Court's interpretation of the Constitution on apportionment. Dirksen in 1965 tried unsuccessfully in Congress to secure a constitutional amendment. Despairing of congressional initiatives, supporters of the Dirksen proposal placed their hopes for an amendment on a convention. But by 1970 the petition drive was still one state short of the thirty-four needed under the two-thirds requirement.

Concerned about the economic impact of the growing federal deficit, thirty-two state legislatures by 1982 had called for a constitutional convention to consider an amendment requiring that the federal budget be balanced. The actions of these legislatures spurred the 97th Congress in 1982 to consider a more limited amendment requiring a three-fifths vote of both chambers to unbalance any future federal budget. President Ronald Reagan, locked in a stalemate with Congress over looming budget deficits, endorsed the balanced budget amendment. The Senate approved it, but it fell forty-six votes short of winning House approval. Although the state convention drive lost steam in 1984, Congress continued to debate the balanced budget amendment into the late 1990s.

The assassination of President Kennedy in 1963 galvanized Congress to propose a constitutional amendment that would allow any vacancy in the vice presidency to be filled quickly. The statutory line of succession to the presidency (after the vice president) starts with the Speaker of the House and then goes to the president pro tempore of the Senate. Both of these posts traditionally have been held by older, and sometimes infirm, members who were not chosen to their posts with the thought that they might someday be president. Nor was the public likely to view them as persons of presidential stature.

Section 1 of the amendment affirms that the vice president becomes president—not just acting president—upon the president's death, resignation, or removal through impeachment. Section 2 provides that whenever a vacancy in the office of vice president exists the president shall nominate a replacement, who becomes vice president upon confirmation by majority vote of the House and the Senate.

Within the first decade of the amendment's ratification, Section 2 was used twice: in 1973 when President Richard Nixon nominated Gerald R. Ford to be vice president after Vice President Spiro T. Agnew resigned, and in 1974 when Ford, who succeeded to the presidency upon Nixon's resignation, nominated Nelson A. Rockefeller to succeed him. For the first time ever, the nation had both a president and vice president who were not elected by the people.

Sections 3 and 4 of the Twenty-fifth Amendment deal with the issue of presidential disability if the president is unable, either temporarily or permanently, to perform his powers and duties. The Constitution's disability provision—Article II, Section 1, clause 6—is vague and ambiguous. It had never been clearly resolved when the disability provision would take effect or who would determine that a presidential disability existed. Clause 6 also gave to Congress the power to determine by legislation who would succeed to the presidency if for whatever reason vacancies arose in both the presidency and vice presidency. Congress enacted succession laws three times (the current line of succession dates from a 1947 law), but it had never addressed, by statute, the procedures that would be followed in the event of a presidential disability.

The disability provisions provided that the vice president would assume the president's powers and responsibilities under either of two situations: (1) if the president informed Congress that he was unable to perform his duties, in which case the vice president would become acting president until the president informed Congress that he was resuming his responsibilities, and (2) if the vice president and a majority of the "principal officers" of executive departments, or another body designated by Congress, determined that the president was incapacitated, in which case the vice president would become acting president until the president informed Congress that his disability had ended. But if the vice president and a majority of top executive officers, or the other designated body, informed Congress within four days that the president remained incapacitated, the vice president would continue as acting president while Congress resolved the issue. Congress had twenty-one days to determine the president's fitness for office, which had to be decided by a two-thirds vote of each chamber.[19]

A joint resolution proposing the Twenty-fifth Amendment was introduced in Congress in January 1965 and approved, with scarcely any opposition, six months later. Ratification by the states was completed February 10, 1967.

Two presidents in the nation's history had become seriously disabled in office: James A. Garfield, who lived for eleven weeks after he was shot in 1881, and Woodrow Wilson, who suffered a severe stroke in 1919 but nevertheless continued to serve as president and completed the last seventeen months of his second term. In each case the vice president did not assume any duties of the presidency for fear he would appear to be usurping the powers of that office.

After President Eisenhower's series of illnesses in 1955, 1956, and 1957, the president and his vice president, Richard Nixon, entered into an unofficial agreement for an orderly, temporary transfer of power should the president again become incapacitated. Nixon would have become acting president after "such consultation as it seems to him appropriate under the circumstances." Presidents Kennedy and Lyndon Johnson made the same understandings with their vice presidents, although some constitutional experts questioned the legality of these arrangements.

Section 3 of the amendment was invoked on July 13, 1985, by President Ronald Reagan just before he underwent an operation at Bethesda (Maryland) Naval Medical Center for removal of a cancerous polyp from his large intestine and two small malignant growths from his nose. Before going into surgery, Reagan temporarily transferred his powers as chief executive to Vice President George Bush by notifying the Speaker of the House and the president pro tempore of the Senate that during his operation he would be "briefly and temporarily incapable of discharging his Constitutional duties." After the operation was over he notified the Speaker and president pro tempore that he was resuming his duties as president. During this eight-hour transfer of power Bush served as acting president.

Reagan had been much more seriously incapacitated in 1981 when he was wounded in an assassination attempt March 30 in Washington, D.C., and subsequently underwent a two-hour operation to remove a bullet from his left lung. Although the president was under anesthesia during the operation, Reagan's advisers and Vice President Bush decided not to invoke the disability provisions. Instead, the vice president substituted for the president unofficially, without appearing to supplant him. Bush had been away from Washington on a speaking engagement at the time of the shooting, and confusion arose as to who, constitutionally, was in charge of the U.S. government in the period before Bush returned. (See "Use of Disability Provisions," p. 392.)

The question of presidential disability arose again briefly in early 1991, two years after Bush had become president. He experienced an irregular heartbeat while jogging at Camp David, Maryland, but doctors quickly determined that he had not had a heart attack. They traced the problem to a thyroid disorder called Graves's disease, a condition diagnosed earlier in the president's wife, Barbara. She was receiving radioactive treatments for the disease, and the president began receiving the same therapy. At no time during the incident was Vice President Dan Quayle called upon to substitute for the president.

Critics charge that the Twenty-fifth Amendment contains several defects. No time limit was placed either on the president to make his nomination for vice president or on Congress to vote to confirm the president's choice. The amendment also does not define who are the "principal officers" of the executive departments, a majority of whom would decide when a president "is unable to discharge the powers and duties of his office," thus allowing the vice president to become acting president. But the biggest loophole, according to the critics, is that it allows the president to challenge the finding of presidential "inability" by forcing Congress to vote on the issue, which the president can win if he receives just one vote more than one-third of members voting in either chamber.

The Vote for Eighteen-Year-Olds

Congress in 1970 enacted legislation lowering the voting age to eighteen beginning January 1, 1971. Although President Nixon signed the measure in June 1970, he stated that he believed the law was unconstitutional because Congress had no power to extend the suffrage by simple statute. It should initiate such action by constitutional amendment, he said.

In 1969 and 1970, even before the voting measure was signed by Nixon, three states—New Jersey, Ohio, and Oregon—already had rejected proposals to lower voter ages. Fifteen more states

---

UNSUCCESSFUL AMENDMENTS IN CONGRESS

Of the numerous constitutional amendments that have been introduced since World War II, Congress has voted in favor of only seven, of which five were subsequently ratified by the required three-fourths of the states and became part of the Constitution (Amendments Twenty-two through Twenty-six). (The Twenty-seventh Amendment—the Madison Amendment—was approved by Congress in 1789 and ratified by the states in 1992.)

Pressure on Congress to approve other changes and additions to the Constitution has been intense. Single issue groups, in particular, have looked to constitutional amendments as a way to achieve their goals. In the 1980s their goals often coincided with those of President Ronald Reagan. These included a constitutional ban on abortions, a balanced budget amendment and the line-item veto, and a constitutional sanction for prayer in public schools.

President George Bush urged Congress to propose an amendment making it a crime to burn or otherwise desecrate the American flag. The Supreme Court had ruled in 1989 and 1990 that such activity was protected by the First Amendment guarantee of free speech.

After the Republicans became the majority in Congress as a result of the 1994 elections, proposed constitutional amendments were voted on in the House or Senate to require a balanced budget, ban flag desecration, impose congressional term limits, restrict Congress's ability to raise taxes, and permit greater religious expression. The Senate Judiciary Committee in 1998 also approved a proposed constitutional amendment designed to bolster the rights of violent crime victims. The measure had the endorsement of President Bill Clinton.

In all, ten proposed amendments have been voted on by one or both houses of Congress since 1978. However, no constitutional amendments were approved by Congress during the Reagan and Bush administrations or during the first six years of the Clinton administration.

Votes on proposed amendments that failed in Congress from 1978 to 1998 follow:

- A ban on busing to achieve school desegregation: rejected by the House in 1979 by seventy-five votes.
- Direct election of the president: passed by the House in 1969; died in the Senate in 1970 by a filibuster (cloture vote failed by six votes); rejected by the Senate in 1979 by fifteen votes.
- A constitutional ban on most abortions: rejected by the Senate in 1982 on a procedural vote; rejected by the Senate in 1983 by eighteen votes.
- Constitutional authorization for prayer in public schools: rejected by the Senate in 1966 by nine votes; rejected by the House in 1971 by twenty-eight votes; rejected by the Senate in 1984 by eleven votes.
- Mandatory limits on spending in congressional campaigns: died in the Senate in 1988 by a filibuster (two cloture votes failed by seven and eight votes, respectively).
- Congressional term limits: rejected by the House in 1995 by sixty-one votes; died in the Senate in 1996 by a filibuster (cloture vote failed by two votes).
- Requirement for a balanced federal budget: passed by the Senate in 1982; rejected by the House in 1982 by forty-six votes; rejected by the Senate in 1986 by one vote; rejected by the House in 1992 by nine votes; rejected by the Senate in 1994 by four votes; rejected by the House in 1994 by twelve votes; passed by the House in 1995; rejected by the Senate in 1995 by two votes; rejected by the Senate in 1996 by three votes; rejected by the Senate in 1997 by one vote.
- American flag desecration ban: rejected by the Senate in 1989 by fifteen votes; rejected by the Senate in 1990 by nine votes; rejected by the House in 1990 by thirty-four votes; rejected by the Senate in 1995 by three votes; passed by the House in 1995; passed by the House in 1997.
- Tax limitation: rejected by the House in 1996 by thirty-seven votes; rejected by the House in 1997 by forty-nine votes; rejected by the House in 1998 by forty-five votes.
- Religious expression: rejected by the House in 1998 by sixty-one votes.

had scheduled referendums on the issue in the November elections. Only four states allowed persons under the age of twenty-one to vote. They were Georgia and Kentucky, eighteen; Alaska, nineteen; and Hawaii, twenty.

On December 21, 1970, the Supreme Court upheld the new law lowering the voting age to eighteen in presidential and congressional elections, but it ruled the change unconstitutional as it applied to state and local elections (*Oregon v. Mitchell*).

The 92nd Congress wasted little time early in 1971 in approving and sending to the states a proposed Twenty-sixth Amendment lowering the voting age in all elections. On March 23 the House approved the amendment by a 401–19 roll-call vote. The Senate had approved the measure March 10 by a 94–0 roll call.

The Twenty-sixth Amendment was ratified by the required number of states by July 1, a record time for approval of a constitutional amendment. The speed of ratification resulted in part from an awareness that, without the amendment, many states would have been faced with the cost and administrative difficulty of keeping separate registration books, ballots, and voting apparatus for federal and for state and local elections. (*See box, Length of Time for Ratification, p. 358.*)

Congressional Pay Raises

Proposed by James Madison and approved by Congress in 1789, the Madison Amendment states: "No law varying the compensation for the services of the Senators and Representatives shall take effect, until an election of Representatives shall have intervened." It was sent to the states in September 1789 as part of a package of twelve, ten of which became the Bill of Rights. Six states had ratified the pay raise amendment by 1792; a seventh did so in 1873 and an eighth more than a hundred years later in 1978. By 1992, more than two hundred years after gaining congressional approval, the amendment was ratified by thirty-three more states. The three-quarters threshold for ratification was reached on May 7, 1992.

Statutes require that once the state legislatures approve a new amendment it be taken to the archivist of the United States, who could declare the amendment constitutional, delay issuing a certification pending guidance from Congress, or issue a conditional certification of ratification pending congressional action.

At first it appeared that Congress would at least exercise its power to review the timeliness question. House Speaker Thomas S. Foley, D-Wash., and Sen. Robert C. Byrd, D-W.Va., a former majority leader and Senate institutionalist, suggested hearings in the Judiciary committees to explore whether too much time had lapsed for the amendment to be valid. Plans for hearings were canceled, however, after the archivist May 13 announced that he found the amendment constitutional. Byrd, considered a stickler for constitutional rectitude, scolded the archivist for not following "historic tradition." When questions arose in the past about the validity of ratification, he said, certification by the archivist or secretary of state was postponed pending congressional discussion and resolution. Nevertheless,

Byrd subsequently acknowledged that the time had come for Congress to accept the amendment, which was publicly popular.

The Senate May 20 approved 99–0 two proposals to recognize the Twenty-seventh Amendment. On the same day, the House voted 414–3 for a resolution supporting the amendment.

Walter E. Dellinger, a professor of constitutional law at Duke University, said the process followed in the Madison Amendment case might "lower the resistance to amending the Constitution." Furthermore, Dellinger said that, ironically, Madison was not enthusiastic about the proposal that now bears his name. When the pay raise language was being debated in the First Congress, concern was expressed that the political popularity of low salaries could preclude good men from entering politics. "'Much inconvenience and very little good would result from this amendment,'" Dellinger quoted a participant in the early debate. "'It might serve as a tool for designing men, they might reduce the wages very low, much lower than it was possible for any gentleman to serve without injury to his private affairs, in order to procure popularity at home.'"[20]

NOTES

1. James MacGregor Burns, Jack W. Peltason, and Thomas E. Cronin, *Government by the People*, 9th ed. (New York: Prentice-Hall, 1975), 67.
2. C. Herman Pritchett, *The American Constitution*, 3rd ed. (New York: McGraw-Hill, 1977), 29.
3. Quoted in Charles Warren, *The Making of the Constitution* (Boston: Little, Brown, 1928), 672–684.
4. Quoted in Warren, *The Making of the Constitution*, 735.
5. Alexander Hamilton, James Madison, and John Jay, *The Federalist Papers*, with an introduction by Clinton Rossiter (New York: New American Library, 1961), 278.
6. Michael Nelson, ed., *Congressional Quarterly's Guide to the Presidency*, 2nd ed. (Washington, D.C.: Congressional Quarterly, 1996), 123–127.
7. Burns et al., *Government by the People*, 64.
8. Background, see Pritchett, *The American Constitution*, 268–287; and Alfred H. Kelly and Winfred A. Harbison, *The American Constitution* (New York: Norton, 1976), 142–143.
9. Pritchett, *The American Constitution*, 288–291, 416–421.
10. Ibid., 219–220.
11. Burns et al., *Government by the People*, 204–205.
12. Pritchett, *The American Constitution*, 293–297, 554.
13. Frederic A. Ogg and P. Orman Ray, *Introduction to American Government* (New York: Appleton-Century-Crofts, 1951), 36.
14. Ibid., 270–273.
15. Ibid., 152–154.
16. Burns et al., *Government by the People*, 73.
17. Ogg and Ray, *Introduction to American Government*, 38.
18. Pritchett, *The American Constitution*, 754.
19. Nelson, *Guide to the Presidency*, 52–55.
20. Laura Michaelis, "Both Chambers Rush to Accept 27th Amendment on Salaries," *Congressional Quarterly Weekly Report*, May 23, 1992, 1423.

SELECTED BIBLIOGRAPHY

Amar, Akhil R. *The Bill of Rights: Creation and Reconstruction*. New Haven: Yale University Press, 1998.

Antieau, Chester J. *The Intended Significance of the Fourteenth Amendment*. Buffalo, N.Y.: Hein, 1997.

Bayh, Birch. *One Heartbeat Away: Presidential Disability and Succession*. Indianapolis: Bobbs-Merrill, 1968.

Bond, James E. *No Easy Walk to Freedom: Reconstruction and the Ratification of the Fourteenth Amendment.* Westport, Conn.: Praeger, 1997.

Caplan, Russell L. *Constitutional Brinksmanship: Amending the Constitution by National Convention.* New York: Oxford University Press, 1988.

Cortner, Richard C. *The Supreme Court and the Second Bill of Rights: The Fourteenth Amendment and the Nationalization of Civil Liberties.* Madison: University of Wisconsin Press, 1981.

Curtis, Michael K. *No State Shall Abridge: The Fourteenth Amendment and the Bill of Rights.* Durham, N.C.: Duke University Press, 1986.

Feerick, John D. *From Failing Hands: The Story of Presidential Succession.* New York: Fordham University Press, 1965.

———. *The Twenty-fifth Amendment: Its Complete History and Applications.* 2nd ed. New York: Fordham University Press, 1992.

Fisher, Louis. *Constitutional Conflicts between Congress and the President.* 4th ed. Lawrence: University Press of Kansas, 1997.

Katz, William L. *Constitutional Amendments.* New York: Franklin Watts, 1974.

Kelly, Alfred H., Winfred A. Harbison, and Herman Belz. *The American Constitution: Its Origins and Development.* 7th ed. New York: Norton, 1991.

Levinson, Stanford, ed. *Responding to Imperfection: The Theory and Practice of Constitutional Amendment.* Princeton, N.J.: Princeton University Press, 1995.

Mansbridge, Jane J. *Why We Lost the ERA.* Chicago: University of Chicago Press, 1986.

Moe, Ronald C. *Presidential Succession.* Washington, D.C.: Congressional Research Service, 1979.

Murphy, Walter F. *Congress and the Court: A Case Study in the American Political Process.* Chicago: University of Chicago Press, 1962.

Nelson, Michael, ed. *Congressional Quarterly's Guide to the Presidency.* 2nd ed. Washington, D.C.: Congressional Quarterly, 1996.

Newman, Roger K., ed. *The Constitution and Its Amendments.* New York: Macmillan, 1999.

Onuf, Peter S., ed. *Ratifying, Amending, and Interpreting the Constitution.* New York: Garland Publications, 1991.

Orfield, Lester B. *Amending the Federal Constitution.* New York: Da Capo Press, 1971.

Poole, Keith T., and Howard Rosenthal. *Congress: A Political-Economic History of Roll Call Voting.* New York: Oxford University Press, 1997.

Pritchett, C. Herman. *The American Constitution.* 3rd. ed. New York: McGraw-Hill, 1977.

———. *Congress Versus the Supreme Court, 1957–1960.* Minneapolis: University of Minnesota Press, 1961.

Silva, Ruth C. *Presidential Succession.* Ann Arbor: University of Michigan Press, 1951.

Sindler, Allan P. *Unchosen Presidents: The Vice-President and Other Frustrations of Presidential Succession.* Berkeley: University of California Press, 1976.

Sundquist, James L. *Constitutional Reform and Effective Government.* Rev. ed. Washington, D.C.: Brookings Institution, 1992.

Vose, Clement E. *Constitutional Change: Amendment Politics and Supreme Court Litigation since 1900.* Lexington, Mass.: Lexington Books, 1972.

West, Robin. *Progressive Constitutionalism: Reconstructing the Fourteenth Amendment.* Durham, N.C.: Duke University Press, 1994.

CHAPTER 11

Power to Select the President

U NDER THE CONSTITUTION, Congress has three key roles in the election of the president and vice president of the United States. First, it is directed to receive and, in joint session, count the electoral votes after they have been certified by the states. Second, if no candidate has a majority of the electoral votes, it is the responsibility of the House of Representatives to choose the president and the Senate to choose the vice president. Third, the Twenty-fifth Amendment, ratified in 1967, gives Congress ultimate responsibility for resolving presidential disability disputes between the president, vice president, and the cabinet.

Although many of the Framers of the Constitution apparently thought that Congress would decide most elections, the House has chosen a president only twice, in 1801 and 1825. But on several occasions in the nation's history presidential campaigns were geared deliberately to throw the election to the House, where each state has one vote and a majority of states is needed to elect the president. Such an outcome was just one of many perceived failings of the Constitution's presidential selection process (Article II, Section 1, clauses 2 and 3).

Except for the Founders, the system for choosing the president has had few defenders. From the very beginning it has caused apprehension and confusion. Besides allowing congressional politics and intrigue to determine the outcome of a presidential election in cases where the electoral vote does not provide a winner, reliance on the electoral college has given the nation three presidents who actually trailed their opponents in the popular vote. (See box, "Minority" Presidents, p. 390.)

As a result of the Constitution's vagueness and ambiguities, the method of selecting the president has changed significantly since 1789. Within a few years it was realized that the original rules for balloting by the electoral college were flawed. In the election of 1800 both the Democratic-Republican presidential and vice presidential candidates received the same number of electoral votes because there was no provision in the Constitution for differentiating between presidential and vice presidential ballots. The political near disaster that resulted led to ratification in 1804 of the Twelfth Amendment requiring electors to vote separately for president and vice president instead of casting ballots for two different presidential candidates. (See "Separate Ballot for Vice President," p. 364.)

But not all the defects in the presidential selection process could have been anticipated by the Framers. Not surprisingly, no guidelines were written into the Constitution for organizing political parties, since the Founders believed that "self-interested factions" endangered the proper functioning and virtues of the Republic. The Framers assumed—incorrectly—that the selection process would transcend petty partisanship. And because factions—their word for special interests, including parties— were bad, in their view, there was no reason to add constitutional guidelines for nominating presidential candidates or election campaigning. Nor did they believe the general public should have the primary voice in these matters.

Despite the introduction of these and many other political factors in modern U.S. presidential election campaigns, and virtually universal suffrage today, the Constitution's electoral college system as modified by the Twelfth Amendment remains intact. Neither the crisis of legitimacy that developed after the Hayes-Tilden election of 1876, in which congressional machinations surrounding the counting of the electoral vote cost Samuel J. Tilden the election even though he won the popular vote over Rutherford B. Hayes, nor the close call in 1968, in which the electoral vote won by third party candidate George C. Wallace almost was enough to throw the election into the House, brought about any constitutional changes.

This was not for lack of trying. Hardly a Congress went by without the introduction of proposals to revise or replace the electoral college. After the 1968 election, Rep. Hale Boggs, D-La., then the House majority whip, said there was a "crying need to amend the Constitution and once and for all get rid of this anachronistic system which every four years puts us in the position of playing Russian roulette with the election of the President of the United States." But despite the continuing anxieties over the existing system, a national consensus on an alternative method has yet to develop.

In addition to its constitutional role in selection of the president and vice president, Congress has responsibility (indeed an increasing one since ratification of the Twentieth and Twenty-fifth amendments) in presidential and vice presidential succession and in cases of presidential disability. The Twentieth Amendment (1933) gives Congress the power to appoint an acting president if both a president-elect and vice president–elect die or, for whatever reason, are found ineligible for the presidency. It also gives Congress the authority to decide how a president is to be selected if the election is thrown into the House and the House's choice for president (under the Twelfth Amendment) dies before taking office. (Before ratification of the Twentieth Amendment there was no provision in the Con-

CONSTITUTIONAL PROVISIONS AND AMENDMENTS GOVERNING PRESIDENTIAL SELECTION, DISABILITY

ARTICLE II

Section 1. The executive Power shall be vested in a President of the United States of America. He shall hold his Office during the Term of four Years, and, together with the Vice President, chosen for the same Term, be elected, as follows:

Each State shall appoint, in such Manner as the Legislature thereof may direct, a Number of Electors, equal to the whole Number of Senators and Representatives to which the State may be entitled in the Congress: but no Senator or Representative, or Person holding an Office of Trust or Profit under the United States, shall be appointed an Elector.

[The Electors shall meet in their respective States, and vote by Ballot for two Persons, of whom one at least shall not be an Inhabitant of the same State with themselves. And they shall make a List of all the Persons voted for, and of the Number of Votes for each; which List they shall sign and certify, and transmit sealed to the Seat of the Government of the United States, directed to the President of the Senate. The President of the Senate shall, in the Presence of the Senate and House of Representatives, open all the Certificates, and the Votes shall then be counted. The Person having the greatest Number of Votes shall be the President, if such Number be a Majority of the whole Number of Electors appointed; and if there be more than one who have such Majority; and have an equal Number of Votes, then the House of Representatives shall immediately chuse by Ballot one of them for President; and if no Person have a Majority, then from the five highest on the List the said House shall in like Manner chuse the President. But in chusing the President, the Votes shall be taken by States, the Representation from each State having one Vote; A quorum for this Purpose shall consist of a Member or Members from two thirds of the States, and a Majority of all the States shall be necessary to a Choice. In every Case, after the Choice of the President, the Person having the greatest Number of Votes of the Electors shall be the Vice President. But if there should remain two or more who have equal Votes, the Senate shall chuse from them by Ballot the Vice President.][1]

The Congress may determine the Time of chusing the Electors, and the Day on which they shall give their Votes; which Day shall be the same throughout the United States.

No Person except a natural born Citizen, or a Citizen of the United States, at the time of the Adoption of this Constitution, shall be eligible to the Office of President; neither shall any Person be eligible to that Office who shall not have attained to the Age of thirty five Years, and been fourteen Years a Resident within the United States. . . .

TWELFTH AMENDMENT
(RATIFIED JUNE 15, 1804)

The Electors shall meet in their respective states and vote by ballot for President and Vice-President, one of whom, at least, shall not be an inhabitant of the same state with themselves; they shall name in their ballots the person voted for as President, and in distinct ballots the person voted for as Vice-President, and they shall make distinct lists of all persons voted for as President, and of all persons voted for as Vice-President, and of the number of votes for each, which lists they shall sign and certify, and transmit sealed to the seat of the government of the United States, directed to the President of the Senate;—The President of the Senate shall, in the presence of the Senate and House of Representatives, open all the certificates and the votes shall then be counted;—The person having the greatest number of votes for President, shall be the President, if such number be a majority of the whole number of Electors appointed; and if no persons have such majority, then from the persons having the highest numbers not exceeding three on the list of those voted for as President, the House of Representatives shall choose immediately, by ballot, the President. But in choosing the President, the votes shall be taken by states, the representation from each state having one vote; a quorum for this purpose shall consist of a member or members from two-thirds of the states, and a majority of all the states shall be necessary to a choice. [And if the House of Representatives shall not choose a President whenever the right of choice shall devolve upon them, before the fourth day of March next following, then the Vice-President shall act as President, as in the case of the death or other constitutional disability of the President.—][2] The person having the greatest number of votes as Vice-President, shall be the Vice-President, if such number be a majority of the whole number of Electors appointed, and if no person have a majority, then from the two highest numbers on the list, the Senate shall choose the Vice-President; a

---

stitution that addressed the circumstance in which a president-elect died or was disqualified for office.)

The Twenty-fifth Amendment, ratified in 1967, provides a specific constitutional framework for appointing the vice president as acting president when the president is temporarily incapacitated. It gives Congress ultimate responsibility for resolving these disability disputes within the executive branch. The Twenty-fifth Amendment also provides an expeditious method of filling vacancies in the vice presidency that gives Congress the authority to confirm the president's choice for the job.

Since the president was given the power to fill vacancies in the vice presidency, it has been used twice—in successive years. First, in 1973 when Vice President Spiro T. Agnew was forced to resign and President Richard Nixon nominated Gerald R. Ford to be vice president. And again in 1974 when Ford, who succeeded to the presidency upon Nixon's resignation, chose former New York governor Nelson A. Rockefeller as vice president. The disability provisions of the amendment were used once. In 1985 President Ronald Reagan invoked the provisions before he underwent surgery. Vice President George Bush served as acting president for about eight hours.

Constitutional Background

The method of selecting the president was the subject of extensive debate at the Constitutional Convention of 1787. Several

quorum for the purpose shall consist of two-thirds of the whole number of Senators, and a majority of the whole number shall be necessary to a choice. But no person constitutionally ineligible to the office of President shall be eligible to that of Vice-President of the United States.

TWENTIETH AMENDMENT
(RATIFIED JANUARY 23, 1933)

Section 1. The terms of the President and Vice President shall end at noon on the 20th day of January. . . .

Section 3. If, at the time fixed for the beginning of the term of the President, the President elect shall have died, the Vice President elect shall become President. If a President shall not have been chosen before the time fixed for the beginning of his term, or if the President elect shall have failed to qualify, then the Vice President elect shall have qualified, declaring who shall then act as President, or the manner in which one who is to act shall be selected, and such person shall act accordingly until a President or Vice President shall have qualified. *(Modified by Twenty-fifth Amendment, see below.)*

Section 4. The Congress may by law provide for the case of the death of any of the persons from whom the House of Representatives may choose a President whenever the right of choice shall have devolved upon them, and for the case of the death of any of the persons from whom the Senate may choose a Vice President whenever the right of choice shall have devolved upon them.

TWENTY-SECOND AMENDMENT
(RATIFIED FEBRUARY 27, 1951)

Section 1. No person shall be elected to the office of President more than twice, and no person who has held the office of President, or acted as President, for more than two years of a term to which some other person was elected President shall be elected to the office of the President more than once. . . .

TWENTY-FIFTH AMENDMENT
(RATIFIED FEBRUARY 10, 1967)

Section 1. In case of the removal of the President from office or of his death or resignation, the Vice President shall become President.

Section 2. Whenever there is a vacancy in the office of the Vice President, the President shall nominate a Vice President who shall take office upon confirmation by a majority vote of both Houses of Congress.

Section 3. Whenever the President transmits to the President pro tempore of the Senate and the Speaker of the House of Representatives his written declaration that he is unable to discharge the powers and duties of his office, and until he transmits to them a written declaration to the contrary, such powers and duties shall be discharged by the Vice President as Acting President.

Section 4. Whenever the Vice President and a majority of either the principal officers of the executive departments or of such other body as Congress may by law provide, transmit to the President pro tempore of the Senate and the Speaker of the House of Representatives their written declaration that the President is unable to discharge the powers and duties of his office, the Vice President shall immediately assume the powers and duties of the office as Acting President.

Thereafter, when the President transmits to the President pro tempore of the Senate and the Speaker of the House of Representatives his written declaration that no inability exists, he shall resume the powers and duties of his office unless the Vice President and a majority of either the principal officers of the executive departments or of such other body as Congress may by law provide, transmit within four days to the President pro tempore of the Senate and the Speaker of the House of Representatives their written declaration that the President is unable to discharge the powers and duties of his office. Thereupon Congress shall decide the issue, assembling within forty-eight hours for that purpose if not in session.

If the Congress, within twenty-one days after receipt of the latter written declaration, or, if Congress is not in session, within twenty-one days after Congress is required to assemble, determines by two-thirds vote of both houses that the President is unable to discharge the powers and duties of his office, the Vice President shall continue to discharge the same as Acting President; otherwise, the President shall resume the powers and duties of his office.

1. Superseded by Twelfth Amendment.
2. Changed by Twentieth Amendment.

---

plans were proposed and rejected before the delegates agreed to a compromise solution. This was incorporated in Article II, Section 1, clause 2.[1] *(See box, Constitutional Provisions and Amendments, p. 378.)*

Among the proposed methods for choosing the president were direct popular election, election by Congress, election by state legislatures, or state election of presidential electors.

Direct election was opposed by those who felt that the people lacked sufficient knowledge of the character and qualifications of potential candidates to make an intelligent choice. Many delegates also feared the citizens of the various states would be unlikely to agree on a single person, usually casting their votes for favorite-son candidates well known to them. Southerners opposed direct election for another reason: the suffrage was more widespread in the North than in the South, where the slaves did not vote.

The Convention also rejected the idea of giving Congress the power to pick the president, largely out of concern that it would compromise executive independence. Similarly, a plan to let state legislatures choose the president was turned down because it was feared the president might feel so indebted to the states as to allow them to encroach on federal authority.

Unable to agree on a plan for selecting the president, the Convention in August 1787 appointed a "Committee on Postponed Matters" to propose a solution. The committee on September 4 suggested a compromise under which each state would appoint presidential electors (collectively known as the electoral college), equal to the total number of its representatives and senators. The electors, chosen in a manner set forth by each state legislature, would meet in their own states and cast votes for two persons. The votes would be counted in Congress, with the candidate receiving a majority elected president and the one receiving the second-highest number elected vice president, an office created for this very purpose. A clear majority of electoral votes was needed to elect. As of the year 2000, 270 electoral votes (out of a total of 538) were needed to be elected.

No distinction was made between ballots for president and vice president. The subsequent development of national political parties and the nomination of tickets for president and vice president caused confusion in the electoral system. All the electors of one party tended to vote for their two nominees. But, with no distinction between the presidential and vice presidential nominees, the danger arose of a tie vote between the two. This actually happened in 1800, leading to a change in the original electoral system by adoption of the Twelfth Amendment. (*See box, Constitutional Provisions and Amendments, p. 378.*)

Only one provision of the committee's plan aroused serious opposition—that giving the Senate the right to decide presidential elections in which no candidate received a majority of electoral votes. Some delegates maintained that the Senate, which already had been given treaty ratification powers and the responsibility to "advise and consent" to all important executive appointments, might become too powerful. Therefore, a counterproposal was accepted, letting the House decide the winner in instances when the electors failed to give a majority of their votes to a single candidate. The interests of the small states were preserved by giving each state delegation only one vote in the House on the roll calls to elect the president.

Congress and the Electoral College

The system adopted by the Constitutional Convention was a compromise born out of the necessity of overcoming major state and regional differences: diverse state voting requirements, the slavery issue, big-state versus small-state rivalries, and the complexities of the balance of power among different branches of the government. It also was apparently as close to direct popular election of the president as the men who wrote the Constitution thought prudent and appropriate at the time. Some scholars have suggested that the electoral college, as it came to be called, was a "jerry-rigged improvisation" that really left it to future generations to work out the best form of presidential selection.[2]

ELECTION OF 1800

The election of 1800 was the first in which the contingent election procedures of the Constitution were put to the test and the president was elected by the House of Representatives.

The Federalist Party nominated John Adams for a second term and chose Charles Cotesworth Pinckney as his running

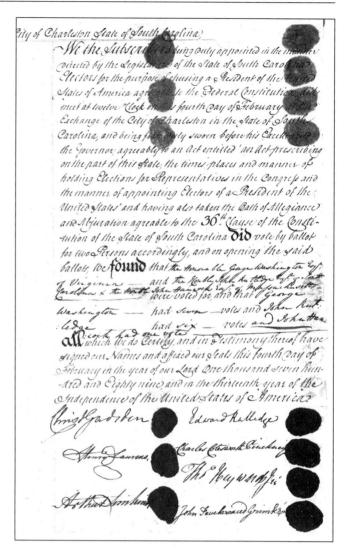

The electors of South Carolina signed this document in 1789, certifying their vote for George Washington to be the nation's first president.

mate. A Democratic-Republican congressional caucus chose Vice President Thomas Jefferson for president and Aaron Burr, who had been instrumental in winning the New York Legislature for the Jeffersonians earlier in 1800, for vice president.

The bitterly fought campaign was marked by efforts in several states to change for partisan advantage the method of selecting electors. In New York, where electors previously had been chosen by the legislature, Alexander Hamilton proposed that Gov. John Jay call the lame-duck Federalist legislature into special session to adopt a proposal for popular election of electors under a district system, thus denying the incoming Democratic-Republicans an opportunity to appoint electors. Jay declined, and in the end the new legislature cast all twelve New York electoral votes for Jefferson and Burr.

The Federalists were more successful in Pennsylvania, another critical state. The state senate, where holdover members maintained Federalist control, refused to renew legislation providing for selection of electors by statewide popular vote. The state's house of representatives, in Democratic-Republican hands, was forced to accept a compromise that gave the Federalists seven electors and the Democratic-Republicans eight.

The electors met in each state on December 4, and the results gradually became known throughout the country: Jefferson and Burr, 73 electoral votes each; Adams, 65; Pinckney, 64; John Jay, 1. The Federalists had lost, but because no Democratic-Republican elector had withheld one electoral vote from Burr, their presidential and vice presidential candidates were tied and the election was thrown into the House.

The lame-duck Congress, with a Federalist majority, was still in office for the electoral count, and the possibilities for intrigue were only too apparent. After toying with and rejecting a proposal to block any election until March 4 when Adams's term expired, some Federalists decided to throw their support to Burr and thus elect a cynical and pliant politician over a man they considered a dangerous radical. Hamilton opposed this move: "I trust the Federalists will not finally be so mad as to vote for Burr," he wrote.

I speak with intimate and accurate knowledge of his character. His elevation can only promote the purposes of the desperate and the profligate. If there be a man in the world I ought to hate, it is Jefferson. With Burr I have always been personally well. But the public good must be paramount to every private consideration.[3]

On February 11, 1801, Congress met in joint session—with Jefferson in the chair—to count the electoral vote. Ending in a tie, the House retired to its own chamber to elect a president. When the House met it became apparent that the advice of Hamilton had not been widely accepted. A majority of Federalists in the House insisted on backing Burr over Jefferson, the man they despised more. Indeed, if Burr had given clear assurances he would run the country as a Federalist he might well have been elected. But Burr was unwilling to make those assurances, and, as one chronicler put it, "no one knows whether it was honor or a wretched indecision which gagged Burr's lips."[4]

In all, there were 106 members of the House at the time, consisting of fifty-eight Federalists and forty-eight Democratic-Republicans. If the ballots had been cast individually, Burr would have been elected, but the Constitution provided that each state cast one vote, with a majority necessary for election. On the first ballot, Jefferson received the votes of eight states, one short of a majority of the sixteen states then in the Union. Six states backed Burr, and the representatives of Vermont and Maryland were equally divided, so their states lost their votes.

Thirty-six ballots were taken before the House came to a decision. Predictably, there were men who sought to exploit the situation for personal gain. Jefferson wrote on February 15, "Many attempts have been made to obtain terms and promises from me. I have declared to them unequivocally that I would not receive the Government on capitulation; that I would not go in with my hands tied."[5]

The impasse was finally broken when Vermont and Maryland switched to support Jefferson. Delaware and South Carolina also withdrew their support from Burr by casting blank ballots. The final vote: ten states for Jefferson, four (all Federalist

CONTINGENT ELECTIONS

Except for the Founding Fathers, few Americans have ever found much to commend in the system of providing for the contingent election of a president by the House. Some comments:

Thomas Jefferson, 1823: "I have ever considered the constitutional mode of election ultimately by the legislature voting by states as the most dangerous blot on our Constitution, and one which some unlucky chance will some day hit."

Martin Van Buren, 1826: "There is no point on which the people of the United States [are] more perfectly united than upon the propriety, not to say the absolute necessity, of taking the election away from the House of Representatives."

Sen. Oliver P. Morton of Indiana, a leading reform advocate, 1873: "The objections to this constitutional provision for the election of the President need only to be stated, not argued. First, its manifest injustice. In such an election each state is to have but one vote. Nevada, with its 42,000 population, has an equal vote with New York, having 104 times as great a population. It is a mockery to call such an election just, fair or republican."

SOURCE: Neal R. Peirce and Lawrence D. Longley, *The People's President: The Electoral College in American History and the Direct Vote Alternative*, rev. ed. (New Haven, Conn.: Yale University Press, 1981), 107.

states from New England) for Burr. Thus Jefferson became president and Burr automatically became vice president.

Federalist James A. Bayard of Delaware, who had played a key role in breaking the deadlock, wrote to Hamilton:

The means existed of electing Burr, but this required his cooperation. By deceiving one man (a great blockhead) and tempting two (not incorruptible), he might have secured a majority of the states. He will never have another chance of being president of the United States; and the little use he has made of the one which has occurred gives me but an humble opinion of the talents of an unprincipled man.[6]

The Jefferson-Burr contest clearly illustrated the dangers of the double-balloting system established by the original Constitution, and pressure began to build for an amendment requiring separate votes for president and vice president. Congress approved the Twelfth Amendment in December 1803, and the states—acting with unexpected speed—ratified it in time for the 1804 election.

JOHN QUINCY ADAMS'S ELECTION

The only other time a president was elected by the House was in 1825. There were many contenders for the presidency in the 1824 election, but four predominated: John Quincy Adams, Henry Clay, William H. Crawford, and Andrew Jackson. Crawford, secretary of the Treasury in the incumbent Monroe administration, was the early front-runner, but his candidacy faltered after he suffered a paralytic stroke in 1823.

When the electoral votes were counted, Jackson had ninety-nine, Adams, eighty-four, Crawford, forty-one, and Clay, thirty-seven. Jackson also led in the popular voting in the eighteen

HOUSE PROCEDURE FOR ELECTION OF JOHN QUINCY ADAMS

The following rules, from Hinds's Precedents of the House, were used in deciding the presidential election of 1824. On February 9, 1825, John Quincy Adams was elected in accordance with these rules. They provide a precedent for future elections of a president, although the House could change the rules.

1. In the event of its appearing, on opening all the certificates, and counting the votes given by the electors of the several States for President, that no person has a majority of the votes of the whole number of electors appointed, the same shall be entered on the Journals of this House.

2. The roll of the House shall then be called by States; and, on its appearing that a Member or Members from two-thirds of the States are present the House shall immediately proceed, by ballot, to choose a President from the persons having the highest numbers, not exceeding three, on the list of those voted for as President; and, in case neither of those persons shall receive the votes of a majority of all the States on the first ballot, the House shall continue to ballot for a President, without interruption . . . until a President be chosen.

3. The doors of the Hall shall be closed during the balloting, except against the Members of the Senate, stenographers, and the officers of the House.

4. From the commencement of the balloting until an election is made no proposition to adjourn shall be received, unless on the motion of one State, seconded by another State, and the question shall be decided by States. The same rule shall be observed in regard to any motion to change the usual hour for the meeting of the House.

5. In balloting the following mode shall be observed, to wit: The Representatives of each State shall be arranged and seated together, beginning with the seats at the right hand of the Speaker's chair, with the Members from the State of Maine; thence, proceeding with the Members from the States, in the order the States are usually named for receiving petitions . . . until all are seated.[1]

A ballot box shall be provided for each State.

The Representatives of each State shall, in the first instance, ballot among themselves, in order to ascertain the vote of their State; and they may, if necessary, appoint tellers of their ballots.

After the vote of each State is ascertained, duplicates thereof shall be made out; and in case any one of the persons from whom the choice is to be made shall receive a majority of the votes given, on any one balloting by the Representatives of a State, the name of that person shall be written on each of the duplicates; and in case the votes so given shall be divided so that neither of said persons

shall have a majority of the whole number of votes given by such State, on any one balloting, then the word "divided" shall be written on each duplicate.

After the delegation from each State shall have ascertained the vote of their State, the Clerk shall name the States in the order they are usually named for receiving petitions; and as the name of each is called the Sergeant-at-Arms shall present to the delegation of each two ballot boxes, in each of which shall be deposited, by some Representative of the State, one of the duplicates made as aforesaid of the vote of said State, in the presence and subject to the examination of all the Members from said State then present; and where there is more than one Representative from a State, the duplicates shall not both be deposited by the same person.

When the votes of the States are thus all taken in, the Sergeant-at-Arms shall carry one of said ballot boxes to one table and the other to a separate and distinct table. One person from each State represented in the balloting shall be appointed by the Representatives to tell off said ballots; but [if they] fail to appoint a teller, the Speaker shall appoint.

The said tellers shall divide themselves into two sets, as nearly equal in number as can be, and one of the said sets of tellers shall proceed to count the votes in one of said boxes, and the other set the votes in the other box.

When the votes are counted by the different sets of tellers, the result shall be reported to the House; and if the reports agree, the same shall be accepted as the true votes of the States; but if the reports disagree, the States shall proceed, in the same manner as before, to a new ballot.

6. All questions arising after the balloting commences, requiring the decision of the House, which shall be decided by the House, voting per capita, to be incidental to the power of choosing a President, shall be decided by States without debate; and in case of an equal division of the votes of States, the question shall be lost.

7. When either of the persons from whom the choice is to be made shall have received a majority of all the States, the Speaker shall declare the same, and that person is elected President of the United States.

8. The result shall be immediately communicated to the Senate by message, and a committee of three persons shall be appointed to inform the President of the United States and the President-elect of said election.

1. Petitions no longer are introduced in this way. This old order of calling the states began with Maine and proceeded through the thirteen original states and then through the remaining states in the order of their admission.

states choosing their electors by popular vote. (Electors in the other six states were chosen by the state legislatures.) Under the Twelfth Amendment, the names of the three top contenders—Jackson, Adams, and the ailing Crawford—were placed before the House. Clay's support was vital to the two front-runners.

From the start, Clay apparently intended to support Adams. But before the House voted, a great scandal erupted. A Philadel-

phia newspaper published an anonymous letter alleging that Clay had agreed to support Adams in return for being made secretary of state. The letter alleged also that Clay would have been willing to make the same deal with Jackson. Clay immediately denied the charge and pronounced the writer of the letter "a base and infamous calumniator, a dastard and a liar."[7] But Jackson and his supporters believed the charges and found their suspicions vindicated when Adams, after the election, did appoint Clay secretary of state. "Was there ever witnessed such a bare-faced corruption in any country before?" Jackson wrote to a friend.[8]

When the House met to vote, Adams was supported by the six New England states and New York and, in large part through Clay's backing, by Maryland, Ohio, Kentucky, Illinois, Missouri, and Louisiana. Thus a majority of thirteen delegations voted for him—the bare minimum he needed for election since there were then twenty-four states in the Union. The election was accomplished on the first ballot, but Adams took office under a cloud from which his administration never recovered.

Jackson's successful 1828 campaign made much of his contention that the House had thwarted the will of the people by denying him the presidency in 1825 even though he had been the leader in popular and electoral votes.

SENATE ELECTION OF VICE PRESIDENT

The Senate has had to decide a vice presidential contest only once. That was in 1837, when Martin Van Buren was elected president with 170 out of 294 electoral votes, while his vice presidential running mate, Richard M. Johnson, received only 147 electoral votes—one fewer than a majority. The discrepancy occurred because Van Buren electors from Virginia boycotted Johnson. (Johnson's nomination had been opposed by southern Democrats because of his long-standing involvement with a mulatto woman.)[9]

The names of Johnson and the runner-up in the electoral vote for vice president, Francis Granger of New York, were sent to the Senate. The Senate adopted a resolution that called for selecting of the vice president by a voice vote in alphabetical order. The Senate elected Johnson, 33–16, over Granger.[10]

PRESIDENTIAL ELECTION CLOSE CALLS

Although only two presidential elections actually have been decided by the House, a number of others—including those of 1836, 1856, 1860, 1892, 1948, 1960, 1968, and 1992—could have been thrown into the House by only a small shift in the popular vote.

The threat of House election was clearly present in 1968, when George C. Wallace of Alabama ran as a third party candidate. For the record, Wallace frequently asserted that he could win an outright majority in the electoral college by the addition of key Midwest and mountain states to his hoped-for base in the Deep South and border states. In reality, the Wallace campaign had a narrower goal: to win the balance of power in the electoral college voting, thus depriving both major parties of the clear electoral majority required for election. In that situation Wallace believed one of the major party candidates would have to make concessions to him in return for enough votes from Wallace electors to win the election.

Wallace made it known that he expected the election to be settled in the electoral college and not in the House. At the end of the campaign it was disclosed that Wallace had obtained written affidavits from all of his electors in which they promised to vote for Wallace "or whomsoever he may direct" in the electoral college.

In response to the Wallace challenge, both major party candidates, Republican Richard Nixon and Democrat Hubert H. Humphrey, maintained they would refuse to bargain with Wallace for his electoral votes. Nixon asserted that the Democratic-controlled House, if the decision rested there, should elect the popular-vote winner. Humphrey said the representatives should select "the President they believe would be best for the country." Bipartisan efforts to obtain advance agreements from House candidates to vote for the national popular-vote winner if the election should go to the House failed. Neither Nixon nor Humphrey responded to suggestions that they pledge before the election to swing enough electoral votes to the popular-vote winner to ensure his election without help from Wallace.

In the end, Wallace received only 13.5 percent of the popular vote and forty-six electoral votes (including the vote of one Republican defector), all from southern states. If Wallace had won a few border states, or if a few thousand more Democratic votes had been cast in northern states barely carried by Nixon, thus reducing Nixon's electoral vote below 270, Wallace would have been in a position to bargain off his electoral votes or to throw the election into the House for final settlement.

Discussion of the electoral college and House election of the president revived once again in 1992 when the independent campaign of Texas business executive H. Ross Perot showed surprising early strength. Perot's campaign faltered, and he won no electoral votes, yet he ended up with 19 percent of the popular vote. The winner, Democrat Bill Clinton, outpolled incumbent Republican president George Bush 43 percent to 38 percent in the popular vote. Clinton won even more decisively in the electoral college, 370–168.

TWO-TERM LIMIT TRADITION

The source of the two-term tradition was Thomas Jefferson, who was the first president to argue that no one should serve more than two terms. Earlier, George Washington had stepped down after two terms, not because of great principle or concern over the office becoming, in Jefferson's words, "an inheritance," but because the first president yearned for "the shade of retirement." The tradition held until 1940, at the start of World War II, when Franklin D. Roosevelt agreed to be "drafted" for a third term. In the 145 years between Washington and Roosevelt, several presidents had indicated they might like to serve for a third term. Except for FDR, however, no president actually ran more than twice. Republican President Ulysses S. Grant was denied renomination for a third term by his party in 1876. Woodrow Wilson wanted a third term but was too ill by 1920 to be seriously considered as a presidential candidate again.

Even though Jefferson's argument made election to a third term unlikely, passage of the Twenty-second Amendment in 1951 had a profound effect on presidential politics. The fact that, before 1951, it was always possible for a president to run for a third

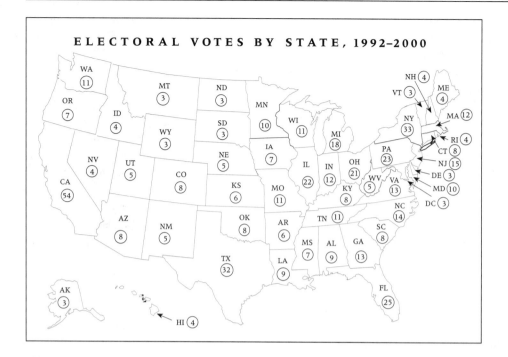

ELECTORAL VOTES BY STATE, 1992–2000

term gave a president added power and influence in his relations with Congress and with special interests in and out of government. The Twenty-second Amendment in many ways makes a two-term president a lame duck in the second term, at least in the last two years of that term. *(See "Presidential Tenure," p. 369.)*

Since passage of the Twenty-second Amendment, two presidents—Dwight D. Eisenhower and Ronald Reagan—publicly questioned the wisdom of the two-term limit. And Reagan supported a short-lived campaign during his second term to repeal the amendment, even though it would not have changed the limitation on his own presidency.

Counting the Electoral Vote

The Constitution in Article II, Section 1, as modified by the Twelfth and Twentieth amendments, gives Congress the right to set the dates for choosing presidential electors, the meeting of the electors in the separate states to cast their ballots for president and vice president, and the official counting of the electoral votes before a joint session of Congress. Congress has changed these dates several times since 1788.

The date for choosing presidential electors has, of course, now been transformed into the nation's general election day. By an act of Congress in 1845, and incorporated in succeeding federal election laws, presidential election day is designated as the first Tuesday after the first Monday in November every fourth year.[11] Voters in most states no longer see the names of the electors on the ballot, only those of the presidential and vice presidential candidates to whom the electors are pledged. Their vote for president is considered a vote for the electors representing that candidate and the candidate's political party. The electors usually are chosen at state party caucuses or conventions or in primary elections. Electors are not required by the Constitution to vote for the candidate they were chosen to represent. In theory they can vote for whomever they like, but electors who have not adhered to the party line have been infrequent (only nine). About a third of the states now require electors to vote for the candidate who won the popular vote in the state, but these laws are of doubtful constitutionality. *(See "Faithless Electors," p. 389.)*

Under current law, dating from 1934, electors meet in their state capitals to cast their votes for president on the first Monday after the second Wednesday in December, and the ballots are opened and counted before Congress on January 6 (the next day if the sixth falls on a Sunday).

The Continental Congress established the procedure for the first election under the Constitution. On September 13, 1788, Congress directed that each state choose its electors on the first Wednesday in January 1789. It further directed that these electors were to cast their ballots on the first Wednesday in February 1789.

In 1792 the Second Congress passed legislation setting up a permanent timetable for choosing electors. Allowing some flexibility in dates, the law directed that states choose their electors within the thirty-four days preceding the first Wednesday in December of each presidential election year. Then the electors would meet in their various states and cast their ballots on the first Wednesday in December. On the second Wednesday of the following February, the votes were to be opened and counted before a joint session of Congress. Provision also was made for a special presidential election in case of the removal, death, resignation, or disability of both the president and vice president.

Under this system, states chose presidential electors at various times. For instance, in 1840 the popular balloting for electors began in Pennsylvania and Ohio on October 30 and ended in North Carolina on November 12. South Carolina, the only state in 1840 still choosing presidential electors through the state legislature, appointed its electors on November 26. But this system, it was argued before passage of the 1872 Uniform Federal Election Day Act, gave some states an "undue advantage" in electing their representatives early. In 1840, for example, news about the results in some states that had already held House elections settled the November presidential election "as effectively as it was afterward done," asserted one of the Act's proponents.

Congress apparently weighed several factors in choosing the month and day for all federal elections. November was pragmatically agreed upon because the weather is still temperate, and farmers would have harvested their crops and were more likely to vote. The first and last days of the month were objected to because they might complicate the closing out of business account books. Sensibility also governed the choice of the day. Religious objections ruled out Sunday and possibly Monday because Monday voting might entail Sunday travel to the polls in rural areas. Thursday was dismissed because it was Britain's election day. Friday was the end of the workweek and Saturday was shopping day. That left Tuesday and Wednesday, but just why Tuesday was chosen remains unclear. One theory argues that it was the day that rural Americans might come to town for court sessions or farmer's markets. The first Tuesday was also rejected because it might fall on the first of the month. Therefore the first Tuesday after the first Monday emerged as Congress's choice.

The next change occurred in 1887, when Congress provided that electors were to meet and cast their ballots on the second Monday in January instead of the first Wednesday in December. Congress also dropped the provision for a special presidential election.

This arrangement remained in effect until the revision enacted in 1934.

DISPUTED ELECTORAL VOTES

The Constitution provides that "The President of the Senate shall, in the presence of the Senate and House of Representatives, open all the certificates, and the votes shall then be counted." But no guidance is offered on resolving political controversies involving the states, such as the handling of disputed electoral ballots. Post–Civil War politics, in particular, severely strained some of the constitutional underpinnings of representative government.

The electoral bargain that settled the presidential election of 1876, in which Republican Rutherford Hayes was elected even though Democrat Samuel Tilden won the popular vote, created one of the country's greatest electoral crisis. (See "Hayes-Tilden Contest," this page.)

Following the 1864 presidential election, Congress—before counting the electoral votes—adopted Joint Rule XXII, which provided that electoral votes that had been challenged in the

joint session could not be counted except by separate votes of both the Senate and House. The rule was pushed by congressional Republicans to ensure the rejection of electoral votes from the newly reconstructed states of Louisiana and Tennessee. Using that rule in 1873, Congress threw out all the electoral votes of Louisiana and Arkansas and three from Georgia.

The rule lapsed at the beginning of 1876, when the Senate refused to readopt it because the House was controlled by the Democrats. Thus, Congress had no rules to guide it after the 1876 election when it became apparent that, for the first time, the outcome of an election would be determined by decisions on disputed electoral votes.

HAYES-TILDEN CONTEST

In the 1876 campaign between the Republican Hayes and the Democrat Tilden, early election night returns indicated that Tilden had been elected. He had won normally Republican Indiana, New York, Connecticut, and New Jersey. Those states, plus his expected southern support, would give him the election. However, by the following morning it became apparent that if the Republicans could hold on to win South Carolina, Florida, and Louisiana, Hayes would be elected with 185 electoral votes to 184 for Tilden. But if a single elector in any of those states voted for Tilden, he would throw the election to the Democrats. Tilden led in the popular-vote count by more than a quarter of a million votes.[12]

The situation was much the same in each of the three contested states. Historian Eugene H. Roseboom described it as follows:

The Republicans controlled the state governments and the election machinery, had relied upon the Negro masses for votes and had practiced frauds, as in the past. The Democrats used threats, intimidation, and even violence when necessary, to keep Negroes from the polls; and where they were in a position to do so they resorted to fraud also. The firm determination of the whites to overthrow carpetbag rule contributed to make a full and fair vote impossible; carpetbag hold on the state governments made a fair count impossible. Radical reconstruction was reaping its final harvest.[13]

Both parties pursued the votes of the three states with a fine disregard for propriety or legality, and in the end double sets of electoral vote returns were sent to Congress from all three. Oregon also sent two sets of returns. Although Hayes carried that state, the Democratic governor discovered that one of the Hayes electors was a postmaster and therefore ineligible to be an elector under the Constitution, so the governor certified the election of the top-polling Democratic elector. However, the Republican electors met, received the resignation of their ineligible colleague, then reappointed him to the vacancy since he had in the meantime resigned his postmastership.

Had Joint Rule XXII remained in effect, the Democratic House of Representatives could have ensured Tilden's election by objecting to any of Hayes's disputed votes. Since the rule had lapsed, Congress had to find some new method of resolving the electoral disputes. A joint committee was created to work out a

Counting electoral votes in Congress is not always just a formality. A special electoral commission is pictured here taking testimony on disputed electoral votes in the 1876 presidential election. Congress gave the election to Rutherford B. Hayes even though Democrat Samuel J. Tilden had a majority of the popular vote.

plan, and the resulting Electoral Commission law was approved by large majorities and signed into law January 29, 1877—only two days before the date scheduled for counting the electoral votes.

The law, which applied only to the 1876 electoral vote count, established a fifteen-member Electoral Commission. It had final authority over disputed electoral votes, unless both houses of Congress agreed to overrule it. The commission was to consist of five senators, five representatives, and five Supreme Court justices. Each chamber was to select its own members of the commission, with the understanding that the majority party would have three members and the minority two. Four justices, two from each party, were named in the bill, and these four were to select the fifth. It was expected that they would pick Justice David Davis, who was considered a political independent, but he was disqualified when the Illinois Legislature elected him to a

seat in the Senate. Justice Joseph P. Bradley, a Republican, then was named to the fifteenth seat on the commission. The Democrats supported his selection because they considered him the most independent of the remaining justices, all of whom were Republicans. However, he voted with the Republicans on every dispute and thus ensured the victory of Hayes.

The electoral vote count began on February 1, and the proceedings continued until March 2. States were called in alphabetical order, and as each disputed state was reached objections were raised to both Hayes and Tilden electors. The question then was referred to the Electoral Commission, which in every case voted 8–7 for Hayes. Subsequently, the Democratic House rejected the commission's decision, but the Republican Senate upheld it, so the decision stood.

As the count went on, Democrats in the House threatened to launch a filibuster to block resumption of joint sessions so that the count could not be completed before inauguration day. The threat was never carried out because of an agreement reached between the Hayes forces and southern conservatives. The southerners agreed to let the electoral count continue without obstruction. In return, Hayes agreed that, as president, he would withdraw federal troops from the South, end Reconstruction, and make other concessions. The southerners, for their part, pledged to respect the rights of blacks, a pledge they proved unable to carry out.

Thus, at 4:00 a.m. on March 2, 1877, the president of the Senate was able to announce that Hayes had been elected president with 185 electoral votes, as against 184 for Tilden. Later that day Hayes arrived in Washington. The following evening he took the oath of office privately at the White House because March 4 fell on a Sunday. His formal inauguration followed on Monday. The country acquiesced. Thus ended a national crisis.

Not until 1887 did Congress enact permanent legislation on the handling of disputed electoral votes. The Electoral Count Act of that year gave each state final authority in determining the legality of its choice of electors. Challenged electoral votes could be sustained by Congress only upon majority vote of both the House and Senate. The act also established procedures to guide Congress in counting the electoral votes.

1969 TEST OF ELECTORAL COUNT ACT

The procedures of the 1887 law relating to disputed electoral votes were used for the first time following the election of 1968. When Congress met in joint session January 6, 1969, to count the electoral votes, Sen. Edmund S. Muskie, D-Maine, and Rep. James G. O'Hara, D-Mich., joined by six other senators and thirty-seven other representatives, filed a written objection to the vote cast by a North Carolina elector, Dr. Lloyd W. Bailey of Rocky Mount, who had been elected as a Republican but chose to vote for Wallace and Curtis E. LeMay instead of for Nixon and Agnew.

Muskie and O'Hara objected to Bailey's vote on the grounds that it was "not properly given" because a plurality of the popular votes in North Carolina had been cast for Nixon-Agnew, and the state's voters had chosen electors to vote for Nixon and Agnew only. Muskie and O'Hara asked that Bailey's vote not be counted at all by Congress.

The 1887 statute stipulates that "no electoral vote or votes from any state which shall have been regularly given by electors whose appointment has been lawfully certified . . . from which but one return has been received shall be rejected, but the two Houses concurrently may reject the vote or votes when they agree that such vote or votes have not been so regularly given." The statute did not define the term "regularly given," though at the time of its adoption concern centered on problems of dual sets of electoral vote returns from a state, votes cast on an improper day, or votes disputed because of uncertainty about whether a state lawfully was in the Union on the day that the electoral vote was cast.

The 1887 statute provided that if written objection to any state's vote was received from at least one member of the Senate and House, the two legislative bodies were to retire immediately to separate sessions, debate for two hours, and decide the issue by vote before resuming the joint session. The act made clear that for the challenge of a disputed electoral vote, or votes, to prevail, both the Senate and House had to sustain the challenge. *(See box, Counting Electoral Votes, p. 388.)*

At the January 6 joint session, the counting of the electoral votes proceeded smoothly through the alphabetical order of states until the North Carolina vote was announced. At that point O'Hara rose to announce the filing of a complaint. The two houses then proceeded to separate sessions, at the end of which the Senate, by a 33–55 vote, and the House, by 170–228, refused to sustain the challenge to Bailey's vote.

Although Congress did not vote in favor of the challenge, the case of the faithless elector helped lead to renewed pressure for electoral college reform. *(See "Electoral College Reform," p. 389.)*

METHODS OF CHOOSING ELECTORS

The Framers of the Constitution intended the selection of the president to be made by the country's most learned and distinguished citizens. These presidential electors—collectively the electoral college—were to be chosen by the states in any manner each state determined. Initially, electors in a majority of the states were selected by the legislatures.

In the first presidential election of 1789, four states held direct, popular elections to choose their electors: Pennsylvania and Maryland in statewide contests, Virginia and Delaware in district elections. In five states the state legislatures picked the electors: Connecticut, Georgia, New Jersey, New York, and South Carolina. Two states, New Hampshire and Massachusetts, adopted a combination of legislative and popular vote methods. (The other two original thirteen states—Rhode Island and North Carolina—had not yet ratified the Constitution.)

In the 1792 election state legislatures chose the presidential electors in nine states, including Vermont, which was admitted to the Union in 1791.

As political parties began to dominate the election process in the early 1800s, manipulation of the system for choosing electors became increasingly widespread. Massachusetts, for example, in 1800 switched from popular voting for electors to selection by the legislature because of recent popular vote successes by the Democratic-Republicans. The Federalists, still in control of the legislature, sought to secure the state's entire electoral vote for its presidential candidate, native son John Adams. New Hampshire did likewise.

Thus until 1832 there were three basic methods for choosing electors: popular vote in statewide contests, popular vote in district contests, and selection by state legislatures.

Initially, most popular-election states provided that electors should be chosen from districts similar to congressional districts, with the electoral vote of a state split if the various districts differed in their political sentiment. This "district plan" of choosing electors was supported by many of the leading states-

COUNTING ELECTORAL VOTES: THE LAW

Following is the complete text of Title 3, Section 15, of the U.S. Code (the Electoral Count Act), enacted in 1887, governing the counting of electoral votes in Congress:

Congress shall be in session on the sixth day of January succeeding every meeting of the electors. The Senate and House of Representatives shall meet in the Hall of the House of Representatives at the hour of 1 o'clock in the afternoon on that day, and the President of the Senate shall be their presiding officer.

Two tellers shall be previously appointed on the part of the Senate and two on the part of the House of Representatives, to whom shall be handed, as they are opened by the President of the Senate, all the certificates and papers purporting to be certificates of the electoral votes, which certificates and papers shall be opened, presented, and acted upon in the alphabetical order of the States, beginning with the letter A; and said tellers, having then read the same in the presence and hearing of the two Houses, shall make a list of the votes as they shall appear from the said certificates; and the votes having been ascertained and counted according to the rules in this subchapter provided, the result of the same shall be delivered to the President of the Senate, who shall thereupon announce the state of the vote, which announcement shall be deemed a sufficient declaration of the persons, if any, elected President and Vice President of the United States, and together with a list of the votes, be entered on the Journals of the two Houses.

Upon such reading of any such certificate or paper, the President of the Senate shall call for objections, if any. Every objection shall be made in writing, and shall state clearly and concisely, and without argument, the ground thereof, and shall be signed by at least one Senator and one Member of the House of Representatives before the same shall be received. When all objections so made to any vote or paper from a State shall have been received and read, the Senate shall thereupon withdraw, and such objections shall be submitted to the Senate for its decision; and the Speaker of the House of Representatives shall, in like manner, submit such objections to the House of Representatives for its decision; and no electoral vote or votes from any State which shall have been regularly given by electors whose appointment has been lawfully certified to accord to section 6[1] of this title from which but one return has been received shall be rejected, but the two Houses concurrently may reject the vote or votes when they agree that such vote or votes have not been so regularly given by electors whose appointment has been so certified.

If more than one return of paper purporting to be a return from a State shall have been received by the President of the Senate, those votes, and those only, shall be counted which shall have been regularly given by the electors who are shown by the determination mentioned in section 5[2] of this title to have been appointed, if the determination in said section provided for shall have been made, or by such successors or substitutes, in case of a vacancy in the board of electors so ascertained, as have been appointed to fill such vacancy in the mode provided by the laws of the State; but in case there shall arise the question which of two or more of such State authorities determining what electors have been appointed, as mentioned in section 5 of this title, is the lawful tribunal of such State, the votes regularly given of those electors, and those only, of such State shall be counted whose title as electors the two Houses, acting separately, shall concurrently decide is supported by the decision of such State so authorized by its law; and in such case of more than one return or paper purporting to be a return from a State, if there shall have been no such determination of the question in the State aforesaid, then those votes, and those only, shall be counted which the two Houses shall concurrently decide were cast by lawful electors appointed in accordance with the laws of the State, unless the two Houses, acting separately, shall concurrently decide such votes not to be the lawful votes of the legally appointed electors of such State.

But if the two Houses shall disagree in respect of the counting of such votes, then, and in that case, the votes of the electors whose appointment shall have been certified by the executive of the State, under the seal thereof, shall be counted. When the two Houses have voted, they shall immediately again meet, and the presiding officer shall then announce the decision of the questions submitted. No votes or papers from any other State shall be acted upon until the objections previously made to the votes or papers from any State shall have been finally disposed of.

1. Section 6 provides for certification of votes by electors by state governors.
2. Section 5 provides that if state law specifies a method for resolving disputes concerning the vote for presidential electors, Congress must respect any determination so made by a state.

---

men of both parties, including Thomas Jefferson, Alexander Hamilton, James Madison, John Quincy Adams, Andrew Jackson, and Daniel Webster.

The district plan, however, tended to dilute the power of the dominant majorities in state legislatures, who found themselves unable to "deliver" their states for one candidate or another. These groups brought pressure to change the electoral procedure, and the states moved toward a winner-take-all popular ballot. Under this system, all of a state's electoral votes went to the party that won a plurality of popular votes statewide.

With the domination of political parties came the adoption of party slates of electors pledged to vote for the parties' presidential candidates. Each party organization believed a statewide ballot was in its best interest, since it provided the opportunity to win all the state's electors and prevent the opposition party from capitalizing on local areas of strength. Under a district election system, such localized strength would give the opposition party a better opportunity of electing some electors. Statewide election contests had the effect of diluting such strength.

By 1804 six of the eleven popular-election states cast their electoral votes under the statewide popular ballot; by 1824, twelve out of eighteen states did so. By 1836 all states except South Carolina had adopted the system of choosing electors statewide by popular vote (South Carolina's legislature chose the electors). The state continued this practice through the election of 1860. Only after the Civil War was popular voting for presidential electors instituted in South Carolina.

Thus, since 1836 the statewide, winner-take-all popular vote for electors has been the almost universal practice. Exceptions include the following:

• Massachusetts, 1848. Three slates of electors ran—Whig, Democratic, and Free Soil—none of which received a majority of the popular vote. Under the law then in force, the state legislature was to choose in such a case. It chose the Whig electors.

• Florida, 1868. The state legislature chose the electors.

• Colorado, 1876. The state legislature chose the electors because the state had just been admitted to the Union, had held state elections in August, and did not want to go to the trouble and expense of holding a popular vote for the presidential election so soon thereafter.

• Michigan, 1892. Republicans had been predominant in the state since the 1850s. However, in 1890 the Democrats managed to gain control of the legislature and the governorship. They promptly enacted a district system of choosing presidential electors in the expectation that the Democrats could carry some districts and thus win some electoral votes in 1892. The result confirmed their expectations, with the Republicans winning nine and the Democrats five electoral votes that year. But the Republicans soon regained control of the state and reenacted the at-large system for the 1896 election.

• Maine, 1972. In 1969 the Maine Legislature enacted a district system for choosing presidential electors. Two of the state's four electors were selected on the basis of the statewide vote, while the other two were determined by which party carried each of the state's two congressional districts. The system is still in force, and has also been adopted by Nebraska.

Since no mention of a statewide, popular election system was ever written into the U.S. Constitution, state legislatures retain the power to specify any method of choosing presidential electors and determine how the electoral votes are divided.

"FAITHLESS ELECTORS"

Throughout U.S. history there have been instances where persons appointed or elected as presidential electors have not voted for their party's candidate for president.

A long-standing criticism of the electoral college system has been the so-called faithless-elector phenomenon. Nothing in the Constitution's provisions providing for selection of the president (Article 2, Section 1, clauses 2, 3, and 4) requires electors to vote in any particular way. Regardless of his or her party affiliation, an elector cannot be forced to vote for the party's candidate for president. In practice, almost all electors do vote for their party's candidate, but legally they are free to vote for whomever they choose.

On at least nine occasions, presidential electors broke from the ranks and voted for a candidate other than their own party's

choice. In none of these instances did the switch alter the election result:

• In 1796 a Pennsylvania Federalist elector voted for the Democratic-Republican candidate, Thomas Jefferson, rather than the Federalist candidate, John Adams. And some historians maintain that three Democratic-Republican electors voted for Adams. The fluidity of political parties in those early years, however, and the reported friendship between Adams and at least one of the electors, made the claim that they were faithless electors one of conjecture.

• In 1820 a New Hampshire Democratic-Republican elector voted for John Quincy Adams instead of his party's nominee, James Monroe.

• In 1948 Preston Parks, a President Harry S. Truman elector in Tennessee, voted instead for Gov. Strom Thurmond of South Carolina, the States Rights Democratic Party (Dixiecrat) presidential nominee.

• In 1956 W. F. Turner, an Adlai E. Stevenson II elector in Alabama, voted for a local judge, Walter E. Jones.

• In 1960 Henry D. Irwin, a Nixon elector in Oklahoma, voted for Sen. Harry F. Byrd, D-Va. Byrd also received fourteen electoral votes from unpledged electors.

• In 1968 Dr. Lloyd W. Bailey, a Nixon elector in North Carolina, voted for George C. Wallace, the American Independent party candidate.

• In 1972 Roger L. McBride, a Nixon elector in Virginia, voted for John Hospers, the Libertarian Party candidate.

• In 1976 Mike Padden, a Ford elector in Washington state, voted for former California governor Ronald Reagan.

• In 1988 Margaret Leach, a Michael Dukakis elector in West Virginia, voted for Dukakis's running mate, Lloyd Bentsen, and gave her vice presidential vote to Dukakis.

ELECTORAL COLLEGE REFORM

The electoral college system used to elect the president and vice president has remained intact for more than two hundred years despite repeated calls for its repeal or modification. The method spelled out in the Constitution has been revised only once—by the Twelfth Amendment—to correct the flaw in voting for president and vice president. That change ensured that electoral votes would be cast separately for president and vice president, thus preventing a recurrence of what happened in the 1800 presidential election, when Democratic-Republican electors inadvertently caused a tie for president by casting an equal number of votes for Thomas Jefferson, whom they wanted elected president, and Aaron Burr, their choice for vice president. *(See "Election of 1800," p. 380.)*

Changes in the system were proposed as early as 1797. Since then, hardly a session of Congress has passed without the introduction of constitutional amendments related to electoral reform. In recent history, the close elections of 1960 and 1968 created a degree of urgency for constitutional changes. Other factors were a series of Supreme Court decisions on apportion-

"MINORITY" PRESIDENTS

Under the U.S. electoral system, there have been seventeen presidential elections (decided by either the electoral college itself or by the House of Representatives) where the victor did not receive a majority of the popular votes cast in the election. Three of these future presidents—John Quincy Adams in 1824, Rutherford B. Hayes in 1876, and Benjamin Harrison in 1888—actually trailed their opponents in the popular vote.

The table shows the percentage of the popular vote received by candidates in the seventeen elections in which a "minority" president (designated by boldface type) was elected.

Year elected	Candidate	Percentage of popular vote	Candidate	Percentage of popular vote	Candidate	Percentage of popular vote	Candidate	Percentage of popular vote
1824	Jackson	41.34	**Adams**	30.92	Clay	12.99	Crawford	11.17
1844	**Polk**	49.54	Clay	48.08	Birney	2.30		
1848	**Taylor**	47.28	Cass	42.49	Van Buren	10.12		
1856	**Buchanan**	45.28	Fremont	33.11	Fillmore	21.53		
1860	**Lincoln**	39.82	Douglas	29.46	Breckenridge	18.09	Bell	12.61
1876	Tilden	50.97	**Hayes**	47.95	Cooper	0.97		
1880	**Garfield**	48.27	Hancock	48.25	Weaver	3.32	Others	0.15
1884	**Cleveland**	48.50	Blaine	48.25	Butler	1.74	St. John	1.47
1888	Cleveland	48.62	**Harrison**	47.82	Fisk	2.19	Streeter	1.29
1892	**Cleveland**	46.05	Harrison	42.96	Weaver	8.50	Others	2.25
1912	**Wilson**	41.84	T. Roosevelt	27.39	Taft	23.18	Debs	5.99
1916	**Wilson**	49.24	Hughes	46.11	Benson	3.18	Others	1.46
1948	**Truman**	49.52	Dewey	45.12	Thurmond	2.40	Wallace	2.38
1960	**Kennedy**	49.72	Nixon	49.55	Others	0.72		
1968	**Nixon**	43.42	Humphrey	42.72	Wallace	13.53	Others	0.33
1992	**Clinton**	43.01	Bush	37.45	Perot	18.91	Others	0.64
1996	**Clinton**	49.24	Dole	40.71	Perot	8.40	Others	1.65

ment and redistricting in the 1960s and the use of unpledged electors in some of the southern states at the height of the civil rights movement in the 1950s and 1960s.

In 1960, for example, uncommitted electors won in the states of Mississippi and Alabama, giving all eight of Mississippi's electoral votes and six of Alabama's eleven votes to Sen. Harry Byrd of Virginia. In recent years there also has been a slight rise in the faithless-elector phenomenon. *(See "Faithless Electors," p. 389.)*

In 1969 President Nixon proposed that Congress take prompt action on electoral college reform. He said he would support any plan that would eliminate individual electors and distribute among the presidential candidates the electoral vote of every state and the District of Columbia in a manner more closely approximating each state's popular vote.

Later that year the House approved, 338–70, a resolution proposing a constitutional amendment to eliminate the electoral college and provide instead for direct popular election of the president and vice president. The measure set a minimum of 40 percent of the national popular vote as sufficient for election and provided for a runoff election between the two top candidates for the presidency if no candidate received 40 percent of

the vote. Under that plan the House no longer would have had a role in the selection of the president.

The proposed amendment also authorized Congress to provide a method of filling vacancies caused by the death, resignation, or disability of presidential nominees before the election was held and a method of filling postelection vacancies caused by the death of the president-elect or vice president–elect.

Although Nixon had favored a proportional plan of allocating each state's electoral votes, he endorsed the House-passed constitutional amendment and urged the Senate to adopt it.

When the proposal reached the Senate in September 1970, senators from small states and the South succeeded in blocking action on it because they feared losing the little advantage they had in the electoral college. Liberal interest groups also argued that minority, union, and urban voters, concentrated (then and now) in the large states, would lose their strategic advantage if these states were no longer as central to presidential candidates' fortunes. The resolution finally was laid aside October 5, following two unsuccessful efforts to cut off a filibuster.

Another major attempt to abolish the electoral college was made in 1977 when President Jimmy Carter proposed a constitutional amendment as part of an election reform package.

Carter called for direct, popular election of the president. He endorsed the proposal approved by the House in 1969. It won approval in the Senate Judiciary Committee in 1977, but opponents threatened a filibuster, blocking action by the Senate.

In 1979 the Senate was allowed to vote on the measure but once again refused to approve Carter's popular-vote plan. The amendment won a majority, 51–48, but this was fifteen short of the two-thirds vote required to approve proposed constitutional amendments. Some northern state senators who were thought to favor the change voted against the amendment because of constituent pressure. As they had in the 1970 reform effort, various minority groups opposed any change, arguing that the electoral college maximized their voting strength because they were concentrated in certain urban areas of some of the large electoral vote states.

The presidential campaigns of seemingly strong independent candidates in 1980 (John Anderson) and 1992 (Perot) briefly renewed concerns that close elections would occur without the benefit of constitutional change. The eventual unsuccessful efforts of these independent bids, however, stilled these fears and no further headway for electoral college reform was made in Congress in the 1990s.

Presidential Disability

Long-standing congressional concern about the implications for the nation of an incapacitated president was removed in 1967 with ratification of the Twenty-fifth Amendment. For the first time, the Constitution now provided a specific method to ensure continuity in carrying out the functions of the presidency if the chief executive became temporarily disabled. The amendment also spelled out procedures to be used in filling vacancies in the vice presidency. *(See "Vice Presidential Vacancies," p. 393.)*

The Constitution, in Article II, Section 1, clause 5, provided that, as in the case of a president's death, resignation, impeachment, and removal from office or "inability to discharge" his responsibilities, the powers and duties of the presidency would be transferred to the vice president. The disability provision was never debated at the Constitutional Convention of 1787 and thus "inability to discharge the Powers and Duties" of the office were never defined. Nor did the original Constitution establish any procedure to determine whether a president was disabled or who would make such a determination.

At least three, and by some studies as many as eleven, presidents who served between 1789 and 1967 were disabled during at least part of their term of office. The three most seriously incapacitated were James A. Garfield, William McKinley, and Woodrow Wilson. Garfield was shot in 1881 and hovered near death for eleven weeks before he died. McKinley lingered for eight days after being shot in 1901. Wilson suffered a serious stroke in September 1919 but served out his term. In all cases, discussions took place within the presidents' cabinets about transferring power to the vice president, but the lack of any constitutional guidelines made their vice presidents reluctant to

PRESIDENTIAL SUCCESSION LAW

Article II, Section 1, clause 5, of the Constitution leaves it to Congress to establish the line of succession to the presidency if the vice president has died, resigned, or otherwise left office.

Congress has enacted succession laws three times in U.S. history. By an act of March 1, 1792, Congress designated (after the vice president) the president pro tempore of the Senate and then the Speaker of the House as the officials who would succeed to the presidency. If those offices were vacant, states were to send electors to choose a new president.

The 1792 law stood until enactment of the Presidential Succession Act of January 19, 1886. The new law changed the line of succession to run from the vice president to the secretary of state, the secretary of the Treasury, and so on through all the cabinet departments in the order in which they were established.

The current line of succession was established by the Presidential Succession Act of 1947 (PL 80-199), subsequently amended to reflect the creation of new cabinet-level departments. It placed the Speaker of the House and then the president pro tempore of the Senate ahead of the cabinet officers. The complete line of succession is as follows:

Vice president of the United States
Speaker of the House of Representatives
President pro tempore of the Senate (by recent tradition the senator of the majority party with the longest period of service)
Secretary of state
Secretary of the Treasury
Secretary of defense
Attorney general
Secretary of the interior
Secretary of agriculture
Secretary of commerce
Secretary of labor
Secretary of health and human services
Secretary of housing and urban development
Secretary of transportation
Secretary of energy
Secretary of education
Secretary of veterans affairs

A different line of executive direction—not of succession to the presidency but of National Command Authority in situations of wartime emergency—was created under the National Security Act of 1947. The command rules are contained in secret presidential orders that each new president signs at the outset of his administration. Among other things, the orders authorize the secretary of defense to act as commander in chief in certain specific, limited circumstances in which neither the president nor vice president is available. Presumably, such circumstances might occur following a nuclear attack on Washington or a foreign assassination plot.

assume the duties of the presidency. In Wilson's case, there was actual doubt about who was running the country in the final seventeen months of his administration. Though not public knowledge at the time, the health of President Franklin Roosevelt deteriorated rapidly in the months before his death in April 1945.[14]

Presidential disability became a pressing national issue in the post–World War II era of nuclear weapons and the cold war. Government leaders became increasingly aware that the United States could no longer afford to be without presidential leadership even for brief periods. After President Eisenhower's series of heart attacks and other illnesses in 1955–1957, the president and Vice President Nixon entered into an unofficial understanding for an orderly, temporary transfer of power if the president again became incapacitated. Nixon would have become acting president after "such consultation as it seems to him appropriate under the circumstances." The informal accord also provided that Nixon could assume such powers and duties on his own initiative if Eisenhower were unable to transfer them voluntarily. Presidents John F. Kennedy and Lyndon B. Johnson entered into similar understandings with their vice presidents. However, various constitutional experts questioned the legality of these arrangements.

A constitutional answer to the disability question was proposed in 1965 when the House and Senate approved the Twenty-fifth Amendment. When the thirty-eighth state ratified the amendment February 10, 1967, it became a part of the Constitution. Although the amendment did not define "disability," it established a set of procedures for determining when a president is disabled and who would make the determination.

The amendment's disability provisions (Sections 3 and 4) provided that the vice president would assume the president's powers and responsibilities under either of two situations: (1) if the president informed Congress that he was unable to perform his duties, in which case the vice president would become acting president until the president informed Congress that he was resuming his regular duties; and (2) if the vice president and a majority of the "principal officers" of executive departments, or another body designated by Congress, determined that the president was incapacitated, in which case the vice president would become acting president until the president informed Congress that his disability had ended. But if the vice president and a majority of top executive officers, or the other designated body—which, for example, Congress could appoint should a determined president fire his cabinet—disagreed with the president's claim that he was no longer incapacitated, Congress would have to decide the issue.

The Twenty-fifth Amendment gives Congress twenty-one days to determine the president's fitness for office. But unless Congress by a two-thirds vote of each chamber sides with the vice president, the president's claim prevails and he resumes his duties and responsibilities as president.

Critics charge that the disability provisions of the Twenty-fifth Amendment contain several defects. For example, a president who is rebuffed by Congress could repeatedly make claims about his fitness, theoretically requiring Congress to vote on the matter every twenty-one days and throwing the government into chaos.

USE OF DISABILITY PROVISIONS

As of 1999 the disability provisions of the Twenty-fifth Amendment had been used only once, in July 1985, when President Reagan underwent surgery for removal of a cancerous polyp from his large intestine and malignant growths from his nose. Responding to criticism that neither he nor the vice president and cabinet had invoked Section 3 of the amendment in 1981 when he was seriously wounded in an assassination attempt, Reagan informed the House and Senate that he would be "temporarily incapable of discharging his Constitutional duties" during the operation. He did not formally invoke the Twenty-fifth Amendment, however, saying he did not believe it applied to such brief periods of disability. Vice President Bush became acting president during the eight-hour transfer of power. After the operation, Reagan notified the Speaker and Senate president pro tempore he was resuming his duties as president.

After the March 30, 1981, shooting, Reagan had undergone a two-hour operation to remove a bullet from his left lung. Although the president was under anesthesia, Reagan's advisers and the vice president decided not to invoke the disability provisions. They discouraged its use on the grounds it could make Reagan appear weak or cause needless public anxiety. Instead, Bush substituted for the president unofficially.

Bush was in Texas on a speaking engagement on the day of the shooting, and confusion arose as to who was in charge of the U.S. government while the president was temporarily unable to function and the vice president was away from Washington. Before Bush returned aboard an air force jet, public statements from the White House indicated that even some cabinet members had been confused.

At a televised press briefing later that afternoon, Secretary of State Alexander M. Haig Jr., confirmed that Reagan was in surgery. Because he was under anesthesia, it was clear that he temporarily was unable to make presidential decisions should a crisis—such as a foreign attack or other national emergency—require them. Attempting to reassure the country, Haig stated that he was in control in the White House pending the return of Vice President Bush, with whom he was in contact.

This assertion was followed by the question, from the press, as to who was making administration decisions. Haig responded, "Constitutionally, gentlemen, you have the president, the vice president and the secretary of state in that order, and should the president decide he wants to transfer the helm to the vice president, he will do so. He has not done that."

Haig was wrong on two counts: First, the Constitution is silent on who follows the vice president in the line of succession. It gives Congress the right to make that determination through legislation, and it has done so on three occasions. The line of succession currently in effect dates from a 1947 law (PL 80-199).

Second, Haig was incorrect about the order of succession designated in that law. PL 80-199 specifies that, following the vice president, the Speaker of the House and then the president pro tempore of the Senate would succeed to the presidency before the secretary of state (followed by the other cabinet secretaries). Haig apparently had confused the 1947 law with an earlier law that did name the secretary of state as next in line after the vice president. *(See box, Presidential Succession Law, p. 391.)*

VICE PRESIDENTIAL VACANCIES

The original Constitution had no procedure for filling the office of vice president after a vice president succeeded to the presidency or caused the office to become vacant by death, resignation, or removal through impeachment.

The Constitution did give Congress the power to pass legislation establishing a line of presidential succession should both the president and vice president die or otherwise leave office at the same time. But the Constitution did not address the potential need to fill a vacancy in the vice presidency.

Between 1789 and the mid-1960s, when the Twenty-fifth Amendment was drafted, the vice presidency became vacant sixteen times, sometimes for long periods. Taken together, the sixteen vacancies left the nation without a vice president for a total of approximately thirty-seven years. (Two subsequent brief vacancies increased the number to eighteen, as of 1999.) Of the eighteen vacancies, seven occurred because the vice president died, two because the vice president resigned, eight because the president died and the vice president succeeded to the presidency, and one because the president (Nixon) resigned and his vice president succeeded him.

It was the assassination of President Kennedy in 1963 that galvanized Congress to propose a constitutional remedy that would allow a vacancy in the vice presidency to be filled quickly. With Kennedy's death, Lyndon Johnson became president and the office of vice president remained vacant for fourteen months. As a senator in 1955, Johnson had had a severe heart attack. With no vice president, the next in line for the presidency was the seventy-two-year-old Speaker of the House, John W. McCormack, D-Mass. The Twenty-fifth Amendment was introduced in Congress in January 1965, after Johnson had won election as president in his own right with Hubert Humphrey as his vice president. The proposed amendment was approved, with scarcely any opposition, six months later. Ratification by the states was completed February 10, 1967.

Section 1 affirms that the vice president becomes president—not just acting president—upon the president's death, resignation, or removal through impeachment. Beginning with John Tyler in 1841, vice presidents assumed the presidency whenever

Both President Gerald R. Ford and Vice President Nelson A. Rockefeller, right, owed their jobs to the passage of the Twenty-fifth Amendment, which outlined how vacancies in the presidency or vice presidency were to be filled in the modern era.

the president died. But they did so on their own volition. The Constitution did not state that the vice president automatically becomes president when the president dies. Section 2 provides that whenever there is a vacancy in the office of vice president, the president shall nominate a replacement, who becomes vice president upon confirmation by majority votes of both the House and the Senate. A potential defect in the amendment is that no time limit is placed on either the president to make his nomination for vice president or on Congress to vote to confirm the president's choice.

Within the first decade of the amendment's ratification, Section 2 was used twice: in 1973 when President Nixon nominated Gerald R. Ford to be vice president after Vice President Agnew resigned, and in 1974 when Ford, who succeeded to the presidency upon Nixon's resignation, nominated Nelson A. Rockefeller to succeed him. Ford became the fortieth vice president of the United States on December 6, 1973, after the House voted to confirm him by a 387–15 vote, the Senate having approved the nomination November 27 by a 92–3 vote. Rockefeller became the forty-first vice president on December 19, 1974, after the House confirmed him by a 287–128 vote. The Senate had approved Rockefeller's nomination December 10 by a 90–7 vote. For the first time ever, the nation had both a president and vice president who were not elected by the people.

With the two highest offices of the land held by nonelected appointees, some members of Congress began to question their wisdom in proposing the Twenty-fifth Amendment, which in effect allowed a disgraced president to appoint his successor. Constitutional amendments were introduced to revise the Twenty-fifth by requiring a special national election for president whenever an appointed vice president became president with more than one year remaining in a presidential term. Although committee hearings were held on the proposal in the Senate, no action was ever taken.

NOTES

1. See Edward Stanwood, *A History of the Presidency from 1788 to 1897* (Boston: Houghton Mifflin, 1898), 1–9.

2. Neal R. Peirce and Lawrence D. Longley, *The People's President: The Electoral College in American History and the Direct Vote Alternative* (New Haven, Conn.: Yale University Press, 1981), 30, citing John P. Roche, "The Founding Fathers: A Reform Caucus in Action," *American Political Science Review* (December 1961): 810.

3. Stanwood, *A History of the Presidency*, 54–73.

4. Peirce and Longley, *The People's President*, 40, citing Sidney Hyman, *The American President* (New York: Greenwood Press, 1954), 128.

5. Arthur M. Schlesinger Jr., ed., *History of American Presidential Elections, 1789–1968* (New York: Chelsea House Publishers and McGraw-Hill, 1971), vol. 1, 133.

6. Eugene H. Roseboom, *A History of Presidential Elections* (New York: Macmillan, 1959), 47.

7. For background, see Stanwood, *A History of the Presidency*, 123–141.

8. Roseboom, *A History of Presidential Elections*, 88.

9. Schlesinger, *History of American Presidential Elections*, vol. 1, 584, 596.

10. Stanwood, *A History of the Presidency*, 187.

11. For background, see Stanwood, *A History of the Presidency*, 20, 38, 203–204, 242, 452; Roseboom, *A History of Presidential Elections*, 246–247.

12. For background, see Stanwood, *A History of the Presidency*, 356–393.

13. Roseboom, *A History of Presidential Elections*, 243–244.

14. See Frank Freidel, *Franklin D. Roosevelt, A Rendezvous with Destiny* (Boston: Little, Brown, 1990), 507–524.

SELECTED BIBLIOGRAPHY

Asher, Herbert B. *Presidential Elections and American Politics: Voters, Candidates, and Campaigns Since 1952.* 4th ed. Chicago: University of Chicago Press, 1988.

Association of the Bar of the City of New York. *Report of the Committee on Federal Legislation: Proposed Constitutional Amendment Abolishing the Electoral College and Making Other Changes in the Election of the President and Vice president.* New York: 1969.

Barbash, Fred. *The Founding: A Dramatic Account of the Writing of the Constitution.* New York: Linden Press/Simon and Schuster, 1987.

Barber, James David, ed. *Choosing the President.* Englewood Cliffs, N.J.: Prentice Hall, 1974.

Beman, L. T. *Abolishment of the Electoral College.* New York: H. W. Wilson, 1926.

Best, Judith. *The Case against Direct Election of the President: A Defense of the Electoral College.* Ithaca, N.Y.: Cornell University Press, 1975.

———. *The Choice of the People: Debating the Electoral College.* Lanham, Md.: Rowman and Littlefield, 1996.

Bickel, Alexander M. *Reform and Continuity: The Electoral College, the Convention, and the Party System.* Rev. ed. New York: Harper and Row, 1971.

Burnham, Walter D. *Presidential Ballots, 1836–1892.* Baltimore: Johns Hopkins University Press, 1955.

Caeser, James W. *Presidential Selection: Theory and Development.* Princeton, N.J.: Princeton University Press, 1979.

Collier, Christopher, and James Lincoln Collier. *Decision in Philadelphia: The Constitutional Convention of 1787.* New York: Ballantine, 1986.

Congressional Quarterly's Guide to U.S. Elections. 3rd ed. Washington, D.C.: Congressional Quarterly, 1994.

Feerick, John D. *From Failing Hands: The Story of Presidential Succession.* Bronx, N.Y.: Fordham University Press, 1965.

Hardaway, Robert M. *The Electoral College and the Constitution: The Case for Preserving Federalism.* Westport, Conn.: Praeger, 1994.

Haworth, Paul L. *The Hayes-Tilden Disputed Presidential Election of 1876.* Cleveland: Burrows, 1906.

Heard, Alexander, and Michael Nelson, eds. *Presidential Selection.* Durham, N.C.: Duke University Press, 1987.

Kuroda, Tadahisa. *The Origins of the Twelfth Amendment: The Electoral College in the Early Republic, 1787–1804.* Westport, Conn.: Greenwood Press, 1994.

Mee, Charles L., Jr. *The Genius of the People.* New York: Harper and Row, 1987.

Nelson, Michael, ed. *Congressional Quarterly's Guide to the Presidency.* 2nd ed. Washington, D.C.: Congressional Quarterly, 1996.

Peirce, Neal R., and Lawrence D. Longley. *The People's President: The Electoral College in American History and the Direct Vote Alternative.* Rev. ed. New Haven, Conn.: Yale University Press, 1981.

Peters, William. *A More Perfect Union: The Making of the United States Constitution.* New York: Crown, 1987.

Sayre, Wallace S., and Judith H. Parris. *Voting for President: The Electoral College and the American Political System.* Washington, D.C.: Brookings Institution, 1970.

Wilmerding, Lucius, Jr. *The Electoral College.* New Brunswick, N.J.: Rutgers University Press, 1958.

Zeidenstein, Harvey. *Direct Election of the President.* Lexington, Mass.: D. C. Heath, 1973.

CHAPTER 12

Seat of Government

T HE CONSTITUTION gave Congress the exclusive right to legislate for the nation's capital. But striking an appropriate balance between federal and local interests has been a continuing problem. The basic question of whether municipal affairs should be handled by Congress or a locally elected government has gone unanswered in Washington since the District of Columbia became the seat of government.

The Constitution is silent on the matter. Article I, Section 8, states only that "the Congress shall have Power . . . To exercise exclusive Legislation in all Cases whatsoever, over such District (not exceeding 10 Miles square), as may, by Cession of particular States, and the Acceptance of Congress, become the Seat of Government of the United States."[1]

Home rule advocates and their foes both have used the constitutional provision to argue their position. The advocates have contended that the framers of the Constitution wanted congressional control only to avoid conflicts between local and federal interests, and that where no conflict existed District citizens could run their own government. For evidence they point to No. 43 of *The Federalist* papers, by James Madison. While writing of the necessity of not leaving the "general government" dependent on the local government for protection, Madison went on to say: "A municipal legislature for local purposes, derived from their own suffrages, will of course be allowed them [the District's residents]."

The District of Columbia

Before the Constitution was adopted, the seat of government was located wherever the Continental Congress met. There were eight such places: Philadelphia, Lancaster, and York in Pennsylvania; Trenton and Princeton in New Jersey; New York City; and Baltimore and Annapolis in Maryland. Throughout the period the nation was governed by the Articles of Confederation, the Continental Congress made a number of futile attempts to agree on a permanent site for the capital.

DECISION ON THE SITE

When the First Congress met in 1789 in New York City a number of cities were already seeking to be the capital. The winner would gain great prestige and perhaps ensure itself a bright commercial future. Kingston, New York, had made the first bid. Others followed from a dozen other towns, including most of those in which the Continental Congress had sat. Shortly before the First Congress adjourned that September 29, the House of Representatives designated a site on the Susquehanna River in Pennsylvania but the Senate voted for Germantown, a community near Philadelphia (later incorporated into the city).

The matter was left in limbo as the lawmakers went home, but an important proposal was pending. The previous December 23, the Maryland legislature had approved a resolution offering land along the Potomac River for a new federal city. And disregarding the First Congress's expressed preference for staying in Pennsylvania, the Virginia legislature on December 3, 1789, passed a resolution that dovetailed with Maryland's; Virginia offered land along the Potomac River adjoining Maryland. The ensuing debate on a "residence act" in the next session of Congress focused on the Maryland-Virginia argument that a Potomac site would be on a navigable waterway, accessible to the trans-Allegheny West, and about midway between New Hampshire and Georgia, the northernmost and southernmost states at that time.

But not only was there competition among various cities for the capital; sectional interests were also strong. New England, in particular, objected to placing the seat of government in a slaveholding area. President George Washington joined fellow Virginians Thomas Jefferson, his secretary of state, and James Madison, then a member of Congress, in advancing the notion that a southern capital was essential to the region's economic future.

Another North-South dispute was brewing at that time, and its resolution contributed to the crafting of a compromise for determining the seat of government. Northerners wanted the new federal government to assume debts that the states had incurred fighting the Revolutionary War. Much of the debt was held by northern financiers in the form of bonds they had purchased from individual creditors at deep discounts. With several states unwilling or unable to redeem the bonds at full value, the investors' best hope lay with the new federal government. Virginia, then the biggest state in size and population, had paid its war debts and insisted that others do likewise.

This impasse was surmounted by a deal Jefferson struck in mid-May with Secretary of the Treasury Alexander Hamilton, the chief advocate of "assumption." According to Jefferson's account, Hamilton agreed to enlist northern backing for a southern site and Jefferson would work to neutralize the objections of his fellow Virginians to assumption.

That agreement cleared the way for Congress on July 16, 1790, to pass the so-called residence act specifying that the seat of government should be in Philadelphia until 1800 and thereafter in "a district . . . on the river Potomac." The next month Congress authorized the federal government to assume the states' Revolutionary War debts.

DEFINITION OF THE BOUNDARIES

The residence act enabled Congress to accept the offers from Maryland and Virginia to cede jurisdiction over land in the yet-to-be designated site and provide $120,000 and $72,000, respectively, for public buildings. As directed by the act, a federal "district of territory, not exceeding ten miles square," would "be located as hereafter directed on the river Potomac" between the mouths of the Eastern Branch (now the Anacostia River) and Conococheague Creek, some seventy miles upriver.

The act empowered President Washington to choose the site, acquire the tract, and appoint commissioners to oversee the building of government facilities. That October he took up his role as agent, and in January 24, 1791, he sent Congress a message stating he had selected "a territory . . . on both sides of the river Potomac to comprehend Georgetown in Maryland and extend to the Eastern Branch." Washington suggested that Congress choose whether the area should extend lower in Maryland and include Alexandria, Virginia, or reach farther north. Without debate, Congress opted for the inclusion of Alexandria, thus placing the southern extremity of the federal district at the mouth of Hunting Creek, just below that port town.

Alexandria and Georgetown, also a port, were the only communities in the district even remotely urban. By an act of March 3, 1791, Congress obligingly redefined the area to accord with Washington's preferences. On March 30 he issued a proclamation specifying the precise boundaries.

NAMING THE CITY

Neither the city nor the entire district had been named. Washington referred to "the federal territory" and "the seat of government." The commissioners he had appointed called it "the city of Washington" and the whole district "the Territory of Columbia." When Congress did apply a name to the city and the district, it did so almost by indirection. An act of Congress approved May 6, 1796, was entitled "An Act Authorizing a Loan for the City of Washington, in the District of Columbia, and for other purposes therein mentioned." But the text of the document merely referred to "the said city."[2]

ACQUIRING LAND: L'ENFANT'S PLAN

It was understood by all parties that what Maryland and Virginia were ceding was governmental jurisdiction only. Owners of land and buildings in the area would retain their property—except for land that would be used for government purposes. It was acquired through an arrangement that Washington himself negotiated with the principal landowners in the portion of the district where the federal city would be built. Laying out the city was entrusted to Major Pierre Charles L'Enfant, a French architect and engineer who had fought with Washington in the Revolutionary War. L'Enfant's design for the city, completed in 1791,

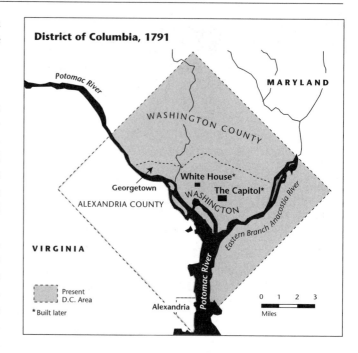

was on a grand scale. A gridiron of streets, each one hundred feet wide, were cut through by even-wider avenues. The avenues radiated from a Federal House (Capitol) on Jenkin's Hill and a President's Palace (White House) one mile away on a ridge west of Tiber Creek near the Potomac. Other public structures and an elaborate system of parks completed the design.

Once L'Enfant determined the exact limits of the federal city, Washington began negotiations with the principal property owners—but withholding much of the information to thwart land speculators. On March 30, 1790, he obtained an agreement to a plan under which all the acreage within the city would be laid off into lots; the landowners would donate alternate lots to the city for streets and other general uses. The rest could be expected to rise in value as the city grew; for whatever the government took for public buildings, the owners would receive outright payment.

Washington's dealings with L'Enfant did not go as smoothly. The city planner would countenance no compromises, which brought him into frequent conflict with local landowners and caused him repeatedly to defy the commissioners who, technically, were in charge of overseeing his work. On one occasion, L'Enfant ordered a large private dwelling of a prominent resident torn down because it would have blocked a view from one of the still-to-be-built avenues. Moreover, L'Enfant insisted on proceeding with development of the new city at a pace that would have forced the government to borrow on a scale it was not prepared to do.

In exasperation, President Washington in February 1792 asked for L'Enfant's resignation and entrusted the supervisory work to Andrew Ellicott, who had surveyed the district's boundaries. Construction began later that year on the White House, the first public building in the new city, and on the Capitol the next year. L'Enfant later prowled the halls of Congress, seeking compensation for his plan for the federal city. He claimed $95,500 but was authorized payments totaling less than $3,000. He died in poverty in 1825. His plan fell into disuse but was revived in 1901 and used as the basis for further development of the city. The layout of present-day Washington bears a striking resemblance to L'Enfant's plan.

GOVERNMENT'S MOVE TO WASHINGTON

The act establishing a federal district on the Potomac stipulated that the government would begin functioning in the new capital on the first Monday in December 1800. By early that year it became clear that the move could be made sooner. So on April 24, 1800, Congress authorized that the president "shall . . . direct the various offices belonging to the several executive departments of the United States, to be removed to the city of Washington, at any time that he shall judge proper, after the adjournment of the present session of Congress."

The first session of the Sixth Congress adjourned in Philadelphia on May 14, 1800, and the next day President John Adams directed his cabinet members to arrange their departmental affairs "so that the public offices may be open in the city of Washington by the 15th of June." This was done, and Philadelphia officially ceased to be the seat of government on June 11. Adams himself arrived in the new capital June 3. The removal of government was not a herculean task; it involved the transfer of 126 government personnel and government records to new quarters on the Potomac.

The new capital presented a doleful scene, as described by Oliver Wolcott, Hamilton's successor as secretary of the Treasury. Wolcott found upon his arrival "few houses in any one place and most of them are small miserable huts, which present an awful contrast to the public buildings." He added: "You may look over an extent of ground nearly as large as the city of New York, without seeing a fence or any object except brick-kilns and temporary huts for laborers." First lady Abigail Adams, coming to Washington that November, found the "President's Palace" lacking in amenities. "We have not the least fence, yard, or other convenience without, and the great unfinished audience room [present East Room] I make a drying room of, to hang the clothes in."[3] The entire district, consisting mostly of pasture land and swamps, was inhabited by only eight thousand people.

The second session of the Sixth Congress, the first session of Congress to be held in Washington, convened November 17, 1800, but for lack of a quorum did not actually sit until November 21. The following March, Thomas Jefferson took the presidential oath of office from the steps of the unfinished Capitol, and after the inauguration walked back to the rooming house where he had been living. Although public buildings continued to rise, waves of discontent with the new city threatened its continued existence throughout that decade and into the next.

During the War of 1812—in the summer of 1814—British troops swept through Washington and burned nearly all of the public buildings, including the White House and Capitol. That fall a special session of Congress met in Washington and consid-

---

SEATS OF GOVERNMENT

Before the selection of Washington, D.C., as the permanent seat of the federal government, Congress met in eight cities in four states. Following are the seats of government under the Continental Congress, the Articles of Confederation, and the Constitution:

CONTINENTAL CONGRESS

Philadelphia	Sept. 5, 1774–Dec. 12, 1776
Baltimore	Dec. 20, 1776–March 4, 1777
Philadelphia	March 5, 1777–Sept. 18, 1777
Lancaster, Pa.	Sept. 27, 1777
York, Pa.	Sept. 30, 1777–June 27, 1778
Philadelphia	July 2, 1778–March 1, 1781

ARTICLES OF CONFEDERATION

Philadelphia	March 2, 1781–June 21, 1783
Princeton, N.J.	June 30, 1783–Nov. 4, 1783
Annapolis. Md.	Nov. 26, 1783–June 3, 1784
Trenton, N.J.	Nov. 1, 1784–Dec. 24, 1784
New York	Jan. 11, 1785–March 2, 1789

CONSTITUTION

New York	March 4, 1789–Aug. 12, 1790
Philadelphia	Dec. 6, 1790–May 14, 1800
Washington, D.C.	Since Nov. 17, 1800

SOURCE: *Biographical Directory of the American Congress, 1774–1989*, 100th Cong., 2nd sess., S. Doc. 100-34 (Washington, D.C.: Government Printing Office, 1989).

---

ered whether to move the government to a more secure place. Speaker Langdon Cheves, D-S.C., cast a tie-breaking vote in the House of Representatives in favor of moving the government for the duration of the war. No sites were specified, but among the possible choices were New York City, Philadelphia, and Lancaster. Local residents, especially land speculators who had bought up much of the district's private property in anticipation of great growth, lobbied Congress to block the relocation. On October 15, the House reversed its position and voted not to leave.

Thereafter, keeping the seat of government in Washington was not seriously questioned, except that after the nation had been extended to the Pacific, a feeble voice was sometimes heard in favor of a more centrally located capital.

RETURN OF ALEXANDRIA TO VIRGINIA

Congress by an act of February 27, 1801, created two counties in the District of Columbia: Washington County in Maryland and Alexandria County in Virginia and provided for the operation of the two counties—though exempting the incorporated towns of Alexandria and Georgetown. That arrangement lasted for four decades. A change began taking shape in 1840, toward the end of Martin Van Buren's presidency. Because a Whig, William W. Seaton, had been elected as Washington's mayor under a system that limited the vote to property holders, the dominant Democrats in Congress initiated a move to extend the franchise to all male adults.

Georgetown and rural parts of Washington County sought to return to Maryland, and Alexandria County to Virginia. The Maryland legislature refused to assume the financial burden of reintegrating Georgetown and the nearby countryside into the state. But later, in 1846, the Virginia Legislature indicated its willingness to take back all of Alexandria County. By an act of July 9, 1846, Congress agreed to retrocede to Virginia the portion of the District of Columbia that lay in that state if the county's residents approved. They did, by a vote of 763–222. President James K. Polk on September 7 proclaimed that Alexandria County was again part of Virginia.

CONSOLIDATION

After the retrocession, the District of Columbia consisted of Washington County and the cities of Georgetown and Washington. The first step toward erasing the inner boundaries of the District was taken in 1861 when Congress established the Metropolitan Police District of the District of Columbia. The act assigned responsibility for law enforcement throughout the District to a board of five presidentially appointed commissioners, three from the city of Washington, one from Georgetown, and one from the county of Washington. The mayors of Washington and Georgetown were ex officio members.

Ten years later, Congress established a territorial government for the District. The act of February 21, 1871, made the entire district a single municipal entity, repealing the city charters of Washington and Georgetown. The final consolidation came under an act of February 11, 1895, merging Georgetown into the city of Washington, which was made coterminous with the District of Columbia.

Changing Forms of Government

Limited self-government was granted to the District soon after the federal government moved to Washington in 1800. Georgetown, which had been governed before 1801 by a popularly elected council and board of aldermen under an appointed mayor, continued to be so governed until 1830. That year Congress authorized Georgetown voters to elect their mayor. Washington County, formerly governed by a so-called levy court whose members were appointed by the governor of Maryland, was governed after February 1801 by a levy court whose members were appointed by the president of the United States.

MAYOR-COUNCIL GOVERNMENT, 1802–1871

Congress in 1802 set up a government for the city of Washington consisting of a mayor appointed by the president and a twelve-member, two-chamber council elected by the people. In 1812 it permitted the council to select the mayor, and in 1820 to let the voters elect him. That form of government continued

until municipal debt and race questions moved Congress to assert full control over the District of Columbia in 1871. Slavery was abolished in the District on April 16, 1862, nearly nine months before President Abraham Lincoln issued his Emancipation Proclamation. In 1867, three years before the Fifteenth Amendment came into effect prohibiting voting discrimination on the basis of race, Congress conferred the franchise "without any distinction on account of color or race" on male citizens twenty-one years and older who had lived in the District of Columbia for one year. President Andrew Johnson vetoed the franchise bill, but Congress quickly overrode his veto.

The city became a haven for black people during and after the Civil War. The 1870 census recorded 43,404 black residents, three times as many as in 1860, constituting one-third of the city's population.[4] Blacks quickly became influential in city politics. When the first city election under the new suffrage law was held in June 1867, many white voters stayed home in protest. Blacks voted solidly for the Republican Party, which they identified with their freedom, giving Republicans control of both chambers of the council. Even after whites returned to the polls in 1868, black votes gave Sayles J. Bowen, the Republican candidate for mayor, a narrow margin of victory.

Bowen launched a series of projects that promptly put the District into financial trouble, and drew blame for the city's mounting debt. Congress refused to bail him out, and in the 1870 election he was deserted by the black electorate. When Bowen's successor fared no better at solving the city's fiscal ills, Congress looked to another form of government for the District.

TERRITORIAL GOVERNMENT, 1871–1874

Alexander Shepherd, a Washington native who had risen from the job of plumber's helper to be the city's leading entrepreneur, persuaded Congress in 1871 to adopt a modified territorial form of government for the District of Columbia. The law provided for a governor appointed by the president; an elected nonvoting delegate in the House of Representatives; a territorial assembly consisting of an eleven-member council appointed by the president and a twenty-two-member house of delegates elected by the people; and a five-member board of public works appointed by the president.

As executive officer of the board of public works, Shepherd set about transforming Washington into a modern city. At his direction, water mains and sewers were laid, streets paved, and parks developed. However, the bill for this work totaled some $20 million, nearly three times the estimate. He left the city bankrupt but habitable.[5]

Shepherd may have been extravagant, but he apparently sought no personal gain. Three congressional investigations into Shepherd's activities found no profit taking by him. One investigation was occasioned by President Ulysses S. Grant's 1873 appointment of Shepherd to the post of governor of the District. Aggrieved taxpayers presented a petition to Congress that led to the creation of a joint congressional committee to investigate District affairs.

Alexander "Boss" Shepherd persuaded Congress in 1871 to adopt a modified territorial form of government for the District of Columbia.

The committee, headed by Sen. William B. Allison, R-Iowa, asserted in its report in June 1874 that the existing government was ridden by graft and financial mismanagement and was a failure. The committee recommended that, for a temporary period, the governorship be replaced by an appointed three-member commission; that the assembly, the board of public works, and the post of delegate in the House of Representatives be abolished; and that Congress perform legislative functions for the District. The investigating committee recommended that Congress appoint a new committee to propose a permanent form of government for the District.

COMMISSION GOVERNMENT, 1874–1967

Allison's committee's basic recommendations were put into effect, but the political strife flared anew when President Grant nominated Shepherd as one of the three new commissioners. The Senate voted down the nomination 6–32; Shepherd, his fortune gone and his name besmirched, moved with his family to Mexico in 1876.

The joint congressional committee that had been appointed to propose a permanent government for the District of Columbia recommended in 1875 that the commission form of government be continued, but with provision for popular election of three of the eight members of the school board. Action on this proposal was bogged down for the next three years over voting rights for District residents.

The commission form of government, without voting rights, was approved in 1878. Underlying the decision to prolong the commission form of government were a hostility to black suffrage and a concern of the business community for a fiscally sound local government. Many white residents of the District preferred to forgo voting rights rather than share them with black residents.

Congress kept tight control over the manner in which Washington developed. In the late 1890s construction of a fourteen-story apartment hotel nine blocks north of the White House caused dismay in Congress, whose members wanted no private buildings in the capital to overshadow government structures. An act of March 1, 1899, limited new residential buildings to five stories or sixty feet in height; buildings of any kind on a residential street to ninety feet; and buildings on a business street to 130 feet. Church spires could go higher with the approval of the District commissioners. As a rule of thumb, no buildings above twelve or thirteen stories were allowed. The height limitations on residential buildings were subsequently modified, but the overall top limit of 130 feet was not relaxed.

During the city's centennial celebration in 1900, the American Institute of Architects held a symposium and concluded that the capital had long departed from L'Enfant's plan and was growing haphazardly. In response, Sen. James McMillan, R-Mich., sponsored a resolution authorizing a committee of experts to make "plans for the improvement of the park system of the District of Columbia." Congress approved the resolution, and appointed to the committee—the so-called McMillan Commission—architects Daniel H. Burnham and Charles F. McKim, landscape architect Frederick Law Olmsted Jr., and sculptor Augustus Saint-Gaudens. They published their report in 1902 and did not confine it to parks; they redefined L'Enfant's plan and set in motion a new era of public building in Washington that marks much of the monumental aspects of the present-day city.

COMMISSIONER-COUNCIL GOVERNMENT, 1967–1974

The commission form of government prevailed in the District of Columbia until 1967. Sentiment for self-government in the nation's capital, by now predominantly black, grew in the civil rights era. In 1961 the Twenty-third Amendment had gone into effect, permitting District voters to cast ballots in presidential elections. The next step, it seemed, was home rule. But moves in Congress to grant home rule to the District were obstructed, mainly by the House District Committee, which long had been under southern control.

President Lyndon B. Johnson's advisers on District affairs persuaded him to make changes in the city's government through his power to submit to Congress government reorganization plans. Such plans take effect unless disapproved by either house within sixty days. On June 1, 1967, Johnson sent to Congress a plan to replace the three-member commission with a single commissioner, an assistant commissioner, and a nine-member city council, all to be appointed by the president and confirmed by the Senate. The new commissioner would have the right to veto the council's action, but the council would be empowered to override his veto by a three-fourths vote.

After a summer of wrangling in Congress, Johnson's plan survived. He nominated Walter E. Washington as commissioner and five council members, all of whom were black, and won Senate confirmation. District residents received a second concession in 1968. Congress, responding to continued pressures for more self-government for the District and taking account of controversies over Washington's educational programs, authorized direct election of an eleven-member board of education. Since 1906 the board had been chosen by judges of the U.S. District Court for the District of Columbia. The new law went into effect April 22, 1968.

LIMITED HOME RULE RESTORED

Johnson's action still fell short of full home rule, which Congress had repeatedly blocked since the 1940s. Then in April 1969, President Richard Nixon asked Congress to enact a fuller measure of home rule. "At issue," Nixon said in his message to Congress, "is whether the city will be enabled to take hold of its future: whether its institutions will be reformed so that its government can truly represent its citizens and act upon their needs."[6]

The House District Committee relaxed its opposition somewhat, approving a bill in 1970 to allow three members of the nine-member council to be elected. But the full House did not approve the measure. The next year the Senate passed a bill for the election of a mayor and an expanded council, but it fell victim to delaying tactics orchestrated by House District Committee Chairman John L. McMillan, D-S.C., and several Republican foes of home rule. The committee failed repeatedly to obtain a quorum to consider any of several self-government proposals, including the Senate bill.

McMillan was defeated in his district's Democratic primary runoff election in 1972. Five other southern Democrats on the committee who generally supported McMillan also lost their bids for reelection or retired. When the committee convened in 1973, its chairman was Charles C. Diggs Jr., a black Democrat from Michigan. Only four southern Democrats remained on the committee; three of them were freshmen. Diggs reorganized the committee, adding a new Government Operations Subcommittee under the chairmanship of Rep. Brock Adams, D-Wash. Adams reported a home rule bill to the full committee despite a boycott of his panel's work sessions by three Republican members.

The full committee approved the bill to authorize an elected mayor and a thirteen-member city council, which would control the city's expenditures and revenues—including federal payments to compensate the city for taxes it cannot impose on federal property. The bill also contained recommendations made by a study commission in 1973 that some duties performed for the District by several federal and quasi-federal agencies be turned over to the local government.

That version proved too liberal for many members of the House. Consequently, Diggs agreed to a compromise version, which won crucial support from William H. Natcher, D-Ky., the powerful chairman of the Appropriations Subcommittee for the District of Columbia. Natcher's endorsement apparently influenced the votes of several members who otherwise were considered unlikely to support the bill. The compromise retained the mayor-council features of the Diggs bill but did not relinquish the existing congressional line-item control over the city's budget. The new bill also authorized the president to take control over the local police force in an emergency, and prohibited the city council from making any changes in the criminal code. A weakening amendment adopted by the House continued the president's authority to appoint local judges. But home rule supporters fended off other debilitating amendments and the House approved the bill October 10, 1973.

Meanwhile, the Senate on July 10 had passed a stronger version, along the lines of the original House committee bill. Aware that its version was unlikely to be approved by the House, Senate conferees agreed to most of the major provisions of the House compromise. The House agreed to the conference report and the Senate cleared the bill December 19. President Nixon signed it into law on Christmas Eve.

The home rule law allowed the mayor to veto an act of the city council. The council could override a veto by a two-thirds vote, but the president then could sustain the mayor's veto. Congress would continue to make annual appropriations for the District as well as set the amount of the annual federal payment. The act said the council could not impose taxes on federal property, amend or repeal any act of Congress affecting the District, reform the city's criminal code until two years after the council was elected, or raise the height limitation on buildings. To ensure its continued control over the District, Congress reserved the right to legislate for the District at any time and established a procedure to use a "legislative veto" to nullify any action taken by the city council.

Congress executed its first veto of a District of Columbia ordinance in 1979: the Senate and the House adopted resolutions disapproving the city's restriction on areas where foreign governments could establish chanceries for their diplomatic missions. The veto resolution did not require the president's signature to take effect. Another measure, to liberalize some criminal penalties in sexual assault cases, was vetoed under the same procedure in 1983. However, the Supreme Court that year overturned the "legislative veto" as unconstitutional and voided such provisions in all laws Congress had enacted, including the district's home rule charter. The next year Congress amended the charter to require that the lawmakers pass, and the president sign, a joint resolution in order to nullify any ordinance enacted by the District. (*See "Separation of Powers," p. 680.*)

Participation in National Politics

On a separate track from the home rule debate was a drive by the District to give its residents a voice in national politics. District voters cast ballots in national and local elections in 1800, and from then until 1874 in local elections only. They did not vote again in a presidential election until 1964. After World War II leaders of both major political parties seemed to favor D.C. voting rights, as did the nation generally.

CONVENTION DELEGATES

The Senate in July 1954, and the House the following month, passed a bill authorizing District of Columbia residents to elect committeemen to represent them in the councils of the national political parties and to elect delegates to the national nominating conventions. President Dwight D. Eisenhower vetoed the bill because it permitted federal employees in the District to engage in partisan political activities, contrary to the Hatch Act of 1939. In 1955 both houses of Congress repassed the bill, but without the objectionable provision. President Eisenhower signed it into law August 12, 1955.

VOTING FOR PRESIDENT

The Constitution provides in Article II, Section 1 for electors in each state to choose the president and vice president. An amendment to the Constitution was required to permit electors from the District. Since 1890 more than sixty-five such amendments were proposed, but none elicited substantial support until Alaska and Hawaii achieved statehood in 1959.[7] The next February the Senate approved a resolution proposing a constitutional revision to let the District participate in presidential elections and elect a nonvoting House delegate. The House balked at accepting a delegate but approved the rest of the resolution. The Senate acquiesced and put forth, for state approval, a constitutional amendment entitling District of Columbia voters to elect three electors for president and vice president—"a number . . . equal to the whole number of senators and representatives in Congress to which the District would be entitled if it were a state, but in no event more than the least populous state."

Kansas on March 29, 1961, became the thirty-eighth state to ratify the Twenty-third Amendment. Ratification was completed in 286 days; only one amendment, the Twelfth, was ratified in a shorter period.

REPRESENTATION IN CONGRESS

District residents had nonvoting representation in Congress briefly in the nineteenth century. The 1871 law that established a territorial form of government let them elect a nonvoting delegate to the House for service on the District of Columbia Committee. Norton P. Chipman, a brigadier general in the Union Army who had settled in Washington after the Civil War, was elected on the Republican ticket in 1871 and remained in the post until it was abolished in 1875 by a change to a commission form of government, as was voted by Congress the previous year.

Bills to reestablish nonvoting representation were introduced repeatedly after the demise of the territorial government, but they made little progress until the 1950s. The Senate passed such bills in 1951, 1953, 1955, 1958, and 1959 only to see them die in the House committee. In 1960 House supporters gained 204 of the 219 signatures needed to discharge the District Committee from further consideration of a home rule bill and bring it to the floor. Their near-success was hailed as a moral victory, but it did not lead to legislation. After the Senate passed a similar measure in 1965, the House approved a bill to set up a complex procedure for determining by referendum whether District residents really wanted suffrage and, if so, what kind they wanted. Differences between the two bills were not reconciled.

President Nixon in 1969 endorsed the idea of a constitutional amendment giving the District voting representation in Congress. He also advocated a nonvoting delegate in the House until the states ratified such an amendment. Legislation providing for a nonvoting House delegate won approval of both houses in 1970 and was signed into law on September 9. Democrat Walter E. Fauntroy, a black Baptist minister, was elected the District's nonvoting delegate on March 23, 1971. He was reelected without significant opposition until 1990, when he ran unsuccessfully for mayor of the District.

The House Judiciary Committee in December 1975 reported a resolution, sponsored by Fauntroy, proposing a constitutional amendment allowing District residents to elect two voting senators and as many representatives in the House as it would be entitled if it were a state. During 1976 Congress extensively debated the proposal. Proponents argued that to continue to deny District residents a voice in Congress amounted to taxation without representation. They pointed out that the residents paid federal taxes, lived under federal law, and served in the armed forces. But opponents countered that permitting members of Congress from the District would open the way for such territories as Guam and the Virgin Islands to demand membership. When it became apparent that the backers could not muster a required two-thirds majority vote to place the proposed amendment before the states for ratification, Fauntroy agreed to support a substitute measure to give the District nonvoting representative in the House immediately and authorize Congress to determine later if the District should be granted senators and an additional House member. That substitute was adopted, but resolution itself still fell short of a two-thirds majority.

Two years later the backers were successful. Congress in 1978 approved a constitutional amendment providing that the District be treated as a state for purposes of congressional and electoral college representation. But state legislatures were reluctant to ratify an amendment that would give another political entity parity with the states in Congress. The amendment died at the expiration of the seven-year ratification period. Only sixteen states, less than half the required number, had approved it.

EFFORTS TO ACHIEVE STATEHOOD

At the same time the amendment backers were working for ratification, another group was pushing the idea of outright statehood for the District. A Statehood Party had been formed in 1969 by Julius Hobson, a District activist, and it pursued statehood even after the 1973 home rule act lessened support for that goal. By 1980 statehood advocates were able to gather enough petition signatures to call for a referendum in the District on the question. The voters were asked to approve a convention to draft a constitution for the District to submit to Congress and thus begin the formal process of seeking admission to the Union as the fifty-first state. Sixty percent of the voters approved.

The convention began its work in January 1982 and completed a draft later that year. The document drew heavy criticism from some city council members as radical and unwieldy, and the voters endorsed it by a slim 53 percent majority. After that the statehood movement lost momentum. The document was redrafted and submitted to Congress, where it lingered without action except in the House District of Columbia Committee. That committee approved it in 1987 but to no avail. The 1980 petition that set statehood in motion also authorized the city council to set elections for interim "shadow" delegates to Congress to lobby for statehood. But those elections were repeatedly postponed.

The statehood effort was undoubtedly hurt by deteriorating relations between the city government and Congress during the latter half of the 1980s. Well-publicized problems of Mayor Marion Barry Jr.—leading to his arrest in January 1990 on drug charges—alienated Congress and virtually eliminated any remaining support for governmental autonomy in the District. Barry, convicted on one charge of cocaine possession, drew a jail sentence. The conviction, though appealed, seemed to doom his political career.

Congress quickly warmed to a new city administration led by Sharon Pratt Dixon, Barry's most vocal critic in the political arena. Barry, in the mayor's office since 1978, did not run for a fourth term in 1990; amid his legal difficulties, he quit the Democratic Party and sought an at-large seat on the city council as an independent candidate, but was rejected by the voters. Dixon, promising to "clean house" if elected mayor, won an upset victory in the city's primary election in September and then went on to a landslide victory in the general election over her Republican opponent.

Fauntroy, vacating the delegate position to run for mayor, was succeeded in the November 1990 election by Eleanor Holmes Norton, who had served in President Jimmy Carter's administration. She promised during the campaign to improve the city's image on Capitol Hill but encountered her own image problems when it was revealed that she and her husband had failed to pay federal income taxes for several years. She attributed the failure to an oversight by her husband, a law school professor, whom she later divorced.

Norton's tax embarrassment caused her no lasting political damage. By 1999 she was serving her fourth consecutive term as D.C. delegate, all the while gaining a reputation on Capitol Hill as a forceful advocate for the residents of Washington.

The statehood movement caught a new breath of life in 1990. The long-delayed election for "shadow" delegates to Congress was held, and the nationally prominent black leader Jesse Jackson Jr., won a seat as a "shadow senator," a post officially unrecognized by Congress but which gave Jackson another public forum. Rep. Stan Parris, R-Va., who had used his ranking position on the House District of Columbia Committee to delay action on statehood, lost his House seat in the November election to Democrat James Moran, who promised to take a more conciliatory attitude toward the District.

At the beginning of the 102nd Congress, Sens. Paul Simon, D-Ill., and Edward M. Kennedy, D-Mass., reintroduced legislation that they had sponsored in the previous Congress to make the District of Columbia the fifty-first state of New Columbia. Statehood foes, meanwhile, tried to preempt the issue by offering legislation to return the District to Maryland or, alternatively, permit residents to vote in Maryland for members of Congress.

In 1992 the House District Committee approved legislation to transform the District into the fifty-first state, called New Columbia, and establish a separate enclave comprising the White House, the Supreme Court, the Capitol, and other federal buildings. Similar legislation was debated on the House floor for the first time in 1993. Although the measure was rejected by 153–277, statehood supporters said they were pleased that it had attracted more than their target total of 150 "yea" votes.

However, statehood proponents suffered a setback that same year when the House amended a new 1993 rule giving the resident commissioner from Puerto Rico and the delegates from the District, American Samoa, Guam, and the Virgin Islands the right to vote on the House floor when the House was considering bills for amendment in the Committee of the Whole, a parliamentary concept designed to speed legislative action. The amended rule provided that, if the delegates' votes made the difference between passage or rejection of a specific bill, an automatic revote would occur in which the delegates could not participate.

The revised rule was adopted to answer charges that delegate voting was unconstitutional and to address the concerns of Republican members. The GOP gain of ten House seats in the 1992 elections could have been halved by giving voting rights to the five delegates, all Democrats.

More bad news for the District surfaced in 1995, when the Republicans took control of both houses of Congress for the first time in forty years. A rule change adopted by the House on Jan. 4, the first day of the new Congress, abolished the chamber's District of Columbia Committee, transferring its jurisdiction to the House Government Reform and Oversight Committee. The House Republicans also abolished the delegates' floor-voting privileges.

View of the Capitol and surrounding congressional and federal buildings. Federal holdings amount to 43.3 percent of the District's land area. Congress votes funds each year to compensate the city for lost taxes and other costs of hosting the federal government.

The same year brought passage of legislation creating a five-member control board—formally called the District of Columbia Financial Responsibility and Management Assistance Authority—to restore order to the city's increasingly chaotic budgetary and financial affairs. The D.C. board was to lose all but oversight power after the city of Washington had posted four consecutive balanced budgets. Anthony A. Williams was appointed as the board's chief financial officer.

FEDERAL PAYMENT TO THE DISTRICT

A key point of contention between Congress and the District government long had concerned the amount of an annual federal appropriation to the city. Since 1878 Congress had voted money from the Treasury for various municipal purposes—to offset the loss of tax revenues the city could not levy on federal holdings. Those holdings amounted to 43.3 percent of the District's land area and hundreds of facilities. As the nation's capital, the city also attracted many other tax-exempt property owners, such as foreign embassies and offices of nonprofit organizations. Moreover, the value of taxable real property had been kept down by a congressional ban on tall buildings.

The federal contribution to the District was set initially in 1878 at one-half of the expenses of the local government. The proportion was cut to 40 percent in 1920. Four years later, Congress abandoned a fixed percentage and started appropriating whatever it chose each year. Since then several attempts to set payment formulas have failed in Congress. In 1965 President Johnson proposed permanent annual payments equal to the real estate, personal property, and business income taxes that the federal government would pay if holdings were taxable. That provision fell victim to the scuttling of a home rule bill. In 1969 President Nixon recommended that the federal payment be equal to 30 percent of the local taxes and the District's other general fund revenues. The Senate approved that proposal in 1970, but the House did not act on it. During the 1973 debate on home rule, the Senate attached a provision setting the federal payment at 40 percent of the local tax base but it, too, failed to become law.

The size, method of calculation, and restrictions on the federal payment became more of an issue in local politics after 1980 than previously. Beginning that year the District's appropriations included a prohibition on spending federal funds for abortion, except in cases of rape or incest or danger to the mother's life. Technically, Congress appropriates the entire budget of the District. All locally raised revenue is paid into the U.S. Treasury; it, together with the federal allocations, is given back to the District. Starting in 1985, abortion foes took advantage of that technicality to prohibit the spending of locally raised funds to provide abortions for indigent mothers. During the latter half of the 1980s the federal appropriation remained at the fiscal 1985 level of $435 million. In early 1991 Congress gave the District an added $100 million in emergency funds. Later in 1991, Congress approved legislation to peg the annual federal payment to a new formula—an amount equal to 24 percent of local revenues through fiscal 1995.

An entirely new approach to federal support of the city of

Washington was adopted in 1997. The key provision in that year's District of Columbia appropriations bill shifted several costly municipal services—including the pension plan for city employees and the prison and court systems—to the federal government. In return, the city was to forgo its annual payment from the federal government, much of which was designed to offset property-tax income lost to tax-exempt real estate.

The bill also stripped Barry, who had returned as mayor in 1995, of much of his power, leaving him in control of only four minor city departments. Many members of Congress blamed Barry for the District's shaky financial condition. Though reduced virtually to a figurehead, Barry remained in place as Washington's chief executive. The unmistakable—if unspoken—message from Capitol Hill was that the mayor's office would not regain its lost authority while Barry was still there.

NEW MAYOR

Given this background, Washington residents were startled by the announcement in February 1998 that the city government had recorded a $186 million budget surplus for the fiscal year ending the previous September. Many local observers credited the unexpected turnaround to work on the financial control board by Williams.

In May 1998 Barry announced that he would not run for a fifth term. Williams entered the mayoral race and easily won the Democratic nomination and the general election. In doing so, he carried every ward in the city, something Barry had never been able to accomplish.

Victory at the polls was not Williams's sole reward. With the support of the financial control board, Congress passed the District of Columbia Management Restoration Act on March 5, 1999, which repealed the 1997 law that had stripped Mayor Barry of much of his powers. The bill restored the management authority over the entire D.C. government to the mayor's office.

Though he quickly established cordial relations with members of Congress who had been critical of Barry, Williams also came under fire during his early months in office. Some members, especially Republicans, faulted his lukewarm support for a tax-reduction package drawn up by the city council. Also, many city residents voiced opposition to his proposal to move the University of the District of Columbia (UDC) from its existing site in a predominantly white section of Northwest Washington to a less affluent neighborhood in the city's largely black Southeast quadrant. Williams later abandoned the relocation plan and apologized to UDC students and faculty at a public meeting on campus.

The new mayor's reputation for personal rectitude also suffered when it was disclosed that as a candidate in 1998 he had failed to report in a timely fashion two consulting jobs for which he was paid $40,000. The D.C. Office of Campaign Finance fined Williams $1,000 for the oversight. The mayor said he was "wrong" not to have reported the income in question and that he would pay the penalty out of his own finances.

Despite these missteps, Williams's popularity remained relatively high—in part because of his willingness to modify or back down from unpopular decisions. Moreover, local political observers noted that a second consecutive District budget surplus—again, credited by many analysts to Williams's work on the financial control board—had enabled the city council to draft its wide-ranging tax-cut plan in the first place. Lower taxes, in turn, raised Washingtonians' hopes of making the city a more attractive destination for both businesses and families.

NOTES

1. Alexander Hamilton, James Madison, and John Jay, *The Federalist Papers*, with an introduction by Clinton Rossiter (New York: New American Library, 1961), 272.

2. Laurence F. Schmeckebier, *The District of Columbia: Its Government and Administration* (Baltimore: Johns Hopkins University Press, 1928), 35–36.

3. Wolcott and Abigail Adams are quoted in *The WPA Guide to Washington D.C.* (New York: Pantheon Books, 1983, a condensed version of *Washington: City and Capitol*, written and compiled by the Federal Writers Project of the Works Progress Administration (Washington, D.C.: Government Printing Office, 1937), 30.

4. Martha Derthick, *City Politics in Washington, D.C.* (Cambridge, Mass.: Harvard University Press, 1962), 38.

5. Ibid., 39.

6. *Public Papers of the Presidents of the United States, Richard Nixon, 1969* (Washington, D.C.: Government Printing Office, 1971), 326.

7. Derthick, *City Politics in Washington, D.C.*, 73.

SELECTED BIBLIOGRAPHY

Alsop, Stewart. *The Center, People and Power in Political Washington.* New York: Harper and Row, 1968.

Bowling, Kenneth R. *The Creation of Washington, D.C.: The Idea and Location of the American Capital.* Fairfax, Va.: George Mason University Press, 1991.

Bryan, Wilhelmus B. *A History of the National Capital.* 2 vols. New York: Macmillan, 1914–1916.

Derthick, Martha. *City Politics in Washington, D.C.* Cambridge, Mass.: Harvard University Press, 1962. (Prepared for Joint Center for Urban Studies, Massachusetts Institute of Technology and Harvard University.)

Green, Constance M. *The Secret City: A History of Race Relations in the Nation's Capital.* Princeton, N.J.: Princeton University Press, 1967.

———. *Washington.* 2 vols. Princeton, N.J.: Princeton University Press, 1963.

Hanson, Royce, and Bernard H. Ross. *Governing the District of Columbia: An Introduction.* Washington, D.C.: Washington Center for Metropolitan Studies, 1971.

Kennon, Donald R., and Richard Striner. *Washington Past and Present: A Guide to the Nations Capital.* 2nd ed. Washington, D.C.: U.S. Capitol Historical Society, 1983.

Porter, J. A. *City of Washington: Its Origin and Administration.* New York: Johnson Reprint, 1973.

Ross, Bernard H. *The Delegate and the District Building: The Potential for Conflict and Cooperation.* Washington, D.C.: Washington Center for Metropolitan Studies, 1971.

Schmeckebier, Laurence F. *The District of Columbia: Its Government and Administration.* Baltimore: Johns Hopkins University Press, 1928.

Tindall, William. *Standard History of the City of Washington from a Study of the Original Sources.* Knoxville, Tenn.: H. W. Crew, 1914.

Young, James. *The Washington Community, 1800–1828.* New York: Columbia University Press, 1966.

CHAPTER 13

Miscellaneous Powers

THE CONSTITUTION GRANTS Congress a number of powers not discussed separately in this volume. Among these are the power to create federal courts below the level of the Supreme Court, to establish uniform rules for the naturalization of citizens, to admit new states into the Union, to establish and maintain a postal system, and to make bankruptcy and patent laws.[1]

The Federal Courts

Congress was given a primary role in the establishment of the federal judiciary. The Constitution states in Article III, Section 1: "The judicial Power of the United States shall be vested in one supreme Court, and in such inferior Courts as the Congress may from time to time ordain and establish." Thus, aside from the Supreme Court, which was established by the Constitution itself, the existence and structure of any lower federal courts were left entirely to the discretion of Congress.

Congress exercised that discretion early in its history. As one of its first acts, it passed the Judiciary Act of 1789, establishing the Supreme Court, three circuit courts of appeals, and thirteen district courts. Thereafter, as the nation grew and the federal judiciary's workload increased, Congress has established additional circuit and district courts.

Legislative authority over the federal courts does not end there. From time to time Congress has made institutional and jurisdictional changes in the federal court system, and on occasion it has reversed specific Supreme Court decisions.

The Senate wields considerable influence in the selection of federal judges, who must win Senate confirmation after being nominated by the president. Both houses share impeachment power, which has been used most often to remove federal judges. (*See Chapter 7, The Senate's Confirmation Power; Chapter 9, Impeachment Power.*)

The Constitution bars Congress from reducing the salaries of federal judges, including Supreme Court justices, but the legislators have absolute control over increases in wages and over appropriations for the federal court system. On one occasion Congress exercised its power of the purse to show its displeasure with Supreme Court rulings. In 1964 legislation authorizing federal pay increases, Supreme Court justices were given $3,000 less than the increase for members of Congress and other top-level federal employees. There was little doubt in anyone's mind that the action was the result of congressional pique over recent Court decisions on such issues as obscenity, school prayer, desegregation, and loyalty-security programs.

Even when Congress does not take deliberate aim at judges, political pressures sometimes lead it to affect the judicial branch in an indirect manner. For much of the 1990s, for example, federal judges received no increase in pay because their salaries were linked in the appropriations process to those of lawmakers, who repeatedly froze their own pay for political reasons. In addition, when the Senate and the White House are controlled by opposing political parties (as has usually been the case in recent decades), senators often balk at approving judicial nominees. This practice sometimes leaves many judgeships vacant, creating a backlog in the courts.

The judicial branch, for its part, is not without influence over Congress—notably through the power of judicial review. Under this power the Supreme Court can nullify an act of Congress if it finds that the law violates the Constitution. (*See Chapter 22, The Supreme Court.*)

JUDGESHIPS

Politics historically has played an important role in the creation of judgeships. In 1801, for example, the Federalist-dominated Seventh Congress created additional circuit judgeships to be filled by a Federalist president. However, the new posts were abolished the following year, when the Jeffersonians came to power in the midterm elections.

Because federal judges are lifelong appointees who hold their offices during good behavior, the power of Congress to abolish judgeships is limited: In creating a new judgeship, Congress can specify that once it becomes vacant, it cannot be filled. The Constitution does not specify how many federal judgeships must be created, or even how many justices must sit on the Supreme Court. Indeed, the number of Supreme Court justices fluctuated in the first century of the nation's history, illustrating the power of Congress over the judicial branch. The Supreme Court was made up of six justices under the Judiciary Act of 1789. Subsequently, Congress changed the size of the Court a number of times: five justices in 1801–02; six in 1802–07; seven in 1807–37; nine in 1837–63; ten in 1863–66; seven in 1866–69; and nine since passage of the Judiciary Act of 1869.

Although the membership of the Supreme Court for more than a century has remained at nine, proposals to change the number of justices have been put forward periodically. The most serious proposal in the twentieth century came not from

Congress but from the White House. In 1937 President Franklin D. Roosevelt set off a public uproar by calling on Congress to increase the Court's membership by adding as many as six justices. The Court had ruled unconstitutional many of Roosevelt's New Deal programs, and critics claimed the president wanted to "pack it" with justices who would support his views. The plan eventually died in the Senate, in part because the Supreme Court became more supportive of New Deal programs. In the 1938 elections Roosevelt tried unsuccessfully to "purge" Democratic members of Congress who opposed the plan.

JURISDICTION

The Supreme Court has limited original jurisdiction, which is the power to hear a case argued for the first time. Article III, Section 2, of the Constitution vested in the Supreme Court original jurisdiction primarily over suits between two states, which may involve such issues as water rights, offshore lands, or disputed boundaries. But the same section of the Constitution granted the Court "judicial power" over all cases arising under the Constitution, federal laws, and treaties. This jurisdiction, however, was appellate—that is, it was limited to review of decisions from lower courts and was subject to "such exceptions and . . . regulations as Congress shall make." Most of the High Court's present jurisdiction is defined by the Judiciary Act of 1925, largely drafted by the Court itself under Chief Justice William Howard Taft.

The 1925 act made the exercise of the Court's appellate jurisdiction largely discretionary, giving the justices more leeway to refuse to review cases. Except for certain limited types of cases in which the Court is still "obligated" to take appeals, the Court is allowed to decide whether lower-court decisions present questions or conflicts of such importance, or are of such a constitutional nature, as to warrant the Supreme Court's consideration.

Only once has Congress curtailed the Supreme Court's jurisdiction as a way of stopping the Court from issuing a decision. In 1868 lawmakers repealed the Court's power to review federal court denials of writs of habeas corpus. This extraordinary action was taken by a Congress dominated by Radical Republicans who wanted to prohibit the Court from reviewing the constitutionality of the Reconstruction Acts of 1867.

Since then Congress has considered legislation to repeal the Court's authority to review specific subjects, such as internal security programs, certain criminal procedures, school desegregation and school prayer, and state laws forbidding abortions. None of these jurisdictional repeal attempts had succeeded by the end of the twentieth century. In recent years, lawmakers have also failed to place restrictions on judges in cases relating to state laws adopted by referendums and prison overcrowding.

REVERSALS

Of all the methods of influencing the Supreme Court, Congress has had most success in reversing individual Court rulings, either through passage of legislation or adoption of constitutional amendments. Four of the twenty-seven amendments to the Constitution were adopted specifically to overrule the Supreme Court's interpretation of that document. The amendments reversed rulings on the ability of citizens of one state to bring suit against another state (Eleventh Amendment); the application of the Bill of Rights to the states, accomplished over many years as a result of numerous Supreme Court decisions (Fourteenth Amendment); the income tax (Sixteenth Amendment); and the eighteen-year-old vote (Twenty-sixth Amendment).

The most frequently used method of reversing the Supreme Court is for Congress to repass a statute after modifying it to meet the Court's objections. This kind of reversal through simple legislation is easily accomplished if the Court has interpreted a statute contrary to the construction intended by Congress. The House and Senate then may pass new legislation clearly setting forth their intention. In many cases of this type the Court will suggest the course the legislation should take to achieve its original purpose or simply indicate that Congress needs to be more explicit.

In 1998, for example, Congress passed a bill allowing credit unions to continue expanding their membership bases, months after the Supreme Court ruled that credit unions lacked the legal authority to accept members and groups that did not have a common bond. But despite repeated efforts throughout the 1990s, congressional conservatives failed to win a majority for a constitutional amendment barring physical desecration of the U.S. flag, which could have nullified a pair of Supreme Court rulings in 1989 and 1990 protecting flag desecration as a form of free speech.

Citizenship and Naturalization

Although it refers to "citizens" in several instances, nowhere does the main body of the Constitution define who is a citizen. The prevailing assumption was that a citizen was a person who was born in the country and who remained under its jurisdiction and protection. This definition, which was followed in England and known as *jus soli*, was in contrast to the common practice of *jus sanguines* followed in the rest of Europe, where citizenship was determined by the nationality of the parents.

This definition was formalized by the Fourteenth Amendment, ratified in 1868 after the end of the Civil War. Its first sentence states: "All persons born or naturalized in the United States and subject to the jurisdiction thereof, are citizens of the United States and of the State wherein they reside."

Designed primarily to confer citizenship on blacks, the Fourteenth Amendment made the concept of *jus soli* the law of the land. This was affirmed and further defined in the case of *United States v. Wong Kim Ark* when the Supreme Court in 1898 declared that—under the Fourteenth Amendment—children born in the United States to resident alien parents were citizens even if their parents were barred from becoming citizens themselves.

Secretary of State Madeleine Albright, left, joins new citizens in reciting the Pledge of Allegiance during a naturalization ceremony at the State Department in 1998. To qualify for naturalization, an alien must have been a resident of the United States for five years and be of good moral character.

Congress may establish whatever condition it deems necessary for citizenship through naturalization. "Naturalization is a privilege, to be given, qualified, or withheld as Congress may determine and which the alien may claim as of right only upon compliance with the terms which Congress imposes," the Supreme Court said in 1931. *(United States v. Macintosh)* *(See box, Absolute Authority over Aliens, p. 408.)*

The Court has held that Congress may exclude an entire class or race of people from eligibility for citizenship and may expel aliens from the country. Upholding a statute expelling Chinese laborers from the country if they did not obtain a residence certificate within a specified time, the Court wrote in 1893 *(Fong Yue Ting v. United States)*:

The right of a nation to expel or deport foreigners, who have not been naturalized or taken any steps towards becoming citizens . . . is as absolute and unqualified as the right to prohibit and prevent their entrance into the country. . . . The power to exclude or expel aliens, being a power affecting international relations, is vested in the political departments of the government, and it is to be regulated by treaty or by act of Congress, and to be executed by the executive authority according to the regulations so established.

EXCLUSIONS

After ratification of the Fourteenth Amendment, Congress enacted laws limiting naturalized citizenship to whites and to blacks of African descent. Citizenship was extended to the residents of some, but not all, of the U.S. territories. The residents of Hawaii became citizens in 1900, those of Puerto Rico in 1917, and those of the Virgin Islands in 1927. But the residents of the Philippines were denied citizenship throughout the period the United States held the islands as a trust territory. Other Asians did not fare any better in winning citizenship through naturalization. The final barriers to their naturalization were not removed until passage in 1952 of the Immigration and Nationality Act, which barred the use of race as a reason for denying citizenship.

Congress has set other conditions for naturalization that have excluded anarchists, members of the U.S. Communist Party, and others who advocate the violent overthrow of the government. To qualify for naturalization, an alien must have been a resident of the country for five years and be of good moral character. This latter phrase has been applied at various times to

ABSOLUTE AUTHORITY OVER ALIENS

The congressional power over aliens is absolute and derives from the fact that the United States is a sovereign nation. That power was recognized by the Supreme Court in 1889 when it upheld an act of Congress barring entry of Chinese aliens into the country.

That the government of the United States through the action of the legislative department, can exclude aliens from its territory is a proposition which we do not think open to controversy. Jurisdiction over its own territory to that extent is an incident of every independent nation. It is a part of its independence. If it could not exclude aliens, it would be to that extent subject to the control of another power.... The United States, in their relation to foreign countries and their subjects or citizens, are one nation, invested with powers which belong to independent nations, the exercise of which can be invoked for the maintenance of its absolute independence and security throughout its entire territory,

the Court wrote in *Chae Chan Ping v. United States* (1889).

Under this authority Congress has barred from entry convicts, prostitutes, epileptics, anarchists, and professional beggars. It has excluded people because of their race, and it has established national origin quotas.

This absolute authority also empowers Congress to regulate to a large extent the conduct of aliens in the country and to provide that aliens convicted of certain crimes may be deported.

The Supreme Court has held that aliens involved in deportation proceedings are entitled to certain constitutional rights, including protections against self-incrimination, unreasonable searches and seizures, cruel and unusual punishment, *ex post facto* laws and bills of attainder, and the rights to bail and procedural due process. *(Kimm v. Rosenberg,* 1960; *Abel v. United States,* 1960; *Marcello v. Bonds,* 1955; *Carlson v. Landon,* 1952; *Wong Yang Sung v. McGrath,* 1950)

But the Court upheld a provision of the 1950 Internal Security Act that authorized the attorney general to keep in jail without bail aliens who were members of the Communist Party pending a decision on whether they would be deported. *(Carlson v. Landon,* 1952)

And although the Court has ruled that the Fourteenth Amendment protects aliens as well as citizens from discrimination, the Court has upheld federal laws that treat aliens and citizens differently.

Because the Constitution gives Congress absolute authority over admission and naturalization, the Court has required Congress only to present some rational basis for making a distinction between citizen and alien or between some aliens and other aliens. *(Mathews v. Diaz,* 1976)

exclude drunks, adulterers, polygamists, gamblers, convicted felons, and homosexuals.

LOSS OF CITIZENSHIP

As early as 1824 the Supreme Court, speaking through Chief Justice John Marshall, declared that there was no difference between a naturalized citizen and one who was native-born. A naturalized citizen, wrote Marshall, "becomes a member of the society, possessing all rights of the native citizen, and standing, in the view of the Constitution, on the footing of a native. The Constitution does not authorize Congress to enlarge or abridge those rights. The simple power of the national Legislature is to prescribe a uniform rule of naturalization, and the exercise of its power exhausts it, so far as respects the individual." *(Osborn v. Bank of the United States)*

With one major exception this statement remains true. Naturalized citizens do enjoy the same rights, privileges, and responsibilities as do native-born citizens. The exception is that naturalized citizens may be denaturalized.

The Supreme Court has repeatedly held that a naturalized citizen may lose citizenship if it was obtained fraudulently. The Court in 1981, for example, held that a Russian native who concealed from immigration and naturalization officials the fact that he had served as a concentration camp guard in World War II must be stripped of his U.S. citizenship, acquired by naturalization in 1970. Concealment of his wartime activities made his admission to the United States under the Displaced Persons Act unlawful and so rendered his subsequent naturalization invalid. *(Fedorenko v. United States)*

Naturalization also may be lost if it is obtained in bad faith. A prime example is the case of *Luria v. United States,* in which the Court in 1913 upheld the denaturalization of a man who apparently never intended to become a permanent resident of the United States at the time he was naturalized. The decision upheld an act of Congress that made residence in a foreign country within five years of naturalization prima facie evidence of bad faith.

EXPATRIATION

The question whether Congress may revoke the citizenship of any citizen, whether naturalized or native-born, has troubled the Supreme Court for a number of years, and it has not yet offered a conclusive answer.

That a citizen may voluntarily expatriate himself has never been questioned. The Court also has held that Congress may stipulate certain acts, the voluntary performance of which would be the equivalent of voluntary expatriation. In 1915 the Court upheld a provision of the Citizenship Act of 1907 providing that any female citizen who married an alien surrendered her citizenship in the United States. *(MacKenzie v. Hare)* That provision was repealed in 1922, but in 1950 the Court ruled that a woman who had voluntarily sworn allegiance to Italy in order to marry an Italian citizen had in essence forsworn her allegiance to the United States and effectively renounced her U.S. citizenship. *(Savorgnan v. United States)*

The issue of whether Congress can revoke American citizenship arose repeatedly under the Immigration and Nationality Act of 1952, which contained a long list of circumstances under which an American would lose citizenship. These included voting in a foreign election, being convicted and discharged from the armed services for desertion during wartime, and leaving or remaining outside the country to avoid military service. In 1958 the Supreme Court upheld the provision revoking citizenship of a person who voted in a foreign election on the ground that the revocation was a necessary and proper means for Congress to exercise its power over foreign affairs. On the same day a divided Court invalidated the provision of the immigration law that revoked the citizenship of persons convicted and discharged from the armed services for desertion. Four members of the majority contended that Congress had no power to revoke citizenship. *(Perez v. Brownell; Trop v. Dulles)*

Five years later, in 1963, the Court struck down the provisions of the immigration act that revoked the citizenship of anyone who left or remained outside the country in order to evade military service. The Court held that Congress had not afforded persons in such circumstances the procedural safeguards required by the Fifth and Sixth Amendments; the Court thus avoided choosing between the powers of Congress and the rights of citizenship. *(Kennedy v. Mendoza-Martinez)*

In 1967 the Supreme Court again divided over the question of Congress's power to revoke citizenship. Five justices argued that Congress did not have that power. "In our country the people are sovereign, and the government cannot sever its relationship to the people by taking away their citizenship," the majority said.

The four justices in disagreement insisted there was nothing in the citizenship clause of the Fourteenth Amendment that denied Congress the power to revoke citizenship under certain conditions. "The construction now placed on the Citizenship Clause rests, in the last analysis, simply on the Court's *ipse dixit*, evincing little more, it is quite apparent, than the present majority's own distaste for the expatriation power," the minority said. *(Afroyim v. Rusk)*

Because of the narrow vote, this decision was not considered definitive, and a subsequent case decided in 1971 only further clouded the picture. *(Rogers v. Bellei)* More than two hundred years after the birth of the nation, the question of congressional power to expatriate citizens is still undecided.

Statehood

Article IV, Section 3, of the Constitution gives Congress the power to admit new states to the Union so long as it does not form a new state by dividing an existing state or by joining parts or all of two or more states without their consent. It also authorizes Congress "to dispose of and make all needful Rules and Regulations respecting the Territory or other Property belonging to the United States."

Five states were formed from land that was originally part of the first thirteen states. In the first four cases—Vermont, Maine, Kentucky, and Tennessee—the ceding states agreed to the division. The fifth State, West Virginia, was formed when the western counties of Virginia that wanted to remain in the Union split away from the rest of the state, which had joined the Confederacy. A special legislature comprised of people from the western counties was convened to give its approval to the split, but Virginia did not formally agree until after the Civil War ended. Texas was an independent nation before its admission to the Union in 1845, and California was carved from a region ceded by Mexico in 1848. The remaining thirty states were all territories before being granted statehood.

Under procedures commonly used, the people of a territory submitted a petition asking for admission as a state. Congress then authorized a convention for the territory to draft a constitution. The constitution was submitted to Congress and the president for approval. Once it had been approved, Congress passed a joint resolution granting statehood, and the president issued a proclamation announcing the admission of a new state into the Union.[2]

Although Congress generally has the power to repeal any statute it passes, it cannot repeal statehood. The Supreme Court has ruled that once a state has joined the Union, its admission cannot be revoked.

SLAVERY AND POLITICS

When the Missouri Territory applied for statehood in 1819, slavery emerged as a serious political and constitutional factor. At the time there were eleven free states and eleven slave states. Northerners in the House of Representatives pushed through an amendment to the statehood resolution that would have prohibited slavery in the new state even though many Missourians were slaveholders. The Senate, dominated by southerners, objected to the amendment, claiming that Congress had no constitutional right to impose such a condition on a new state. The controversy was not resolved until Maine applied for statehood the following year. The Missouri Compromise of 1820 provided for the entry of Maine as a free state and Missouri as a slave state, which maintained the numerical balance between North and South.

With the formal acquisition of Texas in 1846 and the prospect of obtaining more land from Mexico, extension of slavery again became an issue. The controversy over the western lands was settled in 1850 when Congress produced a compromise under which California would enter the Union as a free state and the citizens of the newly organized Utah and New Mexico territories would decide in the future on slavery there.

Further controversy over slavery erupted in 1854 when Congress passed the Kansas-Nebraska Act, which repealed the Missouri Compromise of 1820 and permitted settlers in the Kansas

Some of the greatest debates in Congress have been on statehood questions. Here Henry Clay argues for his Compromise of 1850, which allowed the admission of California into the Union as a free state.

and Nebraska territories to decide in the future whether they wanted slavery there. Conflict over slavery in Kansas led to violence in the territories—and in Congress. During debate on the Kansas statehood bill in 1856, a South Carolina representative used a cane to severely beat Sen. Charles Sumner of Massachusetts at his desk in the Senate chamber. Badly injured, Sumner did not resume his Senate seat until 1859.

STATEHOOD ACTION SINCE THE 1950S

No state has been admitted to the Union since Alaska and Hawaii became states in the 1950s. Both had to overcome obstacles that led to lengthy delays. Southern lawmakers were unwilling to allow four new seats in the Senate from areas unsympathetic to racial segregation. Democrats opposed Hawaii statehood because the territory traditionally voted Republican.

GOP lawmakers opposed Alaska statehood because the territory traditionally voted Democratic. The legislative logjam was finally broken, and Alaska became the forty-ninth state in 1958, followed by Hawaii as the fiftieth state in 1959.

The people of Puerto Rico have been debating about their relationship with the United States almost from the time Congress made the island a commonwealth in 1952. But a clear majority of islanders have never demonstrated that they want to exchange their commonwealth status for statehood or independence.

In 1988 the island's commonwealth and statehood parties agreed to put the status issue to a vote: they wanted Congress to authorize the referendum so that the federal government would be bound by the result. But the referendum legislation died in Congress in 1990, partly because of the absence of a clear majority on either side of the status question. In 1998 the House narrowly passed legislation authorizing the referendum, but the Senate declined to take it up, saying there was not enough time left in the session to adequately address the matter.

Statehood proposals for the District of Columbia have been clouded not only by politics and state interests but also by the intent of the Constitution. Crafters of the Constitution did not want to place the capital of the nation in any state, so the District was carved out of portions of Virginia and Maryland.

A proposed constitutional amendment to give the District of Columbia voting representation in Congress died in 1985; only sixteen state legislatures had ratified that proposal within the seven-year period specified by Congress. The District since 1971 has had a delegate in the House of Representatives who represents the city's interests but cannot vote on the floor.

Following a tradition dating back to 1796, the District of Columbia in 1996 elected a "shadow" senator and a "shadow" representative to lobby for statehood on Capitol Hill. Six territories previously had sent shadow senators to Congress prior to their admission as states: Tennessee, Michigan, California, Minnesota, Oregon, and Alaska. Although not officially members of Congress, these shadow members were often given some privileges, including in one instance (Tennessee) access to the Senate floor. The Senate required that Tennessee and Alaska hold new senatorial elections after their admission to the Union; reelection was not required for shadow senators from the other four states. (See "The District of Columbia," p. 355.)

Other Powers

Other powers granted to Congress by the Constitution include authority to establish a postal system; make bankruptcy, patent, and copyright laws; set standard weights and measures; and punish counterfeiting.

Congress's power over weights and measures has never been seriously challenged, and its power to establish penalties for counterfeiting has proved superfluous because it also may punish counterfeiting under its power to regulate currency. Few restrictions have been placed on Congress's exercise of the other powers. (See box, Control of the Nation's Currency, p. 412.)

BANKRUPTCY

The power to make "uniform laws on the subject of bankruptcies throughout the United States" was exercised only infrequently in the 1800s. Federal laws were enacted in 1800, 1841, and 1867 to meet specific economic crises, but each survived public criticism and political pressure only a few years and then was repealed. In the intervals between the federal laws, state bankruptcy laws were controlling. It was not until 1898 that Congress enacted a general bankruptcy law. That measure, which underwent major amendment in 1938 and 1978, remained in effect as of mid-1999.

Congress generally has interpreted its bankruptcy powers broadly, extending bankruptcy coverage to almost every class of person and corporation, and it has enacted laws to rehabilitate the debtor as well as to provide appropriate relief to creditors. The issue became prominent in the late 1990s, as Congress debated tightening consumer bankruptcy laws to rein in a record number of bankruptcy filings.

PATENTS AND COPYRIGHTS

Congressional authority over patents and copyrights comes from Article I, Section 8, clause 8, of the Constitution, which empowers Congress "to promote the Progress of Science and useful Arts, by securing for limited Times to Authors and Inventors the exclusive Right to their respective Writings and Discoveries."

In fashioning copyright and patent laws, Congress must balance two interests. As described by the Library of Congress, these are "the interest of the public in being protected against monopolies and in having ready access and use of new items versus the interest of the country, as a whole, in encouraging invention by rewarding creative persons for their innovations."[3]

There have been no serious challenges to the right of Congress to set standards and conditions for the granting of patents and copyrights within the constitutional limits. But numerous Supreme Court cases have turned on the question of whether a particular invention meets the standards. This in large measure has made the Supreme Court and not Congress the final judge of what those standards are.

In one case the Court established three tests that an item must pass to be patentable: "Innovation, advancement, and things which add to the sum of useful knowledge are inherent requisites in a patent system which by constitutional command must 'promote the Progress of . . . useful Arts.' This is the *standard* expressed in the Constitution and it may not be ignored." (*Graham v. John Deere Co.*, 1966)

POSTAL POWER

Clause 7 of Article I, Section 8, gives Congress the power "to establish Post Offices and post Roads." Whether this meant that Congress had the power actually to construct post offices and post roads or simply to designate those that would be used as postal facilities was settled in the 1879 *Trademark Cases* when the Supreme Court upheld the government's appropriation of land on which to build a post office. (*United States v. Steffens*)

The postal power has been interpreted to include the authority to ensure the speedy delivery and protection of the mail. (*Ex parte Jackson*, 1878) It was on this principle that the federal government was granted an injunction against leaders of the 1894 Pullman strike that halted mail delivery along with the trains. At the same time, federal troops were sent to Illinois to quell the violence that had erupted. Eugene V. Debs and other labor leaders were convicted of contempt of court for violating the injunction.

CONTROL OF THE NATION'S CURRENCY

The Constitution in Article II, Section 8, gave Congress express power to "coin Money, regulate the Value thereof, and of foreign Coin, and fix the Standard of Weights and Measures." This power has been construed, with one brief but significant exception, to give Congress complete control over the nation's currency.

A national currency did not exist until the Civil War. Then, in 1862 and 1863, Congress passed the legal tender acts, which authorized the printing of paper money or "greenbacks" and made them legal tender for the payment of debts. In 1869 the Supreme Court upheld a federal tax that was intended to drive state bank notes out of circulation and leave a single uniform national currency. (*Veazie Bank v. Fenno*)

In 1870, however, the Court ruled in the *First Legal Tender Case* that Congress had exceeded its authority by making paper money legal tender for the payment of debts incurred before the passage of the laws. (*Hepburn v. Griswold*) The outcry from debtors and the potential economic repercussions from this decision were so great that in the *Second Legal Tender Cases* of 1871 the Court—with two new members—reconsidered and overturned its earlier decision, thus upholding Congress's authority to establish paper money as a legal currency. (*Knox v. Lee, Parker v. Davis*)

Despite its ruling in the *Second Legal Tender Cases,* the Supreme Court in 1872 reaffirmed its 1869 decision that creditors holding contracts specifically calling for payment in gold did not have to accept paper money in payment. As a result, more and more creditors insisted on gold clauses, and eventually they were contained in almost every private contract.

DEVALUATION

In 1933, to counter gold hoarding and exporting, as well as speculation in foreign exchanges, Congress required all holders to surrender their gold and gold certificates to the Treasury in return for an equivalent amount of paper currency. In an effort to raise prices, Congress next devalued the dollar by lowering its value to one thirty-fifth of an ounce of gold.

Congress in a third act then nullified all gold clauses in contracts. The clauses could not be enforced because gold was no longer in circulation, and the statute also prohibited creditors from requiring a higher payment in the devalued currency to make up the value of the gold stipulated in the contract. The nullification

statute was challenged on a number of grounds, but in a series of rulings known as the *Gold Clause Cases,* the Supreme Court in 1935 upheld the absolute power of Congress to regulate the value of currency. (*Norman v. Baltimore & Ohio Railroad Co., United States v. Bankers Trust Co.; Nortz v. United States; Perry v. United States; The Gold Clause Cases*)[1]

The value of the dollar remained fixed at the 1933 level until December 1971, when an international monetary crisis forced President Richard Nixon to devalue the dollar as part of a general realignment of many national currencies. The new exchange rates took effect immediately, even before Congress officially changed the gold value of the dollar. Lawmakers approved a 10 percent devaluation early in their 1972 session, setting the new par value of the dollar at one thirty-eighth of an ounce of gold. As international financial difficulties continued to grow, Congress authorized a further 10 percent devaluation in 1973.

The link between gold and the dollar finally was severed in 1976, when Congress approved changes in the international monetary system that eliminated gold as the standard of international value and permitted currency exchange rates to "float" according to market forces.

DOLLARS AND CENTS

Congress also exercises its control over the currency in more direct ways. In 1985, for example, it authorized the minting of four gold coins in various denominations; the measure gave Americans their first chance to buy new noncommemorative gold coins in more than half a century.

At the other end of the scale, legislation approved in 1974 permitted the secretary of the Treasury to lower the amount of copper contained in the penny whenever the price of copper threatened to make the penny more valuable for its copper content than for its use as a coin. That bill was inspired by rumors of a potential penny shortage as the price of copper climbed. In the 1990s, lawmakers briefly considered replacing the one-dollar bill with a coin but took no action.

1. Joan Biskupic and Elder Witt, *Congressional Quarterly's Guide to the U.S. Supreme Court,* 3rd ed. (Washington, D.C.: Congressional Quarterly, 1997), 132–133.

The Supreme Court upheld the convictions and the use of federal troops in 1895, declaring that the "strong arm of the national Government may be put forth to brush away all obstructions to the freedom of interstate commerce or the transportation of the mails." (*In re Debs*)

The postal power also has been interpreted to allow Congress to bar items from the mails that it deems might defraud the public or injure its morals. The first such case was *Ex parte Jackson*, in which the Supreme Court sustained congressional action barring from the mails certain circulars relating to lotteries.

Congress frequently has invoked its postal power to aid it in

the exercise of its other express powers. In 1910, for example, the Court held that correspondence schools were in interstate commerce, and therefore susceptible to federal regulation, because of their reliance on the mails. (*International Textbook Co. v. Pigg*) In 1938 the Court upheld provisions of the Public Utility Holding Company Act requiring gas and electric utilities to register with the Securities and Exchange Commission, partially on the ground that such holding companies conducted a large and continuous portion of their business through the mails. (*Electric Bond & Share Co. v. Securities and Exchange Commission*)

NOTES

1. This chapter is drawn chiefly from Joan Biskupic and Elder Witt, *Congressional Quarterly's Guide to the Supreme Court,* 3rd ed. (Washington, D.C.: Congressional Quarterly, 1997).

2. General Accounting Office, *Experiences of Past Territories Can Assist Puerto Rico Status Deliberations,* March 7, 1980.

3. Congressional Research Service, Library of Congress, *The Constitution of the United States; Analysis and Interpretation* (Washington, D.C.: Government Printing Office, 1973), 316.

SELECTED BIBLIOGRAPHY

Bell, Roger. *Last Among Equals: Hawaii Statehood and American Politics.* Honolulu: University of Hawaii Press, 1984.

Biskupic, Joan, and Elder Witt. *Congressional Quarterly's Guide to the U.S. Supreme Court.* 3rd ed. Washington, D.C.: Congressional Quarterly, 1997.

Early, Stephen T. *Constitutional Courts of the United States.* Totowa, N.J.: Littlefield Adams, 1977.

Fallon, Richard, Daniel J. Meltzer, and David L. Shapiro. *Hart and Wechsler's The Federal Courts and the Federal System.* 4th ed. Westbury, N.Y.: Foundation Press, 1996.

Fisher, Louis. *American Constitutional Law.* 3rd ed. Durham, N.C.: Carolina Academic Press, 1999.

Pritchett, C. Herman. *The American Constitution.* 3rd ed. New York: McGraw-Hill, 1977.

Swindler, William F. *Court and Constitution in the Twentieth Century: The Old Legality, 1889–1932.* Indianapolis: Bobbs-Merrill, 1969.

———. *Court and Constitution in the Twentieth Century: The New Legality, 1932–1968.* Indianapolis: Bobbs-Merrill, 1970.

Swisher, Carl Brent. *American Constitutional Development.* 2nd ed. Cambridge, Mass.: Houghton Mifflin, 1954.

Congressional Procedures

CHAPTER 14

Party Leadership in Congress

The role of party leaders in Congress changed significantly in the closing two decades of the twentieth century. Leaders must still fulfill their traditional responsibility of managing the internal affairs of the institution, coordinating a legislative schedule, and maintaining personal relationships with colleagues anxious for advancement and sensitive to any perceived slight. But in addition modern party leaders must coordinate and implement massive national fund-raising campaigns for elections, serve as party spokespersons on controversial issues in the era of continuous television reporting and Internet communication, search constantly for popular programs and ideas to use in the next election campaign, and quickly respond to opposing party efforts to do the same things.

The traditional venues of a party leader—the floors of the House and Senate, the Capitol Hill cloakrooms and hideaways, and even the congressional press galleries—can seem isolated and limiting in the face of these ever-increasing demands and expectations that leaders seize control of an agenda for their party's future. With the two major parties in Congress closely divided in numbers, success or failure in these tasks can mean national prominence with the power to legislate as a majority, or relegation to a minority's role in opposition.

Political parties have also changed. Republicans in the House, moving decisively in the 1990s to majority status after decades in the minority, established centralized leadership around conservative values and issues. House Republicans were indebted to Rep. Newt Gingrich of Georgia, Speaker from 1995–1999, for devising a strategy that brought them to power. As Speaker, Gingrich attempted, with mixed results, to redefine the traditional institutional role of the House's presiding officer into a "transformational leader" of a revolution in American society, sometimes at the risk of his power base among House colleagues. Sen. Bob Dole, R-Kan., a more traditional institutional leader, became the first Senate majority leader to win a party's presidential nomination, although he had resigned his Senate seat before formally winning the position as GOP candidate. His successor as majority leader, Trent Lott, R-Miss., a longtime conservative activist when in the House, had first forced his way onto the Senate's leadership ladder to become majority whip and saw the Senate change rapidly with an influx of younger conservatives from the House who had long suffered, along with him, from the frustrations of minority status.

Democrats, who ruled the House continuously from 1955 to 1995 and the Senate for nearly as long (1955–1981; 1987–1995),

had greater difficulty in the 1990s developing a new identity when their longtime base of support in southern states collapsed as members retired, were defeated, or switched to the Republican Party. They were relegated to minority party status in the 1994 elections even as a so-called "New Democrat" from Arkansas, Bill Clinton, occupied the White House, took issues from the Republicans' agenda, and moved the party even further away from its New Deal roots. Democrats elevated younger, telegenic leaders such as Rep. Richard Gephardt, D-Mo., and Sen. Tom Daschle, D-S.D., who were skillful at adapting to the new demands of the information society and constant fundraising requirements. But the congressional Democratic Party had difficulty defining itself as an entity separate from its president, with whom many members had significant policy and personal disagreements. Democratic committee chairs, who had long been rivals of party leaders, lost their positions of power after Republicans took control of the House in the 1994 election, seemingly opening the door to a more centralized leadership style in coping with minority status.

But Democrats are notoriously difficult to lead under any circumstances, sometimes rebuffing ambitious policy activists such as former House Speaker Jim Wright, D-Texas, while criticizing the quieter, consensus styles of longtime Senate majority and minority leader Robert C. Byrd, D-W.Va., and former House Speaker Thomas S. Foley, D-Wash., for lack of dynamism. Democrats often seemed either unsure of goals or unwilling to allow party leaders to act on a common agenda. In complete minority status after the 1994 elections, with the need for political survival and even the search for relevance taking the place of traditional concerns over chairmanships and perks, Democrats had to develop new priorities, including exploiting mistakes and seizing opportunities presented by the new majority, a critical first step on the road back to power.

In the face of all these changes, party leaders in Congress in the twenty-first century will be judged by criteria far different from their predecessors. Some things remain immutable, however: power comes from majority status and leaders who can help their parties obtain, or retain, that status. Although Democrats controlled Congress for nearly forty years, they did not credit party leaders with that achievement. And even for successful campaign strategists such as Gingrich, the most powerful Speaker in nearly a century, the old political adage "what have you done for us lately?" still applies, as Gingrich had to face down an intraparty coup attempt from his leadership colleagues in the summer of 1997, only two years after leading his party to majority status. And then, in 1998, he was in effect deposed after the fall elections when because of his high visibility he was tarred with the failure of the GOP's strategy of attacking President Clinton's character.

Organizational structures evolved over 200 years have made House and Senate leaders at the end of the twentieth century a critical link between the two political parties and the nation's legislative business, between legislators and the president, and between Congress and the voters.

Since the last half of the nineteenth century, when the two-party system became firmly established on Capitol Hill, Congress has been organized on the basis of political party, with each party's congressional leaders seeking to facilitate enactment of their legislative program and to enhance their members' national image and electoral fortunes. Congressional party leaders of 1999, even though they seem so different from predecessors in personality and ideology, represent a long-standing institutional imperative. Congress cannot run itself.

In this partisan struggle the majority party has a distinct advantage, since it controls not only the top leadership posts in both the House and Senate but the legislative committees and subcommittees as well. Through its party leaders and its majorities on the various committees and subcommittees, the majority party is in a position to determine the legislation Congress will consider and when.

The minority party is not powerless, however. Depending on its numbers and coherence, the minority can influence the shape of legislation and the operation of Congress.

The extent to which party leadership can control its rank and file depends on a multitude of factors, among them the personalities and abilities of the individual leaders, the institutional authority at the leadership's disposal, party unity and strength, the willingness of the rank and file to be led, the extent of the president's involvement, and the mood in the country. In the past, particularly in the House, a few party leaders dominated the chamber. Gingrich achieved even greater influence using resources outside Congress, including tax-exempt entities, political action committees, skillful manipulation of media, policy ideas created to generate public appeal, and overarching theories of leadership.

A series of reforms inside and outside Congress changed it markedly from the seniority-driven, hierarchical institution of the 1950s, when House Speaker Sam Rayburn and Senate Majority Leader Lyndon B. Johnson, both Texas Democrats, exercised control over their chambers that was legendary in scope and effectiveness.

Widespread turnover brought into both chambers younger members, less bound by tradition, who objected to being closed out of the process. New rules and procedures made the institution more democratic. Power that resided largely with committee chairmen was parceled out to subcommittees, and the seniority system was weakened. At the same time, election law reforms, the advent of television campaigning, and the expanded role of political action committees in financing campaigns made individual members of Congress less dependent on the political party apparatus for electoral survival.

Leaders must lead in the direction the rank and file wants to go and to involve members in the decision-making process along the way. "In Mr. Rayburn's day," Wright once commented,

about all a majority leader or Speaker needed to do in order to get his program adopted was to deal effectively with perhaps twelve very senior committee chairmen. They, in turn, could be expected to influence their committees and their subcommittee chairmen whom they, in those days, appointed. . . . Well, now that situation is quite considerably different. There are, I think, 153 subcommittees [in Congress]. . . . We have relatively fewer rewards that we can bestow or withhold. I think that basically about all the leadership has nowadays is a hunting license to persuade—if we can.[1]

In more recent times, even as a Republican-controlled Congress has changed the style of operation of the institution, particularly in the House, leadership power is still the power to persuade others to follow.

Congressional Leadership Structure

Although the strategies of leadership have changed substantially over time, the basic leadership structure has remained the same. In the House the leadership consists of the Speaker, who is both the chamber's presiding officer and the majority party's overall leader; the majority and minority floor leaders, who are responsible for handling legislation once it reaches the floor; the assistant floor leaders or whips, who try to convince party members to follow the leadership's program and who serve as the communications nerve center for the parties; and several political party committees that develop strategy, assign members to legislative committees, assist the leadership in scheduling and tracking legislation, and provide campaign assistance to House and Senate candidates.

The Senate has no institutional or party official comparable in power and prestige to the Speaker. The Constitution designates the vice president of the United States as the president, or presiding officer, of the Senate and a president pro tempore to preside in his absence. Neither office, however, has been endowed with any commanding legislative or political authority, and neither has ever played much of a leadership role in the Senate. *(See box, The Senate's Presiding Officers, p. 456.)*

The remainder of the Senate leadership apparatus is similar in structure and function to that of the House.

Of all the party leadership positions in Congress, the only one that has functioned continuously since 1789 is that of Speaker—a post established by the Constitution. Although various members assumed the roles of floor leader and whip from time to time, the positions were not made official in the House until 1899, during a period when parties and partisanship were strong, both in Congress and throughout the country. Formal party leadership positions began to develop in the Senate in the early 1900s, but majority and minority leaders were not officially designated by the party caucuses until the 1920s.

Senate Majority Leader Trent Lott, R-Miss., right, and Senate Minority Leader Tom Daschle, D-S.D., maintained a good working relationship as leaders of opposing parties in the Senate in the mid- to late 1990s.

Top party leaders in both chambers are elected by their respective party caucuses—or conferences, as three of the four are formally named. (Only House Democrats refer to their partisan gathering as a caucus.) Factors such as personal style, geographical balance, and length of service traditionally play an important role in the selection of the leadership. In an age of television news and the "thirty-second sound bite," the ability of leaders to effectively speak for their party and present a legislative program to the nation has taken on new importance; a central component of this task is a talent to use the media adroitly to put forth party messages.

Ideologically, leaders tend to represent the center of their party. In this, as well as in their role as mediators, they usually occupy the "middle ground" as the various factions of the party try to draft legislative compromises that the party and Congress will accept. "As a member of the leadership," said Senate Majority Whip Byrd in 1976, "it is my duty to bring North and South, liberals and conservatives together; to work out compromises. . . . I think it takes a centrist to do that."[2] A conservative when he entered the Senate in 1959, Byrd had moved considerably leftward by the time he was first elected majority leader after the 1976 elections.

But ideological perceptions are often deceiving and can be a product of a specific point in time, and can change rapidly with the shifting political orientation of the parties. For example, Gingrich, often branded a right-wing extremist by Democrats and even by some moderate Republicans when the party was a minority in the House, was later criticized as too centrist by some of the conservatives he helped elect in 1994. In 1999 Trent Lott, the Senate majority leader, who might have been considered on the far right of his party just a few years before, made a comfortable fit with the Republican Conference that had moved toward him politically and added many like-minded legislators. And the demands of institutional leadership and majority responsibility changed these leaders as well, along with their approach to politics.

LEADERSHIP FUNCTIONS

The powers the leaders may exercise and the ways the leadership functions differ in the House and Senate. House rules allow a determined majority to lead, while Senate rules protect minority rights. Yet House and Senate leaders have the same fundamental job: "to bring," as political scientists Roger H. Davidson and Walter J. Oleszek have written, "coherence, direction, and efficiency to a decentralized and individualistic legislative body."[3]

The job has two overlapping, sometimes competing, parts. Leaders, Davidson and Oleszek observe, must constantly balance the needs of Congress as a lawmaking institution against Congress as a representative assembly:

In their "inside" role, party leaders guide institutional activities and influence policy. . . . Good communications skills, a talent for coalition building, tactical and strategic competence, intelligence, parliamentary expertise, and sensitivity to the mood of the membership and of the electorate are important attributes of an effective leader. . . . In their "outside" role, party leaders . . . help recruit candidates for Congress and assist in their campaigns. Leaders also must serve as the party's link to the president, the press, the public, and the partisan faithful.[4]

In their inside role, leaders organize each chamber and each party within the chamber, setting and reviewing committee jurisdictions and assignments and institutional and party rules. Leaders of each party also work together and with their members, usually through the party caucuses, to develop the party's stand on policy issues. Leaders assign individual bills to the appropriate committee or committees and decide how best to handle each bill as it comes to the floor. Once a bill is on the floor, the leadership is responsible for monitoring the debate and using the rules and procedures in ways that will help the party's chances of legislative success. Throughout, establishing and maintaining party unity is an important goal.

Scheduling business on the floor—deciding what will come to the floor when, under what conditions, and in what order—may be the majority leadership's most important institutional task, and is a forceful tool in achieving the party's policy agenda. "The power of the Speaker of the House is the power of scheduling," Speaker Thomas P. "Tip" O'Neill Jr., D-Mass., declared in 1983.[5]

The leadership often schedules floor action for the convenience of members; little business is scheduled in the House on Mondays and Fridays, for example, so that members can return to their districts for long weekends. The leadership may delay action on a controversial bill until it is sure that it has the winning votes, it may bring a controversial bill to the floor quickly to prevent opposition from building, or it may keep a vote going while it tries to recruit or change enough votes to gain victory.

In the Senate, where bills are open to nearly unlimited amendment and debate, the majority leader generally consults with the minority leadership, the floor managers of the bill, and other interested senators to draw up unanimous consent agreements governing floor action on major legislation. These agreements can be quite complicated, stipulating which amendments will be offered, how long they will be debated, and when they will be voted upon. Because a single member can block a unanimous consent agreement, the leaders must take care to ensure an opportunity to speak to all senators who want to be heard on the issue. The procedure is quite different in the House, where all but the most routine bills typically receive a rule for floor consideration. (See "Major Legislation and the Rules Committee," p. 494.)

Building winning coalitions is also essential to effective leadership. In the House this leadership function is aided by expanded whip organizations in both parties, which poll party members on specific issues, inform them of upcoming votes, help persuade them to support the party's cause, and ensure that they show up to vote. Ad hoc task forces also are used in both chambers to build support for specific issues important to the leadership. And for all the partisan rhetoric and real philosophical differences, leaders of both parties try to win support from members of the opposing party on most major legislation and amendments.

In their outside roles, congressional leaders of both parties meet periodically with the president to discuss his legislative agenda, letting him know how their respective memberships are likely to respond to his proposals. The leaders of the same party as the president also generally serve as his spokespersons in the House and Senate, although they remain independent of the president. "I'm the president's friend," Senate Majority Leader Byrd said of President Jimmy Carter. "I'm not the president's man."[6]

MESSAGES THROUGH THE MEDIA

In both inside and outside roles, skilled use of the media has become a prerequisite for success and even for selection as a leader. Despite his relatively short tenure in the Senate when he ran for majority leader in 1988, George J. Mitchell of Maine won the support of many Democrats who thought he would be a more articulate and appealing public spokesperson for Senate Democrats than his opponents.

Leaders in both chambers are routinely available to the news media. The Speaker of the House for many years until 1995 held a press conference before each House session began. The Senate majority and minority leaders gather with journalists on the Senate floor prior to Senate sessions, to announce the schedule and answer questions. Party leaders in both the House and Senate routinely respond to presidential addresses such as the State of the Union message or other speeches calling for legislative action. (See Chapter 19, The Media.)

Use of the media goes beyond simply articulating party positions. Public opinion is one of the main influences on a legislator's vote and fights on the House and Senate floor can be won not only by appealing to members of Congress but also by appealing to their constituents. Dick Gephardt, the future Democratic majority and minority leader, once said: "Being a good legislator means you have to do both. If you are going to pass important legislation, you have to both deal with members and put together coalitions in the country."[7] Tactics both parties use to influence public opinion include floor speeches meant to be picked up by the television news networks, newspaper opinion page pieces written by senior members of key committees, and carefully scheduled appearances on the Sunday morning TV talk shows. Party leaders and members generally in recent years have set up Web sites on the Internet to post their views.

One of the most adroit congressional manipulators of the media was Gingrich, a conservative Republican who arrived in the House in 1979, the same year the national cable network C-SPAN began televising House proceedings. Using that medium to attack and confront the Democratic leadership, and on occasion moderate Republicans, Gingrich soon became a visible presence in the national media and a favorite of conservatives nationwide. "Conflict equals exposure equals power," the future Speaker told a reporter.[8]

The strategy paid off. Gingrich's Conservative Opportunity Society, a group of Republicans he brought together in 1983 to promote similar philosophical and political beliefs, had a significant impact on the shape of the 1984 Republican platform. In 1988 Gingrich filed the formal ethics complaint against Speaker Wright that forced him to resign in 1989. That same year Gingrich was elected minority whip over the preferred candidate of the minority leader. The ultimate victory came after the Gingrich-led GOP won control of the House in the 1994 elections and he was elected Speaker.

TOOLS OF PERSUASION

Although the greater independence of individual members means leaders in both chambers must rely heavily on persuasion and negotiation, they are not without inducements and a few punishments to help coax their colleagues into line. A legislator who votes with his party might be rewarded with a better committee assignment or a visit by party leaders to his district during his reelection campaign. A pet program might be handled by a sympathetic committee or attached to an important bill heading for the floor. Leaders can see that a loyal member gets benefits for his district or state—a tax break for a key industry, a new flood control project, or an exemption from clean air rules. Campaign appearances and funds are also distributed judiciously to encourage loyalty.

In addition there are many services the leadership can offer individual members, what House Speaker O'Neill once called the "little odds and ends":

You know, you ask me what are my powers and my authority around here? The power to recognize on the floor; little odds and ends—like men get pride out of the prestige of handling the Committee of the Whole, being named Speaker for the day. . . . [T]here is a certain aura and respect that goes with the Speaker's office. He does have the power to be able to pick up the telephone and call people. And members oftentimes like to bring their local political leaders or a couple of mayors. And oftentimes they have problems from their area and they need aid and assistance. . . . We're happy to try to open the door for them, having been in the town for so many years and knowing so many people. We do know where a lot of bodies are and we do know how to advise people.[9]

Punishment for disloyal behavior can be subtle or brutal. A member's bid for a local dam or scheme to revamp national education grants could languish in an unresponsive committee. A request to switch committees or add an additional assignment, or travel abroad in a congressional delegation could be denied. Sometimes the threat of punishment may be enough to induce a member to fall into step. In the 104th Congress, Speaker Gingrich threatened to refuse to appoint members to a conference committee and to deny permission for foreign travel as a penalty for supporting a former member who opposed abortion and was running in a primary against a proabortion Republican incumbent. In the 105th Congress he endorsed a proposal that threatened to discipline members holding chairmanships who opposed the GOP position on key procedural votes, such as ordering the previous question or rules from the Rules Committee and sustaining rulings of the chair. In rare cases legislators are stripped of committee seniority or a committee post for repeatedly betraying the party position. After Democratic Rep. Phil

Gramm, Texas, masterminded enactment of budgets proposed by Republican President Ronald Reagan, Democratic leaders in 1983 stripped him of his seat on the House Budget Committee. Gramm resigned his House seat, won reelection as a Republican, and soon rejoined the committee as a GOP member.

Divided government—a president of one party and a Congress of another—has been an important factor in the difficulties political leaders faced in Congress in the last several decades of the century but by no means the only one. Forces within Congress and the country that had been gathering for years exacerbated partisan differences, most especially a resurgence of Republican conservatism that captured control of the GOP starting about 1964. The direct and indirect results of the reforms that Congress had put in place in the 1970s also contributed to challenge of leadership that congressional parties faced. After 1974 Congress was filled with politicians who had never known the era in which backbenchers took care to be seen but not heard. The newcomers owed their seats and careers not to the party apparatus but to constituents, campaign consultants, and election campaign contributors. Gone were the days when their votes were there to be "delivered."

The rise of negative campaign tactics and the thirty-second sound bite made this new generation of politicians see more and more votes as perilous. Many members also concluded that party leaders no longer offered them political cover. "There is a sense that they are out there all by themselves," said Foley, "that if they are not careful, no one will be careful for them."

That undertow of political vulnerability, combined with the diffusion of power that resulted from the 1970s reforms and the leadership's lack of effective tools to keep the rank and file in line, made it difficult to impose the discipline needed to legislate effectively, especially on huge federal budget deficits that overshadowed almost all other considerations until the mid-1990s.

The House Speaker

Widely regarded as the most powerful figure in Congress, the Speaker is the presiding officer of the House of Representatives as well as the leader of the majority party in the House. Since 1947 the Speaker has also been second in line, after the vice president, to succeed the president. "No other member of Congress possesses the visibility and authority of the Speaker," Davidson and Oleszek have written.[10]

The speakership has not always been endowed with such prestige. For the first two decades of Congress, the Speaker was largely a figurehead; not until Henry Clay was elected to the office in 1811 did a Speaker exercise any real leadership in the House. After Clay left the House in 1825, the authority of the Speaker ebbed and flowed, but no Speaker wielded as much influence as Clay until 1890, when Republican Thomas Brackett Reed of Maine used his personal and institutional authority to ensure that the minority could no longer frustrate the legislative actions of a unified majority. (See "Speakers of the House of Representatives, 1789–1999," p. 1100, in Reference Materials, Vol. II.)

The stalemate and gridlock that so often characterized executive-legislative relations in the 1980s and 1990s were blamed in large part on divided government. With the Republicans in control of the White House and the Democrats in control of one or both houses of Congress between 1981 and 1993, and with a Democratic president and Republican Congress beginning in 1995, conflicts between the branches were inevitable.

But control of Congress and the presidency by the same party does not always guarantee cooperation between the two branches. There have been numerous occasions in American history in which determined lawmakers resisted the proposals of their own presidents, and strong-willed presidents disregarded their party leaders in Congress.

LINCOLN, WILSON, THE ROOSEVELTS

Many of the conflicts between the White House and Congress when both were controlled by the same party have come at times of strong presidential leadership. Abraham Lincoln, Woodrow Wilson, and the two Roosevelts—Theodore and Franklin Delano—all had difficulties with their party's congressional leaders, although all four men were largely successful in winning enactment of their programs.

The first important clash of this kind arose during the Civil War, when Republican extremists dominated Congress. In 1861 Congress created a Joint Committee on the Conduct of the War, which went so far as to intervene in military operations. In 1864 Congress sought to undermine Lincoln's liberal reconstruction program by transferring responsibility for reconstruction from the president to Congress. Lincoln pocket-vetoed that bill and, so far as possible, ignored the extremists. He used executive orders to maintain the upper hand, but after Lincoln's assassination Congress achieved the supremacy it was seeking and retained it for more than thirty years.

Theodore Roosevelt was the next strong president to experience difficulty with his party's congressional leadership. Roosevelt clashed sharply with Sen. Nelson W. Aldrich, R-R.I., the unofficial but acknowledged leader of the Senate's Republicans. Aldrich, for example, refused to support the president's bill to regulate railroad rates in exchange for Roosevelt's agreement to drop tariff reform. After relying primarily on Democrats to report the rate bill from the Senate committee, Roosevelt won agreement from William B. Allison of Iowa, the other most influential Republican in the Senate, on judicial review of rate adjustments. This maneuver split the opposition and led to passage of the bill by an overwhelming vote. Aldrich, however, continued to oppose administration measures and occasionally won important concessions from the president.

Although relations between President Wilson and the Democratic congressional leadership generally were good, party leaders sometimes deserted the president on foreign policy issues. On the eve of the opening of the Panama Canal in 1914, both Speaker Champ Clark, Mo., and House Majority Leader Oscar Underwood, Ala., opposed Wilson's request to repeal a provision of a law exempting American vessels traveling between U.S. ports from having to pay canal tolls. The exemption, which Great Britain said violated an Anglo-American treaty, was eventually eliminated despite the opposition of the House leadership.

In 1917 Rep. Claude Kitchin, D-N.C., who had replaced Underwood as majority leader, opposed Wilson when the president asked Congress to declare war on Germany. Later, Clark opposed Wilson's request for military conscription. Near the end of Wilson's second term, relations between Clark and the president were nearly nonexistent.

Although Franklin Roosevelt's overall relations with Congress were as good as or better than Wilson's, he still had problems with his own congressional leadership. During his third term (1941–1945) the Democratic leadership deserted Roosevelt on major domestic issues. In 1944 Senate Majority Leader Alben W. Barkley, Ky., resigned the post when FDR vetoed a revenue bill. The Democrats promptly reelected Barkley, and the bill was passed over the president's veto.

MADISON, JOHNSON, MCKINLEY

Congressional leaders also frequently clashed with less aggressive presidents of their own party. These conflicts usually occurred when Congress attempted to dominate the president by initiating its own legislative program and directives. One of the earliest examples came during the administration of James Madison when Speaker Henry Clay forced the president into the War of 1812 against Britain. Another was Clay's successful attempt to pressure James Monroe into a series of unwanted measures including a revision of the tariffs.

After the Civil War, the Radical Republicans in Congress were able to push through their reconstruction policy over President Andrew Johnson's opposition. In the process they almost managed to remove the president through an impeachment effort that historians record as entirely politically motivated.

The next major clash came in 1898. Speaker Thomas Brackett Reed, R-Maine, a strong isolationist, sought but failed to block three controversial aspects of President William McKinley's foreign policy: war with Spain, annexation of Hawaii, and acquisition of the Philippine Islands. Reed's failure to stop McKinley, which led to his retirement from Congress, was due largely to the popularity of the president's policies, not to the successful application of pressure on congressional leaders by McKinley.

MODERN PRESIDENTS:
JOHNSON, CARTER, CLINTON

In the mid-1960s President Lyndon B. Johnson demanded congressional support of his military policies in Southeast Asia. Although the Democratic Congress generally went along with Johnson's conduct of the war, the majority leader in the Senate, Mike Mansfield, D-Mont., actively opposed the president's military venture virtually from the beginning.

Congress was overwhelmingly Democratic throughout the four years Democrat Jimmy Carter was president (1977–1981). Nevertheless, many of Carter's proposals and the way they were formulated and presented to his party received less than enthusiastic support from the leadership in Congress. Said Majority Leader Robert C. Byrd, D-W.Va., in 1980: "At the leadership meetings, he [Carter] urges certain action and says he hopes he'll have our support. But he can't force it. The president is expected to make his proposals, and we have a responsibility to him and the country to weigh them and act on them only if, in the judgment of the Senate, we should."

President Bill Clinton failed to receive support from both ideological wings of his party on several highly contentious issues during the 103rd Congress, which contributed to loss of Democratic control of both houses for the first time in forty years in 1994. Clinton was distrusted by liberals for his campaign as a "new Democrat" willing to reassess traditional party orthodoxy, while more conservative members worried about his administration's initial liberal policy proposals, such as his support for the rights of gays to remain in military service. However, it was Clinton's controversial plan for a new system of national health insurance that most deeply divided the party and angered the public; it failed to receive floor consideration in either house and undermined Democratic claims that its unified control of both major branches of government would lead to substantial achievements. Many House liberals also deserted Clinton on major crime control legislation in 1994, forcing the president to deal with individual Republicans to assemble a majority for a more conservative bill.

SUCCESS THROUGH BIPARTISANSHIP

Cases in which a party's congressional leadership has cooperated in a substantial way with a president of the other party are less frequent and have dealt mainly with national security and related issues. One example is Republican President Dwight D. Eisenhower, who worked with a Democratic Congress for six of his eight years in office. Yet Democratic congressional leaders cooperated actively and willingly with the White House most of the time. Speaker Sam Rayburn, Texas, who often described himself as a Democrat "without prefix, without suffix, without apology," generally acted as the president's man in the House. During Eisenhower's second term, Rayburn's liberal critics, dismayed over his seeming inattention to traditional Democratic Party causes, began referring to him as an "Eisenhowercrat."

As Senate majority leader, Lyndon Johnson was a firm believer in the bipartisan conduct of foreign policy. In 1980 House Minority Leader John J. Rhodes, R-Ariz., recalled Johnson sitting in on foreign aid conference committee meetings: "He was there, not to ensure the Democratic position would win, but to ensure the administration position would win. He was acting as a broker for the Eisenhower administration. . . . It was often said at that time that 'the president proposes while Congress disposes.' The philosophy is not very popular today, but the people running Congress then were pretty much dedicated to that idea, no matter who the president was."

Ronald Reagan's first year in office was marked by a Republican Senate and a Democratic House more conservative than it had been during Carter's presidency. Working closely with Senate and House Republicans and with conservative Democrats in the House, Reagan was able to put together a string of dramatic victories, including the deepest budget cuts and largest tax reductions ever considered by Congress and a controversial arms deal with Saudi Arabia. In 1986 the Republican president and a divided Congress produced a landmark tax reform bill, largely because both parties saw political gain in passing the bill, and neither wanted to advantage the other party by blocking the reform.

President George Bush won bipartisan support from Congress to use force in the Persian Gulf crisis but it came over the objections of Democratic leaders in both the House and Senate. Bush worked effectively with Democratic leaders in both houses to push through long-delayed legislation in 1990 to strengthen the Clean Air Act.

Clinton won bipartisan support for a number of foreign policy initiatives, including passage of the North American Free Trade Agreement (NAFTA) in the Democratic-controlled House in the 103rd Congress but with Republicans providing the majority of votes; the expansion of NATO; and ratification of a chemical weapons treaty with substantial help from Senate Majority Leader Trent Lott, R-Miss. Congress denied Clinton controversial "fast track" trade negotiating authority in 1997, which was supported by many Republicans, but the president failed to obtain enough support within his own party.

But Republican congressional leaders repeatedly refused to defer to the tradition that politics stops at the water's edge. Clinton's personal difficulties with a variety of scandals intruded on his foreign policy efforts, as when House Majority Whip Tom DeLay, R-Texas, denounced Clinton's alleged behavior as the president was touring African countries in 1998. Later that year, Speaker Newt Gingrich, R-Ga., visiting Israel, made provocative remarks that Clinton officials said harmed Middle East peace efforts. In 1999 the House, in a rare tie vote, defeated a resolution that endorsed the president's policy of bombing Yugoslavia as part of NATO's campaign against that nation's attacks on ethnic Albanians in the province of Kosovo. House Speaker Dennis Hastert of Illinois voted to support Clinton while his deputies pressured other Republicans to oppose the president.

On domestic issues, Clinton vetoed much of the Republicans' ambitious domestic policy agenda in the 104th Congress and resuscitated himself politically by taking advantage of the missteps of the inexperienced new House majority. But he also embraced and reshaped a number of major Republican initiatives, resulting in enactment of a 1996 law repealing the long-standing federal welfare program and a 1997 law that balanced the federal budget the following year for the first time since 1969. Republicans took the lead in enacting a 1996 law making Clinton the first president to exercise a "line item veto" over certain new spending and tax provisions. However, the Supreme Court declared the law unconstitutional in 1998. *(See box, Line-Item Veto Experiment Ended by Supreme Court, p. 530.)*

"Czar" Reed was soon followed by Joseph G. Cannon, R-Ill., the Speaker from 1903 to 1911, whose autocratic control over the House led to a revolt against him in 1910. Ultimately the Speaker's powers as presiding officer were limited by House rules. Changes in the caucus rules of the two political parties also served to lessen the Speaker's authority.

Cannon's tyrannical rule and the rebellion against it had a lasting effect on the office and the men who have held it. Power in the House became concentrated in the hands of the chairmen of the legislative committees until the mid-1970s. The reforms of the 1970s restored many of the Speaker's powers. Yet every Speaker since Cannon who has been an effective House leader has achieved influence chiefly through personal prestige, persuasion, brokerage, and bargaining.

That is not to say that Speakers do not use their authority to achieve their goals. "Tradition and unwritten law require that the Speaker apply the rules of the House consistently, yet in the twilight zone a large area exists where he may exercise great discrimination and where he has many opportunities to apply the rules to his party's advantage," wrote future Senate parliamentarian Floyd M. Riddick in 1949—a statement as true today as it was then.[11]

But in the modern era a Speaker must take care to ensure that his actions have the continued support of a majority of his party. Democrat Jim Wright pushed his leadership close to the limits of its powers and caused resentment by acting without first consulting other party leaders or the rank and file. That exclusion, coupled with his aggressive and sometimes abrasive style, left him politically vulnerable when a challenge to his personal ethics arose. The crisis eventually forced Wright to resign both the speakership and his House seat. Republican Newt Gingrich, the most powerful speaker since Cannon, surmounted political difficulties and personal ethics problems because he enjoyed support from a united party and from colleagues who valued strong leadership. When Gingrich's leadership no longer produced the desired results, the party replaced him in favor of a different approach.

FRAMERS' INTENTIONS

The framers of the Constitution were silent on the role they intended the Speaker to play in the House. The Constitution's only reference to the office is in Article I, Section 2, clause 5, which states, "The House of Representatives shall chuse their Speaker and other Officers." There is no evidence that the Founding Fathers debated this provision.

Two respected authorities on the speakership, Mary P. Follett and Hubert Bruce Fuller, have suggested that this absence of any discussion indicated that the framers thought the Speaker would act as both presiding officer and political leader. "Surely," wrote Follett in *The Speaker of the House of Representatives,* the Speaker could not have been thought of "as a non-political moderator, as a mere parliamentary officer whom it was necessary to dissociate from politics. What [was] intended must be inferred from that with which [the framers] were familiar." Follett's book, published in 1896, is still widely regarded as the authoritative study of the early development of the office.[12]

What the framers knew were the colonial Speakers. In most cases these Speakers were active politicians who not only presided over the legislatures but also used their positions to further their own or their faction's legislative aims. This concept of the office differed sharply from that of the speakership of the House of Commons. The British Speaker was, and still is, a strictly nonpartisan presiding officer. (The term "Speaker" first appeared in the Commons in 1377, when Sir Thomas Hungerford assumed the post. Until the late seventeenth century, the Speaker in England was directly responsible to the Crown. The term was derived from the fact that it was the duty of the presiding officer to interpret the will of the House of Commons to the Crown.)

In any event, because political parties had not yet been formed, the first Speaker, Frederick A. C. Muhlenberg, Pa., was nonpartisan. His duties, as spelled out by the House on April 7, 1789, were to preside at House sessions, preserve decorum and order, announce the results of standing and teller votes, appoint select committees of not more than three members, and vote in cases of a tie, a practice referred to as the Speaker's "casting" vote. By the Second Congress, clearly defined party divisions had begun to develop, and Muhlenberg's successor, Jonathan Trumbull of Connecticut, displayed definite leanings toward President George Washington's legislative program. In 1796 Speaker Jonathan Dayton, a Federalist, twice voted to produce ties that resulted in the defeat of Jeffersonian motions that would have undermined the Federalist-backed Jay Treaty with Britain.

Party affiliation, although weak and more diffuse than in modern times, also became the basis for choosing the Speaker. In 1799 the Federalists elected Theodore Sedgwick of Massachusetts over Nathaniel Macon of North Carolina to the Speaker's post by a vote of 44–38, a margin that reflected that of the Federalists over the Jeffersonians in the Sixth Congress. Sedgwick, according to Follett, "made many enemies by decided and even partisan acts," so many that the Jeffersonians in the Sixth Congress refused to join in the customary vote of thanks to the Speaker at adjournment. At the beginning of the Seventh Congress, the Jeffersonians, now in commanding control of Congress, elected Macon to the speakership by a wide margin.

But throughout the early years, and particularly during Thomas Jefferson's presidency, it was the executive, and not the Speaker, who was the real political and legislative leader in the House. As Washington's Treasury secretary, Alexander Hamilton dominated the Federalist majority even during the First Congress by operating through supporters in Congress who formed what might be considered the first party caucuses. "Instead of being a forum, where every member was a peer and no man led, where great principles of government were evolved through the give and take of unrestricted discussion, Congress as such had become in effect a mere ratifying body," wrote Ralph V. Harlow in 1917. "The real work of legislation was put in shape, not in the legislature, but in secret session of the majority party."[13]

Jefferson's secretary of the Treasury, Albert Gallatin, soon became as adept as Hamilton in guiding administration measures through the party caucus and the House. Jefferson, moreover, carried his control over the legislative branch one step further, picking his own floor leader, who was named chairman of the Ways and Means Committee at the same time. One of these congressional leaders, William B. Giles of Virginia, was actually referred to as the "premier" or "prime minister." There was little room under Jefferson's shadow for a Speaker to carve out an independent leadership role, notes political scientist Ronald M. Peters.[14]

CLAY AND THE SHIFT OF POWER

Executive domination of the House came to an end under Jefferson's successor, James Madison. Although nominally supported by the Democratic-Republican (Jeffersonian) majorities throughout his two terms, Madison soon lost control of the party to a band of young "war hawks," who, affronted by British interference with American trade and shipping, advocated war with England. Henry Clay of Kentucky, who had served brief stints as a senator in 1806–1807 and 1810–1811, entered the House in 1811 as spokesperson for the war hawks who had swept seventy House seats in the elections of 1810. Although only thirty-four and a newcomer, he was elected Speaker on his first day in the House. He would soon become the first Speaker of national prominence and the first to use the position to achieve his own ends.

Clay's great success as presiding officer lay in his personal magnetism. "All testify," wrote Follett, "to the marvelous charm of his voice and manner, which attracted attention, awakened sympathy, and compelled obedience. He had a bold and commanding spirit, which imposed its will upon those around him. He carried all before him with his imperious nature to give him complete ascendancy over his party, and the easy leadership of the House."[15]

Employing to the full his power as Speaker to select committee chairmen and appoint members to committees, Clay immediately filled key positions on the Foreign Affairs, Military Affairs, and Naval Affairs committees with fellow war hawks. On November 29, 1811, less than four weeks after Congress had convened, the Foreign Affairs Committee issued a report recommending that the nation begin immediate preparations for war. President Madison, a leader of the Constitutional Convention and a strong secretary of state under Jefferson, proved to be a weak president. Although he sought a peaceful settlement with England, he was subjected to continuous pressure for war from Clay and the war hawks. Finally, on June 1, 1812, Madison sent Congress a war message. The House voted 79–49 for war three days later.

As congressional historian George Rothwell Brown wrote, in this episode, "Clay had lifted the Speakership of the House to a

Henry Clay was chosen as Speaker on the day he entered the House of Representatives in 1811. A formidable presiding officer, he exerted firm control over the House.

point of new power and responsibility, the Speaker to a place in the state where, backed by party organization . . . he could present to the President a program determining national policy and involving a declaration of war . . . against the pacifist sentiment of the President and most of the Cabinet."[16]

According to Peters, Clay was not a particularly good parliamentarian. Another Speaker, Robert Winthrop, said of him that "he was no painstaking student of parliamentary law, but more frequently found the rules of his governance in his own instinctive sense of what was practicable and proper than in Hatsell's Precedents or Jefferson's Manual."[17] Yet Clay was widely respected for his ability to maintain order on the House floor and to bring into line some of the chamber's more unruly members.

A notable example of these talents occurred during the debate on the proposed declaration of war, when John Randolph, a Virginia Democrat who for years had intimidated House members with his rhetoric, sought to take the floor to oppose the war policy. Clay ruled that Randolph could not speak unless he submitted a motion to the House. Randolph did so, whereupon Clay ruled that he still could not speak until the House considered the motion. The House refused to consider it, and Randolph was denied the floor. Clay frequently resorted to such tactics on important issues. In his six terms as Speaker, none of his rulings was overturned, though many were sustained only by strict party-line votes.

In addition to establishing new standards of order for the conduct of business on the House floor, Clay also helped to establish the committee system. There were ten standing committees in the House in 1810, the year before Clay entered the chamber. When he left the House in 1825 there were twenty-eight.[18] Historians and political scientists disagree about whether Clay fostered the committee system primarily to solidify and advance his own position or to improve the efficiency of the House.

Unlike previous Speakers, Clay remained a vigorous spokesperson for the interests of his congressional district. He was the first Speaker—and one of the few in history—to vote in instances when his vote could make no difference in the result, a practice that has revived under Speakers in the 1990s. Clay's voting practices and his participation in debate set the precedent that Speakers forfeit none of their normal privileges as members.

Clay remained Speaker as long as he was in the House. Although he left his seat twice—in 1814, to help negotiate an end to the War of 1812, and in 1820—he was reelected Speaker as soon as he returned to the House in 1815 and again in 1823. He is the only early Speaker members elected repeatedly "irrespective of their partisan or factional allegiances, their geographic loyalties, or their views."[19]

FROM CLAY TO COLFAX

For the next four decades, as the issue of slavery grew to dominate the national agenda, factional allegiances and geographic loyalties would divide both the country and Congress. In the House the speakership rarely stayed in one man's possession for more than a single term. Of the fourteen Speakers who presided between 1825, when Clay left the House, and 1861, only three—Andrew Stevenson of Virginia, James K. Polk, the future president from Tennessee, and Linn Boyd of Kentucky—served for more than one Congress. Many election contests for the speakership were marked by multiple ballots; it took sixty-three ballots, for example, before Howell Cobb, a proslavery Democrat from Georgia, was elected Speaker in 1849 by a two-vote margin. *(See box, Heated Contests for Speakership, p. 428.)*

Given the brief periods that most of these Speakers served, it is little wonder that none of them achieved the stature and influence of Clay. Stevenson, who served between 1827 and 1834, may have come the closest. Although he lacked Clay's magnetism, he was an able politician, actively promoting Andrew Jackson's program in the House. "No Speaker," wrote Follett, "except perhaps Macon, has been so distinctly the president's man."[20]

Two men, both Republicans, presided over the House during the Civil War, Galusha Grow of Pennsylvania (1861–1863) and Schuyler Colfax of Indiana (1863–1869). But the real leader of the House during this period was Thaddeus Stevens, the leader of the Radical Republicans, who engineered the impeachment of President Andrew Johnson.

Grow was clearly controlled by Stevens, and Colfax, while personally popular, was not a forceful Speaker and was, like Grow, regarded by many as Stevens's man. "Colfax possessed neither will nor mind of his own," said historian Fuller. "Thaddeus Stevens furnished him with these mental attributes."[21]

RISE OF MINORITY OBSTRUCTIONISM

While the speakership may have been a position of little real authority by the time the Civil War began, the emergence of the modern two-party system and a new partisanship in the House was soon to produce two of the most powerful Speakers in history. The first Speaker after the Civil War to add any new authorities to the post was James G. Blaine, R-Maine, one of the founders of the Republican Party and Colfax's successor. As Speaker from 1869 to 1875, Blaine was the first leader since Clay to organize the House in a way that favored his party's program. Blaine successfully manipulated committee assignments to produce majorities favorable to legislation he desired.

As partisan as he was, Blaine nonetheless refused to use the powers of the speakership to stop the variety of obstructionist tactics that the Democrats used to block action on legislation they did not support but could not defeat through the regular procedures. Chief among these tactics were constant demands for roll-call votes and use of the "disappearing" or "silent" quorum, in which members of the minority party refused to answer to their names even though they were present on the floor. Blaine's reluctance to restrict the rights of the minority party may have stemmed in part from his realization that the Republican Party would some day find itself in the minority and wish to avail itself of the same tactics.

When the Democrats won control of the House with the elections of 1874, they elected as their Speaker Michael C. Kerr of Indiana, who died in 1876. They then chose Samuel J. Randall of Pennsylvania, who served as Speaker until 1881 when the Republicans regained control of the House. Randall too refused to curb minority (this time Republican) obstructionism, but he did initiate a thorough revision of the House rules designed "to secure accuracy in business, economy in time, order, uniformity and impartiality."[22] The next such revision did not occur until 1999. Perhaps the most significant of these revisions, which were adopted in 1880, made the Rules Committee a standing, instead of a select, committee. The Speaker retained chairmanship of the committee, a privilege he had enjoyed since 1858.

Republicans controlled Congress for one term (1881–1883), and when Democrats regained control of the House in 1883, they passed over Randall (who opposed the party's low-tariff policy) and elected instead John G. Carlisle of Kentucky, who served as Speaker until 1889. Carlisle was a strong Speaker, deriving much of his authority from his willingness to use his power of recognition to forestall motions he opposed. By asking "For what purpose does the gentleman rise," Carlisle could withhold recognition from any member whose purpose opposed his own.

But like Blaine and Randall before him, Carlisle was reluctant to do anything about minority obstructionism, making him what one commentator called "the slave of filibusters." By the end of his speakership, the minority's use of delaying tactics, coupled with a disappointing legislative record, opened the House to public criticism and demands that the rules be modified "to permit the majority to control the business for which it is responsible," to quote one editorial in the *New York Tribune*.[23]

REED'S RULE

Reform was to come in the person of Thomas Brackett Reed, R-Maine. Reed—a physically imposing man at six feet, three inches and nearly 300 pounds, dressed always in black—was Speaker from 1889 to 1891 and again from 1895 to 1899. In his rulings from the chair in his first months in office, later formally incorporated into the rules and procedures of the House, Reed expanded the powers of the office more than any other Speaker except Clay, in essence establishing the absolute right of the majority to control the legislative process.

Even as minority leader, Reed had deplored minority obstructionism. "The rules of this House are not for the purpose of protecting the rights of the minority," he had said, "but to promote the orderly conduct of the business of the House."[24] The minority's rights were preserved in their right to debate and to vote, Reed argued. The dilatory tactics the minority used controverted the essential function of the House, which was to legislate. Once elected Speaker, he determined to do something about the situation.

The Speaker's decision was risky—his Republicans commanded only a seven-vote majority in the House, 166 to the Democrats' 159—not only to his role as Speaker but also to his future political ambitions. Like Clay and Blaine before him, Reed aspired to the presidency. According to historian Barbara Tuchman, Reed confided his decision to attack the silent quorum to no one, not even to Cannon, his closest lieutenant, in part because no one else would have thought he had any chance of success, in part because he was not sure his own party, including Cannon, would support him.

On January 21, 1890, Reed took his first major step against obstructionism by refusing to consider a member's demand for a teller vote on a motion to adjourn. A few days later he announced his intention to disregard all motions and appeals, even if procedurally correct, if their purpose was simply to delay House business.

Then, on January 29, Reed made his assault on the silent quorum. When the Republicans called up the first of several contested election cases, Charles F. Crisp of Georgia, the Democratic leader who would succeed Reed as Speaker in the next two Congresses, objected to considering the Republican motion. The yeas and nays were ordered, and the vote came to 161 "yeas," two "nays," and 165 not voting—mainly Democrats who while not voting were nonetheless present. When the vote was announced, the Democrats immediately claimed that it was invalid because a quorum (165) had not voted, whereupon Reed

Thomas Brackett Reed was one of the most powerful Speakers in House history. Known as "Czar" Reed, he established the "Reed Rules" to curb Democratic obstructionism in the 1890s.

ordered the clerk to enter the names of those present who had refused to vote. He then ruled that a quorum was present and that consideration of the question was in order.

The House erupted into pandemonium when the quorum count began. Republicans applauded the Speaker. Democrats, wrote historian Tuchman, "foamed with rage. A hundred of them 'were on their feet howling for recognition,' wrote a reporter. 'Fighting Joe' Wheeler, the diminutive former Confederate cavalry general, unable to reach the front because of the crowded aisles, came down from the rear 'leaping from desk to desk as an ibex leaps from crag to crag.' As the excitement grew wilder, the only Democrat not on his feet was a huge representative from Texas who sat in his seat significantly whetting a bowie knife on his boot."[25]

An appeal from the ruling was tabled by a majority of those voting (again with a quorum present but not voting). The following day, the Speaker declined to reconsider the ruling and declared that he would refuse to recognize any member rising to make a dilatory motion. The debate, angry and strident, continued for several more days. At one point, it appeared that a group of irate Democrats were preparing to pull the Speaker out of the Chair. At another point, Democrats decided to leave the chamber, in an effort to deny the Republicans a quorum, but Reed ordered the doors locked, forcing Democrats to hide under their desks and behind screens. Reed was called tyrant, despot, dictator—the epithet that stuck was czar. Throughout it all he re-

At the beginning of every two-year term each party caucus nominates a candidate to be Speaker of the House and the candidate of the majority party wins the office, normally on a straight party-line vote on the House floor. The Clerk of the House from the previous Congress presides until a Speaker is chosen. The Speaker is elected by a majority of members-elect voting by surname for a candidate, a quorum being present. Traditionally, the members nominated for Speaker vote "present" rather than for themselves. The Constitution does not require that the Speaker be a member of the House, but he always has been. Any member may run for Speaker.

But pro forma elections of the Speaker have not always been the case. Before the two-party system became entrenched on Capitol Hill, factions sometimes so splintered the majority party that the election of a Speaker turned into a battle royal. On two occasions, the House departed from precedent and, using special rules, chose Speakers by a plurality vote; but in each case the House by majority vote subsequently passed a resolution declaring the result.

Regional disputes, mainly over slavery, produced at least eleven hotly contested races for the speakership before the Civil War. The first was in 1809, when none of the Democratic-Republican candidates was able to achieve a majority on the first ballot. The election finally went to Joseph B. Varnum of Massachusetts after the South's candidate, Nathaniel Macon, N.C., withdrew because of poor health.

Other battles occurred in 1820, when an antislavery candidate, John W. Taylor, D-N.Y., won on the 22nd ballot; in 1821, when Philip P. Barbour, D-Va., won on the 12th; in 1825, when Taylor recaptured the post on the second ballot; in 1834, when John Bell, Whig-Tenn., won on the tenth vote; in 1847, when Robert C. Winthrop, Whig-Mass., won on the third; and in 1861, when Galusha A. Grow, R-Pa., won on the second.

In four other pre–Civil War instances the House became deadlocked for weeks or months over the election of the Speaker.

1839: NEW JERSEY CONTROVERSY

The first of these prolonged battles began on December 2, 1839, when election of the Speaker hinged on the outcome of five contested House seats in New Jersey. Excluding the five New Jersey members, the party lineup in the House was 119 Democrats and 118 Whigs. Democrats sought to organize the House (and elect the new Speaker) before the contested elections were decided; the Whigs wanted to wait until the elections were resolved.

After much debate the House on December 14 agreed with the Democratic proposal to vote for Speaker before the contested seats were decided. But Democratic leaders were then unable to hold a sufficient number of members in line to name a Speaker. On December 16, Robert M. T. Hunter, D-Va., who had declared himself an independent, was elected Speaker on the 11th ballot.

1849: FREE-SOIL DISPUTE

The next major contest for the speakership developed in 1849, when neither the Whigs nor the Democrats could achieve a majority because the so-called Free-Soil factions in both parties decided to act independently. The resulting deadlock lasted for three weeks and sixty-three ballots.

The Free-Soilers, who opposed expansion of slavery into the territories, wanted to ensure that certain House committees were controlled by antislavery legislators. They thus opposed the election of the leading candidates for Speaker in both parties: Robert C. Winthrop, Whig-Mass., who they felt had been lukewarm on the issue as Speaker from 1847 to 1849, and Howell Cobb, D-Ga., a strong proponent of slavery. Each faction put up its own candidate—at one time there were eleven—preventing either Winthrop or Cobb from winning a majority.

At various points compromise solutions were considered and rejected, including proposals that the Speaker be chosen by lottery and that members receive no salary or mileage reimbursement until a Speaker was elected. Finally, after the 59th vote, the House agreed to elect the Speaker by a plurality, provided that it be a majority of a quorum. On the 60th vote, Cobb led; on the 61st, Winthrop; and on the 62nd, the vote was tied. The issue was decided on the 63rd vote, when Cobb won a plurality of two votes. "The choice of a very pronounced pro-slavery and southern man at this crisis undoubtedly aggravated the struggles of the following decade," Mary P. Follett noted in her authoritative 1896 book on the speakership.

1855: KANSAS AND SLAVERY

Six years later another multifaction battle stemming from the slavery issue delayed election of a Speaker. The specific concern was who would be appointed to the committee investigating the admission of Kansas into the Union: Would the Speaker choose committee members who favored its entry as a free state or as a slave state?

Although antislavery forces held a majority of House seats, their ranks were so split by factions—mostly the new Republican Party and various Free-Soil groups—that they could not unite behind a single candidate. After 129 ballots, the House decided that the candidate receiving the largest number of votes on the 133rd ballot would be declared the winner. On February 2, 1856, Nathaniel P. Banks, American-Mass., was elected with 103 out of the 214 votes cast.

Banks met the expectations of the antislavery forces by giving them a majority on the Kansas investigating committee. The practical effect of that action, Follett observed, "delayed the settlement of the Kansas episode until after 1857, and this gave time for the antislavery forces to organize."

1859: IMPENDING CRISIS

The last of the great pre–Civil War contests over the speakership occurred in 1859. The tone was set on the first day of the session, December 5, when slavery advocates proposed a resolution that anyone who endorsed the sentiments of *The Impending Crisis of the South: How to Meet It*, a book hostile to slavery, was not fit to be Speaker.

The resolution and another introduced the next day were directed at John Sherman, R-Ohio, who had endorsed the book. "The ball thus set rolling," Follett wrote, "the discussion of slavery began, bitter and passionate on one side, eager and vehement on the other. The state of the country was reflected in the struggle for Speaker. The House was the scene of a confusion and uproar which the clerk could not control.... Bitter personal invectives nearly led to personal encounters.... It seemed as though the Civil War was to begin in the House of Representatives."

Sherman led in the early voting, falling only six votes short of a majority on the third ballot. By the end of January, however, Republicans saw that Sherman could not be elected and shifted their support to William Pennington, Whig-N.J., a new and unknown member. On February 1, 1860, after forty-four votes and two months into the session, Pennington was elected with 117 votes, the minimum needed to win. Pennington was the only Speaker other than Henry Clay ever elected to the speakership during his first term. But he did not share Clay's skill. Pennington was defeated for reelection to the House in 1860.

1923: PROGRESSIVE INSURGENCY

The only deadlock over the speakership since the Civil War occurred in 1923, when twenty Progressive Republicans held the balance of power in the House. They put up their candidate, Henry A. Cooper, R-Wis., as a protest against House procedures. After eight inconclusive votes, Nicholas Longworth, R-Ohio, the GOP majority leader, made an agreement with the progressives to liberalize the rules. The next day they threw their support to the Republican candidate, Frederick H. Gillett, R-Mass.

OTHER LEADERSHIP FIGHTS

Since 1923 there have been no floor battles for the speakership. One party has always held a clear majority and has been able to elect its choice on the first ballot. But there have been fights in the party caucuses. In 1933 Democratic Majority Leader Henry T. Rainey of Illinois faced four candidates in his bid to win the nomination in the caucus, which was tantamount to election since the Democrats controlled the House. A northerner and a liberal, Rainey was opposed by the southern establishment that controlled the Democratic Party at the time. But with three of the other four candidates from southern states, Rainey had room to maneuver. He was nominated Speaker in a deal that ensured the southern establishment would continue to be the effective ruling power in the House.

No significant battles for the speakership have developed on the Democratic side since 1933; each time a Democratic Speaker has left office and the party controlled the chamber, the Democratic majority leader has been elevated to the speakership without much ado. In several cases the Democratic Caucus has then elected the party whip to be majority leader. However, this pattern appeared to be ending in the 1970s, as Democratic whips failed to sustain long-term careers in the House. John McFall, D-Calif., lost a race for majority leader in 1976. His successor as whip, John Brademas, D-Ind., was defeated in the 1980 Republican landslide. Thomas S. Foley, the last member to be chosen as whip by appointment, then got back on the ladder, rising to become majority leader and Speaker. However, the next two Democratic whips, Tony Coelho of California and William Gray III of Pennsylvania, resigned from the House before any opportunity of advancement opened up.

The Democratic pattern of leadership succession fell apart most visibly in 1976 when deputy whip Jim Wright of Texas offered himself as an alternative to the bitterly antagonistic front-runners, Caucus Chairman Phillip Burton of California and Richard Bolling of Missouri. Whip John McFall was popular with his fellow Democrats but tainted by his association with the "Koreagate" influence-peddling scandal; he was eliminated from the race on the first ballot. Wright had seemed an unlikely winner when he announced he would enter the contest, but he eliminated Bolling by two votes on the second ballot, and Burton by a single vote on the third ballot.

House Republicans have had more contests for party leader in recent decades. In 1959 Charles A. Halleck of Indiana, a conservative, deposed the more moderate Joseph W. Martin Jr., of Massachusetts, as minority leader. Martin had served as Speaker of the House in 1947–1949 and 1953–1955. Republicans had suffered massive losses in the 1958 elections.

Similarly, Gerald R. Ford of Michigan ousted Halleck as minority leader in 1965 following landslide Democratic election victories. After the 1980 elections Bob Michel of Illinois, the minority whip since 1974, was elected minority leader over Guy Vander Jagt of Michigan.

Minority Whip Newt Gingrich, R-Ga., became Speaker by unanimous vote of the House Republican Conference in 1995 and was elected by a party-line vote in the House as the first Republican Speaker since Joseph Martin left office in 1955. Gingrich's political stature dropped dramatically during his first term as Speaker, and he endured a scare in 1997 as he sought reelection in the face of an ongoing ethics investigation. Despite his party's 227 members in the chamber, Gingrich received only 216 votes for Speaker, three more than the absolute majority required from among members-elect who voted for candidates by surname. Four Republicans voted for other persons, either sitting Republican House members or former Republican members. Five other Republicans voted present, but their actions did not affect the race.

In November 1998, after House Republicans lost seats in the fall election that reduced their majority to a razor-thin margin, Robert L. Livingston of Louisiana challenged Gingrich for the speakership. Gingrich, sensing probable defeat, announced he would resign from Congress. Other top GOP House leaders survived, although Majority Leader Dick Armey of Texas had to fight off tough challenges from other Republican colleagues. Armey finally prevailed on the third ballot—an indication of considerable unhappiness in the ranks over his leadership.

SOURCE: George B. Galloway, *History of the House of Representatives* (New York: Crowell, 1961), 43; Mary P. Follett, *The Speaker of the House of Representatives* (New York: Longmans, Green, 1896; reprint, New York: Burt Franklin Reprints, 1974), 56, 59, 61–62, 95.

mained calm and implacable, and on the fifth day the Democrats conceded, unable to muster a majority to overturn the Speaker's decision.

On February 14, 1890, the House formally adopted new rules incorporating Reed's rulings and other new procedures. The new code, reported by the Rules Committee chaired by Reed, provided that all members must vote unless they had a pecuniary interest in the issue at hand, motions to recess or to fix a date of adjournment would not be entertained when a question was under debate, 100 members would constitute a quorum in the Committee of the Whole, and the Speaker would entertain no dilatory motions. The House adopted the "Reed Rules" after bitter debate. The most controversial of them—counting present but nonvoting members to make a quorum—was upheld by the U.S. Supreme Court in an 1891 test case (*U.S. v. Ballin*).

The Democrats regained control of the House in 1890 with such a convincing majority that they were able to reject the Reed Rules. But Reed had not had his final word on the subject. Though the Democrats after the 1892 elections reverted to the Reed rule that set a quorum in the Committee of the Whole at 100 members, Speaker Crisp refused to count those present but not voting. In his capacity as minority leader, Reed in 1893 and early 1894 organized several Republican filibusters in an effort to force Crisp to count the quorum. These efforts were to no avail until February 1894, when Reed attacked a Democratic-supported measure by calling for one roll call after another and then using the silent quorum tactic to delay action. Despite their majorities the Democrats were unable to muster a quorum on their own, and after two months Crisp was forced to concede; the House adopted a rule allowing the Speaker to declare a quorum when a majority of members were actually present, regardless of whether they answered to their names.

Crisp's tenure is notable in the evolution of the speakership for strengthening the Rules Committee as a tool of the Speaker. Historian Fuller noted that this expanded role for the Rules Committee was a "radical departure from the long-established rules and principles of parliamentary law and practice." He added that the "tyranny of Reed seemed beneficence when Crisp ruled that not even 'the question of consideration could be raised against a report from the Committee on Rules.'"[26]

"CANNONISM"

During their reigns as Speaker, Reed and Crisp centralized power in the House. Not only was the Speaker now able to take effective command of the House, his authority to name the members and chairmen of all committees gave him the power to punish or reward his colleagues. As chairman of the Rules Committee, which had the right to immediate access to the floor, he could control the timing and content of bills to be brought before the House. And with unlimited power of recognition, he could determine in large measure what business would be taken up on the floor of the House. Though these authorities ensured that the House would run efficiently, if abused they could allow a Speaker to tyrannize the House. That is what

happened when "Uncle Joe" Cannon was elected Speaker in 1903.

Regaining control of Congress in 1895, the Republicans returned Reed to the speakership. Having broken with President William McKinley over the intervention in Cuba and the annexation of Hawaii and the Philippines, Reed resigned from the House in 1899. Cannon, who had already lost races for the speakership in 1881 and 1889, hoped to succeed Reed then, but the Republicans instead chose David B. Henderson, R-Iowa, who served two ineffective terms as Speaker before retiring from the House. When he was finally elected Speaker in 1903, Cannon was the oldest representative (sixty-seven) and had served longer (twenty-eight years) than any member yet to head the House of Representatives.

Cannon's first years in office gave little indication of what would develop. The affable Speaker was one of the most popular men in Congress, and in his first term, "his natural kindliness and sense of humor fostered a spirit of amicability that influenced the mood of the House."[27] Though he would eventually rescind it, Cannon even granted authority to the Democratic leader, John Sharp Williams, D-Miss., to assign Democrats to committees, subject to Cannon's veto.

But Cannon was also a devout conservative, unsympathetic to much of the progressive legislation sought by President Theodore Roosevelt and favored by a growing number of liberal Republicans and Democrats in the House. Though he was forced to accept some of these measures—including the Hepburn Act (1905), which strengthened the power of the Interstate Commerce Commission to set railroad rates, the Pure Food and Drug Act of 1906, and the Mann Act of 1910—he also made increasingly arbitrary use of his powers as Speaker to maintain control of the House.

On days set aside for approval by unanimous consent of purely local bills of minor importance, Cannon moved arbitrarily to reward his friends and punish his enemies. "Often on the success of these bills would depend the reelection of many men in Congress," Fuller wrote. The Speaker's "smile and assent made and unmade members, accordingly, as he bestowed or withheld these powerful benefices."[28] Although the seniority system was still not firmly embedded, Cannon's flagrant disregard for it in assigning members to committees further contributed to the chamber's growing irritation with his rule.

But it was Cannon's use, or misuse, of the Rules Committee that most offended his colleagues. Before any committee could report legislation to the full House, the committee had to obtain clearance from Rules, and clearance usually was granted only for those measures that met with Cannon's favor. The Rules Committee's special terms and guidelines for bills to be considered by the House—those acceptable to Cannon—usually placed sharp limits on debate and foreclosed floor amendments. The latter practice enabled Cannon and his associates to attach legislative "riders" (nongermane amendments) in committee that might have been defeated on the floor if brought to a separate vote. But because these riders were frequently attached to annu-

"Uncle Joe" Cannon addresses the House of Representatives. Cannon dominated the House from 1903 until 1910, when Republicans and Democrats revolted against his arbitrary rule.

al appropriations bills, the House usually accepted them rather than kill the entire bill.

Eventually the persistent use of the Speaker's powers to obstruct the legislative will—not of the majority party itself, but of a new majority of members of both parties—sparked a revolt. In March 1909 the House adopted the Calendar Wednesday rule, setting aside time each Wednesday for committee chairmen to call up bills that their committees had reported but that had not been cleared for floor action by Rules. *(See box, Prying Loose Legislation Stuck in Committee, p. 488.)*

At the beginning of a special session that opened a few days later, a group of Republican insurgents joined the Democrats, led by James Beauchamp "Champ" Clark, D-Mo., in a move to curb the powers of the Rules Committee. That effort failed when several Democrats joined the Republican majority in opposition to Clark, and instead the House adopted a weak alternative that made only slight inroads into Cannon's power. Chief among these was the establishment of the Consent Calendar, which set aside two days each month on which individual members could call up minor bills of particular interest to them without prior approval from the Speaker.

In March 1910 the insurgent Republicans found another opportunity to challenge Cannon's iron rule. On March 17, George W. Norris, R-Neb., the leader of the insurgents, took advantage of a parliamentary opening to move for immediate consideration of a reform resolution that would remove the Speaker from the Rules Committee and expand the committee to fifteen members; the members would be chosen by election of the House and would then choose their own chairman. Cannon stalled for two days, while he pondered a point of order that Norris's motion was out of order, until Republican stalwarts who had gone to their districts for St. Patrick's Day returned to the capital. Finally, on March 19, Cannon ruled that Norris's motion was out of order. The returning Republicans were not enough. The House overturned Cannon's decision, 164–182, and then adopted the reform resolution, which Norris had modified, 191–156. The modification set the size of the Rules Committee at ten members, six from the majority and four from the minority.

In what has been described as one of the most dramatic events in the history of the House, Cannon then announced that he would entertain a motion to declare the chair vacant so that the House could elect a new Speaker. But though they were willing to strip him of his powers, most of the Republican insurgents were not willing to unseat him—or to help put a Democrat in the speakership—and Cannon remained Speaker until the term ended in March 1911.

DECLINE OF THE SPEAKER'S POWER

When the Democrats won control of the House in 1911, they named Champ Clark their new Speaker and chose Oscar W. Underwood, D-Ala., as majority leader and chairman of the Ways and Means Committee. They also agreed that the Democratic members of Ways and Means would serve as their Committee on Committees to draw up committee assignments for all Democrats, a move that further weakened the powers of the Speaker. (The Democrats retained that arrangement until 1974, when the power to make committee assignments was transferred to the Steering and Policy Committee. In 1917 Republicans set up their own Committee on Committees.) Both parties now call their committee assignment bodies the "Steering Committee."

The Democrats also retained the Calendar Wednesday and Consent Calendar innovations, as well as a discharge rule, adopted in 1910, which allowed a majority of House members to petition to free legislation bottled up in a committee. A special calendar for private bills was also established.

Because Clark left most of the management of party business to Underwood, the floor leader quickly became the acknowledged leader in the House. "The Speaker became a figurehead, the floor leader supreme," wrote a contemporary observer.[29] Underwood made frequent use of the party caucus to develop unity on legislative issues. Democrats in 1909 had adopted rules that bound all party members to support any party position approved by two-thirds of those Democrats present and voting at a caucus meeting, provided the vote represented a majority of the Democrats in the House. A member could vote against the caucus position only if he considered the position unconstitutional or had made "contrary pledges to his constituents prior to his election or received contrary instructions by resolutions or platform from his nominating authority."

Underwood also used the caucus to develop legislative proposals, which then would be referred to the appropriate committees for formal approval; to instruct committees as to which bills they might or might not report; and to instruct the Rules Committee on the terms to be included in its special orders governing floor consideration on major bills and proposed amendments. The power that had been concentrated in the hands of the Speaker was now transferred to "King Caucus" and the man who dominated it. "Whereas Cannon had often exercised control by keeping unwanted legislation off of the floor," observed Peters, "Underwood sought to control legislation by ensuring a majority vote on the floor. The result was despotism under two different guises."[30]

Rule by caucus worked well as long as Democrats were relatively united on the issues; during President Woodrow Wilson's first term, they were able to enact a large body of domestic legislation. But the Democrats soon began to split over foreign policy, and the effectiveness of the binding caucus had disappeared by the time the Republicans took control of the House in 1919. Once again, however, the Speaker was not the true leader of the House.

The leading contender for the speakership in 1919 was James R. Mann, R-Ill., who had been minority leader since 1911. But many Republicans feared that Mann would try to centralize power in the Speaker's office, so they turned to Frederick H. Gillett, R-Mass., who, like his Democratic predecessor, Champ Clark, declined to assert political leadership. Mann refused the position of floor leader, which was then given to Franklin W. Mondell, R-Wyo. Mann, however, retained substantial influence among House Republicans.

To further ensure decentralization, the Republicans set up a five-member Steering Committee, chaired by the majority leader. The Speaker and the chairman of the Rules Committee were barred from sitting on this committee, though Mondell invited both to attend its meetings, which were held almost daily to discuss party positions and map strategy with committee chairmen and other Republican leaders. "For the most part," Randall B. Ripley reported, "the Steering Committee carried out the wishes of the Republican leaders in the House, even when these were not in accord with the Republican administration." As example Ripley cited Steering Committee opposition that killed a bill to raise civil service pensions despite support from the Coolidge administration, the Senate, and every member of the House Civil Service Committee. Leadership under this system was so diffuse that House Republicans accomplished little during the period. House members, Ripley wrote, "including some committee chairmen, used the loose leadership structure to pursue legislative ends other than those officially sanctioned."[31]

As Speaker from 1925 to 1931, Nicholas Longworth, R-Ohio, sought to centralize power once again in the Speaker's office. Longworth held it "to be the duty of the Speaker, standing squarely on the platform of his party, to assist in so far as he properly can the enactment of legislation in accordance with the declared principles and policies of his party and by the same token to resist the enactment of legislation in violation thereof."[32] One of his first actions was to discipline Republican Progressives; those who had opposed his candidacy for the speakership, and who had also opposed a rules change that made it much more difficult to discharge a bill from committee, found themselves stripped of their committee seniority.

Despite these moves, Longworth as Speaker had few of the powers that enabled Cannon to centralize power in the speakership. He nonetheless was considered an effective Speaker, able, as Peters notes, to wield power and authority not so much by manipulating the rules but "by force of his character." Longworth's style was collegial. While he made little use of the Steering Committee, he established a small group of trusted associates to help him run the House. Though it appeared contradictory given his stand on strong party leadership, Longworth also was willing to deal with the Democrats not only on policy issues but on scheduling business. He and the Democratic leader, John Nance Garner, D-Texas, began the tradition, later made famous by Sam Rayburn, of the "Board of Education"—gatherings in a Capitol hideaway where leaders from both parties met over drinks to work out accommodations on various matters.

THE POWER OF PERSUASION: RAYBURN

Democrats regained control of the House in 1931, a position they lost only twice in the next sixty-four years, in 1947–1949 and 1953–1955. During the first ten years of this cycle, four different Democrats held the speakership. Garner was elected Speaker in 1931. When he became vice president in 1933, he was replaced by Henry T. Rainey of Illinois, who died in 1934. Rainey was followed in 1935 by Joseph W. Byrns of Tennessee, who died in 1936. Byrns's successor, William B. Bankhead of Alabama, served as Speaker until his death in 1940. None of them left a lasting mark on the office. That was to change with the election in 1940 of Majority Leader Rayburn, who served as Speaker until his death in 1961, except for during the two Republican Congresses, when Joseph Martin of Massachusetts held the post.

Rayburn was a strong Speaker—indeed, his reputation reached near mythic proportions in the decades following his death. But the reasons for Rayburn's strength and the style with which he led the House were in sharp contrast to those in play during the Reed and Cannon speakerships.

Rayburn entered the House in 1913, just three years after the revolt against Cannon and at a time when the powers and the stature of the Speaker were at low ebb. By 1940 little real change had been made in the Speaker's powers. The seniority system was well entrenched, which meant that committee chairmen and ranking members could act with a great deal more independence than they could at the turn of the century. In 1940 and for the next two decades most of the chairmen of the major committees were southern Democrats.

At the same time most southern Democrats began to vote with the Republicans on New Deal, and eventually on civil rights, issues, forming a conservative coalition against liberal northern Democrats. Even when the conservative coalition did not form on a particular issue, the thin Democratic majorities could make it difficult for the Democratic leadership to achieve its program. As Rayburn himself put it in 1950, "The old day of pounding on the desk and giving people hell is gone. . . . A man's got to lead by persuasion and kindness and the best reason—that's the only way he can lead people."[33]

A man of great integrity who venerated the House of Representatives, Rayburn dealt with the individual rather than the party. He sought to bind individual members to him through friendship and favors; he did not force Democrats to vote against their conscience or constituency; he played down partisanship, shunning the use of the caucus and other party mecha-

One of the most respected twentieth-century House Speakers was Texas Democrat Sam Rayburn.

nisms that he thought divisive and working with minority leaders, even doing the occasional favor for a rank-and-file member of the minority; he cultivated younger members, advising them "to get along, go along."

Rayburn's preferences were controlling when it came to Democratic committee assignments. In 1948 he obtained the removal from the Un-American Activities Committee of three Democrats who had supported Dixiecrat Strom Thurmond in the 1948 presidential campaign. He saw to it that Democrats named to vacancies on Ways and Means were sympathetic to reciprocal trade bills and opposed to reductions in oil depletion allowances. And he turned the Education and Labor Committee from a predominantly conservative body into a more liberal one.

Despite the active presence of the conservative coalition, Rayburn was able to win House passage of an impressive amount of legislation dealing with both foreign and domestic matters, including two far-reaching civil rights bills. He accomplished his goals by working with the other power centers in the House. Rayburn, writes Peters,

was a man carved for the role he played, yet he was also a shrewd politician who was able to create a political labyrinth in which his own skills would prove most effective. His success lay less in his ability to swing large numbers of votes than in avoiding situations in which that would be necessary. When he wanted legislation stopped, he let others stop it; when he wanted legislation passed, he worked with the committee chairman to get bills that could command a floor majority. . . . [Rayburn's] emphasis upon the virtue of honesty and his reputation for fairness in dealing with members contributed to the creation of an atmosphere of comity in the House that facilitated his leadership. . . . He did not win votes by staring people down; instead, he established a set of expectations about behavior that enabled him to deal for votes when necessary.[34]

TRANSITIONAL SPEAKERS: MCCORMACK, ALBERT

Rayburn's speakership marked the end of an era. In his later years, younger and more liberal Democrats began to demand changes that would lead to the greatest internal reforms in the history of the House. Indeed, Rayburn's last major victory, in 1961, came in a battle to make the Rules Committee, dominated by conservative southerners, more responsive to the will of the Democratic majority. *(See "Major Legislation and the Rules Committee," p. 494.)*

Rayburn's two immediate successors, John W. McCormack, D-Mass., who served as Speaker from 1962 to 1971, and Carl Albert, D-Okla., who was Speaker from 1971 to 1977, had the ill luck to lead the House during a time both of great social and political upheaval within the nation and of great institutional change that neither man was well equipped to manage. McCormack was popular with his colleagues, and like Rayburn, based his leadership on his personal ties to members. But he lacked the persuasive skills of his predecessor and placed considerable reliance on Albert, his majority leader, and on the majority whip, Hale Boggs, D-La.

McCormack's weakness as a leader, coupled with his opposition to reform proposals in the House and his support of President Johnson's escalation of the Vietnam War, frustrated many of the younger, more liberal House Democrats. In 1968 Morris K. Udall, D-Ariz., challenged him for Speaker in the party caucus. McCormack easily won reelection, but soon announced his decision to retire at the end of the Congress.

Albert, too, was generally considered by his colleagues to be a weak leader. His low-key style did not seem suited to the requirements of the times, although any Speaker would have been hard put to guide the House smoothly and firmly through an unparalleled period of internal reform, against the backdrop of U.S. withdrawal from the Vietnam War and the Watergate crisis, which resulted in President Richard Nixon's resignation.

Relations between the Republican president and the Democratic Congress were tense throughout the Nixon presidency. Intent on expanding his power, Nixon acted with minimal consultation with and concern for Congress. His administration was committed to political and economic programs opposed by the great majority of the Democrats. Their first priority was to halt administration plans to revamp or terminate many of the Great Society programs of President Lyndon B. Johnson. The prolonged congressional-executive stalemate that resulted gave rise to frustration in Democratic ranks that found expression, especially in the House, in criticism of the leadership.

Albert also drew criticism from younger and more activist House members for not supporting internal House reforms more vigorously. By the early 1970s a sharp increase in retirements and reelection defeats of much of the "Old Guard" had resulted in a significant infusion of new blood in the House. The average age of House members had crept steadily downward, and most of the new generation were liberal Democrats. With the dramatic turnover in membership—particularly the election of seventy-five new Democratic members in 1974—came pressure for changes in House rules and practices. Reforms adopted by the Democratic Caucus in the early 1970s, particularly in 1971, 1973, and 1974, were to have a substantial effect on the way the House and its leaders would conduct their business.

One set of reforms broke the grip senior members held on the House by subjecting committee chairmen to election by secret ballot. In 1975 the caucus deposed three chairmen. Committee chairmen also were forced to share their powers with quasi-independent subcommittees, some of which were led by junior members. Other changes limited House Democrats to one subcommittee chairmanship, gave the subcommittees their own staffs and guaranteed each party member an assignment on a major committee.

A second set of reforms granted new powers to the Speaker, making that office potentially stronger than at any time since the reigns of Reed and Cannon. The Speaker was given the right to nominate the chairman and all the Democratic members of the Rules Committee, subject to caucus approval, and that panel once again became an arm of the leadership, not the independent power center it had been in the previous three decades. The Democratic Steering and Policy Committee was set up in 1973 to give coherence and strategy to the party's legislative program and was placed firmly under the Speaker's control. At the end of 1974 the committee was given the authority, formerly held by Ways and Means Democrats, to appoint the Democratic members to House committees, subject to caucus approval. Although most of these new powers became available during Albert's tenure as Speaker, he made little use of them, leaving them to his successors to exploit.

THE MODERN SPEAKERSHIP: O'NEILL

In many respects Thomas P. "Tip" O'Neill Jr. of Massachusetts was an unlikely candidate to modernize the speakership. A New Deal liberal, he was to the political left of most of his colleagues. Intensely partisan, he was forced to work with a popular Republican president, Ronald Reagan, and a Republican Senate during six years of his decade as Speaker from 1977 to 1987. A consummate practitioner of inside politics, O'Neill faced demands from rank-and-file Democrats for greater participation in the decision-making process. A less-than-commanding public speaker who reserved his public appearances for his Massachusetts constituents, the new Speaker was called upon to be the national spokesperson for his party. O'Neill once told a reporter that he was one old dog ready to learn new tricks—and he did learn some, giving many more members, especially junior members, leadership responsibilities and becoming a nationally recognized media celebrity. But his reluctance to temper both his liberal beliefs and his partisanship made coalition-building, even within his party, difficult at times.

Genial and enormously popular, O'Neill based his leadership on friendships, doing favors for loyal colleagues, taking care of what he called the "little odds and ends." But O'Neill also took some innovative steps to expand participation of the party rank and file in House affairs, enlarging the whip organization and setting up special task forces to help the leadership develop support and strategy on major legislation. One of O'Neill's most successful ploys was the creation of an ad hoc committee in 1977 to draw up comprehensive energy legislation, a top priority of the Carter administration. Although the tactic worked well in that case, policy differences and objections from the standing committees prevented the Speaker from ever using it again.

O'Neill also made use of several powers the House reforms had bestowed upon the Speaker, including the authority to name the Democratic members of the House Rules Committee. Although O'Neill did not demand unstinting loyalty from the Democrats on Rules, he did expect them to support him on key issues. In response to the Republican minority's penchant for offering floor amendments designed to put Democrats on the spot, O'Neill also came to rely heavily on restrictive rules, those specifying which amendments could be offered on the floor and in what order, as a potent tool to maintain control of debate on the House floor. *(See "Shift Toward Restricted Rules," p. 495.)*

Another tool O'Neill used to help the leadership control the flow of legislation was the authority to refer bills to more than one committee either at the same time or sequentially. The Speaker may also set time limits for committee action, whether a bill is referred to one committee or several. This authority keeps alive bills that otherwise might die in an unfriendly committee.

O'Neill also gave the speakership unprecedented visibility. He was aided by the decision to allow House floor proceedings to be televised to the public, beginning in 1979, and later spurred on by criticisms from his colleagues that he was not effectively articulating Democratic alternatives to President Reagan's legislative agenda. Soon the Speaker's office was issuing a steady stream of press releases trying to mobilize support for Democratic Party positions. Though previous Speakers had met with reporters before every House session, they usually only answered specific questions. Now O'Neill used them to volunteer information about the goals and achievements of House Democrats and to spar with Reagan on the issues.

O'Neill's attempts at public relations won mixed reviews. His sometimes garbled syntax, his physical bulk, shaggy dog appearance, and ever-present cigar were reminiscent of the stereotypical backroom pol, an image that some younger members had hoped the Democratic Party could shed. Nonetheless, O'Neill affected public attitudes on a variety of questions, some more successfully than others. Nothing the Speaker said or did could have headed off support in the nation or in the House for the 1981 Reagan economic program. But on several foreign policy is-

sues, where there was substantial doubt about Reagan's approach, O'Neill helped solidify Democratic opposition and made it credible to the public. For example, by coming out strongly against an expensive and controversial intercontinental ballistic missile, known as the MX missile, and U.S. aid to the Nicaraguan "contras," a guerrilla force that was battling to oust the leftist government of that nation, the Speaker focused media attention on the anti-Reagan position and almost certainly locked in some Democratic votes on those closely fought issues.

Yet O'Neill's speakership was not an unqualified success. His first year in the post seemed to bear out early predictions that he could be the strongest Speaker since Rayburn. But Carter's weak presidency and new militancy on the part of House Republicans combined with O'Neill's own unyielding partisanship to his disadvantage. Unable to keep his Democrats united, he lost several key votes in his first four years.

Ronald Reagan's election in 1980 and the loss of thirty-three House seats only worsened his situation in 1981–1982. Not until House Democrats won twenty-six seats in the 1982 elections was O'Neill able to unite his party in opposition to Reagan's policies. The stalemate that often resulted and the heightened partisan rhetoric that it engendered led to accusations that O'Neill was a heavy-handed partisan and that the Democratic Party had no focus and could not govern. When O'Neill did try to exercise policy leadership on an issue, he was often deserted by one wing or another of his party, as he was in 1983, when a number of Democrats—including Majority Leader Jim Wright and Whip Thomas S. Foley, Wash.—voted against O'Neill to support funding for the MX missile.

Despite these setbacks, O'Neill's speakership was never in any jeopardy. But criticisms of his leadership and the clear frustrations among many House Democrats about the image the party was projecting may have weighed in his decision to retire in January 1987, the end of the 99th Congress.

THE LIMITS OF POWER: WRIGHT

As Speaker from 1987 to June 1989, Jim Wright was determined to give House Democrats the policy leadership many of them had found lacking in O'Neill. "I think there's a creative role for the legislative branch and a leadership role for the Speaker," Wright once said. "The Congress should not simply react, passively, to recommendations from the president but should come forward with initiatives of its own."[35]

But in pursuing his activist agenda for the House, Wright may have overstepped the limits of the speakership's powers at that time, although Speaker Newt Gingrich would later seek to expand the office far beyond anything Wright had attempted. Wright exceeded the bounds of what many Democrats were willing to accept in a leader. He certainly was not what Democrats had expected when they chose him as a balanced compromise for majority leader over the ambitious liberals Phillip Burton and Richard Bolling a decade earlier.

By his second year in the office, Republicans considered him to be the match for Cannon in his treatment of the minority.

Ethics charges forced the resignation of Speaker Jim Wright in 1989. Wright, shown here offering his resignation as Speaker of the House, was the first Speaker in history to give up his post under fire.

Democrats were alienated by his failure to practice the politics of inclusion that had become *de rigueur*. As allegations of financial misconduct lodged against the Speaker by Gingrich developed into a full-blown investigation, Wright found that Democrats who were willing to support him when he—and they—were winning were not as ready to back him on a question of personal ethics. On May 31, 1989, Wright announced that he would give up the speakership effective June 6, becoming the first Speaker to be forced from office at midterm. A month later he resigned his House seat. *(See box, Some Speakers Faced a Trial by Fire, p. 438.)*

Wright was a deputy whip when he ran for majority leader in 1976, winning by a single vote. Had he lost, he would have become chairman of the Public Works Committee. Unlike his three rivals, Wright had few enemies or personal negatives. He had always compromised personal differences when possible, or disagreed gently if he had to. He also had another advantage: as a member of the Public Works Committee, he had done countless small favors, making sure a dam was put up here or a federal building there. And throughout his ten years as majority leader, Wright continued to do the little favors, devoting months of precious time to public appearances and fund-raising missions in districts throughout the country.

Favors notwithstanding, many members felt a sense of un-

ease, even mistrust, about Wright. Private, competitive, at times aggressively partisan, Wright did not inspire the sort of personal affection that O'Neill had drawn. His reputation for oratorical skills was well deserved, but now and again his speech turned florid, his smile disingenuous. "You watch him and you know when he's going to get partisan," GOP leader Bob Michel, Ill., said in 1984. "The eyebrows start to rise. The voice begins to stretch out. And the Republicans say, 'Snake oil is at it again.'"[36] Though such descriptions might be dismissed because they came from the opposition, Democrats were nonetheless concerned about the image Wright might convey to the public.

Despite these misgivings, Wright was not challenged when he ran to succeed O'Neill in 1986. His assertions that he would be a strong, policy-oriented Speaker appealed to his Democratic colleagues who not only wanted to demonstrate that the Democrats could govern but also wanted a record to see them through the 1988 presidential campaign. And Wright was clearly ready. As Speaker, he seemed to suddenly unleash an agenda and a pace of activity he had kept under wraps from his colleagues, and the adjustment was sometimes difficult even for members who professed to want such activism in their leader.

In his acceptance speech Wright laid out an ambitious agenda for the 100th Congress, calling for renewal of the clean water act and a new highway bill and suggesting that the tax rate for the wealthy be frozen at 1987 levels instead of dropping as scheduled, a proposal that some said put him beyond the majority of the Democrats. By the end of the 100th Congress, not only had the clean water and highway bills become law, but Congress had overhauled the welfare system, approved the biggest expansion of Medicare since its creation, and rewritten U.S. trade law. Most of this legislation had passed the House with bipartisan support.

Although Wright's Democratic colleagues took pride in these legislative achievements, many resented being excluded from the process of achieving them. The "Lone Ranger," as Wright was sometimes dubbed, had a record of springing major decisions without consulting key colleagues. His very public involvement in trying to negotiate a peace plan between the Nicaragua government and the contra rebels not only angered the administration and Republicans in the House but unsettled Democrats who feared that they might be held accountable at the polls if the peace process failed.

Wright was also criticized for his aggressive tactics in getting legislation passed. Rules to guide floor debate grew more restrictive; no amendments, for example, were allowed on the clean water and highway bills or on a moratorium on aid to the Nicaraguan contras. Republicans complained that under Wright, many bills were never given hearings and came to the floor of the House without being reported by committee, that substantive legislation was being enacted through self-executing rules (which provide for the automatic adoption of an amendment or other matter upon adoption of the rule), and that the minority was more often denied its right to try to recommit bills.

Wright's support among Democrats was substantially weakened early in 1989 over a proposed pay raise that would have increased congressional salaries by 51 percent. The raise was to take effect if the House and Senate did not veto it by February 9. The initial strategy was to let the pay raise take effect and then to vote on legislation to curb honoraria. But public outrage at the size of the raise—and the fact that it might take effect without a vote in Congress—was overwhelming.

Wright buckled to the pressure, his colleagues believed, failing in his duty to take the heat and protect their interests. He circulated a questionnaire to Democratic members asking whether they wanted a vote scheduled. They viewed this tactic as a major blunder, focusing additional attention on the issue and creating a mechanism that could reveal members' views. This indeed proved to be the case, as members were barraged with demands from the press about how they had filled out the questionnaire. As expected, the pressure proved too great and the questionnaire indicated that a majority of members had asked to have a vote on the issue, whether they really wanted one or not.

After the Senate yielded to the pressure and voted no on the pay raise, Wright scheduled a vote for February 7. When the raise, not surprisingly, was defeated, many Democrats angrily blamed Wright for changing the strategy at the last minute.

Barely a month later, the ethics committee announced that it "had reason to believe" that Wright had violated House rules on financial conduct. In the next few weeks, new allegations of misconduct surfaced, further damaging the Speaker, as did a *Washington Post* story revealing that a top aide to Wright had a criminal record for brutally beating a woman sixteen years earlier. After Wright's attorneys failed to persuade the Ethics Committee to dismiss the charges on technical grounds, the Speaker decided to resign to spare the House the embarrassment of a public investigation of its Speaker. Only days before, Democratic Whip Tony Coelho, Calif., had announced he would resign his House seat in the face of allegations of irregularities in his purchase of a $100,000 junk bond.

Political scientist Ronald Peters observes that "if Wright had not been vulnerable to the ethics charges brought against him, it is unlikely that his Republican opponents could have undermined his support in the Democratic Caucus. However, if Wright had led the House differently, neither Republicans nor Democrats would have had a sufficient motive to seek to unseat him."[37]

Whether a Speaker who worked more closely with his own leadership and his rank and file and who was less openly partisan would have survived the same ethics charges Wright faced is, of course, conjecture. But the Wright episode clearly shows the potential weakness of a Speaker who fails to develop an atmosphere in which consensus building and shared decision-making can flourish in a Democratic Party that had grown used to broad dispersion of power and multiple independent power centers. Wright himself seemed to recognize this. "Have I been too partisan? Too insistent? Too abrasive? Too determined to

have my way?" he asked in his resignation speech. "Perhaps. Maybe so."[38]

While Wright's relatively brief tenure and the circumstances of his departure may make it easy to brand his speakership a failure, a case can also be made that Wright was focused on creating legislative achievements for his party, and was ahead of his time in his willingness to recentralize leadership to respond to an increasingly aggressive partisan opposition. Ironically, the much criticized Central American peace plan, which the Republicans used to help demonize him, may be remembered as Wright's most successful and daring initiative.

However, after Wright's resignation Democrats wanted a respite from what they regarded as excessive activism and controversy and a return to a quieter, more consensual leadership style.

END OF AN ERA: FOLEY

On June 6, 1989, the Democratic Caucus nominated Majority Leader Thomas S. Foley of Washington by acclamation to succeed Wright as Speaker. Better known for bringing together warring factions than for drawing up battle plans, Foley seemed well equipped to help the Democrats—and the House—put the Wright episode behind them; in his first speech as Speaker he called for debate "with reason and without rancor."

Indeed, Foley had the most impressive resume of any House Speaker in decades; he had served in each of the Democrats' major leadership positions in succession—caucus chairmanship (1976–1980), as the last appointed whip (1980–1986), and majority leader (1986–1989). He was also the first Speaker since Rayburn to have been a committee chairman—he had chaired the Agriculture Committee (1975–1981).

A thoughtful and articulate man, Foley was perhaps the first Speaker his Democratic colleagues felt comfortable putting in front of a television camera. With a knack for telling stories and a near-photographic memory that helped him to master the substance of most issues that came before him, Foley was a superb negotiator who was on good terms with most Democrats and a good number of Republicans. "Foley has a talent for listening and knowing what other people want," a veteran leadership aide said.[39] He chaired the task force that drew up the Democratic alternative to the 1985 Gramm-Rudman deficit reduction act. He also chaired the 1989 budget negotiations and was the lead negotiator on a comprehensive aid package for the Nicaraguan contras.

Endowed with a sense of detachment rare among politicians, Foley was a cautious, careful political navigator. "The reality," he said a few weeks before becoming Speaker, "is that in a modern, participatory Congress . . . the responsibility of leadership and the necessity of leadership is to constantly involve members in the process of decision and consensus."[40] He did not like to commit himself early on controversial issues, and he could be as skillful at making the case for the opposing side as for his own. "I think I am a little cursed," he said in 1984, "with seeing the other point of view and trying to understand it." Indeed, he was

SOME SPEAKERS FACED A TRIAL BY FIRE

Service as Speaker of the House would have to be considered the culmination of any politician's career but some leaders must survive a trial by fire to hold on to the post and emerge with their political and personal reputations reasonably intact. Some have succeeded better than others.

Speaker Newt Gingrich, R-Ga., was embarrassed during his reelection campaign for Speaker in 1997 as several Republicans cast their votes for other persons or voted present. He then suffered a historic formal reprimand by his colleagues for ethics violations and later repelled a group of younger conservatives who, with encouragement from other members of Gingrich's leadership team, made an effort to depose him. Gingrich survived because he was in the mainstream of his party conference and lacked popular rivals positioned to take over the post. It did not last. Following surprise GOP election losses in 1998, calls again arose for new leadership, and Gingrich was formally opposed by Robert L. Livingston of Louisiana. Faced with almost certain defeat, Gingrich said he would not stand for Speaker again and would give up his seat in the 106th Congress that was to begin in 1999.

Jim Wright, D-Texas, the only Speaker to be forced out of office during his term, has often been compared to Gingrich in his desire to be a visible national leader and to use the speakership to promote a strong party agenda. But Wright never commanded strong loyalty or personal regard from his party colleagues. The link between them probably also is inevitable given Gingrich's leading role in pummeling Wright with ethics allegations for years before Wright's resignation in 1989. Wright left to avoid formal discipline by the House. Historians will no doubt argue whether the controversy that ended Wright's career was more or less serious than the reprimand, $300,000 fine, and allegations of tax law violations and misleading

the ethics committee that Gingrich endured. There is broad consensus that Gingrich helped to create the political climate for use of ethics charges to demonize opponents, a tactic that his Democratic rivals then turned against him.

NINETEENTH-CENTURY SPEAKERS

In the early nineteenth century, Speaker Nathaniel Macon also came close to being deposed. Macon was one of Thomas Jefferson's most devoted loyalists, and was rewarded for his fealty with Jefferson's support during his election as Speaker in 1801.

But Macon later allied himself with a bitter foe of the president's, John Randolph, who broke with Jefferson over a plan to acquire Florida. Jefferson retaliated against Macon by opposing his reelection as Speaker in 1805. Jefferson's effort failed, but it was a close enough decision that Macon chose not to seek another term as Speaker.

Henry Clay went to the well of the House to defend himself against allegations of impropriety while he was Speaker in 1825. In a published letter in a newspaper, another member accused Clay of cutting a secret deal to support John Quincy Adams for president in exchange for an appointment as secretary of state. Adams had been elected by the House after the popular vote leader, Andrew Jackson, failed to receive a majority of the electoral vote. The scandal died quickly. Clay asked the House to name a special committee to look into the charges, but the member who had made the allegation refused to appear.

John White, Speaker from 1841–1843, came under fire for one of the last speeches he gave before leaving the House in 1845 to take a judgeship in Kentucky. After it was disclosed that a particularly eloquent speech he gave had been plagiarized from former Vice President Aaron Burr, White committed suicide.

---

criticized for being insufficiently partisan and too indecisive. "He sees three sides of every coin," noted one observer.

Foley's honeymoon as Speaker was brief. Republicans were in no mood for an olive branch. Foley's passive leadership style—trying to avoid controversy within the caucus and allowing committee chairmen to compete among themselves, and with the leadership, for influence—allowed him to be overtaken by events at critical points. And he seemed especially ill-suited to confront the accelerating guerrilla warfare against Democrats, and against the institution of Congress itself, led by Minority Whip Gingrich.

Foley was surprised by the scandal that surrounded the House Bank throughout 1992, when it was revealed that hundreds of sitting and former House members had routinely overdrawn their accounts without penalty. Foley had argued for limited disclosure, as recommended by the Committee on Standards of Official Conduct, but could not resist overwhelming public pressure as the Republicans forced the names of members of both parties to be made public. Of the 269 sitting mem-

bers with overdrafts, seventy-seven retired or were defeated in primary or general election bids for the House or other offices. The House Post Office also fell victim to allegations of embezzlement and drug dealing by postal clerks as well as revelations that some members had received special favors, including the ability to convert stamps received by their offices into cash. (Ways and Means Committee Chairman Dan Rostenkowski, D-Ill., later went to prison as a result.)

Foley said that he was not responsible for supervising these House offices, which, indeed, had long operated as quasi-independent patronage operations under the nominal control of the Democratic Caucus. Both the Sergeant at Arms, whom many members blamed for the bank scandal, and the Postmaster ultimately went to prison. The Post Office was eliminated as a separate entity, and Foley finally acceded to a caucus rules change giving him the responsibility for nominating the officers of the House, which he had previously resisted.

Nonetheless, Foley seemed well-positioned for a long career as Speaker. He acted swiftly to shore up support for his reelec-

While James G. Blaine, R-Maine, was Speaker, he was cleared of wrongdoing by a special committee appointed to look into the Credit Mobilier bribery scandal, in which promoters of the Union Pacific Railroad used stock to bribe members of Congress to support federal subsidies for the railroad. But other allegations of graft surfaced in 1876, after Blaine left the Speaker's office due to a change of party control in the House.

Blaine took to the House floor to read from letters that supposedly exonerated him. That quelled efforts to censure him but the scandal did not help his unsuccessful quest for his party's presidential nomination at the GOP convention just months later. Blaine was finally nominated in 1884, but he lost the election to Grover Cleveland.

CANNON: STRIPPED OF POWER

The House in 1910 nearly deposed Speaker Joseph G. Cannon, R-Ill., for his heavy-handed use of power. The revolt against Cannon exploded in response to his spectacular use of the Speaker's powers to reward friends and punish foes. Cannon freely wielded his authority to control who sat on which committee, which bills went to the floor, and who would be recognized to speak.

Democrats made common cause with insurgent Republicans on March 19, 1910, and defeated Cannon on a procedural question that was, in effect, a referendum on his leadership.

The insurgents went on to ram through rules changes that stripped the Speaker of his right to make committee assignments and of his control of the Rules Committee.

Cannon refused to resign as Speaker, but invited a vote on deposing him. Pandemonium broke loose on the House floor, judging from the notation in the *Congressional Record:* "Great confusion in the Hall."

A resolution declaring the Speaker's office vacant was put to a vote—the only time such a vote has been taken—but Cannon survived, 155–192. It suited the political purposes of some to keep Cannon in office: that made it easier to run against "Cannonism" in the 1910 elections. This was perhaps the first time a Speaker had been a major focus in an election campaign. Cannon lost the speakership after Democrats won a majority of House seats for the first time since 1895. Cannon's resistance to political change in the country and within his party, and his increasingly arbitrary style of leadership had cost his office the influence it had long held within the House.

MCCORMACK, O'NEILL

More recently, Speaker John McCormack, D-Mass., retired in 1971 after top aides were accused of using the Speaker's office and name for fraudulent purposes, without McCormack's knowledge. McCormack, in his seventies and under pressure from a restive younger generation of lawmakers, had other reasons for leaving the House when he did.

When Thomas P. O'Neill Jr., D-Mass., became Speaker in 1977, he immediately faced questions raised in connection with the "Koreagate" influence-peddling scandal. The House Committee on Standards of Official Conduct in January 1977 began an investigation into allegations that as many as 115 members—Republicans and Democrats—had taken illegal gifts from South Korean agents. Some people suggested that O'Neill, during a 1974 trip to Korea, had asked Korean rice dealer Tongsun Park to make contributions to House members and their wives. But other members were the principal targets, and in July 1978 the committee issued a statement exonerating O'Neill. The panel said the only thing of "questionable propriety" the Speaker had done was to let Park pay for two parties in his honor.

tion in the Democratic Caucus in 1992, and no challenger emerged as a result of the scandals. In his first four years, he faced the same dynamic of a Democratic House confronting a Republican president as O'Neill and Wright had.

Many Democrats considered Foley too accommodating to the administration of President George Bush. When Democrats won the 1992 presidential election and obtained unified control of the executive and legislative branches for the first time in twelve years, the party nonetheless lost seats in the House. Foley was put in the position of having to pass an ambitious presidential program with a caucus membership that was not united either on policy or in loyalty to the new chief executive.

In pre-inauguration meetings with President-elect Clinton, Foley and other congressional leaders urged him to retreat from some of his commitments as a "New Democrat" candidate, including a promise to press campaign reform legislation on Congress. The new administration also began inauspiciously with highly visible political missteps on numerous issues, most notably President Clinton's proposed health care reform plan,

which never achieved enough support even to reach the floor in the Democratic-controlled Congress. Internal divisions within the party, as well as effective opposition from a highly-unified Republican minority in both chambers, limited the ability of Congress to develop a politically popular legislative record. The widely touted benefits of unified government appeared hollow to much of the public. Clinton's unpopularity also created a backlash against Congress.

Foley himself showed serious weakness in his Washington congressional district for the first time in more than a decade, falling below forty percent of the vote in the state's all-candidate primary in September 1994. He was opposed by an attractive Republican, George Nethercutt, who was not the sort of fringe candidate who sometimes had won GOP nominations to oppose Foley. In addition to vulnerability based on his leadership post, Foley was also attacked for supporting a legal challenge to Washington's newly enacted law, passed by referendum, to impose term limits on the state's congressional delegation. (The U.S. Supreme Court later threw out the law.)

Amid the national Democratic rout in 1994, Foley lost in the general election, only the third such defeat for a sitting Speaker. The last had been Galusha A. Grow, a Pennsylvania Republican, who lost in 1862; his predecessor, William Pennington of New Jersey, had lost in 1860.

The Democratic Party surrendered fifty-two seats and control of the House shifted to the GOP after forty years of Democratic rule. Gracious in defeat, Foley offered cooperation in the transition, but Republicans responded harshly, with warnings to Democratic leaders and outgoing committee chairmen not to shred documents.

After his departure from Congress, Foley joined a law firm and, following the career path of former Senate Majority Leader Mike Mansfield and former Vice President Walter Mondale, was nominated by President Clinton to be ambassador to Japan, a post he assumed in 1997.

TRANSFORMING THE HOUSE AND BEYOND: GINGRICH

Even after his departure from Congress following the 1998 election setback for the GOP, evaluating Newt Gingrich's place in history would have to await future developments in the speakership and the politics of the House. But his mere presence as a Republican Speaker, after forty years of Democratic rule, guaranteed historical recognition. Gingrich's move from freshman to Speaker in only sixteen years, never having chaired a committee or subcommittee, was also unprecedented in the modern era.

Gingrich was clearly a new breed of legislative leader, although his role combined recognizable elements from predecessors of both parties. Among modern Speakers, Gingrich most resembled Wright in his desire to use power. But his control of his party gave him a power unrivaled since the days of Cannon.

Gingrich was elected to the House from an Atlanta, Georgia, district in 1978 after consecutive defeats in 1974 and 1976. In the earlier races, he had campaigned as a more liberal alternative to traditional Georgia Republicans, stressing the importance of civil rights and environmental protection. But in his winning campaign he ran as a conservative promising tax cuts. For the majority of his service prior to becoming Speaker, Gingrich was the only Republican in his state's House delegation. The sea change in southern politics that helped make Republican control of the House possible was illustrated by Georgia's representation in the 104th and 105th Congresses—an eight-to-three GOP advantage.

Unlike other recent leaders of both parties, Gingrich was in no sense a "man of the House," a phrase denoting a quintessential congressional insider that Speaker O'Neill had used to characterize his own service and as the title of his autobiography. It suggested someone who allowed himself to be shaped by the institution around him, by the need to establish relationships with the Senate and the executive branch, by shared personal and political accommodation with colleagues, and by the desire to pass legislation. Indeed, a substantial part of Gingrich's "apprentice-

After surviving a House ethics investigation, Speaker Newt Gingrich of Georgia is sworn in after being reelected by a slim margin to a second term in January 1997.

ship" for the speakership consisted of demonizing Congress, its leaders, the rival political party and almost every aspect of its manner of doing business, and creating issues to use in the future.

For Gingrich, the House was the trophy in a campaign of conquest; once secured, it was to be a vehicle for transforming society, not just through enactment of the principles stated in the 1994 election platform Republicans called the "Contract with America" as well as other legislation, but for ushering in a new era and repudiating the old. Its rules and practices were subservient to this greater purpose. The House seemed almost too small to contain the revolutionary zeal that the new majority, especially its large freshman class from the 1994 election, sought to spread throughout the country.

Gingrich as Speaker conceived of himself as a visionary who could make the House not only a vehicle for passage of legislation but a forum for ideas, principles, and values. Gingrich had these goals early. "The Congress in the long run can change the country more dramatically than the president," he said in a 1979 interview with Congressional Quarterly. "One of my goals is to make the House the co-equal of the White House."[41]

Indeed, for years as a backbencher Gingrich had developed a political philosophy that he felt could lead eventually to Republican control of the House, a conservative but futuristic creed that called for replacing the welfare state with an "opportunity society" in which the rising technological tide of the Information Age would lift the poor to prosperity. Gingrich formed a group of members called the "Conservative Opportunity Society" in 1983 to foster these beliefs and mastered the use of special order speeches and other mechanisms in the House to gain public attention. He also used ethics as an issue not only to dramatize disagreements with his colleagues over ideas but to condemn personally opponents who fought him, most notably Speaker Wright. In 1986 he inherited the chairmanship of GOPAC, a political action committee, and turned it into an instrument to inspire Republican candidates with ideas and strategies for seeking office.

Gingrich was hardly a loyal follower of the House Republican leadership, which he viewed as too passive, too prone to negotiate with Democrats for scraps of influence, and too easily co-opted by the collegialism of the House. Many of his colleagues, including some moderates, came to share these concerns, creating an unlikely coalition that elected Gingrich as minority whip in 1989 over the opposition of Minority Leader Bob Michel of Illinois. Gingrich also opposed policies of Republican presidents that he felt compromised the party's long-term goals, such as the bipartisan 1990 budget agreement between President Bush and the Democratic congressional leadership, which repudiated Bush's "no new taxes" pledge. As polit-

ical scientist Barbara Sinclair has noted, "[Gingrich] was willing to pay the policy cost in order to preserve the message."[42]

Gingrich's Republican colleagues in the 104th Congress were interested not in forming consensus or in shaping his style of leadership, which had helped elect many of them and gave them a program to run on and a list of bills to enact, but in aggressive followership. It was Gingrich's ability to inspire followership in the early days of his speakership that perhaps distinguished his role as a party leader most clearly from the Democrats, whose many factions had developed a distracting sense of self-importance that often made party unity and coherent leadership difficult. And it was the weakening of this loyalty, as Gingrich struggled with the transition from the rhetoric of revolution to the responsibility of governing, that threatened his hold on the speakership in the 105th Congress and ultimately forced him out after four years.

Gingrich united the Republican Conference around the plan of voting on all ten planks of the contract in the first 100 days of the session. The strategy focused the conference and invited a high level of party loyalty, even from less enthusiastic moderates who nonetheless welcomed the title of "chairman" preceding

---

CONTRACT WITH AMERICA

On September 27, 1994, six weeks before the November 8 election, approximately 350 House Republican members and candidates unveiled a ten-point campaign manifesto—they called it their "Contract with America." The event, staged on the Capitol lawn and spearheaded by Minority Whip Newt Gingrich, R-Ga., was aimed at creating a high-profile national platform from which Republicans could attack the Democratic Congress and present their priorities. When the GOP won a major victory in 1994, the contract became the agenda for House Republicans' first 100 days in office in the 104th Congress. GOP leaders promised only that the House would vote on the proposals, not that all would pass or be enacted.

Following are the ten subject areas covered by the contract, as well as the changes in internal House procedures discussed in the contract's preface:

• *Congressional Process.* Require that Congress end its exemptions from eleven workplace laws; and revise House rules to cut committees and their staff, impose term limits on committee chairmen, end proxy voting, and require three-fifths majority votes for tax increases.

• *Balanced Budget Amendment, Line-Item Veto.* Send to the states a constitutional amendment requiring a balanced budget and give the president the power to cancel (line-item veto) any appropriation or targeted tax break.

• *Crime.* Require restitution to victims; modify the exclusionary rule; increase grants for prison construction; speed deportation of criminal immigrants; create block grants to give communities flexibility in using anticrime funds; and limit death row appeals.

• *Welfare.* Cap spending on cash welfare; impose a lifetime five-

year limit on welfare benefits; deny benefits to unwed mothers under age eighteen; and give states new flexibility, including the option to receive federal welfare payments as a block grant.

• *Families and Children.* Require parental consent for children participating in surveys; provide tax benefits for adoptions and home care for the elderly; increase penalties for sex crimes against children; and strengthen enforcement of child support orders.

• *Middle-Class Tax Cut.* Add $500-per-child tax credit; ease "marriage penalty" for filers of joint tax returns; and expand individual retirement account savings plans.

• *National Security.* Prohibit use of U.S. troops in United Nations missions under foreign command; prohibit defense cuts to finance social programs; develop a missile defense system for U.S. territory; and cut funding for United Nations peacekeeping missions.

• *Social Security.* Repeal the 1993 increase in Social Security benefits subject to income tax; permit senior citizens to earn up to $30,000 a year without losing benefits; and give tax incentives for buying long-term care insurance.

• *Capital Gains and Regulations.* Cut capital gains taxes; allow for accelerated depreciation of business assets; increase first-year deductions for small businesses; reduce unfunded mandates; reduce federal paperwork; and require federal agencies to assess risks, use cost-benefit analysis, reduce paperwork, and reimburse property owners for reductions in value as a result of regulations.

• *Civil Law and Product Liability.* Establish national product liability law with limits on punitive damages; make it harder for investors to sue companies; and apply "loser pays" rule to certain federal cases.

their names and gave Gingrich the benefit of the doubt. The contract was drafted to avoid divisive social issues like abortion and school prayer and to focus on unifying conservative themes geared toward economic policy and a reduced role for government, such as balancing the budget, reforming welfare, and curbing unfunded mandates directed at the states. (*See box, Contract with America, p. 441.*)

As Speaker, Gingrich enjoyed remarkable success, at least in his first year, in passing legislation through the House and in shaping a national debate over issues based on the Republicans' message of less government, more tax cuts, and a return of power to the states. He was far less successful in reaping proportionate political credit for himself or for the Republican Party in part because the speakership contained innate limitations as a bully pulpit that no amount of revolutionary zeal could overcome and that Gingrich's often bombastic personality aggravated. It has been axiomatic in American politics in the twentieth century that the nation looks to the president as the nation's chief policy spokesperson and representative of the national values. Indeed, Gingrich became, as polls showed, perhaps the most disliked political figure in the nation, and gave President Clinton a target that helped reinvigorate a presidency some had given up for dead after the 1994 elections. Gingrich's assertiveness was often perceived by the public as arrogance, with a tendency to lecture and to appear overbearing, uncaring, and threatening. By the end of 1995, some polls gave him an approval rating hovering around 30 percent.

Congress shut down much of the government at the end of 1995, refusing to pass new versions of appropriations bills, after Clinton had vetoed the GOP leadership's ambitious domestic policy changes and tax cuts contained in a budget reconciliation bill and various spending measures. Republicans tried to blame Clinton for the ensuing disruption of vital services but it was the president who convinced the country that he was right, and the Republicans had to retreat, pass new appropriations bills, and allow government agencies to reopen. Senate Majority Leader Bob Dole, who was running for president, also appeared eager to repudiate House Republicans and present a more traditional image of responsible governance. The House revolutionaries were placed on the defensive, and the defeat forced Gingrich to reevaluate GOP tactics.

In 1996, Gingrich tried a less confrontational approach, allowing appropriations to pass with fewer controversial riders and obtaining enactment of welfare reform, a major Republican policy goal for decades that Clinton was also eager to use as a centerpiece for his reelection. The public seemed to like the more cooperative style and emphasis on bipartisan legislative achievements, retaining the status quo in the 105th Congress with a slightly reduced GOP House majority.

Gingrich's leadership style could hardly be called consistent, as he careened from one manner of doing business to another during his first three years in power. He experimented with different techniques, sometimes engaging in what his critics called micromanagement, at other times withdrawing from a direct role in the House to focus on the future and long-term political themes. He could be consultative and autocratic in rapid succession.

Part of Gingrich's need for experimentation stemmed from the Republicans' long years in the minority; they had no experience in running the House and many of their members had no significant legislative or political experience to deploy in their new roles. Many senior conservative veterans were regarded with suspicion by the freshmen as insufficiently zealous or too frequently collaborationist in earlier years with the defeated Democrats. Gingrich formed numerous task forces to develop ideas and sometimes let them draft actual legislation, although in the 105th Congress he deferred more frequently to the committee system.

The Speaker's daily press conference, a traditional event that had preceded every House session, became a major media spectacle when Gingrich opened it to television coverage after taking office. But Gingrich quickly ended the event entirely after the press became hostile, asking about his ethics problems or other potentially unfavorable matters, and his own lack of discipline in his comments threatened to shift public focus away from the GOP message.

Democrats, eager for payback against Gingrich for his attacks on Wright, filed dozens of ethics complaints against him. On December 21, 1996, the Speaker admitted, after two years of repeated denials, that he had failed to properly manage the financing of his political activities through charitable foundations. He also conceded giving the ethics committee misleading information in the course of the investigation. The admission spared the Speaker the spectacle of a trial-like proceeding to defend himself before the committee.

In 1997, the election for Speaker was held before the ethics committee submitted its final report and recommendation for punishment. Gingrich barely survived. As the election was being conducted, he was still negotiating for votes with disgruntled Republicans, four of whom defied the Republican Conference to vote for other Republicans while five others voted "present." Gingrich received 216 votes, only three more than the majority required from among members who had voted for candidates for Speaker.

On January 21, 1997, the House for the first time formally reprimanded a Speaker, by a vote of 395 to 28. It adopted the report of the ethics committee that found that Gingrich had brought discredit on the House by failing to seek legal advice regarding the use of tax-exempt foundations for political purposes and for providing inaccurate information to the ethics subcommittee investigating the case. The House also fined Gingrich $300,000 to cover some of the costs of the investigation.

In the fall of 1998, Gingrich decided on a political strategy for the Republicans, criticizing misconduct by President Clinton and attempting to tar the Democrats. A major element of this strategy was Gingrich's action arranging for the immediate release of the report by Special Prosecutor Kenneth Starr describing sexual misconduct, perjury, and other offenses Starr consid-

Speaker of the House J. Dennis Hastert of Illinois, center, confers with House Majority Leader Dick Armey of Texas, right, and House Republican Conference Chairman J. C. Watts of Oklahoma.

ered impeachable. However, the public strategy backfired as the party of the incumbent president gained seats in the House for the first time since 1934 in a midterm election.

The election shattered Gingrich's credibility with his colleagues. One of Gingrich's close colleagues, Appropriations Committee Chairman Bob Livingston of Louisiana, had already been soliciting support for a future speakership campaign. When the election results placed Gingrich's future in immediate jeopardy, Livingston moved immediately to challenge the Speaker, and he demonstrated such broad support that Gingrich within a few days announced he would relinquish his seat in Congress, making way for Livingston.

That, however, lasted only a little over a month before Livingston himself announced his retirement from Congress in the wake of revelations about sexual misconduct in the past.

As a result, the GOP was faced with selecting a new Speaker for the next Congress. It turned, in 1999, to a low-ranking member of the leadership, Rep. J. Dennis Hastert of Illinois, who—it was believed—could best heal the wounds left by Gingrich's contentious tenure.

RETURN TO TRADITION: HASTERT

Hastert was a low-key leader who had been the Republicans' chief deputy whip, an appointive position, during Gingrich's tenure. He was little known by the public although well respected by his colleagues as a quiet but proficient conciliator.

His election was seen as creating breathing space, for the Republicans as well as the House, while both parties sought to calm the rancorous atmosphere in the chamber and to establish

better and—in the words of many members—more civil relations. Hastert maneuvered carefully through the final impeachment proceedings against President Clinton in early 1999, a volatile situation that he inherited, without inflaming the issue more than had already occurred.

Hastert owed his election in no small degree to the perception that higher-ranking members of the Republican leadership possessed the hard-edged contentious approach and public image of Gingrich, a perception the party was desperate to shed.

In the initial months of the 106th Congress, Hastert returned to more traditional House prerogatives, particularly by allowing committees and their chairs more autonomy in developing legislation.

His early leadership success was mixed. In April 1999 the House, in a rare tie vote, defeated a resolution that endorsed the president's policy of bombing Yugoslavia as part of NATO's campaign against that nation's attacks on ethnic Albanians in the province of Kosovo. Hastert voted to support Clinton while his deputies pressured other Republicans to oppose the president. Later the GOP was embarrassed over gun control legislation following a deadly and much publicized shooting at a Colorado high school where fifteen youngsters died.

But by summer, Hastert had better footing as he pushed through the House a major Republican plan for huge tax cuts, which—even though the legislation faced certain death by veto of President Clinton—was designed to position the Republican Party for the 2000 election contests. In doing this, he leaned hard on many colleagues to support him, including Republicans at both ends of the spectrum who wanted much deeper cuts or who argued that reductions should be limited or delayed until other issues such as federal debt reduction and Social Security and Medicare stability were resolved.

House Leadership:
A Hierarchy of Support

The party leadership structure is particularly important in the House because of its size and consequent potential for unwieldiness. In his 1963 study of the House, *Forge of Democracy*, Neil MacNeil described the chamber's leadership organizations as its "priesthood." Though the younger, media savvy, sound-bite quoting, expert fund-raisers who rose to the leadership late in the century might laugh at such a description, the leadership remains a structure separate from other members.

Indeed, over the years, a hierarchy of leaders has been constructed in the House to support the Speaker, and opposing this hierarchy has been another, created by the minority party and led by the 'shadow' Speaker, the leader of the opposition party. With the hierarchy also has been built a vast array of political and party organizations to assist the Speaker and his lieutenants in the complicated task of making the House a viable, responsible legislative body.[43]

THE MAJORITY LEADER

In the modern House, the second in command is the majority leader, whose primary responsibility is to manage the legislative affairs of the chamber. To that end, he or she helps formulate, promote, negotiate, and defend the party's program, particularly on the House floor. A majority leader was not officially designated in the House until 1899, when Sereno E. Payne, R-N.Y., was named to the post. But from the earliest days, the Speaker has appointed someone to help him guide his party's legislative program through the House. Occasionally this person was a trusted lieutenant. More often the chairman of the Ways and Means Committee also served as the floor leader, largely because until 1865 the committee handled both revenues and appropriations and thus the bulk of the legislation that came before the House. Payne, for example, was also chairman of Ways and Means. *(See "House Floor Leaders, 1899–1999" p. 1102, in Reference Materials, Vol. II.)*

After the Appropriations Committee was established, its chairman sometimes served as majority leader. At other times, the Speaker chose a leading rival within the party, presumably either to promote party harmony or to neutralize an opponent. Thus in 1859 William Pennington, R-N.J., the only House member besides Clay to be elected Speaker in his first term, chose as his majority leader his chief rival for the speakership, John Sherman, R-Ohio. And in 1889 Reed named as his majority leader William McKinley Jr., R-Ohio, who had challenged Reed for the speakership and who, like Reed, had presidential ambitions.

The revolt against Cannon in 1910, which stripped the Speaker of many of his powers, also stripped him of the right to name the majority leader. Since 1911 Democratic majority leaders have

been elected by secret ballot in the party caucus. The first two, Oscar W. Underwood and Claude Kitchin, N.C., also chaired the Ways and Means Committee. When the GOP returned to power in 1919, their Committee on Committees named the majority leader, but since 1923 the Republican Conference, as the caucus is called, has selected the majority leader.

Franklin Mondell, Wyo., the Republican floor leader chosen in 1919, had been chairman of the Ways and Means Committee, but he gave up his committee assignments to help the Speaker manage the House. The first Democratic majority leader to give up his committee assignments was Henry T. Rainey, who resigned his seat on the Ways and Means Committee upon his election as majority leader in 1931. Beginning in the 1970s, Democratic majority leaders held leadership-designated slots on both the House Budget Committee and, later, on the Permanent Select Intelligence Committee, in order to be able to intervene when needed in difficult budget negotiations and maintain access to sensitive national security information. However, after the Republican takeover in 1995, the practice was not continued by the new majority; Majority Leader Dick Armey, R-Texas, held no committee assignment.

Underwood, the first elected majority leader, may also have been the strongest majority leader in the history of the House. Champ Clark, the Democrat who succeeded Cannon as Speaker, gave Underwood a free hand to manage both legislation and the party. "Although I am going to be Speaker . . . , I am going to sacrifice the Speaker's power to change the rules," he declared.[44] As a result of Clark's attitude and the limitations placed upon the Speaker's office, Underwood was able to dominate the House through the Democratic Caucus and his chairmanship of Ways and Means, which assigned members to the standing committees. "The main cogs in the machine were the caucus, the floor leadership, the Rules Committee, the standing committees, and special rules," wrote historian George B. Galloway. "Oscar Underwood became the real leader of the House. He dominated the party caucus, influenced the rules, and as chairman of Ways and Means chose the committees."[45]

But changing circumstances in the years following World War I made it more difficult for Underwood's successors to wield such power. Internal party divisions made the caucus ineffective, while strong Speakers such as Longworth and Rayburn elevated the prestige and thus the power of the Speaker. The majority leader eventually came to give up his committee chairmanships and assignments, and between 1937 and 1975 the Rules Committee ceased to be an arm of the leadership. The majority leader under the Democrats was seen as the chief lieutenant to the Speaker, not his rival. The majority leader, Wright wrote in 1976, "must work with the Speaker, in a supportive role, and never against him."[46]

The status of any potential Republican leadership ladder remains problematic in the absence of any long-standing tradition of succession after decades in the minority. Both Majority Leader Armey and Majority Whip Tom DeLay, who assumed their positions in the 104th Congress, were conservatives from one state, Texas. Both also sustained political damage based on differing perceptions of their roles in the alleged "coup" plotted against Speaker Gingrich in the summer of 1997 by younger conservatives dissatisfied by what they considered Gingrich's loss of focus and movement toward moderation, further aggravated by a series of tactical mistakes by the Speaker. The coup may have been more smoke than fire but it created an embarrassing spectacle of members of a now-divided party scheming to remove their leader in the middle of a session and damaged the reputations of the entire top GOP leadership.

Every Speaker between 1900 and 1989, when Foley took office, advanced to that position from either the majority or minority leadership position; Gingrich effectively continued the tradition because he had been the highest-ranking sitting leader of his party—minority whip—as the Republican-controlled 104th Congress organized itself. (Minority Leader Bob Michel had retired in 1995 at the end of the 103rd Congress.) However, the pattern changed with Livingston who was chairman of the Appropriations Committee when he refused the speakership over the personal scandal. At this point, his colleagues turned to and elected Hastert, who was chief deputy whip.

Three of the six Democratic Speakers elected between 1945 and 1989 also served as whip. The exceptions were Rayburn, who was chairman of the Interstate and Foreign Commerce Committee when he was chosen majority leader in 1937; McCormack, who was chairman of the House Democratic Caucus; and Wright, who was a deputy whip and next in line to chair the Public Works Committee when he bid for, and won by a single vote, the floor leader position in 1976.

The duties of the majority and minority leaders are not spelled out in the standing rules of the House, nor is official provision made for them, except through periodic appropriations specifically made for their offices. House rules do provide preference in recognition for the party leaders to offer certain specified procedural motions on the House floor. Both leadership positions are also enumerated in their respective party rules.

In practice, the majority leader's job has been to formulate the party's legislative program in cooperation with the Speaker and other party leaders, to steer the program through the House, to persuade committee chairmen to report bills deemed of importance to the party, and to arrange the House legislative schedule. The majority leader is also the party's field general on the floor, coordinating with the bill's manager and others to anticipate problems before they develop.

Like the Speaker, the majority leader is in a position to do many favors for colleagues—scheduling floor action at a convenient time, speaking in behalf of a member's bill (or refraining from opposing it), meeting with a member's important constituents, or campaigning for a member in his home district. Such favors clearly help the leadership build coalitions and maintain party unity; indeed, the opportunity to campaign for

colleagues has become, in recent years, an opportunity eagerly sought after by party leaders of both parties.

THE MINORITY LEADER

Although individual members occasionally stepped forward to lead the loyal opposition against the majority position on specific bills or issues, the position of House minority leader first became identifiable in the 1880s. Since then the post has always been assumed by the minority party's candidate for the speakership. The titular head of the minority party, or "shadow Speaker" as he is sometimes called, is chosen by the party caucus.

The basic duties of the minority leader were described by Bertrand Snell, R-N.Y., who held the post from 1931 to 1939: "He is spokesman for his party and enunciates its policies. He is required to be alert and vigilant in defense of the minority's rights. It is his function and duty to criticize constructively the policies and program of the majority, and to this end employ parliamentary tactics and give close attention to all proposed legislation."[47] Snell might also have added that if the minority leader's party occupies the White House, he is likely to become the president's chief spokesperson in the House.

Because the minority's role is to counter the legislative program of the majority, or advance the president's legislative agenda if he or she is of the same party, it rarely offers its own comprehensive legislative program. However, given the success of the minority House Republicans' "Contract with America" proposals in unifying the party prior to the 1994 election, this pattern could change.

Michel, the Illinois Republican who became the GOP minority leader in 1981, described his job as twofold: "To keep our people together, and to look for votes on the other side."[48] Michel's greatest success in this regard came in 1981, when Congress, aided by a Republican Senate and a popular president of the same party, passed the Reagan administration's unprecedented budget and tax-cut package. Large-scale defections by conservative Democrats in the House made the Republican successes possible.

But such victories are rare for the minority. "One of the minority leader's greatest problems," wrote Ripley, "is the generally demoralizing condition of minority party status."[49] Minority members want the same things majority members do—information, legislative success, patronage, and the like. When they do not get them, the minority leader is often the target of their frustrations. Throughout his term as minority leader Michel was pushed by younger and more conservative and aggressive colleagues who urged him to turn the House floor into a theater for all-out partisan warfare. The election of Gingrich as minority whip in 1989 accelerated this trend and further eroded remaining patterns of bipartisan cooperation. (See box, *Partisan Tensions in the House*, p. 448.)

Michel did grow increasingly confrontational during Wright's tenure as Speaker, when he, along with most other

It used to be that ambitious House members of both parties yearned to be Speaker and plotted for years to advance their careers and position themselves more advantageously in the leadership. The post of majority leader, or "heir apparent," once attained, virtually guaranteed eventual promotion by acclamation to the speakership. All modern Democratic Speakers had advanced in this fashion. But increasingly in the latter years of the century, prominent members of both parties attempted to leap over colleagues and move up the ladder more quickly than one step at a time. Other members have looked up the ladder and simply retired from politics instead.

REPUBLICANS

The Republicans threw out two top leaders, Joseph Martin of Massachusetts in 1959, and his successor, Charles Halleck of Indiana, in 1965, after election debacles. Both served as minority leaders, and Martin was Speaker in the two postwar Republican-controlled Congresses (1947–1949 and 1953–1955). The bloodletting did not continue after the 1974 Watergate election, in which the GOP lost many seats, because Minority Leader John Rhodes of Arizona had only just assumed the post in 1973 after incumbent Gerald Ford left the House to become the first appointed vice president in history. Speaker Newt Gingrich of Georgia was, in effect, dumped in 1998 after the GOP suffered embarrassing losses in the fall elections.

Bob Michel of Illinois had been minority whip from 1974–1981, and assumed the top post after Rhodes stepped down in 1980. Gingrich had been minority whip from 1989–1995 and gradually assumed much of Michel's authority in his final term.

The race to succeed Gingrich as Speaker began years in advance of any potential opening. Gingrich was limited to four terms of service by a new House rule adopted in 1995, requiring him to vacate the position no later than January 3, 2003, assuming Republicans retained control of Congress. The nominal front-runner, Majority Leader Dick Armey, R-Texas, was not assumed to be a shoo-in for the top job, in part because Republicans did not have a clear leadership ladder after forty years in the minority. Before becoming leader, Armey had been chairman of the House Republican Conference, the third-ranked post in the minority.

Speculation fueled by Gingrich himself of a potential presidential run in 2000 led other candidates to assume that the Speaker would resign prior to embarking on a campaign, creating a vacancy perhaps sometime in 1999. This led to further speculation that Armey would be challenged by Rep. Bill Paxon of New York, chairman of the National Republican Congressional Committee in 1993–1997 and briefly holder of a new post, chairman of the Republican leadership, appointed by Gingrich. Paxon had been ousted by Gingrich following a reported "coup" attempt by junior conservatives in the summer of 1997 but remained widely popular for his campaign strategy and funding work in electing the GOP class of 1994. However, within days of announcing an exploratory and unprecedented campaign to oust Armey as majority leader in the 106th Congress as a means of positioning himself for the speakership upon Gingrich's eventual departure, Paxon suddenly announced that he would not seek reelection in 1998 in order to spend time within his family.

While Paxon jumped off the leadership ladder, Rep. Robert L. Livingston of Louisiana suddenly backed away from political oblivion to seek the speakership. Having announced he would retire in 1998, Livingston suddenly changed his mind and declared not only for reelection but also for the speakership upon Gingrich's eventual departure. He immediately began to line up commitments from colleagues and, as chairman of the powerful Appropriations Committee, was considered a formidable challenger to Armey. Livingston was steeped in the culture of the Appropriations Committee, which often put governance ahead of ideology through enactment of its "must pass" appropriations bills.

The 1998 elections telescoped all maneuvering into a few weeks' time. House Republicans suffered a devastating setback in the off-year races, losing a net of five seats and reducing the GOP majority to a margin so thin that leaders had to hold every party member in line to achieve victory. In the aftermath of this debacle, Gingrich announced he would step down as Speaker and give up his seat, which he had won again in November, in the new Congress.

This propelled Livingston into the role of heir apparent. He was easily nominated by the Republican Conference without opposition, enjoying this status until revelation of past extramarital affairs prompted him to say he would not stand for Speaker and would resign his seat in Congress.

Bruised and embarrassed, Republicans turned to a relative unknown, J. Dennis Hastert of Illinois. Although little known outside Congress, Hastert was the party's chief deputy whip and was seen as a compromise candidate who did not carry the controversial aroma of higher-ranking members such as Armey and Majority Whip Tom DeLay, also of Texas. His selection reinforced the movement away from a guaranteed ladder of leadership succession.

DEMOCRATS

Democrats had endured the most shocking break in their leadership ladder in 1989 when Speaker Jim Wright, D-Texas, resigned in the face of disciplinary action by the ethics committee. His successor as Speaker, Thomas S. Foley, D-Wash., was defeated for reelection in 1994 as the party was losing control of the House, the first such loss by a sitting Speaker since 1862. But the other top leaders—Majority Leader Richard Gephardt of Missouri, who became minority leader, Majority Whip David Bonior of Michigan, who became minority whip, and caucus Vice Chair Vic Fazio of California, who moved up to caucus chairman to fill a vacancy caused by the party's rotation rule for that office—simply remained in place, turning back more conservative challengers who had little support. But Fazio, considered a likely aspirant for majority leader if Democrats regained control of the House, later surprised colleagues in 1998 by announcing his retirement. He faced another in a series of close reelection campaigns that had made political life difficult since an unfavorable 1992 redistricting and also wanted more time for a private life.

Other significant breaks in the leadership ladder for Democrats have occurred in the whip's position, which was frequently, though not always, the stepping-stone to majority leader. Two visible occupants, Tony Coelho of California and William H. Gray III of Pennsylvania, resigned in 1989 and 1991, respectively. Coelho was caught up in a financial scandal and Gray accepted an offer to head the prestigious United Negro College Fund.

Democratic House Minority Leader Richard A. Gephardt of Missouri, left, and Minority Whip David E. Bonior of Michigan discuss campaign finance reform at a 1997 news conference.

House Republicans, believed the Democrats were becoming more brazen in using the rules to deny them their rights. Republicans' intense personal dislike of Wright made this easy. And Michel made a Republican takeover of the House in the 1992 elections—the first to be held after the decennial redistricting—a top priority, working with various Republican groups in the House to develop Republican alternatives on issues such as child care, education, and health policy. Although some judged Michel to be one of the most effective House leaders on either side of the aisle since Rayburn, many Republicans felt a need for the strident partisanship offered by Gingrich and other members of his Conservative Opportunity Society. In 1989 Gingrich defeated Michel's friend and candidate Edward R. Madigan of Illinois, 87–85, to succeed Richard Cheney of Wyoming as minority whip.

"What that says to me," Michel told reporters immediately after Gingrich's election, "is that they want us to be more activated and more visible and more aggressive, and that we can't be content with business as usual."[50] Indeed, as minority whip Gingrich often eclipsed Michel as the Republicans aggressively attacked the majority and planned the strategy that led to the Republican takeover of the House in the 1994 elections.

When Democrats lost control of the House beginning in the 104th Congress in 1995, the new minority leader was Missouri's Richard Gephardt, who had earlier been caucus chairman (1984–1988) and majority leader (1989–1995) and had run unsuccessfully for the party's presidential nomination in 1988. Gephardt was unprepared for his greatly reduced role but had no trouble turning back a token challenge in the caucus from the more conservative Rep. Charlie Rose, D-N.C., who did not offer a strong rationale for running. Democrats, unlike Republi-

cans after previous election disasters in 1958 and 1964, did not take out their anger on party leaders. In contrast to his earlier roles in developing policy and serving as a national party spokesperson, Gephardt now had to devote substantial energy just to the mechanics of obtaining committee assignments for members displaced by the election results and calming various party factions who wanted to assess blame for the election defeat. The press reported that he and Gingrich almost never spoke, inhibiting the development of a sustainable relationship between the majority and minority leaderships under the new regime. Hastert, the new Speaker, in 1999 promised a more collegial relationship.

PARTY WHIPS

The term "whip" comes from British fox-hunting lore; the "whipper-in" was responsible for keeping the foxhounds from leaving the pack. It was first used in the British Parliament in 1769 by Edmund Burke. Though neither party in the House of Representatives designated an official whip until 1897—Rep. James A. Tawney, Republican of Minnesota, was the first—influential members played that role from the outset working to forge consensus on important issues and for particular floor fights.

Unlike the British system, where political parties are well disciplined and a whip's major concern is good party attendance, whips in the U.S. House cajole votes as well as count noses, gather information as well as impart it. "We try to keep our people . . . informed of the leadership's position on things—what they'd like, what we're seeking, what we're trying to do," a member of the Democratic whip organization said. "Not only on policy, but also on scheduling and programming. . . . We pick up static from our people and relay it to the leadership, so that they know what's going on, but we also pick up information from the leadership and convey it back. It's a two-way conduit."[51]

Specifically, whips of both parties help their floor leaders keep track of the whereabouts of party members and lobby them for their votes. Whips also serve as the party's acting floor leaders in the absence of the regular leaders. They handle the mechanics of polling members both on their views on issues and on the stands on specific floor votes, information that the majority leader uses to determine whether and when to bring a bill to the floor. Through weekly whip notices, whips inform members about upcoming floor action, including key amendments.

The whips are also responsible for ensuring that members are present for tight votes. Sometimes, whips and their assistants stand at the door of the House chamber, signaling the leadership's position on a vote by holding their thumbs up—or down. They also put out information sheets to members describing the vote. During recorded votes, a computer on the floor prints out how members have voted. If the vote is close, the whips can use that list as a guide to seek possible vote switches before the result of the vote is announced. Occasionally the whip organization

Any institution that embraces members with competing ideals and philosophies is likely to break down in partisan bickering from time to time. The U.S. House of Representatives may be the premier example.

But political or personal disagreements reached a level of vituperation and nastiness beginning in the 1980s not previously seen in the modern Congress. The gloves came off. The weakening of personal relationships among members and traditions of comity on the House floor accelerated the process. And new members entering the House were less willing to recognize the legitimacy of opposing viewpoints or to allow their respective party leaderships to negotiate as readily with "the enemy."

Some referred to it as "the politics of personal destruction" as opponents were no longer satisfied simply to win an argument and move on, perhaps working together on the next issue. Instead, some sought to destroy a rival both personally and politically, using investigations, demands for special prosecutors, ethics charges, or seemingly any other technique that would garner advantage. Rep. Newt Gingrich, R-Ga., was credited or blamed for pioneering this technique and using it successfully to publicize and escalate partisan tensions in the ethics investigation of Speaker Jim Wright, which led to Wright's resignation.

PARTISAN WARFARE

One other factor that accounted for the increased stridency was divided government—a Congress controlled by one party and a president of the other (1987–1993; 1995–2001), or a Congress split between the parties, as was the case in 1981–1987. Democrats lost control of the White House for twelve years during the Reagan and Bush administrations, and House Republicans had been in the minority from 1955 to 1995. This led to frequent clashes over policy that often left both parties frustrated by the inevitable "half a loaf" results. Members of the Republican minority concluded that they could benefit if they sharpened the conflict and demonstrated strong disagreements between the parties, ultimately forcing the public to make a choice between them, rather than engaging in compromise and bipartisanship that tended to muffle distinctions between the parties.

Partisan tensions escalated rapidly during the first term of Gingrich's speakership (1995–1997) as Democrats raged at their sudden loss of power and Republicans, including many newcomers unschooled in the mechanics of legislating, exulted at their ability to pass quickly most elements of their "Contract with America" legislative agenda that was used effectively in the 1994 election campaign. In doing so, they sometimes ran roughshod over the minority rights that they had long complained Democrats had ignored during that party's long era of House control.

The strain on the House reached a climax during Gingrich's fight for reelection as Speaker in 1997 in the face of ethics charges filed by Democrats. A telephone strategy conference among Gingrich and other Republican leaders dealing with the ethics charges was recorded by private citizens from a cellular phone and was later leaked to the press, allegedly by James McDermott, D-Wash., ranking minority member of the Committee on Standards of Official Conduct, which was investigating Gingrich. McDermott recused himself from further participation in the Gingrich case. Rep. John Boehner, R-Ohio, chairman of the House Republican Conference from whose cell phone the conversation had been recorded, demanded that McDermott resign from the House and later filed a civil lawsuit seeking damages. (As of September 1999, the case was still in the courts.)

The proceedings of the Committee on Standards of Official Conduct, which were usually insulated from direct partisan intervention, broke down as the GOP leadership forced the committee to adopt a timetable for issuing its recommendations that minimized potentially embarrassing public hearings.

In the aftermath of Gingrich's narrow reelection as Speaker and subsequent formal reprimand by the House, both parties made some effort to cool tensions, with mixed results. But numerous investigations of President Bill Clinton and of allegations of campaign finance abuses in the 1996 presidential campaign further exacerbated partisan warfare. The GOP was accused of conducting a vendetta against the president and First Lady Hillary Clinton and abusing its subpoena powers to investigate campaign violations by Democrats while ignoring Republicans. Majority Leader Dick Armey and Whip Tom DeLay, both of Texas, broke precedent by criticizing Clinton in highly personal terms, but Dan Burton of Indiana outdid both by calling the president a "scumbag." The battle culminated in impeachment of the president by a near party-line vote by a lame duck Republican House following an election in which the party unexpectedly lost seats, sparking bitter attacks on the floor.

Gingrich's later action relinquishing the speakership and voluntarily resigning from Congress following surprising GOP losses in the fall 1998 elections removed a flashpoint from House partisan warfare. Eventually Republicans settled on J. Dennis Hastert of Illinois as the new Speaker. Hastert and his party allies, as well as Democrats, promised new efforts at bipartisanship and cooperation. Nevertheless, the closely divided House and the volatile atmosphere in the 106th Congress going into the 2000 elections left in doubt how well these commitments would be fulfilled.

In earlier years, House Speakers Thomas P. "Tip" O'Neill Jr., of Massachusetts, who retired from the House in 1987, and Jim Wright of Texas, who resigned in June 1989, were both highly partisan Democrats who were not comfortable regularly working with Republicans. Republicans were outraged in the early 1980s when the Democrats under O'Neill stacked key committees to deny Republicans representation proportional to their numbers in the House. (Republicans adopted a similar practice when they assumed control with a substantially smaller majority.) Democrats eventually agreed to increase the number of seats on most major committees. In 1985, a drawn-out fight over a contested election in Indiana's Eighth District further embittered Republicans, who walked out of the House chamber *en masse* after the Democratic candidate, Rep. Frank McCloskey, was declared reelected by a four-vote margin. Although O'Neill maintained cordial relations with many Republicans, including Minority Leader Bob

Speaker Thomas P. "Tip" O'Neill Jr.'s partisan quarrel with Newt Gingrich led to the Speaker's words being stricken from the record.

Michel of Illinois, which helped cool passions, his successor, Wright, was unable to do so.

Republicans were even more incensed at what they considered to be Speaker Wright's heavy-handed partisanship. One of the most divisive incidents occurred October 29, 1987, when Wright forced passage of a major deficit-cutting budget reconciliation bill that called for taxes Republicans opposed. The Speaker, who has sole authority under House rules to determine when to announce the result of a vote after the normal time allotment has expired, held the vote open so a Texas ally, Rep. Jim Chapman, could be persuaded to change his vote, making the result 206–205. Angry GOP House members booed Wright after the vote and accused him of stealing their victory. (After assuming the speakership in 1995, Gingrich used this authority to extend voting time for much longer periods to persuade members to change their positions; he said he was following the "regular order" of House practice in doing so. During one such interlude, a Democrat asked Gingrich from the floor whether he was planning to apologize to Wright for the earlier criticism.)

THE GINGRICH FACTOR

Much of the partisan tension was deliberately fomented over a long period of time by a group of Republicans led by Gingrich. Younger Republican conservatives effectively demonized the Democrats not only as political and policy adversaries but also personally as "corrupt" and "evil" in their ultimately successful campaign to seize power in the chamber. Such feelings, and such language, made it virtually impossible for the parties to communicate and hamstrung those who still were willing to attempt bipartisan cooperation.

Since he entered the House in 1979, Gingrich had argued that the badly outnumbered Republican House contingent should forget about compromising to improve Democratic legislation and instead use the chamber as a political forum to express opposition and build political support. To advance his strategy Gingrich and his supporters frequently criticized the Democrats during the "special order" period held after the close of regular business. Like regular business, these proceedings were televised to the nation (although the requirement at the time that the camera remain on the member speaking meant that viewers could not know the chamber was often nearly empty), and Gingrich was soon attracting regular attention not only from conservative viewers but also the national media.

The use of dilatory tactics on the House floor increased. The use of motions to adjourn, demands for roll-call votes on routine matters, and other techniques to disrupt the schedule of the House proliferated. These tactics had been used in the past, usually in response to some specific event that angered the minority or to try to run out the clock for action on legislative business at the end of a session. But more aggressive conservatives such as Gingrich had little concern with the majority's reaction to the frequency of these techniques; nor did they care that they could not win these votes or have significant impact on the end product of legislation. Delaying tactics helped mobilize and unite the minority, created uncertainty in the majority's otherwise firm control of the chamber, attracted the media's notice, and made bipartisan collaboration more difficult.

In 1984 Gingrich endeared himself to Republican conservatives when he humiliated Speaker O'Neill on the House floor. Addressing a nearly empty chamber during the special order period after the close of regular business one night in May, Gingrich denounced Majority Leader Wright and nine other Democrats for writing a conciliatory letter to Nicaraguan leader Daniel Ortega, addressing him as "Dear Commandante" and calling for a settlement between political factions in that country. Gingrich said the letter was undermining U.S. foreign policy. O'Neill retaliated by ordering the television cameras to pan the chamber during special order speeches so that viewers would see that Gingrich and his supporters were addressing an empty chamber.

A few days later, when Gingrich repeated his charges during regular debate, O'Neill took the floor himself to denounce the Georgian's tactics as "the lowest thing that I have seen in my thirty-two years in Congress." That remark, an obvious violation of House rules of decorum, brought a demand from GOP Whip Trent Lott, Miss., that O'Neill's words be "taken down," that is, be reread to the House and examined by the Speaker, who determines whether they should be stricken from the record. Speaker pro tempore Joe Moakley, a Massachusetts Democrat with close ties to O'Neill who was presiding at the time, had no choice but to agree with Lott—the first time the words of a Speaker had been taken down since February 12, 1797, when Speaker Jonathan Dayton of New Jersey was called to order for using "improper language" during debate on the House floor. O'Neill's comment never became part of the official record.

goes to extremes. In 1984, for example, deputy whip Marty Russo, D-Ill., actually carried Daniel K. Akaka, D-Hawaii, onto the House floor in an effort to persuade him to change his vote.

House Republicans have always elected their whip. The Democratic whip was appointed by the Speaker and majority leader until 1986, when the Democratic Caucus elected Tony Coelho of California. In recent decades the Democratic whip position has frequently been a first step toward the speakership. The change to elective status had been demanded and passed years earlier by caucus members who did not want an appointed member to gain the advantage of such an important post, with its potential for advancement on the leadership ladder. But implementation of the new rule was delayed until a vacancy developed in the whip post, which it did when Thomas S. Foley moved up to become majority leader. Members also wanted the whip to act as a liaison between the leadership and the rank and file, and not simply as an enforcer and intelligence gatherer. Coelho shocked his colleagues by resigning suddenly in 1989 in the midst of an ethics controversy that developed simultaneously with, but unrelated to, Speaker Wright's troubles. He was succeeded by the first African American to win a major leadership position, Rep. William H. Gray III of Pennsylvania, who had previously been Budget Committee chairman (1985–1989) and moved up to whip from the chairmanship of the Democratic Caucus. Gray's career was brief, as he also stunned his colleagues by abandoning the leadership ladder in 1991 and accepting a post as head of the United Negro College Fund.

In the last years of Democratic rule in the House, the whip system was expanded into a continuous information-gathering and strategizing mechanism. Congressional scholar Sinclair notes that in the 103rd Congress, with more than ninety-five members involved, the whip system had evolved "from a sporadically active body more inclined to count than persuade . . . into a continuously active organization that perceived persuasion as its central mission."[52]

Coelho and Gingrich were the most influential party whips of the modern era, Coelho for his fundraising skills and Gingrich as a political strategist, which gave them both influence beyond the technical rank of their leadership positions. Tom DeLay of Texas, who became majority whip in 1995, was an aggressive conservative activist who enjoyed considerable success in the 104th Congress in helping pass most elements of the "Contract with America" and other items on the new majority's legislative agenda. His opposite number was Rep. David Bonior, D-Mich., who had served as majority whip from 1991 to 1995 and continued in that role for the minority.

In recent years the politics of inclusion and the need to build coalitions have induced both parties to expand and enhance their whip organizations.

By the late 1980s virtually every bill of significance was given a task force by the Democrats, made up of committee members and noncommittee members with an interest in the issue. The task force's job was to round up support for the bill. Task force members discussed which arguments would work best with which members of Congress and who was best suited to push those points with individual members. Sometimes task forces reached out to unions, trade associations, and others who were lobbying on the issue. If the votes were not there, the task force and key committee members, under the aegis of the leadership, might even tinker with the substance of the legislation to try to reach a compromise acceptable to a majority.

The tactic proved successful in getting legislation through the House and in involving more members, especially junior members, in the process. "It's helped the leadership to get to know the new members and the new members to get to know the leadership," one member told Sinclair. "And it's certainly helped the new members . . . understand the need for leadership and followership. I think the guys who have served on task forces know a lot more about the need for a party structure with some loyalty than those who haven't."[53]

Republicans in the majority also used many of these same techniques. DeLay was heavily criticized for involving outside interest groups more visibly in the process of garnering support for legislation, but Republicans countered that Democrats had always consulted labor and liberal groups.

The whip system of both parties has expanded over time to involve more members in the process and to gather greater amounts of political intelligence. For example, in mid-1999 DeLay had one chief deputy whip, Roy Blunt of Missouri, eight deputy whips, and thirty-one assistant whips. The whip's responsibilities as formally defined by the Republican leadership included floor strategy, counting votes, identifying member concerns, providing information on floor activities, an automatic call system for Republican members, a Republican job bank, and a member ombudsman program.

THE PARTY CAUCUSES

The use of party caucuses—the organization of all members in each party in the House—has waxed and waned since the beginning of Congress. In the Jeffersonian period, the Democratic-Republicans, in conjunction with the president, used the caucus to formulate their party's legislative strategy. During Clay's terms as Speaker, most important legislative decisions were still made in the Democratic-Republican caucus; less than two weeks after being seated in 1813, Federalist Daniel Webster concluded that "the time for us to be put on the stage and moved by the wires has not yet come," since "before anything is attempted to be done here, it must be arranged elsewhere."[54]

The nominees for president and vice president were chosen by congressional caucuses from 1800 to 1824. By the 1830s the importance of the caucuses had diminished, and except to nominate the party's candidate for Speaker at the beginning of each Congress, they met rarely during the next sixty years.

In the 1890s the caucus was revived as a forum for discussing legislative strategy. Speaker Reed used the Republican caucus to a limited extent to discuss policy questions. For the most part, though, the caucus under Reed functioned only to give the party's stamp of approval to decisions Reed had already made. In the early 1900s Speaker Cannon called caucus meetings occasionally but manipulated them much as Reed had. It was not until the revolt against Cannon and the return of control of the House to the Democrats that the caucus was restored to its earlier legislative significance.

The Democratic Caucus

In 1909 the Democrats adopted a party rule that the caucus, by a two-thirds majority, could bind its members on a specific vote. Throughout President Wilson's first term, the Democratic leadership used this rule and the caucus effectively, achieving remarkable party unity on a wide range of domestic legislation. But the party began to split over foreign policy issues, and the caucus fell into disuse in Wilson's second term. The binding caucus rule was used during Franklin D. Roosevelt's first term as well, but subsequently it was invoked only on procedural or party issues, such as voting for Speaker, and the rule was finally abolished in 1975.

In recent decades the Democratic Caucus has been revived. In the late 1960s younger House Democrats with relatively little seniority sought to revitalize the caucus as a means of countering the arbitrary authority exercised by committee chairmen and other senior members. The campaign, led by the House Democratic Study Group, began when Speaker McCormack established regular monthly caucus meetings in 1969, and it gained momentum in the early 1970s. The result was a basic transferal of power among House Democrats and eventually throughout the House.

The most important change modified the seniority system by making committee chairmen subject to secret-ballot election by the caucus. This modification was achieved in steps and took its final form—automatic secret votes on all chairmen—in December 1974. Early in 1975 the caucus rejected three chairmen, a clear signal that all chairmen in the future would be held accountable to their colleagues and could not expect to exercise the absolute powers they had held when the seniority system all but guaranteed them tenure as chairmen. Other chairmen were unseated in 1984 and 1990.

The Democratic Caucus instituted other changes that helped transform the House into a more open and accountable institution. It opened many of its own meetings to the public and the media between 1975 and 1980. It limited House Democrats to one subcommittee chairmanship and guaranteed each party member a seat on a major committee. It also created a "bill of rights" for subcommittees that gave them considerable independence from committee chairmen. On purely party matters it transferred the authority to make committee assignments from the Democratic members of the Ways and Means Committee to a revamped Steering and Policy Committee and placed that committee firmly under the control of the leadership.

Although the Democratic Caucus focused primarily on procedural reforms during this period, it also gave some attention to substantive issues. In 1972, for example, it forced a House vote on a nonbinding, end-the-Vietnam-War resolution. In 1975 it went on record as opposing more military aid to Indochina, and it voted to order the Rules Committee to allow a floor vote on an amendment to end the oil depletion allowance.

These forays into substantive legislation plunged the caucus into new controversy, partly because it was seen as usurping the powers of the standing committees and undermining the committee system. At least that was the argument expressed by conservative Democratic opponents of the resolutions, which were drafted and backed mainly by the party's liberal bloc. The conservatives insisted that caucus meetings, which had been closed, be opened to the public. That killed the role the caucus played as a "family council," which greatly diminished its usefulness.

Occasionally the caucus still took a stand on a legislative matter. In 1978, for example, it voted 150–57 to approve a resolution urging Ways and Means to roll back a planned Social Security tax increase. President Carter and House leaders backed the increase, however, and thwarted the rollback attempt.

The caucus elects a variety of party leaders, including the nominee for Speaker when Democrats hold a majority. Other elected posts in the 106th Congress were the minority leader, whip, caucus chair and vice chair, and chair of the Democratic Congressional Campaign Committee, though in practice that position is filled by nomination of the minority leader. In 1999 the new position of assistant to the leader was created, to be nominated by the leader and then elected by the caucus. Its purpose was to place a woman in a visible spot. The chair and vice chair of the caucus serve two full consecutive terms, the only major positions in the Democratic leadership required under the rules to rotate.

Under the chairmanship of Gillis W. Long, D-La. (1980–1984), the Democratic Caucus once again closed its meetings following substantial losses in the 1980 election. This made it easier to keep party disputes within the family.

Long also set up a Committee on Party Effectiveness early in 1981 to reassess the party's direction after its election losses in 1980; members of the committee covered a spectrum of political opinion, including several rising stars such as Richard Gephardt, who succeeded Long as caucus chairman. Gephardt ran for president in 1988 while holding the post. Gray, the outgoing Budget Committee chairman, succeeded him at the caucus. (Rep. Shirley Chisholm of New York had been caucus secretary, a post at that time traditionally reserved for a woman, in the 1970s. The title was later changed to the more prestigious "vice chair," which, ironically, had the effect of eliminating the automatic claim to it by women members.) When Gray became whip in 1989 after Coelho resigned, the vice chairman, Steny Hoyer of Maryland, was elected to fill the vacancy and was then reelected twice for full terms, ultimately holding the post for five and one-half years. When Democrats lost control of the House in 1994, the party did not hold it against Vic Fazio of California, who was both vice chairman of the caucus and chairman of the Democratic Congressional Campaign Committee. It elevated him to caucus chairman until his retirement from the House at the beginning of 1999.

Representatives and senators are automatically members of their party caucus or conference. Here Democrats assemble for a pep rally on the steps of the Capitol.

The Republican Conference

The counterpart of the Democratic Caucus, the Republican Conference, is the umbrella organization for House Republicans. Like its Democratic counterpart, the conference sets party rules and elects the leadership. In the majority, it chooses its nominee for Speaker, and also elects a majority leader, whip, conference chairman, vice chair, secretary, and policy committee chair. Other than the Speaker, who is limited to four terms under House rules used by the GOP majority, the other positions are not limited.

The conference builds party unity through retreats and other meetings of the rank and file, and helps to identify campaign issues. The conference also produces legislative status reports and research information on issues pending before the House, coordinates use of talk radio, and provides training sessions for members and staff on efficient use of House resources.

The Republican Conference rarely served as a policy-setting body, although in the 1965–1969 period it was used occasionally to develop policy positions for consideration by the party's leadership. Although he did not try to make it an active arm of the

leadership, Minority Leader Michel used the conference as a sounding board to determine the party's position on substantive matters and to communicate the viewpoint of House Republicans to the Republican administration.

The conference occasionally passed resolutions stating House Republican views on particular issues. In what was widely seen as a slap at Republican President Bush, the conference in 1990 approved a resolution opposing any new taxes; Bush had recently renounced his "no new taxes" campaign pledge in an effort to reach agreement with the Democrats on a budget deficit reduction measure.

The Republican Conference was revitalized by Gingrich and often served as the vehicle pressing the GOP leadership to implement the "Contract with America" and other items on its legislative agenda. There were frequent policy discussions, including votes on strategy, such as a conference majority urging continuation of the controversial government shutdown at the end of the 1995 session.

Gingrich also summoned members to conference meetings to explain votes at variance with party policy, such as occurred when defections derailed the 1997 committee funding resolution. The most dramatic conference event of Gingrich's tenure as Speaker was a session in the summer of 1997 at which various party leaders were asked to explain their roles in a reputed coup aimed at toppling the Speaker.

Gingrich set up task forces to develop legislation, and allowed the conference chairman, John Boehner of Ohio, a major strategic role. Boehner was later accused of participating in the coup discussions but his position in the leadership was not challenged at the time. However, he lost his job to J. C. Watts of Oklahoma, 121–93, when Republicans organized for the 106th Congress. One problem with the new Republican leadership structure since the party achieved its majority has been the absence of clear lines of authority on some matters, as Gingrich experimented with different strategies and combinations of party personnel. For example, to reward Rep. Bill Paxon, R-N.Y., who had led the campaign committee successfully to achieve the majority, Gingrich in 1997 created the title of "chairman of the Republican leadership" to give Paxon continuing status among the top leadership. However, several months later Paxon was forced to resign, and the new post was abolished, when his loyalty to the Speaker was questioned in the aftermath of the coup discussions.

MAKING COMMITTEE ASSIGNMENTS

After the House revolt against Cannon in 1910, the power to appoint members of standing committees was taken from the Speaker and vested in the party caucuses. In 1911 the Democratic Caucus delegated the authority to choose the party's committee members to a special Committee on Committees, which was composed of all Democrats on the Ways and Means Committee.

The reforms of the 1970s also affected the committee assignment process. In 1973 the Democratic Caucus expanded the Committee on Committees to include the Speaker, who served as chairman, the majority leader, and the caucus chairman. In December 1974 the caucus transferred the assignment power to the Steering and Policy Committee, which is composed of the Democratic leaders and their appointees and regionally elected members. The Steering and Policy Committee's recommendations were subject to ratification by the caucus, as were those of Ways and Means, but ratification, particularly of committee chairmen, was no longer perfunctory. The policy functions were later split off into another body and the committee assignment function is now performed by the Steering Committee.

In 1917 the Republican Conference also established a Committee on Committees, which traditionally is chaired by the GOP House leader. Committee chairmanships when in the majority, or ranking minority positions otherwise, as well as committee assignments, are subject to approval by the conference. In 1989 Republicans gave their minority leader the same authority to appoint the GOP members of the Rules Committee that Democratic Speakers had obtained for their Rules members in 1974. When Republicans took control of the House in 1995, the committee on committees was called the Steering Committee and was chaired by Speaker Gingrich.

Speakers often have exercised great influence on committee assignments, even when they were not on the panel making the choices. In the late 1920s, for example, Speaker Longworth had four uncooperative members of the Rules Committee replaced with his own choices. In the 1940s and 1950s Speaker Rayburn intervened frequently to influence the makeup of the Ways and Means Committee, which he insisted be stacked with members opposed to reductions in the oil and gas depletion allowance. Rayburn was from Texas, one of the largest oil-producing states. Rayburn also led the effort in 1961 to increase the size of the Rules Committee, which allowed him to engineer the selection of two additional Democrats more amenable to his leadership.

Speaker Gingrich made sure that members of the aggressive and conservative 1995 freshman class received assignments to the most important committees, both to cement their loyalty and spread their activism.

POLICY AND STRATEGY COMMITTEES

During the twentieth century both parties established groups called "steering committees" to assist the leadership with legislative scheduling and party strategy (not to be confused with the entities with similar names in the 1990s that now handle only committee assignments). The Republican Steering Committee, established in 1919, dominated the business of the House until 1925, when power again shifted to the Speaker. Speaker Longworth largely ignored the Steering Committee. In 1949 the committee was expanded and renamed the Policy Committee. The Policy Committee was considered the chief advisory board for the minority leader from 1959 to 1965, when it was replaced in the role by the Republican Conference. In its role after the Republicans assumed majority status in 1995, the Policy Committee issues and disseminates policy statements on issues of concern to the conference, considers policy resolutions, issues reports, and conducts policy forums. It helps develop the legislative agenda for House Republicans.

Democrats established a Steering Committee in 1933, abandoned it in 1956, and reconstituted it in 1962. Its duties and role in the party structure were vague. In 1973 the Democratic Caucus voted to create a new Steering and Policy Committee to give coherence and direction to the party's legislative strategy. In 1974 the caucus gave the new Steering and Policy Committee the authority to make Democratic committee assignments, removing that power from the Democratic members of the Ways and Means Committee. However, this and other periodic efforts by Democrats in later years to create a separate leadership entity to deal with policy floundered on opposition from both party leaders, who thought a new structure hampered their flexibility, and committee chairs, who did not want a potential rival intruding on their turf.

The size of the Steering and Policy Committee expanded over time as additional members of the leadership were added to it. The Speaker was also given the right to make additional appointments of members of his choice, the number of which also increased. The caucus membership at large could seek elective seats from geographic regions.

In 1992, the caucus created a "Speaker's Working Group on Policy Development" to satisfy demands for a separate, smaller entity to deal with policy matters, since the Steering and Policy Committee focused on little besides committee assignments and that was the reason members sought to be on it. Speaker Foley promptly expanded the size of the "Working Group," which made the new entity unwieldy, and it exercised little influence. After becoming the minority in 1995, Democrats created a new, separate Policy Committee.

The Democratic Study Group (DSG), created in 1959, functioned as the primary source of research on legislative issues for the Democrats and exercised considerable influence, particularly during the height of the reform period. It was one of many Legislative Service Organizations (LSOs) that hired staff and used office space in the House funded by members from their office allowances. DSG's legislative reports, which explained the content of bills, and its more political special reports that often had a partisan slant, were widely read even by Republicans. But the DSG and similar entities were effectively abolished in 1995 when the new Republican majority eliminated LSOs and the ability of members to pool resources. This action damaged the Democrats' ability to gather and coordinate legislative information and weakened the party's ability to compete effectively with the Republican Conference, which published similar legislative materials for its own party members. Some of the LSOs lingered in name only, without offices or staff, or reconstituted themselves as entities outside the House relying on other sources of funding. (*See "The Internal Lobbyists: Special Interest Alliances," p. 646.*)

Leadership in the Senate: "We Know No Masters"

Sen. Daniel Webster in 1830 described the upper chamber as a "Senate of equals, of men of individual honor and personal character, and of absolute independence. We know no masters, we acknowledge no dictators."[55] At the time and for several decades thereafter, the Senate had no structured leadership apparatus. Not until the early twentieth century did either party formally designate a leader to oversee and guide its interests in the Senate. Now both parties name a leader and an assistant leader and have a number of party committees to help them formulate policy and strategy and win reelection.

But Webster's words still hold true; the Senate is essentially a collection of individuals, each of whom is a leader in his or her own sphere. The independence of each senator is further ensured by Senate rules, which protect the rights of the minority against the will of the majority. As Ripley has observed, Senate floor leaders are not "automatically invested with a specific quota of power; they still must create much of their own."[56] Effective

leadership in the Senate, even more than in the House, thus depends on the leaders' personal and negotiating skills.

EVOLUTION OF SENATE LEADERSHIP

As with the House, the Constitution did not offer much direction about Senate leadership. Its two references to leadership posts and responsibilities in the Senate (Article I, Section 3) stipulate that the vice president shall be president of the Senate and that the Senate shall choose a president pro tempore to preside in the vice president's absence. Neither of these offices has ever been a very effective leadership position.

Thus legislative leadership was left to individual senators. Here, as in the House, Alexander Hamilton acted much like a stage manager, controlling floor action through his many friends in the chamber. Jefferson and his Treasury Secretary Albert Gallatin exercised as much control over the Senate as they did over the House. Jefferson, wrote Thomas Pickering of Massachusetts, tries "to screen himself from all responsibility by calling upon Congress for advice and direction. . . . Yet with affected modesty and deference he secretly dictates every measure which is seriously proposed."[57]

The first significant move toward party organization did not occur until 1846, when the parties began to nominate members of the standing committees. Until 1823 the Senate had chosen committee members by ballot. That year the Senate turned over the appointment process to the presiding officer. Initially this officer was the president pro tempore, but in 1825–1827 Vice President John C. Calhoun assumed the power. Hostile to the administration of John Quincy Adams, he used the power to place supporters of Andrew Jackson in key positions. In 1828 the Senate amended its rules to return the appointment power to the president pro tem, who, of course, was selected by the Senate itself. In 1833 the Senate reverted to selection by ballot.

By this time the seniority system had begun to develop, and chairmanships of Senate committees rotated less than they had in the past. Parties began to control assignments, committees began to divide along ideological lines, and minority reports began to appear. By 1846 the routine was formalized. When the second session of the 29th Congress met in December, the Senate began balloting for committee chairmen. Midway through the process the balloting rule was suspended, and on a single ballot the Senate accepted the list of committee assignments that had already been agreed upon by the majority and minority. For the most part, that routine has been followed since.

Immediately before and during the Civil War, party authority extended to substantive as well as organizational matters. In 1858, for example, the Democratic Caucus removed Stephen A. Douglas as chairman of the Committee on Territories, despite his seniority, because he had refused to go along with President James Buchanan and the southern wing of the party on the question of allowing slavery in the territories.

With the end of the Civil War, however, party influence on substantive matters declined. By the time Ulysses S. Grant entered the White House in 1869, political parties required unity only on organizational matters. Disputes over committee assignments were settled in the party caucuses, and pressing issues were discussed there, but there was no way to enforce caucus decisions against senators who refused to be bound by a vote of the majority of their caucus. "I am a senator of the United States," Charles Sumner, R-Mass., once declared. "My obligations as a senator were above any vote in a caucus."[58]

Beginning in the 1870s, Republicans sought to strengthen party control of the Senate by appointing a caucus chairman, who was considered to be the party's floor leader, and setting up a Committee on Committees to recommend committee assignments to the caucus and then to the full Senate. But the power of the caucus chairman, then Henry Anthony, R-R.I., was overshadowed by a Republican faction led by Roscoe Conkling of New York that held sway for roughly ten years. Though the faction generally controlled the Committee on Committees, it never controlled the Senate's proceedings. Eventually in the early 1880s, it dissolved as a consequence of a series of unsuccessful feuds with Republican presidents over patronage in New York state.

EMERGENCE OF REPUBLICAN LEADERS

The emergence of another Republican faction in the 1890s led to establishment of a permanent leadership organization in the Senate. The leader of this faction was Nelson W. Aldrich of Rhode Island, who worked in close alliance with William B. Allison of Iowa, Orville H. Platt of Connecticut, and John C. Spooner of Wisconsin. Aldrich had, in the words of one historian, "made himself indispensable to the party organization [in the Senate], rising step by step as the elders passed out, until in the end he made himself the dictator of the cabal which for a time was the master of the government."[59] Already an influence in the Senate, this group took complete control after Allison, as the member with the longest period of Senate service, was elected chairman of the Republican Caucus in March 1897.

Previous caucus chairmen had not seen the office as a vehicle for consolidating party authority, an oversight that Allison and Aldrich were quick to correct. Since the mid-1870s the Republicans had appointed a Steering Committee to help schedule legislative business. Unlike previous caucus chairmen, Allison assumed the chair of this committee and filled it with his allies. For the first time a party organization arranged the order of business in minute detail and managed proceedings on the Senate floor.

Allison also controlled the Committee on Committees. By this time committee chairmanships were filled through seniority, and Allison and Aldrich made no attempt to overturn this practice (to which they owed their committee chairmanships—Allison of Appropriations, Aldrich of Finance). But seniority did not apply to filling committee vacancies, and here the two found an opportunity to reward their supporters and punish their opponents. "Realizing the potentialities for control in the chamber," wrote historian David J. Rothman, Allison and Aldrich "entrenched and tightened personal leadership and par-

ty discipline. Their example would not always be emulated. . . . Nevertheless, they institutionalized, once and for all, the prerogatives of power. Would-be successors or Senate rivals would now be forced to capture and effectively utilize the party post."[60]

Like Speaker Cannon, who dominated the House for much of the same period, Allison and Aldrich were largely successful in imposing their conservative political views upon the chamber. Defeats were rare until President Theodore Roosevelt was able to push a part of his legislative program through Congress. The group retained much of its power even after Allison's death in 1908. Though Allison had held the formal positions of power, Aldrich exercised power through the sheer force of his personality; he was considered by many to be the most powerful man in the Senate. But as the number of Republican insurgents in the Senate increased, the once all-powerful group began to weaken, and it quickly disintegrated after Aldrich retired in 1911.

EMERGENCE OF DEMOCRATIC LEADERS

A centralized Democratic organization in the Senate developed in the same period. Under the leadership of Arthur P. Gorman of Maryland, who served as chairman of the Democratic Caucus from 1889 to 1899, the Democratic power structure was very similar to that put together by Allison and Aldrich. Gorman consolidated his power by assuming all of the party's top leadership posts himself, including floor leader and the chairmanship of both the Steering Committee and the Committee on Committees. He further solidified his control by appointing his political allies to positions of influence.

Historian Rothman has concluded that the Democratic Party structure under Gorman may have been more conducive than the Republican structure to the emergence of an effective and energetic leadership. Rothman notes that Gorman was elected chairman of the caucus not on the basis of seniority, but because of his standing among his colleagues. And Gorman eventually came to appoint the same group of men to the Steering Committee and the Committee on Committees, concentrating power over the party organization in a relatively small number of Democrats. For all but two of his ten years as caucus chairman, however, Senate Democrats were in the minority, and they were often badly divided on substantive issues. As a result Gorman never attained the same degree of power and authority as the Allison-Aldrich team.

EARLY EFFECTIVE LEADERS

Few of the Senate leaders in the twentieth century were particularly effective. One of the stronger leaders was Democrat John W. Kern of Indiana, whose election as caucus chairman in 1913, after only two years in the Senate, was engineered by progressive Democrats after they first deposed conservative Thomas S. Martin of Virginia. The Democratic Steering Committee, appointed by Kern and dominated by the progressives, assigned members sympathetic to President Woodrow Wilson's programs to key committees. The Steering Committee also rec-

THE SENATE'S PRESIDING OFFICERS

The only two Senate leaders mentioned by the Constitution have little effective leadership power. Article I, Section 3 provides that the vice president "shall be President of the Senate, but shall have no vote, unless they be equally divided." It also provides that the "Senate shall choose . . . a President pro tempore, in the absence of the Vice President, or when he shall exercise the office of President of the United States." The Constitution also provides that the chief justice of the United States will preside during an impeachment trial of a president. This has occurred only twice, once in 1868 in proceedings against President Andrew Johnson, and in 1999 in the impeachment trial of President Bill Clinton.

DUTIES OF THE PRESIDING OFFICER

As presiding officer, the principal function of the vice president and the president pro tem is to recognize senators, but this is rarely significant since Senate rules usually require the presiding officer to recognize the senator who first seeks recognition. The presiding officer also decides points of order, subject to appeal to the full Senate; appoints senators to House-Senate conference committees (although it is customary for the presiding officer to take the recommendations of the floor manager of the bill in question); enforces decorum; administers oaths; and appoints members to special committees. The president pro tem may appoint a substitute to replace him in the chair; the vice president may not.

As a senator, the president pro tem may vote on all matters; the vice president may vote only if the Senate is evenly divided on a question, as stipulated by the Constitution, and then only if he is available and chooses to participate.

Such votes may be widely separated in time. Between 1945 and September 1999, when twelve different vice presidents served, only thirty-five such votes were cast; of these, Vice President Albert Gore Jr., D-Tenn., cast four votes, as of September 30, 1999. Four other modern vice presidents, Lyndon B. Johnson, D-Texas (1961–1963),

Gerald R. Ford, R-Mich. (1973–1974), Nelson A. Rockefeller, R-N.Y. (1974–1977), and Dan Quayle, R-Ind. (1989–1993), did not cast any.

THE VICE PRESIDENT AS PRESIDING OFFICER

It is little wonder that the Senate has not placed any real power with the vice president, who is not chosen by the Senate, may not be a member of the majority party in the chamber, and may not be sympathetic with the aims of its majority. Precedent was established by John Adams, who, although in agreement with the majority of the Senate during his terms as vice president (1789–1797), perceived his role simply as that of presiding officer and made little effort to guide Senate action. His successor, Thomas Jefferson (1797–1801), could not have steered the Federalist-controlled Senate even if he had wanted to.

A few vice presidents have attempted to use their position as presiding officer to achieve a partisan purpose, with varying degrees of success. John C. Calhoun, vice president to John Quincy Adams, was hostile to the Adams administration. Taking advantage of an 1823 rule change giving the presiding officer the right to appoint committee members, Calhoun placed supporters of Andrew Jackson on key committees. But he refused to use the authority exercised by earlier vice presidents to call senators to order for words used in debate.

Nelson A. Rockefeller, vice president to Gerald R. Ford, once used his authority to refuse to recognize a senator who wanted to filibuster a Ford administration bill. Senators from both parties were incensed at Rockefeller's action and made it clear that the president's program would suffer if Rockefeller did not desist.

Most vice presidents preside only upon ceremonial occasions or when a close vote on a bill or amendment of interest to the administration is likely to occur. But as president of the Senate, the vice president is well positioned to lobby on behalf of the president's program. Walter F. Mondale, D-Minn., who left his Senate seat to become Jimmy Carter's vice president, proved to be an effective spokesperson for

---

ommended, and the caucus adopted, rules that permitted a majority of committee members to call meetings, elect subcommittees, and appoint conferees. Thus party authority was augmented, and the power of committee chairmen curbed, in a movement that somewhat paralleled the rise of the caucus in the House. (See "Senate Floor Leaders, 1911–1999," p. 1104, in Reference Materials, Vol. II.)

Kern worked hard to push Wilson's progressive program through the Senate, achieving passage of a steep reduction in import duties and imposition of the first income tax under the Sixteenth Amendment, establishment of the Federal Reserve and the Federal Trade Commission, and enactment of antitrust laws, among others. Kern served as leader for only four years (he was defeated for reelection to the Senate in 1916). Yet until the 1950s few other floor leaders of either party attained the effectiveness he had achieved.

Massachusetts Republican Henry Cabot Lodge, who served

as majority leader from 1919 to 1924, managed twice (in 1919 and 1920) to mobilize the Senate to oppose the Treaty of Versailles, which embodied the Covenant of the League of Nations and which Wilson strongly backed. But on other matters, Lodge was not a particularly effective leader, nor were the other Republicans who served in the 1920s.

President Franklin D. Roosevelt was fortunate in having Joseph T. Robinson of Arkansas as the Senate majority leader from 1933 to 1937. Robinson revived the Democratic Caucus, and won agreement from Senate Democrats to make caucus decisions on administration bills binding by majority vote. There is no evidence that Robinson ever made use of the binding rule, but nonbinding caucuses were frequently held to mobilize support. In his four years as majority leader, Robinson pushed through the Senate most of the president's controversial New Deal legislative program, including measures he personally opposed.

the White House on numerous occasions and tried to fill part of the gap caused by Carter's lack of experience in Washington and the absence of any long-standing political or personal relationships with congressional leaders. Vice President Albert Gore wielded even more influence during the Clinton administration, exercising significant power over federal appointments and several key areas of government policy, most notably on government reorganization, technology, and the environment.

THE PRESIDENT PRO TEMPORE

The first president pro tempore, John Langdon of New Hampshire, was elected on April 6, 1789, before John Adams appeared in the Senate to assume his duties as presiding officer. When the first vice president took his seat on April 21, Langdon's service as president pro tem ended. For the next 100 years, the Senate acted on the theory that a president pro tempore could be elected only in the vice president's absence and that his term expired when the vice president returned. (Unlike modern practice, the vice president frequently presided over the Senate in the nineteenth century.) By 1890 the Senate had elected presidents pro tempore on 153 occasions. In the 42nd Congress alone (1871–1873), ten such elections, all of the same senator, were held.

In 1890 the Senate gave the president pro tem tenure of a sort by adopting a resolution stating that "it is competent for the Senate to elect a president pro tempore, who shall hold the office during the pleasure of the Senate and until another is elected, and shall execute the duties thereof during all future absences of the vice president" until the Senate otherwise orders. That practice was still in use in 1999.

By law, the president pro tem is third in line, behind the vice president and the Speaker of the House of Representatives, to succeed to the presidency. Like the Speaker, he is a member of the majority party, and his election, if contested, is usually by a straight party-line vote. By custom the most senior member of the majority party in terms of Senate service is elected president pro tem. Only one of those elected since 1945 did not follow this pattern: Arthur H. Vandenberg, R-Mich., was the second-ranking Republican when elected in 1947.

Before 1945 there were some notable exceptions to the custom. George H. Moses, R-N.H., ranked only fifteenth in party seniority when he was elected president pro tem in 1925, and Willard Saulsbury, D-Del., was still in his first term when elected to the post in 1916.

Strom Thurmond, of South Carolina, who switched to the GOP in 1964, was considered the most senior Republican when he was elected president pro tem in 1981 even though John Tower of Texas had served longer as a Republican. Thurmond, a former Democratic governor, began his Senate service in 1955 after winning election as a write-in candidate, the only senator ever to do so. He resigned the following year and was absent from the Senate for most of 1956 in order to run again, and win, as a Democrat. When Thurmond became a Republican in 1964, the Republican Conference agreed to base his seniority on the date he entered the Senate, not the date he switched parties. Thurmond resumed the president pro tempore post when Republicans regained Senate control in 1995.

Few presidents pro tem in the twentieth century have had much influence on the Senate. One who did was Vandenberg, who was also chairman of the Foreign Relations Committee. Vandenberg "no doubt exerted as much influence in what was done and not done as the Speaker of the House," Floyd M. Riddick, who would later become Senate parliamentarian, wrote in 1949. When Robert C. Byrd of West Virginia became president pro tempore (1989–1995), he liked to preside over complicated procedural situations. As chairman of the Appropriations Committee and a former majority and minority leader, Byrd brought far more stature to the position than could accrue simply through seniority.

Alben W. Barkley of Kentucky, who was elected majority leader after Robinson died of a heart attack in 1937, was also influential with his colleagues, but, like a growing number of Senate Democrats, he did not always support Roosevelt on domestic issues. In 1944 Barkley resigned his leadership post when FDR vetoed a revenue bill. He was promptly reelected by the Democrats, and the bill was passed over the president's veto.

THE JOHNSON YEARS

In the decades immediately after World War II two Republicans were widely acclaimed as effective Senate leaders. "Mr. Republican," Robert A. Taft of Ohio, was the majority leader for only a few months before he died in 1953, but he had been the de facto Republican power in the Senate since the early 1940s, just as Richard B. Russell, Ga., was the real leader of the Senate Democrats. Everett McKinley Dirksen of Illinois, known as the "wizard of ooze" for his florid style, was one of the more colorful personalities to grace the modern Senate. A conservative, he served as minority leader from 1959 until his death in 1969.

Taft and Dirksen employed two different styles—Taft won unity through his intellectual command of the issues; Dirksen won it through negotiation and compromise. Both men centralized the Republican leadership apparatus, controlling the formulation of Republican policy in the Senate and taking an active part in scheduling and setting floor strategy.

Taft and Dirksen may have had great influence among their Republican colleagues but their leadership talents were eclipsed by those of Lyndon Baines Johnson. Johnson, wrote political scientist John G. Stewart, "set for himself no less an objective than *running* the Senate, in fact as well as in theory."[61] Elected minority leader by the Democrats in 1953 after only four years in the Senate, Johnson became majority leader when the Democrats regained control of the Senate after the 1954 elections and

SINCE THAT NEW SENATE LEADER TOOK OVER, WE WILL NEED AT LEAST THREE MINORITY LEADERS ON **OUR** SIDE OF THE AISLE.

A tongue-in-cheek portrayal of the power of Senate Majority Leader Alben Barkley, who held the post from 1937 to 1947.

served in that position until his resignation to become John F. Kennedy's vice president in 1961.

As a leader Johnson quickly became famous—some would say notorious—for his power of persuasion and his manipulative skills. Johnson was adroit at doing favors for and extending courtesies to his colleagues, their families, and staffs, at maneuvering his supporters onto desired committees and keeping his opponents off. He revitalized the Senate Democratic Policy Committee and modified the seniority system to ensure freshman Democrats at least one major committee assignment, a practice the Republicans also eventually adopted. On the floor he exploited to the fullest the majority leader's right of first recognition by the chair to control what was debated and under what terms. He was the first majority leader to make extensive use of unanimous consent agreements to control debate on legislation. He also used night sessions to wear down senators who might, if fresher, choose to engage in extensive floor debate. Perhaps most important, Johnson kept himself informed about the views and positions of his Senate colleagues through an active intelligence operation headed by Robert G. "Bobby" Baker, secretary to the Senate Democrats.

Johnson, whose entire tenure as both minority and majority leader was spent with Republican President Dwight D. Eisenhower in the White House, was also a master of compromise. He made sure to have allies among conservative southern Democrats and Republicans as well as among northern liberals. Like his mentor, House Speaker Sam Rayburn, Johnson worked to pass those elements of Eisenhower's legislative program that did not challenge basic tenets of Roosevelt's New Deal or Harry S. Truman's Fair Deal. As a result Johnson presided over some of the most productive years in Senate history.

The future president was renowned for what came to be known as the "Johnson Treatment," a tactic he carried with him into the White House. Rowland Evans and Robert Novak gave a vivid description in their book, *Lyndon B. Johnson: The Exercise of Power:*

The Treatment could last ten minutes or four hours. It came, enveloping its target, at the LBJ Ranch swimming pool, in one of LBJ's offices, in the Senate cloakroom, on the floor of the Senate itself—wherever Johnson might find a fellow senator within his reach. Its tone could be supplication, accusation, cajolery, exuberance, scorn, tears, complaint, the hint of threat. It was all of these together. It ran the gamut of human emotions. Its velocity was breathtaking, and it was all in one direction. Interjections from the target were rare. Johnson anticipated them before they could be spoken. He moved in close, his face a scant millimeter from his target . . . his eyes widening and narrowing, his eyebrows rising and falling. From his pockets poured clippings, memos, statistics. Mimicry, humor, and the genius of analogy made The Treatment an almost hypnotic experience and rendered the target stunned and helpless.[62]

Johnson's effectiveness lost some of its edge after the 1958 elections added substantially to the Democrats' majority in the Senate. Members began to lose patience with Johnson's intensity; as one observer said, "After eight years of Lyndon Johnson, a lot of senators were just worn out."[63] An influx of liberal Democrats rejected the long-standing notion that junior senators were to be seen and not heard, and they began to chafe under Johnson's centralized leadership. In response Johnson added more caucus meetings and named some freshmen Democrats to the Policy Committee. But calls from younger liberal members for greater inclusion in party matters continued to build.

By all accounts, Johnson was the most effective leader the Senate had ever seen, if not always the most liked. ("I know he comes off with high marks for getting things done, but he was repugnant to me," one senator recalled. "When I dealt with him I always had the feeling that I was standing on a trap door that was waiting to be sprung."[64]) Like the strong leaders before him, he derived his power primarily from his own force of personality, aided by his skill at finding out what his colleagues needed. As one observer put it, Johnson "worked at being better informed than anyone else, and that information then made him better equipped than anyone else to broker many agreements."[65]

Although he made innovative use of a number of institutional tools, such as unanimous consent, Johnson left the structure of the Senate itself largely untouched. When he left, Evans and Novak wrote, it was as though the leadership system he had constructed had never existed.

THE AGE OF COLLEGIALITY

Meanwhile other factors were changing the Senate substantially. Between the 1950s and the mid-1970s, southern domination and the seniority system gave way to a more decentralized, more democratic institution, in which junior members played a greater role. Party leaders on both sides of the aisle eschewed the arm-twisting tactics that Johnson used so effectively and engaged in a more collegial style of leadership, dependent for its success not on the leader's ability to bend the Senate to his will but on his ability to meet the expectations of his colleagues and to facilitate the conduct of Senate business.

Johnson's successor, Mike Mansfield, D-Mont., could not have provided a greater contrast in leadership styles. Known as the "gentle persuader," Mansfield, who served longer than any other majority leader in Senate history (1961–1977), was a permissive, at times even passive, leader. "I rarely asked for votes on specific legislation," Mansfield told political scientist Robert L. Peabody in 1972. "I assumed that these people are mature, that they have been sent back here by their constituents to exercise their own judgment. I will say that if on an issue they are doubtful I would hope that they will give the administration, if it's a Democratic administration, the benefit of the doubt. Or if it's a party matter, that they will give the party the benefit of the doubt. But I don't believe in being pressured myself and I don't pressure other senators. I treat them as I would like to be treated myself."[66]

Though Mansfield was criticized for not being sufficiently partisan and for sometimes failing to provide direction, he was working with a larger, more liberal, and less cohesive group of Senate Democrats than Johnson had led. As congressional scholar Roger Davidson noted, "Most senators flourished under Mansfield's regime, for its very looseness gave them the leeway they needed to pursue their increasingly diverse legislative and career goals."[67]

When Mansfield retired from the Senate at the end of 1976, Democrats chose Robert Byrd of West Virginia as his successor for the first of two cycles as majority leader (1977–1981; 1987–1989). Byrd had been whip from 1971–1977, taking the post on a dramatic secret ballot away from Edward Kennedy, D-Mass., who had been distracted by the consequences of a 1969 accident at Chappaquiddick in Massachusetts, which resulted in the death of a passenger in a car driven by the senator. Byrd was in many ways an old-style Senate personality, but he also had to contend with a rapidly changing body that was more partisan, less patient, and with younger and more independent colleagues even more willing to employ the Senate's rules to press their interests and less susceptible than ever to party discipline. More significantly, Byrd also had to survive and adapt a leadership style to a Senate no longer with a firm Democratic majority, as the Republican Party took control from 1981–1987 and relegated him to minority leader.

While other senators built their careers on national issues and oratorical flair, Byrd was the quintessential insider, working quietly and diligently to build support through a combination of service to his colleagues and knowledge of Senate rules and procedures, skills he honed to near perfection during his six years as Democratic whip. As majority leader he so disadvantaged his opponents through the artful use of his parliamentary talents that the Republicans later hired the parliamentarian Byrd had fired, Robert B. Dove, to improve their procedural strategies. (Dove became Senate parliamentarian again in 1995.)

A more activist leader than Mansfield, Byrd emphasized the need for strong party loyalty and said he wanted to bring about a resurgence of party spirit. He did not see his role as forcing an unpopular measure on his colleagues, who probably would not have accepted such a role in any event, but as trying to find consensus. Byrd tended to go to his colleagues with only the hint of an objective. If a consensus could be found that would attract the necessary number of votes, he would take the bill under his wing. "I talk to senators. I have meetings with senators, I try to stimulate a consensus for a party position on issues where one is necessary," he explained. "By getting a consensus first, senators are more likely to support the leadership."

Byrd had an uneasy relationship with President Carter, who came to the White House in 1977, the year Byrd became majority leader. Byrd seemed to regard Carter as an amateur with little aptitude for the exercise of power. Nonetheless, he repeatedly saved the Democratic administration in difficult legislative situations. Byrd played an indispensable role in the passage of Carter's energy policy package and in the extension of the deadline for ratification of the Equal Rights Amendment, among other matters. He successfully commanded the floor, with Vice President Walter Mondale in the chair to deny recognition to any other senator, to sweep dilatory amendments out of the way and successfully break a postcloture filibuster against the energy legislation by Senate liberals. Perhaps his most dramatic rescue operation came in 1978, when he amassed enough votes to ratify the Panama Canal treaties—giving canal ownership to Panama—through nonstop negotiation with wavering senators, personal diplomacy with Panamanian officials, and last-minute language changes.

Byrd also took steps to help the Senate conduct its business more smoothly, perfecting a track system that allowed controversial measures to be dealt with while noncontroversial legislation was being debated, and instituting periodic scheduled recesses, known as "nonlegislative work periods." Along the way he found time to write and deliver a series of Senate speeches—later published as a book—chronicling the history of the Senate from 1789 to 1989.

Despite his obvious love and respect for the Senate, Byrd was a private man, withdrawn from his colleagues; a former aide once noted that "Byrd was most comfortable in a room by himself."[68] His inability to develop a personal rapport with fellow senators, combined with his emphasis on Senate procedures and prerogatives, meant that though he was respected, Byrd was regarded by some as more of a technician than a leader. Dissatisfaction grew louder after the 1980 elections, when Republicans took control of the Senate and Byrd was relegated to what for him was the uncomfortable role of minority leader.

Byrd worked hard to reunite the party, scheduling weekly luncheon meetings of the Democratic Caucus, which had rarely met during the Carter years, and holding a series of weekend retreats in West Virginia where Democratic senators could work through many of their disagreements. He also set up several task forces to propose Democratic alternatives to President Reagan's legislative proposals.

LEADERSHIP FIRSTS

From the very first, when Oliver Ellsworth of Connecticut exercised "more practical leadership in the day-to-day activities" of the Senate, the upper chamber has had unofficial leaders. But congressional scholars disagree as to who were the first official Senate floor leaders.

Some scholars, among them Randall B. Ripley, hold that the position of floor leader emerged around 1911. The chairmen of the Democratic Caucus—Thomas S. Martin of Virginia from 1911 to 1913 and John W. Kern of Indiana from 1913 to 1917—were clearly the party's leaders in the Senate, although it is unclear that the term "floor leader" was formally applied to either man.

In a 1988 pamphlet on the origins of Senate leadership, Senate parliamentarian emeritus Floyd M. Riddick wrote that neither party's caucus minutes used the term "leader" until 1920, when the Democratic minutes referred to Oscar W. Underwood, D-Ala., as "minority leader." (Underwood had also served two terms as majority leader in the House before being elected to the Senate.) According to Republican Caucus minutes, the first GOP Senate floor leader was Charles Curtis of Kansas (1924).

SOURCE: Walter J. Oleszek, "John Worth Kern," in *First Among Equals,* ed. Richard A. Baker and Roger H. Davidson (Washington, D.C.: CQ Press, 1991), 9–10.

But perceptions lingered that Byrd was too stilted and old-fashioned to be the Senate Democrats' national spokesperson in the age of television. After the 1984 elections Lawton Chiles of Florida challenged Byrd for the leadership post, but lost, 36–11. Never before had anyone challenged an incumbent Democratic leader in the Senate, and it was a sign of simmering discontent that Chiles, a cautious, moderate-to-conservative figure, had chosen to undertake it. J. Bennett Johnston, La., spent much of 1986 preparing to challenge Byrd, but when the Democrats regained control of the Senate, and by a much wider margin than had been expected, he quietly dropped his plans.

In his second tour as majority leader Byrd played the partisan spokesperson that his party seemed to want, rallying the Democrats behind an ambitious legislative agenda meant to show that the Democrats could govern. But criticisms of his leadership style and his media image continued, and in the spring of 1988 Byrd announced that he would retire from the leadership post at the end of the year to take up the chairmanship of the Senate Appropriations Committee and to become president pro tempore, where he was more active than previous occupants, sometimes choosing to preside over complex parliamentary situations where his knowledge of Senate rules was especially valuable. And on the Appropriations Committee, Byrd was in an even better position to direct billions of dollars to his home state. Even in the minority after 1994, Byrd remained an aggressive institutionalist, leading opposition to the enactment of the line item veto in 1996 and challenging it in the Supreme Court. He was ultimately vindicated in 1998 when the Supreme

Court, in a case brought by other persons, declared the law unconstitutional. (*See box, Line-Item Veto Experiment Ended by Supreme Court, p. 530.*)

THE MODERN LEADERSHIP: MITCHELL

The winner in a three-way race to succeed Byrd as majority leader was George J. Mitchell of Maine, unsuccessful Democratic nominee for Maine governor in 1974 and former federal judge. Mitchell was appointed to the Senate to fill the vacancy caused in 1980 by President Carter's appointment of Sen. Edmund Muskie as secretary of state, and did not have to run for election in that year. He quickly caught the notice of his colleagues with his keen memory for detail and his command of facts, particularly on environmental issues. Mitchell further impressed his fellow senators with his political skills when he came from thirty-six points behind to win election to a full term in 1982 with 61 percent of the vote.

Chosen to chair the Democratic Senatorial Campaign Committee for the critical 1986 elections, Mitchell was instrumental in helping the party regain control of the Senate with a wider-than-expected margin. As a reward he was made deputy president pro tempore, a post created for Hubert H. Humphrey, D-Minn., in 1977 and not occupied since. Appointed in 1986 to the joint committee investigating the Iran-contra scandal, the secret sale of U.S. arms to Iran and diversion of some of the profits to "contra" rebel forces in Nicaragua, Mitchell proved himself to be an able performer before national television cameras, a factor considered crucial to his election as majority leader over Louisiana's Bennett Johnston and Daniel K. Inouye of Hawaii.

Mitchell's background left him flexible enough for a variety of tasks awaiting the leader of a rapidly changing body that had just endured two shifts of partisan control. "The role of party leaders has changed so that . . . they have become conciliators who must set broad goals and then prepare themselves for incremental progress that may yield both policy change and eventual political support," *National Journal* reporter Richard E. Cohen has written.[69]

In his first year in the position, Mitchell won high marks for his legislative savvy and administration of the Senate. Toward the end of the session, he managed almost single-handedly to kill a capital gains tax cut sought by the Bush administration, which had passed the House when nearly a quarter of the Democrats there defected from the party position to support it. Early in 1990 he demonstrated the effectiveness of negotiation and persistence, working out a comprehensive compromise with the White House on a clean air bill when it became clear that the committee version could not overcome a filibuster and then fighting to protect the compromise from major amendment. The bill was assembled over a month of extraordinary closed door meetings just off the Senate floor run by Mitchell, who assembled key senators and administration representatives to thrash out details for a package that could be protected by a bipartisan majority coalition. Mitchell attributed his victory on the floor to direct, personal, face-to-face talks with his col-

Effective at opposition or negotiation, Maine Democrat George Mitchell was Senate majority leader from 1989 to 1994.

leagues, urging them to stick with the compromise or see the entire bill collapse under the weight of controversial amendments. Mitchell also cemented his leadership by successfully staring down his predecessor, Byrd, whose efforts to protect coal miners threatened to unravel the bill. Byrd's key floor amendment was defeated by a single vote.

Republicans considered Mitchell partisan but his judicial demeanor often served to mask that aspect of his leadership. His more matter-of-fact debate style was a far cry from the sometimes emotional, florid performances of Johnson, Dirksen, and Byrd. Nonetheless, Mitchell often found the Senate as frustrating as they had. His announcement that he would not seek reelection in 1994 shocked colleagues. He quickly became the front-runner for a vacancy on the Supreme Court in that year, but Mitchell issued a statement asking that he not be considered and noting the importance of his presence as majority leader in trying (ultimately unsuccessfully) to push health care legislation through the Senate.

The result of Mitchell's departure, for Democrats, was loss of his Senate seat to the GOP and another hotly contested leadership fight.

The contest to succeed Mitchell as Democratic leader began as a contest between younger senators close to Mitchell and more senior traditionalists, although like any struggle by secret ballot in a highly personalized body the alliances did not always follow obvious or expected patterns. Mitchell's mantle fell on Sen. Thomas A. Daschle of South Dakota, elected in 1986, who had been made cochairman of the Policy Committee. Because the original senior contender for majority leader, Budget Committee Chairman Jim Sasser of Tennessee, appeared a likely loser in his reelection race, his supporters switched quickly to Christopher Dodd of Connecticut. When the Democrats lost control of the Senate in the 1994 elections, the battle became one over who would become minority leader. Dodd, elected in 1980, had substantial seniority over Daschle. But he lost to Daschle by one vote, 24–23, indicating, as did Mitchell's election, that senators had different criteria than seniority in mind in choosing leaders.

Daschle had served in the House and was attuned to the needs of a media-conscious Senate to develop a united party message. From 1995 to 1999, Daschle enjoyed considerable success as Senate minority leader. Although his Democratic colleagues in the Senate were further reduced to forty-five for the 105th and 106th Congresses—which was also the party's low point in strength during the 1980s—Daschle was able to keep the Democrats together during many cloture votes.

MODERN REPUBLICAN LEADERSHIP

Republican leadership styles in the age of collegiality paralleled those of the Democrats. Hugh Scott of Pennsylvania, who was narrowly elected to succeed Dirksen in 1969, was less assertive but perhaps even more flexible than Dirksen. His leadership of compromise and accommodation was very much like Mansfield's, but Scott was considered a rather ineffective leader. His moderate-to-liberal politics sometimes made it difficult for him to serve as a spokesperson for the Nixon and Ford administrations, and his support, first of U.S. action in Vietnam long after many of his colleagues and constituents had turned against it, and then of Nixon well into the Watergate crisis, further undermined his standing.

Scott, who retired at the end of 1976, was succeeded by Dirksen's son-in-law, Howard H. Baker Jr. of Tennessee. Baker had sought the post twice before, running unsuccessfully against Scott in 1969 and 1971. Baker was best known for adopting an aura of bipartisanship during the televised 1973 hearings of the Senate Watergate Committee, where he served as the ranking Republican to folksy Chairman Sam Ervin, D-N.C., and for asking the famous question "What did the President know and when did he know it?" In 1977 his colleagues, apparently convinced that he would be a more articulate spokesperson for the party, elected Baker minority leader over minority whip Robert P. Griffin of Michigan by a single vote. When the Republicans took over the Senate in 1981, Baker was made majority leader with no opposition.

A relaxed manner and close friendships with many of his Republican colleagues were Baker's principal assets. He was open and accessible to GOP senators of every ideology and was committed to protecting their rights. As majority leader, Baker was able to hold the disparate group of Republicans together on most issues during Reagan's first year in office. But when the economy faltered in late 1981, old divisions between moderate and conservative Republicans reopened, and unity became more difficult to achieve.

Baker's job was increasingly frustrated by the procedural chaos that gripped the Senate. His penchant for accommodation created a situation in which nearly every senator expected the schedule to conform to his or her personal needs. Floor action was delayed by senators who asked for "holds" on legislation—guarantees that a particular matter would not be taken up until the senator was present to protect his or her interests. Baker eventually announced that he would no longer consider holds sacrosanct, nor would he stack votes for the convenience of members who wanted more time to return to their home states. But there was little Baker could do to prevent individual members from tying up the Senate with filibusters and other delaying tactics.

In January 1983 Baker announced that he would retire from the Senate after the 1984 elections. To succeed him as majority leader, Republicans elected Bob Dole of Kansas over four other candidates.

DOLE: SHARP TACTICS, HARD EDGES

After four years of Baker's easygoing stewardship, Republican senators opted for a leader who they thought would restore some discipline and sense of purpose to a chamber increasingly bogged down in procedural chaos.

Five candidates entered the lists: Dole; Ted Stevens, Alaska, the majority whip; Richard G. Lugar, Ind.; Pete V. Domenici, N.M.; and James McClure, Idaho. It was the first time since 1937 that the selection of a Senate majority leader came down to a vote in a party body. On the first ballot, McClure fell out of the race, followed on subsequent ones by Domenici and then Lugar. On the fourth ballot, Dole won, 28–25.

Dole was chairman of the Republican National Committee at the time of the Watergate burglary in 1972 but was forced out of the post at the beginning of 1973 and was never associated with the scandal. "Watergate happened on my night off," he said. Dole, as the nominee for vice president on the Republicans' unsuccessful 1976 national ticket, had suffered a memorable embarrassing moment in debate with the Democratic nominee, Sen. Walter Mondale, D-Minn., by referring to World Wars I and II as "Democrat Wars." It cemented the public image of Dole as a harsh and humorless partisan, which he tried with only mixed success to mellow in later years. He also ran briefly for president in 1980 but dropped out without mounting a serious effort.

However, despite his often glowering persona on national television, in the Senate Dole moved steadily into the position of insider who was willing to negotiate and valued legislative achievement. Dole had a hand in much of the important legisla-

tion of a generation, from taxes to Social Security to civil rights to protections for the disabled. He ably chaired the Finance Committee for four years (1981–1985) before ascending to the leadership, and ultimately Dole was to become the longest serving Republican Senate leader in history (1985–1996).

In addition to his image as a decisive leader, Dole was known as a superb negotiator with an ability to find compromises where others had failed. "You don't try to cram things down people's throats," he once said. "You try to work it out." Many of his colleagues, especially those up for reelection in 1986, thought he would also be willing to stand up to the Reagan White House when needed to protect their political interests. Of the candidates for majority leader, Dole was considered the least likely to toe the White House line on legislation. He had disagreed with President Reagan on issues as diverse as food stamps, civil rights, and tax policy.

That did not mean that Dole was anything less than an aggressive advocate for the administration on a broad range of issues. With a thin 53–47 Republican majority in his first term as majority leader, Dole produced significant victories, helping to pass tax revision, a new immigration law, a new farm bill, and aid to the Nicaraguan contras. Although Dole restored a modicum of discipline to the Senate, some of his methods—lengthy sessions and complicated parliamentary tactics intended to disarm obstructionists—were not popular with his colleagues and in some instances had only minimal effect. Democrats often gleefully used Dole's past image as a tough political hatchet man against him. They successfully ran against the Republicans' conservative budget priorities as well as the weaknesses of many members of the Republican class of 1980, who proved too weak to withstand a campaign without an accompanying presidential landslide.

Dole was relegated to minority leader from 1987–1995. He ran again for the Republican presidential nomination in 1988, winning the Iowa caucuses before losing the New Hampshire primary to Vice President George Bush's better focused effort. As minority leader, Dole was considered a tough partisan who was particularly effective in mobilizing Republicans against President Clinton's 1993 economic stimulus package, which was killed by a filibuster signaling that Republicans would give Clinton no honeymoon.

In his second incarnation as majority leader in 1995 and part of 1996, Dole became the front-runner for the Republican presidential nomination, but as a congressional leader he played second fiddle to Speaker Gingrich during the first session of the 104th Congress. Known to be skeptical of elements of the "Contract with America," Dole was uncomfortable with the House's breakneck pace and what he regarded as careless legislating. However, Dole pushed aggressively for elements of the GOP plan, particularly the constitutional amendment requiring a balanced federal budget that had passed the House for the first time in 1995. Dole's aggressive tactics angered Democrats, who accused him of breaking an agreement by delaying a final vote that would have defeated the proposal, as he tried to secure one

Republican Senate Majority Leader Trent Lott, at podium, holds a press conference with other members of the GOP Senate leadership in 1998.

additional vote. However, the defection of Sen. Mark Hatfield, chairman of the Appropriations Committee and the only Republican to oppose the amendment, killed any chance of it passing and deeply embarrassed Senate Republicans.

After Speaker Gingrich was badly weakened following the fiasco of the two government shutdowns during the winter of 1995–1996, Dole took the initiative to force an end to the controversy and to repudiate conservative House members who wanted to continue the shutdown.

Democrats in 1996 successfully tied down Dole in the Senate, blocking legislation and making him appear frustrated and ineffective. Realizing that trying to run the Senate was incompatible with his ambitions for the White House, Dole surprised his colleagues by resigning not only from the leadership but the Senate itself in the spring of 1996. After losing the presidential election to Clinton overwhelmingly, Dole joined a law firm.

LOTT: PRAGMATIC IDEOLOGUE

Sen. Trent Lott, R-Miss., had crashed his way into the GOP leadership in 1994 by defeating the combative but less conservative incumbent Alan Simpson of Wyoming for majority whip by a single vote. In his new role, there was speculation that Lott would push Dole to the right, but the two leaders moved to put aside their initially uneasy relationship.

Lott became majority leader in mid-1996 after squashing a campaign by his senior Mississippi colleague and longtime rival, Thad Cochran, 44–8. Lott seemed well suited to lead the most conservative Senate since the 1920s, with a 55–45 Republican majority in the 105th and 106th Congresses. He came into office

with high expectations. Once considered a sharp-edged ideologue from his days in the House as minority whip from 1981 to 1989, Lott did not use the Senate's top post, as some thought he would, to transform the chamber into an engine of conservative activism similar to the House. That perception may have been buttressed by an increasing number of conservative Republican senators who had served in the House and agreed with many of the views of Gingrich and the 1994 GOP freshman class.

However, Lott had broad legislative experience that characterized House leadership. He also had an accommodating personal style, unlike the often harsh tones Gingrich took in the House. The nature of the Senate itself made such a strategy impractical. Like many Senate leaders, Lott found that a more successful approach was to accommodate a leadership style to the institution of the Senate rather than to change that body to suit outside constituencies. "Senate majority leaders are so highly constrained by institutional arrangements, the variations we see among them in strategy and tactics are very small," notes political scientist Steven Smith.

The challenge of mustering votes from the minority side in the House gave Lott formidable training for his whip role in the Senate. And it gave him valuable ties to colleagues of both parties, many of whom had since been elected to the Senate.

In office, Lott proved effective at the sort of member-to-member, retail politics that have traditionally sustained cooperation and inoculated leaders from assault in the Senate. The smiling, affable demeanor of Lott, a former cheerleader at the University of Mississippi, provided a stark contrast with the dour, acerbic Dole, generating praise even from Democrats.

Lott did not often employ the all-or-nothing tactics employed by House Republicans in 1995. Faced with an opportunity for legislative achievement at the expense of ideological purity, Lott grabbed it eagerly, overseeing the passage of major legislation to raise the minimum wage, improve the safety of drinking water, guarantee health insurance coverage for displaced workers, and overhaul the nation's welfare system. The fact that some of these initiatives were favored by Democrats and passed over the opposition of conservatives did not prevent Lott from claiming credit for substantial legislative accomplishments and increasing the GOP majority by one in the 1996 election even as the President Clinton was trouncing his predecessor, Dole. Lott's impeccable conservative credentials enabled him to strike deals with Democrats without arousing the mistrust of Republicans, who, he told a reporter, "know where my heart is."

As the 105th Congress neared its end, Lott had not yet become a high-profile national figure, as had Gingrich. With the Speaker weakened politically, it had been anticipated that Lott, with a larger GOP majority in his chamber—at least in percentage terms—would assume a more prominent role as party spokesperson. However, Lott demonstrated no rush to fill such a role. And when he did step forward as a party spokesperson, Lott sometimes was too open for his troops' tastes, as when early in 1998 he called on special prosecutor Kenneth Starr to wrap up his investigation of the Clinton presidency, when many Republicans considered the variety of alleged presidential scandals ripe for lengthy political exploitation. And in the 106th Congress Lott worked with Daschle to ensure that the Senate's prerogatives were protected in the impeachment trial.

Party Support Structure in the Senate

The leadership hierarchy in the Senate is not as strong as that in the House, but the apparatus follows many of the same patterns. The party support structure is composed of party whips, leaders of the party conference, and leaders of other party committees.

PARTY WHIPS

The first whips appeared in the Senate about the same time the floor leader positions were being institutionalized. The Democrats designated J. Hamilton Lewis of Illinois their first whip in 1913; in 1915 James W. Wadsworth Jr., N.Y., was named the first GOP whip.

Although the duties of Senate whips are essentially the same as those of their House counterparts, the whip organizations are much less prominent in the Senate than in the House. For one thing, their functions and duties are less institutionalized, and their organizations much less elaborate. The majority and minority leaders in the Senate also generally assume some of what the whip's responsibilities would be in the House.

Senate whips at times have openly defied their own party leaders. Both parties elect their whips in the Senate, and the political maneuvering entailed in running for the office has some-

times led members to back certain senators for reasons that may have little to do with leadership effectiveness.

A serious breach occurred between Majority Leader Mansfield and Russell B. Long, La., the Democratic whip from 1965 to 1969. The two first clashed in 1966 over Long's proposal for federal subsidies for presidential election campaigns. Long exacerbated the dispute in 1967 by sending a newsletter to constituents in which he listed his disagreements with President Johnson (and Mansfield) on the issue. Mansfield sought to circumvent Long's influence by appointing four assistant whips. Long was defeated for whip by Edward Kennedy in 1969 (although Long eventually won the policy battle in 1971, when Congress finally approved public financing legislation).

Long lost his bid for reelection perhaps as much because he had been insufficiently attentive to the day-to-day details of the whip's job as because of any lingering ill-feeling between him and Mansfield. His successor, Kennedy, was neither a particularly active nor effective whip and was crippled early in his tenure by the auto accident at Chappaquiddick. In 1971 he lost his bid for reelection to West Virginia's Byrd, then secretary of the Democratic Conference.

Alan Cranston, of California, who was elected Democratic whip when Byrd became majority leader, was particularly effective in that post. A liberal able to build bridges to Senate moderates and conservatives, he demonstrated a remarkable ability to sense shifts in sentiments as legislation moved toward the Senate floor and through the years put together numerous winning coalitions.

Senate whips do not move up the leadership ladder as regularly as House whips do. Although Johnson, Mansfield, and Byrd all did so, Cranston did not even seek the leadership spot when Byrd announced he would vacate it in 1989. When Cranston left the Senate in 1993, the more conservative and low-key Wendell H. Ford of Kentucky, who did not run in the 1994 race to replace Mitchell, succeeded him. On the Republican side the whips who moved up to floor leader in recent times have been Dirksen, Scott, and Lott, with Robert Griffin and Ted Stevens trying and losing.

PARTY CONFERENCES

The development of party caucuses (now called conferences) in the Senate paralleled that of the House. In 1846 the party caucus increased in importance by acquiring the authority to make committee assignments. During the Civil War and Reconstruction era, Republicans used the caucus frequently to discuss and adopt party positions on legislation.

In the 1890s Republican leaders Allison and Aldrich used the caucus extensively and effectively. As Rothman observed, "The Republican caucus was not binding, and yet its decisions commanded obedience for party leadership was capable of enforcing discipline. Senators could no longer act with impunity unless they were willing to forgo favorable committee posts and control of the chamber proceedings."[70]

It is unlikely that any Senate Democrats ever were penalized

Helping their members win reelection and wresting seats away from the other party are top priority jobs for party leaders in Congress. Given the ever-mounting cost of House and Senate election campaigns, fund-raising is probably the most valuable service the leadership can provide. In addition to attending fund-raising dinners and receptions in members' home districts or states, many leaders in both parties have established their own political action committees (PACs) that solicit money from unions, corporations, and other contributors, which the leaders then channel to candidates. Commonly referred to as "leadership PACs" or "congressional PACs," these fund-raising tools are formed by ambitious members to help party candidates win seats, expand party representation, and establish a sense of gratitude among beneficiaries when leadership positions are decided.

The major campaign efforts, however, are handled by special party committees set up expressly for the purpose: the Democratic Congressional Campaign Committee (DCCC) and the National Republican Congressional Committee (NRCC) in the House; and the Democratic Senatorial Campaign Committee (DSCC) and the National Republican Senatorial Committee (NRSC) in the Senate. Chaired by members of Congress, these committees help identify candidates to challenge incumbents of the other party or to run for open seats. They brief candidates on the issues and help them with all phases of campaigning, advising—even supplying—campaign managers, finance directors, and press secretaries. They also play an increasingly important role in recruiting candidates.

These committees also raise and disburse millions of dollars. For the 1998 elections, the Democratic committees raised nearly $61 million on behalf of their candidates; the Republican committees nearly $126 million. Millions of dollars in so-called "soft" money were raised separately. (*See Chapter 32, Campaign Financing.*)

The party campaign committees are important to candidates not only as sources of money but also because they attract funding from other contributors. Given the high cost of campaigns and the limits on campaign contributions, a commitment from a congressional party entity can help a candidate cross an important threshold of credibility with other potential sources of funding. The party committees almost invariably give to an incumbent of their party if there is a challenge in the primary, except in unusual circumstances. For example, in 1998, the NRCC worked aggressively to shore up Rep. William Goodling of Pennsylvania, chairman of the House Committee on Education and the Workforce, in a primary against an opponent who had won 45 percent of the vote against him two years earlier. Goodling won the rematch easily. But at the same time, it refused to support Rep. Jay Kim of California for renomination in 1998 after he had pleaded guilty to campaign finance law violations in earlier campaigns, was sentenced to house arrest, and was forced to campaign from Washington, where he had been required to wear an electronic monitoring device. Kim lost in the primary.

Incumbents are routinely asked to contribute to the party committee in their chamber, and also for special purposes, such as hotly contested special elections that may arise in the House.

The party committees often decline to support candidates for an open seat that is being contested in a primary. But if one candidate is believed to be visibly stronger for the general election early intervention can help that candidate win the primary and begin an earlier focus on the general election. With party control of Congress closely divided, especially in the House, such intervention has become much more common. Recruitment activities by the party committees can also be expected to intensify.

To help attract additional funding, the party committees work on selling their candidates to PACs through meetings with the candidates, briefings, even newsletters. Party committees can also play a crucial role by giving a promising challenger money to get his or her campaign off the ground or by channeling funding into a sagging campaign.

Raising campaign funds for one's colleagues is not new. In his book *The Path to Power*, Robert A. Caro writes that in 1940 Lyndon B. Johnson, then in his third year in the House, tapped into Texas oil money, directing it to Democratic colleagues. His endeavors are credited with saving thirty to forty Democratic seats, which kept the House from going Republican. Of course, campaign finance laws, and the amounts of money potentially available, have changed dramatically since then but the leadership's interest has not.

In more recent times, House Majority Whip Tony Coelho, D-Calif., and Senate Majority Leader George J. Mitchell, D-Maine, won their leadership positions in part because of their success in directing their respective campaign committees. Mitchell ran the committee for the 1986 election cycle, when Democrats regained control of the Senate. Similarly, Rep. Bill Paxon, R-N.Y., used his success running the NRCC before the 1994 election, when the Republicans gained control of the House, to position himself for a run for higher office in the GOP leadership before suddenly announcing his retirement in 1998 to spend more time with his family. Indeed, fund-raising for colleagues seems to have become a prerequisite for anyone who wants to join the party leadership. Mitchell's two challengers for the post of majority leader in 1988 both set up PACs to direct campaign funds to colleagues. Mitchell did not set up a PAC but indirectly channeled money to colleagues when asked for advice from other PACs and contributors.

Today, campaign aid is one of the services that leaders are expected to provide their rank and file. It is a service that can also benefit the leadership when the time comes to ask for support for the parties' legislative programs in Congress. More disturbingly, however, the money chase has filtered down to other levels of leadership activities, such as the assignment of members to committees. It is not uncommon for members on the leadership panels making such assignments to examine how financially supportive an applicant for an important legislative committee has been to other, more vulnerable, colleagues.

for not abiding by a binding caucus rule adopted in 1903. But they used the rule to achieve remarkable unity in 1913–1914 in support of President Wilson's legislative objectives. Twenty years later, charged with enacting Franklin Roosevelt's New Deal, Democrats readopted the rule. It was not employed, but frequent nonbinding caucuses were held to mobilize support. Since that time neither party has seriously considered using caucus votes to enforce party loyalty on legislative issues.

Both party conferences elect the various party leaders and ratify committee chairmanship and ranking minority member posts and other committee assignments. After resuming control of the Senate in the 104th Congress, Republicans amended their conference rules to limit service in elected party leadership posts, except floor leader and president pro tempore, to no more than three Congresses. The affected positions would be majority whip, conference chairman and conference secretary, chairman of the policy committee, and chairman of the National Republican Senatorial Committee (NRSC), though that post has traditionally rotated. In recent years both parties have used the conference to collect and distribute information to members, to perform legislative research, and to ratify decisions made by the policy committees. Each conference meets weekly for luncheons to discuss scheduling and strategy. Administration officials sometimes attend their party's sessions.

OTHER PARTY COMMITTEES

The two Senate parties each have a policy committee, a committee on committees (called the Steering Committee by the Democrats), and a campaign committee. Traditionally the Democratic leader chaired the party conference as well as the Policy and Steering committees, giving him significant potential power to control the party apparatus. Breaking with that custom, George Mitchell gave responsibility for the Steering Committee to Inouye and made Daschle cochair, with Mitchell, of the Policy Committee. Daschle continued the practice. The Republican Conference and party committees traditionally are chaired by different senators, thus diffusing power among Senate Republicans.

The first of the party committees to be created was the Committee on Committees, which originated during the Civil War era, when Republicans, then in the majority, used a special panel appointed by their party caucus to make both Republican and Democratic committee assignments. Senate Democrats set up a Committee on Committees in 1879. Committee assignments made by each of these committees are subject to ratification by the respective party conference and the full chamber.

What was, in effect, the first Senate Steering Committee was established in 1874, when the GOP Conference appointed a Committee on the Order of Business to prepare a schedule for Senate floor action. That committee was replaced in the mid-1880s by a Steering Committee appointed by the caucus chairman. Democrats established a Steering Committee in 1879 but abandoned it when the Republicans regained control of the Senate and the legislative agenda. They did not set up another

Steering Committee until 1893 when the Democrats once again controlled the Senate.

In 1947 both parties created policy committees that were assigned the scheduling functions of the old Steering committees. At the same time the Democratic Steering Committee, while retaining its name, was reconstituted as the party's committee on committees. The Policy committees—which prepare material on issues and legislation and discuss broad questions of party policy—have been more or less active, depending on the needs of the party leadership and whether the party was in or out of the majority.

Under Daschle's leadership, for example, the Democratic Policy Committee stepped up its analysis of the issues and put together an ambitious policy agenda for Senate Democrats.

NOTES

1. Christopher J. Deering and Steven S. Smith, "Majority Party Leadership and the New House Subcommittee System," in *Understanding Congressional Leadership*, ed. Frank B. Mackaman (Washington, D.C.: CQ Press, 1981), 288–289.

2. Roger H. Davidson and Walter J. Oleszek, *Congress and Its Members*, 7th ed. (Washington, D.C.: CQ Press, 2000), 184.

3. Ibid., 184.

4. Ibid., 164.

5. Ibid., 185.

6. Richard E. Cohen, "Byrd of West Virginia: A New Job, A New Image," *National Journal*, August 20, 1977, 1295.

7. Richard E. Cohen, "Taking Advantage of Tax Reform Means Different Strokes for Different Folks," *National Journal*, June 22, 1985, 1459.

8. Howard Fineman, "For the Son of C-Span, Exposure Equals Power," *Newsweek*, April 3, 1989, 23.

9. Michael J. Malbin, "House Democrats Are Playing with a Strong Leadership Lineup," *National Journal*, June 18, 1977, 942.

10. Davidson and Oleszek, *Congress and Its Members*, 165.

11. Floyd M. Riddick, *The United States Congress: Organization and Procedure* (Washington, D.C.: National Capitol Publishers, 1949), 67.

12. Mary P. Follett, *The Speaker of the House of Representatives* (New York: Burt Franklin Reprints, 1974), 25–26 (reprint of 1896 edition).

13. George B. Galloway, *History of the House of Representatives* (New York: Crowell, 1961), 20.

14. Ronald M. Peters Jr., *The American Speakership: The Office in Historical Perspective* (Baltimore: Johns Hopkins University Press, 1990), 31.

15. Follett, *The Speaker of the House of Representatives*, 82.

16. George Rothwell Brown, *The Leadership of Congress* (New York: Arno Press, 1974), 37–38 (reprint of 1922 edition).

17. Peters, *The American Speakership*, 35–36.

18. Steven S. Smith and Christopher J. Deering, *Committees in Congress*, 2nd ed. (Washington, D.C.: CQ Press, 1990), 28.

19. Peters, *The American Speakership*, 36.

20. Follett, *The Speaker of the House of Representatives*, 84.

21. Hubert B. Fuller, *The Speaker of the House* (Boston: Little, Brown, 1909), 26.

22. Galloway, *History of the House of Representatives*, 51.

23. Ibid., 132.

24. Ibid., 133.

25. Barbara W. Tuchman, *The Proud Tower: A Portrait of the World before the War: 1890–1914* (New York: Macmillan, 1966), 127.

26. Fuller, *The Speaker of the House*, 244.

27. Peters, *The American Speakership*, 77.

28. Fuller, *The Speaker of the House*, 257.

29. Robert Luce, *Congress: An Explanation* (Cambridge, Mass.: Harvard University Press, 1926), 117.

30. Peters, *The American Speakership*, 94.

31. Randall B. Ripley, *Party Leaders in the House of Representatives* (Washington, D.C.: Brookings Institution, 1967), 101.

32. Galloway, *History of the House of Representatives*, 144.

33. *U.S. News & World Report*, October 13, 1950, 30.

34. Peters, *The American Speakership*, 140–141.

35. John M. Barry, *The Ambition and the Power* (New York: Viking Penguin, 1989), 4.

36. Alan Ehrenhalt, ed., *Politics in America: Members of Congress in Washington and at Home, 1986* (Washington, D.C.: CQ Press, 1985), 1507.

37. Peters, *The American Speakership*, 280.

38. Phil Duncan, ed., *Politics in America, 1990* (Washington, D.C.: CQ Press, 1989), 2.

39. Christopher Madison, "The Heir Presumptive," *National Journal*, April 29, 1989, 1036.

40. Ibid., 1035.

41. *1995 Congressional Quarterly Almanac* (Washington, D.C.: Congressional Quarterly, 1996), I-21.

42. Barbara Sinclair, "Transformational Leader or Faithful Agent? Innovation and Continuity in House Majority Party Leadership: The 104th and 105th Congresses," paper presented at 1997 meeting of the American Political Science Association, Washington, D.C., 9.

43. Neil MacNeil, *Forge of Democracy: The House of Representatives* (New York: McKay, 1963), 87.

44. Peters, *The American Speakership*, 92.

45. Galloway, *History of the House of Representatives*, 108.

46. Barbara Sinclair, *Majority Leadership in the U.S. House* (Baltimore: Johns Hopkins University Press, 1983), 46.

47. Floyd M. Riddick, *Congressional Procedure* (Boston: Chapman & Grimes, 1941), 345–346.

48. Irwin B. Arieff, "Inside Congress," *Congressional Quarterly Weekly Report*, February 28, 1981, 379.

49. Ripley, *Party Leaders in the House of Representatives*, 29.

50. Duncan, ed., *Politics in America, 1990*, 470.

51. Sinclair, *Majority Leadership in the U.S. House*, 57.

52. Sinclair, "Transformational Leader," 20.

53. Barbara Sinclair, "Majority Party Leadership Strategies for Coping with the New U.S. House," in *Understanding Congressional Leadership*, ed. Frank H. Mackaman (Washington, D.C.: CQ Press, 1981), 202.

54. Galloway, *History of the House of Representatives*, 130.

55. Sinclair, *Majority Leadership in the U.S. House*, 96–97.

55. George H. Haynes, *The Senate of the United States: Its History and Practices*, (Boston: Houghton Mifflin, 1938), vol. 2, 1003.

56. Randall B. Ripley, *Power in the Senate* (New York: St. Martin's, 1969), 24.

57. W. E. Binkley, *The Powers of the President* (New York: Russell & Russell, 1973), 52.

58. David J. Rothman, *Politics and Power: The United States Senate 1869–1901* (Cambridge, Mass.: Harvard University Press, 1966), 19.

59. Charles O. Jones, *The Minority Party in Congress* (Boston: Little, Brown, 1970), 48.

60. Rothman, *Politics and Power*, 44.

61. John G. Stewart, "Two Strategies of Leadership: Johnson and Mansfield," in *Congressional Behavior*, ed. Nelson W. Polsby (New York: Random House, 1971), 61–92.

62. Rowland Evans and Robert Novak, *Lyndon B. Johnson: The Exercise of Power* (New York: New American Library, 1966), 104.

63. Roger H. Davidson, "The Senate: If Everyone Leads, Who Follows?" in *Congress Reconsidered*, 4th ed., ed. Lawrence C. Dodd and Bruce I. Oppenheimer (Washington, D.C.: CQ Press, 1989), 280.

64. Ross K. Baker, *Friend and Foe in the U.S. Senate* (New York: Free Press, 1980), 203.

65. Barbara Sinclair, "Congressional Leadership: A Review Essay," in *Leading Congress: New Styles, New Strategies*, ed. John J. Kornacki (Washington, D.C.: CQ Press, 1990), 141.

66. Robert L. Peabody, "Senate Party Leadership: From the 1950s to the 1980s," in *Understanding Congressional Leadership*, ed. Frank B. Mackaman (Washington, D.C.: CQ Press, 1981), 59.

67. Davidson, "The Senate: If Everyone Leads, Who Follows?" in *Congress Reconsidered*, 281.

68. Janet Hook, "Mitchell Learns Inside Game; Is Cautious as Party Voice," *Congressional Quarterly Weekly Report*, September 9, 1989, 2294.

69. Richard E. Cohen, *Washington at Work: Back Rooms and Clean Air* (Needham Heights, Mass.: Allyn and Bacon, 1995), 96.

70. Rothman, *Politics and Power*, 60.

SELECTED BIBLIOGRAPHY

Aldrich, John H. *Why Parties? The Origin and Transformation of Political Parties in America*. Chicago: University of Chicago Press, 1995.

Alexander, De Alva S. *History and Procedure of the House of Representatives*. Boston: Houghton Mifflin, 1916.

Baker, Richard A., and Roger H. Davidson, eds. *First among Equals: Outstanding Senate Leaders of the Twentieth Century*. Washington, D.C.: Congressional Quarterly, 1991.

Baker, Ross K. *Friend and Foe in the U.S. Senate*. New York: Free Press, 1980.

———. *House and Senate*. 2nd ed. New York: Norton, 1995.

Baldwin, Louis. *Hon. Politician: Mike Mansfield of Montana*. Missoula, Mont.: Mountain Press Publishing, 1979.

Barry, John M. *The Ambition and the Power*. New York: Viking Penguin, 1989.

Bolles, Blair. *Tyrant from Illinois: Uncle Joe Cannon's Experiment with Personal Power*. New York: Norton, 1951.

Bolling, Richard W. *House Out of Order*. New York: Dutton, 1965.

———. *Power in the House: A History of the Leadership of the House of Representatives*. New York: Dutton, 1968.

Brown, George Rothwell. *The Leadership of Congress*. New York: Arno Press, 1974.

Burns, James MacGregor. *Leadership*. New York: Harper and Row, 1978.

Busbey, L. White. *Uncle Joe Cannon*. New York: Henry Holt, 1927.

Byrd, Robert C. *The Senate, 1789–1989: Addresses on the History of the United States Senate*. 2 vols. Washington, D.C.: Government Printing Office, 1988.

Chiu, Chang-Wei. *The Speaker of the House of Representatives since 1896*. New York: Columbia University Press, 1928.

Clancy, Paul, and Shirley Elder. *Tip: A Biography of Thomas P. O'Neill, Speaker of the House*. New York: Macmillan, 1980.

Clark, Joseph S. *The Senate Establishment*. New York: Hill & Wang, 1963.

Cohen, Richard E. *Washington at Work: Back Rooms and Clean Air*. Needham Heights, Mass.: Allyn and Bacon, 1995.

Connelly, William F., and John J. Pitney Jr. *Congress' Permanent Minority? Republicans in the U.S. House*. Lanham, Md.: Rowman and Littlefield, 1994.

Cox, Gary W., and Mathew D. McCubbins. *Legislative Leviathan: Party Government in the House*. Berkeley: University of California Press, 1993.

Davidson, Roger H., and Walter J. Oleszek. *Congress and Its Members*. 7th ed. Washington, D.C.: CQ Press, 2000.

Dodd, Lawrence C., and Bruce I. Oppenheimer, eds. *Congress Reconsidered*. 6th ed. Washington, D.C.: CQ Press, 1997.

Evans, C. Lawrence, and Walter J. Oleszek. *Congress under Fire: Reform Politics and the Republican Majority*. Boston: Houghton Mifflin, 1997.

Evans, Rowland, and Robert Novak. *Lyndon B. Johnson: The Exercise of Power*. New York: New American Library, 1966.

Fiorina, Morris P., and David W. Rohde, eds. *Home Style and Washington Work: Studies of Congressional Politics*. Ann Arbor: University of Michigan Press, 1989.

Follett, Mary P. *The Speaker of the House of Representatives*. New York: Longmans, Green, 1896. Reprint. New York: Burt Franklin Reprints, 1974.

Fuller, Hubert Bruce. *The Speakers of the House*. Boston: Little, Brown, 1909.

Galloway, George B. *History of the House of Representatives*. 2nd ed. New York: Crowell, 1976.

Gillespie, Ed, and Bob Schellhas, eds. *Contract with America.* New York: Times Books, 1994.

Hardeman, D. B., and Donald C. Bacon. *Rayburn: A Biography.* Austin: Texas Monthly Press, 1987.

Haynes, George H. *The Senate of the United States: Its History and Practice.* 2 vols. Boston: Houghton Mifflin, 1938.

Hertzke, Allen D., and Ronald M. Peters Jr. *The Atomistic Congress: An Interpretation of Congressional Change.* New York: Sharpe, 1992.

Hinckley, Barbara. *Stability and Change in Congress.* 4th ed. New York: Harper and Row, 1988.

Jones, Charles O. *The Minority Party in Congress.* Boston: Little, Brown, 1970.

Kiewiet, D. Roderick, and Mathew D. McCubbins. *The Logic of Delegation: Congressional Parties and the Appropriations Process.* Chicago: University of Chicago Press, 1991.

Koopman, Douglas L. *Hostile Takeover: The House Republican Party, 1980–1995.* Lanham, Md.: Rowman and Littlefield, 1996.

Kornacki, John J., ed. *Leading Congress: New Styles, New Strategies.* Washington, D.C.: CQ Press, 1990.

Krehbiel, Keith. *Pivotal Politics: A Theory of U.S. Lawmaking.* Chicago: University of Chicago Press, 1998.

Loomis, Burdett A. *The New American Politician.* New York: Basic Books, 1988.

Mackaman, Frank H., ed. *Understanding Congressional Leadership.* Washington, D.C.: CQ Press, 1981.

MacNeil, Neil. *Dirksen: Portrait of a Public Man.* New York: World Publishing, 1970.

———. *Forge of Democracy: The House of Representatives.* New York: McKay, 1963.

Mann, Thomas, and Norman J. Ornstein, eds. *The New Congress.* Washington, D.C.: American Enterprise Institute, 1981.

Mayhew, David R. *Divided We Govern: Party Control, Lawmaking and Investigations, 1946–1990.* New Haven, Conn.: Yale University Press, 1991.

O'Neill, Thomas P., Jr., with William Novak. *Man of the House: The Life and Political Memoirs of Speaker Tip O'Neill.* New York: Random House, 1987.

Palazzolo, Daniel J. *The Speaker and the Budget: Leadership in the Post-Reform House of Representatives.* Pittsburgh: University of Pittsburgh Press, 1992.

Peabody, Robert L. *Leadership in Congress: Stability, Succession and Change.* Boston: Little, Brown, 1976.

Peters, Ronald M., Jr. *The American Speakership: The Office in Historical Perspective.* 2nd ed. Baltimore: Johns Hopkins University Press, 1997.

———, ed. *The Speaker: Leadership in the U.S. House of Representatives.* Washington, D.C.: Congressional Quarterly, 1995.

Ranney, Austin. *Channels of Power.* New York: Basic Books, 1983.

Reedy, George E. *The U.S. Senate: Paralysis or a Search for Consensus?* New York: Crown, 1986.

Riddick, Floyd M. *The United States Congress: Organization and Procedure.* Manassas, Va.: National Capitol Publishers, 1949.

Ripley, Randall B., and Grace A. Franklin. *Congress, the Bureaucracy, and Public Policy.* 5th ed. Pacific Grove, Calif.: Brooks/Cole, 1991.

Robinson, William A. *Thomas B. Reed: Parliamentarian.* New York: Dodd, Mead, 1930.

Rohde, David W. *Parties and Leaders in the Postreform House.* Chicago: University of Chicago Press, 1991.

Rothman, David J. *Politics and Power: The United States Senate, 1869–1901.* Cambridge, Mass.: Harvard University Press, 1966.

Sinclair, Barbara. *Legislators, Leaders, and Lawmaking: The U.S. House of Representatives in the Post Reform Era.* Baltimore: Johns Hopkins University Press, 1995.

———. *Majority Leadership in the U.S. House.* Baltimore: Johns Hopkins University Press, 1983.

———. "Transformational Leader or Faithful Agent? Innovation and Continuity in House Majority Party Leadership: The 104th and 105th Congresses." Paper presented at the meeting of the American Political Science Association, Washington, D.C., August 1997.

———. *The Transformation of the U.S. Senate.* Baltimore: Johns Hopkins University Press, 1989.

Steinberg, Alfred. *Sam Rayburn.* New York: Hawthorne Books, 1975.

Stewart, John. "The Strategies of Leadership: Johnson and Mansfield." In *Congressional Behavior,* edited by Nelson W. Polsby, 61–92. New York: Random House, 1971.

Tuchman, Barbara W. "End of a Dream." In *The Proud Tower: A Portrait of the World before the War: 1890–1914.* New York: Macmillan, 1966.

U.S. Congress. House. *The History and Operation of the House Majority Whip Organization.* 94th Cong., 1st sess., 1975. H Doc 94-162.

U.S. Congress. Senate. *Majority and Minority Leaders of the Senate: History and Development of the Offices of the Floor Leaders.* Prepared by Floyd M. Riddick. 100th Cong., 2nd sess., 1988. S Doc 100-29.

———. *Majority and Minority Whips of the Senate: History and Development of the Party Whip System in the United States Senate.* Prepared by Walter J. Oleszek. 98th Cong., 2nd sess., 1985. S Doc 98-45.

———. *Policymaking Role of Leadership in the Senate* (papers compiled for the Commission on the Operation of the Senate). "Party Leaders, Party Committees, and Policy Analysis in the United States Senate." Prepared by Randall B. Ripley. 94th Cong., 2nd sess., 1976.

Wilson, Woodrow. *Congressional Government: A Study in American Politics.* Boston: Houghton Mifflin, 1885. Reprint. Cleveland: Meridian, 1956.

CHAPTER 15

The Legislative Process

NOWHERE ARE policy and process more intertwined than in the Congress of the United States. They interact at many stages of the legislative drama as skillful senators and representatives use the rules of procedure—fashioned to ensure orderly consideration of legislative proposals—to advance their policy goals.

Bill sponsors tinker with wording to ensure the proposal goes to a sympathetic rather than a hostile committee. The Senate may attach major tax legislation to a House revenue bill, circumventing a constitutional requirement that all revenue bills must originate in the House. Wording of a House rule for consideration of a bill on the floor may greatly constrict the ability of opponents to alter it. Senators may seek to end or continue debate on a proposal in order to position themselves to force action on an entirely unrelated matter. All of these things, and many more, routinely go on in a session of Congress.

On the surface, the actions of Congress appear fairly straightforward. To become law proposed legislation must be approved in identical form in both the House and the Senate. Most legislative proposals are first considered in subcommittee and committee. After reaching the floor legislation is debated, possibly amended further, and approved by the full House or Senate. After both chambers have acted, any differences in the two versions of the legislation must be resolved and the final version sent to the White House for the president's signature, which completes the process. If the president vetoes the legislation, Congress may enact the measure into law by overriding the veto.

Both chambers use procedures to expedite minor and noncontroversial legislation, but negotiating this lawmaking course for controversial measures is complicated and time-consuming. Throughout the process Congress must consider the opinion of the executive branch, constituents, and special interest groups. At any point the bill is subject to delay, defeat, or substantial modification. At each step of the way the bill's proponents must assemble a majority coalition through continual bargaining and compromise. "It is very easy to defeat a bill in Congress," President John F. Kennedy once observed. "It is much more difficult to pass one."[1]

Importance of Rules

Reinforced by more than two centuries of precedent and custom, congressional rules and procedures can speed a bill to final passage or kill it, expand the policy alternatives or narrow them, disadvantage the minority or thwart the will of the majority. *(See box, House and Senate Rules, p. 474.)*

Legislators who know the rules and procedures are better able to influence the legislative process than those who do not. "If you let me write the procedure," Rep. John D. Dingell, D-Mich., once said, "and I let you write the substance, I'll [beat] you every time."[2] Dingell may have exaggerated. No amount of procedural wizardry is ultimately a substitute for having the votes needed to win.

In the House of Representatives, a majority can always find a way to work its will. But in both houses skillful use of the rules can allow a majority to achieve its objectives more quickly, bargain with the other chamber and with the president from strength, and reap maximum political advantage. Ineffective use of the rules, on the other hand, can splinter a potential majority, require unwelcome concessions to opponents, create a potentially damaging record of controversial and divisive votes, and portray a chamber in disarray.

House and Senate rules and procedures differ significantly. Because House actions are intended to mirror the will of a national majority, its procedures are intended to ensure that the majority of the nation's representatives prevail. Because the Senate was designed to check what Thomas Jefferson called the "irregularities and abuses which often attend large and successful legislative majorities," its procedures are intended to ensure that the voice of the individual will be heard. This tradition survived the Senate's radical transformation from a body whose members were originally selected by state legislators to one elected directly by popular vote, starting in 1913. "Senate rules are tilted toward not doing things," Speaker Jim Wright, a Texas Democrat, said in 1987. "House rules if you know how to use them are tilted toward allowing the majority to get its will done."[3]

The sheer size of the House—with 435 members it is more than four times larger than the Senate—requires it to operate in a more orderly, predictable, and controlled fashion than the Senate. Thus the House is more hierarchically organized and has more rules, which it follows more closely. Because debate is restricted and the amending process frequently limited, the House is able to dispose of legislation more quickly than the Senate.

By comparison, the Senate's smaller size allows it to be more personal and informal in its operations. Although the Senate has an elaborate network of rules and procedures, it may ignore or override them to suit the political needs of the moment, often increasing the difficulty of predicting how the Senate may operate at any particular time. However, it most often conducts business (such as deciding what legislation to call up, the length of time for debate, or the number of amendments) by unanimous consent. Each member, even the most junior, is accorded a deference rarely seen in the House, and failure to recognize this could result in paralysis of the chamber's business. The privileges of engaging in unlimited debate—the filibuster—and offering nongermane amendments are cherished traditions in the Senate that are not permitted under House rules. Thus, it is not surprising that the Senate may spend days or weeks considering a measure that the House debates and passes in a single afternoon.

EVOLUTION OF RULES

Congressional rules and procedures are not static but evolve in response to changes within Congress. In the modern era several external developments and internal reforms have led to significant changes in the ways the two chambers conduct their business.

A major change in the 1970s was a new openness in congressional proceedings. For the first time many committees, including Senate-House conference committees, were required to open their meetings to the public; outsiders could sit in as committee members bargained over provisions and language to be included or deleted from bills and resolutions.

Magnified further by the antipolitical atmosphere fostered by the Watergate scandal, which led to the resignation of President Richard Nixon, the emphasis on openness even extended to the traditionally secret meetings of the House Democratic Caucus, the organization of House Democrats. The Caucus, which met in the House chamber, opened the public galleries to visitors and to the press from 1975 to 1980 for certain types of business.

A rules change in the House in 1971 made it possible to record how each individual voted on floor amendments considered in the Committee of the Whole, one of the procedures used to consider legislation. Formerly, the House only recorded the total number voting for or against such an amendment. The rules change meant that members could not vote one way while telling their constituents they voted another. Many of these changes were favored by more liberal members of both parties, who correctly believed that a more open process would weaken long-established power centers in congressional committees, where conservative committee chairmen wielding immense power often frustrated their legislative goals. (See box, Methods of Voting in the House and Senate, p. 496.)

Another major development in the 1960s and 1970s was an increase in the number of amendments offered on the floor of each chamber. Several factors contributed to this development. Constituents and special interest groups pressured individual members to take specific stands on issues of concern to them. Members, with one eye always on reelection, responded in ways to gain them wide recognition with their constituents and in later years with organizations that donated money to their re-election campaigns. Increased opportunities to obtain recorded votes in the House made it much easier to be visibly on the public record. In addition, gradually increasing partisanship in Congress since the 1960s has broken down political norms of earlier eras—exemplified by Speaker Sam Rayburn's admonition to "get along, you have to go along"—which had tended to discourage members who wanted to be considered serious legislators from presenting issues and seeking confrontation solely to score political points.

Within Congress, reductions in the authority exercised by committee chairmen and the rise in importance of subcommittees also contributed to increased amending activity. "Weaker full committee chairmen were less able to mold consensus positions in their committees, making it more likely that disputes among committee members would spill onto the floor," political scientist Steven S. Smith wrote. "Subcommittee chairmen, who assumed more responsibility for managing legislation on the floor, often lacked the experience and political clout" to anticipate and divert floor amendments.[4] Increased coverage of congressional activities by the media, the televising of congressional floor and committee sessions, and members' desire to use this visibility led them to exploit such opportunities through speeches and the amendment process. This combination of diminished committee authority and more assertive members meant that lawmakers in both chambers began to offer more amendments during floor action.

In response leaders in each chamber began to develop ways to limit amendments. In the House that meant writing more restrictive rules to limit amendments that could be offered to some legislation, raising concerns among the minority party that it was being closed out of the debate. In the Senate it meant developing complicated agreements for each major piece of legislation that would reduce the likelihood the Senate would bog down in filibuster and delay, unable to act on important issues in timely fashion.

The number of amendments brought to the House and Senate floors decreased somewhat in the 1980s, partly because of these new strategies and partly because massive federal budget deficits meant that fewer new programs—and therefore fewer amendments to them—were being initiated.

By the mid-1980s the deficit itself—and the special process Congress had devised for dealing with it—had become by far the single most time-consuming issue before Congress. It had also led to the increased use of omnibus bills, the packaging of many, often unrelated, proposals in a single, massive piece of legislation. So-called budget reconciliation measures, for example, revised existing laws touching every aspect of government to bring government programs into conformity with the overall budget plan for the year. In addition, it became common practice to package all or most of the year's appropriations bills in a single piece of legislation. The opportunities to debate and amend these bills were often severely limited.

Rank-and-file House members were particularly affected by this narrowing of their opportunities to influence legislation.

TERMS AND SESSIONS

The two-year period for which members of the House of Representatives are elected constitutes a Congress. Under the Twentieth Amendment to the Constitution, ratified in 1933, this period begins at noon on January 3 of an odd-numbered year, following the election of representatives the previous November, and ends at noon on January 3 of the next odd-numbered year. Congresses are numbered consecutively. The Congress that convened in January 1999 was the 106th in a series that began in 1789.

Prior to 1935, the term of a Congress began on March 4 of the odd-numbered year following the election and coincided with the inauguration of the president (also changed by the Twentieth Amendment to January 20 beginning in 1937), but Congress often did not actually convene until the first Monday in December.

Under the Constitution, Congress is required to "assemble" at least once each year. The Twentieth Amendment provides that these annual meetings shall begin on January 3 unless Congress "shall by law appoint a different day," which it frequently does. For example, before the first session of the 105th Congress adjourned it passed a law, later signed by the president, to reconvene for the second session on January 27, 1998. Each Congress, therefore, has two regular sessions beginning in January of successive years.

The Legislative Reorganization Act of 1970 stipulates that unless Congress provides otherwise the Senate and House "shall adjourn *sine die* not later than July 31 of each year" or, in nonelection years, take at least a thirty-day recess in August. The provision is not applicable if "a state of war exists pursuant to a declaration of war by the Congress." Congress routinely dispenses with this restriction by passing a concurrent resolution. In practice the annual sessions may run the entire year.

Adjournment *sine die* (literally, without a day) ends a session of Congress. Adjournment of the second session is the final action of a Congress and all legislation not passed by both houses expires. However, following adjournment there may still be some delay before legislation that has passed near the end of the session is enrolled and formally presented to the president for action. Members frequently include in the adjournment resolution language to authorize their leaders to call them back into session if circumstances require it. This occurred in 1998 when the House returned to consider impeachment charges against President Bill Clinton.

The president may "on extraordinary occasions" convene one or both houses in special session, or threaten to do so to achieve a political or legislative objective. For example, in 1997 President Clinton threatened to delay the adjournment of the first session of the 105th Congress by calling a special session to consider campaign finance reform legislation. The Senate quickly took up the major legislation but the proposal succumbed to a filibuster.

Within a session either house of Congress may adjourn for holiday observances or other brief periods of three days or less. In a typical week, for example, the Senate or House may meet through Thursday and then, by unanimous consent or by motion, convene on the following Monday. By constitutional directive neither house may adjourn for more than three days without the consent of the other, which they give through passage of a concurrent resolution.

The third session of the 76th Congress was the longest session in history; it lasted 366 days, from January 3, 1940, to January 3, 1941. Four other sessions have lasted 365 days: the first session of the 77th Congress (1941–1942), the second session of the 81st Congress (1950–1951), the first session of the 102nd Congress (1991–1992), and the first session of the 104th Congress (1995–1996).

"What we have now is a technique for returning to a closed system where a few people make all the decisions," said Indiana Democrat Philip R. Sharp.[5]

In the 1980s and 1990s the tough choices posed by the need to reduce the deficit, frustration over the reduced opportunities to enact new programs, the new assertiveness of individual lawmakers, and increased partisanship posed procedural challenges in both chambers. When they were in the minority, House Republicans complained, sometimes bitterly, that the Democratic leadership restricted floor debate and amendments in ways that trampled minority rights. In the minority themselves in both houses starting in 1995 in the 104th Congress, Democrats made the same claims.

Members in both houses complained that it was politically difficult to make tough decisions in open committee meetings, and majority members were reluctant to allow the minority too many opportunities for procedural and political counterattack. An uneasy balance began to evolve between the ideals of process and the realities of politics. Many members of Congress, who were reformers of the 1960s and 1970s criticizing the institutions of Congress, but had risen to power as committee barons in the 1980s and 1990s, were squirming in the limelight under multiple pressures from the public, the press, interest groups, and the opposition party; and these committee chairmen were ready to make some compromises.

A few committees began to close their doors occasionally to the public, although the vast majority of meetings remained open. Conference committees, required by rule to operate in the open unless the full House of Representatives closed them by recorded vote, often finessed the rules by holding one or two open meetings and then having closed subconferences, "caucuses" of conferees and staff negotiations to make the real decisions. These mechanisms proved essential to enact complex legislation such as omnibus budget reconciliation bills potentially involving two dozen committees and hundreds of conferees. In these cases, it was often physically impossible to squeeze all of the conferees into the same room at the same time, and any "meeting" could merely be ceremonial or procedural rather than substantive.

The procedural problems were most acute in the Senate, where individual members could, and often did, bring the chamber to a standstill. Many senators were vocal about their

J. Dennis Hastert accepts the Speaker's gavel in front of the assembled House of Representatives at the start of the 106th Congress in 1999.

dissatisfaction with Senate procedures that let individual members pursue their legislative interests at the expense of the Senate's interests. Washington Republican Daniel J. Evans, a former governor and university president, said frustration with the Senate was a major reason he chose not to seek reelection in 1988. "Somehow we must reach a happy compromise between the tyranny of autocratic chairmen and the chaos of a hundred independent fiefdoms," Evans said.

It is ironic that throughout the 1970s and 1980s, despite the emphasis on deficit reduction, balancing the budget, and the development of new procedures supposedly to enhance the ability to set priorities, little actual progress was made toward these goals. The federal budget deficit and the national debt increased substantially throughout the 1980s. It was almost as if a constant emphasis on reforming the process took the place of the substantive decision making it was meant to enhance. A major budget-reform effort, named Gramm-Rudman-Hollings after its congressional authors, was routinely waived when the political consequences of using it became clearer. Ultimately it had little impact.

Only in the 1990s, when Congress adopted a new budget ethos based on "pay as you go," which required new spending to

be counterbalanced by cuts, did progress toward deficit reduction resume. These accomplishments were made possible by mechanisms and events essentially outside of process—budget "summit" deals negotiated between key executive branch and congressional leaders and then sold to a majority of both chambers as a package, and a booming economy that increased tax revenues.

CHANGE IN LEADERSHIP

It is often easy to forget that for all its powers, rules, and traditions, Congress is dominated by forces beyond its control, such as the shifting will of the electorate. Just when consistent trends and historical patterns observed over several decades in Congress seem ripe for analysis and placement in historical perspective, the political environment can change rapidly.

The evolution of congressional procedures and practices over the thirty years from the end of the 1960s reflected the emergence of a younger, more liberal Democratic congressional membership, especially in the House, who began as insurgents in the 1950s and 1960s, assumed control of both chambers in the 1970s, and became the power brokers and senior committee members of the 1980s and early 1990s. There was a period of brief conservative resurgence in the House following the presidential landslide of Ronald Reagan in the 1980s, which was complemented by Republican control of the Senate from 1981 to 1987. By the early 1990s, with the Democrats back in control of both houses of Congress, however, these GOP inroads on Democratic power seemed transitory and did not leave any fundamental changes in either body.

The Democratic dominance ended abruptly in 1995, as a new Republican majority containing large numbers of young, militant conservatives joined frustrated and angry senior GOP members who had long felt victimized and impotent in their legislative careers. Suddenly Republicans found themselves the guardians of congressional practices that many either knew little about or had railed against for years. Although it remained to be seen whether the Republican Party would adapt the institutions of Congress to its own ends, or break the mold and create a fundamentally different House and Senate, one thing was certain: the rules and procedures that had guided Congress for more than 200 years would continue to evolve.

PITFALLS TO PASSAGE

As President Kennedy said, it is easier to defeat legislation than to pass it. And the route a bill must travel before it wins final approval allows many opportunities for its opponents to defeat or delay it. "Legislation is like a chess game more than anything else," Representative Dingell has said. "It is a seemingly endless series of moves, until ultimately somebody prevails through exhaustion, or brilliance, or because of overwhelming public sentiment for their side."[6]

The first place that a bill might run into trouble is in subcommittee or committee, where the measure is likely to receive its closest scrutiny and most significant modification. That occurs in part because committee members and staff have developed expertise in the subject areas within their areas of jurisdiction and in part because committee consideration gives opponents their first formal opportunity to state how the bill needs to be changed to be acceptable to them, if it can be.

The second place a bill may be delayed is in scheduling for floor action. When, and sometimes whether, a bill is brought to the floor of either the House or Senate depends on many factors, including what other legislation is awaiting action, how controversial the measure is, and whether the leadership judges its chances for passage to be improved by immediate action.

The leadership, for example, might decide to delay taking up a controversial bill until its proponents can gather sufficient support to guarantee its passage. In the Senate, bills often cannot be scheduled much in advance until all of the interested senators have given clearance and "holds" by individual senators or groups of senators have been removed. (A "hold" is a request by a senator to delay action on a matter. The intent may be to delay indefinitely or postpone action until some concern is addressed. A hold carries an implicit threat that a filibuster would begin if the hold is not honored.) Even then, absent a unanimous consent agreement, filibusters are possible unless a supermajority of sixty senators intervenes to move the process forward. However, even if a bill itself is delayed or blocked, that still does not prevent controversial issues from reaching the floor unexpectedly because they can be offered as nongermane amendments to other legislation at almost any time.

The next hurdle a bill must cross is amendment and passage on the chamber floor. The amending process is at the heart of floor debate in both chambers. Amendments have many objectives. Members may offer amendments to dramatize their stands on issues, even if there is little chance their proposals will be adopted. Some amendments are introduced at the request of the executive branch, a member's constituents, or special interests. Some become tactical tools for gauging sentiment for or against a bill. Others are used to stall action on a bill. In the Senate, the majority leader, who has the choice of always being the first to be recognized, may offer amendments to prevent other amendments from being offered, which is called "filling the amendment tree." In the House, where debate is more strictly limited, a member may offer a pro forma amendment, later withdrawn, solely to gain a few additional minutes to speak on an issue.

Still other amendments may be designed to defeat the legislation. One common strategy is to try to load a bill with so many unattractive amendments that it will eventually collapse under its own weight. Another strategy is to offer a "killer" amendment, one that if adopted, would cause members who initially supported the bill to vote against it on final passage. Conversely, amendments known as "sweeteners" may be offered to attract broader support for the underlying measure. And finally, in the House, a motion to recommit the bill back to committee, either to kill it outright or send it back to the floor "forthwith" with additional amendments, gives opponents a

final chance to persuade their colleagues to back away from the proposal or change it significantly.

Legislation that fails to win passage at any of these points in either the House or Senate is likely to be abandoned for the remainder of that Congress. Those bills that survive passage by both houses must still be reconciled through processes that hold a host of additional dangers and delays. The House and Senate may trade the bills back and forth like ping pong balls, adding, subtracting, and modifying provisions; or the legislation may face the conference committee, a temporary panel of House and Senate members established solely to work out the differences between the two chambers on a particular bill. Sometimes known as the third house of Congress, conference committees bargain and compromise until they reach a version of the legislation acceptable to a majority of the conferees of each chamber; sometimes the legislation is substantially rewritten in conference. Occasionally conferees cannot strike a compromise, and the legislation dies.

For a small number of measures the final hurdle is approval by the president. All modern presidents have used the veto threat to persuade Congress to pay attention to the executive viewpoint as it considers specific measures. Because presidents most of the time can muster the necessary support to defeat override attempts in Congress, lawmakers usually try to compromise with the president. Sometimes, however, such efforts fail, and the bill is vetoed.

All of these steps, repeated in endless variation for dozens of major bills, must be completed within the two-year cycle of a single Congress. Any bill that has not received final approval when a Congress adjourns automatically dies and must be reintroduced in the next Congress to begin the entire procedure over again. When a Congress is drawing to a close, the pressure to act can be intense. Lawmakers, who have put off making difficult choices, often find themselves rushing to keep their bills from dying. In a sentiment as apt in the 1990s as it was in the 1820s, Davy Crockett, a legendary frontiersman who served four House terms, once said: "We generally lounge or squabble the greater part of the session, and crowd into a few days of the last term three or four times the business done during as many preceding months."[7]

Controversial and far-reaching proposals are seldom enacted in a single Congress. More often they are introduced and reintroduced, incubating in a legislative cauldron as national sentiment on the issue coalesces and the necessary compromises are struck. The comprehensive revision of the Clean Air Act finally approved in 1990 had been stalled in Congress since 1977—over such controversial issues as acid rain—before the right combination of supporters and political circumstances emerged simultaneously to free it finally. Congress enacted welfare reform in 1996, ending a sixty-one-year federal guarantee and representing the first time a major entitlement program for individuals was transformed into a block grant to states. Republicans had advocated radical changes in welfare for decades, and they revived these ideas as part of the "Contract with America," a

HOUSE AND SENATE RULES

Article I, Section 5, of the Constitution stipulates that "Each House may determine the Rules of its Proceedings." In addition to the standing rules adopted under this authority, the House and Senate each have a separate set of precedents, practices, and customs that guide their conduct of business.

The standing rules of the House are set forth in the *Constitution, Jefferson's Manual, and Rules of the House of Representatives,* or the House Manual as it is commonly called, which is published with revisions during the first session of each Congress. The content is also available on Congress's web site *(See "Congressional Information on the Internet," p. 1146, in Reference Materials, Vol. II.)*

This is the most important single source of authority on the rules and contains voluminous annotations. In addition to the written chamber rules, the document contains the text of the Constitution, portions of the manual on parliamentary procedure that Thomas Jefferson wrote when he was vice president, and the principal rulings and precedents of the House. The formal rules of the Senate are found in the *Senate Manual Containing the Standing Rules, Orders, Laws, and Resolutions Affecting the Business of the United States Senate.*

In the House, on the day when a new Congress convenes, the chamber has no formal rules and thus, no committees, which are created in the rules. It operates under what is called "general parliamentary law," which relies on *Jefferson's Manual* and many House precedents. Prior to opening day, the rules have been drafted by the majority party's conference or caucus; amendments suggested by individual majority members are considered at such party meetings.

Following the election of the Speaker and the administration of the oath of office to members, the proposed rules of the House are offered directly from the floor as a resolution, usually by the majority leader. After one hour of debate, the minority has an opportunity to offer a substitute. After it is defeated, the majority's rules package is then formally adopted, usually on a party-line vote, and becomes effective immediately. Once adopted, House rules continue in force through the Congress, unless further amended, and expire at its end.

Amendments to the rules package on the House floor are not permitted unless opponents can "defeat the previous question," the motion offered by the majority party that has the effect of cutting off debate and forcing a vote on final passage. This has not occurred since 1971, when a conservative coalition of Republicans and southern Democrats defeated the previous question and forced the Democratic leadership to drop a provision for a "twenty-one-day rule," a procedure that would have allowed legislation to reach the floor without action by the Rules Committee.

When Republicans took over the House in 1995 after forty years in the minority, they deviated from the traditional practice by splitting their rules proposal into numerous pieces to highlight what they considered major reforms in the rules. All passed, some by votes largely along party lines, others with substantial bipartisan support. However, in the 105th Congress that began in 1997, Republicans returned to a single rules package. In the 106th Congress, for the first time since 1880, the House recodified its rules, reducing them in number, reorganizing provisions without making substantive changes, and eliminating archaic language.

The Senate, on the other hand, does not readopt its rules at the beginning of a Congress. Since only one-third of the chamber turns over every two years, the Senate considers itself a continuing body. Any proposed changes in existing rules are adopted subject to provisions already in the rules, such as Rule XXII, the cloture rule requiring a supermajority to cut off debate. This interpretation of the Senate's continuing nature was challenged by liberals for years as conflicting with Article I, Section 5 of the Constitution, but their contention that the Senate could cut off debate on proposed rules changes by majority vote at the beginning of a Congress was unsuccessful.

In the controversy leading to the most recent important change

grouping of legislative and philosophical proposals the GOP used in the 1994 elections in its campaign to win control of the House. *(See box, "Contract with America," p. 441.)*

Bill Clinton in his 1992 campaign for the presidency had promised to "end welfare as we know it." But it was only after initial presidential vetoes of Republican bills in 1995 and 1996, the intervention of the nation's governors who were greatly burdened by welfare costs, GOP fears of political reprisals from a partial shutdown of the federal government in late 1995 after a deadlock with Clinton, and Clinton's desire in his 1996 reelection bid to claim a major promise kept that the necessary compromises were reached to ensure enactment.

The legislative process and its various stages seem straightforward enough. Those interested in either passing or defeating legislation will ultimately win, lose, or accept some compromise. However, as noted earlier, sometimes long-standing patterns of congressional behavior, the seemingly fixed interrelationships with other branches of government, and the com-

fortable access to the legislative process enjoyed by a mix of influential special interest groups can shift abruptly with the public mood.

An extraordinary modern example of the effects of a sudden radical change in the traditional approach to legislating occurred during the first few months of the 104th Congress in 1995, after the Republican Party had assumed control of both houses for the first time in four decades. The House Republican majority, apparently sensing a popular mandate after its landslide 1994 victory and gain of fifty-two seats, briefly appeared to be ushering in a new era of "congressional government." The House Speaker seemed to be the nation's "legislator-in-chief." The Senate was relegated to playing second fiddle. The president was widely seen as almost irrelevant. The House worked feverishly to rush the legislative components of its "Contract with America" proposals to the floor, sometimes without even holding hearings or allowing amendments. The House seemed to be all action but little deliberation. While most of these bills

in the cloture rule, the Senate did cast a series of votes in 1975 that appeared to support the right of a simple majority to avoid a filibuster and change Senate rules. But agreement was subsequently reached to change Rule XXII by invoking cloture first by a two-thirds vote. Before doing so the Senate cast procedural votes which, it was argued, reversed this "majority" precedent.

House precedents, based on past rulings of the chair, are contained in three multivolume series: *Hinds' Precedents of the House of Representatives* covers the years 1789 through 1907; *Cannon's Precedents of the House of Representatives* covers from 1908 through 1935; and *Deschler's Precedents of the United States House of Representatives*, volumes one to nine, and *Deschler-Brown Precedents of the United States House of Representatives*, volumes ten to fifteen, cover 1936 through 1999. In addition, *Procedure in the U.S. House of Representatives* is a summary of all important rulings of the chair through 1984. *House Practice: A Guide to the Rules, Precedents and Procedures of the House*, published in 1996, is a single volume by retired House Parliamentarian William Holmes Brown that discusses selected precedents and the operation of current House rules in a less intimidating format and includes material on rules changes following the shift in party control in the 104th Congress.

Riddick's Senate Procedure: Precedents and Practices, by retired parliamentarian Floyd M. Riddick and Alan S. Frumin, who was parliamentarian when the book was last revised in 1992, contains current precedents and related standing rules and statutory provisions through the end of the 101st Congress.

In addition to precedents, each chamber has particular traditions and customs that it follows—recognition of the Senate majority leader ahead of other senators seeking recognition from the chair is an example of such a practice. Moreover, each party in each chamber has its own set of party rules that can affect the chamber's proceedings (Rules of the Republican Conference of the United States House of Representatives, 106th Congress; Rules of the House Democratic Caucus, 106th Congress; History, Rules and Precedents of the Senate Republican Conference).

Many public laws also contain provisions that affect House and Senate procedures. Prominent examples are the Congressional Budget and Impoundment Control Act of 1974; the Balanced Budget and Emergency Deficit Control Act of 1985, better known as Gramm-Rudman-Hollings, after its sponsors; and so-called "fast track" legislation, enacted in previous Congresses but blocked from a House vote on renewal in 1997, which would have forced each chamber to vote on the president's proposed international trade agreements without amendments. Other examples would be numerous statutory provisions, rendered moot by the Supreme Court's 1983 *Chadha* decision, which provided for various schemes of approval or disapproval of actions by the executive branch or independent agencies by either one or both houses.

Such rulemaking statutes obviate the need for each chamber to create special procedures on an ad hoc basis whenever it takes some action on the subject matter dealt with in these laws. Without "fast track," for example, it would be extremely difficult for the president to negotiate credibly with foreign nations without the advance assurance that each chamber would not amend the agreements in potentially unpredictable ways, ultimately rendering them unacceptable to these nations. The existence of procedures set out by law is particularly significant in the Senate, where they serve to limit debate and prevent filibusters. However, such statutes, even though they are laws passed by both chambers and signed by the president, still remain subservient to each chamber's constitutional power to amend its rules at any time. (For example, the House could always adopt a special rule allowing amendments to a "fast track" trade agreement; in the Senate, which h as no equivalent of the House's Rules Committee, any alterations in process would be far more difficult.)

passed, action was delayed on routine but essential legislation in the congressional process, such as the appropriations bills needed to fund government activities and services.

The controversies associated with the ambitious new agenda led to gridlock between the GOP-led Congress and a Democratic president, vetoes of tax and appropriations bills, two shutdowns of some government departments and agencies from December 1995 to January 1996, a near collapse of Republican control of the chamber in the 1996 election, and the easy reelection of the once seemingly crippled President Clinton.

In the 105th Congress that followed in 1997, although many controversial bills were still considered, the multiple, time-consuming steps of the normal legislative process reasserted themselves without the weight of an overarching political agenda or the new theories of governance that had nearly consumed its predecessor. In other words, the more things seemed to have changed, the more they remained the same. Congress still waited for presidential proposals. Committees still mattered. Committee chairmen could still exercise power. The minority could still offer proposals and slow down the process. Members of both parties appeared relieved to fall back on a more predictable, less confrontational way of doing business because the potential rewards of radical change that had proved so tempting two years earlier had led to excessive political risk. In the 106th Congress in 1999, with new Speaker J. Dennis Hastert of Illinois in control, the tight legislative controls were loosened, returning the House to more normal operations it had experienced in the past.

Developing Legislation

Procedures for introducing legislation and seeing it through committee are similar in the House and Senate.

Legislative proposals originate in different ways. Members of Congress, of course, develop ideas for legislation. Assistance in drafting legislative language is available from each chamber's

Office of Legislative Counsel. Special interest groups—business, labor, farm, civil rights, consumer, trade associations, and the like—are another fertile source of legislation. Many of these organizations and their lobbyists in Washington provide detailed technical knowledge in specialized fields and employ experts in the art of drafting bills and amendments. Constituents, either as individuals or groups, also may suggest legislation. A member of Congress may introduce a bill for the administration or a private organization, such as a trade association, and the bill will have "by request" printed on it.

Much of the legislation considered by Congress originates in the executive branch (although key members of Congress may participate in the formulation of administration programs). This is especially true if Congress and the president are of the same political party. However, the periodic emergence of an entirely separate congressional agenda, such as the GOP's 1994 contract, illustrates the ability of Congress to confront the president aggressively and push ahead independently on a vast range of issues. Although Congress may not be dependent on the executive if it wants to pass legislation, the presidential veto usually remains the ultimate arbiter of whatever is enacted into law.

Each year after the president outlines his legislative program, executive departments and agencies transmit to the House and Senate drafts of proposed legislation to carry out the president's program or ideas. These may be introduced by the chairman of the committee or subcommittee having jurisdiction over the subject involved, or by the ranking minority member if the chairman is not of the president's party. The congressional leadership, especially if it is from the opposition party, may designate a group of bills as key legislative initiatives and give them low bill numbers (such as HR 1 or HR 2) to emphasize their importance.

Committees may also consider proposals that have not been formally introduced. The committee may work from its own preliminary text, called the "chairman's mark," and an actual bill is introduced at a later stage. When legislation is heavily amended in committee, all the changes, deletions, and additions, together with whatever is left of the original bill, may be organized into a new bill. Such measures, referred to as "clean bills," are reintroduced, usually by the chairman of the committee, given a new bill number, and formally reported out of committee.

Some committees, such as House Appropriations, usually skip this stage because they have the special power in House rules to originate legislation directly—that is, to draft bills themselves and report the final text to the floor. Only then will the bill be given a bill number.

In an ideal world, cooperation between the two branches throughout the legislative process will smooth out the rough edges in legislation and help ensure that no one is surprised either in committee or on the floor. This assumes, of course, that there is a desire for cooperation. It may appear to be to the political advantage of one branch or the other, or both, to engage in a confrontation; enactment of legislation may not be the primary goal in such circumstances, or even be desired. Someone wants to create an issue, so they pick a fight. Fights involve risks,

so one side must perceive some political reward for taking them. The president often gains the advantage in such situations because of the White House's ability to present a case more clearly and consistently to the public, while Congress has many potential spokespeople of lesser stature who may not all be of the same opinion or able to command attention.

For example, President Harry S. Truman in the midst of his 1948 reelection campaign summoned the GOP-controlled 80th Congress—which he had labeled "do nothing"—back to Washington for a special summer session that produced no legislation of substance. The president then used this inaction—in a situation he created exactly for the purpose—to bolster his campaign themes and aid his uphill reelection fight.

More recently, congressional Republicans disregarded the Clinton administration in pressing their "Contract with America" in 1995. When the president vetoed the omnibus budget reconciliation bill containing the GOP's major tax cut proposals and other key priorities, as well as a number of appropriations bills, both the GOP-controlled Senate and House adopted a strategy of shutting down government departments over the Christmas and New Year's holidays at the end of the first session of the 104th Congress, to try to force him to yield and to better position themselves to retain control of Congress and regain the presidency in 1996. House Speaker Newt Gingrich became the principal spokesperson for this strategy in the public mind, but he was eventually undercut by Senate Majority Leader Bob Dole, a presidential candidate himself, who followed the more traditional precepts of congressional behavior that legislation, especially appropriations bills, were "must pass" matters.

The shutdown strategy was a major political miscalculation and disaster for the Republicans. Congress was blamed for shutting off important government services. The president won the ensuing public relations battle, and Congress had to back down and pass the requisite funding. Gingrich's popularity, as registered in numerous polls, plummeted and his political control of the House weakened. These were examples of pure political calculation, one of which worked while the other failed.

At other times, new issues suddenly emerge unexpectedly, or long-standing controversies finally become highly visible through the media that raises them above the normal din of the legislative process.

INTRODUCTION OF LEGISLATION

No matter where a legislative proposal originates, it can be introduced only by a member of Congress. In the House, a member may introduce any of several types of bills and resolutions by handing them to the clerk of the House or by placing them in a mahogany box near the clerk's desk called the hopper. The member need not seek recognition for the purpose. The resident commissioner of Puerto Rico and the delegates of the District of Columbia, Guam, American Samoa, and the Virgin Islands, none of whom may vote on the floor, also have this right. Senators introduce legislation from the floor during the "morning hour" or other period of the day set aside for doing so, but increasingly they have gone to the House practice of leaving them at the desk. In some cases, such as the example of the House appropriations committee originating legislation, a bill is introduced by the chairman and given a bill number only after committee action has been completed and the bill is ready for floor debate; in this instance, a committee report would also be filed simultaneously.

There is no limit to the number of bills and resolutions members may introduce, nor any restrictions on the time during a Congress when they may do so. It is rare to find a day when Congress is in session when someone does not introduce something. House and Senate bills may have joint sponsorship and carry several members' names. (Before 1967 House rules barred representatives from cosponsoring legislation. Members favoring a particular measure had to introduce identical bills if they wished to be closely identified with the original proposal.) The Constitution stipulates that "all bills for raising revenue shall originate in the House of Representatives," and the House has successfully insisted that it reserves the power to originate appropriation bills as well. All other bills may originate in either chamber.

Major legislation often is introduced in both houses in the form of companion (identical) bills, primarily to speed up the legislative process by encouraging both chambers to consider the measure simultaneously. Sponsors of companion bills also may hope to dramatize the importance or urgency of the issue and show broad support for the legislation. At the beginning of a Congress, members vie to be the sponsors of the first bills introduced and to retain the same bill number in consecutive Congresses on legislation that has not been enacted. The House and Senate majority leadership typically reserve low bill numbers for measures that are key elements of their legislative program. In 1987, for example, House Speaker Wright made sure that his top-priority bills for the session were numbers HR 1 and HR 2. In 1995, Speaker Gingrich gave many "Contract with America" items the first bill numbers assigned, including designating as HR 1 the Congressional Accountability Act, which applied workplace laws in the private sector to Congress (this was S 2 in the Senate), and as H J Res 1 a proposed constitutional amendment to require a balanced federal budget.

Thousands of bills are introduced in every Congress, but most never receive any consideration, nor is consideration expected. Every lawmaker introduces measures for a variety of reasons—to stake out a stand on an issue, as a favor to a constituent or a special interest group, to get publicity, or to ward off political attack. As congressional expert Walter J. Oleszek writes, once such a bill has been introduced, the legislator can claim that he or she has taken action "and can blame the committee to which the bill has been referred for its failure to win enactment."[8]

However, in the House, a number of factors have operated to reduce the number of bills introduced substantially during the 1980s and 1990s. The most significant was a rules change in 1979 that allowed an unlimited number of members to cosponsor any legislation introduced, obviating the need for members to introduce duplicate bills in order to get their names onto them. The effect was immediate, reducing the number of bills introduced from 14,414 in the 95th Congress to 8,456 in the 96th. Since then, the number continued to decline, averaging fewer than 6,000 over the next five congresses.

The modern Congress considers and enacts fewer measures than its predecessors. But it is impossible to measure congressional workload by the number of measures passed. After enactment of the Congressional Budget and Impoundment Control Act of 1974, Congress tended to package many, often unrelated, proposals in lengthy pieces of legislation known as omnibus bills. Each year the House and Senate are required to adopt a budget resolution setting an overall plan for government spending and revenues. They often follow up with another omnibus measure—called a budget reconciliation bill—revising government programs to conform to the overall plan, but this type of legislation is not needed every year.

With the advent of massive budget deficits in the early 1980s Congress repeatedly used the practice of providing funding for most or all government departments and agencies in a single omnibus appropriations bill, known as a continuing resolution. Although Congress used continuing resolutions previously their prominence expanded as legislative delays resulted from ever-increasing complexities of the budget process, rivalries among authorizing committees, disputes between authorizing and appropriations committees, House-Senate conflicts, and the traditional use of thirteen different appropriations bills. The presence of controversy over a particular year's budget does not necessarily mean that a continuing resolution will be required or that final appropriations will not be in place when a new fiscal year begins on October 1. Congress managed to pass all thirteen appropriations bills separately and before the beginning of the new fiscal year as recently as 1994. In 1996, after passing seven appropriations bills but facing delays in six others, Congress placed the remaining ones in an omnibus appropriations bill that was completed on September 30. This was one of the few times since modern federal budgeting began in 1974 that Congress finished all of its spending bills at the start of the new fiscal year.

During the 1980s, the number of commemorative bills—those designating commemorative days, weeks, or months, for example—increased. Commemoratives were introduced as joint resolutions, which required a presidential signature to become law and carried the possibility of a signing ceremony and media coverage. However, their sheer volume was often misrepresented by critics and by the media to ridicule the work product of a Congress whose principal achievements might actually be contained in a massive omnibus budget reconciliation bill and a continuing resolution.

When the Republicans took control of the House in 1995, they prohibited by rule the introduction of commemorative legislation or its consideration in that chamber, which also had the effect of shutting off similar Senate action. The impact of the new rule can easily be seen in the drop in the number of joint

WHEN A SUPERMAJORITY VOTE IS REQUIRED BY CONGRESS

The Constitution created two houses of Congress, each of which could act, with a quorum present, by simple majority vote except with respect to certain extraordinary matters that required support from a supermajority. *Jefferson's Manual* states: "The voice of the majority decides . . . where not otherwise expressly provided." These principles have also applied to actions taken in congressional committees, unless otherwise provided by rule or statute.

The Constitution requires a two-thirds majority vote of *both* the House and Senate to:

• Override a presidential veto
• Pass a constitutional amendment
• Remove political disabilities (14th Amendment)
• Overrule a disabled president's declaration that he is capable of resuming duties (25th Amendment)

The Constitution requires a two-thirds majority in the Senate to:

• Convict in an impeachment trial
• Ratify a treaty

The Constitution requires a two-thirds majority of either the House or the Senate to expel a member.

The House and Senate also have adopted supermajority requirements for various procedural actions. In the House, a two-thirds majority is required to:

• Suspend the rules and pass a measure
• Consider a report from the Rules Committee relating to a rule or special order of business on the same legislative day it is reported to the House
• Dispense with Calendar Wednesday
• Dispense with the call of the Private Calendar

The House in the 104th Congress (1995–1997) adopted rules that also require a three-fifths vote to pass a measure called up from the Corrections Calendar and to pass a federal income tax rate increase.

In the Senate, a two-thirds vote is required to suspend a rule of the Senate (a rarely used procedure) and to invoke cloture and end debate under Rule XXII on any measure to change the rules of the Senate. (Senate rules themselves may be amended by a simple majority.)

The Senate rules otherwise require sixty votes ("three fifths of the senators duly chosen and sworn," assuming no vacancies in the Senate) to invoke cloture under Rule XXII on debate on all other debatable matters including bills, nominations, and motions.

A supermajority of sixty members is also required in the Senate to override various points of order under the Budget Act and to appeal rulings of the presiding officer related to those provisions.

---

resolutions introduced in the House, from 429 in the 103rd Congress to 140 in the 105th, and in the Senate from 232 in the 103rd to 60 in the 105th. The total of public laws enacted declined from 465 in the 103rd Congress to 394 in the 105th, a drop of more than 15 percent.

Bills not enacted die with the Congress in which they were introduced and must be reintroduced in a new Congress if they are to be eligible for further consideration. Resolutions adopted by the House affecting its operations during a Congress also expire automatically; however, similar Senate resolutions may remain in effect, as the Senate considers itself a "continuing body." (The Senate reads George Washington's Farewell Address each year pursuant to a resolution adopted on January 24, 1901.) Nominations pending in the Senate expire at the end of each session of Congress but are usually carried over into the next session of the same Congress by unanimous consent. Treaties pending in the Senate, once submitted by the president, remain pending from one Congress to another; nominations, however, lapse under those conditions and must be resubmitted in the next Congress.

Major legislation goes through changes in nomenclature as it works its way through the legislative process. When a measure is introduced and first printed, it is officially referred to and labeled as a bill. When it has been passed by one house and sent to the other body it is reprinted and officially labeled an act. When cleared by Congress and signed by the president, it becomes a law (and also may still be referred to as an act).

Types of Legislation

The types of measures that Congress may consider and act on (in addition to treaties and nominations submitted by the president to the Senate) include bills and three kinds of resolutions (joint, concurrent, and simple). The first to be introduced is designated as number 1 of its type, and numbers increase with the chronological introduction of additional measures.

Bills are prefixed with HR when introduced in the House and with S when introduced in the Senate, followed by a number assigned to the measure. The vast majority of legislative proposals dealing with either domestic or foreign issues and programs affecting the United States government or the population generally are drafted in the form of bills. These include both authorizations, which provide the legal authority and spending limits for federal programs and agencies, and appropriations, which actually provide the money for those programs and agencies. When passed by both chambers in identical form and signed by the president (or repassed by Congress over a presidential veto), they become laws. The president also may allow a bill to become law without his signature.

Joint resolutions are designated H J Res or S J Res. A joint resolution, like a bill, requires the approval of both houses and (usually) the signature of the president; it has the force of law if approved. There is no real difference between a bill and a joint resolution. The latter generally is used when dealing with a single item or issue, such as a continuing or emergency appropriations bill.

Joint resolutions also are used for proposing amendments to the Constitution. Such resolutions must be approved by two-thirds of both houses. They do not require the president's signature but become a part of the Constitution when ratified by three-fourths of the states.

Concurrent resolutions are designated as H Con Res or S Con Res. Used for matters affecting the operations of both houses, concurrent resolutions must be passed in the same form by both houses, but they are not presented to the president for his signature, and they do not have the force of law. Concurrent resolutions are used to fix the time of adjournment of a Congress or to express the "sense of Congress" on an issue. Some concurrent resolutions, such as the annual congressional budget resolutions setting Congress's revenue and spending goals for the upcoming fiscal year, set rules or other procedures for one or both houses and, as such, can have a substantial impact on all other legislation that Congress considers.

Resolutions, also referred to as simple resolutions, are designated as H Res or S Res. A simple resolution deals with matters entirely within the prerogative of one house of Congress, such as setting the spending levels for its committees, revising the chamber's standing rules, or expressing the opinion of that house on a current issue, and is acted on only by that chamber. A simple resolution is not considered by the other chamber and does not require action by the president. Like a concurrent resolution, it does not have the force of law. However, adoption of resolutions can have effects outside the chamber. For example, the Senate adopts resolutions of ratification for treaties; at the end of the 100th Congress (1987–1989) adoption of a Senate resolution had the effect of carrying over into the next Congress impeachment proceedings against a federal judge. In the House, simple resolutions embody the special orders of business, or "rules," reported by the Rules Committee that set guidelines for floor consideration of legislation.

Bill Referral

Once a measure has been introduced and given a number, it is almost always referred to committee. (Very rarely a member might ask unanimous consent that a bill be taken up for consideration on the House or Senate floor immediately. Such bills are usually either noncontroversial or of great urgency.) The Speaker of the House and the presiding officer in the Senate are responsible for referring bills introduced in their respective chambers to the appropriate committees, but the job is usually left to the House and Senate parliamentarians, respectively.

House and Senate rules require that all bills be read three times before passage, in accordance with traditional parliamentary usage. In the House the first reading occurs when the bill is introduced and printed by number and title in the *Congressional Record*. The second reading occurs when floor consideration begins; often the bill is read section by section for amendment. The third reading comes just before the vote on final passage. Senate rules require bills and resolutions to be read twice, on different legislative days, before they are referred to committee.

The third reading follows floor debate and voting on amendments.

The jurisdictions of the standing committees are spelled out in House Rule X and Senate Rule XXV, and referrals are generally routine—tax bills go to House Ways and Means and Senate Finance, banking bills to the banking committees in both chambers, and so on. However, bills can cover a multitude of subjects that need not have any relationship to each other, which can lead to complications in the referral process.

Many issues that come before Congress cut across the jurisdictions of several committees. Three House committees—International Relations, Commerce, and Ways and Means—might all lay claim to jurisdiction over a trade measure, for example, and the Speaker might refer it to all of them for consideration.

The authors of a bill often try to manipulate or anticipate the referral process to ensure it goes to a sympathetic committee or avoids a hostile one, a consideration that often figures into the manner in which legislation is drafted initially. The mechanics of this strategy have changed over the years, especially in the House, where the rules on committee referral have been modified on several occasions. Prior to 1975, measures introduced in the House could only be referred to a single committee, no matter how many subjects they might encompass. Any bill containing a tax provision, for instance, was always referred to the Ways and Means Committee.

During the reform period of the mid-1970s, in an attempt to prevent some committees from monopolizing legislation, to provide additional opportunities for a larger number of members to participate in the legislative process, and to strengthen the role of the Speaker, House rules were changed to allow the Speaker to refer legislation to more than one committee and to impose time limits on referrals. The Speaker was given several options. The Speaker could refer a bill to several committees at once, which was called a "concurrent" or "joint" referral; refer a bill first to one committee and then later to others, called a "sequential referral"; and send portions of bills to different committees, called a "split referral." As a result, some bills could be referred to numerous committees simultaneously, making it difficult to plot a path for them to the floor. Open warfare often developed among committees that sought opportunities to expand their power by claiming jurisdiction, with the Speaker placed in the middle. The Energy and Commerce Committee under the Democrats, with a mammoth portfolio and chaired by the aggressive John D. Dingell, D-Mich., from 1981 to 1995, was especially noted for its expansive, repeated, and contentious jurisdictional claims.

If necessary, legislation could be rereferred from one committee to another by unanimous consent to correct any errors that arose.

In referring bills, the House Speaker may set deadlines for committee action. At the beginning of the 1983 session Speaker Thomas P. "Tip" O'Neill Jr., D-Mass., announced that in some multiple referrals he would designate one committee the primary committee and might "impose time limits on committees having a secondary interest following the report of the primary committee." The use of multiple referral gave House leaders greater opportunities to bargain with and bring together key legislative players and opened the process to a broader range of views. But multiple referral also created potential additional obstacles for a bill to surmount before it reached the floor. While the referral reforms of the 1970s in the House democratized the process and prevented one committee from monopolizing a particular subject matter, there were distinct negative tradeoffs in terms of increased complexity, confusion, and lack of ultimate accountability for legislation. The House-Senate conference process also was affected, as conferences grew in size to accommodate all the new participants.

Sometimes the subject matter of a bill, or the political situation surrounding it, proved to be so complex that the normal rules could not work. House rules were amended to provide that, in addition to referring bills to more than one committee, the Speaker, with the approval of the House, may set up an ad hoc committee to consider a bill. Speaker O'Neill did that in 1977 when he created a temporary committee to consider President Jimmy Carter's energy package.

When the Republicans took over the House in 1995, they had little stake in the existing system or in the various formal and informal jurisdictional accommodations that had been reached over the years to satisfy key Democrats. They reacted to complaints that the referral process was too confusing by changing the rules again and further enhancing the role of the leadership. The earlier version of the "joint" referral was abolished. Instead the Speaker was required to designate a primary committee to manage the major workload related to a bill; other committees would participate through an "additional initial referral" or through later sequential referrals at the Speaker's discretion, and under possible time limitations.

The Senate usually refers bills to more than one committee by unanimous consent. Bills may be referred to two or more committees concurrently or sequentially, or a bill may be split so that part of it is referred to one committee, part to another. Also, the majority and minority leaders or their designees, acting jointly, may offer a motion providing for a joint or sequential referral. In the Senate multiple referrals may contain a deadline for action by one or more of the committees.

Often, different committees of the House and Senate can claim jurisdiction of the same subject matter, because the committee systems of the two bodies do not coincide. The result can be a dramatically different reception for a measure, depending on the composition of the panel. A classic example of this strategy was the 1963 civil rights bill. The House version was referred to the Judiciary Committee, whose chairman supported the measure. The chairman of the Senate Judiciary Committee, however, opposed it; thus the Senate version was drafted in such a way that it would be referred to the more sympathetic Senate Commerce Committee. (The measure guaranteed minorities access to public accommodations, which fell within the commerce clause of the Constitution.)

IN COMMITTEE

Although the House and Senate handle bills in different ways when they reach the floor, the committee system in both chambers is similar. The standing committees of Congress determine the fate of most proposals. A bill comes under the sharpest scrutiny at the committee stage, in part because committee members and staff frequently are experts in the subjects under their jurisdiction. If a measure is going to be substantially revised that revision usually occurs at the committee or subcommittee level rather than during floor consideration. Committees usually use hearings as the first step of their process, to receive testimony and information. But if legislation moves forward, further revision occurs at meetings where a bill is "marked up" when amendments are offered, debated, and voted on.

Legislation may be disposed of by a committee in several ways:

• It may be ignored if the chairman never puts it on the agenda at a committee meeting, which is by far the most frequent disposition of most legislation.

• It may be approved, or "reported favorably" with or without amendments, which is the normal result for most legislation that is allowed to reach the stage of a committee markup.

• It may be reported "negatively" or "without recommendation," which might still allow full House or Senate consideration. For example, in a highly unusual action the House Rules Committee in 1996 reported a rule providing procedures for consideration of a controversial campaign reform bill "without recommendation," an indication of distaste for the House GOP leadership's decision to schedule floor action on this controversial proposal. (Thirty years earlier, when the committee was still an autonomous power center rather than an arm of the House leadership that it later became, the panel would probably have simply refused to grant a rule.)

• It might be taken up and killed outright through a tabling motion, a rare event but one that occurred in 1997 in the House Judiciary Committee, which used this means to give sponsors of legislation abolishing affirmative action programs a vote while demonstrating that the proposal was not yet ripe for action.

Subcommittee Action

The full committee may decide to consider a bill in the first instance but more often the committee chairman assigns it to a subcommittee for study and hearings. The rules of many committees in the House were amended starting in the 1970s to require the referral of bills to subcommittees, and the House Democratic Caucus adopted a rule urging a greater role on the floor for subcommittees that had initiated major legislation. The Republican-controlled House of the late 1990s, while continuing to use subcommittees, subjected them to greater discipline and control by the leadership in pursuing a party agenda than was true when Democrats were in the majority.

Assigning bills to a sympathetic or unsympathetic subcommittee is one of the ways a committee chairman can influence the legislative outcome. No longer able to dictate committee activities the way they could prior to 1970s procedural reforms, committee chairmen now negotiate with committee members to work out arrangements that will accommodate as many members as possible. But the chairman still controls the committee's funds and can hire and fire most committee staffers. Chairmen therefore are in a position either to promote expeditious action on legislation they favor or to encourage delay and inaction on measures they oppose.

Few bills reach the House or Senate floor without first being the subject of subcommittee hearings. Hearings are used to receive testimony from members of Congress, executive branch officials, policy experts, interest groups, and the general public, and are usually held at the subcommittee level. Testimony may be delivered by witnesses either in person or through written submissions that may later be published as part of the hearing transcript. Most persons who come before committees offer prepared statements, after which they may be questioned by subcommittee members and, on some committees, by staff members.

Hearings are used for a raft of purposes—to gather information, to attract media attention, to test initial reaction to a legislative idea. Full committees will sometimes hold hearings as well on subjects of major public controversy, or when witnesses from the top levels of government are called to testify. Senate hearings in 1997 on alleged campaign finance scandals were held by the full Committee on Governmental Affairs, rather than its investigations subcommittee, and a companion House inquiry was run by the full Committee on Government Reform and Oversight.

Hearings are intended as fact-finding forums to educate both members of Congress and the public about specific problems. They may also be used to assess the degree of support or opposition to a particular bill or to promote support or opposition to a bill both in Congress and among the public. Many hearings are brief and perfunctory. Because demands on legislators' time are so great only a few subcommittee members with a special interest in a subject are likely to participate.

The presence of television, along with controversial subject matter, can attract substantial interest from members even on subjects on which they might not otherwise actively participate. The creation of the Cable Satellite Public Affairs Network (C-SPAN), which usually televises some hearings on any day that Congress is in session, has forced Congress to accommodate the new medium. Television's powerful intrusiveness is coupled with the medium's need for interesting or dramatic events that readily provide heroes and villains and promote controversy. Members with the skill to accommodate these channels of communication to the public have a powerful force to influence the outcome of policy debates. *(See box, Televised Floor Debates Here to Stay, p. 482.)*

The Army-McCarthy hearings in the early 1950s turned public opinion against Sen. Joseph R. McCarthy, R-Wis., who had made a career of accusations of Communist penetration of the

government. Senate Foreign Relations Committee hearings in the mid-1960s, under Sen. J. William Fulbright, D-Ark., mobilized opposition to the Vietnam War. Senate committee hearings in 1973 into a variety of illegal activities in the White House that came to be known collectively as the Watergate scandal, and the ensuing 1974 House Judiciary Committee impeachment proceedings against President Nixon, destroyed the remnants of popular support for Nixon and, in the process, made folk heroes of the committees' chairmen, Sen. Sam Ervin, D-N.C., and Rep. Peter W. Rodino Jr., D-N.J. Televised Senate Judiciary Committee hearings in 1987 helped fuel the controversy over the nomination of Robert H. Bork to a seat on the Supreme Court, moving public opinion decisively against him and ensuring his defeat. Explosive 1991 hearings by the all-male Senate Judiciary Committee on sexual harassment accusations against Supreme Court nominee Clarence Thomas charged a national debate that continued years later. While public opinion about Thomas was sharply divided and he was ultimately confirmed by a 52–48 vote, the most immediate impact of the hearings was to focus more attention on issues of sexual harassment and gender politics in the 1992 political campaigns, contributing to the election of four additional women to the Senate in a period that their supporters called the "Year of the Woman."

In less historic or controversial circumstances, a reasonable amount of national press coverage will result from testimony by popular actors and other celebrities who are active in a particular cause, such as film stars Robert Redford on environmental issues or Elizabeth Taylor on increased AIDS research funding.

Ordinary citizens with good stories to tell can also hit a nerve, especially on subjects of broad public interest. In 1997, House hearings on allegations of abusive tactics against citizens by the Internal Revenue Service (IRS) had such a significant and swift impact that Clinton administration opposition to a reform bill sponsored by House Republicans instantly collapsed and the president endorsed the legislation. Before the president's reversal, the fight seemed to be about the structure of the IRS. With the help of television, the Republicans gained control of the issue and won a political victory far more easily than otherwise might have been possible.

During the 1980s and 1990s, most hearings and meetings of congressional committees occurred in open session, although committees dealing with national security and other sensitive or classified information often close their meetings. The congressional Intelligence committees nearly always meet in closed session. The Senate Armed Services and House Armed Services committees use a combination of open and closed (executive) hearings. Until 1971 the House Appropriations Committee held all its hearings in closed session.

House rules by 1995 made it extremely difficult for most committees and subcommittees to close meetings or hearings except for a few specified reasons relating to national security, use of law enforcement information, or protection of the rights of witnesses testifying. A rules amendment in 1995 liberalized media access to open sessions and made coverage by radio, tele-

TELEVISED FLOOR DEBATES HERE TO STAY

At noon on March 19, 1979, the U.S. House of Representatives made its live television debut. That appearance was the culmination of years of hard work by proponents of the idea. First proposed in 1944 by then-Sen. Claude Pepper, D-Fla., the movement to open the chambers to television cameras took hold only slowly in a body often resistant to change. Indeed, Senate floor action has been televised only since June 1986.

Albert Gore, a Tennessee Democrat who became vice president under Bill Clinton, led the fight for television in the House, where he served from 1977 to 1985, and in the Senate, where he served from 1985 to 1993. "The marriage of this medium and of our open debate have the potential . . . to revitalize representative democracy," Gore said in the first televised speech in 1979, a one-minute address to the House before the regular legislative day began.

Since members can use television to keep up with the action, said political scientist Steven S. Smith in 1989, "(they) are not quite as reliant on a colleague at the door telling them whether to vote up or down."

DAWN OF A NEW AGE

Until the early 1970s, television was just a dream to its proponents. But the arrival in Congress of reform-minded members in the wake of political scandals in the 1970s, particularly the Watergate affair that led to President Richard Nixon's resignation, contributed to an atmosphere more amenable to openness.

In 1977 the Democratic leadership directed the House Select Committee on Congressional Operations to conduct a ninety-day experiment using closed-circuit telecasts of House floor proceedings to members' offices. The experiment was labeled a success, and on October 27, 1977, the House tentatively agreed to go ahead, although it took some time to iron out the details.

In June 1978 news organizations began broadcasting House proceedings over radio, and by March 1979 television had arrived. The Cable Satellite Public Affairs Network (C-SPAN), the private, non-profit cooperative of the cable television industry, was launched in

1979 with the express purpose of televising Congress. House employees remain in control of the cameras.

The Senate proceeded more slowly in bringing in the cameras. Majority Leader Howard H. Baker Jr., R-Tenn., began the effort in earnest in 1981. In February 1986 the Senate passed a resolution to allow television broadcasting.

For a month the Senate permitted closed-circuit transmissions into members' offices, followed by six weeks of public broadcasts. At the conclusion of the six-week test period, the Senate voted to keep the cameras permanently. And on June 2, 1986, the Senate premiered on a second C-SPAN channel.

Senate rules are fairly strict. Cameras are operated by congressional staff and usually remain fixed on a single speaker. Initially the House rules were similar. Since May 1984, however, House cameras began to slowly pan the room during votes and special orders, a period at the end of a daily session when members may speak on various topics, usually to a mostly empty chamber.

When the Republicans took control of the House in 1995, procedures for panning the chamber changed. The camera would focus on individual members talking on benches in the chamber or reading the newspaper, practices which appeared to give some degree of "editorial control" to the camera operators and raised concerns about possible partisan abuse of the television coverage. After protests at the new intrusiveness, Speaker Newt Gingrich ordered that such close-in shots of members who are not directly participating in the business on the floor be stopped, though the cameras still have more mobility than they did under Democratic rule.

THE VIEWING AUDIENCE

The public does watch Congress on television. As of January 1998, C-SPAN had 72.5 million subscribing households who received its cable channel showing House proceedings (C-SPAN1), and 49.5 for its Senate channel (C-SPAN2).

In a survey by Statistical Research Inc. released in January 1997, it was estimated that 22.4 million people watched C-SPAN at some

---

vision, and photographers a right to be exercised by the press, not a privilege to be granted or withheld by committees.

Once the hearings are concluded, the subcommittee may take no action, in effect killing a bill. Or it may "mark up" the bill, considering the contents of each provision and section of the measure, amending some provisions, discarding others, perhaps rewriting the measure altogether. When the markup is finished, the subcommittee reports its version of the legislation, presuming it has not rejected the measure, to the full committee. In some instances, the full committee may exercise its au-

thority to take up the bill directly, bypassing a separate subcommittee markup stage.

Full Committee Action

The full committee may repeat the subcommittee procedures, sometimes even including additional hearings. It may conduct an amending process, especially if the stage of subcommittee action has been bypassed, or it may simply ratify the action of the subcommittee. Frequently the full committee will propose additional amendments to alter the proposal. If the

point each week, with 72 percent watching congressional hearings, 67 percent the House floor, and 64 percent the Senate floor. However, the increase in the number of viewers was less than four percent from a decade earlier.

In 1988 21.6 million households reported watching C-SPAN, which commissioned the survey. The public is not C-SPAN's only audience, though. When Congress is in session it is nearly impossible to find a congressional office without its television tuned to C-SPAN. Congress has its own cable system that carries floor action without C-SPAN graphics or commentary.

Time is a precious commodity for members of Congress. Televised proceedings and committee hearings often allow them to gauge their time better during votes and other floor activities. Members follow the proceedings and committee hearings to keep abreast of the latest developments.

MIXED VERDICTS ON MEDIA IMPACT

Members of Congress and political scientists agree that the cameras are a fixture in the chambers and the public would not allow their removal. "The horror stories that were supposed to happen didn't happen," political scientist Larry Sabato said in 1989.

While passage of rules changes allowing television coverage of floor proceedings was probably inevitable, the ultimate effect on the legislative process at the heart of Congress remains difficult to evaluate. During the 1990s there have been widespread complaints from members about the increasing partisanship and "meanness" in debate, and some observers—both in and out of Congress—blamed the live coverage for encouraging use of floor speeches to produce sound bites for the evening news. A substantive and spontaneous legislative process, it is argued, has too often been sidelined by staged events. Not only television, but the advent of talk radio shows that specialized in inciting listeners, contributed to a debasement of political dialogue.

In the House, use of one-minute speeches for this purpose has become widespread, with outside political committees and interest groups sending suggested remarks for members to recite. Both parties often carefully organize their presentations in this daily forum. The use of charts and exhibits likely to be visible on a television screen has proliferated. Even opposing political candidates have gotten into the act, using excerpts of speeches by House members in campaign commercials, and then attacking them. A House rule prohibits use of the televised proceedings for political purposes, but it is enforceable only against sitting members. Democrats had been considering a proposal to modify this rule, effective with the 104th Congress, to allow members to better defend themselves against opponents who might use excerpts of floor proceedings in potentially misleading ways, but the idea died with the 1994 election that turned over House control to Republicans.

Members of the House held a bipartisan retreat in March 1997, in Hershey, Pennsylvania, as a reaction to the frequent vitriolic floor speeches and intense partisanship of the previous Congress. In a background report on *Civility in the House of Representatives,* political scientist Kathleen Hall Jamieson argued that traditional methods for striking inappropriate language from the *Congressional Record* and letting tempers cool had been rendered obsolete by television. "Not only is it impossible to strike words taken down from the C-SPAN record but the process, designed to enhance civility, may instead diminish it, as the offending Member plays to the cameras. C-SPAN footage also increases the likelihood that moments of incivility will be replayed on the news."

Of course, some of these concerns reflect late-twentieth-century sensibilities about the way a political process should be conducted. In earlier times, members of Congress sometimes fought each other in physical brawls on the floor and had duels with political opponents. So recent instances of incivility, while disturbing, pale in historical comparison.

Most observers of Congress agree that despite all the attention televised debate has generated, Congress survived the television revolution. It was a change the public would have forced eventually if the two houses had not acted. Television made the work of members of Congress more real and immediate to constituents, giving a sense of elected officials that voters often saw only in campaign commercials. In that sense, television strengthened Congress as an institution.

SOURCES: John Schachter, "Congress Begins Second Decade Under TV's Watchful Glare," *Congressional Quarterly Weekly Report,* March 11, 1989, 507–509; C-SPAN News Release, "New Survey: 22 Million Watch C-SPAN Weekly," January 6, 1997; Kathleen Hall Jamieson, *Civility in the House of Representatives* (Philadelphia: University of Pennsylvania, Annenberg Public Policy Center, 1997), Report Series No. 10.

amendments are not extensive, the original bill is "reported with amendments." When the bill comes to the floor, the House or Senate must approve, alter, or reject the committee amendments, before the bill is put to a vote.

If the changes are substantial and the legislation is complicated, the committee chairman or another committee member may introduce a "clean bill," which embodies the proposed amendments. The original bill is then set aside and the clean bill, with a new number, is the version voted out of committee and reported. In addition to expediting floor action, the clean bill procedure also can eliminate problems of germaneness. House germaneness rules require only that amendments offered on the floor, including committee amendments, be pertinent to the bill; the rules do not apply to provisions of the bill itself as introduced. So any amendments made part of a clean committee bill are usually protected from points of order on the floor. (There are exceptions that can be used to delete provisions from bills that include tax or tariff matters not reported by the Ways and Means Committee, and provisions in appropriations bills that violate the jurisdictions of authorizing committees.)

At a House Appropriations Committee meeting, Chairman C. W. Bill Young, R-Fla., standing right, discusses markup procedures with ranking minority member David R. Obey, D-Wis., left.

In 1973 both chambers adopted new rules to encourage more committees to open their markup meetings to the public, and most committee meetings were opened. By 1990, however, there was a discernible trend toward closing some meetings, particularly on controversial bills. Advocates of closed sessions believed that members would make politically difficult decisions more easily in the absence of lobbyists and interested constituents. The minority, which often objected to the decisions made, pressed for greater openness and attacked closed sessions as a symbol of majority arrogance.

When the Republicans assumed control of the House in 1995, they amended rules for the conduct of meetings and hearings to make closed sessions more difficult. For example, the new rules allow a committee majority, by a roll-call vote, to close all or part of a meeting to consider legislation only by determining that an open meeting would endanger national security; compromise sensitive law enforcement information; tend to defame, degrade, or incriminate any person; or violate a law or rule of the House. Arguments to close as a matter of convenience or to satisfy members' desire for privacy no longer carried weight. All meetings and hearings open to the public were also open automatically to broadcast and photographic media, without the need for advance permission.

When a committee votes to approve a measure, it is said to "order the bill reported." Occasionally, a committee may order a bill reported unfavorably or without recommendation. The House Judiciary Committee, for example, voted 19–17 in June 1990 to report without recommendation a proposed constitutional amendment barring desecration of the American flag. In such cases, the committee may be acting only because of overwhelming political pressure to deal with legislation a majority of its members actually disapprove of but feel that they cannot avoid. This situation occurred after the Supreme Court threw out a statute barring the practice on constitutional grounds. The

constitutional amendment later passed the House but failed in the Senate.

But because a committee can effectively kill a measure by not acting on it, committee reports almost invariably recommend passage. Those bills reported favorably have usually been amended to satisfy a majority of the committee's members.

Committee Reports. House rules and Senate custom require that a written report accompany each bill reported from a committee to the floor. The report, written by the committee staff, typically describes the purpose and scope of the bill, explains committee amendments, indicates proposed changes in existing law, estimates additional costs to the government of the recommended program changes, and often includes the texts of communications from department and agency officials whose views on the legislation have been solicited. Committee members opposed to the bill or specific sections of it often submit minority views in a separate section of the report. Bills discharged from a committee prior to formal committee action and brought up on the floor are not accompanied by a written report.

After enactment of the Legislative Reorganization Act of 1970, committees were required to publish in their reports all votes taken on amendments disposed of during markup as well as the vote to report the bill. Only vote totals were required, not the position of individual members on roll calls. Following rules changes in 1995, House committees were also required to publish in the report how members voted individually both on the bill and on any amendments considered and disposed of by roll-call vote, whether successful or not. Committees are required to keep a record of all roll calls and make it available to the public on request, which provides another source of information if a bill has never actually been reported. The Senate has similar, if somewhat looser, procedural requirements. It requires that the results of all votes, including the votes of individual senators, be included in the committee report unless previously announced by the committee.

Reports are numbered, by Congress and chamber, in the order in which they are filed (S Rept 105-1, S Rept 105-2, H Rept 105-1, H Rept 105-2, and onward, with the first number referring to the Congress in which the bill is reported) and immediately printed. The report number and the date the bill was reported formally are also shown on the bill. The reported bill is also printed with any committee amendments indicated by insertions in italics and deletions in stricken-through type.

Sometimes, a House committee will rework legislation well after the time it is reported using the Rules Committee as a means to make final changes to its liking, or to accommodate other committees' interests, or to deal with concerns raised by the leadership. In these cases, the Rules Committee may make a new bill, often referred to as "an amendment in the nature of a substitute," the vehicle for formal debate and amendment on the floor, while retaining the shell of the bill's "HR" number. Adoption of the rule could substitute this new text for the original language, which would never be formally acted on and would disappear entirely once the bill is passed. Or the Rules Committee may allow consideration of a new bill with an entirely new number, making the legislative history of an issue into a tricky maze in which the original bill, along with its committee report, appears to die through lack of House consideration while actually forming the basis of eventual chamber action.

Legislative Intent. In some situations, the language of the report is as important as the bill itself. It has been common practice for committees, including House-Senate conference committees, to write in their reports instructions directing government agencies on interpretation and enforcement of the law. Moreover, courts have relied on these guidelines in establishing what is known as "legislative intent."

Some legal scholars, judges, and members of the Supreme Court have expressed skepticism about relying on these reports because they are not written into law, or relying on floor debate, complaining that Congress is often sloppy in its preparation for floor action. The most prominent and outspoken critic of "legislative intent" in the 1990s was Supreme Court Justice Antonin Scalia. Critics say they prefer to rely on the actual text of the measure as the basis for statutory interpretations. Others counter that divorcing a bill from the circumstances surrounding its passage can lead to misinterpretations.

Legal scholar Robert A. Katzmann of the Brookings Institution notes: "The more authoritative Congress is as to the appropriate use of such material, the more likely that legislative history will have the intended weight. Thus it is imperative that Congress develop means to clarify the use of such materials if courts are to better interpret legislative meaning." Katzmann suggests that Congress take care to use "more precise drafting, more authoritative legislative histories, and refinement of the process of revising statutes."[9]

Lobbyists are also vitally interested in the report language as one way to promote or protect their clients' interests. Many appropriations bills, for example, set out only the amount of money an agency or department might spend. But the accompanying committee report often contains directives on how Congress expects the money to be spent or warnings to bureaucrats not to take certain actions.

House Floor Action: Structured Efficiency

Because of the sheer number of representatives in the House—435—the chamber can appear disorderly, especially at the end of a session, with members milling about in small groups and streaming in and out of the chamber to answer to roll calls. But underlying this general hubbub is a structure for considering legislation that allows the House to act relatively efficiently and expeditiously. (*See box, Dilatory Tactics Are Limited in the House, p. 492.*)

SCHEDULING FLOOR ACTION

Bills can reach the House floor in a number of ways. Most are reported first by a committee. However, there is no requirement in the rules that a bill be reported by or even considered by a committee, or that any report be available for members prior to floor action, unless the bill was in fact actually reported. By unanimous consent, noncontroversial bills and resolutions can even be offered from the floor, considered, and passed without even being formally introduced and given a number first. (They may be given a number when actually called up.) Some bills receive committee consideration but may be called up for a vote without any final committee action or a report being filed. Major legislation, however, nearly always must survive the full stages of committee action culminating in a committee vote and report, and also receive a rule from the Rules Committee before being brought up for action. In practice, even noncontroversial bills brought up under an expedited procedure called suspension of the rules are accompanied by a committee report, or have received some committee action, in order to reassure members that the bill's presence on the floor has legitimacy and that interested members have been given sufficient notice to participate in the process.

After a bill is reported from a House committee and before it is scheduled for floor action, it is placed on one of three legislative calendars: Union, House, or Private. Bills already on the Union or House calendars may also be placed on a "Corrections Calendar" at the Speaker's discretion. Another calendar, Discharge, is used only for motions to discharge committees from consideration of a measure, when such motions have received the signatures of a majority of members on a discharge petition. Each day the House is in session it publishes a Calendar of the House as a formal document that includes all matters on each of the calendars, and also provides a history of action on them by committees, the House and Senate, conferences, and the president.

All bills, including authorization bills, having any effect on

A TYPICAL SCHEDULE IN THE HOUSE

The House conducts different types of business on different days, so its daily routine will vary. However, from week to week, a pattern is usually followed.

• The House convenes early for morning hour debate for five-minute speeches on Mondays and Tuesdays sixty to ninety minutes prior to the formal opening of the day's session, even if that is in the afternoon. No votes or legislative business can occur. The House then recesses until the formal convening of the day's session.

• The chaplain delivers the opening prayer, and a House member leads the chamber in the Pledge of Allegiance.

• The Speaker approves the Journal, the record of the previous day's proceedings. Often a member demands a roll-call vote on the approval of the Journal, which can be used to determine who is present and to allow the leadership to "whip" them on other matters. The Journal vote can also be postponed by the Speaker until later in the day and clustered with other votes that may be occurring.

• After the House receives messages from the Senate and the president and privileged reports from committees, and conducts other similar procedural activities, members are recognized by unanimous consent for one-minute speeches on any topic.

• The House then turns to its legislative business. On Mondays and Tuesdays only, the House usually considers less controversial bills, sometimes dozens at a time, under the suspension of the rules process requiring a two-thirds majority for passage, and recorded votes are postponed until late in the day, or until the next day. Measures that are even less controversial are frequently passed by unanimous consent. A "Corrections Calendar" for the consideration of bills that the Speaker determines would change erroneous actions or regulations by the federal government may be called on the second and fourth Tuesdays of each month. A sixty percent majority of members present and voting is required for passage. The House must call the Private Calendar on the first Tuesday of each month and the Speaker may direct it to be called on the third Tuesday.

• Virtually every bill of any significance is considered under a special rule, reported from the Rules Committee, that sets guidelines for floor action. The rule may be approved with little opposition but the vote can also be a first test of a bill's popularity. If the rule restricts the amendments that may be offered, those members barred from offering amendments may work with opponents of the bill itself to defeat the rule or to defeat the previous question so that amendments to the rule can be offered.

• After the rule is adopted, the House resolves into the Committee of the Whole to consider the bill. The Speaker relinquishes the gavel to another member, who serves as chairman of this "committee" and presides over the activities. Debate time is controlled by the managers of the bill, usually the chairman and ranking minority member of the standing committee with jurisdiction over the measure. (See "Action in the Committee of the Whole," p. 502.)

After time for general debate has expired, amendments that are permitted under the rule may be offered and debated. Debate on an amendment may be for a fixed time. If none is specified in the rule it is conducted under the "five-minute rule," which limits each side to five minutes. However, members may obtain additional speaking time by offering amendments to "strike the last word," a pro forma action that allows additional time for discussion and debate.

Voting may be conducted in three different ways plus variations depending on whether the House or the Committee of the Whole is sitting: by voice, the usual procedure; by division (members stand to be counted but no record of names is kept); or by electronic device (referred to as "the yeas and nays" or a "recorded vote" depending on the parliamentary circumstances). Certain matters in the House require a roll-call vote under the Constitution (for example, to reconsider a vetoed bill) or the rules of the House (for example, passing a general appropriations bill or closing a conference committee meeting to the public). Most electronic votes last fifteen minutes. If several votes in sequence are conducted, the second and any subsequent votes are usually reduced to a minimum of five minutes. (See box, Methods of Voting, p. 496.)

• After the amending process is complete, the Committee of the Whole "rises," and the chairman reports to the Speaker on the actions taken. The House votes on whether to accept the amendments adopted in the Committee, usually a pro forma action. The House then votes on final passage of the bill, sometimes after voting on a motion by opponents to recommit the bill to its committee of origin, which would kill it, or to recommit the bill with instructions to report it back "forthwith" with additional amendments that would be adopted prior to final passage. After final passage, a motion to reconsider is in order but is usually announced as "laid on the table" by the Speaker to save time.

• After the House completes its legislative business, members may speak for up to sixty minutes each under "special orders," with hour speeches limited to four hours evenly divided between the parties (except on Tuesdays). Members must reserve the time in advance but can speak on any topic—often to an almost deserted chamber. Members seeking recognition for short periods of time, such as five or ten minutes, are recognized first, alternating between the parties. In 1994, the House limited the total time available for special orders to prevent sessions from extending too long but special orders cannot extend beyond midnight.

---

the Treasury go on the Union Calendar, which is by far the most important. Technically it is the Calendar of the Committee of the Whole House on the State of the Union, so called because bills listed on it are first considered in the Committee of the Whole and reported back to the House for a final vote on passage. Other types of matters, such as investigative reports approved by committees, may also appear on the Union Calendar even though they will not be considered by the House. Legislation on the Union Calendar may be considered on the floor, debated, and amended in a wide variety of different ways under the rules of the House. (See "Action in the Committee of the Whole," p. 502.)

Matters that have no direct effect on the Treasury are placed on the House Calendar. These bills or, far more commonly, resolutions, generally deal with administrative and procedural matters and are usually not considered by the Committee of the Whole but taken up directly by the House. However, some legislation of great significance, such as constitutional amendments and approval of compacts among states, appear on the House Calendar. Simple and concurrent resolutions also go on the House Calendar, including the concurrent resolution that starts off yearly action on the budget process and special rules reported from the Rules Committee allowing consideration of other legislation. On the floor, matters from this calendar may also be considered in several different ways.

Noncontroversial bills in the past had been placed on the Consent Calendar, but it was not used during the final years of Democratic control of the House that preceded the GOP majority starting in 1995. The leadership and committees preferred to use the "suspension of the rules" process, which is itself often mistakenly referred to as a calendar. The Consent Calendar was replaced in 1995 by the new Corrections Calendar.

The Corrections Calendar is completely under the control of the Speaker and was created by the new Republican majority as a vehicle to promote its political agenda. Bills may be placed there by the Speaker if they are considered noncontroversial and deal with correcting "mistakes" in previously enacted legislation or in government actions or regulations. The Republican Conference considered these types of measures to be a class of legislation that deserved special recognition and easy access to the floor. After putting this new device in place, Speaker Gingrich sought advice from a bipartisan task force he established to advise him on use of the calendar.

The Corrections Calendar may be called on the second and fourth Tuesdays of each month, if desired by the Speaker. The procedure for consideration of these bills is specified in House rules. Debate is limited to one hour, evenly divided between the majority and the minority, and only committee amendments or those offered by the chairman are in order. The minority is allowed to offer one motion to recommit, which may contain instructions providing for consideration of other amendments. Passage of all measures on the Corrections Calendar requires a 60 percent supermajority vote, which effectively prevents the Speaker from using it for consideration of controversial matters. After an initial flurry of partisan strife in 1995, the Corrections Calendar has not been employed frequently, and no measure called up on it had been defeated as of early 1999. If a measure were to fail, it would retain its place on its original calendar and could still be called up later under other procedures in House rules.

Private immigration bills and bills for the relief of individuals with claims against the United States are placed on the Private Calendar. This calendar must be called on the first Tuesday of each month, unless dispensed with by a two-thirds vote or by unanimous consent, which is what usually occurs unless there are a number of bills on the calendar ready for passage. The Pri-

vate Calendar may also be called on the third Tuesday of each month at the Speaker's discretion. If two or more members object to the consideration of a bill it will be recommitted to the committee that reported it, but if there is some concern or uncertainty about a bill it may be passed over "without prejudice" by unanimous consent and still remain eligible for action on a future call of the Private Calendar. Both major political parties appoint several members as "official objectors" to monitor such bills and ensure that only those that have overwhelming support pass using the Private Calendar. Most private bills are called up from the calendar and simply passed by unanimous consent without debate and without a recorded vote, but debate may occur under a procedure that allows any member to speak for five minutes. Amendments may be offered and debated for a maximum of five minutes in support, and five minutes opposed.

The Judiciary Committee handles most private relief bills, which typically deal with various claims against the government, and immigration status. Once enacted, private laws receive separate private law numbers, as opposed to the numeration given to public laws that Congress enacts. The quantity of private bills enacted into law, however, has dropped precipitously since the 96th Congress (1979–1981) when 123 private laws were enacted. In the 102nd (1991–1993), 103rd (1993–1995), and 104th (1995–1997) Congresses, there were twenty, eight, and four respectively. In the 105th Congress (1997–1999) ten became law. Congressional scholar Walter Oleszek has suggested that the transfer of jurisdiction over some of these issues to federal agencies, fears of scandals over favoritism to individuals, and reluctance to disburse federal funds for private concerns in an era of deficit spending led to a decline in popularity of the private law mechanism. As a result, the House does not call the Private Calendar very frequently anymore. *(See box, Private Bills, p. 526.)*

The House also has a Discharge Calendar. It is used to list motions to discharge committees from further consideration of bills or resolutions, when a majority of the total membership of the House—218—signs a discharge petition at the desk in the House chamber. Discharge motions are taken up on the second and fourth Mondays of each month and may be debated for twenty minutes, divided between a proponent and an opponent. If the motion is adopted, the measure discharged will then be considered in a number of possible ways. Since the discharge procedure is rarely attempted, and few discharge petitions obtain the 218 signatures, the Discharge Calendar usually consists of a restatement of the discharge rule followed by a blank page.

Discharge motions that have been filed but have not obtained the requisite signatures can be found in the *Congressional Record*, and Congress's Web sites, along with a current list of signers. *(See box, Prying Loose Legislation Stuck in Committee: Use of Discharge and Calendar Wednesday, p. 488.)*

The five calendars (Union, House, Private, Corrections, and Discharge) are printed in one document titled *Calendars of the United States House of Representatives and History of Legislation*. This calendar is printed daily when the House is in session. The first issue of the week lists in numerical order all House and

The House has two special procedures—the discharge petition and Calendar Wednesday—designed to bring to a vote legislation that has been blocked from floor consideration. Both devices were instituted during the speakership of Joseph G. Cannon, R-Ill. (1903–1911), in an effort to circumvent the near-complete control the dictatorial Speaker held over the legislative agenda. These procedures have been used rarely and are even more rarely successful. However, the threat of using a discharge petition has sometimes been successful in prompting action through the normal legislative process. *(See "Cannonism," p. 430.)*

DISCHARGE PETITION

The House's modern discharge motion was first adopted in 1910, reached approximately its present form in 1931, and was then further modified in the 1990s as public attention to the procedure increased. The discharge petition enables a majority of the membership to bring before the House any public bill blocked in a standing committee. With respect to the Rules Committee, it allows discharge of resolutions proposing changes in House rules and of resolutions providing special rules for consideration of any bill that has been before a standing committee.

While the discharge rule is specifically directed against committees, its use also serves as a check on the majority leadership. This is true because in cases where discharge is attempted a committee is usually working in concert with or at the direction of the leadership. (If the leadership wanted a vote on a measure, it could simply use the Rules Committee to bring it out to the floor.)

The discharge procedure may be used if a bill has been referred to a standing committee for at least thirty legislative days without having been reported. Members also have the option, in such cases, of introducing a special rule providing for consideration of the bill which, if not reported in seven legislative days, becomes subject to discharge. Any member may then file a motion to discharge a committee from further consideration, popularly known as a discharge "petition," which members may sign at the clerk's desk in the chamber whenever the House is in session. Members may withdraw their names until 218—a majority—have signed, at which point the motion to discharge is placed on the Discharge Calendar and the complete list of the names of the signers and the order of their signatures are published in the Calendar and in the *Congressional Record.*

The identity of the members signing a discharge petition was kept secret until 1993. Up to that point, the petition had been considered an internal matter in the House; secrecy was intended to ensure that the process was considered a last resort and to permit quiet efforts to persuade members to withdraw their names and to preserve opportunities to reach a compromise on an issue through the normal legislative process. From time to time, some members would threaten to reveal the names of their colleagues who had or had not signed

a petition, in order to subject them to pressure from outside interest groups. There had been stories of members asking to view a petition, with each memorizing several names and then leaving to write them down until a comprehensive list was obtained.

The sponsors of the 1993 rules change, principally from the Republican minority, intended that it would pressure more members to sign such petitions. They viewed a discharge petition as a legislative mechanism that should be subjected to public scrutiny, much like a member's cosponsorship of a bill. The handful of members publicly opposed to opening the process worried that it might result in the more frequent consideration of irresponsible legislation and undermine the committee system.

Ironically, the resolution to open up the process to public view was only passed after itself being discharged from the Rules Committee. However, no significant changes in the normal legislative process were immediately evident. The names of members signing a discharge petition are published in the *Congressional Record* on a weekly basis and made public by the clerk of the House daily.

A motion to discharge must remain on the Discharge Calendar for seven legislative days before it can be called up for floor action. On the second and fourth Mondays of each month, except during the last six days of the session, any member who has signed the discharge petition may be recognized to move that the committee be discharged. Debate on the motion is limited to twenty minutes, divided equally between proponents and opponents. If the motion carries, any member who signed the petition can move for immediate consideration of the discharged measure, which then becomes the business of the House until it is resolved. Depending on the nature of the measure discharged, it may be considered either in the House or in the Committee of the Whole. If the House postpones action on the discharged measure, it is placed on the appropriate calendar, to be available for potential floor action just as other measures are.

Partly because the process is so cumbersome and time-consuming, and partly because members are usually reluctant to challenge committees so directly, the discharge petition has seldom been successful. Between 1931 and 1998, 540 discharge petitions were filed, but only twenty-six measures were actually discharged. Of these, nineteen passed the House, but only two bills were ultimately enacted into law along with two resolutions changing House rules. The failure to enact more laws suggests that the resistance to such legislation in the normal House legislative process was not purely obstructionist. It often foreshadowed a level of controversy that reappeared again at other stages such as in the Senate or with the president. This made final success very difficult.[1]

Discharge petitions nonetheless can serve a purpose by focusing attention on a particular issue and sometimes forcing the recalcitrant committee to take action. In 1985, after 200 members signed a petition filed by Harold L. Volkmer, D-Mo., to discharge from the

Judiciary Committee a Senate-passed bill weakening federal gun controls, that committee hastily reported out gun control legislation. Ultimately Volkmer's version of the measure passed the House, in part because his discharge petition, which was eventually signed by 218 members, forced the Rules Committee to make his version in order on the floor.

In modern practice, rather than discharge actual legislation, discharge supporters will instead usually target the Rules Committee, especially if they intend to make a serious effort to obtain 218 signatures. They introduce and attempt to discharge a special rule that not only brings up the legislation but does so employing procedures of the sponsors' choosing that provide maximum prospects for passage. (Discharging legislation directly to the floor without a rule can subject it to potentially cumbersome floor procedures that might inhibit passage.)

Constitutional amendments are frequently the subjects of discharge petitions. For example, in 1990, 1992, and 1994 special rules were discharged from the Rules Committee providing for consideration of constitutional amendments requiring a balanced budget. The Judiciary Committee, which had jurisdiction over the amendments, the Rules Committee, and the majority leadership opposed floor action through normal procedures. In each case, the House ultimately fell short of the two-thirds majority required for passage. In 1995 the constitutional amendment was part of the Republicans' "Contract with America" and was reported out of committee and passed by the House using the normal legislative process. It failed by one vote in the Senate, however. The same thing happened again in 1997.

Longtime advocates of discharge quite understandably lost interest in it following the shift in party control and no measures were discharged during the first four years of Republican majorities starting in 1995. But, in another example of partisan turnabout, minority Democrats attempted to discharge campaign finance reform legislation in 1997 over the opposition of the Republican leadership. The effort stalled when Speaker Gingrich promised a vote on the issue in the spring of 1998.

However, Republican supporters of campaign reform who had shunned the discharge strategy later cried betrayal when Gingrich would only allow the issue on the floor using the two-thirds majority suspension process, which would prevent passage of any major legislation. Gingrich also barred action on the most important bipartisan proposal. Denouncing the Speaker for a cynical ploy, they quickly got behind the discharge petition sponsored by Rep. Scotty Baesler, D-Ky., which would have discharged an essentially open rule allowing consideration of the bill with substitute amendments made in order that embodied several major proposals. The rule used a "queen-of-the-hill" process in which, if any substitutes passed, the one receiving the most votes would become the basis for further action. As the petition moved above 200 signatures in April 1998, Gingrich capitulated and promised consideration under an open rule reported by the Rules Committee using a normal legislative process.

CALENDAR WEDNESDAY

Calendar Wednesday is a little-used method for bringing to the House floor a bill that has been blocked by the Rules Committee. Under the procedure, each Wednesday standing committees may be called in alphabetical order for the purpose of bringing up any of their bills that have been reported, except those that are privileged, on the House or Union Calendar. General debate is limited to two hours and action must be completed in the same legislative day. Bills called up from the Union Calendar are debated in the Committee of the Whole with amendments considered under the five-minute rule.

The procedure may be dispensed with at other times by a two-thirds vote and also during the last two weeks of the session if such a time frame is established in advance. In practice Calendar Wednesday is usually set aside prospectively, by unanimous consent, when the House adjourns at the end of the previous week's session.

Several limitations made the process cumbersome to use. Because committees are called alphabetically, those near the end of the list may have to wait several weeks before they are reached, and once a committee has brought up one bill under the procedure it may not bring up another until all other committees have been called. Because the bill must be disposed of in a single day, opponents need only delay to kill the bill.

During the 98th Congress (1983–1985) Republicans regularly objected to dispensing with Calendar Wednesday and forced a call of the Calendar to protest the Democratic leadership's failure to schedule action on legislation they supported, such as school prayer measures and a constitutional amendment calling for a balanced budget. The protests were purely symbolic because the committees to which these measures had been referred had never reported them and the reading clerk simply read the name of each committee in alphabetical order before the House moved on to other business. On January 25, 1984, the Democratic leadership allowed a minor agricultural bill to be considered under the Calendar Wednesday procedure—the first such passage since May 1960. Finding the process as cumbersome and ineffective as its earlier users had, the Republicans eventually stopped objecting to dispensing with Calendar Wednesday.

1. Richard S. Beth, "The Discharge Rule in the House of Representatives: Procedure, History, and Statistics," Congressional Research Service, Library of Congress, March 2, 1990; "The Discharge Rule in the House: Recent Use in Historical Context," Congressional Research Service, Library of Congress, September 15, 1997; "The Discharge Rule in the House: Principal Uses and Features," Congressional Research Service, Library of Congress, February 18, 1999.

most Senate measures that have been reported by committees, with a capsule history of congressional action on each. It also includes a general index and other valuable reference material.

Bills are placed on the calendars in the order in which they are reported. But they do not come to the floor in chronological order; in fact, some never come to the floor at all. The Speaker of the House, working with the majority leader, committee chairmen, and the Rules Committee, determines which bills will come to the floor and when. How the bill will be handled on the floor depends on whether it is noncontroversial, privileged, or major legislation that requires a special rule from the Rules Committee.

Noncontroversial Legislation

The House has two time-saving procedures for passing noncontroversial bills or bills of minor interest—unanimous consent and suspension of the rules.

Unanimous Consent. The House may accomplish almost any action by unanimous consent, but the procedure is most commonly used to act quickly. Sometimes the actions desired can only be accomplished by unanimous consent because there is no readily available motion that can be used to force the matter before the House for debate and vote. In other instances, available motions might waste the time of the House with debate or votes since the matter is noncontroversial.

If the Speaker recognizes a member to make a unanimous consent request it will be granted unless another member objects. The Speaker can prevent a unanimous consent request from being placed before the House simply by withholding recognition, after inquiring "for what purpose does the gentleman rise?"—in effect signifying his own opposition to the request. Unanimous consent requests relating to action on legislation normally must be cleared in advance by the majority and minority or the Speaker will not entertain them. No debate is in order and no vote is held on unanimous consent requests, saving substantial time for the House. However, in order for the House to understand the purpose of a unanimous consent request, in many cases, when the Speaker asks "is there objection?" another member who supports the request will often "reserve the right to object" and yield to the maker of the request for an explanation. Several members may participate in an informal discussion in this manner until a legislative record has been made.

Unanimous consent requests are used dozens of times each day, most commonly to insert material into the *Congressional Record;* to address the House when no legislation is pending, such as during one-minute speeches at the beginning of the day and "special order" speeches at the end; to extend the time a member may speak on an amendment; to obtain a leave of absence from a House session; to discharge committees from consideration of noncontroversial matters and bring them directly to the floor; and to dispose of various motions that could normally be voted on if demanded by any member.

Suspension of the Rules. The suspension procedure is most often used to bring to the floor noncontroversial measures on the Union or House Calendars that have been reported from committee. Additionally, measures never considered by a committee or even those just introduced also may be taken up. The Speaker has total control over bringing legislation to the floor under this procedure, and he invariably recognizes only members of the majority party to offer motions to suspend the rules. However, bipartisan cooperation is required for passage of suspension motions because a two-thirds majority is needed.

Any member may move to suspend the rules and pass a measure, although it is generally a committee or subcommittee chairman, with the concurrence of the ranking minority member, who will be recognized for the purpose. The motion suspends all rules of the House that normally affect consideration of the measure, including referral to a committee and requirements for committee action such as preparation of a committee report. This precludes points of order against the legislation. A suspension motion may be debated for forty minutes and may not be amended from the floor, although amendments are permitted if initially stipulated in the motion. Time is normally evenly divided between the floor manager and a minority member, but any member who opposes a bill under suspension has preference to claim half the time.

Two-thirds of the members present must vote to suspend the rules and pass the measure involved. If a suspension motion is not approved, the measure may be considered later under regular House procedures. In 1979 the House amended its rules to give the Speaker discretion to delay final votes until all the suspension bills scheduled for the day have been debated. The measure then may be called up at some time within the next two days and voted on in succession. The Speaker also was given discretion to shorten the time for each recorded vote to five minutes from fifteen minutes after the first vote in a sequence. These procedures have since become the normal means of considering suspensions.

Motions to suspend the rules are in order on Mondays and Tuesdays of every week, and also during the last six days of the session (but only if such a period has been formally designated by Congress, or in the days preceding the constitutional close of a session on January 3).

The availability of the suspension motion has changed repeatedly over time. Originally in order on any day, in 1847 it was restricted to Mondays only and, in 1880, to the first and third Mondays of each month; in the 93rd Congress (1973–1975) it was made available also on the Tuesdays following those Mondays and, in the 95th Congress (1977–1979) it was amended to its current form. From time to time, especially toward the end of a session, or if Congress is returning to work at midweek, the Rules Committee reports and the House passes resolutions making the motion available at other times as well.

As adjournment nears there usually is a considerable backlog of legislation awaiting action. Members who might have voted against a measure under the suspension procedure earlier in the session because of the bar to floor amendments might in the final days support a suspension motion on the grounds that the unamended measure is better than no measure at all. Conversely, members opposed to a bill under suspension have maximum leverage to force the bill's manager to incorporate amendments in the motion or risk losing it altogether.

Because they require a two-thirds vote to pass, most measures brought up under suspension of the rules are relatively noncontroversial, although there have been notable exceptions. The House declared war on the Axis powers in World War II through passage of joint resolutions under suspension of the rules. Ironically, when the House convened on Monday, December 8, 1941, following the attack on Pearl Harbor the day before, it was neither the first nor the third Monday, and the House needed unanimous consent to use the procedure to consider a declaration of war on Japan. Rep. Jeanette Rankin, R-Mont., the only member ultimately to oppose the joint resolution (she had also voted against American participation in World War I), failed to make a timely objection when she had the chance and was then denied an opportunity to speak. Later in the week, the House followed a similar procedure to deal with Germany and Italy. (Rankin voted "present.")

The Twenty-Fourth Amendment to the Constitution, abolishing the poll tax, was passed by the House using the suspension procedure on August 27, 1962, by a vote of 295–86. On November 15, 1983, an attempt to again pass the so-called "Equal Rights Amendment," which had expired without being ratified by a sufficient number of states, failed to receive the requisite supermajority under suspension of the rules by a vote of 278–147.

In the late 1970s, the Republicans accused the Democrats of using the shortcut procedure to push through some complex or controversial legislation without adequate debate or the opportunity to offer amendments. By 1978 the procedure had become as much of an issue as the bills themselves. The Democrats were highly embarrassed that year when a controversial education aid bill supported by President Carter failed under suspension on a vote of 156–218, in part because members were angry about the large numbers of suspension bills.

In 1979 the Democratic Caucus formalized guidelines that prohibited any bill with an estimated cost of more than $100 million in a single year from being taken up under suspension unless the Democratic Steering and Policy Committee granted a waiver to the Speaker. When the Republicans assumed control of the House in 1995, they continued to use the suspension procedure much as the Democrats had done. The Republican Conference rules largely mimicked the Democratic rules. Major legislation, however, is still sometimes passed under suspension, either because there is substantial bipartisan support for it or because an emergency situation warrants.

The Republican leadership in 1995 used the Rules Committee on several occasions to bring noncontroversial bills to the floor under open rules—bills that might ordinarily have been considered under suspension. An open rule allows any germane amendment to be offered. Ironically, the Democrats complained that the new majority was avoiding the suspension process to inflate artificially the Rules Committee's claims that it was re-

porting a greater percentage of open rules than had been the case previously. The majority used these statistics to bolster its claims to have brought greater openness and fairness to House procedures.

The Democrats staged a series of dilatory tactics in 1997 to protest what they regarded as the Republicans' refusal to schedule a sufficient number of suspension bills offered by Democratic sponsors. They claimed that the Republicans, when in the minority, had been allowed far more access to the process. To retaliate, Democrats opposed a number of suspensions, ensuring their defeat, and forced a series of delays in voting on many others. After tempers had cooled, in an unusual procedure, the bills were finally approved en bloc by unanimous consent on the last day of the session.

Sometimes the suspension process has been used as a safe way to test sentiment on an issue or to allow members to go on the record while avoiding actually passing legislation. For example, in February 1998, following more than a year of bitter partisan strife, the House dismissed an election challenge against Rep. Loretta Sanchez, D-Calif., after failing to find proof of sufficient voting irregularities to question the result. The Republican majority, however, still wanted to make a statement expressing concern about allegations that noncitizens had voted in the election. Their method of doing so was to immediately call up for consideration under suspension controversial legislation that would have required proof of U.S. citizenship for voting. The unsuccessful 210–200 vote for passage demonstrated some House interest in the concept, but the close margin also served as a warning that a full-fledged airing of the issues in the normal legislative process was called for before the bill made a reappearance on the floor.

At other times, however, the majority leadership's absolute control of the suspension process can lead to abuse and possibly even a revolt by the full House. In March 1998 Speaker Gingrich learned an embarrassing lesson about the limits of his ability to manipulate the process for political advantage. Gingrich used motions for suspension of the rules to create a series of "mock" votes to prevent passage of serious campaign finance reform legislation. The Republican leadership had promised to allow consideration of the issue but later balked when it seemed likely that a bipartisan bill they opposed, sponsored by Christopher Shays, R-Conn., and Martin Meehan, D-Mass., which commanded the broadest support, would pass by a simple majority if allowed to reach the floor. The leadership did not command the votes on the floor to bring out an alternative measure reported by the House Oversight Committee, because it lacked the votes to pass a rule for its consideration without also allowing a vote on Shays-Meehan.

Instead, the Speaker abandoned the idea of an open process with a rule, extensive debate, and amendments and chose four bills to take up but only under suspension, which ensured that no controversial matters could pass. Despite the protection of a two-thirds vote, he refused even to allow a vote on Shays-Meehan. Two minor bills did pass easily under suspension but

DILATORY TACTICS ARE LIMITED IN THE HOUSE

The House does not permit the range of dilatory tactics common in the Senate. This is due to its much larger size, which does not permit the same degree of recognition for the interests of individuals; its rules, which limit the ability of members to obtain the floor except for specified purposes and which provide several mechanisms for cutting off debate; and its traditions of bringing business to some conclusion.

The House has a number of rules and practices not used in the Senate that operate to restrict debate:

• The motion for ordering the previous question in the House, which, if adopted, ends all debate and forces an immediate vote.

• The "one-hour rule," which prevents any member from being recognized for more than one hour at a time for debate, or to call up legislation. Business directly before the House, such as a conference report or a special rule from the Rules Committee, can only be considered for one hour unless additional time is granted by unanimous consent, the "previous question" motion ending debate is defeated, or a special rule is passed extending debate time.

• The Rules Committee, which can bring before the House a resolution providing a special rule for a debate and amending process that limits opportunities for delay and can force the House to consider such a resolution.

• An 1890 rule that "no dilatory motion shall be entertained by the Speaker."[1] On January 31, 1890, Speaker Thomas B. Reed ruled: "The object of a parliamentary body is action, and not stoppage of action," in refusing to allow the House to consider a motion to adjourn, one of the few procedural matters directly mentioned in the Constitution. The prohibition also may be applied to other motions including appeals from the ruling of the chair as well as to amendments. Its application is extremely rare.

Despite its rules, the House does not always operate like clockwork. It is possible to delay proceedings by forcing electronic votes on matters that might not otherwise merit one, such as on the Speaker's approval of the *Journal*, or by offering and then forcing electronic votes on motions to adjourn, motions to table, ordering the previous question, moving to rise (end proceedings) in the Committee of the Whole, reconsidering actions taken by the House, and offering resolutions raising questions of the privileges of the House. Sometimes motions long forgotten or almost never seen on the floor, such as Texas Rep. Lloyd Doggett's 1997 motion to "reconsider the vote by which the yeas and nays were ordered" on a pending motion to adjourn, are resurrected to provide additional delaying tactics. Eventually, all of these options will be exhausted after some hours have elapsed and the House can conclude its legislative business.

In an extraordinary example of measures to ensure that the House can conduct its business, on October 8, 1968, the Speaker used his authority in the standing rules to order the doors of the chamber locked so that members could not leave while a quorum call was in progress. The House was attempting to complete the reading of the *Journal*, which had been demanded, so that it could move on to other business. During these proceedings, which lasted into the next day, thirty-three quorum calls delayed action. The House ultimately adopted a motion providing that the doors would be locked until the conclusion of the reading. Once a quorum had been established and with members locked in the chamber, the *Journal* was disposed of and the House got down to business.

Underlying the obscure parliamentary pyrotechnics were questions of the rawest politics. First, the minority Republicans wished to preserve their lead in the 1968 presidential election. Richard Nixon, the GOP nominee, was refusing televised debates with the Democratic candidate, Vice President Hubert Humphrey, and Democrats sought to embarrass Nixon.

The unsuccessful delaying tactics were intended to prevent consideration of a special rule, and, following that, a bill suspending the equal time requirements of the Communications Act of 1934, the enactment of which would have allowed Nixon and Humphrey to debate in the absence of other candidates. While the House went on to pass the bill it did not clear the Senate and was not enacted.

Second, the minority wanted to make a major issue of the Democrats' refusal to consider reform proposals recommended by a 1965–1966 joint committee on the reorganization of Congress prior to final adjournment. Their delaying tactics were a means to draw attention to that issue. (The legislation was not considered until the next Congress when the Legislative Reorganization Act of 1970 was passed.)

The potential for seemingly endless delay through repeated quorum calls was later eliminated by House rules changes in the 1970s.

When unanticipated delays arise, the majority can always employ the Rules Committee to remedy the situation. In 1997, the Democratic minority used delaying tactics on several occasions to signal its displeasure over what it considered the majority's failure to resolve the election challenge filed by former Rep. Robert K. Dornan, R-Calif., against Democrat Loretta Sanchez, who had defeated him in a close race in 1996. In November 1997, Democratic members announced their intention to present nearly two dozen consecutive privileged resolutions—each offered by a different member—in an effort to pressure the majority to dismiss the challenge. Pushing all of these resolutions out of the way, by moving to table each after it had been read but before any debate, would have disrupted the schedule of the House for a considerable period of time.

In a preemptive strike, the majority adopted a resolution from the Rules Committee barring such resolutions for the rest of the session unless offered by either the majority or minority leader. As expected, after its adoption the minority leader chose not to offer all of these resolutions himself. (The Democrats ultimately achieved their objective the following February when the election challenge was dismissed.)

1. Asher C. Hinds, ed. *Hinds' Precedents of the House of Representatives*, vol. 5 (Washington, D.C.: Government Printing Office, 1907), sec. 5713, 358.

two others were overwhelmingly defeated, including the Republican-sponsored omnibus measure that received a humiliating seventy-four votes. With the four votes concluded, the Speaker claimed that he had carried out his commitment for a vote on campaign finance reform.

Instead of burying the issue, however, the plan backfired explosively, energizing a Democratic-sponsored discharge petition on campaign reform legislation that had been languishing for months without significant Republican support. In addition, as outraged Republicans began to sign the petition in the aftermath of the suspension fiasco, the number crept above 200 and it seemed possible that 218 names might quickly be obtained, repudiating the GOP leadership and handing a bipartisan coalition control of the issue on the floor. Gingrich quickly capitulated, promising a new vote on campaign reform under an open process if Republicans would abandon the discharge strategy.

District Day. Another special procedure allowing consideration of certain noncontroversial legislation is "District Day," which was once used to bring up bills under the jurisdiction of the District of Columbia Committee on the second and fourth Mondays of each month. That committee was abolished in 1995 and its legislative jurisdiction and special floor privileges were transferred to the Committee on Government Reform and Oversight. However, "District Day" had already effectively become an anachronism because the District of Columbia Committee reported few bills and the House often dispensed with consideration of legislative business or votes on Mondays, making any use of the special day potentially inconvenient. No bills were called up using District Day in the 104th Congress. The "suspension of the rules" process has become by far the more likely choice for bringing minor legislation affecting the nation's capital to the floor.

Privileged Matters

House Rule XIV provides a detailed order of business for the House each day, which has changed little since 1890. The rule (in slightly shortened form) reads as follows:

First. Prayer by the chaplain.
Second. Reading and approval of the Journal.
Third. The Pledge of Allegiance to the Flag.
Fourth. Correction of reference of public bills.
Fifth. Disposal of business on the Speaker's table.
Sixth. Unfinished business.
Seventh. The morning hour for the consideration of bills called up by committees.
Eighth. Motions to go into Committee of the Whole House on the State of the Union.
Ninth. Orders of the day.

The House routinely ignores this order of business because over time many elements of the rule have become obsolete or different practices more efficiently accomplish the objectives. For example, the morning hour has not been used for decades, and the House, while it often resolves into the Committee of the Whole to debate and amend legislation, arrives there in a manner different from that contemplated by the rule.

The only elements of the order of business that always occur in the House are the first, second, and third. After that, other rules procedures, such as motions to suspend the rules, or special orders of business from the Rules Committee, are used to determine the House's actual agenda. In addition, other informal practices, such as the period at the beginning of the day when the Speaker, at his discretion, recognizes members to speak for one minute, occur routinely but are not mentioned in Rule XIV.

The House operates by putting aside formal rules and making in order other matters in their place. Some observers have described this as the use of "privileged interruptions" in the order of business. This new business derives from the use of other rules of the House, or through the use of resolutions from the Rules Committee, to make legislation "privileged" for consideration, which means it cannot be stopped simply by the objection of a single member. The House must then decide whether it wants to conduct this privileged business. But assuming it does, legislation comes up for debate and votes.

In the House, the term "privilege" may have several meanings. The House's standing rules create privilege for certain measures or motions to come up on the floor, which might depend on the subject matter of the legislation, the committee reporting the measure, or both. For example, general appropriations bills that are reported from the Appropriations Committee may simply be placed before the House, requiring some action be taken as a result. The class of such privileged matters is relatively small compared to the total number of measures that the House considers each year. A bill revising criminal laws, on the other hand, is not privileged because neither the subject matter itself nor the committee that reported it—in this case, Judiciary—have been given any special recognition in the rules for such a purpose. Such a bill may not be brought up unless the rules are suspended to allow it to interrupt the order of business, or unless the House adopts a resolution reported from the Rules Committee to make it privileged. Such a resolution is called a "special rule" or a "rule providing a special order of business." (Not to be confused with "special orders," the speeches members give at the end of a day's session.)

In some cases, not only can committees call up bills they have reported without going first to the Rules Committee, but they can create and report out a measure without even introducing it first. Under House rules, these committees have "leave to report at any time."

Among the most significant types of legislation in this category are:

• General appropriations bills, as well as continuing appropriations resolutions reported after September 15.

• Concurrent budget resolutions reported by the Budget Committee in accordance with the Congressional Budget and Impoundment Control Act of 1974.

• Resolutions providing biennial committee funding and disposing of House election contests reported by the House Administration Committee.

• Measures amending the rules of the House, or providing a "special order" for future consideration of a bill on the floor, reported by the Rules Committee.

• Resolutions dealing with ethics complaints against members reported by the Committee on Standards of Official Conduct.

Most privileged measures must lie over for some short period of time after they have been reported. This includes, for example, one day in the case of special rules from the Rules Committee and committee funding resolutions, and three days for general appropriations bills and the concurrent budget resolution, to give members an awareness of the contents and an opportunity to read the committee report on the legislation.

While "privilege" may convey status to a committee, it does not necessarily automatically convey additional power or political advantage on the floor. Indeed, the Ways and Means Committee lost its power to report legislation as privileged in 1975, but the committee has not suffered a loss in power as a result.

Certain other legislative matters in the House also are considered privileged and may be called up quickly. In this category, for example, are conference reports (after a three-day layover) and any bill vetoed by the president and returned to the House, which may be called up immediately for disposition.

Although a rule is not required to bring privileged legislation to the floor, the managers will often seek a rule anyway to waive the time layover requirements, eliminate points of order that might be lodged against the bill, and restrict or prevent the offering of floor amendments. Appropriations bills, for example, frequently contain authorizing language, which violates House rules. A waiver protects such language from a point of order, which, if upheld, would have allowed any single member to strike the provision.

To prevent floor amendments from unraveling compromises on complex legislation, committees routinely seek rules that permit only specified amendments to be offered on the floor. The Budget Committee, for example, effectively abandoned use of its power to call up budget resolutions as privileged in 1980 because the resolutions would be subjected to perfecting amendments in the Committee of the Whole on virtually any subject large or small without effective restrictions and could remain on the floor for weeks at a time. Instead, using the Rules Committee the leadership can usually pass the measure in only a day or two. Invariably it obtains a rule barring all amendments except a handful of complete substitute budgets offered by the minority party, the Congressional Black Caucus, a coalition of conservative members, supporters of a return to the "Gold Standard," and other identifiable groups. A common tactic used in the 1990s by both parties to embarrass the administration in power was to prepare a substitute labeled as the "president's budget," offer it as an amendment, and then watch it suffer overwhelming defeat.

The increasing use of the Rules Committee to protect even privileged legislation from points of order and a potentially lengthy amendment process is one of the most significant developments of the last two decades. It represents an increase in the ability of House leaders to exert control over virtually every committee and a corresponding loss of power by the House membership at large to alter legislation once it reaches the floor.

Gone are the days when the chairmen of the thirteen appropriations subcommittees, the so-called "College of Cardinals," would pride themselves on drafting their own bills, bringing them to the floor without a rule or consultation with the Speaker, and managing them as they saw fit. Floor time is too limited, and the potential for embarrassing surprises too great, for the kind of uncertainty this style of committee independence might generate, and the majority party has increasingly sought to structure floor action around its agenda rather than the longstanding traditions of committees or the egos of chairmen. In 1997, at a leadership meeting, Speaker Gingrich was reported to have upbraided Appropriations Committee Chairman Bob Livingston, R-La., for allowing a subcommittee chairman, Rep. Sonny Callahan, R-Ala., to make policy decisions on the bill he managed without approval of the leadership. Just a few years earlier, such criticism by a Speaker, along with the concept that the full committee chairman should control a subcommittee chairman, would have been considered an unprecedented assault on the integrity of the Appropriations Committee.

Major Legislation and the Rules Committee

Virtually all major legislation, including privileged bills and any measure considered controversial, is routed through the Rules Committee before going to the floor. The purpose is twofold. First, a special rule makes a bill in order for floor consideration even though it is not at the top of whichever calendar it is on. It might not ordinarily be considered at all without a rule. If bills were called in the order in which they appeared on the House calendars, much significant legislation would never reach the House floor. Second, the special rule sets out the guidelines for floor debate and amendment on the legislation.

Because it controls the flow of legislation from the committees to the full House, the power of the Rules Committee is considerable and its role in the legislative process crucial. The Rules Committee chairman, who is the Speaker's personal choice for the post, has wide discretion in arranging the panel's agenda. The chairman may call an "emergency meeting" of the committee whenever he or she wishes. Scheduling—or not scheduling—a Rules hearing on a bill usually determines whether it ever comes before the House for debate.

In the past the committee has used that power to kill bills it opposed even though they were supported by the majority leadership and a majority of the House. Since the House reforms of the 1970s, however, the Rules Committee has become an arm of the majority leadership and usually works with the Speaker and majority leader to expedite action on measures the leadership favors and to delay or modify measures that might not have sufficient support to pass or have other political problems. The committee and the leadership also consult often on the terms of debate and amendment that will be allowed for each bill.

The House Rules Committee meets in 1997. The Rules Committee has considerable power in controlling the flow of legislation from the committees to the full House.

Rules Committee Hearings. Usually the chairman of the committee or subcommittee that reported a bill requests a rule, technically a House resolution specifying a "special order of business." At Rules Committee hearings the chairman of the legislative committee, supported by the bill's sponsors and other committee members, proposes a rule to the Rules Committee. Members who oppose the bill or who want to offer floor amendments to it also may testify.

Rules Committee hearings also serve as a dress rehearsal for the bill's floor managers. As political scientist Bruce I. Oppenheimer has pointed out, "The Rules Committee dress rehearsal gives them a chance to make errors and recover before going to the floor."[10]

Drafting the Rule. All rules limit the time for general debate on the House floor. The time permitted varies (it is often one hour equally divided between the two parties), depending largely on the extent of controversy surrounding a bill. Many rules also waive points of order against certain provisions of the bill or against specified amendments that are expected to be offered on the floor. This waiver permits the House to violate its own rules by barring any objections to such matters.

During the 1980s the committee granted an increasing number of "blanket waivers," barring all points of order that might be raised against a particular bill. Most blanket waivers were granted for conference reports and for omnibus bills. The committee justified the increase by pointing to the growing number and complexity of procedural requirements, such as those added by the Gramm-Rudman-Hollings deficit reduction law, which made it difficult to specify exactly which rules needed to be waived. Failure to waive a specific rule would give opponents of the bill an opening to challenge it.

Republicans, when in the minority in the House, expressed their displeasure with the trend toward blanket waivers. They "are indicative of the [majority] leadership's willingness to per-

mit committees to circumvent and violate House rules in order to advance their legislative agenda," Rep. Trent Lott, R-Miss., himself a member of the Rules Committee, said in December 1977.[11] Nonetheless, Republicans often did support such waivers when passage of an essential bill, such as a continuing appropriations resolution, was at issue. When Republicans assumed control of the House in 1995, they quickly discovered the wisdom of the approach they previously had so roundly criticized.

Rules also govern amending activity on the floor. The committee traditionally grants three kinds of rules affecting amendments: open, closed, or modified. These terms are not defined in the rules of the House or of the committee, are often used colloquially, and can have different meanings depending on the circumstances and the opinion of the person using the term. An "open" rule usually permits any germane amendment to be offered on the floor at the appropriate time. A rule that bars all amendments, or all but committee amendments, is referred to as "closed," or often pejoratively by its opponents, as a "gag" rule. A "modified" rule generally permits amendments only to certain provisions or sections of the bill, or to specific subjects dealt with in the bill, or only allows certain specific amendments. Sometimes the terms "modified open" and "modified closed" are used as well, and the difference is usually in the eye of the beholder.

Shift toward Restrictive Rules

Until the 1980s the vast majority of rules were open. Closed rules were generally reserved for tax bills and other measures too complicated or technical to be tampered with on the House floor. But in the 1970s a number of developments led the Rules Committee to begin to draft more modified rules that specified which amendments could be offered and often stipulated in what order they would be considered.

For one thing, the decision to allow recorded votes on floor amendments significantly increased the number of amend-

The House and Senate have each developed their own procedures for voting. Guiding them are voting rules spelled out in the Constitution. Most specific are requirements for roll-call votes: "The yeas and nays of the members of either house on any question shall, at the desire of one fifth of those present, be entered on the Journal." This provision also is aimed at preventing secret ballots. It is in the Constitution at Article I, Section 5, Clause 3.

HOUSE

The House has also developed a complex set of rules governing how members make demands on the House floor to have their votes recorded. The House regularly uses three types of votes: Voice, division, and votes recorded by the name of the member ("yeas and nays" or "recorded vote"). Often, the House takes several votes on the same proposition, using the most simple method first and then increasingly more complex voting methods, before a decision is reached. *(See "Action in the Committee of the Whole," p. 502.)*

A voice vote is the quickest method of voting and the type nearly always used first when a proposition is first put to the membership. The presiding officer calls for the "ayes" and then the "noes," members shout in chorus on one side or the other, and the chair decides the result.

If the result of a voice vote is in doubt or a single member requests a further test, a division, or standing vote, may be demanded. In this case those in favor of the proposal and then those against it stand up while the chair takes a head count. Only vote totals are announced; there is no record of how individual members voted. Few issues are decided by division vote. After a voice vote, members will usually skip it and ask for a vote in which members are recorded by name. This kind of vote, which is nearly always taken using the electronic voting system, draws many more members to the chamber. It is called "the yeas and nays" or a "recorded vote" depending on the circumstances in which it is taken, but the result is identical.

Since 1973 the House has used an electronic voting system for recording members' votes. Members insert white plastic cards into one of forty-four voting stations mounted on the backs of chairs along the aisles of the House chamber. When a member punches a button to indicate his position, a giant electronic board behind the Speaker's desk immediately flashes green for "yes" and red for "no" next to the legislator's name. Members may also vote "present," which shows up as a yellow light on the board. Members may change their votes at any time until the result is announced. The Speaker may vote on any matter but, by tradition, rarely does.

The "yeas and nays," provided for by the Constitution, is used only when the House itself is sitting, and never in the Committee of the Whole. This method of voting may be ordered by one-fifth of those present regardless of how few members are actually on the floor. House rules also provide that it may occur automatically whenever a quorum is not present on the floor when the question is put and any member objects to the vote on those grounds. The resulting vote both establishes a quorum and settles the question at issue.

A "recorded vote," provided for by House rules, may be demanded both in the House and in the Committee of the Whole, but it works differently in each case. In the House, it may be ordered upon demand of one-fifth of a quorum of 218, which is forty-four. For example, as a matter of strategy, a member would demand a recorded vote, rather than the yeas and nays, whenever a majority of the members was present on the floor because the requisite number (forty-four) would always be less than one-fifth of those present. In the Committee of the Whole a "recorded vote" is always ordered by twenty-five members.

Once any vote by electronic device begins members have fifteen minutes to record their votes, although an additional two minutes is usually allowed to accommodate latecomers. The voting time is often shortened to five minutes, if a number of votes have been clustered, for each vote beyond the first one; again, an additional two minutes may be allowed. Regardless of the time limit, any member who is in the chamber at the time the result is to be announced has the right to record a vote, or to change one already cast. Once the result has been announced, however, the vote is closed and members may not subsequently vote or change their votes, even by unanimous consent. Often members who miss a vote will insert statements in the *Congressional Record* immediately following the missed vote indicating what their position would have been, though there is no requirement that they do so.

Until 1971, the "yeas and nays" were the only votes on which House members were individually recorded. Votes in the Committee of the Whole were taken by methods that did not record the stands of individual members. Many questions were decided by "teller votes" under which the chair appointed tellers representing opposite sides on a vote and directed members to pass between them up the center aisle to be counted—first the "ayes" and then the "noes." Only vote totals were announced on teller votes.

In the 1960s, members and outside interest groups began to object to unrecorded votes in the Committee of the Whole. They believed that members could not be held accountable for saying one thing to their constituents but voting the opposite way by tellers. Members could effectively hide their votes on key amendments, which were sometimes closely contested and usually determined the final form of the bill, while going on the record on the less controversial matter of final passage in the House. Liberals also believed that their views might have a better chance to prevail against established institutional power centers, which were more conservative, if members were forced to go on record.

"A member can vote for any number of amendments which may cripple a water pollution bill or render ineffective a civil rights bill or fail to provide adequate funding for hospital construction or programs for the elderly, and then he can turn around on final passage and vote for the bill he has just voted to emasculate by amendment," Wisconsin Democrat David R. Obey said of the voting system.

A provision of the Legislative Reorganization Act of 1970 opened the way for "tellers with clerks," more commonly called "recorded teller votes." This procedure, used in 1971 and 1972, made it possible to record the votes of individual members in the Committee of the Whole. When the change first went into effect, members were required to write their names on red or green cards, which they handed to tellers. The consequence of the rules change was very swift; many more members appeared for these votes because absentees could now be noted by name in the *Congressional Record*. After the electronic voting system was installed in 1973, the recorded teller vote process became known simply as a recorded vote. The advent of recorded teller votes, and then the electronic voting system, rendered the old unrecorded teller votes essentially obsolete. However, unrecorded teller voting still remained as a potential fallback option in the rules until its formal abolition in 1993.

When members' votes first began to be recorded in the Committee of the Whole on amendments and other motions, only twenty members were required to stand and demand a recorded vote. This number was later raised to twenty-five in 1979 after some members complained that it was too easy to force votes. But there has been no evidence that the change to twenty-five made any significant difference.

In the Committee of the Whole, unlike the House, there is no means to force a vote automatically by claiming that a quorum (100) is not present; in such cases, a member usually will demand a recorded vote and, pending that, make the point of order that a quorum is not present. By doing so the member gains time to ensure the presence of at least twenty-five supporters when the chair announces whether sufficient support exists for a recorded vote. If a quorum is not present, the chairman will order a quorum call to establish one before determining whether twenty-five members will support the demand for a recorded vote. The chairman has two choices: to order a regular quorum call, which summons all 435 members, whose names are recorded in the *Congressional Record* after the vote; or a "notice quorum call," in which the chair simply stops the proceedings after 100 members have responded and no permanent record of those responding is kept.

In many cases, to save time, enough members will rise informally to indicate their support for a recorded vote while the chair is still counting for a quorum; the point of no quorum will then be withdrawn and a recorded vote will occur. If both the quorum call and then the recorded vote are used the quorum call will be fifteen minutes long, followed, if ordered, by a recorded vote, which the chairman may reduce to five minutes.

Before the electronic voting system was installed, yeas and nays were taken by calling the roll, a time-consuming process in the 435-member House. Each roll call took about half an hour. The Speaker still retains the right to call the roll rather than use the electronic voting system. The old-fashioned method is used when the electronic system breaks down, as it does from time to time. An archaic provision still exists in the rules that allows the Speaker to direct the clerk to "tell" the members by name in the House. In addition, on the opening day of each Congress the clerk calls each member by name to elect a Speaker, since members shout out the name of the person they support. Usually there are only two candidates, one Republican and one Democrat, but the 1997 election was unusual as four Republican members voted for persons other than Speaker Newt Gingrich for reelection because of ethics controversies surrounding him at the time. They voted either for another sitting Republican member or for former House members.

Use of the electronic voting system opened the possibility of "ghost voting" in which an absent member gave his voting card to a colleague. Such instances are exceedingly rare but the House has banned the practice by rule and has disciplined members suspected of violations.

No member may be deprived of his or her right to vote. House rules direct members to refrain from voting on an issue on the House floor if they have a conflict of interest, and also admonish members in a "Code of Official Conduct" (House rule XXIV of the 106th Congress) not to vote on the floor or in committees if they have been convicted of crimes for which a sentence of two or more years imprisonment may be imposed. Compliance with these rules is strictly at the discretion of the member affected; however, convicted members who have continued to vote in such circumstances have been threatened with expulsion.

SENATE

Only two types of votes are in everyday use in the Senate—voice votes and roll-call votes ("yeas and nays"). Standing votes are seldom employed. The Senate does not use the teller vote and has no electronic voting system.

As in the House, the most common method of deciding issues is by voice vote. The presiding officer determines the outcome. Under the Constitution, one-fifth of the senators present must support a demand for a roll call. (Unlike the House, the Senate assumes that an actual quorum—fifty-one—is present when this demand is being made, so a minimum of eleven senators must rise in support. When a request for a roll call occurs immediately after a roll call or a live quorum call has occurred, the number needed is one-fifth of the senators who actually responded, to a maximum of twenty. Informal practices have evolved in which a vote may be ordered by the chair if only a few senators are present and the two parties' floor managers agree.)

Unlike the House, where a demand for a roll-call vote comes only when debate has been concluded and the chair has put the question, senators may demand the yeas and nays on pending business at a time long in advance of the vote. The Senate usually allows fifteen minutes for a roll-call vote, although unanimous consent requests may shorten the voting time in specific situations. The fifteen-minute period also may be extended to accommodate late-arriving senators. Senators who miss a vote cannot be recorded after the result has been announced. However, unlike the House, a senator who voted but was not recorded or was incorrectly recorded may, by unanimous consent, have the proper vote recorded if it would not change the result.

ments offered. Before 1971 only vote totals, not individual votes by members, were recorded on floor amendments in the Committee of the Whole, which made members much more accountable to their colleagues than to their constituents. Once their votes were routinely made public, however, members found it to their advantage to offer and vote for amendments their constituents supported even if those amendments were opposed by the reporting committee. Activist junior Republicans also took advantage of recorded votes to force the Democrats to vote repeatedly on politically sensitive issues such as abortion.

The erosion of seniority and the rise of subcommittees also had its effects. When most bills were managed by the chairman of the committee reporting the bill, or his or her designee, rank-and-file members tended to accept committee bills on the floor, in part because the chairman, and often others on the committee, had developed expertise in the subject area and because members might need cooperation from the chairman in the future. With the increase in the importance of subcommittees in the late 1970s, many bills came to be managed on the House floor by junior members often inexperienced in House procedure and without acknowledged expertise in the subject matter. In these situations, rank-and-file members were less inclined to defer to the subcommittee's judgment and more likely to offer amendments of their own on the House floor.

Consequently, the number of amendments offered on the floor increased substantially. According to political scientists Stanley Bach and Steven S. Smith, the number of floor amendments more than doubled, from 792 in the 92nd Congress (1971–1973) to 1,695 in the 95th Congress (1977–1979) before beginning to decline again.[12] And with this explosion of amendments the Democratic leadership and bill managers found it more and more difficult to know what was likely to be offered on the floor, whether it would win, and how long the whole process might take.

This pressure to regain control over the amending process was reinforced by several other developments.

First, the decision to allow a bill to be referred to more than one committee created a need for mechanisms by which conflicting recommendations could be resolved on the House floor in an orderly fashion. Bills that have been referred to more than one legislative committee can present special problems to the Rules Committee, particularly if the legislative committees report conflicting provisions. To prevent divisiveness, embarrassment, and perhaps defeat on the House floor, Rules will often ask the committees to try to negotiate their differences before a rule is granted. The resulting compromise, rather than the original reported legislation, is then made the basic legislation to be debated and amended on the House floor. This is called "an amendment in the nature of a substitute considered as original text." If negotiations are unsuccessful, the Rules Committee may write a rule that allows members to vote on the alternatives.

Second, many members were eager to open Ways and Means Committee bills, which had traditionally been considered under closed rules, to at least some adjustment on the floor. In 1973 the Democratic Caucus began to require committee chairmen to give advance notice in the *Congressional Record* whenever they intended to seek a closed rule. The caucus also adopted a rule allowing it to instruct Democrats on Rules to vote to make certain specific amendments in order during floor consideration. But after a brief flurry of activity in the 1970s, the power fell into disuse as the Rules Committee became a reliable arm of the party leadership and, as such, more representative of the views of the majority of the caucus.

Third, the increased partisanship in the House beginning in the 1970s erased earlier norms that had inhibited members of the minority from offering controversial proposals purely to embarrass the opposition. These votes created a record that could be attacked by interest groups in their "voting scorecards" and related materials disseminated to their membership. The majority, while it could not prevent all such votes, sometimes moved to restrict amendments to limit the damage.

Fourth, the increased political independence of members from their political parties, and the need to maintain a fund-raising apparatus, encouraged more members to freelance on the floor by offering amendments that might give them greater visibility. In many cases, while such amendments might have accomplished the objectives these members desired, they also might not contribute much of substance to the bill and could delay and distract the House, and the Rules Committee moved to limit them.

As a result of all these factors, the Rules Committee began to draft more rules controlling the amendment process. In the 95th Congress (1977–1979) only 15 percent of the rules reported to the House were closed or restrictive; by the end of the 101st Congress (1989–1991), that number had risen to 55 percent. As part of their broader critique of Democratic dominance of the chamber, Republicans attacked the majority constantly for using restrictive rules to stifle debate and block amendments. Rules that were defined as not being "open" became objects of opprobrium in a battle of dueling statistics, even though use of modified or closed rules might have been appropriate given the complexity and politics surrounding a particular bill.

In the 104th Congress, with a Republican-controlled Rules Committee, the new majority trumpeted important victories for openness in House procedures during consideration of its critical "Contract with America" bills, claiming to have issued open rules 72 percent of the time. The Democratic minority, however, responded that the correct figure was 26 percent. Predictably, each side differed on the definition of "openness" and which legislation should be included in the statistics.

The kinds of restrictive rules vary considerably. The Rules Committee may simply require that amendments will be in order only if they have been printed in the *Congressional Record* in advance of the debate. This practice may actually increase the number of amendments rather than reduce them. "When you see you are fixin' to be cut off and not be able to have an opportunity to offer an amendment you start conjuring up all possible

Pairing was a device members of Congress used to indicate how they would have voted on an issue. Normally, it came into play when a member was absent during a roll call but wanted his position on record. It was accomplished by having the name of a member printed in the *Congressional Record* indicating his position and being "paired" with another member on the opposite side of the issue.

The use of this device was altered in the House under rule changes in 1999. The changes did away with pairing except for so-called live pairs where one of the members was actually present during the vote. The use of pairs continued in the Senate but rarely occurred.

In the past pairs were often considered "gentlemen's agreements" that House and Senate members used to cancel out the effect of absences on recorded votes. *Cannon's Procedure in the House of Representatives* notes that pairs are voluntary agreements between members: "The rules do not specifically authorize them and the House does not interpret or construe them or consider complaints arising out of their violation. Such questions must be determined by the interested members themselves individually."

Two types of pairs were used. A live pair involved a member who was present for a vote and another who was absent. The member in attendance voted and then withdrew the vote, announcing that he or she had a live pair with an absent colleague and stating how the two members would have voted, one in favor, the other opposed. In modern practice, live pairs appeared from time to time in the Senate but were rare in the House. A senator would withdraw his vote, vote "present," and announce he was granting a live pair to accommodate an absent colleague, who is identified by name.

In a specific pair, members in the House and Senate who anticipated being absent notified their cloakrooms and asked to be paired with another absent member on the opposite side of the issue. The staffs developed the pairings, and then the opposing stands of the two members were identified and printed in the *Record*. In the 1999 rules changes, the House abolished use of specific pairs while allowing live pairs to continue.

Pairs were not counted in vote totals. If the vote was one that required a two-thirds majority, creation of a live or specific pair required two members favoring the pending matter and one opposed to it.

Because they were printed in the *Congressional Record* and had a long tradition, specific pairs remained in use even though they had no more weight than any other method of announcing a member's position. A member can ask unanimous consent to insert a statement in the *Record* directly after a vote indicating how he or she would have voted, which is a common practice.

WHEN PAIRS MATTERED

A live pair in the Senate may affect the outcome of a closely contested vote because it subtracts one "yea" or one "nay" from the final tally. In 1986, the "gentleman's agreement" of pairing crashed into hardball politics in a combination of circumstances that result-

ed in the confirmation of Daniel A. Manion as a federal appellate judge.

Manion's nomination reached the floor only after the Judiciary Committee reported it "without recommendation." Senators filibustering against the nomination thought they had a majority and unexpectedly offered to allow an immediate vote to occur. Majority Leader Bob Dole, R-Kan., agreed after three senators opposed to the nomination—Joseph Biden, D-Del., ranking minority member of the committee; Daniel Inouye, D-Hawaii; and Nancy Landon Kassebaum, R-Kan.—were persuaded to grant live pairs to absent Republicans Bob Packwood, Ore., Paula Hawkins, Fla., and Barry Goldwater, Ariz., who, they were told, favored the nomination.

Unexpectedly, Slade Gorton, R-Wash., an expected opponent, voted to confirm Manion after he received a phone call from the White House during the vote promising to nominate a candidate he wanted for a federal district judgeship. Shocked opponents realized too late that their earlier firm majority had been picked apart as the nominee appeared headed for confirmation in a tie vote. Vice President George Bush was available to cast the potential tie-breaking vote in Manion's favor. However, none backed out of their pairs. Minority Leader Robert C. Byrd, D-W.Va., an opponent, switched to vote for Manion to make the final tally 48–46. Byrd, by voting on the prevailing side, was then eligible to move to reconsider the vote, hoping that once the situation had sorted itself out and absentees had returned confirmation could be undone on a later date. Under Senate rules, the confirmation vote was not considered final until that motion was disposed of.

The pairs became controversial because two of the Republican absentees later claimed to have been undecided, even though Manion opponents had been paired with them. Democrats claimed the "gentlemen's agreement" had been abused by the GOP leadership to mislead senators.

When the motion to reconsider was taken up the senators who had granted live pairs to Manion supporters were now free to vote as they wished but the same factors came into play to thwart them yet again. Packwood announced that he opposed Manion and supported reconsideration, Hawkins supported Manion and opposed reconsideration, while Goldwater was again absent but announced his opposition to reconsideration. However, he persuaded his home state colleague, Democrat Dennis DeConcini, who favored reconsideration, to grant him a live pair. Daniel J. Evans, R-Wash., who had voted against confirmation, voted not to reconsider, effectively reversing his position. The result was another tie which, with the final but unneeded addition of Bush's negative vote, produced a 49–50 vote against reconsideration.

Thus, due to incredible luck, skillful manipulation of the pairing process, and senators' reliance on personal relationships with colleagues, Manion was confirmed to a lifetime judicial appointment even though a majority of senators was actually opposed to his nomination.

amendments and you put them in the *Record*," Lott said.[13] But advance notice does help the leadership anticipate floor action and develop strategy to deal with it.

Structured Rules. A structured rule is a rule that can have many different forms. It usually can be anything other than a simple open rule but its principal purpose is to supply a sense of order on the floor as amendments are offered and debated in the Committee of the Whole. Such rules may specify the amendments that can be offered, by whom, and, sometimes, in what order they will be considered. Structured rules may also set time limits on debate for the amendments. Most such rules are restrictive in that they prevent members from offering some amendments. However, structured rules may also be expansive, by making it in order for the House to consider amendments that are not germane to the bill. They may attempt to focus debate around entire substitutes for a bill, rather than numerous minor perfecting amendments; this invariably happens during consideration of the congressional budget resolution, since debate there deals with broad issues of policy and philosophy rather than the nuts and bolts of programs.

While some structured rules are clearly written to give an edge to the legislative proposal preferred by the majority leadership, many of these rules are intended primarily as a way to organize debate on the House floor and to ensure that members are given an opportunity to debate the major amendments and alternatives to a particular bill. In these cases, Bach and Smith have written, "the intent of special rules is to minimize uncertainty about process, not about policy—to control in advance what alternatives will be presented, not what the final shape of the legislation will be."[14]

"King-of-the-Hill" Rules. One of the newer and more creative of the restrictive rules is known as the "king-of-the-hill" or "king-of-the-mountain" rule. It makes in order a series of alternatives to the bill under consideration and provides that even if a majority votes for two or more of the alternatives, only the last one voted on wins.

This procedure circumvents House rules that prohibit amending any portion of a bill that has already been amended. Under the normal rules, if a substitute for a bill is offered and adopted as an amendment, further substitutes or other amendments are precluded and the House moves to final passage. But king-of-the-hill rules allow amendments to continue to be offered.

In cases where the alternative favored by the majority leadership is sure of winning, this procedure provides a means to satisfy various factions within the House by letting them present, and the members vote on, their alternatives. In cases where the outcome is uncertain, positioning the preferred alternative last can give it an edge over its competitors.

"Queen-of-the-Hill" Rules. A king-of-the-hill variation first used in the 104th Congress is sometimes referred to as the "queen-of-the-hill" or "top-vote-getter" rule. As in king-of-the-hill, several substitutes for a bill can be voted on in succession, and a majority vote for any one of them does not result in the

In 1973 the House began using an electronic voting system. Members insert plastic cards in the voting boxes at forty-four stations throughout the chamber and vote "aye," "no," or "present." Their votes are displayed on the wall above the House gallery (top).

termination of the amending process. However, instead of endorsing the last such amendment considered that received a majority, under queen-of-the-hill rules, the amendment that passed with the largest number of affirmative votes, after voting on all substitutes, prevails. If two amendments received an equal number of affirmative votes, the last one voted on wins.

Rules Committee Chairman Gerald Solomon, R-N.Y., argued that king-of-the-hill was flawed because it "allowed lawmakers to be on both sides of an issue and violated the democratic principle that the position with the strongest support should prevail."[15] However, it also could be argued that the new procedure represented less of an innovation than a reaction by the Republican majority against previous Democratic use of king-of-the-hill rules.

Queen-of-the-hill rules, similar to "king-of-the-hill" rules, allow the leadership to appease various factions and allow members to vote on various sides of a question. For example, during consideration in 1997 of a constitutional amendment limiting the number of years a member could serve in Congress, eleven substitute amendments were made in order under the queen-of-the-hill process precisely so that members from particular states could vote for the congressional term limit scheme adopted by those states. (Attempts by states to limit the terms of members of Congress by statute were later thrown out by the U.S. Supreme Court, thus necessitating a change in the U.S. Constitution to accomplish the purpose.) All of the substitutes were rejected, as was the constitutional amendment itself.

Self-Executing Rules. Another innovative mechanism that Rules began to use in the 1980s was the self-executing rule, under which adoption of the rule also resulted in adoption of an amendment or amendments. Self-executing rules were devised originally to expedite consideration of Senate-passed amendments to House bills and to make technical corrections, but they have also been used to enact more substantive and controversial measures.

In 1987, for example, a vote for a rule on a continuing appropriations resolution also had the effect of exempting members of Congress from a controversial pay raise. A vote for a rule on another continuing resolution earlier in the year was also a vote to provide $3.5 billion in humanitarian assistance to Nicaraguan contras fighting the Sandinista government there. The move, which was supported by the leadership of both parties, avoided a direct vote on the controversial issue of continued aid to the contras. The rule was adopted by voice vote.

In 1990, passage of a conference report on a major immigration bill was unexpectedly threatened when opposition developed to one of its provisions, leading to defeat of the rule. A second rule was then prepared and passed that self-executed adoption of a concurrent resolution changing the offending section of the conference report. Once the Senate sent a message that it had adopted the concurrent resolution, the conference report, as newly modified, was immediately available under the terms of the rule for consideration in the House. It then passed.

HOUSE FLOOR PROCEDURES

Procedural differences between the House and Senate are most visible on the chamber floors. Because of its size the House adheres strictly to detailed procedures for considering legislation. These procedures, which limit debate on bills and amendments, are designed to ensure majority rule and to expedite action. Although the opposition can slow legislation from time to time in the House, it usually cannot impede it altogether. In contrast, the much smaller Senate emphasizes minority rights and virtually unlimited debate.

The House tends to operate on a Monday-to-Thursday schedule, with Mondays reserved primarily for noncontroversial legislation considered under shortcut procedures such as suspension of the rules. Sessions occasionally are scheduled for Friday, but that day is often left free so that legislators can return to their districts for the weekend.

Meeting times now vary. Daily sessions may begin at any hour, although earlier daily meetings are common as a session progresses. The day opens with a prayer and the pledge of allegiance, followed by approval of the Journal. Often a member demands a roll-call vote on approval of the Journal. This request may be dilatory in nature, or it may serve to determine which members are present. Once the Journal has been approved, the Speaker recognizes members for one-minute speeches and submission of material to be inserted in the *Congressional Record*. Messages from the president and the Senate are received.

Once this preliminary business is concluded, the House turns to the legislative business of the day. If the House is to take up legislation under its shortcut procedures, it remains sitting as the House, with the Speaker presiding. The rules for considering and passing legislation under these expediting procedures have been described above. Most major legislation, however, comes to the House floor under a special rule and is subject to a much more elaborate procedure. The process involves four steps: adoption of the rule governing debate on the bill; general debate on the bill itself; consideration of any amendments by the Committee of the Whole; and final passage of the bill by the full House.

Adoption of the Rule

Floor action on a major House bill ordinarily begins when the Speaker recognizes the member of the Rules Committee who has been designated to call up the rule for the bill. The rule may be debated for up to one hour, with, by custom, half the time allotted to the minority party. A simple majority is sufficient to adopt a rule.

Rules are seldom rejected. In 1987 the House voted 203–217 to reject the rule for consideration of budget reconciliation legislation because it included the text of a major welfare reform bill. The Democratic leadership realized that it had made a political error by overloading the process with too many divisive issues at once. The Rules Committee immediately revised the rule by dropping the welfare provisions. However, under normal circumstances a rule may not be taken up the same day it is reported unless permitted by a two-thirds vote of the House, and in this case it was unlikely that a two-thirds vote could be mustered. In a rare parliamentary maneuver, Speaker Wright arranged a successful motion to adjourn the House, reconvening it one minute—and one legislative day—later. Although Republicans bitterly complained about Wright's tactics, the House adopted the revised rule.

Opponents may also seek to amend a rule by defeating the "previous question." The previous question, a parliamentary device used only in the full House, is a motion that, if adopted, cuts off all further debate and amendments and requires an immediate vote on the matter at hand. Routinely, the Rules Committee member handling the rule will move the previous question to bring the rule to a vote. If that motion is defeated, the rule is then open to amendment. However, the tactic is very rarely successful, since defeat of the previous question has the effect of turning control of the floor over to opponents of the rule, who are likely to be members from the minority. Even majority members opposed to a rule are loath to do that, preferring instead to vote against the rule itself and have the Rules Committee report out another, while retaining control of the process.

One of the most controversial recent instances of defeat of the previous question on a rule occurred in 1981, when a coalition of Republicans and conservative Democrats blocked a deficit reduction package pushed by the Democratic leadership and substituted instead an alternative containing many elements of President Reagan's legislative program, embodied in the so-called "Gramm-Latta" bill. This conservative coalition defeated the previous question, adopted an amendment to the rule, adopted the revised rule, and went on to successful passage of their version of the legislation. In some instances the leadership may not realize that a rule faces defeat until it actually is being debated on the floor. In 1999, for example, a rule for consideration of the Department of Defense authorization bill was withdrawn during debate when it became clear that defeat was possible.

Action in the Committee of the Whole

Once the rule has been adopted, the House resolves itself into the Committee of the Whole House on the State of the Union to debate and amend the legislation. Not a committee as the word is usually understood, the Committee of the Whole is rather a parliamentary framework to expedite House action. Although all 435 House members are members of the Committee of the Whole, business may be conducted with a quorum of 100 members rather than the 218 members required in the full House.

The Committee of the Whole has no counterpart in the Senate, although for many years the Senate had a "Committee of the Whole" to deal with treaties. The concept developed in the British House of Commons when the Speaker was once considered to be an agent of the king. During periods of strained relations between the king and the lower house of Parliament, the procedure allowed members of Commons to elect a chairman of their own and to discuss matters, particularly matters pertaining to the king's household expenses, without observing the normal restrictions that applied to a formal session of the House of Commons.

The Speaker does not preside over the Committee of the Whole but selects another member of the majority party to take the chair. The Mace is lowered from its position behind the Speaker's chair when the Committee of the Whole sits. *(See box, The House Mace, p. 48.)*

Amendments are debated in the Committee of the Whole under the five-minute rule, which in theory but not in practice limits debate to five minutes for and against the amendment. They may then be voted on by voice vote or by division (standing) vote. There is only one way to obtain a recorded vote on an amendment or any other matter in the Committee of the Whole, unlike the situation in the House, where there are several possibilities. Twenty-five members must stand in support of a demand for a "recorded vote" in the Committee of the Whole. If a quorum is not present a quorum call may be demanded to bring additional members to the floor. To avoid using this time members will often routinely grant a colleague a recorded vote even on matters that have little substantive support. *(See box, Methods of Voting in the House and Senate, p. 496.)*

The Committee of the Whole cannot pass a bill. Instead it reports the measure back to the full House with whatever changes it has made. The House then may adopt or reject the Committee of the Whole's proposed amendments, amend a bill further through a motion to recommit with instructions, recommit it to the legislative committee where it originated, and finally, if the bill is still on the floor, pass or reject it.

Amendments adopted in the Committee of the Whole are always put to a second vote in the full House, which is usually a pro forma voice vote with all amendments considered en bloc. However, if the initial vote on an amendment in the Committee of the Whole was very close, the second vote in the House also may be a recorded vote as the losing side seeks to change the outcome. Sometimes proponents of an adopted amendment will attempt to discourage such reconsideration in the House, or express their displeasure, by threatening to demand recorded votes on all amendments reported back to the House, even of the most minor nature.

In 1993, Republicans led by Rules Committee ranking member Gerald Solomon of New York instituted a practice of demanding a separate recorded vote in the House on every amendment passed by a recorded vote in the Committee of the Whole. They objected to a new House rule passed at the beginning of that Congress granting the four delegates and the resident commissioner from Puerto Rico, all of whom sat with the Democratic Caucus, the right to vote in the Committee of the Whole even though the rule prevented their votes from affecting the outcome. However, these five could not vote in the full House. The minority demanded that more than sixty such votes be rerun without them after the Committee of the Whole rose to report its actions to the House. It desisted only after a federal appeals court ruled that the delegates' participation was constitutional. (A Republican-controlled House revoked these special voting rights in 1995.)

The Committee of the Whole itself may not recommit a bill, although it may recommend to the full House that the enacting clause be stricken—a parliamentary motion that, if adopted, kills the measure. However, the motion to strike the enacting clause is almost never successful, since members desiring to kill the underlying legislation can express themselves more clearly by defeating the rule prior to its consideration, or the bill itself on final passage. The motion to strike the enacting clause is sometimes made anyway because it guarantees five minutes of debate to the maker even under circumstances when debate may not be in order. After the member finishes, he or she withdraws the motion by unanimous consent without a vote. Recommittal must be voted on in the House rather than in the Committee of the Whole.

General Debate

After resolving into the Committee of the Whole, the first order of business is general debate on the bill. General debate, as Oleszek noted, serves both practical and symbolic purposes: complicated or controversial provisions of the legislation may be explained, a legislative record developed for the administrative agencies that administer the bill and the courts that interpret it, a public record built for legislators to campaign on. In the process, Oleszek wrote, general debate "assures both legislators and the public that the House makes its decisions in a democratic fashion with due respect for majority and minority opinion."[16]

But he and other congressional observers have questioned whether general debate actually influences members' views and policy outcomes in an era when there is little time to sit on the House floor or watch the proceedings on television. A 1992 examination of floor procedures by a group of scholars led by Thomas Mann and Norman Ornstein concluded that "General

FORCING A HOUSE VOTE CAN BE CONFUSING

In the House, members who desire a vote in which members are recorded by electronic device on a pending matter can usually get it in one of three ways: by objecting to a vote on the grounds that a quorum is not present; by asking for a recorded vote; or by asking for the "yeas and nays." However, sometimes this may not be as easy as it seems. There are circumstances in which it actually does matter which request is made. (Voting procedures in the Committee of the Whole are different.) *(See box, "Methods of Voting," p. 496.)*

On November 4, 1983, Democrat Henry B. Gonzalez of Texas waited for his turn to be recognized during special order speeches on the floor following the conclusion of legislative business for the day. A few Republican members were finishing up their speaking time as another Democrat presided over the House as Speaker pro tempore. The Democratic leadership wanted the House to remain in session awhile longer so that the Rules Committee could file a report on the floor. The Republicans wanted to prevent that, so Rep. Dan Lungren (R-Calif.) initiated the following proceedings:

LUNGREN: "Mr. Speaker, I move that the House do now adjourn." (The motion to adjourn is highly privileged and must be voted on when made. With the House adjourned, the Rules Committee could not file until the following legislative day, which would delay consideration of any legislation requiring a rule for at least another day beyond that. And adjournment would also prevent Gonzalez from speaking, though Lungren assured him that was not his purpose.)

SPEAKER PRO TEMPORE: "The question is on the motion offered by the gentleman from California . . . The question was taken, and on a division (demanded by Mr. Lungren) there were—ayes 3; noes 1."

GONZALEZ: "I object to a vote on the ground that a quorum is not present."

SPEAKER PRO TEMPORE: "The chair would advise the gentleman from Texas that he cannot do that on an affirmative vote to adjourn, only

on a negative vote." (Gonzalez had run into a rare exception to the normal operation of House rules. The Constitution provides that "a Majority of each [House] shall constitute a Quorum to do Business; but a smaller Number may adjourn from day to day." So a simple majority of the handful of members present could decide that the House would adjourn; had the division resulted in a negative vote, any member could have obtained an electronic vote, calling all members to the House floor, by objecting that a quorum was not present. Since Gonzalez was momentarily outnumbered by the Republicans, the House would adjourn under the constitutional provision unless a vote could be held and bring majority Democrats to the floor. The Speaker pro tempore would ordinarily choose not to participate in a division vote but could do so if his vote changed the outcome.)

GONZALEZ: "Mr. Speaker, I demand a recorded vote."

SPEAKER PRO TEMPORE: "The gentleman cannot get a recorded vote in the House based on the number now present (since there were not forty-four members present to support the demand). Does the gentleman ask for the yeas and nays?"

GONZALEZ: "Mr. Speaker, on that I demand the yeas and nays."

SPEAKER PRO TEMPORE: "Those in favor of taking this vote by the yeas and nays will stand. . . . The yeas and nays were ordered." (Gonzalez, the Speaker pro tempore, and any other Democrats who may have appeared in the chamber during the preceding exchanges constituted one-fifth of those present).

The Democrats had succeeded in ordering a roll-call vote. The fifteen minutes for such a vote allowed enough time for other Democrats to return to the chamber. The final vote on whether to adjourn was: 99 yeas, 120 nays, 1 voting "present," and 213 not voting. So the House did not adjourn, the Republicans were foiled, the Rules Committee filed its report, and Gonzalez got to give his speech after all.

---

debate . . . has become a time of reading prepared statements by the floor managers and is widely considered a filler time between adoption of the rule and voting on amendments, during which members can leave the floor for other activities."[17]

The rules on most bills allot an hour for general debate, although more time may be granted for particularly controversial measures. The allotted time is divided equally between and controlled by the floor managers for the bill. Ordinarily the chairman of the committee or subcommittee that reported the measure acts as the floor manager for the bill's supporters, while the ranking minority member or his designee leads the opposition. If both support the legislation, which often happens, they may allot some of their time to members of their party opposing the bill. A bill that has been referred to more than one committee might have multiple floor managers, each of whom is responsible for the part of the bill that was before his or her committee and each controlling a small chunk of time. The importance of the managers is evident in their physical location on the House floor; they occupy designated seats at tables on either side of the center aisle, and they are permitted to bring several committee staff members onto the floor to assist them.

Floor managers are exactly what their name implies: managers of legislation while it is on the floor of the House, marshaling speakers and support for the majority or minority position. Regardless of his or her personal view on the measure or amendments, the majority floor manager is responsible for presenting the committee's bill in the most favorable light and for fending off undesirable amendments. The mark of a successful majority floor manager is the ability to get a bill passed without substantial change. The minority manager, if opposed to the bill, is expected to line up convincing arguments against the legislation and for amendments, if the rule permits, that would make the measure more acceptable to the opposition.

The Amending Process

Amendments, which provide a way to shape bills into a form acceptable to a majority, may change the intent, conditions, or requirements of a bill; modify, delete, or introduce provisions; or replace a section or the entire text of a bill with a different version. Amendments that seek to revise or modify parts of bills or of other amendments are called perfecting amendments. Amendments that seek to add extraneous matter to the bill under debate are sometimes referred to as "riders." They are far more common in the Senate than in the House, where a rule of germaneness protects the members from unexpected proposals. Riders do appear sometimes on appropriations bills where they may restrict the use of funds for a controversial program under the jurisdiction of an authorizing committee that may not have addressed the issue.

House rules require amendments to be germane, or relevant, to the bill itself. Any member may raise a point of order on the floor that an amendment is not germane but if there is general agreement on the need or desirability of a nongermane amendment it may be protected from a point of order by the Rules Committee.

Riders are often controversial for two reasons: the substantive provisions they contain and the potential that disagreements about them between the House and Senate, or between Congress and the president, will cause a deadlock delaying or preventing enactment of the main bill. Riders are especially visible on so-called "must pass" legislation such as appropriations bills. In 1997, a supplemental appropriations bill providing disaster relief to several states after heavy flooding was delayed because several controversial riders opposed by President Clinton were attached. One of these sought to alter the manner in which the 2000 census was scheduled to be conducted. The president vetoed the bill, and Congress succumbed to public pressure and passed it without the extraneous matters.

Substitute amendments aim at replacing pending amendments with alternatives. A variation of the substitute, known as an amendment in the nature of a substitute, seeks to replace the pending bill with an entirely new measure. The bill reported by the committee frequently is an amendment in the nature of a substitute for the original bill; the rule for its debate typically stipulates that it shall be considered the original bill for purposes of amendment.

Debate on Amendments. Once general debate is completed the measure is read for amendment, which constitutes the second reading of the bill. The special rule usually specifies that each part of a bill must be considered in sequential order. The bill may be read paragraph by paragraph, section by section, or title by title, and amendments are offered to the appropriate part as it is read. Once the reading of that part is completed, amendments to it are no longer in order except by unanimous consent. On occasion the Rules Committee may allow the bill to be considered as read and open to amendment at any point. Alternatively, the floor manager may make a unanimous consent request that the bill be open to amendment. Committee amendments are always considered before amendments offered from the floor.

Debate on any amendment is theoretically limited to five minutes for supporters and five minutes for opponents. Members regularly obtain more time, however, by offering pro forma amendments to "strike the last word" or "strike the requisite number of words." Under the Legislative Reorganization Act of 1970, ten minutes of debate, five minutes on each side, are guaranteed on any amendment that has been published in the *Congressional Record* at least one day before it is offered on the floor (assuming that the amendment is otherwise in order) even if debate has been closed on the portion of the bill to which the amendment is proposed. The change thus ensured that opponents could not block even an explanation of an important pending amendment, but it has also been used on a few occasions as a delaying device by members who have had dozens of amendments to a bill printed in the *Record,* all of which may be called up and debated for up to ten minutes. Committee floor managers encourage members to print their amendments in the *Record,* in order to obtain as complete a picture as possible of the political problems a bill may face. When the Republicans took power in the House in 1995 they began reporting rules that allowed the chairman of the Committee of the Whole to give preference in recognition to members who had preprinted their amendments.

Degrees of Amendments. Provided the special rule on the bill has not imposed specific restrictions, four types of amendments may be pending at any one time: a perfecting amendment to the text of the bill, also called a "first degree" amendment; an amendment to that amendment, which is called a "second degree" amendment; a substitute amendment for the original amendment; and an amendment to the substitute. An amendment to an amendment to an amendment, known as an amendment in the third degree, is barred under House rules.

Amendments to the original amendment are voted on first. Only one first degree amendment is in order at a time, but once it has been disposed of another may be offered immediately. When all amendments to the original amendment have been disposed of perfecting amendments to the substitute amendment are voted on one at a time. The perfected substitute is voted on next, followed by a vote on the original amendment as amended. If the substitute has been adopted, this last vote will be on the perfected original amendment as amended by the perfected substitute. Once an amendment has been offered in the Committee of the Whole its author may only modify it or withdraw it by unanimous consent but may not offer an amendment to it directly. A diagram of a so-called amendment tree and the order in which amendments must be voted on are shown below.

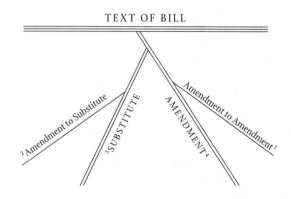

TEXT OF BILL

2 Amendment to Substitute

3 SUBSTITUTE

AMENDMENT 4

Amendment to Amendment 1

House members and staff enter and exit the Capitol during a 1998 vote on telecommunications.

This description may seem complex, but it gives only a hint of the total universe of amending possibilities. It can be mind-boggling when a substitute for the entire bill may be pending along with the base legislation, and such substitute may attract yet another substitute to itself as well as a panoply of perfecting amendments.

More than one vote may be taken on any given amendment. The Committee of the Whole may first take a voice vote and then, if members request, move on to division or recorded votes before finally deciding the questions. First-degree amendments (original amendments as amended) and amendments in the nature of substitutes, as amended, adopted in the Committee of the Whole are subject to roll-call votes after the committee rises and the chamber resumes sitting as the full House. Few roll-call votes actually are taken, and the full House rarely rejects amendments adopted in the Committee of the Whole. Amendments defeated in the Committee of the Whole cannot be offered again at this stage because the previous question has usually been ordered on the bill when the House adopted the rule for its consideration, barring additional amendments or debate once the Committee of the Whole has risen back to the House with its recommendation that the bill as amended be passed.

Action by the Full House

When the Committee of the Whole has completed its work on the bill, it "rises," according to the House's parliamentary terminology. The Speaker returns to the chair and the erstwhile chairman of the Committee of the Whole formally reports the bill to the House, with any amendments that have been adopted, and a recommendation that the bill pass.

If the previous question has been ordered by the special rule governing the bill—the usual procedure—the full House then votes immediately on amendments approved by the Committee of the Whole. As already noted, members may demand a roll call on any amendment adopted in the Committee of the Whole. Amendments not considered separately are approved en bloc by a pro forma voice vote.

Once the amendments have been disposed of the question is on engrossment (the preparation of an accurate version of the bill including all amendments) and third reading, by title only, of the bill. This too is nearly always pro forma. Prior to 1965, any House member could demand that the bill actually be "engrossed," that is, printed on special paper, prior to further proceedings. This was sometimes used as a dilatory tactic.

After engrossment and third reading, a member opposed to the bill may offer a motion to recommit the measure to the committee that reported it. The Speaker will inquire of a member attempting to make the motion whether he or she so qualifies. The Speaker typically asks "Is the (member) opposed to the bill?" and if the response is yes then that member is recognized. In practice, the motion to recommit belongs to the minority party and the Speaker looks first to the floor manager of the minority, then to other minority members of the committee, and then to any other minority member.

There are two kinds of recommittal motions: a nondebatable simple motion to recommit, sometimes called a "straight motion," which kills the bill if it is adopted by sending it back to committee; and a motion to recommit with instructions. The minority often moves to recommit with instructions directing the committee to report the bill back with amendments "forthwith." This tactic offers the minority members one last chance to amend the bill to their satisfaction. The minority may offer any germane amendment as part of its instructions, even one which had previously been offered and rejected in the Committee of the Whole. If the motion to recommit is adopted, the floor manager announces that the committee has reported the bill back to the House with the amendments contained in the instructions. The bill in this case is not literally recommitted to the committee that reported it. The amendment is then voted on again directly; this is usually a pro forma voice vote.

Instructions also can have the effect of removing a bill from the floor, however, if they contain nonamendatory provisions, such as directing the committee in question to hold hearings before bringing the bill back before the House.

The motion to recommit is privileged and the right to offer it is guaranteed by House rules but its use has been regulated by the Rules Committee. From 1934 to 1995 the majority reserved the right to restrict the motion in certain circumstances. The Rules Committee is forbidden by a House rule to report a rule for consideration of a bill or joint resolution that denies the right to offer a motion to recommit. However, a series of precedents was established that construed the rule so that members were guaranteed the right to offer only the "straight motion" to recommit without instructions.

A motion to recommit with instructions was, on occasion, barred by a special rule governing consideration of a bill. This might occur if the majority feared that last-minute amendments could pull apart the support built up for the pending legislation during the original amendment process, or if a minority proposal was considered potentially popular enough to pass. The Republicans, while in the minority for four decades prior to 1995, often used a recommittal motion with instructions to present their alternative to the Democratic-crafted legislation being considered. They roundly criticized the constraints under rules governing recommittals that they considered a denial of basic rights, and frequently appealed rulings of the Speaker on this issue but always lost.

When Republicans gained control of the House in 1995, the new majority effectively wiped out the earlier precedents that had allowed the Rules Committee to prevent a motion to recommit with instructions from being offered to bills and joint resolutions, and amended House rules to guarantee that right to the minority leader or the minority leader's designee. In this respect, the Republicans increased the rights of the Democratic minority beyond what they themselves had enjoyed. However, other parliamentary restrictions may still apply to such a motion, such as the requirement that amendatory instructions be germane to the underlying bill.

A straight motion to recommit is not debatable. A motion to recommit a bill or joint resolution with instructions may be de-

bated for ten minutes, evenly divided, although, since 1985, the majority floor manager—but not the minority floor manager—may ask for up to an hour of debate, which is then divided evenly between the two sides. That change was a direct result of a motion by Rep. Dan Lungren, R-Calif., in September 1984 to recommit the fiscal 1985 continuing appropriations resolution with instructions to add to it a Senate-passed crime bill. The House version of the crime bill had been bottled up in the Judiciary Committee. The motion was debated for ten minutes, and the House, to the majority leadership's embarrassment, adopted it on a vote of 243–166. The continuing resolution was then passed, and the crime package was eventually enacted.

Another example of amending strategy and clever use of the motion to recommit occurred in 1995 when Massachusetts Democrat Edward J. Markey offered a motion to recommit a telecommunications bill, with instructions to include a provision mandating use of V-chip circuitry in televisions to allow parents to control more effectively their children's viewing habits. Markey had earlier offered a perfecting amendment to the bill in the Committee of the Whole to accomplish this, but he had been prevented from getting a direct vote when his proposal was altered by adoption of a second-degree Republican-sponsored amendment. The Republican proposal encouraged, but did not require, the new technology.

However, use of the motion to recommit in the House offered Markey, in effect, a "second bite of the apple" under parliamentary circumstances when a counterproposal could not be offered. Now forced to go on the record in an up-or-down vote on Markey's popular plan, the House effectively reversed its earlier vote and adopted the mandatory requirement.

These victories were unusual because few controversial recommittal motions are ever adopted. A competent majority can usually anticipate and head off such dangers before a bill is reported, or through the amendment process on the floor as they attempted to do, ultimately unsuccessfully, in the Markey case cited above. In recent years, the motion has also become perceived more as a partisan vote in an increasingly partisan House, greatly reducing the minority's chances of success.

In 1981, there was an unusual instance of the majority attempting to seize control of the motion to recommit from the minority. This happened on the Gramm-Latta amendments to a budget reconciliation bill, in which a conservative group of Democrats combined with minority Republicans to seize control of the rule and control the floor debate and amendment process to promote the Reagan administration's legislative agenda. The majority party was effectively cut out of the process, but, once put in the position of being the opponents of the amended bill that was then overwhelmingly supported by Republicans, the Democrats could make a potential claim to the motion to recommit.

Anticipating a last-minute counterattack through a motion to recommit with instructions that might unravel the bill, the Republicans needed to find someone qualified to offer the motion in order to keep it away from the Democrats. Since Republicans were the minority party, the Speaker would still look first to their side to offer the motion. They recruited one of their most liberal members, freshman Claudine Schneider, R-R.I. (1981–1991), to state her opposition to the bill. Schneider then offered a motion to recommit with instructions to amend the bill to reinstate a law guaranteeing semiannual cost-of-living adjustments to federal retirees' pensions. Her action had the effect of using up the single motion permitted under the rules, and on subject matter less controversial and far narrower than many other issues dealt with in the bill. Schneider made her status as a front for her party obvious when she yielded most of her time to the Republican leadership to explain her proposal.

The Democrats attempted to defeat the previous question on Schneider's motion. Ordering the previous question cuts off debate and further amendments to a proposal and forces it to a final vote. Defeating it would have allowed them to gain control of the floor and offer a new instruction with amendments aimed at the heart of the bill's provisions. However, Democratic defections that had allowed the Republicans to control the process throughout continued, and the previous question was ordered on Schneider's motion. With the vote over and the bill safe from further attack, the substance of Schneider's motion became irrelevant, and her motion was rejected by voice vote. Schneider then voted against the bill on final passage, as is customary for a member offering a motion to recommit.

If the motion to recommit is rejected, which it almost always is, the next step is the vote on final passage. If the bill is passed, a pro forma motion to reconsider the final vote is usually offered. A supporter of the bill then offers a counter motion to "lay the motion on the table," or kill reconsideration, thus safeguarding final passage. Or the Speaker will simply say "Without objection the motion to reconsider is laid upon the table." With that, the bill is considered to be formally passed by the House. At this point, the bill officially becomes an "act," although it generally still is referred to as a bill.

An engrossed copy of the bill, including changes made during floor action, is certified in its final form by the clerk of the House and transmitted to the Senate for its consideration. (An engrossed bill in the Senate must be certified by the secretary of the Senate.)

If a similar Senate bill has already reached the House, the rule providing for floor action on the House version might also have included a provision permitting the House to take it up, strike out the text, insert the text of the House-passed legislation, pass the "S" numbered bill and send it back to the Senate to await further amendments or a Senate request for a conference. Or the House itself could ask for the conference first. In these legislative scenarios, the House bill passed earlier would be laid on the table (killed) since it is no longer needed as a vehicle for further proceedings.

Senate Floor Action: Flexibility, Informality

House members elected to the Senate are inevitably struck by the difference in the way the two chambers operate. Although the Senate has an elaborate framework of parliamentary machinery to guide its deliberations, in practice its procedures are far more flexible than those of the House. Almost anything can be done by unanimous consent. That very flexibility also means that a single member can delay or threaten to delay action on a bill until his or her wishes are accommodated or a compromise is struck. The Senate also effects changes in its procedures from time to time, without formally changing its rules, by overruling decisions made by the presiding officer. The result of such a vote can establish a new precedent that would govern future proceedings.

From time to time the Senate reviews its procedures in an attempt to pick up the pace and predictability of action in the chamber. But the Senate is rarely receptive to the proposals for change that come forth from these reviews, largely because they almost always entail curbs on the rights of the individual member.

In 1982 Howard H. Baker Jr., R-Tenn. (1967–1985), then the majority leader, expressed the prevailing attitude: "The Senate is a great institution. It is the balance wheel which keeps democracy on track. It is the framework on which the Republic is constructed. It is the essence of compromise. It is the only place where there is unfettered expression of individual views. It is the last fortress that can be used to defend against the tyranny of a temporary majority. I would not change a thing about that."[18]

SCHEDULING IN THE SENATE

In a chamber devoted to preserving individual rights, the challenge of scheduling floor action can sometimes be formidable. Senators can—and do—insist that the legislation in which they are interested be scheduled for floor action at a time convenient to them. At the same time senators faced with ever-increasing political, constituent, and legislative demands on their time have sought greater predictability in the Senate schedule.

Scheduling in the Senate is primarily the responsibility of the majority leader, who works closely with the majority party's policy committee, committee chairmen, and other partisan colleagues to develop a legislative program acceptable to a majority of the party. Because of the need to secure unanimous consent to bring up a bill, the majority leader also works closely with the minority leader and his staff in working out the schedule. This bipartisan cooperation is in sharp contrast to the House, where scheduling is solely a responsibility of a majority party that has the ability to enforce its decisions by majority vote.

A system based largely on unanimous consent also necessitates that the membership be kept informed about the status of pending legislation. The majority leader regularly begins each session with an announcement of the day's anticipated schedule and concludes it with the likely program for the next session.

THE PRESIDING OFFICER

Members of the House and Senate take turns presiding over floor debate, a job some view as drudgery and others see as an honor requiring finesse and skill. Members may speak on the floor and offer legislation, amendments, or motions for consideration only if the presiding officer permits, or "recognizes," them.

The presiding officer also rules on points of order and delivers other pronouncements that regulate floor debate. Members may appeal, or challenge, the presiding officer's decisions, and, in the House, these rulings can always be overturned by majority vote. Some rulings by the chair in the Senate, related to the budget process, require sixty votes to overturn. In the House, while rulings are occasionally appealed, none has been overturned since February 1, 1938. In the Senate, on the other hand, where procedure is more fluid and often yields to the political needs of senators, rulings of the chair have been appealed and overturned on various occasions in recent decades.

SPEAKER OF THE HOUSE

The presiding officer in the House is called the Speaker, a position designated by the Constitution. When the House convenes to begin a new Congress, it is first presided over by the clerk from the previous Congress. After a quorum is established, the first order of business is to elect the Speaker. The election is nearly always pro forma because the actual decision is made earlier by the majority party's caucus or conference.

The Speaker need not be a member of the House but always has been. In the speakership election in January 1997 in the 105th Congress, two Republican members cast votes for former members of the House to protest the candidacy of Rep. Newt Gingrich, R-Ga., who was seeking reelection as Speaker but was also about to be disciplined for ethics violations.

The Speaker effectively serves as political leader of the majority party and also has rights as an elected representative to participate fully in all activities of the chamber. The Speaker may vote at any time but rarely does, except to break a tie.

By statute, the Speaker is next in line, behind the vice president, to become president of the United States in the event of a vacancy, although this has never occurred. The president pro tempore of the Senate follows the Speaker in order of succession.

The Speaker cannot preside over the House all of the time. When the Speaker is not present, a member of the majority party is designated as Speaker pro tempore, although any member may preside if called to the chair.

Unlike the Senate, in the House the presiding officer has broad authority to choose which member to recognize, and will inquire "for what purpose does the gentleman rise" to ascertain whether he wishes to recognize the member. Members seeking to conduct business made privileged under House rules will have priority in recognition.

When the House is considering bills for amendment in the Committee of the Whole, the Speaker steps down and appoints another member, who is called the chairman, to preside. When sensitive bills are under consideration, the Speaker's choice for the chair usually turns to senior members who are skilled parliamentarians or who are close to the leadership. Sometimes a tradition develops that the same member always presides over a certain bill whenever it comes to the floor. For example, Rep. Dan Rostenkowski, D-Ill. (1959–1995), best known as the longtime chairman of the powerful Ways and Means

---

Whip notices, televised floor proceedings, and an automatic telephone connection to each member's office help the leadership keep the membership informed.

To the extent possible the modern leadership tries to accommodate the schedules of individual senators. Most leaders have acknowledged the frustration inherent in the job. "It is extremely difficult to deal with the wishes of 99 other senators, attempting to schedule legislation," Majority Leader Robert C. Byrd, D-W.Va., said in 1987, "because in almost every case, at any time it is scheduled, it inconveniences some senator."[19]

All legislation reported from Senate committees is placed on the Calendar of General Orders, while all treaties and nominations that require the Senate's "advice and consent" are placed on the Executive Calendar. To consider treaties or nominations, the Senate resolves into "executive session" either by motion or unanimous consent. There are no restrictions on when the Senate may enter executive session. Despite its connotations, the term "executive session" is an open session of the Senate just like any other.

Senate rules require bills and reports on nonprivileged matters to lie over on the calendar for one legislative day before they are brought to the floor. This rule is usually waived by unanimous consent, and the Senate often stays in the same legislative day for a considerable period of time. Another rule requires that printed committee reports be available to members for two calendar days before a measure is debated. It too may be waived by unanimous consent.

The leadership evolved several ways to handle the various scheduling problems it regularly confronts. Different majority leaders have had their own ideas of how best to conduct business while giving their colleagues adequate "down time." In 1988, for example, the Senate worked for three weeks and then took a week off, giving members a set time to return to their states without running the risk of missing votes in the Senate or other legislative work of importance to them. However, this practice did not become institutionalized.

In the early 1970s Majority Leader Mike Mansfield, D-Mont., devised a system that allowed several pieces of legislation to be considered simultaneously by designating specific periods each day when the measures would be considered. The track system, still in use in the 1990s, affected all aspects of Senate procedure. When a filibuster was under way, the filibustered bill occupied one track while the Senate could proceed by unanimous consent to other legislation on the second track. But the ability of the

Committee, was usually named to preside over consideration of the annual defense authorization bill.

VICE PRESIDENT AND PRESIDENT PRO TEMPORE

The Speaker is far more powerful than his counterpart in the Senate, the vice president, who is not a member of the Senate and cannot speak except to recognize senators or make parliamentary rulings.

In the Senate, the presiding officer is always referred to as "Mr. (or Madam) President." The vice president of the United States serves formally as president of the Senate under the Constitution. It once was common for the vice president to preside over floor debates. In the modern Senate the vice president seldom is called in unless his or her vote might be needed if the Senate is evenly divided in order to vote to break a tie. In this case, only an "aye" vote can affect the result because a tie is considered defeat of a pending proposition. The vice president may not vote to create a tie. In theory, the vice president can vote when the Senate is evenly divided on matters requiring a supermajority vote for approval but since the proposition would thereby have been defeated anyway, the vice president could not affect the result. The vice president is rarely called on to vote. Between 1945 and August 1999 only thirty-five such votes were cast.

The "president pro tempore" is a position created by the Constitution and is usually held by the senior member of the majority party in the Senate. This senator has the right to preside in the absence of the vice president but generally the Senate puts a freshman member in the chair. That relieves more senior members of a time-consuming task and gives newcomers firsthand lessons in Senate rules and procedures. Not surprisingly, new senators are heavily dependent on the

parliamentarian for advice. In the Senate, the rules require the presiding officer to recognize "the Senator who shall first address him" if several senators are seeking to speak. However, by custom, the majority and minority leaders are always recognized first if they seek recognition when no one else holds the floor.

Many senators tend to view presiding as drudge work to be avoided, because the job frequently involves presiding over quorum calls that interrupt business while agreements are being worked out privately or senators are coming to the floor. However, some have embraced it and a custom has developed of giving a "Golden Gavel" to those who have presided for 100 hours.

Some House members also actively seek to preside. In an institution as large as the House it is one way for members to increase their visibility. The House puts no premium on giving new members experience in the chair; however, during routine business, it is not uncommon to see them there, visible to their constituents on C-SPAN, the cable network that broadcasts congressional events around the clock.

In both the House and Senate in 1999 only members of the majority party preside. Until 1977 members of each party took turns presiding in the Senate. The bipartisan practice was ended abruptly following an incident the previous year. The presiding officer, Sen. Jesse Helms, R-N.C., a member of the minority, broke with Senate custom by denying recognition to the majority leader, Sen. Mike Mansfield, D-Mont., in favor of conservative Sen. James B. Allen, D-Ala. The Democratic leadership then decided that the majority should retain control of the chair at all times, unless the vice president, who might be a member of the opposite party, decided to occupy it. Republicans continued this practice when they controlled the Senate.

Senate to continue its more routine work also encouraged senators to threaten to filibuster more frequently, since the incentives were much less for the leadership and other senators to try to stop them, and there were few negative consequences for those who filibustered.

The Senate normally recesses from day to day, rather than adjourns. The effect is the same—an end to the day's session—but a recess avoids creating a new legislative day that can, in some circumstances, create unwanted procedural complications when the Senate next convenes. It is not uncommon for the Senate to remain in the same legislative day for weeks or even months at a time.

Unanimous Consent Agreements

The leadership has been most innovative with its use of unanimous consent requests, traditionally the mechanism the Senate uses to expedite business by circumventing its rules. As its name implies, a unanimous consent request may be blocked by a single objection. Once the request is agreed to, however, its terms are binding and can be changed only by another unanimous consent request.

There are two kinds of unanimous consent requests. Simple

requests, which can be made by any senator, usually deal with routine business—asking that staff members be allowed on the floor, that committees be allowed to meet while the Senate is in session, that material be inserted in the *Congressional Record*, and the like. Noncontroversial matters, including minor legislation, private bills, and presidential nominations may be considered by unanimous consent; generally these matters are cleared with the leadership beforehand.

Complex unanimous consent requests set out the guidelines under which a piece of major legislation will be considered on the floor. In some respects like a special rule for guiding debate in the House, these unanimous consent requests usually state when the bill will come to the floor and set time limits on debate, including debate on motions, amendments, and final passage. For that reason they are often referred to as time agreements. Frequently the agreements stipulate that any amendments offered must be germane but, unlike House rules, they cannot prevent a senator from offering a particular amendment because the senator would have to be accommodated somehow to ensure there would be no objection to the request.

Lyndon B. Johnson, D-Texas, began to develop complex unanimous consent agreements during his tenure as majority leader from 1955 to 1960. Such agreements steadily grew more complex and were applied to more legislation. Negotiating a complex unanimous consent agreement can be complicated and time-consuming, involving the majority and minority leaders, the chairman and ranking minority member of the committee and/or subcommittee with jurisdiction for the bill, and any senator who has placed a "hold" *(discussed below)* on or otherwise expressed strong interest in the measure. The leadership tries to negotiate a unanimous consent agreement before the measure comes to the floor, but additional agreements—to limit time spent on a specific amendment, for example—may be fashioned on the floor.

The fundamental objective of a unanimous consent agreement, as Oleszek has observed, "is to limit the time it takes to dispose of controversial issues in an institution noted for unlimited debate."[20] The agreements are also valuable because they bring some predictability to Senate business.

But complex unanimous consent agreements "must not be viewed as rigid restrictions comparable to those found in House special rules," Steven Smith cautions. The need to obtain unanimous consent to ward off a potential filibuster "forces leaders to make concessions before and during floor debate on a scale that would seem quite foreign in the House. As a result, the new use of complex agreements on the floor does not alter the basic principles of Senate floor politics, which remain rampant individualism and the protection of minority rights."[21]

Holds

One scheduling complication the leadership has been unable to do away with is the practice of "holds." A hold is a request by a senator to the party leadership asking that a certain measure not be taken up. The leadership usually respects holds; to do otherwise would likely be self-defeating since the senator could easily block any unanimous consent request to consider the measure.

Most holds are kept confidential and are requested simply so that the senator will be told when the bill is likely to come up. But some senators have used them extensively as bargaining tools, to ensure that they will be able to offer their amendments or to force the leadership to call up some unrelated piece of legislation that otherwise might not have been scheduled for the floor. There have been instances of "rolling holds," in which one

---

A TYPICAL DAY IN THE SENATE

A typical day in the Senate might go like this:

• The Senate is called to order by the presiding officer. The constitutional presiding officer, the vice president, is seldom in attendance. Sometimes the president pro tempore presides over the opening minutes of the Senate session. During the course of the day, other members of the majority party take turns presiding.

• The Senate chaplain delivers the opening prayer and pledge.

• The Pledge of Allegiance is recited.

• The majority and minority leaders are recognized for opening remarks. The majority leader usually announces plans for the day's business, which are developed in consultation with the minority leadership.

• The Senate usually conducts morning business (which need not be in the morning and should not be confused with the "morning hour," so if morning business is put off other business will necessarily precede it). During morning business senators may introduce bills and the Senate will receive reports from committees and messages from the president, and conduct other routine chores. Senators who have requested time in advance are recognized for speeches on any subject.

• The Senate may turn to consider legislative or executive matters. To begin work on a piece of legislation the majority leader normally asks for unanimous consent to call up the measure. If any member objects, the leader may make a debatable motion that the Senate take up the bill. The motion gives opponents the opportunity to launch a filibuster, or extended debate, even before the Senate officially begins to consider the bill. Certain types of measures, such as budget resolutions, omnibus budget reconciliation bills, and reports from House-Senate conference committees, are privileged, and a motion to consider them is not debatable.

Floor debate on a bill is generally handled by managers, usually the chairman and ranking minority member of the committee with jurisdiction over the measure. Most measures are considered under a unanimous consent, or time, agreement in which the Senate unanimously agrees to limit debate and to divide the time in some prearranged fashion. In the absence of a time agreement any senator may seek recognition from the chair and, once recognized, may talk for as long as he or she wishes. Unless the Senate has unanimously agreed to limit amendments, senators may offer as many as they wish. In most cases, amendments need not be germane, or directly related, to the bill.

Most bills are passed by voice vote with only a handful of senators present. Any member can request a roll-call vote on an amendment or motion or on final passage of a measure. Senate roll calls are casual affairs. Senators stroll in from the cloakrooms or their offices and congregate in the well (the area at the front of the chamber). When they are ready to vote, senators catch the eye of the clerk and vote, sometimes by indicating thumbs up or thumbs down. Roll-call votes are supposed to last fifteen minutes but some have dragged on for more than an hour.

• Often, near the end of the day, the majority leader and the minority leader quickly move through a "wrap-up" period, during which minor bills that have been cleared by all members are passed by unanimous consent.

• Just before the Senate finishes its work for the day, the majority leader seeks unanimous consent for his agenda for the next session—when the Senate will convene, which senators will be recognized for early speeches, and specific time agreements for consideration of legislation.

senator withdraws a hold when it is discovered but another then steps in to retain the block in place, and even cases where a Senate staffer has applied a hold in a senator's name.

In the Clinton administration the president and even the chief justice of the United States objected to the practice by conservative senators of placing holds on large numbers of judicial nominations. The practice was not new, just more visible and seemingly more organized. Senators have also placed holds on legislation in behalf of the administration or an interest group. Sen. Jesse Helms, R-N.C., frequently placed holds on ambassadorial nominations to pressure the State Department into adopting policies more to his liking. Sen. Howard Metzenbaum (D-Ohio 1974; 1977–1995) placed holds on all types of legislation, especially during the end of each session as the Senate rushed toward adjournment, to ensure that he was not unpleasantly surprised by unexpected developments.

In 1997 and 1998, the Senate passed a proposal by Sen. Ron Wyden, D-Ore., and Sen. Charles Grassley, R-Iowa, to require senators to identify themselves when using holds, which would make it easier for opponents of a hold to apply pressure to allow consideration of a measure or a nomination. But the proposal was not adopted in the form of a simple resolution, which would have given it immediate effect, but rather as an amendment to another bill. This enabled the reform's opponents to drop the measure in conference, even though the House had no objection to it. In 1999 the majority and minority leaders declared a new policy requiring that senators using holds identify themselves, and banned holds placed by staff.

Other Scheduling Methods

Because the Senate allows nongermane amendments on most legislation, it has little need for procedures to wrest bills out of reluctant committees. A member may simply offer the legislation blocked by a committee as an amendment to another measure being considered on the floor. There are, however, three other ways that a senator may bring a bill to the floor, although none of them is used with any frequency.

First, all measures introduced in the Senate, including House-passed bills, must be read twice on successive legislative days before they are referred to committee. If any senator objects to the second reading of a bill, it is placed immediately on the calendar. This tactic was used to avoid sending the House version of the 1964 civil rights legislation to the Senate Judiciary Committee, which opposed it.

The Senate may also vote to suspend the rules by a two-thirds vote, but the procedure bears little relation to the similarly named House practice and has little practical use. While approval of the motion requires a two-thirds vote, it only suspends a rule but does not simultaneously pass a measure. The motion, and the measure, also remain subject to potential filibusters.

Finally, the Senate may discharge a bill from committee. The motion to discharge, which is debatable, must be made during morning hour. However, morning hour is rarely used in the Senate, and, even if it were, opponents would have ample opportunities to delay and render the discharge procedure inoperative. If debate is not completed by the time morning hour ends, the motion is placed on the calendar, where it can be subjected to another series of delays.

SENATE FLOOR PROCEDURES

While the Senate's rules establish elaborate procedures to conduct certain types of business, in practice many of these rules are either ignored or altered by unanimous consent. This is because efforts to invoke the formal rules may prove too cumbersome, provoking retaliation from opponents. The purported cure for a parliamentary stalemate or obstacle may prove to be worse than the disease. And some of the rules simply do not work.

The Senate may set a standard daily meeting time for noon but it frequently alters its meeting times by unanimous consent each day to accommodate the demands of the daily workload and the scheduling needs of individual senators who wish to be present for particular items of business. The Senate chaplain gives an opening prayer, the Pledge of Allegiance is recited, and the previous day's Journal is approved. A rules change in 1986 made approval nondebatable, although amendments to correct the Journal may still be offered and filibustered. The majority leader and then the minority leader are recognized for brief periods. Usually they discuss the Senate's schedule for the day.

What happens next depends on whether the Senate is beginning a new legislative day. If the Senate recessed at the end of its previous session, it may proceed immediately to any unfinished business. If it adjourned, it must begin a new legislative day, which, after the opening preliminaries, requires the Senate to enter a two-hour period called "morning hour" (though this is almost always waived by unanimous consent). During that period members conduct what is known as "morning business"—introducing bills, filing committee reports, and receiving messages from the House and the president.

In the second hour, or at the conclusion of morning business, members may move to consider any measure on the calendar. This motion is not debatable, in theory, but in practice efforts to employ it to avoid a filibuster have been thwarted by the use of other provisions of the rules, making this "shortcut" effectively obsolete. After morning hour, because a motion to consider a nonprivileged measure is debatable, opponents of a measure have found ways to tie up the morning hour with other business and votes to prevent the leadership from forcing it up.

In an attempt to avoid a certain filibuster on the fiscal 1988 defense authorization bill on May 13, 1987, Majority Leader Byrd sought to call up the bill during morning hour. But before he could do that, the Journal of the previous day's proceedings had to be approved. Republicans requested a roll call on approval of the Journal and then used more arcane procedural tactics, demanding time to explain their individual votes and calling for votes on excusing them from voting, to further slow the proceedings. By the time the ensuing wrangle over the rules between Byrd and the Republicans had been untangled, seven roll-

SENATE PROCEDURES USED TO THWART SUBSTANTIVE ACTIONS

In a notable example in 1997 of the impact of Senate rules on debate and amendment strategy on controversial legislation, Senate Majority Leader Trent Lott, R-Miss., agreed to call up major campaign finance reform legislation, the so-called "McCain-Feingold bill" for proponents John McCain, R-Ariz., and Russell Feingold, D-Wis. As the most heavily promoted campaign reform vehicle in the Senate that bill would have banned "soft money" contributions to political campaigns—a method of support for candidates that fell outside the legal restrictions on contributions—and curbed "issue ads," often presented on television and radio by special interest advocacy groups that in many election contests were aimed more at electing or defeating candidates than at promoting debate on issues.

The legislation was certain to be filibustered, with Lott and Sen. Mitch McConnell, R-Ky., among its principal opponents. But supporters, consisting of the Democratic minority and a handful of Republicans, hoped that by getting the bill to the floor they could attract enough media attention and popular support, and work out compromises through the amendment process, to gain legislative momentum and overcome this obstacle.

Action stalled when the Republican leadership insisted on offering an amendment that would have required labor organizations, banks, or corporations to secure voluntary authorization from their members before using any membership dues, initiation fees, or other payments to fund political activities. They called the proposal the "paycheck protection act." Democrats, allied with labor and the primary beneficiaries of financial support from union leaders, filibustered against this amendment, knowing its adoption would prevent them from supporting the bill on final passage. Indeed, that was exactly the outcome Republicans were seeking as each side tried to blame the other for the failure to reform the nation's widely criticized and ineffective campaign finance laws. In the meantime most Republicans continued to filibuster the bill itself.

These stark partisan and ideological cleavages, exacerbated by the Senate's loose amendment rules and reliance on a sixty-vote supermajority needed to stop a filibuster, prevented compromise and smothered direct consideration of the legislation even as campaign finance scandals implicating both parties were being played out daily in highly publicized committee hearings in both chambers and on the front pages of major newspapers.

However, in the amending process of the Senate, which allows unrelated amendments to be offered to virtually any piece of legislation, hope springs eternal and often prevents the permanent demise of an issue. McCain-Feingold was resuscitated when its proponents threatened to attach it to other legislation as an amendment, and to filibuster if the majority leadership used its prerogatives to prevent this course of action. They blocked a major transportation reauthorization bill, which contained billions of dollars for highway construction and mass transit operations throughout the country, until an agreement was reached to allow a more direct vote on campaign finance reform in 1998.

But when the issue returned to the floor for a week in February 1998 the political and procedural dynamics remained essentially unchanged. In this case, Lott presented "paycheck protection" as the base bill; McCain-Feingold was a substitute.

While supporters of McCain-Feingold demonstrated a majority for their proposal and in opposition to "paycheck protection," they got nowhere near the sixty votes required to end debate. Nor were there actual votes on adoption of the various proposals. Instead, as is often the case in the Senate, procedural votes were employed as a safe test of strength; each side retained its full rights to filibuster if it did not get its way.

McConnell failed to table McCain-Feingold, 48–51. Sen. Olympia Snowe, R-Maine, proposed an amendment to the McCain-Feingold substitute to prohibit use of labor or corporate money to broadcast campaign ads shortly before a primary or general election. This was intended to weaken the appeal of "paycheck protection" and win over additional moderate Republicans to support cloture. It failed to do that, but a tabling motion to kill it failed 47–50. Snowe's amendment was then adopted by voice vote. Another effort to table McCain-Feingold, as amended, failed 48–50. A cloture vote on the McCain-Feingold substitute failed, 51–48. Lott could not obtain cloture on his paycheck protection base bill, 45–54, failing even to secure a simple majority.

All of the key votes, except for Snowe's amendment, were on either tabling motions or cloture. No direct votes were permitted on McCain-Feingold or the Lott bill. Lott then used his leadership prerogative to be recognized to offer multiple amendments and motions to recommit—to "fill the amendment tree"—with his proposals, which effectively precluded other senators from offering anything else and prevented further action on the bill.

---

call votes had occurred, the period for morning hour had long since expired, and the motion to call up the defense bill was once again debatable. Future majority leaders were thus put on notice that a similar parliamentary maelstrom could erupt if the use of the morning hour to circumvent a filibuster were ever attempted again.

Morning Business

The Senate rarely conducts morning business and the morning hour as stated in its rules because the formal procedures are too cumbersome and, as discussed above, do not really work to help the leadership avoid filibusters. However, it can conduct morning business at any time by unanimous consent.

The decision to adjourn or recess at the end of the day is made by unanimous consent or by motion, usually by the majority leader. The leadership generally prefers to recess from day to day because it can maintain greater control over the daily schedule. Senators seeking to delay action on a measure, however, may push for adjournment because the convening of a new legislative day offers them more opportunities to slow Senate deliberations.

If the Senate has recessed and there is no morning hour

when it next reconvenes, it may still conduct morning business by unanimous consent. Within morning hour, morning business may be followed by the call of the Calendar of General Orders. During this procedure, which is almost always set aside by unanimous consent, the chair calls each bill in the order in which it appears on the calendar. If objection is raised to considering the bill, the chair moves on to the next measure. No senator may speak for more than five minutes on any one bill during the call of the calendar.

Morning hour may be followed by a period when members are given permission to speak for brief periods on virtually any topic. The Senate next turns to any unfinished business. If there is none, or if it is set aside by unanimous consent, the Senate may then take up new business.

Most major bills are brought up under unanimous consent agreements worked out in advance by the leadership. If a member objects to a unanimous consent request, the leadership may decide to renegotiate the consent agreement or it may move that the Senate take up the bill. Because most such motions are debatable, a filibuster could be launched against the bill before it is even technically on the floor. Motions to proceed to consider some measures, such as House-Senate conference reports, are not debatable, though the conference reports themselves may be filibustered once they become the pending business.

Floor Debate

Once a bill is brought to the floor for consideration, floor managers take over the task of guiding the legislation through the amendment process and final passage. As in the House, the chairman and ranking minority member of the committee or subcommittee with jurisdiction for the bill act as the majority and minority floor managers. Floor managers play much the same role in the Senate as they do in the House, mapping strategy for passing the bill, deflecting debilitating or undesirable amendments, offering amendments to attract additional support, and seeing that members in favor of the bill turn out to vote for it.

On measures brought to the floor under a unanimous consent agreement, the time allotted for debate is usually divided evenly between the two opposing sides. The chair gives preferential recognition first to the majority manager and then to the minority manager, who, if they control time, yield it to other senators. If there is no time agreement, any senator may seek recognition from the chair. Once recognized, in the absence of a time agreement, a senator may speak as long as he or she likes and on any subject, unless he or she violates the rules of the Senate. A senator may yield temporarily for the consideration of other business, after asking unanimous consent to do so without losing the floor, or to another senator who wants to ask a question, but he or she may not parcel out time to other members as floor managers in the House typically do and as Senate managers may when time is controlled. Typically, senators yielded to find ways to make broader statements within the guise of asking their questions.

The Senate does not consider bills in a Committee of the Whole or set aside a period for general debate before the amending process begins. Amendments are in order as soon as the bill is made the pending order of business.

Debate in the modern Senate is a far cry from debate during the Senate's "Golden Age," when great orators like Daniel Webster, John C. Calhoun, and Henry Clay fought an eloquent war of words over slavery and states' rights. While a few issues still engender lively debate on the floor, Senate speeches are seldom spontaneous; most are prepared by staff and read to an often nearly empty chamber or inserted, unread, in the *Congressional Record*. "Floor debate has deteriorated into a never-ending series of points of order, procedural motions, appeals and waiver votes, punctuated by endless hours of time-killing quorum calls," Sen. Nancy Landon Kassebaum, R-Kan. (1978–1997), wrote in the *Washington Post*. "Serious policy deliberations are a rarity. 'Great debate' is only a memory, replaced by a preoccupation with procedure that makes it exceedingly difficult to transact even routine business."[22]

"There is dialogue and debate, but most of it does not take place on the floor under public scrutiny," Sen. Paul Simon, D-Ill. (1975–1997), said in 1985.[23]

Comparatively few limits are placed on the debate that does occur on the Senate floor. Most unanimous consent agreements limit the time to be spent debating amendments and on debatable motions, points of order, and appeals of rulings. Some agreements also limit the overall time that the entire bill, including amendments, may be debated. A few statutes, such as the 1974 budget act, also effectively prohibit unlimited debate on such matters as budget resolutions and budget reconciliation bills. A motion to table, if adopted, also serves to cut off debate on an amendment or motion, but does not affect the right to offer additional amendments. And under Rule XXII, the filibuster rule, sixty senators may vote to invoke cloture, limit debate to a potential maximum of thirty hours, require amendments to be germane. The "previous question" motion, which brings debate to a close in the House, is not used in the Senate.

Senate rules bar members from speaking more than twice on the same subject in the same legislative day. This has not been an effective limit on debate, however, because each amendment is considered a different subject, and the "two speech rule" was effectively gutted by a Senate vote in 1986 overturning a ruling of the presiding officer after the issue of enforcing the rule was raised. The so-called "Pastore Rule" adopted in 1964, named after Sen. John O. Pastore, D-R.I., requires debate to be germane for the first three hours following the morning hour on a new legislative day, or after pending business has been laid before the Senate on any calendar day. However, the morning hour is almost never used; on other days, while the three-hour time is still tracked, the rule has not been enforced and has little practical impact today.

As in the House, the Senate presumes that a quorum is present until a member suggests otherwise. During floor debate a

At a Senate Budget Committee hearing, Chairman Pete Domenici, R-N.M., discusses the White House's proposed federal budget with Olympia Snowe, R-Maine.

senator will often suggest the absence of a quorum. This is a tactical maneuver designed to occupy time while the leadership negotiates a procedural agreement or to give a senator time to reach the floor to speak or to offer an amendment. Except in limited circumstances, the presiding officer is not permitted to count the senators on the floor to see whether a quorum really exists, as the House does, but must proceed to a call of the roll. When the reason for requesting the quorum call is resolved—that is, when the negotiation is completed or the senator is in the chamber and ready to proceed—the call may be suspended by unanimous consent.

This sort of quorum call differs from a "live" quorum, where a member insists upon a majority of the members actually appearing on the Senate floor. By refusing to answer the roll call, opponents of a bill or an amendment can delay action or even try to deny the Senate a quorum—in the absence of a quorum no business or debate may take place and the Senate must wait for one to appear, direct the sergeant at arms to obtain the presence of absentees, or adjourn.

A dramatic example of an attempt to force a quorum to appear occurred in 1988 during debate on a controversial campaign finance bill. To break a Republican filibuster, Majority Leader Byrd sought to keep the Senate in session all night. Republicans countered by calling for repeated live quorums and then refusing to come to the floor. That forced Democrats to keep enough members present to maintain the quorum needed for the Senate to remain in session. When the Democrats came up short around midnight, Byrd resorted to a motion directing the sergeant at arms to arrest absent senators and bring them to the floor. The sergeant at arms arrested Sen. Bob Packwood, R-Ore., after forcing his way into the senator's office, and escorted him to the entrance of the Senate chamber. When Packwood refused to go in under his own steam, two Capitol police lifted the senator and carried him feet first into the Senate chamber. Byrd had established his quorum, but he was ultimately unable to break the filibuster and the bill died.

The Amending Process

The flexibility that marks the Senate's rules of procedure also characterizes its amending process. When a bill is taken up for consideration on the Senate floor, it is not read for amendment by section, or title, as in the House, where amendments to the beginning of the bill are offered first, and so on. Any part of the measure is open immediately to amendment in the Senate, so the subject matter of debate may shift repeatedly while the bill is on the floor. Unlike the House, the Senate is not bound by a five-minute rule governing debate on amendments. Unless limited by a unanimous consent agreement or cloture, debate on amendments may continue until no senator seeks recognition to offer further amendments. The majority leader can obtain recognition at any time no other senator has the floor, to try to advantage his party's positions on a pending bill.

Tax legislation is particularly susceptible to nongermane amendments for a special reason. The Constitution requires revenue measures to originate in the House, a stipulation that restricts the Senate to amending House-passed bills that contain tax provisions. The Senate cannot simply add a tax provision to a House-originated measure that does not contain any. If the Senate attempts to circumvent the constitutional restriction and send a tax provision to the House on its own, the House will "blue slip" the legislation—adopt a resolution as a question of the privileges of the House sending the offending matter back to the Senate without action. Despite this constitutional stricture, the Senate, nonetheless, takes the initiative on tax issues from time to time under its constitutional power to amend all tax bills as it may all other House-passed measures. It even may act first on its own tax bill and add the provisions later as an amendment to a House-passed tax bill.

A noteworthy example occurred in 1982, when Congress approved a $98 billion tax increase that the House considered for the first time when it took up the conference report on the bill. The tax increase was required by the fiscal 1983 budget resolution. The House Ways and Means Committee took no action, in part because its members were unable to agree on what should go into a revenue-raising package and in part because Democrats wanted to force Republican President Reagan to share some of the blame for raising taxes in an election year. The Republican-led Senate Finance Committee wrote a bill raising revenue and then attached it to a minor tax bill the House had passed in 1981. After the Senate passed its version, the full House agreed with the Ways and Means Committee's recommendation to go straight to conference on the House-passed bill as amended by the Senate.

Moreover, amendments need not be germane, except in the case of general appropriations bills (this restriction was gutted by Senate votes in 1995 but restored in 1999), bills on which cloture has been invoked, concurrent budget resolutions, budget reconciliation bills, and measures regulated by unanimous consent agreement. And the number of amendments that may be offered is rarely limited. Unanimous consent requests may disallow nongermane amendments but they seldom limit the number of germane amendments that may be offered. Once cloture is invoked, the Senate may consider only germane amendments. When a cloture petition is filed, senators anticipating that cloture may be invoked on a measure and wishing to protect their rights must submit first-degree amendments by one o'clock in the afternoon on the day following the submission of the petition and second-degree amendments by one hour prior to the beginning of the cloture vote.

The right of senators to offer nongermane amendments is a primary means of ensuring that legislation does not get bottled up in an unsympathetic committee. In 1983, for example, Senate Finance Committee Chairman Bob Dole, R-Kan., vehemently opposed a proposal to repeal a provision of the 1982 tax bill that required tax withholding on interest and dividends. But when proponents of repeal threatened to attach it to important jobs and Social Security legislation, the Senate leadership agreed to allow it to be offered as an amendment to an unrelated trade bill.

When the Senate requires that amendments be germane the test is stricter than that in the House. An amendment in the Senate is considered germane only if it deletes something from the bill, adjusts a figure up or down, or restricts the scope of the bill. An amendment is considered nongermane if it in some way expands the scope of the bill, no matter how relevant the subject matter of the amendment may be to the underlying legislation. An amendment adding a fourth country to a bill granting most-favored-nation trade status to three countries would be just as nongermane as an amendment revising the criminal code.

A sponsor may modify or withdraw an amendment at any time before a roll-call vote is ordered on it or it becomes the subject of a unanimous consent agreement. The amendment may then be modified or withdrawn only by unanimous consent. (In the House, members may modify or withdraw their amendments only by unanimous consent during consideration in the Committee of the Whole.) A sponsor may agree to modify an amendment to make it more acceptable to a greater number of senators. If a senator has offered an amendment simply to make a point, he or she may choose to withdraw it before it comes to a vote. Amended language cannot be changed again unless the change is part of an amendment that also changes other unamended parts of the legislation.

Amendments offered by the reporting committee are taken up before other amendments. Often, the Senate by unanimous consent agrees to the committee amendments en bloc, particularly if the amendments are extensive, and then provides that the bill as amended is to be "considered as an original text for the purpose of further amendment." Or, as is frequently the case with appropriations bills, the Senate might agree en bloc to all but one or two of the committee amendments, which are then considered separately. Such amendments are themselves open to amendment and must be disposed of before other unrelated amendments are proposed.

As in the House, the principles governing consideration of amendments in the Senate are similar: legislation may be amended in the first and second degree, which means that a proposed amendment to a bill may itself be amended; and again, substitutes may also be proposed for pending amendments as well as for the bill itself.

The Senate process, however, is more complex in its treatment of the precedence of different types of first- and second-degree perfecting amendments and substitutes. It differs somewhat from the House process in the order in which they may be offered. Another difference is the ability of senators to modify their amendments virtually at will, and, in some cases, to offer second-degree amendments to their own amendments. The majority leader, who always has priority of recognition, has sometimes used these tactics to offer several proposals himself and close off the "amendment tree" to opponents.

In voting on amendments, the Senate makes frequent use of a procedural device known as tabling to block or kill amendments. When approved, a motion to "lay on the table" is considered the final disposition of that issue. The motion is not debatable, and adoption requires a simple majority vote. In the Senate, a motion to table is usually offered after an amendment has been debated, rather than as a means to prevent debate. By voting to table, a senator can appear to avoid being recorded directly on a controversial amendment to a politically sensitive issue, though the substantive result is the same. (Although the House also has a motion to table, it is not in order in the Committee of the Whole and thus cannot be used to prevent consideration of amendments offered there. In the House, the motion is most commonly used to block any debate on "hostile" motions or resolutions—that is, those not supported by the majority leadership—that might otherwise be debatable and whose consideration would, unless tabled, give the minority party control of the floor.)

Like the House, the Senate has available motions to recommit a bill under consideration on the floor to a committee, which would terminate action on it. The Senate may also choose to recommit a bill to a committee with instructions to take certain actions, such as to report back "forthwith" with amendments, and such a motion if adopted would immediately bring the bill back to the floor in an altered form. The Senate motion to recommit is more flexible than its House equivalent, because it can be offered at any point during consideration of a measure, not just at the end of the amendment process, can be offered more than once, may be amended by proposing instructions or by offering amendments to instructions offered in the initial motion, and may be proposed by any senator without preference to those in the minority. The motion also has precedence over the offering of amendments.

Filibusters and Cloture

In its most extreme form, the Senate's tradition of unlimited debate can turn into a filibuster—the deliberate use of extended debate or procedural delays to block action on a measure supported by a majority of members. Filibusters once provided the Senate's best theater. Practitioners had to be ready for days or weeks of freewheeling debate, and all other business was blocked until one side conceded. In the modern era, drama is rare. Disappointment awaits visitors to the Senate gallery who expect a real-life version of Jimmy Stewart's climactic oration in the 1939 movie, *Mr. Smith Goes to Washington*. They are likely to look down on an empty floor and hear only the drone of a clerk reading absent senators' names in a mind-numbing succession of quorum calls. Often today's filibusterers do not even have to be on the floor, nor do the bills they are opposing. *(See box, Dilatory Tactics: As Old as the Senate, this page.)*

Despite the lack of drama, filibusters are still effective weapons. Any controversial legislation that comes to the floor without a prearranged time agreement is vulnerable to fili-

DILATORY TACTICS: AS OLD AS THE SENATE

The Senate was just six months old in 1789 when delaying tactics were first used, by opponents of a bill to locate the nation's capital on the Susquehanna River. By 1840 dilatory debate was so common that Henry Clay of Kentucky was demanding "a rule which would place the business of the Senate under the control of a majority."

The first full-fledged filibusters occurred the next year, when Democrats and Whigs squared off first over the appointment of official Senate printers and then over the establishment of a national bank. Slavery, the Civil War, Reconstruction, and ex-slaves' voting rights in turn sparked the increasingly frequent and contentious filibusters of the nineteenth century. Because the Senate repeatedly rejected efforts to restrict debate, the majority's only recourse was to win unanimous consent for a time limit on considering a bill, on a case-by-case basis.

Minor curbs on debate were adopted early in the twentieth century. But they did not hinder Republican filibusterers from killing two of President Woodrow Wilson's proposals to put the nation on a war footing—bills in 1915 concerning ship purchases and in 1917 to arm merchant ships.

As a political scientist in 1882, Wilson had celebrated "the Senate's opportunities for open and unrestricted discussion." After the 1917 defeat, he railed, "The Senate of the United States is the only legislative body in the world which cannot act when the majority is ready for action. A little group of willful men . . . have rendered the great government of the United States helpless and contemptible."

On March 8, 1917, the Senate yielded to public outcry and adopted a cloture rule (Rule XXII), which required a vote of two-thirds of those present to end debate. The rule's framers predicted it would be little used, and for years that was the case.

The first successful cloture motion came in 1919, ending debate on the Treaty of Versailles, which nonetheless failed to be ratified.

Nine more motions were voted on through 1927, of which three succeeded. Over the next thirty-five years, until 1962, only sixteen were voted on and not one was adopted.

In large part that reflected the politics of civil rights. Southern Democrats successfully filibustered legislation against the poll tax, literacy tests, lynching, and employment discrimination by building an anticloture coalition that included westerners and some Republicans. In 1949 proponents of the right to filibuster gained a further advantage when they were able to amend Rule XXII to require a two-thirds vote of the total Senate membership to invoke cloture. That change occurred after a coalition of northern Democrats and moderate Republicans sought to make it easier for the majority to invoke cloture.

Undaunted by its failure, a liberal-moderate coalition sought to ease Rule XXII nearly every time a new Congress convened. A key strategy was to assert the right of a majority to amend Senate rules at the beginning of a Congress. They received support from sympathetic vice presidents Richard Nixon, Hubert Humphrey, and Nelson Rockefeller. Filibuster supporters maintained that the Senate was a "continuing body" not subject to wholesale revision with each new class of senators who, after all, constituted only one-third of the chamber.

In 1959 Rule XXII was amended back to provide for limitation of debate by a vote of two-thirds of the senators present and voting, with the vote to occur two days after a cloture petition was submitted by sixteen senators. If cloture was adopted, further debate was limited to one hour for each senator on the bill itself and on all amendments affecting it. Amendments that were not germane to the pending business and dilatory motions were out of order. The rule applied both to regular legislation and to motions to change the Standing Rules of the Senate.

buster; success is most likely near the end of the session, when a filibuster on one bill may imperil action on other, more urgent legislation. Filibusters may be intended to kill a measure outright, by forcing the leadership to pull the measure off the floor so that it can move on to other business, but they are often mounted to force a compromise on the measure. Time is such a precious commodity in today's Senate that individual members who even threaten to hold a bill hostage to lengthy debate can usually force compromises on the measure, either in committee or on the floor.

Filibusters have always generated intense controversy. Supporters view filibusters as a defense against hasty or ill-advised legislation and as a guarantee that minority views will be heard. Detractors contend that filibusters allow a minority to thwart the will of a majority and impede orderly consideration of issues before the Senate.

Silencing a Filibuster. A filibuster can be ended by negotiating a compromise on the disputed matter or by mustering a determined supermajority of senators to shut it off. Since 1917 the Senate has also been able to vote to invoke cloture to cut off a filibuster, though the supermajority required to do so has changed over the years.

The procedure to end a filibuster is contained in Senate Rule XXII. This cumbersome procedure requires sixteen senators to sign a cloture petition and file it with the presiding officer of the Senate. Two days later, and one hour after the Senate convenes, the presiding officer establishes the presence of a quorum and then poses the question: "Is it the sense of the Senate that the debate shall be brought to a close?" If three-fifths of the Senate (sixty senators) votes in favor of the motion, cloture is invoked. (A two-thirds majority of those present and voting, which would be sixty-seven senators if all were present, is needed to invoke cloture on proposals to amend the Senate's standing rules, including Rule XXII. This means that an even larger majority would be needed to change the rule. In practice, it puts an almost impossible task in front of advocates of ending the cloture rule entirely and creating a situation of simple majority rule in the Senate.)

Slowly, the anticloture coalition began to dissolve. In 1964 the Senate for the first time invoked cloture on a civil rights bill, cutting off the longest filibuster in Senate history. A year later cloture was approved for another civil rights measure, the Voting Rights Act, and in 1968 a filibuster on an open housing bill was cut off.

In 1969, the Senate came close to eviscerating the cloture rule, as Vice President Humphrey ruled that the Senate could end debate on a rules change by a majority vote at the beginning of a new Congress. However, the Senate promptly overruled Humphrey.

By the early 1970s the liberals' victories on civil rights had cooled their ardor for cloture reform. Moreover, they had become the ones doing much of the filibustering—against President Nixon's Vietnam policies, weapons systems, and antibusing proposals.

In 1973, for the first time in years, the new Senate did not fight over the cloture rule. But in 1975 the liberals tried again—and won. After the Senate seemed ready on a series of procedural votes to adopt the principle that a simple majority could change the rules at the beginning of a Congress without having to invoke cloture, senators opposed to cloture reform agreed to relax the supermajority requirements if this precedent were overturned. Under Rule XXII as amended, three-fifths of the total membership of the Senate, or sixty votes, could shut off a filibuster—seven votes less than was needed under the old rule if every senator voted. (A two-thirds vote of those present and voting was still required to cut off debate on proposed rules changes.)

The 1975 revision made it easier for a majority to invoke cloture. But much of the revision's success relied on the willingness of the senators to abide by the spirit as well as the letter of the chamber's rules. When cloture was invoked on a particular measure, senators had generally conceded defeat and proceeded to a vote without further delay.

But in 1976 conservative James B. Allen, D-Ala., began violating this unwritten rule of conduct and finding ways around the existing restrictions. By capitalizing on a loophole that permitted unlimited postcloture quorum calls, parliamentary motions, and roll-call votes on amendments introduced before cloture was invoked, Allen was able to delay a vote on the issue itself for far longer than the hour allotted to him under the 1959 rules revision. In 1977, with Vice President Mondale presiding, Majority Leader Robert C. Byrd took the floor to have ruled out of order dozens of amendments filed by liberal Senators Howard Metzenbaum, D-Ohio, and James Abourezk, D-S.D., who were staging a postcloture filibuster on energy legislation, a major legislative priority of the Carter administration. The vice president refused to entertain appeals of his rulings or to recognize anyone other than the majority leader. Mondale and Byrd were subsequently criticized for heavy-handed and arbitrary tactics, but their actions stood amid indications that the Senate's tolerance for delaying tactics pushed to a potentially infinite degree was waning.

The Senate closed the postcloture loophole in 1979, when it agreed to an absolute limit on such delaying tactics. The rule provided that once cloture was invoked, a final vote had to be taken after no more than 100 hours of debate. All time spent on quorum calls, roll calls, and other parliamentary procedures was counted against the 100-hour limit. In 1986 the Senate reduced that limitation to thirty hours. The change, enacted as part of the Senate's decision to allow live television coverage of its floor action, was intended to quicken the pace of the proceedings.

Republican control of the Senate in 1981–1987, and since 1995, pretty much eliminated interest by liberals in further changes in the cloture rule. Indeed, the filibuster became an important tool used by Democrats to restrain Republican presidents and, later, to block key parts of the political agenda of House Republicans.

There is no limit on how long a filibuster must go on before a cloture petition can be filed. "Years ago, even Lyndon Johnson wouldn't try to get cloture until after a week," Sen. Strom Thurmond, R-S.C., said in 1987. "But now, after one day, if the leaders see you are really going to fight, they'll apply cloture immediately."[24] Thurmond's record for the longest filibuster by a single individual—twenty-four hours and eighteen minutes on a 1957 civil rights bill (which became law despite his efforts)—is likely to stand in the modern era.

Nor are there any limitations on the number of times the Senate can try to invoke cloture on the same filibuster. "There used to be an unwritten rule that three [cloture votes] was enough," said Robert B. Dove, who was Senate parliamentarian during periods of Republican control in the 1980s and 1990s.[25] But in 1975 the Senate took six cloture votes in a futile effort to cut off debate on a dispute over a contested Senate seat in New Hampshire. And in 1987–1988, the Senate took eight cloture votes to shut off a Republican filibuster of a campaign spending bill before conceding defeat and shelving the measure.

Increased Use of Filibusters. For most of the Senate's history, the filibuster was used sparingly and for the most part only on legislative battles of historical importance, such as peace treaties and civil rights matters. Since the mid-1970s, the Senate has seen a significant increase in its use. Members, Sen. Thomas F. Eagleton, D-Mo., said in 1985, "are prepared to practice the art of gridlock at the drop of a speech or the drop of an amendment."[26] Indeed, in some cases the majority leader, aware of potential controversy surrounding a bill, may offer a motion to proceed to its consideration and then immediately file for cloture on that motion to get a more accurate sense of the intensity of the opposition; if sixty votes are not available, he or she may not attempt to advance the legislation further.

Ironically, a change in Senate rules that made it easier to invoke cloture to cut off a filibuster coincided with their increased use. In 1975, after years of trying, Senate liberals succeeded in pushing through a change in the Senate's cloture rule. Instead of two-thirds of those voting (sixty-seven if all senators are present), three-fifths of the membership, or sixty senators, could invoke cloture on a filibuster.

Several factors account for the increase. More issues come

CONGRESSIONAL RECORD

The *Congressional Record* is the primary source of information about what happens on the floors of the Senate and House of Representatives. Published daily when Congress is in session, the *Record* provides an officially sanctioned account of each chamber's debate and shows how individual members voted on all recorded votes.

The *Record* is not the official account of congressional proceedings. That is provided in each chamber's Journal, which reports actions taken but not the accompanying debate. But the *Record* is often used by the courts to determine legislative history—what Congress intended when it passed a law. The status of tapes of televised broadcasts of House and Senate proceedings in such situations is undetermined.

By law the *Record* is supposed to provide "substantially a verbatim report of the proceedings." Exchanges among legislators can be quite lively and revealing, though watching Congress on television conveys far more of the flavor and atmospherics governing debate than reading the *Record*. Until recent years, there was broad discretion to edit remarks for the *Record*, fixing grammatical errors or even deleting words spoken in the heat of floor debate. Speeches not given on the floor were often included, although both the House and Senate have tightened rules about "inserting remarks," as the process is known. There have been complaints from time to time that this practice had been abused. The full texts of bills, conference reports, and other documents, rarely read in full on the floor, are often printed in the *Record*.

When Republicans took control of the House in 1995, the rules were changed to limit alterations that members might make "only to technical, grammatical and typographical corrections," which prohibited removal of remarks actually made. Written statements can still be inserted in the *Record*, even within the text of actual remarks made by a member, as long as they appear in a distinctive typeface. The new stringency was ruled to apply even to the Speaker, who had customarily refined rulings made from the chair after the fact to ensure clarity. Now the Speaker's actual comments appear verbatim.

The Speaker often inserts written material into the *Record*, especially at the beginning of a Congress, to elaborate certain practices that he will follow in recognizing members, referring bills, and on other subjects.

HISTORY

Before 1825 reports of congressional debates were sporadic. In 1789–1790 Thomas Lloyd of New York took down congressional debates in shorthand. Four volumes exist of his *Congressional Register*. Between 1790 and 1825 debate in the House was reported haphazardly by some of the better newspapers. Senate debates scarcely were reported at all. In 1834 Gales and Seaton published the first of forty-two volumes of *Annals of Congress*, which brought together material from newspapers, magazines, and other sources on congressional proceedings from the First through the Twelfth Congress (March 3, 1789, to May 27, 1824).

From 1824 through 1837 Gales and Seaton published a *Register of Debate*, which directly reported congressional proceedings. In 1833 Blair and Rives began to publish *The Congressional Globe*, but debates were still not reported systematically until 1865, when the *Globe* took on a form and style that later became standard. When the government contract for publication of the *Globe* expired in 1873, Congress provided that the *Congressional Record* would be produced by the Government Printing Office.

PROCEEDINGS

The *Record* contains four sections. Two of them, the proceedings of the Senate and of the House, are edited accounts of floor debate

before the Senate, making time an even scarcer commodity than in the past. More issues are controversial, and in a period of divided party rule between Congress and the White House, which has prevailed much of the time since the 1970s, more partisan. In addition, constituents and special interest groups put more pressure on members, and members are more apt to pursue their political goals even if it means inconveniencing their colleagues. In the 1990s, filibusters and threats of filibuster were common weapons of senators hoping merely to spotlight or change as well as delay or kill legislation.

The track system, which allows the Senate to set aside a filibustered measure temporarily while it considers other legislation, also may have contributed to the heightened use of filibusters. "For senators peripheral to the fight on a filibustered measure, separate tracking made filibusters more tolerable, made them less resentful of the filibustering senators, and even may have reduced the incentive to vote for cloture," Steven Smith wrote. "And for the filibustering senators, tracking may have improved the chances of success and reduced the costs of filibustering."[27]

The Rise and Fall of the Postcloture Filibuster. Traditionally, filibusterers bowed to the inevitable in the face of a successful motion to invoke cloture, abandoning any further attempts to delay action on the disputed measure. After the Senate made it easier to invoke cloture in 1975, however, a postcloture filibuster quickly appeared. The tactic took advantage of the fact that the hour allotted each senator did not count time spent on procedural motions and that all germane amendments filed before cloture was invoked were in order. By filing dozens of amendments, demanding roll calls and quorum calls, and engaging in other parliamentary procedures, senators could delay final action for days or weeks.

The postcloture filibuster was developed largely by James B. Allen, a conservative Democrat from Alabama. But two northern liberals, James G. Abourezk, D-S.D., and Howard M. Metzenbaum, D-Ohio, exploited the tactic fully in 1977, tying up the Senate for two weeks after cloture had been invoked on a bill to deregulate natural gas. The postcloture debate was ended only after the presiding officer, Vice President Walter Mondale, in close consultation with Majority Leader Byrd, took the then-

---

and other action taken in each chamber. A member may request "unanimous consent to extend my remarks at this point in the *Record*," or to include extraneous matter, at any time he or she is able to gain recognition on the floor. When the request is granted, and it almost always is, a member may include a statement, newspaper article, or speech, which will appear in the body of the *Record* where the member requested.

Until March 1978 there was no way to tell whether a lawmaker had actually delivered his or her remarks or had them inserted. Since then, inserted remarks are indicated in the House proceedings by a different typeface; in the Senate they are denoted by black dots, or bullets. If a member read only a few words from a speech or article, it would appear in the *Record* as if the member had delivered it in its entirety. As noted, the House in 1995 restricted this practice to require all undelivered remarks to appear in a separate typeface.

Since 1979 time cues have marked House floor debate to show roughly when a particular discussion occurred. Senate proceedings have no indication of time.

EXTENSIONS OF REMARKS

In addition to inserting material, senators and representatives are given further space to extend their remarks. By unanimous consent, they may add such extraneous material as speeches given outside Congress, selected editorials, or letters. Such material may also be included in the body of the *Record* by unanimous consent if a representative or senator prefers.

DAILY DIGEST

The fourth section of the *Record* is the Daily Digest, which summarizes House and Senate floor action for the day as well as Senate and House committee meetings and conferences. It also notes

committee reports filed and the time and date of the next House and Senate sessions and all committee meetings. The last issue of the Digest in the week lists the program for the coming week, including legislation scheduled for floor action if it has been announced, and all committee meetings. At the beginning of each month the Digest publishes a statistical summation of congressional activity in the previous month. An index to the *Record* is published semimonthly.

COSTS

About 9,000 copies of each day's issue of the *Record* are printed. In fiscal 1997 the total cost came to $18.9 million. An annual subscription cost $295 in 1998; an individual copy cost $2.50. Until 1970 a subscription cost only $1.50 a month. The *Record* is also available on microfiche.

Rules require that any insert of more than two pages include an estimate of printing costs by the Government Printing Office. One of the most expensive inserts appeared in the issue of June 15, 1987, when Rep. Bill Alexander, D-Ark., inserted 403 pages covering three and a half years of congressional debate on an amendment barring military aid to the antigovernment contra guerrillas in Nicaragua. Estimated cost of the insertion: $197,000.

COMPUTER ACCESS

The public can gain free access to the daily *Congressional Record* through Internet web sites run by the U.S. Government Printing Office (*http://www.access.gpo.gov*) and the "Thomas" service provided by the Library of Congress (*http://thomas.loc.gov*). (See *"Congressional Information on the Internet," p. 1146, in Reference Materials, Vol. II.*)

extraordinary step of recognizing only Byrd, ruling amendments offered by the two senators out of order and refusing recognition to appeal his rulings. While these actions stood, effectively killed the filibuster, and ensured passage of the president's energy legislation, their arbitrary nature disturbed some senators since they placed "ends" (passage of a bill) ahead of "means" (each senator's right to use the rules).

In 1979 the Senate moved formally to eviscerate the postcloture filibuster by including all time spent on procedural activities as well as on substantive debate against each senator's allotted hour. That put a 100-hour cap on postcloture debate. Senators were also barred from calling up more than two amendments until every other senator had an opportunity to call up two amendments. And the presiding officer was authorized to rule clearly dilatory motions out of order. In 1986 the Senate agreed to cap postcloture debate at thirty hours. Senators could still be recognized for an hour, but the time was allocated on a first-come, first-served basis. Any senators who had not yet been recognized at the end of thirty hours were each entitled to receive ten minutes.

Final Senate Action

Once debate and voting on all amendments has ended and no senator wishes to speak, a final vote on the pending legislation is taken. Senate observers are often surprised to discover that most bills pass by voice votes with only a handful of senators present. Any member, however, can request a roll call on final passage and the Senate nearly always grants such a request.

After the final vote is announced, the Senate must dispose of the routine motion to reconsider before a bill is considered finally passed. A senator who voted for the bill (or who did not vote) moves to reconsider the vote; a second senator who voted for the bill moves to table the motion to reconsider, and the tabling motion is almost always adopted, usually by voice vote. In the House, the Speaker in order to save time usually says, "Without objection, the motion to reconsider is laid upon the table."

Final Action: Resolving Differences

Before a bill can be sent to the White House for the president's signature, it must be approved in identical form by both chambers of Congress.

There are three ways of resolving differences between the two houses: one chamber may yield to the other and simply accept its amendments; amendments move back and forth between the two houses until both agree; or a conference committee may be convened. The strategy that is used can be determined by many factors—the nature of the legislation, the time of year it is being considered, and the desire to avoid procedural entanglements.

On many noncontroversial measures the second chamber may simply agree to the version approved by the first chamber. When that occurs, no further legislative action is required, and the bill can be submitted to the president.

On virtually all major legislation, however, the second chamber approves a version that differs, sometimes radically, from the measure adopted by the first chamber. (Often the second chamber already has a similar measure under consideration.) When that happens, the second chamber has two options. It may return the bill to the chamber of origin, which then has the choice of accepting the second chamber's amendments, accepting them with further amendments, or disagreeing to the other version and requesting a House-Senate conference. Or, less frequently, the second house itself may request a conference.

Sometimes one chamber accepts major amendments made by the other to avoid further floor action that might jeopardize the bill. That occurred on a bill involving Alaskan lands in the postelection session of 1980. Democratic sponsors of the House version bill knew that they would face a Republican-controlled Senate in 1981 as a result of the election, and that any conference agreement would face a successful filibuster from the newly energized Senate minority in the lame-duck session. As a result, the House grudgingly accepted the Senate version, which did not contain as many environmental protections, rather than risk ending up with no bill at all.

Often, after both chambers have passed different versions of the same measure, members and staff of the House and Senate committees with jurisdiction for the bill informally work out a compromise that one house adopts as an amendment to the other chamber's version. The latter chamber then agrees to the version as amended, avoiding a conference and clearing it for the president.

Just as neither chamber may offer amendments beyond the second degree, neither chamber may amend the other's amendments more than twice. Like other rules, however, this one can be waived and sometimes is. The budget reconciliation act of 1985 was shuffled between the two chambers nine times before agreement was finally reached the following year.

It should be noted that many bills pass one chamber of Congress never to be considered in the other. Those measures, as well as any on which the House and Senate are unable to reconcile their differences, die at the end of the Congress.

CONFERENCE ACTION

Sen. Joel Bennett Clark, D-Mo., once introduced a resolution providing that "all bills and resolutions shall be read twice and, without debate, referred to conference." He was joking, of course, but his proposal highlights the crucial role of conference committees in drafting the final form of complex and controversial legislation. Everything the bill's sponsors worked for and all the efforts exerted by the executive branch and private interests to help pass or defeat it can be won or lost during these negotiations. Some of the hardest bargaining in the entire legislative process takes place in conference committees, and frequently the conference goes on for days, weeks, even months, before the two sides reconcile their differences.

During floor consideration of a bill members may adopt certain tactics solely to better position themselves for the bargaining and compromise that is the hallmark of all conference nego-

House and Senate negotiators meet in conference to work out the final shape of a major transportation funding bill.

tiations. A senator, for example, may demand a roll call on a particular amendment to demonstrate to the House the Senate's solid support for the amendment—or its solid opposition. A committee may add some provisions to its version that can be traded away in conference. Or it may deliberately keep out a provision it knows the other chamber favors, again to have something to trade in conference. A floor manager may agree to an amendment, especially if he or she can persuade the sponsor not to ask for a recorded vote, knowing that it can be dumped in the conference.

Once in conference, conferees generally try to grant concessions only insofar as they remain confident the chamber they represent will accept the compromises. That is not always possible, however. The threat of a Senate filibuster on a conference report, for example, may influence House conferees to drop a provision that they believe too many senators might find distasteful. Time also may be a factor, especially at the end of a Congress when delay might cause a bill to die in conference.

Calling a Conference

Either chamber can request a conference once both have considered the same legislation. Generally, the chamber that approved the legislation first will disagree to the amendments made by the second body and request that a conference be convened. Sometimes, however, the second body will ask for a conference immediately after it has passed the legislation, assuming that the other chamber will not accept its amendments. The distinction can be important, since the chamber that requests the conference nearly always, by custom, acts last on the conference report. Depending on the political situation, this may have strategic importance affecting the legislation's chances for final passage.

Both chambers technically must go to conference on a single bill. Thus one chamber often takes up the other's version of the measure, strikes everything after the enacting clause, and substitutes its version for everything but the other chamber's bill number. Both versions can then be considered by the conference committee. Measures raising revenue and making appropriations that are sent to conference always have an "HR" designation. A conference cannot change the number of the bill committed to it or create a different-numbered bill.

A conference cannot take place until both chambers formally agree that it be held. The Senate usually requests or agrees to a conference by unanimous consent. However, a motion to do so is debatable and may be filibustered. In the House this action generally is taken by unanimous consent or, since 1965, by motion, if authorized by the committee managing the legislation and if the floor manager is recognized at the discretion of the Speaker for that purpose. Before 1965, if there was objection to unanimous consent, the House could go to conference only if it suspended the rules with a two-thirds majority or if the Rules Committee granted a rule that the House could adopt by majority vote. On some occasions, the Rules Committee refused to report a rule allowing a conference, which gave the conservative coalition that often controlled that committee prior to its expansion in 1961 another means of blocking legislative action.

Selection of Conferees

The two chambers have different rules for selecting conferees, or "managers," as they are formally called, but in practice both follow similar procedures. House rules grant the Speaker of the House the right to appoint conferees, but the Speaker usually does so only after consultation with the minority leader and the chairman and ranking minority member of the committee having jurisdiction over the legislation. As in the selection of members of standing committees, the minority selects its choices for conferees, which, by custom, are appointed by the Speaker without change. Once appointed, conferees normally

LEGISLATIVE ANOMALIES

Peculiar situations have arisen occasionally as Congress searches for an appropriate manner to achieve a new or unique result. And even if Congress cannot find one, it may do what it wants to anyway. Here are several examples.

In 1978 Congress attempted a new form of legislative enactment to extend the time permitted for ratification of a constitutional amendment. The so-called Equal Rights Amendment (ERA), passed by Congress in 1972 and intended to enhance women's rights, carried within it a seven-year time limit for ratification by the requisite three-fourths of the states. It would die on March 22, 1979, unless ratified by thirty-eight states. Congress had first set time limits on amendment ratifications beginning in 1917 to ensure that the initial proposal of an amendment and its ultimate ratification were roughly contemporaneous.

With the deadline nearing Congress wanted to keep the amendment alive to see if several additional states might ratify the amendment. A joint resolution was passed extending the life of the amendment by thirty-nine additional months, until June 30, 1982. Congress first had determined, by simple majority, that a two-thirds vote was not required for passage of the time-extension. (It also would have been more difficult to obtain a two-thirds vote in 1978 than in 1972 because the amendment had become far more controversial after its passage.)

Once passed by both houses, the joint resolution was sent to President Jimmy Carter, who proceeded to sign it even while raising doubt that he had any role in the process and questioning whether the joint resolution was really a law. The Archivist of the United States, who received the joint resolution next, did not give it a public law number but instead notified the states of its existence. A federal judge ruled in 1981 that Congress had acted improperly but the question became moot when additional states failed to ratify the amendment even under the extended timetable. The Supreme Court dis-

missed the case as moot in 1982 and vacated the lower court's decision, leaving the ultimate validity of the congressional action in constitutional limbo.

Other examples of unusual legislative actions have involved constitutional amendments. Congress does not need to take any formal action once an amendment has been ratified. In 1868, however, Congress passed a concurrent resolution to declare that the Fourteenth Amendment to the Constitution had been ratified by the requisite number of states. In 1992, reeling from scandals and low public approval ratings, members rushed to identify themselves with the so-called Madison Amendment to the Constitution, which required that an election intervene before any congressional pay raise could take effect. The amendment, originally proposed by Congress in 1789, suddenly reemerged in 1978 after more than a century in limbo since the last time a state legislature had approved it, to begin a flurry of new ratifications. Previous historical concerns by Congress about contemporaneous enactment of constitutional amendments were thrown to the winds as members rushed to embrace what was still one of the most popular forms of Congress-bashing—denying themselves pay raises.

Each house passed a concurrent resolution stating that the new Twenty-Seventh Amendment was properly ratified, but neither house passed the concurrent resolution adopted by the other. Not satisfied with that, the Senate also adopted a simple resolution declaring ratification of the amendment. Adding to the confusion, the Archivist of the United States had already declared the amendment ratified on May 18, 1992, before Congress acted.

In 1998, as Congress awaited the results of an investigation by special prosecutor Kenneth Starr into scandals involving the Clinton administration, rumors of possible impeachment proceedings waxed and waned on Capitol Hill with each passing news cycle. Under the Constitution, the House by majority vote can initiate articles

---

serve throughout the conference process, but often, particularly on complex legislation that has conferees from several committees, the Speaker routinely announces changes in the composition of the conference. These actions usually reflected an error in the initial appointment that might not properly have reflected committee jurisdictions on a particular issue.

However, in 1993, the House amended its rules to give the Speaker formal authority to replace any conferee whenever he wished, obviating the need for a unanimous consent request required in earlier practice. While the new power has rarely been used for any substantive purpose, it does give the leadership substantial power in any conference negotiation and restrains conferees from bringing back a conference report likely to face defeat. Conferees technically may be named or replaced only by the Speaker, not by a Speaker pro tempore, except by unanimous consent.

Senate rules allow the chamber as a whole to elect conferees, but that rarely happens. The common practice is for the presiding officer, by unanimous consent, to appoint conferees on the

recommendation of the appropriate committee chairman and ranking minority member. The process of going to conference and appointing conferees is debatable, however, and provides another potential choke point for opponents of a measure.

Those members who are usually selected as conferees are the chairmen of the committee(s) that handled the legislation, the ranking minority member(s), and other members of the committee(s) most actively involved. If a subcommittee has exercised major responsibility for a bill, some of its members may be chosen. Seniority once governed the selection of conferees, but it is quite common today for junior members in each chamber to be chosen, especially if they are particularly knowledgeable about or interested in the bill. Occasionally a member from another committee with expertise in the subject matter of the bill may be named to the conference, or one who sponsored a major amendment adopted on the floor.

Sometimes there have been questions about whether conferees are likely to uphold the chamber's position on key points in conference deliberations. There have also been charges that a

of impeachment that would result in a trial by the Senate, where a two-thirds majority is required for conviction and removal from office. Until 1998 only one president, Andrew Johnson (1865–1869) had ever been impeached, but he was acquitted by a single vote in the Senate. Richard M. Nixon (1969–1974) was believed to have faced certain impeachment, conviction, and removal from office had he not resigned first.

That changed in 1998 when the Republican-led House late in the year, following elections in which the GOP lost seats, approved articles of impeachment against President Bill Clinton, forcing the issue to the Senate. The Senate in 1999 took up the articles but voted not to convict the president. *(See "President Bill Clinton," p. 343.)*

In the course of this, members in both chambers—but particularly the Senate—looked for ways to express strong disapproval of Clinton's actions involving a female White House intern and his response to legal proceedings that grew out of the matter. Senate Majority Leader Trent Lott, R-Miss., suggested a "censure" of the president by Congress if the charges against Clinton were insufficient for impeachment conviction. The Senate had done this before, to President Andrew Jackson in 1834, in a political dispute over the Bank of the United States, whose reauthorization Jackson had vetoed. He later directed U.S. funds be removed from the bank and deposited in state banks. Bank supporters in Congress and Jackson's bitter enemies then arranged a presidential censure, but the action carried no legal weight and was never repeated by any future Congress. The Constitution does not recognize any punishment other than impeachment and removal from office. Jackson's allies later expunged the censure from the Senate Journal. In 1999, once conviction of Clinton was defeated, the idea of censure was not raised again.

Presumably, if Lott's suggestion were to be followed either House could initiate a concurrent resolution to censure the president or act separately by simple resolution, but such measures would not be privileged for consideration in either chamber and would be subject to a filibuster in the Senate.

The Senate reached back to rewrite history again in 1997. In 1996 the House had passed a conference report containing continuing appropriations funding government agencies. However, to deal with possible Senate opposition the House also passed the funding as a separate bill that the Senate might amend if it chose to do so. Ultimately, the Senate passed both bills; the conference report was sent to the president and signed into law. However, instead of simply killing the unnecessary separate bill, it was passed without amendment by a roll-call vote and the Daily Digest of the *Congressional Record* noted that it was cleared for the president. However, this did not happen. The Senate never sent a message to the House formally notifying it of the bill's passage, which prevented the House from enrolling it for presentation to the president, as required. Presumably, had this been done, the president could simply have disposed of the bill with a quiet pocket veto. With the bill in limbo, the 104th Congress expired, preventing any enrollment.

Nevertheless, Rep. David Skaggs, D-Colo., concerned with setting a precedent that a bill passed in identical form by both houses of Congress could be kept from the president by direction of the majority leadership of one chamber, called Majority Leader Lott demanding an explanation. He also inserted a letter to Lott and a history of the incident into the *Record*.[1]

In response, in February 1997, Senate Majority Whip Don Nickles, R-Okla., rose on the floor to ask unanimous consent to amend the Senate Journal of the preceding Congress to state that the bill had been indefinitely postponed.

---

1. "Concerning a Congressional Failure to Comply with the Constitution during the 104th Congress," *Congressional Record*, January 7, 1997, E2.

---

chairman might have stacked a conference with members favoring his or her position rather than the position of the chamber majority. A member may have voted for final passage but still have opposed key amendments during committee or floor action. Each chamber has remedies in such situations that restrain conferees—motions to instruct conferees, motions to recommit a conference report, the filibuster in the Senate, and the Speaker's power to change conferees in the House.

The increase in the size of conference committees led to ways to limit the role of some conferees, particularly those who are not members of the principal committee of jurisdiction. General conferees have overall responsibility for the whole bill. "Additional" conferees consider and vote only on specific subjects or sections of the legislation. "Exclusive" conferees are the sole negotiators for their chambers on specified subjects or sections. Members who are general conferees may vote on the same issues as additional conferees but may not participate in the areas reserved for exclusive conferees unless they are also so named.

The number of conferees each chamber selects does not have to be the same. A majority in each delegation will be from the majority party in the chamber, however. That requirement means that each chamber must name at least three conferees on each bill, but there is no upper limit. Bills that have been referred to more than one committee usually entail large conferences because conferees are selected from each of the committees of jurisdiction.

Twenty-three committees, for example, sent conferees to the conference committee on the omnibus trade bill enacted in 1988. Budget reconciliation bills generally engender some of the largest conferences because they may affect the jurisdictions of almost every House and Senate committee. More than 250 conferees from both houses were appointed as conferees on the 1981 budget reconciliation bill, for example. Such large conferences usually divide up into smaller working groups, or subconferences, that deal only with specific parts of the bill. In more recent years, Congress has moved in the opposite direction, sometimes limiting conferences to as few as three members from a chamber—the chairman, another majority member, and the ranking minority member—to expedite the process and ensure leadership control.

Conferees in both the House and Senate are expected to support the legislative positions of the chamber they represent. In an effort to ensure that its conferees would uphold its position, the House in 1974 modified its rules on conferees selection. The revised rule said that "the Speaker shall appoint [as conferees] no less than a majority of members who generally supported the House position as determined by the Speaker." A further revision, in 1977, said that "the Speaker shall name members who are primarily responsible for the legislation and shall, to the fullest extent feasible, include the principal proponents of the major provisions of the bill as it passed the House." Some of these changes were intended to further strengthen the Speaker and to give him authority to resist demands by committee chairmen that might not be in the majority's interest. The Speaker's conference appointments may not be challenged in the House. The 1993 rules change giving the Speaker power to name and replace conferees at will has effectively limited the independent power of conferees, individually or collectively, to actively defy the majority party's agenda.

In 1995, Speaker Gingrich used his appointment power in a new way to highlight divisions in the minority over legislation headed to conference. For example, on one occasion he appointed a conservative Democrat, Rep. Gary A. Condit of California, to a conference on legislation relating to curbing unfunded federal mandates to the states and localities. In another, conservative Rep. Mike Parker, D-Miss., was appointed a conferee on the concurrent budget resolution. (Parker later switched parties.) These members had been passed over by Minority Leader Richard Gephardt when the Democrats announced their choices from among more senior members. But Gingrich did not violate the custom of allowing the minority exclusive power over its choices; the slots he gave to these Democrats were taken from the Republicans' own allotment.

Political scientist Barbara Sinclair described the process in choosing conferees for the 1995 budget reconciliation bill, which was later vetoed by President Clinton. The Republican Party leadership in both houses sought to ensure close control over the bill, both to achieve a satisfactory result and to conclude negotiations quickly. The conference consisted of forty-three senators in twelve subgroups and seventy-one House members in fourteen subgroups. "Had Gingrich not assertively exercised the Speaker's discretion . . . the House delegation could easily have been much larger. . . . Gingrich chose whenever possible members who could do double duty because they served on the Budget Committee and another concerned committee. A subgroup of eight House members had authority over the entire bill and included . . . a number of party leaders—Majority Leader Dick Armey of Texas, Majority Whip Tom DeLay of Texas, and Conference Chairman John A. Boehner of Ohio on the Republican side and Minority Whip David Bonior on the Democratic side. In the Senate, the group of three that had authority over the entire bill was confined to the Budget Committee leaders. The oth-

er subgroups consisted of members from committees with provisions in the bill and had authority over those provisions only."[28]

Instructing Conferees

Either chamber may try to enforce its will by instructing its conferees how to vote in conference, but the rules do not obligate the conferees to follow the instructions. The Senate rarely instructs its conferees but the practice may be becoming more common. In both chambers, conferees may be instructed just prior to their appointment by the chair. In the House, they may be instructed again, day after day, if they have failed to report after twenty calendar days have elapsed. (One day's advance warning must be given in the House of the intention to offer such motions, along with the exact wording.)

Efforts to instruct conferees may reflect the degree of support in the chamber for certain provisions in either the House or Senate versions of a bill. Depending on the circumstances, votes to instruct may serve as warnings that conferees had better not stray too far from the language the chamber originally approved or they may have just the opposite intent and signal receptivity to a provision originated in the other chamber. In the House motions to instruct are often used to react to Senate provisions that the House, under its germaneness rules, would never have had the opportunity to consider.

The potential political advantages of forcing a vote on a motion to instruct have led to its frequent use in the House. In a 1997 example of the tactics involved as the House prepared to go to conference, Rep. Steny Hoyer, D-Md., offered a motion to instruct conferees on the Treasury-Post Office appropriations bill that directed conferees to increase funding for the Exploited Child Unit of the National Center for Missing and Exploited Children. As ranking minority member of that subcommittee, Hoyer had the right to priority of recognition to offer the motion, and under the rules only a single such motion was permitted. Hoyer's motion was not in dispute but was intended to prevent a vote on the far more controversial issue of a cost-of-living pay adjustment for members of Congress, which was scheduled to take effect automatically the following year. The pay raise was authorized by existing law and the subject matter of the appropriations bill was unrelated to it. The Senate version of the bill, however, contained an amendment prohibiting the raise.

If the House voted to instruct its conferees to agree to the Senate pay ban, it would become nearly impossible for the House conferees to oppose the Senate language. This was exactly what pay-raise opponent Rep. Linda Smith, R-Wash., hoped to achieve, but she had no right to be recognized to offer the motion. Instead, she sought to seize control of it from Hoyer by defeating the previous question, the motion in the House that ends debate and forces a vote on the pending matter. Had that motion lost, Smith could then have been recognized to amend Hoyer's motion without violating the rule that only a single motion could be offered. In the end, Hoyer won as the House ordered the previous question by a vote of 229–199, then easily passed his original language. Members who had supported the previous question could shield themselves from attack by critics of congressional pay raises by claiming to have supported a procedural motion, or by claiming that they wanted to help exploited children. In conference, the Senate receded from its pay-ban amendment, and the raise was allowed to take effect. When the conference report passed, press coverage at the time made much of the idea that Congress had "voted itself a pay raise" when in fact the raise did not require any vote. Congress had simply refused to take action to change existing law.

As noted, the minority party has preference to offer motions to instruct conferees in the House when the House first votes to go to conference. When such motions again become available to any member if the conferees have not reported after twenty days have elapsed, again it is the minority that is most likely to take the initiative in attempting to influence the conference. The minority has used the right to offer motions to instruct to embarrass the majority, or to force repeated votes on controversial issues. For example, during the 103rd Congress, the Republican minority offered numerous motions to instruct as a conference on major crime legislation dragged on for months. The tactic was so effective, and annoying, that the then-Democratic majority considered changing House rules for the next Congress to restrict such motions, but the subsequent shift in party control prevented any action.

Authority of Conferees

Theoretically House and Senate conferees are limited to resolving matters in disagreement between the two chambers. They are not authorized to delete provisions or language that both chambers have agreed to or to draft entirely new provisions. This is called staying "within the scope" of disagreements between the two chambers. When the disagreement involves numbers, such as the level of funding in appropriations bills, conferees are supposed to stay within the amounts proposed by the two houses.

In practice the conferees have wide latitude, except where the matters in disagreement are very specific. If one chamber has substituted an entirely new version of the bill for that approved by the other chamber—which is nearly always the case on major bills, except for appropriations—the entire subject is technically in disagreement, and the conferees may draft an entirely new bill if they so choose. In such a case, the Legislative Reorganization Act of 1946 stipulates that they may not include in the conference version of the bill "matter not committed to them by either house." But they may include "matter which is a germane modification of subjects in disagreement." For appropriations bills, the Senate had long used specific amendments to a House-passed bill rather than sending a complete substitute back, but this practice may now be changing for the sake of convenience.

In the Senate, scope requirements were often ignored or difficult to enforce. They may even be dead as a result of a 1996 vote overruling a decision of the chair that matter contained within a conference report was beyond the scope of the confer-

ence (which it obviously was). The result may further enhance the bargaining power of conferees at the expense of individual members of their respective chambers, if future conferences are conducted in a parliamentary environment where the Senate conferees can agree to virtually anything and the House conferees can as well as long as they have leadership support and a friendly Rules Committee on their side.

The House has long objected to the inclusion in conference reports of Senate-passed amendments that are not germane. Because conference agreements may not be amended on the floor of either chamber, the House was often put in a "take-it-or-leave-it" situation, forced either to accept a nongermane amendment it may never have debated or to recommit or vote down the entire conference report, including provisions it favored. A series of rules changes in the 1970s, including one in 1972 that allows the House to take separate votes on nongermane amendments in conference reports, has given the House some leverage both in conference and on the Senate floor. Senate floor managers sometimes tried to turn away nongermane floor amendments by arguing that they might prevent the entire bill from winning approval in the House.

However, in more recent practice, the trend has been toward allowing conferees, with the concurrence of the leadership, greater flexibility to negotiate and present conference reports that produce the desired policy results, irrespective of procedural inadequacies. The House leadership has worked with the committees to protect conference reports from points of order and possible dismemberment on the floor by having the Rules Committee waive points of order, such as the germaneness of Senate provisions or the inclusion of legislation on appropriations bills. Indeed, by the end of the 1990s it had become more common to waive all points of order, including scope.

Appropriations bills used to return from conference with hundreds of "amendments in disagreement" at the insistence of the House. Disposition of compromise language on these amendments was considered separately after the House had adopted the conference report. Most of these amendments were reported in "technical disagreement," which meant there were technical violations of House rules involved, and an agreement was not placed in the body of the conference report to avoid potential points of order against the entire report. The conferees actually had reached agreement on these issues, but each such item was theoretically subject to separate debate and votes to ratify the decisions and even potentially to additional amendment. Of course, sometimes there were substantial issues in "true disagreement" that the two chambers sent back and forth until an agreement was reached. Both houses had to reach final agreement on all of these amendments to conclude action on a bill and send it to the president.

After the Republicans took control of Congress in 1995 they stopped this practice, insisting that conferees reach agreement on all issues whenever possible before returning to the floor. Every provision was placed within the body of the conference report and, in the House, was protected by a rule waiving points

A private bill in Congress is legislation intended for the benefit of a specific individual or entity rather than the general public. At one time, hundreds, even thousands, of these would be enacted into law during a Congress but in recent decades the number has dropped dramatically.

Private legislation is used essentially as a court of last resort because those seeking relief must have exhausted all reasonable administrative and judicial procedures before asking Congress to intercede on their behalf. Courts and federal administrative agencies can make decisions based only on interpretations of public laws; Congress reserves to itself the privilege of aiding some parties who, for various reasons, are seen as deserving of special treatment. Most private bills deal with claims against the federal government and immigration and naturalization matters. Their titles usually begin with the words "For the relief of. . . ."

A fine line sometimes separates public and private bills. House parliamentarian Asher C. Hinds offered the following explanation in his 1907 *Precedents of the House of Representatives:* "A private bill is a bill for the relief of one or several specified persons, corporations, institutions, etc., and is distinguished from a public bill, which relates to public matters and deals with individuals only by classes." As an example, Hinds cited bills benefiting soldiers' widows: a bill that granted pensions to soldiers' widows as a class would be a public bill, but a bill that granted a pension to a particular soldier's widow would be a private bill.

The history of private bills dates at least from Roman times when they were called *constitutionis privilegia,* privileges accorded to specified individuals. They came to Congress by way of the English Parliament. The first private bill was passed by Congress September 24, 1789, and signed by President George Washington five days later. The bill gave seventeen months' back pay at the rank of captain to the Baron de Glaubeck, a foreign officer in the service of the United States.

FLUCTUATING USAGE

Private bill usage has fluctuated over the years, largely because changes in federal law have made exceptions for individuals more necessary sometimes and less necessary other times. For example, when Congress passed legislation giving people other avenues to pursue their claims against the government the numbers would decline, or if Congress enacted a stricter immigration law the numbers would jump.

Ten private bills were enacted into law in the First Congress (1789–1791), the same number enacted in the 105th Congress (1997–1999). But over those more than two hundred years the numbers varied substantially. For example, there were 6,248 private laws enacted in the 59th Congress (1905–1907) but only 234 enacted in the very next Congress. There were 457 enacted in the 80th Congress (1947–1948) and 1,103 in the 81st Congress.

In modern times there has been a sharp decline in the use of private bills. Since the early 1980s, the totals have dropped to double—sometimes single—digits. There were eight private bills enacted in the 103rd Congress (1993–1994), only four in the next Congress, and then the ten in the 105th Congress.

REASONS FOR DECLINE

There have been several reasons for the decline in the use of private bills.

The most important of these is that Congress has taken steps over the years to limit the need for private bills. These steps have included the establishment of the U.S. Court of Claims (now the U.S. Court of Federal Claims) with the authority to decide certain claims cases and to issue advisory reports on private bills when requested by the House or Senate. Congress also has approved a series of public laws authorizing executive agencies to act on other cases previously handled by Congress. Title IV of the 1946 Legislative Reorganization Act, known as the Federal Tort Claims Act, provided for settlement of certain claims by executive agencies and U.S. district courts. Another title of the 1946 act provided for the correction of military records by civilian review boards. When passage of the Immigration and Nationality Act of 1952 resulted in a marked increase in requests for relief from immigration restrictions, Congress adopted amendments easing some of the restrictions or authorizing the attorney general to do so.

Congressional scholar Walter J. Oleszek noted in *Congressional Procedures and the Policy Process* additional reasons for the decline in private bills. Scandals involving private bills have resulted in tighter procedures for their consideration and have contributed to the drop-off. Members are reluctant to assign staff to handle private bills because they can be so time-consuming and the claims can sometimes be incorrect or fraudulent. Budget deficits in the 1980s and much of the 1990s also made it more difficult for members to focus on the needs of just one individual or entity while they were cutting back on programs for the general public.

TYPES OF BILLS

The two kinds of private legislation that Congress deals with most often are claims and immigration cases. Before 1950 private bills dealing with land claims, military justice, and pensions were more common.

A total of seventy-four private bills were referred to the House Judiciary Subcommittee on Immigration and Claims in the 105th Congress—thirty-four claims bills and forty immigration bills. One claims bill and nine immigration bills were eventually enacted.

The Constitution provides in Article I, Section 8, clause 1, that "the Congress shall have Power . . . to pay the Debts . . . of the United States." This provision has been construed broadly to include not only legal but also moral obligations. Bills introduced in Congress for payment of private claims against the government include refund cases that aim to wipe out individuals' obligations to give back money the government paid them in error; waiver cases that allow the government to honor a claim after the government's obligation has expired; and tort (wrongful act, injury, or damage) claims not covered by the Federal Tort Claims Act of 1946.

Private laws are also used to provide relief to aliens because public immigration and naturalization laws do not cover all hardship cases. Private laws permit them to come to the United States, to remain here, or to become citizens, even though they technically may not be eligible.

ENACTMENT PROCESS

The general course of a private bill, from introduction to presidential approval, is much the same as that of a public bill. But there are some important differences.

A private bill generally is initiated at the request of the individual, company, group, or locality that stands to benefit from its enactment. By contrast, public laws usually originate in the executive branch or in Congress itself. The intended beneficiary of a private bill may get in touch with a member directly or use an intermediary, such as a lawyer or lobbyist, to present the facts and considerations believed to justify the introduction of a bill.

Virtually all private bills are referred to the House or Senate Judiciary committees. Once a private bill is reported out of committee, it is placed on the Private Calendar in the House and on the Calendar of Business in the Senate.

In the House, the Private Calendar, also known as the Calendar of the Committee of the Whole House, must be called on the first Tuesday of the month (unless dispensed with by a two-thirds vote or moved to another day by unanimous consent) and may be called on the third Tuesday at the Speaker's discretion. In the Senate, private bills may be taken up on any day after the conclusion of the morning hour.

The House uses a formal system of objectors to monitor private bills. The majority and minority leaders each select three party members to serve as objectors who will screen the bills for controversial provisions. They also answer questions that arise during floor consideration.

A bill must be on the Private Calendar for at least seven days before it can be called up for floor consideration. If one House member objects to a bill's consideration, the bill is passed over for later consideration. If two or more object, the bill is recommitted, a procedure that usually kills the bill.

Bills passed over for later consideration may be pulled together into an omnibus bill, which is given preference over other bills when the Private Calendar is called on the third Tuesday. When such an omnibus bill is passed, the bills within it are considered to have been passed separately. This type of omnibus bill, however, has rarely been used in recent decades.

When a private bill is taken up on the floor, it is considered in "the House as in Committee of the Whole," which means the House is operating under a combination of procedures from the general rules of the House and rules of the Committee of the Whole. No time is allotted for general debate and amendments are considered under expedited procedures.

As with public bills, once a private bill has been passed in identical form by both chambers, it is sent to the president. If the president signs it into law, the measure is given a private law number. Vetoes of private bills are handled in the same manner as vetoes of public bills. There may be an immediate vote to override or sustain the veto, the vote may be postponed to a fixed date, or the veto message may be referred to a committee. Committee referral in effect kills the bill in most cases.

ABUSES OF THE SYSTEM

Private bills occasionally have given rise to impropriety, or at least the appearance of it.

A newspaper investigation in 1969, for example, produced accusations of wrongdoing in the introduction of hundreds of private immigration bills to help Chinese seamen stay in the United States. Knight Newspapers reported evidence that New York lawyers and Washington lobbyists had been getting $500 to $2,500 for each Chinese immigration bill involved. The disclosures resulted in a preliminary investigation by the Senate ethics panel into allegations that some senators or their aides received gifts and campaign contributions for introducing bills to help Chinese ship-jumpers escape deportation. Senate leaders moved to put an end to the practice of allowing staff aides to introduce private bills.

Rep. Henry Helstoski, D-N.J., was indicted by a federal grand jury in 1976 on charges that he solicited and accepted bribes in return for introducing bills to delay deportation of Chilean and Argentinian aliens living illegally in the United States. The indictment alleged that Helstoski received "at least" $8,735 for his sponsorship of the immigration bills. But the charges were thrown out after the Supreme Court ruled in *United States v. Helstoski* that, because of the Constitution's grant of immunity to members of Congress under the speech and debate clause, federal prosecutors could not use any evidence relating to Helstoski's legislative acts against him. *(See box, Congressional Immunity, p. 688.)*

The power to introduce private immigration legislation proved ruinous to the members of Congress caught in the FBI's Abscam operation in 1980. Agents of the FBI, posing as Arab sheiks or their representatives, asked the members to introduce private bills to permit wealthy "Arabs" to enter the United States in exchange for money. Although the investigation turned up no evidence of bills actually introduced on behalf of the fictitious Arabs, the videotapes and recorded conversations of the members and the government agents were enough to end seven congressional careers. *(See "Abscam Investigation," p. 953, Vol. II.)*

of order. The result was a considerable simplification of the conference procedure and represented another step back from the rules changes of the 1970s, which had sought to preserve opportunities for individual members to modify conference reports that might contain some violation of House rules.

After the mid-1970s, the growing power of the House leadership of both parties at the expense of committees, as well as the creation of committee memberships more representative of their respective parties, decreased the importance of procedural protections for the membership as a whole because the ability of committees and conferees to defy the majority was drastically curtailed.

During the reform period of the 1970s, many members of the House felt the Senate's loose amendment procedures gave it a distinct advantage over the House in conferences. Since the Senate's adoption in 1985 of the "Byrd Rule" barring extraneous matters in budget reconciliation bills, however, many in the Senate feel the pendulum has swung back the other way. The Byrd Rule allows points of order against any matter in a reconciliation bill that violates the rule, including major provisions in a conference report that might have survived from the House version, unless sixty votes waive the point of order.

The House has complained bitterly that its ability to legislate on reconciliation bills and to negotiate in conference has been restricted because conferees on the bill risk rejection of their entire product if it includes a provision that violates the Senate rule and cannot command sixty votes. The Senate argues that the Byrd Rule is vital to protect the Senate tradition of unlimited debate because reconciliation bills, by statute, are immune to filibusters. In the absence of the Byrd Rule, the House could use conference reports on such bills to force the Senate to act on matters that might be filibustered if considered separately outside the budget process.

If conferees find they are unable to reach agreement they may report their failure to reach agreement to the parent chamber and allow the full House or Senate to act as it wishes; if neither chamber is willing to yield the legislation will die.

House rules allow conferees to be discharged and replaced by new conferees if they fail to reach agreement within twenty calendar days (or within thirty-six hours of their appointment during the last six days of a session), but this authority is rarely invoked.

Adoption of the Conference Report

When a majority of the conferees from each chamber have reached agreement on a bill, conference committee staff—generally the staff of the committees with jurisdiction over the measure—writes a conference report indicating changes made in the bill and explaining each side's action. If the two sides have been unable to reach a compromise on particular House or Senate amendments, those amendments are reported "in disagreement" and are acted on separately after the conference report itself has been agreed to.

The conference report must be signed by a majority of conferees from each chamber and submitted in document form to each house for approval. Minority reports or statements of minority views are not permitted, though sometimes a member will note next to his signature "except section ___" or a similar notation indicating partial disapproval. Until the 1970 Legislative Reorganization Act required House and Senate managers to prepare a joint explanatory statement discussing the specific changes made by the conferees, the conference report was printed only in the House, together with an explanation by the House conferees. The joint statement ensures that both houses have the same interpretation of the actions taken by the conferees, in addition to having an identical bill text. Although the conference report is supposed to be printed in the Senate, that requirement is frequently waived by unanimous consent. The report is always published in the *Congressional Record*. House rules also require that conference reports lie over three days before the House takes them up. The Senate requires only that copies be available on each senator's desk.

Each chamber must vote on a conference report as a whole. No new amendments may be considered. The Senate can still filibuster a conference report. In the House, conference reports may be called up at any time after the three days have expired. This requirement has been increasingly waived in the 1990s, either by unanimous consent or through adoption of a rule. Often members are forced to consider huge bills with little notice or even without access to the written text of the legislation. In 1997, for example, members complained that copies of huge budget reconciliation/tax reduction legislation, which was supposed to lead to a balanced federal budget, were not available except for a few copies in the hands of the floor managers. In perhaps a portent of things to come in the use of technology by Congress, the Republican leadership responded by advising members to check for the legislation on the Speaker's Web site.

For complex legislation, the House Rules Committee is usually asked to report a rule waiving points of order. Protection from points of order may be critical because a point of order against the conference report—for example, that it contains matter beyond the scope of the disagreements committed to conference—would, if sustained, kill the conference report immediately without any vote and return the bill to its parliamentary status prior to the conference. There may be no time for a new conference, and the result would be the death of the legislation.

The house that agreed to the other chamber's request to go to conference on a bill acts first on the conference version. This procedure, followed by custom rather than by rule, is sometimes ignored; the Senate, for example, asked for the conference on the 1981 tax cut, and it acted first on the conference report.

Which chamber acts first or last can occasionally influence the outcome. The chamber to act first has three options: it can agree to the conference report, reject it, or recommit it to the conference committee for further deliberation. Once the first chamber has acted, however, the conference committee is dissolved, and recommittal is no longer an option. The second chamber must vote the conference report up or down.

The pressure on reluctant members to support a report that the other chamber has already approved can be intense. Rep. Jack Brooks, D-Texas, counted on that intense lobbying when he maneuvered in 1979 to have the House take up the conference report creating the Department of Education after the Senate had already agreed to it. Brooks's strategy worked; the House, which had originally approved creation of the department by a four-vote margin, agreed to the conference report with fourteen votes to spare.

While the conference version of the bill must be approved or rejected in its entirety by both bodies, in the House exceptions are made for nongermane Senate amendments. Unless a special rule has waived all points of order, any member of the House may make the point of order that a particular section of a conference report contains nongermane material and move to reject the offending language. Forty minutes of debate, equally divided between opposing sides, is allotted for such motions. If the motion carries, the nongermane material is deleted, the conference report is considered as rejected, and the House may go on to approve the remaining text of the conference report, minus the deletion, as a further amendment to the bill. The bill as amended must then go back to the Senate, which can either accept the amendment by the House, reject it, amend it further, or ask for a new conference.

If conferees have been unable to agree on any of the amendments in disagreement, separate votes are taken in both houses to resolve the differences. One chamber may insist on its amendment, or it may move to "recede and concur" in the other chamber's position. Occasionally the amendment in disagreement will be returned to conference for further compromise efforts.

Conference reports are seldom rejected, in part because legislators have little desire to begin the entire legislative process all over again and in part because members tend to defer to the expertise of the conferees, just as they tend to defer to the recommendations of the legislative committees. If a bill dies once it has reached conference, it is more likely that conferees have been unable to reach a compromise before the end of the Congress. That is what happened to the 1990 campaign finance bill.

Sometimes the House Rules Committee has been asked to make changes in a pending conference report through the device of allowing passage of a concurrent resolution "changing the enrollment of a conference report." These changes, for example, might be altering the text to enhance chances for passage or to correct errors discovered after passage. If the Senate also passes such a concurrent resolution, the conference report is modified by the enrolling clerk and ultimately sent to the president in its new, "improved" form.

FINAL LEGISLATIVE ACTION

After both houses have given final approval to a bill, a final copy of the bill, known as the enrolled bill, is prepared by the enrolling clerk of the chamber in which the bill originated, printed on parchment-type paper, and certified as correct by the secretary of the Senate or the clerk of the House, depending on which chamber originated the measure. No matter where the bill originated, it is signed first by the Speaker of the House and then by the vice president or president pro tempore of the Senate, and sent to the White House.

The president has ten days (not counting Sundays) from the day he receives the bill to act on it. In modern practice, an enrolled bill may be sent to the president even as the Congress that passed it is expiring, and the president still may act on it even though a new Congress has convened. If he approves the measure he signs it, dates it, and usually writes "approved" on the document. The Constitution requires only the president's signature.

A bill may become law without the president's signature in one of two ways. If the president does not sign a bill within ten days (Sundays excepted) from the time he receives it, the bill becomes law provided the Congress that passed it is in session. A bill may also become law without the president's signature if Congress overrides a veto.

When the president signs some bills, especially major legislation, he may stage a signing ceremony at the White House or some other appropriate location to draw attention to the new law and to honor its congressional sponsors and other supporters. The president, in such circumstances, uses numerous pens to affix his signature to the document and passes them out to his audience.

Another variation of the method of presidential signing might be called the "yes, but . . ." approach. During the 1980s, Presidents Ronald Reagan and George Bush occasionally issued "signing statements" when they approved some bills, objecting to certain provisions as unconstitutional and stating that they would ignore them. Members of Congress have sometimes voiced objection to such actions as inappropriate, but executive officials in recent years have argued that the president had a right to state an executive branch interpretation for the courts to consider in a potential legal action, just as Congress did when it made "legislative history." However, there is no evidence that courts have given such presidential statements any weight.

The idea was not new, and had appeared occasionally in more radical forms. In 1842, President John Tyler sent Congress a message noting that he had signed a bill and that it had been filed with the Secretary of State with "an exposition of my reasons for giving it my sanction." Tyler was promptly criticized for this action by Rep. John Quincy Adams of Massachusetts, a former president (1825–1829), who successfully moved to have a select committee examine the matter. Adams later filed a critical report from the select committee, which also submitted a resolution warning ". . . of evil example for the future." The resolution was not, however, adopted by the House. The select committee noted in its report that it

can find . . . no authority given to the President for depositing in the Department of State an exposition of his reason for signing an act . . . and most especially none for making the deposit in company with the law . . . unless disavowed and discountenanced . . . its consequences may contribute to prostrate in the dust the authority of the very law which the President has approved with the accompaniment of this most extraordinary appendage, and to introduce a practice which would transfer the legislative power of Congress itself to the arbitrary will of the executive.

A House committee also criticized President Andrew Jackson for an 1830 action when he had signed a bill and then written on the bill itself his views as to its meaning, views not shared by many in Congress.[29]

The Veto Power

If the president does not want a bill to become law he may veto it by returning it to the chamber in which it originated without his signature and with a message stating his objections. If no further action is taken the bill dies.

The Constitution provides that Congress may attempt to enact the bill into law "the objections of the president to the con-

---

LINE-ITEM VETO EXPERIMENT ENDED BY SUPREME COURT

Congress's historic enactment in 1996 of a law giving the president a "line-item veto" began a short-lived experiment with a power that Republicans had long sought for the executive branch. The line-item veto lasted only until June 1998, when the Supreme Court declared it unconstitutional.

The Line-Item Veto Act, which took effect on January 1, 1997, gave the president the power to strike out, or "cancel," dollar amounts of discretionary spending, new "direct spending," and certain forms of new tax benefits in bills signed into law. Congress could vote to pass the item(s) again, but the president could then use his constitutional veto power to kill this legislation, forcing Congress to find a two-thirds majority to override the veto in the normal manner.

Proponents of the line-item veto, generally political conservatives opposed to government spending and programs, argued that the overwhelming majority of state governors possessed the line-item veto in some form and that it had proved to be a useful tool in controlling expenditures. They responded to constitutional concerns by arguing that there was a long history of presidential action declining to carry out spending passed by Congress, and that Congress could properly delegate authority to the president to declare cancellations of spending authority.

Opponents argued that the Constitution clearly required that bills be approved or rejected by the president in their entirety, not in pieces. They said that the new procedure gave the president the power to change laws after their enactment—in effect, to make laws, a power reserved exclusively to Congress—and to leave on the statute books truncated laws in a form that Congress might never have chosen to enact. The most fundamental argument, however, went to the balance of power between Congress and the executive branch. Opponents warned that a line-item veto would upset this balance among the branches of government by ceding too much political power to the president while Congress considered legislation. Beyond the basic principle, they feared the executive branch would have enormous leverage to offer to withhold cancellations if members backed unrelated presidential priorities.

OPERATION OF THE LINE-ITEM VETO

The 1996 law allowed the president to look not only at the specific language of new spending and tax laws but to examine other elements of the legislative package that described these laws, including tables, charts, or explanatory text included in the statement of the managers accompanying a conference report. In other words, the president was allowed to locate spending wherever it tried to hide, subject to limitations of the act. If an item of spending could be clearly identified, the president could only cancel the entire amount (not simply reduce it in part).

It was anticipated that the president's use of the line-item veto would focus on appropriations bills, since there are thirteen of them that contain discretionary spending. But when President Bill Clinton first employed his new power in 1997, appropriations bills had not yet reached his desk. Consequently, he targeted other forms of spending defined by the law—new direct spending and limited tax benefits contained in the Balanced Budget Act and the Taxpayer Relief Act of 1997.

The president was allowed to use the line-item veto to cancel items of "new direct spending," which encompassed any new entitlement programs Congress passed. (He could not attack existing entitlements.) The president was also allowed to block "limited tax benefits," a provision that was put into the law to satisfy members who believed that tax benefits were just as much a form of spending as appropriations and deserved the same treatment.

The law allowed the president to target federal tax benefits that went to one hundred or fewer beneficiaries and in certain other limited situations. The Joint Committee on Taxation of Congress also could have included a statement in legislation specifying which provisions qualified as limited tax benefits, and if it did so the president would have been able to examine only those provisions. If it did not, he could have examined the whole bill to make a determination based on definitions in the act.

The president had to use the line-item veto within five days (excluding Sundays) of his signature on a bill or forfeit the power. He could not use it on bills he allowed to become law without his signature. If he used it, he had to send a message to Congress enumerating the items he had chosen and including other information, such as the impact on the federal budget and the specific states and congressional districts affected. The effect of sending the message was to immediately "cancel" the item in question.

THE PRESIDENT AS FISCAL GUARDIAN

Presidents dating back to Ulysses S. Grant (1869–1877) have advocated a line-item veto for themselves or their successors. President Clinton had long supported a line-item veto, a version of which he employed at the state level as Arkansas governor. It finally sprang to life as part of the Republicans' "Contract with America" in the 104th Congress.

The intellectual concept behind the law was that Congress had demonstrated many times it could not restrain its urge to spend. In an era of huge and seemingly ever-expanding and intractable deficits, Congress needed to be held in check by the president, who was—in this concept—defined as an opponent of waste and "pork barrel" politics. The idea of the president as a fiscal disciplinarian and opponent of increased spending was without historical foundation, but it fit especially well into the political rhetoric of the 1980s and early 1990s, when a Congress usually controlled by liberal Dem-

trary notwithstanding." A two-thirds vote of those present and voting in both chambers is required to override a veto. There must be a quorum present for the vote, which must be by roll call, and whether the two-thirds majority is achieved is determined only from the number of "yea" and "nay" votes. Those who vote "present" are not considered.

Despite the Constitution's provision that Congress "shall

proceed to reconsider" veto messages, the language has been interpreted to give each chamber various procedural options under its rules that do not require an immediate vote to override or sustain the veto. In the House, a vetoed bill is usually handled in one of four ways:

• It may be called up and debated for one hour, after which a vote on an override is held.

---

ocrats faced conservative Republican presidents Ronald Reagan and George Bush. Historically, there were many presidents of both parties—including such unquestioned conservatives as Dwight D. Eisenhower and Richard Nixon—who backed huge spending programs.

Once the new law was passed, however, times had changed. The Republican Congress postponed the effective date until after the 1996 election to prevent President Clinton from using it during his first term. Clinton was reelected, and when the historic moment for the unveiling of the first line-item veto finally came in 1997, it was a Democratic president facing off with a Republican Congress that controlled the purse strings and had its own spending and tax reduction priorities. Instead of huge deficits, federal red ink was decreasing each year and a large and growing budget surplus was anticipated as early as fiscal 1998.

CLINTON V. CONGRESS

When President Clinton employed the new tool to cut spending he opposed, he was accused of playing politics by Republicans in Congress. Some said that the administration was using veto threats to bargain with members on unrelated issues, such as the renewal of "fast track" authority for trade agreements. In other words, the dreaded fears of line-item veto opponents that the law would give a president unprecedented political leverage might actually prove to be true. Some earlier veto proponents switched sides and suggested repeal of the law.

In reality, the line-item veto was used sparingly in its debut. Clinton employed it eighty-two times in 1997, for an estimated savings of $1.9 billion over five years. But this was only about two-tenths of a percent of the $9 trillion the federal government was estimated to spend during that time.

In addition to the entitlement and tax provisions that Clinton had initially targeted to unveil his new power, and which became the basis for Supreme Court review in 1998, he canceled items on nine of the appropriations bills enacted in 1997. The cancellations represented a tiny amount of total spending in each bill.

In another court case, Judge Thomas P. Hogan, who was to later declare the line-item veto unconstitutional, blocked on statutory grounds Clinton's use of a line-item veto to kill a provision allowing federal employees to change pension plans. The administration agreed that the veto had been improperly cast, since the provision did not fit the definition of spending items the president could cancel, and the provision was restored as law.

In 1997, following procedures in the act, Congress passed a bill to reinstate all of the president's cancellations of $238 million for items in a military construction appropriations bill. This had been Clinton's most controversial use of the new power and was the only time

he was seriously challenged within Congress. The president admitted that some cancellations he made in the bill had been in error, but he vetoed the restoration bill that would have undone all of them. Both houses easily overrode him, the Senate in 1997 and the House following the convening of the second session of the 105th Congress in 1998.

VETO DECLARED UNCONSTITUTIONAL BY COURT

Two federal district judges agreed that the law was unconstitutional in decisions in 1997 and 1998. The Supreme Court turned back the first challenge to the law, in *Byrd v. Raines*, in 1997. The Court did not rule on the line-item veto's constitutionality because it said that the members of Congress who brought the lawsuit lacked legal standing to do so. The president had not actually used the line-item veto yet at that point.

The second case combined *City of New York v. Clinton* and *Snake River Potato Growers Inc. v. Rubin*, which were responding to the president's actual use of the line-item veto, enabling the new plaintiffs to argue directly that they had been injured by its use.

On February 12, 1998, Federal District Judge Hogan ruled that the line-item veto was unconstitutional. The Clinton administration immediately appealed his decision to the Supreme Court. On June 25, 1998, in a 6–3 decision, the Court upheld the lower court ruling, affirming the unconstitutionality of the veto.

The majority of the Court ruled that Congress had gone beyond the Constitution in allowing the president the power to cut out individual elements within a single spending bill. In a sense, this veto gave the president an unconstitutional role in altering legislation. Justice John Paul Stevens wrote for the majority:

There is no provision in the Constitution that authorizes the President to enact, to amend, or to repeal statutes. . . .

If the Line-Item Veto Act were valid, it would authorize the President to create a different law—one whose text was not voted on by either House of Congress or presented to the President for signature. . . .

If there is to be a new procedure in which the president will play a different role in determining the final text of what may "become a law," such change must not come by legislation but through [constitutional] amendment."

After the decision was announced, congressional supporters of the line-item veto immediately vowed to press the search for a constitutional means of giving such power to the president. With the end of the federal deficit, the main impetus for the line-item veto, and the unhappiness of many members of Congress over President Clinton's use of the veto, most analysts felt that Congress's experiment with sharing its legislative power would not be repeated any time soon.

Stymied often by vetoes by President George Bush, House Democratic leaders display their view of the president's veto pen at a 1991 press conference.

• It may be immediately referred back to its committee of origin by motion, with the expectation that it will remain there and no veto override vote will ever be held.

• It may be referred back to committee to be "parked" for awhile, awaiting a decision on scheduling a future override vote. The committee may not amend the bill but could theoretically hold further hearings on it to generate or increase public support for an override. (A motion on the floor to discharge a vetoed bill from a committee is privileged and may be made by any member each day.)

• It may remain at the Speaker's table but with further action postponed to a later date, either by motion or unanimous consent.

The last two options may be employed either to gain additional time to assemble the needed two-thirds majority or to schedule a vote closer to the next election for maximum political visibility. A vetoed bill may not be amended in any manner, only repassed or rejected.

In the Senate, if a vetoed bill is not considered immediately on receipt, the majority leader is normally permitted to bring it up at any time. A vetoed bill may be subject to a filibuster, but this rarely occurs because if there is any realistic chance of overriding the veto the bill's supporters would almost certainly have at least the sixty votes needed to end the filibuster. If they did not, there would be little point in taking up the bill at all. Vetoed bills are normally considered subject to a time agreement arrived at by unanimous consent.

The Senate has used another procedural mechanism, the "motion to reconsider" (the meaning of which differs from the Constitution's use of the same word), to give itself two chances to override a veto. In 1987, following President Reagan's veto of a major highway and mass transit funding bill, the House overrode but the Senate appeared about to sustain the veto by a single vote, with all senators voting, as a previously undecided Sen. Terry Sanford (D-N.C.) voted "nay." Majority Leader

Robert C. Byrd changed his vote to "nay" before the result was announced, making the final vote 65–35, to vote on the prevailing side and be eligible under Senate rules to make a motion to reconsider the vote. His action kept the vetoed bill on parliamentary life support until the following day, when Sanford changed his mind, the Senate adopted Byrd's motion to reconsider the earlier vote, and then the Senate finally overrode the veto by a 67–33 vote.

This is an excellent example of occasional disparity in the practices of the two houses even on such a supposedly fixed constitutional procedure as a veto override. House precedents would have barred a motion to reconsider the result of a veto override vote. Under Senate precedents, had the veto initially been overridden, no motion to reconsider would have been permitted as the bill would have effectively left the chamber and become law.

If the first house to act fails to override the veto, the bill is dead and the matter ends there. If the vote to override succeeds, the measure is sent to the second house. If the veto is overridden there, the bill becomes law without the president's signature; otherwise, the veto stands and the bill is dead. The attempt to override can occur at any time during the Congress that passed the legislation. For example, a vote in the House on overriding President Reagan's veto of a protectionist textile bill was delayed from December 1985 to August 1986, when the veto was finally sustained.

The Pocket Veto

The Constitution also provides that a bill shall not become law if "Congress by their adjournment prevent its return." The president can then "pocket veto" the bill since he does not have an opportunity to return it to Congress for further consideration. Unlike the veto specifically provided for in the Constitution, which is sometimes called a "return veto" because it is returned to Congress without the president's signature and with a statement of his objections, a pocket veto is accomplished wholly by inaction. However, it has become a common practice in recent years for the president, at his discretion, to issue a statement called a "memorandum of disapproval" with such pocket vetoes explaining the reason for his refusal to sign, and Congress has published these in the *Congressional Record*.

The president clearly may pocket veto any bills that are still awaiting his approval when Congress adjourns *sine die*. The Supreme Court ruled in the 1929 *Pocket Veto Case* that the president may pocket veto a bill when Congress has adjourned its first session *sine die* fewer than ten days after presenting it to him for its approval. But whether it is proper for the president to pocket veto bills during congressional recesses of more than three days or between sessions of the same Congress when the two houses have made arrangements to receive presidential messages is still unsettled in the law.

Federal courts have ruled such pocket vetoes to be unconstitutional, but the Supreme Court has not made a definitive ruling on the issue. President Gerald Ford, after losing a case in a federal appeals court, entered into a consent decree agreeing to use the "return veto" during intersession and intrasession adjournments where each house had provided for the receipt of such messages. The Supreme Court in 1987 threw out a federal appellate court ruling against an intersession Reagan pocket veto as moot *(Burke v. Barnes)*, without reaching the merits of the issue. President Bush raised these issues again in two pocket vetoes during his term. President Clinton, through his first six years in office, did not use a pocket veto.

Sometimes Congress has refused to recognize a purported "pocket veto" and has treated it as a "return veto" and conducted a vote to override it, leading to further confusion. In the second session of the 93rd Congress (1974), for example, President Ford returned a bill to Congress without his signature while asserting that he had pocket vetoed it during an adjournment of the House to a day certain. However, each house treated it as a return veto and then proceeded to override. The bill was sent to the Archives to receive a public law number. The administrator of General Services, on advice from the Justice Department, refused to promulgate the bill as law. Without acquiescing in this interpretation, both houses then passed an identical bill that the president signed.

The House has authorized its clerk, and the Senate its secretary, to receive veto messages when either body is in recess when a veto message arrives. Both houses have asserted that this procedure allows them to properly receive the vetoes while awaiting the reconvening of the receiving chamber for formal action. But presidents have not accepted this mechanism as a means of restricting their broad claims of authority to issue pocket vetoes.

NOTES

1. Walter J. Oleszek, *Congressional Procedures and the Policy Process*, 4th ed. (Washington, D.C.: CQ Press, 1996), 20.

2. *National Review*, February 27, 1987, 24.

3. Janet Hook, "Speaker Jim Wright Takes Charge in the House," *Congressional Quarterly Weekly Report*, July 11, 1987, 1486.

4. Steven S. Smith, *Call to Order: Floor Politics in the House and Senate* (Washington, D.C.: Brookings Institution, 1989), 9.

5. *Congressional Quarterly Almanac 1986* (Washington, D.C.: Congressional Quarterly, 1987), 33.

6. *Washington Post*, June 26, 1983, A14.

7. Quoted in *Congress A to Z: A Ready Reference Encyclopedia*, 2nd ed. (Washington, D.C.: Congressional Quarterly, 1993), 180.

8. Oleszek, *Congressional Procedures*, 4th ed., 93.

9. Robert A. Katzmann, *Congress and Courts* (Washington, D.C.: Brookings Institution, 1997), 64–65.

10. Bruce I. Oppenheimer, "The Changing Relationship between House Leadership and the Committee on Rules," in *Understanding Congressional Leadership*, ed. Frank H. Mackaman (Washington, D.C.: CQ Press, 1981), 217.

11. Walter J. Oleszek, *Congressional Procedures and the Policy Process*, 3rd ed. (Washington, D.C.: CQ Press, 1987), 127.

12. Stanley Bach and Steven S. Smith, *Managing Uncertainty in the House of Representatives: Adaptation and Innovation in Special Rules* (Washington, D.C.: Brookings Institution, 1988), 28.

13. Janet Hook, "GOP Chafes Under Restrictive House Rules," *Congressional Quarterly Weekly Report*, October 10, 1987, 2452.

14. Bach and Smith, *Managing Uncertainty in the House of Representatives*, 73.

15. Oleszek, *Congressional Procedures*, 4th ed., 149.

16. Ibid., 169.

17. Thomas E. Mann and Norman J. Ornstein, *Renewing Congress: A First Report* (Washington, D.C.: Brookings Institution and American Enterprise Institute, 1992), 49.

18. Smith, *Call to Order*, 243.

19. Jacqueline Calmes, "Byrd Struggles to Lead Deeply Divided Senate," *Congressional Quarterly Weekly Report*, July 4, 1987, 1422.

20. Oleszek, *Congressional Procedures*, 4th ed., 210.

21. Smith, *Call to Order*, 128.

22. Nancy Landon Kassebaum, "The Senate Is Not in Order," *Washington Post*, January 27, 1988, A19.

23. Oleszek, *Congressional Procedures*, 4th ed., 231.

24. Jacqueline Calmes, "'Trivialized' Filibuster Is Still a Potent Tool," *Congressional Quarterly Weekly Report*, September 5, 1987, 2120.

25. Ibid.

26. Smith, *Call to Order*, 97.

27. Ibid., 96.

28. Barbara Sinclair, *Unorthodox Lawmaking: New Legislative Processes in the U.S. Congress* (Washington, D.C.: CQ Press, 1997), 202.

29. Asher C. Hinds, ed., *Hinds' Precedents of the House of Representatives*, vol. 4 (Washington, D.C.: Government Printing Office, 1907), sec. 3492, 336–338.

SELECTED BIBLIOGRAPHY

Bacchus, William I. *Inside the Legislative Process*. Boulder, Colo.: Westview Press, 1983.

Bach, Stanley, and Steven S. Smith. *Managing Uncertainty in the House of Representatives: Adaptation and Innovation in Special Rules*. Washington, D.C.: Brookings Institution, 1988.

Berman, Daniel M. *How a Bill Becomes a Law: Congress Enacts Civil Rights Legislation*. New York: Macmillan, 1966.

Bessette, Joseph M. *The Mild Voice of Reason: Deliberative Democracy and American National Government*. Chicago: University of Chicago Press, 1994.

Birnbaum, Jeffrey H., and Alan S. Murray. *Showdown at Gucci Gulch*. New York: Random House, 1987.

Brady, David W. *Critical Elections and Congressional Policy-Making*. Stanford, Calif.: Stanford University Press, 1988.

Brown, William H. *House Practice: A Guide to the Rules, Precedents and Pro-*

cedures of the House. Washington, D.C.: Government Printing Office, 1996.

Cannon, Clarence, ed. *Cannon's Precedents of the House of Representatives.* 6 vols. Washington, D.C.: Government Printing Office, 1936.

Connelly, William F., Jr., and John J. Pitney Jr. *Congress' Permanent Minority.* Lanham, Md.: Rowman, 1994.

Cooper, Joseph, and G. Calvin Mackenzie. *The House at Work.* Austin: University of Texas Press, 1981.

Davidson, Roger H., and Walter J. Oleszek. *Congress and Its Members.* 7th ed. Washington, D.C.: CQ Press, 2000.

———. *Governing: Readings and Cases in American Politics.* Washington, D.C.: CQ Press, 1987.

Deering, Christopher J., and Steven S. Smith. *Committees in Congress.* 3rd ed. Washington, D.C.: CQ Press, 1997.

Democratic Study Group, House of Representatives. "A Look at the Senate Filibuster." DSG Special Report, June 13, 1994.

Deschler, Lewis. *Precedents of the House of Representatives.* Washington, D.C.: Government Printing Office, 1977– .

Deschler, Lewis, and William H. Brown. *Procedure in the House of Representatives.* Washington, D.C.: Government Printing Office, 1982; 1987 supplement.

Dodd, Lawrence C., and Bruce I. Oppenheimer, eds. *Congress Reconsidered.* 6th ed. Washington, D.C.: CQ Press, 1997.

Eidenberg, Eugene, and Roy D. Morey. *An Act of Congress: The Legislative Process and the Making of Education Policy.* New York: Norton, 1969.

Evans, C. Lawrence, and Walter J. Oleszek. *Congress Under Fire.* Boston: Houghton Mifflin, 1997.

Fenno, Richard. *Congressmen in Committees.* Boston: Little, Brown, 1973.

Fiorina, Morris P. *Divided Government.* New York: Maxwell Macmillan, 1992.

Fox, Harrison W., Jr., and Susan W. Hammond. *Congressional Staffs: The Invisible Force in American Lawmaking.* New York: Free Press, 1979.

Froman, Lewis A., Jr. *The Congressional Process: Strategies, Rules, and Procedures.* Boston: Little, Brown, 1967.

Galloway, George B. *The Legislative Process in Congress.* New York: Crowell, 1953.

Hawkins, Betsy W. *Setting Course: A Congressional Management Guide.* 6th ed. Washington, D.C.: Congressional Management Foundation, 1996.

Hinckley, Barbara. *Less Than Meets the Eye: Foreign Policymaking and the Myth of the Assertive Congress.* Chicago: University of Chicago Press, 1994.

Hinds, Asher C., ed. *Hinds' Precedents of the House of Representatives.* 11 vols. Washington, D.C.: Government Printing Office, 1907–1941.

Jewell, Malcolm E., and Samuel C. Patterson. *The Legislative Process in the United States.* 4th ed. New York: McGraw-Hill, 1985.

Johnson, Charles W. *Constitution, Jefferson's Manual, and Rules of the House of Representatives.* 104th Cong., 2nd sess., 1997. House Doc. 104-272.

Katzmann, Robert A. *Courts and Congress.* Washington, D.C.: Brookings Institution, 1997.

King, David C. *Turf Wars: How Congressional Committees Claim Jurisdiction.* Chicago: University of Chicago Press, 1997.

Kingdon, John W. *Congressmen's Voting Decisions.* 3rd ed. Ann Arbor: University of Michigan Press, 1989.

Kornacki, John J., ed. *Leading Congress: New Styles, New Strategies.* Washington, D.C.: Congressional Quarterly, 1990.

Krehbiel, Keith. *Information and Legislative Organization.* Ann Arbor: University of Michigan Press, 1991.

Luce, Robert. *Legislative Procedure: Parliamentary Practices and the Course of Business in the Framing of Statutes.* Boston: Houghton Mifflin, 1922. Reprint. New York: Da Capo Press, 1972.

Malbin, Michael J. *Unelected Representatives.* New York: Basic Books, 1980.

Mann, Thomas E., and Norman J. Ornstein. *The New Congress.* Washington, D.C.: American Enterprise Institute, 1981.

———. *Renewing Congress: A First Report.* Washington, D.C.: Brookings Institution and American Enterprise Institute, 1992.

———. *Renewing Congress: A Second Report.* Washington, D.C.: Brookings Institution and American Enterprise Institute, 1993.

Nickels, Ilona B. *Parliamentary Reference Sources: An Introductory Guide.* Washington, D.C.: Congressional Research Service, 1986.

Oleszek, Walter J. *Congressional Procedures and the Policy Process.* 4th ed. Washington, D.C.: CQ Press, 1996.

Ornstein, Norman J., ed. *Congress in Change: Evolution and Reform.* New York: Praeger, 1975.

Ornstein, Norman J., Thomas E. Mann, and Michael J. Malbin. *Vital Statistics on Congress, 1997–1998.* Washington, D.C.: Congressional Quarterly, 1997.

Parker, Glenn R., ed. *Studies of Congress.* Washington, D.C.: CQ Press, 1985.

Parker, Glenn R., and Suzanne L. Parker. *Factions in House Committees.* Knoxville: University of Tennessee Press, 1985.

Peabody, Robert L., and others. *To Enact a Law: Congress and Campaign Financing.* New York: Praeger, 1972.

Price, David. *Who Makes the Laws?* Cambridge, Mass.: Schenkman, 1972.

Redman, Eric. *The Dance of Legislation.* New York: Simon and Schuster, 1973.

Reid, T. R. *Congressional Odyssey: The Saga of a Senate Bill.* New York: Freeman, 1980.

Riddick, Floyd M., and Alan S. Frumin. *Riddick's Senate Procedure: Precedents and Practices.* Rev. ed. 101st Cong., 2nd sess., 1992. Senate Doc. 101-28.

Rieselbach, Leroy N. *Congressional Reform.* Washington, D.C.: CQ Press, 1986.

Ripley, Randall B. *Congress: Process and Policy.* 4th ed. New York: Norton, 1988.

Sheppard, Burton D. *Rethinking Congressional Reform: The Reform Roots of the Special Interest Congress.* Cambridge, Mass.: Schenkman, 1985.

Siff, Ted, and Alan Weil. *Ruling Congress: How House and Senate Rules Govern the Legislative Process.* New York: Grossman, 1975.

Sinclair, Barbara. *Unorthodox Lawmaking: New Legislative Processes in the U.S. Congress.* Washington, D.C.: CQ Press, 1997.

Smith, Steven S. *The American Congress.* Boston: Houghton Mifflin, 1995.

———. *Call to Order: Floor Politics in the House and Senate.* Washington, D.C.: Brookings Institution, 1989.

Stein, Robert M., and Kenneth N. Bickers. *Perpetuating the Pork Barrel: Policy Subsystems and American Democracy.* New York: Cambridge University Press, 1995.

Strom, Gerald S. *The Logic of Lawmaking: A Spatial Theory Approach.* Baltimore: Johns Hopkins University Press, 1990.

Sullivan, Terry O. *Procedural Structure: A Success and Influence in Congress.* New York: Praeger, 1984.

Tiefer, Charles. *Congressional Practice and Procedure: A Reference, Research, and Legislative Guide.* Westport, Conn.: Greenwood Press, 1989.

U.S. Congress. House. *Manual on Legislative Procedure in the U.S. House of Representatives.* 6th ed. Washington, D.C.: Government Printing Office, 1986.

U.S. Congress. House. Committee on Government Reform and Oversight. *Minority Rights, Prerogatives and Protections in the Committee on Government Reform and Oversight.* Prepared by the Minority Staff. Washington, D.C.: Government Printing Office, 1997.

U.S. Congress. Senate. Committee on Rules and Administration. *Senate Manual Containing the Standing Rules, Orders, Laws, and Resolutions Affecting the Business of the United States Senate.* Washington, D.C.: Government Printing Office, 1967– .

Vogler, David J. *The Third House: Conference Committees in the United States Congress.* Evanston, Ill.: Northwestern University Press, 1971.

Whalen, Charles, and Barbara Whalen. *The Longest Debate: A Legislative History of the 1964 Civil Rights Act.* Washington, D.C.: Seven Locks Press, 1985.

Wright, Gerald C., Leroy N. Rieselbach, and Lawrence C. Dodd, eds. *Congress and Policy Change.* New York: Agathon Press, 1986.

CHAPTER 16

The Committee System

THE COMMITTEE SYSTEM in Congress has been under assault so frequently, and for so long, that it is important to remember that committees still matter:

• They continue to perform important work that cannot be duplicated elsewhere in Congress.

• They operate in open view under the microscope of extensive coverage by television and the press.

• They endure despite efforts to weaken their chairmen, rotate chairmen out of office, and transfer committee powers to political party bodies or ad hoc entities.

Members of Congress seem to agree. No reform proposals are more abundant than those that would reform or even eviscerate the existing committee structures and jurisdictions of the House and Senate. Nonetheless, despite periodic changes in the institution, the committee system at the end of the twentieth century had remained basically intact for the last fifty years. Although scholars and participants alike still see many deficiencies in the system, members clearly believe that it works and that experimentation with other means of processing legislation should be attempted only incrementally and with careful monitoring.

Committees are the infrastructure of Congress. They are where the bulk of legislative work is done—where expertise resides, where policies incubate, where most legislative proposals are written or refined, where many necessary compromises are made, where the public can make its views known, where members of Congress build influence and reputations.

Committees have enormous power, especially in the House of Representatives. They hold hearings, conduct investigations, and oversee government programs. They initiate bills, approve and report legislation to the floor, control most of the time for debate on the floor, have preference in offering amendments, and take the lead in representing their chamber in conferences with the other house. They can kill measures through inaction or defeat. In the Senate, where individual senators' prerogatives may hold sway over collective interests and where the ability to offer amendments is practically unlimited, committees can be more readily bypassed and do not perform the same "gatekeeper" role in determining access to the floor. Still, the ability of committees to influence the ultimate disposition of an issue remains substantial.

It is difficult—at times virtually impossible—to circumvent a committee that is determined not to act. A bill that has been approved by a committee may be amended when it reaches the House or Senate floor, but extensive revisions generally are more difficult to achieve at that stage. The actions of the committees, or their failure to act, more often than not give Congress its record of legislative achievement or failure.

Congressional expert Walter J. Oleszek has observed that the rules and precedents of both chambers reinforce committee prerogatives. Because "committee members and their staffs have more expertise on matters within their jurisdiction than members of Congress as a whole, the fundamental outlines of committee decisions generally will be accepted."[1]

Committees in Transition

As Congress approaches the twenty-first century, it is readily apparent that committees lack the clout they once did. They are no longer the imperial "little legislatures" of political science literature that once so dominated the presentation of legislation to Congress and set the agenda, from floor action through presidential action. Committees are affected by the same factors that transformed the broader operations of Congress and the relationships between politicians and the American public. Changes in membership, shifts in power in relation to the leadership, the evolution of new rules and procedures, demands of partisan political agendas, extensive media coverage, and the availability of new sources of information and technology have all served to alter the balance of power within Congress. Sometimes these changes have pulled the institution in opposite directions over relatively short periods of time.

During the 1970s, reforms initiated earlier by a new generation of younger, activist Democrats came to fruition with the election of the large 1974 class of "Watergate babies," as they were known after their election in the wake of the political scandal that drove President Richard Nixon from office. Their numbers provided the votes to complete an institutional revolution that weakened committee chairmen, dispersed power to subcommittees, strengthened the leadership, increased accountability to the House Democratic Caucus, and fostered the growth of staff on both sides of the Capitol. Power was diffused and rival power centers emerged. Many lawmakers no longer deferred to committees on the details of legislation. Floor challenges to committees became more common once members had gained the expertise and staff needed to make independent judgments.

Unchallenged in previous Congresses, committee leaders be-

The organizations of the House's two political parties—the Republican Conference and Democratic Caucus—exercise complete control of committee assignments, committee chairmanships, and ranking minority member positions. Committee assignments and seniority rankings are ratified by the House through the adoption of privileged resolutions offered by direction of the parties and may be altered at any time.

The longtime Democratic majority from 1955–1995 created an increasingly complex system to resolve competing claims for committee chairmanships and assignments while giving members hope that they would be considered fairly for important posts at some point in their careers. Party leadership exercised considerable influence over the process but sometimes could be effectively pushed or challenged by the general membership, depending on the salience of the issue involved. Many of the major committee-related reforms of the 1970s, for example, along with the principal efforts to unseat conservative committee chairmen, were driven by younger, more liberal members, sometimes over leadership opposition or passive acquiescence.

The Republican minority, without real power, quarreled with the Democrats over committee ratios, sued them unsuccessfully in court, offered its reform proposals on the House floor at the organization of each new Congress, and developed a critique of Democratic control that gradually became the "forty years of corruption" theme used successfully in the 1994 elections.

During the reform period of the 1970s, the Democratic Caucus had threatened to intrude on committee independence and to direct action on legislative matters by instructing committee members, but this quickly sparked a counterreaction and the caucus initiatives did not last long. Changes in committee chairmanships and memberships accomplished the objective of ensuring greater responsiveness to the caucus using more traditional means.

However, the activist tradition reemerged in 1993 with a demand by junior members to discipline subcommittee chairmen who had voted against President Bill Clinton's budget reconciliation legislation, which had passed by only two votes over unified Republican opposition. But the effort faded rapidly after liberals had vented their anger.

The Republican Conference, once in the majority in 1995, immediately assumed an aggressive posture. The conference, new to power, had little tradition of deferring to committees that it had not controlled for forty years. The GOP conference had an activist agenda coming out of the 1994 election campaign and wanted action as quickly as possible.

Far more than the Democrats, the Republican leadership, led by Speaker Newt Gingrich, R-Ga., who was credited with masterminding the campaign for majority status, was deferred to by a party containing many members with little political experience. The Speaker intervened freely in the legislative process, sometimes reaching down to the level of dictating subcommittee chairmen and subcommittee agendas. He exercised far greater influence over the committee system than Democratic leaders could have ever dreamed of. Demands were even made for individual dissenters to explain to the conference their votes against the party's positions on the floor. For example, a handful of rebellious members who voted against, and helped defeat, the rule for consideration of the 105th Congress's committee funding resolution in 1997 were called upon to explain themselves. Later in the year senior members of the GOP leadership were forced to explain their knowledge of and roles in a celebrated and unsuccessful effort to replace Gingrich as Speaker.

COMMITTEE ASSIGNMENTS

The two parties developed rules dividing the various committees into different classifications, to ensure a fair distribution of desirable committee assignments, and mechanisms to distribute committee and subcommittee chairmanship and ranking minority member posts. Both parties consider the Appropriations, Commerce, Rules, and Ways and Means committees as "exclusive," meaning that no member of one of them may serve on any other committee. There are also various "grandfather clauses" allowing certain members to escape these restrictions. In addition, members of exclusive committees are allowed to serve on committees on House Administration, Standards of Official Conduct, and the Budget, which is required by House rules to have some members from Appropriations and Ways and Means.

Members who are not awarded exclusive posts—meaning most members of the House—usually serve on two standing legislative committees. Exceptions are sometimes made when the majority party needs members on less desirable panels to ensure its numerical control. The Democrats grappled for years with the problem of "temporary" members serving on committees, principally to fill vacancies that other members did not want and to provide proxy votes to the committee chairman. Temporary assignments were often denounced by reformers, but in the absence of any rules governing committee sizes, the caucus realized it could not dispense with the practice entirely. Indeed, the Democratic leadership sometimes encouraged it by promising politically vulnerable members additional assignments.

The Republicans in 1995 passed new rules in the House itself purporting to regulate and rationalize the number of committee and subcommittee assignments, restricting members to two standing committees and four subcommittees. But they soon found themselves in the same bind as the Democrats, further complicated by the fact that the new majority had deprived itself of the convenience of proxy voting. Quickly, exceptions to the rules again began to be made. *(See box, Proxy Voting, p. 552.)*

ROLE OF MAJORITY AND MINORITY RULES

The voluminous House Democratic Caucus rules, when that party last controlled the House, illustrated the importance of process for regulating the many ways in which power was dispersed. Because committee and subcommittee chairmanships, assignments, and seniority represented raw power and could make or break members' careers, the application of the rules assumed tremendous importance. Indeed, the existence of increasingly complex rules became essential to maintain a balance between different factions, to let members feel they were being treated fairly, and to settle contests for important posts with highly structured competition. They provided checks and balances among the leadership, the committees, and the general caucus membership.

Committee chairmen held great power, but there were mechanisms that could remove them and allow others to run against them directly in the caucus. The Steering Committee dominated by the Democratic leadership could almost always get its way in selecting members of the most important committees, but other candidates could run from the floor. Members could bid by order of seniority for subcommittee chairmanships on their committees, but challengers could announce opposition, run elaborate campaigns to reject the senior members on secret ballots, and then, if successful, claim the posts themselves.

The caucus rules reflected decades of adjustments and accommodations made for different reasons at different times. Eventually, they became so filled with multiple classifications of committees and with service and chairmanship limitations, all further layered with exceptions geared to specific individuals, that the system became increasingly difficult to comprehend and administer. Issues such as the proper size of committees and their jurisdictional workloads, which might have been used to distinguish between "major" as opposed to "non-major" committees, were often ignored and took a back seat to the political needs of members or the leadership's desire to grant special favors.

After Democrats became a minority in 1995 and lost their power to control committee ratios and a legislative agenda, the need for such a complex rules structure diminished. Members had less interest in their share of a minority with little power, which opened the way for a further enhanced leadership role in the committee as-

signment process and even returned some power to the former committee chairmen, now the ranking minority members. The new decisions that had to be made reflected ways to limit the pain of minority status, rather than to distribute additional rewards, so members were more willing to leave such decisions to the leadership's discretion.

The most important rules change by the new Democratic minority weakened the so-called "subcommittee bill of rights" created during the reform period of the mid-1970s that had allowed each subcommittee chairman the right to hire one staffer. The Republican majority in 1995 dramatically cut back the number of committee staff, claiming that it was making a one-third cut. That change, along with minority status, so decimated available Democratic staff positions that it made less sense to guarantee staff to ranking subcommittee members and created an argument for recentralization so that the core committee staff had enough resources to function. A new rule allowed each committee's Democratic caucus to decide the staff allocations and some chose to return control over them all to the ranking minority member.

The Republican Conference rules remained far simpler because in the minority complex rules had not been needed. So when majority status finally came, the leadership found itself with fewer existing constraints. Republicans had never undergone the relentless push for democratization reflected in Democratic rules fights over more than two decades, with their complex procedures guaranteeing bidding rights for subcommittee chairmanships and assignments, and battles over expanding ways to discipline committee chairmen. Republican Conference rules give the Steering Committee the right to nominate candidates for committee chairs, without regard to seniority, until a nominee is approved. They also give committee chairmen the right to take the initiative in selecting subcommittee chairmen and members, subject to modification by the full committee caucus, which allows the chairmen greater influence over assignments.

The first years of the House Republican majority starting in 1995 emphasized party discipline and the need to enact the party's political and legislative agenda. Strict adherence to party rules, seniority, and accommodations with individuals were of secondary importance and were dispensed with when they interfered with the primary objectives.

If the Republicans retain the majority for a substantial period, however, it seems inevitable that pressures for dispersion of power and "sharing the wealth" will eventually complicate their internal party processes just as they did with the Democrats.

Committees are where the bulk of legislative work is accomplished. Here the Senate Labor and Human Resources Committee meets in 1997.

came accountable for their actions and could be ousted by a vote of their party. This happened to Democratic committee chairmen six times in the House between 1975 and 1990, though never in the Senate. (No Democratic committee chairman or ranking minority member was removed by vote of the caucus after 1990.) Indeed, House reformers struggled repeatedly over a period of more than twenty years to find better ways to control, restrict, discipline, or challenge chairmen, and to remind them that they were always under scrutiny. No ideal formula ever emerged, and committees and their leaders remained imperfect vehicles for fulfilling the aspirations of their fellow politicians. Some prominent leaders, such as former Ways and Means Committee Chairman Dan Rostenkowski, D-Ill., maintained an often tense relationship with substantial segments of their party membership.

Committees routinely shared their once exclusive domains with other committees, particularly in the House, through the use of bill referrals to more than one committee. Committees had to comply with timetables for action set by the House Speaker. The traditional authorizing committees found their power diluted, if not eclipsed, by the Appropriations and Budget committees as Congress had less time for floor action on committee initiatives. Summits, task forces, and other ad hoc groups were convened on occasion to handle controversial issues as traditional channels worked less well. Massive pieces of omnibus legislation often were used to conduct the most important business and on occasion were the only way to get work done. Congressional leaders tried to orchestrate a changing legislative process that sometimes seemed out of control.

As the decade of the 1970s closed, the committee structure was still firmly entrenched in Congress, but much of the power and prestige that had been held by the full committees had been transferred to the subcommittees and to a new, larger corps of chairmen, especially in the House. Subcommittees took on the institutional characteristics and vested interests of their parent committees. People began to talk about "subcommittee government" instead of "committee government" on Capitol Hill.

This empowerment of subcommittees led to a decentralization of power and to heavier legislative workloads for members of both houses. Critics noted a slowing down of the legislative process. "On balance, Congress has become more decentralized, more responsive to a multitude of forces inside and outside its halls, and, as a result, more hard pressed to formulate and enact coherent, responsible public policies," wrote Leroy N. Rieselbach.[2]

So great was the proliferation of subcommittees that limits on their number were set in both chambers. Other changes and accommodations were made as well.

By the mid-1990s, before a recentralization of power in the House undermined their autonomy, subcommittees were widely blamed for the inability of Congress to act coherently on major issues. Of course, other factors—the increasing political independence of members from their parties, weak congressional leadership, multiple jurisdictional requirements, and increased partisanship in both houses—also created unpredictable obstacles in the traditional paths to legislative achievement.

The mix of historic precedents and contemporary reforms placed committees in a state of flux. "[L]ike other institutional features, congressional committees are dynamic rather than static. Indeed, in a variety of small ways committees change almost constantly," political scientists Christopher J. Deering and Steven S. Smith observed.[3] On the one hand, committees were still the central players in the legislative process. Yet committees were also much less autonomous than they were just a few decades earlier.

When Republicans gained control of both chambers of Congress in the 1994 elections, for the first time in four decades, many of the common patterns of congressional organization were disrupted. The new majority had a well-defined political and legislative agenda but inherited traditional legislative institutions to enact it. The role of committees and subcommittees, relationships between committees and the leadership, and seniority all became subordinate to the need to build a record that would allow continued GOP control of Congress; committees and their procedures had little claim to legitimacy based merely on past history.

After the Republican takeover, House committees initially were eclipsed by the leadership using the Republican Conference, the organization of all House GOP members, and ad hoc task forces as vehicles to drive a conservative policy agenda known as the "Contract with America" that Republican candidates had used with great success in the 1994 elections. When committees did consider contract legislation early in 1995, their actions were often pro forma, while the Democratic minority's ability to offer amendments and debate the proposals in committee were sometimes curtailed to an unusual degree. "I am a transmission belt for the leadership," said Judiciary Committee Chairman Henry Hyde. "Either I don't live up to the Contract, or I move faster than both I and the Democrats want."[4]

In the 105th Congress, starting in 1997—following a series of legislative defeats at the hands of President Bill Clinton and his allies and the GOP's near loss of their House majority in the 1996 election—the value of the committee process became more apparent to Republican leaders and attempts to bypass it were less blatant. A less impatient GOP took more time to learn how to use the traditional tools of committee leadership.

Nevertheless, some changes in the relationship between Congress and its committees did occur. It is unquestioned that by 1999 committees were much less the independent power centers than they were thirty years earlier. Committees now served many political masters who were no longer reluctant to crack the whip to obtain the legislative performance desired. There also was no doubt that the party leadership would go around committees to attain important political goals.

After attaining the majority in 1995, Republicans were well positioned after four decades in a minority to reexamine practices to which they had never been wedded and that might not serve their particular needs. After assuming the speakership, Newt Gingrich, R-Ga., made and unmade committee leaders at will, even influencing subcommittee chairmanship selections. Nevertheless, it was not certain by 1999 whether the changes Republicans made in the conduct of House business would take hold for the long-term, or how quickly such institutionalization

might occur. Some observers wondered if Congress—and the House in particular—had entered a period of instability in the late 1990s with the use of a more ad hoc "ends justify the means" style of legislating.

Evolution of the System: Growth and Reform

Congressional committees became a major factor in the legislative process by evolution, not by constitutional design. Committees are not mentioned in the Constitution. The committee concept was borrowed from the British Parliament and transmitted to the New World by way of the colonial legislatures, most notably those of Pennsylvania and Virginia. But the committee system as it developed in Congress was modified and influenced by characteristics peculiar to American life.

In the early days of the Republic, when the nation's population was small and the duties of the central government were carefully circumscribed, Congress had little need for the division of labor that today's committee system provides. A people who viewed with grave suspicion the need to delegate authority to elected representatives in Washington were served by a Congress that only grudgingly delegated any of its own powers to committees.

In the earliest Congresses, members were few in number and their legislative workload was light. Temporary committees served their needs. But as the nation grew and took on more complex responsibilities and problems, Congress had to develop expertise and the mechanisms to deal with the changing world. And so, from a somewhat haphazard arrangement of ad hoc committees evolved a highly specialized system of permanent committees.

Standing committees were institutionalized and multiplied in the nineteenth century. Efforts in the twentieth century to consolidate the burgeoning committee system—especially through the 1946 Legislative Reorganization Act—served to strengthen the streamlined committees and their leaders. So overriding did the influence of committees in the legislative process become that scholars over the years called them "little legislatures"[5] and their chairmen "petty barons."[6]

None of this could have been foreseen during the First Congress, when many of the "Founding Fathers" served and took major roles in every issue that came along. In the early Congresses, legislative proposals were considered first in the Senate or House chamber, after which a special or select committee was appointed to work out the details of the legislation. Once the committee submitted its report on the bill, it was dissolved. Approximately 350 such committees were created during the Third Congress alone.[7]

As legislation increased in volume and complexity, permanent ("standing") committees gradually replaced select committees, and legislation was referred directly to the committees without first being considered by the parent body. This proce-

---

DATES COMMITTEES WERE ESTABLISHED

Only committees in existence in 1999 are listed. Where major committees have been consolidated, the date cited is when the component committee was established first. Names in parentheses are those of current committees where they differ from the committees' original names.

HOUSE

1789—Rules (originally as select committee; became permanent in 1880)
1789—Enrolled Bills (House Administration)
1795—Commerce and Manufactures (Commerce)
1802—Ways & Means
1805—Public Lands (Resources)
1808—Post Office and Post Roads (Government Reform)
1808—District of Columbia (Government Reform)
1813—Judiciary
1813—Pensions and Revolutionary Claims (Veterans' Affairs)
1816—Expenditures in Executive Departments (Government Reform)
1820—Agriculture
1822—Foreign Affairs (International Relations)
1822—Military Affairs (Armed Services)
1822—Naval Affairs (Armed Services)
1837—Public Buildings and Grounds (Transportation and Infrastructure)
1865—Appropriations
1865—Banking & Currency (Banking and Financial Services)
1867—Education & Labor (Education and the Workforce)
1941—Select Small Business (Small Business)
1958—Science & Astronautics (Science)
1967—Standards of Official Conduct
1974—Budget
1977—Select Intelligence

SENATE

1789—Enrolled Bills (Rules & Administration)
1816—Commerce and Manufactures (Commerce, Science & Transportation)
1816—District of Columbia (Governmental Affairs)
1816—Finance
1816—Foreign Relations
1816—Judiciary
1816—Military Affairs (Armed Services)
1816—Naval Affairs (Armed Services)
1816—Post Office and Post Roads (Governmental Affairs)
1816—Public Lands (Energy & Natural Resources)
1825—Agriculture (Agriculture, Nutrition & Forestry)
1837—Public Buildings and Grounds (Environment & Public Works)
1842—Expenditures in Executive Departments (Governmental Affairs)
1867—Appropriations
1869—Education & Labor (Labor & Human Resources)
1913—Banking & Currency (Banking, Housing & Urban Affairs)
1950—Select Small Business (Small Business)
1958—Aeronautical & Space Sciences (Commerce, Science & Transportation)
1970—Veterans' Affairs
1975—Budget
1976—Select Intelligence
1977—Indian Affairs

NOTE: Both the House and Senate Select Intelligence committees are permanent committees, but for reasons relating to congressional rules on committee organization they are called select committees.

SOURCES: *Constitution, Jefferson's Manual and Rules of the House of Representatives* (105th Congress); *House Practice;* George Goodwin Jr., *The Little Legislatures: Committees of Congress* (Amherst: University of Massachusetts Press, 1970).

---

dure gave the committees initial authority over legislation, each in its specialized jurisdiction, subject to subsequent review by the full chamber.

The House led the way in the creation of standing committees. The Committee on Elections, created in 1789, was followed by the Claims Committee in 1794 and by Commerce and Manufactures and Revision of the Laws committees in 1795. The number had risen to ten by 1810. The next substantial expansion of committees did not occur until the administration of President James Monroe (1817–1825). Between the War of 1812 and the Civil War the standing committee system became the standard vehicle for consideration of legislative business by the House, but it was not yet fully exploited as a source of independent power. The dramatic growth of the House and its workload contributed to the institutionalization of committees. House Speaker Henry Clay of Kentucky also found a responsive committee

system helpful to his policy goals and thus encouraged the creation of committees.[8]

The Senate was slower in establishing standing committees. In the first twenty-five years of its existence, only four standing committees were created, and all of them on the whole were more administrative than legislative. Most of the committee work fell to select committees, usually of three members, appointed as the occasion demanded and disbanded when their task was completed. These occasions were so frequent that during the session of 1815–1816 between ninety and one hundred select committees were appointed. Frequently, however, related legislation would be referred to special committees already in existence, and the same senators often were appointed to committees dealing with similar subjects.

In 1816 the Senate, finding inconvenient the appointment of so many ad hoc committees during each session, added eleven standing committees to the existing four. By 1863 the number had grown to nineteen.[9] But prior to the Civil War committees still played a relatively small role in the Senate.

COMMITTEE MEMBERSHIP

Each chamber developed its own method of making appointments to the committees. The rule established by the House in 1789 reserved to the whole House the power to choose the membership of all committees composed of more than three members. That rule gave way in 1790 to a rule delegating this power to the Speaker, with the reservation that the House might direct otherwise in special cases. Eventually, however, the Speaker was given the right to appoint the members as well as the chairmen of all standing committees, a power he retained until 1911. The principle that the committees were to be bipartisan, but weighted in favor of the majority party and its policies, was established early.

In making committee appointments and promotions certain principles governed the Speaker's choices. The wishes of the minority leaders in filling vacancies going to members of their party usually were respected. Generally, seniority—length of service on the committee—and factors such as geographical distribution and party loyalty were considered. But the Speaker was not bound by such criteria, and there were cases where none of those factors outweighed the Speaker's wishes. Despite complaints and various attempts to change the rule the system remained in force until 1911, when the House again exercised the right to select the members of standing committees. *(See "Committee Assignments," p. 566.)*

In the Senate assignment to a committee was made by vote of the entire membership until 1823. Members wishing to serve on a particular committee were placed on a ballot, with the choicest committee assignments going to those receiving the most votes. The senator with the largest number of votes served as chairman.

By the 1820s, however, a number of difficulties with the ballot system had become evident. The arrangement proved tedious and time-consuming and provided no guarantee that the party in control of the chamber would hold a majority of seats on the committee or retain control of the committee chairmanships in the event of a vacancy. Several times in the ensuing years the Senate amended its rules to provide for appointment to committees by a designated official, usually the vice president or president pro tempore. However, abuse of the appointment power and a transfer of power between parties compelled the Senate to return to use of the ballot.

In 1823 senators rejected a proposal that the chairmen of the five most important committees be chosen by the full Senate, and that the chairmen then have the power to make all other committee assignments. The Senate instead amended the standing rules to give the "presiding officer" authority to make committee assignments, unless otherwise ordered by the Senate. Since Daniel D. Tompkins, vice president during the administration of James Monroe, scarcely ever entered the chamber,

committee selection was left to the president pro tempore, who in effect had been chosen by and was responsible to the Senate majority leadership. But when the next vice president, John C. Calhoun, used the assignment power with obvious bias the Senate quickly and with little dissent returned to the election method to fill committee vacancies.

This time the chairmen were picked by majority vote of the entire Senate; then ballots were taken to select the other members of each committee, with members' rank on the committee determined by the size of their plurality. The Senate in 1828 changed the rules to provide for appointment to committees by the president pro tempore, but in 1833 it reverted to selection by ballot when control of the Senate changed hands. Since 1833 the Senate technically has made its committee assignments by ballot, although the last time a formal ballot appears to have actually been taken—on assigning new committees to Sen. Wayne Morse of Oregon, a Republican-turned-independent—was in 1953.

To avoid the inconveniences inherent in the ballot system it became customary between 1833 and 1846 to suspend the rule by unanimous consent and designate an officer (the vice president, the president pro tempore, or the "presiding officer") to assign members to committees.

The method of selecting committee members in use today was—with some modification—developed in 1846. In that year a motion to entrust the vice president with the task was defeated, and the Senate proceeded under the regular rules to make committee assignments by ballot. But after six chairmen had been selected, a debate began on the method of choosing the other members of the committees. At first, several committees were filled by lists—arranged in order of a member's seniority—submitted by the majority leader. After a number of committees had been filled in this manner the ballot rule was suspended and the Senate approved a list for the remaining vacancies that had been agreed upon by both the majority and minority leadership.[10]

Since 1846 the choice of committees usually has amounted to routine acceptance by the Senate of lists drawn up by special committees of the two major parties (in 1999 the Committee on Committees for the Republicans and the Steering Committee for the Democrats).

INCREASE IN STANDING COMMITTEES

The standing committee system, firmly established in the first half of the nineteenth century, expanded rapidly in the second half. Several factors influenced the role of committees, Smith and Deering wrote.

First, dramatic economic, geographic, and population growth placed new and greater demands on Congress, which responded with more legislation and new committees. Second, further development of American political parties and the increasing strength of congressional party leaders, especially in the late nineteenth century, led to an even greater integration of congressional parties and committee systems. Third, members of Congress, first in the Senate and then in the House, came to view service in Congress as a desirable long-term career, which in

The Rules Committee is among the most powerful committees in the House. Often described as the gatekeeper to the floor, the committee works with the majority leadership to control the flow of legislation and set the terms of floor debate. The Speaker and minority leader nominate all of its members. Because the majority party in recent decades has always insisted on holding a "two-to-one-plus-one" ratio in the committee's membership, even if it controls only a small majority in the House, an occasional defection on a vote does not affect its control.

GRANTING A RULE

Controversies have occurred frequently throughout the House's history over the function of the Rules Committee in the legislative process: whether it should be a clearinghouse (or traffic cop) for legislative business, the agent of the majority leadership, or a superlegislative committee editing the work of the other committees.

For major bills, the committee writes a resolution, or "special rule" that, subject to the approval of the House, sets the time limit on general debate, and regulates how the bill may be amended.

Before granting a rule, the committee usually holds a hearing at which only members of the House are able to testify. The chairman of the committee reporting the bill usually requests the kind of rule desired. Members testify for and against the bill and to ask that their amendments be made eligible for consideration. The hearing procedure is usually informal, with members being added to or dropped off the witness list on a continuing basis. The committee usually will listen to any member who wishes to be heard. It may then either grant a rule immediately or meet again later after controversies and strategies have been considered privately.

When the committee orders a rule reported, the chairman and ranking minority member decide who will manage the one hour of House floor debate on it. Once the rule is filed on the House floor, it may be considered on the next legislative day, or even on the same day if a two-thirds majority of the House votes to do so.

In many cases, the committee will restrict amendments. It may forbid all amendments; allow only amendments proposed by the legislative committee that handled the bill; allow only certain specified amendments; allow only amendments that are printed in the *Congressional Record* prior to their consideration on the floor; or allow only amendments that can be called up within a fixed time limit.

On complex bills, the committee may create its own original text, called "an amendment in the nature of a substitute," that incorporates provisions desired by the various committees to which a bill might have been referred or represents a compromise. The committee may also propose perfecting amendments to a bill, which it "self-executes" within the proposed rule—that is, adoption of the rule automatically adopts the amendments, even before the bill is formally considered on the floor.

CHANGING ROLE OF THE COMMITTEE

Established in 1789, Rules originally was a select committee authorized at the beginning of each Congress. Because the rules of one Congress usually were readopted by the next, this function was not initially of great importance, and for many years the committee never issued a report.

In 1858 the Speaker was made a member of the committee, and in subsequent years Rules gradually increased its influence over legislation. The panel became a standing committee in 1880, and in 1883 began the practice of issuing rules—special orders of business—for floor debate on legislation. Other powers acquired by the committee over the years included the right to sit while the House was in session, to have its resolutions considered immediately, and to initiate legislation on its own.

Before 1910 the Rules Committee worked closely with the leadership in deciding which legislation to allow on the floor, and was often chaired by the Speaker himself. But in the Progressive revolt of 1910–1911 against the arbitrary reign of Speaker Joseph G. Cannon, R-Ill., a coalition of Democrats and insurgent Republicans succeeded in enlarging the committee and excluding the Speaker from it. Alternative methods of bringing legislation to the floor while avoiding the committee—the Discharge Calendar, Calendar Wednesday, and the Consent Calendar (repealed in 1995)—were created and added to standing rules. *(See box, Prying Loose Legislation, p. 488.)*

By the late 1930s the committee had come under the domination of a coalition of conservative Democrats and Republicans. From then until the 1970s it repeatedly blocked or delayed liberal legislation. Opposition to the obstructive tactics led, in 1949, to adoption of the "twenty-one-day rule." It allowed a committee chairman whose panel approved a bill to call it up on the House floor if the Rules Committee failed to act within twenty-one days of receiving a request to grant a rule. The Speaker was required to recognize the chairman for this purpose. Two years later, after the Democrats had lost twenty-nine seats in the midterm elections, the House repealed this procedure. Although used only eight times, the threat of its use was credited with prying other bills out of the Rules Committee.

HOUSE REVOLT

After the Rules Committee in the 86th Congress (1959–1961) blocked or delayed measures that were to later become key elements in the new Kennedy administration's legislative program, Democratic reformers pressured Speaker Sam Rayburn, D-Texas, to act against it. In 1961 the House by a 217–212 margin agreed to enlarge the committee from twelve to fifteen members. That gave Rayburn and the incoming administration a delicate eight to seven majority on most issues coming before the committee.

Nevertheless, dissatisfaction continued, and following a 1964 Democratic election sweep the twenty-one-day rule was revived. The new version adopted by the House in 1965 gave the Speaker discretion whether to recognize a committee chairman to call up legislation. The new rule, employed successfully only eight times, was abandoned in 1967 following Republican gains in the 1966 midterm elections.

The House adopted a rule in 1965 that curbed the committee's power to block conferences on legislation. Before 1965 most bills could be sent to a conference committee only through unanimous consent, suspension of the rules, or adoption of a special rule from the Rules Committee. The change made it possible to send any bill to conference by majority vote of the House if the committee that reported the bill authorized such a motion and the Speaker recognized a member to make it.

Despite repeal of the twenty-one-day rule in 1967, the committee continued generally to pursue a stance more accommodating to the leadership. Several factors contributed to the committee's less conservative posture. First, it had lost its chairman of twelve years, Rep. Howard W. Smith, D-Va., who was defeated in a 1966 primary election. Smith was a skilled parliamentarian and the acknowledged leader of the House's conservative coalition, a voting alliance of Republicans and southern Democrats. He was replaced by Rep. William M. Colmer, D-Miss., who was unable to exert the high degree of control over legislation that Smith had exercised. In addition, new rules governing committee procedures reduced the arbitrary power of the chairman. The rules took from the chairman the right to set meeting dates, a power Smith frequently had used to postpone or thwart action on bills he opposed.

Another effort to revive a twenty-one day rule in 1971 failed when a conservative coalition blocked the Democrats' rules package on the House floor at the opening of the Congress and passed an amendment excising the provision.

Effective leadership control over the Rules Committee finally came when the Democratic Caucus voted in December 1974 to give the Speaker the power to nominate all of its Democratic members, subject to caucus approval. Using this power, Speaker Carl Albert of Oklahoma nominated liberals to fill two vacant positions. The Republican leader later acquired the same power over GOP members.

Although the committee's power remains immense, the loss of influence by its members as individuals has reduced the panel's attractiveness as an assignment. Ambitious members seeking power in the institution, or a base to aid their constituencies, will look to committees such as Appropriations, Commerce, and Ways and Means. The era of recent Rules Committee members considered powerful in their own right, such as chairmen Howard Smith, D-Va., and Richard Bolling, D-Mo., is probably over.

RESTRICTIVE RULES

No matter who was Speaker, the panel was used increasingly to limit amendments and debate on the House floor, provoking an outcry from Republican members usually in the minority. Democratic leaders argued that the Rules panel was an essential tool of a well-managed House. Such limits, they argued, helped focus debate on central issues, weed out dilatory amendments, and still ensure that major alternatives were considered. The Republicans themselves, despite decades of complaints about the committee, adopted and even expanded some of these restrictive practices when they took control in 1995.

Use of more complex rules also reflected institutional changes that had little to do with a deliberate strategy of closing off amendments. After 1974, when House rules were changed to allow more than one committee to handle a bill, the Rules Committee had to set guidelines for resolving conflicts and eliminating overlap when several committees marked up a single bill. Moreover, faced with huge budget deficits and waning public enthusiasm for government programs in the 1980s, the House considered fewer authorizing bills, the sort of legislation that had usually received an open rule. Increasingly, authorizing legislation was folded into omnibus measures, which usually were not entirely open to amendment.

ERA OF RAPID CHANGE

The chairmanship of the Rules Committee turned over several times in the 1970s and 1980s, accommodating a variety of diverse personalities in an era of rapidly increasing partisanship in the House. Leadership influence, cemented by the Speaker's power to select all Democratic members, ensured that the committee would operate as a loyal instrument of the Democratic Caucus. *(See box, Rules Committee Seniority, p. 546.)* When party control shifted in 1995, ranking Republican member Gerald B. H. Solomon of New York, an aggressive partisan, assumed the chairmanship. Former Democratic chairman Joe Moakley of Massachusetts stayed on as the leader of a four-member Democratic minority.

The Republican-controlled Rules Committee became a more visible forum for advocates of changes in House rules, though the majority had already implemented its most controversial proposals directly on the floor during the first two days of the 104th Congress. The committee held hearings on issues such as how changing technologies would affect the operations of the House in the twenty-first century. Under the Democrats, the committee had largely shunned institutional oversight. It left nearly all such activities to be handled privately in the Democratic Caucus, out of concern by the leadership that hearings or other formal action on controversial matters in a public setting might prove divisive or provide Republicans with a forum to launch attacks. This posture effectively marginalized the Rules Committee as a vehicle for dealing with institutional problems in the years preceding the loss of Democratic control of the House.

Solomon acted quickly in response to leadership directives to modify, or repeal, long-standing institutional practices when they inhibited achieving the majority's political agenda. For example, in 1995, the Rules Committee abolished the moribund Consent Calendar and substituted the more politically promotable Corrections Calendar as a vehicle to attack government regulations. In 1995 and 1997 it gave the staff of the Government Reform and Oversight Committee, which was investigating scandals in the Clinton administration, the power to take depositions from witnesses under oath. In 1997 it overrode GOP rules changes passed just two years earlier limiting the number of subcommittees in order to give Government Reform an extra one to deal with controversy surrounding conduct of the year 2000 census. And in 1997 it repealed a long-standing rule, inspired by the excesses of the McCarthy era, that had given witnesses appearing at House committee hearings under subpoena the right to bar photographs and television and radio broadcasts of the proceedings.

turn gave more personal significance to congressional organization, particularly the committee systems.[11]

The number of standing committees reached a peak in 1913, when there were sixty-one in the House and seventy-four in the Senate. The House Appropriations, Rules, and Ways and Means and the Senate Finance committees, in particular, exercised great influence; some others were created and perpetuated chiefly to provide members with offices and clerical staff.

Initial efforts to consolidate the House committee system occurred in 1909, when six minor committees were dropped. Two years later, when the Democrats took control, six superfluous committees were abolished.

In 1921 the Senate reduced the number of its committees from seventy-four to thirty-four. In many respects this rationalization of the committee structure was simply the formal abandonment of long-defunct bodies such as the Committee on Revolutionary Claims. The House in 1927 reduced the number of its committees by merging eleven expenditures committees, those dealing primarily with oversight, into a single Committee on Expenditures in the Executive Departments.

The next major overhaul of the committee structure took place in 1946 with enactment of the Legislative Reorganization Act. By dropping minor committees and merging those with related functions, the act achieved a net reduction of eighteen in the number of Senate committees (from thirty-three at that time to fifteen) and of twenty-nine in the number of House committees (from forty-eight at that time to nineteen). The act also defined in detail the jurisdictions of each committee and attempted to set ground rules for their operations.

For the next three decades, until a partial reorganization of Senate committees in 1977, only minor changes were made in the committee structure in Congress. During that period many of the achievements of the 1946 act were weakened by the creation of additional committees as well as the proliferation of subcommittees.

In 1993, the House began a modest cycle of reexamination of its committee system. It abolished four constituent-dominated select committees, temporary entities that had acquired seemingly permanent status.

In 1995, following a shift in party control from Democrats to Republicans, the House abolished three minor standing committees: District of Columbia, Post Office and Civil Service, and Merchant Marine and Fisheries.

In the 106th Congress, 1999–2001, the House had nineteen standing committees and one permanent select committee; the Senate had seventeen standing committees, two permanent select committees, and two "special committees." There were also four joint committees.

The Legislative Reorganization Act of 1946, in fact, had led to an explosion at the subcommittee level. The number of subcommittees grew gradually after its passage, reaching more than one hundred in the House and more than eighty in the Senate by 1964. Smith and Deering found that: "The growth in the number of subcommittees had roots in the practical problems

involved in managing larger and more complex workloads, in the desire of larger numbers of senior members for a 'piece of the action,' and in isolated efforts on individual committees to loosen the grip of chairs on committee activity."[12] In 1999 there were eighty-seven subcommittees in the House, and sixty-seven in the Senate.

But the creation of a larger network of subcommittees in the years following the 1946 act did not mean that power automatically gravitated there. Until the early 1970s, most House committees were run by chairmen who were able to retain much of the authority for themselves and a few trusted senior members, while giving little power to junior members or subcommittees.

THE SENIORITY SYSTEM

As the committee system grew so too did a system that awarded power on committees to the member with longest service on the committee. Seniority—status based on length of service, to which are attached certain rights and privileges—pervades nearly all social institutions. But in no other political group has its sway been stronger than in the United States Congress.

Despite frequent references to a "seniority rule" and a "seniority system," observance of seniority in Congress was never dictated by law or formal ruling. It developed as a tradition. The formal rules simply stated that the House or Senate should determine committee memberships and chairmen. *(See box, Seniority Under Fire, p. 554.)*

Seniority on Capitol Hill is based on the length of service in Congress, referred to as congressional seniority, or on the length of consecutive service on a committee, called committee seniority. As the system developed in both houses, it affected the assignment of office space, access to congressional patronage, and deference shown members on the floor. But seniority was most apparent—and important—in the selection of committee chairmen and in filling vacancies on committees, although state and regional considerations, party loyalty, legislative experience, and a member's influence with his or her colleagues always were important factors in making committee assignments.

Seniority had been relatively unimportant in the early years of Congress, when political parties were weak, turnover of congressional membership was frequent, and congressional careers were brief.

By 1846, however, party control had become so firm that committee assignment lists supplied by the parties were approved routinely. With party domination of assignments, the principle of seniority also appeared. Seniority came to be applied both to committee assignments and to advancement within a committee.

The seniority principle caught hold earlier in the Senate than in the House. As the Civil War neared, southern Democrats, who dominated Senate committee chairmanships, "supported the hardening of seniority to protect their position so that they could defend slavery," Randall B. Ripley wrote.[13] During the Civil War and Reconstruction period, between 1861 and

Many southern Democrats who opposed the national party programs held committee chairmenships in the decades following World War II, thanks to seniority. Sen. James. O. Eastland, D-Miss., who chaired the Senate Judiciary Committee from 1956 to 1978, was notorious for bottling up civil rights bills sought by party leaders.

1875, Democrats virtually disappeared from Congress, and Republican senators disregarded seniority in committee assignments. But when Democrats began to reappear in the Senate, the Republican majority returned to the seniority system to keep peace among party members. Republican leaders found they had to rely on the support of all their party colleagues, Ripley wrote. And one way to gain this support was to agree to an "automatic and impartial rule for committee advancement. The leaders of the party thus helped institute this limit on their own power."[14]

As committees developed into powerful, autonomous institutions, committee chairmen assumed ever greater powers over legislation. So great was their influence that Woodrow Wilson in 1885 could write: "I know not how better to describe our form of government in a single phrase than by calling it a government by the chairmen of the standing committees of Congress."[15]

In the House committee chairmen and the evolving seniority system suffered a temporary setback during the speakership of Joseph G. Cannon, R-Ill., in the early 1900s. The period from the Civil War to 1910 had seen the gradual development of an all-powerful Speaker. Through his power to name committee members and chairmen, the Speaker was able to control legislation, grant favors or impose political punishments, and ride roughshod over the minority party. "Czar" became a title the press frequently bestowed on the Speaker.

Finally, in 1910–1911, insurgent Republicans in the House, led by Nebraska's George Norris, combined with Democrats to strip Speaker Cannon of much of his power. The Speaker could no longer name committee members, chair or even serve on the Rules Committee, or hold unchallenged control over recognizing representatives who wished to bring legislation to the floor. *(See "Cannonism," p. 428.)*

The successful revolt against Cannon returned the right to appoint committee members and chairmen to the political party structures, but it was several decades before the seniority system was strictly followed.

The gradual lengthening of congressional careers had much to do with the dominance of seniority, which was solidified by the Legislative Reorganization Act of 1946. The consolidated committees produced by the act had wider jurisdictions than before and their chairmen gained greater power.

The Democrats' almost unbroken dominance in Congress during the fifty years after World War II meant relatively little turnover in their membership and long tenure for chairmen elected from the Democrats' safest seats—those in the South and in predominantly urban areas often dominated by party machines. These men grew increasingly unrepresentative of the party as younger members were elected in the political landslides of 1958 and 1964. Many of these younger members came to be identified with advocacy of new social programs, civil rights and, later, opposition to the Vietnam War.

Members who were out of step with their party's program or with the mood of the country, because of advanced age, ideology, or both, chaired important committees thanks to seniority. James O. Eastland, D-Miss., chairman of the Judiciary Committee from 1956 to 1978, routinely tried to bottle up civil rights bills and initially opposed the appointment of Thurgood Marshall to the federal judiciary. A party loyalist, Sen. Carl Hayden, D-Ariz., became chairman of the Appropriations Committee at age seventy-eight and served until he was ninety-one, setting a record for longest service in Congress, fifty-six years (counting both House and Senate service). Emanuel Celler, D-N.Y., longtime House Judiciary Committee chairman and liberal stalwart, ended his career as an opponent of the proposed constitutional amendment providing equal rights for women and lost a primary to a liberal feminist in 1972. F. Edward Hebert, D-La., a strident supporter of military programs and the Vietnam War who chaired the Armed Services Committee, opposed the appointment of African Americans and women to his committee. When antiwar liberals Ronald V. Dellums, D-Calif., an African American, and Patricia Schroeder, D-Colo., forced their way onto the committee in 1973, Hebert provided only one chair for them in the committee hearing room, until the leadership intervened. He saw his career ended by the 1974 Democratic freshmen after he referred to them condescendingly as "boys and girls."

Sen. Strom Thurmond, R-S.C., the oldest person ever to serve in Congress, holds the record for Senate service (1955–1956, 1956–); he chaired both the Judiciary and Armed Services committees at different times and serves as president pro tem-

RULES COMMITTEE SENIORITY

For decades, few committees illustrated the importance of seniority more vividly than did the House Rules Committee. Rep. Thomas P. "Tip" O'Neill Jr., D-Mass., a longtime committee member before giving up his seat in 1973 to become majority leader, joked that he had served for eighteen years on the panel (1955–1973) and had moved from eighth to fifth in seniority; in the party leadership, on the other hand, O'Neill was appointed to the post of majority whip in 1971 and moved up to become Speaker after only six years.

The Rules Committee had once been a strong arm of the majority party leadership, chaired by the Speaker himself, until the revolt against Speaker Joseph G. Cannon, R-Ill., resulted in his removal from the committee in 1910. *(See "Cannonism," p. 428.)*

For most of the decades after that until the early 1960s, Rules served as a power center for conservatives opposed to the Democratic congressional leadership and presidential administrations. Its independence began to be curbed beginning in 1961, when its size was expanded, and continued in the 1970s with party rules changes giving the Speaker control of Democratic appointments.

From 1949 until 1979, except for a two-year interval when Republicans ran the House, the Rules Committee was chaired by two elderly Democrats from the rural South and three others who came out of big-city machine politics. They were: Reps. Adolph Sabath of Chicago (chairman in 1949–1953), who died at age eighty-six while still chairman; Howard W. Smith of Virginia (chairman in 1955–1967), leader of the southern bloc in the House, who at age eighty-three was upset in his party's 1966 primary; William M. Colmer of Mississippi (chairman in 1967–1973), who retired from Congress upon reaching age eighty-two; Ray J. Madden of Gary, Ind. (chairman in 1973–1977), who became chairman at age eighty and was defeated in the Demo-

cratic primary four years later; and James J. Delaney of New York City (chairman in 1977–1979), who succeeded Madden for one Congress.

"Judge" Smith, as he was known, was so antagonistic to liberal Democratic programs and worked so well with Republicans that Speaker Sam Rayburn, D-Texas, reluctantly agreed in 1961 to increase the committee's size to fifteen, from twelve. The new 10–5 party ratio (instead of 8–4) diminished the prospect of tie votes, when Smith and Colmer had voted with Republicans to create a deadlock. Rayburn agreed to "pack" the Rules Committee with two additional Democrats willing to vote for programs of the newly elected administration of John F. Kennedy. The passage in 1974 of a Democratic Caucus rule giving the Speaker the power to nominate the chairman and all other Democratic members of the Rules Committee finally secured full control of the committee for the party leadership. *(See box, House Rules Committee Functions as Arm of Majority Leadership, p. 542.)*

Richard Bolling, D-Mo., chairman from 1979–1983 and the most significant figure to head the committee since Smith, was recognized as one of the ablest legislators in the House and was one of only a handful of Rules Committee members in recent decades who had significant expertise and interest in the rules and structure of the institution. He had chaired the Select Committee on Committees in the 93rd Congress (1973–1974), which proposed a number of significant reforms but is perhaps best remembered for its radical, and unsuccessful, scheme to reorganize the House committee system and limit members' committee assignments. A power broker in his own right who had run unsuccessfully for majority leader, and the author of several books on Congress, Bolling served as a link between the committee's jurisdictional responsibilities for the structure of the House

---

pore (1981–1987; 1995–), third in line for the presidency. Rep. Jamie Whitten, D-Miss. (1941–1995), holds the record for House service; Whitten chaired the Appropriations Committee from 1979–1993.

The lengthy terms served by these men testify to the growing careerism in Congress that gradually also spread to members who could rely on mastery of the media, campaign skills, and a strong fund-raising base to compensate for an unsafe seat. But tenure and age made it increasingly difficult for elderly members to adjust to changing political climates and younger, more demanding, and less deferential colleagues.

With the long tenure of senior members, a generation gap developed. Roger H. Davidson observed:

In 1973 the average House committee chairman was 66 years old and had almost 30 years of congressional service behind him; the average Senate chairman was 64 years old and had 21 years' experience. Not only did such a situation squander talent in the mid-seniority ranks, but it eventually generated frustration and resentment.[16]

The gap between leaders and backbenchers, covering not only age but also region, type of district, and ideology, "lay at

the heart of the Democrats' seniority struggles in the 1970s," Davidson wrote.

The regional imbalance in top committee posts was especially irksome to Democratic liberals. In 1973 the six chairmen of the most powerful committees in Congress—those dealing with taxes, appropriations, and the armed services—came from just four states in the south central part of the country: Louisiana, Arkansas, Mississippi, and Texas. Congress was ready for change.

1970S REFORM MOVEMENT

Frustration with the existing system led by the late 1960s to concerted demands for reforms. As Smith and Deering noted:

These demands were especially strong among junior members and some long-standing liberal Democrats, who found their efforts to shape public policy stymied by their more conservative senior colleagues. . . . These members, and the outsiders whose causes they supported, were concerned about issues that were not receiving active committee consideration and did not fall easily into existing committee jurisdictions. A nascent environmental movement, opposition to the Vietnam conflict, and a continuing interest in civil rights legislation placed new challenges before congressional committees.[17]

and its other role as a loyal processor of special rules to promote the majority's agenda.

After Bolling retired for health reasons, the committee entered a period of drift. With its perceived loss of influence came reduced desirability as a committee assignment. Would-be power brokers now had little room to operate. Relatively junior members were recruited to fill vacancies because there was less need for the leadership to require members to serve an apprenticeship elsewhere to see if they had the temperament for the job. Committee size varied from the fifteen established by Rayburn in 1961, to sixteen from 1975–1985, then back to thirteen.

There was an effort in 1983 to persuade octogenarian Rep. Claude Pepper, D-Fla., not to assume the chairmanship, but Pepper quickly dismissed that suggestion. The Speaker named him and he held the post until his death in 1989, when he was the House's oldest member. Pepper was regarded as an ineffective chairman whose principal interest remained issues affecting elderly Americans, which he had long championed. Other Democratic members assumed more visible roles to fill the vacuum. Rep. Joe Moakley, D-Mass., an O'Neill protégé who served as chairman from 1989 to 1995, restored a sense of order to the committee's role in reporting special rules and coordinating business with the leadership. But the committee largely sat on the sidelines during controversies over whether, and how, to reform the House and over how to respond to the Republicans' increasingly effective institutional attacks on Congress and the Democratic Party in the 1980s and 1990s. When Democrats lost control of the House in 1994, Moakley stayed on as ranking minority member.

Despite—or possibly because of—the 1974 Democratic Caucus rule giving the Speaker the power to nominate all Democrats on the Rules Committee, the seniority system continued to be followed rigidly. Speakers always appointed the senior Democratic member as chairman and reappointed all serving members. Ironically, instead of opening the door for membership changes, the rule may have had the opposite effect; with leadership control of the committee secured, the threat of potential removal controlled committee votes without the need for violations of seniority, which might have seemed threatening to the rest of the caucus.

The pattern of the Republican minority's assignment process on the Rules Committee, by contrast, began to evolve to reflect its more aggressive, partisan role and the minority's increasing willingness to use its limited resources more effectively. The minority leader, like the Speaker, exercised the power to select his party's membership. For years, the most visible Republican member of the committee, even though he was not the senior member, was Minority Whip Trent Lott, R-Miss., who served as the leadership spokesperson on the committee until his election to the Senate in 1988. The seniority tradition was formally breached during the 1990s, and the weakening of the practice had important consequences when the party finally took over the House.

In 1991 Republicans moved aside their longtime ranking minority member, 75-year-old James H. (Jimmy) Quillen, R-Tenn., and replaced him with Gerald B. H. Solomon, R-N.Y., a younger, more aggressive partisan who had served on the committee for only two years. Solomon was made chairman in 1995 by Speaker Newt Gingrich, R-Ga., and was a vigorous advocate for the "Contract with America" and the party's conservative agenda. Solomon retired from Congress in January 1999 and was succeeded by David Dreier, R-Calif., who at age 47 was the youngest member to chair the panel.

The reformist trend in Congress on domestic policy was greatly accelerated by the election of President John F. Kennedy in 1960, which focused responsibility for the obstruction of liberal policy goals squarely on congressional impediments within the congressional majority party.

Rule by seniority reigned supreme until the early 1970s. At that time, Democrats had controlled both houses of Congress for all but four years since 1933. Then, changing circumstances caught up. The principal change was the election to Congress of dozens of new members—persons who had little patience with the admonition to newcomers, credited to Speaker Sam Rayburn, that "to get along, go along." New members, who did not have much influence in the Senate or House, joined forces with disgruntled incumbents, who had chafed under the often heavy-handed rule of arbitrary chairmen. Thus, in the late 1960s and early 1970s a revolt began that was to undermine the seniority system and lead to numerous other procedural changes that redefined the role and power of committees and their chairmen.

The 1970s revolt began in the House as membership turnover accelerated and the proportion of younger, first- and second-term members increased. These lawmakers demanded fundamental changes in the way Congress—and particularly the committees—operated. Major changes in Democratic Caucus rules and, to a lesser extent, in the standing rules of the House and the Senate, diluted the authority enjoyed by committee chairmen and other senior members and redistributed the power among the junior members.

The newcomers balked at the traditions of apprenticeship and deference to committee leaders, congressional scholar Leroy Rieselbach pointed out.

Moreover, many of these new members found it electorally advantageous to run for Congress by running against Congress, . . . to criticize the legislative establishment and upon arriving in Washington to adopt a critical, reformist view of congressional structure and procedure. Finally, the new electoral circumstances that protected most incumbents from November surprises at the polls—effective personal campaign organizations and the ready availability of funds from the proliferating political action committees . . .—gave new members the independence they needed to pursue their own political agendas, agendas that included reform.[18]

On the House side, the newcomers breathed life into a dormant Democratic Caucus and gave would-be reformers the votes they needed to effect change. The reform movement took off in the 1970s. The single most important factor that undermined the chairmen's authority was the decision by Democrats in both chambers to allow chairmen to be elected by their party's caucus. The change came gradually, beginning in 1971. By 1975 Democrats had adopted rules providing for secret-ballot election of the top Democrats on committees. A secret vote was automatic in the House and held at the request of 20 percent of Senate Democrats. That year three House chairmen were ousted in caucus elections. (Others followed in 1984 and 1990).

The election requirement made chairmen accountable to their colleagues for their conduct. Caucus election of committee chairmen was only one of a number of changes that restricted the chairmen's power. Committees were required under the 1970 Legislative Reorganization Act to have written rules. In 1973 House Democrats adopted a "bill of rights" that reinforced subcommittee autonomy. And before the decade was over, the committee system had been radically restructured. The era of the autocratic committee chairman who answered to no one was over. Junior and minority party members of Congress now had positions, privileges, and resources earlier members had been denied. Committee operations and votes were opened to the public eye. (*See box, Congress Adapts to "Sunshine" Reforms, this page.*)

In later years House Democrats gave members of each committee the power to determine the number of subcommittees

---

CONGRESS ADAPTS TO "SUNSHINE" REFORMS

In the late 1990s, Congress continued the process of adapting to demands for greater public access to its proceedings that began with so-called "sunshine" rules in the 1970s requiring open committee and conference committee meetings. The media also gained virtually unfettered access to committee hearings and meetings.

The initial sunshine reforms were part of an effort to improve Congress's image, which had suffered dramatic reversals after a series of widely publicized scandals. They were further accelerated by the public's disgust for excessive government secrecy as revealed by the Watergate scandal in the 1970s that led to the resignation of President Richard Nixon. Proponents maintained that open meetings helped protect the public interest and made lawmakers more accountable to the electorate.

During the 1980s, there was some retreat from the reforms, including votes by a number of key panels to close their doors during consideration of major legislation. Votes to close committees had to be conducted in open session by roll-call vote with a quorum present. The House Ways and Means Committee, perhaps the most heavily lobbied committee in the House, chose to close its doors to write such landmark legislation as a historic tax-overhaul bill in 1985 and trade and catastrophic illness insurance bills in 1987. Ways and Means Chairman Dan Rostenkowski, D-Ill., argued: "It's just difficult to legislate. I'm not ashamed about closed doors. We want to get the product out." Other panels—notably House Appropriations subcommittees—also met privately to draft legislation. Sometimes committees' decisions were made by small groups of members behind the scenes, then ratified in open session. Defenders of closed sessions argued that committee members were more open, markups more expeditious, and better laws written away from lobbyists' glare.

However, efforts to institutionalize a pattern of exceptions to the rules failed in the face of continuing public suspicions about the operations of Congress and the ability of special interest groups to influence the legislative process. In 1995, after Republicans took control of the House, the rules were further amended to prevent committees from closing their sessions merely for the sake of convenience. Committees wishing to close had to determine by roll-call vote that disclosure of testimony or other matters to be considered would endanger national security, compromise sensitive law enforcement information, or would tend to defame, degrade, or incriminate any person. The House Committee on Standards of Official Conduct was exempted from these requirements in 1997.

SUNSHINE RULES

The Legislative Reorganization Act of 1970 took the first steps toward more open committee meetings and hearings and required that all House and Senate committee roll-call votes be made public. The House in 1973 voted to require that all committee sessions be open unless a majority of the committee voted in public to close them. The Senate adopted a similar rule in 1975. Both chambers in 1975 voted to open conference committee sessions, unless a majority of the conferees of either chamber voted in public to close a session. The House amended this rule in 1977 to require a recorded vote by the full House to close a conference committee meeting. Conferences have been closed for legislation dealing with sensitive intelligence and national security matters.

BROADCASTS

While the Senate had a long tradition of broadcasting hearings, the House did not sanction such broadcasts until passage of the 1970 reorganization act. In 1974 it decided to allow broadcasts of markup meetings as well. The Senate left decisions on broadcast coverage to its committees. The House for many years set more stringent standards for broadcast coverage of hearings or bill-drafting sessions, considering it a special privilege to be granted or denied, but the House was eventually forced to stop nit-picking requests for media access. House rules were amended in 1995 to require that all open committee sessions be opened to press coverage, including radio and television broadcasts, without the need for special permission. Televised broadcasts of floor debate began in the House in 1979 and in the Senate in 1986. (*See box, Televised Floor Debates Here to Stay, p. 482.*)

their committee would have. Most committees were required to have subcommittees. Because of concerns over their proliferation, even on minor committees, the number of subcommittees was subsequently further limited by caucus rule, and, after the Republican takeover in 1995, by House rule. However, in later years Republicans loosened these restrictions.

Staffing prerogatives were extended to members other than the chairman. This change made members less subservient to the chairman by giving them professional staff help on legislative issues.

Both chambers also tried to limit the influence of chairmen and other senior members by restricting the number of chairmanships and committee slots that any one member could hold.

REVIVAL OF THE DEMOCRATIC CAUCUS

In the late 1960s, the House Democratic Study Group (DSG), a legislative service organization within the House funded collectively by a group of liberal members, accelerated the drive to overhaul the seniority system and open House procedures. The outlook for the DSG agenda brightened with the revival of regular meetings of the House Democratic Caucus in 1969 following a challenge to the reelection of Speaker John W. McCormack, D-Mass. The retirement of McCormack at the end of the 1970 session deprived the dominant committee chairmen of a powerful ally at the top of the House leadership structure and opened the way for younger liberals to operate more freely under his successor, Carl Albert, D-Okla.

The caucus revival meant that moderate and liberal Democrats elected to the House in the 1960s or earlier, who were frustrated by the operation of a committee system that tended to freeze them out of power, at last had a vehicle to change House procedures. Their actions were directed at undercutting the power of committee chairmen and strengthening the role of the subcommittees, where the opportunity lay for them to gain a greater role and make an impact on the legislative process.

The drive had a sharp generational edge. Many middle-ranking Democrats elected in the late 1950s and 1960s were allied against the senior members and the leadership. Between 1958 and 1970, 293 Democrats entered the House. Between 1970 and 1974, another 150 Democrats were elected. From this group, many of whom tended to be more moderate or liberal than their predecessors, sprang pressure for reform. This influx of Democrats—especially the seventy-five members of the "Class of 1974," otherwise known as the "Watergate babies"—provided the votes needed to effect change.

HARBINGERS OF REFORM

Though it preceded the period of sustained reform by more than a decade, the fight for expansion of the size of the Rules Committee in 1961 represented a sign of things to come. Speaker Sam Rayburn, D-Texas, allied himself with the incoming Kennedy administration to break the conservative coalition that frequently stymied the majority's ability to bring legislation to the floor or to go to conference with the Senate. By a vote of 217

to 212, with many conservative Democrats opposing Rayburn, the House increased the size of the committee from twelve (an 8–4 party ratio) to fifteen (a 10–5 party ratio). Chairman Howard W. Smith, D-Va., and William M. Colmer, D-Miss., had often joined the Republicans to create a tie, paralyzing legislative action. The new configuration, with two additional Democrats handpicked by Rayburn, prevented that and gave the Speaker greater assurance that Rules would not routinely stymie the party's more activist legislative agenda. But the leadership's control of the committee was still far from assured.

The push for further reforms in the early 1960s led to the creation in 1965 of a Joint Committee on the Organization of Congress, headed by Sen. A. S. Mike Monroney, D-Okla., and Rep. Ray J. Madden, D-Ind. The following year the panel recommended a wide-ranging set of reforms including proposals to curtail the powers of committee chairmen, to limit committee assignments, and to increase committee staff resources. However, unlike the reforms of 1946, there was no immediate consensus about the joint committee's work, and it was not immediately enacted in the years that followed.

Some of the committee's procedural recommendations were enacted into law in the Legislative Reorganization Act of 1970. Its recommendations opened the processes of Congress to greater public view and fostered participation in key decisions by more members but it did not directly attack the power bases of senior members. The law encouraged open committee proceedings, required that committees have written rules, required that all committee roll-call votes be made public, allowed radio and television coverage of committee hearings, and safeguarded the rights of minority party members on a committee. The law made only minor revisions in the committee structure itself, and it left the seniority system intact, after the House rejected two proposals to modify the system. Perhaps its most significant change for the House of Representatives was a provision requiring recorded teller votes in the Committee of the Whole, which forced members to vote publicly on key amendments and undermined the control of proceedings by senior committee members who had once stage-managed legislation with sparse attendance on the floor.

Although the 1970 law had limited effects, it marked a turning point in the reform movement, signaling an end to an era when committee chairmen and senior members could block reforms and the beginning of nearly a decade of change. Because the reform goals of the two chambers were different and the pressure for change was greatest in the House, subsequent attempts at change took the form of intrachamber reform efforts rather than bicameral action. That was perhaps inevitable because, in the House, the next steps in reform became more intensely personal through political assault on committee chairmen and others deemed unresponsive to the caucus, the undermining of chairmen's power bases, and, in some cases, actual removal from leadership positions.

Loosening the grip of seniority was seen as a crucial step toward changing committee operations. The issue of committee seniority was treated as strictly a party matter. Democratic leaders feared that if seniority changes were proposed through legislation instead of through party rules, a coalition of members of both parties could upset the majority party's control of the legislative program. When changes in seniority were offered as amendments on the floor of the House and Senate, they consistently had been defeated.

The "go-it-alone" strategy for congressional reform has prevailed for each chamber ever since. The most recent attempt at bicameral coordination—the 1993 Joint Committee on the Organization of Congress—failed at least in part because in an atmosphere of increased tension between the houses the bicameral structure created another layer of obstacles to be overcome.

HOUSE COMMITTEE CHANGES

The first blow to seniority in the House came when both parties decided that the selection of committee leaders no longer had to be dictated by seniority. In January 1971 the House Democratic Caucus voted to adopt modest changes recommended by its Committee on Organization, Study, and Review, created in 1970 to examine the party's organization and the seniority system. The committee was headed by Julia Butler Hansen, D-Wash.

The principal changes agreed upon were:

• The Democratic Committee on Committees, composed of the Democratic members of the Ways and Means Committee, would recommend to the caucus nominees for the chairmanship and membership of each committee, and such recommendations did not have to follow seniority. (The committee's power was transferred in December 1974 to the Steering and Policy Committee, a leadership entity.)

• The Committee on Committees would make recommendations to the caucus, one committee at a time. Upon the demand of ten or more caucus members, nominations could be debated and voted on.

If a nomination were rejected, the Committee on Committees would submit another nomination.

• In an important breakthrough for midcareer Democrats, the caucus decided that no member could chair more than one legislative subcommittee. That change made it possible to break the hold of the more conservative senior Democrats on key subcommittees, and it gradually made middle-level and even some junior Democrats eligible for subcommittee chairmanships. The rule in its first year gave sixteen Democrats who came to the House after 1958 their first subcommittee chairmanships.

House Republicans also in 1971 agreed that the ranking Republican on each committee would be selected by vote of the Republican Conference, which is made up of all House Republicans, and not automatically selected by seniority. They also bypassed Armed Services Committee member Alvin O'Konski, R-Wis., who was next in line to be ranking member, by allowing the more senior Minority Whip Les Arends, R-Ill., to take the

post even though party rules would have prevented him from holding both jobs. In 1973, the Republican Conference confirmed moderate Frank Horton of New York as ranking member of the Government Operations Committee, deflecting a challenge from the junior but more conservative John Erlenborn of Illinois. (While Republicans have on rare occasions bypassed seniority, unlike the Democrats they have never formally ousted a committee leader in a vote of the full conference.)

House Democrats in January 1973 altered their chairmanship selection procedures by allowing a secret-ballot vote on any committee chairman when 20 percent of the caucus demanded it. The expectation was that votes would be taken on all candidates. (This cumbersome procedure was replaced in 1974 by an automatic secret vote.) In 1973 all the chairmen survived, as did the seven ranking Democrats marked for elevation by the retirement of their predecessors.

Subcommittee Rights

The House Democratic Caucus in January 1973 adopted a "subcommittee bill of rights." The new caucus rules created a party caucus for Democrats on each House committee and forced the chairmen to start sharing authority with other Democrats. Each committee caucus was granted the authority to select subcommittee chairmen (with members allowed to run for chairman based on their seniority ranking on the full committee), establish subcommittee jurisdictions, set party ratios on the subcommittees to reflect the party ratio of the full committee, write the committee's rules, provide a subcommittee budget, and guarantee all members a major subcommittee slot where vacancies made that possible. Each subcommittee was authorized to meet, hold hearings, and act on matters referred to it.

Under the bill of rights, committee chairmen were required to refer designated types of legislation to subcommittees within two weeks. They no longer could kill measures they opposed by pocketing them, at least not at the subcommittee stage.

Compromise Hansen Plan

Further procedural changes, along with minor committee jurisdictional shifts, were approved by the House in 1974 in a new package of recommendations put forward by Hansen's study committee. The Hansen plan was a substitute for a much broader bipartisan proposal, drafted by a select committee headed by Rep. Richard Bolling, D-Mo. The Bolling committee's call for wholesale restructuring of the committee system had triggered a flood of protests from chairmen and committee members who would have been adversely affected. It was decisively rejected in favor of the Hansen substitute, which made some jurisdictional shifts—such as giving the Public Works Committee control over more transportation matters—but mainly retained the existing committee structure dating from 1946.

Under the Hansen plan, each standing committee's permanent staff, beginning in 1975, was increased from six to eighteen professionals and from six to twelve clerks, with the minority party receiving one-third of each category. And in what would prove to be the most controversial provision, the plan gave the minority party control of one-third of a committee's investigative staff funding. As the 94th Congress convened to adopt its rules, the Democratic Caucus engineered repeal of the one-third provision for investigative staffing before it could take effect. However, each side received more staffing and subcommittee chairmen and ranking members were allowed to hire one staff person each to work directly for them on their subcommittees.

In other changes, which also took effect in 1975, committees with more than fifteen members (increased to those with more than twenty members by the Democratic Caucus in 1975) were required to establish at least four subcommittees. This change was directed at the Ways and Means Committee, which had operated without subcommittees during most of the sixteen-year chairmanship of Wilbur D. Mills, D-Ark. It also created an important precedent in that it institutionalized subcommittees in House rules for the first time.

Committees with more than fifteen members (increased to those with more than twenty in 1975) were required to set up an oversight subcommittee or to require their legislative subcommittees to carry out oversight functions.

In addition, the Hansen plan gave the Speaker new powers to refer legislation to more than one committee and banned proxy voting in committee. (In 1975 proxy voting was effectively restored by the Democratic Caucus and remained in effect for twenty years until Republicans took control in 1995. Under the 1975 amendments to the House rules each committee could decide in its own rules whether to allow proxies, and most did; proxies were allowed on a specific issue or on procedural matters, and they had to be in writing and given to a member, among other requirements.) *(See box, Proxy Voting, p. 552.)*

More Blows to Seniority

Further changes in House committee operations unrelated to the Hansen plan were made in late 1974 and early 1975 by the Democratic Caucus after the party's overwhelming victory in post-Watergate elections resulted in a two-to-one majority. Meeting in December 1974 to organize for the next Congress (as had been required under the Hansen plan), Democrats decided to require a secret-ballot vote on the election of each committee chairman. The new procedure allowed competitive nominations for chairmen if the original Steering Committee nominee was rejected. Democrats immediately made use of their new rule by deposing three committee chairmen. *(See box, Seniority Under Fire, p. 554.)*

In other changes the Democratic members of the Ways and Means Committee were stripped of their power to select the party's members of House committees; this authority was transferred to a revamped Democratic Steering and Policy Committee, chaired by the Speaker. Many of the other members served in the leadership or were appointed by the Speaker, along with members elected from specific geographic regions. Over time, both the size of the Steering Committee and the number of leadership-influenced appointments increased. At the same time the caucus increased the size of the Ways and Means Committee from twenty-five to thirty-seven members, a change designed to give the committee a more liberal outlook and thus make it more likely to support party-backed proposals on tax revision, health insurance, and other issues.

In actions affecting the independence of subcommittees, the caucus directed that the entire Democratic membership of each committee, rather than the chairman alone, was to determine the number and jurisdiction of a committee's subcommittees. The Democratic caucus of each committee drafted and approved a committee's rules, which incorporated the number, size, and jurisdiction of its subcommittees. And the caucus specified that no Democratic member of a committee could become a member of a second subcommittee of that committee until every member of the full committee had chosen a subcommittee slot. (A grandfather clause allowed sitting members on subcommittees to protect two subcommittee slots, but this protection for the second subcommittee slots was eliminated in 1979.)

One group of subcommittees always had been semiautonomous—the powerful units of the House Appropriations Committee. The thirteen subcommittees were organized to parallel the executive departments and agencies, and most of the annual budget review was done at that level. The staggering size and complexity of the federal budget required each subcommittee to develop an expertise and an autonomy respected and rarely challenged by other subcommittees or by the full committee. Because of the panels' special role the caucus decided that, like full committee chairmen, all nominees for chairmen of these subcommittees would have to be approved by the Democratic Caucus. (Nominees for Appropriations subcommittee chairmen were selected by the membership of each subcommittee, with members bidding for a subcommittee chairmanship in the order of their seniority on the subcommittee.)

The Speaker's powers were further buttressed by allowing him to select the Democratic members of the Rules Committee, subject to caucus approval.

In a change adopted by the Democratic Caucus in December 1976, the chairmen of the Ways and Means and Appropriations committees were stripped of their power to nominate members from their committees to serve on the Budget Committee; that power was transferred to the Democratic Steering and Policy Committee.

In December 1978 the House Democratic Caucus voted to prohibit, as of the next Congress, a committee chairman from serving as chairman of any other standing, select, special, or joint committee; some chairmen were exempt because they were required by law to also chair joint committees.

PROXY VOTING

Proxy voting in House committees was abolished in 1995 as part of the Republican majority's new rules package. It continues to be used in Senate committees and in House-Senate conferences by members from both chambers. Proxy voting is not permitted on the floor of the Senate or House.

Proxies permit one committee member to authorize another to cast votes for that person in the member's absence. The device is a convenience for members of Congress caught between conflicting demands of busy schedules, which often include more than one committee or subcommittee meeting at the same time. A proxy is nearly always given to a committee or subcommittee chairman, or, if the member differs from the chairman on an issue, to another member who is on the same side of the issue as the absentee. Although proxy voting may seem an innocuous practice, it was the bane of the minority party in Congress and a target of reformers for years.

Controversy over proxy voting focused principally on the House, where one member could cast many proxies. The practice is viewed less harshly in the Senate because of the large number of committee and subcommittee assignments held by each senator and the tradition of accommodating the convenience of individuals. In addition committees do not have the same power or importance in the Senate.

HOUSE

Proxy voting was an important tool for the majority in operating committees because it allowed members to cope with multiple simultaneous scheduling commitments while ensuring that political control could not slip away to a well-organized minority that might concentrate its strength at a single location for a "sneak attack" on the majority. In this respect, proxy voting was simply a means of ensuring majority control over committees as subunits of the House and preventing such control from succumbing to whims of committee scheduling or flukes of member absences.

Proxy voting was denounced by the minority members and reform advocates outside the House for encouraging absenteeism and irresponsibility. Perhaps more significantly, it tended to discourage efforts to improve the coordination of the scheduling of committee and subcommittee meetings as well as to reduce the number of subcommittees and member assignments.

Before 1970 the use of proxies was regulated by custom or by guidelines established by individual committees and differed from committee to committee. Some committees never used them. Before the power of House chairmen was diminished by the Democratic Caucus in the 1970s, proxy voting reinforced their domination of committees. A chairman had little trouble procuring and using proxies, while opponents actually had to appear, and in significant numbers, to change the outcome on a key vote unless they were capable of organizing themselves around a proxy campaign as well.

The Legislative Reorganization Act of 1970 was the first measure to alter proxy voting. That act prohibited proxy voting unless a committee's written rules specifically allowed it, in which case it was limited to a specific bill, amendment, or other matter. Proxies also had to be in writing, designating the person on the committee authorized to use them.

In October 1974, as part of the Select Committee on Comittees' resolution making changes in the committee system, the House voted 196–166 to ban proxy voting entirely, effective at the beginning of the subsequent Congress. But the ban never took effect. The Democratic Caucus, voting this time without the Republicans, modified the ban before the 94th Congress convened in 1975 to adopt House rules on a party-line vote. The revision once again gave committees the authority to decide whether to permit proxy voting. If a committee allowed proxy voting, it was to be used only on a specific measure or matter and related amendments and motions. General proxies, covering all matters before a committee for either a specific time period or for an indefinite period, were prohibited, except for votes on procedural matters. As before, they had to be in writing, with a member designated to cast the proxies. The proxy vote also had to be dated and could not be used to make a quorum.

During its brief consideration of reform proposals recommended by the Joint Committee on the Organization of Congress as adjournment approached in 1994, the House Rules Committee considered amendments to the rules that would have further restricted or abolished the practice of proxy voting. With several Democrats reportedly considering support for such reforms the committee recessed and never resumed the markup, preventing any votes on the joint committee's proposals.

Each House Democrat was limited to five subcommittee seats on House standing committees. In 1987 waivers to the five-subcommittee rule—which had become routine—were barred in most cases, but the change proved ineffective. In order to maintain effective control of a subcommittee, it was sometimes necessary to add members who might violate the assignment limit. Attempts to restrict subcommittee assignments were frequently disregarded, especially when the leadership supported exceptions.

In addition, the caucus decided that the bidding for subcommittee chairmanships would be based on a member's seniority rank on the full committee, with the exception of Appropriations subcommittee chairmen.

Decline of Reform Zeal

Toward the end of the 1970s while there were occasional important struggles over who would occupy committee and subcommittee chairmanships, the broad agenda for House reform among Democrats abated. Liberals who dominated the Democratic Caucus had gotten virtually everything they wanted, the leadership had been strengthened in its relationships with chairmen, and junior members who served long enough were as-

Ironically, following the abolition of proxy voting when House rules were adopted in January 1995, the Republicans endured immediate political pain for their decision. They were forced to conduct numerous simultaneous committee meetings and House floor votes to ensure prompt passage of the legislative agenda promised in the election campaign, while struggling to maintain voting control with the narrowest House majority in forty years. Although pleas by a few members for a return to proxy voting were not heeded, the Republicans eventually loosened some of the other restrictions they had passed on the number of committee and subcommittee assignments members might hold, so they would be able to place enough majority members in the right places to ensure control.

SENATE

For Senate committees the 1970 act provided little restraint on the use of proxies. The law said proxy votes could not be used to report legislation if committee rules barred their use. If proxies were not forbidden on a motion to report a bill, they nevertheless could be used only upon the formal request of a senator who planned to be absent during a session. To prevent the use of general proxies, Senate rules bar the use of a proxy if an absent member "has not been informed of the matter on which he is being recorded and has not affirmatively requested that he be so recorded." Proxies cannot be counted toward the quorum needed for reporting legislation.

In addition to proxy voting, some Senate committees permit polling—holding an informal vote of committee members instead of convening the committee. Such votes usually are taken by sending a voting sheet to committee members' offices or by taking members' votes by telephone.

Because Senate rules require a quorum to be present for a committee to report legislation, polling is supposed to be restricted to issues involving legislation that is still pending before the committee, to matters relating to investigations, and to internal committee business.

If polling is used to report a matter, any senator can challenge the action by raising a point of order. Such was the case in December 1980 when opponents of a Carter nominee for a federal judgeship charged that the nomination had not been properly reported be-

cause the Judiciary Committee had approved it by a written poll. The issue was dropped and the nominee was approved when Judiciary Chairman Edward M. Kennedy, D-Mass., gained Republican support by agreeing not to push other Carter lame duck judicial nominations pending in the committee.

FROM PROXY VOTING TO A CYBER-CONGRESS?

Neither chamber of Congress has ever allowed members to vote by proxy on the floor, and the House has disciplined members who used another's voting card to cast votes in his absence. But in recent years some members raised the issue of voting from other locations, as long as it was concurrent with voting on the floor and their votes could be verified through a secure system. Improving technology could, at some point, allow members of Congress working in their states or districts to participate in real time in congressional debates.

Members broached these ideas as a way of enhancing their personal convenience and allowing them to perform more of their congressional functions, but perhaps at the expense of Congress's broader purposes. The concept of representation and the role of members of Congress has changed in the latter part of the twentieth century as Congress stayed in session longer and members had less time to spend time in their districts. The demands of campaign fund-raising and the need for direct constituent contact at town meetings and other events increased pressure on congressional schedules. Members also had less time to spend with their families.

Congress traditionally fears change and has resisted even modest technological intrusions. Both chambers long resisted television. The House in 1995 banned the use on the floor of any personal electronic office equipment, including cellular telephones and computers. The Senate, similarly, banned the use of laptop computers on the grounds that they would disrupt floor proceedings and distract senators.

Critics of the use of technology to allow absent members to legislate say this development would contradict the very essence of Congress, which requires an interaction of legislators face to face. In addition, the Constitution requires that Congress "assemble" to exercise its power. It is doubtful that video-conferencing or a "Congress-Online" could qualify.

sured of eventually acquiring the titles of subcommittee chairs along with increased staff resources. There were no important constituencies left to satisfy; with a sharply reduced House majority and policy divisions between the party's liberal and conservative factions during and after the presidency of Republican Ronald Reagan (1981–1989) other subjects dominated the caucus's attention.

The more self-satisfied attitude was reflected in a less than hospitable reception accorded to some of the limited reform efforts that emerged in this period. A House Commission on Administrative Review, headed by Rep. David Obey, D-Wis.,

concluded that members had too many committee assignments and that existing committee jurisdictions were too confused. But its recommendations for improving committee operations went down to defeat in October 1977. The House also declined to consider its proposals to change the administrative operations of the House.

The House in March 1979 once again set up a Select Committee on Committees to recommend how to improve the House's internal organization and operations. But the effort proved to be little more than lip service to the idea of reform, since substantive changes would have proved too threatening to

Both political parties in the House and Senate in the 1970s decided that seniority—status based on length of service—should no longer be the sole determinant in selecting committee leaders. The House took substantive steps to implement this reform, while the Senate did not. But even the threatened use of this authority gave rank-and-file members a potent weapon.

The House Democratic Caucus shook the foundations of the committee structure by ousting three autocratic chairmen in 1975. It was a watershed that redirected the flow of institutional power in the House. The caucus rules required an automatic yes-or-no vote on a candidate for a chairmanship nominated by the Steering and Policy Committee if the nominee was either the incumbent chairman or the senior Democrat seeking the post if the chairmanship was vacant. Other candidates were only allowed to run if the chairman or senior member were rejected by the Steering Committee, or by the full caucus. In 1992, the rules were further liberalized to allow others to run directly if fourteen or more members opposed the nomination of the chairman or senior member in the Steering Committee, or if fifty members signed a petition.

The House Republican Conference took a somewhat different approach to seniority. There were few direct challenges to ranking minority committee members because those posts had little power relative to the chairmanships controlled by the majority. Moderate Rep. Frank Horton, R-N.Y., was challenged as ranking minority member of the Government Operations Committee in 1972 by conservatives supporting Rep. John N. Erlenborn, R-Ill. Horton easily won confirmation in an up-or-down vote. In 1992, an attempt by the Steering Committee to nominate Rep. Paul Gillmor, R-Ohio, as ranking member of the House Administration Committee over incumbent Rep. William M. Thomas, R-Calif., whose relations with the leadership were sometimes testy, was rejected by the conference.

Upon taking power of Congress in 1995, however, the GOP immediately demonstrated it was less concerned about seniority than the Democrats. Speaker Newt Gingrich, R-Ga., hand-picked chairmen of the Appropriations, Commerce, and Judiciary committees, bypassing senior members. Rep. Carlos Moorhead, R-Calif., senior member of both the Commerce and Judiciary committees, was denied either chairmanship. Moorhead retired in 1997. Rep. Joseph M. McDade, R-Pa., was denied the Appropriations chairmanship in 1995 because he was under a federal indictment for corruption. Gingrich then skipped over the next two senior members to select Rep. Robert Livingston, R-La., as chairman. After McDade was acquitted, however, Livingston remained chairman and McDade had to be satisfied with the title of vice chairman and a subcommittee chairmanship. He announced his retirement at the end of the 105th Congress.

HOUSE CHAIRMEN OUSTED

In 1971 House Democrats and Republicans decided that seniority need not be followed in the selection of committee leaders. In 1973 Democrats permitted one-fifth of their caucus to force a vote on a nominee for committee chairman, and in 1974 that vote became automatic for all nominees.

Rank-and-file Democrats in January 1975 asserted their new power by unseating three incumbent chairmen: Armed Services Committee Chairman F. Edward Hebert of Louisiana; Agriculture Committee Chairman W. R. Poage of Texas; and Banking, Currency, and Housing Committee Chairman Wright Patman of Texas. Hebert and Poage were both replaced by the next ranking Democrat on their committees, but, in yet another blow to the seniority system, the fourth-ranking Democrat on the Banking Committee, Henry S. Reuss of Wisconsin, was elected to succeed Patman. The autocratic manner in which the three chairmen had run their committees was primarily responsible for their downfall.

In 1984 the Democratic Caucus voted narrowly to remove elderly Melvin Price of Illinois from the chairmanship of the Armed Services Committee and replace him with Les Aspin of Wisconsin, the panel's seventh-ranking Democrat, despite an impassioned plea in behalf of Price from Speaker Thomas P. "Tip" O'Neill Jr., D-Mass. Many Democrats had complained that Price's infirmity allowed the Republican minority to exercise effective control of the conservative panel.

Aspin nearly suffered the same fate two years later. Many liberal Democrats were distressed at what they considered his betrayals on several controversial defense issues. Aspin lost his chair in early January 1987 in a yes-or-no vote in the Democratic Caucus on his reelection, with no other name on the ballot. But two weeks later, pitted against three other committee members, Aspin won it back on the third ballot over the more conservative Rep. Marvin Leath of Texas.

Democrats ousted two committee chairmen in December 1990, as they organized for the 102nd Congress. Public Works Chairman Glenn M. Anderson, D-Calif., and House Administration Chairman Frank Annunzio, D-Ill., were regarded as weak, ineffective leaders. They were rejected and then replaced by younger Democrats: Rep. Robert A. Roe of New Jersey, the second-ranking Democrat on Public Works, defeated third-ranking Rep. Norman Y. Mineta of California (who would become chairman in the next Congress); and Rep. Charlie Rose of North Carolina, the third-ranking Democrat on House Administration.

Use of caucus rules to challenge committee chairmen usually was at the behest of the rank-and-file membership and was often unsuccessfully opposed by some in the party leadership, who feared disruptions from ongoing competition for committees and subcommittee posts. There were important exceptions, however.

In the most significant recent contest, Rep. David Obey, a senior member of the Appropriations Committee and one of the House's most aggressive and partisan liberals, benefited from the weakening of the seniority tradition in 1994 when Chairman William H. Natcher, D-Ky., became terminally ill. Obey, the fifth-ranking member, was supported by the leadership and easily won a vote of the Steering and Policy Committee to succeed Natcher as "acting chairman" over the third-ranking Democrat, Neal Smith of Iowa, who argued that he deserved the post as a veteran liberal who had served for thirty-five years. Obey automatically assumed the chairmanship upon Natcher's death.

SUBCOMMITTEE CONTESTS

In 1973 Democrats allowed their party members on each committee to select subcommittee chairmen. Previously, they had been picked by the committee chairman. In 1975 Democrats decided that all subcommittee chairmen on the Appropriations Committee should be subject to election by the full Democratic Caucus; on the highly decentralized Appropriations panel it was argued that those subcommittee chairmen were as powerful as most chairmen of legislative committees. In 1990, the rule was also applied to subcommittee chairmen on the Ways and Means Committee.

The seniority system suffered another reversal in January 1977 when the Democratic Caucus for the first time rejected a sitting subcommittee chairman of the Appropriations Committee. The target was Robert L. F. Sikes of Florida, the longtime chairman of the Military Construction Subcommittee who had been reprimanded by the House the year before for conflicts of interest.

Democratic caucuses on other committees have also ousted subcommittee chairmen or rejected senior members who had been heirs apparent. Several of these contests were significant in influencing party policies for years to come. In 1975, on the then–Interstate and Foreign Commerce Committee, Rep. John Moss, D-Calif., ousted Rep. Harley Staggers, D-W.Va., from the chairmanship of the Oversight subcommittee. Staggers's loss was an especially significant slap at the seniority system since he was also chairman of the full committee. In 1979, on the same committee, Rep. Henry Waxman, D-Calif., defeated the more senior and conservative Rep. L. Richardson Preyer, D-N.C., for the vacant chairmanship of the important Health subcommittee after a bitter contest focusing on allegations that Preyer's status as heir to a pharmaceutical fortune created a potential conflict of interest, and complaints about Waxman's campaign contributions to other committee Democrats.

Perhaps the strangest contest occurred in 1981 on the then–Foreign Affairs Committee. Rep. Michael Barnes, D-Md., a second-term liberal, challenged the conservative subcommittee chairman Rep. Gus Yatron, D-Pa., for his post on the Western Hemisphere subcommittee. With Yatron perceived as vulnerable, Rep. Dan Mica, D-Fla., a conservative, also decided to run. Mica had been elected to the House and the committee along with Barnes but had been ranked ahead of him in the committee's order of seniority determined by lot. When the voting began by secret ballot, caucus rules required a yes-or-no vote on each candidate, who bid for a chairmanship in order of full committee seniority until the post was filled. Yatron lost by one vote, which was known to be Mica's. Angered by Mica's opportunism, Yatron then voted against him, resulting in Mica's defeat by one vote. Barnes, who bid next, was then easily elected chairman and led Democratic opposition to the Reagan administration's policies in the region.

SENATE ADHERES TO SENIORITY

The Senate also decided in the 1970s that seniority should not dictate the choice of committee leaders. Senate Republicans adopted the policy in 1973 and the Democrats in 1975. Yet the Senate continued to adhere to the seniority tradition, and in the smaller body longtime personal relationships among senators also worked to smooth over arguments that ideology should be a more significant determinant of chairmanships.

In 1977, in the most visible attempt to undermine seniority, the liberal-dominated Democratic Conference took a secret ballot vote on all nominees for chairmen, with opposition centering on Finance Committee Chairman Russell Long of Louisiana. He won overwhelmingly, 42–6.

A battle in 1987 over the position of ranking minority member on the Foreign Relations Committee was settled primarily on the issue of seniority. The contest was between Jesse Helms, R-N.C., and the more moderate Richard G. Lugar, R-Ind. The situation was somewhat unusual because Lugar had been chairman of the Foreign Relations panel for the previous two years while the Republicans controlled the Senate. Helms tended to North Carolina issues as chairman of the Agriculture Committee. But when the Senate reverted to the Democrats, Helms, who had joined the Foreign Relations panel the same day as Lugar, decided he wanted the position of ranking Republican on the committee and claimed seniority by virtue of his four years of longer service in the Senate.

Under the rules of the Senate Republican Conference, each committee chooses its top ranking member, subject to confirmation by the entire conference. Republicans on the Foreign Relations Committee nominated Lugar as ranking member, but the full Republican Conference rejected him, 24–17. Helms—and the seniority system—won out. Lugar then became ranking minority member of the Agriculture Committee, and both he and Helms became chairmen of these committees when Republican Senate control resumed in 1995.

The apparent personal animus between Helms and Lugar lingered, and the fallout from their contest had interesting repercussions for years to come. Lugar led the opposition to Helms' refusal in 1997 to hold a confirmation hearing for William Weld, a moderate Republican nominated as ambassador to Mexico. In an unprecedented action, a committee majority forced Helms to schedule a meeting at which they intended to discuss the Weld nomination, but Helms successfully used his chairmanship powers to deny most other senators, including Lugar, a chance to speak. Lugar, in turn, threatened to use his powers as Agriculture chairman against North Carolina tobacco interests.

Despite dramatic conservative gains in the Republican Conference, more moderate senators continue to rely on seniority to obtain and keep important positions on committees. Sen. Mark O. Hatfield, R-Ore., a veteran liberal, was not removed as Appropriations Committee chairman during the 104th Congress after he cast the lone—and decisive—vote to kill a balanced budget constitutional amendment, and Sen. John H. Chafee, R-R.I., assumed the chairmanship of the Environment and Public Works Committee. In the 105th Congress, a rumored challenge to Sen. James M. Jeffords, R-Vt., for the open chairmanship of the Labor and Human Resources Committee by conservative Sen. Dan Coats, R-Ind., never developed.

a wide variety of entrenched interests. When the panel, chaired by Jerry M. Patterson, D-Calif., closed its doors in April 1980, it left behind barely a trace of its thirteen-month-long effort to change the House committee system. Only one of its recommendations—a plan to create a separate standing committee on energy to untangle overlapping committee jurisdictions—went to the House floor, where the proposal was promptly gutted. In place of the select committee's plan, the House merely decided to rename its Commerce Committee as the Energy and Commerce Committee and to designate that panel as its lead committee on energy matters.

The Patterson committee's other recommendations had included proposals to limit subcommittee assignments as well as the number of subcommittees. The committee said the proliferation of subcommittees had decentralized and fragmented the policy process and had limited members' capacity to master their work. The Patterson committee report emphasized that on no other issue concerning committee reform had it found greater agreement than that there were too many subcommittees in the House of Representatives and that members had too many subcommittee assignments.

There were few major rules proposals considered after the 1970s. Over a twenty-year period, Democrats continued to make a series of incremental adjustments in House floor rules that gave the Speaker power to postpone and cluster certain votes, to eliminate "ordering a second" (a potentially dilatory additional vote) on motions to suspend the rules, and to abolish the vestiges of nonrecorded teller voting. Giving the leadership the ability to coordinate a more rational floor schedule, it was argued, would enhance the ability of committees to conduct business with fewer interruptions.

House Democrats in January 1981 amended their caucus rules to limit the number of subcommittees and similar committee subunits that could be established by standing committees. Under the new rule, the Appropriations Committee was allowed to retain all of its thirteen panels, but all other standing committees were restricted to a maximum of either eight (if the standing committee had at least thirty-five members) or six (for smaller committees). In 1992, Democrats amended the caucus rules further to limit most committees to a maximum of five subcommittees, but, in a gesture to the importance of placating individuals and avoiding sacrifice, they also guaranteed that no subcommittee chairman would lose a post.

One subject—administrative reform of the House—was never effectively addressed by the Democratic Caucus because it was not perceived to involve real power and most members had little awareness of it. Nevertheless, the issue would eventually surface with a series of scandals in the 1990s that helped to undermine the Democratic House majority.

The Joint Committee on the Organization of Congress, created for the first session of the 103rd Congress, was structured similarly to previous joint committees whose work had achieved some success with the legislative reorganization laws in 1946 and 1970. But ultimately that was all it had in common with them.

For example, the joint committee discussed many ideas for reform of the committee system in the House but accomplished little except the compilation of diverse proposals. There was little appetite in the House for significant change among Democrats, and Republicans were anxious to take credit for the idea of reform and to use the theme of institutional corruption in the next campaign. The Democratic leadership wanted the issue to go away, while simultaneously claiming public credit for working on it. They continued to make commitments to consider the committee's recommendations on the House floor in 1994, scheduling a "reform week" late in the second session that never came to pass.

The joint committee foundered over bitter partisanship in the House and poisonous bicameral relations when Senate Republicans angered Democrats by employing filibusters against Clinton administration proposals. House Democrats refused to consider enhanced minority rights for Republicans, such as a guarantee that the minority could offer amendatory instructions in the motion to recommit bills to committees, unless the Senate agreed to reforms in the filibuster, anathema to key senators from both parties. These issues were difficult enough without the addition of changes in committee structure and jurisdiction.

After the 103rd Congress expired, party control of both chambers shifted and reforms again became a unicameral, partisan initiative, this time in GOP hands. In 1995, the House abolished the District of Columbia, Merchant Marine and Fisheries, and Post Office and Civil Service committees, three minor panels whose absence had little effect on the operation of the chamber.

SENATE COMMITTEE CHANGES

While most of the attempts to reorganize the committee system in the 1970s were directed at the House, the Senate committee system was altered in 1977 by the first comprehensive committee consolidation in either house since passage of the 1946 reorganization act. Earlier in the decade the Senate had adopted important procedural changes involving committees. Later attempts to use another bicameral vehicle, the 1993 Joint Committee on the Organization of Congress, to implement new reforms ultimately failed.

Committees and committee assignments are much less important in the work of the chamber and in determining the course of a member's career than in the House. In the Senate, the parties also control the assignment process, but some assignment limitations that do exist are actually set out in the rules. Consequently, proposed reforms might open the door to the delicate subject of amendments to Senate rules. The Senate often prefers instead to adjust committee structure and assignment issues by creating new exceptions, irrespective of the rules, that benefit individual senators while taking nothing away from anyone else. Each party also privately determines policies affecting its own members, which has the advantage of avoiding messy floor debate and keeps the parties out of each other's affairs.

Challenges to Seniority

The Senate had struck the first successful blow to the seniority system in the post–World War II period. As Senate minority leader in 1953, Lyndon Johnson proposed that all Democratic senators be given a seat on one major committee before any Democrat was assigned to a second major committee. The proposal, which became known as the "Johnson Rule," was a stunning blow to seniority. But it had the backing of Sen. Richard Russell of Georgia—the powerful leader of the southern Democratic bloc that dominated the Senate for years—and was approved by the Democratic Steering Committee that made Democratic committee assignments in the Senate. It was fitting that Johnson had successfully staged the breakthrough because he was a junior senator, chosen as his party's leader while still in his first Senate term. He had served six terms in the House, however, and had become a protégé of House Speaker Rayburn.

Later, Senate Republicans adopted the same party rule, first informally in 1959 and then through the Republican Conference in 1965.

In 1971, under renewed pressure to modify the seniority system, Senate Democrats and Republicans agreed to further changes. Majority Leader Mike Mansfield, D-Mont., announced that a meeting of the Democratic Conference would be held at the request of any senator and any senator would be free to challenge any nomination by the Steering Committee of a committee chairman. Republicans adopted a proposal that a senator could be the ranking minority member of only one standing committee. (After the GOP took control of the Senate in 1981, Republicans applied the same rule to the selection of committee chairmen.)

The Senate rejected a major challenge to the seniority system in 1971 when it blocked, on a 48–26 vote, a resolution that would have permitted the selection of committee chairmen on some basis other than seniority. The resolution had provided that in making committee assignments "neither [party] conference shall be bound by any tradition, custom, or principle of seniority."

But in 1973 Senate Republicans decided to choose their top-ranking committee members without regard to seniority. Republicans adopted a plan to limit the seniority system by having members of each standing committee elect the top-ranking Republican on that committee, subject to approval by a vote of all Senate Republicans.

And in 1975 Senate Democrats also voted to choose committee chairmen without regard to seniority. A secret ballot would be taken whenever one-fifth of their conference requested it. The provision was first used in 1977 when twelve senators made a request for a secret ballot, though several of them said they still intended to support the committee chairmen. Unlike the changes underway in the House, the new rule failed to reveal any significant dissatisfaction with the traditional seniority system even on a secret ballot, as only a handful of votes were cast against any chairmanship nominees. Sen. Russell Long, D-La., supposedly a longtime target of reformers, was easily renominated by a 42–6 vote. Appropriations Committee Chairman John McClellan, D-Ark., received an identical tally. Majority Leader Robert C. Byrd, D-W.Va., later forced a separate Senate vote on Long's election as chairman to demonstrate what he called the democratic nature of Senate rules. Long won 60–0.

Also in 1975, junior senators obtained committee staff assistance for the first time. A new rule authorized them to hire up to three committee staffers, depending on the number and type of committee assignments they had, to work directly for them on their committees. In the past, committee staff members had been controlled by the chairmen and other senior committee members.

1977 Committee Reorganization

The 1977 Senate reorganization consolidated a number of committees, revised jurisdictions of others, set a ceiling on the number of committees and subcommittees on which a senator could serve or chair, gave minority members a larger share of committee staff, and directed that schedules for committee hearings and other business be computerized to avoid conflicts. The organizational and procedural changes were the product of a special panel, chaired by Sen. Adlai E. Stevenson III, D-Ill.

One of the biggest organizational changes was the consolidation of most aspects of energy policy, except taxes, in one committee. Although the final result fell short of the Stevenson committee's goals for consolidating and merging committees, three committees were abolished: District of Columbia, Post Office, and Aeronautical and Space Sciences, as well as the joint committees on Atomic Energy, Congressional Operations, and Defense Production. (The decision to end the joint committees was a unilateral Senate action. The House continued the Congressional Operations panel as a select committee for another two years.) Special interest groups were able to preserve several other committees slated for extinction, such as Small Business.

Changes also were made in Senate committee procedures.

Senate reformers, like their House counterparts, were concerned with the proliferation of committees and subcommittees. In 1947 most senators served on two or three subcommittees. By the 94th Congress (1975–1977) they held an average of eleven assignments on subcommittees of standing committees.[19] Stevenson's Temporary Select Committee to Study the Senate Committee System stated in its report:

Proliferation of committee panels means proliferation in assignments held by Senators. And the burdens and frustrations of too many assignments, whatever the benefits, produce inefficient division of labor, uneven distribution of responsibility, conflicts in the scheduling of meetings, waste of Senators' and staff time, unsystematic lawmaking and oversight, inadequate anticipation of major problems, and inadequate membership participation in committee decisions.[20]

As part of the 1977 reorganization, the Senate prohibited a senator from serving as chairman of more than one subcommittee on any committee on which he or she served. This, in effect, placed an indirect cap on subcommittee expansion by limiting the number of subcommittees of any committee to the number of majority party members on the full committee.

House and Senate negotiators meet in a budget reconciliation conference in 1997.

With certain exceptions, each senator was limited to membership on two major committees and one minor committee. Each senator was limited to membership on three subcommittees of each major committee on which he or she served (the Appropriations Committee was exempted from this restriction). And each senator was limited to membership on two subcommittees of the minor committee on which he or she served.

Though it was not made a requirement, the Senate adopted language, similar to the practice in the House, stating that no member of a committee should receive a second subcommittee assignment until all members of the committee had received their first assignment.

The Senate also prohibited a senator from serving as chairman of more than one committee at the same time; prohibited the chairman of a major committee from serving as chairman of more than one subcommittee on the senator's major committees and as the chairman of more than one subcommittee on his or her minor committee; prohibited the chairman of a minor committee from chairing a subcommittee on that committee; and prohibited a senator from chairing more than one of each of his of her major committees' subcommittees.

The Senate in addition required the Rules and Administration Committee to establish a central computerized scheduling service to keep track of meetings of Senate committees and subcommittees and House-Senate conference committees.

Finally, the Senate required the staff of each committee to reflect the relative size of the majority and minority membership on the committee. On the request of the minority party members of a committee at least one-third of the staff of the committee was to be placed under the control of the minority party, except that staff deemed by the chairman and ranking minority member to be working for the whole committee would not be subject to the rule.

1980s Reform Attempts

Frustration with Senate procedures ran high in the 1980s, but despite several serious proposals for reform no major changes were achieved by the end of the decade.

A 1983 report by former Sens. James B. Pearson, R-Kan., and Abraham Ribicoff, D-Conn., urged major changes in the Senate structure and procedures, including restrictions on subcommittees and a reduction in the number of committees. Under their plan, subcommittees would not have been permitted to report legislation. Nor would the panels have been staffed, a move aimed at eliminating what they saw as time-consuming specialization at the subcommittee level.

The following year another Temporary Select Committee to Study the Senate Committee System, chaired by Dan Quayle, R-Ind., recommended, among other things, strictly limiting the number of committee and subcommittee assignments each senator could have. The panel called for the strict enforcement of the existing rule allowing senators to serve on two major committees and one minor committee.

The Senate Rules and Administration Committee in 1988 proposed changes in committee and floor procedures. To reduce the number of competing demands on senators' time, the panel proposed allowing subcommittees to hold only hearings, thus requiring all legislative drafting sessions to be held at the full committee level.

In 1993, the Joint Committee on the Organization of Congress proposed a variety of ideas to revise committee structure, assignments, and procedures, although it did not recommend abolition of any existing committee. Among its proposals: limiting senators to three committees; restricting major committees (called "super A" and "A") to three subcommittees (except Appropriations) and minor "B" committees to two subcommittees; limiting senators to service on two subcommittees per "A" com-

Congress historically has resisted limiting the length of time members may serve on committees. To do so, it was argued, would detract from the expertise that committees possess in dealing with complex legislation. Limitations also would disrupt the concept of seniority that provides a stable mechanism for determining committee leaders over long periods of time and avoiding power struggles.

However, in 1995, the new Republican majorities in the House and Senate took important steps toward legitimizing term limitations for top committee posts. They not only amended House rules at the beginning of the 104th Congress to place a three-term service limit on all committee and subcommittee chairs but placed a four-term limit on the speakership. The House rules changes were effective immediately.

The Senate's term limitation was a Republican Conference rule, not an amendment to the chamber's rules. It was adopted prospectively to limit full committee chairmen to six years of service, and the clock began to run only in 1997.

The three-term/six-year chairmanship limits were a significant movement away from seniority and toward a broader sharing of power in Congress.

The "Contract with America," a GOP political agenda used in the 1994 elections, contained a proposal for a constitutional amendment requiring term limits on service in Congress itself. However the amendment was easily defeated in 1995 and 1997 when brought to a vote. *(See box, Contract with America, p. 441.)*

Whether the changes would hold up was uncertain. Many things could happen in the interim that would prevent the new rules from taking effect. Because they were created by Republican majorities, any shift in party control back to the Democrats would very likely result in numerous changes in the rules, including possible repeal or modification of term limits. At the very least the effective date would be postponed to accommodate a new generation of Democratic committee chairmen. The new House rule does not apply to ranking minority members of committees and subcommittees, and the Democratic Caucus in 1997 overwhelmingly rejected a proposal to implement a term limitation through the party's caucus rules. The Republicans themselves could have second thoughts as the deadline approaches. They would face wholesale replacements of committee leadership as a new presidential administration was taking office and possible retirements by departing chairmen, creating vacant seats that might endanger control of the House.

Reformers in the past have argued for even broader committee service limitations for the entire House membership to break up entrenched oligarchies on committees and encourage members to explore new interests across the jurisdictional spectrum. The idea never attracted significant support because by disrupting seniority it removed the most significant source of stability and predictability for members as they planned their congressional careers. There were also legitimate questions about how any wholesale rotation would work when hundreds of members might be affected at once.

The use of term limits in very limited circumstances is not new in Congress, however. Two House standing committees—Budget and Standards of Official Conduct—have employed term limits since their inception. The Budget Committee, which is supposed to have a broad range of membership, including mandatory representation from the Appropriations and Ways and Means committees, began with a two-term limit and gradually expanded to three terms, then to four terms in the 104th Congress. Technically, the rule limits members to no more than four terms out of six successive Congresses, thus preventing them from leaving the committee and quickly being brought back. The chairman can serve for an additional term, if necessary, to allow him a minimum of two terms in that post. But Republicans weakened the chairmanship rule by allowing Kasich to hold the post continuously after 1995.

The Democrats refused to adopt the new four-term limit, retaining the three-term limit in their caucus rules and making Budget the only committee in Congress in which each party uses a different term limit. The Democrats' decision did not represent a judgment of the appropriate length of service on the committee; instead, they sought to use the already scheduled three-term rotation to create some vacant seats to give to members because so few committee assignments were available under the ratios created by the new Republican majority.

In the case of the Standards Committee, term limits have varied. Effective in 1999 a service limitation of no more than three Congresses in any period of five successive Congresses was imposed. However, there is no demand for service on the committee. The size of the committee was fixed at fourteen by the Ethics Reform Act of 1989, but the controversy associated with the committee's workload made that number unrealistic; only ten seats were occupied in each of the 104th, 105th, and 106th Congresses. Rules changes in 1997 allowed twenty members who do not serve on the committee—ten from each party—to serve in a pool from which members could be drawn to join regular committee members in filling subcommittees to investigate ethics violations.

The lone House select committee, Permanent Intelligence, originally had a six-calendar-year service limitation, which was changed to four-terms-out-of-six successive Congresses in 1995, as had been recommended by the Joint Committee on the Organization of Congress. Proponents of term limits had argued at the committee's inception that a limitation would refresh the membership and prevent it from being coopted by the intelligence community. The rule was also amended to allow a member selected as chairman in his or her fourth Congress of service to be eligible to serve for a fifth term if reappointed as chairman, in order to ensure greater continuity of the committee's work. Due to defects in the operation of the original six-year rotation rule, there had been criticism that the committee had been weakened because nearly all of its chairmen (except the first) had been effectively limited to only two years in that post and could not establish strong and stable working relationships with executive branch entities.

The Senate does not employ rotation on any of its standing committees, so the shifting members of the House Budget Committee face a Senate counterpart with long-term permanent membership. (The Senate chairman in 1999, Pete V. Domenici of New Mexico, also held the post during an earlier period of Republican Senate control in the 1980s.) The Senate Select Intelligence Committee, however, has an eight-year limit that the House has now essentially copied.

mittee (except Appropriations) and one per "B" committee; requiring bipartisan leadership approval and a Senate recorded vote for extra assignments; allowing majority and minority leaders to make committee assignments, subject to party rules; setting meeting days for the various classifications of committees to reduce scheduling conflicts; and barring use of proxies if they affected the result of a vote.

The Joint Committee's recommendations were reworked by a Republican task force appointed by incoming Majority Leader Bob Dole, R-Kan., in 1994, which called for Senate floor action on:

• Barring major committees (except Appropriations) from having more than five subcommittees in the 104th Congress and four in the 105th (as opposed to the limit of three proposed by the joint committee). Senate rules have no limits.

• Barring senators from serving on more than two major and one minor committee, a provision already in the Senate rules but often ignored.

• Abolishing joint committees.

• Abolishing committees deemed too trivial or unpopular with senators to continue to exist, but defining them only as any committee that dropped to less than 50 percent of the membership it had in the 102nd Congress.

• Allowing proxy voting only if it did not affect the outcome of a committee vote.

None of these proposals was adopted, but Republicans in the 104th Congress later considered several proposals in their party conference. Most significantly they approved a six-year term limit on committee chairmen, to begin in 1997, that would also apply if Republicans returned to minority status. Democrats

---

CONFERENCE COMMITTEES

The conference committee is an ad hoc joint committee appointed to reconcile differences between Senate and House versions of pending legislation. The conference device, used by Congress since 1789, had developed its modern form by the middle of the nineteenth century. *(See "Conference Action," p. 520.)*

Before a bill can be sent to the president, it must be passed in identical form by both chambers. Whenever different versions of the same bill are passed, and neither chamber is willing to yield to the other or make modifications by sending a bill back-and-forth, a conference becomes necessary to determine the final shape of the legislation. It is unusual for the Senate or House to reject the work of a conference committee.

In the past, conference committees were composed of senior members of the committees that handled the bill. This remains generally true today, but there are opportunities for junior members to be appointed and occasionally even members who were not on a committee that originally reported the bill. Conferees are appointed by the Speaker and the presiding officer of the Senate on the recommendations of the committee chairmen and ranking minority members, subject to influence by the respective party leaderships. Although the chairmen, by tradition, have played the principal role in picking conferees, in the House the Speaker retains the substantive power to make the appointments, subject only to the restrictions in Rule I, clause 11, that he "shall appoint no less than a majority of Members who generally supported the House position as determined by the Speaker . . ." and "shall name Members who are primarily responsible for the legislation and shall, to the fullest extent feasible, include the principal proponents of the major provisions of the bill as it passed the House." The Speaker's appointments may not be challenged on a point of order for alleged violations of these criteria.

Recent Speakers have intervened more frequently to select members they want to serve as conferees and to bar those they do not. Speaker Newt Gingrich, R-Ga., even appointed members of the Democratic minority to serve in conference slots reserved for the majority in order to highlight differences within the minority.

In 1993, the House changed its rules to give the Speaker the power, after a conference has been appointed, to appoint additional conferees and to remove conferees as he wishes. Before then, any changes in the composition of a conference after its appointment had required unanimous consent. While the change by 1999 had no dramatic impact on the operation of conferences, it effectively prevented conferees from defying the will of the majority leadership. Largely because of complexities in the House created by multiple referrals of bills to different committees and the increasing use of massive omnibus bills to deal with budget and tax matters, the size of conference delegations increased during the 1980s and in subsequent years. Scholars Walter Oleszek and C. Lawrence Evans have noted that committee chairs in the 1980s often demanded positions on conferences from Democratic Speakers, who often found it politic to accommodate them. In 1981, for example, more than 250 members of Congress participated in a conference on a budget reconciliation bill, making it the largest conference in history. The conference split up into fifty-eight subgroups to consider various sections of the legislation.

It is possible that 1995 rules changes in the House requiring a primary committee be designated for each bill, rather than the previous practice of joint referrals, may swing the trend back toward less complex conference structures. Evans and Oleszek have observed that the new rule gave Speaker Gingrich "the procedural rationale for resisting chairs' demands for conference slots."[1] Data indicates that, for legislation in conference which received multiple referrals, the average size of the House delegation dropped from 42.7 members to 29.1 between the 103rd and 104th Congresses.

CONDUCTING A CONFERENCE

There need not be an equal number of conferees (or "managers," as they are called) from each house. Each house's delegation has a single vote, which is determined by a majority vote of its conferees. Therefore, a majority of both the Senate and House delegations must agree before a provision emerges from conference as part of the final bill. Both chambers permit proxy voting in conferences.

Both parties are represented on conference committees, with the majority party having a larger number, and a majority of conferees

would not be affected. Unlike the House, which wrote term limits into the chamber's rules in 1995, the Senate did not ammend its rules to incorporate the proposal. The Republican Conference also mandated a secret-ballot vote by Republican members of a committee in nominating a candidate for chairman and required a chairman, if indicted for a felony, to step aside temporarily until the matter was resolved. *(See box, Term Limits on Committee Chairmenships and Service, p. 559.)*

The Committee Structure

There are three principal classes of committees in Congress:

• Standing committees, by far the most important and most numerous, with permanently authorized staff and broad legislative mandates.

• Select or special committees that have a limited jurisdiction, may be restricted to an investigative rather than a legislative role, and may be temporary in that they are authorized to operate for a specific period of time or until the project for which they are created has been completed.

• Joint committees that have a membership drawn from both houses of Congress and usually are investigative or housekeeping in nature.

Conference committees, a special variety of joint committee, serve only on an ad hoc basis to resolve differences in Senate and House versions of the same legislation. *(See box, Conference Committees, p. 560.)*

Below the committee level are a plethora of subcommittees that are functional subdivisions of the committees. Like the full committees they are composed of members of the majority and

from each house must sign the conference report. In the past, conference committees met on the Senate side of the Capitol, with the most senior senator presiding, but this custom is no longer followed. Conferences now meet anywhere in the House, Senate, or Capitol complexes, with members of either house presiding, though the role is largely honorific. For certain legislation considered on an annual basis, such as appropriations bills and the congressional budget resolution, the chairmanship alternates between the chambers.

Most conference committees met in secret until late 1975 when both chambers amended their rules to require open meetings unless a majority of either chamber's conferees vote in open session to close the meeting for that day. In 1977 the House amended its rules further to require open conference meetings unless the full House voted by recorded vote to close them. That rule was never adopted by the Senate but in practice Senate conferees have always gone along with the representatives on those occasions—limited to defense and intelligence agency bills—when the House has voted to close a conference committee. Despite the "sunshine" rules, committees have found various ways to avoid negotiating in public, including the use of informal sessions, separate meetings of each delegation with staffers as go-betweens, and meeting rooms too small to accommodate all who wish to attend.

Conferees may be "instructed" by the House, just before they are appointed and while they are meeting, although the instructions are not binding and are sometimes ignored. When conferees are about to be appointed, the principal manager for the minority is usually recognized to offer a motion to instruct, and sometimes a motion may be offered pro forma in order to prevent another member from offering a less desirable proposition. The House also has a rule that allows any member, with preference for recognition again going to the minority party, to offer a motion to instruct its conferees or to dismiss them if a conference has not reported after twenty calendar days. This form of motion to instruct may be offered repeatedly by any member until the conferees finally report. This motion has sometimes proved a useful device for the minority to bring attention to a conference's failure to act or to force the House to vote for or

against legislative provisions proposed in the Senate. The Senate rarely instructs its conferees, but there have been some indications the practice may be becoming more popular.

After conferees reach agreement, they sign a conference report and submit it and a statement of managers providing a detailed explanation of their actions to each chamber. Unlike a bill reported by a House or Senate legislative committee, conferees who disagree may not include any "minority views." Sometimes conferees who sign the report but object to certain provisions include a notation, such as "except section XXX," next to their names, but these caveats have no substantive effect. When conferees are unable to agree, the bill may die in conference if they take no formal action. Sometimes conferees file a report incorporating only matters on which they have agreed, leaving out others on which they disagree to await further negotiation or additional votes on the floor of each house to see if one chamber or the other will compromise. On rare occasions conferees formally report "in disagreement" and await further amendments by both houses.

Once their report is approved by the first of the two houses to consider it, the conference committee automatically is dissolved and the report goes to the remaining house for a vote. If either chamber rejects the conference report, the legislation remains before it in the form it existed prior to its commitment to conference, to await additional amendments or a new conference. The first chamber to consider the report also has the option to "recommit" it to conference, usually with instructions, to change an unacceptable provision. This action has the effect of rejecting the initial conference report but does not require the appointment of a new conference. The conferees may simply resume meeting. However, it may endanger chances for a new agreement if the other chamber refuses to accede on the issue in question. If an agreement is reached on the issue in dispute the filing process is repeated. In the Senate, conference reports may be filibustered like other legislation.

1. C. Lawrence Evans and Walter J. Oleszek, "Procedural Features of House Republican Rule," paper presented at a conference at Florida International University, Miami, January 31, 1998, 16.

minority parties in roughly the same proportion as the party ratios on the full committees.

Beginning in the 1970s additional mechanisms were developed to consider legislation apart from the traditional committee structure. Appearing principally in the House, these include the creation of ad hoc committees by the chamber to deal with complex legislation within the normal jurisdiction of several committees. This mechanism requires formal approval by the House and should be considered a variation of a multiple referral.

On the other hand, the use of informal leadership task forces to develop or refine legislation occurs outside the committee process entirely, at least until the bill is ready to be considered more formally.

STANDING COMMITTEES

The standing committees are at the center of the legislative process. Legislation usually must be considered and approved in some form at the committee level before it can be sent to the House or Senate for further action. *(See Chapter 15, The Legislative Process.)*

The 1946 reorganization act organized the Senate and House committees along roughly parallel lines, although eventually divergences emerged. One of the act's purposes was to eliminate confusing and overlapping jurisdictions by grouping together related areas. The authorizing committees (as distinct from the Appropriations committees) generally were regrouped to follow the major organizational divisions of the executive branch.

SUBCOMMITTEES

Most standing committees have a number of subcommittees that provide the ultimate division of labor within the committee system. Although they enable members of Congress to develop expertise in specialized fields they often are criticized on grounds that they fragment responsibility, increase the difficulty of policy review, and slow down the authorization and appropriation process.

Subcommittees play a much larger role in the House than in the Senate. In the House, subcommittees usually are responsible for hearings and the first markup of a bill before a measure is sent on to the full committee. In the Senate, subcommittees may hold hearings but the full committee generally does the writing of legislation. And, Deering and Smith write, "on nearly all Senate committees the work of subcommittees on important legislation is shown little deference by the full committees."[21]

Subcommittees also vary in importance from committee to committee. Some, especially the Appropriations subcommittees in both chambers, have well-defined jurisdictions and function with great autonomy. Much of their work in both the House and Senate is often endorsed by the full committee without significant change, though, as noted, both the desire and the capacities of individual members to intervene in the legislative process have dramatically increased over time.

A few committees such as House Ways and Means and Senate Finance long resisted the creation of subcommittees even though there were logical subdivisions into which their work could be divided. Subcommittees were established by the Finance Committee in 1970, and by Ways and Means only in 1975

A House subcommittee meets to mark up a bill to improve regulation at the Food and Drug Administration.

after the House Democratic Caucus voted to require them. The subcommittee requirement was established in part because of dissatisfaction with the power and performance of Ways and Means Chairman Wilbur Mills. But these subcommittees, unlike those on the Appropriations Committee, never became autonomous legislative power centers because tax bills were put together as a unified package that required negotiations with all members of the full committee.

Ways and Means subcommittee chairmen became subject to caucus election in 1990 after two chairmen defied the leadership on tax legislation in 1989. However, none of the chairmen were ever seriously challenged for reelection to their positions.

After Republicans took over the House in 1995, committee chairmen exercised greater influence in the selection of subcommittee chairs than had been the case under the Democrats, subject to approval by GOP members of the committee.

The House and Senate Budget committees were among the few panels that had no subcommittees in the 105th Congress. Under Democratic control, the House panel had task forces that allowed a variety of members to chair oversight hearings on subjects of interest and to justify additional staffing but they were not integral to the committee's work.

SELECT AND SPECIAL COMMITTEES

Select and special committees are established from time to time in both chambers to study special problems or concerns, such as population, crime, hunger, or narcotics abuse. On other occasions, they deal with a specific event or investigation. Major investigations have been conducted by select committees such as the Senate panel that investigated the Watergate scandal in 1973–1974 and the House and Senate panels that jointly investigated the Iran-contra affair in 1987.

The size and life span of select and special panels usually are fixed by the resolutions that create them. In most cases, they have remained in existence for only a short time. Ordinarily they are not permitted to report legislation although there are exceptions, such as the 1973–1974 Select Committee on Committees chaired by Rep. Richard Bolling, D-Mo. However, much of Bolling's work was rejected. When the House reexamined itself again with a new Select Committee on Committees in 1979–1980, chaired by Rep. Jerry Patterson, D-Ca., it withheld legislative authority from the panel. Some of these committees, however, such as the Special Aging Committee in the Senate, have gone on continuously and are, for all intents and purposes, permanent. *(See box, House Abolishes Select Committees, p. 564.)*

Unlike most select committees, the Intelligence committees in both chambers have legislation referred to them and consider and report legislation to the chamber. But this is a special case, as the committees are effectively permanent entities. The Intelligence panels' subject matter is much narrower than that of most standing committees. In the House the panel is maintained as a select committee and appointed by the Speaker to insulate it from the normal political competition of the committee assignment process. Speakers have complained of being deluged by requests from members to serve. In 1995, House rules were amended to make the Speaker himself an ex officio member of the House panel, replacing the majority leader in this role. The new rule replaced an earlier one adopted in 1989 that had given the Speaker the right to attend the committee's meetings and to receive access to its information.

JOINT COMMITTEES

Joint committees are permanent panels created by statute or by concurrent resolution that also fixes their size. Of the four functioning in the 106th Congress (1999–2001), none had the authority to report legislation. The Joint Economic Committee is directed to examine national economic problems and review the execution of fiscal and budgetary programs. The Joint Committee on Taxation, made up of senior members of both parties from the House Ways and Means and Senate Finance committees, serves chiefly to provide a professional staff that long enjoyed a nonpartisan reputation on tax issues. When the Republicans assumed control of both houses in 1995, the new majority used it as a resource to develop its agenda for enacting major tax cuts. The other two joint committees deal with administrative matters: the Joint Committee on Printing oversees the Government Printing Office and the Joint Committee on the Library oversees the Library of Congress and works of art in the Capitol.

Chairmanships of joint committees generally rotate from one chamber to another at the beginning of each Congress. When a senator serves as chairman the vice chairman usually is a representative and vice versa. The last joint committee to have legislative responsibilities was the Joint Committee on Atomic Energy, which was abolished in 1977.

The most recent temporary body, the Joint Committee on the Organization of Congress, which existed in 1993 to propose reforms in the operations of the House and Senate, adopted a report that was never formally acted upon in either house.

AD HOC COMMITTEES

The Speaker of the House has the authority to create ad hoc committees, if approved by a vote of the House, to consider legislation that might be within the jurisdiction of several committees. Membership of such ad hoc committees would come from committees that would otherwise have exercised legislative jurisdiction. This authority, created in 1977, has been used twice, most notably in the 95th Congress to handle consideration of major energy legislation proposed by the Carter administration.

In 1995 the new Republican majority extended this idea to oversight, giving the Speaker the power to propose, subject to a House vote, the creation of ad hoc oversight committees to review specific matters within the jurisdiction of two or more standing committees. While aggressive use of oversight to investigate the Clinton administration became one of the new majority's priorities, it was conducted through the standing committees with efforts at coordination by the leadership. Through the

HOUSE ABOLISHES SELECT COMMITTEES

The rise and sudden fall in 1993 of the supposedly temporary House panels known as select committees was a small but significant illustration of the inability of House Democrats to conduct oversight of the committee system. In the 1980s and 1990s it became increasingly difficult for the majority party to get rid of these entities once they had come into existence. They acquired virtually permanent status.

The initial urgency that was often used to justify the creation of a select committee to study an issue and hold hearings was quickly transformed into an argument that the subject matter was important enough to require an ongoing panel. Once established, abolition would have constituted a slap at interest groups, such as the elderly or children's lobbies, which viewed the select committees as friendly forums tailor-made to promote their issues.

In fact, the subject matter may have been a secondary consideration. Select committees were regarded as a prestigious reward for the member chairing the committee, who controlled a staff and budget, and as patronage for the Speaker, who appointed the chairman and all other members of such committees. Moreover, members could chair subcommittees of the select committees, even if they already chaired other subcommittees on their permanent committee assignments, because the select subpanels were usually outside the multiple-chairmanship restrictions in Democratic Caucus rules.

Attempts to abolish select committees, or even to conduct oversight of their usefulness, were regarded as challenges to a comfortable status quo. Two of the five select committees in existence at the end of the 102nd Congress existed as part of the rules of the House. Three others were reestablished by resolutions reported from the Rules Committee at the beginning of each Congress and passed by the House, and their funding was folded into the annual resolution which provided money for most standing committees.

Following the 1992 election, however, the push for reform of Congress was gaining momentum as a result of scandals in the operation of the House. Members of the large new freshman class were looking for potential targets. The Republican minority proposed a raft of changes in the structure and operations of the House, many of them quite radical, but in the renewed climate of public scrutiny some Democrats were also looking for at least a symbolic way to support reform without causing major disruptions.

Four select committees, each without legislative jurisdiction, proved to be vulnerable:

• Permanent Select Committee on Aging. Created in 1975, it was made a permanent part of the House rules and was recreated automatically on the opening day of each Congress, along with the Permanent Select Committee on Intelligence, which had legislative jurisdiction. The Aging panel had sixty-eight members, making it larger than any other House committee, a staff of thirty-seven, and a budget of $1,542,240 in 1992.

• Narcotics Abuse and Control. Created in 1976, it had thirty-five members, a staff of eighteen, and a budget of $729,502 in 1992.

• Children, Youth and Families. Created in 1983, it had thirty-six members, a staff of eighteen, and a budget of $764,593 in 1992.

• Hunger. Created in 1984, it had thirty-three members, a staff of sixteen, and a budget of $654,274 in 1992.

The Democratic Caucus, meeting in December 1992 to organize for the next Congress, eliminated the Select Committee on Aging from House rules as a permanent body, effectively abolishing it and requiring it to seek renewal and survive a House floor vote just like the other select committees. The proposal slipped through in part because the chairmanship was vacant, so there was no incumbent to be displaced, and no clearly designated successor. Reps. William J. Hughes, D-N.J., and Marilyn Lloyd, D-Tenn., were competing at the time to get Speaker Thomas S. Foley's nod for the position. And few believed the rules change seriously threatened the panel.

Once the 103rd Congress convened in 1993, the Rules Committee reported separate resolutions recreating the four select committees. However, the first to be considered by the House, the popular anticrime narcotics panel, went down to a surprising defeat by a vote of 180–237. An unusual coalition of opponents consisted of near-unanimous Republicans, a small number of Democratic reformers, and a group of committee chairmen and other senior members. Members of the latter group had always regarded the existence of the select committees as an implicit slap at the standing committees, which had the actual legislative jurisdiction, for inattention to these issues, and a source of competition for media coverage and financial resources. They had long waited for an opportunity to get rid of them.

Surprisingly, the large class of freshman Democrats, many of whom had been elected on pledges to reform Congress, strongly supported the narcotics panel chaired by senior Ways and Means Committee member Charles B. Rangel, D-N.Y., a member of the Congressional Black Caucus.

Defeat of the narcotics committee surprised the Democratic leadership. Despite an attempt by the Rules Committee to reverse the result by repackaging all of the select committees in a single resolution to try to maximize support from the combination of special interest constituent groups that wanted them, it quickly became apparent that their time had passed in the House and no new floor vote was ever held. Rep. Tony Hall, D-Ohio, went on a hunger strike to protest the abolition of that committee, which he had chaired.

Only the Permanent Select Committee on Intelligence, created in House rules, which reports the intelligence authorization bill and is really a legislative committee but with members appointed by the Speaker rather than elected by the House, survived. Some members had advocated abolishing the panel and creating a joint committee with the Senate to reduce the number of members involved in intelligence issues and the possibility of security leaks. When Republicans assumed control of the House in 1995, they retained the select committee, increased the term of service on the rotating panel, and even added the Speaker as an ex officio member.

end of 1998, no ad hoc oversight committees had been created by the House.

TASK FORCES

Task forces operating outside the committee system are not mentioned in the rules of the House and usually have no official status. (Some committees have created task forces within themselves that perform certain functions of subcommittees.) They are groups of members working collectively for a specific purpose, usually by appointment of party leadership. Both the majority and minority have used task forces, mostly to work within the respective party caucuses. In some cases the task forces produce a useful product that can be further developed, perhaps as a bill referred to a committee. In others, their creation is intended as little more than another title on a member's stationery. When the Democrats controlled the House there were some complaints from legislative committees that task forces were becoming too visible, but this represented more of an institutional jealousy than reaction to substantive work by task forces.

On rare occasions task forces have played the principal role in creating legislation, most notably in enacting the Ethics Reform Act of 1989 that restricted honoraria and secured enactment of a long-delayed pay raise for members. In the House the bill was written by a bipartisan Leadership Task Force on Ethics and introduced by the Speaker himself. In 1995 Speaker Gingrich created a bipartisan task force on the Corrections Calendar to develop issues that might be considered using that new mechanism. In 1997 a bipartisan task force developed proposals to reform the ethics process in the House after the existing process had created tremendous partisan divisions in reprimanding and fining the Speaker for ethics violations at the beginning of the session. However, its recommendations were substantially changed by the House.

The Republican leadership from 1995 to 1998 dramatically increased the use of task forces of Republican members to prepare legislation and for other purposes. The practice had the advantage, from the point of view of the leadership, of maximizing its control over an issue and simplifying the legislative process by reducing controversy surrounding such issues as committee jurisdiction. On the other hand, the practice was attacked because much of the work was conducted outside the normal protections of public hearings and written committee reports that allow access by other members, the media and the public. Task forces in the 104th and 105th Congress, the two after the Republican Party gained full control of Congress in the 1994 elections, were criticized for meeting in secret, giving too much influence to lobbyists allied with the majority, and weakening the committee system.

COMMITTEE SIZES, RATIOS

The 1946 reorganization act set not only the jurisdiction of congressional standing committees but also their size. Fifty years later, however, the size of committees in both chambers was usually settled through negotiations between majority and minority party leaders. The House dropped nearly all size specifications from its rules in 1975; in the 106th Congress (1999–2001), only the Permanent Select Committee on Intelligence had one. Senate standing rules in 1997 still included committee sizes, necessitating some adjustments at the beginning of a Congress. Each chamber in effect endorses leadership decisions on committee sizes, as well as party ratios, when it adopts resolutions making committee assignments.

One potential disadvantage of the system in the House in 1999 is that committees consist of the number of members who happen to be assigned to them throughout the Congress, with little consideration given to a committee's optimal size. The largest committee in either house in the 106th Congress was the popular Committee on Transportation and Infrastructure with a huge and often unmanageable seventy-five members. One reason for its recent popularity was the expectation that Congress would pass well-funded multiyear highway, mass transit, and aviation program reauthorizations.

Congressional scholars Deering and Smith found that modern House Democratic leaders had expanded committee sizes to meet member demand and maintain party harmony. The authors found less pressure for committee expansion in the Senate, because most senators held two major committee assignments. They also found that senators generally were less concerned with their committee assignments than were their House colleagues.[22]

The standing rules of each chamber are silent on the matter of party ratios on committees. The Senate traditionally has more or less followed the practice of filling standing committees according to the strength of each party in the chamber. The House, on the other hand, has been less inclined to allocate minority party representation on committees on the basis of the relative strength of the two parties.

Under Democratic control that party's caucus rules stipulated that committee ratios be established to create firm working majorities on each committee and instructed the Speaker to provide for a minimum of three Democrats for every two Republicans, although this did not always occur. (The House and Senate committees dealing with ethics matters have equal party representation with the chairman from the majority party in the chamber.)

Democrats in the House felt little need to accommodate their political opposition, especially on exclusive House committee assignments such as Appropriations, Rules, and Ways and Means. House Republicans in the 1980s complained bitterly of mistreatment by Democrats and argued that the Democrats had been in the majority for so long that they had become arrogant in the use of power. Fourteen Republicans filed a lawsuit in 1981 after the defeat of their attempts on the floor to change the party ratios on four key committees—Appropriations, Budget, Rules, and Ways and Means—to reflect the gains made by their party in the November 1980 congressional elections. Republicans charged the Democrats with unconstitutionally discriminating against GOP members and their constituents when they set the party ratios. The case was dismissed by the U.S. District Court for the District of Columbia in October 1981, and the Supreme Court refused to review it in February 1983. In response to the angry Republican protests Democratic leaders in 1985 agreed to give Republicans more seats on most major committees.

When the Republicans took control in 1995, however, these earlier stands were quickly overlooked, given the necessity of controlling the tools of legislative power. The party copied the Democrats' practices of ensuring domination of important committees, even though its majority was far smaller than the ones the Democrats had enjoyed. Even on a housekeeping committee such as House Administration, the leadership took more direct responsibility for sensitive issues involving internal management of the House and expanded their party's ratio of control in the 105th and 106th Congresses to two-to-one (six to three), exceeding ratios previously employed by the Democrats.

THE CHAIRMAN'S ROLE

Each committee is headed by a chairman, who is a member of the majority party of a chamber. A chairman's power once resulted from the rigid operation of the seniority system under which a person rose to a chairmanship simply through longevity in Congress. The unwritten seniority rule conferred a committee chairmanship on the member of the majority party with the longest continuous service on the committee. As long as the chairman's party retained control of Congress he or she normally kept this position; if control passed to the other party he or she changed places with the ranking member of that party. The seniority system, intermittently observed from the mid-1800s, took firm hold in the Senate after the Civil War. It became entrenched in the House within a few decades of the 1910 revolt against the all-powerful speakership of Joseph Cannon, R-Ill.

In Congress at the end of the 1990s, most chairmen were still usually the most senior member of the committee in terms of consecutive service. However, because of the Democratic Caucus reforms of the 1970s and the new powers enjoyed by Speaker Gingrich under House Republicans, this was no longer an ironclad rule in that chamber. In the 104th Congress, the House adopted a new rule limiting committee and subcommittee chairs to a maximum service of three terms. The impact of the provision would be felt beginning in 2001 (provided the GOP held onto the majority). In 1995, Senate Republicans adopted a party rule, effective in 1997, to limit committee chairmen to three terms.

Even with the many changes, committee chairmen remained powerful figures on Capitol Hill, especially in the Senate, although they still had to answer to fellow party members. At the full committee level, the chairman calls meetings and establishes agendas, schedules hearings, coordinates work by subcommittees, chairs markup sessions, files committee reports, acts as floor manager, recommends conferees, controls the committee budget, supervises the hiring and firing of staff, and serves as spokesperson for the committee and the chairman's party in the

Republican Chairman Bill Archer of Texas, left, confers with ranking Democrat Charles D. Rangel of New York during markup of trade legislation before the House Ways and Means Committee in 1997.

committee's area of expertise. Committees can establish rules that permit the full committee chairmen to issue subpoenas on behalf of the committee in the conduct of an investigation. For example, use of the authority by the chairmen of the Government Reform and Oversight and Education and the Workforce committees in the 105th Congress sparked bitter partisan controversies.

The committee's ranking minority member may also be an influential figure, depending to some degree on the person's relationship with the chairman. Where the two do not get along, or the committee has a partisan tradition, the minority can be marginalized. The ranking member assists in establishing the committee agenda and in managing legislation on the floor for the minority, nominating minority conferees, and controlling the minority staff. The ranking member serves as spokesperson for the committee's minority members. In the Senate, the ranking minority member benefits, as do all senators, from the powerful rules and traditions that require them to be consulted. Chairmen and ranking minority members often sit "ex officio" on all subcommittees of their committee of which they are not regular members.

Committee Assignments

The rules of the House and Senate state that the membership of each house shall elect its members to standing committees. In the House all rules, committees, and assignments from the previous Congress effectively expire on January 3 of each odd-numbered year, and committees cannot function until they are recreated in the rules on opening day and members are reappointed. That sometimes can create an extended hiatus if the next Congress convenes late in January, during which committees and subcommittees cannot meet because they do not yet exist. Sometimes the committees try to get around this by inviting witnesses for "forums" that allows the returning committee members to gather and discuss issues or informally question witnesses as "guests."

Senate committees remain in existence in that "continuing body" with members being carried over from the previous Congress while they await a full complement of new members. The committees retain full power to act.

The committee assignment procedure takes place at the beginning of every Congress and throughout the next two years as vacancies occur. There are numerous changes at the beginning of every Congress, as members switch committee assignments, seeking posts of either greater power or greater personal interest to them. Incumbent members are nearly always permitted to retain their existing assignments unless the party ratio changed substantially in the preceding election or partisan control of the chamber shifted. In the House in 1995 dramatic committee ratio changes were involuntary after Republicans gained control in the 1994 election. Republicans assumed control of all committees and reduced the number of Democratic seats. Both parties also faced the problem of reassigning members who had served on three committees that were abolished. The Democrats were forced to remove several members each from the Appropriations, Ways and Means, and Rules committees. The caucus guaranteed these members their old seats back as soon as vacancies developed. By the beginning of the 105th Congress in 1997, all of the dislocated members who wanted to had been returned to their old assignments.

Representatives of the two parties negotiate on committee assignments and party ratios in advance and then submit the committee rosters to their party caucuses and finally the full chambers. The key decisions are made in each party's committee on committees with caucus and floor approval basically pro forma. There are always some adjustments in each new Congress in both chambers to take into account the recent election results, member preferences, and the shifting demands that the ebb and flow of issues place on committee workloads. With some exceptions the method currently in general use was adopted by the Senate in 1846 and by the House in 1911.

In the House nothing in the rules guarantees members any committee assignments. However, in practice each member who wants to serve on a committee has at least one assignment. Since committee assignments originate from political parties, members who switch parties automatically lose their seats under House rules. The Republicans, who have benefited from most party switches since the 1970s, have made a point of allowing their new recruits to retain their old posts, usually with seniority, or have given them even more desirable assignments to help them win reelection. (This does not always work; Rep. Greg Laughlin, R-Texas, a 1995 party switcher who was placed on the prestigious Ways and Means Committee, lost the nomination in the subsequent Republican primary.)

Even Rep. Bernard Sanders of Vermont, a self-proclaimed socialist and the House's only independent member since 1991, received two assignments when there was a Democratic majority in the House. When the Republicans controlled the House in 1995, and thereafter, his seats came out of the Democrats' minority allotment. Sanders was even allowed to become the ranking minority member of House subcommittees in the 105th and 106th Congresses, even though he was not a member of the Democratic Caucus, because no Democratic committee members sought to block him.

Until 1995 the number and types of committees and subcommittees on which any member might serve were left almost entirely to the discretion of the Republican Conference and the Democratic Caucus, which presented privileged resolutions to the House electing committee members. House rules were largely silent and the Rules Committee played no role in this process. As part of its rules changes in the 104th Congress, the Republican majority limited each member to a maximum of two committee and four subcommittee assignments. However, almost immediately exceptions started to be made. The party realized that while rules and formulas for organizing committees sounded good when talking about reform, they were less important than the need to retain effective numerical control of committees and satisfy members' political needs.

Only rarely is a committee seat taken away to punish a member. The last attempt to do this involved a House committee at the start of the 98th Congress in 1983. The Democrats attempted to discipline Phil Gramm, D-Texas, for leaking details of their secret caucuses on the Budget Committee in the previous Congress to the Reagan administration. The Steering and Policy Committee did not renominate Gramm to the Budget Committee. He promptly resigned from the House and was reelected as a Republican, and was then returned to the committee. (See box, *Loss of Committee Positions as Punishment, p. 568.*)

In the 104th Congress Appropriations Chairman Bob Livingston, R-La., removed conservative freshman Mark Neumann, R-Wis., from the powerful Defense Appropriations subcommittee because Neumann opposed Republican spending priorities. The outcry from the huge freshman class, however, proved so intense that Speaker Gingrich had to mollify Neumann with an additional committee assignment on the Budget Committee, bumping a senior member off to make room.

THE SENIORITY FACTOR

Both parties in each chamber generally follow seniority in positioning members on committees and in filling vacancies, with new members being ranked at the bottom of their committees. However, starting in 1974 the House Democratic Caucus began the practice of occasionally bypassing seniority if a chairman had been nonresponsive to party policies. (See box, *Benefits of Seniority, p. 570.*)

More recently, some conservative Senate Republicans, once in the majority after the 1994 elections, argued that fealty to party policy should play a more significant role in determining

LOSS OF COMMITTEE POSITIONS AS PUNISHMENT

Stripping a member of his or her position on a committee as a punishment for political heresy has been resorted to occasionally on Capitol Hill. In 1866, for example, three Senate Republican committee chairmen were dropped to the bottom of their committees for failing to vote with the Radical Republicans on overriding a presidential veto of a civil rights bill.

In 1859 the Senate Democratic Caucus removed Stephen A. Douglas, D-Ill., from the chairmanship of the Committee on Territories because he refused to go along with President James Buchanan and the southern wing of the party on the question of slavery in the territories.

In 1923 Sen. Albert B. Cummins, R-Iowa, lost his chairmanship of the Interstate Commerce Committee in a fight with the Progressive wing of his party. But the next-ranking Republican, Sen. Robert M. La Follette, R-Wis., was then passed over because of his unpopularity with the regulars of the party, and the chairmanship was given to the ranking Democrat, Ellison D. Smith, D-S.C.

Members of the Progressive wing of the Republican Party in the House also were denied the fruits of seniority in this period after they put up their own candidate for Speaker in 1925. Two of their leaders were ousted from their committee chairmanships for having campaigned as La Follette Progressives, and nine GOP members from the Wisconsin delegation who voted with the insurgents' candidate for Speaker were either dropped to the bottom rank on their committees or moved to less prestigious committees. La Follette had been the Progressive Party's candidate for president in 1924.

In 1965 and 1969 the House Democratic Caucus dropped three southern Democrats to the bottom of their committees because two of them had campaigned for presidential candidate Sen. Barry Goldwater, R-Ariz., in 1964 and the other for former Alabama governor George C. Wallace (American Independent) in 1968.

Another southern Democrat who had supported Goldwater in 1964, Sen. Strom Thurmond, S.C., avoided party discipline by switching to the Republican Party. Republicans rewarded him by allowing him to carry over his seniority rights to the GOP side of his committees.

In 1983 House Democrats stripped conservative Rep. Phil Gramm of Texas of his seat on the Budget Committee because of his two-year collaboration with the White House in supporting President Ronald Reagan's budget. Gramm's apostasy was especially aggravating to the Democratic leadership because he had been placed on the committee with the strong support of Majority Leader Jim Wright, D-Texas, after Gramm had given assurances that he would be a team player. Gramm resigned from Congress, switched to the Republican Party, and won his seat back in a special election. And then the Republicans put him right back on the Budget Committee.

In 1995, some conservative Senate Republicans advocated stripping Sen. Mark O. Hatfield, R-Ore., of his chairmanship of the Appropriations Committee because he had cast the lone Republican—and deciding—vote which defeated a balanced budget amendment to the Constitution. The amendment was a major element in the new Republican majority's legislative agenda and had earlier passed the House for the first time. After debate in the Republican Conference, no action was taken against Hatfield. He retained the chairmanship but announced shortly thereafter that he would not seek reelection.

chairmanships. The criticism was aimed at Senate Appropriations Committee Chairman Mark Hatfield, R-Ore., in 1995 after he cast the deciding—and only—Republican vote against a balanced budget constitutional amendment on the Senate floor, a vote that resulted in defeat of the long-cherished GOP proposal. The Republican Conference declined to discipline Hatfield.

Sometimes arcane questions of congressional seniority can even play a role in presidential politics. In 1995, it was known that Sen. Phil Gramm, R-Texas, a candidate for the party's presidential nomination, wanted an open seat on the prestigious Finance Committee. However, the front-runner, Majority Leader Bob Dole, R-Kan., reportedly urged more senior senators to claim available seats to block Gramm. Since Republican senators can claim such posts in order of seniority, Gramm was, at least momentarily, stymied. He did finally gain a seat on the committee later in the Congress.

Members who stay on the same committee from one Congress to another are given the same seniority ranking they had in the previous Congress unless a death, resignation, or retirement on the committee allows them to move up a notch. But if members, even senior members, transfer from one committee to another they are ranked at the bottom in seniority on their new committees. There are exceptions to these rules in unusual circumstances. The five Democratic House members and the two Democratic senators who switched to the Republican Party in 1995 were given some seniority on their new committee assignments or carried their existing seniority with them on the same committee. This helped newly minted Republican Senators Ben Nighthorse Campbell of Colorado and Richard Shelby of Alabama move through the ranks so quickly that they found themselves committee chairmen as the 105th Congress began.

As a rule members of Congress remain on their major committees throughout their careers, gradually working their way up in seniority. Those who do wish to switch, usually to one of the exclusive committees in the House (Appropriations, Commerce, Rules, Ways and Means) or the "Super A" committees in the Senate (Armed Services, Appropriations, Finance, Foreign Relations) make the effort very early in their careers before they accumulate too much seniority on their original assignments and lose the incentive to leave. If a member continues to be reelected and does not have an equally successful, ambitious, and younger colleague ahead of him or her on the committee roster, that member usually can expect to become a chairman or ranking minority member.

Changes in Democratic Caucus rules in the House beginning during the 1970s were therefore extraordinarily controversial, not only because they allowed far greater ease in challenging the reelection of chairmen but because in certain circumstances a junior member who challenged a chairman successfully could jump over others less daring. The defeat of a chairman by the right opponent at a particular time could affect not only the career of the ousted chairman but the long-term futures of other members who might be bypassed. The most dramatic instance of this occurred when seventh-ranking Les Aspin, D-Wis., ousted Chairman Melvin Price, D-Ill., of the Armed Services Committee in 1984. Price lost, 118–121, on the first up-down vote, which then opened the process for other candidates to run against each other. Aspin then defeated second-ranking Charles E. Bennett, D-Fla., also effectively jumping over four other senior, and older, Democrats who either would not contest the chairmanship because they respected the seniority tradition and backed Bennett or could not because they did not have the political strength to compete. If Aspin had not run and won at that time, it is possible that some of these members would have achieved the chairmanship through seniority in later years.

A similar example occurred in 1994 when David Obey, D-Wis., ranked fifth on the Appropriations Committee, won a contest over Neal Smith of Iowa, the third-ranking Democrat. Chairman William H. Natcher, D-Ky., and the second-ranking Democrat, former Chairman Jamie L. Whitten, Miss., had been incapacitated by illness. Smith's defeat was used by his Republican opponent as a sign of his ineffectiveness and he lost his bid for reelection. In addition the elderly Sidney Yates of Illinois, ranked fourth, was effectively removed from any chance of succession.

Many factors are involved in the decisions of the party leadership in assigning new members to committees, but once the member has the seat seniority remains the most important single factor in determining his or her advancement on that committee.

In the Senate the Democratic committee roster is drawn up by the Democratic Steering Committee, whose chairman and members are appointed by the party leader. The Senate Republican committee roster is drawn up by the Republican Committee on Committees, which is appointed by the chairman of the Republican Conference. Republican Party leaders are ex officio members.

The committee assignment process in the House, with 435 members, four delegates, and a resident commissioner involved, can be quite complex in itself and is made more so by mechanisms to ensure that various factions are fairly represented. The Democrats have had basically the same system since 1974. The Republicans have used different methods but by the mid-1990s had a system that was similar in many respects.

The Democratic committee roster is drawn up by the party's Steering Committee, a far larger body than its Republican counterpart. The Steering Committee is chaired by the minority leader (or Speaker, if in the majority). In the 106th Congress it consisted of the whip; caucus chairman; caucus vice chairman; chairman of the Democratic Congressional Campaign Committee; a cochairman of the Steering Committee; two vice chairmen of the Steering Committee; four chief deputy whips; a freshman class representative; twelve members appointed from equal regions; ten members appointed by the leader (or Speaker); and the ranking members of the Appropriations, Budget, Commerce, Rules, and Ways and Means committees. The number of leadership-appointed members has increased steadily. Each member has only one vote. (From 1911 until 1974 Democratic committee assignments were made by the Democratic members of the Ways and Means Committee.) An exception applies to the Democratic members of the Rules and House Administration committees. In 1974, the caucus rules gave the Speaker (or minority leader, after the 1994 elections) the power to nominate all party members of Rules. House Administration was included under this provision in 1994. Nominations to all standing committees are subject to ratification by the caucus.

Republican committee nominations in the House are determined by the party's Steering Committee, which is chaired by the Speaker. In the 106th Congress it also consisted of the floor ("majority") leader; whip; chief deputy whip; conference chair; policy committee chair, vice-chair, and secretary; National Republican Congressional Committee (campaign committee) chair in the 105th and 106th Congresses; the chairmen of the Appropriations, Budget, Rules, and Ways and Means committees; nine members elected from geographic regions; one "small state" representative; and one member each from the class elected to the 104th, 105th, and 106th class.

The two parties' systems diverge as the Republicans allocate additional voting strength to the Speaker and floor leader and make allowances for the needs of small states. (The Democrats' approach was to allow the party leader to appoint additional members to the committee.) The Speaker receives five votes and the floor leader two. The Speaker can give away up to two of his votes to other members he may appoint to the committee; Gingrich gave these to the vice chair and secretary of the Republican conference. If members elected to represent the nine regions come from states that have four or more Republican members, a "small state" group will be triggered to elect a member to Steering. The "small state" group will be composed of states that have three or fewer Republican members.

The Rules Committee and House Administration are again exceptions. GOP members of those committees are nominated by the Speaker (or minority leader, as the case may be).

Once the committee rosters are approved by the two parties in each chamber, they are incorporated in resolutions and put to votes before the full chambers. With approval usually automatic the votes merely formalize recommendations by the two parties and the party ratios previously negotiated by the leadership. Neither party interferes with the individual committee assignments made by the other; to attempt to do so would be a serious violation of comity. However, the minority may not attempt to exceed the allotment of seats on any committee

BENEFITS OF SENIORITY

There are three kinds of "seniority" in Congress:

- Seniority within the chamber among the entire House or Senate membership
- Seniority within a political party in the chamber
- Seniority on a committee

The second and third kinds are linked, because members are chosen for service on committees by the political parties and listed in order of seniority only with others from the same party. Members elected to a committee at the same time are then ranked in order of their full chamber seniority.

Seniority within the House and Senate as a whole is of limited importance but it helps determine who has access to the most desirable office space and a few other privileges. Representatives and senators choose their offices by order of chamber seniority. Senior members also have the right to claim a limited number of suites in the Capitol building itself as private "hideaways" for their personal use, which provides extra space and reduces the need to return to their regular offices after voting.

The most important leadership positions in Congress—House Speaker and Majority Leader of the Senate—have never been filled on the basis of seniority. *(The Seniority System, p. 544.)*

SENATE SENIORITY

The most senior member of the majority party in the Senate is elected automatically to the virtually powerless office of president pro tempore, a position mentioned in the Constitution. The president pro tempore has the right to preside in the absence of the president of the Senate (the vice president of the United States) and may often be from the opposite party as the vice president. This senator may wield substantial influence in another role because his longevity would almost certainly also make him chairman of a committee. In the 105th Congress, president pro tempore Strom Thurmond,

R-S.C., chaired the Armed Services Committee. His Democratic predecessor was Sen. Robert C. Byrd, D-W.Va., who was simultaneously Appropriations Committee chairman and before that a former majority and minority leader. By law the president pro tempore is next in the line of succession to the presidency after the Speaker of the House.

The seniority system has its greatest impact within each political party for determining rank on committees.

Senators and representatives are given a seniority ranking vis-à-vis party colleagues in their chamber at the beginning of each two-year term of Congress.

Senate rank generally is determined according to the official date of the beginning of a member's service, which is January 3 except in the case of a new member sworn in after Congress is in session. For those elected or appointed to fill unexpired terms, the date of appointment, certification, or swearing-in determines the senator's rank.

When senators are sworn in on the same date, custom decrees that those with prior political experience take precedence. Counted as political experience, in order of importance, are any previous Senate service, service as vice president, House service, service in the president's cabinet, and service as a governor. In the past a senator who was retiring or was defeated for reelection occasionally left office a few days before the end of his term, allowing his successor to be appointed and thereby gain a few days' seniority over other freshman senators. In 1980, however, Senate Republicans and Democrats, acting separately, eliminated the principal advantages of this practice. Members appointed to fill out the remaining days of their predecessors' terms no longer were given an edge in obtaining their choice of committee assignments.

If all other factors are equal, senators are ranked by the population of their state in determining seniority.

Within each state delegation in the Senate the member who as-

awarded to it by the majority or its assignment resolution would be rejected on the floor. On several occasions House Republicans, when in the minority, forced votes on Democratic committee assignments to protest what they regarded as excessively advantageous majority committee ratios on some committees. In 1995 the Democrats responded in kind by forcing a vote on the assignment of party-switcher Greg Laughlin, R-Texas, to the Ways and Means Committee, which further expanded the majority's ratio there from that set at the beginning of the 104th Congress. In 1997, the Republicans moved to table (kill) a Democratic committee assignment resolution when they believed the minority was attempting to increase its strength on a committee without permission, but after brief discussion the misunderstanding was cleared up and an embarrassing vote avoided.

PLUM ASSIGNMENTS

In both chambers committee assignments are extremely important to members. The Senate, with fewer political selection procedures and proportionately more plum seats than the House, tends to see less maneuvering, lobbying, and horse-trading for desired committee slots. There are fewer members competing for influence and looser floor rules than in the House. Each senator therefore has a greater chance to affect legislation of all stripes.

In the House influence often is closely related to the committee or committees on which a member serves. Moreover assignment to a powerful committee virtually guarantees large campaign contributions.

Just wanting to be on a committee is not enough. In most cases members have to fight for assignments to the best com-

sumed office first, regardless of party, is always referred to as "the senior senator from (state)" while the other is "the junior senator."

HOUSE SENIORITY

In the House being the most senior member carries no formal status, although by custom the member with the longest period of consecutive service, irrespective of party, administers the oath of office to the Speaker when a new Congress convenes. In the 105th Congress that was Rep. John D. Dingell, D-Mich. The most senior member from each state may sometimes be referred to as the "dean of the delegation," regardless of party, and in some state delegations may preside over delegation meetings if any are held.

Rank in the House generally is determined by the official date of the beginning of a member's service, January 3, except when a representative is elected to fill a vacancy. In such cases the date of election determines the rank. When members enter the House on the same date they are ranked in order of consecutive terms of House service. Any former members returning to the House are ranked above other freshmen, starting with those with the most previous terms of service. Experience as a senator or governor is disregarded.

These factors are taken into account when committee assignments are made by each party to decide the order of seniority in which members will rank along with others of their party on each committee.

Members chosen to fill an open seat on a committee always rank below those who served in the previous Congress and are being reappointed, except in very unusual circumstances. For example, several Democratic members who switched to the Republican Party in the 104th Congress received seniority while remaining on the same committee or moving to a new one. Often when several vacancies on a committee are being filled by each party's Steering Committee at the same time, a junior member may be chosen before a more senior member wins a seat. In the committee roster the member with more House seniority would nonetheless be ranked ahead of the other.

Other procedures have evolved to deal with members who have equal seniority in the House. If several members of equal seniority win seats on the same committee at the same time, the order in which they are ranked could have significant consequences decades later. In 1993 Rep. Norman Y. Mineta, D-Calif., was nominated to fill the vacant chairmanship of the Public Works and Transportation Committee because he had been ranked first on the Democratic committee list by lot ahead of Rep. James L. Oberstar, D-Minn., in 1975 when both were freshmen. At that time Oberstar had actually been selected first by the Steering Committee. Twenty years later the Democratic Caucus changed the rule so that, in cases such as this, members of equal seniority would be ranked in the order they were selected in the Steering Committee.

Neither party gives formal recognition to prior service on a committee as a factor in seniority. In the 105th Congress, however, Republicans gave Rep. Bob Smith, R-Ore., not only seniority but the chairmanship of the Agriculture Committee. Smith, who had retired from the House and the committee in 1995, was promised the chairmanship if he agreed to return and ensure continued GOP control of the House seat after his one-term successor became embroiled in scandal. With his mission accomplished Smith declined to run again in 1998. Democrats also rewarded a former member who was returning to the House, Rep. David Price, N.C., (1987–1995, 1997–), who wanted back the Appropriations Committee seat he had lost with his election defeat. While the Democratic Caucus in the 104th Congress had agreed to eventually restore seats to incumbents ousted from their committees by party ratio changes, Price did not qualify because he was not a member in that Congress. Nonetheless, on Appropriations he was ranked ahead of Rep. Chet Edwards, D-Texas, a sitting member who was switching committee assignments to join Appropriations.

mittees. In each chamber a few committees are considered most powerful and difficult to get on. But congressional leaders often have to go looking for "volunteers" to serve on less attractive panels.

Traditionally the premier House committees sought by representatives have been Appropriations, Rules, and Ways and Means, although the attraction of Rules under the Democrats was reduced after its members were nominated directly by the Speaker and lost much of their power to operate and vote independently. In the 1980s members also avidly sought seats on Budget and Energy and Commerce (now simply Commerce). In the 1990s Public Works and Transportation (now Transportation and Infrastructure), often either desired or reviled by members for its traditional "pork barrel" programs, regained popularity so quickly that there were jokes that the public seats in the committee room would have to be removed to accommodate all of the new members.

In the Senate the most popular committees traditionally have been Appropriations and Finance. Both the Budget Committee and Armed Services have also been in demand. Foreign Relations, once considered highly prestigious, fell steadily in influence and desirability after the defeat of Chairman J. William Fulbright, D-Ark., in 1974 because of a series of weak chairmen and its continuing inability to pass major authorization bills. After Republicans took control in 1995 activist conservative Chairman Jesse Helms, R-N.C., was credited with helping to revive the committee, but it never regained its former stature.

While other panels wax and wane, Appropriations, Finance, and Ways and Means have never been wholly eclipsed because they control the flow of money into and out of federal coffers.

Seniority still plays a major role in the power structure of both houses of Congress. In 1998 by virtue of his seniority Strom Thurmond, R-S.C., was president pro tempore of the Senate and chairman of the Armed Services Committee, but in 1999 he chose to give up his committee post.

In the 1980s and 1990s these taxing and spending committees were thrust to the center of action more than ever before by Congress's increasing tendency to pile most of its legislative work onto a handful of fiscal measures.

Committee Procedures

Committee procedures are regulated by Senate and House rules that incorporate many of the provisions in the Legislative Reorganization Acts of 1946 and 1970 and other measures. In many cases these rules serve to protect minority rights and the rights of witnesses at committee hearings.

One of the basic goals of the 1946 act was to standardize committee procedures in regard to holding regular meeting days, keeping committee records and votes, reporting legislation, requiring a majority of committee members to be in attendance as a condition of transacting committee business, and following set procedures during hearings.

The 1946 rules were not uniformly observed by all committees. The continuing dissatisfaction with committee operations led in the 1970 reorganization act to further efforts to reform committee procedures, particularly to make them more democratic and accountable to the membership and the public. The House has more restrictive provisions than the Senate but the majority still has broad flexibility in running a committee's business.

Senate and House committees are required to establish and publish rules of procedure. Each chamber's standing committees must also fix regular meeting days, although chairman are authorized to call additional meetings and set an agenda.

The rules also must contain procedures under which a com-

mittee majority may call a meeting if the chairman fails to do so, even though use of such a procedure would be a serious affront to a chairman. House rules also allow a committee majority using this process to place items of its choosing on the agenda.

An attempt to undercut a chairman's authority over committee meetings actually was made in the Senate Foreign Relations Committee in 1997 after Chairman Jesse Helms, R-N.C., declared his refusal to hold a hearing on President Clinton's nomination of Massachusetts governor William Weld to be ambassador to Mexico. Helms was adamantly opposed to the liberal Weld, even though he was a fellow Republican, for a variety of philosophical reasons. It appeared likely that a majority of both the committee and the Senate would confirm Weld if allowed to vote. A committee majority was able to force Helms to convene a meeting but was unable to take control of the agenda away from him. With the Senate parliamentarian sitting near him, Helms allowed no debate on the Weld nomination and spent most of the meeting denouncing his opponents. The episode illustrated how little Senate traditions have changed despite reforms of the rules. Senators are still unwilling to push powerful colleagues too far.

Committees were required by the 1970 act to keep transcripts of their meetings and to make public all roll-call votes. In the House the rules require that information about committee votes be made available to the public at the committees' offices. The committees are directed to provide a description of each amendment, motion, order, or "other proposition" voted on, the name of each committee member voting for or against the issue, and the names of those present but not voting. The rules also require that the results of all votes to report legislation be published in the committee reports.

In 1995 the rules were further amended to require that on all votes conducted in a committee markup on a reported bill or other matter reported to the House the report contain the number of votes cast for or against and how individual members voted.

In the Senate the rules are less specific. They require that a committee's report on a bill include the results of roll-call votes on "any measure or any amendment thereto" unless the results have been announced previously by the committee. Senate rules require that in reporting roll-call votes the position of each voting member is to be disclosed.

The rules stipulate that it is the chairman's "duty" to see to it that legislation approved by his or her committee is reported. And there are procedures by which a committee majority may force a bill out of committee if the chairman refuses to bring it up for consideration or to report it after the committee has acted favorably. The rules prohibit a committee from reporting any measure unless a majority of its members are actually present. Members were allowed time to file supplemental and minority views for inclusion in committee reports, but in the House Republicans restricted the minority's longstanding rights to have three full days following the vote on reporting a bill to submit them. In 1997 the rule was amended to reduce the time by counting the day in which the committee ordered a bill reported as the first day.

House rules require committees and subcommittees to announce hearings at least one week in advance unless the chairman and ranking minority member jointly, or the committee itself by vote, sets a shorter period. A Republican proposal to give this power to the chairman alone was successfully resisted by the minority in 1995. In most circumstances committees are required to conduct meetings and hearings in open session and to require witnesses to file written statements in advance. The rules allow minority party members to call witnesses during at least one day of hearings on a subject.

Jurisdictional Conflicts

Most bill referrals to committees are routine matters handled by the parliamentarians of each chamber. Committee jurisdictions outlined in each chamber's rules as well as precedents and public laws normally dictate where a bill is sent. But sometimes things are not quite so clear-cut.

Jurisdictional disputes between and among committees have been evident since the inception of the standing committee system. The Legislative Reorganization Act of 1946 attempted to eliminate the problem by defining each committee's jurisdiction in detail. But the 1946 act was not able to eliminate the problem.

As early as 1947 a fight broke out in the Senate over referral of the controversial armed forces unification bill. In the House the measure had been handled by the Committee on Executive Expenditures (now the Government Reform Committee), which had jurisdiction over all proposals for government reorganization. But in a Senate floor vote that chamber's Armed Services Committee successfully challenged the claim of the Expenditures Committee (now the Governmental Affairs Committee) to jurisdiction over the bill.

Such problems have continued to arise because the complexities of modern legislative proposals sometimes make it impossible to define jurisdictional boundaries precisely.

In the House the problem has been aggravated by a failure to restructure the committee system to meet new developments and national problems. The problem of conflicting and overlapping jurisdictions became acutely obvious in the 1970s as Congress attempted to formulate a coherent energy policy. When President Jimmy Carter in 1977 submitted his comprehensive national energy program the impending jurisdictional tangle forced Speaker Thomas P. "Tip" O'Neill Jr., D-Mass., to establish an ad hoc energy committee to review the work of five House committees and to guide energy legislation through the House. (An attempt to consolidate energy responsibilities in one committee as the Senate had done in 1977 was soundly defeated in the House in 1980.)

Occasionally when the opportunity arises a bill is drafted in such a way that it will be referred to a committee favorable to it.

The 1963 civil rights bill, for example, was worded somewhat differently in each chamber so that it would be referred to the Judiciary Committee in the House and the Commerce Committee in the Senate. Both panels were chaired by strong proponents of the legislation, while the chairmen of the House Interstate and Foreign Commerce Committee (now the Commerce Committee) and the Senate Judiciary Committee were opposed to the legislation. Congressional expert Oleszek noted that "careful drafting therefore coupled with favorable referral decisions in the House and Senate prevented the bill from being bogged down in hostile committees."[23]

Most bills, however, are subject to strict jurisdictional interpretation and rarely open to the legerdemain given the 1963 civil rights bill or the special handling the Speaker was able to give the 1977 energy bill. Oleszek observes:

Committees guard their jurisdictional turfs closely and the parliamentarians know and follow precedents. Only instances of genuine jurisdictional ambiguity provide opportunities for the legislative draftsman and referral options for the Speaker and the presiding officer of the Senate to bypass one committee in favor of another.[24]

MULTIPLE REFERRAL

The practice of multiple referral has been permitted in the Senate by unanimous consent, although it is used less frequently there than in the House, which did not permit the practice until the rules were amended in 1975. In that year the Speaker was permitted to refer a bill to more than one committee.

There were three types of multiple referrals: joint, when several committees considered a bill at the same time; sequential, when a bill was referred first to one committee, then to another, and so on; and split, when parts of a bill were referred to different committees. The most common method was joint referral; split referral was the least used. The Speaker was also given the authority subject to House approval to create an ad hoc committee to consider legislation when there were overlapping jurisdictions.

In 1977 the Speaker was permitted to impose reporting deadlines on the first committee or committees to which a bill was referred. In 1981 Speaker O'Neill announced that in making multiple referrals he would consider not only the content of the original bill but also amendments proposed by the reporting committee. And in 1983 the Speaker announced that he had the authority to designate a primary committee on jointly referred bills and impose time limits on other committees after the primary committee issued its report.

Since 1975 the number of multiple referrals has grown significantly in the House, and so has the importance of multiply referred bills. "In one form or another multiple referral is now employed on a multitude of significant legislation and exists as a prominent feature of congressional operations," wrote Melissa P. Collie and Joseph Cooper.[25]

Collie and Cooper interpreted the arrival of multiple referral in the House "as a signal that committee turf is no longer what it has been cracked up to be." They contended that legislators have

Because Republicans were in the majority in both houses in the 106th Congress (1999–2001), they chose all committee and subcommittee chairmen, while the Democrats selected ranking minority members. House practices are determined by the rules of the Republican Conference and Democratic Caucus, although the rules of the House stipulate certain requirements. The Senate guidelines are governed by the chamber's standing rules, with some party regulations. The guidelines below cover the principal assignment practices, but not every possible rule, contingency, or exception.

HOUSE REPUBLICANS

The Republicans, through their conference, divide the House committees into two categories: exclusive and nonexclusive. Exclusive committees are Appropriations; Commerce; Rules; and Ways and Means. Nonexclusive committees are almost everything else: Agriculture; Armed Services; Banking and Financial Services; Education and the Workforce; International Relations; Judiciary; Transportation and Infrastructure; Budget; Government Reform; House Administration; Resources; Science; Small Business; and Veterans' Affairs.

The Committee on Standards of Official Conduct is not classified and members may serve on it, as well as House Administration, irrespective of their other committee assignments. This practice technically violates a House rule sponsored by Republicans in the 104th Congress that limited all members to service on no more than two standing committees. In order to ensure that members serve on these less desirable, internal housekeeping panels, the Republicans got around the House rule by simply having the House vote to approve the additional committee assignments.

Republicans serving on an exclusive committee may not serve on any other standing committee, with the exception of the House Administration, Standards, and Budget committees. (The Budget Committee is required by House rules to have members from the Appropriations and Ways and Means committees). GOP membership on the Budget Committee includes three members each from the Appropriations and the Ways and Means committees. (Other GOP Budget members include one member appointed by the Republican leadership.)

Chairmen of full committees are recommended by the Steering Committee without regard to seniority and are voted on by secret ballot of the conference. However, the Speaker nominates the chairman and other Republican members of the Rules and House Administration committees, subject to conference approval. If any nominee is rejected by the conference, the Steering Committee, or Speaker, as the case may be, must make a new nomination until one is approved. Development of procedures for the selection of Republican subcommittee chairmen and members is at the discretion of the chairman of a committee, unless a majority of the GOP members of the full committee disapproves.

No Republican may serve as the chairman of more than one standing committee or subcommittee of a standing committee, although chairmen of the Standards and House Administration committees are exempt from the restriction. The chairman of the Appro-priations Committee is not permitted to head a subcommittee of that committee. A subcommittee chairman of a standing committee may chair a subcommittee of the Permanent Select Committee on Intelligence. A 1995 House rules change limits committee and subcommittee chairmen to three terms in these positions.

HOUSE DEMOCRATS

The rules of the Democratic Caucus have many similarities to the House Republican Conference procedures but are more complex. The same committees are classified as exclusive or nonexclusive. Members assigned to an exclusive committee may be on no other standing committee, but Budget, House Administration, and Standards are again the exceptions. Two Democrats each from the Appropriations Committee and the Ways and Means Committee serve on the Budget Committee, as well as one leadership member appointed by the minority leader. (When the Democrats controlled the House, the majority leader always occupied this slot.)

Minority members of the Permanent Select Committee on Intelligence and joint committees are selected by the minority leader and then appointed by the Speaker.

No Democrat may serve on more than two nonexclusive committees, with exceptions allowed for House Administration and also for Standards.

Democrats are nominated to serve on most committees by the Steering Committee, subject to Democratic Caucus approval. Members of the Rules and House Administration committees are nominated by the minority leader subject to caucus approval.

The rules of the caucus are more restrictive than those of the House regarding service on the Budget Committee. Democratic Budget Committee members may serve for only three terms out of every five consecutive terms, instead of the four-of-six terms permitted in House rules and used by Republicans. Exceptions to this limitation include the Democratic leadership–designated member of the Budget Committee, who may stay indefinitely, as well as the ranking minority member, who may stay on for an additional two years, if required, in order to serve a second term in that position.

Democrats are limited to one full committee ranking minority member position. They may not simultaneously rank on another full, select, permanent select, special, ad hoc, or joint committee. Ranking minority members of a standing committee may not rank on any subcommittee, but the ranking members of the House Administration and Standards Committee are exempted. The ranking member of the Appropriations Committee may rank on a subcommittee of that committee. No Democrat may rank on more than one subcommittee of a committee or select committee with legislative jurisdiction. Ranking minority members of the following nonexclusive committees, which were previously classified as "major committees" prior to a 1995 rules change, may not serve on any other committee: Agriculture, Banking and Financial Services, Education and the Workforce, Judiciary, Armed Services, and Transportation and Infrastructure.

Most nominations for ranking minority members are made by the Steering Committee and without regard to seniority, though it is extremely rare for Steering to take the initiative to reject an incumbent. (It most recently did so in the 105th Congress, nominating John LaFalce of New York as ranking minority member of the Banking Committee instead of incumbent Henry B. Gonzalez of Texas. Gonzalez then challenged him before the caucus. With a third candidate also in the race, Gonzalez finished first on the initial ballot, but lacked a majority. LaFalce then withdrew and Gonzalez was confirmed for another term. The caucus votes on all nominations individually by secret ballot.)

Exceptions to the practice of Steering Committee nominations are the Rules Committee and House Administration Committee ranking members, who are nominated by the minority leader, and the ranking member of the Budget Committee, who is selected from among members choosing to run for the position on the floor of the caucus.

Subcommittee ranking members of the Appropriations Committee also are voted on by secret ballot in the party caucus. The committee caucus may use subcommittee seniority as the criterion in nominating candidates for subcommittee chairmen. Beginning with the 102nd Congress (1991–1993), subcommittee ranking members of the Ways and Means Committee also have been ratified by the Democratic Caucus.

On other committees, ranking subcommittee members are elected by the Democrats on their committee. (Special rules allow such choices to be brought before the full caucus for a vote if they are especially controversial, but this has never been done.) Committee members are entitled to bid for subcommittee ranking memberships in the order of their seniority on the full committee, with members choosing which subcommittee they would bid for, and an up-or-down vote is then held on that member's candidacy. If a candidacy is rejected, under a 1995 rules change the next member in order of committee seniority can bid for any open subcommittee ranking post; before the change, the committee had to fill the post selected by the rejected candidate before moving on.

SENATE REPUBLICANS AND DEMOCRATS

The Senate divides its committees into "major" and "minor" committees in its Rule XXV—although those words are not actually used in the rule. Major committees are Agriculture, Nutrition, and Forestry; Appropriations; Armed Services; Banking, Housing, and Urban Affairs; Commerce, Science, and Transportation; Energy and Natural Resources; Environment and Public Works; Finance; Foreign Relations; Governmental Affairs; Judiciary; and Labor and Human Resources. Minor committees are Budget; Rules and Administration; Veterans' Affairs; Small Business; Aging; Intelligence; and Joint Economic. Committees on Ethics, Indian Affairs, and the Joint Committee on Taxation are also considered minor committees but do not count toward the service limits outlined in the paragraph below, nor does membership on any joint committee that a senator is required by law to serve on.

Senate rules also regulate both service and chairmanships, but chamber rules may be supplemented or superseded by party rules,

sometimes resulting in variations in practice from one Congress to the next. Exceptions are also granted to individual senators from various rules.

Senators sit on two major committees and may serve on one minor committee. Party practices limit senators to service on only one of the so-called elite or "Super A" committees—Appropriations, Armed Services, Finance, and Foreign Relations, although there have been exceptions. Senators are limited to membership on three subcommittees of each major committee on which they serve (the Appropriations Committee is exempt from the limit) and on two subcommittees of their minor committee. The chairman or ranking minority member of a committee may serve as an ex officio member without a vote on any subcommittee of that committee. There are numerous exceptions to these rules that protect senators who would have been in violation at the time they took effect. By agreement of the majority and minority leaders, the membership of a committee may be temporarily increased above the size limits set by the rules— but by no more than two members—in order to maintain majority party control, and any senator serving on a committee for this purpose would be allowed to serve on three major committees.

Both parties guarantee their members one seat on a major committee before any member receives a second top assignment.

The Senate requires that membership on the Select Intelligence Committee be rotated. No senator may serve on the committee for more than eight successive years.

A senator generally may serve as chairman or ranking minority member of only one standing, select, special, or joint committee, though again there may be exceptions, especially with regard to service on joint committees. A Republican Conference rule effective in 1997 limits GOP senators to no more than three Congresses of service as a committee chairman.

Under Senate rules, the chairman of a major committee may serve as chairman of only one subcommittee among all of his or her major committees and one subcommittee of his or her minor committee. The chairman of a minor committee may not serve as chairman of any subcommittee on that committee; he or she may chair one subcommittee of each of his or her major committees. A senator who does not otherwise chair a committee may chair only one subcommittee of each committee on which he or she serves.

The Senate Republican Conference's Committee on Committees makes committee assignments on major committees and the Rules and Administration Committee. Other assignments are made by the majority leader. Members of each Senate committee elect the chairmen of their committee by secret ballot subject to the approval of the Republican Conference. Votes in the Committee on Committees and in the conference are also by secret ballot.

Senate Democratic committee assignments and nominations for ranking minority members are made by the Steering Committee and circulated to all Senate Democrats. A party rule adopted in 1975 provides for a secret ballot vote on an individual nominee for chairman (or ranking member) if requested by 20 percent of the Senate's Democrats.

surrendered their exclusive autonomy over legislation for access to all legislation to which they have claims.[26]

The growth of multiple referrals in the House affected key aspects of the legislative process, including the Speaker's prerogatives, the work of the Rules Committee, floor proceedings, and relations with the executive branch and interest groups. It encouraged members, committees, and staff aides to negotiate with one another rather than acting separately as traditionally done, according to scholars Roger Davidson, Oleszek, and Thomas Kephart. "More importantly, the procedure at the same time has greatly augmented the powers of the Speaker and the Rules Committee, by strengthening their role in centralizing and coordinating the House's workload. That may well be the most profound effect of the multiple-referral procedure."[27] However these changes came with a price of greater complexity in the legislative process as bills had to be tracked through multiple locations and battles among committees over jurisdiction and the type of referrals they would receive, creating controversies that the Speaker was often called upon to mediate.

When Republicans assumed control of the House they instituted changes intended to streamline the process and reduce such distractions.

Joint referrals were replaced in 1995 in the House by a procedure that required the Speaker in cases in which more than one committee had a jurisdictional claim to designate a committee as the "primary" committee for consideration. Other committees could be granted secondary or sequential referrals with time limits at the Speaker's discretion. This is sometimes called "additional initial referral," perhaps to ease the loss of status by the other committees involved. The change was not radical inasmuch as the Speaker already had the power to designate a committee as the primary panel in cases of multiple referrals even though he rarely did so. The change did have the effect of simplifying the referral process and placing greater responsibility in the primary committees. It also reduced the intense competition among committees for referrals that sometimes had produced distracting jurisdictional wars among chairmen and staff during the period of Democratic rule, with the Speaker in the middle.

SPENDING RIVALS

The relationships between the Appropriations and authorizing committees traditionally have provided striking illustrations of intercommittee rivalries. Authorizing committees handle bills allowing funding, but usually only the Appropriations committees are permitted to consider the actual spending permitted for federal agencies and programs. There are exceptions for certain instances of "direct spending" approved by committees, such as entitlement programs authorized by permanent law.

The Appropriations committees are theoretically barred by the standing rules from inserting legislative provisions in their appropriations bills but they habitually do so, often out of necessity. Indeed, while the other committees often grumble about the usurpation of their authority by the appropriators, the committees also often cooperate because they must rely on the appropriations process to include provisions regulating the programs they administer if the normal authorization bills cannot be enacted.

The creation of the House and Senate Budget committees in 1974 added yet another dimension to committee rivalries. The new committees were charged with the task of preparing two congressional budget resolutions (later reduced to only one when the original procedure proved impractical) setting out and enforcing goals for spending and revenues in the next fiscal year and later years. They also were to monitor the revenue and spending actions of the House and Senate.

As the country became increasingly preoccupied with budget deficits in the 1980s, the power relationships among these various committees started to shift. The authorizing committees went from proposing various new programs to a fallback position of defending existing ones. "Squeezed between the budget resolution and appropriations stages there is little time left for debating the recommendations of the authorization committees," Oleszek observes. "As a result these panels have lost influence to the Appropriations and Budget committees."[28]

The Appropriations committees also benefited in the 1980s from Congress's increasing reliance on omnibus continuing appropriations resolutions that were used when legislators almost routinely failed to pass some or all of the individual appropriations bills. These bills in the 1980s and 1990s became vehicles for authorizing legislation. As a result, Deering and Smith note:

appropriators gained a voice in shaping legislation that they otherwise would not have had, particularly in conference. And the continuing resolutions gave appropriators—as well as other members through appeals to appropriators and through floor amendments—an opportunity to pursue legislative matters without the consent and cooperation of the affected authorizing committee.[29]

Yet the Appropriations committees also lost influence. They had to share power with party and budget leaders in negotiating budget resolutions and then had to operate within the rigid constraints of those resolutions.

Smith and Deering summed up the power shifts:

As partisan conflict over budget priorities intensified and produced policy stalemates among the House, Senate, and White House, both appropriations and authorizing committees lost autonomy. Party and Budget Committee leaders became central to resolving the conflict. Normal legislative procedures were ignored, set aside temporarily, and in some cases directly altered. All committees learned new legislative tricks to minimize the damage to programs they wanted to protect, but most could not avoid deep encroachments on their traditional autonomy. . . . Thus, in the quite unsettled power structure of Congress, leaders and budget committees fared well, appropriations committees survived but were injured, and authorizing committees took strong blows to their autonomy.[30]

But the Budget committees have had their ups and downs. After being considered power centers with seats carefully balanced, especially in the House, among various other committees and factions, they lost attraction as a committee assignment for members as available funds for discretionary government pro-

Senate Banking Committee members gather for the markup of banking legislation. The stack of papers in front of each senator are amendments to the legislation.

grams were squeezed out in the face of growing deficits. Members preferred the power of awarding funds for programs to other colleagues and to constituents but balked at the pain of searching for cuts year after year. Adoption of a budget resolution each year was often delayed by broad disagreements among the parties or between Congress and the president. Rep. Martin Russo, D-Ill., who rotated off the House Budget Committee in 1991, found service there so painful that he rejoiced, he said, that "my sentence is over."

After party control switched in the House in 1995 the Budget Committee regained visibility under the chairmanship of Rep. John Kasich, R-Ohio, a close ally of Speaker Gingrich. It also benefited from rules changes that expanded the committee's jurisdiction over the structure of the budget process itself. But once again factors beyond the control of Congress were bringing matters full circle. By the end of 1999 a soaring economy was pouring such huge amounts of tax revenue into the federal Treasury that a budget surplus was certain and promised to continue for years. This shifted debate to a subject members of Congress understood better: how to spend or cut taxes.

BUDGET SUMMITRY

The frequent use in the 1980s of executive-legislative budget conferences to work out fiscal issues added yet another twist to the power relationships. Authorizing and appropriations committees—already wary of a budget process that had shifted some of their control over tax and spending issues to the Budget committees—viewed the high-level talks, where budget decisions were further centralized, with even greater suspicion.

A 1989 budget-summit deal collapsed in part because chairmen of key committees required to enact the plan were not involved in crucial negotiations. The tax-writing committees were given a revenue-raising target without any agreement on how the figure would be attained.

Attempting to avoid a replay, congressional and White House

leaders involved key committee chairmen in a 1990 budget summit from the start. Although the authorizing committee chairmen were still excluded, the congressional negotiating team included the chairmen and ranking members of the tax-writing and Appropriations committees in both the House and Senate, along with the Budget committees and other congressional leaders.

After intermittent talks beginning in May 1990, two dozen congressional and White House negotiators in September went into seclusion at Andrews Air Force Base outside Washington, D.C., for what they hoped would be a final round of budget talks. A budget agreement ultimately was reached by eight congressional and administration officials.

But many members of Congress were not pleased with an agreement reached by a handful of leaders in secrecy away from Capitol Hill, a process that seemed to some observers to cast aside the committee system and political accountability. Many committee chairmen in the House were up in arms about provisions of the agreement that trod on their turf. More than half of the committee chairmen voted against the budget, along with seven of the thirteen Appropriations subcommittee chairmen. The summit agreement went down to humiliating defeat in the House, leading to a three-day shutdown of the government.

The budget crisis finally was resolved and the resulting budget reconciliation package boded further power shifts in the budget process. The new law gave the executive branch closer scrutiny of legislation as it was being crafted. But whatever the near-term outcome, the rivalries among the spending committees were certain to continue.

Oversight Mandate

In addition to their lawmaking function, committees bear important responsibilities for overseeing implementation of the laws already on the books. Congress has given the executive branch broad authority over the vast array of agencies and programs it has created. As the range of activities of the federal government has grown so too has the need for Congress to oversee how the executive branch administers the laws it has passed. Oleszek explains:

A thoughtful, well-drafted law offers no guarantee that the policy intentions of legislators will be carried out.... The laws passed by Congress are often general guidelines, and sometimes their wording is deliberately vague. The implementation of legislation involves the drafting of administrative regulations by the executive agencies and day-to-day program management by agency officials. Agency regulations and rules are the subject of "legislative oversight"—the continuing review by Congress of how effectively the executive branch is carrying out congressional mandates.[31]

Congress did not officially recognize its responsibility for oversight until enactment of the 1946 Legislative Reorganization Act. That law mandated that the House and Senate standing committees exercise "continuous watchfulness of the execution by the administrative agencies" of any laws under their jurisdiction. The 1946 law divided oversight responsibilities into three areas: the legislative or authorizing committees were to review government programs and agencies, the Appropriations committees were to review government spending, and the committees currently named House Government Reform and Senate Governmental Affairs were to probe for inefficiency, waste, and corruption in the federal government. But, as Oleszek points out, "to some degree all committees perform each type of oversight."[32]

Since enactment of the 1946 law Congress has passed several measures affecting oversight activities. In the 1970 Legislative Reorganization Act Congress increased staff assistance to all House and Senate committees, recommended that committees ascertain whether programs within their jurisdiction should be funded annually, and required most committees to issue oversight reports every two years.

Congress acted in 1974 to improve its oversight procedures when it passed the Congressional Budget and Impoundment Control Act. That act strengthened the role of the General Accounting Office (GAO) in acquiring fiscal, budgetary, and program-related information from federal agencies, authorized the GAO to establish an office to develop and recommend methods by which Congress could review and evaluate federal programs and activities, and authorized committees to assess the effectiveness of such programs and to require government agencies to carry out their own evaluations.

Congressional committees have a variety of ways of exercising their oversight responsibilities. The traditional and most obvious way is through normal legislative procedures. Congress can examine government activities through committee hearings and investigations ranging from routine reviews to such highly publicized probes as the 104th Congress's investigations of personnel firings at the White House travel office, access by Clinton administration officials to FBI files on former Republican White House staffers, and the Whitewater real estate deal involving President and Mrs. Clinton, and the 105th Congress's hearings on campaign finance law violations in the 1996 election and IRS abuses of taxpayers' rights.

It is often difficult to interest members in conducting routine oversight over government agencies unless there are visible political rewards for those participating. Oversight does not involve obtaining funds for projects or trading favors with colleagues. When the House mandated that most committees create subcommittees specifically devoted to oversight, the panels often became the last chosen in the internal subcommittee assignment bidding process and were often chaired by junior members.

There were some powerful members who vigorously pursued oversight agendas and employed the full range of Congress's investigative powers, in recent years most notably Rep. John D. Dingell, D-Mich., who chaired both the House Energy and Commerce Committee (1981–1995) and its oversight subcommittee. He conducted highly publicized investigations ranging across his committee's vast legislative domain, which he frequently fought to expand. After Democrats lost control of the House in 1995, in order to make more key subcommittee posts available for other members Dingell and most other committee ranking minority members were barred from also ranking on any subcommittee. Even though he no longer could control a committee or subcommittee agenda, Dingell vigorously but unsuccessfully fought the change, arguing that it needlessly downgraded the conduct of committee oversight and left it to junior members who either did not care or lacked the expertise to investigate effectively.

Committees can use their subpoena powers broadly to demand information from government agencies and even hold executive officials in contempt for failure to comply, subject to approval by the parent chamber. The House voted several times during the 1980s to hold executive branch officials in contempt, most notably Anne Gorsuch, the administrator of the Environmental Protection Agency during the Reagan administration.

In 1996 the House Government Reform and Oversight Committee voted to hold White House counsel Jack Quinn in contempt for refusing to respond to a committee subpoena for documents, generating controversy over whether a committee had the authority to vote contempt without first giving the person cited a chance to appear and offer some defense. The majority determined that it had the power to proceed; after the vote, White House compliance was obtained and no House vote on contempt was held.

The use of the contempt power may become a first resort, rather than a last, in highly charged, partisan confrontations between the branches over information. Late in 1997 Attorney General Janet Reno was threatened with contempt by the committee, even before she testified, when it was learned that the Department of Justice would not supply a copy of a memorandum from the director of the FBI to Reno reportedly outlining why he disagreed with her decision not to appoint an independent counsel to investigate allegations of improper fund-raising by the president, vice president, and others during the 1996 election campaign.

Alleged scandals in the Clinton administration provided many opportunities for congressional oversight and substantial media coverage. Republicans seemed to have concluded that by weakening the Democratic president, political prospects might improve for enactment of their legislative agenda.

The GOP leadership, especially in the House, took on a major new role in selecting topics for committees to examine. Leadership intervention extended so far as selecting subcommittee chairmen and obtaining additional funds for investigations and expenses in the biennial committee funding resolution passed by the House, and even afterwards

For example, in the 105th Congress Speaker Gingrich recommended that additional funds be allocated for the Education and the Workforce Committee to use to investigate organized labor. The money was subsequently provided on a party-line vote of the House Oversight Committee (which became the House Administration Committee in 1999), with no House vote required, using new House rules that allowed a "reserve fund" of extra money in the committee funding resolution that the Speaker could direct to special projects. Democrats called this a "slush fund," claiming that it undermined the requirements of fiscal discipline and advance planning that the committee funding resolution was supposed to place on committee activities. They also argued that the investigation was a sham intended as retribution to organized labor for its massive spending to overturn the Republican majority in the 1996 election. The Democrats demanded unsuccessfully that the full House vote on all such reallocations of funds. Republicans countered that flexibility was essential in the conduct of congressional oversight to deal both with new issues and expansions of previously planned investigations, and that Congress should not be straight-jacketed by funding priorities made very early in a two-year cycle.

Special reports required from agencies, investigations by agencies' inspectors general, audits by the GAO, and studies by congressional support agencies are other oversight tools. The substantial growth in reports required by Congress has triggered some complaints within both the executive branch and Congress that legislative committees are attempting to "micromanage" administrative details. The 104th Congress passed a "Reports Elimination Act" in response to these complaints to reduce the number of reports required but the traditional tension between the legislative and executive branches concerning oversight is unlikely to be relieved simply by paperwork reduction.

The legislative veto had been a popular oversight mechanism since 1932, when Congress began attaching to various statutes provisions giving one or both chambers or individual committees authority to veto government actions, regulations, and orders. The Supreme Court threw out the legislative veto in the 1983 *INS vs. Chadha* decision on the grounds that Congress could only exercise such power through the enactment of legislation presented to the president for signature or veto. Some of these provisions continue to exist in statutes, however, and can occasionally still be used under the rules of each chamber to make a political point, even though they no longer have legal effect. For example in 1998 Rep. Tom Campbell, R-Calif., used a provision of the War Powers Act to force a House vote on a concurrent resolution purporting to force withdrawal of U.S. troops from a peacekeeping mission in Bosnia. (The resolution was reported adversely from committee and defeated on the floor.) In 1999, similar votes occurred relating to NATO's military action against Serbia. Since *Chadha*, Congress has either rewritten many of these laws to pass constitutional muster or has found other informal ways to continue to exercise its influence.

Congress also has at its disposal nonstatutory controls, such as informal contacts between executive officials and committee members and staff, and statements made in committee and conference reports as well as statements during hearings and floor debates. Davidson and Oleszek observe: "Although there is no measure of their usage, nonstatutory controls may be the most common form of congressional oversight."[33]

NOTES

1. Walter J. Oleszek, *Congressional Procedures and the Policy Process,* 4th ed. (Washington, D.C.: CQ Press, 1996), 121.

2. Leroy N. Rieselbach, *Congressional Reform* (Washington, D.C.: CQ Press, 1986), 110.

3. Christopher J. Deering and Steven S. Smith, *Committees in Congress,* 3rd ed. (Washington, D.C.: CQ Press, 1997), 2.

4. Oleszek, *Congressional Procedures and the Policy Process,* 4th ed., 112.

5. George Goodwin Jr., *The Little Legislatures: Committees of Congress* (Amherst: University of Massachusetts Press, 1970).

6. Woodrow Wilson, *Congressional Government: A Study in American Politics* (Boston: Houghton Mifflin, 1885; Cleveland: Meridian Books, 1956), 59.

7. George B. Galloway, *Congress at the Crossroads* (New York: Crowell, 1946), 88.

8. Deering and Smith, *Committees in Congress,* 3rd ed., 26.

9. Galloway, *Congress at the Crossroads,* 139–144; Goodwin, *The Little Legislatures,* 11–12.

10. George H. Haynes, *The Senate of the United States* (Boston: Houghton Mifflin, 1938), vol. 1, 273–277.

11. Steven Smith and Christopher J. Deering, *Committees in Congress,* 2nd ed. (Washington, D.C.: CQ Press, 1990), 33.

12. Ibid., 42.

13. Randall B. Ripley, *Power in the Senate* (New York: St. Martin's Press, 1969), 23.

14. Ibid., 47.

15. Wilson, *Congressional Government,* 82.

16. Roger H. Davidson, "Subcommittee Government: New Channels for Policy Making," in *The New Congress,* ed. Thomas E. Mann and Norman J. Ornstein (Washington, D.C.: American Enterprise Institute, 1981), 105–108.

17. Deering and Smith, *Committees in Congress,* 3rd ed., 33.

18. Rieselbach, *Congressional Reform,* 45–46.

19. Norman J. Ornstein, Thomas E. Mann, and Michael J. Malbin, *Vital Statistics on Congress: 1997–1998* (Washington, D.C.: Congressional Quarterly, 1998), 123.

20. Senate Temporary Select Committee to Study the Senate Committee System, *First Report, with Recommendations; Structure of the Senate Committee System: Jurisdictions, Numbers and Sizes, and Limitations on Mem-

berships and Chairmanships, Referral Procedures, and Scheduling, 94th Cong., 2nd sess., 1976, 6.

21. Deering and Smith, *Committees in Congress,* 3rd ed., 141.

22. Ibid., 78–81.

23. Walter J. Oleszek, *Congressional Procedures and the Policy Process,* 3rd ed. (Washington, D.C.: CQ Press, 1989), 87.

24. Ibid., 88.

25. Melissa P. Collie and Joseph Cooper, "Multiple Referral and the 'New' Committee System in the House of Representatives," in *Congress Reconsidered,* 4th ed., ed. Lawrence C. Dodd and Bruce I. Oppenheimer (Washington, D.C.: CQ Press, 1989), 248.

26. Ibid., 254.

27. Roger H. Davidson, Walter J. Oleszek, and Thomas Kephart, "One Bill, Many Committees: Multiple Referrals in the U.S. House of Representatives," *Legislative Studies Quarterly* 13, 1 (February 1988), 4.

28. Oleszek, *Congressional Procedures and the Policy Process,* 3rd ed., 76.

29. Deering and Smith, *Committees in Congress,* 3rd ed., 201.

30. Smith and Deering, *Committees in Congress,* 2nd ed., 211.

31. Oleszek, *Congressional Procedures and the Policy Process,* 4th ed., 300.

32. Ibid., 301.

33. Roger H. Davidson and Walter J. Oleszek, *Congress and Its Members,* 7th ed. (Washington, D.C.: CQ Press, 2000), 327.

SELECTED BIBLIOGRAPHY

Cooper, Joseph. *Congress and Its Committees: A Historical Approach to the Role of Committees in the Legislative Process.* New York: Garland, 1988.

Davidson, Roger H. "Subcommittee Government: New Channels for Policy Making." In *The New Congress,* edited by Thomas E. Mann and Norman J. Ornstein, 99–133. Washington, D.C.: American Enterprise Institute, 1981.

Davidson, Roger H., and Walter J. Oleszek. *Congress and Its Members.* 7th ed. Washington, D.C.: CQ Press, 2000.

Deering, Christopher J., and Steven S. Smith. *Committees in Congress.* 3rd ed. Washington, D.C.: CQ Press, 1997.

Dodd, Lawrence C., and Bruce I. Oppenheimer, eds. *Congress Reconsidered.* 6th ed. Washington, D.C.: CQ Press, 1997.

Elving, Ronald D. *Conflict and Compromise: How Congress Makes the Law.* New York: Simon & Schuster, 1995.

Endersby, James W., and Karen M. McCurdy. "Committee Assignments in the U.S. Senate." *Legislative Studies Quarterly* 21 (1996): 219–234.

Evans, C. Lawrence. *Leadership in Committee: A Comparative Analysis of Leadership Behavior in the U.S. Senate.* Ann Arbor: University of Michigan Press, 1991.

Evans, C. Lawrence, and Walter J. Oleszek. *Congress Under Fire.* Boston: Houghton Mifflin, 1997.

Fenno, Richard F., Jr. *Congressmen in Committees.* Boston: Little, Brown, 1973.

Galloway, George B. *Congress at the Crossroads.* New York: Crowell, 1946.

Goodwin, George, Jr. *The Little Legislatures: Committees of Congress.* Amherst: University of Massachusetts Press, 1970.

Groseclose, Tim, and Charles Stewart. "The Value of Committee Seats in the House, 1947–1991." *American Journal of Political Science* 42 (April 1998): 453–474.

Hall, Richard L. *Participation in Congress.* New Haven, Conn.: Yale University Press, 1996.

Hall, Richard L., and C. Lawrence Evans. "The Power of Subcommittees." *Journal of Politics* 52 (May 1990): 335–355.

Haynes, George H. *The Senate of the United States.* 2 vols. Boston: Houghton Mifflin, 1938.

Hinckley, Barbara. *The Seniority System in Congress.* Bloomington: Indiana University Press, 1971.

Katz, Jonathan, and Brian Sala. "Careerism, Committee Assignments, and the Electoral Connection." *American Political Science Review* 90 (March 1996): 21–33.

Kiewiet, D. Roderick, and Mathew D. McCubbins. *The Logic of Delegation: Congressional Parties and the Appropriations Process.* Chicago: University of Chicago Press, 1991.

Krehbiel, Keith. *Pivotal Politics: A Theory of U.S. Lawmaking.* Chicago: University of Chicago Press, 1998.

Krehbiel, Keith, Kenneth A. Shepsle, and Barry Weingast. "Why Are Committees Powerful?" *American Political Science Review* 81 (September 1987): 929–945.

Longley, Lawrence D., and Walter J. Oleszek. *Bicameral Politics: Conference Committees in Congress.* New Haven, Conn.: Yale University Press, 1989.

Maltzman, Forrest. *Competing Principals: Committees, Parties, and the Organization of Congress.* Ann Arbor: University of Michigan Press, 1997.

McConachie, Lauros. *Congressional Committees.* New York: Crowell, 1898.

McGown, Ada C. *The Congressional Conference Committee.* New York: Columbia University Press, 1927.

Munson, Richard. *The Cardinals of Capitol Hill: The Men and Women Who Control Federal Spending.* New York: Grove Press, 1993.

Oleszek, Walter J. *Congressional Procedures and the Policy Process.* 4th ed. Washington, D.C.: CQ Press, 1996.

Ornstein, Norman J., Thomas E. Mann, and Michael J. Malbin. "Committees." Chap. 4 in *Vital Statistics on Congress: 1997–1998.* Washington, D.C.: Congressional Quarterly, 1998.

Parker, Glenn R., and Suzanne L. Parker. *Factions in House Committees.* Knoxville: University of Tennessee Press, 1985.

Reeves, Andree E. *Congressional Committee Chairmen: Three Who Made an Evolution.* Lexington: University of Kentucky Press, 1993.

Rieselbach, Leroy N. *Congressional Politics: The Evolving Legislative System.* 2nd ed. Boulder, Colo.: Westview, 1995.

Robinson, James A. *The House Rules Committee.* Indianapolis: Bobbs-Merrill, 1963.

Shepsle, Kenneth A. "The Changing Textbook Congress." In *Can the Government Govern?* edited by John E. Chubb and Paul E. Peterson, 238–266. Washington, D.C.: Brookings Institution, 1989.

———. *The Giant Jigsaw Puzzle: Democratic Committee Assignments in the Modern House.* Chicago: University of Chicago Press, 1978.

Shepsle, Kenneth A., and Barry R. Weingast. "The Institutional Foundations of Committee Power." *American Political Science Review* 81 (June 1987): 85–104.

Strahan, Randall W. *New Ways and Means: Reform and Change in a Congressional Committee.* Chapel Hill: University of North Carolina Press, 1990.

Unekis, Joseph K., and Leroy N. Rieselbach. *Congressional Committee Politics: Continuity and Change.* New York: Praeger, 1984.

U.S. Congress. House. Committee on Rules. *A History of the Committee on Rules: 1st to 97th Congress, 1789–1981.* 97th Cong., 2nd sess., 1982. Committee Print.

U.S. Congress. House. Select Committee on Committees. *Final Report of Select Committee on Committees.* 96th Cong., 2nd sess., 1980. H Rept 96-866.

U.S. Congress. Senate. Committee on Rules and Administration. *Report on Senate Operations 1988.* 100th Cong., 2nd sess., 1988. Committee Print 129.

U.S. Congress. Senate. Temporary Select Committee to Study the Senate Committee System. *First Report, with Recommendations; Structure of the Senate Committee System: Jurisdictions, Numbers and Sizes, and Limitations on Memberships and Chairmanships, Referral Procedures, and Scheduling.* 94th Cong., 2nd sess., 1976. S Rept 94-1395.

Van Beek, Stephen D. *Post-Passage Politics: Bicameral Resolution in Congress.* Pittsburgh: University of Pittsburgh Press, 1995.

CHAPTER 17

Congressional Staff

THOUSANDS OF PEOPLE work for Congress, a generally faceless mass of mostly young people who are an integral part of the legislative process. For the public, congressional staff members are represented by the voices at the other end of phone calls to members' offices, or the blurred faces behind members at televised congressional committee meetings. Staffers are drawn to Capitol Hill by the exciting prospect of being at the epicenter of important political, social, and economic issues, by the idealistic hope of making a difference in public service, and—often—by raw ambition.

Staff members cannot vote, but their imprint is everywhere—on legislation, politics, and public policy. The influence of congressional staff members is vast—too vast, say critics who believe they wield excessive power and cost too much tax money. But legislators reply that staffs provide the expertise on complex issues that members could never master alone.

Although thousands of people work for Congress, the term *congressional staff* as the term is commonly used applies to men and women who work for committees or for individual members. Capitol Hill staffers may be policy and legal experts—these usually work for congressional committees—or they may be versed in running an efficient office for a member, helping constituents, and doing whatever they can to get their bosses reelected. Members rely heavily on staff during all stages of the legislative process. Some staffers draft legislation, negotiate with lobbyists, and plot strategy for floor action. These "entrepreneurial staffers," a phrase coined by David Price, a political scientist and member of the House, are given considerable responsibility for legislative decision making, with members of Congress backstopping their efforts.[1]

Faced with more complex issues, more technical legislation, and more demanding constituents, members apparently have encouraged the growth of entrepreneurial staff.

Many members of Congress also view staff—especially large staffs—as a symbol of prestige and importance. To some members, the larger the staff, the more powerful a member appears. Similarly, many staffers feel that the more powerful the committee or member they work for, the more powerful they are.

Postwar Waves of Staff Expansion

Congressional staffs have become large and diverse only in the half-century since World War II. That worldwide conflict and the Great Depression before it in the 1930s transformed the United States into a global power and an increasingly complex society. With those changes came an unremitting need in Congress for assistance in understanding and legislating on issues of the postwar world.

Huge increases in the size of congressional staff came in two waves: after a landmark congressional reorganization in 1946 and during a period of internal reform in the 1970s that changed many of the traditional ways in which Congress operated. As the size of staff increased, so did the cost of running Congress, which by 1999 was more than $2.6 billion. By comparison, the cost in 1960, when adjusted to the value of 1999 dollars, was $667 million, only about a quarter of the actual number for 1999. Although the 1999 figure includes some congressional support agencies not in existence in 1960, the magnitude of the increase still holds. About one-half of the 1999 total is devoted to House and Senate operations, with the largest share going for staff salaries. *(See Table 28-2, p. 797, and Table 28-3, p. 800, Vol. II.)*

Congress has more staff members than any other national legislature. About 16,500 aides work directly for its 540 voting and nonvoting members (including the delegates from American Samoa, the District of Columbia, Guam, and the Virgin Islands, and the resident commissioner from Puerto Rico). By comparison, the Canadian parliament, with slightly more than 400 senators and members of parliament, employs about 2,500 staff members, down about 25 percent over the past five years.[2]

Another 7,000 or so congressional employees are "support staff." They work for the Library of Congress, General Accounting Office, Congressional Budget Office, and the other large agencies of the legislative branch. This chapter deals primarily with personal and committee staffs; the support groups are covered separately. *(See Chapter 26, Supporting Organizations.)*

Although the forces that helped push staff size to record heights remain strong, actual growth stopped in the 1980s and 1990s because of budget cuts and reductions of committee staff that to an extent emerged from changing political control and attitudes on Capitol Hill. It is not likely, however, that Congress will significantly shrink its bureaucracy back to the pre-1970 levels.

EXPLAINING STAFF GROWTH

Congressional staffs expanded steadily after enactment of the 1946 Legislative Reorganization Act but most dramatically after the Legislative Reorganization Act of 1970. In 1947 House and Senate committees had 399 aides; by 1999 the number had reached 2,281, including standing, special, and select committees, an increase of almost 500 percent. (The high point in com-

Maryland senator John Marshall Butler and his entire staff pose in the 1950s. Congressional staff sizes ballooned in the 1960s and 1970s.

mittee staff occurred in the mid- to late 1980s—around 3,000.) Similarly, in 1947 House and Senate personal staffs numbered 2,030; in 1999, about 11,500.

Significant staff growth began in the 1960s but accelerated dramatically in the 1970s in response to institutional reform and increasing member responsibility to voters. The rapid growth began to level off in the late 1970s, although the actual numbers reached a peak in the 1980s.

At the end of the 1990s the total number of personal congressional staff was at about the same level as two decades earlier, even with declines during the decade. Although committee staff declined by about a third in the 104th Congress (1995–1997) from levels in the 103rd Congress, the overall staff levels have been more stable.[3] *(See Figure 17-1, p. 583.)*

The significant growth in staff after World War II was caused by congressional efforts to be more independent of the executive branch, the growing number of complex legislative issues, competition among committees, and increased constituent mail and services.

Staff growth—especially committee staff—after the 1970 Reorganization Act was linked to congressional reform efforts at the beginning of that decade. The period was noteworthy for the election of more activist members, the decline of the congressional seniority system, more intense lobbying efforts by special interests, and a growing sense that junior and minority party members should get fairer treatment than they had received in the past. House committee staffs were almost three

times as large in 1979 as they were in 1970, and Senate committee staffs doubled over the same time period.[4] In the House the increase stemmed largely from the creation of many more subcommittees—opening up positions of authority to the members who would chair them. Subcommittee chairmen were given the authority to hire staff, a prerogative previously jealously guarded by the full committee chairmen.

In the Senate the passage of S Res 60, allowing senators—often more junior in status—to hire personal staff members to help with committee work, accounted for much of the staffing growth in that chamber.

The relationship between Congress and the executive branch also was a factor in staff growth during the 1970s. Before the mid-1960s Congress still depended to a large extent on the executive branch for information and advice on existing programs and legislative proposals. But growing distrust of the executive branch, partially the result of the Vietnam War and, in the 1970s, the Watergate scandal that drove President Richard Nixon from office, prompted Congress to hire more and better-qualified committee staff to monitor and evaluate executive branch performance as well as to provide independent analysis of issues and proposals. In addition, the larger staff increased Congress's capacity to initiate more legislation rather than depend heavily on executive branch agencies.

Also during the 1970s there was a vast expansion in White House and executive office staff. As the executive branch grew, Congress felt greater urgency to create its own bureaucracy as a

Figure 17–1   Congressional Staff, 1891–1997

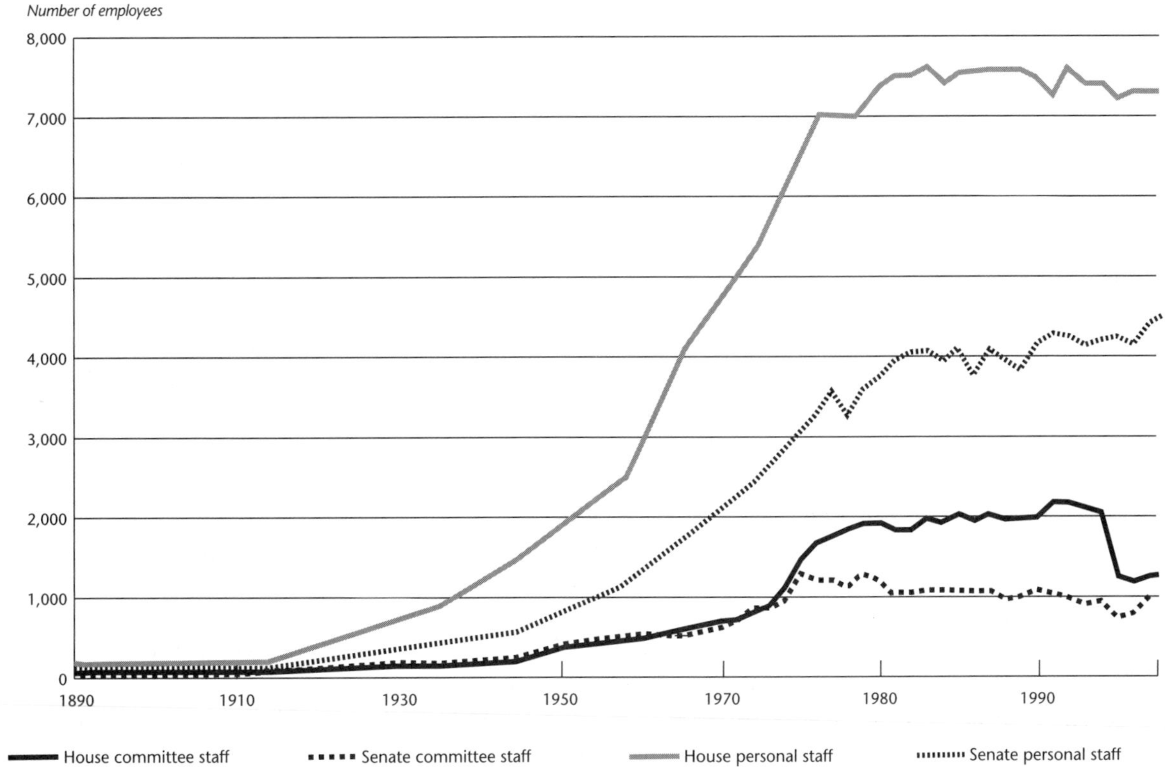

Number of employees

| House committee staff | ▪▪▪▪▪ Senate committee staff | House personal staff | ▪▪▪▪▪▪▪▪ Senate personal staff |

Source: Norman J. Ornstein, Thomas E. Mann, and Michael J. Malbin, *Vital Statistics on Congress, 1997–1998* (Washington, D.C.: Congressional Quarterly, 1998), 135, 139.

counterbalance. Sen. Daniel Patrick Moynihan, D-N.Y., termed this process the "Iron Law of Emulation": "Whenever any branch of government acquires a new technique which enhances its power in relation to the other branches, that technique will soon be adopted by those other branches as well."[5]

Similarly, the growth of special interest groups in Washington contributed to an increase in Capitol Hill staff as members sought better assistance in evaluating the claims and proposals of the proliferating groups representing business, labor, environment, and citizens. Sen. James Abourezk, D-S.D., argued that "an active, if sometimes redundant, congressional staff is imperative" to protect the public interest in the face of the often powerful "private constituencies that influence Congress."

All of these factors added up, in the minds of members, to more work, longer days, more difficult issues, and larger controversies. Although some indicators of the congressional workload—the number of bills introduced, reported, and passed; the number of votes taken; and the number of subcommittee and committee meetings—decreased in the 1990s, the workload remained heavy. The decrease in the number of bills reflected Congress's penchant, developed in the 1980s and into the 1990s, for using omnibus bills, one big package containing many separate bills. In addition, until the late 1990s, the budget deficit restrained members from considering any legislation that cost a lot of money.

The number of committee and subcommittee meetings may

have decreased, but contentious confirmation hearings in the Senate, rooted in the increased partisanship characterizing Washington politics from the 1970s on, became especially time-consuming as members and interest groups used the process as a vehicle to debate social and political issues such as abortion and race relations. Congressional and executive ethics investigations also added to the committee workload.

At the end of the century, Congress was closely divided between Republicans and Democrats, with the GOP holding a razor-thin voting margin—but no real operating majority—in the House. This, too, contributed to a lower work profile as each side was able to thwart the other's initiatives. As a result, both parties looked forward to the 2000 elections—when there also would be a White House race without an incumbent—to capture a commanding majority that would permit carrying forward a full-fledged party program. If that were to occur, the role and size of staff were likely to start growing once again.

EMPLOYMENT PRACTICES

Until the latter years of the century, congressional aides—for all the power and prestige they possessed—were treated differently than the vast majority of American workers. For the most part, federal labor, safety, and health laws did not cover staffers. After Congress was criticized for being unable to live under the laws it passed for others, lawmakers in 1995 enacted a workplace compliance bill, known as the Congressional Accountability

Act, which applied eleven federal labor and antidiscrimination laws to most congressional employees. *(See box, Congress and Workplace Compliance, p. 602.)*

Still, even with these new protections, and for all the glamour of working in Congress, aides often face long hours, cramped quarters, and the sometimes capricious demands of the politicians at whose pleasure they serve. Women and African Americans are at a particular disadvantage: studies of congressional hiring patterns reveal that they tend to be concentrated in low-paying jobs. According to a 1998 study of House personal staffs, even though women make up 57 percent of employees, they are overrepresented in lower-paying jobs and underrepresented in higher-paying ones. The same study also found that black House staff members receive 87 percent of the pay of their white counterparts and make up 5.9 percent of the total staff, while Hispanic staffers earn 70 percent of the salaries of white staffers. These differences in average salary largely stem from the positions held by minority staff compared with those held by white staff.[6]

In 1999 the *National Journal,* a Washington, D.C., news magazine, reported that only about 27 percent of congressional top staff positions were held by women, based on a survey of about 300 top committee and leadership posts. The Senate had more—33 percent—than the House, at 20 percent.

Evolution of the Congressional Staff

During the early years of Congress, senators and representatives were reluctant to admit they required staff assistance, either in the committees or in their own offices. According to William L. Morrow, in his book *Congressional Committees,* "Legislators were considered more erudite than most citizens and they believed any suggestion for staff assistance might be interpreted as a lack of confidence in their ability to master their jobs."[7]

Congressional staffing began as clerical assistance. Harrison W. Fox Jr. and Susan Webb Hammond noted in their 1977 book, *Congressional Staffs,* that the term *clerk-hire* was applied in the early days to the account used to pay personal staffers.[8] The term remained common in the decades that followed even though both chambers moved to consolidate accounts and give members more flexibility in hiring staff.

Until the 1820s standing committees were few and far between. Even though more were created, members handled business without paid assistance. Congress rejected requests to employ permanent committee clerks until about 1840 when, after pleas by committee chairmen, some clerical help was permitted in emergencies on a per diem or hourly basis. Funds for these part-time assistants were made available through special appropriations.

In 1856 the House Ways and Means and Senate Finance Committees became the first to obtain regular appropriations for full-time clerks. Appropriations for other committees followed, but their staffing generally was limited to persons hired for housekeeping duties, such as stenographers and receptionists. Members or their personal aides (who were still paid out of members' own pockets) usually handled substantive committee work and bill drafting. The number of committee employees continued to increase gradually, however. By 1891 committee staff numbered forty-one in the Senate and sixty-two in the House.

The turn of the century, wrote George B. Galloway, a specialist on Congress with the Library of Congress for many years, found Congress adding line items to appropriations acts specifying funds for the standing committees of the House and Senate. The first comprehensive pay bill authorizing appropriations for all legislative employees, including committee clerks, was enacted in 1924. That act appropriated $270,100 for 141 Senate committee clerks and $200,490 for 120 House committee employees.

Senators were first authorized to hire personal aides in 1885, at a pay rate of six dollars a day. The House passed similar provisions in 1893. Before this time, members who were not committee chairmen either worked without personal assistance or paid aides with personal funds.[9]

In the late nineteenth century, an ill-defined line, in practice and by statute, separated committee and personal staffs. Clerks appointed by committee chairmen to assist on committee business often worked on the chairmen's district business as well. Some superfluous committees were kept in business to provide chairmen with clerk services and to provide the offices that accompanied a committee bureaucracy.

Distinctions between the duties of committee employees and members' personal staff remained blurred well into the twentieth century. Under provisions of the Legislative Pay Act of 1929, for example, when a senator assumed leadership of a committee, the three senior clerks of his office staff became ex officio clerk and assistant clerks of that committee. Furthermore, the act stipulated that the clerical staff of a Senate committee also would serve as secretarial workers for its chairman.

Personal staffs did not increase much in size between the turn of the century and World War II. In 1946 representatives were authorized to employ five aides and the average Senate office had six staffers. Committee staffs also did not expand greatly; in 1943 Senate committees employed 190 aides; House committees, 114.[10]

BIRTH OF THE MODERN CONGRESS: THE 1946 REORGANIZATION ACT

The organization of the modern Congress—its procedures, organization, structure, staffing—dates, by most accounts, from the Legislative Reorganization Act of 1946.

As early as 1941, senators and representatives realized that congressional operations—including staffing procedures and the committee structure—required modernization to deal with the challenges faced by the national government in the wake of the Great Depression and in the face of the looming world war. Members pointed out that the growing congressional workload placed too heavy a burden on them and their staffs. In addition, improved communications and transportation permitted voters to ask more of elected officials, thereby increasing constituency casework. And from the depression-inspired New Deal days of the 1930s onward, issues and legislation became more complex as the federal government expanded.

Faced with more complex legislation, Congress realized it lacked staff with technical knowledge and skills; it had to rely instead on the executive branch and private groups for specialized assistance and help with drafting bills. Members, then, began to fear that their excessive dependence on the executive branch would make Congress a secondary, rather than a coequal, institution in the national government. This apprehension was underscored by a warning issued in 1942 by President Franklin D. Roosevelt, who was frustrated with delays in enacting key administration proposals: "In the event that Congress fails to act, and act adequately, I shall accept the responsibility, and I shall act."[11]

Congress, however, did not have money to expand its staff; the United States was entering World War II:

[In 1941] of every seven dollars it authorized the federal government to spend, Congress spent only one cent on itself. Its thirty-two-hundred-member staff was predominantly clerical and custodial, with not more than two hundred persons who could be considered legislative professionals. [Members] were often required to use their office clerks as the principal staff of any committee they chaired, thus ignoring professional competence as the foundation for committee staffing.[12]

The lack of professional staff, however, was to an extent self-inflicted. Members were reluctant to increase their own funding lest the public view them as unable "to carry traditional legislative burdens."[13] In 1941, for example, senators balked when Sen. A. B. "Happy" Chandler, D-Ky., suggested allowing each senator one "research expert." Senior members who chaired committees objected to adding specialists to the clerical ranks, fearing it might establish a cadre of political assistants who could eventually compete for their bosses' jobs.[14]

Nevertheless, as frustrations rose with the workload and institutional ineffectiveness, Congress passed legislation in 1944 creating the Joint Committee on the Organization of Congress to study the organization, operation, and staffing of the House and Senate; House, Senate, and committee interaction; and congressional–executive relations. Two years later Congress incorporated most of the committee's recommendations into the Legislative Reorganization Act of 1946.

The central elements of the 1946 act reduced the number of standing committees in the Senate from thirty-three to fifteen and in the House from forty-eight to nineteen, and authorized the hiring of professional committee staff. Senators were assigned two committees instead of as many as nine. Representatives served on one committee instead of five. Each committee's jurisdiction was more strictly defined.

Congress also tried in the reorganization to separate the roles of committee and personal staffs by specifying that the former "shall not engage in any work other than committee business, and no other duties may be assigned to them."

The House and Senate Appropriations Committees and the Joint Committee on Taxation had begun building nonpartisan professional staffs in the 1920s. According to political scientist Michael J. Malbin, the success of those staffs led Congress in 1946 to institutionalize the practice by allowing each standing committee to hire a total of ten staff members—four professional and six clerical—selected "solely on the basis of fitness to perform the duties of office."[15] The professional staff provided expert knowledge on a subject while the clerical staff supplied nonpolicy administrative and secretarial support. Although the terminology has changed some, and other names—such as investigative, associate, or temporary—have come into use, this broad distinction continued in 1999.

In 1946 the Appropriations committees were permitted to determine their staff needs by majority vote. Thus the total number of committee aides allowed under the 1946 act was 340, plus the additional staffers hired by the Appropriations committees.

The Joint Committee on the Reorganization of Congress also recommended that each member be allowed to hire an administrative assistant for his or her personal staff. Although this recommendation was dropped from the final act because of House resistance, it was instituted separately by the Senate shortly after the act's passage.[16]

Under the 1946 act, majority party members were responsible for hiring and firing committee staff, although in practice committees usually delegated that power to the chair, who often consulted with the senior minority party member. Normally, chairmen obtained most staff funding from the House Administration and the Senate Rules and Administration committees.

In two other important reforms, the 1946 act expanded the Legislative Reference Service (now the Congressional Research Service) and created senior specialist positions in subject areas roughly equivalent to those of the standing committees. The specialists received salaries comparable to those of their counterparts in the executive branch. In addition, the act expanded the bill-drafting service available through the Office of the Legislative Counsel.

Although members thought the 1946 act improved staffing procedures, concern about staff quality remained. By 1948 ninety-three senators had appointed administrative assistants, but some senators complained that unqualified personal secretaries had been promoted. Some members also felt that committees were not always using the staffing authority or hiring well-trained experts.[17]

REFORM ERA: REORGANIZATION ACT OF 1970

By 1965 a new joint committee was looking into the concerns about the quality and availability of staff that had arisen since

LAWS AND RULES GOVERNING THE HIRING OF STAFF

Since 1946 Congress has approved the following major laws and regulations that affect the hiring and placement of congressional staff:

LEGISLATIVE REORGANIZATION ACT OF 1946

This act established a permanent complement of professional staff for all standing committees and directed that staff be appointed on the basis of merit and not political affiliation. The latter directive is not always observed because committees prefer to hire their own Democratic or Republican "experts." Under the act, committees were allowed to hire four professional staff aides and six clerical aides. Although a provision recommending that each member hire an administrative assistant on his personal staff was dropped from the act, the Senate instituted the reform later that year.

POSTAL RATE–FEDERAL PAY LAW OF 1967

This 1967 postal rate–federal pay law contained a ban on nepotism. It prohibited public officials, including members of Congress, from hiring, appointing, promoting, or advancing relatives in the agency in which the officials serve. The ban did not include relatives already employed, nor did it prevent an official in one agency or chamber of Congress from seeking to obtain employment for a relative in another agency or chamber.

LEGISLATIVE REORGANIZATION ACT OF 1970

This act increased from four to six the number of professional aides that could be employed by most standing committees of the House and Senate. The minority party was authorized to hire two of them and one of the six clerical aides. Committees were permitted to provide training for staff and to hire consultants. The act also required that one-third of House investigative staff funds be allocated to the minority (this provision was deleted in 1971 by the House Democratic Caucus).

HOUSE COMMITTEE AMENDMENTS OF 1974

Changes adopted in 1974 tripled the staffs of most House standing committees. The number of professional aides went from six to eighteen and of clerical employees from six to twelve, with the minority party allowed to appoint one-third of each category. (The latter provision was killed in 1975.)

HOUSE DEMOCRATIC CAUCUS ACTION OF 1975

In 1975 the House Democratic Caucus overturned the 1974 House committee reorganization plan that had given Republicans one-third of investigative staff. Instead, it increased the number of statutory staff working on subcommittees by allowing subcommittee chairmen and ranking minority members to hire one staff person each to work on their subcommittees. The increase of up to twelve aides (since standing committees are permitted a total of six subcommittees) was considered to be an overall increase in committee staff to forty-two statutory aides. The actual number of committee aides permitted by statute remained at thirty, however.

HOUSE RESOLUTION 359

In 1979 the House approved a rules change that permitted representatives to hire up to four additional employees if their jobs fit into one of the following five categories: a part-time employee; a "shared" employee; an intern; a temporary employee hired for three months or less; or a person who replaced an employee on leave without pay. This brought the total number of House personal staffers in a member's office to eighteen full-time and four part-time. (There are no limits on the number of Senate personal staff.)

SENATE RESOLUTION 60

The Senate in 1975 adopted S Res 60 authorizing senators to hire up to three staffers, called associate staff, to help them with their committee work. The resolution permitted each senator to hire up to three committee assistants. S Res 60 later was changed from a Senate rule to a statute, which forms the basis for the legislative assistance allowance now provided to all senators regardless of their committee leadership posts.

SENATE COMMITTEE AMENDMENTS OF 1977

Legislation enacted in 1977 to reorganize Senate committees required committee staffs to be in proportion to the number of majority and minority members on each standing committee. The measure directed that a "majority of the minority members of any committee may, by resolution, request that at least one-third of the funds of the committee for statutory, investigative, and clerical personnel . . . be allocated to the minority members."

SENATE RESOLUTION 281

Approved in 1980, S Res 281 directed each Senate committee, except the Select Committee on Ethics, to submit a single budget for all expenses anticipated for the fiscal year. (Money requested by the Ethics Committee comes from the Senate contingent fund.) The resolution eliminated the distinction between statutory and investigative committee staffs, which previously had separate budgets, and the change itself made it much easier to get a true picture of actual Senate committee expenditures.

CONGRESSIONAL ACCOUNTABILITY ACT OF 1995

In 1995 Congress passed legislation that ended exemptions from workplace laws that both chambers long enjoyed. The law established an Office of Compliance for employees to file grievances regarding an alleged violation but also allowed eventual recourse to the courts. (See box, *Congress and Workplace Compliance, p. 602.*)

COMMITTEE CUTS

At the beginning of the 104th Congress in 1995, Republicans revised House rules (H Res 6) to change the way the House conducted business. One change was the restructuring of committees, with a directive that committee staff be reduced by one-third. Moreover, no committee was permitted more than five subcommittees, except the Appropriations Committee, the Government Reform and Oversight Committee, and the Transportation and Infrastructure Committee. The rules also gave control of staff hiring for subcommittees to the full committee chairman. Subcommittee chairmen and ranking members no longer had the authority to hire one staffer each.

LEGISLATIVE BRANCH APPROPRIATIONS ACT, FISCAL 1999

A provision of this act gave the Senate Appropriations Committee the authority to determine its own staffing needs and budget. The committee had been exempt from the annual funding process from 1946 to 1981, when the Senate's overall biennial funding process was applied to it like other panels. The House Appropriations Committee has continuously had such funding independence since 1946.

HOUSE AND SENATE SUPPORT OFFICES

In its day-to-day operations Congress is supported by the offices and staffs of the clerk of the House, the secretary of the Senate, the House and Senate sergeants at arms and parliamentarians, and the House chief administrative officer, among others.

The functions of the clerk of the House and the secretary of the Senate are administrative as well as quasi-judicial. The full chamber elects each official, who usually is the nominee of the majority party. These officials normally remain in their posts until that party loses control of the chamber (although each house retains the power to remove its officials).

The clerk and secretary perform a wide range of tasks. They process all legislation; prepare the "Daily Digest" and periodic reports for the *Congressional Record;* record and print bills and reports; compile lobby registration information; and supervise, respectively, the House and Senate libraries and the document rooms.

Other administrative functions that used to rest with the clerk are now the responsibility of the House chief administrative officer (CAO), a position dating from 1992. The chief administrator's office furnishes stationery supplies, electrical and mechanical equipment, and office furniture; disburses the payroll; and supervises repair services. The position initially was titled director of nonlegislative and financial services. In the Senate, these tasks are undertaken by the secretary.

Although promoted as nonpartisan, the nonlegislative and financial services idea elicited sharp criticism from House Republicans. They charged it was a Democratic cover-up for various House scandals that had erupted around that time. Later, when the Republicans took control of the House in 1995, the CAO was created (and the earlier director position eliminated) as part of a package of rules changes. The CAO is nominated by the Speaker and elected by the full House, making it essentially a party position.

The House and Senate sergeants at arms do not wear uniforms, but they are the police officers of their respective chambers. They attend all House and Senate floor sessions and are responsible for enforcing rules and maintaining decorum, ensuring the security of buildings and visitors, and supervising the Capitol police. In addition, the House sergeant at arms is in charge of the mace, a traditional symbol of legislative power and authority. *(See boxes, U.S. Capitol Police, p. 744, Vol. II; The House Mace, p. 48.)*

The House and Senate sergeants at arms also introduce the bearers of all messages, official guests, and members attending joint sessions; supervise doormen and pages; issue gallery passes; and perform a variety of custodial services. On the House side the doorkeeper performed these duties until 1995, when the position was abolished.

The parliamentarians of the House and Senate sit in on all sessions to advise the presiding officers on parliamentary procedures. They help refer legislation to committees, and they maintain compilations of the precedents of each chamber.

The House and Senate chaplains are officers of their respective chambers. The chaplains open each day's session with a prayer and provide other religious services to members, their families, and congressional staff.

The Office of the Senate Legal Counsel advises and represents senators, committees, officers, and staffers on legal matters related to official Senate work and civil proceedings.

The House Office of the Law Revision Counsel develops and updates an official classification of U.S. laws. The office periodically prepares and publishes a new edition of the *United States Code,* including annual cumulative supplements of newly enacted laws.

---

the landmark 1946 reorganization law. The committee focused on increasing the number of personal and committee staff, expanding staff with scientific and technical expertise, increasing pay to attract more qualified candidates, and providing more staff for the minority.

Five years later Congress passed the Legislative Reorganization Act of 1970. That law:

• Increased from four to six the number of permanent professional staff employees authorized for each standing committee. Two of the six professional staffers, in addition to one of six permanent clerical staffers provided under previous law, were to be reserved for the exclusive use of the committee's minority party members. That provision did not apply to the House and Senate Appropriations Committees or to the House Committee on Standards of Official Conduct. Equally important, the 1970 changes established a procedure by which a committee could seek annual funding for additional staff, which later led to substantial growth in staff that came to be called investigative or temporary. In the decades that followed, the bulk of committee staff fell under these, rather than statutory, categories.

• Authorized standing committees, with the approval of the Senate Rules and Administration Committee or House Administration Committee, to provide staff members with specialized training.

• Authorized salary levels for Senate committee staff personnel comparable to those of House committee staff personnel.

• Redesignated the Legislative Reference Service in the Library of Congress as the Congressional Research Service; redefined its duties to better assist congressional committees by providing research and analytical services, records, documents, and other information and data, including memorandums on proposed legislation; and expanded its staff resources.

• Allowed the minority party one-third of a House committee's investigative funds (for temporary staff). (The House voted in 1971 to disregard this provision. It was revived in 1974, killed in 1975, and taken up again in 1989.) By 1999 most House committee and subcommittee staffs were considered investigative, although funds for them were provided through biennial resolutions. *(See "Committee Staffs," p. 590; "Partisanship and Minority Staffing," p. 593.)*

CHANGES IN 1974–1979

The expansion of committee and personal staffs continued into the 1970s, pushing Congress toward what would become, in the mid-1980s, the high-water mark in support staff numbers.

House Committee Staffing

Another change in House committee staffing levels occurred in 1974 when the number of permanent professional staff employees was increased to eighteen and the number of clerical aides to twelve. This brought the total number of permanent committee aides to thirty, where it remained in 1999. At the request of the minority party, up to ten of these thirty professionals within each committee can be assigned to the minority.

In addition to permanent statutory staff, House—as well as Senate—committees continued to rely heavily on temporary or investigative aides. At first these employees were funded annually, but by 1999 they were provided under biennial resolutions covering a full Congress, increasing their resemblance to regular statutory employees. Even though temporary employees, they often remain with a committee year after year.

House Subcommittee Expansion

The 1970s reform movement throughout Congress fed the growth of House committee staff. A principal goal of reformers was to break the iron grip of seniority and the power held by a handful of the most senior members—usually full committee chairs. Reformers sought to diffuse this power by creating new enclaves—subcommittees—where that power could be exercised and to give protection in the rules to those entities.

In 1973 the House Democratic Caucus adopted a "subcommittee bill of rights" empowering each committee's majority caucus to determine subcommittee chairmen, jurisdictions, and budgets. In 1974 the House required all committees with more than fifteen members to establish at least four subcommittees, a threshold changed to twenty members by the caucus in 1975. The changes during these years also gave subcommittee leaders the right to staff support paid from committee funds. These significant moves institutionalized House subcommittees to an unprecedented degree. Then, as the power of subcommittees grew, so did their staffs. By the late 1970s the number of staffers working for subcommittees equaled the number assigned to full committees in the 1960s.

A further change in House practices adopted in 1975 affected the growth of subcommittee staff. The new rule allowed subcommittee chairmen and the ranking minority member on each panel to hire one staff person each to work directly for them on their subcommittee business.

The 1970 changes were dramatic, increasing staff by about 650 percent. Congressional scholars Christopher J. Deering and Steven S. Smith noted that in 1970 twelve House committees had no separate subcommittee staff. Of the seven that did, only Appropriations and Government Operations functioned under clearly decentralized systems in which a subcommittee staff

TABLE 17-1 Congressional Committee Staffs

From 1935 to 1999 the committee staffs in Congress expanded and then shrank. The table below lists the number of statutory and investigative staff members of standing committees (special and select committees are not included). Staff growth in both chambers began after the Legislative Reorganization Act of 1946 but accelerated in the 1970s. The highest number of staff positions in the House was recorded in 1991, 2,201, and in the Senate in 1975, 1,277. The House numbers began to decline in the early 1990s and dropped dramatically in 1995 when the Republicans took control after winning the 1994 elections. In the Senate the numbers began to decline in the late 1970s, stabilizing at around 1,000–1,100 through the 1980s, with a further drop in the 1990s.

The personal staff of members also increased during these years but, unlike committee staffs, stabilized in the 1990s rather than dropping. (See Table 17-3, p. 590.)

Year	House	Senate
1935	122	172
1947	167	232
1960	440	470
1965	571	509
1970	702	635
1975	1,460	1,277
1979	1,909	1,269
1980	1,917	1,191
1985	2,009	1,080
1990	1,993	1,090
1995	1,246	732
1999	1,238	805

SOURCES: Harrison W. Fox Jr. and Susan Webb Hammond, *Congressional Staffs: The Invisible Force in American Lawmaking* (New York: Free Press, 1977); Norman J. Ornstein, Thomas E. Mann, and Michael J. Malbin, *Vital Statistics on Congress, 1999–2000* (Washington, D.C.: American Enterprise Institute, 1999), 135.

worked almost, if not entirely, exclusively for the subcommittee chair. By the end of the decade, in 1979, only three House committees with subcommittees had not created separate staffs.[18]

The movement to separate and distribute staffs to subcommittees continued in the new decade where it peaked between 1985 and 1988. After that, the percentage of committee staff assigned to subcommittees in the House started to drift downward, reaching a point in 1995, after the Republican takeover, not seen since the late 1970s. (See Table 17-2, p. 589.)

Senate Committee Staffing

Whereas House subcommittee staff grew nearly 650 percent in the 1970s, Senate subcommittee staff grew less than 50 percent. In 1979 just two committees, Judiciary and Governmental Affairs, employed nearly three-fourths of the Senate's subcommittee staff.

Senate subcommittee staff did not grow so quickly because the Senate retained far more centralized staffing arrangements than the House. By the late 1990s a few specialized Senate committees, including Budget, Select Committee on Intelligence Activities, and Small Business, had no subcommittees.

TABLE 17-2 Staff Allocated to Subcommittees

A major reason for committee staff growth in the 1970s and later was the proliferation of subcommittees, particularly in the House. This table shows, for selected Congresses, the increasing number and percentage of staff working on subcommittees. The numbers began to decline in the 1990s, accelerated by the Republican takeover of both chambers of the 104th Congress.

| | Subcommittee Staff Allocation | | | |
| | House number | Percentage | Senate number | Percentage |
Congress				
91st (1969–1970)	461	23.2	504	42.1
94th (1975–1976)	1,083	32.8	859	32.1
97th (1981–1982)	1,507	39.8	906	32.5
100th (1987–1988)	1,545	45.8	790	37.3
103rd (1993–1994)	1,719	40.5	985	31.2
104th (1995–1996)	1,090	38.0	777	26.1

SOURCE: Christopher J. Deering and Steven S. Smith, *Committees in Congress*, 3rd ed. (Washington, D.C.: CQ Press, 1997), 167.

Nevertheless, the Senate—like the House—moved to provide better staffing for members. A key event occurred in 1975 when the Senate authorized an increase in committee staff in response to the complaints of junior senators. They wanted, according to Sen. Bob Packwood, R-Ore., "the same access that the senior senators do to professional staff assistance." Senators were allowed to hire up to three staffers, called associate staff, depending on the type and number of committees assigned each senator.

That change (S Res 60) was intended to prevent a senator who already had staff on a committee from getting more staff for that committee. Thus it benefited primarily junior senators who had been excluded from separate staff on their committees because of their low-seniority status. The plan cut into the traditional power base that senior members enjoyed through their control of committee staff and was opposed by many of them for that reason. Over time S Res 60 increased staff for all senators.

The 1975 change also required senators to certify that their new aides worked only on committee business. The funds to pay for the additional committee aides were merged with senators' general clerk-hire funds, allowing members to use the money as they wished but thereby undermining the original premise for personal committee staff. In addition, today most of these staffers work out of senators' personal offices and often are difficult to distinguish from the legislative assistants on senators' personal staffs.

Senate Subcommittees

Senate committees, unconstrained by rules requiring separate subcommittee staff, varied widely in their staffing. Committees such as Governmental Affairs, Judiciary, and Labor resembled House committees in allowing subcommittee leaders to appoint staff. Others, such as Armed Services and Banking,

did not appoint separate staffs but assigned certain subcommittee responsibilities to full committee staff members, giving the staff assistant two masters—the full committee chair and the subcommittee chair. In some committees, such as Agriculture, there was little meaningful differentiation among committee staff and usually little separate subcommittee activity, particularly with respect to drafting legislation.[19]

Growth of Personal Staffs

Like committee staff, the number of personal assistants to senators and representatives continued to grow throughout the 1970s and 1980s until the numbers stabilized in the Senate and gradually declined in the House during the 1990s. In 1997 almost 7,300 personal staffers were working for members of the House and just over 4,400 for senators. In 1999 Houses members could hire up to eighteen full-time and four part-time aides in their Washington and district offices. There was no Senate limit other than that imposed by the funds available to a senator. (*See Table 17-3, p. 590.*)

Before 1979 a representative could hire a maximum of eighteen personal aides, with no exceptions. In July of that year the House approved a rules change permitting members to add up to four more staffers to their payrolls—without counting them toward the ceiling of eighteen—if their jobs fit into one of five categories:

1. A part-time employee, defined as one who does not work more than fifteen full working days a month or who is paid $1,270 a month or less.

2. A "shared" employee—an employee, such as a computer expert, who is on the payroll of two or more members simultaneously.

3. An intern in the member's Washington office, defined as an employee hired for up to 120 days and paid $1,160 a month or less. In 1998 the minimum salary in a representative's personal office was $1,200 a month.

4. A temporary employee, defined as a staff member hired for three months or less and assigned a specific task or function.

5. A person who temporarily replaces an employee on leave without pay.

A senator's personal staff was enhanced primarily through the adoption in 1975 of S Res 60, which allowed hiring a personal staffer to do work connected with the senator's committee assignments.

STAFF CONTRACTION IN THE 1980S AND 1990S

Even with these changes, the staff began to contract during the 1980s and on through the next decade. One factor in the slowdown of staff expansion was the effort begun by Republican president Ronald Reagan in 1981 to shrink the size of the federal government. The total executive staff, including the White House and related support groups such as the National Security

TABLE 17-3 Personal Staffs in Congress

Similar to the growth of committee staffs, personal staffs began to increase in the late 1960s, reaching their height in the 1980s. But unlike committee staffs, which declined under budget and political pressures, personal staffs stabilized from the late 1980s on. (See Table 17-1, p. 588.)

Year	House	Senate
1935	870	424
1947	1,440	590
1957	2,441	1,115
1967	4,055	1,749
1972	5,280	2,426
1977	6,942	3,554
1980	7,371	3,746
1982	7,511	4,041
1984	7,385	3,949
1986	7,920[a]	3,774[a]
1988	7,564	3,977
1990	7,496	4,162
1992	7,597	4,249
1994	7,390	4,200
1996	7,288	4,151
1999	7,216	4,272

NOTE: a. Senate figures reflect the period immediately after congressionally mandated staffing cuts in legislation known as the Gramm-Rudman bill. House figures are for the entire fiscal year, thus averaging post–Gramm-Rudman staffing levels with previous, higher ones.

SOURCES: Harrison W. Fox Jr. and Susan Webb Hammond, *Congressional Staffs: The Invisible Force in American Lawmaking* (New York: Free Press, 1977); Norman J. Ornstein, Thomas E. Mann, and Michael J. Malbin, *Vital Statistics on Congress, 1999–2000* (Washington, D.C.: American Enterprise Institute, 1999), 131.

Council, had peaked at 5,639 in 1972; by 1988, Reagan's last year in office, the staff had dropped to 1,645. The staff grew slightly during the succeeding term of President George Bush, reaching 1,855 in 1992. Democratic president Bill Clinton moved into the White House with the promise of cutting staff. By 1997, the first year of his second term, White House staff had declined to 1,565.[20]

Lawmakers in Congress—especially Republicans, who had taken over the Senate—echoed Reagan, calling for a reduction of the congressional bureaucracy. Thus both the House and Senate cut committee budgets 10 percent in 1981. The Republican-controlled Senate led the way, cutting its committee staffs by 14 percent. More than half the cuts, however, came from a single committee, Judiciary.[21] The Democratic House felt pressure to follow suit.

In 1981 political considerations forced the House Democratic leadership to combine investigative funds for all committees in a single package. Until then, the House had taken up each committee's budget one at a time on the House floor. Given the Republican move to trim congressional budgets, Democrats feared that funds for some committees might suffer further cuts if each committee's request was considered individually.

House Democrats cut committee staffs by around 10 percent

at the start of the 103rd Congress in 1993, primarily by abolishing four temporary select committees. But major reductions came only after Republicans took control of Congress in 1995. As part of their "Contract with America," the GOP's political platform in the 1994 elections, House Republicans cut committee staff by more than a third. Senate Republicans, who controlled that chamber, also reduced committee staff, although not as much.

Because personal staff for individual members of Congress are evenly distributed regardless of party, cuts in committee aides allowed GOP leaders in 1995 to claim credit for a significant overall staff reduction while minimizing damage to individual lawmakers, the majority of whom were now Republican. Most of the committee staff cuts forced by the GOP that year affected the now-minority Democrats, largely through dismissal of former Democratic majority staff. Republicans then limited the number of staffers hired to replace those previously serving Democrats.[22]

Some critics complained that staff reductions were too severe. The Republicans "went too far in downsizing committee staffs, hurting their ability to advance their own agenda," wrote a former GOP staff aide in 1996.[23] And in the opinion of Sen. Robert C. Byrd, D-W.Va., staff reductions had affected "the ability of members to adequately address issues of national importance which arise in Congress every day."[24]

Committee and Personal Staff: What They Do

As legislative activities and work have expanded, paralleling growth in the executive branch, Congress has changed as an institution. The legislative staff has changed as well, becoming larger and less collegial, more expert oriented, and often more activist. Theses changes reflect the demands made on staff as Congress has faced more complex issues and, increasingly in the last decades of the century, more sharply partisan divisions on both domestic and international problems. But one matter remained as true at the end of the century as in 1946 when Congress adopted its major post–World War II reorganization: members of the Senate and House need the support and advice of staff, both on committees and in their own offices, to carry out their jobs.

Staff is roughly divided into two types: those who work for a committee, usually serving either the majority or minority party on the panel, and those who work in a member's office serving that person's requirements. As noted earlier, staffers in a member's office may be assigned to work on the issues that are before the committee on which the member serves. But even without this close link, all members have someone on staff to handle legislative issues.

COMMITTEE STAFFS

While congressional committees vary in their organization, most at one time had dual staffs—one professional and one clerical. By the end of the 1990s, however, this distinction had all but disappeared in Congress.

Yet the work to be done has not fundamentally changed. Certain staff members are responsible for the day-to-day running of the committee and assisting the members and other staff colleagues who concentrate on substantive issues. Some of the routine tasks include keeping the committee calendar up to date, processing committee publications, referring pending bills to appropriate executive branch offices for comment, preparing the bill dockets, maintaining files, announcing hearings and contacting witnesses, opening and sorting mail, and—increasingly—preparing or updating electronic data, including committee Web sites. Other staff members handle committee policy and legislative matters, including legal and other types of research, public relations, statistical and other technical work, and drafting and redrafting legislative language and amendments.

All of these staffers are a committee's statutory, or permanent, staff. Their positions are established by rules of the House or Senate or by law and are funded annually in the legislative branch appropriations bill. Committees also hire additional personnel for special work. These so-called "investigative" employees are considered temporary, but they often remain with the committees for extended periods.

Although permanent staff funding and investigative staff funding were once handled separately, by 1999 both chambers had eliminated the distinction to gain better financial control over staff costs. Senate committees now submit all funding requests in one budget document to the Rules and Administration Committee for review.

As noted earlier, permanent House committees are entitled to thirty staffers paid out of statutory funds. Most of the committees put their highest-paid staff in this category and not under the investigative budget, which is reviewed by the House Administration Committee. Over the years, investigative employees have accounted for much of the increase in committee staff costs, as the budgets for these aides are flexible. In addition to staff salaries, House investigative budgets include money for office equipment, consultants, publications, and travel within the United States.

House investigative budgets do not include funds for hiring statutory staff or for printing expenses, stenographic costs, foreign travel, stationery, and some communications expenses. The investigative total also does not include funding for the House Appropriations or Budget Committees, both of which are included directly in the annual legislative appropriations bill and are not limited to thirty statutory staffers. The House Appropriations Committee in the 106th Congress had more than 150 staff members. (Its counterpart in the Senate had seventy as of September 1998.)

Committees seeking additional investigative help may use the services of legislative or executive branch agencies under rules employed by the housekeeping committees in both chambers. The congressional General Accounting Office, the Treasury

A committee aide consults with Sen. James M. Jeffords, R-Vt., right, chairman of the Senate Health, Education, Labor and Pensions Committee, during a committee markup session.

Department, and the FBI, among others, frequently are called on for assistance.

Functions

While committee responsibilities vary, most staff perform these basic functions:

Planning Agendas. Staffers help chairmen set committee agendas, select issues to consider, schedule hearings and bill markups, and plan floor action.

Organizing Hearings. Staffers set up hearings on legislation and issues under the committee's jurisdiction. Aides select witnesses, prepare questions, inform the press, brief committee members, and occasionally substitute for members who cannot attend hearings, often asking questions prepared by the absent legislator. Even when the chairman is present, senior aides with special knowledge sometimes question witnesses on technical subjects.

Oversight and Investigations. Staff members conduct original research on issues, which often takes the form of critiques of existing legislation, court decisions, and current practices. Aides on the Armed Services and foreign policy committees, for example, often travel to areas or countries about matters the committee is considering. Sometimes staffers hold regional hearings outside Washington, D.C.

Bill Markup and Amendment Drafting. Staff aides assist in marking up (amending) bills by explaining technical provisions, outlining policy questions, analyzing proposed changes following committee decisions, and incorporating decisions in successive revisions of the bill. They also often serve as liaison among the Office of the Legislative Counsel in each chamber, committee members, government agencies, and special interest groups during the drafting of legislation. *(See box, Legislative Counsel, p. 759, Vol. II.)*

Preparing Reports. Committee reports that accompany bills sent to the full chamber are almost entirely written by staff. Often the reports are the only information available to noncommittee members when the House or Senate considers a bill. Staff aides consult with the chair or the majority party members about information and emphasis in the report. Minority party members and opponents of a bill often file "minority views," usually drafted by the committee's minority staff members. Reports generally have a standard format that includes three basic ingredients: an explanation and interpretation of the bill and its background; a section-by-section analysis of the provisions of the bill; and a comparison of the bill with existing law. Most reports also include an estimate of the legislation's cost. *(See Chapter 15, The Legislative Process.)*

Preparing for Floor Action. Top aides most familiar with the legislation often accompany the committee chairman or another sponsor of the bill when the legislation is debated in the Senate or House. They advise the bill's supporters and sometimes help prepare amendments. They also may draft a script for the bill's managers to follow during the floor debate, including opening and closing remarks.

Conference Committee Work. The staffs of corresponding committees in each chamber work together on the preparation of conference reports and in resolving differences in legislation initially considered by those committees and subsequently passed by the House and Senate.

Liaison with Executive Branch, Special Interests. Staff aides communicate frequently with executive branch officials and lobbyists on legislative proposals before the committee. Some members regard this activity as the most consequential of all staff work. Representatives of special interest groups, particularly those that have Washington, D.C., offices, often provide staff aides with detailed information and answers to questions.

Press Relations. Committee staffers also perform press-related tasks. They alert reporters to upcoming hearings, markup sessions, and floor action on committee-reported measures. Aides answer questions from the press and public, provide background information on legislation before the committee and on recent committee decisions on legislation, and write press releases. In addition, they make committee members accessible to the media and generally work to obtain favorable publicity for the committee.

CONGRESSIONAL INTERNS

For years, members of Congress have been assisted by temporary employees known generally as congressional interns. The origins of the practice are obscure, but it probably began when members hired students of American government or the sons and daughters of constituents to work in their offices during the summer. This diverse and informal method of employment expanded greatly during the 1960s.

Congressional interns vary widely in their experience and their office responsibilities. Younger ones may undertake clerical tasks, help to answer mail, or conduct visitors around the Capitol. Those with more experience may be assigned to constituent casework, draft speeches and reports, or help committee staff.

Interns may be paid from a member's annual staff allowance or other funds available to the office, but many are not paid at all. Those under private internships are paid by their sponsors. The Congressional Fellowship program of the American Political Science Association, for example, brings each year a few dozen experienced journalists, teachers, and government officials to Congress. Employees of federal agencies may be assigned to Congress for a time if necessary. Many student interns receive academic credit for their work from their colleges and universities.

SOURCE: Harrison W. Fox Jr. and Susan Webb Hammond, *Congressional Staffs: The Invisible Force in American Lawmaking* (New York: Free Press, 1977), 137–138.

Recruitment and Tenure

The chairman or the top-ranking minority party member of a committee selects most committee employees, as a perquisite of office, subject only to nominal approval by the full committee.

From surveys and interviews with committee staff, certain generalizations about committee professionals emerge. They are relatively young, although not as young as personal office staffers, and most are male. The majority of aides have advanced degrees, particularly law, and many have previous experience in the executive branch. Although congressional scholars have, since the 1970s, observed a trend toward career development in committee staff positions, staff experience does decline sharply in periods of shifting party control, such as in 1995 when Republicans took control of the House for the first time in nearly four decades. The same phenomenon occurs when committee leadership posts change frequently, which may occur when a senior member retires or is defeated.

Congressional aides accept positions knowing there is no job security. Employees' tenure is subject to the whims of the chairman or member who hired them, and aides can be fired with or without cause. As one Capitol Hill observer pointed out, "Staff members all have friends whose chairman retired, switched committees, or was beaten, leaving them with a new chairman wanting to 'clean house.' They all know competent people who were fired without warning because the boss sensed a slight, or just felt it was time for a change."[25]

Power of Committee Staff

Congress's reliance on staff assistance prompts some observers to call these individuals unelected representatives. As senators and representatives spend more time on policy issues, constituency service, and campaign fund-raising, they delegate additional responsibilities to staff professionals, many of whom have advanced degrees and considerable experience and come to Capitol Hill hoping to make substantive policy decisions. The extent of that influence is often debated.

In his 1988 book, *The Power Game,* journalist Hedrick Smith quoted members who said they were highly dependent on their aides. House Majority Whip Tony Coelho, D-Calif., said: "When I leave a meeting, I don't have time to do the follow up. . . . The staff controls that meeting, that issue. I don't have time to make phone calls, to listen to the lobbyists. What is power? Information. Follow-through. Drafting an op-ed article."

Smith quotes some senators as bemoaning the trend toward communication through aides. William S. Cohen, then a Republican senator from Maine and later President Clinton's secretary of defense, said: "More and more you are dependent on your staff. There is so much competition among staffs, fighting over issues, that sometimes you'll call a senator and ask, 'Why are you opposing me on this?' and he'll say, 'I didn't know I was.' And you'll say, 'Well, check with your staff and see.'"[26] Interestingly, Cohen was succeeded in the Senate by Susan Collins, one of his staff aides.

Others believe staff influence is exaggerated. After Senate Majority Leader Howard H. Baker Jr., R-Tenn., retired and joined a Washington law firm, he said he was amazed that lobbyists paid so much attention to staff aides. "I was struck by the fact that [lobbyists] had list after list of people on the staff they'd gone to see. . . . I think part of it is an illusion. . . . [W]hen I met with most committee chairmen every Tuesday morning around the conference table in my office, I saw how it worked. They would really go at it hammer and tongs on particular items within their jurisdiction. So I think the impact of staff is overrated. But God knows, there's enough of them, they generate enough memos, and I know they attract lobbyists and lawyers like flies."[27]

Some observers see positive results in the empowerment of staff. By initiating policy, the staffs help Congress retain its vitality and independence from the executive branch. According to political scientist Malbin: "Most other national legislatures do not give individual members similar staff resources; most legislatures depend on their cabinets for almost all policy initiatives. Congress is not so passive today, thanks largely to its staff."[28]

Partisanship and Minority Staffing

Partisanship of committee employees has long been controversial. The 1946 Legislative Reorganization Act did not apportion the professional committee staff between the chairman and the ranking minority member. The act simply stated that "staff members shall be assigned to the chairman and ranking minority member of such committee as the committee may deem advisable." Committees interpreted that provision in different ways, but generally the chairman's preferences dictated the number—if any—of aides made available to minority party members. The result was that for the most part the minority had little or no staff support to assist in developing proposals to counter the program of the majority. Because Democrats were the majority most of the years after 1946, this meant that Republicans were at a disadvantage in advancing their own ideas.

In the 1960s Republicans began to press for formally recognized and permanently authorized minority staffing. Newspaper columnist Roscoe Drummond succinctly gave the GOP argument in 1961:

If the Republican members of Congress are ever to be in a position to clarify, expound, and defend their stand on the major issues . . . and to advance constructive alternatives of their own, they must get a steady flow of adequate, reliable, competent research and information from an adequate, reliable, and competent professional staff. This staff must be in the service of the minority, selected by the minority, and working for it.[29]

Historically, another problem facing minority staff was inequitable treatment. Sometimes minority staffers were paid less than their counterparts working for the majority. In addition, minority senators and representatives often waited longer than majority members to appoint staff. This remained true at the end of the 1990s.

In the 1970s several changes were made in minority staffing. The 1970 Legislative Reorganization Act provided that at least three full-time minority staff aides were to be assigned to most committees of the House and Senate. Since then, however, the two chambers have traveled somewhat different paths in their approaches to minority staffing.

House. In January 1971 the House voted to delete the provisions of the 1970 Legislative Reorganization Act allocating one-third of committee investigative funds—those used to hire part-time professionals and otherwise to assist members—to the minority side. The Democratic Caucus had voted to bind all House Democrats to vote for the deletion, a move that infuriated Republicans and emphasized the importance members attach to congressional staffing. Although the GOP did eventually win additional staffing, the highly partisan Democratic actions fed Republican discontent. That discontent led in the 1980s and early 1990s to Republican vilification of the majority for its arrogant and unrestrained use of its power, which contributed to the GOP takeover of the House in the 1994 elections.

The minority staffing issue resurfaced in late 1974, as representatives debated a proposal to reorganize House committees. That plan called for giving Republicans ten of thirty staff members assigned to committees by statute and one-third of the investigative staff allotted to subcommittees by the House Administration Committee. But when the Democratic Caucus met in January 1975, a resolution was introduced to nullify the one-third minority investigative staff guarantee. The caucus agreed to a compromise that allowed subcommittee chairmen and top-ranking minority members to hire one staff person each to work on their subcommittees—up to a maximum of six subcommittees—but dropped the one-third minority investigative staff guarantee. House rules permitted standing committees a total of six subcommittees. Although the staff increase applied specifically to subcommittees, the revision was widely billed as an increase of twelve in the number of statutory committee employees. The actual number of committee employees permitted by statute remained at thirty.

The minority staffing compromise produced one of the most significant changes of the many revisions made in House rules during the 1970s. Incorporated into the rules on January 14, 1975, the compromise was seen as crucial to strengthening the subcommittees and giving House minority members a meaningful opportunity to influence legislation. Dispersing power among committee members and reducing the authority of House committee chairmen also meant dispersing control over committee staffs and budgets.

The idea of allocating one-third of investigative staff to the minority came up again in 1989. This time, House Democrats agreed to let the minority have at least 20 percent of committee investigative staff positions, with an eventual goal of one-third. By 1999, in the wake of party control shifts and changes in House committee staffing procedures, more than half of the committees in that chamber allotted at least 30 percent of their staff positions to the minority, which by then was the Democrats.

Senate. As part of the Senate's 1975 change in committee staffing (S Res 60), all minority members were authorized to hire up to three personal committee aides, except for those who already had staff appointment authority on a particular committee. In 1977 a Senate committee reform resolution (S Res 4) directed that committee staffs be allocated in proportion to the number of the majority and minority members on a standing committee. The measure further specified that a "majority of the minority members of any committee may, by resolution, request that at least one-third of the funds of the committee for statutory, investigative, and clerical personnel . . . be allocated to the minority members." The reform resolution set a four-year timetable for Senate committees to provide one-third staffing to the minority.

Majority–Minority Staff Cooperation. The degree of cooperation between the majority and minority staffs varies among committees. It is difficult to be nonpartisan on Capitol Hill, and most staffers have party or philosophical preferences. Even more important, most staffers work for a single member or the majority or minority committee leadership and must act in accordance with their wishes. A few committees—Appropriations, ethics, and Joint Taxation, among others—have traditions of professional nonpartisan staffing. But that tradition has faltered somewhat in recent years.

From the late 1940s to the late 1970s the Senate Foreign Relations Committee had a bipartisan staff that served all committee members. In 1979, however, a group of Republican senators led by Jesse Helms of North Carolina, S. I. Hayakawa of California, and Richard G. Lugar of Indiana requested and received separate minority staff. In 1981, when Republicans took control of the Senate, the partisan staffing arrangement continued.

Political science scholar Michael Malbin, who studied the Joint Taxation Committee in the late 1970s, found there the benefits of nonpartisan staffing. These aides served as the principal staff on tax legislation for both the House Ways and Means and Senate Finance Committees. On all major issues likely to be considered by the two committees on tax-related measures, the joint committee aides outlined the political interests of both major parties. This information was published before the committees met to allow all members of the House and Senate, the press, and the public to understand the issues and political implications of committee deliberations.[30]

Washington journalists Jeffrey H. Birnbaum and Alan S. Murray, who followed the passage of the 1986 Tax Reform Act in their book, *Showdown at Gucci Gulch,* painted a similar picture:

> [The staffers of the joint committee] were not beholden to any single member. Their job was not political, and their bosses were many. . . . [They] served as a reservoir of in-house expertise for the entire Congress, especially the two tax-writing committees. Joint Tax aides shaped and analyzed every change in tax law proposed by their bosses and often came up with suggestions themselves. Their revenue estimates on the changes were gospel. In tax reform, an exercise driven by revenue estimates and income-distribution charts, Joint Tax pronouncements were crucial.[31]

In the 1990s, however, growing partisanship—particularly in the House—altered this respect for comity on certain committees as some members argued that the Joint Taxation Committee, as well as other panels that have had traditions of nonpartisan staffing, had moved toward partisanship. For example, during a 1997 House Appropriations Committee debate, Rep. Vic Fazio, D-Calif., attempted to eliminate the extra funding that would have allowed the Joint Taxation Committee to increase its staff by twelve. Fazio claimed the panel had swerved from its nonpartisan roots to become an advocacy arm for the Republican majority in charge of the House Ways and Means Committee.[32]

The tradition of nonpartisanship also broke down in the House Committee on Standards of Official Conduct (commonly known as the House ethics committee) during the panel's investigation of House Speaker Newt Gingrich, R-Ga., in the 104th Congress. The panel always had depended on members to put their politics aside for the sake of maintaining the honor of the House's self-policing system, but the poisonous political atmosphere that prevailed in the House during the 1990s, in part stemming from Gingrich's attacks on Democrats for

Rep. John Edward Porter, R-Ill., seated right, works on a spending bill with his personal staff.

many years, caused Democrats—as they saw it—to respond in kind.

PERSONAL STAFF

Members of the House are entitled to withdraw funds from the chamber's clerk-hire allowance to run and staff their offices. The clerk-hire funds are divided equally among representatives. For senators, the money is divided according to their state's population.

The characteristics of personal staff vary greatly from those of committee staff. A former House legislative assistant (LA), Mark Bisnow, has painted a vivid picture of personal aides:

House LA's tend to be young, commonly in their twenties; theirs can be an entry-level professional position requiring no previous Hill experience. . . . (Committee staffers, in contrast, tend to be more specialized, and therefore older and of greater experience.) Their workaday world is informal and often frenetic. . . . Fifty-to-sixty hour work weeks are not unusual. Under constant time pressure and a multitude of urgent assignments, LA's typically switch among projects and topics by the half hour; they learn to write quickly, think politically, and argue combatively. In crowded offices, their desks nudged up against each other in ways that would affront a fire marshal, they do their own typing, photocopying, and phone-calling. They then suspend any calm reflections until things settle down again at six or seven or eight o'clock at night.[33]

But, like committee staff, personal staffers have little job security. Their tenure is up to the member who hired them.

Personal staffs are set up differently in each congressional office, although clear patterns exist. Whether a representative or senator chooses to emphasize constituent service or legislation probably makes the biggest difference in how the office is organized. A member's personality is another factor.

Most congressional offices have an administrative assistant (AA), a legislative director, legislative assistants, caseworkers, and at least one press secretary. Many also have an office manager, appointments secretary, legislative correspondent, and systems or computer manager.

The administrative assistant, sometimes called the executive assistant or chief of staff, often serves as the member's alter ego and chief political adviser, keeping him or her abreast of district and Capitol Hill politics. The AA also usually directs and supervises the staff, or shares these supervisory responsibilities with others who manage the legislative staff in Washington, the clerical staff, and staff in the state or district offices.

Functions

In the modern Congress no senators or representatives try to manage their activities entirely unassisted. Members generally depend on staff to handle the routine work of a congressional office. Reliance on staff is underscored by this picture of a member's typical day:

On a normal day, a senator or [representative] has two and sometimes three simultaneous committee hearings, floor votes, issues caucuses, meetings with other congressmen from his state or region, plus lobbyists, constituents, and press to handle. He will dart into one hearing, get a quick fill-in from his staffer, inject his ten minutes' worth and rush on to the next event, often told by an aide how to vote as he rushes onto the floor. Only the staff specialist has any continuity with substance. The member is constantly hop scotching.[34]

Constituent Service. A congressional office today more closely resembles the customer service department of a large company than the typical legislative office of an earlier period. Until World War I a single clerk handled a member's entire correspondence. In those days congressional mail usually involved awarding rural mail routes, arranging for Spanish-American War pensions, sending out free seeds, and, occasionally, explaining legislation.[35]

Today a major responsibility of personal staffs, especially in the House, is responding to the myriad constituent requests from a member's state or district. For example, staffers untangle bureaucratic snarls in collecting Social Security or veterans' benefits; answer questions about student loans and similar programs; help home state or district organizations obtain federal grants; respond to constituent questions and comments on legislative and national issues by mail and e-mail; and produce newsletters and other mailings to keep constituents informed of their boss's activities. *(See "Casework," p. 617.)*

Such services are important not only for the benefits they provide to constituents but also for the benefits they bring to the relationship between a member of Congress and a voter. According to former congressional staffer Bisnow,

[Constituent service] is often considered one of the more beneficial things congressmen do, but the motivation goes beyond mere charity; personal touches typically matter to voters as much as larger issues of ideology, voting record, or even public reputation. As a result, constituents occupy almost deified status in the eyes of Hill offices, a flotilla of paid aides poised to handle their problems. Too bad for a challenger who can do nothing more than walk the district at his own expense.[36]

Junior members of Congress tend to pay more attention to constituent services than more senior members, and House members spend more time on casework than senators. In both chambers, however, senior legislators are likely to receive proportionately more casework requests than junior members, in part because they are better known to the public and, being senior, presumably are more powerful and thereby better equipped to resolve constituents' problems.[37] Senators often receive casework requests from outside their home states, particularly if they are prominent national figures; representatives rarely do.

With the recent explosion of Internet resources, congressional staff are able to communicate more easily through Web sites and e-mail with an increasing number of politically active constituents. One member's systems administrator described this phenomenon in 1997:

Measured by the e-mail responses some Hill offices are getting, technology has made contacting a member of Congress easier than ever. It has something to do with the speed and ease of sending e-mail, as opposed to sitting down to pen a letter. And e-mail, unlike U.S. mail,

TABLE 17-4 Congressional Staffs in House District and Senate State Offices

A sizable portion of the personal staff of a senator or representative is assigned to work in district or state offices rather than in Washington. For the House the percentage of staff in district offices has grown steadily over the years, reflecting in part the importance of direct contact with constituents. In the Senate the percentage has grown as well but is a smaller share of the entire staff and has not grown as much as House staff assigned to districts.

	House employees	Percentage of personal staff in district offices	Senate employees	Percentage of personal staff in state offices
1972	1,189	22.5	303	12.5
1978	2,317	33.4	816	25.0
1980	2,534	34.4	953	25.4
1985	2,871	38.1	1,180	28.8
1990	3,027	40.4	1,293	31.1
1995	3,459	48.1	1,278	30.1
1997	3,209	44.1	1,366	31.0
1999	3,192	44.2	1,414	33.2

SOURCE: Norman J. Ornstein, Thomas E. Mann, and Michael J. Malbin, *Vital Statistics on Congress, 1999–2000* (Washington, D.C.: American Enterprise Institute, 1999), 133, 134.

doesn't cost 32 cents a pop. There's a whole group that has emerged that would not be politically active in any way if they didn't have a computer. They've grown politically active through e-mail. We've never gotten a letter from them.[38]

The emphasis on constituent services is reflected in the increase in personal staff working in a member's district or state office. In 1999 senators deployed a third of their staff to their state offices—up from 12.5 percent in 1972. Representatives sent 44 percent of their aides to their districts in 1999, as opposed to 22.5 percent in 1972. Members contend that the field offices have lower staff salaries and lower overhead and are more convenient for constituents, local and state officials, and regional federal officials.[39] Caseworkers may be called research assistants or staff assistants. Their operations may be centered in either the member's Washington office or the state/district office. *(See Table 17-4, this page.)*

Legislation. Lawmaking is the primary task of members of Congress. In undertaking this task, members rely on their legislative assistants for substantive and political guidance as they weave their way through the daily thicket of complex, interdependent issues. More committee meetings are held than a member can prepare for or attend. Other members, federal officials, special interest groups, and sometimes even White House staff must be consulted before decisions are made, and often floor debates last well into the evening.

To juggle these demands, a member must depend heavily on staff throughout the legislative process. Specifically, legislative assistants work with members to draft bills and amendments and recommend policy initiatives and alternatives. LAs also monitor committee sessions that members cannot attend and may prepare lawmakers' speeches and position papers. In many offices, LAs are supervised by a legislative director, normally the senior legislative assistant.

In Senate offices, which have more staffers, a team of LAs often will specialize in different issues. Members of the House may rely simply on one or two LAs to handle legislation. In some cases the member delegates legislative correspondence and personally takes care of monitoring pending legislation.

Other Duties. Casework and legislation are only some of the chores handled by personal staffers. The press secretary serves as the member's chief spokesperson to the news media. Press aides compose news releases about legislative issues and newsworthy casework or federal grants, write newsletters, and organize press conferences. Because they deal almost exclusively with hometown media outlets, some House press aides are based in the district offices rather than in Washington. Where there is no press secretary, press relations are handled by the administrative assistant or a legislative assistant. Senators, who receive more national publicity and represent larger areas than members of the House, often have several deputy press secretaries or assistant press staff.

The office manager, who often is the second-level manager in a congressional office, is in charge of handling clerical functions.

The appointments secretary, called the executive secretary or scheduler in some offices, normally handles personal appointments and travel arrangements for the member. An executive secretary who has been in a member's office for some time often exercises direct or indirect control over other staff members.

The legislative correspondent drafts responses to letters about pending legislation. In some offices, the LA may draft letters in a particular subject area; in others, the legislative correspondent drafts letters for the LAs regardless of the subject.

The systems manager coordinates the member's computerized correspondence operations and often the e-mail and Internet homepage setup and maintenance. Given the enormous amount of mail members of Congress receive each year, correspondence operations have become an important function.

Relations with Committee Staff

Besides the help they get from personal aides, senior senators and representatives are assisted on legislative matters by staffs of the committees and subcommittees on which they serve. In addition, all senators since 1975 have been authorized up to three aides to help with their committee business. The chairman of a standing committee actually has two staffs. It is not unusual for an aide to do both committee work and personal casework for a member, no matter which payroll he or she is on.

Recruitment and Tenure

Representatives and senators hire their own personal aides. Although House and Senate employment offices are available, most hiring is based on informal contacts, but word of mouth and just plain luck are important as well. Potential staffers may seek out members who are involved in particular issue areas,

who are known to pay well, who are from a certain area of the country, or who have a particular ideological bent. Conversely, members may hire staffers for some of the same reasons.[40] In recent years members with private business backgrounds have used the congressional employment offices and even newspaper ads to solicit job applications.

In seeking knowledge and experience, members must decide whether to hire from the state or district, or from Washington circles. This is an especially delicate problem for first-term members who may have limited Washington contacts and who feel indebted to their campaign staff and stress cultivating state and district contacts. A staffer who came to Washington with newly elected senator Pete Domenici, R-N.M., said he soon realized how important it is to strike a balance when hiring staff:

> We had a lot of people we felt we had to hire from the campaign. We brought a lot of them with us. . . . The big mistake we made was that we did not hire anyone who knew the Senate. . . . I had to check ten offices every time I wanted to find out how you did something. It was insane.[41]

A staffing study conducted by the Congressional Management Foundation urged new House members to balance applicants' knowledge of constituencies and Washington politics in choosing their Hill staff. According to the study:

> Most members find it essential that at least one senior staffer be from the district to advise on the local political ramifications of positions and actions. Hiring all, or virtually all, of your Washington staff from the district, however, may cause your office to go through a long learning curve. Many freshman offices advise hiring an experienced office manager and an experienced legislative staffer. An experienced manager will save months of muddling through in the crucial phase of establishing your office. Similarly, an experienced legislative staffer can guide your inexperienced legislative staff.[42]

Party loyalty of staff, while important, may be a secondary consideration to many representatives and senators when making hiring decisions. "It may be [that members] consider their aides already self-screened: If someone wants to work for them, their politics must be compatible."[43] But loyalty does count and on occasion turns up in startling ways. In 1999 Republican Michael P. Forbes, who represented the First District of New York, switched to the Democratic Party, saying that the GOP "has become an angry, narrow-minded, intolerant and uncaring majority, incapable of governing at all, much less from the center, and tone-deaf to the concerns of a vast majority of Americans." His staff as loyal Republicans declined to go with him, resigning en masse two days after his announcement and forcing the Democrats to quickly put together a temporary replacement group of aides.

QUALIFICATIONS OF HILL STAFFERS

Congressional staffers in the modern Congress are more qualified than ever before and come increasingly from professional rather than political backgrounds, giving members better information for decisions. Yet some Capitol Hill employees, especially those with long service, believe many staffers see their

A Senate aide helps move boxes of evidence delivered from the House of Representatives in 1999 during the presidential impeachment trial.

jobs as way stations on the road to other opportunities—that is, employment on the Hill helps prepare them through training, experience, and contacts for other careers, often in the private sector at much larger salaries. Once, legislative work was a career, even a cause. As one staffer put it: "It used to be a way of life. Now it's a job."

Despite the presence of many highly qualified staffers on the Hill, actual congressional staff experience declined in the 1990s, according to a study by the Congressional Management Foundation. For example, in 1998 personal staff members on the House side had an average of 2.7 years of experience in their current jobs, a 27 percent decline from 1992. Personal staff on the Senate side in 1997 had 2.8 years of experience in their current position. In 1993 it was 3.5 years.[44] Foundation executive director Rick Shapiro attributed the House decline to the fast turnover of lawmakers: "As member experience declines, the experience they bring with them is going to decline."[45]

The 1998 study also showed that the average length of time House aides worked in Congress was 4.9 years, indicating that employees may transfer to new offices once their employers

leave. "I think this is a cause for concern," said Shapiro. "Ask any CEO if you can run an effective institution when your employees are leaving their jobs every 2.7 years, and the answer is no. Can you create an effective team? No. Can you create an effective institution? No."[46]

Sarah M. Martin, a staffer who worked on Capitol Hill for forty years, explained the change: "When I first started work here, you got to know everybody on the Hill. We were almost one family, really. We helped each other out, no matter what the party affiliation." Now, she said, "It's more time-consuming. The bigness—especially with the subcommittees—has broken up the closeness between members and their personal staffs and the committee staffs. People are out to advance themselves, to prove their worth, rather than to find a career. There's a lot of selfish motivation."

The Cost and Pay of Congressional Staff

The steady expansion of congressional staffs stemming from the 1946 and 1970 Legislative Reorganization Acts contributed significantly to the higher cost of running Congress. The expansion of House and Senate committees from 399 aides in 1947 to 2,043 in 1999 and personal staffs from 2,030 to about 11,500 drove up costs. For example, in fiscal 1960, approximately $12.3 million was appropriated for permanent committee and investigative staffs in both the House and Senate. By fiscal 1999 the amount was more than $175.9 million.[47]

The expansion of personal staffs also produced a substantial increase in the funding needed to run a member's office. In 1970 each representative was entitled to an annual clerk-hire allowance of $149,292 for a staff not to exceed fifteen employees for a district under 500,000 persons, or $157,092 for a staff not to exceed sixteen employees for a member representing a larger district. In 1979 the annual clerk-hire allowance for a staff of up to twenty-two employees was $288,156. By 1999 the allowance for the same number of staff had risen to $632,355.[48]

HOUSE ALLOWANCE

Since November 1995 representatives have paid for staff salaries, office expenses, and official mail out of their single "members' representational allowance." In 1999 this allowance averaged $952,777, including a base office expense allowance of $122,500. By 1999, the clerk-hire allowance of each House member was $632,355 a year, which members could use to hire up to eighteen full-time and four nonpermanent aides in their Washington and district offices. The clerk-hire allowance represented an increase of $393,775 since 1977. When adjusted for inflation, however, the 1999 amount was slightly lower in current purchasing power. The increase in the staff allowance mainly benefited junior members, who lacked the committee staff assistance enjoyed by their senior colleagues.

The representational allowance also includes travel funds for each member calculated by the distance between the District of Columbia and the farthest point in a member's district, as well as funds for rental of district office space. Funding for official mail is based on the number of non-business addresses per district. The average mail allowance in 1999 was $113,299. As of 1998 there was no longer a limit on the amount members may spend on mail, although there are many regulations on content. Because these three allowances have effectively been combined, members who wish to pay their staff more in salaries than the clerk-hire allowance can reduce other official expenses accordingly. Conversely, unused staff salary funds or travel money can be used to send more mail to the district. *(See "Official Allowances," p. 791, Vol. II.)*

SENATE ALLOWANCE

Three allowances make up senators' official personnel and office expense account: the administrative and clerical assistance allowance; the legislative assistance allowance; and the office expense allowance.

The administrative and clerical assistance allowance varies with the size of the senator's state. For 1999 the annual allowance ranged from $1,210,967 for states with fewer than 5 million residents to $2,157,222 for states with more than 28 million.

Senators may hire as many aides as they wish within their allowance. In practice, the range of employees is from thirteen to seventy, depending on the size of the state and the salary level; the "average" senator employs more than forty staffers.

In 1975 senators were provided a separate allowance to hire personal staffers for specialized work on a senator's committees, up to a maximum of three committee assignments. Although initially limited to senators without other staff support on com-

mittees, the fiscal 1978 appropriations bill for the legislative branch gave this additional legislative assistance allowance to all senators along with the administrative and clerical allowance, thereby making the Senate clerk-hire allowance actually two separate allowances. In 1999 each senator was authorized $396,477 for legislative assistance in addition to the regular clerk-hire allowance.

The original intent of the 1975 change was to give junior senators assistance in meeting their committee responsibilities. But because there no longer is any limit on the number of staff that can be employed, senators can use their legislative aides for either committee or personal staff work and appoint as many staff as funds will permit.

The office expense allowance, like the clerk-hire allowance, is governed by a formula, in this instance based primarily on the distance between Washington, D.C., and the senator's home state, and the population of the senator's state. In 1999 this allowance for senators ranged from $127,384 to $470,272.[49]

CHANGES IN STAFF SALARIES

The salaries of committee employees increased dramatically in the decades after World War II. In 1945 House employees were listed under "clerk-hire" categories with an annual base pay of $2,500. The 1970 Legislative Reorganization Act converted the "base pay" system of the House into a monthly salary system and raised the compensation levels of committee employees. In 1999 the highest-paid committee aides in the House received an annual salary of approximately $132,100; in the Senate, $134,015. Staffers on the House and Senate Appropriations panels are tra-

A late night at the congressional office: Majority Whip Tom DeLay, R-Texas, and his staff work at 10 p.m. to prepare for a House floor debate.

ditionally the highest paid. In 1999 forty-nine House Appropriations Committee aides earned over $100,000; ten Senate Appropriations staffers were above that level.[50]

Both the House and the Senate are required by law to report the salaries, allowances, and expenses paid to members and members' personal and committee staffs. The "Statement of Disbursements of the House" (known before 1993 as the "Report of the Clerk of the House") is issued quarterly; the "Report of the Secretary of the Senate," every six months. (Both reports are available to the public through the House and Senate Document rooms.)

Committee staff receive the same cost-of-living increases and insurance and retirement benefits as do other Capitol Hill employees. Vacation and sick leave policies vary according to committee.

Few regulations are available to guide members in setting pay rates for their personal aides, but there are ceilings on pay levels. In 1999 personal staff in the House and Senate could earn up to $132,159 annually, although few aides in either chamber are paid this much. And there is a minimum pay level: $1,200 per year in the House and $1,689 in the Senate, salaries normally intended for interns and part-time employees. Congress also is regulated by the minimum wage requirement, which in 1999 was $5.15 an hour.

Within these parameters, however, salaries and benefits for personal staff are left to the discretion of each member of Congress. Formal policies on working hours, vacation time, sick leave, and maternity leave also vary from office to office. In 1995 Congress included the Fair Labor Standards Act in its workplace compliance bill, which applied to the legislative branch eleven federal labor and antidiscrimination laws. However, the Office of Compliance, created with the workplace compliance bill to carry out the statutes, decided to exempt from overtime pay requirements many of the legislative employees who often work longer hours. The Compliance Office maintained that the overtime policy reflected standards found elsewhere in the government and in many private businesses.

Most House and Senate employees, like all federal employees, qualify for annual salary increases, or cost-of-living adjustments (COLAs). Unlike for most federal employees, however, the additional earnings are not automatically included in congressional staffers' paychecks. Instead, they are added to the members' committee and personal payroll funds, to be paid out to staff members only at the discretion of the Hill employer. Members, committee chairmen, or administrative officers can choose among giving their employees the increase, using the money to hire more staffers, or returning the money to the Treasury at the end of the year.

The salaries of some congressional staff—such as the clerk of the House, secretary of the Senate, parliamentarians, House counsel, and legislative counsel—are set by statute. Thus their salaries (and raises) are funded by legislative appropriations and, like those of senators and representatives, are normally assured. But if the pay of officers gets too close to that of members, they will not get an annual adjustment unless members also accept adjustment for their pay. (*See Chapter 27, Pay and Honoraria.*)

Congressional Staff: Ethics and Legalities

The highly charged political atmosphere on Capitol Hill leads inevitably to close public scrutiny of the personal conduct of members and staff. The result more often than not is controversy and conflict and, perhaps later, changes in rules and procedures.

Three of the most prominent ethics and legality issues emerging in the last fifty years have been congressional compliance with laws governing other public as well as private workers, use of staff at public expense for political—particularly election—purposes, and nepotism. Workplace compliance, as it was usually called, was addressed forthrightly in 1995 but only after years of struggle by reformers. Political use of staffers remains a ticklish issue as members and their aides walk a blurred line between appropriate committee or personal staff work and efforts to help get the boss reelected. Finally, the nepotism issue has faded almost from sight after a few high-profile scandals.

WORKPLACE COMPLIANCE

Until nearly the end of the twentieth century, members of Congress exempted themselves from most of the civil rights laws and other worker protection standards that they, by law, imposed on other employers. This policy earned Congress the unwelcome epithet as "The Last Plantation."

Members argued that their employment practices should not be regulated like those of a private business because Congress's work was political. Defenders of no regulation believed elected officials must be free to choose staffers who would be loyal to them. Many members also believed the principle of separation of powers would be violated if the executive branch had the power to enforce employment laws in the legislature. But the exemptions from laws governing most other employers eventually became a target of reformers inside and outside Congress, who attacked the practice as a failure of Congress to live under the very laws it passed.

When legislation to subject Congress to the labor laws governing private sector employment stalled in 1994, the House at first changed its rules to impose the compliance requirements on members. But in 1995 the newly Republican-controlled Congress moved further, passing as its first bill the Congressional Accountability Act. This legislation, which applied eleven federal labor laws to all congressional employees, replaced a haphazard mix of voluntary rules and internal protections for congressional staff. It also allowed congressional employees to take claims to federal court after an initial mediation and counseling stage. Many members remained skeptical of allowing employees to hail them into court, particularly during an election campaign, but supporters said this enforcement mechanism was essential to allow meaningful redress under the law. Nevertheless,

ETHICS RULES FOR CONGRESSIONAL STAFF

Like members of Congress, House and Senate employees must abide by certain ethics rules. These restrictions deal with honoraria, outside income, gifts, travel, financial disclosure, and post-employment lobbying. Most of the rules were amended in 1989 when Congress passed the Government Ethics Reform Act and again in 1995 when Congress adopted new gift rules. *(See "1995 Changes in Gift Rules," p. 981, Vol. II.)*

HONORARIA

As of January 1, 1991, members and staff of the House were prohibited from accepting honoraria. House employees could request, however, that charitable contributions be made in their name in lieu of honoraria for speeches and appearances. Charitable contributions, which were limited to $2,000 per speech, appearance, or article, could not be made to any organization that benefited the person who spoke or any of his or her relatives, nor could the House employee seek tax advantages from the contribution. In mid-1991 the Senate, in return for a pay raise, also eliminated honoraria for members and staff, although charitable contributions could be made.

OTHER OUTSIDE INCOME

Senior staff in the House—employees compensated at or above the GS-16 salary level—were barred from keeping more than 15 percent of the Executive Level II salary, $136,700 in 1999, in outside earned income; from being paid for working or affiliating with a law or other professional firm (they were allowed to teach for pay if the House Committee on Standards of Official Conduct approved); and from serving on boards of directors. Outside earned income included "wages, salary, fees, and other amounts paid for personal services, as opposed to items such as interest, rents, dividends, and capital gains, which represent a return on investments."

Also as of 1991 senior staff in the Senate were subject to a cap on outside income that was equal to or more than 15 percent of their Executive Level II salary.

GIFTS

In 1995 the Senate placed a $50 limit on gifts that senators and employees could receive. The rules placed a $100 annual limit on gifts from any one source. Senators and staff could accept unlimited gifts from family members and close friends but had to get approval from the ethics committee for gifts valued at more than $250. House members could no longer accept any gifts, unless the items were of nominal value. Members could still accept unlimited gifts from family and friends, but gifts valued at more than $250 required ethics committee approval. At the beginning of the 106th Congress in 1999, the House voted to permit its members to accept gifts valued at up to $50 as well.

The 1995 gift ban rules replaced rules approved in 1991 that allowed senators, representatives, and their employees to accept up to $250 in gifts annually. Members and staff did not have to count gifts worth $100 or less. The rules, which eased those passed less than two years earlier under the Ethics Reform Act of 1989, eliminated almost all requirements to disclose the receipt of gifts.

Under the 1989 rules, House members and staff were limited to $200 in gifts. Senators and their staff were prohibited from receiving gifts totaling more than $100 a year from anyone with a direct interest in legislation or gifts totaling more than $300 a year from anyone else but relatives. In both chambers, "nominal" gifts worth less than $75 were exempted.

TRAVEL

House staff could not receive more than thirty days of lodging a year from someone other than a relative. If the hospitality was extended more than four days, the employee had to ensure that it was in fact personal—not corporate-financed or being claimed as a business expense. Private sources could pay travel expenses for no more than four days of domestic travel and seven days for international trips (travel time was excluded for both categories). Travel expenses also could be paid for one accompanying relative. The House Committee on Standards of Official Conduct could waive gift and travel restrictions in "exceptional circumstances."

Private sources could pay travel expenses of Senate staff for no more than three days of domestic travel and seven days for international trips (both limits excluded travel time). The travel expenses for an accompanying spouse also could be paid.

FINANCIAL DISCLOSURE

The Government Ethics Act of 1989 for the first time brought all three branches of government under the same financial disclosure law, although each branch continued to be responsible for administering requirements for its own employees. The new rules on financial disclosure became effective with the reports due in 1991. Income of more than $200 from any source had to be reported. Gifts worth less than $75 did not have to be reported.

Employees who had charitable contributions made on their behalf in lieu of honoraria had to disclose the source and amount of the contributions. The charities receiving such contributions had to be disclosed in confidential reports to the House Committee on Standards of Official Conduct. In addition, the source and amount of any honoraria received by the spouse of a reporting individual had to be disclosed.

Travel reimbursements, including an itinerary and dates of travel, also had to be reported.

Finally, within thirty days after leaving office staffers were required to file a "termination report" containing complete financial disclosure information for the previous year up to the date of departure.

POSTEMPLOYMENT LOBBYING

Effective January 1, 1991, former House and Senate staff members (those at the GS-17 salary level or above) were barred for one year after leaving employment from lobbying the member, office, or committee for which they had worked. In 1999 an attempt to extend the postemployment ban to two years failed to win approval in a House–Senate conference committee. Leadership staff members were barred from lobbying the members and employees of the leadership for the chamber in which they served.

CONGRESS AND WORKPLACE COMPLIANCE

The first bill enacted by the Republican-led 104th Congress (1995–1996) was S 2, which amended eleven federal labor and antidiscrimination laws to apply specifically to Congress and its related offices. Among other things, the Congressional Accountability Act allowed congressional employees to take claims to federal court after an initial mediation and counseling stage. The amended laws were:

• Civil Rights Act of 1964—prohibited discrimination in employment on the basis of race, color, religion, sex, or nationality.

• Occupational Safety and Health Act of 1970 (OSHA)—set safety regulations for workplaces.

• Age Discrimination in Employment Act of 1967—prohibited workplace discrimination against people age forty and older.

• Rehabilitation Act of 1973—provided federal aid for a variety of programs for disabled workers and for the training of personnel to work with the disabled.

• Americans with Disabilities Act of 1990—prohibited workplace discrimination against people with disabilities.

• Family and Medical Leave Act of 1993—set criteria for unpaid parental and medical leave for employees seeking to spend time with children or ailing family members.

• Fair Labor Standards Act of 1938—dealt with minimum wage and mandatory overtime or compensation for employees who worked more than forty hours per week, as updated in 1989. (The minimum wage was increased again in 1996.)

• Employee Polygraph Protection Act of 1988—restricted the use of polygraph tests of employees by employers. The use of legal lie detector tests by the Capitol police was not affected by application of this law.

• Worker Adjustment and Retraining Notification Act of 1988—required a sixty-day advance notice of a plant closing or large layoffs of permanent workers.

• Veterans Re-employment Act of 1994—required employers to rehire for the same or similar position returning veterans who left their jobs after being called into military service.

• Labor-Management Dispute Procedures—a part of the *United States Code* (Chapter 71 of Title V) that established procedures for resolving federal labor-management disputes.

OFFICES COVERED

Congressional offices and officers covered by the 1995 Congressional Accountability Act were:

• Each office of the House and Senate, including each office of a member and each committee
• Each joint committee
• Office of Technology Assessment
• Capitol police
• Congressional Budget Office
• Office of the Architect of the Capitol
• Senate and House restaurants and gift shops
• Botanic Garden
• Office of the attending physician
• Capitol Guide Service
• Office of Compliance.

members could still fire, or refuse to hire or promote, anyone for "political incompatibility."

The statutes to which Congress made itself subject included the Civil Rights Act of 1964, which prohibited discrimination in employment on the basis of race, color, religion, sex, or nationality, and the Occupational Safety and Health Act of 1970, which set safety rules for workplaces. Other statutes included the Americans with Disabilities Act of 1990, which prohibited workplace discrimination against people with disabilities, and the Family and Medical Leave Act of 1993, which allowed unpaid leave to care for sick family members. *(See box, Congress and Workplace Compliance, this page.)*

Even before the 1995 legislation, the House did attempt to create procedures allowing employees to file complaints alleging mistreatment by supervisors, including members of Congress. An Office of Fair Employment Practices was set up in-house, under supervision of the clerk of the House, to handle complaints. Critics, however, said internal policing was inherently flawed. In fact, the complaint procedures were rarely used, which critics attributed to employees' fear of retribution, including firing, if they spoke out.

The 1995 Congressional Accountability Act addressed this issue squarely by setting up clear complaint procedures. Under this act, both House and Senate employees with grievances must go through a formal complaint, mediation, and hearing process conducted by the newly created Compliance Office. Employees must request private counseling by the office within 180 days of the alleged violation. No later than 15 days after the counseling phase, which is normally 30 days, the aggrieved employee who wants to proceed must file a request for mediation with the office. Mediation typically involves communication among all the parties involved in the case. If unsatisfied, the employee can file a formal complaint with the office to request a hearing and a decision by a hearing officer, or abandon the internal review process and file a civil lawsuit in U.S. District Court or in the District of Columbia District Court. Appeals are permitted if the parties are not satisfied with the hearing officer's decision. An aggrieved party not satisfied with the final court decision can appeal it to the U.S. Court of Appeals for the Federal Circuit. A final appeal can be made to the U.S. Supreme Court.[51] Employees may go to the courts first only if the claim is based on the Constitution, rather than the statutes of the 1995 law. Before 1995, court action was another main avenue for settling congressional employment grievances.

One important event that increased pressure for an employee rights law was a precedent-setting congressional job discrimination suit based on the Constitution that was settled out of court in 1979 for an undisclosed sum of money. The suit was filed in 1974 against former representative Otto E. Passman, D-La., by one-time aide Shirley Davis.

The case established the constitutional right of a congressional employee who claims sex discrimination to sue a member of Congress for damages. The out-of-court settlement, however, left undecided the question of whether the Constitution's

"Speech or Debate" clause (Article I, Section 6) provides a member of Congress with immunity from job discrimination suits in at least some circumstances. This clause protects members from court suits for actions taken in Congress as part of their official duties.

The suit filed by Davis against Passman initially was thrown out of court by a federal district judge, who ruled that no existing law provided Davis with protection from job discrimination by a member of Congress. On appeal, however, the Supreme Court ruled that the Constitution itself gives individuals the right to sue members of Congress, regardless of the provisions of any particular statute, for alleged constitutional violations.[52]

In its decision, the Court dealt only with Davis's right to sue Passman, not the merits of her complaint. The case was then sent back to the lower federal courts to be decided on the merits, but the out-of-court settlement was announced before the courts acted. Nevertheless, the specter of future court actions by employees, under the precedent of the Passman case, helped to buoy the case of reformers seeking a statutory employment protection law.

LEGISLATIVE WORK VERSUS POLITICS

The issue of employing congressional staff for political gain invariably comes up at election time when incumbents are accused of using staffers to help in their reelection campaigns.

When members return home to campaign they take with them the customary entourage of staff aides, who must juggle their political work with their status as government employees paid with federal tax dollars. No specific federal law forbids congressional staff to perform political duties, but the practice is somewhat limited by rules in the House and, to a lesser extent, in the Senate.

Personal staff members may play an important role in the reelection campaigns of their members of Congress. House rules allow a House employee to work on a campaign—compiling mailing lists and organizing fund-raisers, for example—if assigned congressional duties also are being fulfilled. The Senate has no formal procedures to govern the practice.

A former congressional aide commented in 1990 on the fine line between legislative work and politics:

[Congress] by its nature is so intensely political that it becomes a practical impossibility to say in many instances where the discharge of official duties leaves off and aspirations to higher office (or reelection) begin. A congressman and his staff, for example, are not supposed to use office typewriters, photocopy machines, and phone lines to solicit financial contributions for election campaigns, but who is to judge their ulterior motives in taking positions, proposing bills and amendments, writing speeches, or issuing press releases that happen to be of value in both legislative and campaign contexts?[53]

To avoid being criticized for using government-paid staff to work on their campaigns, incumbents seek legitimacy, or the appearance of legitimacy, through several different approaches. "Because of what has gone under the bridge in the past, people are more aware and more careful," said one legislative aide who took a 50 percent pay cut in 1978 to help his boss, Sen. Robert P.

As Sen. Daniel Patrick Moynihan, D-N.Y., makes his way with congressional aides to a committee meeting, a lobbyist hands him literature.

Griffin, R-Mich., in his unsuccessful effort to win a third term. "My sense is that everybody is overly sensitive and overly paranoid about it."[54]

In some cases House and Senate staffers go on vacation or temporarily take themselves off the government payroll. Others try to mix their congressional job with election campaign duties and agree to a cut in pay to reflect the reduction in their congressional work. Others remain on the payroll to avoid losing benefits but claim to put in a full day of constituent service at the member's district office before going to campaign headquarters to help their boss in the reelection bid. Nonetheless, staffers "simply doing their ordinary job is a large contribution in itself."[55]

Supreme Court Case

In March 1981 the Supreme Court let stand an appeals court ruling that said it was up to Congress to determine whether and under what restraints congressional aides may double as campaign workers. The Court's decision appeared to clear the way for a senator or representative to keep staff aides on the government payroll even when they were working almost exclusively on the member's reelection campaign.

The 1981 appeals court ruling was issued in a 1977 suit brought by former Federal Election Commission attorney Joel D. Joseph against Sen. Howard W. Cannon, D-Nev., and Chester B. Sobsey, Cannon's $40,000-a-year administrative assistant. Joseph charged that Sobsey had remained on the Senate payroll from March 1975 through November 1976 while working for Cannon's reelection.

The suit also claimed that Cannon's approval of Sobsey's salary payments under those circumstances constituted a fraudulent claim against the government. But the appeals court held that to judge the legality of Cannon's actions would violate the Constitution's separation of powers doctrine. Only the House and Senate can judge such "political questions," the appeals court ruled.

The appeals court based much of its ruling on the conclusion that Congress itself had set no hard-and-fast standard that would have enabled Cannon to determine where to draw the line between Sobsey's official duties and his political chores. Existing rules governing staff campaign work were lenient and subject to differing interpretations. In the past both chambers had been extremely reluctant to police their members' use of staff in political campaigns. Indeed, Congress had never allowed its own staffers to be restricted by the Hatch Act, which prohibits civil service employees from participating in partisan political activities.

Today, under House regulations staff members, while not permitted to contribute cash to a campaign, may assist a member's reelection effort so long as their assigned congressional duties also are being fulfilled. Those duties are set by each member, as is the amount of vacation time granted. "If they are on their own time, they can do all the politicking they want," said a spokesman for the House Committee on Standards of Official Conduct.

Senate restrictions are even more lax. One House aide, who took himself off the payroll in 1978 to manage a Senate campaign, said: "The Senate rules have big wide holes in them large enough to let just about anybody work in the campaign from the federal staff."

The guiding document on the subject is a Senate Rules and Administration Committee report of October 17, 1977, which states that "other than actual handling of campaign funds, the Senate has not imposed any restrictions on the participation of a member of a senator's staff in that senator's reelection campaign." Several weeks after the 1981 appeals court decision in the Cannon case, the Senate Select Committee on Ethics proposed incorporating into the Senate ethics code a 1977 ruling by the committee declaring that senators should remove from their congressional payrolls staffers who undertake political work to the detriment of their official Senate duties. But the full Senate never acted on the proposal.

Flexibility of Staff Use

Unlike the House, which does not allow personal staff to solicit and receive campaign contributions, the Senate provides that three members of each senator's staff may be designated for that purpose. In fact, in Cannon's Supreme Court case, the senator argued that he had designated Sobsey as one of the staffers allowed to solicit and receive campaign funds.

The use of congressional staff on a campaign offers an enormous advantage to members over their challengers, who must use their own campaign funds to finance staff support. But it is difficult to differentiate political activities from legislative work that is also usable in an election campaign. Some activities, such as managing a campaign, raising money, and dealing with poll results, are clearly political. But casework, speech writing, and preparation of responses on particular issues fall into a gray area.

Most of those engaged in campaign efforts at high levels are the administrative assistants. An AA is usually a member's top congressional aide and the one having the most political as well as legislative experience.

In close races it is not unusual to find a massive shift of personnel from congressional work to the campaign. Because this shift offers an obvious target for an opponent, staff members in these contests almost always leave the government payroll.

In 1985 the Senate Ethics Committee issued an "interpretive ruling" (No. 402) stating that an unnamed senator's personal secretary could receive pay from the campaign committee for off-hours work she did for the senator's reelection. The secretary had been designated to receive campaign contributions for the senator.

In 1986 the House ethics committee investigated complaints that Rep. Mac Sweeney, R-Texas, was threatening to fire staff members who refused to perform campaign activities. The

Speaker Tom Foley's staff, pictured here in 1989, included his wife, seated beside him; under the nepotism rule, she served without pay as his chief of staff.

committee said it found no evidence of impropriety and it took no further action.

House Minority Whip Newt Gingrich, R-Ga., later Speaker, was investigated by the House ethics committee in 1989–1990 for suggestions that he improperly used his congressional payroll for political purposes. The *Atlanta Business Chronicle* reported in its July 24, 1989, issue that Gingrich had given large, but temporary, year-end pay raises to staff members when they returned to his congressional office after taking leave without government pay to work on his campaign in the 1986 and 1988 elections. Gingrich denied any wrongdoing and said he was being chastised for a legitimate practice that is widespread on Capitol Hill—members giving their staff year-end bonuses. The investigation of Gingrich, which included other charges, was dropped in March 1990.

QUESTIONABLE HIRING PRACTICES

Nepotism has been a recurring problem in Congress. Some members have used their staff allowances to hire relatives and, in effect, supplement their own incomes.

On May 20, 1932, the House adopted a resolution providing that: "The Clerk of the House of Representatives is hereby authorized and directed to keep open for public inspection the payroll records of the disbursing officer of the House." The resolution was adopted without debate. Few members on the floor understood its import. The next day, however, newspapers published stories based on examinations of the disbursing officer's

records. They disclosed that ninety-seven members of the House devoted their clerk-hire allowance, in whole or in part, to paying persons having the same names as their own. Presumably these persons were relatives. The names were published, and "nepotism in Congress" became the subject of wide public discussion. At that time, however, nepotism was not illegal or even a violation of the standing rules.

Senate payroll information did not become available for public inspection until twenty-seven years later. On June 26, 1959, the Senate by voice vote adopted a resolution requiring the secretary of the Senate to make public the name, title, salary, and employer of all Senate employees. The resolution was the outgrowth of critical newspaper stories on the withholding of payroll information, coupled with additional disclosures of congressional nepotism.

A few years later nepotism became a problem for Rep. Adam Clayton Powell Jr., D-N.Y., in a case that was one of a series of events leading to a landmark Supreme Court decision on qualifications of members of Congress. Soon after marriage in December 1960, Powell employed his Puerto Rican wife, Yvette Marjorie Flores, as a paid member of his congressional office staff. Mrs. Powell remained in Puerto Rico after the birth of a son in 1962 but continued to draw a $20,578 annual salary as a clerk whose job was to answer mail from Spanish-speaking constituents.

In 1964 the House adopted a resolution aimed specifically at the Powell situation: it forbade members to hire employees who did not work either in the member's home district or in the member's Washington, D.C., office. (That provision was made permanent in 1976.) Mrs. Powell, however, continued to live in Puerto Rico. Following a select committee investigation of that and other charges against Powell, the House on March 1, 1967, voted to exclude him from the 90th Congress. The Supreme Court ruled later, however, that the House action was unconstitutional, and Powell returned to Congress in 1969. *(See "Powell," p. 921, Vol. II.)* In 1967 Congress approved a measure to curb nepotism in federal employment. The measure, added to a postal rate–federal pay bill, prohibited public officials, including members of Congress, from appointing or trying to promote the appointment of relatives in the agency in which the officials served. The ban covered all officials, including the president, but it did not cover relatives already employed. And it did not prevent an official in one agency or chamber of Congress from seeking to obtain employment for a relative in another agency or chamber.

The *U.S. Senate Handbook and the House Members' Congressional Handbook,* prepared for all new members and updated periodically by the Senate Rules and Administration Committee and the House Administration Committee, lists twenty-seven classifications of relatives whose employment by representatives and senators is prohibited by law. Certification that an employee is related to a member of Congress must be made on payroll authorizations by the employing member or by the committee or subcommittee chairman.

In 1995 and 1996 the conservative Landmark Legal Foundation requested that the ethics committee investigate whether House Democratic Whip David E. Bonior of Michigan violated nepotism rules by employing his wife. The ethics committee eventually found no substance to the nepotism charge; Bonior said his wife worked in his office four years before they were married in 1991 and thus was exempt from the ban.[56]

NOTES

1. Michael J. Malbin, *Unelected Representatives: Congressional Staff and the Future of Representative Government* (New York: Basic Books, 1980), 28.

2. Paul S. Rundquist, "Congress and Parliaments," *CRS Review* (March 1989): 32.

3. Norman J. Ornstein, Thomas E. Mann, and Michael J. Malbin, *Vital Statistics on Congress, 1997–1998* (Washington, D.C.: CQ Press, 1998), 129.

4. Ibid., 139.

5. Hedrick Smith, *The Power Game: How Washington Works* (New York: Random House, 1988), 282.

6. Bradley S. Keare, *1998 House Staff Employment Study* (Washington, D.C.: Congressional Management Foundation, 1998), 3, 93–94.

7. William L. Morrow, *Congressional Committees* (New York: Scribner's, 1969), 52.

8. Harrison W. Fox Jr. and Susan Webb Hammond, *Congressional Staffs: The Invisible Force in American Lawmaking* (New York: Free Press, 1977), 15.

9. Ibid.

10. Ibid., 20.

11. Richard A. Baker, *The Senate of the United States: A Bicentennial History* (Malabar, Fla.: Krieger, 1988), 89–90.

12. Lindsay Rogers, "The Staffing of Congress," *Political Science Quarterly* 56 (March 1991): 1–2.

13. Robert C. Byrd, *The Senate, 1789–1989: Addresses on the History of the United States Senate* (Washington, D.C.: Government Printing Office, 1988), 538.

14. Baker, *Senate of the United States,* 89–90.

15. Michael J. Malbin, "Delegation, Deliberation, and the New Role of Congressional Staff," in *The New Congress,* ed. Thomas E. Mann and Norman J. Ornstein (Washington, D.C.: American Enterprise Institute, 1981), 138.

16. Byrd, *The Senate, 1789–1989,* 550.

17. Fox and Hammond, *Congressional Staffs,* 22.

18. Christopher J. Deering and Steven S. Smith, *Committees in Congress,* 3rd ed. (Washington, D.C.: CQ Press, 1997), 166.

19. Ibid.

20. Lyn Ragsdale, *Vital Statistics on the Presidency: Washington to Clinton* (Washington, D.C.: CQ Press, 1998), 266–268.

21. Ornstein et al., *Vital Statistics on Congress, 1997–1998,* 139.

22. Lawrence C. Dodd and Bruce I. Oppenheimer, *Congress Reconsidered,* 6th ed. (Washington, D.C.: CQ Press, 1997), 379.

23. Bruce Bartlett, "Downsizing Staff with Painful Results," *Washington Times,* November 22, 1996, A18. Cited in Roger H. Davidson and Walter J. Oleszek, *Congress and Its Members,* 7th ed. (Washington, D.C.: CQ Press, 2000), 219.

24. U.S. Congress, *Congressional Record,* daily ed., 105th Cong., 1st sess., July 30, 1996, S9117. Cited in Davidson and Oleszek, *Congress and Its Members,* 220.

25. Malbin, "Delegation, Deliberation, and the New Role of Congressional Staff," 151.

26. Smith, *Power Game,* 284, 289–290.

27. Ibid., 285.

28. Malbin, "Delegation, Deliberation, and the New Role of Congressional Staff," 170.

29. Quoted in Kenneth Kofmehl, *Professional Staffs of Congress* (West Lafayette, Ind.: Purdue Research Foundation, 1962), 212.

30. Malbin, *Unelected Representatives,* 170–187.

31. Jeffrey H. Birnbaum and Alan S. Murray, *Showdown at Gucci Gulch: Lawmakers, Lobbyists, and the Unlikely Triumph of Tax Reform* (New York: Vintage Books, 1987), 217, 214.

32. *CQ Almanac, 1997* (Washington, D.C.: Congressional Quarterly, 1998), 9–59.

33. Mark Bisnow, *In the Shadow of the Dome: Chronicles of a Capitol Hill Aide* (New York: Morrow, 1990), 91.

34. Smith, *Power Game,* 282.

35. Stephen Isaacs, "The Capitol Game," *Washington Post,* February 16–20, 22–24, 1975.

36. Bisnow, *In the Shadow of the Dome,* 76.

37. Davidson and Oleszek, *Congress and Its Members,* 152.

38. Christoper Swope, "Mr. Smith E-mails Washington," *Congressional Quarterly Weekly Report,* November 29, 1997.

39. Ornstein et al., *Vital Statistics on Congress, 1997–1998,* 128–129; Davidson and Oleszek, *Congress and Its Members,* 155.

40. Fox and Hammond, *Congressional Staffs,* 49.

41. Richard F. Fenno Jr., *The Emergence of a Senate Leader: Pete Domenici and the Reagan Budget* (Washington, D.C.: CQ Press, 1991), 4–5.

42. David Twenhafel, ed., *Setting Course: A Congressional Management Guide,* 4th ed. (Washington, D.C.: Congressional Management Foundation, 1992), 30.

43. Bisnow, *In the Shadow of the Dome,* 131.

44. Keare, *1998 House Staff Employment Study,* 3; Thomas J. Klouda, *1997 Senate Staff Employment: Salary, Tenure, Demographics, and Benefits* (Washington, D.C.: Congressional Management Foundation, 1997), 3.

45. Guy Gugliotta, "House Aides' Experience Drops, 'Pay Gap' Grows," *Washington Post,* November 12, 1998, A19.

46. Ibid.

47. Paul Dwyer, "Legislative Branch Appropriations for Committee and Personal Staff and Agency Contributions: FY 1960–FY 1984," Congressional

Research Service report, February 14, 1984; Paul Dwyer, "Appropriations for FY 1999: Legislative Branch," Congressional Research Service report, October 27, 1998.

48. Norman J. Ornstein, Thomas E. Mann, and Michael J. Malbin, *Vital Statistics on Congress, 1984–1985* (Washington, D.C.: American Enterprise Institute, 1984), 132; Norman J. Ornstein et al., *Vital Statistics on Congress, 1991–1992* (Washington, D.C.: CQ Press, 1992); Paul Dwyer, "Salaries and Allowances: The Congress," Congressional Research Service report, June 27, 1999, 3.

49. Dwyer, "Salaries and Allowances: The Congress," 6.

50. Abigail Reese, "Six-Figure Staffers See Their Ranks Grow by 3%," *www.rollcall.com*.

51. *Congress and the Nation Vol. IX, 1993–1996* (Washington, D.C.: Congressional Quarterly, 1998), 892–893.

52. *Davis v. Passman*, 442 U.S. 228 (1979).

53. Bisnow, *In the Shadow of the Dome*, 192.

54. Christopher Buchanan, "Campaigning by Staff Aides Is Still a Common Practice," *Congressional Quarterly Weekly Report*, October 28, 1978, 3116.

55. Bisnow, *In the Shadow of the Dome*, 192.

56. *Congress and the Nation Vol. IX*, 902.

SELECTED BIBLIOGRAPHY

Baker, Richard A. *The Senate of the United States: A Bicentennial History.* Malabar, Fla.: Krieger, 1988.

Birnbaum, Jeffrey H., and Alan S. Murray. *Showdown at Gucci Gulch: Lawmakers, Lobbyists, and the Unlikely Triumph of Tax Reform.* New York: Vintage, 1987.

Bisnow, Mark. *In the Shadow of the Dome: Chronicles of a Capitol Hill Aide.* New York: Morrow, 1990.

Byrd, Robert C. *The Senate, 1789–1989: Addresses on the History of the United States Senate.* Washington, D.C.: Government Printing Office, 1988.

Cooper, Joseph, and G. Calvin Mackenzie. *The House at Work.* Austin: University of Texas Press, 1981.

Cummings, Frank. *Capitol Hill Manual.* 2nd ed. Washington, D.C.: Bureau of National Affairs, 1984.

Davidson, Roger H., and Walter J. Oleszek. *Congress and Its Members.* 7th ed. Washington, D.C.: CQ Press, 2000.

Deering, Christopher J., and Steven S. Smith. *Committees in Congress.* 3rd ed. Washington, D.C.: CQ Press, 1997.

Fenno, Richard F., Jr. *The Emergence of a Senate Leader: Pete Domenici and the Reagan Budget.* Washington, D.C.: CQ Press, 1991.

———. *The Making of a Senator: Dan Quayle.* Washington, D.C.: CQ Press, 1989.

———. *The Presidential Odyssey of John Glenn.* Washington, D.C.: CQ Press, 1990.

Fox, Harrison W., Jr., and Susan Webb Hammond. *Congressional Staffs: The Invisible Force in American Lawmaking.* New York: Free Press, 1977.

Francis, Charles C., and Jeffrey B. Trammell, eds. *The Almanac of the Unelected: Staff of the U.S. Congress.* 2nd ed. Washington, D.C.: Almanac of the Unelected, 1988.

Hawkins, Betsy W. *Setting Course: A Congressional Management Guide.* 6th ed. Washington, D.C.: Congressional Management Foundation, 1996.

Jones, Rochelle, and Peter Woll. *The Private World of Congress.* New York: Free Press, 1979.

Kofmehl, Kenneth. *Professional Staffs of Congress.* 3rd ed. West Lafayette, Ind.: Purdue University Press, 1977.

Malbin, Michael J. "Delegation, Deliberation, and the New Role of Congressional Staff." In *The New Congress*, ed. Thomas E. Mann and Norman J. Ornstein. Washington, D.C.: American Enterprise Institute, 1981.

———. *Unelected Representatives: Congressional Staff and the Future of Representative Government.* New York: Basic Books, 1980.

Miller, James A. *Running in Place: Inside the Senate.* New York: Simon and Schuster, 1986.

Morrow, William L. *Congressional Committees.* New York: Scribner's, 1969.

Ornstein, Norman J., Thomas E. Mann, and Michael J. Malbin. *Vital Statistics on Congress, 1997–1998.* Washington, D.C.: Congressional Quarterly, 1998.

Redman, Eric. *The Dance of Legislation.* New York: Simon and Schuster, 1973.

Reid, T. R. *Congressional Odyssey: The Saga of a Senate Bill.* New York: Freeman, 1980.

Smith, Hedrick. *The Power Game: How Washington Works.* New York: Random House, 1988.

U.S. Congress. House. Committee on House Administration. *New Member Orientation Handbook.* Washington, D.C.: Government Printing Office, 1988.

Wolpe, Bruce C. *Lobbying Congress: How the System Works.* Washington, D.C.: Congressional Quarterly, 1990.

PART IV

Pressures on Congress

CHAPTER 18

Constituency Pressures

"MEMBERS OF CONGRESS are inevitably caught in a crossfire of competing expectations," political scientist R. Douglas Arnold wrote in 1981. "They are national legislators, charged with such exalted goals as furthering the national interest, providing for the common defense, and promoting the general welfare. They are also local representatives, elected by and accountable to narrow geographic constituencies, and held responsible for protecting and advancing myriad local interests."[1]

Since the First Congress convened in 1789, the dual roles of Congress—making laws and responding to constituents' demands—have compelled lawmakers to balance great national issues against vital local concerns. As an ever-expanding legislative agenda made serving in Congress a full-time job, members came under increasing pressure to help constituents deal with an increasingly complex government that had more and more effect on their daily lives.

Members of Congress must deal with conflicting demands on their time and attention. Some legislators base their careers on meticulously caring for the interests of their state or district. A few—usually those with safe seats and sufficient seniority to have earned committee chairmanships or leadership posts—can devote nearly full attention to national issues.

In deciding which legislation to support or oppose, most legislators—especially representatives, who must stand for reelection every two years—continually weigh demands of their constituencies against their conscience, their understanding of the issues, and the pressures created by the broader political context. On major issues, allegiance to the party, pressure from congressional leaders, the influence of politically powerful national lobbies, and the persuasive powers of the president can compel senators and representatives to vote against their constituents' opinion—or at least to sidestep issues.

Nevertheless, it is constituents—not the president, the congressional leaders, or the national lobbyists—who hold the ultimate power. Whatever factors legislators consider in making specific decisions, they cannot ignore for long the voters who elected them. As successful politicians who were elected largely because of their skill at dealing with constituents, most senators and representatives are adept at courting public favor in their home states or districts. And as party organizations have lost power at the grass roots, legislators have come to rely more heavily on constituent services to ensure the continuing loyalty of the voters who have the power to turn them out of office.

Most members today keep themselves before the voters' eyes through frequent trips back home, newsletters and mass mailings, press coverage, and diligent casework on the part of their staffs. Most also lobby vigorously for federal projects and funds that will benefit their states and districts.

Representation: Members and Constituents

Representation is at the center of legislators' relationships with their constituents. With a few exceptions, when state legislatures tried to instruct senators how to vote on certain issues, members of Congress have always determined for themselves how closely they would try to represent the interests of their constituents. (See box, Early Notions of Representative Government, p. 612.)

In his "Speech to the Electors of Bristol," the British statesman Edmund Burke identified two styles of representation: the trustee, who is a free agent and follows personal convictions, principles, judgments, and conscience; and the delegate, who consults with constituents and follows their wishes. Few members of Congress follow only one style or the other; most are what political scientists refer to as "politicos," who assume a particular style of representation depending on the circumstances. As scholars Roger H. Davidson and Walter J. Oleszek noted in Congress and Its Members, "Most lawmakers develop sophisticated ways of thinking about the choices they make, distinguishing those for which they can play the Trustee from those for which the Delegate mode is expected or appropriate."[2]

On some matters, constituents' opinions may set boundaries that a lawmaker cannot cross. A representative from an agricultural district, for example, could not support policies that would lower the price for local crops. Even on non–income-related matters, legislators must be responsive to views that are broadly held or held with great intensity. When issues are low profile, relatively mundane, or of interest to only a few of their constituents, however, members have considerably more freedom to vote as they see fit. As political scientist David C. Kozak noted,

constituency heat and constituency relevance may be the dividing line between a member's use of a trustee or a delegate style. When input is received from constituents . . . or constituency interests are on the line . . . the legislator is more apt to be a delegate. When these factors are absent for the individual members—even though there may be more controversy within the Congress—there is a greater likelihood that the member will be a trustee.[3]

EARLY NOTIONS OF REPRESENTATIVE GOVERNMENT

The relationship between a member of Congress and his or her constituents is the crux of self-government in the United States. Only the vitality of that relationship ensures that government by the laws enacted in Congress is also government by the people. Notions of effective representation have changed, however, as the country has grown and its government has become more complex.

Before the American Revolution, the colonists were English subjects represented, at least in theory, in the English Parliament. It was precisely against the fictitious character of this representation that the colonists rebelled.

INSTRUCTION OF HOUSE MEMBERS

The frustration of being subject to a government in which they did not participate impressed upon the colonists the importance of exercising continuous control over the government. That desire for control was reflected in the first American experiments with a representative national government: under the Articles of Confederation that preceded the Constitution, members of Congress considered instructions from their state legislatures to be binding. And several state constitutions explicitly recognized the right to instruct members of Congress and state legislators.

Some sought to extend this control to the newly created House of Representatives. In the first session of the First Congress, a proposed amendment to the Bill of Rights would have guaranteed the right of the people to instruct their representatives. The preponderance of opinion, however, held that representatives should act on their own initiative, as trustees, and not merely as agents for their constituencies.

Thomas Hartley of Pennsylvania, for example, argued that Congress itself was the best judge of legislation and that binding instructions would make it impossible to accommodate various viewpoints. James Madison did not believe that members of any one constituency could speak for all the people. And Roger Sherman of Connecticut, implied that instructions would turn representatives into messenger boys. The amendment was never approved.

INSTRUCTION OF SENATORS

Circumstances differed in the Senate, which was deliberately separated from the voters. Until the passage of the Seventeenth Amendment, in 1913, which required direct election of the Senate, the Senate's constituents were not the people but the state governments, whose legislators elected the senators. Since the voters could not show their preferences for U.S. senators, the state legislators enjoyed great freedom in selecting them and sometimes adopted the practice of instructing the senators they had elected.

Insofar as senators were considered ambassadors of their states, the practice of giving them instructions seemed perfectly natural. The size and operation of the state legislatures made the practice of instruction a simple matter. Although senators generally obeyed instructions, state legislatures, not surprisingly, were more inclined than the senators themselves to consider their wishes binding on their senators' actions.

The distinction between senators' and representatives' responsibility to their state legislatures was evident in the formula commonly used to provide direction to members of Congress. Instructions

adopted by the Tennessee General Assembly in 1840 offer an example: "That our Senators to Congress be *instructed* and our Representatives *requested* to vote against the chartering by Congress of a National Bank" [italics added].

Before the Civil War, southern state legislatures frequently instructed senators to assert states' rights, but the Union victory in 1865 settled the national divisions that had given force to that practice. According to historian George H. Haynes, more senators were instructed by state legislatures during the 1868 impeachment trial of President Andrew Johnson than on any other issue that had ever come before the Senate. But with that exception, senators after the Civil War came to feel as free as representatives to disregard legislatures' instructions.

In 1913, with passage of the Seventeenth Amendment, senators were freed entirely from the constraints of legislatures and became representatives of—and accountable to—the voters in their states. Because of their longer terms and usually larger and more diverse constituencies, senators generally enjoyed more freedom to vote their conscience than did House members. For members of both houses, however, the task of balancing national interests and local concerns grew more formidable as the country emerged as a world power and the federal government expanded into new economic and social arenas.

In modern times, certain technological, scientific, and political forces have combined to alter our notions of representative government in ways that are almost certain to have ramifications in the twenty-first century. None of these forces are likely to return either chamber of Congress to the status of the Senate before 1913; nevertheless, by the end of the 1990s, they had produced among senators and representatives an unprecedented level of attentiveness to voters' concerns.

Politicians who are either in office or seeking office now make routine use of modern scientific polling to gauge the attitudes of constituents—a practice sometimes supplemented by the organization of focus groups to coax out additional information. Despite the claims of critics that too many members use these methods blindly to tailor their actions to voters' latest attitudes, political necessity suggests that the use of such techniques is not likely to diminish. Potentially even more far-reaching is the immense growth of electronic communications—particularly the Internet—which, beginning in the late 1990s, gave an immediacy to political contact that had never before existed.

A few outspoken advocates of the application of electronic communication to politics went so far as to suggest that it could lead to national referendums at the click of a computer key. Although both politicians and scholars of politics consider this a dangerous approach to decision making in a representative government, other observers point to the increasing popularity at the state level of the initiative and referendum, which circumvent elected officials—especially the legislatures—by putting issues, even proposed laws, directly on the popular ballot during elections.

SOURCES: George B. Galloway, *History of the House of Representatives* (New York: Crowell, 1969); and George H. Haynes, *The Senate of the United States*, 2 vols. (Boston: Houghton Mifflin, 1938).

STYLE OVER SUBSTANCE

On most questions, legislators have considerable freedom to exercise their own judgment. First, because lawmakers often share many of the views and attitudes of their constituents, agreement between members and their constituents is more usual than disagreement. Second, although the demographics and other characteristics of a constituency may influence the issues to which legislators give priority, those characteristics do not necessarily determine how members will vote on those issues. Thus, a representative from a district with a large ethnic minority might become a champion of immigration reform, while a senator from a western state might concentrate on natural resources policies. Similarly, the committees on which legislators seek membership are often determined by the constituency that they serve.

Other factors also enable a legislator to act more like a trustee and less like a delegate. Given the sheer number of legislative decisions made between elections, senators and representatives do not depend heavily on public support for any one vote; the exceptions are the few issues of overriding importance to the electorate. And as legislation has become increasingly complex, members have much more information and expertise than most of their constituents—a circumstance that gives lawmakers more leeway to explain to constituents why they voted as they did.

Perhaps most important, however, few constituents have extensive knowledge of or care deeply about many issues: their judgment of a legislator is more likely to be based on his or her personality than on the legislator's stance on issues. In many cases, if a lawmaker can make a convincing case for his or her voting decisions, constituents will continue to extend their support even if they disagree with the position the legislator took on one or two issues. "If constituents do not agree with the member's conclusions," Davidson and Oleszek wrote, "they may at least respect the decision-making style."[4]

Consequently, legislators take care to present themselves to their constituents in such a way as to encourage the voters' trust. This presentation, which varies from lawmaker to lawmaker, is what political scientist Richard F. Fenno Jr. has called "home style." Davidson and Oleszek identify the three principal ingredients of trust:

Qualification, the belief that legislators are capable of handling the job, a critical threshold that nonincumbents especially must cross; identification, the impression that legislators resemble their constituents, that they are part of the state or region; and empathy, the sense that legislators understand constituents' problems and care about them.[5]

Two essential elements in the development of this sense of trust are (1) service to the district or state and to individual constituents and (2) communications with constituents.

In addition to providing service to constituents as a means of gaining their trust, legislators may emphasize service for another reason. Although some lawmakers represent states or districts that have a single dominant interest, few constituencies are as homogeneous as they once were. When states or districts are divided by economic, cultural, or other differences, legislators must attend to a wide range of problems and attempt to build coalitions among diverse groups. And from time to time, members may be forced to take stands on issues about which their constituents are deeply divided. To bridge the differences and to offset the risks involved in occasionally voting against the views of at least some of their constituents, members try to strengthen their ties to the voters through visits home, casework, and other constituent services.

VULNERABILITY IN ELECTIONS

In the 1980s, all but a handful of House members who ran for reelection were returned to Washington. Although proportionately more senators were defeated, incumbents in both chambers became exceedingly difficult to unseat, and in many cases the opposing party could not even find a challenger willing to make the race against a popular incumbent. The polls continued to reflect strong advantages for incumbents in the 1990s. Even during the Republican landslide of 1994, only 15 percent of the Democratic members who ran for reelection were defeated. Of course, some incumbents, sensing their vulnerability, may have retired rather than face the prospect of defeat.

Political scientists disagree about the precise factors that account for this high rate of incumbency: the many perquisites and resources available to members, incumbents' higher name recognition among the voters, and incumbents' greater ability to raise campaign funds are all important. But most legislators believe that their reelection depends, in large part, on the effectiveness of their communications with and service to their constituents. As one administrative assistant told an interviewer, "You're elected to be a legislator, but casework and [public works] projects keep you elected."[6] "There's no bigger message than when you come within an eyelash of losing an election," said Ray H. LaHood, an adviser hired by House Minority Leader Robert H. Michel, R-Ill., after Michel was nearly defeated in 1982. "But if you can deliver the pork and take care of problems, that's more important to local people and office holders than whether you are for the ERA [Equal Rights Amendment], abortion, or the budget."

Representatives, who face the voters every two years, campaign almost constantly. Senators, even though they serve six-year terms, are more likely to encounter serious challengers and must also stay in close touch with their electorates. Members who won narrow victories—or whose margins declined from previous levels—feel particular pressure to court constituents' support if they want to stay in Congress.

That pressure was evident following the 1990 elections, when a wave of anti-incumbent sentiment swept the country. Only fifteen House members were ousted from office, but fifty-three members were reelected by their narrowest margins ever. The percentage of incumbents winning by "safe" margins (55 percent of the vote or more), has declined steadily, from nearly 90 percent in the late 1980s to 65.9 percent in 1994. While this trend reversed modestly in 1998, many members read the narrowing margins as a warning that they could not ignore.

Four years before becoming Speaker, Georgia Republican Newt Gingrich was reelected by the smallest margin of any incumbent in 1990. He learned from the experience and began spending more time in his Georgia district and less time traveling across the country for other Republicans. "They wanted to see me more at home, more involved in local activities," he said early in 1991. "If they want me, here I am."

Serving Constituents: Communications and Casework

Through media appearances, newsletters, mass mailings (print and electronic), and visits home, senators and representatives continuously cultivate the image that they wish to present to voters. At the same time, communications from and meetings with constituents help to keep members apprised of issues of concern to voters. To demonstrate their concern, most members assign staff—both in Washington and in their state or district offices—to help constituents who have specific problems deal with the federal bureaucracy.

STAYING IN TOUCH

Although staying in touch with a state or district no doubt has its benefits at the ballot box, legislators also believe that providing services to constituents is something that is expected of them. In a 1977 survey conducted by the House Commission on Administrative Review, representatives were asked what functions they thought they were expected to perform as individual members of Congress. Not surprisingly, nearly all of them—87 percent—mentioned legislative responsibilities. But nearly as many—79 percent—also mentioned constituent services. "The American people, with the growth of the bureaucracy, feel nobody cares. The only conduit a taxpayer has with the government is a congressional office," one member said.[7]

While House members are most closely associated with casework, senators understand its political value. Alfonse M. D'Amato, a three-term Republican senator from New York, was dubbed "Senator Pothole" because of his concern for—and success in addressing—individual and community needs. One state legislator, bemoaning D'Amato's eventual defeat in 1998, had special praise for the senator: "It really seemed that no one in Al's office felt too important to worry about our local needs. That's not the way it is when you deal with most senators' offices."

Touching base with the voters on the courthouse steps, Sen. Howard H. Baker Jr., R-Tenn., center, shares a joke with constituents in 1973.

In December 1998, before the House voted on the impeachment of President Bill Clinton, Christopher Shays, R-Conn., holds a town meeting with constituents in Norwalk to gauge their opinion of how he should vote. Contrary to his party, Shays voted against impeachment.

Another 43 percent of survey respondents listed education and communication among their responsibilities. "Staying in contact with the people in my district," one member told the commission. "Answering the mail. That's my first priority, because it may well be their only contact with the office. You let them know you represent them. I have hearings, personal appearances, and seminars in my district. I go to the important charitable functions." Another member said,

I think a congressman has a duty to educate the public. You present both sides of an issue to your district and you try to persuade them to the way that you think is correct. I invite public participation in my decision-making process. I think I can teach my people why certain programs . . . are right and important. Sometimes they convince me.[8]

A classic case of consulting with constituents occurred in 1998, during the House's consideration of impeachment articles against President Clinton. In considering whether to vote for the articles, Republican moderate Christopher Shays of Connecticut held a marathon "town meeting" during which he sought, and received, his constituents' views on the subject. In the end, Shays ignored the position of his party leadership, joining four other Republicans in voting against impeachment.

Letters from Home

Each year, Americans send members of Congress millions of letters and postcards requesting assistance or urging support for particular positions on issues before the House and Senate. In 1995, according to an estimate from the House Postmaster's office, congressional offices located in the Capitol building received a total of 29 million pieces of mail. By 1998, the volume had fallen by about one-third, to approximately 20 million. Although there is no hard evidence to explain the reduction, it is likely that the growing use of electronic mail—in 1999, between one hundred and three hundred messages during an ordinary (no major issue pending) day—accounts for at least some of the decrease in the use of regular mail. Despite its high volume, the mail remains an inexact gauge of constituents' sentiment. Among the comparatively few Americans who ever write to their representatives and senators, the well educated, prosperous, and politically active are overrepresented. Furthermore, constituents are more likely to write to members with whom they agree than to those with whom they take issue.

Some letters to members reflect the thoughtful views of knowledgeable citizens who are concerned about particular issues. Letters from personal or political friends have the greatest impact. Highly organized grassroots lobbying campaigns on the part of interest groups inspire a great deal of legislative mail, not to mention telegrams and telephone calls. Sometimes this "inspired mail" takes the form of printed postcards. Identical letters indicate that the writers have been supplied with the message. Other communications generated by interest groups, such as forwarded e-mail and patched-through telephone calls, can be identified through recurring phrases or arguments, or even by their timing.

Most members give such communications less weight than they accord to spontaneous communications that reflect individual thought. Nevertheless, inspired mail provides at least some measure of an issue's importance to certain constituents. And it may contain an implied threat: if an organization can prompt people to write, it may also be able to deliver their votes. (Political scientists disagree about the ability of interest groups to actually deliver votes.)

Popular presidents can also generate considerable grassroots pressure on members. In 1981, for example, President Ronald Reagan's televised pleas for support for his economic plan generated an enormous volume of letters and phone calls.

Although constituent mail distorts the electorate's opinion to some degree, legislators treat it with respect for two reasons: first, other sources of information are inadequate; second, legislators are aware that the overrepresented views are likely to be held by the more active, informed, influential, and organized voters—those whose votes, and perhaps campaign funds or efforts, may depend on a legislator's stand on the issues in question.

No senator or representative has time to read all the mail. Ordinarily, only complex matters and letters from friends or the politically influential are referred to the member. Some lawmakers ask to see all significant case mail or all mail concerning legislation, and many members review the responses written by staff members before they sign them.

Members and their staffs often develop standard answers to inquiries on uncomplicated matters, and routine requests may be handled by a staff member authorized to use the member's signature. Thoughtful, concerned letters from constituents are likely to prompt careful replies. If the issue is complex, the response may include additional materials—a speech or article, a committee report, or a bulletin from an executive agency. Some members prepare "issue packets" on controversial subjects.

Many members periodically tabulate the opinions expressed in their mail on important issues, though inspired mail may be discounted or tabulated separately. Many House and Senate offices keep records on all correspondents, noting the subjects of their letters. Such files may provide addresses for special mailings, among other purposes.

Office Visits

Constituents may travel to Washington specifically to discuss legislation with their senators or representatives or to seek assistance on matters of personal concern. But most visitors from home are tourists who stop by the member's office, often as part of a group: typical visitors include high school classes, convention delegates, and tours led by organizations in the home state or district. Visitors may take advantage of this opportunity to discuss their views and concerns with a legislator or staff, but they are more likely to seek information and assistance as tourists in the nation's capital.

Knowing the importance of the impression that such visitors will take home, the staff generally welcomes them, providing booklets and brochures about Washington tourist attractions and the federal government and sometimes preparing calendars of events as well. Staff may also hand out passes to House and Senate visitors' galleries and arrange special tours of the White House and some executive agencies.

Unless they are hard-pressed for time, members are likely to meet with visitors who ask to see them. Legislators may arrange to be photographed with a group of constituents, giving them copies of the photos to take home. Some lawmakers even conduct groups on tours of the Capitol or sponsor luncheons with them. Others attempt to keep time spent with visitors to a minimum.

On the Home Front

As the nation's business has grown more complex and legislative sessions have increased in length, members of Congress have come to be in Washington nearly full time. Because most own or rent housing in or near the capital city and move their families there, to a great extent Washington becomes "home." Thus, it is all the more important for legislators to demonstrate that they have not lost touch with the people who sent them to Washington in the first place.

A number of the perquisites of office assist legislators to stay in touch with their constituents. One of these is a travel allowance, which enables members to return frequently to their states or districts. While there, lawmakers often attend fundraising and other political events and travel about the state or district, meeting with groups of constituents about their particular concerns. In addition, nearly all senators and representatives have state or district offices; some even have mobile offices that travel from town to town. (See "Office Allowances," p. 791, Vol. II.)

The division of labor between the district or state office and the Washington office varies widely. Some members handle substantial amounts of casework out of their home offices, especially if regional offices of federal agencies are located nearby. Others prefer to deal with all casework in Washington and to use the district or state office primarily for public relations work or to keep track of events back home.

Another valuable perquisite is the congressional frank, the privilege of mailing letters and packages under members' signatures without being charged for postage. In the mid-1990s, Congress altered its procedure for funding franked mail, eliminating the separate line items for mail and other expenses and replacing them with a general office allowance that legislators could use for staffing, office supplies, and mail in such proportions as they saw fit. For 1999, the total appropriation for these allowances was $385 million. Most House offices estimated that they would send out between 750,000 and 1 million pieces of franked mail during the 106th Congress (1999–2001).

Members use their franking privilege to send mass mailings to their constituents. It is not uncommon for members to insert politically useful material into the *Congressional Record* so that it can be reproduced and mailed under frank. Members also use the frank to mail regular newsletters that paint an upbeat picture of their activities in Washington, solicit constituents' opinions, and demonstrate concern for the problems of the state or district. However, there are limits on when items such as newsletters can be mailed out. In the House, for example, they may not be mailed within 90 days prior to an election.

Congressional newsletters vary in frequency, format, tone, and content. They may come out weekly, fortnightly, monthly, or quarterly. The format ranges from photocopied sheets attached by staples to polished photo-offset publications embellished with photographs—often of the member—and other graphics. Some newsletters adopt a chatty tone, and others are written more formally. Content varies from brief legislative rundowns to the extensive analysis of a single issue. The member's work is usually highlighted, and items of special interest to the state or district are often discussed.

The party organizations in the House and Senate operate radio and television facilities in which members can prepare programs at fraction of the cost that would be charged by private facilities. Some members tape weekly, biweekly, or monthly reports to constituents and ship the programs to radio or television stations and cable television channels in their states and districts, which are often willing to air such programs. Legislators may also tape short commentaries on major news events or items of local interest to fit into local newscasts. Interviews, lasting anywhere from five to thirty minutes and often including an executive from a federal agency, are a popular format for discussing issues of concern to constituents. (See "Influence of Local Television," p. 632.)

Senators and representatives also employ modern technology—the computer, the fax, and sophisticated telephone services—to stay in touch with constituents. Lawmakers use computers to print and address their mail and to target mailings to specific categories of recipients—for example, all those constituents who have indicated an interest in a particular issue. They use fax machines and telephones to transmit press releases and other materials directly to press and other offices in their states and districts.

CASEWORK

To have a senator or representative intercede on their behalf with an administrative agency of the federal government may be the most memorable contact that many Americans have with Congress. Although few members may relish that part of the job, virtually all of them acknowledge that prompt and effective casework pays off in election support. As one member put it, "A near idiot who has competent casework can stay in Congress as long as he wants, while a genius who flubs it can be bounced very quickly."[9]

Casework is a modern phenomenon. Before 1900, when Congress was in session only half the year, legislators did not have their own Washington, D.C., offices, the population was smaller, and requests for help on particular problems were rare and required little time or effort. The volume of private requests increased as education became more widespread, the population grew, and communication became easier. But it was the expansion of the federal government into many areas directly affecting citizens' private lives that led to an explosion in the volume of requests for constituent services. First during the Great Depression, and again in the 1960s and 1970s, the federal government enacted dozens of programs offering benefits and entitlements aimed directly at individuals.

The variety of casework is almost unlimited, the distinction between major and minor cases is imprecise at best, and classification standards vary from office to office. Nevertheless, in 1999 House members estimated their average yearly caseload at about one thousand major cases (those requiring at least a few hours of work) and three thousand minor cases. Senators from small states averaged three thousand to five thousand major cases; senators from New York and California, in contrast, handled between forty thousand and sixty thousand such cases.

Typical requests concern military service, Social Security benefits, veterans' affairs, immigration, passports, unemployment claims, and problems arising from federal aid programs, such as those that assist with housing. The character of the requests may also be affected by the characteristics of the particular state or district: agricultural districts, for example, generate casework related to acreage quotas and delayed crop subsidy checks.

Although much casework involves complaints, a significant portion consists of requests for assistance in approaching federal agencies. Constituents seek government contracts, loans, grants, jobs, and patents, among other benefits. They may ask only to be referred to the appropriate agency; or, at the extreme, they may ask their legislator to appear before an agency to argue the merits of a specific claim. Some constituents seek introductions to federal officials, ranging from the secretary of Treasury to the "right person" in the Pentagon with whom to discuss the purchase of surplus goods.

Many "cases" are simply requests for information about legislation, government programs and regulations, and even tourist information about Washington. One popular request has given rise to a routine procedure: because schools and other organizations often ask for an American flag that has flown over the Capitol building, members purchase flags from the House stationery room, which are then hoisted over the Capitol on a special flagpole put up for the purpose. When the flag is sent out, it is accompanied by a letter from the clerk's office certifying that the banner has flown over the Capitol as requested by the specified individual or group. (See box, Raising the Flags, p. 740, Vol. II.)

Casework Procedures

Staff handle most casework. At both the Washington and home offices, at least one member of a senator's or representative's staff specializes in casework. Assistants who are skilled in handling constituents' relationships with federal agencies are highly valued; in some offices, staff members may specialize in problems relating to specific federal agencies; in others, all caseworkers handle requests of all types.

A telephone call to the appropriate agency is often sufficient, especially when the request is for information only. More complex matters, or those requiring a record of the transaction, are usually addressed through a letter to the agency. The member's staff often forwards to the constituent a copy of the agency's reply.

To cope with the volume of constituents' problems, federal

Pat Danner, D-Mo., left, talks with a voter in her home state. Members of Congress spend considerable time and resources looking after the needs of constituents.

agencies and the three military services have liaison offices to assist members of Congress. Often, the problem will be addressed first by agency's regional office and taken up in Washington only if the regional office is unable to resolve it to the member's satisfaction.

A legislator's intervention in a constituent's case increases the chances of a prompt and favorable response, but members usually get involved only when a case is particularly difficult or when it involves a friend, an important supporter, an influential figure in the state or district, or large numbers of constituents.

How far members may properly go in intervening with federal agencies on behalf of constituents—particularly campaign contributors—has long been the subject of debate. The issue came under particular scrutiny in 1991, after a Senate Ethics Committee investigation of five senators who had intervened with federal banking regulators on behalf of California savings and loan executive Charles H. Keating Jr. Keating, along with his associates, had contributed $1.5 million to the campaigns and political causes of the five senators.

In April 1991, a Senate-appointed bipartisan task force developed a set of recommendations which, after approval by the full Senate, became section 43 of the *Senate Manual.* The new section provides that senators may "assist petitioners before executive and independent government officials and agencies." Appropriate assistance includes requesting information or a status report; urging prompt consideration of a matter; arranging appointments; and expressing (the senator's) opinions. Senators may even urge reconsideration of an agency response "which the member believes is not reasonably supported by statutes, regulations, or considerations of equity or public policy." Sec-

tion 43 makes clear, however, that a senator's intervention may not be tied to campaign contributions either to the senator or to the senator's party. Chapter 7 of the House ethics manual contains similar provisions. The House rule stresses that off-the-record communications may not be made in an effort to influence a matter that is the subject of a "formal proceeding."

Most members of Congress believe that casework is essential to reelection; many consider it more important in gathering votes than their positions on legislative matters. As long as they do not outrage the people of their state or district by consistently or blatantly ignoring their opinions on controversial issues, the senators and representatives who carefully tend to constituents' requests are considered very hard to beat.

By helping individual constituents with matters of immediate concern, lawmakers can build up a substantial personal following. According to the House Commission on Administrative Review, 15 percent of all adults surveyed said that they or members of their family had sought assistance from their House member, and two-thirds of them were satisfied with the response. Satisfied constituents not only have little incentive to abandon an incumbent for a challenger, but they are also likely to tell their family and friends how helpful the representative or senator was.

In closely contested races, a strong personal following can make the difference between victory and defeat—especially because when personal loyalty cuts across party lines. In fairly homogeneous districts, where rival candidates are likely to agree on basic legislative matters, a member's effectiveness in serving constituents' interests may be the principal election issue. Given the potential payoff, it is no wonder that many members use newsletters and visits to their state or district to actively solicit casework from their constituents. Moreover, any candidates seeking to replace an incumbent are unlikely to have a comparable means of making individual voters take note of them. Some political scientists and other observers have argued that this advantage of incumbency contributes to the lack of competition in House races.

Controversy over Casework

In addition to giving incumbents a decided edge over challengers, casework has been criticized on several other grounds. Some observers have warned that the growing volume of requests for help threatens to divert congressional staffs from other duties. Lawmakers themselves complain that dealing with constituents' requests interferes with legislative responsibilities. "Legislation takes a back seat," one House member told the House Commission on Administrative Review in 1977.

It can be neglected without any immediate adverse impact on a congressman. He can miss a committee hearing, not be on the floor, neglect material necessary for an informed decision, and who's ever gonna know? But he cannot avoid, except at the risk of the peril of constituent hostility, responding to constituent requests. So constituent requests take a priority over legislation. You have a turning upside down of what the priorities ought to be.[10]

Critics of casework also assert that when legislators use friendly contacts or "go to the top," they undermine the orderliness, efficiency, and even impartiality of the executive branch. Others suggest that constituents who are more important to a member's reelection efforts may receive faster or better treatment than other constituents who ask for help.

Such allegations are difficult to prove or disprove empirically. Moreover, casework may produce legislative benefits. The investigation of a constituent's problem has sometimes led to formal congressional oversight of an executive agency and to the passage of legislation to correct problems in the administration of a law. Proposals to turn over all casework to an independent, nonpartisan ombudsman or to achieve economies of scale by centralizing casework in a single congressional office have found little support among members of Congress, who could no longer take credit for helping their constituents.

Serving the State or District: Pork-Barrel Politics

Public works projects—and their value as a means of winning support from voters—are nearly as old as Congress itself. Virtually all legislators try to protect their electoral bases through the time-honored use of "pork-barrel" politics, by means of which Congress distributes federal public works, facilities, grants, and other government benefits across the American landscape. A legislator who secures the construction of a dam in a home state or district or obtains a defense contract for a local weapons manufacturer contributes directly to the livelihood of both business and labor. And the lawmaker with a reputation

---

ORIGIN OF A PHRASE

Although lawmakers have indulged in pork-barrel politics from the beginning of the Republic, the phrase itself is more recent. According to columnist and etymologist William Safire, the term can be traced to "the pre–Civil War practice of periodically distributing salt pork to the slaves."

Safire quotes a 1919 magazine article: "Oftentimes the eagerness of the slaves would result in a rush upon the pork barrel, in which each would strive to grab as much as possible for himself. Members of Congress in the stampede to get their local appropriation items into the omnibus river and harbor bills behaved so much like the Negro slaves rushing the pork barrel, that these bills were facetiously styled 'pork barrel' bills."

SOURCE: William Safire, *Safire's Political Dictionary*, 3rd ed. (New York: Ballantine, 1978), 553.

---

for "bringing home the bacon" is hard to beat. (*See box, "Origin of a Phrase," this page.*)

To the voters, the benefits of pork are tangible and unambiguous in a way that most campaign issues are not. Those who benefit from federal projects that can be attributed to the efforts of their legislators may feel that contributing time and money toward members' reelection is merely a practical investment in their own well-being. Similarly, constituents in an ailing economy may put heavy pressure on their senators and representatives to bring home some federal projects or risk being ousted from office.

CUTS OF PORK

Congress cannot specify exactly where every dollar of federal money goes, and outlays for most programs are allocated on the basis of formulas that are written into law. But in the case of federal public works programs, which concentrate expenditures in specific geographic areas, Congress itself still designates the precise location of each project. And while executive agencies are responsible for granting contracts and siting new federal facilities, senators and representatives often influence those decisions as well.

Traditionally, "pork" has been identified with public works projects such as roads, bridges, dams, and harbors. Water projects are particularly popular, even when the costs ultimately outweigh the benefits. As R. Douglas Arnold has noted, the local benefits of water projects

are visible, concentrated, and easily traceable to a congressman's actions, so that voters and group beneficiaries know precisely whom to reward. The costs, on the other hand, are borne by millions of anonymous taxpayers, who have little incentive to organize in opposition because each pays but a few dollars for all water projects.[11]

As the economy and the country have grown, the variety of public works projects has expanded. Environmentalists, who often opposed traditional public works projects, now push legislators to undertake sewer projects and waste-site cleanups and to

FEDERAL "PORK-BARREL" SPENDING FOR LOCAL PUBLIC WORKS

Public spending for local projects is nearly as old as the nation itself. One of the first acts of the First Congress in 1789 was to take over maintenance of all lighthouses—and to order that a new one be built to protect the Chesapeake Bay. Within a few years, lighthouse bills included long lists of new facilities at specific locations.

In 1806, Congress got into the highway business by authorizing surveys for a "national road" from Cumberland, Maryland, to Wheeling, West Virginia. Two years later, Albert Gallatin, President Thomas Jefferson's secretary of Treasury, outlined ambitious plans for a network of roads and canals to tie together and help develop the country, which was rapidly expanding westward.

The question soon arose whether such "internal improvements," as they were called, were primarily in the national interest or primarily of benefit to local residents. This distinction posed difficulties for many Congresses and a number of presidents.

In his 1815 State of the Union message, President James Madison asked Congress to support roads and canals but said that he thought a constitutional amendment was necessary first. The following year, relying on two existing clauses in the Constitution—the commerce clause and the clause authorizing Congress to "establish post offices and post roads"—Congress passed a bill that called for profits from the National Bank to be used for internal improvements. Madison vetoed the bill on constitutional grounds. In 1822 James Monroe vetoed a road bill for similar reasons, arguing that federal support "should be confined to great national works only, since if it were unlimited it would be liable to abuse and might be productive of evil."

Monroe's successor, John Quincy Adams, owed his election to the House of Representatives—and was therefore in no position to exercise veto power over internal improvements bills. Shortly before Adams took office in 1825, Speaker Henry Clay had outlined his "American System," which was based on setting high tariffs to pro-

tect eastern industry and using the proceeds to develop western roads, canals, and harbors. Two bills enacted in Adams's first year opened the way for federal public works: one provided $30,000 for surveys of roads and canals, and the other appropriated $70,000 for clearing snags and sandbars from the Ohio and Mississippi Rivers.

While much of the debate on these bills, as recorded in the *Annals of Congress*, focused on their constitutionality, members foresaw many of the dangers and advantages of the pork-barrel system. Sen. Thomas Hart Benton of Missouri, for example, tried to ensure that Congress got credit by offering an amendment that would have specified the routes of roads and canals. "It is wrong to give the executive the vast increase of patronage which the general provisions of this bill will confer upon him," Benton argued.

A future Speaker, Virginia Democrat Andrew Stevenson, worried openly that later Congresses would dole out public works projects unfairly: "Does not every impartial mind see that the resources of the nation, derived from all, would be used for local rather than national objects, and that favorite portions of the Union would receive the benefits, whilst other parts could not participate?" One member who thought the bills unconstitutional nevertheless tried to add two rivers because, the *Annals* reported, "if it did pass he wished his own constituents to receive their due proportion of expenditure."

Andrew Jackson, the next president, was assertive in fighting projects that he did not consider national in scope, vetoing several bills. Succeeding presidents followed this same principle. Congress responded by bundling together long lists of projects in the hope of building coalitions large enough to overturn a veto. In an 1854 veto message, President Franklin Pierce suggested that Congress "make appropriation for every work in a separate bill, so that each one shall stand on its own independent merits," a suggestion that has been conspicuously ignored.

---

construct parks, solar energy laboratories, and fish hatcheries, among other projects. The Clean Water Act reauthorization enacted in 1987, for example, included special cleanup programs for the Chesapeake Bay, the Great Lakes, and Boston Harbor. (The last of these—worth $100 million—was regarded as a parting gift to Thomas P. "Tip" O'Neill Jr., D-Mass., the former House Speaker who had retired after the 1986 elections.) *(See box, Federal "Pork-Barrel" Spending for Local Public Works, this page.)*

In the 1980s, tight federal budgets induced legislators to earmark appropriations for many academic research grants and facilities, bypassing the usual competitive procedures for awarding funding for such purposes. Such earmarking was necessary, its supporters argued, because the competitive process favored elite universities over less prestigious institutions. "Do we make a big university bigger, or do we provide . . . the sons and daughters of coal miners [and] farmers an equal break?" Sen. Daniel K. Inouye, D-Hawaii, asked during a 1990 debate on funding for defense research grants. Critics countered that earmarked pro-

jects were mostly a testament to the sponsors' political pull and overlooked questions of merit. "It is a matter of diverting research funds from high-quality research to lesser quality research," Sen. John C. Danforth, R-Mo., said in response to Inouye's argument.

Because of the billions of dollars and thousands of jobs involved, members of Congress take great interest in Department of Defense decisions on the location of military bases and the assignment of weapons procurement contracts. Influential legislators—indeed entire state delegations—have often cooperated to win military installations and defense contracts for their state—or, in times of fiscal austerity and military downsizing, to head off base closings or the cancellation of contracts.

As chairman of the House Armed Services Committee from 1965 to 1971, Democratic Rep. L. Mendel Rivers was well positioned to obtain an impressive array of military installations for his South Carolina district. These included the big Charleston shipyard, a naval weapons station, a Polaris submarine base, an air force base, the Parris Island marine corps recruit depot, a

HIGH ON THE HOG

If there was a golden age of pork, it was the 1870s and 1880s. According to Senate historian Richard A. Baker, during those decades, senators tended to be party bosses "sent as messengers to see what they could get for their states." The biggest political problem was how to dispose of a huge Treasury surplus built up by high protectionist tariffs.

Debate on the periodic rivers and harbors bills often amounted to a long parade of senators and representatives rising in succession to add their own projects, with little opposition. In the midst of one such spectacle in 1873, a representative asked facetiously, "Would it be in order to move an amendment appropriating $10,000 for every bay, harbor, creek, and inlet known in the United States?"

The presidential election of Republican Rutherford B. Hayes in 1876 owed much to pork. Hayes was chosen by an electoral commission over the top vote-getter, Democrat Samuel J. Tilden, partly because Hayes promised to help the South, which had been frozen out of patronage and public works since the end of the Civil War. (See "Hayes-Tilden Contest," p. 385.)

The following year, in rebellion against the alleged parsimony of the Appropriations Committee, the House stripped that panel of control over the prized rivers and harbors bill; and in 1883, it created the Committee on Rivers and Harbors. Five years later, Rep. Charles Addison Boutelle, a Maine Republican, noted that of the $20 million in the bill, $13.3 million went to states represented on the committee. "The ardent affection with which these gentlemen of the . . . Committee are attached to each other is a sight for gods and men," he said.

A LOSING BATTLE

Modern-day presidents have had no less difficulty holding down spending on pork-barrel projects. In 1959, when President Dwight D. Eisenhower vetoed a spending bill because of water projects that had been added on Capitol Hill, Congress resorted to a favorite tactic: it cut all projects by 2.5 percent rather than kill any. Eisenhower vetoed that measure as well, but his veto was overridden.

In 1977 President Jimmy Carter proposed eliminating or modifying thirty-five water projects on the grounds that they were wasteful or environmentally damaging. Not only did Congress reject most of his suggestions; but the episode also soured Carter's relations with Congress and weakened his presidency. In 1978 Carter's veto of a public works bill created a stalemate on new projects that lasted until 1986. Although Carter was by then out of office, one of his earlier recommendations—to increase user fees at projects—was eventually approved.

President Ronald Reagan fared no better. Reagan began 1987 by vetoing two public works bills as pork-barrel spending; both vetoes were overridden. On one of them, a highway and mass transit authorization bill that contained more than 120 special "demonstration projects," some of the top GOP leaders, including House Minority Leader Bob Michel of Illinois, deserted their president on the override vote because of projects that the bill made available to their districts.

Even the conservative Republicans who took over the House from Democrats in 1995 were unable to resist the attractions of spending that benefited their districts. Despite their flamboyant rhetoric after the 1994 election upset, in which Republicans outlined plans for eliminating dozens of programs and even entire departments, four years later many GOP members acknowledged how difficult cutting federal spending really is. In a study of 1994 spending-cut promises, the Cato Institute, a conservative Washington think tank, found that many of the programs targeted by the GOP were actually receiving more money in 1999 than they had five years earlier.

---

marine corps air base, an army supply station, and two naval hospitals. In 1969 the Charleston Chamber of Commerce estimated that the military installations alone accounted for more than $317 million in payrolls and that 55 percent of the area's payrolls came from defense industries attracted to the area.

Once federal installations are in place, legislators and their constituents strenuously resist any effort to close them down. In 1976, to protect a major air force base in Maine, William S. Cohen, then a representative (later to become Secretary of Defense in the Clinton Administration), and Tip O'Neill, then House majority leader, succeeded in pushing through legislation that required time-consuming environmental impact studies of any base slated for closure. The legislation proved so effective that no major military bases—including some that were clearly obsolete—were closed in the United States for more than a decade.

In 1988 Congress passed legislation that set up an independent commission to recommend which bases should be closed or sharply reduced in size; the law also required Congress to accept or reject the commission's report in its entirety. The strategy worked: in response to the commission's recommendations, Congress agreed to shut down thirty-five major bases and ninety-five minor ones. But political habits die hard: in protest against the impending closure of the air force base in Plattsburgh, New York, Senators Alfonse M. D'Amato and Daniel Patrick Moynihan delayed a key vote on nominations for the commission. Eventually, the base was closed. Representative G. V. "Sonny" Montgomery, D-Miss., had better luck. In an effort to preserve the naval air station located in Meridian, Montgomery attended nearly every meeting of the commission. His persistence was rewarded: in 1995 the commission voted seven to one to keep the base open.

COMPETITION FOR FUNDS

Appropriations bills have long been a favorite vehicle for pork-barrel projects. As the federal budget tightened in the 1980s, the pool of available funding dwindled, intensifying the competition among legislators to get their pet projects into spending bills. Some members believe that the increased competition provided a benefit by improving the quality of the projects that received approval. "I don't think we get as many bad projects," Rep. Vic Fazio, D-Calif., a member of the House Appropriations Committee, said in 1987. Others disagreed, contending that the tighter competition simply pushed off the list the projects that had been sponsored by less well connected members. "We are not seeing a tightening up of the process at all," Rep. Robert S. Walker, R-Pa., said. "Those with the clout use the clout to get what they want, and merit selection never enters into the thinking."

In 1992 George E. Brown Jr., D-Calif., then chair of the House Science, Space, and Technology Committee, won a short-lived antipork victory on the House floor. Brown moved to cut $95 million—earmarked for university buildings projects—from an energy and water appropriations bill, arguing that the funds should be authorized only after a competitive selection process. The funds had been added to the final version of the bill during the House-Senate conference and benefited the home states of some of the conferees. After the House voted to cut the funds, supporters of the projects arranged to have them added to a defense appropriations bill, where they remained despite Brown's objections. "We always try to help as many members as we can," said John P. Murtha of Pennsylvania, then chair of the House Appropriations subcommittee that wrote the defense appropriations bill.

Critics of pork-barrel spending especially lamented the massive $216 billion, six-year surface transportation plan signed into law in June 1998. Sen. John McCain, R-Ariz., critical of the money earmarked by lawmakers for pet projects, called the legislation "the largest pork barrel spending bill ever written." Members who controlled the purse strings saw their districts and states benefit the most. House Transportation and Infrastructure Committee Chairman Bud Shuster, R-Pa., the main force behind the bill, delivered $110 million in special road projects to his district—about eight times what the average representative got for his or her district. Other members of his committee secured more than $40 million in funds above the average.[12]

Later that year, after hammering out an agreement on the omnibus appropriations bill for fiscal year 1999, Republican Whip Tom DeLay of Texas announced that the process of including funding for pet projects would continue until "the members are happy." But not all the members were happy: many of DeLay's Republican allies failed to share his Murtha-like sentiments: "How can a fiscal conservative vote for this?" fumed Rep. Mark Sanford, R-S.C. Even a veteran Democrat, Indiana's Lee Hamilton, called the process "an abomination."

Nevertheless, most legislators view their efforts to distribute federal funds back home as a legitimate aspect of their jobs. They apply the term "pork-barrel" to the individual projects of other members, if they use the term at all. But critics continue to complain that Congress is overly influenced by parochial concerns and should be more attuned to national needs.

Presidents, given their national constituencies, are likely to evaluate federal budgets and spending measures from a broader perspective than are members of Congress. Both Jimmy Carter and Ronald Reagan tangled with Congress over pork-barrel spending. Reagan's successor, George Bush, continued to attack congressional spending, calling on Congress to vote on specific "items of pork" instead of concealing them within huge multibillion-dollar appropriations bills. "Funds for local parking garages, $100,000 for asparagus-yield declines, meat research, prickly pear research," Bush complained in 1992. "The examples would be funny if the effect weren't so serious."

Presidential opposition may count for something, but it is Congress that determines how much will be spent, where, and for what purpose. Thus, local politics and divvying up the pork will always play a role in federal spending decisions. Former Rep. Douglas H. Bosco captured the legislative perspective:

All of us go begging to the Appropriations Committee for water projects or different things we want in our district. . . . It isn't easy to vote to cut one of these bills because a lot of times you're fearful that the next time you go asking for something, the door will be slammed in your face.

PORK-BARREL POLITICS

Whether projects are meritorious or not, the most time-honored rule of pork-barreling is that any member who gets a project is duty-bound to support the rest of the bill. Although legislators have occasionally balked at implied threats that their own projects would be jeopardized if they failed to support other projects, most go along with the system. Committee leaders are in particularly advantageous positions both to secure federal funds for their own states or districts and to reward other members for their votes. In his first year as chairman of the Senate Appropriations Committee, former Democratic majority leader Robert C. Byrd secured more than $400 million for his state of West Virginia, and that sum did not include millions more for the state's share of federal programs for which Byrd was a leading proponent, such as rural airport subsidies, coal research, and flood control. In 1990–1991, Byrd also used his position in Congress to obtain some seven thousand federal jobs for his state by creating new government offices or transferring existing offices from Washington to West Virginia.

Used skillfully, pork can "grease the wheels" to allow smooth passage of complex or controversial legislation. During consideration of the 1986 tax reform legislation, for example, lawmakers were swamped with requests from business constituents and others for special breaks to ease the transition from the old to the new tax laws. In the House, these requests for so-called transition rules were controlled by Ways and Means Committee Chairman Dan Rostenkowski, D-Ill., who made it abundantly clear that members who did not follow his lead on the bill would not receive transition rules for their constituents. "There were probably sufficient votes to pass the tax bill [in the House]," said Robert T. Matsui, D-Calif., a member of the Ways and Means Committee, "but the transition rules assured its passage. I don't think there's any doubt about that." Much the same pattern occurred in the Senate and again in conference, where large chunks of the legislation were rewritten. The final package contained about seven hundred transition rules, many giving a break to just one corporation, university, or other beneficiary, at a cost to the Treasury of about $10.6 billion over five years.

Some members of committees use their power to dispense favors as a means of achieving broader influence in Congress. From his long-standing perch on the House Public Works Committee, Jim Wright, D-Texas, was able to do countless favors—small and large—for other members. To some extent, the chits were called in when Democrats elected him majority leader in 1976.

The political aspects of the pork-barrel system have always troubled its critics, who would prefer to see federal funds distributed more impartially. Critics also charge that pork-barrel projects are often wasteful, especially when they are awarded primarily for politically strategic reasons. But there seems little likelihood that legislators will turn away from the pork barrel. Many of them agree wholeheartedly with the view of a former representative: "As long as the money is going to get apportioned," he said in 1987, "I'd like to see as much of it get apportioned in my district as possible."

NOTES

1. R. Douglas Arnold, "The Local Roots of Domestic Policy," in *The New Congress,* ed. Thomas E. Mann and Norman J. Ornstein (Washington, D.C.: American Enterprise Institute, 1981), 250.

2. Roger H. Davidson and Walter J. Oleszek, *Congress and Its Members,* 3rd ed. (Washington, D.C.: CQ Press, 1990), 128–129.

3. David C. Kozak, *Contexts of Congressional Decision Behavior* (Lanham, Md.: University Press of America, 1984), 211–212.

4. Davidson and Oleszek, *Congress and Its Members,* 136.

5. Ibid., 135.

6. Bruce Cain, John Ferejohn, and Morris Fiorina, *The Personal Vote: Constituency Service and Electoral Independence* (Cambridge, Mass.: Harvard University Press, 1987), 79.

7. Thomas E. Cavanagh, "The Two Arenas of Congress," in *The House at Work,* ed. Joseph Cooper and G. Calvin Mackenzie (Austin: University of Texas Press, 1981), 65.

8. Cavanagh, "Two Arenas of Congress," 66.

9. Ibid.

10. Cavanagh, "Two Arenas of Congress," 69.

11. Arnold, "Local Roots of Domestic Policy," 256.

12. Alan K. Ota, "Highway Law Benefits Those Who Held the Purse Strings," *CQ Weekly,* June 13, 1998, 1595.

SELECTED BIBLIOGRAPHY

Anderson, John B. *Congress and Conscience.* Philadelphia: Lippincott, 1970.

Arnold, R. Douglas. "The Local Roots of Domestic Policy." In *The New Congress,* edited by Thomas E. Mann and Norman J. Ornstein, 250–287. Washington, D.C.: American Enterprise Institute, 1981.

Bernstein, Robert A. *Elections, Representation, and Congressional Voting Behavior: The Myth of Constituency Control.* Englewood Cliffs, N.J.: Prentice Hall, 1989.

Bianco, William T. *Trust: Representatives and Constituents.* Ann Arbor: University of Michigan Press, 1994.

Browne, William P. *Cultivating Congress: Constituents, Issues, Interests, and Agricultural Policymaking.* Lawrence: University Press of Kansas, 1995.

Cain, Bruce, John Ferejohn, and Morris Fiorina. *The Personal Vote: Constituency Service and Electoral Independence.* Cambridge, Mass.: Harvard University Press, 1987.

Cavanagh, Thomas E. "The Two Arenas of Congress." In *The House at Work,* edited by Joseph Cooper and G. Calvin Mackenzie, 56–77. Austin: University of Texas Press, 1981.

Clapp, Charles L. *The Congressman: His Work as He Sees It.* Washington, D.C.: Brookings Institution, 1963.

Davidson, Roger H. *The Role of the Congressman.* New York: Pegasus, 1969.

Davidson, Roger H., and Walter J. Oleszek. *Congress and Its Members.* 7th ed. Washington, D.C.: CQ Press, 2000.

Fenno, Richard F. Jr. *Home Style: House Members in Their Districts.* Boston: Little, Brown, 1978.

Ferejohn, John. *Pork Barrel Politics: Rivers and Harbors Legislation, 1947–1968.* Palo Alto, Calif.: Stanford University Press, 1974.

Fiorina, Morris. *Congress: Keystone of the Washington Establishment.* 2nd ed. New Haven, Conn.: Yale University Press, 1989.

———. *Representatives, Roll Calls, and Constituencies.* Lexington, Mass.: D.C. Heath, 1974.

Galloway, George B. *History of the House of Representatives.* 2nd ed. New York: Crowell, 1976.

Gellhorn, Walter. *When Americans Complain: Governmental Grievance Procedures.* Cambridge, Mass.: Harvard University Press, 1966.

Hale, George E., and Marion Lief Palley. *The Politics of Federal Grants.* Washington, D.C.: CQ Press, 1981.

Haynes, George H. *The Senate of the United States: Its History and Practice.* Boston: Houghton Mifflin, 1938.

Jacobson, Gary. *The Politics of Congressional Elections.* 4th ed. Boston: Little, Brown, 1997.

Johannes, John R. "Casework in the House." In *The House at Work,* edited by Joseph Cooper and G. Calvin Mackenzie, 78–96. Austin: University of Texas Press, 1981.

———. *To Serve the People: Congress and Constituency Service.* Lincoln: University of Nebraska Press, 1984.

Kingdon, John W. *Congressmen's Voting Decisions.* 3rd ed. Ann Arbor: University of Michigan Press, 1989.

Kozak, David C. *Contexts of Congressional Decision Behavior.* Lanham, Md.: University Press of America, 1984.

Matthews, Donald R. *U.S. Senators and Their World.* Chapel Hill: University of North Carolina Press, 1960.

Mayhew, David R. *Congress: The Electoral Connection.* New Haven, Conn.: Yale University Press, 1974.

Miller, Clem. *Member of the House.* New York: Scribner's, 1962.

Miller, James A. *Running in Place: Inside the Senate.* New York: Simon and Schuster, 1986.

Norton, Philip, and David M. Wood. *Back from Westminster: British Members of Parliament and Their Constituents.* Lexington: University Press of Kentucky, 1993.

Olson, Kenneth G. "The Service Function of the United States Congress." In *Congress: The First Branch of Government,* edited by Alfred de Grazia, 337–374. Washington, D.C.: American Enterprise Institute, 1966.

Parker, Glenn R. *Homeward Bound: Exploring Changes in Congressional Behavior.* Pittsburgh: University of Pittsburgh Press, 1986.

———. "Members of Congress and Their Constituents: The Home-Style Connection." In *Congress Reconsidered,* 4th ed., edited by Lawrence C. Dodd and Bruce I. Oppenheimer, 171–193. Washington, D.C.: CQ Press, 1989.

Polsby, Nelson W. *Congressional Behavior.* New York: Random House, 1971.

Rothenberg, Lawrence S. *Linking Citizens to Government: Interest Group Politics at Common Cause.* New York: Cambridge University Press, 1992.

Tacheron, Donald G., and Morris K. Udall. *The Job of the Congressman: An Introduction to Service in the House of Representatives.* 2nd ed. Indianapolis: Bobbs-Merrill, 1970.

Wright, James. *You and Your Congressman.* Rev. ed. New York: Capricorn Books, 1976.

CHAPTER 19

The Media

A MONG THE MANY sources of pressure on Congress, the press stands out because of the ambivalence it provokes among legislators. On the one hand, senators and representatives must cope with constant and sometimes critical media scrutiny, which may include unwelcome investigations into the lawmakers' personal lives. At the same time, members of Congress depend on the media as a tool to further their own political ambitions and to inform their constituents.

Since the early 1970s, four factors have intensified the pressure of media coverage on members of Congress. First, reforms enacted in the 1970s opened more of congressional activities than ever before to both the press and the public. Almost all House and Senate committees conduct much of their work in public sessions. Reporters and lobbyists often crowd around while conference committees hammer out final decisions on compromise legislation. Both the House and the Senate record members' votes on most questions during floor debate on legislation. And floor action in both chambers is transmitted to millions of households via C-SPAN, the Cable Satellite Public Affairs Network.

Second, since the Watergate scandal of the early 1970s, the Washington press corps has remained on the alert for official misconduct in Congress as well as in the White House. This interest intensified during the Clinton sex scandals of the late 1990s, when the press gave increasing attention to extramarital affairs and other aspects of legislators' private lives.

Third, since the 1980s, television—especially local television—has had a much greater presence on Capitol Hill than ever before. The ability to send and receive television signals by satellite enabled local television stations to cover daily events in the nation's capital. It also allowed the political parties to set up their own television studios and broadcast their points of view to constituents.

Fourth, throughout the 1990s, new technologies, such as fax machines and the World Wide Web, intensified media coverage of Congress by vastly expanding options for the rapid distribution of information. When Congress began posting all its bills on the World Wide Web, reporters gained access to a considerable resource for tracking legislative actions. And when news organizations set up Web sites and began faxing or e-mailing afternoon news updates to subscribers, lawmakers responded in kind: since the mid-1990s, every congressional committee and almost every member of Congress has created a Web site. Members' Web sites typically contain a biography, statements on major issues, press releases, and descriptions of key legislative initiatives; committee Web sites contain information about hearings, markups, and major bills. As early as 1997, then-Speaker Newt Gingrich's Web site was accessed 20,000 times a day.

The combination of these four factors—congressional reforms, Watergate, increased television coverage, and new technologies—has made it possible for the press, constituents, and political opponents to watch lawmakers' actions more closely than ever before. Today, about seven thousand journalists, photographers, and technicians are accredited to the House and Senate press galleries—an increase of 40 percent since the late 1980s. Many members of this group work for specialized publications that focus on particular issues. Two newspapers, *The Hill* and *Roll Call,* cover the nonlegislative actions of Congress in depth, targeting an audience of lawmakers, staff aides, and lobbyists. Yet most Americans are informed of only a few of the events that occur on Capitol Hill: of the dozens of hearings, meetings, and debates that occur in Congress each day, only one or two are likely to receive attention in most newspapers or in radio and television broadcasts.

Despite the greater openness in Congress, reporters must still cultivate senators, representatives, and their staffs to discover what goes on backstage and to be able to explain the subtle pressures that shape the legislative process. Legislators, in turn, use contact with the media as an opportunity to seek favorable coverage in the hope of not only improving their image among their constituents but also increasing their influence among Washington colleagues.

Members of Congress use a variety of methods to attract favorable press coverage: they distribute press releases and videotapes, issue weekly news columns, appear on television interview shows, create their own cable television programs, grant personal interviews to reporters, give floor speeches on major issues, and hold press conferences and briefings for journalists. Occasionally, a member may draw widespread attention by conducting a highly publicized hearing or investigation. Younger members of Congress, more accustomed than older legislators to television and its potential, are particularly adept in the use of that medium.

As recently as the 1950s, few senators and virtually no representatives formally designated staff members as press secretaries. Today, nearly all lawmakers employ press officers, often former journalists, to handle relations with reporters. Congressional committees also hire press secretaries and may even set

Controversy attracts the press. Here dozens of reporters gather in the Senate press gallery awaiting news from the impeachment trial of President Bill Clinton in 1999.

up separate press information offices to communicate the majority and minority viewpoints. Press secretaries steer journalists to knowledgeable staff members, set up interviews with members of Congress, and provide much of the background information that reporters use to write Capitol Hill stories. They also create printed press releases and videotaped "interviews" with their bosses; these are directed at both national and local media and are often timed to meet press deadlines or to make the evening television news. Press secretaries are accorded so much power that, very often, the "quotes" ascribed to lawmakers were in fact written by press secretaries and may never even have been uttered by the members.

Senators' and representatives' efforts to obtain press coverage are largely directed at the news outlets in their states or districts, where the audience is likely to be the members' constituents and the coverage more extensive and more favorable than what can be obtained through the national media. Few legislators receive regular attention in the national media, and those who do generally hold leadership positions or have assumed leadership on a particular issue; the exceptions are members who are caught up in a scandal. Senators generally receive more national attention than House members. Legislators who are seeking the presidency receive national attention, but their faces fade quickly from the nation's television screens when they are no longer in contention for the highest office in the land.

Nonetheless, more and more legislators look for opportunities to attract national as well as local press coverage. "A member of Congress has to court two constituencies," a veteran Senate press secretary explained. "The constituency that sends him here and the constituency he has to work with. As a general rule, the home-state press has got to be any smart member's priority." But, he added, "the national press can be very effective in getting your views across to people you work with."[1]

The Washington Press Corps: Unforeseen Power

The power that the nation's news media—and the Washington press corps in particular—now wields in the American governmental process was not envisioned by the men who founded the federal government. The Constitutional Convention of 1787 worked behind closed doors, as had the Continental Congress that ran the country during the Revolutionary War. The Constitution itself omitted any guarantee of freedom of speech or the press.

But even as the Constitution was being drafted, momentum was building to open legislative sessions to the press and the public. By 1789, when the new government was established, English papers were regularly printing the proceedings of the House of Commons; some state legislatures were also open to the public. Soon after it was formed, the fledgling federal government moved to ensure that its conduct of the nation's business would be subject to the scrutiny of an independent press.

EARLY FIGHT FOR FREEDOM OF THE PRESS

As first conceived, the American form of government provided no legal protection for a press bent on perusing the activities of government officials. Thomas Jefferson, who was in France at the time of the Constitutional Convention, criticized this omission. In early 1787 he wrote from Paris:

The people are the only censors of their governors; and even their errors will tend to keep these to the true principles of their institution. To punish these errors too severely would be to suppress the only safeguard of the public liberty. The way to prevent these irregular interpositions of the people is to give them full information of their affairs thru the channel of the public papers, & to contrive that those papers would penetrate the whole mass of the people. The basis of our government being the opinion of the people, the very first object should be to keep that right; and were it left to me to decide whether we should have a government without newspapers or newspapers without a government, I should not hesitate for a moment to prefer the latter.[2]

The main opposition to a guarantee of press freedom came from Alexander Hamilton, who wrote in *The Federalist* No. 84:

What signifies a declaration that "the liberty of the press shall be inviolably preserved"? What is the liberty of the press? Who can give it any definition which would not leave the utmost latitude for evasion? I hold it to be impracticable; and from this, I infer that its security, whatever fine declarations may be inserted in any Constitution respecting it, must altogether depend on public opinion, and on the general spirit of the people and of the government.[3]

At the Constitutional Convention, Hamilton was able to repel attempts by James Madison and George Mason to add to the Constitution a bill of rights that included a guarantee of freedom of the press. But Madison and Mason won the struggle in 1791, when Virginia became the necessary eleventh state to ratify the Bill of Rights. Among its other protections, the first of these ten amendments stipulated that Congress should make no law abridging freedom of the press.

During the first decade of the Republic, the rivalry that had developed between Jefferson and Hamilton intensified, as did the conflict between their opposing concepts of government. Both Hamilton, the leader of the Federalist Party, and Jefferson, the leader of the Democratic-Republican Party, relied heavily on the press to advance their own views of government. The result was an era of partisan journalism in which each side used party organs to attack the other. The vigorous press battle, fought mainly in the Federalist *Gazette of the United States* and the Republican *National Gazette* and later the *Aurora*, culminated in the several Alien and Sedition Acts passed by the Federal Congress in 1798. One of the main purposes of these acts was to curb the Democratic-Republican press, in part by threatening to deport its journalists who had been born abroad and were not yet naturalized.

Although no one was in fact deported under the Alien Act (which was never enforced and expired in 1800), several newspapermen were fined and some were sent to prison under the Sedition Act. Under this act, it was a crime, punishable by up to two years' imprisonment and $2,000 in fines, to speak, write, or publish any "false, scandalous, and malicious" writing against the government or its high officials with "intent to defame the said government." All journalists convicted under the act were pardoned, however, when Jefferson became president on March 4, 1801, the day after the act expired. Congress eventually reimbursed the journalists for the fines they had paid.

EARLY PRESS COVERAGE OF CONGRESS

Like freedom of the press, newspaper coverage of Congress was not envisioned by the Founders of the Republic. But on April 8, 1789, at its second session, the House of Representatives opened its doors to the public and the press. In 1790, four seats in the chamber were set aside expressly for members of the press. The Senate conducted its business behind closed doors until December 1795, when galleries built specifically for the public were opened.

The early congressional reporters functioned more like stenographers, recording floor proceedings and paraphrasing floor speeches for their readers. Beginning in 1802 Samuel Harrison Smith, editor of a Democratic-Republican paper, the *National Intelligencer,* obtained permission from the Democratic-Republican House Speaker to make and publish stenographic reports of House debates; Smith had been denied such permission the year before, when the House was evenly divided between Federalists and Democratic-Republicans. For years, the reports in the *Intelligencer* were the only printed records of congressional proceedings; the paper became the official organ of the Democratic-Republican administration and remained so until John Quincy Adams became president in 1825, when the *National Journal* became the official organ. Under the presidency of Andrew Jackson, the *Globe* was the administration organ, and it remained so through the Van Buren administration.

Each of these three papers also received lucrative government printing contracts, a practice that ended in 1860 with the establishment of the Government Printing Office. For a time, the owners of the *Intelligencer* did a thriving business by publishing the debates and proceedings of Congress in book form under the title *Register of Debates*. In the 1830s, the *Globe* began to publish a similar book called the *Congressional Globe,* and the *Register of Debates* eventually ceased publication. In time, the *Congressional Globe* developed a form and style for reporting congressional debate that became standard. In 1873, when its contract expired, the publication ceased to exist, and the Government Printing Office began to publish the *Congressional Record.*

The Washington press corps began to develop in the late 1820s, when correspondents wrote letters to their home newspapers commenting on congressional proceedings and social events in the nation's capital. Newspapers at the time were closely allied to political parties and individual politicians, and capi-

ATTACKS ON THE PRESS

Despite the constitutional guarantee of freedom of the press, Congress sometimes has attempted to intimidate reporters and editors and to discredit their papers' editorial policies.

One of the most noteworthy cases occurred in 1915, when a Senate committee chaired by Thomas J. Walsh, D-Mont., probed the motives of the *New York Times* in publishing editorials opposing an administration bill to authorize purchase of foreign ships interned in American harbors at the start of World War I. Both the editor in chief and the managing editor answered the committee's questions about the *Times's* financial backing and its news and editorial policies. At the conclusion of the hearings, editor in chief Charles Ransom Miller said:

I can see no ethical, moral or legal right that you have to put many of the questions you put to me today. Inquisitorial proceedings of this kind would have a very marked tendency, if continued and adopted as policy, to reduce the press of the United States to the level of the press in some of the Central European empires, the press that has been known as the reptile press, that crawls on its belly every day to the foreign office or to the government officials and ministers to know what it may say or shall say—to receive its orders.[1]

Another major confrontation occurred in 1936, when the House Committee on Military Affairs subpoenaed a *Washington Herald* reporter who had linked Rep. John J. McSwain, D-S.C., a member of the committee, to a group of war surplus speculators. The reporter, Frank C. Waldrop, declined to answer the committee's questions on the ground that the panel was proceeding improperly "pursuant to a threat of its chairman and without legislative purpose." The committee subsequently called off its inquiry.

An even stormier episode took place in 1953, when the Senate Permanent Investigations Subcommittee, chaired by Joseph R. McCarthy, R-Wis., questioned *New York Post* editor James A. Wechsler on his paper's editorial policy. During the hearing McCarthy launched a lengthy attack on Wechsler's editorial page, claiming that it "always leads the vanguard . . . against anyone who is willing to expose Communists in government." At the close of the hearing, Wechsler retorted that he regarded the proceeding "as the first in a long line of attempts to intimidate editors who do not equate McCarthyism with patriotism." The Wechsler incident produced much public animosity toward McCarthy and the committee, and congressional committees thereafter were more wary about subpoenaing reporters.

In 1971 Congress and the news media clashed again, after CBS broadcast on television a controversial and award-winning documentary, "The Selling of the Pentagon," which portrayed an elaborate public relations campaign by the Defense Department. Some legislators criticized the program, charging that the film had been edited to alter the meaning of certain remarks, Vice President Spiro T. Agnew said the documentary was "a clever propaganda attempt to discredit the defense establishment."

After CBS President Frank Stanton refused to supply the House Interstate and Foreign Commerce Investigations Subcommittee with film outtakes from the production that had not been used in the broadcast, the committee voted to cite him and CBS for contempt of Congress. The full House, however, refused to go along, voting 226–181 to kill the panel's contempt citation.

1. Alan Barth, *Government by Investigation* (New York: Viking, 1955), 185.

---

tal reporters wrote—usually under pseudonyms—highly opinionated pieces that supported the positions of whatever party their paper backed.

By the end of nineteenth century, newspapers—or at least their reporters—were less closely identified with political parties, and a more independent and objective approach to journalism began to take hold. Interviews of legislators became standard procedure. Newspapers no longer reported full floor proceedings as they had in the early years of the Republic. "The press galleries as a rule are comparatively free of occupants," said a Washington reporter in 1903. "Washington has become so fruitful in gossip and scandal, and intrigue, political and otherwise, that in contrast the ordinary debates can prove exceedingly dry reading."[4]

THE MODERN PRESS CORPS

Although the Capitol Hill press corps grew steadily in the first decades of the twentieth century, three factors caused the number of reporters covering the federal government to swell. First, beginning with the New Deal, the federal government took on vastly larger responsibilities, which it sustained for

more than fifty years. The larger and more complex federal government had to be covered by a larger press corps. Second, as the federal government increased in complexity and size, the number of specialized publications covering particular areas of federal policy rose. Third, the advent of entirely new media—radio, television, and the World Wide Web—not only changed how news is covered but brought a new cadre of reporters and technicians to Washington.

Of the seven thousand journalists, photographers, and technicians currently accredited to the Senate and House press galleries, only a relative handful cover Congress full-time. Congress has given reporters themselves responsibility for deciding who qualifies for membership in the press galleries. Accreditation is straightforward for working journalists, but congressional rules prohibit gallery members from lobbying or doing paid promotion work.

The House and Senate wings of the Capitol, completed in 1857, included special press galleries just above and behind the dais in each chamber. Today, each chamber has four separate press galleries for daily newspapers and news services, periodicals, radio and television correspondents, and photographers.

A media stakeout: journalists press Speaker Newt Gingrich for comment on budget issues as he makes his way to his office in the Capitol in 1998.

Each gallery is staffed by congressional personnel and furnished by Congress with telephones, fax machines, and other equipment. Studios just off the House and Senate floors offer facilities for television and radio broadcasts. Unlike the spectators who sit in the public galleries above the other three sides of each chamber, journalists are permitted to take notes as they observe floor proceedings; however, they are not permitted to use tape recorders when they are sitting above the chambers.

The House and Senate office buildings also house press rooms for the use of reporters who are covering committee sessions or members of Congress. Most congressional committees, especially those that draw major media attention, reserve press tables for reporters attending hearings or legislative drafting sessions. While lobbyists and ordinary citizens wait in long lines with no guarantee of getting a seat, reporters receive favored treatment: they are ushered into committee rooms and provided with printed copies of testimony, members' remarks, draft bills, and committee reports. In rare cases, when conference committee meetings are held in particularly small rooms, seating may be so limited that one reporter will be asked to file a "pool" report for members of the press who cannot get into the room.

Since the early 1900s, House and Senate committees have followed a policy of holding public hearings on most major legislation. Some exceptions are made, notably when panels hear testimony on classified matters from defense or intelligence officials. Until the 1970s, committee markup sessions (in which legislators vote to amend or approve proposed bills) were closed to the press as well as to the public. Under reforms passed in the 1970s, markup sessions in both chambers are required to be open un-

less committee members vote specifically to bar reporters. Even the meetings of conference committees, which resolve differences between House and Senate versions of bills, were opened to reporters.

By the mid-1980s, the push for openness on Capitol Hill had begun to fade, and more committees closed their doors to the press and public more often. Asked in 1987 about closed-door sessions, Ways and Means Committee Chairman Dan Rostenkowski, D-Ill., said, "It's just difficult to legislate [in open meetings]. I'm not ashamed about closed doors. We want to get the product out." Another Ways and Means Democrat, Don J. Pease of Ohio, usually voted against closed meetings but acknowledged their value: "I hate to say it, but members are more willing to make tough decisions on controversial bills in closed meetings."[5]

After taking control of Congress in 1995, however, Republicans placed greater emphasis on open proceedings, at least in the House. House Appropriations Committee Chairman Robert L. Livingston, R-La., made sure that reporters received, for the first time, copies of staff summaries that listed key areas of agreement and disagreement between House and Senate appropriations negotiators. House Speaker Gingrich, R-Ga., ordered the texts of bills and legislative reports to be put on the World Wide Web, fulfilling a pledge he had made after the GOP's 1994 sweep: "Information . . . [will be] available to every citizen in the country at the same moment that it is available to the highest-paid Washington lobbyist."[6]

Senators, in contrast, continued to make some important decisions in private. For example, the Finance Committee closed its doors during negotiations on a major tax package in 1997.

And during a portion of the 1999 impeachment trial of President Clinton, senators ordered the television cameras to be turned off so that they could debate in private.

When a markup or conference on an important bill is closed, reporters often gather outside the doors to the committee room in what is called a "stakeout," hoping to elicit information from legislators as they enter and leave the room. Reporters also stake out strategy meetings held by Republican and Democratic caucuses and major meetings attended by top party leaders.

National Coverage:
A Focus on the Institution

The reporters who cover Capitol Hill work for a highly varied communications industry—newspapers, news services, newsletters, magazines, radio and television stations and networks, and on-line publications—that range in focus from the national to the local level. In addition, several hundred journalists in Washington represent foreign newspapers, magazines, and broadcasters.

In the United States, the national media provide most of the widely distributed news about Congress. National news organizations include the Associated Press, Reuters, Bloomberg, and other wire services; three large daily newspapers, the *Washington Post,* the *New York Times,* and the *Wall Street Journal;* the major commercial television networks—ABC, CBS, NBC, and Fox; cable television networks such as CNN and MSNBC; National Public Radio; and three weekly news magazines, *Time, Newsweek,* and *U.S. News & World Report.*

In addition, two government affairs journals, *Congressional Quarterly Weekly* and *National Journal,* offer detailed coverage of congressional activities through a variety of media—weekly magazines, morning newsletters, and afternoon fax and e-mail bulletins. Two newspapers, *Roll Call* and *The Hill,* cover nonlegislative activities such as leadership battles and political campaigns. Specialized publications such as *Aviation Week,* the *Chronicle of Higher Education,* the *Journal of Commerce,* and a host of newsletters and reports cover particular areas of federal policy making. Public television's *Jim Lehrer's News Hour,* the networks' Sunday talk shows, and programs such as ABC's *Nightline* often interview legislators and cover issues that are before Congress.

Most national media assign reporters to full-time congressional beats. Correspondents who cover particular agencies or issues come to Capitol Hill periodically for congressional hearings or debates on matters of interest to their audience. By and large, the major news organizations concentrate on legislative activities and Congress as an institution rather than on individual legislators. In many cases, lawmakers are not even the main focus of a story. Instead, a news report on a hearing will concentrate on a key witness, such as a cabinet secretary, or on a celebrity who is testifying on behalf of a favorite cause.

Legislators are often asked for their reaction to a presidential announcement or action. Chris Matthews, press aide to Speaker Thomas P. "Tip" O'Neill Jr., D-Mass., once described Congress as "the Hamburger Helper to the White House Story."[7] Members of Congress have long complained about the president's ability to dominate the news that comes out of Washington, contending that the disparity in media attention shifts the balance of power toward the president and away from Congress. Even after Republicans took control of Congress in 1995—and President Clinton found himself telling reporters that he was still "relevant"—the White House nonetheless continued to dominate the news coverage, an advantage that helped Clinton best GOP leaders in the 1995 battle over the budget.

The national press, especially the television networks, generally gives more coverage to senators than to House members. "We tend to go for the senators because there are fewer of them," said a producer for one of the Sunday network talk shows. They are more well known nationally and tend frankly to speak out more on national policy than members of the House."[8] In addition to having fewer members, the Senate includes celebrities and presidential hopefuls. Moreover, it is the Senate, not the House, that considers treaties and approves presidential nominees, tasks that generate the sort of controversy that makes news.

Senators who buck their party leadership or lead fights for major legislation tend to gain media attention. Sen. John McCain, R-Ariz., for example, found himself much in demand by the press after taking on GOP leaders in the late 1990s over campaign finance reform. But the attention seems to fall on just a few senators. Brookings Institution scholar Stephen Hess found that in 1983, just ten senators received 50 percent of the national coverage (Hess counted mentions on three network news programs, three Sunday interview shows, and five newspapers).[9]

On occasion, individual House members do garner significant coverage. The outspoken Gingrich, for example, drew media attention by making biting remarks about well-known liberals, ranging from President Clinton to the comedian Woody Allen. But Gingrich paid a price for his time in the spotlight, eventually becoming deeply unpopular with the public and resigning in 1999 after GOP election setbacks in 1998.

Generally, neither representatives nor senators receive much sustained coverage. House Judiciary Committee Chairman Henry Hyde, R-Ill., enjoyed brief celebrity during the Clinton impeachment effort but gained little attention thereafter. Similarly, members who run for president, such as 1992 candidates Sen. Tom Harkin, D-Iowa, and Sen. Bob Kerrey, D-Neb., tend to fade from the national spotlight after their campaigns fold.

INCREASINGLY AGGRESSIVE
INVESTIGATIONS

Provided that they are quoted accurately and shown in a positive light, most legislators welcome national media attention, no matter how brief. National coverage can turn members of Congress into celebrities almost overnight—and end political careers just as abruptly. Since Watergate, Washington investigative journalists have uncovered misconduct on the part of a number of legislators, prompting House and Senate ethics investigations, criminal proceedings, and in some cases resignations from Congress. House Ways and Means Committee Chairman Wilbur D. Mills, D-Ark., for example, once the unquestioned master of congressional tax legislation, lost that post and eventually retired from public life after a series of highly publicized incidents in 1974 involving a striptease dancer. Two years later, Rep. Wayne L. Hays, D-Ohio, the powerful chairman of the House Administration Committee and the Democratic Congressional Campaign Committee, resigned after the *Washington Post* reported that he had kept a mistress on the House payroll.

Intensive coverage of alleged misconduct has contributed to the downfall of several lawmakers since then. One of the most notable examples was House Speaker Jim Wright, D-Texas, who was forced to resign the speakership and his House seat after the House Ethics Committee announced that it had found reason to believe that Wright had violated House rules on financial conduct. The investigation was undertaken after Gingrich raised questions about Wright's conduct during a televised floor speech.

Throughout the 1980s and early 1990s, reporters focused increasing attention on the personal lives of legislators, sometimes leading to highly embarrassing revelations. A newly aggressive style of journalism was unveiled in 1988, when a group of *Miami Herald* reporters, pursuing rumors of infidelity, staked out the Washington townhouse of presidential candidate Sen. Gary Hart, D-Colo., and saw Hart and model Donna Rice emerge early in the morning. The incident caused Hart to withdraw from the race. In 1992, the *Seattle Times* ended the career of Sen. Brock Adams, D-Wash., by reporting that he had sexually harassed eight young women in a series of incidents that dated back two decades.

While taking fire for publicizing such information, news organizations have also been criticized for holding back. In 1996, when Sen. Bob Packwood, R-Ore., was locked in a tight reelection battle, the *Washington Post* decided against running allegations of sexual harassment against Packwood. Oregon voters were furious when the story came out after the election, and Packwood was eventually forced to resign.

The emergence of on-line journalism and the extensive coverage of the sex-related scandals that engulfed Clinton in his second term sparked a sort of journalistic "open season" when it came to the private lives of elected officials. Gossipy Web sites run by cyberjournalists such as Matt Drudge reached millions of people, spreading stories of sexual indiscretion and compelling mainstream reporters to follow up on the rumors. During the tense investigation in 1998 of Clinton's extramarital affair with a White House intern, even rank-and-file lawmakers found themselves being asked by reporters whether they were faithful to their spouses, while high-profile legislators—including Judiciary Committee Chairman Hyde—were forced to acknowledge having committed adultery.

Media scrutiny of Congress reached unprecedented levels when *Hustler* magazine publisher Larry Flynt offered $1 million for evidence of sexual indiscretions on the part of lawmakers. In December 1998, House Speaker-designate Livingston, resigned after Flynt uncovered allegations that Livingston had had sexual affairs.

Some reporters find this sort of journalism as repellent as lawmakers do. A 1990 survey by the Pew Research Center found that growing numbers of journalists were concerned that the lines had blurred between reporting and commentary, and that the media were driving news about scandals rather than merely reacting to events. But with news organizations locked into an around-the-clock competition to be the first to put up the latest scandal on their Web sites, some news experts believe that journalism will continue to become increasingly aggressive. Harvard University professor and former television correspondent Marvin Kalb told the Washington Post: "I see no incentives that would drive journalism in a different direction. Quite the contrary."[10]

Local Coverage: Spotlight on Legislators

As noted earlier, most legislators, particularly House members, are likely to receive more extensive—and less critical—coverage from the media in their states and districts. Nearly all of the nation's 9,000 newspapers, 13,000 radio stations, and 1,600 broadcast television stations, along with major cable stations and on-line servers, carry some congressional news, but they usually rely on wire services, television networks, or Washington bureaus for most of their national coverage.

Some daily newspapers based in major cities—for example, the *Los Angeles Times,* the *Dallas Morning News,* and the *Chicago Tribune*—operate respected Washington bureaus. Large newspaper chains—such as Newhouse, Gannett, Knight-Ridder, and Cox—maintain Washington bureaus that cover the news for the papers owned by the chains. Some newspapers and television and radio stations have one- or two-person Washington offices, while others rely on "stringers" who report for a number of separately owned papers. Local television coverage of Congress has grown significantly with the advent of satellite technology, which allows coverage of breaking news in distant locations.

A FAVORABLE IMPRESSION

Because most local papers and broadcasters stress the local or regional angles of Washington news—for example, how legislation or regulation affects the region, what the local senator or representative has to say on an issue—local coverage tends to focus on the individual legislator. With fewer resources at their disposal, local newspapers and broadcast stations are less likely than the national media to look at legislative issues in depth or to pursue time-consuming investigations; they are also more likely to use the press releases and videotapes supplied by the legislators themselves. Consequently, local coverage also tends to be more favorable than national coverage: members of Congress who court the local press can significantly influence the way that they are portrayed to their constituents.

TELEVISING CONGRESS

Congress for years resisted live televised coverage of its daily proceedings, fearful that cameras would prompt grandstanding or erode the dignity of its operations. Now routine, the gavel-to-gavel broadcasts of floor action have not caused major changes in the way Congress works. Instead, television has proven to be politically expedient, as members gain public exposure when national and local news programs air excerpts from floor debates. The broadcasts have also allowed members to follow floor action from their offices.

The House was first to open its chamber to television, in 1979. The Senate held out until 1986. A year later, even senators who once opposed television applauded the results. "It seems to be an unalloyed success at this point. . . . Our fears were unfounded," said Sen. J. Bennett Johnston, D-La., who had been a vocal opponent.

Long before broadcasts of floor debate, television had captured dramatic events on Capitol Hill. Presidential State of the Union messages were televised from the packed House chamber. Senate committee hearings were opened to cameras several times, enabling viewers to watch the Kefauver probe of organized crime and the Army-McCarthy investigations in the 1950s, testimony on the Vietnam War in the 1960s, and the Watergate hearings in 1973. The House banned cameras from committee sessions until 1970; in 1974 it won a large national audience for committee sessions on impeachment of President Richard Nixon.

Unlike committee hearings, which are open to cameras from accredited news organizations, each chamber keeps close control over broadcasts of floor action, using cameras owned by Congress and operated by congressional staff. Although the recordings are not edited, the coverage provides only a limited view of floor action, usually focusing on the rostrum or on the member who is speaking. The cameras are operated by remote control from basement studios under each chamber. Senators speak from their desks; representatives go to one of two lecterns in the House well or use the tables on either side of the central aisle. When votes are in progress, the cameras show the full chamber, with information about the vote superimposed on the screen. Recordings of House and Senate floor action cannot be used for political or commercial purposes. On rare occasions, this practice has been violated, usually for political reasons. *(See box, Partisan Tensions in the House, p. 448.)*

Although networks and local television stations use excerpts from the recordings, the only gavel-to-gavel broadcast is on a cable network, Cable Satellite Public Affairs Network (C-SPAN). In addition to its floor coverage, C-SPAN selectively broadcasts other major congressional events, such as noteworthy committee hearings, press conferences, and the like. In 1999 an estimated 22 million people watched C-SPAN each week.

Moreover, Washington correspondents for local and regional media rely on the legislators that they cover, and their staffs, to keep them informed not only of congressional action but also of executive or regulatory decisions that may affect the local community. As a veteran Washington reporter wrote, a local correspondent "is almost compelled to keep the lines to the congressional office open and friendly. If they are not, he can be effectively frozen out of major news stories."[11]

Local television may be even less judgmental than local newspapers. "Some local programs do contain a thoughtful look at legislation, and some members of Congress do provide a useful service in interpreting the issues of the day or in explaining their relevance to the district," wrote Cokie Roberts, a congressional reporter for National Public Radio and ABC. "But in all honesty, most members' statements are presented without criticism, and the gathering of comment might make P. T. Barnum blush."[12]

While favorable local coverage may please lawmakers, it worries some journalists. In recent years, tight-budgeted news organizations such as Thomson Newspapers have slashed their Washington bureaus so severely that smaller newspapers and television stations sometimes run unedited press releases. In consequence, voters may be at a disadvantage when trying to judge their senator or representative. "An ever-growing portion of the Fourth Estate is relying entirely on canned Congressional news," warned a 1990 article in the *Washington Journalism Review*.[13]

INFLUENCE OF LOCAL TELEVISION

There is little doubt that technological advances have made television a more potent tool of self-promotion for media-savvy legislators, especially House members. Legislators have always been able to get their share of coverage at parades and ribbon cuttings in their states or districts. Today, satellite technology allows incumbents to be seen "at work"—in their offices, in front of the Capitol, at hearings, or (via C-SPAN) on the House or Senate floor. Legislators can serve as instant analysts of the day's headline events, explaining the local impact of federal actions—including those in which their own involvement was remote.

Although the number of correspondents covering Capitol Hill for local television stations has increased, lawmakers do not have to rely on independent broadcast stations. Some have their own cable television shows, although these programs tend to attract far fewer viewers than the local news. In addition, the Democratic and Republican campaign committees in both the House and Senate now operate sophisticated recording studios whose camera crews can tape a member at a Capitol Hill hearing, a downtown luncheon speech, or nearly anywhere else a camera is permitted. One favorite format is an "interview" in which the member responds to questions from a press aide; the member then distributes the video tape to small local stations back home, many of which have limited resources and welcome this source of "news" from Washington.

Senate Minority Leader, Tom Daschle, D-S.D., consults with his press secretary, Marc Kimball, left, before giving an interview in the Democrats' "Intensive Communications Unit" on Capitol Hill.

Junior members from closely contested districts with small or medium-size television markets tend to be the most strongly drawn to the Capitol's broadcast facilities. One member who fits that profile, Rep. Kenny Hulshof, R-Mo., hosts a half-hour show each month on a cable station in Columbia, the district's largest city and Hulshof's home. He also holds a telephone conference each week with radio stations back home and periodically hooks up with local television stations so that they can get footage of him discussing the issues of the day.

Such arrangements are helpful for both lawmakers and news editors. For Hulshof, the goal is "to help educate the folks back home on what we do. . . . I've been treated very fairly back home by the media, who have been content to just report the facts."[14] Dick Aldrich, the news assignment editor with KRCG-TV, in Jefferson City, Missouri, says that he welcomes Hulshof's interest in television. "He's trying to manage the information aspect of this," Aldrich said. "But we get the information we need, so we don't mind it too much."[15]

Not all members receive frequent local television coverage. Big-city television stations have neither the time nor the resources to cover the many House members from their media markets. In New York City, where close to three dozen representatives compete for time on the same local news programs, House members are lucky to receive television news coverage more than a couple of times a year.

Legislators from the wide-open rural spaces, mainly in the West, have different problems: television stations in lightly populated media markets may be too small to support large-scale news departments, and constituents may get their television signals from stations in other districts or even other states. In such cases, a member's own satellite feeds may be of little use. Legislators for whom television coverage is impractical and lawmakers (often older members) who are uncomfortable with it rely on newsletters and personal appearances to stay in touch with their constituents. Even the media stars acknowledge that television cannot substitute for a personal presence in a district or state.

Media Influence on Congress: Assessing the Impact

It would be hard to overstate the media's impact on Congress. Had it not been for intense press scrutiny, powerful lawmakers such as Livingston and Packwood would probably not

A 1906 magazine series on "The Treason of the Senate" spurred adoption of the Seventeenth Amendment, providing for direct election of senators.

ing the Pure Food and Drug Act of 1906. That year *Cosmopolitan* magazine published "The Treason of the Senate," a series of articles by David Graham Phillips that linked many leading senators to large corporations and political machines. The resulting furor cost a number of members reelection and led to the adoption of the Seventeenth Amendment, which requires that senators be elected by voters rather than by state legislatures.

After World War I, some news correspondents worked closely with opposition senators to help tip the scales against Senate ratification of President Woodrow Wilson's Treaty of Versailles. During the 1920s, investigative reports prompted the congressional action that exposed the Teapot Dome scandal and led to criminal convictions for Secretary of the Interior Albert B. Fall and other officials of President Warren G. Harding's administration.

Media coverage of the Vietnam War, the antiwar movement, and the Senate Foreign Relations Committee's hearings on the war significantly influenced public opinion and eventually helped turn congressional opinion against the war. Press investigations of the Watergate break-in and subsequent cover-up, as well as coverage of the Senate Watergate Committee hearings and House Judiciary Committee impeachment proceedings, led to the resignation of President Richard Nixon in 1974.

Savvy legislators can sometimes harness the media to help whip up support for their initiatives. In 1997, for example, Senate Finance Committee Chairman William V. Roth, R-Del., held a series of hearings that included emotional testimony about alleged abuses by the Internal Revenue Service (IRS). The allegations provoked a storm of media condemnations of the IRS, forcing the Clinton administration to accept legislation that revamped the agency and boosted taxpayers' rights.

EFFECT ON LAWMAKERS

In addition to affecting the issues that legislators take up, media coverage has changed the way that legislators do business. Perhaps the most obvious change is the expanding role of television advertising in political campaigns: given the expense involved, lawmakers must spend ever-increasing amounts of time raising money.

Television coverage has had other effects as well. Because of the immediacy and power of television images, members cannot easily take stands on national issues that differ greatly from those of their constituents. And the brevity of television coverage may lead members to oversimplify issues or to focus only on problems and solutions that are easy to understand. To receive coverage, political scientist Timothy E. Cook wrote, legislators "may have to choose issues that fit reporters' requisites—fresh, clear-cut, easily synopsized, affecting as large a portion of the news audience as possible, and packaged with reforms that seem able to resolve the problems."[16]

The political process has become increasingly geared toward sound bites—so much so that a growing number of lawmakers come from the ranks of broadcast journalists. Sen. Rod Grams, R-Minn., a former news anchorman, said that after facing near-

have resigned. Even when an issue does not originate with the media, assiduous coverage can magnify the issue's importance and increase public awareness of it. Both directly, through editorials, and indirectly, by helping to shape public opinion, news organizations put pressure on Congress to act.

One of the most vivid examples of such pressure occurred in the late 1890s, when newspaper reports by New York City's "yellow press" helped push the United States into the Spanish-American War. For months, the *New York World,* which was owned by Joseph Pulitzer, and the *New York Journal,* which was owned by William Randolph Hearst, tried to outdo each other with reports of Spanish atrocities in Cuba, then Spain's possession. President William McKinley attempted to keep the United States out of war, but the wave of hysteria whipped up by the papers eventually overwhelmed both the president and Congress. When the U.S. battleship *Maine* was sunk in Havana harbor in 1898, press reports blamed the Spanish; though Spanish complicity was never proved, Congress declared war.

In the early 1900s, a number of investigative articles by magazine reporters—eventually referred to collectively as "muckrakers"—resulted in a large body of reform legislation, includ-

monthly evaluations on the basis of Nielsen ratings, the prospect of facing reelection just once every six years seemed "like a breeze."[17]

Televising Congress has also created more of an incentive for lawmakers to use the floor to appeal to voters or to generate support for a cause. Andrew Jay Schwartzman, president of the Media Access Project, a public interest law firm that promotes the public's First Amendment rights, said that C-SPAN has created "a tremendous opportunity for some of the more articulate, telegenic, earnest or crazed members, including a number without a whole lot of general influence or seniority, to be able to frame the debate or generate grass-roots interest in an issue."[18]

Indeed, Gingrich ascended to the speakership partly because of his masterly use of television. In the 1980s, while their party was the minority, Gingrich and other House Republicans pioneered the use of C-SPAN for one-minute speeches during special orders to vocalize complaints about the Democratic majority. C-SPAN thus provided House Republicans with a forum to build grassroots support for their cause outside Washington. According to Stephen Frantzich, co-author of *The C-SPAN Revolution*, "Newt Gingrich probably wouldn't be speaker without C-SPAN."[19]

For some legislators, getting national media coverage is part of a strategy to increase their influence with their colleagues; but most members believe that influence within Congress is less the result of media attention than of sustained hard work. "I think you earn your spurs with your colleagues not so much because the press quotes you a lot but because you know what you're talking about," said Hyde, whose colorful and pointed one-liners made him a favorite among reporters even before the Clinton impeachment hearings.[20]

In fact, highly quotable lawmakers are not always successful in their legislative careers. In 1998 Rep. John A. Boehner, R-Ohio, was upset in his bid to be reelected as chairman of the House Republican Conference, even though he was a leading spokesperson for the party. Noting that the great majority of members receive no sustained press attention, Stephen Hess, in *The Ultimate Insiders: U.S. Senators in the National Media,* argued that use of the national media to build legislative support is an overrated tactic:

Trying to use the media to get legislation through Congress is a Rube Goldberg design based on (A) legislator influencing (B) reporter to get information into (C) news outlet so as to convince (D) voters who will then put pressure on (E) other legislators. Given all of the problems inherent in successfully maneuvering through the maze, no wonder that legislative strategies are usually variations of (A) legislator asked (E) other legislators for their support through personal conversations, "Dear Colleague" letters, caucuses, or other means.[21]

Although the goal of congressional leaders is to work simultaneously behind the scenes and through the media, in practice that is nearly impossible. When Gingrich tried to do both, he found himself under fire—from friends and foes alike—for making rash comments to the press. Similarly, Senate Majority Leader Trent Lott, R-Miss., has been criticized for remarks he has made to reporters, including his initial condemnation of a bombing campaign in Iraq in 1998. Perhaps it was no coincidence that House Republicans in 1998 elected Illinois's Dennis

During Senate Foreign Relations Committee hearings, press photographers position themselves between the senators and witness table.

CONGRESSIONAL NEWS LEAKS

Many veteran Washington politicians, in both the executive and legislative branches, are masters of selectively leaking confidential information to the press. But Congress, historically more open in its dealings with reporters, may contribute more than its share of leaks.

Leaks can serve many purposes: to raise an alarm about proposed government action, to set the stage for further maneuvering, to take first credit for significant developments, or simply to embarrass the political opposition. As journalists began covering Congress and the executive branch more intensively—and as more members of Congress gained access to secret or classified briefings and documents—Capitol Hill became fertile ground for reporters seeking inside information.

While legislators frequently attempt to use news leaks for their advantage, Congress has long been plagued by improper or injudicious release of information received in confidence. As early as 1812 Nathaniel Rounsavell, editor of the Alexandria, Virginia, *Herald*, was cited for contempt of Congress for refusing to answer questions about leaks from a secret House session. During the Civil War the Radical Republicans on the Joint Committee on the Conduct of the War publicized information gathered in closed sessions when it suited their purposes.

In the 1990s, the Senate Watergate Committee was plagued by leaks during its highly publicized investigation into the Nixon White House scandal. "The committee did not invent the leak," said Howard H. Baker Jr., R-Tenn., the vice chairman of the panel, "but we elevated it to its highest art form."

James Hamilton, who served on the committee's legal staff and later wrote a book on congressional investigations, noted that the "coverage of the [Watergate] committee investigations was marked by strenuous competition among newsmen for confidential information. For a reporter to obtain a major leak was viewed in the press as a

badge of honor."[1] Hamilton said leaks were sometimes unfair to the people under investigation. But he acknowledged that Watergate—and many other major investigations—might not have been undertaken without the independent investigations of the press.

SECRET REPORT DISCLOSURE

A particularly embarrassing leak occurred in 1975, when the New York–based *Village Voice* printed excerpts of a select committee's report on its investigation of the intelligence community. The excerpts were printed after the House had voted to block release of the report on the ground that it contained classified material that might be damaging if made public. The newspaper had obtained the report from CBS reporter Daniel Schorr.

In its first formal investigation, the House Committee on Standards of Official Conduct subpoenaed Schorr and three editors of *New York* magazine, the parent publication of the *Village Voice.* Nine times Schorr refused to answer questions by members of the ethics panel about how he acquired the secret report, citing First Amendment guarantees of freedom of the press. By a 5–6 vote, the committee voted against recommending that Schorr be cited for contempt of Congress, but in its report called Schorr's role in the leak "a defiant act in disregard of the expressed will of the House." The committee said that it was "not axiomatic . . . that the news media is always right and the government is always wrong."

IRAN-CONTRA LEAK

As the Schorr incident illustrated, the source of a reporter's leaks are rarely revealed. But in July 1987 Sen. Patrick J. Leahy, D-Vt., announced that he had resigned from the Senate Select Committee on Intelligence in January after he violated committee rules by giving a reporter access to a draft report on the Iran-contra affair.

The document, which Leahy gave to an NBC television correspon-

Hastert to be their Speaker: a man with little television presence, Hastert has considerable experience working "on the inside" to advance legislation.

Nevertheless, for party leaders, merely being on the inside may not be enough. The first leader to find that out was House Speaker "Tip" O'Neill, an inside player who had shunned the media throughout his political life. However, after Republicans won control of the White House and the Senate in 1980, O'Neill became the top Democratic leader in Washington and found that he was expected to be his party's chief spokesperson. O'Neill's transformation into a media celebrity and news source reflected, in part, his recognition that the modern rank and file is less susceptible to arm twisting than it is to public opinion.

EFFECT ON THE INSTITUTION

How the press portrays Congress shapes what the public thinks of the institution. The national media's attention to (some would say preoccupation with) congressional miscon-

duct has no doubt served to lower Congress's prestige in the eyes of many voters. Media coverage of legislative action may also contribute to the consistently low approval ratings that Congress receives in public opinion polls. Particularly when an issue is contentious, a political institution that reaches decisions through consensus and compromise can appear to be indecisive and slow to act.

Despite their need for press coverage, most lawmakers think that the press does not do a good job. A 1998 study by the Pew Research Center found that 77 percent of members of Congress rate press coverage as "poor" or "fair." The lawmakers and other public officials surveyed "name the media as a prime culprit in public distrust of government," the report concluded.[22]

At times, the cynicism of reporters has exasperated lawmakers. Shortly after the GOP sweep in 1994, Gingrich emerged from a White House session with Clinton that he termed "a great, positive meeting." When a reporter asked what issue was likely to cause a partisan rupture, Gingrich retorted: "Couldn't

dent early in January, was a draft preliminary report on the Iran-contra matter compiled in December 1986 by the Intelligence Committee staff. At that time Republican control of the Senate—and thus of the Intelligence Committee—was in its final weeks. Democrats on the committee complained that the report was incomplete and contained inaccuracies. On January 5, 1987, with Democrats now ensconced as the majority, the panel voted not to release the document.

The White House then charged that the Democrats were suppressing the report because it found no direct evidence that President Ronald Reagan had been aware that Iran arms sales money had been diverted to the contra guerrillas fighting Nicaragua's leftist government. Leahy said he allowed a reporter to look at part of the draft "to show that it was being held up because there were major gaps and other problems with it, and not because of a desire to embarrass the president."

Information from the committee report was revealed and a copy of the document displayed on an NBC newscast on January 11. Two days later Leahy resigned from the intelligence panel. During a joint hearing of the Senate and House Iran-contra committees July 19, Rep. Dick Cheney, R-Wyo., cited Leahy's statement as proof that "there was legitimate cause for concern that Congress could not keep a secret, and a lot of evidence that . . . various members of Congress had in fact been responsible for sensitive leaks." In response, William S. Cohen, R-Maine, vice chairman of the Senate Intelligence Committee and a member of the Senate Iran-contra panel, declared that Leahy's resignation had been "a very strong signal" that the Intelligence Committee would not tolerate unauthorized disclosures.

CLARENCE THOMAS HEARINGS

In October 1991 the issue of sexual harassment took center stage as the Senate Judiciary Committee conducted explosive hearings into allegations that Supreme Court nominee Clarence Thomas had harassed a former aide, Anita Hill.

The committee originally did not plan to pursue the allegations, which Hill had made confidentially. But two reporters—Timothy Phelps of Newsday and Nina Totenberg of National Public Radio—publicized her story, embarrassing the all-male panel into seeking testimony from both Thomas and Hill. The reporters refused to divulge how they got their information, although it seemed clear that the leak must have come from a lawmaker or staff aide on the committee.

Furious Republicans demanded an investigation into the leak. Less than two weeks after the harassment stories ran in early October, Senate Majority Leader George J. Mitchell, D-Maine, announced that he would order an investigation. "I don't know what happened, but I'm going to try to find out," Mitchell said in a stern floor speech. "And if I can determine the identity of the person who did it, I'm going to try to see that the person is appropriately punished."

Totenberg faced scathing attacks from conservatives who accused her of bias. She engaged in a heated exchange with Sen. Alan Simpson, R-Wyo., on *Nightline*, then cursed Simpson after the show when he followed her to her car and railed at her for violating journalistic ethics. Despite the raw feelings, the Senate dropped its investigation in March 1992, with Phelps and Totenberg refusing to divulge how they got their information. By this time, Thomas was already on the Supreme Court, and senators were inclined to move on. Simpson even escorted Totenberg to the Radio and Television Correspondents dinner in March. "We would like to find who in the Senate staff violated the Senate rules," Simpson said. "But she [Totenberg] should be protected fully in her willingness to say nothing."[2]

1. James Hamilton, *The Power to Probe: A Study of Congressional Investigations* (New York: Random House, 1976), 287.

2. "Soup to Sources at Radio-TV Dinner," *Washington Post*, March 20, 1992.

you try for 24 hours to have a positive optimistic message, as though it might work?"[23]

On the other hand, local media coverage may be one reason that incumbent legislators are hard to beat when they seek re-election. As Michael J. Robinson suggested in a 1981 study, "The media, by treating Congress poorly but its incumbents relatively well, may be strengthening incumbents but weakening their institution."[24]

Within Congress itself, the combination of flagging party discipline and intensely media-conscious members could contribute, as Robinson noted, to "a Congress that is less likely to get along with itself, more likely to focus on higher office, less likely to behave as a group than as a disjointed collection of individuals."[25] As Congress became steadily more partisan in the 1990s—culminating in the extraordinary spectacle of the House impeaching the president by a nearly party-line vote—both journalists and the public seemed to share Robinson's assessment. A poll by the Pew Research Center found that journalists, by a slight plurality, feel that by covering the personal and ethical behavior of public figures as they do, they drive controversies rather than just report the news.[26] In a 1987 speech, Sen. Nancy Landon Kassebaum, R-Kans., said that the legislative process had been damaged because

government must now operate under the microscope of the news media. That can make the outlandish claim and the fervent war cry seem to be the most effective tools for a successful campaign for or against an issue. The frequent victim of such tactics is effective government, the ability and the willingness to accommodate and shape a consensus.

But the media can hardly be asked to shoulder all the blame for partisan conflict and a lack of consensus; such problems have plagued Congress for most of the nation's history. On the contrary, the neutral coverage provided by C-SPAN, which allows millions of Americans to watch lawmakers in action, seems to be spurring an ever-growing feeling of cynicism. "Congress started [televising its proceedings] under the premise that to know us is to love us," Frantzich said. But, he added: "The data shows that familiarity breeds contempt."[27]

NOTES

1. Nadine Cohodas, "Press Coverage: It's What You Do That Counts," *Congressional Quarterly Weekly Report,* January 3, 1987, 30.

2. William Grosvenor Bleyer, *Main Currents in the History of American Journalism* (Boston: Houghton Mifflin, 1927), 103.

3. Hamilton, Alexander, James Madison, and John Jay, *The Federalist Papers,* with an introduction by Clinton Rossiter (New York: New American Library, 1961), 514.

4. F. B. Marbut, *News from the Capital: The Story of Washington Reporting* (Carbondale: Southern Illinois University Press, 1971), 136.

5. Jacqueline Calmes, "Few Complaints Are Voiced as Doors Close on Capitol Hill," *Congressional Quarterly Weekly Report,* May 23, 1987, 1059.

6. *Congressional Quarterly Almanac, 1994* (Washington, D.C.: Congressional Quarterly, 1995), 35-D.

7. Doris A. Graber, *Mass Media and American Politics,* 5th ed. (Washington, D.C.: CQ Press, 1997), 291.

8. Cohodas, "Press Coverage," 32.

9. Stephen Hess, *The Ultimate Insiders: U.S. Senators in the National Media* (Washington, D.C.: Brookings Institution, 1986), 11.

10. David S. Broder and Dan Balz, "A Year of Scandal with No Winners," *Washington Post,* February 11, 1999, A1.

11. Ray Eldon Hiebert, ed., *The Press in Washington* (New York: Dodd, Mead, 1966), 15.

12. Cokie Roberts, "Leadership in the Media and the 101st Congress," in *Leading Congress: New Styles, New Strategies,* ed. John J. Kornacki (Washington, D.C.: CQ Press, 1990), 94.

13. Mary Collins, *Washington Journalism Review,* 1990 (cited in *Impact of Mass Media,* 3rd ed., ed. Ray Eldon Hiebert (New York: Longman Publishers), 305.

14. Jeffrey L. Katz, "Studios Beam Members from Hill to Hometown," *Congressional Quarterly Weekly Report,* November 29, 1997, 2946.

15. Ibid.

16. Timothy E. Cook, *Making Laws and Making News: Media Strategies in the U.S. House of Representatives* (Washington, D.C.: Brookings Institution, 1989), 121.

17. Frank Ahrens, "Camera-Ready Politicians," *Washington Post,* October 29, 1998, D1.

18. Juliana Gruenwald, "C-SPAN: From Novelty to Institution," *Congressional Quarterly Weekly Report,* November 29, 1997, 2948.

19. Ibid., 2949.

20. Cohodas, "Press Coverage." 29.

21. Hess, *Ultimate Insiders,* 103.

22. "Public Appetite for Government Misjudged: Washington Leaders Wary of Public Opinion," Pew Research Center for the People and the Press, April 17, 1998, 4.

23. Joseph N. Cappella and Kathleen Hall Jamieson, *Spiral of Cynicism* (New York: Oxford University Press, 1997), 4.

24. Michael J. Robinson, "Three Faces of Congressional Media," in *The New Congress,* ed. Thomas E. Mann and Norman J. Ornstein (Washington, D.C.: American Enterprise Institute, 1981), 93.

25. Ibid., 95.

26. "Striking the Balance," Pew Research Center for the People and the Press, 1999, 17.

27. Gruenwald, "C-SPAN," 2948.

SELECTED BIBLIOGRAPHY

Blanchard, Robert O., ed. *Congress and the News Media.* New York: Hastings House, 1974.

Broder, David S. *Behind the Front Page: A Candid Look at How the News Is Made.* New York: Simon and Schuster, 1987.

Cappella, Joseph N., and Kathleen H. Jamieson. *Spiral of Cynicism: The Press and the Public Good.* New York: Oxford University Press, 1997.

Clark, Peter, and Susan H. Evans. *Covering Campaigns: Journalism in Congressional Elections.* Stanford, Calif.: Stanford University Press, 1983.

Cook, Timothy E. *Making Laws and Making News: Media Strategies in the U.S. House of Representatives.* Washington, D.C.: Brookings Institution, 1989.

Davidson, Roger H., and Walter J. Oleszek. *Congress and Its Members.* 7th ed. Washington, D.C.: CQ Press, 2000.

Fenno, Richard F. *Home Style: House Members in Their Districts.* Boston: Little, Brown, 1978.

Garay, Ronald. *Congressional Television: A Legislative History.* Westport, Conn.: Greenwood Press, 1984.

Graber, Doris A. *Mass Media and American Politics.* 5th ed. Washington, D.C.: CQ Press, 1997.

———, ed. *Media Power in Politics.* 3rd ed. Washington, D.C.: CQ Press, 1994.

Graber, Doris A., Denis McQuail, and Pippa Norris, eds. *The Politics of News: The News of Politics.* Washington, D.C.: CQ Press, 1998.

Hamilton, James. *The Power to Probe: A Study of Congressional Investigations.* New York: Random House, 1976.

Hess, Stephen. *Live from Capitol Hill! Studies of Congress and the Media.* Washington, D.C.: Brookings Institution, 1991.

———. *The Ultimate Insiders: U.S. Senators in the National Media.* Washington, D.C.: Brookings Institution, 1986.

———. *The Washington Reporters.* Washington, D.C.: Brookings Institution, 1981.

Leonard, Thomas C. *The Power of the Press: The Birth of American Political Reporting.* New York: Oxford University Press, 1986.

Linsky, Martin. *Impact: How the Press Affects Federal Policymaking.* New York: Norton, 1986.

Mann, Thomas E., and Norman J. Ornstein. *Congress, the Press, and the Public.* Washington, D.C.: Brookings Institution, 1994.

Marbut, F. B. *News from the Capital: The Story of Washington Reporting.* Carbondale: Southern Illinois University Press, 1971.

Ranney, Austin. *Channels of Power: The Impact of Television on American Politics.* New York: Basic Books, 1983.

Ritchie, Donald A. *Press Gallery: Congress and the Washington Correspondents.* Cambridge, Mass.: Harvard University Press, 1991.

Roberts, Cokie. "Leadership and the Media in the 101st Congress." In *Leading Congress: New Styles, New Strategies,* edited by John J. Kornacki, 85–96. Washington, D.C.: CQ Press, 1990.

Robinson, Michael J. "Three Faces of Congressional Media." In *The New Congress,* edited by Thomas E. Mann and Norman J. Ornstein, 55–96. Washington, D.C.: American Enterprise Institute, 1981.

Schudson, Michael. *Discovering the News: A Social History of American Newspapers.* New York: Basic Books, 1978.

Smith, Hedrick. *The Power Game: How Washington Works.* New York: Random House, 1988.

Vermeer, Jan Pons, ed. *Campaigns in the News: Mass Media and Congressional Elections.* Westport, Conn.: Greenwood Press, 1987.

CHAPTER 20

Internal Pressures

T HE 535 MEMBERS of Congress—100 senators and 435 representatives—often come under intense pressure to side with their colleagues from the same party, region, or special caucus. These internal pressures, which may be formal or unspoken, and often occur out of public view, are essential for Congress to get its work done. Indeed, internal congressional dynamics sometimes overshadow outside pressure from constituents, lobbyists, the media, and the president.

As Congress has changed, however, so have the ways in which internal pressures are brought to bear on its members. Until the 1960s, legislators usually found it in their best interest to follow the advice often given by the legendary House Speaker Sam Rayburn, D-Texas: "To get along, you have to go along." A member who cooperated with the leadership was often rewarded with a choice committee assignment, a coveted public works project, or a display of personal approval from the leadership, any of which could enhance the member's prestige and effectiveness. By the same token, a member who defied the leadership on important issues might be relegated to a minor committee, denied the benefits of "pork-barrel" appropriations, and shunned by the leadership.

Beginning in the 1960s, however, and continuing until approximately 1990, several factors combined to make individual members of Congress less dependent on their political parties and party leaders, and therefore less responsive to traditional pressure tactics. Two important developments were the growing role of television in congressional campaigns and the rise of special interest groups who were armed with political action funds for favored candidates. As members found that they could campaign more effectively as independent-minded powers in their own right, party allegiances weakened. Legislators no longer owed their seats to the party apparatus but to their constituents, their political consultants, and their campaign contributors.

During the 1970s, Congress itself reduced the price of acting independently. Structural and procedural reforms eroded the arbitrary power of senior party members, broadened the influence of subcommittees, and made the processes that determined committee assignments and the selection of committee chairs more democratic.

Although senior party members did not regain the power that they had enjoyed earlier in the twentieth century, the decade of the 1990s saw a resurgence of party discipline as a major source of internal pressure, particularly in the House. After

narrowly taking control of the House in 1995, Republicans spent months voting in lockstep on contentious issues. With the chamber split closely between the two parties and the number of conservative southern Democrats greatly diminished, members came under as much pressure as ever to support their party—pressure that reached its apex in 1998 when the House took the extraordinary step of impeaching President Bill Clinton on a nearly party-line vote. *(See "President Bill Clinton," p. 343.)*

Modern party leaders may have fewer disciplinary tools than their predecessors, but they can still count on institutional loyalties and call in personal debts as they try to forge majorities on legislation. Committee and subcommittee chairs, members of state delegations and regional and special interest caucuses, and even personal friends influence members' votes by offering specialized knowledge or personal advice on issues. Party allegiances and political horse trading still play important roles in the legislative process, as does the unwritten code—still followed in both chambers—that forbids legislators from allowing personal differences to disrupt congressional work.

Parties and Party Leaders: Formal Pressures in Congress

The nation's Founders did not anticipate the role that political parties would come to play at all levels of the national government. The Constitution made no provision for partisan leaders to organize the House and Senate and discipline legislators. Nevertheless, for the two centuries of Congress's existence, party ties have largely determined how members acquired power and used it, and party affiliation remains a significant influence on legislators' actions. In a 1981 study of House leadership, Robert L. Peabody concluded that a House member's party identification—as a Republican or a Democrat—was the single most reliable factor for predicting how the member would vote. By the late 1990s, party identification appeared to be even more important to members—despite the fact that voter identification with a particular political party had weakened steadily throughout the century.[1]

In fact, despite the diminished power of the leadership and the party, the rate at which members voted with their party increased throughout the 1980s, driven by the dynamics of a divided government. With the White House controlled by Republicans and Congress largely run by Democrats, partisan battles erupted over many issues. The GOP takeover of Congress in

From 1995 to 1999, Tom DeLay, R-Texas, right, served as majority whip and David E. Bonoir, D-Mich., left, as minority whip. Among their primary duties, whips try to influence party members to follow the leadership's program.

1995 spurred an extraordinary surge in partisan fighting. In 1995 senators voted with their parties 68.8 percent of the time and House members 73.2 percent of the time—the highest level since at least the 1950s, when *Congressional Quarterly* began tracking such voting patterns.[2]

Political scientists attributed the polarization of Congress in the 1980s and 1990s to the relative absence of political moderates and to the emergence of two distinct ideological camps separated by passionate differences on emotional issues such as abortion, school vouchers, environmental regulation, and the minimum wage.

House Republicans offered another explanation, claiming that they had to stick together and pass legislation in order to maintain their fragile majority. "We've been on the outside looking in as a minority for the last 40 years," said Sherwood Boehlert, R-N.Y., a leading moderate. "We'd like to maintain majority status in the next generation at least."[3]

By 1998, the party unity vote rate was down to about 56 percent in both chambers, but the drop in the rate appears to have been driven by a lack of major bills rather than by any lessening of partisan differences. Roger Davidson, a congressional scholar at the University of Maryland, said that Congress in the late 1990s was in the midst of the most partisan era since the days of Reconstruction. "There is a very deep chasm between the parties," he said.[4]

PARTY LEADERSHIP

Over the years, both parties in both chambers have devised similar leadership structures to develop the party's position on issues before Congress and to create support for that position. In the modern Congress, the leaders of the two parties are assisted by whip organizations and party committees that can bring to bear a variety of pressures, both subtle and overt, on the party's rank and file.

On the House side, the most powerful leader is the Speaker, who is both the presiding officer and the leader of the majority party. He is nominated by his party's caucus or conference, then elected by the whole House in what is customarily a party-line vote.

The Speaker's duties, which spring from the Constitution and from the rules and traditions of the House, include presiding over House sessions, recognizing members to address the House, deciding points of order, referring bills and reports to the appropriate committees and House calendars, appointing the House conferees for House-Senate conferences on legislation, and appointing members of select committees (the Speaker wields considerable influence within the party's committee on committees, which assigns party members to standing committees).

Both the majority and minority parties in the House and Senate appoint officials to shape and direct party strategy on the floor. These majority and minority leaders, as they are called, devote their efforts to forging voting majorities to pass or defeat bills. The House majority leader ranks just below the Speaker in importance. In the Senate, the majority leader is the most powerful officer because neither the vice president nor the president pro tempore holds substantive power over proceedings in the chamber. Majority floor leaders have considerable influence over the scheduling of debate and the selection of members to speak on bills.

In both chambers, each party appoints a whip and a number of assistant whips to assist the floor leader to execute the party's legislative program. The whip's main job is to canvas party members on a pending issue and give the floor leader an accurate picture of the support or opposition that can be expected for the measure. Whips are also responsible for ensuring that party members are on hand to vote. And at the direction of the floor leader, whips may apply pressure to party members to make certain that they follow the leadership line.

Both parties rely on caucuses of party members (called *conferences* by Republicans in both houses and by Senate Democrats) to adopt party positions on legislation, set party rules, and elect party leaders. House Democrats also make committee chairs subject to secret-ballot election by the caucus. During the 1990s, both Democratic and Republican leaders in the Senate made extensive use of party conferences and caucuses to discuss party strategy and air members' proposals and grievances.

The two parties also maintain committees in each chamber to assist the party leadership and to enable more party members to participate in the leadership process. Steering committees help with floor tactics and recommend the order in which measures should be taken up; policy committees research proposed legislation and recommend party positions. (The two functions may be combined in a single committee.) *(See Chapter 14, Party Leadership in Congress.)*

Congressional reforms of the mid-1970s reduced the power of committee chairs, distributing some authority among subcommittee chairs and shifting other powers to the leadership. In 1995 House Republicans imposed six-year term limits on committee chairs, further weakening their position. Occasionally, legislators will attempt to dethrone a committee chairman who appears to be out of step with the party membership or unable to continue to lead. In 1995, when Mark O. Hatfield, R-Ore., voted against a constitutional amendment to balance the budget, two Senate conservatives attempted to punish Hatfield by trying to strip away his position as chair of the Senate Appropriations Committee. Although Hatfield retained the chairmanship, he announced his retirement soon after the attempt to remove him.

Nonetheless, the chairs of full House and Senate committees wield strong influence not only over the members of their panels but also over the full membership on the floor; moreover, they are positioned to hold considerable sway over legislation within their purview. At the full committee level, chairs call meetings, establish agendas, schedule hearings, preside over markup sessions, act as floor managers, recommend conferees, control committee budgets, oversee the hiring and firing of committee staff, and often act as spokespeople for their committee and political party in the areas of their expertise. Committee members who hope to have their legislative proposals considered favorably generally take care to enlist the support of their committee chairs.

CHANGING LEADERSHIP STYLES

Like pressure tactics, congressional leadership styles have changed with the times. In the 1890s, Thomas Brackett Reed, R-Maine, exerted such control over House proceedings during his tenure as Speaker that he became known as "Czar Reed." "No company of soldiers in the regular army was ever more thor-

---

PRESSURES FOR PARTY UNITY

Even though voters identify far less with political parties than they used to, legislators are siding with their party leadership as much as ever. If anything, party unity grew stronger during the 1990s, in part because the Republican takeover of the House in 1995 sparked new partisan tensions in that body, while the increased use of the filibuster in the Senate meant that the minority party could block most initiatives as long as its members remained unified. The fact that one party has controlled the White House and the opposing party has controlled Congress for much of the past three decades has further bred sharp partisan differences on major domestic and foreign issues.

Those differences have been reflected in the party unity scores Congressional Quarterly calculates by studying votes in which a majority of Democrats opposed a majority of Republicans. Democrats on average supported their party on 64 percent of the partisan votes in 1960, 57 percent of the votes in 1970, 68 percent of the votes in 1980, 81 percent in 1990, and more than 82 percent in 1998.

The pattern was similar for Republicans. Republicans on average supported their party on 68 percent of the partisan votes in 1960, 58 percent in 1970, 70 percent in 1980, 74 percent in 1990, and 86 percent in 1998.

SOURCES: *Congressional Quarterly Almanac* (Washington, D.C.: Congressional Quarterly, selected years); Alan K. Ota, "Partisan Voting on the Rise," *CQ Weekly,* January 9, 1999, 79.

---

oughly drilled" than were the Republicans under Reed, recalled James Beauchamp "Champ" Clark, D-Mo., Reed's contemporary, who was himself Speaker of the House from 1911 to 1919. "Time and again I have seen Mr. Reed bring every Republican up standing by waving his hands upward; and just as often, when they had risen inadvertently, I have seen him make them take their seats by waving his hands downward."[5]

Little more than a decade after Reed's tenure ended, a coalition of Democrats and progressive Republicans ended the dictatorial reign of Speaker Joseph G. Cannon, R-Ill., and stripped the office of the Speaker of many of its powers. Since then, even though some of those powers have been restored, congressional party leaders have relied on persuasion, negotiation, and the distribution of favors to line up support for party positions. In both the House and Senate, leaders have preserved their control by sensing what most members think and taking care of their political needs.

A party leadership position can be frustrating, particularly in the Senate, where a single member can thwart, or at least delay, the will of the majority. Howard H. Baker Jr., R-Tenn., who was majority leader from 1981 through 1984, complained that leading the Senate was like trying "to push a wet noodle."[6] Robert C. Byrd, who was the Senate Democratic leader from 1977 through 1988, once said that if he were asked to name his occupation he would reply "slave."[7]

Leaders in the House have more means of controlling the

rank and file than their Senate counterparts do. But they must take care to lead in the direction in which their members want to go. In 1997, after surviving a coup staged by disgruntled conservatives, House Speaker Newt Gingrich, R-Ga., promised to listen more closely to his colleagues.

DISTRIBUTION OF FAVORS

Although House and Senate leaders may not be able to twist arms in the way that their predecessors sometimes did, they are not without powerful tools for persuading members to follow their lead. One of the most important of these is the favor. Favors take many forms—awarding a better committee assignment; ensuring that a member's district receives special benefits, such as public works projects; assisting with campaign funding; or distributing what Speaker Thomas P. "Tip" O'Neill Jr., D-Mass., called the "little odds and ends." By distributing enough favors to members, leaders accumulate a significant number of chits that they can call in when a close vote is expected on an important bill.

The master of this tactic was Speaker Sam Rayburn, a Texas Democrat who carefully cultivated his personal popularity among other legislators throughout his forty-eight-year career in the House. In his book *House Out of Order,* Rep. Richard Bolling, D-Mo., a Rayburn protégé, wrote:

There was hardly a member, however strong a political opponent, for whom [Rayburn] had not done a favor—securing a more desirable committee assignment, obtaining a federal project to help in a difficult reelection campaign, an appointment to a board or commission for prestige purposes, or the assignment of extra space. Rayburn knew that the speakership had been shorn of much of its substantive power. Therefore, he built up, in place of it, a vast backlog of political IOUs with a compound interest.[8]

Expressions of friendship toward fellow lawmakers also help congressional leaders stack up IOUs. Senate leaders, for example, make a particular effort to schedule votes for the greatest convenience of members. Or a leader may schedule action on a particular bill—even one that has no chance of becoming law—so as to maximize publicity for the measure's sponsor. In the House, the Speaker may enhance a member's influence and prestige through an appointment to lead a special task force. Rep. J. Dennis Hastert, R-Ill., was elected Speaker in 1999 partly because he made a practice of "constituent service"—performing countless favors for his Republican colleagues. While such favors clearly help the leadership build coalitions and party loyalty, they also seem to be expected by the rank and file.

DISTRIBUTION OF COMMITTEE ASSIGNMENTS

When a congressional leader resorts to exercising overt pressure, the "carrot-and-stick" technique is one of the most effective: leaders promise prestigious committee assignments to members who cooperate and assign undesirable ones to those who do not. One of the first and most severe applications of this approach occurred in 1858, when Sen. Stephen A. Douglas, D-

Ill., was removed from the chairmanship of the Committee on Territories for failure to follow the Democratic stand on the expansion of slavery.

In the twentieth century, in 1965 the House Democratic caucus stripped two legislators—Albert W. Watson of South Carolina and John Bell Williams of Mississippi—of their committee seniority for supporting the Republican presidential candidate in the 1964 election. Watson left the Democratic Party, resigned his seat, and was reelected as a Republican. The loss of seniority cost Williams the chairmanship of the House Interstate and Foreign Commerce Committee, which he would have been in line to receive in 1966, upon the retirement of Chairman Oren Harris, D-Ark.

More recently, such methods have not always been effective. In early 1983, as punishment for two years of collaboration with the White House in support of President Ronald Reagan's budget, the House Democratic Steering and Policy Committee stripped Rep. Phil Gramm of Texas of his seat on the Budget Committee. Gramm promptly resigned from the House, switched parties, won his seat back as a Republican—and received a Republican appointment to the Budget Committee. In 1995 Republican leaders attempted to punish Rep. Mark Neumann, R-Wis., for repeatedly voting against GOP spending priorities. But when they moved to demote Neumann from the Appropriations National Security Subcommittee to the less prestigious Military Construction Subcommittee, Neumann's fellow freshmen protested. The leadership backed down, giving Neumann a prestigious Budget Committee seat.

No other leader in the history of Congress was more proficient at the strategic use of committee assignments than Lyndon B. Johnson, the Senate Democratic leader in the 1950s. When Sen. John C. Stennis, D-Miss., supported Johnson's effort to censure Sen. Joseph R. McCarthy, R-Wis., for misconduct in his stormy probe of suspected Communists in government, Stennis was quickly rewarded with a seat on the prestigious Appropriations Committee. Sen. J. Allen Frear Jr., D-Del., a conservative who took a moderate position at Johnson's behest on a number of important bills, was quickly awarded a place on the Finance Committee, whereas Sen. Paul H. Douglas, D-Ill., a strong liberal but a Johnson foe, waited for nine years to be named to that panel.

House reforms in the mid-1970s, while generally giving legislators more independence, strengthened the Speaker's control over committee assignments, albeit not to the extent that Speaker Cannon had enjoyed in the early 1900s. In a December 1974 caucus, House Democrats transferred authority to assign committee seats among party members from the Democratic members of the Ways and Means Committee to the newly revived Democratic Steering and Policy Committee. That panel, with half of its seats filled by the party leadership or members appointed by the Speaker, generally honors party leaders' commitments. "In the process of overseeing committee assignments," Robert Peabody pointed out, "a Speaker has one of his best opportunities to reward the party faithful and to build credit toward future needs."[9]

When Republicans took over the House in 1995, Speaker Gingrich enjoyed considerable power over committee assignments, which he used to bypass senior legislators in line for top committee posts in favor of members whom he saw as more assertive and conservative, such as Robert L. Livingston, R-La., who was chosen to chair the Appropriations Committee. Gingrich, who consolidated power as no other Speaker had since Joseph Cannon, became the spokesperson for the GOP's national agenda while overruling committee chairs and taking an unusually active role in appropriations and tax policy. Thanks in part to his use of committee assignments, Gingrich commanded nearly absolute loyalty among the Republican rank and file.

DISTRIBUTION OF PUBLIC WORKS PROJECTS

Like the award of good or bad committee assignments, the selective distribution of public works projects is an effective means of pressuring legislators to follow the party line. Such projects can serve as powerful means of persuasion: legislators' political success or failure is based at least partly on how much "pork" they can win for their state or district. *(See Chapter 18, Constituency Pressures.)*

One of the masters of this method was House Transportation Committee Chairman Bud Shuster, R-Pa. In 1997, as he was beginning work on a six-year omnibus transportation bill that would include public works funds for every congressional district in the nation, Shuster won House passage of legislation to change the budget rules in a way that would benefit road projects. Powerful members of the Budget Committee from both parties opposed the measure, but Shuster picked up support from the hundreds of Republican and Democratic representatives who wanted his committee to approve projects in their districts. Shuster even successfully stood up to Speaker Gingrich, insisting that other spending priorities be pared back in order to accommodate his transportation preferences.

Members of appropriations committees are also well situated to wield influence by helping other members obtain funds for parochial projects. Each year, legislators approach the chairs of appropriations subcommittees to plead for funds for specific projects. Some chairmen regularly receive more than one hundred such requests and take great pains to let members know how many of the requests were honored. "Appropriations is the key spot," House Appropriations Committee member Mickey Edwards, R-Okla., said in 1987. "Members need you and come to you for help. If you're not on Appropriations, you are really at the mercy of other people."[10]

Party leaders can also be influential. Lyndon Johnson, for example, frequently used the distribution of public works funds to win votes on important Senate bills. When Johnson needed northern votes on a compromise version of the 1957 civil rights bill, he won support from Sens. Margaret Chase Smith, R-Maine, and Frank Church, D-Idaho, by securing appropriations for important reclamation projects in their states. Later in the year, when the civil rights bill came up, both senators voted with Johnson.[11]

Congressional support for the system remains high, although it is an easy target for newspaper editors and legislators who want to rail against Congress's profligate ways. The system is based on the members' presumption that, over time, they can win approval for projects in their state or district. Leaders of the appropriations and transportation committees may be especially generous with their own regions, but they must also distribute projects to a sufficient number of members to ensure their continued backing. "Actually, the committees must treat others fairly if they seek to maintain those huge congressional majorities that allow them to overpower presidents who occasionally veto public works bills," R. Douglas Arnold wrote in a 1981 American Enterprise Institute study.[12]

DISTRIBUTION OF CAMPAIGN FUNDS

As congressional campaigns become increasingly expensive, party leaders are finding that they can exert considerable pressure on members through promises of financial aid. Gingrich was perhaps more adept at this tactic than any previous leader. Beginning in the late 1980s, he controlled a political action committee (PAC) called GOPAC, which was created to cultivate local and state politicians for eventual congressional races. Upon becoming Speaker, Gingrich appeared at fund-raisers across the country to help members raise reelection funds.

But Gingrich also used his financial clout to punish errant members. In 1996 he canceled fund-raisers in the districts of several legislators who had defied his directive to vote to reopen the federal government—which the Republican Congress had shutdown in a budget duel with President Clinton. One of those members, Rep. John Hostettler of Indiana, responded with a letter in which he told the Speaker, "I cannot allow my fundraising to be tied in any way to specific votes." Hostettler invited Majority Leader Dick Armey of Texas to visit his district instead, and Armey accepted.[13]

Both the Democratic and Republican parties have Senate and House campaign committees that identify candidates to challenge incumbents from the other party, brief candidates on the issues, parcel out funds to assist with campaigns, and help party members with all phases of campaigning. These campaign committees are important to candidates not only as sources of funding in their own right but because their imprimatur often helps attract money from other contributors, particularly PACs *(See Chapter 32, Campaign Financing.)*

The distribution of campaign funds can be an important tool for congressional leaders. Just as Lyndon Johnson mastered the other facets of party leadership, he was also able to mold the Senate Campaign Committee into an effective instrument of control. In their book *Lyndon B. Johnson: The Exercise of Power,* Rowland Evans and Robert Novak wrote:

De facto control of the Campaign Committee's funds was one of Johnson's least obvious but most effective tools in building his network [of supporters]. He controlled the distribution of committee funds through both its chairmen—first Earle Clements, D-Ky., and later George Smathers, D-Fla.—and through its secretary, Bobby Baker. More often than not, the requests for campaign funds were routinely made to Baker, and the money was physically distributed by him. Johnson further tightened his control when Clements was named the committee's executive director after his Senate defeat in 1956. Johnson got the most out of the committee's limited funds—at that time a mere four hundred thousand dollars—by shrewdly distributing them where they would do the most work. In the small mountain states like Idaho, a ten-thousand dollar contribution could change the course of an election. But in New York or Pennsylvania, ten thousand dollars was the merest drop in the bucket. Johnson and Baker tried to reduce contributions to Democrats in the industrial Northeast to the minimum. Because senators seldom bite the hand that feeds them, these Westerners were naturally drawn into the Johnson network, while the Eastern liberals tended to remain outside.[14]

In recent years, party leaders and influential committee chairmen have established their PACs—called leadership PACs—which raise money from individuals and other PACs and then make contributions to other candidates' campaigns. With more fund-raising clout than junior members or challengers, the leaders are able to raise far more money than they themselves need for their next campaign. And they are top drawing cards at fund-raisers for other candidates.

Friendly Persuasion:
Pressures from Colleagues

Two important internal influences on legislators' actions are the unwritten—but generally understood—code of congressional behavior and members' personal relationships with their colleagues. Pressure may also be exerted through "Dear Colleague" letters and "logrolling"—the exchange of votes to achieve particular goals.

CONGRESSIONAL CODE OF CONDUCT

Most lawmakers share similar expectations about how they and their colleagues ought to behave. For example, members are expected to devote their time to legislative and constituent work and not seek personal publicity at the expense of those obligations. Members are also expected to treat colleagues with personal courtesy, keep their word once an agreement is reached, reciprocate favors, and defer to colleagues on matters affecting their district or state. These and other behavioral norms, described in a 1960 study of the Senate by Donald R. Matthews, are not always observed: in fact, violations of some of these principles have increased substantially in the last three decades.[15] Nevertheless, the unwritten code remains the basis for the type of behavior expected of the members of both the House and Senate.

Peer pressure is the principal enforcement mechanism. For example, late in the 1982 lame-duck session, when Jesse Helms and John P. East undertook a filibuster against a proposal to raise the gasoline tax—delaying action on the bill for more than a week—the two GOP senators from North Carolina made themselves unpopular with even their Republican colleagues. At one point, when East refused to yield the floor, S. I. "Sam" Hayakawa, R-Calif., sarcastically asked whether East believed that the opinions of other senators did not matter. "If such is the case . . . why does he demean himself by associating himself with clods and peasants like us?" Helms's refusal to let the Senate vote on the gas tax and go home prompted Alan K. Simpson, R-Wyo., to say, "Seldom have I seen a more obdurate, more obnoxious performance."[16] The Senate finally broke the filibuster, leaving the two North Carolinians with little more than the lingering displeasure of their colleagues.

Indeed, such dilatory tactics often backfire. Neither Sen. Ernest Hollings, D-S.C., who delayed the end of the 103rd Congress over trade legislation, nor Sen. Edward M. Kennedy, D-Mass., who delayed the end of the 104th over a labor provision, were able to win much support for their causes. Another senator who often used delay tactics, Democrat Howard M. Metzenbaum of Ohio, was unapologetic: "The Senate custom is to go along to get along. But I don't do that. If I'm not the most popular guy in the Senate—well, I can live with that."[17] It takes a legislator with a thick skin to be willing to risk the scorn of senatorial colleagues, and Metzenbaum acknowledged that his reputation had led some members of his own party to vote against him on occasion. More often, an obstinate senator is quietly persuaded by colleagues to give in to the will of the majority.

Adhering to the more traditional custom, Sen. Rick Santorum, R-Pa., declined to stall a Republican-drafted farm bill in 1996 even though he strongly opposed provisions in it that continued the sugar price-support program. Instead of siding with Democrats and voting "no," which would have sunk the measure, Santorum voted "present." As a result, Republicans were able to pass the landmark measure, which a reluctant President Clinton signed into law. For Santorum, a highly conservative member from a moderate state, the payoff came in the form of support from his GOP colleagues as he neared a challenging re-election bid.

PERSONAL RELATIONSHIPS:
SOCIAL TIES AND EXPERTISE

The influence of personal relationships among lawmakers, though powerful, often escapes notice. On the surface, a conservative Republican and a liberal Democrat may appear to have little basis for cooperation on a piece of legislation. But if the two members play tennis together every weekend, share the same hobby, or belong to the same health club or parent-teachers' association—or if their spouses have been friends for many years—the web of social connections can create a strong bond that carries over into their work. Two influential senators—Utah Republican Orrin Hatch and Massachusetts Democrat Ted Kennedy—forged a close friendship that enabled them to overcome their very considerable philosophical differences and work together on such measures as a proposed cigarette tax.

Before a committee meeting, senators enjoy a light moment. Personal and social relationships among members are an important influence on their behavior. From left to right are Sens. Robert F. Bennett, R-Utah; Robert C. Byrd, D-W.Va.; and Ben Nighthorse Campbell, R-Colo.

Senate Majority Leader Trent Lott, R-Miss., strengthened his bonds with three Republican senators with divergent political views—John Ashcroft of Missouri, Larry E. Craig of Idaho, and James M. Jeffords of Vermont—by forming the "Singing Senators" quartet. The group serenaded listeners at a variety of party and public functions and, in 1997, journeyed to Nashville to record a compact disk of country and gospel songs.

Even without overt lobbying, members sometimes influence their colleagues through the weight of their expertise on a particular issue. As Sen. Edmund S. Muskie, D-Maine, once put it, "Real power [in the Senate] comes from doing your work and knowing what you're talking about. Power is the ability to change someone's mind."[18] For example, the views of Sen. Sam Nunn, D-Ga., on defense matters were often highly influential with many of his Democratic colleagues, who respected his expertise in the field. Moreover, Nunn's credentials as a pro-military Democrat could provide "cover" for other Democrats, who could follow his lead without worrying about being branded as soft on military matters. Along the same lines, Republicans affirmed the views of Sen. Bill Frist, R-Tenn.—a highly respected former heart surgeon—to protect themselves from being tagged as out of step with health care reform issues.

Members with specialized expertise can also wield influence across the aisle. During the 1986 debate on a major tax overhaul measure, GOP Sen. Charles E. Grassley of Iowa told the *Wall Street Journal* that he often took his voting cues from Democratic Sen. Bill Bradley of New Jersey, who was regarded as a trailblazer on the issue. Grassley said that there was always "another factor to consider: How does Bradley look at this?"[19]

"DEAR COLLEAGUE" LETTERS

"Dear colleague" letters—a more overt way of attempting to influence colleagues—are most often used by a legislator who hopes to attract as many cosponsors as possible for legislation being prepared for introduction. The form letter generally includes a brief description of the legislation and a plea for support. In hopes of winning favorable treatment for the measure, a legislator who gathers a substantial number of cosponsors for a piece of legislation will often trumpet that fact to the leadership and, through press releases, to constituents back home.

LOGROLLING

Because of the diversity of interests in both the House and Senate, members often trade votes to attain legislative goals. This bargaining strategy—known as *logrolling*—has been practiced in Congress since the early days of the Republic and in state legislatures before that. The term originated in the nineteenth century, when neighbors helped each other roll logs into a pile for burning.

A classic example of logrolling occurred in 1964, when liberal House Democrats voted for wheat and cotton subsidies in return for rural conservatives' support for a new food stamp program. Both bills were passed April 8, the food stamp measure by a 229 to 189 roll call vote and the wheat-cotton bill by a vote of 211 to 203. The Johnson administration had arranged the trade after both bills appeared to be foundering in the House.[20]

In the 1980s, with efforts to reduce the federal budget deficit commanding high priority, members bargained with each other to distribute the impact of spending cuts. As Roger H. Davidson and Walter J. Oleszek have noted, "In a hostile fiscal environment, logrolling is often aimed at equalizing sacrifices rather than distributing rewards."[21] But when budget surpluses returned in the late 1990s, members struck deals that simultaneously boosted spending for Democrat-backed social programs and met the Republicans' goal of cutting taxes.

Many students of government defend logrolling as a legitimate means of enabling legislators to protect their constituency's interests. As longtime House journalist Neil MacNeil put it,

In the inside struggle to set the House's stance on a question of public policy, rarely has the decision involved for the individual Representative a moral choice between right and wrong. . . . Normally on legislation, there has always been an area of possible compromise, legitimate compromise, and this possibility has caused the bargaining implicit in the formulation of almost all legislation. The adoption of even an amendment of seemingly little or no consequence sometimes has provided the votes needed to pass an entire bill.[22]

Political scientist Nelson W. Polsby, another defender of logrolling, notes that cooperative effort of this sort in Congress "dilutes the power of the most entrenched, and enhances tremendously the powers of all [members], however low on the totem pole."[23]

The Internal Lobbyists:
Special Interest Alliances

Congress, as a representative institution, gives full play to the myriad regional, cultural, economic, and ethnic differences that characterize the American people. Like-minded Republicans and Democrats in both houses often work together to pursue common policy goals. And members who have opposing viewpoints but who hail from the same state or region often band together to promote legislation that would benefit their particular constituents.

The granddaddy of such alliances was the Conservative Coalition. For more than six decades, beginning in the 1930s, Republicans and southern Democrats joined on the House and Senate floors to influence, and occasionally dominate, economic and social policy debates. Another effective coalition of many years' standing was the Democratic Study Group (DSG), which liberal and moderate Democrats established in 1959 to counter the Conservative Coalition. In succeeding years, House members sharing similar political philosophies created other organizations, such as the House Wednesday Group and the Conservative Opportunity Society.

In the past few decades, as party discipline declined and special interest groups took an increasingly active role in politics, senators and representatives began forming more coalitions, many of them highly organized, to articulate and pursue particular goals that they shared. African American, Hispanic, and women lawmakers organized caucuses not only to ensure that the interests of minorities and women were placed before Congress but also to increase their own influence within Congress. And during the 1970s, as regional rivalries intensified over energy and economic policy, caucus organizations proliferated to advance the causes of industrial states, energy-producing regions, specific industries, and many other economic and social interests. In the 1990s, with the House closely divided between Republicans and Democrats, caucuses such as the moderate "Blue Dog" Democrats and the Conservative Action Team (CAT) wielded significant clout because House leaders needed their support to ensure a bare majority on the floor.

Until 1995, the most prominent caucuses were known as legislative service organizations (LSOs) and received annual dues from their members. Many of these more than two dozen organizations, such as the Congressional Black Caucus, were active in pursuing Democratic goals. When the GOP took over the House, Republicans transferred the $4 million budgeted yearly for the LSOs back to the members' offices, forcing the LSOs to close down their operations. Several, such as the DSG, which issues analyses of proposed legislation, had to privatize; others simply continued to operate as before—except that, like the 150 or so more minor caucuses, they were now run out of members' offices, without special staff. "That's our whole point: They could continue to function," said Rep. Pat Roberts, R-Kans., who led the fight to eliminate the funding. "To have them taxpayer-funded was not necessary."[24]

By the late 1990s, senators and representatives had set up close to 200 special interest caucuses, and most legislators belonged to at least one of these groups, which ranged from the House Footwear Caucus to the Congressional Coalition on Population and Development, and from the Pro-Life Caucus to the Congressional Travel and Tourism Caucus. *(See box, Multitude of Interests Are Represented in Special Caucuses, p. 648.)*

The emergence of special caucus groups, especially in the House, has partly filled a void left by the weakening of party leadership. Caucuses give members an opportunity to exchange information and participate in formulating policy on matters that are of interest to them and their constituents. Caucuses can also help marshal support for common positions. Functioning almost as internal interest groups, many caucuses lobby committees and individual legislators to gain support for particular causes. Caucuses sometimes send representatives to testify at hearings, and some draft specific legislative proposals. Critics contend, however, that special interest alliances contribute to the splintering of legislative authority and hamper efforts to shape compromise legislation.

THE CONSERVATIVE COALITION

The Conservative Coalition was the most potent congressional alliance for much of the twentieth century. The coalition never had a staff or formal organization, but between the 1930s and the early 1990s, Republicans and southern Democrats often cooperated to exert powerful influence in both chambers of Congress. After Republicans became the congressional majority in 1995, House GOP leaders no longer needed Democratic help to pass major initiatives. The coalition faded, and voting became rigidly partisan.

The coalition developed when southern Democrats, disillusioned with the economic policies of the New Deal, began banding together with Republicans to defeat or weaken President Franklin D. Roosevelt's proposals. Under the guidance of Democrat Howard W. Smith of Virginia, the powerful chairman of the House Rules Committee, and Republican leader Joseph W. Martin Jr., Mass., and his successor, Charles A. Halleck, Ind., the coalition dominated the House in the 1950s and in the early 1960s, defeating many Kennedy administration initiatives. It was less powerful in the Senate but still had an important impact on legislation.

David W. Brady and Charles S. Bullock III, describing the Conservative Coalition in a 1981 study, noted that

one of the most striking features about the influential and long-lived coalition is that it meets almost none of the procedural or organizational criteria for coalition building. There are no whips, no formal leaders, no inducements to members in the form of choice committee assignments or patronage.

In its 1950s heyday, Brady and Bullock reported, the coalition developed its position through brief meetings between House Rules Committee Chairman Smith and the Republican leaders. Because its purpose was usually to block liberal legislation, the coalition could function without an elaborate organization. Be-

Joseph W. Martin, R-Mass., swears in the 83rd Congress in 1953. During the 1940s and 1950s, Martin, who only served four years as Speaker, was one of the de facto leaders of the Conservative Coalition—the potent alliance of Republicans and southern Democrats.

cause of the success of the coalition, Brady and Bullock wrote, "the voting alliance begun in 1937 between southern Democrats and Republicans has greatly reduced the ability of the majority Democratic Party to function as a governing party."[25]

The coalition did not spring into action on every House and Senate roll call vote but only on major economic or social issues. Neil MacNeil explained how the coalition took shape before an important House vote:

The Republican strategists conferred with the southern Democratic tacticians, and together they agreed on a joint plan of action. The secret of success was for [Republican leader] Martin to permit the southern Democrats to carry the fight on the House floor. They would make the main speeches, they would make the motions, they would offer the substitutes and the amendments. The design was to encourage Democrats to join the opposition. . . . The technique, once learned, proved a major weapon in the conservative coalition's arsenal. Martin used it against Roosevelt measures and Truman measures and Charles Halleck used it against Kennedy bills. It was no accident that Phillip Landrum of Georgia, a conservative Democrat, offered the Eisenhower labor bill in 1959 or that James C. Davis of Georgia, even more conservative than Landrum, offered the Eisenhower airport construction bill. Both had been chosen by Halleck and Smith as the southerners most likely to encourage other Democrats to join the conservative cause.[26]

The coalition lost strength in the House in the 1964 Democratic landslide that resulted in congressional passage of President Johnson's Great Society programs. Although it recouped some of its losses in the late 1960s, the election of new and younger members of Congress prevented the coalition from re-

gaining its former level of power. The newer members tended to seek legislative compromises rather than to resort to the obstructive tactics that had worked so well for the coalition. This shift in strategy reflected the increasing moderacy of the southern electorate: migration from the North and the enfranchisement of black residents prompted southern politicians of both parties to become more sensitive to civil rights and other social issues.

The coalition enjoyed a resurgence in the early 1980s, providing the backbone of congressional support for President Reagan's conservative economic, defense, and social policies. Bolstered by Republican election gains in 1980, the coalition in 1981 outpolled northern Democrats on 92 percent of the recorded House and Senate votes in which the two groups faced off. That record surpassed the 89 percent success rate the coalition had achieved in 1957, the first year *Congressional Quarterly* began studying the congressional voting patterns.[27]

Later in the 1980s, however, the coalition's influence diminished once again. Abandoning its traditional allegiance to the Democratic Party, the South became a Republican bastion in the 1990s, shifting the national balance of power between the two political parties. Propelled by their Dixie base, Republicans swept to congressional majorities in 1994 and established a mostly southern leadership team headed by House Speaker Gingrich of Georgia and Senate Majority Leader Lott of Mississippi.

The surviving southern Democrats—especially those from predominantly black congressional districts—became more lib-

MULTITUDE OF INTERESTS ARE REPRESENTED IN SPECIAL CAUCUSES

Informal congressional groups, or special caucuses, have proliferated on Capitol Hill throughout the last three decades. These voluntary alliances, unlike formal leadership and party groups, are not formally recognized by chamber rules. Although new House rules in 1995 ended the practice of funding the more prominent caucuses through member dues, the organizations have continued to operate without special staff. Some groups are little more than a circle of lunch-table companions, while others wield considerable influence over the congressional agenda.

The Congressional Research Service (CRS) counted at least 178 informal groups in the 105th Congress. Of these, seventy were registered as congressional member organizations with the Committee on House Oversight, meaning that they consisted of members from the House or from both chambers who shared official resources. Following is a list of House groups and congressional member organizations:

101st Congressional Democratic Caucus
African Trade and Investment Caucus
Albanian Issues Caucus
Animal Welfare Caucus
An Artistic Discovery
Bipartisan Drug Policy Working Group
Bipartisan Freshman Campaign Finance Reform Task Force
Commuter Caucus
Congressional Advisory Panel to Reduce Teen Pregnancy
Congressional Air Power Caucus
Congressional Automotive Caucus
Congressional Aviation and Space Caucus
Congressional Bearing Caucus
Congressional Biomedical Research Caucus
Congressional Boating Caucus
Congressional Border Caucus
Congressional Caucus on Armenian Issues
Congressional Caucus on Hellenic Issues
Congressional Caucus on India and Indian-Americans
Congressional Census Caucus
Congressional Children's Caucus
Congressional Children's Working Group
Congressional Coalition on Population and Development
Congressional Coastal Caucus
Congressional Dialog on Vietnam
Congressional Electricity Caucus
Congressional Family Caucus
Congressional Farmland Protection Caucus
Congressional Fatherhood Promotion Task Force
Congressional Footwear Caucus
Congressional Friends of Animals
Congressional Gaming Caucus
Congressional Grace Caucus
Congressional Human Rights Caucus
Congressional Jobs and Fair Trade Caucus
Congressional Manufactured Housing Caucus
Congressional Manufacturing Task Force
Congressional Member Organization for the Arts
Congressional Mining Caucus
Congressional Missing and Exploited Children's Caucus
Congressional Narcotics Abuse and Control Caucus
Congressional Native American Caucus
Congressional Pro-Choice Caucus
Congressional Steel Caucus
Congressional Task Force Against Anti-Semitism
Congressional Task Force on International HIV/AIDS
Congressional Task Force on Tobacco and Health
Congressional Task Force to End the Arab Boycott

Congressional Travel and Tourism Caucus
Congressional U.S.–Former Soviet Union Energy Caucus
Congressional Ukrainian Caucus
Congressional Urban Caucus
Congressional Working Group on China
Conservative Action Team
Conservative Opportunity Society
Constitutional Caucus
Constitutional Forum
Democratic Budget Group
Democratic Freshman Class
Democratic Task Force on Hunger
Depot Caucus
Diabetes Caucus
Education Caucus (House)
Export Task Force
Forestry 2000 Task Force
Great Lakes Task Force
House Army Caucus
House Beef Caucus
House Bicycle Caucus
House Cancer Awareness Working Group
House Impact Aid Coalition
House Intercity Passenger Rail Coalition
House Medical Technology Caucus
House Pro-Life Caucus
House Reading Caucus
House Renewable Energy Caucus
House Republican Israel Caucus
House Trails Caucus
House Working Group on Mental Illness and Health Issues
Information Technology Working Group
Insurance Caucus
Interstate 69 Mid-Continent Highway Caucus
Law Enforcement Caucus
Long Island Sound Caucus
Mainstream Conservative Alliance
Minor League Baseball Caucus
National Guard and Reserve Components Caucus
National Retail Sales Tax Caucus
New Democrat Coalition
Northeast Agricultural Caucus
Northern Border Caucus
Older Americans Caucus
Porkbusters Coalition
Portuguese American Caucus
Progressive Caucus
Public Pension Reform Caucus

Republican Class of the 100th Congress
Republican Education Caucus
Republican Freshman Class
Republican Housing Opportunity Caucus
Republican Sophomore Class
Results Caucus
Rural Health Care Coalition
Social Security Caucus

Sustainable Development Caucus
The Coalition (Democratic)
Tuesday Group
United Nations Working Group
Upper Mississippi River Task Force
Wednesday Group
Western Caucus

The Senate, with fewer members, has fewer caucuses. The 1998 CRS survey turned up twenty-nine Senate organizations, including several that paralleled the House member organizations:

Bipartisan Senate Task Force on Fatherhood Promotion
Centrist Coalition
Concerned Senators for the Arts
Friends of Portugal
Grassley-Dorgan Farm Policy Coalition
Jewelry Task Force
Northeast-Midwest Senate Coalition
Science and Technology Caucus
Senate (Republican) Steering Committee
Senate Anti-Terrorism Caucus
Senate Auto Caucus
Senate Beef Caucus
Senate Cancer Coalition
Senate Children's Caucus
Senate Coastal Coalition

Senate Delta Caucus
Senate Drug Enforcement Caucus
Senate Medical Technology Caucus
Senate National Guard Caucus
Senate NATO Observer Group
Senate Republican Freshman Class
Senate Republican Task Force on Health Care
Senate Rural Health Caucus
Senate Steel Caucus
Senate Sweetener Caucus
Senate Textile Steering Committee
Senate Tourism Caucus
Senate Transit Caucus
Western States Senate Coalition

Additional bicameral groups listed in the CRS report included:

Republican Class of the 100th Congress
Ad Hoc Congressional Committee for Irish Affairs
Ad Hoc Steering Committee on Telehealth
American Automotive Performance and Motorsports Caucus
Bipartisan Regulatory Reform Caucus
California Democratic Congressional Delegation
Congressional Alcohol Fuels Caucus
Congressional Asian Pacific Caucus
Congressional Biotechnology Caucus
Congressional Black Caucus
Congressional Caucus for Women's Issues
Congressional Caucus on Hong Kong
Congressional Coalition on Adoption
Congressional Coast Guard Caucus
Congressional Committee to Support Writers and Journalists
Congressional Competitiveness Caucus
Congressional Empowerment Caucus
Congressional Fire Services Caucus
Congressional Friends of Human Rights Monitors
Congressional Health Care Quality Task Force
Congressional Heart and Stroke Coalition
Congressional Hispanic Caucus
Congressional Internet Caucus
Congressional Leaders United for a Balanced Budget
Congressional Members Organization on Terrorism and
   Unconventional Warfare

Congressional Oil and Gas Forum
Congressional Peanut Caucus
Congressional Pork Industry Caucus
Congressional Prevention Coalition
Congressional Property Rights Coalition
Congressional Soybean Caucus
Congressional Sportsmen's Caucus
Congressional Task Force on Organ and Tissue Donation
Congressional Western Water Caucus
Education Caucus (bicameral)
Federal Government Service Caucus
Friends of Ireland
House/Senate International Education Study Group
House/Senate Steering Committee on Retirement Security
Long Island Congressional Caucus
Mississippi River Caucus
National Security Caucus
Naval Mine Warfare Caucus
New York State Congressional Delegation
Northeast-Midwest Congressional Delegation
Peace Accord Monitoring Group
Religious Prisoners Congressional Task Force
Renewal Alliance
Tennessee Valley Authority Congressional Caucus
Vietnam Era Veterans in Congress

eral and more loyal to their party. In consequence, GOP leaders made fewer attempts to court southern Democrats, focusing instead on gaining the support of moderate northeastern legislators who might otherwise enter into coalitions with Democrats.

By the late 1990s, the Conservative Coalition had become moribund. In 1998 the coalition's votes were not essential to the passage of any significant bill. That same year, the coalition made its presence felt on less than 8 percent of House votes. In the Senate, southern Democrats left their party and voted with Republicans on only eight votes—too few to be statistically significant.

Strikingly, the House showed that it could take the most momentous step possible—the impeachment of President Clinton—with the votes of only four southern Democrats. But the Senate in 1999 could not pick up a single southern Democrat to convict the president.

OTHER PARTY GROUPS

As noted earlier, the success of the Conservative Coalition helped spark the creation of the Democratic Study Group (DSG). Established to counter the informal Conservative Coalition's power to block liberal legislation, the DSG set up a formal research and coordinating organization for House Democrats with moderate and liberal leanings. The DSG played a supporting role in program initiatives sponsored by Democratic administrations from 1961 to 1969, supplying crucial votes for the passage of major education, civil rights, and other social welfare legislation.

The DSG was the prototype for other intraparty alliances within the House, among Republicans as well as Democrats. In 1963, for example, Republican moderates set up the House Wednesday Group to develop constructive opposition at a time when Democrats controlled the White House and Congress.

In the mid-1980s, a small band of conservative House Republicans formed a group called the Conservative Opportunity Society to call public attention to what they considered to be the weak and wayward policies of the Democratic majority. The group used whatever parliamentary maneuvers it could to frustrate—and occasionally defeat—the Democrats. Generally, the group took its message straight to the electorate via C-SPAN, the cable television network that provides gavel-to-gavel coverage of House floor proceedings. Often, after regular legislative business had been completed for the day, members of the Conservative Opportunity Society took to the floor to make televised speeches. These "special orders," sometimes lasting several hours, enabled the conservatives to draw distinctions between their views and those of the majority Democrats—often by focusing on what the members characterized as the evils of the Democratic majority.

Despite the demise of the Conservative Coalition and the privatization of the DSG in the 1990s, a new generation of caucuses cropped up that wielded considerable influence. In 1998, the Conservative Action Team—a group of about forty conservative House Republicans—lobbied top leaders to pass a tax cut worth hundreds of billions of dollars. Although the conserva-

tives failed to get the plan through the House, they helped lay the groundwork for a greater emphasis on tax cuts in the following year. On the other side, the Tuesday Group, a loose-knit organization of about fifty moderate Republicans, worked to curtail plans to cut taxes and scale back government regulations.

With the House closely divided between the two parties throughout most of the late 1990s, the caucuses found themselves with increasing leverage. When Republicans had a majority of only about twenty seats in the 105th Congress, for example, they had to win the support of both moderate and conservative caucuses in order to muster a floor majority. For their part, Democrats worked hard to maintain the support of one of the most prominent caucuses, the "Blue Dog" Democrats, a moderate group that sided with Republicans on some fiscal issues.

In the Senate, caucuses also found themselves with increased leverage because most legislation required a sixty-vote supermajority for passage—meaning that top leaders had to satisfy all factions. An informal group of moderate Republican senators, including John H. Chafee of Rhode Island and Olympia J. Snowe of Maine, blocked tax cuts in 1998 and saw to it that the GOP placed greater emphasis on Social Security. The following year, moderate Republicans thwarted efforts to convict President Clinton of the offenses for which he had been impeached, depriving the more conservative Republicans of the majority that they needed to remove the president from office. (Even if all Senate Republicans had closed ranks, Democratic support for the president would have prevented the Senate from achieving the two-thirds majority necessary to remove Clinton.)

MINORITY GROUPS

Ethnic and minority groups have often banded together when Congress considered issues of particular importance to them. Italian Americans, Polish Americans, Irish Americans, and others have periodically spoken in unison on specific matters. Black, Hispanic, and women legislators have formed organized caucuses.

The Congressional Black Caucus, which includes nearly every black legislator, is one of the most effective of all caucuses. When it was formed in 1969, the caucus had only nine members, who had little role in the congressional power structure. By 1998, thirty-nine House members belonged to the caucus. At times, the mostly Democratic caucus has drawn support from black legislators across the aisle, although the only black Republican in the House in the late 1990s, J. S. Watts of Oklahoma, refused to join the caucus.

In the 1980s, pressure from the caucus led the Democratic leadership to appoint black legislators to the most powerful House committees. A measure of the caucus's success was the election, in 1985, of William H. Gray III, a black Pennsylvania Democrat, as chairman of the Budget Committee, an important and highly visible post. Gray went on to win election as Democratic whip in 1989, the third-highest leadership post in the House, before retiring from Congress in 1991 to become president of the United Negro College Fund.

Legislatively, the caucus lobbied for an economic agenda that would help the poor, who are disproportionately black, and for legislation that would strengthen and enforce civil rights laws. A major victory was the passage, in 1986, of legislation imposing economic sanctions on South Africa. Members of the Congressional Black Caucus, who are among the House's most liberal lawmakers, denounced GOP cuts to poverty programs in the 1990s and emerged as some of President Clinton's most passionate defenders during the impeachment proceedings in 1998.

The Congressional Hispanic Caucus, which had seventeen members in 1998, is much less cohesive than the Congressional Black Caucus. Caucus members range from conservative to liberal and rarely take a unanimous position.

Women House members formed a caucus in 1977, but they reorganized it in 1981 as the Congressional Caucus on Women's Issues and opened it to men. In 1998, the bipartisan group claimed fifty members. Among other activities, the caucus supports legislation to improve the economic status of women.

STATE AND REGIONAL ALLIANCES

State delegations in Congress have always worked together informally for common purposes. Some delegations meet regularly, perhaps for a weekly breakfast or lunch, to talk over state and national issues. These meetings are often monitored and sometimes attended by the party leadership. Delegations also may collaborate to capture their share of federal grants and projects, to back colleagues for important committee positions, and to support party leadership candidates. Within large delegations whose members have similar constituencies, legislators with specialized expertise are often able to sway part, if not all, of the state group.

The ideological makeup of a delegation often matters less than the common need of members to direct more federal funding to their home states. When it came to a major battle over highway funds, for example, Sen. Connie Mack, R-Fla., said in 1997, "It moves away from the ideological debate into one of 'How does my state do?'"[28] In the 1980s and 1990s, the Texas House delegation was extremely powerful, particularly during Jim Wright's tenure as Speaker (1987–1989) and Dick Armey and Tom DeLay's tenures as GOP majority leader and majority whip, respectively, in the mid- to late 1990s.

In a study of state delegations, Alan Fiellin found that "[a] division of labor, corresponding to the committee structure of the House, develops in some groups and provides benefits for the individual." He added:

By virtue of his informal ties, the New York Democrat, for example, has ready access to committees of which he is not a member. Individual members may, and do, use group connections to check on the status and prospects of legislation in committees other than their own. In the absence of personal ties with members of most House committees, the task of quickly getting trustworthy information on the work of many committees would be most difficult. The New York Democrat may save many hours of legwork, reading and anxious deliberation by holding a brief conversation with a like-minded colleague who knows the material and has previously sifted through it.[29]

State party delegations in the House can be an effective means of applying pressure to support the party's position on an issue. Votes may be swayed at delegation meetings, and—at the very least—the party's whip organization has the means to gauge the delegation's sentiment on pending issues. Political divisions within state delegations are usually submerged to common state interests.

A sense of shared interests may also carry over to regional issues, leading states to work together on matters of concern. As noted earlier, regional differences over economic and energy policies in the 1970s and 1980s spawned several congressional alliances. The 150-member Northeast-Midwest Congressional Coalition took active stands against policies that its members thought would harm industries and consumers in the regions that the coalition represented. For instance, the coalition pushed for policies that would provide industrial states with a larger share of federal funding. It opposed power-marketing administrations, which provided subsidized electricity to other regions, and coal severance taxes in western states, which raised energy costs in the Northeast and Midwest. Other regional alliances in Congress took opposing positions.

It is worth noting that the interests of one regional coalition do not necessarily conflict with the interests of another. In the 1990s, for example, the Northeast-Midwest coalition pressed for legislation designed to control so-called invasive species—plants and animals from overseas that wreak havoc on ecosystems in the Great Lakes and elsewhere. Much of the legislation, including the National Invasive Species Act, passed in 1996, was noncontroversial.

FUNDING CHANGES

Unlike the official party caucuses, for which Congress directly appropriates funds, the unofficial caucuses used to depend on member dues to cover expenses. (Caucuses without separate offices or staff did not usually require support from dues.) Dues were transferred to the caucuses from legislators' office expenses and salaries, but in 1995, Republicans barred members from using taxpayer-financed office accounts to fund caucuses.

Some caucuses were forced to make difficult adjustments. The Congressional Black Caucus, for example, had to rely on the personal aides of a few members, rather than on a full-time staff, to assemble alternative federal budget plans that promoted social spending while cutting defense funding. Rep. Major R. Owens, D-N.Y., who oversaw the caucus's budget plan in 1995, said that the new rules had increased the pressure on personal staff and hindered the group's ability to speak with one voice.

Groups such as the Environmental and Energy Study Conference, which prepares in-depth legislative reports, were forced to privatize their operations. Nevertheless, many of the reconfigured caucuses appear to have made a smooth transition. In the year after its funding was eliminated, the Congressional Caucus for Women's Issues was "alive and well," according to cochairwoman Constance A. Morella, R-Md. "If it's important, you will find a way to survive," she said.[30]

NOTES

1. Robert L. Peabody, "House Party Leadership in the 1970s," in *Congress Reconsidered*, 2nd ed., ed. Lawrence C. Dodd and Bruce I. Oppenheimer (Washington, D.C.: CQ Press, 1981), 138.

2. *Congressional Quarterly Almanac, 1995* (Washington, D.C.: Congressional Quarterly), C-8.

3. Ibid., C-10.

4. Alan K. Ota, "Partisan Voting on the Rise," *Congressional Quarterly Weekly Report*, January 9, 1999, 79.

5. Champ Clark, *My Quarter Century of American Politics*, vol. 2 (New York: Harper & Bros., 1920), 294.

6. "Changing Times Make Senate Hard to Lead," *Congressional Quarterly Weekly Report*, December 1, 1984, 3024.

7. Roger H. Davidson, "The Senate: If Everyone Leads, Who Follows?" in *Congress Reconsidered*, 4th ed., ed. Lawrence C. Dodd and Bruce I. Oppenheimer (Washington, D.C.: CQ Press, 1989), 275.

8. Richard Bolling, *House Out of Order* (New York: Dutton, 1965), 68.

9. Peabody, "House Party Leadership," 143.

10. Janet Hook, "The Influential Committees: Money and Issues," *Congressional Quarterly Weekly Report*, January 3, 1987, 19.

11. Rowland Evans and Robert Novak, *Lyndon B. Johnson: The Exercise of Power* (New York: New American Library, 1966), 128–130, 137.

12. R. Douglas Arnold, "The Local Roots of Domestic Policy," in *The New Congress*, ed. Thomas E. Mann and Norman J. Ornstein (Washington, D.C.: American Enterprise Institute, 1981), 257.

13. Phil Duncan, ed., *1998 Politics in America* (Washington, D.C., Congressional Quarterly, 1997), 530.

14. Evans and Novak, *Lyndon B. Johnson*, 103–104.

15. Donald R. Matthews, *U.S. Senators and Their World* (New York: Vintage, 1960).

16. *Congressional Quarterly Almanac, 1982* (Washington, D.C.: Congressional Quarterly), 4.

17. Alan Ehrenhalt, "In the Senate of the '80s, Team Spirit Has Given Way to the Rule of Individuals," *Congressional Quarterly Weekly Report*, September 4, 1982, 2179.

18. Bernard Asbell, *The Senate Nobody Knows* (Garden City, N.Y.: Doubleday, 1978), 210.

19. Jeffrey H. Birnbaum, "Progress of the Tax Bill Enhances Reputation of Sen. Bill Bradley," *Wall Street Journal*, June 4, 1986, 24.

20. Randall B. Ripley, *Party Leaders in the House of Representatives* (Washington, D.C.: Brookings Institution, 1967), 132–135.

21. Roger H. Davidson and Walter J. Oleszek, *Congress and Its Members*, 7th ed. (Washington, D.C.: CQ Press, 2000), 279.

22. Neil MacNeil, *Forge of Democracy: The House of Representatives* (New York: David MacKay, 1963), 273.

23. Nelson W. Polsby, *Congress and Presidency* (Englewood Cliffs, N.J.: Prentice-Hall, 1964), 39.

24. Jonathan Salant, "LSOs Are No Longer Separate, But the Work's Almost Equal," *Congressional Quarterly Weekly Report*, May 27, 1995, 1483.

25. David W. Brady and Charles S. Bullock III, "Coalition Politics in the House of Representatives," in *Congress Reconsidered*, 188, 201.

26. MacNeil, *Forge of Democracy*, 283–284.

27. For annual Congressional Quarterly studies of Conservative Coalition voting, see *Congressional Quarterly Almanac*, 1957–1998.

28. David Hosansky, "Lawmakers Brace for Battle over Highway Funding," *Congressional Quarterly Weekly Report*, February 1, 1997, 294.

29. Alan Fiellin, "The Functions of Informal Groups in Legislative Institutions," *Journal of Politics* (February 1962): 72–91.

30. Salant, "LSOs No Longer Separate," 1483.

SELECTED BIBLIOGRAPHY

Arnold, R. Douglas. "The Local Roots of Domestic Policy." In *The New Congress,* edited by Thomas E. Mann and Norman J. Ornstein, 250–287. Washington, D.C.: American Enterprise Institute, 1981.

Barnett, Marguerite Ross. "The Congressional Black Caucus." In *Congress Against the President,* edited by Harvey C. Mansfield Sr., 34–50. New York: Praeger, 1975.

Bibby, John F., and Roger H. Davidson. *On Capitol Hill.* Hinsdale, Ill.: Dryden, 1972.

Bolling, Richard. *House Out of Order.* New York: Dutton, 1965.

———. *Power in the House: A History of the Leadership of the House of Representatives.* New York: Dutton, 1968.

Cigler, Allan J., and Burdett A. Loomis. *Interest Group Politics.* 5th ed. Washington, D.C.: CQ Press, 1998.

Clapp, Charles L. *The Congressman: His Work as He Sees It.* Washington, D.C.: Brookings Institution, 1963.

Clark, Champ. *My Quarter Century of American Politics.* 2 vols. New York: Harper & Bros., 1920.

Clark, Joseph S. *Congress: The Sapless Branch.* New York: Harper & Row, 1964.

Clausen, Aage R. *How Congressmen Decide: A Policy Focus.* New York: St. Martin's, 1973.

Davidson, Roger H., and Walter J. Oleszek. *Congress and Its Members.* 7th ed. Washington, D.C.: CQ Press, 2000.

Evans, Rowland, and Robert Novak. *Lyndon B. Johnson: The Exercise of Power.* New York: New American Library, 1966.

Fenno, Richard F. Jr. "The Internal Distribution of Influence: The House." In *The Congress and America's Future,* 2nd ed., edited by David B. Truman, 63–90. Englewood Cliffs, N.J.: Prentice-Hall, 1973.

Ferber, Mark F. "The Formation of the Democratic Study Group." In *Congressional Behavior,* edited by Nelson W. Polsby, 249–269. New York: Random House, 1971.

Fiellin, Alan. "The Functions of Informal Groups in Legislative Institutions." *Journal of Politics* (February 1962): 72–91.

Galloway, George B. *History of the House of Representatives.* 2nd ed. New York: Crowell, 1976.

Hammond, Susan Webb. "Congressional Caucuses in the Policy Process." In *Congress Reconsidered,* 4th ed., edited by Lawrence C. Dodd and Bruce I. Oppenheimer, 351–371. Washington, D.C.: CQ Press, 1989.

Hinckley, Barbara. *Stability and Change in Congress.* 4th ed. New York: Harper & Row, 1988.

Jones, Charles O. *Party and Policy-Making: The House Republican Policy Committee.* New Brunswick, N.J.: Rutgers University Press, 1964.

Kingdon, John W. *Congressmen's Voting Decisions.* 3rd ed. Ann Arbor: University of Michigan Press, 1989.

MacNeil, Neil. *Forge of Democracy: The House of Representatives.* New York: David McKay, 1963.

Matthews, Donald R. *U.S. Senators and Their World.* New York: Vintage Books, 1960. Reprint, New York: Norton, 1973.

Mayhew, David R. *Party Loyalty among Congressmen.* Cambridge, Mass.: Harvard University Press, 1966.

Miller, James. *Running in Place: Inside the Senate.* New York: Simon and Schuster, 1986.

Oleszek, Walter J. *Congressional Procedures and the Policy Process.* 3rd ed. Washington, D.C.: CQ Press, 1988.

Schneider, Jerrold E. *Ideological Coalitions in Congress.* Westport, Conn.: Greenwood Press, 1979.

Shelley, Mack C. *The Permanent Majority: The Conservative Coalition in the United States Congress.* Tuscaloosa: University of Alabama Press, 1983.

Sinclair, Barbara. *Majority Leadership in the U.S. House.* Baltimore: Johns Hopkins University Press, 1983.

———. *The Transformation of the U.S. Senate.* Baltimore: Johns Hopkins University Press, 1989.

Smith, Steven S. *Call to Order: Floor Politics in the House and Senate.* Washington, D.C.: Brookings Institution, 1989.

Sullivan, Terry O. *Procedural Structure: Success and Influence in Congress.* New York: Praeger, 1984.

U.S. Congress. House. *History of the House of Representatives, 1789–1994.* Washington, D.C.: Government Printing Office, 1994.

CHAPTER 21

The President

DESPITE THE SEPARATION of powers set out in the Constitution, the chief executive today is also the "chief legislator." Except in times of war, presidents, wrote Bertram M. Gross, "are now judged more by the quality of the legislation they propose or succeed in getting enacted than by their records as executives."[1]

Because their political fortunes are at stake, presidents, some more skillfully than others, employ all the powers at their disposal to persuade a majority in Congress, directly or indirectly, to support their legislative program. Presidents lobby Congress directly and through their aides. They seek to influence Congress indirectly by appealing to public opinion and special interest groups for support. They use government jobs, federal contracts, and other forms of patronage as bargaining tools with members of Congress. They provide legislators with constituent services, campaign aid, and social courtesies to build goodwill and loyalty. They threaten to veto bills, and when all else fails, they do veto them.

A president unskilled at the art of persuasion and applying pressure to legislators is likely to experience difficulties and frustrations in dealing with Congress. But the success of any president's persuasive powers depends on many factors, some of which are beyond the president's control. These include the strength of Congress itself, whether the same party controls the White House and Congress, the popularity of the president and the president's program, and whether the issue is foreign or domestic.

The Constitution provides that the president should "from time to time give to the Congress Information of the State of the Union, and recommend to their Consideration such measures as he shall judge necessary and expedient." The Constitution also gives the president appointment powers, the power to make treaties with the advice and consent of the Senate, the authority to convene Congress "on extraordinary Occasions," and the right to veto legislation.

To these bare bones, Congress has attached other obligations. The most important of these is the requirement that the president send Congress an annual budget message, setting forth the administration's plans for taxes and spending.

In the twentieth century Woodrow Wilson was the first president to take an active role in proposing and drafting legislation. Wilson was also a master of virtually all the arts of pressure—direct lobbying, public opinion, and patronage—and he won passage of several landmark bills, including the laws creating the Federal Reserve and the Federal Trade Commission. But when Wilson failed to persuade the public of the need to join the League of Nations after World War I, he was also unable to persuade the Senate to approve the treaty creating the League.

In putting forth a broad economic program to cope with the Great Depression, Franklin D. Roosevelt, during the 1930s, dominated the legislative agenda more than any previous president. To win passage Roosevelt used every means at his disposal, vetoing more bills than any other president, using patronage to the fullest extent, lobbying Congress, and molding public opinion with his "fireside chats." As a result Roosevelt created the expectation in Congress and among the public that the president would in fact be the chief legislative leader.

Indeed, in 1953, his first year in the White House, Dwight D. Eisenhower was criticized for neglecting to offer a legislative program. In 1954 he moved to correct that failure, and every president since has proposed an annual legislative program to Congress, usually through the annual State of the Union message.

No president has ever come to office more schooled in the ways of Congress than Lyndon B. Johnson. He had worked at the Capitol for thirty-two years—as a secretary, member of the House, senator, Senate minority leader, majority leader, and vice president. In 1965, with President Johnson using all his vast powers of persuasion, Congress in a single year passed the most sweeping domestic program since Franklin Roosevelt, including aid to schools, voting rights, health care for the aged, rent supplements for the poor, and freer immigration.

Yet Johnson knew that success was fleeting. "I have watched the Congress from either the inside or the outside, man and boy, for more than forty years," he remarked early in 1965, "and I've never seen a Congress that didn't eventually take the measure of the president it was dealing with."[2]

Johnson's prosecution of the unpopular war in Vietnam, a worsening economy, and racial violence that erupted every summer from 1964 to 1968 cost Johnson much of his public and congressional support, and the president did not run for reelection in 1968.

Richard Nixon's election that year began an unprecedentedly long period of divided government. Republicans held the White House for twenty of the thirty-two years between 1969 and 2000, while Democrats controlled the House until 1995 and the Senate for all but the first six years of the Reagan administration and since 1995. Between 1789 and 1954, control of the White House and Congress had been divided between political parties for only eight years.

PRESIDENTIAL APPEARANCES BEFORE CONGRESS

Only sixteen of the forty-two presidents have appeared personally before Congress to promote their legislative programs. George Washington set a brief precedent in 1789 when he addressed the members on the occasion of his first annual message. John Adams stood before Congress six times, but successor Thomas Jefferson dropped the practice of personal appearances.

From 1797 until 1913—when Woodrow Wilson delivered his first annual message—twenty-five presidents never addressed Congress.

Wilson's return to the custom of Washington and Adams was controversial. Some members mocked it as the president's "speech from the throne." But Wilson went on to appear twenty-six times, establishing a record. Since Wilson all presidents have addressed Congress except Herbert Hoover. Since Truman, annual messages have been called State of the Union messages.

Following is a list of the appearances by presidents before Congress through October 1999 (appearances are before joint sessions unless otherwise indicated):

President	Number of Appearances	Occasions
Washington	10	8 annual messages (1789–1796); 2 inaugural addresses (1789, 1793—second inaugural before Senate only)
John Adams	6	4 annual messages (1797–1800); inaugural address, relations with France (1797)
Wilson	26	6 annual messages (1913–1918); tariff reform, bank reform, relations with Mexico (1913); antitrust laws, Panama Canal tolls, relations with Mexico, new tax revenue (1914); impending rail strike (1916); "Peace without Victory" (Senate only), breaking relations with Germany, arming of merchant ships, request for war declaration against Germany (1917); federal takeover of railroads, "14 points" for peace, peace outlook, need for new revenue, request for ratification of women's suffrage amendment (Senate only), armistice (1918); request for approval of Versailles treaty (Senate only), high cost of living (1919)
Harding	7	2 annual messages (1921–1922); federal problems (1921); 2 on the Merchant Marine, coal and railroads (1922); debt (1923)
Coolidge	2	1 annual message (1923); George Washington's birthday (1927)
Roosevelt	16	10 annual messages (1934–1943); 100th anniversary of Lafayette's death (1934); 150th anniversary of First Congress, neutrality address (1939); national defense (1940); declaration of war (1941); Yalta conference report (1945)
Truman	17	6 State of the Union messages (1947–1952); prosecution of the war, submission of UN charter (Senate only), Congressional Medal of Honor ceremony, universal military training (1945); railroad strike (1946); Greek-Turkish aid policy, aid to Europe (1947); national security and conditions in Europe, 50th anniversary of the liberation of Cuba, domestic issues and civil rights (1948); steel industry dispute (1952)
Eisenhower	7	6 State of the Union messages (1953–1954; 1957–1960); Middle East (1957)
Kennedy	3	3 State of the Union messages (1961–1963)
Johnson	8	6 State of the Union messages (1964–1969); assumption of office (1963); Voting Rights Act (1965)
Nixon	7	4 State of the Union messages (1970–1972, 1974); Vietnam policy (1969—separate addresses to House and Senate); economic policy (1971); Soviet Union trip (1972)
Ford[a]	6	3 State of the Union messages (1975–1977); assumption of office, inflation (1974); state of the world (1975)
Carter	6	3 State of the Union messages (1978–1980); energy program (1977); Middle East talks at Camp David (1978); SALT II arms control treaty (1979)
Reagan	11	7 State of the Union messages (1982–1988); 2 budget addresses (1981); Central America (1983); U.S.-Soviet summit (1985)
Bush	5	3 State of the Union messages (1990–1992); budget address (1989); Persian Gulf crisis (1991)
Clinton[b]	8	6 State of the Union messages (1994–1999); budget address, health policy reform (1993)

a. On October 17, 1974, President Gerald R. Ford testified before the Subcommittee on Criminal Justice of the House Judiciary Committee on his pardon of former president Richard Nixon for crimes possibly committed during the Watergate affair.

b. Through October 1999. Note also that Presidents Reagan, Bush, and Clinton each gave a speech to Congress within weeks of their inauguration. This speech, while not technically a State of the Union address, served the outline the new president's broad legislative agenda.

SOURCES: Congressional Research Service, Library of Congress, *Congressional Record;* Public Papers of the Presidents; *Congressional Quarterly Weekly Report* (various issues).

Nixon did not fare well with the Democratic Congress. Within fifteen months of his inauguration, Congress rejected two of his nominees for the Supreme Court. In 1971 Nixon set "Six Great Goals" for his administration, but by the end of his first term Congress had approved only one.

In Nixon's second term Congress cut off funding for the Vietnam War and enacted the War Powers Resolution over Nixon's veto, imposing the first congressional limits on a president's powers to act in international emergencies. Angered by Nixon's refusal to spend money as it had directed, Congress also put limits on the president's power to impound appropriations. Facing almost certain impeachment and removal from office for his role in Watergate, Nixon resigned the presidency in 1974.

Heightened partisanship also plagued Presidents Ronald Reagan, George Bush, and Bill Clinton. Bush was stunned early in his presidency when the Senate refused to confirm his nomination of former Sen. John Tower, R-Texas, as secretary of defense. In late 1990 Bush was embarrassed when even House Republicans refused to support a budget deal his administration had negotiated with congressional leaders from both parties. But with Democratic support, Congress passed the deficit reduction plan. Similarly, despite growing partisan acrimony, the Clinton administration worked with the Republican-controlled Congress in 1996 and 1997 to enact major legislation, including welfare reform and a balanced budget. Fierce partisanship roared back, however, during Clinton's impeachment ordeal in 1998–1999.

Having a Congress of the president's own party is no guarantee of success, however. Jimmy Carter had a Democratic House and Senate, but he was inept at pressuring Congress, either directly or through public opinion. Although he eventually won a few significant legislative victories, Congress rejected or drastically changed many of Carter's major proposals.

Nor does opposition control of Congress necessarily spell a president's defeat. In 1981 Reagan put together a coalition of Republicans and southern Democrats to force his tax and spending plans through a House controlled by Democrats. Bush achieved a crucial victory early in 1991 when Congress, over the objections of its Democratic leaders, formally authorized the president to use force to eject Iraq from Kuwait.

As political scientist David Mayhew wrote in *Divided We Govern*, "There is something more than just having your party in power in all three places. You've got to know [how] to build political coalitions that work, that pull together, that sustain policies that you as President effectively articulate."[3]

Presidential Influence on Congressional Elections

For the most part, members of the president's party in Congress are more inclined to support the administration's legislative initiatives than are the partisan opposition. Therefore, among the most potentially effective exercises of presidential party leadership are those that influence the election of members of the president's party to Congress. Presidential coattails, midterm campaigning, fund-raising, and strong approval ratings for the chief executive all influence the partisan composition of Congress from election to election.

COATTAILS

"Presidential coattails" is the voting phenomenon by which voters attracted to a presidential candidate tend to cast their ballots in congressional elections for the nominees of the president's party. In turn, the coattails effect presumably translates into increased presidential support in Congress. Because shared party affiliation produces a predisposition to support the president, an increase in the ranks of the congressional partisans should increase presidential support. In addition, those members who have ridden into office on the president's coattails should be particularly grateful and thus more inclined to be supportive.

This theory of presidential coattails as an influence on Congress is, however, both highly questionable and difficult to test. In the first place, not all presidents even have coattails when they are elected. In the post–World War II presidential elections, several presidents were associated with minimal changes in the size of the congressional parties. Moreover, there is also the possibility of reverse coattails. On four occasions—1956, 1960, 1988, and 1992—the elected president's party actually lost seats in the House, while in 1972, 1984, 1988, and 1996, the party lost seats in the Senate.

It is not uncommon for presidential nominees to run behind the congressional party nominees in their states and districts. For example, in 1960, Democratic presidential nominee John F. Kennedy, a Massachusetts Catholic who had taken a strong campaign stand on civil rights, ran behind the party's congressional and senatorial nominees throughout the South. Conversely, the party's 1976 nominee, Jimmy Carter of Georgia, trailed the party ticket in many northern states and districts. Harry S. Truman and Bill Clinton (twice) were elected president without popular vote majorities while their congressional party counterparts clearly out polled them in states and districts.

The Democrat's domination of Congress in the post–World war II era also complicates the coattails effect theory. The Democrats took control of both houses of Congress in the 1948 election, when Truman won by a narrow margin. They relinquished control in 1952 when Dwight D. Eisenhower won the presidency, but in 1954 the party reestablished majority control in the House and maintained it until 1994, losing the midterm elections to a resurgently conservative Republican Party. After twenty-six years, the GOP also gained control of the Senate in 1980, the year Ronald Reagan won the presidency, but six years later, the Democrats returned to power in the upper house and maintained control of both houses until the watershed 1994 midterm elections.

Only the elections of Truman and Eisenhower coincided with shifting party control of both chambers; Reagan's coincided with shifting party control of only one. While the gains and

President Dwight D. Eisenhower poses with congressional leaders in the 1950s.

losses of the president's party in the other post–World War II presidential elections affected the size of existing party majorities, they had no bearing on the partisan nature of the majorities themselves. George Edwards, a political scientist who has studied the coattails effect concluded that it has had a minimal influence on congressional elections for some time; he attributes this result primarily to decreasing competitiveness in congressional districts. In other words, safe seats, from districts carefully drawn by state legislators eager to protect their parties and incumbents, have become a pervasive presence in Congress and thus reduce presidential opportunities to influence electoral outcomes. This decline of the coattails effect weakens the president's ability to exercise strong party leadership in Congress.

MIDTERM CAMPAIGNING

The Constitution mandates that midway through the president's term, elections be held for the entire House and one-third of the Senate. The president, by campaigning for his party's candidates in these elections, may influence the partisan composition of Congress. Midterm campaigning is one of the most overt examples of the chief executive's party leadership, when the president puts aside a nominal above-partisanship stance to

assume that role. Among the forms this activity can take are public speeches, statements, and gestures of support for the party ticket (including the announcement of projects and programs that directly benefit a candidate's state or district); personal appearances in key districts and states on behalf of selected party congressional nominees by the president and others in the executive branch; access to the national party's organizational and financial resources; and, of course, fund-raising for individual candidates as well as the national and state party organizations.

Presidential fund-raising has taken on heightened significance in recent years, particularly as campaigns for national office have become increasingly expensive and very large sums of money are needed to mount a credible campaign even for a House seat. One estimate puts the amount that President George Bush raised in 1990 at $80 million for the Republican congressional elections. Immediately after his inauguration President Clinton took the lead in raising an estimated $41 million for the national party to use in the 1994 midterm elections.

Midterm campaigning emerged under Woodrow Wilson in 1918 as a new dimension of presidential party leadership when the president directly urged the voters to vote Democratic and to thus demonstrate support for his foreign policy initiatives in the wake of World War I. The supposedly nonpolitical Eisenhower, according to his biographer Stephen Ambrose, initially viewed participation in midterm campaigns as improper and unlikely to succeed; but, swayed by dire predictions of an electoral debacle for the Republicans in the 1954 elections, Eisenhower took to the campaign trail, covering more than 10,000 miles and giving forty speeches. Despite his efforts, the Democrats regained control of both houses.

In 1962 President Kennedy campaigned even more strenuously for his party's nominees and since then, presidential midterm campaigning has become an important component of the president's party leadership. However, these exercises are no guarantee of success at the polls. In fact, one abiding axiom of American electoral politics is that the president's party loses seats in the House in midterm elections (although there have been exceptions). The Senate record is less clear, but significant gains in either chamber are not the norm.

The outcome of 1994 elections demonstrated the vulnerability of the president's party to midterm losses. President Clinton, despite his then low popularity ratings, was extraordinarily energetic in campaigning for Democratic nominees. He presented the campaign as a referendum, pitting his leadership and policies against those of his Republican predecessors. The elections, instead of providing Clinton with any mandate, transferred majority control of both houses of Congress to a resurgent Republican Party.

The 1998 midterm elections witnessed many Democratic congressional candidates avoiding contact with Clinton, who despite achieving record high job approval ratings, was reeling from the sex and perjury charges that would later result in his impeachment. There were also charges by some congressional candidates that the president was not distributing campaign funds from the national party to specific Democratic candidates. Nevertheless, the Democrats managed to shrink the size of the Republican majority in the House by five seats, an outcome that subsequently forced the party's firebrand leader and House Speaker, Newt Gingrich of Georgia, to resign the speakership and his seat. Not since 1934 had the president's party gained seats during midterm elections.

Whatever the reasons behind the almost consistent pattern of midterm losses for the president's party, midterm campaigning appears to be more of an effort to minimize losses than to maximize gains. One of the most visible exercises of presidential party leadership thus appears, on the surface at least, to be one of the least productive.

When one party controls the presidency and another controls at least one chamber of Congress, midterm campaigning carries potentially severe disadvantages for presidential legislative leadership. An active partisan campaign by the president can serve to inflame the opposition, making subsequent bipartisan appeals by the chief executive hollow or ineffective. In addition, some presidents have found members of the opposition party to be more consistently supportive of their programs than members of their own party; presidents are thus reluctant to campaign strenuously, if at all, against these friendly enemies.

Presidents sometimes delegate parts of their midterm campaign efforts to their vice presidents and other high-ranking members of the executive branch. President Eisenhower asked Richard Nixon to campaign in the 1954 and 1958 elections and Nixon, as president, assigned his vice president, Spiro Agnew, in 1970 to the same task. In 1998 Vice President Al Gore played an active role in a number of congressional campaigns, and First Lady Hillary Rodham Clinton campaigned vigorously and effectively in several contests important to the Democrat's congressional fortunes, notably (and successfully) the New York Senate race.

Presidential Lobby: More Open, Elaborate

Since the birth of the Republic, presidents have lobbied Congress, in person or indirectly through aides, cabinet officers, and others. Careful of the form if not the substance of separate powers, early presidents kept their congressional lobbying discreet. In recent years, presidential lobbying has become more open and more elaborate.

George Washington visited the Senate to try to win its advice and consent to an American Indian treaty. Washington expected to force quick action, but Congress declined to cooperate. After that, the first president stayed away from the Capitol, except to deliver annual messages. Instead, he sent Secretary of State Thomas Jefferson and Treasury Secretary Alexander Hamilton for private talks on foreign and fiscal matters. Hamilton became so influential that the House established its committee on Ways and Means to defend against him.

When Jefferson became president, he used a series of Virginia representatives, starting with William B. Giles, as his eyes, ears, and hands in Congress.

In this century Woodrow Wilson made his lobbying as discreet as possible. His chief congressional lobbyist was Postmaster General Albert Burleson, a Texas Democrat who had quit the House to take the cabinet job. With postmasterships and post offices at his disposal, Burleson had considerable influence over members of Congress.

At Burleson's suggestion, Wilson enlisted another Texas Democrat, John Nance Garner, to act as his confidential lobbyist inside the House. Garner was a member of the Ways and Means Committee and later was to become Speaker and vice president. The Wilson-Garner relationship was hidden from the House Democratic hierarchy. Supposedly on private business, Garner left Capitol Hill twice a week by streetcar, got off near the White House, entered through a side door, and was ushered into Wilson's private study where he reported to the president.[4]

But Wilson knew how to apply pressure in person, too. In pursuit of tariff revision, he dropped by congressional committee meetings. In the Senate, every Democrat voted for the tariff bill. Also, he revived the practice, abandoned by Jefferson, of giving the State of the Union address in person.

Franklin Roosevelt used White House aides James Rowe, Thomas G. Corcoran, and Benjamin Cohen to exert pressure on Congress. As their official duties included drafting legislation, they were natural choices to lobby to get bills enacted. Postmaster General James A. Farley was also the Democratic national chairman. Farley used the postal and the political powers to influence votes in Congress. Harry S. Truman used White House assistants Clark Clifford and Charles Murphy in part-time legislative liaison roles.

In not publicly identifying their congressional lobbyists, Neil MacNeil wrote, "Wilson, Roosevelt, and Truman . . . kept up a pretense of staying within the traditional strictures of the assumed independence of the President and the Congress. They felt the need for such intimate contact with the members of Congress, but they hesitated to offend the sensibilities of the House and Senate as institutions."[5]

Beginning with Dwight D. Eisenhower, presidents have appointed full-time legislative liaison officers to their White House staff. In addition, all federal departments now have their own congressional liaison forces. The practice began in 1945, when the War Department created the office of assistant secretary for congressional liaison, centralizing congressional relations that had been handled separately by the military services.

Eisenhower, as one observer put it, "had little aptitude for or interest in congressional relations, and did not involve himself in detailed consideration of them. . . . The skill and experience of his [congressional liaison] staff was therefore all the more important to his presidency. . . ."[6] Eisenhower named his deputy chief of staff, Wilton B. "Jerry" Persons, a retired major general who had been a congressional lobbyist for the army during World War II, to head the first White House Office of Congressional Relations. Persons was succeeded by Bryce Harlow, who had served Eisenhower in a variety of capacities. Legislators, wrote Eric L. Davis, "soon came to see that a commitment on the part of either of these men was the equivalent of a commitment from the president himself."[7]

KENNEDY-O'BRIEN LIAISON TEAM

President John F. Kennedy sought to beef up the liaison function, appointing his longtime associate Lawrence F. O'Brien as chief lobbyist and giving O'Brien full authority to speak for him on legislative matters. O'Brien was given coequal rank with other top White House aides and was assigned aides for both the House and Senate. MacNeil reported that "to even the most influential Senators who telephoned Kennedy in the first weeks of his Presidency, the President had a stock reply: 'Have you discussed this with Larry O'Brien?'"[8]

At the outset of the Kennedy administration, O'Brien organized a series of cocktail parties, all held in House committee rooms, where he sought to meet House members on a purely social basis. Later, O'Brien invited House members in groups of fifty for coffee at the White House with Kennedy. For committee

Lawrence F. O'Brien was the chief presidential lobbyist during the administration of John F. Kennedy. O'Brien had full authority to speak for the president on legislative matters.

chairmen, he set up private discussions with the president. At a dinner with the Democratic Study Group, a bloc of about one hundred House liberals, O'Brien promised that the president would support them for reelection if they backed his legislative program. "The White House certainly remembers who its friends are," he said, "and can be counted on to apply significant assistance in the campaign."[9]

Clearing their activities with O'Brien, cabinet officials sought to cultivate congressional leaders. Defense Secretary Robert S. McNamara courted House Armed Services Committee Chairman Carl Vinson, D-Ga., Vinson's Senate counterpart Richard B. Russell (also a Georgia Democrat), and other key members of the House and Senate military committees. Treasury Secretary Douglas Dillon kept in close touch with House Ways and Means Committee Chairman Wilbur D. Mills, D-Ark. Agriculture Secretary Orville L. Freeman consulted frequently with congressional leaders on the president's farm program. Other cabinet officers and their liaison staffs made similar contacts.

Kennedy and O'Brien made extensive use of the congressional liaison offices of the cabinet departments and executive agencies, first formalized under Eisenhower. When an administration bill was introduced in Congress, the department involved was given prime responsibility for getting the measure through subcommittee and committee. When the bill neared House or

Senate floor action, O'Brien and his corps of White House lobbyists joined forces with the agency liaison teams. There were about thirty-five agency lobbyists working during the Kennedy-Johnson era although not all of them devoted full time to legislation. The Kennedy tactics were often successful in removing major legislative obstacles, but the obstacles appeared so frequently that the president's program foundered in Congress.

LIAISON UNDER JOHNSON

The liaison system Kennedy nurtured paid dividends during the administration of Lyndon B. Johnson. Loyal Democrats had picked up a working majority of seats in the 1964 election, and with O'Brien still supervising the liaison job, almost all of the old Kennedy measures sailed through Congress. Even when Johnson appointed O'Brien postmaster general, he continued as chief White House lobbyist, after Johnson himself.

More than any other modern president, Johnson was his own best lobbyist. The former Senate majority leader often looked at proposed legislation from the perspective of Congress and gave his liaison staff a role in policy making. Beyond that, as political scientist Charles O. Jones wrote, "Johnson wanted to know everything that affected or might potentially affect his legislative program. Not only was the knowledge itself important to him in judging what to do, how, and when, but he had a reputation to uphold."[10] Johnson himself said that "there is but one way for a president to deal with Congress, and this is continuously, incessantly, and without interruption."[11]

NIXON AND FORD

Johnson's successor, Richard Nixon, had no taste for such intimate dealings with Congress, and the fact that he was a Republican president facing a Democratic Congress did nothing to smooth relations. Bryce Harlow served as Nixon's chief lobbyist for two years, returning to the White House after eight years of lobbying for the Procter & Gamble Co. In 1970 Harlow's team helped win a notable victory on funds to deploy a controversial antiballistic missile system, but the Nixon administration lost critical battles over two Supreme Court nominations and over restrictions on its southeast Asia policy.

When Harlow left after two years, William E. Timmons, who had served in various Senate and House offices, shared responsibility for the liaison staff with former House member Clark MacGregor, R-Minn., and then became chief lobbyist in July 1972. Harlow and the president had been close, but with Harlow's departure there was a noticeable difference in Nixon's dealings with his lobbying staff. Timmons had to have an appointment to see the president and was often kept waiting. "Nixon didn't like politicians, and that included congressmen," Rep. Barber B. Conable Jr., R-N.Y., said in 1975. "The result was that these [congressional liaison] people became second-class citizens as far as the rest of the White House staff was concerned."

In June 1973 Nixon brought on Harlow and former representative Melvin R. Laird, R-Wis., as presidential counselors and plenary ambassadors to Congress, mostly to help deflect the gathering Watergate crisis. Timmons and his staff continued the day-to-day legislative lobbying operations, but the liaison staff had lost much of its effectiveness.

Timmons remained chief legislative liaison for the first few months of Gerald R. Ford's presidency. When Timmons resigned at the end of 1974, Ford promoted Max L. Friedersdorf to the position. A former newspaper reporter, Friedersdorf had been an administrative assistant to a House member and a congressional relations officer with the White House Office of Economic Opportunity.

Ford, who had been House minority leader before being elected vice president by Congress, enjoyed good personal relations with senators and representatives. Like Johnson before him, Ford took an active interest in the White House lobbying operation, but, unlike the Johnson operation, much of Ford's effort was aimed not at promoting new programs and policies but at lining up the votes necessary to block the Democratic Congress from overriding the president's veto. Ford vetoed sixty-six bills during his brief term in office; only twelve of them were overridden.

PROBLEMS FOR CARTER

A newcomer to Washington, President Jimmy Carter got off to a bad start with Congress by appointing a fellow Georgian and an equally inexperienced hand, Frank B. Moore, as his chief lobbyist. Moore quickly offended congressional sensibilities by failing to return phone calls, missing meetings, and neglecting to consult adequately about presidential appointments and programs. He broke with precedent by organizing his twenty-member staff around issues rather than geographical groups of legislators. That arrangement hampered vote trading as well as the development of good working relationships between the liaison staff and legislators. As a former Carter aide explained, a White House liaison officer "is no longer in a position to discuss a sewage treatment plant in the context of a foreign aid vote, because the liaison aide who handles foreign aid does not also handle environmental issues."[12]

Six months after taking office, Carter reorganized his liaison team by geography and added several Washington veterans, including William H. Cable, a respected House staffer who was put in charge of lobbying the House. Moore also adopted some of Lawrence O'Brien's techniques for pushing major bills through Congress, including close coordination of White House and department lobbyists and personal intervention by the president before key votes. The White House also began using computers to analyze each legislator's past votes and target support for the future. These "task force" techniques were used to help persuade Congress to stop development of the B-1 bomber, ratify the Panama Canal treaties, and revise the civil service system.

After its shaky start, the Carter liaison team also learned to work through the Democratic leadership in the House and Senate. Carter himself met with the leaders every Tuesday. But according to most observers, Carter's team never recovered totally from the damage its early ineptness caused on Capitol Hill or from the president's own disdain for legislative politics.

REAGAN AND BUSH

Attention to detail was one of the factors that set President Ronald Reagan's legislative lobbying team apart from the Carter team. Headed initially by Friedersdorf, the liaison team helped Reagan to build a reputation for a winning way with Congress during his first year, thanks mainly to a few major showdowns on the budget, tax cuts, and the sale of Airborne Warning and Control System (AWACS) radar planes to Saudi Arabia.

During 1981 House liaison Kenneth M. Duberstein became known as an effective, discreet, and partisan go-between. When

Friedersdorf stepped down at the end of the year, Reagan turned the chief lobbyist's job over to Duberstein. Duberstein left in late 1983 and was succeeded by M. B. Oglesby Jr., a former White House aide. Oglesby was followed in 1986 by William L. Ball III, an assistant secretary of state for legislative and intergovernmental affairs and a former administrative assistant to Sen. John Tower.

According to his aides, Reagan genuinely enjoyed the lobbying side of his job. In December 1985, following his landslide re-election victory, Reagan again demonstrated his almost mystical powers of political salesmanship. He was able to persuade fifty-four House Republicans to switch their votes in favor of a rule that paved the way for passage of a major tax reform bill. In addition to a blitz of phone calls and White House visits with indi-

---

REACHING CONGRESS THROUGH OUTSIDE GROUPS

Modern presidents have taken special steps to build goodwill with special interest groups, to win both their electoral support and their support of the president's program in Congress. Interest groups, wrote Bradley H. Patterson Jr., "can multiply [the president's] influence—to their memberships, and through their memberships to the Congress. With skillful staff work, the president can . . . enlist those organization leaders to help in squeezing out just the few votes needed in House or Senate to move his highest priority objectives." [1]

The first official White House public liaison chief was William Baroody Jr., who served in the administration of Gerald R. Ford. But appealing to nongovernment sources of support was not new to the White House. Thomas G. Corcoran, for example, marshaled his extraordinarily wide contacts in and out of government on behalf of Franklin D. Roosevelt's programs.

Clark Clifford, adviser to Harry S. Truman, suggested what has become a standard strategy of public liaison operations—capitalizing on the glamour of the White House. In a lengthy memo, quoted by Patrick Anderson in *The President's Men,* Clifford proposed that Truman invite "labor leaders . . . to the White House to flatter them." But he warned that such consultations should be on "general issues. To invite advice on specifics, and then not follow it, is to court trouble." [2]

Late in Richard Nixon's second term, Baroody proposed creation of a separate office for interest group contacts. It was President Ford who carried out the suggestion, appointing Baroody to the new position. Baroody launched a series of meetings, large and small and often publicized, between the president and top administration officials and various outside organizations and leaders. The sessions were held both at the White House and in "town hall" meetings around the country. Baroody's goal was to end the president's isolation and to counter Watergate-generated distrust of the president and government.

President Jimmy Carter's first public liaison chief, the outspoken Midge Costanza, occasionally gave the appearance of opposing Carter rather than building support for him, and by 1978 she had been replaced by Anne Wexler, a respected political operative.

Wexler sought to demonstrate benefits of explaining proposed legislation to as many groups as possible "including those that were not necessarily Carter loyalists." She believed that interest groups had to be involved "in the development of policy at the earliest stages" and that they should be kept involved. The payoff was twofold. First, within the White House, Wexler said, "our input was often critical on what was going to fly" in Congress. Second, she said, "we were able to present Congress with pretty good evidence that certain issues had broad-based support."

During the Reagan administration it was Wayne Valis, a deputy to public liaison chief Elizabeth Dole, who organized the massive telephone campaign that clinched congressional approval of the president's budget and tax package. According to Bradley Patterson, Valis and his office supplied 1,100 companies and organizations with names, numbers, and information. "We had matched Reagan maneuver for maneuver until the phones started ringing off the wall," one House Democratic leader told the *Washington Star.* "The telegrams we could withstand, but not that damn Alexander Graham Bell." [3]

President Bill Clinton understood that outside support, especially from the business community, would be important for passing his 1993 deficit-reduction package. He recruited allies from among liquor manufacturers and research-intensive companies by providing their industries with favorable treatment in his tax proposal. Stuart Eizenstat, former Carter domestic policy advisor, recognized the president's political savvy: the plan "touched some important positive buttons in the corporate community, so that you have some people who have an equity interest in the package." [4] Clinton appreciated that "equity interests" often result in active lobbying campaigns on Capitol Hill.

1. Bradley H. Patterson Jr., *The Ring of Power: The White House Staff and Its Expanding Role in Government* (New York: Basic Books, 1988), 201.

2. Patrick Anderson, *The President's Men* (New York: Doubleday, 1968), 120.

3. Patterson, *The Ring of Power,* 210.

4. *National Journal,* March 6, 1993, 570.

SOURCE: Adapted from Elizabeth Wehr, "Public Liaison Chief Dole Reaches to Outside Groups to Sell Reagan's Programs," *Congressional Quarterly Weekly Report,* June 6, 1981, 975–978. Unless otherwise noted, quotes are taken from that source.

vidual members, Reagan made a rare journey to Capitol Hill where he met for nearly an hour in a closed-door session with House Republicans.

After the first year, however, Reagan and his liaison team faced increasing difficulty winning majority support in Congress. Many of the votes Reagan did win on issues such as defense spending and foreign policy were by paper-thin margins and came only after the president agreed to substantial concessions. A loss of twenty-six Republican seats in the House in the 1982 elections, the Democrats' takeover of the Senate in 1986, Reagan's lack of a focused legislative agenda after the first year, partisan differences over the growing budget deficit, and the revelation of the Iran-contra affair all contributed to divisiveness between the White House and Congress.

George Bush, a former House member from Texas, personally knew most members of Congress and enjoyed contacts with them; even as president he occasionally worked out in the House gym. The thoughtful personal gesture—a birthday greeting or a get-well wish—was the hallmark of both the president and his liaison team, which was headed by Frederick D. McClure, a former aide to Senator Tower and a Senate lobbyist for Reagan.

Bush's cabinet and top staff also lobbied actively in their areas of interest and expertise. Secretary of State James A. Baker III spent hundreds of hours negotiating an agreement on aid to the anticommunist contra rebels in Nicaragua on Capitol Hill, Bush's first major legislative victory. Secretary of Defense Dick Cheney lobbied on defense issues, White House Chief of Staff John Sununu on clean air legislation, and Office of Management and Budget Director Richard G. Darman on the budget and taxes.

In 1990, however, Bush prevailed only 46.8 percent of the time on congressional votes on which he took a position. That was the second lowest presidential support score recorded since Congressional Quarterly began the vote study in 1953. (The lowest was 43.5 percent, recorded by Reagan in 1987.) Like Nixon, Ford, and (for his final two years) Reagan, Bush faced a Democratic and highly partisan Congress. He also paid substantially more attention to foreign affairs than to domestic issues. Some observers, however, also attributed Bush's problems with Congress to the president's failure to set a legislative agenda. "He's like the captain of a ship who can read longitude and latitude well but doesn't know where his port or destination is," said Steve Bell, a former Republican staff director of the Senate Budget Committee.

CLINTON

Bill Clinton arrived with two distinct differences from his predecessor Bush: Clinton had an almost overabundant domestic legislative agenda, but he had almost no familiarity with the inner workings of Congress. As a "New Democrat," he appeared to be a president who would lead the Democratic Party away from its perceived liberal leanings and toward the political center. However, his espousal, like that of Carter, of "no-party" politics deprived him, as it had Carter, of deep-seated party loyalty that could translate into effective legislative support. And similar to Carter, Clinton had been governor in a southern state where the Republican opposition was, at best, token and not a vital factor in legislative liaison.

Clinton's first two years in office were marked by narrow but noteworthy successes that relied on two distinct leadership strategies evolved from his gubernatorial experience in Arkansas. In the first instance, his budget proposal passed without the vote of a single Republican member of Congress because he was personally able to mobilize the support of the Democratic majorities in both chambers. But this support came at a price: the congressional Democrats advanced their own special interests in negotiations with Clinton in return for their support of his fiscal package. In the second strategy, Clinton actively courted Republican votes to win passage of the North American Free Trade Agreement (NAFTA), a measure opposed by many prolabor Democratic legislators, who subsequently felt alienated from their nominal party chief.

By Clinton's second year, these conflicts intensified and he was unable to muster either partisan or bipartisan support for the centerpiece of his ambitious legislative agenda, health care reform. Clinton's political standing steadily eroded from this point and led to the watershed midterm election of 1994 in which the Republicans took control of both houses of Congress for the first time in forty years. In 1995, however, Clinton's political fortunes revived as he pursued the policy of "triangulation" that positioned his administration between the extremes represented in Congress by the Republican majority, with its conservative bent, and the liberal Democratic minority.

Clinton's style (largely mirrored by his staff) in the early dealings with Congress reflected a youthful, inexperienced, zealous approach. The White House was often caught unprepared for many of the political conflicts that bombarded the new administration. It had to scramble frantically to mend fences and repair political damage, sometimes succeeding in snatching a victory from the jaws of defeat, sometimes not, and in the cases of health care reform and gays in the military, suffering serious political setbacks inside and outside Washington.

Little firm organizational direction came from the top and Clinton, again like Carter, attempted to micromanage every important decision and thus spread himself too thin over too many issues. As a result, Clinton had to rework his staff system several times in the first two years, the first overhaul coming only 107 days after his inauguration. Later he would tap former House member and Washington insider Leon Panetta to be his chief of staff, and relations with Congress both regularized and improved.

Clinton placed primary emphasis on domestic policy and in his early dealings with Congress showed an extraordinarily high degree of personal involvement in pushing his legislative agenda. The president frequently telephoned members of Congress and hosted them at White House functions to flatter their egos and to press his case. His first legislative liaison was Howard

Paster, who had worked as a legislative aide in Congress, then as a private lobbyist representing such diverse clients as labor unions and the National Rifle Association. Paster would leave after one year, ostensibly citing burnout but really, according to reporter Bob Woodward, because he was unhappy with the White House's uncoordinated approach to legislators and policy making. He was succeeded by Patrick Griffin, a former top aide to Sen. Robert Byrd, D-W.Va.

While Clinton's liaison office actively cultivated strong ties with members of Congress, the president relied heavily on a multipronged approach, enlisting top aides and advisers, as well as cabinet secretaries, Vice President Al Gore, and First Lady Hillary Rodham Clinton. However, many of these relationships would be severely hampered as the president dealt with impeachment in 1998–1999; the administration's legislative concerns virtually grounded to a halt as the president fought successfully to keep his office.

Moving Congress by Going to the People

When even the most skillful direct pressure fails, presidents often turn to the public for help in moving Congress. Going over congressional heads to the people has always required cultivation of reporters and others responsible for gathering and transmitting the news. Today, radio and television permit a president to go over reporters' heads, too, in marshaling public opinion.

Of the early presidents, Andrew Jackson was one of the most skillful at public relations. Jackson arranged to have official documents leaked to his favorite newspapers. According to James E. Pollard, Jackson "knew what he wanted, he meant to have his way, and he was fortunate in finding journalists devoted to him and capable of carrying out his desires."[13]

Lincoln found himself on the defensive with Congress in regard to his war policies. But he overcame congressional opposition with public support, generated by the stories he passed out to reporters and editors and by letters he wrote that found their way into print. The press also published Lincoln's eloquent speeches. While Lincoln "paid some heed to the sanctity of military secrets, he declined to worship at that shrine," wrote George Fort Milton. "He knew that the people had ears, whether the walls had them or not, and took advantage of every appropriate occasion to tell his innermost thoughts."[14]

Andrew Johnson was the first president to grant a formal interview to the press. He gave twelve exclusive interviews, most of them on his troubles with Congress over Reconstruction.[15] But press coverage failed to generate enough public sympathy to save Johnson from impeachment by the House. Indeed, some of Johnson's more intemperate speeches provoked two of the eleven articles of impeachment. He escaped conviction in the Senate by a single vote.

Theodore Roosevelt made himself easily available to reporters. Credited with having invented the "background" press conference, Roosevelt launched "trial balloons" to test public opinion before deciding on a course of action. Under Roosevelt the White House began issuing regular news releases.

Roosevelt saw the White House as a "bully pulpit," to be used to mobilize public support. "People used to say of me that I . . . divined what the people were going to think," Roosevelt once said. "I did not 'divine'. . . . I simply made up my mind what they ought to think, and then did my best to get them to think it."[16] Eager to show the American flag abroad, Roosevelt sent the U.S. battleship fleet around the world, even though the navy lacked funds to pay for the cruise. The public was so impressed with this display of American naval power that Congress lost no time in appropriating the necessary funds.

Woodrow Wilson began the practice of holding regular and formal press conferences. Until the war in Europe took most of his time, Wilson met the press an average of twice a week. But Wilson was most effective with his appeals directly to the public. Several weeks after his inauguration, he issued a statement attacking the "extraordinary exertions" of special interest groups to change his tariff bill. "The newspapers are filled with paid advertisements," he said, "calculated to mislead the judgment of public men not only, but also the public opinion of the country itself."[17]

While Wilson succeeded in having his way with the tariff, the technique failed him in 1919 when he conducted a whistle-stop tour of the country to drum up support for the League of Nations. He was followed by a "truth squad" of senators opposed to the league. In the end, the Senate rejected the Treaty of Versailles, which contained the Covenant of the League.

Although Calvin Coolidge has gone down in history as "Silent Cal," during his five years in office, he was considered one of the nation's most popular presidents. Assuming office after the scandal-plagued Warren Harding died unexpectedly in 1923, Coolidge quickly exhibited a knack for public relations; he held over 520 press conferences while president. More importantly, he made full use of the new medium of radio, which he used effectively to enhance his image. He told one legislator, "I am very fortunate I came in with the radio. I can't make an engaging, rousing, or oratorical speech to a crowd as you can . . . but I have a good radio voice, and now I can get my messages across to them without acquainting them with my lack of oratorical ability." One historian noted that Coolidge's astute use of the airwaves in the period following Harding's death greatly helped his bid for the 1924 Republican presidential nomination and his eventual victory.

FDR: MASTER OF THE ART

Like his distant relative Theodore, Franklin Roosevelt viewed the president as more than a chief executive. "The presidency is not merely an administrative office. That is the least of it," he said during the 1932 campaign. "It is pre-eminently a place of moral leadership."[18]

Probably no other president has used the news media so skillfully as FDR. He showered attention on White House reporters, holding 998 press conferences during his 145 months in

President Franklin D. Roosevelt used radio broadcasts from the White House, known as "fireside chats," to shape public opinion and pressure Congress.

office. According to Pollard, Roosevelt "was on an unprecedented footing with the working press. He knew its ways, he understood many of its problems and he more than held his own in his twice-weekly parry and thrust with the correspondents."[19]

But it was in the radio that Roosevelt found a powerful new tool for shaping public opinion and pressuring Congress. At the end of his first week in office, Roosevelt went on the radio to urge support for his banking reforms. He addressed a joint session of Congress, too. His reforms were passed that very day.

Similar radio messages followed, and they became known as "fireside chats." According to political scientists Sidney Milkis and Michael Nelson, these radio talks "were a revolutionary advance in presidential use of the mass media. Calvin Coolidge and, less successfully, Hoover had spoken on the radio, but only to broadcast fixed, formal pronouncements."[20] They were effective, as Arthur M. Schlesinger Jr. put it, because they "conveyed Roosevelt's conception of himself as a man at ease in his own house talking frankly and intimately to neighbors as they sat in their living rooms."[21]

According to Wilfred Binkley, Roosevelt "had only to glance toward a microphone or suggest that he might go on the air again and a whole congressional delegation would surrender. They had no relish for the flood of mail and telegrams they knew would swamp them after another fireside chat to the nation."[22]

So Congress went on, in the spring of 1933, to approve a spate of Roosevelt proposals, pausing to change scarcely so much as a comma. At the time, the president's program was known as the "Roosevelt Revolution," but Roosevelt said he preferred "New Deal." In Roosevelt's first hundred days, Congress approved the bank bill, a 25 percent cut in government spending, farm relief, public works, relief for the states, and the Civilian Conservation Corps, among other important measures. Although pushing through legislation got much tougher later on, Roosevelt still won passage of the Trade Agreements Act, Social Security, and the Public Utilities Holding Company Act.

TELEVISION BECOMES IMPORTANT

President Eisenhower permitted his news conferences to be filmed and then televised, after occasional editing for national security reasons by the White House. President Kennedy permitted live telecasts of his news conferences. For the first time the public saw the actual questions and answers as they occurred, unedited. While these TV encounters with the press helped to make Kennedy popular, they were not sufficient to pressure Congress into passing his legislative program.

President Lyndon B. Johnson was a master at moving legislators in person. But he often appeared stiff before television cameras. One biographer said Johnson "projected an image of feigned propriety, dullness, and dishonesty" in his public speeches.[23] But his televised address to Congress on voting rights in 1965 proved that he could move the people, too.

The war in Vietnam finally soured Johnson's public and congressional relations. In 1966 Congress showed that TV could be as powerful a weapon against a president as for him. When the administration asked for more money to conduct the war, the Senate Foreign Relations Committee turned its televised hearing into a full-scale debate on the war itself.

President Nixon tried to go over the heads of the Washington press corps, which he regarded as hostile, by occasionally holding press conferences outside of the capital. He also tried to generate public support through prime-time televised speeches, with mixed results. His televised veto of a Labor-HEW money bill in 1970 brought 55,000 telegrams down on the Democratic House, which upheld the veto. But Nixon's TV appearances failed to erase Watergate from the public mind. On November 17, 1973, Nixon told a startled nation: "I am not a crook." Meanwhile, the Senate Watergate Committee's televised hearings and the House Judiciary Committee's televised impeachment proceedings undermined public support for Nixon. He resigned the presidency August 9, 1974.

President Gerald R. Ford took office promising an "open administration." Indeed, at the end of 1975, the National Press Club praised him for conducting twenty-four news conferences in nineteen months in office, compared with Nixon's thirty-seven in five and a half years. But the club criticized White House Press Secretary Ron Nessen for being unprepared and devious in his briefings.

Jimmy Carter campaigned as a Washington outsider and continued to cultivate that populist image after he took office. Carter's inaugural parade walk along Pennsylvania Avenue, his radio "town meetings," fireside chats, and blue jeans—all conveyed to the people through television—failed, however, to generate enough support in the country to move his program through Congress. "We used to be frightened to death that he would go over the top of Congress and appeal directly to the people," said Rep. Timothy Wirth, D-Colo., "but there's not enough cohesion in his program to do that. There's no reason to feel threatened."[24]

An exception was the televised signing, in March 1979, of the peace treaty between Israel and Egypt, following the Camp David summit meeting, which Carter called in 1978. That ceremony played a part in persuading an otherwise stingy Congress to increase foreign aid to Israel and Egypt.

President Ronald Reagan, a former actor, enjoyed early success with TV. He became known as the "Great Communicator" for his ability to project his ideas to audiences, both in person and via the electronic media. In May 1981 Reagan made a televised address to a joint session of Congress to appeal for passage of his budget package, one that cut social spending and increased spending for defense. It was Reagan's first public appearance following the March 30 attempt on his life. A few days after the address, the Reagan budget easily passed the Democratic House. Speaker Thomas P. O'Neill Jr., D-Mass., called the Reagan effort "the greatest selling job I've ever seen."

High-profile speeches on Central America, and especially Nicaragua, became a staple of the Reagan administration. Reagan delivered at least one nationally televised speech asking for congressional support of his Central America policies annually from 1983 to 1988, except in 1987.

Reagan continued to rely on his strategy of appealing directly to the American people, despite the somewhat diminished effectiveness of that strategy over time. In April 1985, for example, Reagan made a televised address supporting a fiscal 1986 GOP Senate budget plan. The public response was mixed, contrasting sharply with the overwhelming support Reagan received following his 1981 budget speech. His plea for action failed to move the Senate to consensus.

Reagan was also the first president to face a now-common problem: the decline in the audience for presidential speeches that occurred when cable TV and video tape players offered viewers more choices.

Reagan generally did not perform so well in nationally televised news conferences as he did delivering speeches. He often made misstatements and appeared confused on the issues. Reagan's meetings with the press were infrequent, compared with his predecessors', and complaints arose about his inaccessibility. Reagan held twenty-six news conferences in his first term in office, compared with Carter's fifty-nine.

The good-natured persona that Reagan projected contributed to his personal popularity. His faculty for walking away from criticism apparently unaffected was matched by an ability to escape serious blame for setbacks and embarrassments that occurred during his administration. Rep. Patricia Schroeder, D-Colo., bestowed the title of the "Teflon president" on Reagan. Blame, it seemed, would not stick to him. As Bruce Buchanan wrote, "It became an article of faith among journalists on the presidency beat that the public simply would not stand for harsh treatment of this president. . . . Consequently, Reagan's press has been noticeably less critical than Carter's was."[25]

In his presidency, George Bush abandoned much of the stage managing that had accompanied every Reagan appearance. Less comfortable with formal speeches than Reagan had been, the new president had a penchant for informal news conferences often convened at the spur of the moment.

Bill Clinton, a highly effective speaker to live audiences, limited the number of formal prime-time speeches from the Oval Office. During the 1992 presidential debates, Clinton had proved highly adept at talking directly to audiences, particularly in "town meeting" settings where he fielded a wide variety of questions from those attending; too, he was far better than Reagan and Bush in dealing with the media's questions in press conferences.

He also delivered several memorable State of the Union addresses, memorable more for the circumstances under which they were delivered and their very delivery, perhaps, than for their content. One came in January 1998, six days after the first reports of his extramarital affair with a twenty-two-year-old White House intern, Monica Lewinsky, and possible illegal attempts in covering it up. His confident demeanor and well-articulated legislative agenda helped reverse a downward trend in his approval ratings, to the consternation of the Republican-controlled Congress. On January 19, 1999, Clinton (despite much advice to the contrary from congressional leaders) chose to deliver his State of the Union address under even more dramatic conditions: he was being tried by the Senate on perjury and obstruction of justice charges stemming from the Lewinsky case that had been brought by the House in its impeachment vote.

In both situations, the president reached beyond the immediate audience to demonstrate that he was doing the job he had been elected to do despite his difficulties with Congress. This proved an effective strategy as his job approval ratings in the aftermath of both speeches were high and strong while those of Congress and its Republican majority continued at a low ebb.

Patronage: Favors for Votes

Another means to exert pressure on Congress is patronage—the president's power to fill government jobs, award government contracts, and do other political favors. Patronage can create a debt that is repaid by voting the president's way on legislation. At least it creates an atmosphere of friendly familiarity between the president and members of Congress. "Broadly conceived, patronage involves not only federal and judicial positions, but also federal construction projects, location of government installations, offers of campaign support, availability of strategic information, plane rides on Air Force One, White House access for important constituents, and countless other favors both large and small," wrote Roger H. Davidson and Walter J. Oleszek. "The actual or potential award of favors enables presidents to amass political IOUs they can cash in later for needed support in Congress."[26]

In this century civil service and postal reform have reduced the number of jobs the president has to fill. But award of government contracts and other favors remains a powerful lever in the hands of presidents.

How effective patronage is as a pressure tool is a matter of debate. Sen. Everett M. Dirksen of Illinois, a Republican leader in the 1960s, called patronage a "tremendous weapon," adding that "it develops a certain fidelity on the part of the recipient."[27] But Rep. Paul J. Kilday, D-Texas, said in 1961 that a legislator usually has one hundred applications for every job. Said Kilday: "You make ninety-nine fellows mad at you and get one ingrate."[28]

George Washington thought that government jobs should be filled by "those that seem to have the greatest fitness for public office." The framers of the Constitution, meanwhile, sought to protect members of Congress from the president's patronage power. The Constitution says: "No Senator or Representative shall, during the Time for which he was elected, be appointed to any civil Office under the Authority of the United States, which shall have been created, or the Emoluments thereof shall have been increased during such time; and no Person holding any Office under the United States, shall be a member of either House during his Continuance in Office."

"In other words," wrote Rep. DeAlva Stanwood Alexander, R-N.Y., in 1916,

a legislator was not to be induced to create an office, or to increase the emoluments of one, in the hope of an appointment; nor was the Executive able to appoint him while he continued in Congress. But in prac-

President Ronald Reagan entertains Republican members of Congress in front of the White House.

tice these constitutional limitations neither preserved the legislator's independence nor restrained executive influence. In fact, the President's possession of an ever-increasing patronage has enabled him at times to absorb the legislative branch of Government.[29]

While the Constitution forbids legislators to hold other federal jobs, it does not forbid appointment of his or her friends, family, and supporters. With the emergence of political parties in the first decade of government under the Constitution, party loyalists started demanding federal jobs.

SPOILS SYSTEM: CREATED, PERFECTED

The inauguration of Thomas Jefferson in 1801 marked the first change in political parties at the White House. The new president found himself surrounded by Federalist Party office-holders appointed by Washington and John Adams. Jefferson replaced enough of the Federalists with Democratic-Republicans to ensure, he said, a more even distribution of power between the parties.

But if Jefferson modestly initiated the spoils system, one which allows victors to appoint their own people to public office, it was Andrew Jackson, twenty years later, who perfected and justified it. According to Martin and Susan Tolchin, Jackson was "the first to articulate, legitimize, and translate the spoils system into the American experience."[30] The spoils system engendered power struggles. Jackson had a House controlled by his own Democratic Party and a Senate in the hands of the opposition Whigs. The president and Congress spent much of their time fighting over patronage.

In the Senate Jackson was challenged by John Tyler and John C. Calhoun, who led the battle against confirming some of the president's appointees and conducted a formal inquiry into the extent of federal patronage. Calhoun said that "patronage made government too big: if this practice continued, he warned, states' rights would be crushed under the force of an ever-expanding federal bureaucracy. His investigation revealed the shocking fact that the 60,294 employees of the federal government, together with their dependents and other pensioners, made up a payroll of more than 100,000 people dependent on the federal treasury."[31]

President Lincoln used patronage to promote a constitutional amendment abolishing slavery. Unsure whether enough states would ratify the amendment, Lincoln sought to hasten the admission of a new state, Nevada. The Nevada bill was bogged down in the House when Lincoln learned that the votes of three members might be up for bargaining. When Assistant Secretary of War Charles A. Dana asked Lincoln what the members expected in return for their votes, Lincoln replied: "I don't know. It makes no difference. We must carry this vote. . . . Whatever promises you make, I will perform." Dana made a deal with the three representatives, and Nevada entered the Union. The new state then voted for the Thirteenth Amendment.[32]

President William McKinley appointed members of Congress to commissions, thus skirting the constitutional prohibition against members holding other federal offices. McKinley appointed them to make peace with Spain, settle the Bering Sea controversy, set the boundary between Alaska and Canada, arrange a commerce treaty with Great Britain, and gather information on Hawaii. McKinley asked the Senate to confirm senators named to the Hawaiian commission, but it declined to do so.

Perhaps the most successful dispenser of patronage ever to hold the presidency was Woodrow Wilson, who made patronage an important instrument of his party leadership. Although patronage jobs had been cut back severely under President Grover Cleveland, as part of his civil service reform, Wilson used what patronage was left with maximum effect. According to the *New York Sun*, Wilson's use of patronage

was never better illustrated than last Saturday, when at four o'clock, it became apparent that the senators from the cotton-growing states of the South had effected a coalition with the Republican side to kill the war-revenue bill or suspend it until legislation was put into the measure for the relief of the cotton planters. Immediately a strong arm was extended from the White House which promptly throttled the movement within thirty minutes after the fact of the revolt became known to Postmaster General Burleson, with the immense post-office patronage of the country at his disposal. . . . When the test came, four hours later, three of the eight revolters faltered and the scheme collapsed.[33]

PATRONAGE AND MODERN PRESIDENTS

The next Democrat in the White House, Franklin Roosevelt, also made effective use of his patronage power. His patronage chief, Postmaster General James Farley, asked congressional patronage seekers questions such as, "What was your preconvention position on the Roosevelt candidacy?" and "How did you vote on the economy bill?" If a member was asked to vote for a presidential measure against local pressures, the matter was put "on the frank basis of quid pro quo."[34]

The Eisenhower administration used patronage more as a stick than a carrot. The president's patronage dispenser, Postmaster General Arthur Summerfield, frequently set up shop in the office of House Minority Leader Charles A. Halleck, R-Ind., and berated Republican representatives who broke party ranks. Insurgents were warned that key jobs such as postmasterships might be cut back unless they got behind the president's program. The president himself sought to broaden the spoils, however, by removing some 134,000 classified jobs from the Civil Service.

Presidents John F. Kennedy and Lyndon B. Johnson both assigned the task of dispensing patronage to John Bailey, chairman of the Democratic National Committee. Although clever use of patronage swayed votes on several key bills, Kennedy preferred the pressure of direct lobbying. Johnson was a master at dispensing jobs and other favors. He invited members of Congress to the White House for tête-à-têtes, danced with the wives, telephoned them on their birthdays, and invited them to his Texas ranch.

Richard Nixon presided over the dissolution of a large piece of the president's patronage empire when he signed a bill that converted the 141-year-old Post Office Department into a politically independent government corporation, the U.S. Postal Service. While the main reason Congress passed the bill in 1970 was to solve the postal system's money problems, the measure ended the power of politicians to appoint or promote postmasters and other postal workers.

Although the number of federal jobs that may be filled by presidential appointment has been reduced, presidents may still fill judgeships, federal marshal and attorney positions, and customs collector posts. And presidents still have a number of other patronage powers that can help build goodwill among members of Congress, including the location of pork-barrel projects, awards of federal contracts, and support for legislation that will aid a particular constituency. "The principal reason why President Reagan kept the widely criticized Clinch River breeder reactor in the budget was that it was in Tennessee, represented by Senate Majority Leader Howard Baker," noted George C. Edwards III. [35] Bill Clinton proved particularly adept at reaching out to interest groups through announcements of federal grants or programs and also by appointing people long associated with major national interests or representing important electoral constituencies to high positions in the government. His appointment of Bruce Babbitt as secretary of the interior, for example, proved popular with environmentalists.

Presidents have shown varying degrees of skill at handling the small change of patronage. Kennedy, Johnson, Ford, Reagan, Bush, and Clinton all seemed to enjoy informal conversation with members of Congress. Nixon and Jimmy Carter were not so comfortable in these personal meetings. Tales of the Carter administration's ineptness at dealing with Congress are legion. Two Massachusetts Republicans, for example, Elliot L. Richardson and Evan Dobelle, were named ambassador-at-large and chief of protocol, respectively, at the State Department. Speaker O'Neill was furious when he learned through the press that the two men from his state had been appointed. Or, as a congressional staffer said, "When Jerry Ford would sign a bill, he'd use nice metal pens with his name on them, and then he'd pass them out to the members who had worked on the bill. But Carter signs bills with a felt-tip pen, and then he puts the pen back into his pocket."[36]

Veto Threat: The Ultimate Weapon

When surprise parties, free tickets, government contracts, jobs, lobbying, and appeals to the public all fail to move Congress, a president may resort to his most powerful defensive weapon: the veto.

A president uses the veto not only to try to kill unpalatable bills but also to dramatize policies and to try to force Congress to compromise on issues the president cares about. Short of a veto itself, a presidential threat to veto legislation is a powerful form of lobbying.

The Constitution says that any bill Congress passes must go to the president. The president must either sign it or send it back to Congress with his objections. A two-thirds vote of each house is required to override a veto. The Supreme Court ruled in 1919 that two-thirds of those voting, assuming there is a quorum, rather than two-thirds of the total membership, is enough for an override.

The veto is powerful because a president usually can muster the support of at least one-third plus one member of a House or Senate quorum. Woodrow Wilson said the veto power makes the president "a third branch of the legislature."

From 1789 through 1999, presidents vetoed more than 2,500 bills, and Congress overrode slightly more than 100. *(See box, Vetoes and Vetoes Overridden, p. 669.)* About 60 percent have been regular vetoes; 40 percent have been pocket vetoes, which cannot be overridden because they occur after Congress has adjourned. Thus only about 7 percent of regular vetoes have been overridden.

The concept of *veto* (I forbid) originated in ancient Rome as a means to protect the plebeians from injustice at the hands of the patricians. Roman tribunes, representing the people, were authorized to veto acts of the Senate, dominated by the patricians. English rulers were given absolute veto power, and in 1597 Queen Elizabeth I rejected more parliamentary bills than she accepted. The English monarch's veto, which cannot be overridden, is still nominally in effect but has not been used since 1707.

Early American presidents conceived of the veto as a device to be used rarely and then only against legislative encroachment on the prerogatives of another branch of government. Washington vetoed only two bills; Adams and Jefferson, none. Although Madison and Monroe vetoed eight bills between them, they cited constitutional grounds for doing so in all except one case. John Quincy Adams did not veto a bill.

JACKSON'S VIEW OF VETO

The concept of the veto underwent a marked change under Andrew Jackson, who vetoed twelve bills (more than all six of his predecessors put together), mostly because he took issue with their content or purpose. Jackson, who also use the pocket veto for the first time, believed the president could reject any bill that he felt was injurious to the nation. "One implication of Jackson's interpretation of the veto power," according to Sidney M. Milkis and Michael Nelson, "was that Congress now had to consider the president's opinion about bills before enacting them or else risk a veto."[37]

Jackson's most noteworthy veto was of a bill to recharter the Bank of the United States, which Jackson considered a creature of special interests. Jackson's veto message was "a landmark in the evolution of the presidency," Binkley said. "For the first time in American history, a veto message was used as an instrument of party warfare. Through it, the Democratic Party, as the Jacksonians were now denominated, dealt a telling blow to their opponents, the National Republicans. Though addressed to Congress, the veto message was an appeal to the nation. Not a single opportunity to discredit the old ruling class was dismissed."[38]

President John Tyler's veto of a tariff bill in 1843 brought on

POCKET VETO CONTROVERSY

Under the procedure outlined in the Constitution, the president must veto a bill and return it within ten days of its receipt to the chamber where it originated. The bill automatically becomes a law if the president has not returned it within that time—with one exception. Under the Constitution, a bill does not become law if "Congress by their adjournment prevent its return." In such a case, the president can "pocket veto" the bill, since he does not have an opportunity to return it to Congress, together with his objections, for further consideration. (The image is that of the president putting a bill in his pocket and leaving it there.)

Controversy has long surrounded the issue of whether "adjournment" meant only the final adjournment of Congress—which is call adjournment *sine die*—or also applied to interim adjournments, such as those between sessions or recesses during sessions. In the *Pocket Veto Case* of 1929, the Supreme Court held that the issue was not the kind of adjournment but whether the adjournment prevented the president from returning a vetoed bill to Congress. That ruling in effect meant that the pocket veto was appropriate during any adjournment.

Less than ten years later, the Court narrowed the broad sweep of its 1929 ruling, holding that the House and Senate could designate agents to receive vetoed bills during short recesses. Designations of such agents, usually the clerk of the House and secretary of the Senate, meant that the president was not prevented from returning a vetoed bill to the chamber of origin. This ruling, in the case of *Wright v. United States* effectively restricted pocket vetoes to final adjournments of Congress.

And there the matter rested until 1970, when President Richard Nixon pocket vetoed a medical training bill during a congressional recess. The bill had passed both chambers by nearly unanimous votes, indicating that Congress would have overridden a regular veto. Ruling on a suit brought by Sen. Edward M. Kennedy, D-Mass., the U.S. Court of Appeals for the District of Columbia in 1974 declared that the president had improperly used his pocket veto power. A second case decided by the same court in 1976 broadened the ruling to prohibit the president from pocket vetoing a bill

during adjournments between sessions of the same Congress. In both cases the court ruled that the pocket veto was invalid because both the House and Senate had approved agents to receive veto messages during the interim period. The Nixon administration declined to appeal the cases to the Supreme Court.

Despite these lower court rulings, the pocket veto remained a contentious issue. In 1981 and 1983 President Ronald Reagan pocket vetoed bills between the first and second sessions of the 97th and 98th Congresses. In August 1985 a U.S. federal appeals court ruled that Reagan's use of the pocket veto was unconstitutional because Congress had appointed officials to receive the messages. The Supreme Court, in reviewing the case in 1987, left the issue unresolved by declaring the case moot because the provisions of the vetoed law had no effect beyond 1984.

President George Bush confused the issue further when in 1989 and again in 1991 he pocket vetoed minor measures during congressional recesses. Bush maintained that a pocket veto was in order any time Congress adjourned for more than three days. In both cases, however, Congress considered the pieces of legislation enacted into law because of the president's failure to return the bills. (After adjournment of the first session of the 101st Congress in November 1989, Bush had also pocket vetoed a bill to let Chinese students stay in the United States, but he also returned the bill to Congress, saying he was doing so because of questions arising from recent court decisions. Whether the pocket veto would have stood if Congress had overridden the veto was never tested; the Senate sustained the veto at the beginning of the second session. This veto has been recorded by Congress as a regular veto.)

In 1990 legislation to allow use of the pocket veto only after *sine die* adjournment was introduced and reported in the House, but no further action was taken and the measure died with the end of the 101st Congress. What constitutes constitutional application of the pocket veto thus may remain a point of contention between Congress and the White House until the Supreme Court takes up the issue again.

---

the first attempt by Congress to impeach a president. An impeachment resolution, introduced in the House by Whig members, charged the president "with the high crime and misdemeanor of withholding his assent to laws indispensable to the just operation of the government." When the impeachment move failed, Henry Clay proposed a constitutional amendment to enable Congress to override the president's veto by a simple majority instead of the required two-thirds. The president's right of veto gave him power equal to that of almost two-thirds of Congress, Clay said, adding that such power would ultimately make the president "ruler of the nation."[39]

USE OF VETO AFTER THE CIVIL WAR

When, after the Civil War, President Andrew Johnson vetoed a bill to protect the rights of the freed slaves, Congress passed

the measure over his head—the first time Congress had overridden the president's veto on a major issue. The civil rights bill was only the first of a number of measures to be passed over Johnson's veto. Among others was the Tenure of Office Act, which led indirectly to Johnson's impeachment. When Johnson refused to abide by the provisions of the act, which prohibited the president from removing appointed officials from office until their successors had been confirmed by the Senate, the House initiated impeachment.

During the rest of the nineteenth century, presidents used the veto mainly to prevent corruption through the passage of private bills. Grover Cleveland vetoed 584 bills (346 directly and 238 by pocket veto), including 301 private pension bills, which previous presidents had signed routinely. While meant to discourage fraudulent claims, Cleveland's use of the veto incurred

VETOES AND VETOES OVERRIDDEN, 1789–1999

From 1789 through September 1999, presidents had vetoed a grand total of 2,540 bills, with all except 59 of the vetoes occurring in the years after Abraham Lincoln's presidency. Congress overrode on 106 of the vetoed bills.

The presidents who vetoed the most bills were Franklin D. Roosevelt (635 during his twelve years in the White House) and Grover Cleveland (584 during two terms). Andrew Johnson had the most vetoes overridden (15 of the 29 bills vetoed).

Until 1969 presidents usually vetoed more private bills than public bills. President Dwight D. Eisenhower, for example, vetoed 81 public bills and 100 private bills. President Richard Nixon reversed the trend, vetoing only 3 private bills during his years in office. Presidents Gerald R. Ford, Jimmy Carter, and Ronald Reagan vetoed a total of 12 private bills in their combined fourteen and a half years in the White House.

Before 1936 the distinction between public and private bills was hazy, with some bills now considered public designated as private and vice versa. After 1936, if a bill was listed in the bill status section of the *Digest of Public General Bills*, Congressional Quarterly categorized it as public; if not, the bill was classified as private.

The *Digest* first was published by the Library of Congress for the 74th Congress, 2nd session (1936). By then, however, three years of Roosevelt's first term in office had elapsed. Consequently, a reliable breakdown of vetoes by public and private bills was not feasible.

The table below shows the number of private and public bills vetoed by each president, the type of veto used, and the number of vetoes overridden.

Under Article I, Section 7 of the Constitution, the president has ten days (Sundays excepted) after receiving a bill passed by Congress to sign the measure into law or veto it, returning it to Congress with his objections. Congress can override a veto by a two-thirds vote of each chamber. Any bill neither signed nor vetoed within those ten days "shall be a law . . . unless the Congress by their adjournment prevent its return, in which case it shall not be a law."

| President | Public and Private Bills | | | | President | Public and Private Bills | | | |
	Total vetoes	Regular vetoes	Pocket vetoes	Vetoes overridden		Total vetoes	Regular vetoes	Pocket vetoes	Vetoes overridden
Washington	2	2	0	0	B. Harrison	44	19	25	1
J. Adams	0	0	0	0	Cleveland (2nd term)	170	42	128	5
Jefferson	0	0	0	0	McKinley	42	6	36	0
Madison	7	5	2	0	T. Roosevelt	82	42	40	1
Monroe	1	1	0	0	Taft	39	30	9	1
J.Q. Adams	0	0	0	0	Wilson	44	33	11	6
Jackson	12	5	7	0	Harding	6	5	1	0
Van Buren	1	0	1	0	Coolidge	50	20	30	4
W.H. Harrison	0	0	0	0	Hoover	37	21	16	3
Tyler	10	6	4	1	F.D. Roosevelt	635	372	263	9
Polk	3	2	1	0	Truman	250	180	70	12
Taylor	0	0	0	0	Eisenhower	181	73	108	2
Fillmore	0	0	0	0	Kennedy	21	12	9	0
Pierce	9	9	0	5	Johnson	30	16	14	0
Buchanan	7	4	3	0	Nixon[b]	43	26	17	7
Lincoln	7	2	5	0	Ford	66	48	18	12
A. Johnson	29	21	8	15	Carter	31	13	18	2
Grant[a]	93	45	48	4	Reagan	78	39	39	9
Hayes	13	12	1	1	Bush[c]	44	29	15	1
Garfield	0	0	0	0	Clinton[d]	27	27	0	2
Arthur	12	4	8	1					
Cleveland (1st term)	414	304	110	2	Total	2,540	1,475	1,065	106

a. Veto total listed for Grant does not include a pocket veto of a bill that apparently never was placed before him for his signature.

b. Two Nixon pocket vetoes, later overturned in court, are counted as regular vetoes.

c. Two Bush pocket vetoes, attempted during recesses, are not counted since Congress considered the bills enacted into law because of Bush's failure to return them. Another bill that Bush claimed to have pocket vetoed is counted as a regular veto since the veto was sustained by Congress.

d. Through September 1999.

SOURCES: *Presidential Vetoes, 1989–1994*, compiled by the Senate Library under the direction of Martha S. Pope, secretary, and Gregory Harness, librarian (Government Printing Office, 1994); and Congressional Quarterly.

the wrath of veterans' groups. Cleveland's veto record stood until Franklin Roosevelt, who disapproved 635 bills, 372 directly and 263 by pocket vetoes. Nine Roosevelt vetoes were overridden. *(See box, Private Bills, p. 526.)*

Under Roosevelt, vetoes increased both in absolute numbers and in relation to the number of bills passed. That, according to Professors Wilfred Binkley and Malcolm Moos, reflected the growing complexity of America, which in turn was reflected in legislation. While Cleveland focused his vetoes on private pensions, Roosevelt took in the full range of issues. Until Roosevelt, no president had vetoed a revenue bill, and it was assumed that precedent exempted tax bills from the veto. Roosevelt first vetoed a revenue bill during World War II.

Presidents Harry S. Truman and Dwight D. Eisenhower continued to make extensive use of the veto. Truman used it to safeguard organized labor against industry and agriculture. When, during the coal and rail strikes of 1946, Congress passed a bill restricting strikes, Truman vetoed it, and Congress sustained the veto. The votes to sustain came mainly from members representing big cities. In 1947 Truman vetoed the Taft-Hartley Labor Act, claiming it was unfair to labor. By then, however, Republicans were in control of Congress, and, with help from conservative Democrats, the veto was overridden.

During his second term Eisenhower used the veto and the veto threat to defeat or limit social programs favored by the Democrats, who controlled Congress. To fight liberal measures, Eisenhower put together a coalition of the Republican minority and conservative southern Democrats. In 1959, for example, he vetoed two housing bills and another to promote rural electricity. Congress was unable to override any of the three vetoes. That same year Eisenhower used the threat of veto to defeat Democratic proposals for school aid, area redevelopment, a higher minimum wage, and health care for the aged.

MODERN PRESIDENTS AND THE VETO

Presidents John F. Kennedy and Lyndon B. Johnson seldom had to use the veto or threaten it. They were activist presidents whose main interest lay in getting their programs through a Congress controlled by their own party. But in 1965 Johnson vetoed a military construction authorization bill that required advance congressional review of presidential decisions to close military bases.

Like Eisenhower, Republican presidents Richard Nixon and Gerald R. Ford used the veto and its threat to prevent enactment of Democratic programs. Nixon often justified his vetoes on grounds that the bills were inflationary. When Congress passed a Labor-HEW appropriations bill that exceeded his request by $1.1 billion, Nixon vetoed it on national radio and TV. The Democratic House sustained the veto. Congress also sustained him on his vetoes of bills authorizing funds for the war on poverty and for manpower training and public service jobs. But in 1973 Congress overrode Nixon's veto of legislation to limit the president's power to commit armed forces abroad without congressional approval.

Ford made extensive use of the veto and the veto threat during his two and a half years in the White House. Although the former House minority leader was personally popular on Capitol Hill, Ford and the Democratic majority in Congress disagreed on the proper approach to take to the flagging economy and on energy policy. Through the veto and the veto threat, Ford exacted compromises on several key issues, including an extension of the 1975 tax cut, emergency employment, housing subsidies, and energy policy. Altogether, Ford vetoed sixty-six measures; Congress overrode twelve of them.

Jimmy Carter was the first president since Truman to have a veto overridden by a Congress controlled by his own party. In 1980 Carter disapproved a debt-limit bill because it included a section killing an import fee he had imposed on foreign oil. Only a handful of senators and representatives, all Democrats, voted to sustain the veto. Later that year Congress again overrode the president's veto, this time of a bill to increase salaries of doctors at veterans hospitals.

Ronald Reagan pocket-vetoed thirty-four bills, almost as many as he vetoed through regular methods. Congress overrode nine of the thirty-seven regular vetoes. Reagan often used or threatened to use the veto on budget-related matters and on foreign policy issues.

In one of the most stunning blows to Reagan's presidency, Congress in October 1986 overrode the president's veto of a measure imposing economic sanctions against South Africa. The vote was the first override of a veto on a major foreign policy issue since 1973, when Congress enacted the War Powers Resolution into law over President Nixon's veto.

Reagan did not always follow through on his veto threats, and in some cases he vetoed bills in the face of hopeless odds. When he vetoed a 1987 water projects bill heavily laden with local pork-barrel projects, he openly acknowledged that he would not be sustained.

George Bush, on the other hand, used vetoes and veto threats to great effect. Like other recent Republican presidents, faced with a Democratic-controlled Congress, Bush used the veto to block measures that he viewed as expanding the role of government as well as those that did not reflect his budgetary priorities. Only one of his forty-four vetoes was overridden during his term. Bush also issued around 60 veto threats per year, often not to kill legislation but to stimulate serious bargaining.

Bill Clinton did not veto a bill from the Democratic-controlled Congress in the first two years of his first term, but this stance changed dramatically after Republicans took over both houses of Congress in 1995. Clinton used his veto power first in rejecting a GOP plan to cut $16.5 billion from the previously passed 1995 budget, defending traditionally liberal Democratic programs for education, the environment, and housing. He then vetoed, over the course of 1995, ten other spending bills thwarting the new Republican majority's campaign promises (their "Contract with America") to reduce the size of government and balance the budget. Clinton used vetoes and the

The veto gives the president formidable power in negotiating with Congress. Here President Bill Clinton, using the pen that Lyndon Johnson used to sign Medicare into law in 1965, vetoes legislation that he argued would have drastically cut Medicare spending.

threat of vetoes to counteract what he branded the "extremism" of the new congressional leaders.

One Clinton veto, prompted by a provision in a budget that cut the growth in Medicare spending, led to a partial shutdown of the federal government. After the public placed the primary blame for this shutdown and a subsequent one on the Republican Congress, Clinton's political fortunes began to revive. Many political observers believed that Clinton's adroit handling of the budget stalemate with Congress greatly aided his reelection in 1996.

Ironically, Democrat Clinton was the initial beneficiary of the Republican-favored Line-Item Veto Act, which took effect in January 1997. The law gave a president the power to strike out or "cancel" dollar amounts of discretionary spending, new "direct spending," and certain forms of new tax benefits signed into law. Congress could vote to pass the item(s) again, but the president could then use his constitutional veto power to kill this legislation, forcing Congress to find a two-thirds majority to override the veto in the normal manner. *(See box, Line-Item Veto, p. 174.)*

Clinton used this new power sparingly but opposition quickly formed on political and legal grounds. In February 1998 the Supreme Court in *Clinton v. City of New York* declared the act unconstitutional because, in the words of the decision, "There is no provision in the Constitution that authorizes the President to enact, to amend, or to repeal statutes."

NOTES

1. Bertram M. Gross, *The Legislative Struggle: A Study in Social Combat* (New York: McGraw-Hill, 1953), 101.

2. Rowland Evans and Robert Novak, *Lyndon B. Johnson: The Exercise of Power* (New York: New American Library, 1966), 490.

3. Walter J. Oleszek, "The Context of Congressional Policy Making," in *Divided Democracy: Cooperation and Conflict between the President and Congress,* ed. James A. Thurber (Washington, D.C.: CQ Press, 1991), 96.

4. Neil MacNeil, *Forge of Democracy: The House of Representatives* (New York: David McKay, 1963), 253–254.

5. Ibid.

6. Nigel Bowles, *The White House and Capitol Hill: The Politics of Presidential Persuasion* (Oxford: Oxford University Press, 1987), 16.

7. Eric L. Davis, "Congressional Liaison: The People and the Institutions," in *Both Ends of the Avenue: The Presidency, the Executive Branch, and Congress in the 1980s,* ed. Anthony King (Washington, D.C.: American Enterprise Institute, 1983), 61.

8. MacNeil, *Forge of Democracy,* 257.

9. Ibid., 260.

10. Charles O. Jones, "Presidential Negotiation with Congress," in *Both Ends of the Avenue: The Presidency, the Executive Branch, and Congress in the 1980s,* ed. Anthony King (Washington, D.C.: American Enterprise Institute, 1983), 108.

11. Doris Kearns, *Lyndon Johnson and the American Dream* (New York: Harper and Row, 1976), 236–237.

12. Louis Fisher, *The Politics of Shared Power: Congress and the Executive* (Washington, D.C.: CQ Press, 1981), 50.

13. James E. Pollard, *The Presidents and the Press* (New York: Macmillan, 1947), 147.

14. George Fort Milton, *The Use of Presidential Power* (Boston: Little, Brown, 1944), 131, 133.

15. Pollard, *The Presidents and the Press,* 413.

16. George C. Edwards III, *The Public Presidency: The Pursuit of Popular Support* (New York: St. Martin's, 1983), 38.

17. Pollard, *The Presidents and the Press,* 645.

18. Edward S. Corwin and Louis W. Koenig, *The Presidency Today* (New York: New York University Press, 1956), 63.

19. Pollard, *The Presidents and the Press,* 773.

20. Sidney M. Milkis and Michael Nelson, *The American Presidency: Origins and Development, 1776–1998,* 3rd ed. (Washington, D.C.: Congressional Quarterly, 1999), 266.

21. Arthur M. Schlesinger Jr., *The Coming of the New Deal* (Boston: Houghton Mifflin, 1958), 559.

22. Wilfred E. Binkley, *President and Congress* (New York: Vintage Books, 1962), 305.

23. Edwards, *The Public Presidency*, 40.

24. Roger H. Davidson and Walter J. Oleszek, *Congress and Its Members* (Washington, D.C.: CQ Press, 1981), 306–307.

25. Bruce Buchanan, *The Citizen's Presidency: Standards of Choice and Judgment* (Washington, D.C.: CQ Press, 1987), 12.

26. Roger H. Davidson and Walter J. Oleszek, *Congress and Its Members*, 7th ed. (Washington, D.C.: CQ Press, 2000), 299.

27. Ibid.

28. MacNeil, *Forge of Democracy*, 247–248.

29. DeAlva Stanwood Alexander, *History and Procedure of the House of Representatives* (Boston: Houghton Mifflin, 1916), 378–379.

30. Martin Tolchin and Susan Tolchin, *To the Victor: Political Patronage from the Clubhouse to the White House* (New York: Random House, 1971), 323.

31. Ibid., 325.

32. Alexander, *History and Procedure of the House*, 379.

33. Ibid., 381–382.

34. Binkley, *President and Congress*, 301.

35. George C. Edwards III, *At the Margins: Presidential Leadership of Congress* (New Haven, Conn.: Yale University Press, 1989), 85.

36. Davis, "Congressional Liaison," 77.

37. Milkis and Nelson, *The American Presidency*, 121.

38. Binkley, *President and Congress*, 86.

39. Ibid., 119, 120.

SELECTED BIBLIOGRAPHY

Alexander, DeAlva S. *History and Procedure of the House of Representatives.* Boston: Houghton Mifflin, 1916.

Binkley, Wilfred E. *Powers of the President.* New York: Doubleday, 1937.

———. *President and Congress.* New York: Vintage Books, 1962.

Binkley, Wilfred E., and Malcolm C. Moos. *A Grammar of American Politics: The National Government.* New York: Knopf, 1958.

Bond, Jon R., and Richard Fleisher. *President in the Legislative Arena.* Chicago: University of Chicago Press, 1990.

Bowles, Nigel. *The White House and Capitol Hill: The Politics of Presidential Persuasion.* New York: Oxford University Press, 1987.

Buchanan, Bruce. *The Citizen's Presidency: Standards of Choice and Judgment.* Washington, D.C.: CQ Press, 1987.

Chubb, John E., and Paul E. Peterson, eds. *Can the Government Govern?* Washington, D.C.: Brookings Institution, 1989.

Collier, Kenneth. *Between the Branches: The White House Office of Legislative Affairs.* Pittsburgh: University of Pittsburgh Press, 1997.

Congressional Quarterly. *The Washington Lobby.* 5th ed. Washington, D.C.: Congressional Quarterly, 1987.

Corwin, Edward S. *The President, Office and Powers, 1787–1957.* New York: New York University Press, 1984.

Corwin, Edward S., and Louis W. Koenig. *The Presidency Today.* New York: New York University Press, 1956.

Davidson, Roger H., and Walter J. Oleszek. *Congress and Its Members.* 7th ed. Washington, D.C.: CQ Press, 2000.

Denton, Robert E., Jr., *The Primetime Presidency of Ronald Reagan: The Era of the Television Presidency.* New York: Praeger, 1988.

Edwards, George C., III. *At the Margins: Presidential Leadership of Congress.* New Haven, Conn.: Yale University Press, 1989.

———. *The Public Presidency: The Pursuit of Popular Support.* New York: St. Martin's, 1983.

———, John H. Kessel, and Bert A. Rockman, eds. *Researching the Presidency: Vital Questions, New Approaches.* Pittsburgh: University of Pittsburgh Press, 1993.

Evans, Rowland, and Robert Novak. *Lyndon B. Johnson: The Exercise of Power.* New York: New American Library, 1966.

Fisher, Louis. *Constitutional Conflicts between Congress and the President.* 4th ed. Lawrence: University Press of Kansas, 1997.

———. *The Politics of Shared Power: Congress and the Executive.* 4th ed. College Station, Texas: Texas A&M University Press, 1998.

Gross, Bertram M. *The Legislative Struggle: A Study in Social Combat.* New York: McGraw-Hill, 1953.

Grossman, Michael Baruch, and Martha Joynt Kumar. *Portraying the President: The White House and the News Media.* Baltimore: Johns Hopkins University Press, 1981.

Herring, Edward P. *Presidential Leadership: The Political Relations of the Congress and Chief Executive.* Westport, Conn.: Greenwood Press, 1972.

Hess, Stephen. *Organizing the Presidency.* 2nd ed. Washington, D.C.: Brookings Institution, 1988.

Johnson, Cathy M. *The Dynamics of Conflict between Bureaucrats and Legislators.* Armonk, N.Y.: Sharpe, 1992.

Johnson, Haynes. *In the Absence of Power: Governing America.* New York: Viking, 1980.

Jones, Charles O. *The Presidency in a Separated System.* Washington, D.C.: Brookings Institution, 1994.

Jones, Charles O. *Separate but Equal Branches: Congress and the Presidency.* 2nd ed. New York: Chatham House, 1999.

Kernell, Samuel. *Going Public: New Strategies of Presidential Leadership.* 3rd ed. Washington, D.C.: CQ Press, 1997.

King, Anthony, ed. *Both Ends of the Avenue: The Presidency, the Executive Branch, and Congress in the 1980s.* Washington, D.C.: American Enterprise Institute, 1983.

Korn, Jessica. *The Power of Separation: American Constitutionalism and the Myth of the Legislative Veto.* Princeton, N.J.: Princeton University Press, 1996.

Light, Paul C. *The President's Agenda: Domestic Policy Choice from Kennedy to Clinton.* 3rd ed. Baltimore: Johns Hopkins University Press, 1999.

Lowi, Theodore J. *The Personal President: Power Invested, Promise Unfilled.* Ithaca: Cornell University Press, 1985.

MacNeil, Neil. *Forge of Democracy: The House of Representatives.* New York: David McKay, 1963.

Mezey, Michael L. *Congress, the President, and Public Policy.* Boulder, Colo.: Westview Press, 1989.

Milkis, Sidney M., and Michael Nelson. *The American Presidency: Origins and Development, 1776–1998.* 3rd ed. Washington, D.C.: Congressional Quarterly, 1999.

Milton, George F. *The Use of Presidential Power.* Boston: Little, Brown, 1944.

Nelson, Michael, ed. *Congressional Quarterly's Guide to the Presidency.* 2nd ed. Washington, D.C.: Congressional Quarterly, 1996.

———. *The Presidency and the Political System.* 5th ed. Washington, D.C.: CQ Press, 1998.

Neustadt, Richard E. *Presidential Power and the Modern Presidents: The Politics of Leadership from Roosevelt to Reagan.* New York: Free Press, 1990.

Patterson, Bradley H., Jr. *The Ring of Power: The White House Staff and Its Expanding Role in Government.* New York: Basic Books, 1988.

Peterson, Mark A. *Legislating Together: The White House and Capitol Hill from Eisenhower to Reagan.* Cambridge, Mass.: Harvard University Press, 1990.

Pollard, James E. *The Presidents and the Press.* New York: Macmillan, 1964.

Schlesinger, Arthur M., Jr. *The Imperial Presidency.* Boston: Houghton Mifflin, 1989.

Spitzer, Robert J. *President and Congress: Executive Hegemony at the Crossroads of American Government.* Philadelphia: Temple University Press, 1993.

Sundquist, James L., ed. *Back to Gridlock: Governance in the Clinton Years.* Washington, D.C.: Brookings Institution, 1995.

Thomas, Norman C., and Joseph A. Pika. *The Politics of the Presidency.* 4th ed. Washington, D.C.: CQ Press, 1997.

Thurber, James A., ed. *Divided Democracy: Cooperation and Conflict between the President and Congress.* Washington, D.C.: CQ Press, 1991.

Tolchin, Martin, and Susan Tolchin. *To the Victor: Political Patronage from the Clubhouse to the White House.* New York: Random House, 1971.

Watson, Richard A. *Presidential Vetoes and Public Policy.* Lawrence: University Press of Kansas, 1992.

CHAPTER 22

The Supreme Court

Congress and the supreme court are separate but interdependent branches of the federal government. The Supreme Court defines the limits of congressional authority, while Congress confirms the president's appointments to the Court, sets its jurisdiction, pays its bills, and holds the power to impeach its justices. Through the power of judicial review, the Court may weigh acts of Congress against the Constitution and nullify those in conflict. Thus, within a legal framework, the Court often exercises policy-making functions that otherwise are held solely by the two elected branches of government, the legislative and executive.

"Every discussion of the Supreme Court refers to the central tension between the Court as a political institution making national policy and the basic principles of representative government," writes law professor David Adamany.[1] The tension arises from the very structure of a federal government that was created to achieve checks and balances among the three branches. The tension resulting from this interplay of power has often brought Congress and the Supreme Court into periods of sharp, and sometimes bitter, confrontation.

The Constitution does not expressly grant the Court the right to review acts of Congress, but the Court assumed this power in its earliest years and asserted it explicitly during the chief justiceship of John Marshall (1801–1835). The Court used the power to invalidate laws passed by Congress only twice before the Civil War but has wielded it much more frequently since then—sometimes to protect the powers of the states, other times to protect the economic rights or civil liberties of individuals. By September 1999, the Court had ruled unconstitutional a total of 150 laws. That number included twenty-eight laws during the chief justiceship of William H. Rehnquist (1986–), while the Court had a majority of justices ostensibly committed to a philosophy of "judicial restraint." (*See "Acts of Congress Held Unconstitutional," in Reference Materials, p. 998, Vol. II.*)

The Court has also used its power of judicial review, however, to support and strengthen the powers of Congress. The Marshall Court expansively construed Congress's power to enact laws under the Constitution's "necessary and proper" clause and protected Congress's power to regulate interstate commerce against encroachments by the states. The Court through history has sustained most congressional decisions concerning taxes, spending, and currency. It has generally avoided interference with Congress's power to regulate its own affairs or to conduct investigations.

Just as the Court has used its judicial review powers to influence the shape of federal legislation, so Congress has tried from time to time to use its powers to shape the Court's political or ideological makeup or to respond to the outcomes of particular rulings. Congress can influence the Court in three general ways: through selection, confirmation, and impeachment of individual justices; through institutional and jurisdictional changes; and through direct reversal of specific Court decisions. Congress has exercised some of these powers frequently, others only rarely.

The Senate's "advice and consent" power gives Congress a role in the selection and confirmation of justices. Although Congress has only limited influence over a president's choice of a Supreme Court nominee, the Senate has taken its power to confirm appointees very seriously. Of the 148 nominations to the court, 28 have failed to win confirmation—some because of partisan politics, others because of legal philosophy, and at least two because of questions about their qualifications. Even though the president gets to make a new selection, the Senate's rejection of a nominee can have significant effect. After Robert Bork was defeated for confirmation in 1987, President Ronald Reagan turned to a somewhat less conservative judge, Anthony M. Kennedy, who won confirmation unanimously.

Congress's impeachment power creates a potential check on the conduct of justices while in office, but it has been of only limited significance. Only one justice has been impeached—Samuel Chase in 1804—and he was acquitted. Another justice, Abe Fortas, resigned in 1969 under threat of impeachment. But efforts to impeach Chief Justice Earl Warren in the 1950s and Justice William O. Douglas in 1970 failed.

The Constitution gives Congress the power to limit the Court's jurisdiction, and Congress theoretically can affect the Court's workload through its power to create and define the jurisdiction of lower federal courts. But Congress has not been successful in using these powers to influence the Court's decisions. Critics of the Court's decisions have often responded with proposals to curb its power over specific types of cases, but Congress has done so only once—with limited effect. Proposals have also been made to require a two-thirds majority or unanimous vote to declare federal or state laws unconstitutional, but none has ever been approved. As for the lower federal courts, the First Congress exercised the constitutional power to create a federal court system, and Congress for the most part has tended to expand rather than shrink their jurisdiction.

The Supreme Court has the final check on the work of Congress and the president: it can declare legislation unconstitutional.

More important, Congress can try to reverse the effects of specific Supreme Court decisions by exercising its normal lawmaking powers. Congress can reverse a particular Court ruling by legislation if the decision is based on statutory construction or interpretation. A Court decision based on a constitutional provision can also be overturned, but only by a constitutional amendment approved by two-thirds majorities in both houses of Congress and then ratified by three-fourths of the states. The first constitutional amendment after the Bill of Rights—the Eleventh, ratified in 1795—overturned a Supreme Court decision. Three other amendments have reversed rulings by the Court—most recently, the Twenty-sixth, guaranteeing eighteen-year-olds the right to vote. Lawmakers in recent years have proposed other constitutional amendments to reverse rulings on such issues as reapportionment, school busing, and abortion, but they have failed.

Congress can more readily reverse a Supreme Court decision if the ruling is based on statutory grounds. The first such reversal came in 1852; one scholar has recently counted more than 120 such reversals in the period 1967–1990.[2] Generally, the Court acquiesces in legislative overrides. On occasion, however, it has refused to go along with congressional efforts to circumvent a Court ruling. In one recent example, Congress passed a law in 1993 aimed at overturning a decision three years earlier making it harder to protect religious practices from state laws. But the

Court in 1997 ruled the law unconstitutional, saying Congress had no power to change the Court's interpretation of the Constitution.

Judicial Review

The Constitution itself describes the Supreme Court's powers in Article III with a minimum of detail and makes no explicit mention of the power of judicial review. Two sections, however, give some textual basis for judicial review. Article III states that "the judicial Power of the United States" extends to "all cases . . . arising under this Constitution, the Laws of the United States, and Treaties made, or which shall be made, under their Authority." In addition, the so-called supremacy clause states that the Constitution, laws, and treaties "shall be the supreme Law of the Land; and the Judges in every State shall be bound thereby, any Thing in the Constitution or Laws of any State to the Contrary notwithstanding" (Article VI, Section 2).

Despite the limited elaboration in the Constitution, few scholars today believe that the Framers intended to deny this power to the Supreme Court. The concept of judicial review was relatively well established in the colonies. The Privy Council in London had reviewed the acts of the colonies for compliance with English law before the Revolution. Several state courts had voided state laws inconsistent with the new state constitutions.

In addition, the records of the Constitutional Convention and the debates over ratification of the Constitution provide additional support for judicial review.

The Constitutional Convention considered but rejected a proposal that the Supreme Court share with the president a veto power over acts of Congress. The objection appeared to center not on judicial review but on the prospect of the Court's becoming involved in enactment of a law that it would later be required to enforce. In supporting the proposal, however, delegate George Mason said that judicial review would be a "restraining power" against enactment of "unjust and pernicious laws" by the legislature. Another delegate, Nathaniel Gorham, said, "All agree that a check on the Legislature is necessary." By contrast, according to records of the convention compiled by Max Farrand, only two delegates expressed reservations about judicial review.[3]

Nonetheless, Philip B. Kurland, a University of Chicago law professor, notes that the Framers also had concerns about a strong judiciary because in colonial America the judiciary had been "the handmaiden of the crown."[4] Moreover, they did not want to alarm the states, which remained wary of sharing additional power with the federal government. Still, both James Madison and Alexander Hamilton supported the concept of judicial review in *The Federalist,* the collection of essays written by them and John Jay urging the states to ratify the Constitution. Hamilton played down the importance of the judiciary by describing it as "the least dangerous branch" of the new federal government. But he also explicitly envisioned the courts' power to nullify acts contrary to the Constitution. Limitations on power, he wrote in The *Federalist* No. 78, "can be preserved in no other way than through the medium of courts of justice, whose duty it must be to declare all acts contrary to the manifest tenor of the Constitution void."

EARLY DEVELOPMENTS

After ratification of the Constitution, the First Congress promptly passed the Judiciary Act of 1789, setting up a federal system of district and appellate courts and determining that the Supreme Court would consist of six members. The act, in Section 25, also fortified the Constitution's supremacy clause by granting the Supreme Court authority to hear and decide appeals from state courts in cases where (1) a federal law or treaty was questioned and a state court decided against its validity, (2) a state law was upheld against federal authority, or (3) a litigant claimed a right or privilege under a federal statute, treaty, or the Constitution that was denied by a state.

With that specific grant of authority from Congress, the Supreme Court assumed the arbiter's role of deciding constitutional questions—first in state matters. The Court's first important use of that power against the states, however, provoked a loud outcry and resulted in a constitutional amendment overturning the ruling. The 1793 ruling stemmed from a suit over a debt brought in federal court by two South Carolinians against the state of Georgia. The state argued that the Court had no authority to hear the case, but the Court ruled in *Chisholm v. Georgia* that the suit was properly brought and that Georgia had defaulted.

The ruling "fell upon the country with a profound shock," wrote historian Charles Warren. "The vesting of any such jurisdiction over sovereign states had been expressly disclaimed . . . by the great defenders of the Constitution, during the days of the contest over its ratification."[5] The decision itself was never implemented, and Congress promptly moved to protect the states from suits in federal court by proposing what was to become the Eleventh Amendment. The amendment, ratified by the states in 1798, prohibits a resident of one state from suing another state in a federal court without that state's consent.

The Court's first assumption of the power of judicial review over acts of Congress, by contrast, was undramatic. The 1796 ruling *Hylton v. United States* upheld the validity of a federal tax on carriages. The decision occasioned little comment since it did not overturn the law. Moreover, the Supreme Court initially seemed relatively unimportant alongside the president and Congress. The first chief justice (John Jay) and one of the original associate justices (John Rutledge) left the bench for more attractive opportunities in state government. During the Court's first decade, the 1790s, it decided only about fifty cases.

THE MARSHALL COURT

The rise of the Court's prestige and power came during Marshall's long tenure as chief justice. Marshall, appointed by the Federalist president John Adams shortly before leaving office, "dominated the Court to a degree unmatched by any other justice," writes Ohio State University professor Lawrence Baum.[6] Marshall was sworn in February 4, 1801, the second day of the Court's first term in Washington, the new national capital. He served for thirty-four years, until his death at age seventy-nine, and guided the Court to bold assertions of power that placed it on an equal footing, in fact as well as in name, with the legislative and executive branches.

The most famous decision of the Marshall era, *Marbury v. Madison,* came just two years after he became chief justice. That ruling on February 24, 1803, for the first time struck down an act of Congress as unconstitutional. Ironically, the immediate effect of the decision was to nullify a provision expanding the Court's appellate jurisdiction and to give President Thomas Jefferson, an opponent of Marshall's, a political victory in a dispute over judicial appointments by Adams in his last days in office.

Marshall used the opinion, however, to assert in unmistakable language the Court's power to declare acts of Congress unconstitutional. "It is emphatically the province and duty of the judicial department to say what the law is," Marshall wrote. "[A] law repugnant to the constitution is void," he concluded, "and . . . *courts,* as well as other departments are bound by that instrument." The precedent had been clearly established. Since then, the right of judicial review has gone virtually unchallenged.

Two of Marshall's other opinions are especially noteworthy

MARBURY V. MADISON

The Supreme Court's first ruling striking down an act of Congress as unconstitutional stemmed from a dispute over judicial appointments between the two political factions that formed in the early years of the new national government: the Federalists and the Jeffersonian Republicans. The Federalists had held power under President John Adams following George Washington's two terms as chief executive. But Adams lost his bid for reelection in a four-way contest that ended with a vote by the House of Representatives in 1801 choosing Thomas Jefferson as the next president.

In one of his final acts in office in 1801, Adams filled several newly created judicial posts with loyal Federalists. The commissions were made out and signed, but Adams's secretary of state, John Marshall, failed to deliver some of them before Adams officially left office at midnight, March 3, 1801. Marshall was still serving as secretary of state even though Adams had already appointed him to the Supreme Court as chief justice.

Jefferson accused his predecessor of filling the judiciary with "midnight judges" and ordered his secretary of state, James Madison, not to deliver the commissions. William Marbury, who had been appointed justice of the peace for the District of Columbia, was one of those whose commissions were being withheld. Later that year he went before the Supreme Court, where Marshall now presided, and asked it to issue a judicial order—called a writ of mandamus—to require Madison to hand over the commission. Marshall refused to disqualify himself from the case despite his personal interest in it. In fact, it was Marshall who delivered the opinion for the Court in *Marbury v. Madison* on February 24, 1803.

Marshall agreed that Marbury was entitled to his commission, but explained that the Court had no jurisdiction in the case. In passing the Judiciary Act of 1789, Congress had given the Court so-called original jurisdiction to hear petitions for writs of mandamus without any lower court acting first on the case. But Marshall said the Constitution gave the Supreme Court original jurisdiction only over "cases affecting ambassadors, other public ministers and consuls, and those in which a state shall be party." In other cases the Court was given only appellate jurisdiction. Congress had no power, Marshall concluded, to enlarge the Court's original jurisdiction so that it could hear a case before any other court.

Under the guise of handing his Jeffersonian foes a political victory, Marshall had laid the cornerstone of federal judicial power. This assertion of authority to strike down unconstitutional legislation attracted little comment at the time. The Jeffersonians were critical instead of Marshall's comment that if the Court had jurisdiction, Marbury should have been granted the order he sought. Jefferson wrote a friend years later that Marshall and the other Federalist justices had "intentionally gone out of their way to rule on points unnecessary for the decision, and he regarded it as a deliberate assumption of a right to interfere with his executive functions."[1]

1. Letter of Jefferson to William Johnson, June 12, 1823, cited in Charles Warren, *The Supreme Court in United States History* (Boston: Little, Brown, 1922), vol. 1, 245.

---

in establishing both the Court's and Congress's authority. The first, *McCulloch v. Maryland,* came in 1819 and upheld the constitutionality of Congress's creation of the second Bank of the United States. The ruling barred the state of Maryland from enforcing a tax on the bank, but Marshall first had to contend with the state's argument that Congress had no power under the Constitution to establish the bank. In rejecting the argument, Marshall construed expansively Congress's authority to enact "all Laws which shall be necessary and proper" for the execution of its constitutional functions (Article I, Section 8). "Let the end be legitimate, let it be within the scope of the constitution, and all means which are appropriate, which are plainly adapted to that end, which are not prohibited, but consistent with the letter and spirit of the constitution, are constitutional," he wrote.

Five years later, Marshall laid the basis for Congress's expansive use of its power to regulate interstate commerce. The 1824 decision in *Gibbons v. Ogden* struck down a New York steamboat monopoly law on the ground that it conflicted with a federal coastal licensing law. Marshall explained that power over commerce, including navigation, was "one of the primary objects" in the formation of the new national government. Congress had "complete" power to regulate commerce between the states, he said, although the states retained authority to regulate "completely internal commerce."

THE TANEY COURT

Marshall's death in 1835 gave President Andrew Jackson, who was favorably inclined toward states' rights, an opportunity to put his stamp on the Supreme Court. Jackson's choice for chief justice was his former secretary of the Treasury, Roger B. Taney, who served for nearly three decades until his death in 1864. Under Taney, the Court struggled to define the limits between federal and state regulation of commerce, eventually settling on a doctrine that gave the states more power than Marshall's formulation had recognized. The Court had an even more difficult time with the growing sectional conflict over slavery. The issue resulted in the Court's second decision nullifying an act of Congress: the Dred Scott decision, perhaps the most controversial and criticized ruling in the Court's history.

The Court's 1857 decision *Scott v. Sandford* ruled that Congress had acted unconstitutionally in passing the Missouri Compromise, the 1820 package of laws that had admitted Missouri as a slave state but barred slavery in the territories north of Missouri's southern boundary. Congress had actually repealed the law in 1854 when it passed the Kansas-Nebraska Act, giving newly admitted states the right to decide whether to permit slavery. But the validity of the Missouri Compromise arose in a suit by a slave, Dred Scott, who had been taken by his former master from the slave state of Missouri into territory made free

In the 1857 Dred Scott decision, Chief Justice Roger Taney, shown here, said that Congress had no authority to limit the extension of slavery. The decision aroused great resentment in the North and damaged the Court's reputation.

under the 1820 law. After returning to Missouri, Scott sued to establish his freedom on the ground that his sojourn in free territory had made him a free man. The Missouri Supreme Court held that he had indeed gained his freedom when he was on free soil but had lost it when he returned to a slave state.

At the time Scott sued for his freedom, his master was a citizen of New York; the case could now be considered by a federal court as a controversy between citizens of different states—if Scott were declared a citizen of Missouri. The Supreme Court held that no Negro could be a citizen, and therefore the federal courts had no jurisdiction. Chief Justice Taney went further to assert that Scott was a slave because the Missouri Compromise had been unconstitutional. Taney said Congress had no authority to limit the extension of slavery, although he never said precisely why.

The Dred Scott decision aroused tremendous resentment in the North, especially among members of the newly organized Republican Party whose cardinal tenet was that Congress should abolish slavery in all of the territories. Seventy years later, Charles Evans Hughes, who was later to serve as chief justice himself, called the ruling one of the Court's "self-inflicted wounds."[7] The decision was effectively reversed immediately after the Civil War by the adoption of the Thirteenth and Four-

teenth Amendments, which abolished slavery and guaranteed the rights of citizenship to "all persons born or naturalized in the United States."

RECONSTRUCTION AND REACTION

Congress and the Court came into frequent conflict in the decades following the Civil War. The Court repeatedly used its power to declare acts of the Reconstruction era unconstitutional. The rulings stunted Congress's efforts to implement provisions of the post–Civil War amendments guaranteeing civil rights to the newly emancipated slaves and other African Americans. The Court also initially overturned, but then changed its mind and upheld, laws making paper money legal tender for all debts. In addition, the Court in 1895 blocked Congress from enacting a federal income tax—a decision overturned by the Sixteenth Amendment.

The so-called *Legal Tender Cases* stemmed from Congress's decision during the Civil War to authorize the issuance of paper money or "greenbacks" to finance the war. It refused to hear a case challenging the decision during the war, but then agreed after the war's end to rule on the issue. The case was argued in 1867, reargued in 1868, and decided a full two years later, in 1870. By a 4–3 vote, the Court held that greenbacks could not be used to pay debts contracted before passage of the 1862 legislation. After the appointment of two new justices by President Ulysses S. Grant, the Court agreed to reconsider the issue and then voted 5–4 in 1871 to uphold the law. "The degree of the necessity for any congressional enactment . . . is for consideration in Congress, not here," wrote Justice William Strong, one of Grant's appointees.

The Court proved less supportive of congressional action on other Reconstruction era issues. In 1867—in the first ruling to strike down a law passed by Congress on a 5–4 vote—the Court barred loyalty oaths for former Confederate supporters to practice law or serve in federal office. In succeeding decades, the Court issued five rulings between 1876 and 1906 striking down civil rights laws passed by Congress. The most important of the rulings came in 1883 in five companion cases collectively called the *Civil Rights Cases*. The 8–1 decision struck down provisions of the Civil Rights Act of 1875 that made it a crime for anyone to deny equal access to public accommodations such as hotels, theaters, and railroads on account of race. The Court said the Fourteenth Amendment did not authorize Congress to enact laws against private racial discrimination. Other decisions overturned civil rights provisions aimed at protecting blacks from retaliation by private groups such as the Ku Klux Klan, safeguarding the right to vote as guaranteed by the Fifteenth Amendment, and guaranteeing blacks equal rights with whites to "make and enforce" contracts.

The Court's narrow view of federal powers in the second half of the nineteenth century extended to other areas as well. For example, the Court in 1870 struck down a congressional ban on the sale of inflammable naphtha as "a mere police regulation." The disputes became more dramatic as Congress began responding to pressure from populists, progressives, and organized labor to take a more active role in regulating social and economic affairs. In the first of many such clashes, the Court in 1895 overturned a newly enacted federal income tax on the ground that it violated the constitutional requirement that taxes be apportioned among the states according to population. Public opinion was strongly opposed to the ruling, but Congress and the states needed eighteen years to complete ratification of the Sixteenth Amendment overturning the decision.

THE *LOCHNER* ERA

The income tax ruling was one of many probusiness rulings the Court issued overturning on constitutional grounds laws passed by Congress or the states during a conservative era that stretched from the 1880s to the mid-1930s. The period is often called "the *Lochner* era," after a 1905 decision, *Lochner v. New York,* striking down a state law setting hours for bakers. Most of the justices of this era—many of them previously lawyers for railroads or corporations—brought to the Court a deep suspicion of government regulation of business. The Court held firmly to those views, despite some spirited dissenters in its ranks, until President Franklin D. Roosevelt was able to forge a more liberal majority in his second and third terms in office.

Although the *Lochner* case concerned a state rather than a federal law, the Court's rationale cast doubt on the ability of either Congress or the states to regulate economic affairs. The ruling struck down a law prohibiting bakeries from requiring employees to work more than sixty hours a week or ten hours a day. The law, the Court said in a 5–4 decision, interfered with the freedom of contract of the bakeries as well as that of the bakery employees. In a famous dissent, Justice Oliver Wendell Holmes Jr. complained, "The Constitution is not intended to embody a particular economic theory."

The *Lochner* decision was implicitly overruled in a 1917 decision that upheld a somewhat similar Oregon law. But the Court's solicitude for property rights remained strong and produced a dramatic clash with Congress over the issue of child labor. Twice the Court struck down acts of Congress to restrict use of child labor in plants and factories. In the first of the decisions, *Hammer v. Dagenhart,* the Court in 1918 held that a law prohibiting interstate shipment of goods produced with child labor was unconstitutional because Congress was attempting to regulate manufacturing rather than commerce. Congress responded the same year with a 10 percent excise tax on goods manufactured with child labor, but the Court struck down that law too in a 1922 decision that termed the law an infringement on states' rights. Congress sought to overturn the rulings with a constitutional amendment, but it fell short of ratification.

The Court's concern for property rights reached its high-water mark during the chief justiceship of William Howard Taft (1921–1930). The Taft Court declared twenty-two acts of Congress unconstitutional, including a minimum wage for the District of Columbia, worker compensation laws for sailors and other maritime workers, and a variety of business tax provi-

sions. Taft died in 1930 and was succeeded by Charles Evans Hughes, who had previously served as an associate justice from 1910 to 1916. Hughes had a greater concern for civil liberties than did other conservatives, but he shared Taft's abhorrence of government intervention in the economy. The result was continuing conflicts with Congress and with President Roosevelt over economic measures aimed at lifting the country out of the Great Depression.

THE NEW DEAL AND THE COURT

The clashes over the federal government's power in economic affairs reached the point of constitutional crisis in the 1930s. President Roosevelt's New Deal programs included an array of economic measures passed by a largely supportive Congress in an effort to get the nation's economy growing again. The Court, however, viewed the measures with deep suspicion. In a period of fewer than two years, the Court in 1935–1936 struck down eleven laws as unconstitutional. Frustrated, Roosevelt in 1937 proposed a so-called Court-packing plan to try to win the right to make additional appointments to the Court. Congress rejected the proposal, but deaths and retirements over the next four years gave Roosevelt the opportunity anyway to give the Court a majority more favorably inclined toward congressional intervention in economic affairs.

The New Deal laws struck down by the Court included such key parts of Roosevelt's program as the National Industrial Recovery, Agricultural Adjustment, and Bituminous Coal Conservation Acts. In one of the first and most important of the decisions, *Schechter Poultry Corp. v. United States,* the Court on May 27, 1935, struck down the industry code provisions of the National Industrial Recovery Act on the ground that they amounted to an unconstitutional delegation of power by Congress to private industry bodies. The agricultural law, which authorized payments to farmers for keeping land out of production, was struck down in January 1936 as an improper use of Congress's spending powers to regulate manufacturing. The coal mining law was similarly held unconstitutional in May 1936 as an improper regulation of manufacturing rather than commerce.

The decisions were politically unpopular, but the Court insisted that it was merely enforcing the constitutional limits on Congress's powers. After his landslide reelection, however, Roosevelt in 1937 proposed a judicial "reorganization" measure to increase the number of justices to as many as fifteen by creating one new seat for each justice who, upon reaching the age of seventy, declined to retire. Congress shelved the plan amidst a public outcry over the evident attempt to curb the Court's independence. But with the proposal dormant, the Court itself switched directions in a series of decisions upholding New Deal measures between late March and late May 1937. Hughes and Justice Owen Roberts joined with three dissenters from the earlier cases to form 5–4 majorities for upholding state minimum wage laws and three federal acts: the National Labor Relations Act, a federal unemployment compensation law, and the Social Security Act for old age benefits.

In addition, Justice Willis Van Devanter, a New Deal opponent, announced his retirement on May 18, giving Roosevelt his first appointment to the Court. He selected a strong New Dealer from Congress, Alabama senator Hugo L. Black. By 1941 retirements and deaths allowed Roosevelt to name six other justices and to elevate a New Deal supporter, Harlan Fiske Stone, to chief justice. After 1937 the Court gradually repudiated earlier limits it had placed on Congress's exercise of the commerce power and discarded the dual federalism concept that federal power was limited by states' rights.

INDIVIDUAL RIGHTS

The Rooseveltian transformation of the Court—sometimes called the Revolution of 1937—appeared to have firmly established a broad construction of congressional powers to regulate economic affairs. At the same time, the Court began to show greater concern for individual rights in civil rights and civil liberties cases, most dramatically in the racial desegregation and criminal procedure decisions under Chief Justice Earl Warren (1953–1969). The most dramatic of these decisions involved state rather than federal laws, but the Warren Court also struck down many laws passed by Congress as violations of individual rights. Moreover, the Court continued to closely scrutinize federal laws challenged on individual rights grounds under Warren's more conservative successor as chief justice, Warren E. Burger.

Congress and the Court clashed on the issue of national security. Congress and the executive branch established a web of antisubversive laws and regulations at the beginning of the cold war following World War II. In the 1950s the Court generally upheld these laws, but a solid liberal majority struck down several provisions in the 1960s as violations of freedom of speech and association. Among the laws invalidated was one that subjected Communist Party members to prosecution for failing to register as members of a subversive organization.

The Warren Court's civil rights revolution began with its 1954 school desegregation decision, *Brown v. Board of Education.* The ruling came in companion cases involving racially segregated public school systems in four states. In a less well-known companion case, *Bolling v. Sharpe,* the Court on the same day invalidated school segregation laws passed by Congress since 1862 for the District of Columbia. The Court held that the due process clause of the Fifth Amendment included an implicit equal protection requirement applicable to federal legislation just as the Fourteenth Amendment's equal protection clause applied to the states. The Burger Court later used the principle as the basis for striking down provisions of some federal benefit programs as illegal sex discrimination.

The Warren Court's criminal procedure rulings of the 1960s included several that struck down federal laws. It overturned on self-incrimination grounds tax law provisions used in prosecuting gambling, firearms, and drug offenses. In 1968 the Court also invalidated the death penalty provision of the Lindbergh Kidnapping Act, on the ground that it penalized the right to jury trial by allowing imposition of the death penalty only if

The Supreme Court came under congressional fire during the tenure of Chief Justice Earl Warren for its decisions on school desegregation, school prayer, and other issues.

recommended by a jury. Later, the Burger Court in 1978 invalidated a portion of the Occupational Safety and Health Act allowing warrantless inspections of workplaces.

Congress was also affected by another of the Warren Court's expansions of individual rights: the so-called one-person, one-vote reapportionment and redistricting rulings. In a series of rulings beginning with the 1962 decision *Baker v. Carr,* the Court held that federal courts could hear challenges to malapportioned legislative districts and that states had to create roughly equal districts for both chambers of their legislatures. The rulings primarily affected state legislatures, but the Court under both Warren and Burger also required state legislatures to draw congressional districts with close to equal populations. In addition, the Burger Court in 1986 also ruled that federal courts could entertain challenges to political gerrymandering even if legislative districts met the one-person, one-vote test. But the Court upheld the state legislative districting plan challenged in the case, *Davis v. Bandemer,* and did not delve further into redistricting issues until a new issue presented itself in the 1990s: racial gerrymandering.

Both the Warren and Burger Courts struck down a handful of congressional enactments on free speech grounds. Some of the laws were relatively minor—for example, provisions barring demonstrations on the Capitol grounds (1972) or in front of the Supreme Court (1983). But the Court created a major expansion of free speech doctrine—and left Congress with a major political headache—with a 1976 ruling striking down parts of a newly enacted campaign finance reform law. The decision in *Buckley v. Valeo* struck down limits on campaign spending and on the amount of money that candidates could contribute to their own campaigns. The ruling sharply limited Congress's ability to fashion new campaign finance legislation, a politically treacherous issue even without constitutional constraints.

SEPARATION OF POWERS

The Burger Court took a more limited view of the judiciary's role in some areas than the Warren Court had done, but it still handed down controversial decisions in areas such as abortion, women's rights, and freedom of speech that often brought it into conflict with Congress. The sharpest conflicts with Congress, however, came in an area that had received little attention since the New Deal: separation of powers. In the most important of these rulings, the Court in 1983 ruled unconstitutional a device known as the "legislative veto" that Congress had used to control decisions by regulatory and executive branch agencies. The decision swept aside provisions that Congress had added over time to as many as two hundred laws.

Three years later, the Court cited separation of powers principles in striking down part of another congressional enactment: the Gramm-Rudman-Hollings balanced budget act.

The legislative veto decision, *Immigration and Naturalization Service v. Chadha*, ruled unconstitutional a practice that allowed one house of Congress—or sometimes a single committee—to veto new regulations by regulatory agencies or executive branch departments. The practice dated to the 1930s and had been used with increasing frequency in the antiregulatory climate of the late 1970s. Presidents had challenged the practice as a violation of separation of powers, but Congress paid no attention. The issue reached the Supreme Court when an alien facing deportation challenged the one-house legislative veto that Congress had included in the 1952 Immigration and Nationality Act.

By a 7–2 vote, the Court held that the practice violated the principle of "bicameralism"—the requirement that Congress can make law only by passing identical bills in each chamber, the House and the Senate. The one-house veto, Chief Justice Burger wrote, violated "the Framers' decision that the legislative power of the Federal Government be exercised in accord with a single, finely wrought and exhaustively considered, procedure." Burger acknowledged that legislative vetoes might be convenient for Congress but said that "convenience and efficiency are not the primary objects—or the hallmarks—of democratic government." Four years later, the Court limited the impact of the decision somewhat by ruling that in most cases elimination of a legislative veto would not require nullification of the underlying law containing the provision.

The ruling on the budget law, *Bowsher v. Synar* (1986), nulli-

fied one part of a law that Congress had passed to try to control growing budget deficits. The law gave the comptroller general, an officer of Congress, power to specify spending reductions that the president was to carry out. That provision, the Court ruled, impermissibly infringed on the president's power to execute the laws.

The Burger Court also breathed new life into states' rights issues, though the rulings had limited impact. The Warren Court had rebuffed states' rights challenges to federal laws even when Congress legislated in areas traditionally regulated by the states. In one such case, the Warren Court upheld the Voting Rights Act of 1965, which established federal oversight of voting practices in states with a history of racial discrimination. But in 1970 the Court held unconstitutional a new law lowering the voting age in state elections. The decision was rendered moot the next year, however, by ratification of the Twenty-sixth Amendment lowering the voting age to eighteen in federal and state elections. In a second decision, the Court in 1976 held by a 5–4 vote in *National League of Cities v. Usery* that Congress had exceeded its power to regulate commerce when it placed state and local government employees under federal wage and hour laws. But in 1985 the Court reversed itself on the issue and upheld federal coverage for state and local workers when one of the justices in the majority in the earlier decision, Harry A. Blackmun, changed his position.

THE REHNQUIST COURT

President Ronald Reagan's selection of William Rehnquist, an avowed believer in judicial restraint, to become chief justice in 1986 seemingly presaged an era of increasing deference to Congress. But the conservative majority forged by later appointments by Reagan and his Republican successor, George Bush, proved to have an activist streak that created new areas of conflict with Congress. In the 1990s the Court invoked states' rights and a limited view of Congress's commerce clause powers to strike down several congressional enactments. In addition, the Court unsettled congressional redistricting with a series of rulings that limited state legislators' discretion to consider race in drawing district lines.

The Rehnquist Court also acted, however, to uphold congressional prerogatives in two important cases that divided the lawmakers themselves. In 1995 the Court struck down state laws setting term limits for members of Congress. Term limits could be imposed only by a constitutional amendment, the Court ruled in *U.S. Term Limits, Inc. v. Thornton*. Three years later, the Court overturned a law, the Line Item Veto Act, that Congress itself had passed to give the president the power to delete individual items from congressional spending measures. The act violated the Constitution, Justice John Paul Stevens wrote in *Clinton v. City of New York*, by giving the president "the unilateral power to change the text of duly enacted statutes."

In its earliest years, the Rehnquist Court did side with Congress in several closely watched constitutional confrontations. It upheld laws providing for preventive detention of some defen-

President Ronald Reagan announces the retirement of Chief Justice Warren Burger, right, in 1986. He nominated Justice William Rehnquist, second from right, to the post of chief justice and Antonin Scalia, left, as associate justice.

dants and barring abortion counseling by organizations receiving federal funds. The Court also upheld two congressional enactments that were challenged on separation of powers grounds. In *Morrison v. Olson* (1988) the Court rejected a constitutional challenge to the independent counsel law. The next year, in *Mistretta v. United States*, it upheld the creation of the federal Sentencing Commission with power to set binding sentencing guidelines for federal criminal defendants.

The redistricting decisions came in suits brought mostly by white voters challenging plans approved by state legislatures under pressure from the U.S. Justice Department. The plans concentrated African American or Hispanic voters in some House districts to increase the chances of the election of minority representatives. In the first of the cases, *Shaw v. Reno*, the Court in 1993 first held that such redistricting schemes could violate the equal protection rights of white voters. Two years later, in *Miller v. Johnson*, the Court refined the ruling to hold that a state could not use race as "the predominant factor" in drawing district lines unless it had a compelling interest for doing so and the districts were narrowly tailored to serve that interest. The rulings forced legislatures in three states—Georgia, North Carolina, and Texas—to redraw district lines and spawned challenges in several other states that were ruled on by lower federal courts.

Several decisions in the mid-1990s raised doubts about Congress's power to legislate in areas touching on traditional state prerogatives. In one, *Lopez v. United States* (1995), the Court struck down a law making it a federal crime to possess a firearm within one thousand feet of a school. Writing for the Court, Rehnquist said that upholding the law "would bid fair to convert congressional authority under the Commerce Clause to a general police power of the sort retained by the States." Two years later, the Court nullified part of the Brady handgun control law requiring local law enforcement agencies to conduct background checks on prospective gun purchasers. "[T]he Federal Government may not compel the States to implement, by legislative or executive action, federal regulatory programs," Justice Antonin Scalia wrote. Both decisions came on 5–4 votes; in his dissent in the *Lopez* decision, Justice Stephen G. Breyer said the ruling would thwart Congress's ability "to enact criminal laws aimed at criminal behavior that . . . seriously threatens the economic as well as the social well-being of Americans."

In a series of decisions, the Court also acted to limit Congress's ability to authorize private suits against state governments by people seeking damages for violations of federal laws. In the first of the decisions, *Seminole Tribe of Florida v. Florida* (1996), the Court ruled that Congress could not use its general legislative powers to authorize damage suits against state governments in federal courts. Three years later, in *Alden v. Maine,* the Court said Congress also could not authorize suits to enforce federal laws in a state's own court system. In two other cases decided the same day, the Court also limited Congress's power to provide for private suits against state governments to enforce the due process and equal protection provisions of the Fourteenth Amendment. All four cases were decided by 5–4 votes.

The Court also acted to safeguard its own prerogatives from congressional infringement by striking down a law that Congress passed to try to overturn a recent Court ruling on religious freedom. The 1993 law, the Religious Freedom Restoration Act, made it easier for religious groups to be exempted from state laws that interfered with their religious practices. The act was aimed at overturning the Court's 1990 decision that generally barred such exemptions. But the Court in 1997 said Congress had gone beyond its power by attempting to make "a substantive change in constitutional provisions" as determined by the Court.

Writing for the Court in *City of Boerne v. Flores,* Justice Anthony M. Kennedy invoked Marshall's famous precedent in defending the judiciary's authority. "[T]he courts retain the power, as they have since *Marbury v. Madison,* to determine if Congress has exceeded its authority under the Constitution," Kennedy said.

Congress vs. the Court

The Constitution gives Congress some significant powers to use to influence the course of the Supreme Court's decisions or to overturn a particular ruling. The Senate's power to confirm justices determines who actually sits on the Supreme Court, and Congress has the ultimate power to remove a justice through impeachment. Congress has the authority under the Constitution to make "exceptions" to the Court's appellate jurisdiction (Article III, Section 2), and it can also impose other institutional changes, such as altering the size of the Court. Finally, Congress's ordinary lawmaking powers allow it to overturn a Court decision based on statutory grounds or to propose—for ratification by the states—a constitutional amendment to overturn a ruling on a constitutional issue.

THE CONFIRMATION PROCESS

The Senate first used its constitutional "advice and consent" power to reject a presidential nominee for the Supreme Court during George Washington's presidency and defeated a total of twenty-two nominations before 1900. Presidents had greater success with Supreme Court nominations in the twentieth century. The Senate turned down only six nominees in the 1900s. But the confirmation process has become more rigorous. Supreme Court nominees now are expected to appear before a Senate committee and face close questioning on their personal and professional qualifications and their legal philosophy.

Partisan politics underlay most of the Senate's rejections of Supreme Court nominees before 1900. Washington's selection of John Rutledge to be chief justice in 1795 was defeated because of Rutledge's criticism of the Jay Treaty with England. Senate Whigs defeated Andrew Jackson's choice of his secretary of the Treasury, Roger B. Taney, to be associate justice in 1835 and tried but failed to block Taney again when Jackson chose him as chief justice. On the eve of the Civil War, the Senate defeated President James Buchanan's nomination of Jeremiah S. Black because his views on slavery were unacceptable to northern Republicans. After the Civil War, the Senate defeated Ulysses S. Grant's choice of Ebenezer R. Hoar because Hoar had supported civil service reform and opposed the impeachment of President Andrew Johnson.

Legal philosophy became a more important factor in the Senate's consideration of Supreme Court nominees in the twentieth century. Four of the six unsuccessful nominees in the 1900s failed in part because of the Senate's disagreement with the nominees' views on legal issues. Successful nominees have also encountered close questioning and in some cases forceful opposition because of their legal philosophies. In addition, the Senate has given greater scrutiny to nominees' records in public life. Two of the Court's members in the 1990s—Chief Justice William H. Rehnquist and Justice Clarence Thomas—were narrowly confirmed only after senators vigorously cross-examined them about allegations of improper conduct. Rehnquist was charged, among other things, with seeking to discourage African Americans from voting as a Republican campaign worker in Arizona; Thomas underwent a tumultuous confirmation hearing in 1991 over charges of sexual harassment of a former aide.

The pattern of ideological battlegrounds was set in the early decades of the century. Woodrow Wilson's 1916 nomination of Louis D. Brandeis, a longtime consumer and labor activist and the first Jew to be chosen for the Court, was strongly opposed by business interests in a campaign tinged with anti-Semitism; he was nonetheless confirmed, 47 to 22. In 1930 progressive-minded senators opposed President Herbert Hoover's selection of Charles Evans Hughes as chief justice on the ground that he was too conservative; Hughes was confirmed, 52 to 26.

The current pattern of intensive hearings on Supreme Court nominees developed more slowly. Harlan Fiske Stone was the first Supreme Court nominee to testify before a Senate committee. He appeared in 1925 to answer questions about his role as attorney general in a criminal investigation of a member of the Senate and went on to win confirmation, 71 to 6. Felix Frankfurter, a Harvard Law School professor, was persuaded to go before a Senate committee in 1939 to answer questions about his membership in the American Civil Liberties Union. As late as the 1950s, hearings were typically perfunctory, however. Only in the 1960s, with the nominations of Abe Fortas and Thurgood Marshall, did confirmation hearings take on their current character of a close and often critical examination of the nominee's record and views.

Interest groups have also played an increasingly important part in the nomination process. The first of the unsuccessful nominees in the twentieth century, John J. Parker, was rejected 39 to 41 in 1930 after a campaign waged by the American Federation of Labor and the National Association for the Advancement of Colored People, which accused him of insensitivity to racial and labor issues as a federal judge in North Carolina. An array of liberal interest groups contributed to the defeat of three others: successive nominees Clement F. Haynsworth and G. Harrold Carswell in 1969 and 1970, and Robert Bork in 1987. Conservative advocacy groups played a part in Fortas's rejection as chief justice in 1968 and then, following the Bork nomination, rallied to help Thomas win confirmation in 1991.

Fortas, already an associate justice, was nominated by Lyndon Johnson in 1968 to succeed Earl Warren as chief justice; Johnson named Homer Thornberry, a federal judge in Texas, to take Fortas's seat. Fortas was questioned about his support of liberal Warren Court decisions. In addition, Republicans hoped a GOP president could appoint the next chief justice. The nomination was withdrawn when supporters failed to break a Republican–southern Democratic filibuster. Warren then stayed on as chief justice for another year, so there was no vacancy on the Court for Thornberry to fill. And Fortas resigned in 1969 amidst pressure from Republican lawmakers over ethics charges.

Haynsworth, a federal appeals court judge in North Carolina, was President Richard M. Nixon's second Supreme Court nominee in 1969, following his selection of Warren E. Burger as chief justice. Senate Democrats, retaliating for the treatment of Fortas, accused Haynsworth of failing to disqualify himself from cases in which he had a financial interest; many also regarded him as too conservative on legal issues. He was defeated in November 1969 by a vote of 45 to 55. Nixon then turned to Carswell, a federal trial judge in Florida with a less distinguished record than Haynsworth's. He went down to defeat, 45 to 51, after senators of both parties questioned his legal credentials and evidence emerged of his opposition to racial integration as a lawyer and judge.

Bork, a federal appeals court judge with a strongly conservative legal ideology, was nominated to the Court in 1987 by President Ronald Reagan, just one year after Rehnquist had survived a bruising confirmation hearing to gain elevation to chief justice, 65 to 33. Senate Democrats, fearful that Bork could help cement a conservative majority on the Court, depicted his views as out of the mainstream and accused him of a "confirmation conversion" when he softened them somewhat in his testimony. He was defeated 42 to 58, with six Republicans joining all but two Democrats in voting against him. Reagan next turned to another federal appeals court judge, Douglas H. Ginsburg, but he withdrew before being formally nominated when it was disclosed that he had smoked marijuana while a law school professor.

Thomas, a prominent black conservative serving on the federal appeals court in Washington, faced a similar ideological fight when President George Bush nominated him to the Court in 1991. Democrats and liberal interest groups again feared his confirmation would give conservatives a solid majority on the Court; in particular, abortion rights groups viewed him as a possible fifth vote for overturning the landmark *Roe v. Wade* (1973) decision, which recognized a woman's constitutional right to an abortion. With Thomas steadfastly refusing to answer questions about his views on abortion, the Senate Judiciary Committee sent the nomination to the floor without a recommendation on a 7 to 7 tie vote.

The committee was forced to reopen hearings, however, when news reports disclosed that a law professor, Anita Hill, had accused Thomas of sexually harassing her while she worked for him at the Equal Employment Opportunity Commission in the early 1980s. Hill repeated her accusations under oath, followed by Thomas, who vehemently denied the charges and denounced the hearing as a "high-tech lynching." With no conclusive resolution of the charges, senators appeared to hold to their previous views on the nomination; Thomas won confirmation, 52 to 48, with strong support from Republicans and scattered votes from Democrats, mostly from southern states with large African American populations.

In the wake of the Thomas hearings, senators of both parties voiced hopes that the confirmation process could be less acrimonious. Hearings in 1993 and 1994 for President Bill Clinton's two nominees, Ruth Bader Ginsburg and Stephen G. Breyer, proved to be less contentious. But senators questioned both about their legal views, and Breyer was examined about a potential conflict of interest in his ownership of stock in the British insurance syndicate Lloyd's of London. Ginsburg was confirmed by a vote of 96 to 3; Breyer, after pledging to divest himself of his holdings in insurance companies, was also confirmed, 87 to 9.

IMPEACHMENT OF JUSTICES

A Supreme Court justice can be removed from office only through impeachment by the House of Representatives and conviction by two-thirds of the Senate. Only one justice, Samuel Chase, has ever been impeached; he was acquitted of charges of injudicious behavior in a politically charged Senate trial in 1805. Two other justices have faced serious attempts at impeachment. Abe Fortas resigned in 1969 while some House members were considering an impeachment inquiry into charges of financial misconduct. And William O. Douglas was the subject of two House impeachment investigations, in 1953 and 1970, but both ended with no charges. In addition, Chief Justice Earl Warren faced scattered calls for his impeachment during the 1950s and 1960s, but the House never opened a formal inquiry.

Chase, a radical Federalist appointed to the Supreme Court in 1796, became the target of a Republican impeachment attempt because of his openly partisan conduct on and off the bench, including his handling of the sedition trial of a Republican printer, his campaigning for President John Adams's reelection in 1800, and his criticism of President Thomas Jefferson's administration to a Baltimore grand jury in 1803. After Jefferson complained of the grand jury speech, the Republican-controlled House voted 73 to 32 along party lines to impeach Chase in 1804. Republicans held twenty-five of thirty-four seats in the Senate—more than enough for conviction. But Chase was acquitted of all charges. The closest vote concerned the Baltimore grand jury speech: eighteen to sixteen for conviction. After the trial, President Jefferson criticized impeachment as "a farce which will not be tried again."[8] Today, scholars view Chase's acquittal as an important milestone in protecting the Court from partisan attacks.

Fortas resigned May 14, 1969, just ten days after *Life* magazine reported that in January 1966—five months after his appointment to the Court—Fortas had accepted $20,000 from a family foundation established by Louis E. Wolfson, a multimillionaire industrialist, as an adviser to the foundation. Later in 1966 Wolfson was indicted and subsequently convicted of selling unregistered securities. According to the magazine, Fortas returned the money to the foundation in December 1966 and severed his connection with it.

Fortas said he did not consider the money an inducement to influence the Wolfson case. But the statement did not reassure many members of Congress. On May 11, Rep. H. R. Gross, R-Iowa, prepared articles of impeachment against Fortas to present to the House if he did not resign. Two days later, Rep. Clark MacGregor, R-Minn.—apparently with the Nixon administration's blessing—proposed that the Judiciary Committee investigate the matter. The following day Fortas submitted his resignation to Nixon. In a letter of explanation to Chief Justice Warren, Fortas said he had done nothing wrong but that the controversy would "adversely affect the work and position of the Court."

The first impeachment attempt against Douglas stemmed from his decision on June 17, 1953, to stay the execution of convicted atomic spies Julius and Ethel Rosenberg. A House member introduced a resolution of impeachment the next day, but the issue dissipated when the full Court overturned Douglas's action one day after that. The second attempt, in 1970, was led by Rep. Gerald R. Ford of Michigan, the House Republican leader, and followed shortly after the two rejections of President Nixon's nominees to the Court in 1969 and 1970.

Ford brought three charges against Douglas. The most serious was that the justice had assisted as a paid adviser in the establishment of a foundation by an industrialist with gambling interests; the help, Ford charged, amounted to unauthorized practice of law. In addition, Ford complained that Douglas had failed to disqualify himself from an obscenity case involving a publisher of a magazine that had paid Douglas $350 the previous year for an article he had written. Ford also asserted that Douglas's book *Points of Rebellion* could be construed as advocating the violent overthrow of the existing political order. After months of hearings and deliberations, a special House subcommittee adopted a formal report by a 3 to 1 vote saying that Douglas had done nothing unethical or illegal.

Court-Curbing Proposals

Congressional critics of the Supreme Court throughout history have accused the Court of usurping its own lawmaking powers. The early Anti-Federalists (or Jeffersonians) accused the Court of nullifying the Constitution by strengthening federal power at the expense of the states. Democrats more than a century later accused the Court of attempting to impose its own economic views by striking down the New Deal recovery program. In more recent times, critics of the Warren Court contended that its sweeping decisions were exercises in lawmaking, while some Rehnquist Court decisions have been denounced as improperly infringing on Congress's legislative powers under the Constitution.

Many of these movements resulted in congressional efforts to curb the Court's power. Congress has considered a variety of bills or proposed constitutional amendments to require that the Court muster more than a majority vote to declare a law unconstitutional, to allow the removal of a justice if both Congress and the president agree to such action, and to deny the Court jurisdiction to hear certain types of cases. The only proposals to be adopted, however, have been limited ones—such as those changing the size of the Court, delaying the opening of the Court's term, or, in one instance, removing its authority to hear appeals in one category of cases.

The first congressional move against the Court came in 1802, when a newly elected Congress, dominated by Jeffersonians, abolished sixteen federal circuit court judgeships created the previous year by a Federalist-controlled Congress and filled by appointees of President John Adams shortly before he left office. To delay Supreme Court decisions in several controversial cases, including at least one challenging the abolition of the new judgeships, Congress enacted legislation postponing the Court's term for fourteen months, until February 1803. When the Court did rule, it upheld the power of Congress to abolish the new courts.

Other attempts to curb the Federalist bench were less successful, including the Jeffersonians' failure to remove Justice Samuel Chase through impeachment in 1805. Two years later, the Jeffersonians were unable to obtain support for a constitutional amendment to limit the tenure of federal judges and let the president, upon a two-thirds vote of each house, remove them. In 1831 congressional Democrats (who evolved from the old Jeffersonians) tried unsuccessfully to repeal Section 25 of the Judiciary Act of 1789, which authorized the Supreme Court to review state court judgments, and to initiate a constitutional amendment to limit the tenure of federal judges.

After the Civil War, a Republican-controlled Congress that sought to remove President Andrew Johnson from office kept him from appointing any justices by reducing the Court's size from ten to seven members as vacancies occurred. Once Johnson left office, Congress raised the membership to nine, the size it has since remained.

President Franklin D. Roosevelt is lampooned for trying to push his Court-packing plan through Congress in 1937.

Congress engaged in a more direct attack on the Court's powers during Johnson's presidency by enacting legislation to remove the Court's jurisdiction to review certain writs of habeas corpus. The issue arose after the Court heard arguments from an anti-Reconstruction newspaper editor in Mississippi, William H. McCardle, challenging his detention by the state's military government on charges of disturbing the peace. To try to avert a decision on the legality of the military government in the former Confederate states, Congress passed a law to remove the Court's appellate jurisdiction in habeas corpus cases and specifically to prohibit the Court from acting on any pending appeals. The Court, after hearing arguments on the validity of the law, upheld the act in 1869 and dismissed McCardle's appeal. (*Ex parte McCardle*) Congress later reinstated the Court's jurisdiction over habeas corpus cases.

Other congressional attacks on the Court came in the early decades of this century from critics of its decisions protecting property rights. In 1923 Sen. William E. Borah, R-Idaho, introduced a bill to require concurrence by seven of the nine justices to invalidate an act of Congress. The next year Sen. Robert M. La Follette, R-Wis., proposed a constitutional amendment pro-

viding that a statute once struck down by the Supreme Court could be declared constitutional and immune from further Court consideration by a two-thirds majority of both houses of Congress. Neither the Borah bill nor the La Follette proposal won strong support.

Congress, in fact, helped preserve the Court's independence in 1937 when it shelved Franklin Roosevelt's "Court-packing" proposal. Roosevelt's bill would have authorized additional appointments to the Court for each justice over the age of seventy. The press, public, and Congress itself responded with strong opposition to Roosevelt's transparent attack on the Court's prerogatives. The fate of the proposal was sealed after Chief Justice Hughes sent Congress a letter stating that the Court was "fully abreast of its work" and that the addition of new justices would actually slow rather than speed the Court's work.

A new era of tension between Congress and the Court began with the Warren Court's period of judicial activism in the 1950s and 1960s. It drew congressional criticism for rulings limiting the scope of congressional internal security investigations, outlawing school segregation and mandatory school prayer, requiring reapportionment of state legislatures, and enlarging the rights of criminal suspects. The rulings provoked repeated attempts in Congress to curb the Court's power or overturn the rulings directly.

One Court-stripping proposal was offered in 1957 by Sen. William E. Jenner, R-Ind. Jenner's bill would have removed the Court's jurisdiction over five categories of cases, including those involving congressional investigations and federal or state antisubversive laws. The bill drew support from Republicans as well as southern Democrats opposed to the Court's school desegregation decisions. To try to improve its chances for passage, Jenner softened the bill a year later to bar jurisdiction only in one limited area and to merely overturn the Court's rulings in others. The revised bill reached the Senate floor in August 1958 but was killed by a tabling motion, 49 to 41.

The school prayer decisions in 1962 and 1963 touched off congressional opposition that persisted into the 1990s. After constitutional amendments to overturn the rulings failed, some lawmakers offered instead bills to limit the federal courts' power to hear such cases. Court-stripping bills reached the Senate floor four times between 1976 and 1985 but gained majority support only once, in 1979. The measure did not win House approval.

The reapportionment and criminal procedure rulings of the 1960s also prompted a variety of efforts to overturn the decisions by legislation or constitutional amendment. In addition, Congress demonstrated its displeasure with the Court in 1964 by reducing a planned pay increase for the justices from $7,500 to $4,500.

Criticism of the Court abated somewhat after Warren retired in 1969 and was replaced by Burger. But the Burger Court soon drew fire from Capitol Hill for its decisions upholding the use of busing for school desegregation in 1970 and guaranteeing women a right of abortion in 1973. Congressional critics of abortion and busing tried—as had school prayer proponents earlier—to overturn the decisions with constitutional amendments. The Senate blocked an antiabortion amendment in 1976, and the House defeated an antibusing amendment in 1979. Opponents of busing and abortion then turned to Court-stripping legislation but foundered amidst disagreement over Congress's powers to limit the Court's jurisdiction.

The various efforts for Court-stripping proposals continued through the early 1980s, but they were strongly opposed by, among others, the American Bar Association and the Conference of Chief Justices, a group including all fifty state chief justices. The chief justices described the proposals in January 1982 as "a hazardous experiment with the vulnerable fabric of the nation's judicial system." Stripping the Supreme Court of jurisdiction over certain subjects, the state chief justices warned, would result in "divergence in state court decisions, and thus the United States Constitution would mean something different in each of the fifty states."

The Rehnquist Court drew criticism from some lawmakers, advocacy groups, and legal scholars for some of its decisions in the 1990s striking down acts of Congress as going beyond its legislative powers. None of the rulings prompted efforts to curb the Court's jurisdiction, however—in part because Republicans controlled both houses of Congress after 1994 and generally shared the Rehnquist Court's goal of curbing federal power in favor of the states.

Reversing the Court

Congress and the states have succeeded only four times in many attempts to ratify constitutional amendments to overturn Supreme Court decisions. The failed efforts include recent attempts to overturn or limit some of the Court's most controversial rulings in such areas as abortion, school prayer, and reapportionment. Congress can act on its own, however, to reverse or circumvent the effect of a Supreme Court decision based on statutory grounds by passing a new law or amending an existing statute. The Court retains the authority, though, to interpret any new law or constitutional amendment. Typically, the Court bows to the will of Congress, but in some cases its rulings have either thwarted Congress's goals or over the years presented Congress with unintended and unanticipated results.

CONSTITUTIONAL AMENDMENTS

The first constitutional amendment overturning a Supreme Court decision came in the United States' first decade under the new Constitution and buttressed the powers of the states against those of the national government. The Court, ruling in a case called *Chisholm v. Georgia* (1793), upheld the authority of federal courts to hear a suit brought by two South Carolinians against the state of Georgia over a debt. States saw the ruling as an infringement of their once sovereign status. A year later, the House and the Senate overwhelmingly approved what was to become the Eleventh Amendment. The amendment, ratified in 1795, denied federal courts jurisdiction over "any suit in law or equity, commenced or prosecuted against one of the United States by Citizens of another State, or by Citizens or Subjects of any Foreign State."

The amendment emerged in the 1990s as a potentially significant barrier to Congress's power to give private citizens the power to sue states as parts of federal regulatory schemes. The Court in 1989 narrowly upheld a citizen suit provision in a federal toxic waste cleanup statute. But in 1996 the Court overturned that decision and held, in *Seminole Tribe of Florida v. Florida,* that Congress could not authorize private suits against states even to enforce rights granted by federal law.

Congress acted to overturn two important Supreme Court decisions on the Fourteenth Amendment, ratified in 1868, three years after the end of the Civil War. The amendment effectively overturned the Court's infamous Dred Scott ruling, which had denied citizenship to African Americans. All persons "born or naturalized in the United States" are citizens of the United States and of the states where they reside, the amendment stated. In

The Supreme Court in the mid-1990s. From left to right: Clarence Thomas, Antonin Scalia, Sandra Day O'Connor, Anthony M. Kennedy, David H. Souter, Stephen G. Breyer, John Paul Stevens, William H. Rehnquist, and Ruth Bader Ginsburg.

addition, the amendment provided that states could not pass any law to "abridge the privileges and immunities" of any citizen, "deprive any person of life, liberty, or property, without due process of law," or "deny to any person . . . the equal protection of the laws." That provision overturned the Court's ruling in *Barron v. Baltimore* (1836) that the Bill of Rights did not apply to the states.

The Court relied on the Fourteenth Amendment's due process clause in several cases in the late nineteenth century to rule state regulatory schemes unconstitutional infringements of property rights. Then in the twentieth century the amendment emerged as the source of the Court's rulings extending the Bill of Rights' protections to suspects and defendants in state criminal cases and as the basis of the Court's decisions barring racial segregation. In addition, the Court relied in part on the due process clause in its 1973 decision *Roe v. Wade*, overturning state restrictions on abortions.

The Sixteenth Amendment, ratified in 1913, overturned the Supreme Court's decision in *Pollock v. Farmers' Loan & Trust Co.* (1895), which struck down a federal income tax law. In that case the Court held that a tax on income from real estate was a direct tax, which under the Constitution had to be apportioned by

population (Article I, Section 9). The decision was highly unpopular with laborers and farmers. In elections in following years the voters returned to Congress more and more Democrats and progressive Republicans who supported enactment of a federal income tax. In 1909 Republicans countered a Democratic-backed bill with a proposed constitutional amendment, thinking that it would not win ratification from the states. Contrary to expectations, however, the required number of state legislatures ratified the amendment in fewer than four years.

The last of the amendments overturning Supreme Court decisions was the Twenty-sixth, ratified in 1971, which lowered the voting age to eighteen for all federal, state, and local elections. The amendment stemmed from a law that Congress passed in 1970, seeking to establish the lower voting age by statute. The Court ruled in December 1970 that Congress had authority to lower the voting age for federal elections but not for local and state balloting (*Oregon v. Mitchell*). States, facing the administrative difficulty of maintaining separate voter rolls for state and federal elections, backed an amendment to establish the lower voting age for all elections. Congress acted quickly to approve the proposal, and the amendment was ratified on July 1, 1971, just three months and seven days after it was submitted.

CONGRESSIONAL IMMUNITY

The Supreme Court has given a broad but not unlimited interpretation to the immunity that members of Congress enjoy under the Constitution's speech or debate clause. This provision in Article I, Section 6, states that in all cases except treason, felony, and breach of the peace, senators and representatives are "privileged from Arrest during their Attendance at the Session of their respective Houses" and that "for any Speech or Debate in either House, they shall not be questioned in any other Place."

In its first ruling on this clause, in *Kilbourn v. Thompson* in 1881, the Court refused to limit the clause's protection to "words spoken in debate," but held instead that it protected "things generally done in a session of the House by one of its members in relation to the business before it."

Ninety-one years later in 1972, in *Gravel v. United States,* the Court held that this same immunity protected congressional aides if the conduct in question would be protected if performed by the member himself. However, the Court said neither a member of Congress nor an aide to a member would be protected if he or she violated an otherwise valid criminal law in the course of preparing for legislative action.

In 1966 the Supreme Court held in *United States v. Johnson* that in prosecuting a former member of Congress for taking a bribe, the executive branch could not inquire into the member's motive for making a floor speech, even if the speech was allegedly made as part of an unlawful conspiracy.

Six years after that decision in 1972, however, the Supreme Court held in *United States v. Brewster* that the government could prosecute a member of Congress on charges that he had taken a bribe in return for a vote, so long as the government could conduct the prosecution without inquiring into the legislative actions or their motives in order to make its case.

The Court has protected members of Congress against charges that they violated the privacy of individual citizens by publishing their names in a committee report and against charges that they used committee subpoenas to impede citizens in the exercise of their constitutional rights. *(Doe v. McMillan,* 1973; *Eastland v. United States Servicemen's Fund,* 1975) But in 1979 the Court held in *Hutchinson v. Proxmire* that congressional immunity did not protect a member from libel suits for allegedly defamatory statements he made in press releases and newsletters, even though the releases contained statements originally made on the Senate floor.

Of the unsuccessful attempts to overturn Supreme Court decisions by constitutional amendment, only one came close to ratification: an effort to overturn rulings that invalidated laws passed by Congress to restrict the use of child labor. The first of the decisions, in 1918, held unconstitutional a law prohibiting the shipment in interstate commerce of goods manufactured with child labor. The Court said the law exceeded Congress's power under the interstate commerce clause. When Congress responded with a heavy tax on goods made with child labor, the Court in 1922 held that measure unconstitutional as well.

Congress then approved a constitutional amendment in 1924 to authorize federal legislation on the subject. By 1938 twenty-eight states had ratified the amendment, eight short of the number needed. The amendment became unnecessary in 1941, however, when the Court itself reversed its prior ruling.

Congress has refused to approve other proposed amendments to overturn Court decisions. A reapportionment amendment to give states authority to apportion one house of their legislature on a basis other than population fell seven votes short of the two-thirds majority needed in the Senate in 1965 and again in 1966. An amendment to permit voluntary student participation in prayers in public schools fell nine votes short of a two-thirds majority in the Senate in 1967 and twenty-eight votes short of the needed majority in the House in 1971. Many proposals have been made to overturn the *Roe v. Wade* abortion rights decision and have failed in part because congressional supporters disagreed on the best approach. One proposal reached the Senate floor in 1983; it would have declared simply, "A right to abortion is not secured by this Constitution." The measure failed on a 49–50 vote, well short of the two-thirds majority needed.

STATUTORY REVERSALS

Congress first reversed the Supreme Court by legislation in 1852. In that year the Court ruled that a bridge across the Ohio River obstructed interstate commerce and had to be raised or torn down. Congress immediately passed a law declaring that the bridge was not an obstruction and that ships had to be refitted to pass under the bridge. The Court in 1856 sustained the law.

Through the years, the Court has similarly bowed to the will of Congress in such confrontations, many of them on much broader issues. Congress, for example, responded to decisions by the Court limiting the power of the Interstate Commerce Commission with a law in 1906 specifically authorizing the agency to adjust unreasonable and unfair railroad rates. The Court in 1910 upheld the law and, four years later, also sustained a second statute authorizing the commission to set original rates as well. A more protracted clash stemmed from the Court's ruling in 1908 that some labor union practices violated federal antitrust laws. Congress tried in the Clayton Act of 1914 to give unions an antitrust exemption, but the Court in 1921 ruled that some union practices still ran afoul of antitrust law. Congress sought to undo that decision in 1932 with the Norris-LaGuardia Act, and the Court in 1938 went along with the legislative override.

The Court and Congress clashed on a series of other issues during the New Deal era. Between 1934 and 1936, the Court struck down six major acts passed by Congress as part of President Franklin D. Roosevelt's economic recovery program. The Court became more liberal on economic issues beginning in

1937. Congress then revised five of the six laws the Court had declared invalid and enacted a new law, the National Labor Relations Act, to substitute for the other measure, the National Industrial Recovery Act. Between 1937 and 1940 the Court sustained all the new acts.

Congress prevailed in another major dispute only after the passage of considerable time. The Court in 1885 had ruled unconstitutional the Civil Rights Act of 1875. The justices said that Congress, in attempting to prohibit racial discrimination in public accommodations such as hotels, theaters, and railroads, had exceeded its authority under the Thirteenth and Fourteenth Amendments. Eighty years later, Congress sought to reverse the ruling, this time justifying the Civil Rights Act of 1964 under its power to regulate interstate commerce. Six months after the statute was signed into law, the Court unanimously upheld its constitutionality.

In the 1980s Congress and the Court again clashed over civil rights issues. The Court began to restrict some civil rights laws just as congressional support for civil rights was increasing. Twice during the decade Congress reversed individual decisions by the Court. In 1982 it passed a law that overturned a decision two years earlier limiting the application of the Voting Rights Act to intentionally discriminatory practices. In 1988 Congress overturned a decision from four years earlier that had narrowed the effect of a 1972 law prohibiting sex discrimination at schools receiving federal aid. Then in 1991 Congress passed an omnibus job discrimination measure intended to reverse a series of five decisions in 1989 that had made it harder for plaintiffs to win employment discrimination suits.

The Warren Court found itself under persistent attacks from members of Congress on a number of issues, but most efforts to overturn major decisions fell short. Congress did include in the Omnibus Crime and Safe Streets Act of 1968 several provisions aimed at overturning liberal criminal procedure decisions, but the effect of the provisions has been largely symbolic. The legislation sought to overturn the famous *Miranda* ruling on police interrogation by providing that "voluntary" confessions were admissible in federal courts even if suspects had not been warned of their rights. A separate provision, seeking to overturn the 1957 decision *Mallory v. United States*, provided that confessions were admissible without regard to any delay in the suspect's arraignment. A third provision stated that lineup evidence was admissible even if a suspect did not have a lawyer present, contradicting a 1967 decision, *United States v. Wade.* The Court itself defused the lineup issue with a 1972 decision that limited the impact of its original ruling. As for the provisions on confessions, they did not apply in state courts, where most prosecutions occur, and have been largely ignored in federal courts.

Congress tried in 1993 to overturn a Court decision in another area, religious freedom, only to be decisively rebuffed by the Court four years later. The Religious Freedom Restoration Act sought to make it harder for states to enforce general laws that interfered with religious practices. The law was aimed at reversing a 1990 decision, *Employment Division v. Smith,* that found the use of peyote for religious purposes to be prohibited by a state's antidrug laws. The Court, ruling in a challenge to the 1993 law brought by state and local government groups, said Congress had gone beyond its statutory power by trying to overturn a ruling on constitutional ground. "The power to interpret the Constitution," the Court wrote, "remains in the judiciary."

NOTES

1. David Adamany, "The Supreme Court" in *The American Courts: A Critical Assessment,* ed. John B. Gates and Charles A. Johnson (Washington, D.C.: Congressional Quarterly, 1991), 5.
2. William N. Eskridge Jr., "Overruling Statutory Precedents," *Georgetown Law Journal,* vol. 76 (1988), 1361–1439.
3. Max Farrand, *The Records of the Federal Convention of 1787* (New Haven, Conn.: Yale University Press, 1911).
4. Philip B. Kurland, "The Origin of the National Judiciary," in *This Constitution: Our Enduring Legacy,* American Political Science Association and American Historical Association (Washington, D.C.: CQ Press, 1986), 88.
5. Charles Warren, *The Supreme Court in United States History* (Boston: Little, Brown, 1922), vol. 1, 96.
6. Lawrence Baum, *The Supreme Court,* 6th ed. (Washington, D.C.: CQ Press, 1998), 23.
7. Charles Evans Hughes, *The Supreme Court of the United States* (New York: Columbia University Press, 1928), 51.
8. Letter of Jefferson to Spencer Roane, Sept. 6, 1819, cited in Warren, *The Supreme Court,* vol. 1, 295.

SELECTED BIBLIOGRAPHY

Abraham, Henry J. *Justices, Presidents, and Senators: A History of the U.S. Supreme Court Appointments from Washington to Clinton.* New York: Rowman and Littlefield, 1999.

Baum, Lawrence. *The Supreme Court,* 6th ed. Washington, D.C.: CQ Press, 1998.

Berger, Raoul. *Congress v. The Supreme Court.* Cambridge, Mass.: Harvard University Press, 1969.

Bickel, Alexander M. *The Least Dangerous Branch: The Supreme Court at the Bar of Politics.* 2nd ed. New Haven: Yale University Press, 1986.

Biskupic, Joan, and Elder Witt. *Congressional Quarterly's Guide to the U.S. Supreme Court,* 3rd ed. Washington, D.C.: Congressional Quarterly, 1997.

Breckenridge, Adam C. *Congress against the Court.* Lincoln: University of Nebraska Press, 1970.

Corwin, Edward S. *The Constitution and What It Means Today.* 4th ed. Revised by Harold Chase and Craig Ducat. Princeton, N.J.: Princeton University Press, 1978.

———. *The Doctrine of Judicial Review: Its Legal and Historical Basis and Other Essays.* Princeton, N.J.: Princeton University Press, 1914. Reprint. Gloucester, Mass.: Peter Smith, 1963.

Davis, Horace. *A Judicial Veto.* Boston: Houghton Mifflin, 1914. Reprint. New York: Da Capo Press, 1971.

Epstein, Lee, and Jack Knight. *The Choices Justices Make.* Washington, D.C.: CQ Press, 1998.

Epstein, Lee, and Thomas G. Walker. *Constitutional Law for a Changing America: Institutional Powers and Constraints.* 3rd ed. Washington, D.C.: CQ Press, 1998.

Epstein, Lee, and Thomas G. Walker. *Constitutional Law for a Changing America: Rights, Liberties, and Justice.* 3rd ed. Washington, D.C.: CQ Press, 1998.

Ervin, Sam J., Jr. *Role of the Supreme Court: Policy Maker or Adjudicator?* Washington, D.C.: American Enterprise Institute for Public Policy Research, 1970.

Eskridge, William N. *Dynamic Statutory Interpretation.* Cambridge, Mass.: Harvard University Press, 1994.

Forte, David F. *The Supreme Court in American Politics: Judicial Activism vs. Judicial Restraint.* Lexington, Mass.: D. C. Heath, 1972.

Friedman, Leon, and Fred L. Israel, eds. *The Justices of the United States Supreme Court.* 5 vols. New York: Chelsea House, 1997.

Harris, Richard. *Decision.* New York: Dutton, 1971.

Hughes, Charles Evans. *The Supreme Court of the United States.* New York: Columbia University Press, 1928.

Jackson, Robert H. *The Struggle for Judicial Supremacy: A Study of a Crisis in American Power Politics.* New York: Random House, 1941.

Kahn, Ronald. *The Supreme Court and Constitutional Theory: 1953–1993.* Lawrence: University Press of Kansas, 1994.

Krislov, Samuel. *Supreme Court in the Political Process.* New York: Macmillan, 1965.

Maltese, John A. *Selling of the Supreme Court Nominees.* Baltimore: Johns Hopkins University Press, 1995.

Moore, Blaine F. *Supreme Court and Unconstitutional Legislation.* New York: Columbia University Press, 1913. Reprint. New York: AMS Press, 1968.

Morgan, Donald G. *Congress and the Constitution: A Study of Responsibility.* Cambridge, Mass.: Harvard University Press, 1966.

Murphy, Walter F. *Congress and the Court.* Chicago: University of Chicago Press, 1962.

O'Brien, David. *Storm Center: The Supreme Court in American Politics.* 4th ed. New York: Norton, 1996.

Pritchett, C. Herman. *Congress vs. the Supreme Court, 1957–1960.* Minneapolis: University of Minnesota Press, 1961. Reprint. New York: Da Capo Press, 1973.

Schmidhauser, John R. *The Supreme Court and Congress: Conflict and Interaction, 1945–1968.* New York: Free Press, 1972.

Warren, Charles. *The Supreme Court in United States History.* 2 vols. Boston: Little, Brown, 1926.

CHAPTER 23

Lobbying

AMERICA IS NO LONGER a nation. It is a committee of lobbies," Charles Peters, the curmudgeonly editor of the *Washington Monthly,* wrote in 1978. "Politicians no longer ask what is in the public interest, because they know no one else is asking. Instead they're giving each group what it wants."[1] The complaint is not a new one. Political scientist and presidential campaigner Woodrow Wilson said in 1912, "The government of the United States is a foster child of the special interests. It is not allowed to have a will of its own."

As such comments imply, the term *lobbying* has a pejorative connotation. In his *Political Dictionary,* columnist William Safire traces the political use of the term to the midseventeenth century, when citizens would use a large anteroom, or lobby, near the English House of Commons to plead their cause to members of Parliament. By 1829, the phrase *lobby-agents* was being applied to special favor-seekers who hovered in the lobby of the New York Capitol in Albany. By 1832, the term had been shortened to *lobbyist* and was widely used in the U.S. Capitol. "In the U.S. during the politically venal 1800s, lobbying and lobbyists earned a bad name from which their professional descendants today, no matter how pure in motive and deed, have yet to clear themselves completely," Safire wrote.[2]

Lobbyists have been referred to collectively as the Third House of Congress since the nineteenth century. Today, lobbying in all its various forms permeates every aspect of American government: from citizens buttonholing their representative at a Fourth of July picnic to grassroots organizations so vast that, like the American Association of Retired Persons (AARP), they have their own zip code. The White House has a staff of lobbyists who communicate the president's desires to Congress; senators and representatives lobby each other; even lobbies lobby each other.

Political reformers have long called for drastic measures to hobble special interests. After an investigation of lobbying in 1935, Alabama Sen. Hugo L. Black concluded,

Contrary to tradition, against the public morals, and hostile to good government, the lobby has reached such a position of power that it threatens government itself. Its size, its power, its capacity for evil, its greed, trickery, deception, and fraud condemn it to the death it deserves.

Despite the deep dismay of the future Supreme Court justice, lobbying has grown only more vigorous in the intervening decades. Why?

By now it seems clear that lobbying has become integral to the governance of a vast and complex democracy. Through lobbying, ordinary citizens make their wishes known to their legislators, the wronged and the needy call attention to their problems, the issues of the day are brought to public attention, and the potentially damaging consequences of legislation are brought to light in time to forestall harm. As government has grown in size and complexity, citizens all over the country have taken comfort in the existence of specialists whose job it is to act as intermediaries with those who are in positions of power.

In short, it is in large part through lobbying that government gets its information. The idea that lobbying performs a vital function in a democracy fits in with the classic theory of political science known as pluralism; according to this theory, much of the strength of American democracy comes from the interplay of different forces that compete with and balance each other. In this view, the compromises, "deals," and ideological complexity of American governmental decision making lead to diversity, flexibility, and stability in governance.

Those academics who have a less benign view of lobbying argue that interests with the most power or the most money usually get what they want. A slightly less cynical view holds that even a robust interplay among claimants who are roughly equal in influence cannot take adequate account of all viewpoints. In his 1981 farewell address, President Jimmy Carter warned that the proliferation of single-interest groups was "a disturbing factor" that "tends to distort our purposes, because the national interest is not always the sum of all our single or special interests."

As it grew in size and sophistication, the lobbying profession lost much of the stigma that it had acquired in the course of past scandals. But while it has often been difficult to point to the direct influence of lobbying on a particular piece of legislation, concern lingers that some individuals and groups may have too much sway in Congress. For example, House Republicans came in for strong criticism when it was alleged that after gaining the majority in 1995, they permitted some lobbying groups to virtually merge with committee staffs in drafting key legislative provisions. Only a few years earlier, the resignations of House Speaker Jim Wright of Texas and Democratic Whip Tony Coelho of California—as well as the defeat of several prominent incumbents—had been at least partly tied to the legislators' cozy relationships with lobbyists for savings and loan operators.

Although it is easy to pass laws prohibiting bribery or the most obvious forms of influence peddling, even the most virtuous legislator would concede the difficulty of drawing a clear line

Since the nineteenth century, lobbyists have been known collectively as the Third House of Congress. Shown here is the lobby of the House of Representatives during passage of the 1866 civil rights bill.

between improper conduct and legitimate communication. Lobbying derives from basic American rights, and any efforts to control it risk entanglement with constitutional liberties. As a result, there are few legislative restrictions on lobbies or the way that they operate. The first comprehensive lobbying law was enacted in 1946, and although there have been other piecemeal changes since then, the standard approach has been to monitor lobbyists' activities and reveal them publicly when they go too far.

Constitutional Protection

"Congress shall make no law . . . abridging the freedom of speech or of the press; or the right of the people peaceably to assemble and to petition the Government for redress of grievances." That language in the First Amendment to the Constitution protects the essence of lobbying, which is nothing more than addressing Congress "for redress of grievances."

James Madison, in *The Federalist* (No. 10) saw one advantage of a strong central government as its ability

to break and control the violence of faction. . . . By a faction, I understand a number of citizens, whether amounting to a majority or minority of the whole, who are united and actuated by some common impulse of passion, or of interest, adverse to the rights of other citizens, or to the permanent and aggregate interests of the community.

Madison's hopes to the contrary, faction has characterized American government since its earliest days. And the stronger a faction—be it canal builders, Civil War pensioners, farmers, or senior citizens—the more it has turned to Congress to secure its interests.

In the early years of the Republic, the ties between legislators and private interests were quite direct. While Congress forbade bribery of judges in 1790, bribing a legislator was not illegal until 1853. In addition to making direct payments, outside interests could hire members to do their legal work. In the 1830s, when President Andrew Jackson was battling with the Bank of the United States, Sen. Daniel Webster of Massachusetts was one of the bank's biggest defenders. On December 21, 1833, Webster complained to bank president Nicholas Biddle: "My retainer has not been renewed or refreshed as usual. If it is wished that my relation to the Bank should be continued, it may be well to send me the usual retainers." The bank also seems to have made sizable loans to other officials, including James Monroe and Henry Clay.

In the mid-1800s the legislative successes of financier-socialite Samuel Ward, self-proclaimed "King of the Lobby," triggered a congressional investigation. In the Crédit Mobilier affair, during the Grant administration, twelve members of Congress were accused of taking stock in return for helping the Union Pacific railroad obtain huge land grants. By the closing years of the nineteenth century, the image of lobbyists was so bad that President William McKinley had to tell his friend and political mentor, Mark Hanna: "Mark, I would do anything in the world for you, but I cannot put a man in my cabinet who is known as a lobbyist."

The excesses of the era led to a series of sporadic reforms that began in 1907 with the banning of campaign contributions from banks and corporations. Recognizing that the Constitution guarantees anyone the right to seek help from Congress, reformers had to settle for disclosure—principally through 1946 legislation that required lobbyists to register with Congress and to make basic information about their activities available to the public. The political scandals of recent decades, combined with soaring campaign costs and contribution levels, have raised public expectations that legislators would behave with integrity. Lobbyists themselves banded together into an organization, the American League of Lobbyists, that promotes its own code of conduct.

GROWTH OF LOBBYING

Despite the deep and pervading ambivalence with which the profession is regarded, lobbyists have been drawn to Washington by the opportunity to make money and dabble in power. Their legions grew steadily after the New Deal of the 1930s, when growth in federal spending and the expansion of federal authority widened the areas in which changes in federal policy could spell success or failure for special interests.

In the 1970s a series of congressional reforms opened most committee meetings to the public, weakened the seniority system, required more votes to be inscribed in the public record, and increased the power of subcommittees. As power that had once been concentrated in the party leadership and committee chairs was distributed among many legislators—and even among the ranks of professional staffers, which had swelled throughout the 1960s—organized interests found that they had to influence more people to get something accomplished. The increase in the number of access points for influencing legislation led to the growth of large, multifaceted lobbying firms; the proliferation of Washington-based trade associations; and the expansion in size and number of corporate lobbying offices. Outfitted with the latest technology and supplied by an ever-increasing number of databases, these offices have become sophisticated communications centers that not only perform the traditional role of lobbying organizations—gaining access to members of Congress and their aides—but also track thousands of regulations, place advertisements, generate mail and telephone calls from constituents, and arrange to have representatives appear on radio or television programs or be quoted in newspapers.

Because of the vague—and many say unenforceable—laws governing the registration of Washington lobbyists, it is impossible to determine their exact number. One way to get a rough indication of growth in the number of lobbyists, however, is to look at growth in the number of lawyers. Although not all lawyers are lobbyists, it is known that between 1973 and 1999, the membership of the District of Columbia Bar Association tripled; at least some of this growth can likely be attributed to the lobbying profession. In addition to attorneys, lobbying requires a phalanx of political consultants, representatives of foreign governments and interests, legislative specialists, consumer advocates, trade association representatives, and government affairs specialists. The office of the Clerk of the House reported in 1999 that the number of registered lobbyists was just under 7,900; the office assumes, however, that the actual number of people who met the law's threshold for lobbying was much higher. (By way of comparison, the District of Columbia Bar Association reported that 48,237 lawyers were active in the district that same year.) Given First Amendment protections, it is almost impossible to devise a scheme under which every lobbyist would be compelled to register.

Lobbying Techniques: Increasing Sophistication

In the hallway outside the committee room, more lobbyists stand nervously, like so many expectant fathers crowded into the waiting room of a maternity ward. These hallway loiterers include the top ranks of Washington's tax lobbying world—men and women who are paid $200, $300, even $400 an hour to influence legislators and preserve tax benefits worth millions of dollars to their anxious clients. . . . A few of the lobbyists huddle around the back door of the committee room, hoping to catch a senator coming in or going out, hoping for one last chance to make a pitch before the vote. The desperation in their voices makes it clear that big money is at stake. Their expensive suits and shiny Italian shoes give this hallway its nickname: Gucci Gulch."[3]

The sweeping overhaul of the tax code enacted in 1986 brought out the big guns of the lobbying world. But the lobbyist who earns hundreds of dollars an hour is not necessarily the most effective. In 1973, for example, David Saks was a retired furniture salesman who had never finished high school. When his wife, Reba, tried to use a pay phone to make a call from a department store in Baltimore, Maryland, and found that the telephone would not work with her hearing aid, David set out to do something about it. Barraging Capitol Hill with telephone calls, organizing a cadre of hearing-aid users, patiently explaining the problem to staff aides and members—but never giving a dime to a congressional candidate or golfing with a committee chairman—David Saks found pay dirt at the end of his tenacious fifteen-year odyssey: in 1988, he won passage of legislation that outlawed the sale of telephones that were not equipped for use by callers with hearing aids.

At the other extreme are the "superlobbyists" whose telephone calls never go unreturned. Jack Valenti, president of the Motion Picture Association of America and the top-paid lobbyist in 1989, received a reported salary of $672,590—thanks to his well-established reputation for dealing skillfully with Congress.

LOBBYISTS' POINTS OF ACCESS: WHERE OPPORTUNITY KNOCKS

When the roll is called on a major issue in Congress, lobbyists can be found packed into the lobbies directly off the floor of the House and Senate chambers. Via a doorkeeper, they can send their calling cards to members on the floor, often bringing someone out to discuss strategy, or they can buttonhole members on their way from the elevators to the floor.

But by the time an issue is ready for a vote, it is usually too late for a lobbyist to have much influence. Mark O. Hatfield, R-Ore., a chairman of the Senate Appropriations Committee, put it bluntly: "Neither do I appreciate lobbyists who jump out from behind the marble columns outside the Senate to give me one last pitch before I vote on an issue. They should have done their work beforehand."

The real work of lobbying is done far earlier in the legislative process. Not only is it good politics to avoid surprising members at the last moment, there are important strategic reasons for beginning lobbying efforts early in the legislative process. First, the fewer the people who are involved in making policy decisions, the fewer the people a lobbyist needs to persuade. Second, once legislative language is set in print, it is usually easier to defend than it is to change. So, while the focus may be on a crucial vote, most lobbying is a continuous process.

THE DRAFTING STAGE

Lobbyists often suggest subjects for legislation to members. It is common for the well-prepared lobbyist to offer a draft bill or amendment to a legislator. The effort is usually well received if the member is carefully selected, and the draft language is skillfully written and does not appear overly self-interested. This is another area in which former members and staff people can be especially helpful to clients; they know how to prepare a bill both technically and with an eye toward political ramifications. Most congressional offices jealously guard their legislative prerogatives, but the frenetic pace of Capitol Hill leaves little time for most members to create their own initiatives. Doing some outside "staff work" for them can make the differ-

ence between getting an organization's proposal before a committee or having it passed over for lack of preparation time.

IN COMMITTEE

"Congress in its committee rooms is Congress at work," Woodrow Wilson wrote in 1885. Although committee work has grown much more open to public scrutiny in the ensuing century, lobbyists' sway still is greatest at the committee level. There, the heightened interest of staff and members in a certain industry or topic, and the frequent byplay between members and lobbyists, makes for a community of interest.

Some lobbying firms hire former congressional staff aides to improve their access to specific committees—particularly the tax-writing and Appropriations committees, which do much of their business behind closed doors.

The key stages of committee activity include:

Hearings. Committee staff often look to lobbyists to suggest witnesses to present their side of a case. Lobbyists are well equipped to help witnesses prepare testimony.

A key part of the lobbyist's job is to attend hearings, both to keep track of arguments by supporters and opponents of the bill and to listen carefully to members' comments for clues as to how they might vote. It would be a poor lobbyist who did not know how to get a copy of the hearing transcript to review it later.

Markups. Lobbyists often find themselves included in strategy sessions to determine how many votes can be counted on for a bill. They frequently are consulted in drafting of bills and may suggest language for amendments to strengthen or weaken a particular section. If a lobbyist wants to forestall a markup, he or she might try to persuade members simply to be somewhere else so the committee will not have a quorum to proceed. This can be a tricky maneuver, however. Many members are uneasy about missing important legislative meetings. They forfeit an opportunity to be involved in leg-

---

By 1998, Valenti was said to be earning over $1 million a year. But he was not alone in the "seven-figure" category. Robert Klies, former Chief of Staff to the Joint Committee on Taxation, left Capitol Hill for a reported $1 million salary lobbying for PricewaterhouseCoopers.

Other lobbyists get their clout from the numbers of people they represent. With 28 million members, the American Association of Retired Persons (AARP) could boast in 1990 that it was the nation's second-largest organization—after the Roman Catholic Church. AARP had its own zip code and eighteen registered lobbyists, yet it could not prevent its own members from rising up in 1989 and forcing the repeal of a bill that had been enacted just one year before with strong AARP support: a measure to shield 33 million elderly and disabled Americans from "catastrophic" medical bills.

Professional lobbyists most often come from backgrounds in law, public relations, business, and industry. Still others have ex-

perience as former legislators, government officials, or congressional staff aides. Some lobbyists, often highly accomplished in their own right, have the added advantage of being, quite literally, part of the congressional family. Tommy Boggs, who—along with Valenti, Klies, and others—was said to earn more than $1 million a year lobbying during the late 1990s, is the son of Hale and Lindy Boggs, both of whom served in the House. His father was the majority leader until his death in an airplane accident on October 16, 1972. Other prominent lobbyists have also had strong family ties to Congress. Linda Daschle, the wife of Senate Minority Leader Tom Daschle, and Randy DeLay, the brother of House Majority Whip Tom DeLay, lobbied successfully for clients in transportation-related industries in the late 1990s. "I don't know how much it helps being related to someone up here," said one House committee counsel, "but I guess it kind of gets your attention when someone with a name like Daschle gives you a call." To avoid any appearance of impropriety, how-

islative decisions and leave themselves open to charges of neglect of duty. To make such a request usually requires a long-standing relationship between the lobbyist and member. Even then, the request could well be denied.

Reports. The committee's report on a bill, usually written after the markup, frequently is more important to an interest group than the bill itself—not only because members can read it more closely in deciding how to vote, but also because federal agencies and judges often rely on the report to determine how to apply a law. Lobbyists regularly suggest data or examples for inclusion in these reports.

A lobbyist on the losing end of a markup may try to get members to file dissenting views that would be printed along with the report.

ON THE FLOOR

Preparation. It is almost impossible for a lobbyist to speak directly with all 535 members of Congress in advance of a floor vote, but lobbyists are an integral part of most efforts to round up votes. For major bills, lobbyists sometimes are included in whips' meetings as floor leaders try to compare vote counts and make assignments. Broad-based lobbies make sure that constituents who favor their position will deluge members' offices with mail, e-mail, telegrams, telephone calls, and personal visits.

If a lobbying group opposes a bill, it might try to find a strategically placed ally—a member of the House Rules Committee or one of the party's leaders—who could hold up floor action or at least influence the procedures under which it would be considered. In the Senate, any member can place an informal (and secret) "hold" on a bill, and the signal that it would create time-consuming controversy, even a full-scale filibuster, often is enough to keep the majority leader from bringing it up. For all but the most major legislation, this is an especially effective tactic near the end of a session, when floor time is scarce.

Votes. On the day of a vote, a lobbying group may try to pack the galleries with its supporters. While the rules of both chambers forbid demonstrations, clever strategists can find ways to offer silent witness. During 1988 consideration of a bill that could affect the disabled, for instance, lobbyists filled the galleries and office buildings with supporters in wheelchairs. In the late 1990s, members were exposed to graphic depictions of unborn fetuses as they walked across the Capitol grounds to cast votes on abortion-related issues.

Lobbying groups usually make it a point to station staff not only outside the chamber to make last-ditch pleas, but also to have aides in the galleries to watch how members vote and to note members who had not yet voted, in case time remained to bring them there.

Floor colloquies are sometimes arranged by lobbyists intent on influencing the legislative history of a bill. These prearranged formal dialogues between members might be an attempt to show that a bill provision should not apply to a particular industry.

FINAL ACTION

Conference Committees. Negotiations between House and Senate conferees provide an opportunity for savvy lobbyists to work quietly but effectively to settle a controversy, dismantle an onerous provision, or slip in an exception or "transition rule" that would exempt an individual company. Since conference committees usually meet in tight quarters (and do most of their negotiations in private or over the telephone), these provide the greatest challenge to a lobbyist's access.

Veto Strategy. A lobbying group that loses its case in Congress can always look to the president for a veto.

Repeal. It rarely happens, but Congress occasionally has reversed itself when public outrage mounted against an enacted piece of legislation. In 1988 Congress passed a massive rewrite of the Medicare law. The new program would have required most seniors to pay more money "up front" in exchange for more generous "catastrophic" coverage. When seniors learned about the increased expenditures they deluged Congress with mail and visits. The year-old law was repealed in 1989.

---

ever, Daschle took a personal oath to avoid lobbying the Senate when she became a lobbyist in 1997.

USING THE PROCESS TO ADVANTAGE

Successfully ushering legislation through Congress has always been much more difficult than preventing passage, which requires no more than a single subcommittee blockade or a crippling amendment. This developed by design. The bicameral structure of the legislative branch and the constitutional separation of powers give a considerable natural advantage to defensive lobbying efforts. Political scientist David B. Truman wrote that these structures "operate as they were designed, to delay or obstruct action rather than to facilitate it."[4] *(See box, Lobbyists' Points of Access, p. 694.)*

Even the losers can almost always salvage something. In 1970, when they were defeated in their attempts to preserve cigarette manufacturers' freedom to air radio and television advertise-ments, tobacco interests managed to move the effective date back by one day, to January 2, 1971—a change that allowed one last round of advertisements during football bowl games and late-night talk shows.

If an interest group loses a round in Congress, it can continue the fight with the agency that is charged with implementation or in the courts. Congress is often too busy to concern itself with the details necessary to fully execute the laws it has written, and sophisticated lobbyists are well aware that executive branch officials often have a great deal of leeway in policy implementation. In examining the tobacco industry's attempts to thwart the advertising restrictions, A. Lee Fritschler and James M. Hoefler noted that "It can reasonably be argued that the master-servant view of the relationship between legislators and bureaucrats . . . is no longer tenable from either the practical or legal side."[5]

It is not at all uncommon for lobbying organizations to recoup at the regulation-writing stage much of what they have lost in Congress. Lobbyists also know that within a year or two, they can resume the struggle on Capitol Hill. The process sometimes continues indefinitely. Over the long term, interest groups strive to create a sympathetic or at least neutral attitude among those who have the power to affect their particular interests.

DIRECT LOBBYING

At one time, lobbying may have been conducted by a persuasive soloist pleading a case to a senator or representative; but most of today's lobbyists depend far less on personal contacts and the cultivation of individual style than on highly coordinated, indirect techniques made possible by modern means of communication.

As noted earlier, the congressional reforms of the 1970s worked to enlarge the job of Washington lobbyists, who had to develop new techniques for communicating effectively with a much broader range of members and staff. As access to legislators became easier to obtain, more groups formed to protect or enlarge their turf, and competition among lobbyists increased —sometimes to the point where so many lobbyists were pushing so hard on a bill that it was virtually impossible for members to iron out a compromise.

Lobbyists using the direct approach continued to meet with members of Congress and their staffs, provide in-depth information, and give testimony at congressional hearings. But their methods grew more sophisticated, relying more on information than on personal connections. One legislative aide observed: "I think there's a new breed of lobbyist around. There's less of the slap-on-the-back, 'I've been dealing with you for fifteen years, let's go duck hunting' kind of approach. Now it's, 'Here's a twenty-page paper full of technical slides, charts showing the budget impact, a table on how it meets the threat situation, and some language in case you'd like to introduce an amendment.'"

Nevertheless, despite changes in lobbying techniques since the early 1970s, most legislators, staff, and lobbyists agree that effective, face-to-face presentation of the facts remains the number one staple of the lobbying profession. Said one legislator, "Sooner or later they have to look us in the eye and convince us that what they want makes sense—politically and substantively."

Access Essential

To communicate with power brokers, an advocate first needs access to them. Whether a lobbyist is a partner in a Washington law firm or an employee of a union, he or she will more often than not already have close ties to Congress. (*See box, Ex-members as Lobbyists, this page.*) No consensus exists on whether it is contacts that ultimately count, but many lobbying firms believe that hiring staff with insider credentials is a good investment. Charles Black, a one-time campaigner for presidential candidate Ronald Reagan and a member of a political consulting firm, put it this way:

EX-MEMBERS AS LOBBYISTS

When members retire from Congress, or are retired by the voters, many of them remain in Washington to work as lobbyists rather than return to their roots.

In some cases former members become permanently associated with a single organization whose views they share. Others work for a wide range of employers. They enjoy distinct advantages over their competitors, but their experience does not automatically make them effective. A 1989 book profiling 125 key Washington lobbyists included only three who had served in Congress.

"Former members have, to a large degree, what other lobbyists spend years attaining," remarked Sen. John McCain, R-Ariz. He was speaking of access—to former colleagues, to information, to the inner workings of Congress. "Aside from access, they are no more or less effective, but the key to getting something done in this town is access."

Ex-members get their phone calls returned. They get special attention in the scheduling of witnesses. Former members also enjoy lifetime entrée to private sanctums of Capitol Hill—the gyms, the members' dining rooms, and the cloakrooms. The most valued privilege is that of striding directly onto the floor to buttonhole an ex-colleague. This is useful for maintaining acquaintances and visibility, although many members consider it tacky to exploit the privilege.

In the House of Representatives, use of the floor is governed by House Rule XXXII and a chair ruling in 1945 by Speaker Sam Rayburn, D-Texas. Under the "Rayburn rule," a former member is forbidden the privilege of the floor at any time the House is debating or voting on legislation in which he or she is interested, either personally or as an employee of some other person or organization.

The Senate has some restrictions on lobbying by former members, but their effect is largely symbolic because Senate rules cannot be enforced against those who have left the institution. On the other hand, the Senate's atmosphere discourages salesmanship by outsiders, senators say.

Ex-members get varying grades on their knowledge of the legislative process and the substance of legislation—usually commensurate with their involvement when they served in Congress. Many organizations find former staff members more useful in these legislative areas. Often former members work in tandem with lobbyists who are experts on substance; the ex-member makes the appointment and introduction, but the specialist makes the pitch.

The so-called revolving door for alumni was slowed somewhat by ethics legislation enacted in 1989. For the first time, members of Congress were prohibited from lobbying in the legislative branch for a year after leaving office. (*See Chapter 35, Ethics and Criminal Prosecution, and box, 'Revolving Door Slowed,' p. 979, Vol. II.*)

No. 1 is the access—to get them in the door and get a hearing for the case. The second thing is the development of the case and how to present it. Knowing the individuals personally, knowing their staffs and how they operate and the kind of information they want. . . . That kind of personal knowledge can help you maximize the client's hearing.

Personal ties count for a great deal in the small world of the House and perhaps even more in the clubby Senate. The National Federation of Independent Business keeps a ready list of members who know senators and representatives personally and can make a case if called on by the federation. Lobbying firms often make a point of employing both Democrats and Republicans. Firms may also hire "silver bullet" lobbyists who can be counted on for access to just one committee or even one key member. Another practice is to openly hire the friends of a particular member in order to get the legislator's ear.

The Washington social circuit is a time-honored means of gaining access to power. Some lobbyists become well known, even notorious, for giving lavish dinner and cocktail parties, although legislation in the latter years of the 1990s put something of a damper on this approach. Effective January 1, 1996, House and Senate rules limited the value of gifts, including sit-down meals, that members may accept. (*See Chapter 27, Pay and Honoraria.*)

The sheer size of the interest group represented—as in the case, for example, of the senior citizens' lobby—is another advantage in opening doors. A large group that speaks out loudly and vehemently, as the National Rifle Association does, increases its chances of gaining the ear of legislators.

Finally, prestige alone may provide a strong incentive for lawmakers and their staff to open their doors. The Business Roundtable, a group composed of the chief executive officers of major corporations such as General Motors, IBM, and AT&T, can feel confident that when its members speak, legislators will listen.

Information and Expertise

Access is essential, but the skillful presentation of knowledge is also crucial: lobbyists have traditionally provided information and expertise to hard-pressed members and committees. Congressional staffs rarely have the resources to gather their own data and examples, and an outside group that can offer reliable data to a committee or legislator can frame the issue, a critical step in formulating a solution. However, successful lobbyists are cautious about presenting information, striving not only to be accurate and complete but also to alert legislators to any negative aspects of the policy being advocated. "The greatest mistake a lobbyist can make is to mislead a member of Congress," said Charles O. Whitley, a North Carolina Democrat who became a lobbyist after leaving Congress.

A thorough lobbyist provides the committee and its professional staff with extensive background and technical information on the issue of interest, precise legislative language for a proposed bill or amendment, lists of witnesses for hearings, and the name of a possible sponsor for the bill. Such help is especially useful during the consideration of highly technical legislation.

As power diffused throughout the committee system and sunshine laws and rules opened markup sessions, hearings, and conferences to the public, lobbyists were no longer left hovering outside closed doors; instead, they could be right in the thick of things, watching every move—and in many cases suggesting legislative language and compromise positions. Recorded votes on amendments and open access to the names of the members who introduced them enable lobbyists to closely monitor legislative action and apply pressure where it is most needed.

Despite the reforms of the 1970s, some of the committees whose actions are most critical to economic interests—the tax committees and some appropriations subcommittees—continued to mark up their bills in closed session. The chairmen defended this practice on the grounds that it was impossible to gain compromise on money issues when lobbyists were present. In 1988, by threatening to force open meetings and public votes on a whole range of issues, one Connecticut senator forced the Senate Banking Committee to accept a set of provisions on a banking-reform bill that would affect the home-state insurance industry.

Most lobbyists today carefully avoid approaches that could be interpreted as threatening or as constituting excessive pressure. A member's adverse reaction could lead to unfavorable publicity or even to a congressional investigation. Political scientist Donald R. Matthews described the lobbyists as "sitting ducks—their public reputation is so low that public attack is bound to be damaging. . . . To invite public attack, or even worse, a congressional investigation, is, from the lobbyist's point of view, clearly undesirable." Matthews added:

It is the threat of and use of these countermeasures which help explain why so little lobbying is aimed at conversion. A lobbyist minimizes the risks to his job, the cause which he serves, and his ego by staying away from those senators clearly against him and his program. For, of all types of lobbying, attempts at conversion are most likely to boomerang.[6]

INDIRECT LOBBYING

In conjunction with direct lobbying, many organizations use indirect lobbying techniques—grassroots mobilization, media campaigns, and financial contributions—to influence legislators.

Grassroots Power

Nearly every large company, trade association, or public interest group of any stature has developed its own grassroots network to ensure that what its Washington lobbyists say is reinforced by an outpouring from constituents. For interests that lack such a network, a thriving industry has developed that promises clients that it can take a whisper of public interest and amplify it into a roar of public pressure.

A petition containing more than five million names was presented to Congress in 1932, seeking changes in the Volstead Act, the national prohibition law.

Traditional grassroots lobbying methods include maintaining a steady stream of communication—written and oral—with the lawmaker, even when no specific favor is being demanded; inviting legislators to visit local establishments when Congress is in recess; and maintaining frequent and skillful contact with local newspapers and television stations. For established lobbying groups, such tools are not new; what's new is the magnitude, sophistication, and rapidity of the communications technologies on which they now rely.

A fact of modern lobbying is that constituent pressure rarely springs spontaneously from the public. Genuine grassroots support is often amplified by a carefully orchestrated campaign on the part of a special interest group—which may include a professional public relations effort—and occasionally by the persuasive tactics of a union or an employer.

Sometimes lobbying groups do not wait for legislation to be introduced before cranking up a grassroots campaign. In late 1988, real estate agents spread the word that Congress "might" eliminate the tax deduction for the interest paid on home mortgages. Congress was flooded with protests—even though no member would admit to having even thought of such a proposal. This preemptive strike made sure that no member would.

The oldest and most widely used instruments of the grassroots lobbying campaign remain the postage stamp and the telegraph wire. As one veteran congressional administrative assistant observed, "Congress still runs on a paper trail. If we can touch, we believe it. If we can't, we don't." Computer technology and high-speed, low-cost telegram services have enabled interest groups to target mail and telegraph communications where they will do the most good.

Beginning in the early 1990s, technological innovation made two new forms of constituent-to-member communications available to grassroots organizers: telephone patch systems and e-mail. Telephone patch systems enabled concerned citizens to call a toll-free number and be directly connected to a targeted lawmaker's line. For some constituents, e-mail made communications even simpler: during House consideration of the impeachment charges against President Bill Clinton, for example, e-mails outnumbered incoming phone calls by large margins, with many congressional offices receiving an estimated 10,000 to 15,000 e-mails per day. Referring to the e-mail bombardment, one administrative assistant noted, "The hard part was to know which ones came from our district. Usually it was about 10 percent and we tried to answer each one of those." In the Senate, the impeachment trial brought the daily number of incoming e-mails up from 70,000 to 80,000 to 500,000, backing up the Senate computers and requiring an upgrade of the equipment.

Mass Media Campaigns

Mass media campaigns—through radio, television, newspapers, or magazines—are another popular indirect lobbying technique. The campaigns may be designed either to stir up grassroots support or to influence legislators directly. For example, thoughtful editorials in well-known and even in obscure newspapers in members' districts often impel readers to write their member of Congress. And in the late 1980s, to beat back efforts to raise the minimum wage, business lobbyists met regularly with newspaper editors from across the country. The resulting editorials that favored the lobbyists' point of view were arranged by state, gathered into two thick volumes, and sent to every member of Congress.

Perhaps the most controversial media-based lobbying campaign was undertaken in 1994, when the Health Industry Association of America ran a series of television commercials in opposition to Clinton's health care reform proposals. The advertisements depicted a young couple—"Harry and Louise"—discussing the legislation and worrying aloud about its complexity and strong reliance on government administration. Many Capitol Hill observers said that the Harry and Louise commercials were crucial in sealing the fate of Clinton's legislation.

Legislators have often protested that the media campaigns have misled and even panicked constituents. But even when legislators believed that the public did not understand the issue—as was the case with health care coverage for catastrophic illness, which many senior citizens mistakenly believed would cost them large amounts of money—members found that they could not change public opinion.

Financial Support

Campaign contributions to members of Congress serve two important functions for lobbying organizations: first, political support can encourage a senator or representative to back the group's legislative interests; second, it can help to ensure that legislators who are friendly to the group's goals remain in office. (*See Chapter 32, Campaign Financing.*)

Although corporations and labor unions have been barred from making direct contributions to campaigns for federal office (since 1907 and 1943, respectively), contributors have found numerous ways to get around the restrictions. Labor pioneered the practice of creating separate political arms, such as the AFL-CIO's Committee on Political Education, which collect voluntary contributions from union members and their families and use the money to help elect senators and representatives favorable to the labor cause. Unions can also legally endorse candidates.

Similarly, corporations can organize political action committees (PACs) to seek contributions from stockholders and executive and administrative personnel and their families. Corporate

PACs proliferated after the Federal Election Commission's Sun-PAC decision in 1975, which allowed business PACs to solicit not only stockholders but employees as well, vastly expanding the potential to raise money. Slightly more than one-quarter of the $776 million raised by candidates during the 1997–1998 election cycle came from business-sponsored PACs.

Prior to the Republican takeover of Congress in 1995, Democrats and Republicans did about equally well in raising money from corporate PACs. Although Republicans hoped that business PAC managers would follow their ideological—that is, Republican—leanings, pragmatism was the stronger force. This was especially true in House races, where Democrats benefited from more than 50 percent of the business money. By 1998, however, after three years of GOP control, Democrats received only one-third of the corporate PAC contributions to House and Senate races. Pragmatism and ideology had merged.

Contributing to a member's federal campaign treasury is only the most visible means of providing financial support; despite regulations governing campaign contributions, there are many cracks through which money can flow into the system. Many members, for example, operate state campaign committees that are not governed by federal law. And the 1970s saw the rise of leadership PACs, through which members of Congress raised funds not for their own campaigns but for those of colleagues, who might remember the assistance when it came time to elect party leaders.

By the late 1990s, party officials had learned to appreciate the value of "soft money"—funds that could be used for "party building" but that could not directly support national campaigns (state and local campaigns could be funded by these monies). Under 1979 amendments to the Federal Election Campaign Act, as long as the funds were to be used for party building, corporations, labor unions, and other organizations can contribute to parties directly from their treasuries without going through a PAC. And although such contributions have to be reported, there is no limit on their amount. The importance of all of this was magnified when the sponsors of leadership PACs began to raise their own form of soft money: because of a loophole in the federal law, the sponsors could claim that contributors to leadership PACs were exempt from reporting requirements as well as from contribution limits. Thus, these PACs could receive unlimited amounts of money from undisclosed sources.

What few teeth were left in the federal campaign finance law were further dulled when the Supreme Court decided in 1996 that political parties could spend unlimited amounts to support the election of specific candidates as long as these expenditures were not coordinated with the candidates' own campaigns. The Court, however, left intact limits on direct contributions: the national parties and their campaign committees could only give $5,000 directly to House candidates and $17,500 to Senate candidates.

In approaching the typical legislator, a pressure group has no need to announce outright that future political support or op-

WHEN MAY MEMBERS OF CONGRESS INTERVENE IN AGENCY DELIBERATIONS?

The Senate and the House of Representatives have similar rules controlling the circumstances and the manner in which their members may contact federal agencies on behalf of "petitioners." In neither body is a member explicitly prohibited from representing a petitioner's cause solely for the reason that the petitioner has contributed to the legislator's campaign(s).

The Senate Manual permits senators to assist "petitioners" before government agencies in order to

• Request information or a status report.
• Urge prompt consideration.
• Arrange for interviews or appointments.
• Express judgments.
• Call for reconsideration of an administrative response that a member believes is not reasonably supported by statutes.

The manual is explicit with regard to special favors for contributors: "The decision to provide assistance . . . may not be made on the basis of contributions . . . or promises of contributions or services, to a member's political campaigns or to other organizations in which the member has a political, personal or financial interest." The Senate Select Committee on Ethics has further cautioned against diminishing the reputation of the Senate by acts that *appear* to be influenced by campaign contributions or other benefits provided by petitioners. The House Committee on Standards of Official Conduct has a similar prohibition. Neither Senate nor the House bars its members from soliciting contributions from organizations they have "done appreciable favors" for in the past. What is key is that even the appearance of a quid pro quo must be avoided.

The House Ethics Manual permits representation for the same purposes as noted above for the Senate. The House also makes clear that ex parte communications—off-the-record communications that attempt to influence the outcome of *official* proceedings pending at federal agencies—are absolutely prohibited.

The Senate and the House each caution members against the use of undue pressure when communicating with federal agencies. The House committee notes that "federal court opinions discourage inordinate pressure on officials charged by law with responsibility for making administrative decisions." The committee advises that a member "should consider expressly assuring administrators that no effort is being made to exert improper influence."

position depends on how the member votes on a particular bill—or on whether, over time, the member acts favorably toward the group. Lawmakers understand without being told that when the vital interests of some group are at stake, a vote in support of those interests will ordinarily gain the group's friendship and future support, and a vote against them will result in enmity and future opposition.

Pressure Groups: Many and Varied

In his 1951 study of interest groups, David Truman warned that the use of general terms, such as *business, labor,* or *agriculture* to refer to groups that share similar interests risked implying "a certain solidity or cohesion with the groups that may not exist." Equally dangerous is the temptation to ascribe to a group an interest that it does not have. Truman cited the difficulties of the person "who tried to reconcile the Farmers' State Rights League of the early 1920s with other 'farm' organizations" and who "would have been dealing in fact largely with a group of cotton mill operators who assumed this guise to work against the proposed child labor amendment to the Constitution."[7] Despite such warnings, students of political processes often find it useful to be able to distinguish between the major lobbying groups.

Thus, with Truman's caveat in mind, this section describes some of the most powerful, successful, or enduring examples of American lobbying interests.

BUSINESS GROUPS

The business lobby no longer wields the singular power over members of Congress that individual business magnates did during the Gilded Age. Business has fought bitter but losing battles against child labor laws, antitrust legislation, workers' compensation, the minimum wage, Social Security, and Medicare. Nevertheless, their importance to the nation's economy enables business groups to continue to exert considerable influence on legislative decisions, and business executives usually find the doors wide open when they go to Capitol Hill to press their case directly with senators or representatives. Major businesses maintain their own lobbying staffs, hire major lobbying firms to represent them, or both.

Trade groups range from agglomerations representing major business sectors, such as the American Petroleum Institute or the American Bankers Association, to pools of smaller and more obscure businesses that cannot afford a Washington presence of their own.

Through trade associations, business executives in similar fields meet to share resources and exchange information. And trade groups often devote the bulk of their resources to completely nonpolitical activities, such as gathering statistics, setting technical standards for their products, sponsoring product research, or developing marketing ventures. But their most visible function is lobbying.

In Washington, the maxim *e pluribus unum* has special meaning for business. By banding together, even the smallest businesses can afford to keep a full-time specialist on guard to protect their legislative interests. Corporate giants find that what looks like special pleading from one firm seems more like economic common sense when backed by a broad grouping of businesses. Businesses acting together are backed by the weight of an "industry position" and by the ability to mobilize the strengths of individual members. According to one corporate representative, "In this town [Washington, D.C.], your competitors are nearly always your allies."

The advantages of a unified front notwithstanding, one trade association often finds itself in opposition to another. When trucking industry lobbyists realized in 1990 that increased taxes on diesel fuel were inevitable, they focused their energy on ensuring that the taxes would be applied to railroads as well—a move that the trucking industry saw as crucial in maintaining competitiveness.

An even broader range of interests is represented by long-established business federations, such as the U.S. Chamber of Commerce, the National Association of Manufacturers, the Business Roundtable, the National Federation of Independent Business, and the National Small Business Union. By teaming up with one or more of these business federations, trade associations can gain access to the staff, meeting space, communication networks, and money that are required to get a lobbying campaign going. Affiliation with a business federation also offers added visibility—which helps move an issue up on the congressional agenda. When an avowedly probusiness administration holds the White House, as during the Reagan and Bush administrations, business federations gain even more clout.

The two best-known groups representing big business are the National Association of Manufacturers (NAM) and the U.S. Chamber of Commerce. Established in 1894 to expand foreign trade opportunities, NAM soon became a national counterforce to the developing labor union movement and, in the 1930s, to President Franklin D. Roosevelt's New Deal. As of 1999, NAM's 14,000 companies and subsidiaries represented only 3 percent of manufacturing companies, but the association claimed that its members represented three-quarters of the nation's industrial output.

The Chamber of Commerce was founded in 1912, at the urging of President William Howard Taft and with the help of NAM. As of 1998, the chamber had a staff of 990 at its Washington office and its membership included doctors, farmers, and some 215,000 business members, many of whom also belong to local, state, or regional chambers.

Both NAM and the Chamber of Commerce rely on "issue managers," who have expertise in specific areas such as taxes, and on generalists to handle direct lobbying in Washington. But their geographically dispersed membership base makes these organizations especially well positioned to employ grassroots techniques. NAM relies on a network of policy committees of between fifty and four hundred members to iron out its positions—and to be on call for contacting members.

In 1974 corporate executives decided to cash in on their considerable personal power by forming the New York–based Business Roundtable. Designed to give the biggest businesses more clout, the roundtable included two hundred chief executive officers of America's largest corporations, such as General Motors, Du Pont, IBM, and AT&T. The group's main strategy is to send business leaders to conduct direct, behind-the-scenes lobbying of legislators.

In a lobbying effort on behalf of management and labor, the chief executive officer of Bethlehem Steel rallies steelworkers at the Capitol to encourage Congress to pass a bill limiting steel imports.

Because small-business leaders felt that their concerns were not being adequately addressed by the broader business coalitions, they banded together and, like their larger counterparts, adopted increasingly aggressive lobbying tactics. The two major small-business groups were founded at about the same time, the National Federation of Independent Business (NFIB) in 1943 and the National Small Business Union (NSBU) in 1937; in 1986, the NSBU merged with a newer group, Small Business United, but the expanded organization elected to retain the NSBU name.

The NFIB, the larger of the two organizations, had more than 600,000 members in 1998. The NFIB has two principal legislative goals: to obtain passage of legislation that helps small businesses and to fight what the group considers excessive federal regulation. The organization establishes policy by polling its members five times a year about specific issues; it then lobbies according to the preferences that members express. During the 1994 debate on the Clinton administration's health care reform proposal, NFIB emerged as an exceptionally influential lobbying force. Concerning provisions that would have compelled virtually all employers to provide health insurance for their employees, NFIB argued that many of its members could not afford the costs of such a requirement: as one beleaguered congressional staffer said, "I think every business owner in our district got to us on that one."

In 1980, tired of being caught in the crossfire between their larger and smaller brethren, the executives of one hundred mid-sized corporations formed the American Business Conference to promote the interests of high-growth and high-technology companies. The conference's goals are sometimes opposed to those of large businesses: for example, it fought fiercely against protectionist trade policies.

Because of the breadth of the interests that they represent, business groups have their shortcomings. For example, the trade associations have to protect the interests of their weakest members, who are often more conservative than the larger firms. Similar differences may distinguish local chapters from their national-level organizations: House members often complain that although they are in close sympathy with the local chapters of groups such as the Chamber of Commerce, the national organizations are rigidly ideological.

When a single business dominates a region or state, its most eager lobbyists may be legislators themselves. In the 1970s and 1980s, for instance, Seattle-area representatives pushed hard for federal assistance to enable the threatened Boeing Corporation to continue building airplanes. In 1989, when the Department of Defense decided to phase out the F-14 fighter jet, which was built by the Grumman Corporation, of Bethpage, New York, House Democrats and Republicans from Long Island met each Wednesday to devise a campaign to keep the planes in production for the sake of 5,600 jobs. One member of the Appropriations Committee lobbied his colleagues on that panel; a Ways and Means Committee member who had earlier led arms-control fights attempted to defuse liberal opposition; a former Grumman engineer marshaled technical data; and two Republicans concentrated on getting their colleagues to oppose the administration's position. These efforts won the construction of eighteen more airplanes.

LABOR

The craftsmen and laborers of early America embraced the young country's ideals of freedom—which to them meant "every man his own master." Unions, virtually nonexistent in the eighteenth century and weak in the nineteenth, gained prominence only as the Industrial Revolution's effects on the worker became evident.

In 1935 the Wagner Act offered labor unions the protected right to bargain collectively. Union membership grew from fewer than 3 million in 1933 to about 9 million in 1939, and this upward trend continued into the following decade. During World War II, many labor union officials learned how to operate effectively in Washington when they were brought to the capital to serve on the War Labor Board. These developments helped set the stage for the emergence of organized labor as an important pressure group.

The unions' large membership, considerable strength in urban centers, substantial financial resources, and organizational know-how made them a formidable force. Organized labor not only conducted grassroots campaigns to influence public opinion but also undertook direct lobbying of Congress, executive branch leaders, and often the president.

Yet organized labor has never been homogeneous or completely unified: expressions such as "labor victory" and "labor defeat" imply a cohesiveness that rarely exists. Although the unions' ability to bring their members to the polls on Election Day underlies much of their political clout, the election of Ronald Reagan as president in 1980 and 1984, against almost unanimous labor opposition, demonstrated that unions could no longer "deliver" the votes of blue-collar workers. And union membership itself has declined: after peaking at 35 percent of the labor force in the 1950s, it was down to about 14 percent by the late 1990s.

The largest umbrella organization for organized labor has its headquarters one block from the White House and around the corner from its frequent opponent, the Chamber of Commerce. The American Federation of Labor, founded in 1881, merged in 1955 with its rival, the Congress of Industrial Organizations, to form the AFL-CIO. By 1991, the AFL-CIO was a federation of about 150 separate affiliate unions, ranging from white-collar workers—including teachers and government employees—to blue-collar workers in construction or in the trades. The mammoth federation represented about 16.2 million members in 1998, but its numbers had been in decline until 1987, when it got a 13 percent boost by readmitting the International Brotherhood of Teamsters, Chauffeurs, Warehousemen, and Helpers of America, which had been expelled in 1957 for corruption.

Many unions, most notably the AFL-CIO, maintain large research and publication staffs that contribute substantially to the development and popularization of policy proposals in the areas of labor and social welfare. Yet it was the unions' willingness to use political action that probably had a greater impact on their effectiveness. Both the AFL and the CIO maintained political arms; when the two federations merged, their political committees united as well, resulting in the creation of COPE: the AFL-CIO Committee on Political Education. The term *political action committee* came from the CIO's political action committee, which was formed in 1943. By the 1980s, nearly every large union maintained a PAC.

Much of the Great Society legislation of the 1960s, under President Lyndon B. Johnson, was the product of lobbying by organized labor. And, after initial ambivalence, the major unions supported the reforms of the civil rights era. The irony that has frustrated many union lobbyists is that labor has been less successful on issues that directly affect union members than on issues that are related to general social welfare.

The unions jumped into political action in 1947, when they

tried to defeat the Taft-Hartley Act. Although labor won the first round, when President Harry S. Truman vetoed the measure, it lost the next, when Congress overrode the veto. Labor lost again in 1959, failing to prevent passage of the restrictions on union activity in the Landrum-Griffin Labor-Management Reporting and Disclosure Act. The unions suffered yet another loss in 1966, when a Senate filibuster blocked legislation to repeal Section 14B of Taft-Hartley, under which states were permitted to enact "right-to-work" laws that sanctioned nonunion shops.

In 1976 labor saw a long-sought victory turn to defeat when President Gerald R. Ford vetoed a bill that would have allowed a union with a grievance against a single employer to picket and close down an entire job site. Ford's successor, the labor-backed Democrat Jimmy Carter, did no better; in 1977, the House unexpectedly defeated a similar bill. President Reagan, who cemented the animosity of labor unions when he fired 11,400 striking air traffic controllers in 1981, successfully vetoed 1985 and 1987 measures designed to protect the American textile industry. When George Bush became president in 1989, labor aggressively pushed a long list of pent-up desires: another textile bill, an increase in the minimum wage, mandatory unpaid leave for workers with new babies or sick relatives, and the easing of restrictions on political activity by federal workers. Bush vetoed them all, and despite Democratic majorities in both chambers, the 101st Congress (1989–1991) failed to get the two-thirds necessary to override any of the vetoes.

Both union members and lobbyists contend that one reason for labor's failure to win on its own issues was the perception that it was a special interest; whereas when it campaigned for social legislation, labor successfully portrayed itself as a public interest lobby.

Over the years, many legislators lost their fear of union retaliation against an antilabor vote as they realized that union members did not always vote as their leaders wanted them to on Election Day. On social (as opposed to economic) issues, the rank and file tended to be less liberal than their leaders, particularly during the 1980s, when the country experienced a general shift to the right.

Labor leaders strove to recapture influence by reexamining their lobbying techniques. For years they had depended on close ties to powerful committee chairmen and party leaders, but as power dispersed throughout Congress, labor often found itself outflanked by business interests' indirect lobbying techniques. In the early 1990s, the unions tried to revive their own grassroots appeal. They also began to pay greater attention to Republicans, but this strategy did not last long. By 1996, after one Congress under Republican control, organized labor decided to launch a high-profile, high-stakes campaign to help Democrats regain majority status in the House. The effort was unsuccessful in wresting control from Republicans and only partially successful in helping to elect some Democrats in targeted districts.

ENVIRONMENTALISTS

The American conservation movement began in the 1800s as an effort to protect land, mostly in the West, from unregulated and rapacious use. An ardent conservationist, President Theodore Roosevelt succeeded in the early 1900s in making the protection of natural resources a national issue. Even in Roosevelt's day, the lines were already drawn between the protectors of the environment and the advocates of technological progress.

Two world wars and a national depression turned the country's attention to achieving technological superiority and economic stability, and concern about the environment was limited to a fairly docile group of wilderness lovers, bird watchers, and garden club members. Eventually, however, their concern came to be shared by forward-looking scientists who saw the hazards that were inherent in technological and scientific development.

In the 1960s and 1970s, due in part to a number of widely publicized environmental disasters, such as the Santa Barbara oil spill and the poisoning of wildlife by pesticides, the conservation movement began to embrace broader issues of public health and safety. New groups sprang up, each with their own cause and tactics, and joined—however tenuously—with the older, more traditional organizations.

The staid National Wildlife Federation, founded in 1936, increased its membership nearly eightfold between 1972 and 1999 to 4 million members, many of them blue-collar workers interested in preserving hunting and fishing habitats. The federation became the informal moderator of the Washington conservation community, sponsoring conferences and strategy sessions aimed at increasing harmony among the various groups. By the end of the 1990s, the federation had targeted five core areas of interest: endangered habitats, sustainability, stewardship of grazing lands, water quality, and wetlands preservation.

The more militant Environmental Action, founded in 1970, had twenty thousand members in the late 1990s and more of a focus on urban issues such as air pollution, toxic substances, and alternative energy. Environmental Action conducted campaigns against the "Dirty Dozen" members of Congress and the "Filthy Five" corporate polluters.

The middle ground is populated by groups as broad in appeal as the 500,000-member Sierra Club, which was founded as a California hiking club in 1892 and is notable for the bottom-up process it uses to set its agenda; as specialized as the 35,000-member Solar Lobby, which promotes renewable energy sources; as middle-of-the-road as the Conservation Foundation, a think tank sponsored by foundations, corporations, and the government; and as contentious as the two major environmental law firms, the Natural Resources Defense Council (NRDC) and the Environmental Defense Fund (EDF).

From the 1960s through the 1980s, environmental groups sparked a legislative explosion, pushing Congress to enact numerous environmental laws and the regulatory apparatus to interpret and enforce them. The laws governed air and water pol-

LOBBIES RATE MEMBERS

Like a book of baseball records, a published rating of Congress based on selected votes can start as many arguments as it settles. In recent years, it seems as if every spectator has a scorecard.

In 1942 the *New Republic* caused a minor furor by publishing a list of legislators' "plus" and "minus" votes on President Franklin D. Roosevelt's foreign policy. It was entitled "A Congress to Win the War." Members with heavy "minus" scores objected, calling it a "purge list" for those who advocated neutrality prior to Pearl Harbor. And they ripped into the recently formed group responsible for the scoring: the Union for Democratic Action.

Five years later, reconstituted as Americans for Democratic Action (ADA), that group began producing an annual rating of legislators on both foreign and domestic policy. The National Farmers Union published its first study in 1919 and began an annual voting record in 1948. The AFL-CIO has played the rating game since the two labor organizations combined in 1955. The Americans for Constitutional Action began compiling a "conservative" index in 1958, later joined by the American Conservative Union.

Following are some of the organizations that have published voting records or ratings, either annually or for a complete Congress:

Business. U.S. Chamber of Commerce, Competitive Enterprise Institute, National Association of Manufacturers, National Federation of Independent Business.

Conservatives. American Conservative Union, Americans for Constitutional Action Research Institute, Liberty Lobby.

Liberals. Americans for Democratic Action.

Consumer Affairs. Consumer Federation of America, National Taxpayers Union, Public Citizen.

Defense/Foreign Policy. American Committee on Africa, American Security Council, Coalition for a New Foreign Policy, Council for a Livable World, SANE/FREEZE.

Education. American Federation of Teachers, National Education Association, U.S. Student Association.

Environment. Citizen/Labor Energy Coalition, Clean Water Action Project, Critical Mass Energy Project, Environmental Action, Friends of the Earth, League of Conservation Voters, Sierra Club.

Labor. AFL-CIO; many labor unions.

Rural/Farm. American Farm Bureau Federation, National Farmers Organization.

Other Political Activists. Citizens Committee for the Right to Keep and Bear Arms, Common Cause, Handgun Control Inc., Leadership Conference on Civil Rights, National Abortion Rights Action League-Political Action Committee, National Association for the Advancement of Colored People, National Association of Social Workers, National Council of La Raza, National Council of Senior Citizens, National Gay and Lesbian Task Force, National Organization for Women, National Rifle Association, National Right to Life Committee, National Women's Political Caucus, The Woman Activist.

HOW ACCURATE? HOW USEFUL?

Many political scientists use ratings by interest groups only reluctantly. At best, interest group ratings provide a kind of shorthand identification, a one-sentence abstract of a given politician's thinking on the full range of public issues. At worst, the numbers can oversimplify the differences. A member can vote for every amendment intended to "gut" a bill and still get credit from a supporting organization by voting for the measure on final passage. Also, most rating systems do not account for voting in committee and in subcommittee. Yet, these are frequently the most important votes that a member can cast on a measure.

Nevertheless, the political community continued to find them useful. "Ratings are the single most effective way to tell where someone stands on the political spectrum," said Ann Lewis, former director of Americans for Democratic Action. The ratings are especially important to political action committees (PACs). PAC managers, even if they are aware of shortcomings, often place great weight on these rating systems in making their contributions decisions.

Many members kept close track of their ratings by groups with a hold on their constituencies. Staff aides said that members often seemed to go out of their way to avoid getting a perfect score from a group, so they would not appear to be in the thrall of any particular interest.

On the other hand, on a major vote the knowledge that it would be used as a litmus test could be enough to sway votes. On key votes on the 1990 rewrite of the Clean Air Act, for instance, members whipping the vote on an amendment stationed themselves near the doors where members entered the chamber and warned them that the vote would count in scorecards used to determine whether members were "for" or "against" the environment. Some interest groups even passed out fliers warning members that a particular vote would be included in their ratings. During the 1994 votes in the House on banning assault weapons, lobby groups on both sides of the issue were equally aggressive in reminding members that their votes would be weighted heavily in ratings reports that would be sent to "millions" of group supporters.

lution; forest, range, and coastal land management, including strip mining; pesticides and toxic substances; and endangered species.

Although the Reagan administration stalled most new initiatives, it did not succeed in rolling back any significant environmental legislation. Moreover, the Reagan years proved to be an organizational boon to environmental groups: despite failing to push much of their agenda through Congress, they made effective use of Reagan's environmental policies—which favored oil drilling and nuclear power and found their emblem in James Watt, Reagan's high-profile interior secretary—to raise funds and increase their membership. President Bush distinguished himself from his predecessor by embracing the environmental spirit: during his administration, a massive rewrite of air pollution legislation raced through the 101st Congress with relatively little opposition—especially considering that it probably had direct effect on more Americans than the income tax laws.

Environmentalists used the same sophisticated techniques that labor and business did: phone banks and computerized direct mail to mobilize constituents; door-to-door canvassing by volunteers; mass mailings and visits from constituents to impress Congress; and coalition building to increase the effectiveness of lobbying efforts. They also sponsored research and publications that heightened public concern; the EDF, for example, specialized in cost-benefit analyses that appealed to the pragmatists in both industry and government. Establishing its PAC in 1982, the Sierra Club is one of the few environmental groups that contributes directly to candidates, but other groups often provide skilled organizers and campaign workers to help elect sympathetic legislators.

Environmentalists also mastered the art of cashing in on public sympathies. With most voters identifying themselves as "pro-environment," the groups found that rating legislators on an "environmental scorecard" was an effective means of swaying their votes. The board of the League of Conservation Voters, which consisted mostly of leaders from other environmental groups, selected the votes on which members would be rated. Often, the news that a particular floor vote would be included in the ratings was enough to bring undecided members over to the environmentalists' side—particularly when members themselves spread the word as they lobbied colleagues. *(See box, Lobbies Rate Members, p. 704.)*

Environmental groups often divide lobbying efforts according to their special interests or contacts. In the 1980s, the Sierra Club spearheaded action on the oil industry and on coastal protection; the EDF led the way on clean air; the National Audubon Society focused on wildlife, pesticides, and groundwater contamination; and the NRDC addressed public health. In the late 1990s, the Sierra Club emphasized ensuring the health of national forests and preserves, such as the Everglades. The 300,000-member EDF advocated economic incentives as a means of addressing environmental concerns.

FARMERS

After the end of World War II, small, traditional family farms were overtaken by vast changes. The number of farmers steadily declined, the average size of farms increased, land prices rose rapidly, and large corporations and cooperatives became increasingly important in what came to be known as agribusiness. As farmers' lives changed, so did the work of the agricultural lobbyist. What had been a "people's lobby" slowly became an interest group, subject to much the same public suspicion and criticism as other special interests.

The National Grange, established in 1867, originally offered isolated farm families a sense of community as well as an organizational framework for political activity. The Grange supported Congress's formation, in 1887, of the Interstate Commerce Commission, which regulated the rail freight rates that were critical to the farmers' success. The National Grange, the Federal Farm Bureau Federation, and the National Farmers Union formed the basic historical unit of the powerful farm lobby.

Organized at the national level in 1919, the American Farm Bureau Federation (AFBF) claimed a membership of nearly 5 million member families by the late 1990s and is the most geographically diverse of the farm groups. With its federated system of organization—bureaus in every state and in Puerto Rico—it enjoys the benefit of wide-ranging political clout. At the same time, like most political associations, it is occasionally hamstrung by the need to balance competing interests among its members: in the case of the federation, these are commodity interests. Often considered the voice of more prosperous farmers, the federation has championed such issues as the elimination of inheritance taxes. It also argued for moderate implementation of the Food Quality Protection Act, a 1996 measure that was intended to curb the use of selected pesticides.

The National Farmers Union (NFU), formed in 1902, has pushed for a more active government role in maintaining farm prices, supported the concept of parity, and worked to protect the food stamp and federally subsidized school lunch programs. The NFU claimed about 1 million member families, mostly in the Great Plains, the Midwest, and the Pacific Northwest. It is regarded as the most liberal of the "supergroups" and was one of the first groups to advocate the preservation of family farms.

The National Grange faded as a political force during the last few decades of the twentieth century, but it maintained a voice as a conservative farm group. A more active group, the National Farmers Organization (NFO), grew out of a 1950s protest that, at its most militant stage, organized milk dumping and pig executions to dramatize the low prices for farm products. Over time, the NFO became less combative and more of a service organization, bargaining to secure contracts between farmers and distributors.

The militant strain of farm populism is represented by the American Agricultural Movement (AAM). Organized by a group of Colorado wheat producers in 1977, it gained national attention in 1978–1979, when "tractorcades" invaded the nation's capital to protest President Carter's farm policy. While the tactic generated sympathy for the plight of family farmers, the property damage inflicted by the tractors also caused resentment. The group established a formal Washington presence and brought celebrities, such as country singer Willie Nelson, to Washington to testify for its cause. In 1983 and 1988, concerned about increases in freight rates for farm products, the AAM joined with railroads to defeat a proposal to build slurry pipelines to move coal; and in 1987, it helped to win easier access to credit for farmers. But the AAM lost in its major push, a 1985 effort to win direct government control of production.

The farm lobby is strengthened by many single-commodity farm organizations, such as the Associated Milk Producers, the National Wool Growers Association, and the American Cattlemen's Association. Commodity wholesalers and distributors also have lobbyists working in their behalf in Washington. Congress gave several commodity groups a major boon in the 1980s, when it passed legislation requiring consumers to pay for formal efforts to promote the consumption of pork, dairy products, beef, wool, cotton, and other goods. These "checkoff" programs generated tens of millions of dollars for advertising campaigns that were closely tied to producers' groups.

By the late 1990s, farm subsidy programs that had been in place for decades were proving expensive for taxpayers and not very helpful to the farmers whom they were intended to benefit. Bad weather and reduced demands for exports lowered yields, pushing prices up and creating the worst possible economic conditions for farmers. Higher prices led to reduced subsidies, and diminished yields cut overall farm income. Opponents of the existing subsidy programs took the opportunity to push for a move from subsidies to a fixed-payment system. The Freedom to Farm bill, enacted in 1996, did just that. The bill applied a complex formula to provide farmers with direct, fixed payments that were scheduled to diminish over a period of seven years. In exchange for the gradual reduction in payments, farmers received larger payments in 1996 and 1997 than they would otherwise have been eligible for; they also gained greater flexibility in deciding what crops to plant.

The AFBF was adamant in its support for the bill. Dean Kleckner, president of the federation, offered an unvarnished view: "There will be a lot of dead bodies politically if there is no farm bill," he announced when it appeared that some nonfarm issues had temporarily jeopardized the Freedom to Farm bill. In 1998 Congress passed an additional measure that sweetened the benefits for most farmers.

During the middle and late 1990s, another farm issue, the regulation of tobacco products, came to national prominence when a series of lawsuits, many initiated by state attorneys general, sought to hold the tobacco companies liable for the costs of tobacco-related illnesses. In an effort to cut its potential losses, the industry agreed to a financial settlement that also called for Food and Drug Administration (FDA) regulation of tobacco but prohibited action for twelve years. A Senate bill that would have made FDA regulation immediate was defeated in that body in 1998.

PUBLIC INTEREST GROUPS

In his fear of faction, James Madison did not envisage the events of the latter part of the twentieth century, when the public interest itself would become the focus of lobbying conducted by groups borrowing freely from the techniques first developed by lobbyists for narrow economic interests. By 1990, some 2,500 organizations calling themselves public interest groups collected $4 billion annually in contributions and claimed to represent 40 million citizens.

Those who find themselves in conflict with "public interest" groups deride the use of that term, but it remains common usage. In his 1977 book *Lobbying for the People: The Political Behavior of Public Interest Groups,* Jeffrey M. Berry offered this definition: "A public interest group is one that seeks a collective good, the achievement of which will not selectively and materially benefit the membership or activists of the organization."[8] (This definition encompasses many lobbying groups discussed elsewhere in this chapter, such as those focusing on environmental issues, religion, and civil rights.)

Several older groups set the pattern for the later proliferation of public interest groups. The nonpartisan League of Women Voters, founded in 1920 to educate women on the use of their newly won franchise, soon extended the scope of its activities to include the political education of the general public. The league sponsored debates between candidates during several presidential elections, and it lobbied in the 1970s for the passage of the Equal Rights Amendment and the Clean Air Act.

A broad-based group with a more pointed political agenda was the Americans for Democratic Action (ADA), founded in 1947 to "formulate liberal domestic and foreign policies." Best known for its annual ratings of legislators' votes on issues of concern to the group, the ADA also maintains a lobbying staff in Washington. Its conservative counterpart, the American Conservative Union, was founded in 1964 and began rating lawmakers in 1971.

Two of the most well-known public interest groups are Public Citizen, established in 1971 by lawyer-activist Ralph Nader, and Common Cause, founded in 1970 by John Gardner, a former cabinet secretary. Though both groups share the general goal of increasing citizens' influence over political, economic, and social concerns, each has areas of specialty within that framework. Public Citizen acts as an umbrella organization to address a wide range of concerns that reflect Nader's interests: auto safety, consumer protection, insurance, medicine, nuclear power, aviation, pension rights, drug and food safety, product liability, occupational health and safety, and pesticide control. Common Cause focuses on issues of political structure and procedure—although in the early 1980s, after consulting four thousand members in a special poll, it detoured into arms control before returning to "good government" issues such as campaign finance and ethics laws. In the 1990s, Common Cause focused increasingly on the reform of campaign financing laws.

Both groups undertake direct lobbying in Washington and maintain sophisticated grassroots lobbying operations. But unlike many other special interest groups, neither organization endorses candidates or makes campaign contributions. Gardner viewed Common Cause as a vehicle offering interested private citizens, working in concert, an opportunity to influence decisions in Washington—just as business organizations and labor unions do. It uses an insider-outsider strategy, with experienced Washington lobbyists working the halls of Congress while state and local chapters pressure legislators from their home bases. Congress Watch, a Public Citizen organization devoted to legislative affairs, employs policy specialists who register to lobby on specific issues, such as freedom of information, consumer protection, and health and safety.

Both groups are characterized by a grassroots emphasis. Common Cause developed an indirect lobbying operation that

In 1985 lobbyists opposing the development of the MX missile gather on the steps of the Capitol before taking their agenda to members of Congress.

could galvanize its members—numbering 250,000 in 1999—to write or call their senators or representatives when significant issues arose. During congressional elections, the organization took out advertisements in the local media that attacked individual legislators for their stands on issues such as campaign finance. Those tactics—and the fact that Common Cause initiated the ethics complaint that led to the resignation of House Speaker Jim Wright, in 1989—alienated some of the group's traditional allies in the Democratic Party, and its vigorous and repeated attacks on the current campaign financing system further damaged its relations with members of both parties.

The primary objective of the Nader organization's grassroots efforts is to spark local action on local problems, and the group is often more effective at the state than the national level. Nader often urges the audiences at his speeches to become more directly involved in public affairs; he himself has taken a high-profile role in state ballot initiatives, including a successful 1988 California drive to mandate a rollback of auto insurance rates. Pub-

lic Citizen has also been willing to make pragmatic alliances, forming a united front with trial lawyers in the 1980s to combat industry's drive to revamp product liability laws nationwide.

The largest of the activist groups is Citizen Action, which was founded in Cleveland in 1979; a decade later, the organization changed its name to The Citizen Action Foundation and relocated its headquarters to Washington, D.C. By the late 1990s, the foundation claimed 3 million members. The group's priorities include environmental conservation, campaign finance, health care, and legal reforms.

Public interest organizations have their own think tank and training center, the Advocacy Institute, founded in 1984 by David Cohen, a former president of Common Cause, and Michael Pertschuk, head of the Federal Trade Commission under President Carter.

CIVIL RIGHTS GROUPS

Civil rights groups represent a range of interests—African Americans, Hispanics, women, and free speech advocates, among others. In dealing with Congress, these groups present a united front through the Leadership Conference on Civil Rights. Formed in 1950, the conference includes representatives from labor groups, women's rights organizations, organizations for disabled people, senior citizens' organizations, and faith-based groups. Its representatives can elbow their way into the back rooms of the Capitol to influence the wording of major legislation. In 1987 the conference led the fight that defeated the nomination of Robert H. Bork to the Supreme Court.

Formed in 1909, the National Association for the Advancement of Colored People (NAACP) was created, in part, to attempt to resolve ideological disputes—principally, acquiescence versus militancy—among black intellectuals. The NAACP was gradually transformed from a loose-knit group of intellectuals into a national policy-making body with membership in the thousands—and, once the civil rights movement was in full swing—considerable prestige in Washington. The NAACP was credited with formulating a strategy for combating racism that relied on two principal means: the use of marches and nonviolent protests to appeal to the conscience of white America and the prosecution of civil rights cases in the courts.

Under the leadership of Martin Luther King Jr. of the Southern Christian Leadership Conference (SCLC), other civil rights groups eventually added the NAACP's grassroots tactics to traditional lobbying efforts. In the 1960s, the civil rights movement produced two of the largest demonstrations ever assembled in the nation's capital—the 1963 March on Washington for Jobs and Freedom, in which more than a quarter of a million people participated and at which King delivered his famous "I have a dream" speech; and the 1968 Poor People's Campaign, during which an estimated three thousand people camped near the Lincoln Memorial for fifty-six days.

As the oldest and best known civil rights organization, the NAACP was long seen as the leader in the fight for equality, but by the mid-1990s it was burdened with debt and had been badly crippled by a tangled leadership fight. Nevertheless, it did retain some influence, and by 1999, it had reemerged as a major force under new leaders—including Kweisi Mfume, a former House member. It took on businesses over minority hiring, led a legal attack against gun dealers, and vigorously assailed the major television networks for the scarcity of black characters in the primetime programs. Observers felt that this new vigor represented the return of the NAACP to the major role it had held for decades in promoting the interests and rights of African Americans.

Another influential organization, the National Urban League, was founded just one year after the NAACP. Originally known as a social welfare organization that appealed primarily to middle-class blacks, the league eventually became an important voice for the impoverished underclass of America's large cities.

Other highly visible civil rights groups included the Congress of Racial Equality (CORE) and the Student Nonviolent Coordinating Committee (SNCC). Although the militant "black power" groups, the Black Panthers and the Black Muslims, gained significant media attention, for the most part these groups rejected traditional means of achieving power in Washington, and they had little influence after the height of the civil rights movement.

By the 1980s, the conservative Reagan and Bush presidencies forced civil rights groups to swim against a tide of budget cuts, adverse court decisions, resentment against affirmative action, and public indifference. But the phrase *civil rights* had acquired an aura of sanctity that gave even presidents pause: in 1982, civil rights groups secured passage of a new voting rights bill, and in 1988—over a Reagan veto—they gained the reversal of several Supreme Court decisions. Even after Republicans took control of Congress in 1995, the movement had sufficient political strength to protect affirmative action programs against legislation that was intended to reduce their scope and effectiveness.

Through the League of United Latin American Citizens (founded in 1929), the National Council of La Raza (1968), and the Mexican American Legal Defense and Educational Fund (1967), Hispanics emulated the organizing and lobbying tactics of groups such as the NAACP.

Among the most active defenders of civil rights in Washington and across the country is the American Civil Liberties Union (ACLU). Founded in 1920, the ACLU is known for its courtroom prowess in defending political speech across a broad spectrum, from communism to nazism. In the 1970s, when its leaders saw that the end of the Warren Court would bring a decline in judicial activism, the ACLU consciously stepped up its efforts to affect the drafting as well as interpretation of laws. Its Washington office expanded dramatically, and the group played a major role in legislation affecting such areas as secret intelligence, immigration, drug testing, criminal justice, and privacy.

Women's rights groups gained significant influence on Capitol Hill in the 1970s and 1980s. Although they pulled up short in their major drive, to achieve ratification of the Equal Rights Amendment, groups such as the National Organization for Women, formed in 1966, continue to be important voices on abortion and employment issues.

STATE AND LOCAL GROUPS

Faced with the growing complexity, power, and financial might of the federal government, municipal, county, and state officials found the need to have formal representation in Washington. State and local government lobbies boomed when President Johnson's Great Society initiative began funneling vast amounts of federal funds into domestic programs. They had another growth spurt in the 1980s when they had to muster a defense against federal regulations, federal mandates requiring states to provide more support for social programs, and cuts in federal entitlements and grants. Because of local and state officials' political savvy, party ties, and grassroots connections, the intergovernmental lobby stands as a powerful force.

The center of state activity in Washington can be found in the Hall of the States, the office building four blocks from the Capitol where individual states and organizations of state officials have their offices. Many representatives of state interests find that the dormitory-like atmosphere of the building facilitates the easy exchange of information—although some powerful states, such as Texas, prefer to keep their contacts to themselves.

State offices monitor grants, track the legislative process, and keep an eye on regulations. In 1999 only one-third of the states did not have their own Washington offices; these were principally central and western states whose congressional delegations were small enough to coordinate among themselves. Some state offices are directly tied to the current governor and change hands with every election; others represent the entire state bureaucracy. Texas's office is a separate agency of state government. Sometimes regarded as political plums, the Washington jobs are vulnerable to budget cuts: in 1989, for example, incoming governor Evan Bayh abolished Indiana's office.

Although state offices are in competition for federal funds, states, like corporations, see the advantage of presenting a united front to Congress. In 1908 the nation's governors pioneered the collaborative approach by founding the National Governors' Conference, which later became the National Governors' Association (NGA). The NGA's annual Washington meetings are significant political events, often drawing major speeches from the president. The 1988 overhaul of federal welfare programs resulted from several years of work that, largely through the efforts of the NGA, managed to bring together liberal Democrats and conservative Republicans. Eight years later, welfare reform moved much further when, with NGA support, welfare was effectively turned over to the fifty state governments and states were granted nearly full responsibility for determining eligibility and benefit standards.

In 1975 state legislatures formed their own organization, the National Conference of State Legislatures. Cities are represented by the National League of Cities, formed in 1924, and by the more urban-dominated U.S. Conference of Mayors, which was founded in 1932. Counties have their own organization, the National Organization of Counties, which is affiliated with a host of subgroups representing county health officials, parks and recreation directors, welfare directors, and other local government officials. The heads of local government agencies often have their own organizations, from the International Association of Chiefs of Police, a major force on gun control and crime issues, to the National American Court Clerks Association.

Some private lobbyists specialize in helping state officials find their way through the maze of the federal bureaucracy or in helping national companies keep track of what is going on in the states. A tobacco company, for instance, would have to scramble to keep up with the smoking restrictions and cigarette tax proposals under consideration in state legislatures. State and local governments and the private sector are not always at odds, however, and often create coalitions to address issues such as highway and transit funding, taxes, municipal bonds, public housing, and health policy.

FOREIGN GOVERNMENTS

The United Nations may be headquartered in New York, but the hub of international activity is Washington. Afghan resistance leaders, religious factions from Northern Ireland, right- and left-wing guerrilla groups from Latin America and Africa, eastern European governments seeking economic and technical assistance: virtually any foreign faction sends emissaries to the U.S. Congress and administration, as do purely economic interests—Australian meat producers, Chilean fruit shippers, and Japanese auto manufacturers.

Like other interest groups, foreign nations and economic interests seek help from the city's law firms, political consulting firms, and prominent individuals—and, like other interests, they want lobbyists with the best possible connections. Unlike lobbyists for domestic clients, however, those who work for foreign clients are required by separate legislation to register with the Justice Department and to report their fees from foreign clients. In 1999, 531 agents for foreign governments were registered under the Foreign Agents Registration Act as actively representing the interests of foreign nations. (See "Lobbying Regulations," p. 716.)

Acting as an agent for a foreign government carries something of a stigma, and excessively vigorous lobbying can create a backlash, particularly when Americans feel threatened by another country. "Japan's lobbyists manipulate America's political and economic system," charged Pat Choate, a former executive of TRW Corp., in a 1990 book that estimated Japanese interests spent at least $100 million a year to burnish their country's image.

On the other hand, some foreign governments are the beneficiaries of enthusiastic support from domestic groups. One of the most savvy and influential of all lobbying organizations is the American Israel Public Affairs Committee (AIPAC), founded in 1951. The group originally focused exclusively on Congress to counter what it perceived as pro-Arab leanings in the State Department. In the late 1980s, it shifted its focus to the White House—a move that did not sit well with some congressional Democrats. While Israel's supporters were an important source of political donations, AIPAC made no donations itself, although critics claimed that it secretly coordinated millions of dollars from other PACs. Although AIPAC failed to stop the sale of radar surveillance planes to Saudi Arabia in 1981, that was a rare defeat.

Because Congress seldom challenges the president on foreign affairs issues, developing nations often choose lobbying firms that have close ties to the administration in power. A rare rebuff of a president was engineered in 1985 when TransAfrica persuaded Congress to override President Reagan's veto of economic sanctions against South Africa.

SENIOR CITIZENS

In the 1920s, the Fraternal Order of Eagles lobbied state legislatures to set up pension plans; and in 1929, following extensive lobbying by the Eagles, California launched the nation's first mandatory pension system. Running as a Democrat for governor in 1934, novelist Upton Sinclair made an increase in the meager state benefit ($23 monthly) a cornerstone of his unsuccessful campaign.

The push for a nationwide pension, headed by California physician Francis Townsend, began in the early 1930s. The Townsend movement agitated for creation of the Social Security system, which Franklin Roosevelt adopted as his own cause. But Congress did not really face overt lobbying from an organized age-based group until after creation of Medicare in 1965. Within twenty years, however, senior citizens had become one of the most powerful political forces in America. Their influence comes from two sources: first, older Americans communicate actively with their political representatives; second, they vote in huge numbers.

By the mid-1990s, the oldest members of the enormous baby boom generation were poised to join the ranks of retirees—a group that will swell by millions over the coming decades. By the late 1990s, the two most serious and contentious issues that confronted Washington were how to finance and retain (not to mention expand) the Medicare and the Social Security benefits that had been promised to older citizens.

Although many senior citizens' organizations try to avoid overtly partisan politics, the political vigor of their members makes them a force to be reckoned with whenever legislation affecting older Americans comes up. Never was this power more evident than in 1984, when President Reagan and congressional leaders worked out a plan to control the federal deficit by limiting domestic and defense programs. Fearing repercussions from even a tiny nick in Social Security benefits, rank-and-file members of Congress abandoned the proposal entirely. Five years later, President Bush and congressional leaders had to sit by in embarrassment as a major expansion of medical benefits for

When Congress contemplated taking up the volatile issue of overhauling Social Security in 1998, senior citizens mobilized to get their voices heard. The elderly have become perhaps the most powerful force in America.

"catastrophic" illness was repealed—only a year after it had been enacted with great fanfare—because of agitation from senior citizens about how much they would have to pay for it.

In both these cases, the pressure on Congress came primarily from spontaneous grassroots protests, not from campaigns organized by major lobbying groups. But several groups rode the tide of protest: chief among them in the 1980s was the National Committee to Preserve Social Security and Medicare, a group founded by James Roosevelt, Franklin Roosevelt's eldest son and

a U.S. representative from 1955 to 1965. Members of Congress complained that this group used scare tactics to panic uninformed senior citizens and to raise funds for itself.

The largest lobbying group in America is far less confrontational. The American Association of Retired Persons—which officially changed its name to its initials alone, AARP, in 1999—was founded in 1958 by the National Retired Teachers Association. The AARP had 1 million members in 1968; by 1998, almost half of all Americans over fifty years of age—32.5 million people—belonged to it. Any organization so vast would have trouble reconciling different viewpoints, and the AARP has sometimes been hampered by dissension or unable to persuade its own membership on an issue—as occurred, for example, when the "catastrophic" health care program the group had strongly backed was repealed. But this sort of embarrassment is more the exception than the rule.

Throughout the 1980s and 1990s, the AARP proved an effective advocate for the protection of benefit levels for Medicare and Social Security and for legislation to prohibit age discrimination. Recognizing the AARP's potential clout, other interests attempted to woo its support on issues that ranged from campaign finance reform to telephone deregulation. With the rapid growth in the percentage of those who are sixty-five and older, the "gray lobby" seems destined to remain one of Washington's most powerful.

EDUCATION GROUPS

Although local government has historically had primary responsibility for education, the idea that the federal government should help support education is an old one, dating from the post-Revolutionary years when Congress set aside land in every township in the Northwest Territory to provide sites for public schools. In 1862 Congress established a system of land-grant colleges for the agricultural and mechanical arts.

The federal government made large financial contributions to higher education through the post–World War II GI Bill and its successor laws. But only after the Soviet Union demonstrated its superior technical skills by launching Sputnik, in 1957, did Congress step in with direct aid to local primary and secondary schools. Through two bills—the Elementary and Secondary Education Act and the Higher Education Act, both of 1965—the decade of the 1960s (particularly under the administration of former schoolteacher Lyndon B. Johnson) brought the greatest extension of federal aid to education.

As Congress enlarged the federal role in school funding, many education groups set up offices in the capital. The American Federation of Teachers (AFT) moved to Washington from Chicago, where it had been chartered by Samuel Gompers in 1916. The exclusive fifty-four-member Association of American Universities (AAU) established its national office in Washington in 1962. The National School Boards Association, founded in 1940, set up a Washington office in 1966. Teachers and educational institutions of almost every type are represented in Washington, along with parents, libraries, and school administrators.

School librarians and school secretaries each have their own group, as do college governing boards, college registrars, and college business officers. In addition, dozens of colleges and universities have their own Washington representatives, some of whom work through state delegations or congressional networks of alumni to get funding specifically for their institution.

Teachers form the largest and most politically active of the education groups, and the two largest organizations are often fierce rivals: the AFT, which in 1999 placed its membership at more than a million teachers, other professionals, and support staff; and the National Education Association (NEA), which claims a membership of almost 2.5 million.

Founded in the nineteenth century, for most of its history the NEA was a staid professional society dominated by school administrators. Eager to maintain a professional image, it refrained from collective bargaining and had little involvement in politics. But during the 1960s, a new breed of young teachers began to move the organization toward militancy, which had been the hallmark of the AFL-CIO–affiliated AFT. Using typical union tactics, such as strikes and collective bargaining, local NEA affiliates began to push school authorities for better pay and working conditions. As the organization became more like a teachers' union, school administrators began to pull out, and in 1972 administrators and principals seceded to form separate organizations. The NEA officially became a union in 1979 when it agreed to register under the Landrum-Griffin Act, which regulates union practices.

The NEA made a major move into national politics in 1972 when it sought to influence the outcome of several congressional elections. The organization became a force in presidential politics four years later when it endorsed Jimmy Carter after he voiced support for one of the group's long-standing goals: the establishment of a Department of Education. Congress established the department after Carter became president and later ignored several attempts on the part of President Reagan—who wanted to drastically reduce the federal role in education—to abolish it.

In 1999 both the AFT and NEA took positions in opposition to school vouchers; privatization; and "Ed-Flex" authority, which would have expanded the use of block grants for education and permitted states greater flexibility in public school spending. Reflecting its broader, noneducation-related membership, the AFT also worked hard to pass patients' rights legislation. Although the AFT and the NEA had historically devoted much of their energy to claiming credit for the accomplishments of the rival group, in 1990 they began to talk of joining forces; as of September 1999, merger talks were continuing but had not achieved a final resolution.

Despite their many common interests, the various education groups sometimes find themselves in conflict, particularly when they are compelled to compete for scarce funds. Black colleges and community colleges, for example, rarely benefit from programs that are essentially designed to meet the needs of large universities. And when the budget pressures of the 1980s intensified competition for funding, colleges and universities began approaching legislators directly to persuade them to designate (or "earmark") funding for specific schools. The 99th Congress (1985–1987) set aside more than $330 million for close to a hundred research projects at more than fifty campuses. The AAU, upset that the earmarking had bypassed traditional competitive procedures (in which funds are awarded on the basis of merit as determined through peer review), called for a moratorium on the acceptance of earmarked funds.

SINGLE INTEREST LOBBIES

The 1970s witnessed an explosion of groups that focus their energies on a single issue—a strategy that sometimes enlarges their influence far beyond their numbers. Often, single interest groups appear to be less oriented to pragmatic political accommodation than to waging a high-principled fight that leaves little room for compromise. They carry considerable weight, however, because many of their supporters go to the polls with only one thing in mind: how a candidate stands on the issue that is dearest to their hearts.

After the historic *Roe v. Wade* Supreme Court decision in 1973 effectively legalized abortion, antiabortion groups waged a strenuous campaign to overturn the decision. Although strongly motivated by religious considerations, they quickly mastered the art of political influence, pressuring local and national candidates through demonstrations, letter-writing campaigns, and sophisticated lobbying efforts. The best-known group is the National Right to Life Committee, which in 1991 had three thousand local chapters and a $13 million Washington operation.

With the Supreme Court closely divided on the issue in 1987, abortion rights supporters worked hard to prevent the confirmation of Reagan nominee Robert Bork in the belief that if Bork made it to the Court he would help overturn *Roe v. Wade.* Although Bork was rejected, the close divisions on the Court continued throughout the 1990s, keeping the stakes high for everyone involved in this issue. Two years after the Bork nomination, for example, the *Webster v. Reproductive Health Services* decision, which returned to state governments some control over abortion, again galvanized supporters of abortion rights. The National Organization for Women, the National Abortion Rights Action League, and Planned Parenthood worked together, with some success, to persuade many state politicians and members of Congress to modify their stands on abortion.

One of the most entrenched and vocal single interest groups is the National Rifle Association (NRA). Believing that the Northerners had been put to shame during the Civil War by the Southerners' superior shooting, former Yankee officers established the NRA to improve marksmanship among the citizenry. Ulysses S. Grant was an early NRA president, and military men led the NRA throughout its first century.

Over the years, the group came to promote, and later to defend, the role of guns in American culture. Widely regarded as a totem of American manhood, guns continue to symbolize independence in many parts of the country. A certain reverence for

The lobbying efforts of single-interest groups often leave little room for compromise. Here proponents and opponents of abortion gather on the steps of the Supreme Court.

the role of guns in our culture gives NRA members a bond that is more than political and makes them extraordinarily responsive to their leaders' requests for help.

By the late 1960s, as a violence-weary Congress moved toward passage of the 1968 Gun Control Act, the gun lobby was a formidable, if still unsophisticated, force. Protests by gun owners succeeded in significantly weakening the 1968 law, but NRA leaders viewed passage of even the watered-down bill as a major defeat. In the succeeding years, tension built up between the "old guard" NRA leadership and a more militant faction that demanded a professional and uncompromising political organization. Two overtly political groups, the Citizens' Committee for the Right to Keep and Bear Arms and the Gun Owners of America, were formed in 1975. In response to demands from its membership, the NRA established an Institute for Legislative Action; and in 1977, militants took over the organization, routing the old-line advocates of marksmanship and wildlife conservation.

With its network of state and local gun clubs linked to a ganglion of sophisticated computers, the NRA is often cited as a model lobbying organization. It can target mass mailings overnight to any state, congressional district, or state legislative district. But technologically sophisticated grassroots techniques have become standard weaponry in modern lobbying: what distinguishes the NRA is a membership that is linked by a hobby that reinforces identification with the organization even when the legislative front is quiet.

The 1990s proved to be a turbulent time for the NRA. In the wake of several high-profile shooting incidents, including some

on public school grounds, gun control resurfaced as a major public issue. In 1994, with support from the Clinton administration and over the NRA's strong opposition, Congress passed two important pieces of gun control legislation. The first, the Brady Bill—named after President Reagan's press secretary, Jim Brady, who was seriously wounded in an assassination attempt on Reagan in 1981—requires a five-day waiting period for handgun purchases. The second measure banned the sale of certain semiautomatic rifles classified as assault weapons. Despite these setbacks, the NRA remained exceptionally powerful. That same year, it claimed credit for helping to defeat several Democrats who had voted for the "anti-gun" legislation, thus helping Republicans gain control of Congress for the first time in forty years.

In 1999, following several more high-profile shootings, including the particularly violent spree at a high school in Littleton, Colorado, that left fifteen dead, Congress again faced strong pressure for additional controls on the sale of weapons. No legislation was passed, but the issue was expected to play a prominent role in future election races.

In the late 1980s, groups devoted solely to animal rights burgeoned. Traditional groups such as the Humane Society and the American Society for the Prevention of Cruelty to Animals were joined by more militant organizations that used slogans such as "a rat is a pig is a dog is a boy" to protest the use of animals for food and for research. Adherents of animal rights groups continue to be among the most prolific sources of letters to congressional offices.

CHURCHES

From the American Revolution, to the abolition of slavery, to Prohibition, to the Vietnam War, churches have played a central role in the history of American political debate. In the 1970s, most of the lobbying conducted by churches was carried out in alliance with liberal groups, but the conservative spirit of the 1980s led to a wave of activism among religious fundamentalists, who took on issues such as school prayer. Meanwhile, the mainstream denominations found themselves split by the volatile issues of abortion and homosexuality.

Although churches can jeopardize their privileged tax status if they devote a substantial portion of their wealth and human resources to lobbying, *substantial* is a vague enough term to provide plenty of room for churches to testify, persuade, and cajole. Although many of the established churches have their own lobbying operations in Washington, they generally steer clear of election campaigns and have no political action committees, relying instead on their newsletters and magazines to get their message out to the lay and clerical grass roots. Unlike the mainstream denominations, many churches of the evangelical right set up formal lobbying and campaign finance arms, although they carefully separate these organizations to preserve the churches' tax status. *(See box, Charities, Lobbying, and Tax Status, p. 714.)*

The U.S. Catholic Conference, which was established after World War I to cope with immigration issues and became one of the largest and most active religious lobbies, derives its legislative positions from papal encyclicals and rulings by the synods of American bishops. Representatives of Catholic hospitals, schools, and charities also lobby Congress.

In the 1980s, church-based groups focused on issues such as welfare, the nuclear arms race, international human rights, and U.S. policies in Central America and South Africa. One of the most active liberal organizations is the American Friends Service Committee, which was formed in 1917 to further Quaker beliefs, including conscientious objection to war and a commitment to improving the living conditions of the poor.

Throughout much of the 1990s, the 2-million-member Christian Coalition, founded by television evangelist and one-time presidential candidate Pat Robertson, became closely identified with many Republican congressional leaders. Ralph Reed, the coalition's executive director, resigned his position in 1997 to pursue a career as a political consultant working almost exclusively for conservative Republican candidates and causes. The coalition mixed traditional evangelical conservative positions—such as bans on human fetal-tissue research, on abortions in military hospitals, and on "partial-birth abortions"—with support for apparently more secular concerns such as a balanced budget and tax-favored accounts to promote savings for educational expenses. Critics noted that church-affiliated schools stood to be among the beneficiaries of these education accounts—a fact that the coalition did not attempt to conceal in its lobbying for the provision.

PROFESSIONAL ASSOCIATIONS

Independent professionals—doctors and lawyers, for example—are often important leaders in their communities. And by presenting a united front to Congress, they can influence national policy.

Doctors, who are often important campaign contributors, have plenty of political muscle. To ensure that the local connection is made clear, the American Medical Association (AMA) arranges to have contributions delivered to lawmakers in person by a physician (preferably the member's family doctor) who is also a constituent.

The expansion of federal involvement in health care brought the AMA to focus its attention on Washington. And as doctors discovered that federal policies could favor one medical specialty over another, other physicians' groups grew active as well: the American College of Physicians, for example, opened a Washington office in 1980 and became a major source of campaign funds in its quest to represent internists in their frequent tugs-of-war with surgeons.

The AMA fought bitterly against Medicare and has historically resisted anything that smacked of "socialized medicine." In 1977, for example, it helped to defeat President Carter's top priority, the containment of hospital costs. But by the 1980s, the federal government had reached so deeply into health care—principally through Medicaid and reimbursement rates for hospitals and physicians—that the AMA had to take a more practical stance in negotiations on complex bills.

Nevertheless, by 1999, important changes in the nation's medical system, in which more and more decisions were being made by businesspeople working for managed care groups, pushed a new breed of doctors toward the model of organized labor long established in manufacturing and other areas. Physicians began lobbying Congress for legislative changes that would allow doctors and other health care professionals who contract independently with health insurance plans to form collective bargaining units. Significantly, the AMA endorsed the move and made it part of its legislative agenda.

Politics is close to the lifeblood of the Association of Trial Lawyers of America. Trial lawyers tend to be articulate, aggressive, and affluent—and many of them have gone on to become members of Congress. They have been deeply involved in politics as fund-raisers and campaign managers, most often under the Democratic banner. In the 1980s and 1990s, trial lawyers fought a broad coalition of manufacturers to a standstill over proposals to reform liability laws.

COALITION LOBBYING

The concerted exercise of influence is as old as government itself, but the use of coalitions in lobbying accelerated after World War II. As early as 1950, the House Select Committee on Lobbying Activities reported that "The lone-wolf pressure group, wanting nothing more from other groups than to be left unmolested, is largely a thing of the past." By the 1980s, coalition

Since 1934 Congress has severely restricted lobbying by charities and other nonprofit groups that receive tax-deductible contributions from the public. There is no total ban, but a nonprofit group must be careful in how much lobbying it does or it can lose its tax-exempt status—as happened to the Sierra Club.

The 1934 legislation prohibited tax deductions for contributions to an organization when a "substantial part" of its activities consisted of "carrying on propaganda, or otherwise attempting to influence legislation." Defining those terms has been a tricky task for legislation and regulations of the Internal Revenue Service (IRS) ever since.

In 1976 Congress included provisions on tax-exempt lobbying in its overhaul of the tax code. These gave organizations an option: they could elect to be judged by the IRS on the broad standard of the 1934 law, or they could choose to follow specific guidelines that established a sliding scale of how much money could be spent on lobbying and placed limits on how it could be spent. In 1990, after four years of review, the IRS issued regulations to clarify the standards.

The rules applied principally to "public charities" governed by Section 501(c)(3) of the Internal Revenue Code, which granted tax-exempt status to nonprofit charitable, religious, scientific, cultural, or educational groups, and to groups engaged in "testing for public safety" or in preventing cruelty to children or animals. They did not govern churches, which have special status under the First Amendment, or private foundations, which have stricter guidelines.

RULES OF THE ROAD

For groups that elected to follow the specific guidelines, the following regulations applied:

Amounts Spent. An organization was allowed to spend a portion of its funds on lobbying activities according to a sliding scale based on the amount of money it spent in a year to accomplish its major purpose—ranging from 20 percent of the first $500,000 to 5 percent of amounts over $1.5 million. There was a total cap of $1 million, meaning that a charity that spent more than $17 million on its regular activities could spend no more than $1 million on lobbying.

Excess. An organization that spent only slightly more than its permitted amount would have to pay an excise tax on the excess amount; only if an organization exceeded its spending limit by more than 50 percent over a four-year period would it lose its tax-exempt status.

Types of Activities. Of the amount spent on lobbying, only a quarter of the total could be spent on grassroots activities; the rest would have to be spent on direct lobbying—communicating directly with members or their staffs. Indirect lobbying included communications to members of the organization or the general public that referred to specific legislation, gave a viewpoint, and encouraged the recipient to take action, such as to write to a legislator. Advertisements in mass media on highly publicized legislation did not have to include a call to action to qualify, if it was scheduled within two weeks of legislative action.

Legislative activities included state and federal bodies and applied to referendums; they did not cover executive agencies.

Exceptions. If a charity was faced with legislative action that would affect its existence, its powers, or its tax status, it could communicate with members and legislators without limit. Also exempt was material that qualified as nonpartisan analysis or broad social policy advocacy.

"PIGGYBACK" LOBBYING ORGANIZATIONS

After Sierra Club members lost the ability to deduct their contributions because of the organization's aggressive lobbying in the 1960s, they ousted the director—but it was for policy reasons, not financial ones. The organization found that its funding did not dry up; members apparently were willing to make donations even if they could not be deducted.

Many other activists found in the 1980s that they could be just as aggressive in lobbying without running afoul of the tax laws. They did so by establishing separate "piggyback" organizations to do their lobbying for them. Under Section 501(c)(4) of the tax code, a "social welfare" organization could retain its nonprofit status (paying no tax on its income) and engage in unlimited lobbying, just so contributors did not deduct their contributions on their tax forms. The parent organization was not supposed to fund the lobbying group directly, but it could share office space and assist in fund-raising (taking advantage of low postage rates for nonprofits to do so). In 1999 the Christian Coalition was denied 501(c)(4) status by the IRS. The Christian Coalition was deemed to be more than a "social welfare" organization in the context of the regulations. It was engaged in campaign support activities—mostly for Republican candidates running in southern states and districts. The regulations prohibit this sort of "substantial" political activity for qualifying organizations. In an interesting parallel to the Sierra Club incident, the Christian Coalition announced major shakeups in its senior management structure shortly after the exemption was denied.

Many well-known activist groups, including the American Civil Liberties Union, Americans for Democratic Action, National Abortion Rights Action League, and the American Conservative Union, took advantage of the piggyback structure. The Sierra Club set up its own Sierra Club Legal Defense Fund which, unlike the parent organization, could accept tax-deductible contributions.

lobbying had become commonplace: the ad hoc coalition, the working group, the alliance, the committee—these became the typical structures of all but the most obscure lobbying campaigns.

The explosive growth of the lobbying profession as it attempted to comprehend and restrain government activism vastly increased the number of voices that were competing for the ear of Congress. One advantage for lobbyists and legislators alike was that collective lobbying allowed conflicting aims to be sorted out before Congress was approached—much the same way that lawyers settle a case out of court—allowing Congress to focus its effort only on those disagreements that could not be ironed out ahead of time.

Ad hoc lobbying coalitions are often composed of a mix of corporate, association, and business federation lobbyists, as well as unions and any other interests that can be enticed into a marriage of convenience. Some strange liaisons have resulted. The American Civil Liberties Union, for example, allied itself with cigarette manufacturers and Madison Avenue advertising firms to oppose restrictions on tobacco advertising. Fierce competitors and even adversaries can often be persuaded to join in a common cause. In 1996 computer manufacturing giants Apple, IBM, and Compaq joined forces with Microsoft, Netscape, and other organizations to form the Data Coalition. The coalition created a formidable front in opposition to telephone company demands to increase the charges for access to phone lines.

These temporary alliances do their initial work away from Capitol Hill, within a community that has its own committees, leadership, staff, communications network, service organizations, and culture. Coalition members contribute time, legal assistance, and funds to cover printing and mailing costs, depending on their resources and their stake in the battle.

An important advantage of a coalition is the opportunity to share political assets: for example, a group that has close ties to one type of legislator can secure access for coalition partners who do not enjoy such connections. Groups can also benefit from the appeal of their partners' policy arguments. When Congress was working to revise the tax code in the 1980s and 1990s, a coalition of U.S. companies and the Commonwealth of Puerto Rico lobbied to maintain tax incentives designed to attract manufacturing facilities to Puerto Rico. The coalition arrangement allowed the companies to use Puerto Rico's economic need as justification for maintaining the incentives while enabling the commonwealth to benefit from corporate access to Congress. Although compromises were required, the coalition succeeded in preserving much of the favorable tax treatment.

To secure the advantages afforded by membership in a coalition, lobbies sometimes go to great lengths to lobby other lobbies. In 1989, hoping to win the support of ordinary citizens in their drive to be freed of the regulatory shackles that prevented them from offering information services, the "Baby Bell" telephone companies courted both the AARP and consumer groups.

Ideally, before a lobbyist approaches a lawmaker, compromises have been made within the coalition, legislation has been drafted to satisfy a wide range of allies, priorities have been assigned, a strategy has been mapped out, and congressional sponsors for the bill have been identified. Lobbyists representing coalitions are likely to approach members in teams of two or three—perhaps with one individual representing the member's state or district—selected to dramatize the breadth of support for, or opposition to, the legislation.

Although labor organizations, consumer groups, environmentalists, arts and education advocates, charities, and many other groups make short-term alliances, business groups demonstrate superior mastery of the technique—thanks, in part, to the combination of money and a naturally cohesive political outlook. A historic example of the broad business coalition was the protectionist bloc, which in 1930 succeeded in raising protective U.S. tariffs to their highest point ever. Half a century later, powerful business coalitions again rallied to support President Reagan's 1981 program of major tax reductions and the far-reaching revision of the tax code in 1986.

More specialized coalitions have formed for narrower purposes. The Function 250 Coalition took its name from the nondescript title of the space and science portion of the federal budget. In 1990 an Expiring Provisions Coalition formed to garner support for the renewal of tax breaks (for expenditures such as research and development, low-income housing, and student assistance) that were due to run out at the end of the year.

Coalition politics can be fragile. "It's kind of like a bunch of foxes right now—circling the henhouse, warily eyeing each other," said a lobbyist who was part of one coalition that was attempting to bring together disparate groups. Allies on one issue can become opponents on the next. A drive for protection against textile imports, for example, divided the normally cohesive agricultural community: wool growers and cotton producers supported import quotas, but other commodity groups opposed them for fear of foreign retaliation against American farm exports.

When a coalition fails to achieve its objectives, it can disintegrate rapidly. In 1990 energy producers and users united to oppose any tax on energy, but when it became clear that the trucking industry was the likely target for raising revenues, principally through taxes on diesel gasoline, truckers quickly began pushing to ensure that diesel taxes applied to railroads as well; producers of home heating oil approached legislators from the Northeast to attempt to win an exemption; and oil producers were at odds with oil importers. On the other hand, a coalition that had formed to support the sale of the government-owned Conrail freight railroad to the Norfolk Southern Corporation endured even after Norfolk Southern gave up in the face of congressional opposition in 1986. The coalition went on to push successfully for the privatization of the railroad through a public stock offering.

Lobbyists stand by in the hallway as a House subcommittee marks up a bill. Congressional efforts to regulate lobbying have focused on disclosure rather than control.

Lobbying and the Law

Although lobbying is protected by the First Amendment guarantees of freedom of speech, abuses have led to periodic efforts by Congress to regulate lobbying. In 1876, during the 44th Congress, the House adopted a resolution requiring lobbyists to register with the clerk of the House, but the bill did not become law. Beginning in 1911, with the 62nd Congress, federal lobbying legislation was debated in practically every session. Yet by 1991 only one comprehensive lobbying regulation law and a handful of more specialized measures had been enacted, and even these were generally ignored. It was not until 1995 that Congress, responding to pressure from both voters and the press, put in place significant reform legislation designed to close many of the existing loopholes.

LOBBYING REGULATIONS

The principal approach of regulation has been to require disclosure rather than control. Thus, several laws required lobbyists to identify themselves, their employers, and their legislative interests, and to report how much they and their employers spend on lobbying. But the definitions were unclear, the enforcement minimal, and the impact questionable.

As noted earlier, one reason for the relative absence of limitations on lobbying is the difficulty of imposing effective restrictions without infringing on the constitutional rights to free speech, press, assembly, and petition. Other reasons include (1) the concern that restrictions would hamper legitimate lobbying without curbing serious abuses and (2) the lobbies' consolidated and highly effective opposition to more regulation. Another possible factor is the desire on the part of some members of Congress to keep the doors open to future lobbying careers.

The two major laws affecting lobbying are the Foreign Agents Registration Act of 1938 and the Federal Regulation of Lobbying Act of 1946; both are discussed in the subsections that follow. Another area that indirectly influences lobbying practices is campaign financing. The ability to promise support or opposition, and to back up a promise of support with campaign contributions, is one of the most effective devices available to pressure groups in their efforts to influence Congress. Precisely for this reason, Congress has tried on several occasions to limit campaign contributions from corporations, organizations, and individuals in connection with federal elections. Although some limits on gifts to congressional campaigns were passed, they were struck down by the courts as unconstitutional. *(See Chapter 32, Campaign Financing.)*

The following subsections offer brief descriptions of the lobbying laws in chronological order.

Utilities Holding Company Act

Section 12(I) of the Public Utilities Holding Company Act of 1935 requires anyone employed or retained by a registered holding company or a subsidiary to file information with the Securities and Exchange Commission (SEC) before trying to influence Congress, or the SEC itself on any legislative or administrative matter affecting any registered companies. Required information includes the subject matter in which the individual is interested, the nature of the individual's employment, and the amount of compensation.

Merchant Marine Act

Section 807 of the Merchant Marine Act of 1936 requires any persons employed by or representing firms affected by various federal shipping laws to file information with the secretary of commerce before attempting to influence Congress, the Commerce Department, or federal shipping agencies on shipping legislation or administrative decisions. Required information includes the subject matter in which the individual is interested, the nature of the individual's employment, and the amount of compensation.

Foreign Agents Registration Act

Enacted before World War II amid reports of Fascist and Nazi propaganda circulating in the United States, the Foreign Agents Registration Act of 1938 (FARA), as amended, requires anyone in the United States who represents a foreign government or principal to register with the Justice Department. Exceptions are allowed for purely commercial groups and certain other categories. Passage of the act brought to public view many groups, individuals, and organizations that were perhaps not lobbying Congress directly but that did undertake propaganda activities ultimately capable of affecting national policy.

The Justice Department publishes a lengthy annual directory of firms and individuals who have registered as foreign agents. Although being compelled to register under the act carried a certain stigma and the filing requirements could be onerous, some lobbying firms eventually came to view being listed as a status symbol.

FARA was amended repeatedly—for example, in 1939, 1942, 1946, 1950, 1956, 1961, 1966, and 1995—without changing its broad purposes, which had more to do with controlling political propaganda than with tracking normal lobbying activities. The 1966 amendments were intended to clarify and strengthen the act by imposing stricter disclosure requirements for foreign lobbyists; broadening the scope of activities that trigger the requirement to register; requiring foreign agents to disclose their status as such when contacting members of Congress and other government officials; and prohibiting both campaign contributions on behalf of foreign interests and contingency fees (in which the fee is based upon the success of political activities) for contracts.

In 1974 the Justice Department toughened its enforcement policy to encourage foreign agents to submit more detailed and accurate reports on their activities. Nevertheless, the General Accounting Office reported in 1990 that half of the lobbyists who had registered had not fully disclosed their activities and that more than half of the registrations were late.

In 1995 Congress again amended FARA to close a number of loopholes. The amendments made clear that foreign entities with substantial interests in lobbying organizations were required to register. An existing exemption for domestic subsidiaries of foreign companies was revoked, and organizations lobbying for foreign commercial interests were required to register with the House, the Senate, or both. The new law also prohibited former employees of the Office of U.S. Trade Representatives, from lobbying for foreign interests after departing from government service.

Federal Regulation of Lobbying Act

The Federal Regulation of Lobbying Act was passed as part of the Legislative Reorganization Act of 1946. The lobbying provisions of the act did not in any way directly restrict lobbyists' activities: they simply required any person who was hired by someone else for the principal purpose of lobbying Congress to (1) register with the secretary of the Senate and the clerk of the House and (2) file quarterly financial reports to inform Congress and the public of his or her lobbying activities. Organizations that solicited or received money for the principal purpose of lobbying Congress did not necessarily have to register, but they did have to file quarterly spending reports with the clerk of the House, detailing how much they spent to influence legislation.

In 1954, in *United States v. Harriss*, the Supreme Court upheld the constitutionality of the 1946 lobbying law but narrowly interpreted its key aspects. Since then the measure has commonly been described as "more loophole than law."

One loophole opened by the decision concerned the expenditure—versus the collection or receipt—of money. As interpreted by the Court, the law did not cover individuals or groups that spent money to influence legislation unless they also solicited, collected, or received money for that purpose. Another loophole arose from the use of the term *principal purpose*. A number of organizations (including, for nearly thirty years, the National Association of Manufacturers) held that because influencing Congress was not the principal purpose for which they collected or received money, they were not covered by the law, regardless of what kinds of activities they engaged in.

The Court held, in addition, that an organization or individual was not covered by the law unless the method used to influence Congress included direct contact with legislators. Thus, groups or individuals who confined their activities to influencing the public were not subject to the 1946 law. To demonstrate how organizations were making use of this loophole, the public interest group Common Cause publicized the fact that banking interests had reported only one-fourth of the $2 million that they had spent to arouse public opinion against a 1982 law requiring taxes to be withheld on interest and dividends.

The 1954 decision left vague precisely what kind of contacts with Congress constituted "lobbying" for the purposes of the law's registration and reporting requirements. The law specifically exempted testimony before a congressional committee; and in 1950, in *United States v. Slaughter*, a lower federal court held that this exemption applied also to those helping to prepare the testimony. Other direct contacts were presumably covered, but a gray area soon emerged, with some groups contending that their contacts with members of Congress were informational and could not be considered subject to the law.

Another weakness was that the law applied only to attempts to influence Congress; it did not cover administrative agencies, the executive branch, or congressional staff. (Lobbying activities by former executive branch officials were restricted somewhat by the 1978 Ethics in Government Act, and 1989 legislation extended restrictions to former members of Congress and their staffs.)

The law also left it up to each group or its lobbyists to determine what portion of total expenditures to report as spending for lobbying. As a result, some organizations whose Washington office budgets ran into the millions of dollars reported spending only very small amounts on lobbying, contending that the remainder was spent on research, general public information, and other matters. Other organizations, interpreting the law quite differently, reported spending a much larger percentage of their total budgets on lobbying. The result was that some groups (such as Common Cause) gained reputations as "big lobby spenders" when they were simply reporting more fully than other groups that spent just as much.

Compounding its other weaknesses was the fact that the 1946 law did not designate anyone to investigate the truthfulness of lobbying registrations and reports or seek enforcement of the law's requirements. The House clerk and Senate secretary were not directed or empowered to investigate the reports they received, nor could they compel anyone to register. Because violations were a crime, the Justice Department had the power to prosecute offenders, but Congress gave no mandate to the department to investigate reports. In fact, the Justice Department eventually adopted a policy of investigating only when it received complaints, and there were only six prosecutions between 1946 and 1980. In 1983 a Justice Department official told a Senate committee that the law was "ineffective, inadequate, and unenforceable." In 1989 the president of the American League of Lobbyists noted that out of the tens of thousands of lawyers, public affairs professionals, and other consultants in Washington, fewer than 6,000 lobbyists were registered with Congress.

What lobbying registrations there were could be found in the official *Congressional Record* and in a private journal, the *Congressional Quarterly Weekly Report*. Many lobbyists regarded the listings as cheap advertising.

Legislation to tighten the disclosure laws made headway in later Congresses without achieving enactment. Finally, in 1995, Congress approved a number of important changes to the existing law. First, the definition of what qualified as lobbying was expanded to include contact with congressional staff and executive branch policy makers. These were important additions: most lobbyists acknowledge that the vast majority of their lobbying efforts focus on congressional staff—who, even if they do not make the final legislative decisions, are at least the conduits of the information and requests that legislators consider before setting policy. Executive branch agencies originate much of the legislation ultimately enacted by Congress and put into effect many regulations that are similar to legislation.

Registration requirements were amended to cover any person who spends 20 percent or more of his or her time lobbying in a given six-month period, though individuals who earn less than $5,000 and organizations that spend less than $20,000 during the reporting period are exempt from the registration requirement. Grassroots lobbying campaigns and tax-exempt organizations, such as churches, are also exempt.

"Revolving-Door" Restrictions

Under the 1978 Ethics in Government Act, top executive branch officials are barred, for one year after leaving government, from representing anyone before their former agency; officials are permanently barred from lobbying on issues that are directly related to their former areas of responsibility. A 1988 law restricts former Pentagon officers' involvement in procurement contracts for defense contractors. And 1995 legislation prohibits former officials of the Office of U.S. Trade Representative from ever representing foreign governments.

In 1988 Congress approved legislation that, for the first time, extended limitations on postemployment lobbying to former members of Congress and congressional staff; the bill also tightened the restrictions on executive branch officials. Claiming that the measure was so restrictive that it would discourage people from entering government service, President Ronald Reagan pocket-vetoed the bill. But virtually identical provisions were enacted the following year as part of a broad pay and ethics package. Under the 1989 law, members and officers of Congress are barred from lobbying the legislative branch for one year after leaving office. Staff members are barred, for one year after leaving office, from lobbying the member, office, or committee for which they had worked. Of course, as long as they do not present themselves personally to former colleagues during the prohibition period, none of these requirements prohibit former legislators or staffers from designing and directing lobbying campaigns.

Restrictions on Appropriations Lobbying

In 1989, angered by reports that private consultants were drumming up projects for universities that they then lobbied Congress to fund, Senate Appropriations Committee Chairman Robert C. Byrd, D-W.Va., succeeded in rushing into law a provision that cast a wider net around attempts to lobby for federal appropriations. The Byrd amendment requires recipients of federal grants, contracts, or loans greater than $100,000 to file information on the names of, and fees paid to, any lobbyists hired in pursuit of funds from Congress or the executive branch. The provision also prohibits recipients of such funds from using federal money to lobby for contracts, grants, or loans.

LOBBYING INVESTIGATIONS

Public opprobrium has been as strong a force as the law in keeping lobbyists in check. Congresses in which major scandals have led to public investigations of lobbying practices have been more frequent than Congresses in which lobbying legislation was enacted. Although congressional hearings have been used to prepare the way for new regulations, more often they have been used to determine the cleansing effect of sunshine on those who try, behind closed doors, to influence policy. The following are summary accounts of selected major lobbying investigations.

Business Lobbying, 1913

The first thorough investigation of lobbying was undertaken by the Senate in 1913 in response to President Woodrow Wilson's charge that the National Association of Manufacturers and other protectionist groups had undertaken a massive, grassroots lobbying effort against his tariff program. Denouncing an "insidious" lobby that sought to bring on a new tide of protectionism, Wilson said,

I think the public ought to know that extraordinary exertions are being made by the lobby in Washington to gain recognition for certain alterations in the tariff bill. . . . Washington has seldom seen so numerous, so industrious, or so insidious a lobby. . . . There is every evidence that money without limit is being spent to sustain this lobby. . . . The government ought to be relieved from this intolerable burden and the constant interruption to the calm progress of debate.

The Senate hearings disclosed that both the interests seeking high tariff duties and those seeking low duties, such as the sugar refiners, had spent large amounts on entertainment and other lobbying activities. After the hearings, a lobby registration bill was introduced, but farm, labor, and other special interests warded off a vote on it.

Also in 1913, Col. Martin M. Mulhall, a lobbyist for the National Association of Manufacturers, published a sensational account of his activities in a front-page article in the *New York World*. Among other disclosures, Mulhall claimed to have paid "between $1,500 and $2,000" to help Rep. James T. McDermott, D-Ill., in return for legislative favors. A four-month inquiry by a select House committee found that many of Mulhall's allegations were exaggerated. The panel established that Mulhall had set up his own office in the Capitol, paid the chief House page $50 a month for inside information, received advance information on pending legislation from McDermott and House Republican leader John W. Dwight, N.Y., and influenced the appointment of members to House committees and subcommittees. The committee exonerated six of the seven House members implicated by Mulhall but recommended that McDermott

be disciplined. The House adopted the panel's recommendations but stopped short of expelling McDermott, who resigned in July of 1914 and was reelected to another two-year term in November of that year.

Tax and Utilities Lobbying, 1927

Interest in lobbying activities was rekindled in the 1920s after the American Legion and other veterans' groups obtained passage of a bonus bill over the veto of President Calvin Coolidge.

In 1927 an investigative committee under Sen. Thaddeus H. Caraway, D-Ark., conducted extensive public hearings on lobbying efforts. One of the immediate reasons was the pressure being applied to the Ways and Means Committee for repeal of the federal estate tax. The American Taxpayers League brought more than two hundred witnesses, including one governor and many state legislators, to Washington to testify. All travel expenses were paid, and some of the witnesses received additional compensation. Congress also objected when the Joint Committee of National Utility Associations established Washington headquarters to block a proposed Senate investigation of utility financing. The joint committee succeeded in having the investigation transferred to the Federal Trade Commission; although that agency took its assignment seriously and gave the issue of utility financing a thorough going-over, its findings were inconclusive.

At the end of its investigation, the Caraway committee recommended a sweeping registration bill. It defined lobbying as "any effort in influencing Congress upon any matter coming before it, whether it be by distributing literature, appearing before committees of Congress, or seeking to interview members of either the House or Senate." A lobbyist was defined as "one who shall engage, for pay, to attempt to influence legislation, or to prevent legislation by the national Congress." The Senate passed the bill unanimously but a House committee pigeonholed it.

Despite the failure of the Caraway bill, the Senate Judiciary Committee's report on the measure contributed greatly to the public's knowledge of lobbying. According to the committee report, about 90 percent of the three to four hundred lobbying associations listed in the Washington telephone directory were "fakes" whose aim was to bilk unwary clients. These groups purported to represent scientific, agricultural, religious, temperance, and anti-Prohibition interests, among others. "In fact," the committee report said, "every activity of the human mind has been capitalized by some grafter." The committee estimated that $99 of every $100 paid to these organizations "go into the pockets of the promoters." Caraway asserted that one of the lobbyists had collected $60,000 in one year from business interests simply by writing them every time a bill favorable to business was passed and claiming sole credit for its passage.

Naval Armaments, 1929

The next congressional probe of lobbying came in 1929, when a Senate naval affairs subcommittee looked into the activities of William B. Shearer, who represented shipping, electrical, metals, machinery, and similar concerns interested in obtaining larger appropriations for navy ships and blocking limitations on naval armaments. Shearer initiated his own exposure when he filed suit in the New York courts to recover $257,655—which, he claimed, the New York Shipbuilding Co. owed him for lobbying services he had performed in Washington and at the Geneva naval limitation conference of 1927. Testimony showed that shipbuilding interests had indeed sent Shearer to Geneva, where he did everything he could to torpedo an agreement. Following the conference, at which no agreement was reached, Shearer had led lobbying efforts to obtain larger naval appropriations and subsidies for the merchant marine. His other activities included preparing pro-navy articles for the Hearst newspaper chain; writing articles for the 1928 Republican presidential campaign, in which he characterized peace advocates as traitors; and writing speeches for the American Legion and like-minded lobbying groups.

Utilities Lobbies, 1935

A decade of congressional concern about the influence of private utilities led to a stormy 1935 probe of that industry's lobbying activities. Although Congress had instructed the Federal Trade Commission (FTC) to investigate utility lobbying nine years earlier, the two-year FTC probe had been largely inconclusive.

When intensive lobbying threatened to emasculate an administration bill to regulate utility holding companies, President Franklin D. Roosevelt sent Congress a special message describing the holding companies as "private empires within the nation" and denouncing their lobbying techniques. The bill's congressional supporters demanded an investigation to determine how far the lobbying had gone.

A special Senate investigative panel was set up under the chairmanship of Hugo Black, an administration stalwart who later became an associate justice of the Supreme Court. Following a sometimes raucous hearing, Senator Black concluded that the utilities had spent about $4 million in an attempt to defeat the bill and had engaged in massive propagandizing to convince the public that the legislation was an iniquitous invasion of private rights and a sharp turn toward socialism. Among other findings, Black's panel stated that the utilities had financed thousands of phony telegrams to Congress, using names picked at random from telephone books.

Amid the furor over the telegrams, Congress passed the Public Utilities Holding Company Act, which required that utility lobbyists register with and report their activities to the Securities and Exchange Commission. The House and Senate also passed separate bills requiring registration of lobbyists. Although a compromise version of the bills was initially agreed upon, the House ultimately rejected the compromise and final adjournment came before a new agreement could be reached. The defeat of the registration measure was attributed to the combined efforts of hundreds of lobbyists.

Munitions Lobby, 1935

Another 1935 Senate investigation looked into the activities of the munitions lobby. The Special Committee Investigating the Munitions Industry, headed by Gerald P. Nye, R-N.C., uncovered bribery and arms deals in Latin America and Great Britain, prompting sharp responses from leaders there. (See "Nye Munitions Inquiry," p. 269.)

Further Studies, 1938 and 1945

In 1938 the Temporary National Economic Committee, which Congress set up at President Roosevelt's request under the chairmanship of Sen. Joseph C. O'Mahoney, D-Wyo., included lobbying among its areas of study. The Joint Committee on the Organization of Congress, established in 1945, studied lobbying activities along with other matters pertaining to Congress. On the basis of that committee's recommendations, in 1946 Congress passed the Legislative Reorganization Act, which included the Federal Regulation of Lobbying Act.

Omnibus Lobbying Probe, 1950

In 1950 a House Select Committee on Lobbying Activities headed by Frank M. Buchanan, D-Pa., investigated the lobbying activities of a wide range of organizations. The probe had been prompted largely by President Harry S. Truman's assertion that the 80th Congress was "the most thoroughly surrounded . . . with lobbies in the whole history of this great country of ours." Truman said that "There were more lobbyists in Washington, there was more money spent by lobbyists in Washington, than ever before in the history of the Congress of the United States. It's disgraceful." Most of the publicity centered on the efforts of the Committee for Constitutional Government to distribute low-cost or free "right-wing" books and pamphlets designed to influence the public.

To determine more accurately the amount of money spent to influence legislation, the House investigative committee requested detailed information from two hundred corporations, labor unions, and farm groups. Replies from 152 corporations showed a total of $32 million spent for this purpose from January 1, 1947, through May 31, 1950. More than one hundred of these corporations had not filed reports under the Federal Regulation of Lobbying Act of 1946. Reports from the thirty-seven that had filed showed expenditures of $776,000—less than 3 percent of the amount that had been reported by respondents when they filled out the committee's questionnaire. In releasing the survey results, Chairman Buchanan emphasized that it covered the activities of only 152 of the country's half million corporations. "I firmly believe," he said, "that the business of influencing legislation is a billion-dollar industry."

The Buchanan committee recommended strengthening the 1946 lobbying law but no action was taken.

Omnibus Lobbying Probe, 1956

In 1956, under the chairmanship of John L. McClellan, D-Ark., the Senate Special Committee to Investigate Political Activities, Lobbying, and Campaign Contributions conducted a major lobbying inquiry. The inquiry was sparked by an alleged campaign contribution to Francis H. Case, R-S.D., in connection with a vote on a natural gas bill.

After a long investigation, in 1957 McClellan introduced a new lobbying registration bill designed to replace the 1946 act. The bill proposed to tighten the existing law by making the comptroller general responsible for enforcement (the 1946 act included no provision for an administrator); eliminating a loophole that required registration only for those organizations or individuals whose "principal purpose" was lobbying; extending the law to cover anyone who spent $50,000 or more per year on grassroots lobbying; and eliminating an exemption for individuals who merely testify on proposed legislation.

The bill was opposed vigorously by the U.S. Chamber of Commerce and was criticized on certain points by the National Association of Manufacturers, the Association of American Railroads, and the American Medical Association—although the AMA endorsed the measure as a whole. The bill did not reach the floor and died with the close of the 85th Congress.

Retired Military Officers, 1959

In 1959 the House Armed Services Subcommittee on Special Investigations held three months of hearings on (1) the employment of former army, navy, and air force officers by defense contractors and (2) the effect of the retired officers' influence on the award of government contracts to their new employers. The subcommittee found that more than 1,400 retired officers with the rank of major or higher—including 261 of general or flag rank—were employed by the top one hundred defense contractors.

In its report in 1960, the subcommittee said that "the coincidence of contracts and personal contacts with firms represented by retired officers and retired civilian officials sometimes raises serious doubts as to the objectivity of these [contract] decisions." Congress largely accepted the subcommittee's recommendations for tighter restrictions on sales to the government by former armed services personnel.

Foreign Lobbyists, 1962

Lobbying in connection with the Sugar Act of 1962 led the Senate Foreign Relations Committee to launch an investigation of foreign lobbies and the extent to which they attempted to influence U.S. policies. At the request of Foreign Relations Committee Chairman J. William Fulbright, D-Ark., and Sen. Paul H. Douglas, D-Ill., the Finance Committee, which had jurisdiction over the sugar bill, had queried sugar lobbyists on their arrangements with their employers, most of which were foreign countries. A compendium of the answers showed that some payments to sugar lobbyists had been based on the size of the sugar quotas granted by Congress.

Hearings conducted some months later by the Foreign Relations Committee produced evidence that some lobbyists also lobbied their own clients. Fulbright disclosed, for example, that

Michael B. Deane, a Washington public relations representative hired by the Dominican Sugar Commission, had apparently given the commission exaggerated and inaccurate reports. Deane admitted that he had reported falsely that the president invited him to the White House and that he had talked with the secretary of agriculture. Deane said that he occasionally gave himself "too much credit" but that "one tends to do that a little bit when they have a client who is outside of Washington."

The Fulbright probe continued well into 1963; at its conclusion, Fulbright introduced a bill to tighten registration requirements under the 1938 Foreign Agents Registration Act. The bill passed the Senate in 1964 but died in the House. It was revived in the 89th Congress and enacted in 1966.

"Koreagate," 1978

In 1976 the *Washington Post* disclosed a Justice Department probe of reports that South Korean agents dispensed between $500,000 and $1 million a year in cash and gifts to members of Congress to help maintain "a favorable legislative climate" for South Korea. Tongsun Park, a Washington-based Korean businessman and socialite, was named as the central operative. Shortly after the story appeared, Park fled to London, where he remained until August 1977. He then went to Korea but eventually returned to the United States to testify at House and Senate hearings on Korean influence peddling.

By 1978 the House and Senate ethics committees had ended their probes without recommending any severe disciplinary action against colleagues linked to the scandal. The House investigation, which began in early 1977 with reports that as many as 115 members of Congress had taken illegal gifts from South Korean agents, ended in October 1978 with a vote to impose the mildest form of punishment—a reprimand—on three Democrats: John J. McFall and Edward R. Roybal, both of California, and Charles H. Wilson of Texas. The Senate concluded its Korean investigation in October 1978 with a report that recommended no disciplinary action against any incumbent or former senator.

As a result of the Justice Department investigation, two former representatives were prosecuted for taking large sums of money from Tongsun Park: Richard T. Hanna, D-Calif., pleaded guilty to a reduced charge and went to prison, and Otto E. Passman, D-La., was acquitted in 1979.

A separate investigation of U.S.-Korean relations conducted by the House International Relations Subcommittee on International Organizations concluded that the South Korean government had sought to bribe U.S. officials, buy influence among journalists, and rig military procurement contracts to win support for what the panel called the "authoritarian" government of President Park Chung Hee. In its final 450-page report, released in November 1978, the subcommittee said that in addition to its legal and extra-legal lobbying efforts, the South Korean government frequently pursued policies that were antithetical to U.S. interests—most notably, an effort to develop nuclear weapons, a campaign that the subcommittee said that South Korea had abandoned by 1975.

"Abscam," 1980

In 1980 a senator and six House members were indicted for taking bribes from undercover FBI agents who posed as wealthy Arabs seeking congressional help in obtaining federal grants, gambling licenses, real estate, contracts, or immigration assistance. Ethics committees in both the House and Senate investigated; although many legislators criticized the FBI's "sting" tactics, the videotaped evidence was strong. Sen. Harrison A. Williams Jr., D-N.J., was convicted of criminal charges, as were the six indicted House members. One of the House members, Michael "Ozzie" Myers, D-Pa., was formally expelled—the first expulsion in more than a century—and several others resigned to avoid expulsion. *(See "Abscam Investigation," p. 953, Vol. II.)*

Reagan Presidential Aides, 1986–1988

Two high officials of the Reagan White House were convicted of federal charges for lobbying activities that they had engaged in after leaving the administration. Although these convictions were obtained by a special prosecutor and principally concerned lobbying at the White House, Congress did play a role.

After resigning as Reagan's deputy chief of staff in May 1985, Michael K. Deaver gained notoriety when he immediately opened a lucrative Washington public relations firm, with clients ranging from defense contractors to the governments of Canada, South Korea, and Saudi Arabia. In addition to having held an official position, Deaver was a confidant of both the president and his wife, Nancy Reagan. A report by the General Accounting Office (GAO) in May 1986 concluded that Deaver appeared to have violated the 1978 law barring government officials from lobbying their former agencies for a year after leaving the government. A few days after the GAO report was released, Deaver defended himself at an inquiry of the House Energy and Commerce Subcommittee on Oversight and Investigations. The subcommittee subsequently voted seventeen to zero to turn evidence of Deaver's possible perjury and obstruction of justice over to a special prosecutor, who was named within the month. In 1987 Deaver was found guilty of charges that he had lied both to the subcommittee and to a grand jury investigating his lobbying activities.

Until his resignation in January 1982, Lyn Nofziger had been head of the White House Office of Political Affairs. A close associate of Reagan confidant (and later attorney general) Edwin W. Meese III, Nofziger was implicated in a widespread probe of influence peddling for Wedtech, a small military contractor in New York that had become wealthy through political connections. In 1988 Nofziger was convicted of illegal lobbying for exploiting his connections within a year of his departure from government, but an appeals court overturned the conviction in 1989.

In 1987 Congress used the Deaver and Nofziger cases to help push through, over Reagan's opposition, an extension of the special prosecutor law. The following year, Reagan vetoed legislation that would have imposed new restrictions on lobbying by high government officials and members of Congress after they had left office; the same provisions were enacted in 1989 as part of a broader pay and ethics package.

Foreign Money and Campaign Finance Abuses, 1997–1998

The Senate Governmental Affairs Committee, led by Chairman Fred Thompson, R-Tenn., and ranking minority member John Glenn, D-Ohio, conducted months of hearings on alleged campaign finance abuses. Most of the allegations centered on Democratic National Committee fund-raising for President Clinton's 1996 reelection campaign, but some also focused on the activities of Haley Barbour, former Chairman of the Republican National Committee (RNC). Although the committee uncovered many highly suggestive facts, it was unable to prove wrongdoing in most instances.

A key target of the investigation was John Huang, an associate of the Riadys, a powerful Indonesian family that runs the Lippo Group, a major banking and insurance conglomerate. A skilled fund-raiser, Huang became a Commerce Department official in 1994, working in the department's international economic policy section and receiving top security clearances. Republican committee staff later alleged that he had used his position to obtain sensitive material, which he then passed on to Lippo.

Huang eventually moved to the Democratic National Committee, where he focused on raising money from Asian Americans. While his success at fund-raising was impressive, his tactics seemed more than questionable. Committee staff found that much of the money he raised had come through "straw" donors who were later reimbursed by foreign nationals. Concealing the source of contributions is illegal—as are contributions from foreign sources.

The most high-profile series of allegations centered on a 1996 event held at the Hsi Lai Buddhist Temple in California. Much of the money raised at this event had ostensibly come from nuns, but later investigations revealed that the nuns were merely straw donors: the real donors were temple officials who used the nuns as conduits to launder their contributions. Because Vice President Al Gore attended the event, and because the law prohibited fund-raising on the property of tax-exempt religious organizations, the event became a focal point for much committee and media attention. Claiming that he was unaware that the event was a political fund-raiser, Gore denied any knowledge of illegal practices. The majority report took strong issue with Gore's claim, asserting that "the vice president was well aware that the event was designed to raise money."

The committee also examined allegations that illegal contributions had been made in exchange for access to the president. Large contributors were invited to have coffee in the White House with President Bill Clinton. On one such occasion, it appeared, once again, that the underlying contribution came from foreign sources—this time a bank in Bangkok. Adding to the appearance that the Clinton White House was, at best, unconcerned with the technicalities of campaign finance law was the

Sens. Fred Thompson, R-Tenn., left, and John Glenn, D-Ohio, ran the Senate Governmental Affairs Committee that investigated campaign finance abuses from 1997 to 1998.

allegation that Huang used these coffees to solicit campaign contributions. Raising money on federal property is illegal.

Republican fund-raising practices were not immune from criticism by committee members, especially Democrats. Allegations were made that RNC Chairman Haley Barbour had arranged for a Hong Kong business executive to "lend" the National Policy Forum, a conservative organization directed by Barbour, over $2 million. The forum, in turn, gave the money to the RNC for use in 1994 congressional campaigns. All of this might have passed legal scrutiny, but the forum eventually defaulted on the debt. If the default had been agreed to, or even anticipated, at the time the loan was originally granted, a strong case could be made that what Barbour had actually arranged was an illegal contribution from a foreign source.

Despite these and other well-supported allegations, the hearings resulted in little more than two differing reports, one from the Republican members and one from the Democrats. No immediate finance reforms were enacted.

NOTES

1. Charles Peters, "The Solution: A Rebirth of Patriotism," *Washington Monthly,* October 1978, 37.

2. William Safire, *Safire's Political Dictionary* (New York: Ballantine, 1980), 383.

3. Jeffrey H. Birnbaum and Alan S. Murray, *Showdown at Gucci Gulch: Lawmakers, Lobbyists, and the Unlikely Triumph of Tax Reform* (New York: Random House, 1987), 3.

4. David B. Truman, *The Governmental Process* (New York: Knopf, 1964), 354.

5. A. Lee Fritschler and James M. Hoefler, *Smoking and Politics,* 5th ed. (Upper Saddle River, N.J.: Prentice-Hall, 1996), 129.

6. Donald R. Matthews, "Senators and Lobbyists," in *Congressional Reform,* ed. Joseph Clark (New York: Harper & Row, 1964), 194–196.

7. Truman, *Governmental Process,* 65.

8. Jeffrey M. Berry, *Lobbying for the People: The Political Behavior of Public Interest Groups* (Princeton, N.J.: Princeton University Press, 1977), 7.

SELECTED BIBLIOGRAPHY

Almanac of Federal PACs. Washington, D.C.: Amward Publications, 1990– .

American Lobbyists Directory. Detroit: Gale Research, 1990– .

Baumgartner, Frank R., and Beth L. Leech. *Basic Interests: The Importance of Groups in Politics and in Political Science.* Princeton, N.J.: Princeton University Press, 1998.

Beacham, Walton, ed. *Beacham's Guide to Key Lobbyists: An Analysis of Their Issues and Impact.* Washington, D.C.: Beacham Publishing, 1989.

Berry, Jeffrey M. *The Interest Group Society.* 3rd ed. New York: Longman, 1997.

———. *Lobbying for the People: The Political Behavior of Public Interest Groups.* Princeton, N.J.: Princeton University Press, 1977.

———. *The New Liberalism: The Rising Power of Citizen Groups.* Washington, D.C.: Brookings Institution, 1999.

Biersack, Robert, Paul S. Herrnson, and Clyde Wilcox. *After the Revolution: PACs, Lobbies, and the Republican Congress.* Boston: Allyn and Bacon, 1999.

Birnbaum, Jeffrey H. *The Lobbyists: How Influence Peddlers Get Their Way in Washington.* New York: Times Books, 1992

Birnbaum, Jeffrey H., and Alan S. Murray. *Showdown at Gucci Gulch: Lawmakers, Lobbyists, and the Unlikely Triumph of Tax Reform.* New York: Random House, 1987.

Clawson, Dan, Alan Neustadtl, and Denise Scott. *Money Talks: Corporate PACs and Political Influence.* New York: Basic Books, 1992.

Choate, Pat. *Agents of Influence.* New York: Knopf, 1990.

Cigler, Allan J., and Burdett A. Loomis. *Interest Group Politics.* 5th ed. Washington, D.C.: CQ Press, 1998.

Crawford, Kenneth G. *The Pressure Boys: The Inside Story of Lobbying in America.* New York: Arno Press, 1974.

Deakin, James. *Lobbyists.* Washington, D.C.: Public Affairs Press, 1966.

Etzioni, Amitai. *Capital Corruption: The New Attack on American Democracy.* New York: Harcourt Brace Jovanovich, 1984.

Foundation for Public Affairs. *Public Interest Profiles, 1988–1989.* Washington, D.C.: Congressional Quarterly, 1988.

Green, Mark J. *The Other Government: The Unseen Power of Washington Lawyers.* Rev. ed. New York: Norton, 1978.

Hall, Donald R. *Cooperative Lobbying: The Power of Pressure.* Tucson: University of Arizona Press, 1969.

Hall, Richard. *Participation in Congress.* New Haven, Conn.: Yale University Press, 1996.

Hansen, John M. *Gaining Access: Congress and the Farm Lobby.* Chicago: University of Chicago Press, 1991.

Hayes, Michael T. *Lobbyists and Legislators: A Theory of Political Markets.* New Brunswick, N.J.: Rutgers University Press, 1984.

Heinz, John P., et al. *The Hollow Core: Private Interests in National Policy Making.* Cambridge, Mass.: Harvard University Press, 1993

Herrnson, Paul S., Ronald G. Shaiko, and Clyde Wilcox, eds. *The Interest Group Connection: Electioneering, Lobbying, and Policymaking in Washington.* Chatham, N.J.: Chatham House, 1998.

Hrebenar, Ronald J. *Interest Group Politics in America.* 3rd ed. Armonk, N.Y.: Sharpe, 1997.

Jackson, Brooks. *Honest Graft.* Rev. ed. Washington, D.C.: Farragut, 1990.

Jacobs, Jerald A., ed. *Federal Lobbying.* Washington, D.C.: Bureau of National Affairs, 1989.

Levitan, Sar A., and Martha R. Cooper. *Business Lobbies: The Public Good and the Bottom Line.* Baltimore: Johns Hopkins University Press, 1983.

Malbin, Michael J. *Parties, Interest Groups, and Campaign Finance Laws.* Washington, D.C.: American Enterprise Institute, 1980.

Milbrath, Lester W. *The Washington Lobbyists.* Chicago: Rand McNally, 1963.

Noonan, John T., Jr. *Bribes: The Intellectual History of a Moral Idea.* Berkeley: University of California Press, 1984.

Olson, Mancur. *The Logic of Collective Action.* Cambridge, Mass.: Harvard University Press, 1965.

Ornstein, Norman J., and Shirley Elder. *Interest Groups, Lobbying, and Policymaking.* Washington, D.C.: CQ Press, 1978.

Parker, Glenn R. *Congress and the Rent-Seeking Society.* Ann Arbor: University of Michigan, 1996.

Richardson, Jeremy J., ed. *Pressure Groups.* New York: Oxford University Press, 1993.

Sabato, Larry J. *PAC Power: Inside the World of Political Action Committees.* New York: Norton 1984.

Schlozman, Kay L., and John Tierney. *Organized Interests and American Democracy.* New York: Harper and Row, 1986.

Thompson, Margaret S. *The "Spider Web:" Congress and Lobbying in the Age of Grant.* Ithaca, N.Y.: Cornell University Press, 1985.

Truman, David B. *The Governmental Process.* 2nd ed. New York: Knopf, 1971.

Walker, Jack L. *Mobilizing Interest Groups in America: Patrons, Professions, and Social Movements.* Ann Arbor: University of Michigan, 1991.

Washington Representatives. Washington, D.C.: Columbia Books, 1990– .

Wolpe, Bruce C., and Bertram J. Levine. *Lobbying Congress: How the System Works.* 2nd ed. Washington D.C.: Congressional Quarterly. 1996.

Wright, John R. *Interest Groups & Congress: Lobbying, Contributions, and Influence.* Boston, Mass.: Allyn and Bacon, 1996.

Zorack, John L. *The Lobbying Handbook.* Washington. D.C.: Professional Lobbying and Consulting Center, 1990.

Index

Kosovo, 86–87, 190, 240–241, 423, 443
CFE treaty, 215–216
establishment, 207–208
expansion, 243
North Korea, 192
Northeast-Midwest Congressional Coalition, 651
Northwest Ordinance, 26, 32
Norton, Eleanor Holmes, 402, 845, 851
Notice quorum calls, 497
Novak, Robert, 458, 643–644
NRA. *See* National Rifle Association
Nuclear nonproliferation treaty, 208–209, 216
Nuclear Regulatory Commission, 326
Nuclear test ban treaty of 1963, 208
Nuclear test ban treaty of 1996, 217–218
Nuclear weapons. *See also* Arms control
lab espionage, 245
plant safety, 756
Nullification doctrine, 97, 308
Nunn, Sam
arms control treaties, 211, 215, 216
strategic defense initiative, 212–213 (box)
congressional pay, 775
election, 786
Haiti mission, 196
prestige, 645
Nussbaum, Bernard, 277
Nye, Gerald P., 269, 720
Nye Committee, 251, 269

O

Oakar, Mary Rose, 961
Oaths of office
members of Congress, 918, 919
Speaker, 571 (box)
Oberstar, James L., 571 (box)
Obey, David R.
on amendment voting, 496
Appropriations chair, 554, 569
committee reform, 553
ethics reforms, 75, 948
O'Brien, Lawrence F., 658–659
Objectors, 53, 487, 527
O'Connor, John J., 62–63, 118
O'Connor, Sandra Day
appointment, 296
majority-minority districts, 817, 909–910
Occupational Safety and Health Act of 1970, 602, 602 (box), 679
Occupational Safety and Health Administration, 327
O'Daniel, W. Lee, 290
Ogden, Aaron, 309
Ogg, Frederic A., 164
Ogilvie, Donald G., 158–160
Oglesby, M. B., Jr., 660
O'Hara, James G., 387
O'Hare, Michael V., 931
Oil and natural gas
Persian Gulf War, 231–232
pipeline regulation, 314
O'Konski, Alvin, 550
Olds, Leland, 291
Oleomargarine, 318 (box)
Oleszek, Walter J.
on budget process, 191
on committee system, 535, 573, 576
on conference committees, 560 (box)
on foreign policy powers, 185
on general debate, 502
on incumbents' advantage, 866
on legislative process, 477
on logrolling, 645
on multiple committee referral, 576

on oversight mandate, 578–579
on party leadership, 419–420
on patronage, 665
on private laws, 487, 526
on representation style, 611, 613
on Senate confirmation procedures, 303
on Speaker's role, 421
on unanimous consent agreements, 510
on War Powers Resolution, 236
Olmsted, Frederick Law, Jr., 399, 737
Olney, Richard, 224–225, 314
O'Mahoney, Joseph C., 720
OMB. *See* Management and Budget, Office of
Omnibus bills
amendment limits, 470
appropriations, 66, 126, 169, 477
committee clout, 576
pork-barrel projects, 620 (box)
blanket waivers, 495
conferences, 471, 560 (box)
private bills, 527
Omnibus Crime and Safe Streets Act of 1968, 689
One-hour rule, 46, 492
O'Neill, June E., 758
O'Neill, Thomas P. "Tip" Jr.
budget deficit control, 175
career, 546 (box)
censure procedures, 936, 937
committee chair challenge, 554
committee jurisdiction, 573
congressional pay, ethics, 779, 948
foreign travel, 789
majority leader, 66
partisan trends, 77, 78, 448–449
patronage, 667
pork-barrel projects, 620, 621
on Reagan public relations, 664
as Speaker, 72, 76, 434–435, 440, 642
Koreagate scandal, 439 (box)
multiple referral, 479–480, 573
press relations, 636
on Speaker's powers, 420, 421
staff, 630
TV coverage of House, 78
Onion, John, Jr., 972
Open/closed proceedings
appointments confirmation, 289–290, 304
caucus meetings, 451, 475 (box)
committees, 470, 471, 481–482, 484, 573, 629–630
Appropriations, 161–162, 481, 629
Armed Services, 481
Intelligence committees, 481
investigations, 266
lobbyists, 697
Ways and Means, 154
witness protections, 69
conference committees, 470, 471, 561 (box)
Constitutional Convention, 16
earliest sessions, 626–627
journal publication, 22
Senate history, 92, 115 (box), 130
impeachment procedures, 339, 630
treaty consent, 202
"sunshine" reforms, 74, 548 (box), 625
Open rules, 491, 495
Operation Desert Shield/Storm, 180
Oppenheimer, Bruce I., 495
Oppenheimer, J. Robert, 292
Organized Crime in Interstate Commerce, Senate Special Committee to Investigate, 270–271
Organized Crime Control Act of 1970, 257
Ornstein, Norman, 502–503

Ortega, Daniel, 196, 449
Ostrogorski, Moisei, 102
Ott, Attiat F., 164–165
Ott, David J., 164–165
Ottinger, Richard L., 875
Oversight
ad hoc committees, 563
congressional investigations, 249–250, 577–579
subpoena power, 256
constituent casework, 617–619
executive privilege, 258–264
GAO role, 755–757
lobbying, 718
federal agency intervention, 700 (box)
policy implementation, 695–696
staff functions, 591
subcommittee reforms, 551
Overton, John H., 924 (table), 925
Owen, Ruth B., 921 (table)
Owens, Major R., 651

P

Pacheco, Romualdo, 847
Packwood, Bob
campaign finance reform, 140, 885
ethics investigation, 139, 915, 971
press coverage, 631, 633
resignation, 924 (table), 927–928, 943
forced quorum, 514
Gramm campaign aid, 972–973
paired voting, 499
on Senate staff, 589
PACs. *See* Political action committees
Padden, Mike, 389
Paez, Richard A., 305
Pages, 802–803 (box), 937
Paine, Thomas, 9
Paired voting, 499
Panama, 138, 194, 236, 237
Panama Canal tolls, 422
Panama Canal treaties, 133, 188, 198, 200 (box), 202, 212–215, 301, 459
Panetta, Leon, 661
Pappas, Tom, 966
Pardons, 30, 331
Park, Tongsun, 439 (box), 721, 937, 938, 946, 952–953
Parker, John J., 286 (table), 290, 683
Parker, Mike, 524
Parks, Preston, 389
Parliamentarians
bill referral, 479, 573
functions, 587 (box)
nominations, 302
precedents guide, 475 (box)
presiding officers aid, 509 (box)
Parris, Stan, 402
Parties. *See* Political parties
Partisanship. *See also* Bipartisanship
committee chair functions, 566
committee staffing, 593–595
congressional supporting organizations, 757, 758, 759
contested House elections, 836
gerrymanders, 77, 891, 903 (box), 908–909
House trends, 77–78, 448–449
recommittal motions, 506
restrictive rules, 470, 498
impeachment trials, 85–87, 331, 335, 344–347
investigative committees, 251, 266 (box)
Clinton probes, 277–280
judicial appointments, 682
legislative reorganization, 556
news media impact, 483 (box), 636–638